VOLUME FIVE
FUNGI—HUGO

THE BRITISH
ENCYCLOPEDIA

IN TEN VOLUMES
ILLUSTRATED

THE BRITISH ENCYCLOPEDIA

ILLUSTRATED

With an Introduction by
CYRIL NORWOOD, M.A., D. Litt.,
Headmaster of Harrow

Prepared under the general editorship
of J. M. Parrish, M.A. (Oxon.), John R.
Crossland, F.R.G.S., and Angelo S.
Rappoport, Ph.D., B. ès L., with the
specialist assistance and contributions
of over 100 experts

VOLUME
FIVE

ODHAMS PRESS LIMITED
LONDON, W.C. 2

Printed in Great Britain

KEY TO PRONUNCIATION

The method of marking pronunciations here employed is either (1) by marking the syllable on which the accent falls, or (2) by a simple system of transliteration, to which the following is the Key :

VOWELS

ā, as in *fate*, or in *bare*.

ä, as in *alms*, Fr. *âme*, Ger. *Bahn* = á of Indian names.

á, the same sound short or medium, as in Fr. *bal*, Ger. *Mann*.

a, as in *fat*.

ạ, as in *fall*.

a, obscure, as in *rural*, similar to *u* in *but*, e in *her* : common in Indian names.

ē, as in *me* = *i* in *machine*.

e, as in *met*.

ė, as in *her*.

ī, as in *pine*, or as *ei* in Ger. *mein*.

i, as in *pin*, also used for the short sound corresponding to ē, as in French and Italian words.

eu, a long sound as in Fr. *jeûne* = Ger. long *ö*, as in *Söhne*, *Göthe* (Goethe).

eu, corresponding sound short or medium, as in Fr. *peu* = Ger. *ö* short.

ō, as in *note*, *moan*.

o, as in *not*, soft—that is, short or medium.

ö, as in *move*, *two*.

ū, as in *tube*.

u, as in *tub* : similar to ė and also to *a*.

ụ, as in *bull*.

ü, as in Sc. *abune* = Fr. *û* as in *dû*, Ger. *ü* long as in *grün*, *Bühne*.

ů, the corresponding short or medium sound, as in Fr. *but*, Ger. *Müller*.

oi, as in *oil*.

ou, as in *pound* ; or as *au* in Ger. *Haus*.

9

CONSONANTS

Of the *consonants*, b, d, f, h, j, k, l, m, n, ng, p, sh, t, v, z, always have their common English sounds, when used to transliterate foreign words. The letter c is not used by itself in re-writing for pronunciation, s or k being used instead. The only consonantal symbols, therefore, that require explanation are the following :

ch is always as in ri*ch*.

d, nearly as *th* in *th*is =Sp. *d* in Ma*d*rid, etc.

g is always hard, as in *g*o.

h represents the guttural in Scotch lo*ch*, Ger. na*ch*, also other similar gutturals.

ņ, Fr. nasal *n* as in bo*n*.

r represents both English *r*, and *r* in foreign words, which is generally much more strongly trilled.

s, always as in *s*o.

th, as *th* in *th*in.

th, as *th* in *th*is.

w always consonantal, as in *w*e.

x =ks, which are used instead.

y always consonantal, as in *y*ea (Fr. *ligne* would be re-written lēny).

zh, as *s* in pleasure =Fr. *j*.

THE BRITISH ENCYCLOPEDIA

VOLUME V

FUNGI (fun'ji), a very large division of cryptogamous or flowerless plants, comprising not only the different kinds of mushrooms and toadstools, but also a large number of minute parasites, such as mildews, rusts, and smuts, and also the various moulds, yeasts, dry-rot, &c. They agree with the Algæ in being thallophytes, but differ in their mode of nutrition; they possess no chromatophores, and thus live either as saprophytes on dead organic matter, or as parasites at the expense of a living host. Most of the diseases of plants are due to the attacks of parasitic Fungi; but the useful work done by the saprophytic forms, as scavengers which prevent the accumulation of animal and vegetable debris, more than compensates for the destruction wrought by the parastic species. Though many Fungi are edible, others are highly poisonous, and the importance of the whole class as a source of food is small.

The plant-body of Fungi nearly always consists of a richly branched system of delicate filaments—septate in the higher groups, non-septate in the lower forms—called a *mycelium*; this form of thallus, combining large exposure of surface with great power of rapid penetration in all directions, is admirably suited to the needs of plants growing, as most Fungi do, in a solid organic medium.

The reproductive organs of Fungi are various, but generally take the form of minute *spores* produced in incredible numbers and readily scattered by the wind; great quantities of the spores of the common species are always floating in the atmosphere, hence the inevitable appearance of moulds on stale bread or other suitable media if these are left exposed to the air and kept sufficiently moist. Sexual reproduction is prevalent among the more primitive types (Phycomycetes), but in the higher groups becomes reduced or altogether lost.

The classification of Fungi is attended by many difficulties, and the prevailing systems are necessarily more or less artificial. The principal subdivisions, with examples, are as follows: (1) *Phycomycetes*, or Lower Fungi.—Mycelium typically non-septate (or absent). Reproductive methods various. Sexual organs prevalent. Asexual spore often motile. Largely aquatic Fungi. Examples: *Chrysophlyctis endobiotica* (wart-disease of potato); *Phytophthora infestans* (potato-blight); *Mucor Mucedo* (common or black mould). (2) *Eumycetes*, or Higher Fungi.—Mycelium septate. Sexuality usually reduced or absent. Asexual spores never motile. Almost all terrestrial Fungi. There is one stereotyped form of

Examples of Fungi. From left to right:
1. Bulbous Agaric. 2. Shaggy Caps. 3. Buff Gilled Red Cap. 4. Common Helvela.

principal reproductive organ, viz. either the *ascus*, a tubular sac containing eight *ascospores*, or the *basidium*, a club-shaped organ budding off four *basidiospores* from its upper end. Both ascospores and basidiospores are *carpospores* formed as the result of a reduction division. (a) *Ascomycetes.*—Principal reproductive organ the ascus. Examples: *Sphærotheca Castagnei* (hop-mildew); *Eurotium Aspergillus glaucus* and *Pencillium crustaceum* (common green and blue moulds); *Claviceps purpurea* (ergot of rye); *Dasyscypha Willkomii* (larch-canker); *Morchella esculenta* (edible morel); *Saccharomyces cerevisiæ* (beer-yeast). (b) *Basidiomycetes.* —Principal reproductive organ the basidium. Examples: *Ustilago Avenæ* (oat-smut); *Puccinia graminis* (wheat-rust); *Polyporus betulinus* (birch-polyporus); *Merulius lacrymans* (dryrot); *Agaricus campestris*) mushroom). (3) *Fungi Imperfecti.*—Fungi of which the compete life-cycle is not yet known; most of these are probably stages in the life-histories of Ascomycetes. Examples: *Fusarium Lycopersaici* (sleeping-disease of tomato); *Helminthosporium gramineum* (stripe disease of barley). Fungi abound in almost every part of the earth. They are rarest in deserts and in the polar regions; few marine species are known.—BIBLIOGRAPHY: De Bary, *Morphology and Physiology of the Fungi*; Marshall Ward, *Diseases of Plants*; Tubeuf, *Diseases of Plants;* Massee, *British Fungus Flora*; Eriksson, *Fungoid Diseases of Agricultural Plants.*

FUNGICIDE, any substance used, usually in the form of a spray, to combat the attacks of parasitic Fungi on cultivated plants. Among the best are Bordeaux mixture (slaked lime and copper sulphate), powdered sulphur, and Paris green (an arsenical compound).

FUNKIA, a genus of plants of the lily family, cultivated for the beauty of their large leaves and often lilac or white flowers.

FUR AND FUR TRADE. Fur is the fine soft hairy covering of certain animals, especially the winter covering of animals belonging to northern latitudes. The term fur is sometimes distinctively applied to such coverings when prepared for manufacture into articles of dress, while the name of peltry is given to them in an unprepared state or when merely dried. The animals chiefly sought after for the sake of their furs are the beaver, raccoon, musk-rat, squirrel, hare, rabbit, the chinchilla, bear (black, grey, and brown), otter, sea-otter, seal, wolf, wolverine or glutton, marten, ermine, lynx, coypou (nutria), polecat (fitch), opossum, and fox.

Preparation. Drying is the only preparation required by skins before being sent to the market. This prevents their putrefaction, and is effected by exposure to the heat of the sun or of a fire. The small skins are sometimes previously steeped in a solution of alum. When stored in large quantities, they must be carefully preserved from dampness, as well as from moths. The fur-dresser, on receiving a skin, first subjects it to a softening process. He next cleans its under-surface from loose pieces of the integument by scraping it with an iron blade. Finally, the fur is cleaned and combed, after which the skin is ready to be cut into any required shape.

History of Trade. Furs for Europe were formerly supplied largely by Russia, which produces a great quantity, especially in the Asiatic portion of her territory. Austria, Turkey, and Scandinavia also yield a certain quantity. The fur trade of America has long been highly important, and several great trading companies have engaged in it, of which the Dutch East India Company was first. The French early took up the fur trade in Canada, and their chain of forts and trading-posts at one time extended from Hudson Bay to New Orleans. Quebec and Montreal were at first trading-posts.

In 1670 Charles II granted to Prince Rupert and others a charter empowering them to trade exclusively with the aborigines of the Hudson Bay region. A company, then and after called the *Company of Adventurers of England trading into Hudson Bay*, was formed, which for a period of nearly two centuries possessed a monopoly of the fur trade in the vast tract of country known as the Hudson Bay Territory. In the winter of 1783–4 another company was formed at Montreal, called the *Northwest Fur Company*, which disputed the right of the Hudson Bay Company, and actively opposed it. After a long and bitter rivalry the two companies united in 1821, retaining the older name.

The monopoly which had hitherto been enjoyed by the original company about Hudson Bay was now much extended; but in 1868 an Act of Parliament was passed to make provision for the surrender, upon certain terms, of all the territories belonging to the company, and for their incorporation with the Dominion of Canada. In 1869 the surrender was carried out, Canada paying £300,000 to the company by way of compensation. The company still possesses large stretches of valuable land, and many houses, forts, and posts in the region formerly belonging to it. Its operations have even extended beyond British America into the United States and to the Sandwich Isles and Alaska. It employs a large staff of agents, traders, and Indian hunters. Some of its posts are situated far north, almost approaching the Arctic Ocean.

The trade in furs conducted by citizens of the United States has been extensive, but in a greater degree the result of individual enterprise than of the management of gigantic corporations. The Alaska Fur Company holds two of the Aleutian Islands in lease from the United States Government with the sole right of killing yearly not more than 100,000 fur-seals. The two great European centres to which furs are brought are London and Leipzig. St. Louis, U.S.A., is also a great fur market.

FURCA, or **FURCAHORN,** an Alpine mountain in Switzerland, canton of Valais, west of St. Gothard; height 9,935 feet, containing the glacier in which the Rhône has its source. The summit of the Furca Pass is 7,992 feet high.

FURCRÆA, a genus of plants, ord. Amaryllidaceæ, closely allied to Agave; some species yield a fibre known as Mauritius hemp.

FURIES (Gr. *Eumenides* or *Erinnyes*, Lat. *Furiæ* or *Diræ*), goddesses who were originally personifications of the curses pronounced upon guilty criminals. Different ages looked upon these goddesses in different ways. The name Erinnyes means 'goddesses who hunt,' while Eumenides was a euphemistic expression, meaning 'kindly ones.' At Athens they were sometimes also called Semnai or 'venerable ones.' The crimes which they punished were failing to honour father and mother, perjury, murder, and violation of the laws of hospitality or of the rights of suppliants. They were supposed to be able to destroy all peace of mind, and to make their victim either childless or unfortunate in his children.

In the *Eumenides*, the concluding play of the *Oresteia* of Æschylus, the poet brought a chorus of twelve furies upon the stage. This magnificently conceived play describes the reconciliation between the older gods and the newer ones, and ends with the Furies consenting to share a sanctuary with Athene. Æschylus describes them as being dressed in black, having serpents in their hair, and blood oozing from their eyes. Some later writers limit their number to three, and give them the names of Tisiphone, Alecto and Megæra. The sacrifices offered to them consisted of black sheep and a mixture of honey and water. No wine was offered.

FURLOUGH, leave of absence. The term denotes specifically the absence from military duty of the rank and file by permission of the commanding officer for periods exceeding six days on full pay; passes may be endorsed with permission to wear civilian clothes.

FURNACE, a chamber or structure arranged for the utilization of heat generated by the combustion of fuel or by means of an electric current. The word is also sometimes used in a more general sense for combustion chambers, for example, in connection with boilers, arrangements for house heating, baking pottery or bread, but is more particularly used for the structures arranged for the smelting of ores or for the melting or heat treatment of metal.

In the construction of furnaces the following objects are kept in view: (1) to obtain the greatest quantity of heat from a given quantity of fuel; (2) to prevent the dissipation of heat after it is produced; (3) to concentrate the heat and direct it as much as possible to the substance to be acted upon; (4) to be able to regulate at pleasure the necessary degree of heat, and have it wholly under the operator's control. Furnaces vary considerably in design, according to the nature of the operation to be carried out in them, and according to the nature of the fuel to be used. They may be arranged for the combustion of solid fuels such as wood, charcoal, coke, or anthracite; for liquid fuels such as crude natural oils, distilled oils, tar, &c.; or for gaseous fuel such as coal-gas, pro-

Fury (from a painted vase)

duce-gas, waste, furnace gas, &c. In special cases they are arranged for the utilization of electrical energy by means of induction, resistance, and the arc.

The method of applying the heat generated to the work in hand varies considerably, and may consist of direct heating, where the material comes into direct contact with the solid fuel, as in the case of a smith's hearth, and also in the case of blast-furnaces, in which ore and the fuel are charged into one chamber. Direct heating may consist of the flame or products of combustion only coming in contact with the material, as in reverberatory furnaces, in which the fuel is burnt in a separate part or chamber and the flames reverberate from the roof over the material. Indirect heating is utilized in those cases in which crucibles are used, or in which it is desirable to keep the material out of contact with the solid fuel and the products of combustion. In these cases the heating is carried out by conduction or radiation through the walls of the containing vessel, as in crucible-, muffle-, and retort-furnaces.

Furnaces are generally classified according to their form or design, and although not strictly speaking furnaces, *heaps* and *piles* may be considered as the simplest form, as these undoubtedly constituted the oldest form of heating arrangement. These forms are still used to some extent for the preparation of charcoal and coke, in which a portion of the charge itself is burnt to generate the heat; they are also used for the calcination and roasting of certain ores. For this purpose the material is mixed with the necessary fuel and piled up, passages being left for the purposes of draught.

A *stall* is an improvement on the open heap, and generally consists of a rectangular space surrounded on three sides by brick walls, the top and front being left open. In some cases flues and chimneys are arranged in the walls for the regulation of the draught. These structures were formerly used for the preparation of coke, and are now used for calcining ores, burning lime, &c. The material is charged into the space together with layers of fuel as required, and the front is bricked up as the filling proceeds. This structure offers a certain protection from the weather, and ensures more uniform combustion.

Shaft-furnaces consist of vertical walls, either circular or rectangular in cross-section, in which the height is several times the diameter or length of the narrower side. The material is charged in at the top, and the product removed from the bottom either in the solid or liquid form. The fuel used in shaft-furnaces is usually solid, and is mixed with the charge to be treated or added in separate layers during the charging. Oil or gas is sometimes used as fuel in these furnaces, and recently powdered coal has also been used, these fuels being injected at the bottom of the shaft. The air necessary for the combustion of the fuel is admitted at the bottom, either by natural draught or under pressure, through suitably placed tuyeres.

Shaft-furnaces may be conveniently subdivided into three classes, viz. kilns, cupolas, and blast-furnaces. Kilns are relatively short and wide, and are chiefly used for calcining ore, limestone, &c., during which operations a very high temperature is not required, the burnt product being removed in the solid state. Cupolas are also relatively low furnaces, circular in shape, with a small diameter. They are used for the melting of pig-iron in foundry practice and in

Bessemer steel plants. The fuel used is coke, and low-pressure blast is admitted. The bottom of the furnace, where the molten iron accumulates, is called the nearth or well, and is provided with tap-holes for the withdrawal of the iron and slag. The bottom of these furnaces is usually closed with a hinged plate of cast iron, which can be lowered to empty the cupola after a run.

Blast-furnaces are shaft-furnaces in which ores and metallurgical products are smelted with high-pressure blast, and the products, consisting of metal or metalliferous substance with slag, are tapped out in the liquid state.

Reverberatory furnaces are those in which the material to be heated or smelted is charged into one part of the furnace, known as the hearth or laboratory, separated from the part in which the fuel is burnt, known as the fire-place. The necessary heat is obtained from the products of combustion of the coal, oil, or gas used as fuel.

Reverberatory furnaces are frequently fitted with arrangements for the utilization of the heat of the waste gases. When the air required in the furnaces is passed through pipes around which the hot waste gas from the furnace is passed, it is known as a recuperative furnace, or a furnace worked on the counter-current system. When the hot waste gases are made to heat large chambers filled with chequer brickwork on their way to the chimney, the heat stored up in these chambers being subsequently used to pre-heat the air, or air and gas, used in the furnace, it is known as a regenerative furnace. This type of furnace is largely used in the manufacture of steel (Siemens furnace), in zinc retorts, &c.

Crucible Furnaces are those in which the material to be treated is contained in crucibles, which are vessels made of fire-clay, plumbago, &c. The crucibles may be heated by being embedded in solid fuel such as coke, which is burnt in a short shaft-furnace arranged with fire-bars at bottom. These furnaces, known as wind- or pot-furnaces, are frequently sunk below ground-level to facilitate the charging and removal of the crucibles. Similar furnaces are arranged for gaseous firing, and may be fitted with regenerators.

Muffle-furnaces are arranged for the heating of charges out of contact with the fuel or products of combustion. They are largely used for the roasting of sulphide ores, when it is desirable to obtain a gas rich in sulphur dioxide for the manufacture of sulphuric acid. Muffle-furnaces are also used for the heating of various metals, for example, copper, and as heating furnaces for steel-hardening processes.

Retort-furnaces are similar to muffle-furnaces and gas-retorts, and are used in the metallurgy of zinc, and for the extraction of arsenic. A continuous furnace is one in which the material is charged at one end and withdrawn at the other end, charging and withdrawal taking place continuously. This type of furnace is used in the roasting of sulphide ores, and when the charge is moved along by means of rakes worked by machinery, it is known as a mechanical furnace. Continuous heating furnaces are also much used for the heating of ingots in the forge. These are arranged so that the ingots may be charged cold at the flue end, and moved slowly down to the withdrawal door on water - cooled pipes by hydraulic pushers. On reaching the door at the fire-place end the billets should have acquired the temperature necessary for the operation. *See* BLAST-FURNACE; ELECTRO-METALLURGY.

FURNEAUX ISLANDS (fèr'nŏ), also called **FLINDERS**, a group belonging to Tasmania, at the east end of Bass Strait, Flinders Island being the largest. The inhabitants, who number about 600, procure a living by seal-fishing and preserving mutton-birds, a species of petrel. The islands are named after Tobias Furneaux, the officer who was second in command in Captain Cook's second voyage (1773).

FURNES (fûrn, Fl. *Veurne*), a town in Belgium, not far from the North Sea and the French frontier, at the junction of several canals. It has two ancient churches and an interesting town hall. In early times Furnes was an important stronghold. It was bombarded by the Germans 24th–27th Oct., 1914. In 1920 it received the Croix de Guerre. Pop. 8,000.

FUR'NESS, a district of N.W. Lancashire, forming part of what is called the Lake District. Furness Abbey is a noble ruin situated 1 mile s. of Dalton-in-Furness, comprising the church walls, chapter-house, refectory, and guest hall, the whole giving evidence of the former magnificence of the structure. It was founded in 1127 by Stephen, afterwards King of England.

FURNESS, Baron. English ship-owner. Born 23rd April, 1852, Christopher Furness entered business life and in 1877 established at West Hartlepool his own line of steamers. This became the great firm of Furness, Withy & Co., and later he was associated with others of the large industrial undertakings of Durham. In 1895 he was knighted, and in 1910 was made a peer. He had been Liberal M.P. for Hartlepool, 1891-95 and 1900-10. He died 10th Nov., 1912. His son, Marmaduke, who succeeded to his title, was made a viscount in 1918.

FURNISS, Harry, British caricaturist, author, and lecturer, born at Wexford in 1854, died 1925. He came to London at the age of nineteen, and began to contribute drawings and sketches of a humorous character to the principal illustrated papers. In 1884 he joined the staff of *Punch*, and became one of its most popular illustrators. He invented the legendary Gladstone collar which made him famous, and illustrated the works of Dickens (1910) and Thackeray (1911). In 1894 he left *Punch* and started a weekly paper of his own, *Lika Joko*. An admirable lecturer, he lectured in Great Britain, the United States, Australia, and Canada on the *Humours of Parliament*. His works include: *Confessions of a Caricaturist* (1901), *Harry Furniss at Home* (1903), *How to draw in Pen and Ink* (1903), besides novels and plays for the cinematograph.

FURNITURE, furniture indicates the intimate habits of the user, and its study enables the student to gauge the plane on which the men who made it stood. The historian includes social habits and concomitant details in his exposition of the past. Hence the study of the domestic furniture of man and its evolution is parallel with the study of his social progress throughout the various epochs. In general, great art conceptions, whether in architecture, painting, or furniture, were contemporaneous with a great productive period in literature. The Renaissance in art, which began at Florence in the fourteenth century, was at first a literary movement. Art has always been the handmaid of literature, and applied art, such as the fashioning of furniture, is a mirror held to the social culture of a nation.

In a review of ancient furniture, Egypt, as the oldest known civilization, takes a foremost place. The survival of so many examples of furniture is due to the preservative properties of an excessively dry climate, and in addition papyri and mural paintings have depicted furniture and its use. Ancient Egyptian furniture was painted, inlaid with fine woods or ivory or glass, and sometimes plated with gold. It is of great antiquity; there is a wooden coffin of Men-kau-ra, a king of the fourth dynasty, about 3,633 B.C., at the British Museum. From what is known of early Egyptian furniture, the craftsmen must have possessed hammers, chisels, axes, gouges, awls, and possibly some form of lathe.

FURNITURE

A.—Chippendale Cabinet.   B.—Throne of Ancient Rome.   C.—15th Century Coffer.   D.—Late 17th Century Canopied Bed.   E.—16th Century French Dresser

Egyptian furniture is solid in construction, with garish Eastern colouring. The human figure was used, and animal forms with limitations. Sphinxes as supports and terminal ornaments, and animal feet to chairs and couches are prototypes which descended to later schools. Coffers, caskets, couches with sphinx supports (reproduced under the First Empire period of Napoleon), folding stools, and dolls and toys are preserved, including a crocodile with moving jaw. The principal collections of Egyptian furniture are in the British Museum, the Louvre, Paris, the Leyden Museum, the Berlin Musuem, and the museum at Cairo.

Babylonian. Of Babylonian furniture, and of the subsequent Assyrian epoch, few remains exist. The forms are mostly recorded in the sculpture of the period. The Babylonians were the creators as artists and the Assyrians the conquerors; the parallel holds good in relation to the Romans, who similarly appropriated the arts of the Greeks whom they governed. At the British Museum there is a plaster cast of Gudea, a king of Babylon about 2,500 B.C., and an Assyrian bronze throne shows feet of animal form as in earlier Egyptian design. An Assyrian throne (*circa* 880 B.C.) has rams' heads as terminals. This ornamentation was used later by the Romans, and also by the Adam brothers in the eighteenth century. The Bible has many references to Jewish furniture, but Judæan work was largely derivative from Egypt and Assyria, and nothing is preserved, although there is the golden candlestick with its seven branches from the temple at Jerusalem, carried away as spoil by the Romans, and shown in the carving on the Arch of Titus at Rome.

Greek. Greek furniture is mainly known from sculpture. Seated figures, six centuries before Christ, at the British Museum, show the form of chair then in use, with mortises and tenons accurately reproduced in the marble. Drawing upon other earlier sources, the Greeks evolved a distinct type of furniture, from which succeeding ages have adapted many designs. Simplicity of outline marks the period.

The great period of Greek art began in the fifth century, and lasted over two hundred years. The chairs can be adjusted to many angles; modern designers have found inspiration in these ancient models. The chairs of the Empire period of the early nineteenth century were duplicates of these sculptured prototypes, and the arch for the back, a noticeable feature, has become permanent in modern chairs designed for comfort. The chair of Poseidippos, the writer of comedies, first half of third century before Christ, in the Vatican, appears to be quite as comfortable as the modern library chair.

Roman. The excavations at Herculaneum and Pompeii in the eighteenth century enabled the Roman house with its domestic furniture to be reconstructed. The Naples Museum shows many examples of bronze furniture exhibiting winged sphinxes, and lion supports to tables, and elaborate ornament with wreaths, and the predominant feature of the animal foot. Couches in bronze have turned ornaments. (The same style reappeared in Stuart days in brass candlesticks and in turned walnut legs to chairs.)

In Roman furniture there was an amplification of ornament supplanting the beauty and simplicity of the Greek design. The materials employed were gold, silver, bronze, ivory, marble, and wood, and these were decorated by carving, damascening, veneering with coloured woods, or inlaying with precious stones. The peculiar markings of veneer has names such as *tigrinus*, resembling a tiger, and *apiatus*, like a swarm of bees. Tortoiseshell was used, and horn was stained, thus anticipating Boule, the great French cabinet-maker, by many centuries.

Various. After the seat of empire was removed from Rome, the Byzantine style arose in Constantinople, from A.D. 321 till about 1204. Of thirteenth-century work is the Coronation chair made for Edward I, now at Westminster Abbey. The carved lions supporting this chair are modern, and were regilded at the time of Queen Victoria's jubilee in 1887. It was during the thirteenth and fourteenth centuries that mediæval art in Europe reached its zenith. But the finesse of Gothic wood-carving did not touch England till after its adoption on the Continent.

At the Cluny Museum, Paris, a rich collection of Gothic coffers of the fifteenth and sixteenth century is exhibited, and one example of the end of the thirteenth century is noticeable for its finely carved panels. At the Landesmuseum, Zurich, a representative series of old Swiss chests shows fifteenth and sixteenth century types based on German work. Some of the sixteenth-century chests are Italianate in character. At St. Saviour's Church, Southwark, is a fine chest of the sixteenth century, inlaid with marquetry. In Holland the chest was made of oak, walnut, *lignum-vitæ*, or some other wood imported from the Dutch East Indies.

The *kas* was the receptacle for household linen, and the great *kasten* was mounted on wooden ball feet, the prototype of the modern wardrobe.

English. In England the great effects of the Renaissance in art were derived from the Continent. The change from Gothic or Mediæval work to the classic styles of ancient Greece and Rome had its origin in Italy. The early Tudor days under Henry VII saw the dawn of the Renaissance in England. Renaissance art made a change in architecture, and a corresponding change took place in furniture. Foreign workmen were employed by the Church and by the nobility in embellishing cathedrals and churches and feudal castles. Flemish woodworkers settled in England, and the harmonious blending of the designs of the Italian and Flemish schools resulted in the growth in England of the style known as Tudor. A comparison of the examples of Italian Renaissance of the fourteenth and fifteenth centuries with Elizabethan and domestic furniture shows the guiding influence.

In general details of technique the English styles have a close affinity with the art of the Netherlands as derived from Italy. The spiral turned legs and columns, the strap frets cut out and applied to the various parts, are outstanding features. As a chronological record of details of technique, it may be recorded that in the reign of Henry VII (1485–1509) hutches (the old term for cupboards), credences (tasting-tables; It. *credenza*, a shelf or buffet), and a panelled or box chairs all showed Gothic motives in their arches or tracery. Linen-fold panelling remained till 1550, that is, throughout the reign of Henry VIII.

About this date Gothic designs disappeared until revived by Chippendale and others in the middle of the eighteenth century. Oak was the main wood used in all Tudor and early Stuart furniture. In the reign of Edward VI inlay was first used in England to decorate furniture, and chests with drawers came into use, but not general use. Elizabethan furniture is rich in elaborate and massive carving. Caryatides (female figures used as supports), and Atlantes (male figures of similar use), and grotesque masks are features in the massive decoration of tables and bedsteads. Bulbous legs to tables are noticeable, and strap-work, found also in the silver of the period, is prominent. Inlay of coloured woods was popular, though there is a coarseness in its use not comparable with contemporary Italian and Continental examples. Inlays representing buildings, a feeble echo of fine Italian marquetry, such

as the Nonesuch chest (a representation of Nonesuch House, one of Elizabeth's seats), were very popular. Panelled-back chairs were introduced with a cresting (cresting is a term applied to the ornamental work which finishes the upper part, as in a chair back).

In the reign of James I furniture underwent little change, although he is the monarch who gave the term Jacobean to English styles prevalent mainly in later reigns. In general there was a leaning to tapestry. The Mortlake tapestry factory was founded about 1620, and upholstered chairs and stools were made for noble families. Wooden seats had hitherto been considered as sufficient. Sir John Harrington, writing in 1597, asserts that "the fashion of cushioned chayrs is taken up in every merchant's house." Leather seats and backs of finely tooled work richly gilded had been imported from Spain. The insanitary rush floor had been superseded by wood, and carpets came into general use in Elizabeth's day. Even pillows, deemed by the hardy yeomanry as only fit "for women in child-bed," found a place in the elaborately carved Tudor bedstead.

The Stuart or Jacobean styles are varied. The term Jacobean includes the reigns of James I (1603–25), Charles I (1625–49), the Commonwealth period (1649–60), and the reign of Charles II (1660–85), James II, and William and Mary (ending in 1702). Practically a century covers various types, commencing with the continuance of oak, and embracing the adoption of walnut and the beginning of elaborate and nearly modern styles.

In the reign of Charles I chests with drawers became popular, and applied baluster ornament was frequently used in them. Spiral twists for chairs were first used about 1635, and at the same time flap tables with folding legs, which later developed into elaborate gate-leg tables, were introduced. In Charles's reign leather-backed and seated chairs, studded with brass nails, were noticeable. These are most frequently termed Cromwellian chairs, but they originated in or about 1645. During the Civil War little furniture was made.

Under Puritan influence the carved representation of the human figure disappeared. Iconoclasts abominated the style, and it was as much anathema as it was to the Mohammedans, who never used the human figure in their carving, but resorted to geometric design, as exhibited in Hispano-Moresque work at the Alhambra and elsewhere. Table settles and table chairs, a mechanical combination, were introduced under the Common-

FURNITURE

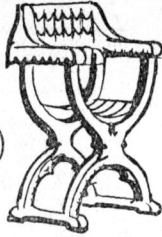

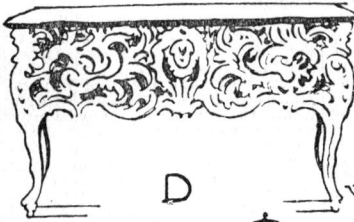

A.—Egyptian Chair.   B.—French Fauteuil.   C.—Seat from Roman Bath.   D.—Early Louis Quinze Commode.   E.—16th Century Oak Chair—French.   F.—17th Century Chair.   G.—Cabinet of Georgian Period

wealth, but there is little else to record in furniture.

Under Charles II and his brother James II quite a variety of fashions came uppermost. The pendulum swung from sobriety to licence, and a great stimulus was given to inventiveness and originality in design. Moreover, some of the Royalists who had been forced to fly the country introduced new ideas from the Continent.

The first introduction of caned backs and seats took place in the reign of King Charles II, when the heavy wood framing and carving of the earlier styles was still very pronounced. Under James II the wood ornament gave place to lighter caning more freely used, and to padded or upholstered seats. Chairs with upholstered wings and arms came into use about 1685. Under William and Mary walnut became dominant, and in consequence greater freedom was possible in fashioning the softer wood. Elaborate scrolls and carved splats were frequent. Fiddle-splats and serpentine stretchers to chairs, and cabriole legs and ball feet, came into England under Dutch influence. Marquetry was introduced from Holland, and a pattern known as 'sea-weed' is noticeable in cabinets and clockcases. Grandfather clocks came into general use about 1700, and tall-boy chests of drawers appeared at the same time, and continued for over a hundred years in constant fashion. Lacquer furniture, also an importation from Holland, became the vogue, and continued through later reigns. It is the most un-English of all classes of furniture, but it had a vogue in the eighteenth century, and has of late years been unaccountably revived.

The reign of Queen Anne is indubitably the age when walnut was supreme. Her reign actually was from 1702 to 1714, but the term "Queen Anne" is applied to furniture made before and after this period. It is somewhat generic. This period is one of solid and sober workmanship. Club feet are noticeable in the chairs; shell and pendant ornament on knees of cabriole legs came into use. The cabriole leg had established itself until Chippendale replaced it with his straight leg in Chinese manner. Certain tall cabinets with drop-down fronts with nests of drawers are associated with this period, and the arched pediments in architectural form. This style has been largely duplicated by modern cabinet-makers.

The reigns of the first two Georges ended in 1760. As an approximate half-century, the period offers interesting points till the rise of Chippendale. Various factors appeared before Thomas Chippendale seized the results and made them his own.

The eagle's head ornament in 1714 lasted some twenty-five years. The shell ornament became established in the following years. In 1720 the lion's mask ornament and lion's paw feet became fashionable for some fifteen years. In 1725 mahogany was a favourite wood, and, being softer than walnut, was capable of finer design. Splats of chairs began to be pierced; top-rails of chairs and settees became hooped with carved crestings. The duty was removed from mahogany in 1733, and from that date the great Mahogany period began. The silver designs of the George II period should be studied with those of the furniture. French influence was strong, both upon the metal-worker and the cabinet-maker. The great epoch of Louis XIV had a decided influence in England.

Books of designs were published by English cabinet-makers which showed derivative influences, such as those of William Jones (1739) and William Kent (1743), and Ince and Mayhew's *Household Furniture* (1743). Rapidly innovation succeeded innovation; the Chinese taste in lacquer panels showed colour in competition with form. Chinese geometric ornament and pagoda pediments came uppermost. The Gothic style also had a vogue. In 1750 ribbon-back chairs, a derivation from French models, came into popular use. In 1753 Chippendale was busy in his workshops at St. Martin's Lane focussing all these styles and forming his own eclectic one. In 1754 he published the first edition of his *Gentleman and Cabinet Maker's Director*. Ladder-back chairs at this date were made, and straight-legged chairs came into fashion. On the return of Sir William Chambers, the architect, from China, the Chinese style gained further publicity. Lattice-work, fretwork, and applied fret were in constant use. Chinese lanterns in mahogany hung in noblemen's mansions.

In 1757 Chambers published his *Designs of Chinese Buildings, Furniture, Dresses, Machines, and Utensils*, and he built the pagoda at Kew.

But contemporaneous with this movement, and almost antagonistic to it, came the Classic revival. Wedgwood in Staffordshire was producing his gods and goddesses in pottery. Roman and Greek cameo designs were applied to furniture. Robert Adam, the Scotsman, one of three brothers, had returned from Italy to revolutionize the arts of furnishing and of architecture. It was in vain that Ince and Mayhew, in 1762, published an echo of other styles, and Chippendale came out with his third edition of the *Director* in 1762. Robert Adam was appointed architect to the king, and the great classic revival began. Chippendale unfortunately reverted to Gothic banalities, and produced some of his worst work, although collectors still give great prices for this. But about 1770 Chinese styles went out of favour and Gothic became less fashionable.

In 1768 Matthias Lock had published several books on furniture, but nothing of importance appeared to influence the main stream of design. At the same date certain chairs with straight top-rails were designed by Adam and executed by Chippendale. The two schools here merged, and records go to show that Adam and Chippendale worked together in design and execution. The firm Thomas Chippendale & Co., or Chippendale and Haig, executed cabinet-work where marquetry was one of the important features. The divergence of Chippendale from his original and brilliant conceptions, where ornament was dependent on form, to his later period, where he accepted the newer dicta that ornament might gain from colour, is interesting, and shows his extraordinary versatility.

With the promulgation of his *Director* Chippendale made a style that was copied by cabinet-makers throughout the country. There is cottage Chippendale made by village joiners, where in elm and yew and beech and sycamore his models were carried out with native touches of delightful originality. Such work is eagerly bought by collectors. In Ireland there was a school which imitated in mahogany some of Chippendale's designs. This work is heavy, and very readily distinguishable from Chippendale's prototypes.

As a masterly adapter Chippendale stands supreme. His ball-and-claw feet and his spacious seats he borrowed from the Dutch, or from earlier Georgian furniture under Dutch influence. He translated the heavy walnut splats of early Georgian days into terms of mahogany. He realized how much of the Louis XIV ornament was suitable to English domestic furniture. In his ribbon-back chairs he assimilated the flowing ornament of the Louis XVI period. But his adaptations became original under his hand, and, tempered by French subtleties, they are robust and sturdy. His Chinese fretwork in the angles of his chairs and tables was in obedience to the Chinese taste.

But symmetry was Chippendale's own gift. He knew to a nicety how much ornament a structure would bear. The splats in his chairs are of such graceful and perfect dimensions, in proportion to the open spaces, that no would-be imitator was able to copy them. He was the prince of chair designers; and for the first time in the history of English furniture Continental designers turned their eyes to this country in admiration of the new styles being produced.

Up to the days of Thomas Chippendale, whether it be the age of oak or the age of walnut, the terms Tudor, Jacobean or Stuart, Anglo-Dutch (under William and Mary), Anne, or early Georgian are names applied by modern connoisseurs to various styles. After Chippendale furniture began to be classified by the particular designers or makers. For half a century the styles of Chippendale held sway, from 1730 to 1780. The Hepplewhite school may be said to reckon from about 1775 to 1795, and the Sheraton designs covered a period from about 1790 to 1805, and behind all there was the paramount classic influence of the brothers Adam, with their absorption of classicism and forms coincident with the later French styles beginning to become chaste and severe.

It is impossible to put aside the contemporaneous influences the great French cabinet-makers had upon design, under the four great periods Louis XIV, Louis XV, and Louis XVI, followed by the great classic revival known as the First Empire period. In a measure this cannot be said to be domestic furniture. It had an architectural outlook. It was designed as a factor in certain schemes of decoration of sumptuous palaces. Removed from Fontainebleau and Versailles, such pieces of grandiloquent art as are exhibited at the Wallace Collection and elsewhere are jewels torn from their settings. But as an influence such unparalleled mastery of technique has found no equal in any other country.

André Charles Boule (1642–1732), succeeded by his four sons, founded an *atelier*, and under Louis XIV introduced his splendour of veneered work in ebony inlaid with tortoiseshell and brass, set in massive metal mounts. The *Louis Quatorze* period extends from the days of Charles I to the reign of Anne. The *Louis Quinze* style (1715–74) is represented by commodes with chased and bronzed gilt mounts by Caffieri, when the cabriole leg and swirling forms of ornament were pronounced. The chaster cabinet work of Riesener is found in the Louis XVI period, when the style became more restrained, and in France the style of Sheraton is termed *Louis Seize à l'Anglaise.*

In middle and late eighteenth-century days books of designs by

London cabinet-makers were published for the use of the trade. They served to consolidate styles and promulgate ideas to lesser men. In 1788 Hepplewhite published his contribution to the literature. The grace and beauty of form is a noticeable feature of the Hepplewhite style. The wheat-ear on chair backs is a favourite design which has stood the test of time.

An examination of the Hepplewhite volume, *The Cabinet-Maker and Upholsterer's Guide, or Repository of Designs for Every Article of Household Furniture, from Drawings by Hepplewhite & Co., Cabinet-Makers* (1788), shows the clarity of Hepplewhite's interpretation. He stood between Chippendale's magnificent impossibilities and Sheraton's seizure of form embellished with colour. In a measure Hepplewhite is the golden mean between two opposite schools. He leaned to form, but he essayed efforts in colour, as in satin-wood with painted panels.

Sheraton was not a practical master cabinet-maker. He was a designer. He came to London as a journeyman cabinet-maker. He opened a stationer's shop in Soho, and became in turn Baptist preacher, author, and teacher of drawing, all these occupations being equally unremunerative. His is a name which posterity recognizes as the founder of a school, derivative though it may have been.

A deep-rooted idea seized France at the Revolution that the modern Republic should emulate the fame of Athens and of Rome. The First Consul appeared with a laurel wreath around his head, posing as Cæsar. This style, which threw aside all the characteristics of former periods, came to be known as the First Empire. At Malmaison and at Fontainebleau there are many examples. The influence on English furniture lasted up to the first quarter of the nineteenth century.

A later style, which has been termed the Regency, as being associated with the period from 1811 when the Prince of Wales was appointed regent when George III became insane, may really be merged with the George IV period (1820–30) and the William IV period to 1837. During these years a decadence set in. With the declining classic modes, the transition into the banalities of the hooped-back Windsor chair, and the ineptitudes of cabriole legs with upholstered seats, there lingered certain forms of chair with curved back of quasi-classic form, where fine brass inlay in floral design was introduced with fine effect. Many of these chairs were made in the eastern counties till up to a later date.

During the Early-and Mid-Victorian period (from 1837 up to 1887) furniture showed no signs of continuing its great traditions. When sumptuous pieces were made, they were so overloaded with ornament as to be repulsive. The same applies to Victorian silver-plate. The period was poor in inventive design, and it was not until the 'eighties that artistic impulses were stirred, under the guidance of William Morris and others, to revert to simpler and more beautiful forms. Old furniture was preserved, and collecting it became a common hobby. The public taste has been educated mainly by colonies of artists who have striven to influence trade productions. Gate-leg tables, simple farmhouse chairs in yew, with fiddle-splats or wheel-backs, graced many a studio of the late 'seventies and early 'eighties before popular opinion was won over and the fashion for old oak on the one hand, and the late eighteenth-century mahogany schools on the other, set in.

The early part of the twentieth century was marked by no particular originality, though the beauty of old English furniture was generally recognized. Since the War, however, a new and entirely original school has come into being, largely influenced by the modern trend in art and architecture. Solid geometric forms, absence of ornament, purity of line are its distinguishing features, while black and white, colours and silver are often employed with striking effect. When, in recent years, chromium-plated steel furniture came into use, the modern style adapted itself quite naturally to the new medium.

The charm of this school, and its claim to rank as a "period," rests on a sound æsthetic basis. Perhaps never before has furniture been so thoroughly at one with the artistic principles of the age. In the best modern furniture there is little to find fault with, whether from the point of view of beauty or use.—BIBLIOGRAPHY: J. H. Pollen, *Ancient and Modern Furniture and Woodwork*; W. M. Flinders Petrie, *History of Egypt*; P. Macquoid, *History of English Furniture*; A. Hayden, *Chats on Old Furniture; and Chats on Cottage and Farmhouse Furniture*; Lady Dilke, *French Furniture*; F. Litchfield, *Illustrated History of Furniture*; H. D. Eberlein and Abbot M'Clure, *The Practical Book of Period Furniture*.

FUR′NIVALL, Frederick James, English philologist, born at Egham, in Surrey, 1825; educated at University College, London, and Trinity Hall, Cambridge; died in 1910. He was called to the Bar in 1849, but devoted his life chiefly to the study of early and middle English literature; and was mainly instrumental in establishing the Early English Text Society (1864), the Chaucer Society (1868), the New Shakespeare Society (1874), the Browning Society (1881), the Shelley Society (1881), and the Wyclif Society (1882). He was also honorary secretary of the Philological Society, and he edited numerous works, chiefly through the medium of some of these societies, notably the Six-Text edition of Chaucer's *Canterbury Tales* (1868–75).—Cf. F. J. Furnivall, *A Volume of Personal Record*.

FURSE, Dame Catherine, British organizer, born 23rd Nov., 1875. A daughter of John Addington Symonds, she married in 1900 the painter C. W. Furse. Through her efforts the Voluntary Aid Detachments, established in 1909, developed their activities at the outbreak of the European War. For some time Mrs. Furse was in France, where she organized the work of the Aid Detachments, but in 1915 she returned to England and became commandant-in-chief of the V.A.D.'s. In 1917 she was appointed Director of the Women's Royal Naval Air Service, and made a G.B.E. She published *Ski-running* in 1924.

FUR-SEAL, a name given to several of the Otariidæ or 'eared' seals which have a dense covering of fine underfur. The best known and most valuable is the fur-seal or sea-bear (*Otaria ursina*) of some of the islands connected with Alaska, especially St. Paul's and St. George's, where it breeds. See SEAL; *also* FUR AND FUR-TRADE.

FÜRST (fûrst), Julius, Orientalist, born of Jewish parents at Zerkowo, Poland, 1805, died at Leipzig 1873. He devoted himself to philological science, and early showed a marvellously extensive acquaintance with Rabbinical literature. He obtained an appointment as lecturer in the University of Leipzig in 1839, and in 1864 was promoted to the rank of professor. He was the author of numerous works all connected with Oriental philology, chief among which were his *Concordantiæ Librorum Sacrorum Veteris Testamenti Hebraicæ et Chaldaicæ*, and his *Hebrew and Chaldee Lexicon*. From 1840 to 1851 he edited *Der Orient*, a journal devoted to Jewish language, literature, history, and antiquities.

FÜRSTENWALDE (fûrst'en-väl-dè), a town of Germany, in Prussia, 30 miles E.S.E. of Berlin, on the right bank of the Spree. It has a brick church of the fourteenth century, and manufactures of woollen and

linen cloth, electric lamps, machinery, and glass. Pop. 23,168.

FÜRTH (fürt), a town of Germany in Bavaria, 5 miles W.N.W. of Nuremberg, at the confluence of the Pegnitz with the Rednitz. It has important and varied manufactures, including mirrors, picture-frames, jewellery, gold-leaf, lead pencils, spectacles, and machinery. Gustavus Adolphus was defeated by Wallenstein in 1632 at Alte Veste, near Fürth. The first steam railway opened in Germany, in 1835, was between Fürth and Nuremberg. Pop. (1925), 74,195.

FURTWAENGLER, Wilhelm, German musician, born in Berlin, 25th Jan., 1886, the son of Adolf Furtwaengler (1853-1907) the archæologist, he early gained a musical reputation, and while yet a young man conducted operas and concerts at Breslau, Zurich, Münich, Strasbourg, Lubeck, Mannhein, Berlin, Frankfort and Vienna. In 1922 he became Director of the Berlin Philharmonic Concerts, and from 1922–28 directed Gewanhaus concerts at Leipzig. He conducted the Philharmonic Orchestra in New York, 1925–27, and Philharmonic concerts in Vienna, 1927–30. He has also conducted in London.

FURZE (A.Sax. *fyrs*), whin, gorse, the common name of the species of the genus Ulex, nat. ord. Leguminosæ. Twelve species have been described, two of which are natives of Britain. The common furze (*U. europæus*) is a well-known low shrubby plant, often very abundant in barren, heathy, sandy, and gravelly soils throughout the west of Europe. The stem is generally 2 or 3 feet high, much branched, and most of the leaves are converted into spines. The flowers are solitary and yellow. It often covers exclusively large tracts of country, and makes a splendid appearance when in flower. It is used as fuel, and sometimes the tops of the branches are used (especially the young tops) as fodder for horses and cattle, after having been beaten or bruised to soften the prickles. The dwarf-furze (*U. nanus*) is found in many parts of the British Isles.

FUSAN, a seaport in Korea, at the south-east extremity of the peninsula. It is the terminus of the railway from Seoul, and is a treaty port. The trade is in cotton, silk, Japanese goods, rice, petroleum, &c. Cod and herring fisheries are extensive. The harbour is good and has been greatly improved. Pop. 113,000 (including about 38,000 Japanese).

FU-SANG, a country referred to in the Chinese work, *Lung Wei Pi Shu.* The trees of Fu-sang are said to be a thousand feet high. Some writers believe that California is referred to.

FUSA'RIUM, a genus of Fungi Imperfecti, including several parasitic species, the most dangerous of which is *F. Lycopersici*, causing the 'sleeping-disease' of the tomato.

FUSA'RO, LAKE OF (the ancient Acherusia Palus), a small Italian lake on the Peninsula of Baiæ, 11 miles w. of Naples. It is supposed to have been the harbour of ancient Cumæ and is still celebrated for its oysters.

FUSE, a tube filled with combustible matter, used in blasting, or to explode shells, mortars, or bombs. There are many varieties in use, such as the fuse used in mining and quarrying, which usually consists of a tube filled with a slow-burning composition, which gradually burns down to the charge; the **concussion** and **percussion fuses** for hollow projectiles, which explode the charge when an object is struck; the **electric fuse**, which is ignited by the passage of an electric spark through it; and **time** or **mechanical fuses**, used in some forms of torpedo, and with such explosives as dynamite and gun-cotton. *See* FUSE, ELECTRIC.

FUSE, ELECTRIC, a device for preventing damage in an electric circuit when the current happens to exceed a safe value. The fuse consists of a wire or strip of metal forming part of the circuit, and so designed in material and dimensions that it carries the ordinary current without being damaged, but melts, fuses, or 'blows' whenever the current becomes too large.

Fuses are generally made of copper, zinc, tin, or lead, or of alloys of these metals, and are usually mounted in a non-inflammable open case of porcelain or metal. The fuse must be of sufficient length to prevent the formation of an arc when the circuit is broken, at least 1 inch to 1½ inches even for low-pressure currents up to 5 ampères. For currents of more than about 600 ampères, fuses are unsuitable, as they have to be bulky to carry such currents, and the molten metal may become dangerous when the fuse blows. Automatic circuit-breakers, though more expensive, are preferable for large currents, and even for small currents when overloads are frequent.

FUSEE', the cone or conical part of a watch or clock, round which is wound the chain or cord. It is a mechanical contrivance for equalizing the power of the mainspring; for as the action of a spring varies with its degree of tension, the power derived from the force of a spring requires to be modified according to circumstances before it can become a proper substitute for a uniform power. In order, therefore, to correct this irregular action of the mainspring, the fusee on which the chain or catgut acts is made somewhat conical, so that its radius at every point may be adapted to the strength of the spring.

FUSELI (fū'se-li), **John Henry** (original name *Füssli*, or *Fuessli*; fūs'lē), a painter, born in 1741 or 1742 at Zürich, died at London, and was buried in St. Paul's Cathedral, 1825. He was educated for the Church, but a political pamphlet written by him and Lavater led to his taking refuge in England in 1765, bent on a literary career. On the advice of Sir Joshua Reynolds he devoted himself to art, went to Italy, and studied there for nearly nine years. He was elected A.R.A. in 1788, R.A. in 1790, lecturer on painting in 1799, and keeper of the Royal Academy in 1804. Among his notable pictures are his contributions to Boydell's *Shakespeare Gallery*, and forty-seven pictures from Milton.

FUSEL-OIL, a liquid of disagreeable odour obtained during the rectification of alcohol from fermentation of sugars and starches. Alcohol produced from potatoes contains the largest amount of the oil, and the constituents and quantity vary according to the source of alcohol and the method of distillation. Fusel-oil distils mainly at temperatures between 105° and 136° C., and consists chiefly of two alcohols, isoamyl alcohol and secondary butyl carbinol, mixed with small quantities of propyl-, butyl-, isobutyl-alcohols, &c. These higher alcohols are deleterious to health, hence their removal from alcohol is necessary if the alcohol is to be used for the preparation of beverages.

FUSIBLE METAL, an alloy, usually of lead, tin, and bismuth, but sometimes containing cadmium also, in such definite proportions as to melt at a given low temperature. The alloy containing lead 32, tin 16, and bismuth 52 melts below the boiling-point of water. In steam-engines, a plug of fusible metal screwed into the crown of the fire-box, so as to melt and allow the steam to blow out the fire if the water gets too low. It is also used for safety-plugs in water-pipes placed in the ceilings of public buildings, or large stores, so that in the event of fire, when the temperature rises, the safety-plugs melt and water is instantly sprayed into the room.

FUSIBLE PORCELAIN, a silicate of alumina and soda obtained from cryolite and sand, fused and worked as glass.

FUSILIERS (Fr. *fusilier*, from *fusil*, gun, musket), formerly soldiers armed with a fusil or light flint-lock musket closely resembling a carabine. The name is given to several regiments in the British army, which differ from other regiments of the line chiefly in the busby worn by officers and other ranks when in full-dress.

FUSING-POINT, or **MELTING-POINT,** the temperature at which a solid melts or liquefies; the temperature at which the solid and liquid phases are in equilibrium. Potassium melts at 144° F., tin at 450°, lead at 622°, zinc at 786°, silver at 1,764°, gold at 1,947°, while cerium and platinum require the temperature of the oxyhydrogen blow-pipe to melt them. Small amounts of impurities always lower the melting-point of a substance.

FUSION, the conversion of a solid body into the liquid state by direct heat, as distinguished from solution, in which the effect is produced by means of a liquid. It is difficult, however, to draw a line between the two, for the main difference is in the temperature, and when a flux is employed all distinction disappears. The term is specially applied to the action of heat on the metals, but it is extended to any solid matter; thus the passage of ice into water at 32° F. is true fusion. There are bodies, like carbon, lime, magnesia, zirconia, and other metallic oxides, which are practically infusible at the temperature attained by the ordinary sources of heat.

FUST, Johann, a goldsmith of Mainz, associated with Gutenberg and Schöffer in connection with the origin of printing. He probably died of the plague in 1466. *See* PRINTING.

FUSTEL DE COULANGES, Numa Denis, French historian, born in Paris in 1830, died in 1889. He was educated in Paris, studied for some time in Athens, and was professor at Strasbourg from 1860 to 1870. In 1878 he became professor at the Sorbonne, and from 1880 to 1889 he was professor at and director of the École Normale. His works include: *Histoire des institutions politiques de l'ancienne France* (1875–92), *La Gaule Romaine* (1888–91), *Questions Historiques* (1893), &c. His most famous work, however, is his *La Cité antique* (1864), wherein he endeavoured to prove, in a somewhat exaggerated way, that the development of the ancient states of Greece was mainly based on religion.

FUSTIAN (O.Fr. *fustaigne*, from *Fustāt*, a suburb of Cairo), a cotton or mixed linen and cotton fabric with a pile like that of velvet but shorter. It includes corduroy, moleskin, and velveteen.

FUSTIC, the wood of the *Chlorophora tinctoria*, a tree of the mulberry order growing in the West Indies. It is a large and handsome tree, and the timber, though, like most other dye-woods, brittle, or at least easily splintered, is hard and strong. It is extensively used as an ingredient in the dyeing of yellow, and is largely imported for that purpose.

Young Fustic is the wood of the *Rhus cotinus* or Venice sumach, a South European shrub with smooth leaves and a remarkable feathery inflorescence. It yields a fine orange colour, which, however, is not durable without a mordant.

FUTHORK (fu̇'thork), the name given to the earliest or runic alphabet in use among the Teutonic or Germanic nations of Northern Europe, so called from its first six letters, f, u, th, o, r, k. Three runic alphabets have been recognized. *See* RUNES.

FUTURE ESTATE. At common law the only kinds of future estates possible were vested and contingent remainders, which were interest in land which waited for and depended upon the determination on some particular (that is, smaller) estate, e.g. it was impossible to give the fee-simple to A until some event, and then to B. All that could be done was to give an estate less than the fee-simple to A and, on the happening of some event, the fee-simple to B, B being said to be entitled to the remainder, but it was possible before the Statute of Uses to give an *equitable* interest until a certain event, or after the happening of some event, such estates if created by means of a use or trust being called springing or shifting uses, and if created by will an executory devise.

After the Statute of Uses the use carried the legal estate and such equitable interests became legal. Since the Law of Property Act, 1925, a legal remainder cannot be created and all kinds of future interests, which could before 1926 be created either in law or in equity, may be created by way of equitable interests.

FUTURISM, a term often loosely applied to the modern movement in art as a whole, but properly describing the doctrines of a group of Italian (mainly Milanese) painters, sculptors, and poets, first published in 1909 in a manifesto signed by F. T. Marinetti, the poet and chief inspirer of the group, and amplified in subsequent manifestos. They hold that every object is the momentary outcome of continuously acting forces, which are indicated by the object's shape. These forces the artist represents by lines on his canvas; and by arranging them to clash, harmonize, or intermingle, he claims to express various states of mind, such as chaotic excitement, happiness, or interest. Colour the Futurists use arbitrarily to assist in conveying these sensations.

The most orthodox of the group is Luigi Russolo; Carlo D. Carra and Giacomo Balla mainly produce descriptive catalogues on canvas, in attractive colour. The work of Umberto Boccioni, both painter and sculptor, is similar, but more attractive in design. Gino Severini, the best known of the Futurists, was formerly notable for his gay and fanciful colour patterns. Of late, he has turned to Cubism, and has even produced some purely academic work. As a movement, Futurism has produced no lasting effect; but some of its doctrines are shared by the English Vorticists.—BIBLIOGRAPHY: U. Boccioni, *Pittura, Scultura Futuriste*; prefaces to *Catalogues of Futurist Exhibitions* in London, 1913 and 1914. In 1920 Marinetti issued *I Manifesti del futurismo* in four vols. in Milan.

FYFFE, Charles Alan, British historian, born in 1845, died in 1892. He was educated at Balliol College, Oxford, was bursar of University College, then studied law, and was called to the Bar in 1876. In the Franco-Prussian War of 1870 he was correspondent for *The Daily News*, and is said to have sent the first account of the battle of Sedan that appeared in print. During the Commune he was nearly shot as a spy. He wrote a *History of Greece* (1875), but is best known for his *History of Modern Europe* (1880–90).

FYLDE (*Fylde*). District of Lancashire. Situated between the estuaries of the rivers Ribble and Wyre, it is mainly an agricultural area.

FYNE (fin), **LOCH,** an arm of the sea in Scotland, in the county of Argyle, running northwards from the Firth of Clyde for about 40 miles. Its depth varies from 12 to 50 fathoms. It is particularly celebrated for its herrings.

FYRD (fürd), in Anglo-Saxon England the military array or land force of the whole nation, comprising all males able to bear arms. The array of the fyrd of each shire was left to the ealdorman.

FYT (fīt), **John,** a Flemish painter and etcher, born at Antwerp in 1609, died there 1661. His subjects were chiefly game, hunting-pieces, dogs, fruit, flowers, and on occasion he painted animals in the pictures of his contemporaries, such as Rubens and Jordaens. His technical skill was great, and his production large. He published three series of etchings of animals.

FYVIE, village of Aberdeenshire. It has a station on the L.N.E. Rly. 38 miles from Aberdeen, and was once a burgh. Here is Fyvie Castle, one of the finest houses in Scotland, restored on a grand scale by Lord Leith of Fyvie. It occupies the site of a castle built in the 12th century or earlier. Pop. 3,180.

FYZABAD, or **FAIZABAD,** (fī-zä-bäd'), a town, British India, in what was formerly the Kingdom of Oude, on the Gogra, 78 miles E. of Lucknow. It was the scene of one of the outbreaks in the Indian Mutiny. Pop., including cantonments, 56,620.

G

G, the seventh letter in the English alphabet. English *g hard* is a guttural mute, the 'voiced' or soft or sonant sound corresponding to the 'breathed' or hard or surd sound *k* (or *c* hard). This sound of *g* is what the letter always has before *a* (except in *gaol*), *o*, *u*, and when initial also before *e* and *i* in all words of English origin, and when final. The *soft* sound of *g*, or that which it more commonly has before *e*, *i*, and *y*, as in *gem*, *gin*, *gymnastics*, is a palatal sound the same as that of *j*, and did not occur in the oldest English or Anglo-Saxon.

G, in music, (a) the fifth note, and dominant of the normal scale of C, called also *sol*; (b) the lowest note of the grave hexachord; in the Guidonian system *gamma ut*; (c) a name of the treble clef, which is seated on the G or second line of the treble staff, and which formerly had the form of G. Notable compositions in this key are: two of Haydn's symphonies; Beethoven's quartet No. 2, the overture to his '*Ruins of Athens*,' and several sonatas; Mozart's symphony; and Mendelssohn's concerto in G minor.

GABA TEPE, a headland on the west coast of Gallipoli. It was on the narrow beach here that the Australian and New Zealand Army Corps made their famous landing on the morning of 25th April, 1915. *See* GALLIPOLI.

GABBRO, a name given by von Buch to an Italian rock consisting essentially of diallage and lime felspar altered to saussurite. It is now applied to any coarsely crystalline igneous rock consisting of a pyroxene and a lime-soda or lime-felspar. The rugged Cuchullin Hills of Skye are largely formed of gabbro.

GABELLE, a name originally given in France to every kind of indirect tax, as on wine and cloth, but at a later period specially applied to the tax upon salt, which, after being frequently imposed as a temporary means of raising money, became under Charles V a permanent impost. Under Henry II nine provinces and three counties purchased perpetual exemption from the tax, but it was only finally suppressed in France by the Constituent Assembly in 1790. About that time, out of 38,000,000 livres raised by farmers-general from this tax 7,000,000 at most came into the Treasury.—Cf. A. Gasquet, *Précis des institutions politiques de l'ancienne France.*

GABES, city and port of Tunis. It stands on the Gulf of Gabes, an opening of the Mediterranean Sea, and is about 200 miles from the city of Tunis. Nearby are enormous salt lakes. Its ancient name was Tacape. Pop. 20,000.

GABLE, pointed or triangular part of the outer wall of a building, at the end of the steeply pitched roof of the Gothic style. It corresponds to the pediment of classical architecture. In many examples of secular Gothic buildings, in Belgium for example, the gable end of the roof is adorned with numerous pinnacles, and ornamented barge-boards are added to the decorative design. Fine examples of ornamented gables are seen also in Tudor buildings.

GABLONZ (gä'blonts),now **JABLONEC,** a town in Bohemia, Czechoslovakia, on the Neisse, famous for its glass industry (imitation pearls and glass ornaments of all kinds). Special instruction is given for this and the bronze manufactures in technical schools. Pop. 33,855.

GABON', THE, or **M'PONGO,** an estuary on the west coast of Africa, opening from the Gulf of Guinea immediately north of the equator. Several rivers discharge themselves into it. The Gabon territory forms part of French Equatorial Africa (French Congo). The chief tribes are the M'pongwa or Gabonese, the Fans, who carry on an active trade with Europeans in ivory, copal, ebony, and dyewoods. The vast swamps render the climate unhealthy, but inland rise some considerable hills with dense jungle-like woods, the abode of the gorilla. The chief station is Libreville. There are several English trading-posts along the estuary (Glass Town, Olemi, &c.), and mission stations of several nations.

GABORIAU, Emile, a French novelist, born 1833, died in Paris 1873. After contributing to the smaller Parisian journals short sketches published under the titles *Ruses d'Amour*, *Les Comédiennes Adorées*, &c., he achieved a considerable success by his novel *Dossier No. 113* (1866). He continued to work this vein in a series of clever stories dealing with crime and its detection: *Le Crime d'Orcival*, *L'Affaire Lerouge, Les Esclaves de Paris, La Vie Infernale, La Corde_au Cou,* and *L'Argent des Autres.*

GAB'RIEL ('hero or man of God'), according to Biblical history, the angel who announced to Zacharias the birth of John, and to Mary the birth of the Saviour. In Jewish mythology he is one of the seven archangels. The rabbins say he is the angel of death for the Israelites, and according to the *Talmud* he is a prince of fire, who presides over thunder and the ripening of fruits. In Mohammedan theology he is one of the four angels employed in writing the divine decrees, and the angel of revelation, in which capacity he dictated the *Koran* to Mohammed.

GAD ('a troop'), one of the twelve tribes of Israel, which took its name from Gad, the son of Jacob and Zillah. At the time of the exodus the tribe numbered 45,650 men of twenty years old and upwards; and as being a pastoral tribe they were assigned a

Gad fly

rich district in Gilead between Reuben and Manasseh. (*See* JOSH. xiii, 24–28.)

GADAMES. See GHADAMES.

GAD'ARA, an ancient city of Palestine, in the Decapolis, about 6 miles S.E. of the Sea of Galilee. It played an important part in the struggles against Antiochus, Alexander Jannæus, and Vespasian, and fell into decay only after the Mohammedan conquest.

GADDI, (1) **Gaddo,** born about 1260, died about 1310, a Florentine painter and worker in mosaic. He was a friend of Cimabue and Giotto, and to him mosaics in the cathedral of Florence and in S. Maria Maggiore, Rome, are ascribed.—(2) **Taddeo,** son of preceding, born 1300, died about 1366, painter, mosaicist, and architect. Instructed by his godfather Giotto, whose assistant he was for twenty-four years, he became one of the most important of his master's successors. He is represented by decorations in S. Croce and S Maria Novella, Florence.—(3) **Agnolo,** son of Taddeo, born after 1333, died 1396. His style was based on that of his father and Giotto, and a reputed visit to Venice has led to his being called

founder of the Venetian school.—(4) **Giovanni,** brother of Agnolo, a painter who died young.

GADE (gä'de), **Niels Wilhelm,** one of the leading Scandinavian composers, born in 1817 at Copenhagen, died in 1890. In 1841 he gained the prize of the Musical Union by his overture entitled *Echoes of Ossian*. He was supported during his studies abroad by a royal stipend, and in 1844 was appointed to succeed Mendelssohn in the direction of the Gewandhaus concerts at Leipzig. In 1850 he was appointed musical director to the King of Denmark, and in 1876 received a life pension. His works, which are Mendelssohnian in character, include seven symphonies, several overtures, sonatas, and quintets; a lyrical drama —*Comala*; a religious cantata—*The Crusaders*, which he conducted at Birmingham in 1876; and an opera— the *Nibelungen.*

GADFLY, two-winged flies of the family Tabanidæ. The females possess piercing mouth-parts, and suck the blood of horses and cattle, causing them much annoyance. They also attack human beings. The large gadfly (*Tabanus bovis*), an allied species (*T. autumnalis*), and the cleg (*Hæmatopota pluvialis*) are especially troublesome. They frequent woods in the neighbourhood of water. The name is sometimes wrongly given to the *warble-flies* (or bot-flies).

GAD'IDÆ, a family of soft-finned fishes, many of which are of economic importance, such as cod (*Gadus morrhua*), haddock (*G. æglefinus*), whiting (*G. merlangus*), hake (*Merluccius vulgāris*), and ling (*Molva vulgāris*). See COD.

GAD'OLINITE, a mineral, a silicate of yttrium, generally containing oxides of cerium, lanthanum, glucinum, and sometimes of other bases. It is usually found in dull, amorphous masses disseminated through granite; is black, or very dark green, with a resinous lustre. It was named after the mineralogist Gadolin, professor at Åbo, 1785–1822.

GADSHILL, an eminence in the county of Kent, on the Gravesend road, 3½ miles north-west by west of Rochester. In olden times there were woods on either side of the ascent, and these used to be the lurking-place of highwaymen. Shakespeare, in *Henry IV*, makes it the scene of the robberies of Prince Hal and Falstaff. Charles Dickens spent the last years of his life (from 1860 to 1870) at Gadshill House close by.

GADWALL', the common name of *Chaulelasmus streperus*, a species of duck not so large as the mallard, with long pointed wings and a vigorous and rapid flight. North America as far down as South Carolina is its favourite habitat; but it also ranges through the northern half of the Old World. It is not often found in Britain and Ireland.

GAEKWAR, or GAIKWAR (gīk-wär). *See* BARODA

GAELIC (găl-ik), the name of a Celtic language spoken in the Highlands of Scotland, Ireland, and the Isle of Man. Gadhel or Gael is the only name by which those who speak the Gaelic language are known to themselves. By way of distinction the Highlanders of Scotland call themselves Gael Albinnich (Gaels of Albin), and in their Celtic language the people of Ireland call themselves Gael Erinnich (Gaels of Erin). *See* CELTIC CIVILIZATIONS; CELTIC LITERATURE.

GAËTA(gà-ā′tả; anciently**CAIETA**), a strongly fortified seaport town of South Italy, province of Caserta, on the Gulf of Gaëta, the seat of a bishop, 45 miles north-west of Naples. It is a place of great antiquity, was a favourite resort of the wealthy families of Rome, and since the fifth century has had a prominent place in the history of Italy, and especially in that of the Kingdom of Naples. Francis II, the last Bourbon King of Naples, was besieged at Gaëta by Garibaldi in 1860. Pop. 6,000.

GÆTULIA, the ancient name of an extensive region of Africa, on the southern slope of Mount Atlas. It corresponds to the modern Biledulgerid, the southern part of Morocco,

Gadshill
Home of Charles Dickens

and the northern part of the Sahara. It was inhabited by warlike tribes, who are supposed to have been the ancestors of the modern Tuaregs of the Sahara oases.

GAFF, a spar used in ships to extend the upper edge of fore-and-aft sails which are not set on stays. The

fore-end of the gaff, where it embraces the mast, is termed the *jaw*, the outer end the *peak*. The jaw forms a semicircle, and is secured in its position by a jaw-rope passing round the mast.

Gaff

GAILLAC (gả-yák), a town of Southern France, department of Tarn, on the right bank of the Tarn. It exports a good red table-wine, the district abounding in vineyards. Pop. 7,740.

GAILLARDE (gả-yärd; It. *Gagliarda*), a lively Italian dance, in triple time; also called, from its alleged origin, *Romanesque*. It is mentioned by Shakespeare, *Twelfth Night*, i, 3, 129, and *Henry V*, i, 2, 252.

GAINSBOROUGH, Thomas, English painter, born at Sudbury, in Suffolk, 1727, died in London 1788. He was trained under the engraver Gravelot and the painter Hayman, and worked for a short time in London. He then returned to Suffolk, and married, in 1746, Margaret Burr, who brought with her a competence. In 1760 he went to Bath, and at once became a popular and successful portrait painter.

In 1774 he moved to London, and shared with Reynolds and Romney the patronage of the fashionable world. An original member of the Royal Academy, he contributed regularly to its exhibitions until 1783, when a dispute over the hanging of a picture caused his refusal to exhibit further. His portraits and landscape (in which latter his naturalism makes him a pioneer) are marked by a subtle handling of tone, and a delicate feeling for colour, which put him in the front rank of English artists.—BIBLIOGRAPHY: Sir W. Armstrong, *Gainsborough and his place in English Art*; W. T. Whitley, *Thomas Gainsborough*.

GAINSBOROUGH, a market town, England, county of Lincoln, 19½ miles north-west of the town of Lincoln, on the Trent, which is navigable by vessels of from 150 to 200 tons, and is connected with the main canal system. An aegre or bore comes up the Trent here twice a day. Among the chief buildings are the parish church, the town hall, and the old hall or manor-house, containing the rooms of the literary and scientific institute—a quaint building. There are oil-mills, breweries, rope-walks, foundries and malt-houses. Water is obtained from artesian wells. Gainsborough gives its name to a parliamentary division of the county (Parts of Lindsey). (Pop. (1931), 18,684.

GAIRDNER, James, historian, was born in 1828 at Edinburgh, where he

Thomas Gainsborough

received his education, died in 1912. In 1864 he entered the Public Record Office, and in 1859 became an Assistant Keeper. He edited, for the Master of the Rolls, *Memorials of Henry VII* (1853), and *Letters and Papers of the Reigns of Richard III and Henry VII* (1861–3), and on Professor Brewer's death was appointed to succeed him as editor of the *Calendar of State Papers of Henry VIII* (London, 1862–1905). He also edited the *Paston Letters* (1872–5, with supplementary volume, 1900), *Historical Collections of a Citizen of London, Three Fifteenth Century Chronicles*; and was the author of the *Houses of Lancaster and York* (Epochs of Modern History Series), *The Life and Reign of Richard III*, *England* (Early Chroniclers of Europe Series), *Studies in English History* (with Spedding), *Henry VII*, *The English Church in the Sixteenth Century to the Death of Mary* (1902), and *Lollardy*

and the Reformation in England (1908 –11); besides writing numerous articles in the *Dictionary of National Biography*. He was an LL.D. of Edinburgh, and was made a C.B. in 1900.

GAIRDNER, Sir William Tennant, sanitary reformer and physician, was born in Edinburgh in 1824, died in 1907. Like his younger brother James (q.v.), he was educated in his native town. In 1845 he took his M.D. degree at the university, and won a gold medal, and from 1846 to 1862 was connected with the Edinburgh Royal Infirmary as resident medical officer and pathologist. In the latter year he was appointed to the chair of medicine in Glasgow University, which he held until his resignation in 1900.

The publication in 1862 of his book *Public Health in relation to Air and Water* led to his appointment as medical officer to the city of Glasgow, an entirely new post, during his tenure of which (1863–72) epidemics were combated and the sanitary arrangements of the city completely revolutionized. He was made a K.C.B. in 1898, and was honorary physician-in-ordinary to the king in Scotland. He is the author of *Clinical Medicine* (1862), *Lectures to Practitioners* (with Dr. J. Coats, 1888), *The Physician as Naturalist* (1889), and *The Three Things that Abide* (1903).

GAIRDNER, lake of Australia. It is in the south of the state of South Australia, and is a salt water lake. It is about 100 miles long, and its extreme breadth about 40 miles.

GAIRLOCH, opening of the Atlantic on the west coast of Scotland. It runs for about 7 miles into the county of Ross and Cromarty. At its head is the village of Gairloch, a tourist resort.

GAIUS, a Roman lawyer of the time of Adrian and Antoninus Pius, of whose life very little is known. Of his numerous works, his *Institutes* are particularly important; first, as having been for centuries, down to the time of Justinian, one of the most common manuals of law; secondly, as having been the foundation of the official compendium of the law which occupies an important place in the reform of the judicial system by Justinian: and thirdly, as the only tolerably full, systematic, and well-arranged source of the old Roman law. The bulk of the work in MS. was discovered in 1816 by Niebuhr. An English translation by E. Poste appeared in 1885.—Cf. J. Ortolan, *Législation romaine*.

GALACTOSE ($C_6H_{12}O_6$), a sugar formed together with glucose when milk-sugar or lactose $(C_{12}H_{22}O_{11})$ is boiled with dilute acids.

GALAGO (ga-lă'go), the native name of a genus of lemurs found in Africa. The species, which are nocturnal in their habits, have long hind-legs, great eyes, and large membranous ears. The great galago (*G. crassicaudatus*) is as large as a rabbit. They live in trees, and are sought after as food in Africa.

GALAHAD, SIR, the son of Lancelot and Elaine in the Arthurian romances. He was the noblest of the Knights of the Round Table, a model of purity and chivalry. Having set out on the quest of the Holy Grail, Sir Galahad redressed all wrongs and grievances which he came across on his journey. He is the hero of Walter Map's *Quest of the Holy Grail*.

GALAN'GA, or GALANGAL ROOT, a dried rhizome brought from China and used in medicine, being an aromatic stimulant of the nature of ginger. It is mostly produced by *Alpinia officinarum*, a flag-like plant about 4 feet high, with narrow lanceolate leaves and simple racemes of white flowers. The greater galangal is the rhizome of *A. Galanga*.

GALA P'AGOS (the Spanish for 'tortoises'), a group of thirteen islands of volcanic origin in the North Pacific Ocean, about 600 miles west of the coast of Ecuador, to which they belong; area, 2,868 sq. miles. The most important are Albemarle, 75 miles long by 15 miles broad, and rising 4,700 feet above the sea; Indefatigable, Chatham, Charles, James, and Narborough. Of these some are used by the Republic of Ecuador as penal settlements. Many of the fauna and flora of the islands are peculiar to them, the most remarkable being a large lizard and the elephant tortoise. Pop. (1931), 2,000.

GALASHIELS (gal-a-shēlz') a burgh in Scotland, one of the Hawick district of parliamentary burghs, in the county of Selkirk, on both sides of the Gala, about a mile above its confluence with the Tweed, 4 miles from Melrose, and 33 miles S.S.E. of Edinburgh. It is noted for its manufactures of tweeds, plaids, shawls, and woollen yarns. The town, which is of rather irregular construction, lies in a narrow valley, and is about 2 miles long. Pop. (1931), 13,102.

GALATE'A, in classic mythology, the daughter of Nereus and Doris, who rejected the suit of the Cyclops Polyphemus and gave herself to the Sicilian shepherd Acis. The monster, having surprised them, crushed Acis beneath a rock. (*See* Austin Dobson's *Tale of Polypheme*.) *Galatea* is also

the name of a statue said to have been endowed with life by Venus at the prayer of the sculptor Pygmalion. This story, which is derived from Ovid, *Metamorphoses*, x, 243, is the subject of a well-known comedy by Sir W. S. Gilbert, produced in 1871.

GALATIA, the ancient name of an extensive region in Asia Minor, so called from its Gallic inhabitants, who in the first place formed part of the invading hordes of Gauls under Brennus in the third century B.C. These were compelled by Attalus, King of Pergamos, to settle within well-defined limits between Paphlagonia, Pontus, Cappadocia, Lycaonia, Phrygia, and Bithynia. With the Gauls were intermingled a considerable proportion of Greeks; hence the inhabitants were often called Gallogræci, as well as Galatians.

GALATIANS, EPISTLE TO THE, one of the most important epistles of St. Paul, written probably about A.D. 56, soon after his second visit to Galatia, recorded in *Acts*, xviii, 23. It was directed against the spread of Judaistic practices in the Galatian churches, and especially against the practice of circumcision. It has been the subject of numerous commentaries, by Luther, Winer, Meyer, Ellicott, Alford, Drummond, and others.—Cf. article in *Encyclopædia Biblica*.

GALATZ, or GALACZ, a town and port of Rumania, in Moldavia, on the left bank of the Danube, between the confluence of the Siret and Prut. It consists of an old and a new town, the latter on a hill dominating the river and commanding a fine view of the Balkans. The harbour, accessible to vessels drawing 15 feet, is well frequented, and an emporium of trade between Austria, Russia, and Constantinople. The trade was formerly entirely in the hands of the Greeks, but now many British and other foreign houses have established themselves.

The chief exports are grain (principally maize), wine, planks and deals, and tallow. The imports are chiefly British manufactures, sugar, tin plates, iron and steel, coal, oil, fruits, tobacco, fish, glass-ware, leather, coarse cloth. When made a free port in 1834, it had only 8,000 inhabitants, but the population now is 101,148. It ceased to be a free port in 1883.

GALA WATER, river of Scotland. It rises in Midlothian, and flows S. from the Moorfoot hills, for 21 miles through Roxburghshire and Selkirkshire. It joins the Tweed just below Galashiels.

GAL'AXY (*Via Lactea*, or Milky Way), in astronomy, that long luminous track which is seen at night stretching across the heavens from horizon to horizon, and which, when fully traced, is found to encompass the heavenly sphere like a girdle. This luminous appearance is occasioned by a multitude of stars so distant and blended as to be separately distinguishable only in telescopes. At one part of its course it divides into two great branches, which remain apart for a distance of 150° and then reunite; there are also many other smaller branches that it gives off. At one point it spreads out very widely, exhibiting a fan-like expanse of interlacing branches nearly 20° broad; this terminates abruptly and leaves here a kind of gap. At several points are seen dark spots in the midst of some of the brightest portions; one of the most easily distinguished of these dark spots has long been known as the 'coal-sack.'

The appearance of the Milky Way shows that our sun is nearly in its medial plane, and probably not far proportionately from its centre. Some astronomers believe that the spiral nebulæ, of which the Great Nebula in Andromeda is to our view the largest, are external galaxies, and that our galaxy seen from one of them would present merely the appearance of a spiral nebula.

GALBA, Servius Sulpicius, Roman emperor, successor of Nero, born 3 B.C. He was made prætor (A.D. 20), and afterwards Governor of Aquitania, and in A.D. 33 was raised to the consulship through the influence of Livia Drusilla, the wife of Augustus. Caligula appointed him general in Germany, and Claudius sent him in A.D. 45 as proconsul to Africa, his services there obtaining him the honours of a triumph. He then lived in retirement till the middle of Nero's reign, when the emperor appointed him Governor of Hispania Tarraconensis, but soon after ordered him to be secretly assassinated. Galba revolted; the death of Nero followed (A.D. 68), and he himself was chosen emperor by the prætorian cohorts in Rome. He went directly to Rome, but soon made himself unpopular by cruelty and avarice, and he was slain in the forum in A.D. 69 at the age of seventy-two.

GAL'BANUM, or **GALBAN** (Gr. *chalbane*, Heb. *khalab*, to be fat), a fetid gum resin procured from at least two species of umbelliferous plants, which are probably *Ferula galbaniflua* and *F. rubricaulis*. It consists of the 'tears' of gum resin which exude spontaneously from the stem, especially in its lower part and about the bases of the leaves. It is brought from the Levant, Persia, and India, and is administered internally as a stimulating expectorant. It is also used in the arts, as in the manufacture of varnish. It is supposed to be yielded by other umbellifers, among which are named *Ferulāgo galbanifěra, Opoidiagalbanifera,* and *Bubon Galbanum.*

GALCHAS, a number of tribes dwelling on the plateaus and in the valleys of Kohistan, in Ferghana, and on the basins of the Amu Darya and Zarafshan. They are of Aryan stock linguistically, and physically seem to belong to the Celtic-European or Alpine race. They are brachycephalic, have blue, brown, or grey eyes, aquiline noses, black, chestnut or red hair, and white or brown complexions. They are mostly Sunni-Mohammedans by religion.—BIBLIOGRAPHY: Ripley, *Races of Europe*; Charles Eugene D'Ujfalvy de Mezoe-Koevsd, article in *Revue d'Anthropologie* (1879).

GALDOS, Benito Perez, Spanish novelist, born on one of the Canary Islands in 1845, died in 1920. He studied law at Madrid, but soon turned to literature, and at first devoted himself to the patriotic historical story. He thus produced in 1871 his first novel, *La Fontana de Oro*, which was followed by a series of novels under the general title of *Episodios nacionales* (20 vols., 1872-80). Among his other works are: *Doña Perfecta, Gloria, Tormento, Tristana,* &c. He also wrote dramas: *La Realidad, Los Condenados, Electra,* &c. The production of *Electra* was prohibited on account of its anticlerical tendencies.

GALE, a plant of the genus Myrĭca, nat. ord. Myricaceæ. Sweet gale or bog-myrtle (*M. Gale*) is a shrub from 1 to 3 feet high, which exhales a rather pleasant aromatic odour, and grows on wet heaths abundantly. In America the name is applied to an allied plant, *Comptonia asplenifolia. See* CANDLEBERRY.

GALE'MYS. *See* MUSK-RAT.

GALEN, properly **CLAUDIUS GALENUS,** a Greek physician, born A.D. 130 at Pergamus, in Asia Minor. He is called Gallien by mediæval writers. His father, Nicon, an architect and mathematician, gave him a careful education, and he studied under physicians in Smyrna, Corinth, and Alexandria, afterwards visiting Cilicia, Phœnicia, and Palestine. He returned in 158 to Pergamus, where he received a public appointment, but five years later went to Rome, and there acquired great celebrity by his cures.

Driven thence by envy, he again travelled for some time and resumed his labours in his native town, but was soon after invited to Aquileia by the Emperors Marcus Aurelius and Lucius Verus (A.D. 169). He followed Marcus Aurelius to Rome, and appears to have remained there for some years before finally retiring to Pergamus. The closing part of his life, however, is obscure. One Arabic writer says that he died in Sicily, and Suidas states that he died at the age of seventy, and accordingly in the year A.D. 200 or 201; but it is not improbable that he lived longer.

The writings attributed to Galen include eighty-three treatises acknowledged to be genuine, forty-five manifestly spurious; nineteen of doubtful genuineness, and fifteen commentaries on different works of Hippocrates, besides a large number of short pieces and fragments, probably in great part spurious. The most valuable of his works were those dealing with anatomy and physiology, and he was the first to establish the consultation of the pulse in diagnosis and prognosis. Till the middle of the sixteenth century his authority in medicine was supreme.—Cf. N. F. J. Eloy, *Dictionnaire historique de la médecine*, s.v. *Galien*.

GALE'NA (Pb S), mineral sulphide of lead, found both in masses and crystallized in cubes, often combined with octahedra; its colour is bluish-grey, like lead, but brighter; lustre metallic; soft, but brittle, breaking along its cleavage-planes parallel to the faces of the cube; specific gravity, 7·5; effervesces with nitric and hydrochloric acids. When pure, it contains about 86·6 per cent of lead and 13·4 of sulphur, but some silver is generally present, and the commercial value of the ore depends greatly on the amount. Antimony, zinc, iron, and bismuth may be present. In the British Isles, galena often occurs in the Carboniferous Limestone, as in Derbyshire. Among the most famous deposits are those of the silver-producing districts of Leadville, Colorado; Utah; Idaho; Burma; and the Broken Hill districts of New South Wales and Rhodesia.

GALE'NA, a town of the United States, in Illinois, near the borders of Wisconsin, in the great lead region, situated on both sides of the Fevre River, 6 miles above its junction with the Mississippi. Pop. 4,742.—Another Galena, also named from lead-mines, is in the south-east of Kansas. Pop. 4,835.

GA'LENISTS, the name of the body of controversialists who, appealing to the authority of Galen, opposed the introduction of chemical and alchemical methods of treatment into medicine. They adhered to the ancient formulas, which prescribed preparations of herbs and roots by infusion or decoction, while the chemists professed to extract essences and quintessences by calcination, digestion, or fermentation. Neither body possessed a monopoly of the truth, and modern medicine combines the better elements in each method.

GALEOP'SIS, the generic name of the hemp-nettles, a genus of plants, of the nat. ord. Labiatæ, characterized by the equally five-toothed calyx. They are herbaceous plants with square stems, usually clothed with sharp bristly hairs, nettle-like leaves on long stalks, and red, white, or yellow labiate flowers. There are about twelve species, three of which are natives of Britain. The handsomest of these (*G. versicolor*) is abundant in Scotland, especially in the Highlands; it has showy yellow flowers, with a broad purple spot on the lower lip.

GALERIE DES GLACES, a famous gallery in the Palace of Versailles. It is one of the most magnificent rooms in the world, is 240 feet long, 40 feet wide, and 42 feet high, is profusely ornamented, and is lighted by seventeen large windows. It derives its name from the huge mirrors which are on one side of the room, opposite and corresponding to the number of windows on the other. The ceiling was painted by Charles Lebrun (1619–1690). Until the Revolution balls and fêtes were given in the Galerie des Glaces, and during the Second Empire a ball was given here in Aug., 1855, in honour of Queen Victoria. On 18th Jan., 1871, King William I of Prussia was proclaimed German Emperor in the Galerie des Glaces, and on 28th June, 1919, the German delegates signed the Peace Treaty with the Allies in this apartment.

GALERIUS, a Roman emperor. *See* MAXIMIANUS II.

GALESBURG, a city of the United States, in Knox county, Illinois. It has railroad workshops, iron-foundries, and manufactures of agricultural implements. Knox College and Lombard University are situated here. Pop. 28,830.

GALEUS, the genus including topes, small sharks of the family Carchariidæ. The common tope (*Galeus canis*) is abundant in British seas. It is 4 to 6 feet long, and feeds on small fishes and various invertebrates on the sea-bottom.

GALICIA (Pol. *Halicz*), a former province of the Austrian Empire, since 1919 absorbed in Poland and Ukraine (q.v.). It is bounded by Podolia,

Volhynia, Bessarabia, and the Carpathians; has an area of 30,321 sq. miles, and a pop. of 8,211,770.

Physical Features. The great physical features of the country are, in a manner, determined by the Carpathians, which form a long and irregular curve on the south, and send out branches into Galicia. Farther to the north the hills subside rapidly, and finally merge into vast plains. It has several considerable rivers, those in the west being affluents of the Vistula, those in the east, of the Danube and Dniester.

Climate and Animals. The climate is severe, particularly in the south, where more than one of the Carpathian summits rise beyond the snow-line. The summers are very warm but comparatively short. The soil in general is fertile, and yields abundant crops of cereals, hemp, flax, and tobacco. The domestic animals include great numbers of horned cattle, and a fine hardy breed of horses. Sheep are in general neglected; but goats, swine, and poultry abound, and bee-keeping is practised on a large scale. Bears and wolves are still found in the forests; and all the lesser kinds of game are in abundance.

Productions. The minerals include marble, copper, calamine, coal, iron, petroleum, and rock-salt. Only the last two are of much importance. Rock-salt is particularly abundant. The most important mines have their central locality at Wieliczka. Manufactures have not made much progress. The spinning and weaving of flax and hemp prevail to a considerable extent on the confines of Silesia. Distilleries exist in every quarter.

The Roman Catholics and the Greek Catholics are the chief religious bodies. The chief educational establishments are the University of Lemberg (Lwow) and that of Cracow. The principal towns are Lemberg, the capital, and Cracow.

History. After being the field of continuous strife between Russians, Poles, and Hungarians, Galicia continued a Polish dependency from 1382 until the first partition of Poland, in 1772, when it was acquired by Austria. Until 1918 Galicia was one of the Cis-Leithan provinces of the Austrian Empire, and was represented in the *Reichsrath* by 63 Deputies, while the affairs peculiar to itself were deliberated and determined upon by its own *Landtag* or Diet. During the European War Galicia was the scene of heavy fighting and of extended operations by the Russians. Since 1919 it has been a part of Poland. *See* GALICIAN CAMPAIGN; POLAND; UKRAINE; EUROPEAN WAR.

GALICIA, one of the old provinces of Spain, situated in the north-west, and bounded north and west by the Atlantic, south by Portugal, and east by the old provinces of Asturias and Leon. It is now divided into the provinces of Coruña, Lugo, Orense, and Pontevedra; area, 11,254 sq. miles. Its broken coast, which has a length of about 240 miles, lies open to the Atlantic, and there are several fine natural harbours, of which Ferrol is one of the finest naval ports in Europe.

The surface is mountainous, and the proportion of good arable land limited; but fruit, particularly apples and pears, nuts, walnuts, and chestnuts, is abundant; and the culture of the vine is common in all the lower districts. The higher mountain slopes are generally covered with fine forests, which feed large herds of swine, and afford haunts to boars and wolves. Both manufactures and trade are insignificant. The chief town is Santiago de Compostella. The natives (Gallegos) speak an uncouth patois, which other Spaniards scarcely understand. The peasantry are very poor, and many leave for service in other parts of Spain. Pop. 2,125,000.—Cf. W. Wood, *A Corner of Spain*.

GALICIAN CAMPAIGN. One of the first acts of the Russian Empire after the declaration of war in 1914 was to invade the Austrian province of Galicia. In the beginning this invasion was successful, Przemysl being invested by 24th Sept., and a rapid advance made towards Cracow and the Carpathians. By the 28th Krosno had been captured, and the Dukla Pass occupied. The Austrians now took the offensive, drove the Russians back to the River San, and forced them to raise the siege of Przemysl (11th Oct.). In that and the following month the Russians, in their new position, not only withstood the Austrian attacks, but forced their army to retreat on Cracow, and by 12th Nov. were again investing Przemysl, and thrusting the Austrians from the line of the Dunajec.

The Austrians now began an offensive from Cracow but were severely defeated, and, by the end of the month, all the Carpathian passes were again in Russian hands. In December a further Russian attempt was made on Cracow, but owing to a vigorous Austro-German counter-stroke from the direction of Hungary this was unsuccessful. At Przemysl, meanwhile, the Austrians were making violent but ineffectual sorties from the town, and the year ended with an Austrian retreat and the reoccupation of the Carpathian passes by the Russians.

In Jan., 1915, the Russian army was aligned along the Carpathians as far as Bukovina, and was successfully repelling Austrian attacks; on 22nd March the Russians captured Przemysl, but lost it, together with most of their other gains, in June, and finally, after some intermittent successes, took up a new position (Grodek) covering Lemberg. On the last day of the year the Russian general, Ivanoff, started another offensive on a front of 250 miles, from the Pripet marshes in Poland through Galicia to the Rumanian frontier, in which both sides claimed successes. By the end of March, 1916, this offensive had died down—partly owing to the thaw—and in April General Brusiloff succeeded Ivanoff.

In June a fresh offensive was again started on the same front, and by August the Russians claimed to have

the River Jordan, on the south by Samaria, on the west by the Mediterranean Sea and Phœnicia, and on the north by Syria and the Mountains of Lebanon. It was in some sense the cradle of Christianity, Nazareth, Cana, Capernaum, Nain, and other places being intimately associated with the life of Christ. The inhabitants of this province, who were mostly farmers or fishermen, on account of their ignorance were despised by the Jews, who, by way of contempt, called Christians, at first, *Galileans*. At present Galiee is one of the ten districts of Palestine.

GALILEE, a portico or chapel annexed to a church, used for various purposes. In it public penitents were stationed, dead bodies deposit-

Sea of Galilee

taken nearly 400,000 prisoners and some 400 guns, besides capturing the fortresses of Lutsk, Buczacz, Czernowitz, and others. In August Rumania entered the war, and by September her armies were in touch with the Russians. The year closed with heavy fighting in favour of the Austro-Germans.

During the first half of 1917 the Germans were particularly active in Galicia, and the Russians were gradually forced back, Kalusz, 30 miles s.w. of the River Dniester, being evacuated in July. This was the beginning of the end. The Russian troops became insubordinate, with the natural result that the retreat degenerated into a rout, and by the end of the month the remaining Russian troops were once more beyond their own frontier and Galicia wa clear. *See* EUROPEAN WAR.

GAL'ILEE, in the time of Jesus Christ, the most northern province of Palestine, bounded on the east by

ed previously to their interment, and religious processions formed; and it was only in the galilee that in certain religious houses the female relatives of the monks were allowed to converse with them, or even to attend divine service. The only English buildings to which the term galilee is applied are attached to the cathedrals of Durham, Ely, Lincoln, Salisbury, and Wells.

GALILEE, SEA OF, also called Sea of Chinnereth or Chinneroth, and the Lake of Gennesaret or Tiberias, a pear-shaped freshwater lake in Central Palestine, 12½ miles long by 7½ miles broad. It was apparently formed by subsidence attended with volcanic disturbance; and is 682 feet below the level of the Mediterranean. On the east the coasts are nearly 2,000 feet high, deeply furrowed by ravines but flat along the summit. The whole basin is bleak and monotonous, and has a scathed volcanic look, the cliffs and rocks along the shore being of hard porous basalt. At the time of Christ there were on its shores nine flourishing cities, of which seven are now uninhabited ruins, while Magdala and Tiberias are both in a poverty-stricken condition. The lake still abounds in fish, but the fishery is neglected.—Cf. G. A. Smith, *Historical Geography of the Holy Land.*

GALILEI (găl-i-lă′ē), **GALILEO**, a most distinguished Italian physicist, born 18th Feb., 1564, at Pisa, died 8th Jan., 1642. His father, Vincenzo Galilei, a nobleman of Florence, procured him an excellent education in literature and the arts, and in 1581 he entered the University of Pisa.

At nineteen the swinging of a lamp in Pisa Cathedral led him to investigate the laws of the oscillation of the pendulum, which he subsequently applied to the measurement of time;

Galileo

and in 1586 the works of Archimedes suggested his invention of the hydrostatic balance. He now devoted his attention exclusively to mathematics and natural science, and in 1589 was made professor of mathematics in the University of Pisa. In 1592 he was appointed professor of mathematics in Padua, where he continued eighteen years, and his lectures acquired European fame. Here he made the important discovery that the spaces through which a body falls, in equal times, increase as the numbers 1, 3, 5, 7. If he did not invent he improved the thermometer, and made some interesting observations on the magnet.

To the telescope, which in Holland remained not only imperfect but useless, he gave a new importance. He noted the irregularity of the moon's surface, and taught his scholars to measure the height of its mountains by their shadow. A particular nebula he resolved into individual stars, and conjectured that the Milky Way might be resolved in the same manner.

His most remarkable discovery was that of Jupiter's satellites (1610), and he observed, though imperfectly, the ring of Saturn. He also detected the sun's spots, and inferred, from their regular advance from east to west, the rotation of the sun, and the inclination of its axis to the plane of the ecliptic. In 1610 Cosmo II, Grand-Duke of Tuscany, appointed him grand-ducal mathematician and philosopher, and with increased leisure he lived sometimes in Florence, and sometimes at the country seat of his friend Salviata, where he gained a decisive victory for the Copernican system by the discovery of the varying phases of Mercury, Venus, and Mars.

In 1611 he visited Rome for the first time, where he was honourably received; but on his return to Florence he became more and more involved in controversy, which gradually took a theological turn. The monks preached against him, and in 1616 he found himself again obliged to proceed to Rome, where he is said to have pledged himself to abstain from promulgating his astronomical views. In 1623 Galileo replied to an attack upon him in his *Saggiatore*, a masterpiece of eloquence, which drew upon him the fury of the Jesuits.

In 1632, with the permission of the Pope, he published a dialogue expounding the Copernican system as against the Ptolemaic. A congregation of cardinals, monks, and mathematicians, all sworn enemies of Galileo, examined his work, condemned it as highly dangerous, and summoned him before the tribunal of the Inquisition. The veteran philosopher was compelled to go to Rome early in 1633, and was condemned to renounce upon his knees the truths he had maintained. At the moment when he arose, he is said (but this is doubtful) to have exclaimed, in an undertone, stamping his foot, "*E pur si muove!*" (and yet it moves!). Upon this he was sentenced to the dungeons of the Inquisition for an indefinite time, and every week, for three years, was to repeat the seven penitential psalms of David.

After a few days' detention his sentence of imprisonment was commuted to banishment to the villa of the Grand-Duke of Tuscany at Rome, and then to the archiepiscopal palace at Sienna. He was afterwards allowed to return to his residence at Arcetri, near Florence, where he employed his last years principally in the study of mechanics and projectiles.

The results are found in two important works on the laws of motion, the foundation of the present system of physics and astronomy. At the same time he tried to make use of Jupiter's satellites for the calculation of longitudes; and though he brought nothing to perfection in this branch, he was the first who reflected systematically on such a method of fixing geographical longitudes. He was at this time afflicted with a disease in his eyes, one of which was wholly blind, and the other almost useless, when, in 1637, he discovered the libration of the moon. Domestic troubles and disease embittered the last years of Galileo's life. His remains were ultimately deposited in the church of Sta Croce, at Florence. A complete edition of Galileo's works appeared in 20 volumes at Florence, 1890–1909.— BIBLIOGRAPHY: P. Chasles, *Galileo Galilei*; Sir David Brewster, *Martyrs to Science, or the Lives of Galileo, Tycho Brahe, and Kepler*; J. J. Fahie, *Galileo; his Life and Work*; W. W. Bryant, *Galileo.*

GAL'INGALE, a name applied to a kind of sedge, the *Cyperus longus*, or to its tubers, which contain a bitter principle, and have tonic and stomachic properties. They also yield a perfume. *See* CYPERUS.

GAL'IPOT, or FRENCH TURPENTINE, the long, soft, stalactitic pieces of resin which form down the sides of the *Pinus maritima* by evaporation of part of the volatile oil.

GALL, Franz Joseph, the founder of phrenology, born in 1758 in Tiefenbrunn, in Baden, died in 1828. He studied medicine, and practised at Vienna as a physician, where he made himself favourably known by his *Philosophisch-medicinische Untersuchungen* (1791). After a series of comparisons of the skulls both of men and animals, he advanced the theory that it was possible to locate definitely twenty mental faculties.

For some time he confined himself to lecturing on the subject, first in Vienna, and afterwards in his travels through Germany. He then accompanied Dr. Spurzheim, in 1807, to Paris, where he published with his friend, in 1810, the *Anatomie et physiologie du système nerveux en général, et du cerveau en particulier*; and in 1812 his own *Des dispositions innées de l'âme et de l'esprit, ou du matérialisme*. Spurzheim also published, in London, a work upon his own and Gall's discoveries, which met with severe criticism but extended their views, and at least gave an impulse to the accurate anatomical study of the brain. *See* PHRENOLOGY

GALL, ST. (Ger. *St. Gallen*), a northeastern frontier canton in Switzerland, abutting on Lake Constance; partly bounded by the Rhine, and enclosing the canton of Appenzell. Its area is 785 sq. miles. In the south it is one of the loftiest Alpine districts of Switzerland, and in other quarters is more or less mountainous. It belongs wholly to the basin of the Rhine, in the valley of which the climate is comparatively mild, while in the mountainous districts it is very rigorous. Wood and good pasture are found on the mountains; on the lower slopes and valleys, vines and orchard fruits, and corn, maize, hemp, and flax are grown. The manufactures are chiefly cotton and linen goods, particularly fine muslins. The constitution is one of the most democratic in Switzerland. The canton sends fifteen representatives to the National Council. German is the language spoken. Pop. (1930), 286,362.

GALL, ST. the capital and the see of a bishop, is situated on the Steinach, 2,165 feet above sea-level. It contains an old cathedral, now completely modernized, and an old abbey partly converted into public offices, but containing also the bishop's residence and episcopal library with valuable manuscripts. The manufactures consist chiefly of cotton goods, more especially embroidered muslins and prints; and the town is the entrepôt both for its own canton and those of Appenzell and Thurgau. It is of ancient origin, having grown up around the abbey of St. Gall, founded by an Irish monk of that name about the beginning of the seventh century. This abbey for several centuries held one of the highest places in the Benedictine order. Pop. (1930), 63,947.

GALLAIT (gä́l-lä), **Louis**, Belgian historical painter, born 1810, died 1887. He studied at his native town Tournai, Antwerp, and Paris, where he acquired a name by his portraits as well as his genre and historical paintings. Among his earlier pictures of note were: *Christ restoring Sight to a Blind Man*; followed by the *Temptation of St. Anthony*; *The Dead Bodies of Counts Egmont and Horn*; *The Prisoner's Family*; *The Last Moments of Count Egmont*; *Alva signing Death-warrants*; and lastly (1882), *The Plague at Tournai*. His work is popular and melodramatic, and of no great artistic interest.

GALLAND (gä́l-äṅ), **Antoine**, a French Oriental scholar, born in Picardy in 1646, died in 1715. He is principally known for his translation of the *Arabian Nights' Entertainments* (in 12 vols., 1704–17), the first into any European language. Among his other writings are a *Treatise on Medals and Coins*; *Tableau de l'empire Ottoman*; *De l'origine du café*; *Paroles remarquables, bons mots et maximes des orientaux*; and the *Contes et fables*

Indiennes de Bidpaï et de Lokman. In 1709 he was appointed professor of Arabic at the Collège Royal at Paris, and died while engaged in translating the *Koran.*

GALLAS, or **OROMA** (*Ilm' orma,* Sons of the Brave), a numerous and powerful Ethiopian race, chiefly inhabiting a territory in East Africa, lying south of Abyssinia proper. They are members of the Hamitic race, and are closely akin to the earliest inhabitants of Egypt. Their colour varies from a deep black to a brownish yellow; stature tall; bodies spare, wiry, and muscular; nose often straight, or even arched; lips moderate; hair often hanging over the neck in long twisted plaits. They are handsome and brave, but ferocious and cruel, cunning and faithless. They leave the plains to their horses,

Maltese Galley

sheep, and cows, while they themselves cultivate the mountains. There are, however, wandering Gallas mainly occupied in hunting and slave-dealing. Their language is spoken over a considerable area stretching south to the equator. The northern Gallas, nominally under Abyssinia, are partly Mohammedans, partly Christians; the southern Gallas are heathens. There are many tribes, generally under an elected chieftain.— BIBLIOGRAPHY: Stanford, *Africa* (vol. i); P. M. de Salviac, *Les Galla.*

GALL-BLADDER is a pear-shaped sac situated on the under surface of the right lobe of the liver. It acts as a reservoir for the bile from the liver. Gallstones may accumulate in the gall-bladder and lead to serious results requiring surgical interference.

GALLE (gal), a seaport near the south-west extremity of Ceylon, on a low, rocky projecting point of land. It is well built, has a good harbour, and fine scenery adjoining. It is a coaling-station for steamers, but has been superseded by Colombo as a port of call for mail steamers. Pop. (1931), 38,424.

GALLEON, large Spanish vessel of the 15th–17th centuries. With a lofty stem and stern, and often with three or four gun decks, it served both for warfare, as in the Spanish Armada, and for transporting treasure from the Indies.

GAL'LERY, in architecture, a long, narrow room, the length of which is at least three times its width, often built to receive a collection of pictures. Among the most renowned European art galleries are those of the Louvre at Paris, that of Versailles, the National Gallery in London, the Pitti and Uffizi Galleries at Florence, the Dresden Gallery, the Real Museo of the Prado at Madrid, the Hermitage at Petrograd, the gallery of Berlin, the gallery of the Museo Borbonico at Naples, and those at Venice, Antwerp, and Turin. The term gallery is also sometimes applied to what is more properly termed a corridor, likewise to a platform projecting from the walls of a building supported by piers, pillars, brackets, or consoles, and, in churches, theatres, and similar buildings, to the upper floors going round the building next the wall. Among well-known glass-roofed galleries are those of Naples, Milan, Brussels, and of the Palais-Royal, Paris. In many German cities there are galleries which are really streets roofed with glass.

GALLEY, a low, flat-built vessel with one deck, and navigated with sails and oars, once commonly used in the Mediterranean. The common galleys varied from 100 to 200 feet in length, those of smaller sizes being known respectively as half-galleys and quarter-galleys. They carried as many as twenty oars on each side, each oar worked by one or more men, and they had commonly two masts with lateen sails. Raised structures in the stern, and even in the prow, were not uncommon. These, however, were more fully developed in the kind of galley known as the *galleass,* which carried three masts, from 200 to 300 rowers, and sometimes twenty guns. France formerly had a number of galleys for service in the Mediterranean, in which convicts were forced to labour. In the British navy galley is the name of the captain's boat, or a similar boat built for speed under oars. The term galley is also applied to the ships of the ancient Greeks and Romans, especially to their war-ships, which were propelled chiefly by oars.—Cf. Holmes, *Ancient and Modern Ships.*

The term is used in Printing for the wooden or metal frames used for receiving the type after it has been set. Proofs taken from this are called **Galley-proofs.**

GALL-FLY, a name for several hymenopterous insects of the family Cynipidæ, which form the disease products known as galls, each species seeming to be addicted to a particular plant and a particular part of the plant. The tumour or gall is due to the morbid action of an irritating fluid deposited with the egg of the insect. Oaks are especially liable to attack. The well-known 'oak apple' is caused by *Cynips quercus folii*; 'oak spangles' on the backs of leaves are due to *Neuroterus fumipennis* and other species. The shrubby oak (*Quercus infectoria*) of Syria is attacked by *C. gallæ tinctoriæ*, which gives rise to the hard gall or gall-nut which is chiefly used in commerce. The hairy gall of the rose, called a *bedeguar*, is the work of *Rhodites rosæ*. The larvæ in this, as in the oak gall, do not come out till the following spring. *See* GALLS.

GALLI - CURCI Amelita, Italian singer, born in Milan, 18th Nov., 1890, her pure soprano voice was largely self-trained. She made her début as Gilda in *Rigoletto* in Rome, 1909, and has appeared at the Chicago Opera House and the Metropolitan Opera House, New York. In 1924-25 she toured Great Britain, where she had previously attained a great reputation on the strength of her gramophone records.

GALLIARD, an old dance for two persons. In triple time, it was very popular in the 16th and 17th centuries. The minuet is said to have sprung from it.

GALLIC ACID ($C_7H_6O_5$), an acid which derives its name from the gall-nut, whence it was first procured by Scheele in 1786. It exists in the seeds of the mango, has been found besides in many other plants, in acorns, colchicum, divi-divi, hellebore root, sumach, tea, walnuts, &c., and is a decomposition product of tannic acid. It crystallizes in brilliant colourless prisms, with an astringent taste. It colours ferric salts of a deep bluish-black. It is of extensive use in the art of dyeing, as it constitutes one of the principal ingredients in all the shades of black, and is an important mordant. It is well known as an ingredient in ink, and when heated yields pyrogallol and carbon dioxide. *See* INK; DYEING.

GAL'LICAN CHURCH, a distinctive name applied to the Roman Catholic Church in France. The peculiarity of the Gallican Church and of Gallicanism consists not in any diversity of doctrine or practice from those generally held and observed by Roman Catholics in other countries, but in the maintenance of a greater degree of independence of the Papal see, more especially by denying the validity of many of the decretals issued since the time of Charlemagne, and refusing to allow the Pope to interfere with the civil jurisdiction of the State and the sovereign rights of the Crown.

The freedom asserted in this respect was increasingly recognized by the Pragmatic Sanctions of 1269 and 1438, and was still more clearly established by the Quatuor Propositiones Cleri Gallicani (Four Propositions of the French Clergy), drawn up in convocation by the French clergy in 1682. These were: (1) The Pope in secular matters has no power over princes and kings, and cannot loose their subjects from allegiance to them. (2) He is

Gall fly

subject to the decrees of a general council. (3) His authority in France is regulated by fixed canons and the laws and customs of the kingdom and Church. (4) In matters of faith his decision is not unalterable (*irréformable*).

During the Revolution the Gallican Church practically disappeared, and though Napoleon extorted from Pius VII a concordat for its re-establishment, no agreement was arrived at as to its organization. With the return of the Bourbons the bishops deprived by Napoleon were restored, and a new concordat concluded in 1817; but its unpopularity led the Government to exact from ecclesiastics an expression of adherence to the articles of 1682. The July revolution in 1830 gave full freedom to all denominations, and a clause was inserted in the Constitutional Charter expressly declaring that each person professes his religion with equal liberty, and obtains for his worship the same protection. Subsequently, and especially since the Vatican Council of 1870, the position of the Gallican Church towards the Popes has essentially changed, and the older Gallicanism may now be said to be represented by the Old Catholics of France. *See* FRANCE.—BIBLIOGRAPHY: Jervis, *The Gallican Church and the Revolution*; Le Roy, *Le Gallicanisme au XVIIIe siècle*; P. Sabatier, *France To-day: its Religious Orientation*.

GALLIENI, Joseph Simon, French soldier, born at St. Béat, in Haute-Garonne, 24th April, 1849, died 26th May, 1916. Educated at St. Cyr, he fought in the Franco-German War, and was sent in 1878 to Senegambia, where he extended French influence. He afterwards served in the Sudan and in Tonquin. In 1896 he was appointed Governor-General of Madagascar, and was raised to the rank of general of division in 1899.

During the European War, in the critical days of Aug., 1914, when the

Galliot. Early nineteenth century

French Government had to leave the capital for Bordeaux, Gallieni was appointed military governor of Paris, and organized the defence of the city. Appointed Minister of War on 28th Oct., 1915, he remained in office only a few months. Retiring on 17th March, 1916, he died at Versailles two months afterwards. On the 12th April, 1921, the Chamber of Deputies conferred upon him posthumously the title of *Maréchal de France*. He wrote: *Deux campagnes au Soudan Français, La Pacification de Madagascar*.

GALLIE'NUS, Publius Licinius, a Roman emperor, associated with his father Valerianus until the capture of the latter by the Persians in A.D. 260, when Gallienus continued to reign alone. His empire was limited by the revolt of most of the legions in the provinces, who chose their commanders as Cæsars, and thus gave rise to the period known as the 'Time of the Thirty Tyrants.' Though given up to pleasure, he defeated the Goths in Thrace and Postumus in Gaul, and

forced Aureolus, whom the legions of Illyria had proclaimed emperor, to take refuge in Milan. While making preparations to reduce that town, he himself was assassinated A.D. 268.

GALLIFFET, Gaston Alexandre Auguste, Marquis de, Prince de Martignes, French general, born in Paris 23rd Jan., 1830, died in 1909. Entering the army in 1848, he fought with distinction in the Crimea, in Italy in 1859, and in Mexico in 1863. During the Franco-Prussian War he commanded the 3rd Chasseurs d'Afrique, and distinguished himself by his cavalry charge at Sedan. The Commune having been declared in Paris, Galliffet was sent to suppress the rising, and employed the most rigorous measures and frightful severity to the Communard prisoners. This severity was subsequently the subject of continual bitter attacks upon him. He was made a member of the Superior War Council in 1885, but retired and entered the Chamber of Deputies in 1894. He was War Minister in 1899 in Waldeck-Rousseau's Cabinet.

GAL'LINULE (Lat. *gallinula*, dim. of *gallina*, hen), a name for aquatic birds belonging to the family Rallidæ or rails, genera Gallinula and Porphyrio. They are good swimmers, though they are not web-footed, but have the toes furnished with a narrow membrane. The common gallinule, moor-hen, or water-hen (*G. chloropus*), is the only British species, and it has a wide range through Europe, Asia, and Africa. It is black, with a red frontal shield. Allied species are found in most parts of the world, Porphyrio including handsome blue birds native to Africa and Madagascar, and also ranging from the Mediterranean region to South China and Polynesia.

GAL'LIOT (O.Fr. *galiote*), a Dutch or Flemish vessel for cargoes, with very rounded ribs and flattish bottom, with a mizzen-mast placed near the stern, carrying a square main-sail and main-top-sail, a forestay to the main-mast (there being no foremast), with fore-stay-sail and jibs.

GALLIP'OLI (ancient CALLIPOLIS), a seaport of Southern Italy, in the province of Lecce, on a rocky peninsula in the Gulf of Taranto, 47 miles south-east of Taranto. It is fortified, and has a cathedral, dating from 1629, a productive tunny fishery and a good harbour, from which large quantities of olive-oil are exported. Pop. 14,500.

GALLIP'OLI (ancient CALLIPOLIS), a town of Greece, formerly belonging to Turkey, on a peninsula of the same name at the north-east end of the Dardanelles, 128 miles W.S.W. of Constantinople. It was once fortified, but is now in a generally dilapidated condition, with no edifice of note except the bazaars. It has manufactures of cotton, silk, and morocco leather, and two harbours, one formerly used as a station for the Turkish fleet, and the other for trade, chiefly in corn, wine, and oil. It was the gate by which the Turks entered Europe (1357), and in the Crimean War the Allied forces landed there (1854). Pop. about 35,000.

GALLIPOLI CAMPAIGN. After Turkey had entered the European War on the side of the Central Powers on 29th Oct., 1914, it was at first considered possible to secure the passage of the Dardanelles—and thus open communication with Russia—by means of a purely naval bombardment, which duly took place early in 1915, commencing on 15th Feb. When it became evident that this attempt was doomed to failure, it was abandoned in favour of a combined naval and military operation, in which an army was to land on the Gallipoli Peninsula supported by the guns of the Allied fleets.

This army was to consist, as did the fleet, of combined British and French formations, and the original force which carried out the actual landing was composed of a French division of Territorials and Senegalese under General d'Amade, the British 29th Division of the Regular Army, the Royal Naval Division, and the Australian and New Zealand Army Corps. All told this force numbered some 120,000 men.

Allied Landing. The harbour of Mudros, in the Island of Lemnos, had for some little time been used by the navy as a base, and here supplies and munitions were brought in huge quantities, nothing whatever being procurable locally; this place had now to serve as the base for the combined force, and it was here that the transports carrying the Expeditionary Force made their rendezvous, and from here that they started at midnight of the 24th-25th April, 1915, *en route* for the selected landing-places on the Peninsula.

These landing-places were six in number, and the principal ones were known as 'V' Beach, 'W' Beach, 'X' Beach, and Gaba Tepe. The landings were to take place at dawn. The troops selected for 'V' Beach were the Dublin Fusiliers, the Munster Fusiliers, two companies of the Hampshire Regiment, and the West Riding Field Company, Royal Engineers; the greater part of these were on the collier *River Clyde.*

At 'W' Beach the Lancashire Fusiliers and the Worcester Regiment landed, and at 'X' Beach the Royal Fusiliers and some of the Anson Battalion, R.N.D. Gaba Tepe, afterwards known as Anzac, some 8 miles N.E. of Beach 'Y' on the Ægean side, was reserved for the Australians and New Zealanders. The French Expeditionary Corps landed at Kum Kale, on the Asiatic side of the straits. In addition to these landings there were two smaller beaches on the Peninsula where troops also landed, known as 'Y' and 'S'.

The net result of the various landings was the establishment of a British line across the very point of the peninsula. Then followed the advance on Krithia, wherein the Expeditionary Force was assisted by long-range fire from H.M.S. *Queen Elizabeth.*

From 1st to 4th May was fought the first battle of Krithia, a succession of attacks and counter-attacks, and after a lull of two days the second battle of Krithia began on 6th May. This had as a possible ultimate objective the heights of Achi Baba, and resulted in an advance by the 29th Division and the French—who had by now landed troops at 'V' Beach—of some 1,000 yards.

From the 9th to 19th May there was very heavy fighting at Gaba Tepe or Anzac, wherein General Bridges, commanding the Anzac Corps, was killed. Small advances also took place elsewhere. On 4th June, after some days of varying successes and reverses, a further general attack on Krithia was begun. This, known as the third battle of Krithia, was carried out by the 29th, 42nd (arrived since the landing), and Royal Naval Divisions, and the French, and resulted in a gain of 500 yards.

On the 21st the French gained ground on the right, and on the 27th the British divisions executed a brilliant piece of work near Krithia, capturing several lines of trenches and fortified posts, and almost succeeding in turning the Achi Baba position. This operation was the means of adding another 1,000 yards depth to our territory.

The month ended with the repulse of heavy Turkish attacks at Anzac and a further French success on the right. The Allies were now in crying need of reinforcements, which, though they were on their way, had not yet materialized. The want of them made impossible a further most necessary attack in force, which might conceivably have had decisive results: wanting these reinforcements, the most the Allies could do was to hold on to what they had gained until the arrival of fresh troops made a new venture feasible.

In the meanwhile a very heavy Turkish attack was defeated by the 29th and Royal Naval Divisions, and for the rest of the month attacks and counter-attacks succeeded each other without any outstanding results. By the end of the month the British losses were given as nearly 50,000 to date, while the Turks were said to have lost 20,000 (killed and prisoners) in the space of five days' fighting.

Landing at Suvla Bay. Early in August the long-expected reinforcements had arrived at the base, and the time was ripe for putting a new plan into execution. This was to land troops at Suvla Bay (north of Anzac) to deal with the Turkish right, while the Anzacs struck at their centre, and the English and French Divisions dealt with their left. The surprise landing duly took place at Suvla on 6th Aug., but, though the landing was made good, the plan in its entirety proved a costly failure, and resulted in little but very heavy losses, the attack finally dying away on the 12th. Nine days later a second attempt was made from Suvla—the immediate objective being Anafarta—but with no better success.

Early in September the Turks attempted a night attack in force on the Australians near Anafarta, but were repulsed with very heavy losses. For the remainder of the month operations were mainly confined to artillery and air-craft, the Turks having strengthened their positions by denuding their fortresses at Adrianople and Chatalja of their heavy armament. During this month the 10th British and the French Divisions were withdrawn, and the question of complete evacuation was being discussed by the Cabinet, and in November Lord Kitchener made a tour of the southern front to see for himself and advise. In the meanwhile Sir Charles Monro had replaced Sir Ian Hamilton as Commander-in-Chief in Gallipoli on 16th Oct.

Evacuation of Gallipoli. During November—on the 15th—the 156th Brigade of the 52nd Division made a highly successful attack on the Turkish position. This, brilliant feat as it was, could not alter the general state of affairs, and the final decision to evacuate was taken. Casualties up to the end of November had been 112,000, besides sick; and on 20th Dec., almost eight months to the day since the original landings, Suvla and Anzac were evacuated under cover of an attack from Cape Helles. Losses in this evacuation were three men wounded.

By the 9th Jan., 1916, the evacuation of the Peninsula was completed by the withdrawal from Cape Helles of the remaining troops with only one casualty. It was, of course, impossible to remove all the stores and munitions which had accumulated on the various beaches, and before evacuation they were prepared for burning, and it is said that the blaze created when they were lighted was the first intimation the Turks had of our withdrawal. However this may be, the fact remains that the withdrawal and embarkation of a large army from open beaches and without casualties shows a marvellous organization.

The official dispatches dealing with this campaign were published in London as follows: 5th July (Hamilton); 4th Aug. (De Robeck, naval); 20th Sept. (Hamilton); 6th March, 1916, (Monro). Casualties up to 11th Dec., 1915, were officially given as 25,000 all ranks dead, 75,000 wounded, 12,000 missing. In addition there was much sickness, no fewer than 96,000 having been admitted to hospital.— Cf. Sir Ian Hamilton, *Gallipoli Diary*. *See also under* EUROPEAN WAR.

GALLIPOLI OIL, a coarse olive-oil used in Turkey-red dyeing and for other purposes, and prepared from olives grown in Calabria and Apulia, the latter being considered the best. The oil is conveyed in skins to Gallipoli, where it is clarified and shipped in casks.

GAL'LIUM, a rare malleable metal, discovered by spectrum analysis in 1875 by De Boisbaudran in the zinc-blende of Pierrefitte in the Pyrenees. It is of a bluish-white colour, has a brilliant lustre, and is fused by the mere warmth of the hand. In its properties it is related to aluminium.

GALLIWASP, the *Celestus occiduus*, a species of lizard about 1 foot in length, and remarkably stout and plump. Its general colour is brown. It is a native of the West Indies, and is particularly common in Jamaica, where it is much dreaded, though without reason.

GALLON, a standard measure of capacity (fixed in 1824 by Act of George IV), containing 277·27384 cubic inches, being equal to 4 quarts or 8 pints. In England formerly three different gallons were in use, the old corn-gallon of 268·8 cubic inches, the old wine-gallon of 231 cubic inches, and the old beer-gallon of 282 cubic inches. The gallon of 231 cubic inches has been adopted as the standard of the United States.

GAL'LOWAY, a district in the south-west of Scotland, now regarded as embracing Wigtownshire and Kirkcudbright, and returning one member to Parliament. It has given name to a breed of horses and one of cattle.

GALLOWS, wooden frame used for executing sentence of death by hanging. It is formed of two upright posts and a cross-beam, from which depends the execution rope; or, of a single upright with a projecting beam. The latter form served more particularly for the gibbet, upon which bodies of criminals, after execution, were suspended.

Until 1868, gallows were erected in public places, as at Newgate and Tyburn. See EXECUTION.

GALLS, gall-nuts or nut-galls, a vegetable excrescence produced by the deposit of the egg of an insect in the bark or leaves of a plant. The galls of commerce are produced by a species of Cynips (see GALL-FLY) in the tender shoots of the *Quercus infectoria,* a species of oak abundant in Asia Minor, Syria, and Persia. They are spherical and tubercular, and vary in magnitude from the size of a pea to that of a hazel-nut. White, green, and blue varieties are recognized, the latter kinds being the best. They are inodorous, but are strongly astringent from the tannin and gallic acid which they contain, and which are their chief products.

Gall-nuts are extensively used in dyeing and in the manufacture of ink, and they are also frequently used in medicine. They are chiefly imported from Aleppo, Tripoli, and Smyrna. The Chinese galls, or *woo-pei-tsze,* differ from the foregoing in that they are really an unusually massive kind of crust or cocoon, such as the aphides form on the surface of a plant; the tissues of the plant are not affected. Since the opening of the Japanese ports these have been imported in considerable quantities to Britain.

GALL'STONES. See CALCULUS.

GALLUS, Roman emperor. Trebonianus Gallus first became prominent as the leader of a Roman army in the region of the Danube. After Decius had been killed in battle in that area, in A.D. 251, Gallus was proclaimed Emperor. He made peace with the Goths and marched to Rome. In 253 he was killed by his own soldiers.

GALSTON, burgh and market town of Ayrshire. It is on the River Irvine, 5 miles from Kilmarnock, on the L.M.S. Rly. There are some industries, and in the neighbourhood are coal mines. Pop. (1931), 4,601.

GALSWORTHY, John, British novelist and playwright, was born at Coombe, Surrey, in 1867. He was educated at Harrow, and New College,

Oxford, where he took a second class in the jurisprudence schools. He was called to the Bar in 1890, but did not practise much. His career as author may be said to have begun with the publication of a volume of tales, called *The Villa Rubein,* in 1900.

His best-known novels and tales are: *The Island Pharisees* (1904), *The Country House* (1907), *The Dark Flower* (1915), *The Forsyte Saga* (comprising *The Man of Property, The Indian Summer of a Forsyte, In Chancery, Awakening,* and *To Let*), *Captures* (1923), *The White Monkey* (1924), *The Silver Spoon* (1926), *Caravan* (1927), *Swan Song* (1928), *A Modern Comedy* (1929), *On Forsyte 'Change* (1930). His plays include: *The Silver Box* (1906), *Joy* (1907), *Strife* (1909), *Justice* (1910), *The Pigeon* (1912), and *The Skin Game* (1920), *Loyalties* and *Windows* (1922), *The Forest, Old English* (1924), *The Show* (1925), *Escape* (1926), *Exiled* (1929), and *The Roof* (1929).

He published two collections of essays, *A Sheaf* (1916) and *Another Sheaf* (1919), dealing with questions of the day. His plays are well constructed, and also deal in a sincere manner with contemporary problems. *The Silver Box* exposes some of the weaknesses of our system of administering justice, and *Strife* deals with the relationship between masters and men.

Galsworthy received the Order of Merit in 1929, and the Nobel Prize in 1932. He died in 1933.

GALT, Sir Alexander Tilloch, son of John Galt, the novelist, born in 1817, died 1893, a Canadian financier and statesman. He entered the Canadian Parliament in 1849, was Minister of Finance of the Dominion of Canada in 1867, and represented Canada on the Halifax Fishery Commission in 1877. From 1880 to 1883 he was High Commissioner of the Dominion in England.

GALT, John, Scottish novelist, born at Irvine in Ayrshire in 1779, died in 1839. He went to London in 1804, printed an epic on the *Battle of Largs,* and tried both commerce and the legal profession; but, failing in each, went abroad for some years. On his return in 1812 he published his *Voyages and Travels,* his *Letters from the Levant,* a *Life of Cardinal Wolsey,* and a volume of tragedies. He then became a contributor to the *Monthly Magazine* and other periodicals, and wrote a tragedy, *The Witness,* a *Life of Benjamin West,* and a romance— *The Wandering Jew.*

His *Ayrshire Legatees* (1820), with its humorous descriptions of Scottish middle and low life, indicated the true scope of his faculty, and it was followed by his *Annals of the Parish* (1821), *The Provost* (1822), *Sir Andrew Wylie* (1822), and *The Entail* (1823). These were perhaps his best works, though his writings comprised about fifty novels, twenty dramas, and other works. He went out to Canada as superintendent to the Canada Company in 1826.

GALT, a town, Ontario, Canada, on the Grand River. It is an industrial centre having flour and woollen mills, and iron works for which electric power is supplied by Niagara Falls, and is served by the C.N. and C.P. Railways. The city is named after John Galt. Pop. 14,006.

GALTON, Sir Francis, English traveller and anthropologist, grandson of Erasmus Darwin, and cousin of Charles Darwin, was born near Birmingham in 1822, died in 1911. He received his earlier education at King Edward's School, Birmingham, and afterwards studied medicine at the Birmingham Hospital and King's College, London. After graduating at Trinity College, Cambridge, he travelled to the White Nile, and subsequently (1850–2) explored Damaraand Ovampo-lands, then unknown countries. He published an account of his experiences in his *Narrative of an Explorer in Tropical South Africa,* and receive one of the gold medals of the Royal Geographical Society. His *Art of Travel, or Shifts and Contrivances in Wild Countries* (1855), went through five editions in seventeen years.

He was a member of the Meteorological Council from its formation in 1868 until 1901, and his *Meteorographica* (1863) contained much original work in this branch of science. From 1869 he devoted himself largely to questions connected with heredity, and published the following important works: *Hereditary Genius: its Laws and Consequences* (1869); *Experiments in Pangenesis* (1871); *English Men of Science: their Nature and Nurture*(1874), *Inquiries into Human Faculty and its Development* (1883); *Natural Inheritance* (1889), *Finger Prints* (1893); and *Finger Print Directory* (1895). He wrote also *Essays in Eugenics* (1909), and published *Memories of my Life* (1908). He was knighted in 1909. In 1886 he received the Royal Society's gold medal, and in 1902 the Darwin medal, besides similar honours.

GALTYMORE, mountain of Ireland. In the county of Tipperary, it is the highest summit of the Galtee range, having an altitude of 3,015 feet.

GALVANI, Luigi, Italian physician and physiologist, born at Bologna 1737, died 1798. He practised medicine in Bologna, and was in 1762 appointed professor of anatomy at the university. He gained repute as a comparative anatomist; but his fame rests on his theory of animal electricity, enunciated in the treatise *De Viribus Electricitatis in Motu Musculari Commentarius,* published in 1791. Twenty years before the publication of this treatise he had been making experiments on the relations of animal functions to electricity. In 1797 he was deprived of his chair for refusing to take the oath of allegiance to the Cisalpine Republic, but was restored to it in less than a year. *See* GALVANISM.

GALVANIC BATTERY. *See* VOLTAIC CELL.

GALVANISM, the production of electricity by means of the galvanic battery. The name is derived from Galvani, professor of anatomy at Bologna, who observed that the limbs of a dead frog could be caused to move by the contact of metals. His experiments attracted the attention of Volta, professor of natural philosophy at Pavia, who shortly afterwards invented the galvanic or voltaic battery.

GALVANIZED IRON, a name given to sheets of iron coated with zinc by a non-galvanic process, the iron being first cleansed by the action of dilute sulphuric acid, and then plunged into a bath of melted zinc covered with sal ammoniac. So long as the coating is entire, and so long as it is not exposed to corrosive substances, galvanized iron is very durable, and it is capable of resisting the corrosive action of the atmosphere.

GALVANOMETER, an instrument employed to detect and measure electric currents. The term is generally confined to those laboratory instruments which depend for their action on the electro-magnetic effect of current.

Tangent Galvanometer. The simplest form of current-measuring instrument consists of a circular coil of wire of one or more turns of known radius, with a compass-needle pivoted at the centre of the coil. The instrument is set up with the plane of the coil vertical and in the magnetic meridian. On passing a current through the coil, the needle is deflected from its position of rest: the strength of the current is proportional to the tangent of the angle of deflection. To find the absolute strength of the current, the tangent of the deflection is multiplied by the galvanometer constant, a number found by dividing the product of the earth's horizontal magnetic field and the radius of the coil by 2π times the number of turns of wire in the coil ($\pi = 3.1416$ nearly). The current thus measured is in absolute units, and these are converted into ampères by multiplying by 10. For accuracy, a short needle is required; the angle of deflection is read off a circular scale, divided in degrees, by means of a long light pointer fixed to the needle at right angles to its length.

Reflecting Galvanometer. A more sensitive current detector is made by largely increasing the number of turns of wire in the coil, and by using an optical method of measuring the angle of deflection. The 'needle' consists of several short lengths of thin watch-spring, tempered and magnetized, and cemented to the back of a light circular mirror about a centimetre in diameter. The mirror is suspended by a strand of silk at the centre of the coil, with the short magnets horizontal and with like poles to the same side. The position of the needle is found by reflecting the rays of a glow-lamp from the mirror to a horizontal scale pasted or etched on a strip of ground glass placed about 1 metre in front of the mirror. If the mirror is slightly concave, a sharply defined, vertical line of light is focussed on the scale. A control magent is placed near the instrument to regulate the zero position of the 'spot of light,' and to neutralize part of the magnetic control of the earth on the needle.

On passing a weak current through the galvanometer, the needle is deflected, and the spot of light moves along the scale; since the reflected beam turns through twice the angle turned through by the mirror, and is also equivalent to a pointer 1 metre long, a very small deflection of the needle system may be detected. By passing a current of known strength through the galvanometer, and observing the deflection of the spot of light, it can be found how many micro-ampères are required to deflect the spot of light through one division of the scale when at 1 metre distance from the mirror. This number is called the figure of merit or sensitiveness of the galvanometer. The instrument was devised and used by Thomson (Lord Kelvin) during the laying of the Atlantic cable. It is subject to disturbance by external magnetic forces, a disadvantage from which the next type is free.

Moving-coil Galvanometer. The moving system is a small coil suspended between the poles of a strong, permanent horse-shoe magnet. The current is led to and from the coil by means of wires above and below, which also hold the coil in position and supply the forces which control the rotation of the coil. When the suspended coil carries a current, it becomes a magnet whose axis is perpendicular to the lines of force of the permanent magnet, and it rotates into a position in which the forces causing rotation are balanced by the effect of torsion in the suspending wires. The deflection of the coil is measured, as previously described, by lamp, mirror, and scale, or in some cases by means of a pointer and scale. The motion of the light coil is practically 'dead-beat,' i.e. the spot of light moves to

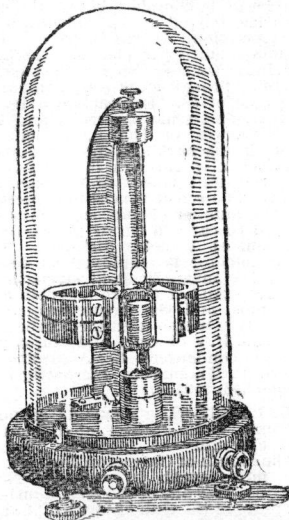

Dead-beat D'Arsonval Reflecting Galvanometer

its position of rest without swinging to and fro about that position like a compass-needle. Some forms of this instrument have a sensitiveness of about $\frac{1}{100}$ micro-ampère per division on a scale at 1 metre distance.

String Galvanometer. The moving coil is replaced by a flexible vertical silvered glass fibre or 'string' fixed at its ends. When the current is passed through the string, the latter moves across the lines of force in the air-gap between the poles of the magnet. The poles are perforated in the direction of the lines of force, and a micro-scope, which fits into one perforation, is focussed on the string; the eyepiece of the microscope contains a scale on which the deflection of the string may be measured. This type was invented by Einthoven, of Leyden, and is capable of detecting currents of the order of a sixty-thousandth of a micro-ampère.

Ballistic Galvanometer. The construction of this instrument is similar to that of the reflecting galvanometers, except that the needle or moving-coil is made relatively much heavier. The galvanometer is used primarily for measuring quantities of electricity by noting the throw of the spot of light caused when the electricity is discharged through the galvanometer. With a slowly moving system, it may be assumed that the discharge is complete before the system has moved appreciably from its zero position. It can then be shown that a quantity of electricity, whose discharge causes a throw of the moving system through $a°$, is proportional to the sine of $\frac{1}{2}a$. In practice a lamp, mirror, and scale are used, and the sensitiveness of the instrument is found by discharging a known quantity of electricity through it and noting the resultant throw of the spot of light. The sensitiveness is expressed by the number of microcoulombs required to cause a throw of one scale division at 1 metre distance. The galvanometer is employed to determine the magnetic field strength in the pole-gaps of electro-magnets and dynamos, and the magnetic quality of steel; it is also used for comparing the E.M.F.'s of cells and the capacities of condensers. *See* AMMETER.—Cf. S. P. Thompson, *Electricity and Magnetism* (1915).

GAL'VESTON, a city and seaport of Texas, United States, at the north-east extremity of Galveston Island, at the mouth of Galveston Bay, about 450 miles south by west of New Orleans. It is one of the most flourishing ports in the Gulf of Mexico. Large quantities of cotton are shipped, the export being over 3 million bales annually. The chief buildings are the custom and market houses, the town hall, a number of churches, including a Gothic Episcopal church and Roman Catholic cathedral, and the Roman Catholic University of St. Mary. Immense loss of life and damage to property was caused by a hurricane in 1900. Pop. (1930), 52,938.

GAL'WAY, a seaport of the Irish Free State, province of Connaught, capital of county of same name, at the mouth of the Corrib, in Galway Bay, 126½ miles west of Dublin. It consists in its older parts of narrow, irregular streets with antique houses, crowded with a pauper population; in the more modern parts it is spacious and well built. Besides numerous churches and chapels it has three monasteries and five nunneries. The town house and county hall and University College are amongst its best buildings. The manufactures are insignificant, and the trade, though once important, is no longer worthy of its excellent harbour. The chief exports are agricultural produce and marble. There are mills for sawing and polishing marble, a brewery, and a distillery. Galway was a parliamentary borough until 1918. Pop. (1926), 14,223.

GALWAY, the county, which is washed by the Atlantic, has an area of 2,375 sq. miles, of which one-eighth is under crops. In the north-west, or district of Connemara, it is rugged and mountainous; in the east, level but extensively covered with bog; and in the south, fertile and tolerably well cultivated, producing wheat, barley, and oats. Lough Corrib, which lies wholly within it, dividing the county into the east and west districts, is the third largest lake in Ireland. The minerals include lead, limestone, marble, and beautiful serpentine. The fisheries are valuable, but much neglected. The principal manufactures are coarse woollens and linens. The population by the Irish Free State census taken in 1926 was 169,366.

GALWAY BAY, a large bay on the west coast of Ireland, between County Galway on the north and County Clare on the south, about 30 miles in length and from 20 to 7 miles in breadth. Across its entrance lie the Aran Islands, and there are numerous small islands in the bay itself.

GAMA, Dom Vasco Da, the first navigator who made the voyage to the East Indies by the Cape of Good Hope, was born in 1450 at Sines, Portugal, of a noble family, died in 1524. His voyage had been projected under John II, and his successor, Emmanuel the Fortunate, having fitted out four vessels, appointed Gama commander-in-chief. He sailed from Lisbon on 8th July, 1497, and, doubling the Cape, visited Mozambique, Mombaza, Melinda, and Calicut, returning to Lisbon in 1499. For this exploit he was named Admiral of the Indies and received the title of Dom, with an annual pension and extensive privileges in Indian commerce.

In the year 1502 he was placed at the head of a powerful fleet, with which he provided for the security of future voyagers by founding establishments at Mozambique and Sofala. He also inflicted signal reprisals on the town of Calicut, where the Portuguese residents had been massacred, and established the first Portuguese factory in the Indies. He re-entered Lisbon in 1503, and passed the next twenty years in obscurity. In 1524 he was appointed Viceroy of India by King John III, but his administration lasted only three months, his death taking place at Goa in the December of that year.—Cf. G. Correa, *The Three Voyages of Vasco da Gama and his Viceroyalty* (Hakluyt Society Publications).

GAMA'LIEL, the name of two men mentioned in Bible history, of whom the first, Gamaliel, the son of Pedahzur (*Num.* i, 10; ii, 20; vii, 54, 59; x, 23), was prince or head of the tribe of Manasseh. The other and better-known Gamaliel is mentioned twice in the *Acts of the Apostles*, as a learned doctor of the law, of the sect of the Pharisees. From *Acts* xxii, 3, we learn that he was the preceptor of St. Paul; the other reference (*Acts* v, 34) records his famous advice to the Sanhedrin as to their treatment of the Apostles. According to tradition Gamaliel became a Christian, and was baptized by St. Peter and St. Paul.

GAMBET'TA, Léon Michel, a French orator and statesman, born in 1838 at Cahors, of a family of Genoese extraction, died in 1882. He was educated for the Church, but finally decided in favour of the law, and, repairing to Paris, became a member of the Metropolitan Bar in 1859. In Nov., 1868, he gained the leadership of the Republican party by his defence of Delescluze, a noted republican. In 1869, having been elected by both Paris and Marseilles, he chose to represent the southern city; and in the Chamber of Deputies showed himself an irreconcilable opponent of the empire and its measures, especially of the policy which led to the war with Prussia. On the downfall of the empire, after the disaster of Sedan in 1870, the Government of National Defence was formed, in which Gambetta was nominated Minister of the Interior. The Germans having encircled Paris, he left that city in a balloon, and set up his head-quarters at Tours, from which, with all the powers of a dictator, he for a short time organized a fierce but vain resistance against the invaders.

After the close of the war he held office in several short-lived ministries, and in Nov., 1881, accepted the premiership. The sweeping changes proposed by him and his colleagues speedily brought a majority against him, and after a six weeks' tenure of office he had to resign. The accidental discharge of a pistol caused his death at Paris on 31st Dec., 1882. On the 11th of Nov., 1920, the anniversary of the armistice concluded with Germany after the European War, the heart of Gambetta was brought to Paris in solemn procession and interred in the Pantheon.—BIBLIOGRAPHY: J. Reinach, *Léon Gambetta*; F. Harrison, *Léon Gambetta, a Positivist*; P. B. Gheusi, *Gambetta*; *Life and Letters*; P. Deschanel, *Gambetta*.

GAMBIA, a British Crown Colony and Protectorate in West Africa. The Crown Colony consists of the island of St. Mary, on which Bathurst, the capital, stands; area, 4 sq. miles; pop. 10,000. The Protectorate has an area of 4,130 sq. miles, and a population of 210,000, and forms a long, narrow strip surrounded by the French territory of Senegal. It includes the small kingdom of Barra, near the mouth of the river. The chief exports are ground-nuts, rubber, and palm kernels. The exports to the United Kingdom, for 1931, amounted to £20,185.

GAMBIA, a river of West Africa, rising in a mountainous district in Futa Jallon and flowing north-west

Gambetta

and west to the Atlantic, through French and British territory; length, 1,000 miles. It is navigable for 300 miles by small vessels.

GAMBIER, Baron, English sailor. Born at New Providence, Bahamas, 13th Oct., 1756, James Gambier joined the navy at the age of 11, and received rapid promotion. He distinguished himself in command of the *Defence* on 1st June, 1794, and next year became one of the Lords of the Admiralty. He commanded the fleet which bombarded Copenhagen in 1807, and for that was raised to the peerage. In command of the Channel fleet in 1809, he refused to support Lord Cochrane in his attempt to destroy the French fleet in the Basque Roads by fireships. For this he was court-martialled, but was acquitted. He died 19th April, 1833.

GAMBIER ISLANDS, a group of small coral islands in the South Pacific belonging to France. A French mission station was formed on the largest island, Mangareva, in 1834. Pop. about 500.

GAMBIR (*Uncaria Gambia*), a climbing shrub of the Malay Archipelago, ord. Rubiaceæ, the leaves and twigs of which yield, when boiled, the genuine catechu or terra japonica, a powerful astringent substance, used medicinally and for tanning.

GAMBLING, or **GAMING**, the practice of indulging in games involving some element of chance or hazard with a view to pecuniary gain. In many countries such games, and the collateral practices of betting on events or taking shares in lotteries, are legally prohibited or restricted as frequently associated with fraud and as themselves demoralizing. At other times Governments, tempted by the prospect of gain, have openly encouraged gambling by licensing gaming-houses, or instituting lotteries under their own authority. (*See* LOTTERY.) In France public gaming-tables were suppressed from 1st Jan., 1838, but lotteries are still sometimes carried on. Previous to the formation of the former German Empire gambling was encouraged in both of the ways referred to in several of the principalities of Germany. Baden-Baden, in the former Grand-Duchy of Baden, and Homburg, in Hesse-Homburg, were the two most famous resorts in Europe of the frequenters of gaming-tables. After the formation of the empire in 1871 gaming was suppressed in these places (31st Dec., 1872), and since that time the principality of Monaco has become the last public resort of this species of gambling.

In Great Britain gaming has been the subject of numerous enactments. Henry VIII made proclamation against certain games, including dice, cards, and bowls, and prohibited the keeping of any common house for unlawful games under penalties of 40s. per day for keeping the house, and 6s. 8d. per time for playing in it. By an Act of Charles II (1663) any person fraudulently winning money by gaming is to forfeit treble the amount, and any person losing more than £100 at cards or dice on credit at one sitting is not bound to pay, and the winner forfeits treble the amount. Under Anne all notes, bills, and bonds given for money won by gaming were decreed void, and any person paying a loss of more than £10 might recover it within three months as a common debt; or if the loser did not sue, any other person might do so. In the reign of William IV such notes were declared void between the parties, but not in the hands of purchasers or endorsers.

By Acts of George II keepers of public-houses were punishable for permitting gaming, and the games of faro, hazard, roulette, and all other games with dice, except backgammon, are prohibited under penalties. An Act of 1845, while repealing some of the previous Acts, and exempting games of mere skill, including billiards and dominoes, inflicts the penalty of £100 (afterwards increased to a maximum of £500) on any person keeping a gaming-house, with the alternative of six months' imprisonment. Cards and other games may of course be played in private houses, but not in gaming-houses, or in such a way as to constitute a nuisance. Persons playing or gaming in public places may be punished as rogues and vagabonds. Penalties are inflicted for keeping billiard or bagatelle tables without a licence.

Lotteries and raffles are illegal (but art union lotteries are excepted). Persons fraudulently winning money by gaming shall be deemed guilty of obtaining it by false pretences. No suit-at-law can be brought against a loser for money won at play or to recover money so lost, or to recover a deposit from a stakeholder; but this does not apply to prizes at any lawful sport. Later Acts provide that betting-houses shall be considered gaming-houses. The present state of the law in Great Britain is defined by the Street Betting Act of 1906. (*See* BETTING.) Any person found in a gaming-house who shall give a false name or address is liable to a fine of £50.—Cf. W. Coldridge and C. V. Hawksford, *The Law of Gambling, Civil and Criminal*.

GAMBOGE (from *Camboja* or *Cambodia*), a concrete, vegetable, inspissated juice or sap, or gum-resin, yielded by several species of trees. The gamboge of European commerce appears to be mainly derived from *Garcinia Hanburii*, a diœcious tree with handsome laurel-like foliage and small yellow flowers, found in Cambodia, Siam, and in the southern parts of Cochin-China. This substance is contained chiefly in the middle layer of the bark of the tree; it is obtained by incision, and issues in the form of a yellowish fluid, which, after passing through a viscid state, hardens into the gamboge of commerce. It consists of a mixture of resin with 15 to 20 per cent of gum.

Gamboge is used in painting, staining, and lacquering. As a drug it has drastic purgative properties, but is seldom administered alone. In doses of a dram or even less it produces death. Other species of Garcinia yield a similar drug. The so-called American gamboge is the juice of *Vismia guianensis* and other South American species.

GAME LAWS, laws relating to the killing of certain wild animals pursued for sport, and called game. Formerly in Britain certain qualifications of rank or property were needed to confer the right to kill game; but this was altered by the Game Act of 1831, and now anyone is qualified to kill game who has taken out a proper inland revenue licence, and every one must hold such a licence whether he is to kill game on his own land, or on that of another with his permission. The law differs somewhat in England, Scotland, and Ireland, but the animals specially designated as game are hares, pheasants, partridges, grouse, black-game, and bustards; while hares and rabbits are also spoken of as 'ground game.'

Close Seasons. No one is allowed to kill winged game during a part of the year called the *close season*, which for partridges begins on 2nd Feb. and ends on 31st Aug., for pheasants is from 2nd Feb. to 30th Sept., for grouse from 11th Dec. to 11th Aug., for black-game from 11th Dec. to 19th Aug. The close-season was established for humanitarian reasons, to allow the birds to breed; but the season ends on different days for different birds merely to enable sportsmen to have an abundance and a variety of game. Hares are also protected during the months March-July.

Penalties. Any person killing game on Sunday or Christmas Day is liable to a fine of £5. Generally, a game licence is also necessary to enable a person to kill deer, woodcocks, snipe, quails, landrails, and rabbits. A person who kills game without a licence is liable to a penalty of £20 (for breach of the excise laws). Whoever trespasses by day in pursuit of game, or any of the above-mentioned animals (though he may possess a game licence), is liable to the fine of £2, and when five or more go together each is liable to the penalty of £5. Night-poaching is a graver matter; the first offence renders the guilty party liable to imprisonment with hard labour for three months, and to find security for good behaviour.

Licences. The duties on licences for killing or dealing in game are excise duties, and are regulated as follows: for a licence to each person for taking or killing any game whatever, if taken after 31st July and before 1st Nov., to expire on 31st July following, £3; if to expire on 31st Oct. of the same year, £2; from 1st Nov. to 31st July, £2; if for a continuous period of fourteen days alone, £1; licence to deal in game, £2.

A person holding a game licence does not require a gun licence.

By an Act of 1880 every occupier of land has a right, as inseparable from and incident to the occupation of the land, to kill and take ground-game (hares and rabbits) thereon, concurrently with any other duly authorized person, all agreements in contravention of this right being declared void. Game laws of greater or less strictness are in force in many other countries. In Canada and the United States the chief restrictions are in regard to killing wild animals during the breeding season.—BIBLIOGRAPHY: Warry, *Game Laws of England*; Marchant and Watkins, *Wild Birds Protection Act*; Oke, *Game Laws* (5th edition, 1912).

GAMES, a name of certain sports or amusements carried on under regular rules and methods, as with cards or dice, billiards, tennis, &c. Among the ancients there were public games or sports, exhibited on solemn occasions, in which various kinds of contests were introduced.

The Grecian games were national festivals attended by spectators and competitors from all parts of Greece, the chief being the Olympic, Pythian, Nemean, and Isthmian. They consisted of chariot races, running, and wrestling and boxing matches, and victory in one of these contests was esteemed one of the highest achievements of a Greek citizen.

The Roman games (*ludi*) were held chiefly at the festivals of the gods. They might, however, be exhibited by private persons to please the people, as the combats of gladiators, theatrical representations, and combats of wild beasts in the amphitheatre. *See also* such articles as ATHLETIC SPORTS; BILLIARDS; CHESS; CRICKET; FOOTBALL; &c.; *also* CHILDREN'S GAMES.

GAMETES, in botany, a general term denoting sexual cells, such as the spermatozoids or ova of Ferns and other oögamous plants, or the two similar cells (isogametes) which conjugate with one another in the case of *Spirogyra* or *Mucor*. See FERNS; ZYGOTE.

GAMETOPHYTE, the phase in the life-history of a plant which terminates with the production of gametes, e.g. the Moss-plant or the prothallus of a Fern.

GAMMA RAYS, one of the emanations from certain radio-active substances. They include electro-magnetic waves more penetrating than X-rays and of smaller wave length. They are given out by some forms of radium, thorium and actinium.

GAMOPETALOUS FLOWERS, those which have the petals cohering, as the primrose, foxglove, deadnettle, &c., in fact, all such as belong to the sub-class known as gamopetalous or sympetalous Dicotyledons.

GAM'UT, or GAMMUT, in music, the entire series of musical tones in the natural order of ascent or descent. With the musicians of the eleventh century A represented the lowest note in their instruments, and a lower note having been introduced, the Greek gamma (Γ) was taken to represent it. From its prominent place as first note of the scale its name was taken to represent the whole. This system of

Gandhi

musical notation was invented in the tenth century by Guido Arezzo, a Benedictine monk.

GANDAK', or GUNDUCK, a river of Northern India, rising in the Himalayas and entering the Ganges; length, 400 miles.

GANDAMAK', a place in North-Eastern Afghanistan, where a treaty with Britain was signed in 1879. *See* AFGHANISTAN.

GANDHI, Mohandas Karamchand, Indian Nationalist. Born in India, 2nd Oct., 1869, he studied law in London, and then returned to practise as a barrister in Bombay. In 1893 he was in S. Africa, where he led his fellow countrymen in their opposition to the legislation directed against them. His methods were successful, and he became known as a leader of the nationalist movement, which gained a good deal of strength after the World War.

In 1919 Gandhi acted as the spokesman of those who objected to British rule in India, and was soon recognized as their leader. He organized a boycott of British goods, and started the movement known as non-co-operation. In 1922 he was arrested for sedition and sentenced to a term of imprisonment; but in 1924, having still four years to serve, he was released. After a period of quiet he renewed his agitation in 1930, his violent speeches, in which he urged the expulsion of the British from India, leading again to his arrest. He was, however, soon released, and at Delhi he made an agreement with the Viceroy, promising, in return for a large measure of self-government for India, to call off the boycott. In spite of this, he continued to make demands for India which to Englishmen seemed impossible. In 1931 he came to London to attend the Round Table Conference, but was arrested and imprisoned shortly after his return to India. Mrs. Gandhi also was arrested and sentenced to six months' imprisonment. In September, 1932, Gandhi by a prolonged fast endeavoured to force the hand of the Government. In May, 1933, he again fasted, on this occasion as a protest against the religious tabu of "untouchability." To his followers Gandhi is the mahatma, or master.

GANDIA, a town and port of Spain, in the province and 34 miles south by east of Valencia, on the Alcoy. It is walled and well built, with a handsome Gothic church and a fine palace of the Dukes of Gandia. Pop. 12,639.

GANDO, a former sultanate of the Western Sudan, intersected by the Niger, and inhabited chiefly by Fellatahs, with a capital of the same name. It is most fertile. Mohammedanism is the prevalent religion. Since 1898 the territory has been merged in the colonies of Nigeria, and in Dahomey and Upper Senegal.

GANESA (ga-nā'sa), an Indian god, the son of Siva and Párvati, represented by a figure half man half elephant, having an elephant's head. He is the god of prudence and good luck, and is invoked at the beginning of all enterprises. There are not many temples dedicated to him, and he has no public festivals, but his image stands in almost every house.

GANGES (gan'jez), a river of Hindustan, one of the greatest rivers of Asia, rising in the Himalaya Mountains, in Garhwál state, and formed by the junction of two head-streams, the Bhagirathi and the Alaknanda, which unite at Deoprag, 10 miles below Srinagar, 1,500 feet above sea-level. The Bhagirathi, as being a sacred stream, is usually considered the source of the Ganges, rising at the height of 13,800 feet, but the Alaknanda flows farther and brings a larger volume of water to the junction. At Hardwar, about 30 miles below Deoprag, the river fairly enters the great valley of Hindustan, and flows in a south - easterly direction till it discharges itself by numerous mouths into the Bay of Bengal, after a course of about 1,540 miles.

During its course it is joined by eleven large rivers, the chief being the Jumna, Son, Ramganga, Gumti, Gogra, Gandak, and Kusi. In the rainy season the flat country of Bengal is overflowed to the extent of 100 miles in breadth, the water beginning to recede after the middle of August. The Ganges delta has the Hugli on the west, the Meghna on the east, and commences about 200 miles, or 300 miles by the course of the river, from the sea. Along the sea it forms an uninhabited swampy waste, called Sunderbunds, or Sundarbans, the whole coast of the delta is a mass of shifting mud-banks. The westernmost branch, the Hugli, is the only branch commonly navigated by ships. The Meghna, or main branch, on the east is joined by a branch of the Brahmaputra.

Some of the principal cities on the Ganges and its branches, ascending the stream, are Calcutta, Mursheda-bad, Behar, Patna, Benares, Allahabad, Cawnpore, and Faruckabad. The Ganges is navigable for boats of a large size nearly 1,500 miles from its mouths, and it forms a great channel for traffic. It is an imperative duty of the Hindus to bathe in the Ganges, or at least to wash themselves with its waters, and to distribute alms, on certain days. The Hindus believe that whoever dies on its banks, and drinks of its waters before death, is exempted from the necessity of returning into this world and commencing a new life. The sick are therefore carried to the bank of the Ganges, and its water is a considerable article of commerce in the remoter parts of India.

GANGES CANAL, UPPER, a lateral canal in Northern India (United Provinces) constructed for purposes of irrigation and supplementary navigation, extending on the right of the Ganges from Hardwar to Cawnpore.—The **Lower Ganges Canal** is a sort of continuation of the Upper, intended for irrigation purposes. The Upper Canal was opened in 1854, and the Lower Canal in 1878. The total length is about 700 miles, and the total cost of the works has been about £5,000,000.

GANG'LION, in anatomy, an enlargement occurring somewhere in the course of a nerve, and containing nerve cells in addition to nerve filaments. There are two systems of nerves which have ganglia upon them. First, those of common sensation whose ganglia are near to the entry of the nerve into the spinal cord. Secondly, the great sympathetic nerve, which has ganglia on various parts of it. In the invertebrates ganglia form the central nervous system, and are distributed through the body in pairs, one for each ring of the body, connected by fibres as in the figure. The cerebral ganglia of vertebrates are the

Ganesa

brain itself, and the masses of grey matter at the base of the brain, as the optic thalamus.

GANGPUR', a native state of Bengal, in Chota Nagpur, consisting mainly of hills, forest, and jungle; area, 2,492 sq. miles; pop. about 300,271.

GANGRENE is the death of a considerable area of body tissue. It is known as dry gangrene when the tissues involved were previously drained of fluid, and moist gangrene when the part is full of fluid. In the latter condition putrefaction frequently appears, as the moisture is favourable to the growth of putrefactive germs. Amputation or removal of the affected part is necessary. Anything that lowers or destroys the vitality of living tissues favours the development of gangrene, as seen by its appearance in certain diseases, in the senile and debilitated, or following the application of certain substances to the skin.

GANGWAY, a narrow platform or bridge of planks along the upper part of a ship's side for communication fore and aft; also a sort of platform by which persons enter and leave a vessel.

In the House of Commons the gangway is a passage across the House, which separates the Ministry and Opposition with their respective adherents, who sit on seats running along the sides of the House, from the neutral or independent members, who

Gannet (Sula bassāna)

occupy seats running across. Hence, the phrase *to sit below the gangway*, as applied to a member, implies that he holds himself as bound to neither party.

GANISTER, or **CROWSTONE,** a hard sandstone found in Yorkshire, Derbyshire, Lancashire, &c., mainly in association with the Lower Coal Measures. Ground down, it is used to make furnace-hearths, and, mixed with clay, to line Bessemer converters.

GANJAM, a town of India, in the Madras Presidency, formerly capital of the district of the same name, near the coast of the Bay of Bengal. It was at one time a flourishing place; but the town declined after the epidemic of 1815, when Berhampur became the headquarters. Pop. 5,100. The principal arm of the Ganjam River, which enters the sea to the south of the town, is about one-third of a mile broad.—The district, one of the five Circars, is one of the most productive

under the Madras Presidency, yielding rice, cotton, sugar, rum, and pulse. Area, 8,380 sq. miles; pop. 1,896,803.

GANNET, the solan goose, a bird of the genus Sula (S. bassāna), the type of a family (Sulidæ) of aquatic birds, related to cormorants and pelicans. It is about 3 feet in length, and 6 feet in breadth of wings from tip to tip; the whole plumage a dirty white, inclining to grey; the eyes a pale yellow, surrounded by a naked skin of a fine blue colour; the bill straight, 6 inches long, and furnished beneath with a kind of pouch.

The gannets are birds of passage, arriving in Great Britain about March and departing in August or September, their movements being partially determined by those of the herring, on which they feed. They migrate to the southward in the winter, and appear on the coast of Portugal. In the breeding season they retire to high rocks on unfrequented islands—the Hebrides, Orkneys, St. Kilda, Ailsa Craig, and the Bass Rock. The nests are generally formed of seaweed. The female lays only one egg, though, if it be removed, she will deposit another. The young, which are much darker than the old birds, remain in the nest until nearly their full size, becoming extremely fat. In St. Kilda they form part of the food of the inhabitants, being taken by men lowered from the top of the cliffs. A number of related species, known to sailors as 'boobies,' range through the warmer parts of the ocean.—Cf. J. H. Gurney, *The Gannet; a Bird with a History.*

GAN'OIDS (Ganoidei), the second order of fishes according to Agassiz. This artificial group is now broken up into three distinct orders. The species of this order are chiefly characterized by angular, rhomboidal, polygonal, or circular scales composed of horny or bony plates covered with a thick layer of glossy enamel-like substance.

The ganoids were most numerous in Palæozoic and early Mesozoic times, but are now represented by eight genera: (1) Crossopterygii: Polypterus, the bichir, represented by a single species occurring in rivers of tropical Africa; Calamoichthys, the reed-fish, found in Old Calabar. (2) Chondrostei: Acipenser, represented by the sturgeon; Scaphirhynchus, best known by the so-called shovelnosed sturgeon of the Mississippi basin, but also represented in Eastern Asia; Polyodon, the paddle-fish of the Mississippi; and Psephurus, native to the great rivers of China. (3) Holostei: Amia, the bow-fin (A. calva), common in the fresh waters of central and southern North America, and distinguished by the possession of flexible overlapping scales; Lepidosteus, including the garfish or bony pike of the North American rivers and lakes.

GANTUNG PASS, a wild pass in the Western Himalayas between Bussahir in the Punjab and Tibet. It is covered with perpetual snow, and is 18,295 feet in height.

GAN'YMEDE (-mēd), in Grecian mythology, the son of Tros and of Callirrhoë, daughter of Scamander. Zeus sent his eagle to carry him off from Mount Ida to Olympus, where he held the office of cup-bearer to the immortals in succession to Hebe. He was also represented as the genius of the fertilizing and life-giving Nile.

GAPER-SHELL, a bivalve mollusc, the *Mya arenaria,* common on the British coasts. It has an oblong shell, and burrows in sand and mud, where it is sought after for bait. The otter shell (Lutraria) is closely related.

GAPES, a disease of fowls and other Rasorial birds, arising from the presence in the windpipe of small parasitic worms (*Fasciola tracheālis*) which cause the bird continually to open its beak. They may be dislodged with an oiled feather, or by mixing a little Epsom salts with the food.

GAPON, Father, Russian priest and revolutionary, born at Biliki, government of Poltava, in 1870, died in 1906. On account of his revolutionary views he was not allowed by the Governmentof the Tsar to take charge of a parish. He became a prominent leader of the revolutionary movement in Russia in 1905, when the great strikes broke out and 12,000 Putilov workmen ceased work. Gapon led the deputation to Tsarskoe Selo to see the Tsar on the famous Red Sunday in 1905. He was saved by his friends and escaped to London, but subsequently disappeared, and it is still doubtful whether he committed suicide or was executed at Petrograd by the revolutionary party whom he had betrayed. —Cf. Gapon, *The Story of my Life.*

GAR'ANCIN, or **GARANCINE,** the product obtained by treating pulverized madder, previously exhausted with water, with concentrated sulphuric acid at 100° C. (212° F.), and again washing with water. The residue thus obtained is found to yield better results in dyeing than madder itself.

GARAY (gå'rĭ), Janos, Hungarian poet, born in 1812, died blind in 1853. He studied at Pesth, where he held a minor post in the public library. His heroic poem *Csatár* (1834) was succeeded by a number of dramas, mostly historical, the chief being *Arbocz* (1837), *Orszǵgy Ilona* (1837), and

Bátory Erzsébet (1840). His cycle of historic ballads, showing Uhland's influence, was published in 1847, under the title *Arpádok,* and his lyric poems *Balatoni Kagylok* (Shells from Lake Balaton) in 1843. His last work was an historical epic, *Szent László* (St. Ladislaus), published 1850.

GARBLER, formerly an officer of the city of London, vested with power to enter any shop or warehouse to examine drugs and spices, and garble (i.e. sift out the coarse parts, dirt &c.) and make clean the same or see it done.

GARBO, Greta, Swedish film actress. Greta Gustafsson was born 18th Sept., 1905, in Stockholm, and at the age of fourteen began work in a department store. In 1922 she began to work in films, and later joined a Dramatic School. She played in *Gosta Berling's Saga* under the direction of Mauritz Stiller, and changed

Ganymede

her name to Garbo. After a picture in Germany she went to Hollywood, with Stiller, and made her first picture, *The Talent.* There followed *The Tempiress, The Flesh and the Devil, Love, The Divine Woman, Anna Christie, Romance, Inspiration, Mati Hari* and *Grand Hotel.*

GARCILASO DE LA VEGA (gàr-thē-là'sō; properly **GARCIAS LASO DE LA VEGA**), called the *prince of Spanish poets,* born at Toledo in 1500 or 1503, died in 1536. He went in his youth to the Spanish court, and in 1529 distinguished himself in the Spanish corps serving against the Turks in Austria. An intrigue with a lady of the court led to his imprisonment on an island in the Danube, where several of his poems were composed.

In 1529 he was engaged in the expedition against Soliman, and in 1535 in that against Tunis. He was made commander of thirty companies of infantry in 1536, and accompanied the imperial army against Marseilles, but was mortally wounded in attempting to scale a tower near Fréjus. He died at Nice, and was buried at Toledo. His name is associated with that of his contemporary Boscan in the impetus given to Spanish literature by the imitation of the Italian poetic style as exemplified in Petrarch, Ariosto, and Sannazaro. His works, which consist of eclogues, epistles, odes, songs, and sonnets, are graceful and musical. His poems were first published in 1543.

GARCILASO DE LA VEGA, or **GARCIAS LASO DE LA VEGA,** historian of Peru, surnamed the Inca, son of Garcilaso de la Vega, one of the conquerors of Peru, and a princess of the race of the Incas; born at Cuzco, Peru, in 1530 or 1540. Having fallen under the groundless suspicion of the Spanish Government, he was sent home in 1560, and died in 1616 or 1620. His great work on the history of Peru is in two parts: the first entitled *Los Comentarios Reales que tratan del Origen de los Incas* (Lisbon, 1609); the second, the *Historia general del Perú* (Cordova, 1616). He wrote also *Historia de la Florida* (Lisbon, 1609).

GARCINIA, the genus of plants to which the mangosteen and gamboge belong, nat. ord. Guttiferæ.

GARD, a department of Southern France, abutting on the Gulf of Lyons; area, 2,270 sq. miles. The north and west are occupied by the Cevennes and their branches, sloping gradually into a fertile plain, the coast-line of which is so low as to form extensive swamps and salines. The drainage belongs partly to the Garonne, but chiefly to the Rhône, which forms the east boundary. Within the department the chief river is the Gard. The rich lower districts produce a large quantity of wine, and are noted for silk-culture. Large quantities of salt are made; and lead, coal, iron, &c., are worked. There are silk, woollen, and cotton manufactures. Nîmes is the capital. Pop. (1931), 406,815.

GARD, PONT DU, a fine Roman aqueduct, in Gard, 10 miles from Nîmes, joining two mountains, and passing over the Gardon. It has three tiers of arches, and is 160 feet high. *See* AQUEDUCT.

GARDA, or **BENA'CO, LAKE** (It. *Lago di Garda*; the *Benácus Lacus* of the Romans), the largest lake in Italy, belonging to the Alpine region, 32¼ miles long north to south, 3 to 11 miles broad, greatest depth, 902 feet, 213 feet above sea-level. The Sarca, almost its only affluent, enters at its north end, and it is drained by the Mincio, which issues from its south-

east end, near Peschiera. It is well stocked with fish. Steamboats ply on it, and its shores are covered with villas.

GARDAYA (går-dä'yå), or **GHARDAIA,** name of a territory and of a town of Algeria, in the Sahara. The town is surrounded by a wall flanked with towers and entered by ten gates. Pop. of territory (1931), 144,366; of town, 11,000. *See* BENI-MZÂB.

GARDE ÉCOSSAISE (gärd ä-kos-āz), the Scottish guard in the service of the Kings of France, first instituted on a regular footing by Charles VII, who in 1453 selected a hundred Scottish archers to form a special body-guard in recognition of the service of the Scottish soldiery in the Hundred Years' War. There was also another company of a hundred Scots placed at the head of a regular army of fifteen companies of 100 lances each, which was organized. This body was commanded by Scots of the highest rank. James VI, and his sons Henry and Charles, and James II when Duke of York, held in succession the rank of captain in it.

GARDELEGEN, town of Germany. It stands on the Mulde, and on the railway line from Hanover to Berlin. Here, during the Great War, the Germans set up a camp for prisoners of war. In 1915 about 11,000 men were interned, and great distress was caused by epidemics of typhus and other diseases. The German treatment of the prisoners in this camp was the subject of a special report drawn up by the British Government in 1916.

GARDE NATIONALE (nà-syo-nál), a guard of armed citizens instituted at Paris on the 13th of July, 1789, for the purpose of preserving order and protecting liberty. At first it numbered 48,000 men, but was increased to 300,000 when it was organized throughout the whole country. Acting as a Royalist and reactionary force, it was crushed by Napoleon in 1795. It was reorganized by the Directory and by Napoleon, and again under the Bourbons, to whom, however, it was a source of such disquietude that it was dissolved by a Royal Ordinance in 1827.

Under Louis Philippe it was resuscitated in its old form, and contributed to his overthrow. In 1851 the National Guard was again reorganized, but in 1855 it was dissolved. In 1870 the National Guard of Paris was again formed for the defence of the city against the Prussians. The resistance of a section of the guard to the decree of disarmament issued under M. Thiers led to the insurrection of the Commune, at the close of which the guard was declared dissolved by the National Assembly (1871).

GARDE NATIONALE MOBILE, a body constituted by Napoleon III in 1868, on the suggestion of Marshal Niel, to form bases of regiments to supplement the regular army. It was called into action in 1870–1, but was too badly organized to be efficient.

GARDEN CITIES, the term for cities or centres of population which would have much garden-ground as one of their features. They are the expressed result of an attempt to remedy the evils of overcrowding in large towns, one means of starting them being by getting manufacturers to move their works out of the towns into the country, and erecting sanitary dwellings suited for their employees, care being taken to leave plenty of open spaces among the dwellings, thus combining the advantages of town and country.

One of the earliest practical essays of the kind was the model village of Port Sunlight, not far from Birkenhead, erected by Messrs. Lever Bros. for their employees. Mr. George Cadbury subsequently placed an estate at Bournville, near Birmingham, in the hands of trustees, and expressed his willingness to advance his workpeople and others money for building on right principles, a certain amount of land being for ever kept clear round each dwelling. Mr. Joseph Rowntree, early in 1905, established a Garden Village Trust at Earswick, near York; but the first Garden City proper is the outcome of a scheme outlined by Mr. Ebenezer Howard in 1898.

An estate of nearly 4,000 acres was acquired at Letchworth, near Hitchin, in 1903, by the Garden City Association, Ltd.; water and sewage arrangements were seen to at once, and the supply of roads, railway, gas, and other facilities followed. Several firms have moved their works there, and a number of well-to-do people have secured sites for residences. Each dwelling has its own garden, and roughly three-quarters of the estate is to be devoted, in perpetuity, to small holdings, parks, &c. A feature of many of these schemes and also of Garden Suburbs is provision for co-operative ownership and administration of the estates by the tenants.

An analogous movement is that for the erection of Garden Suburbs, which are not intended to be complete economic entities like Letchworth, but are designed to provide dwelling-places in healthy and beautiful surroundings on the outskirts of large cities and towns. The best-known Garden Suburb is that at Golders Green, which is built on an extension of Hampstead Heath, and is known as 'Hampstead Garden Suburb,' but a number of other such suburbs are already in existence, and many of the local schemes to remedy the housing shortage felt in 1919 at the close of the European War are on Garden Suburb lines. A large scheme has been carried out at Welwyn, in Hertfordshire, and the Welwyn Garden City has a station on the L.N.E. Railway.

The success of the movement for building garden cities and suburbs must, however, be measured not only by the number of actual Garden Cities and Suburbs in existence, but also by the general improvement in the situation and design of artisan and middle-class houses which is already manifesting itself as a result of the growth of civic pride fostered by the movement, and also by the desire of private undertakers of building not to be outdone by the associations whose competition they now have to meet.

The movement has spread from England to the Continent, and both France and Germany can show creditable examples of Garden Cities. The pioneers of the movement have been enabled to see, even in their own lifetime, a great improvement in the standard of living. To promote the movement, the Garden Cities and Town Planning Association was founded in 1899, with offices at 3, Gray's Inn Place, London, W.C.1.— Cf. C. B. Purdom, *The Garden City.*

GARDEN CITY, on Long Island (U.S.A.), is 20 miles from New York.

GARDE′NIA, a genus of trees and shrubs, nat. ord. Rubiaceæ, natives of tropical Asia and Africa, bearing beautiful white or yellowish flowers of great fragrance. *G. florida* and *G. radicans* are well known in Britain as Cape jasmine, though natives of Japan.

GARDENING (as a career). The possibilities of employment after a horticultural training include nursery gardening, landscape gardening, positions with fruit, flower and vegetable growers, occasional openings in connection with public parks and botanical gardens, and sub-inspectorships under the Ministry of Agriculture. To begin market gardening in a small way, capital amounting to about £1,000 to £1,500 is required.

The highest qualifications to be obtained are the London B.Sc. in Horticulture, and the National Diploma in Horticulture held by the Royal Horticultural Society with the approval of the Board of Agriculture. Other examinations held by the Royal Horticultural Society are:

The General Examination (Juniors and Seniors).

The Teachers' Examination in School and Cottage Gardening (Preliminary and Advanced).

Training for the horticultural examinations is best taken at a college, such as the Royal Horticultural Society's School at Wisley, Surrey, for men (two years' course). Practical experience with a horticulturist is extremely helpful, a premium usually being required. Both sexes are admitted to University College, Reading, and the Royal Botanic Society's School of Gardening in London.

A list of Horticultural Colleges for both men and women, and a syllabus of examinations, may be obtained from the Secretary, Royal Horticultural Society, Vincent Square, Westminster, S.W. 1.

GARDEN-SPIDER, also called **DIADEM,** or **CROSS-SPIDER,** the *Epeira diadema,* a common British spider the dorsal surface of which is marked with a triple yellow cross. It forms a beautiful geometric web.

GARDEN-WARBLER, (*Sylvia hortensis*), a migratory song-bird visiting Britain from the end of April to September. It is rather less than 6 inches long, the head and upper surface greenish-brown, the under surface brownish-white.

GARDINER, Samuel Rawson, English historian, born in 1829, died in Feb., 1902. Educated at Winchester and Christ Church, Oxford, he was for some years professor of modern history at King's College, London, but resigned in 1885. He specially devoted himself to the period of English history beginning with the accession of James I, and gave a full and impartial account of the events of the time, based on the original documents. The first section comes down to the outbreak of the Civil War (1603–42), the second deals with the Civil War (1642–9), the third with the Commonwealth and Protectorate. He also wrote: *Cromwell's Place in History, Oliver Cromwell,* and a *Student's History of England.*

GARDINER, Stephen, an English prelate, son of John Gardiner, a cloth-merchant of Bury St. Edmunds. He was born in 1493 at Bury St. Edmunds, and died in 1555. In 1520 he took the degrees of D.D. and LL.D. at Cambridge, where he became master of Trinity Hall. He passed at this time by the name of Dr. Stephens. Having become secretary to Wolsey and a favourite with the king, he was dispatched to Rome in 1528 to forward Henry VIII's divorce, and on his return was appointed Secretary of State, and in succession Archdeacon of Norwich and Leicester, and Bishop of Winchester. He also went on various embassies to France and Germany. Although he supported the king in renouncing the authority of the Pope, he opposed the doctrines of the Reformation, and took an active part in the passing of the Six Articles and in the prosecution of Protestants. He was successful in contriving the fall of his opponent Cromwell, but failed to injure Catherine Parr, and fell into disfavour.

During the reign of Edward he was imprisoned in the Fleet, deprived of his bishopric, and afterwards imprisoned in the Tower from 1548–53, but Mary restored him to his bishopric, and appointed him Lord Chancellor. He officiated at her coronation and marriage, became one of her chief advisers, and took an active part in the persecutions at the beginning of the reign, maintaining also the illegitimacy of Elizabeth. His works include: *De Vera Obedientia* (1534), a defence of the king's supremacy; *A Necessary Doctrine of a Christian Man* (1543); *Sacrament of the Aulter* (1551); and some tracts.—BIBLIOGRAPHY: Cassan, *Lives of the Bishops of Winchester*; R. W. Dixon, *History of the Church of England.*

GARDNER, Ernest Arthur, English archæologist, born in London in 1862. Educated at the City of London School and at Caius College, Cambridge, he explored in 1885 Naucratis, a Greek colony in Egypt, and was Craven student from 1887 to 1889. Director of the British School of Archæology at Athens from 1887 to 1895, he became Yates professor of archæology at University College, London. In 1910 he was elected first public orator of London University. During the European War he saw service at Salonika. His works include: *Introduction to Greek Epigraphy* (1887), *A Handbook of Greek Sculpture* (1896–7), *Ancient Athens* (1902), *The Inscriptions of Attica* (1905), *Religion and Art in Ancient Greece* (1910), *Six Greek Sculptors* (1910), *The Art of Greece* (1925). In 1931 he contributed to *Art of Egypt Through the Ages.*

GARFIELD, James Abram, an American general and statesman, the twentieth President of the United States, born in Ohio on 19th Nov., 1831, died 19th Sept., 1881. He worked on a farm till his fourteenth year, but acquired a good education, studied law, and in 1859 was elected to the Ohio state Senate. In 1861 he entered the army, was appointed colonel, became chief of staff to Rosecranz, and major-general of volunteers.

In 1863 he was elected to Congress

and resigned his command. He sat in nine Congresses for the same constituency, serving on important committees, and winning ground no less by strong intelligence than uncompromising honesty. In 1880 he was elected to the Senate, and in the same year became President of the United States. Many reforms seemed about to be inaugurated, when he was shot by a disappointed office-seeker named Guiteau, in the railway station at Washington. He lingered eighty days, dying at Long Branch.—Cf. Lossing, *A Biography of James A. Garfield*.

GARFISH, SEA-PIKE, or **GAR-PIKE** (*Belŏne vulgāris*), a fish, known also as the *sea-needle*, making its appearance on the English coasts in summer, a short time before the mackerel. It is long and slender, sometimes 2 or 3 feet in length; the head projects forward into a very long, sharp snout; the sides and belly are of a bright silvery colour, and the back green, marked with a dark purple line. The bones are of a bright-green colour.

The name Garfish or Gar-pike is also given to other species of Belŏne, and to a ganoid fish of the genus Lepidosteus, found in the fresh waters of America. *See* BONY-PIKE.

GARFORTH, urban district of Yorkshire (W.R.). It is 7 miles from Leeds, on the L.N.E. Rly. The principal industry is coal mining. Pop. (1931) 3,774.

GAR'GANEY (*Anas querquedūla*), a species of duck called also 'summer

Garfield Memorial, Cleveland, Ohio

teal,' from its habit of visiting Britain in summer, and from its close kinship to the common teal. It is widely spread through the eastern hemisphere.

GARGA'NO (Lat. *Gargānus*), a group of pine-clad mountains in South Italy, province of Foggia, forming the spur of the boot in the Italian peninsula projecting into the Adriatic. The loftiest summit is Calvo, 5,295 feet.

Garfish (*Belŏne vulgāris*)

GARGAN'TUA, the hero of Rabelais' satire (*Gargantua and Pantagruel*), so named from his father exclaiming "*Que grand tu as!*" "How large (a gullet) thou hast!" on hearing him cry out, immediately on his birth, "Drink, drink!" so lustily as to be heard over several districts. It required 900 ells of linen for the body of his shirt, and 200 more for the gussets, 1,100 cow-hides for the soles of his shoes, and he picked his teeth with an elephant's tusk. *See* RABELAIS.

GARGLE is a wash for the throat. To use a gargle about half a fluid ounce (one tablespoonful) of the fluid to be used should be taken into the mouth and, with the head well thrown back, allowed to pass into the throat. Air should then be expelled through the fluid to enable the fluid to come in contact with all the walls of the passage. Gargles are more effective in chronic throat conditions, and should not be used in very acute throat infections.

GAR'GOYLE, in Gothic architecture, a projecting spout for throwing the water from the gutter of a building, usually of some grotesque form, such as the head or figure of an animal or monster. Among famous gargoyles are those of Notre Dame in Paris.

GARHWÁL (gar-hwäl'), or **GURHWAL,** a district of India, in the United Provinces, bounded on the north by Tibet, east by Kumáun, south by Bijnaur district, and west by the Garhwal state; area, 5,612 sq. miles; pop. 485,186. There are good roads, and a considerable trade with Tibet.

GARHWÁL, or **TEHRI,** a native Indian state under British protection, west of the district of the same name; area, 4,500 sq. miles; pop. 318,482. Chief town, Tehri; chief rivers, the Alaknanda and other headwaters of the Ganges. A large part is covered with forests, which include valuable *deodar* tracts, leased to the British Government in 1864.

GARHWALIS, the inhabitants of a hilly tract of country in the Lower

Gargoyle, St. Cuthbert's, York. Fifteenth century

Himalayas, some 5,500 sq. miles in extent, and bounded on the north by Tibet. Garhwalis are small lightly-built men, and furnish a two-battalion regiment—the 39th Garhwal Rifles—to the Indian Army. As soldiers they are intelligent, law-abiding, and loyal. By religion they are Hindus. Unlike the Gurkha, whom in some respects he resembles, the Garhwali is not much given to sport or voluntary exercise of any kind. He is, however, capable of standing great fatigue and showing the maximum of endurance on little food; moreover, he is exceptionally steady in danger. The Garhwali uniform is similar to that of the Gurkha Rifles, and, like them, they wear short knickerbockers leaving the knees bare, and slouch hats instead of the usual pagri or turban.

GARIBAL'DI, Giuseppe, Italian patriot and hero, the son of a poor fisherman, was born at Nice 1807, and died on 2nd June, 1882, He got little education, and for a number of years was a sailor on various trading vessels. In 1834 he became a member of the 'Young Italy' party, and being condemned to death for his share in the schemes of Mazzini, escaped to Marseilles, took service in the fleet of the Bey of Tunis, and finally went to South America. In the service of the Republic of Rio Grande against the Brazilians he became known as a brilliant leader, and with his famous Italian legion he subsequently gave the Monte Videans such effective aid against Buenos Ayres as to earn the title of 'hero of Monte Video.'

In 1848 he returned to Italy, raised a band of volunteers, and harassed Austrians until the cessation of hostilities and re-establishment of the Austrian supremacy in Lombardy. He then retired to Switzerland, but in the spring of 1849 proceeded to Rome to support Mazzini's republic. He was appointed to command the forces, but the odds were overwhelming, and after a desperate defence of thirty days Garibaldi escaped from Rome with 4,000 of his followers. In the course of his flight his wife Anita died from fatigue and privations. He reached the United States, and was for some years in command of a merchant vessel. He then purchased a part of the small Island of Caprera, off the north coast of Sardinia, and made this his home for the rest of his life. The subscriptions of his admirers enabled him afterwards to become owner of the whole island.

In the war of 1859, in which Sardinia recovered Lombardy, Gari-

Giuseppe Garibaldi

baldi and his Chasseurs of the Alps did splendid service; and on the revolt of the Sicilians in 1860 he crossed to the island, wrested it after a fierce struggle from the King of Naples, recrossed to the mainland and occupied Naples, where he was proclaimed Dictator of the Two

Sicilies. It was now feared that Garibaldi might prove untrue to his motto —*Italy and Victor Emmanuel*—but he readily acquiesced in the annexation of the Two Sicilies to Italy, and, declining all honours, retired to his island farm. In 1862 he endeavoured to force the Roman question to a solution, and entered Calabria with a small following, but was taken prisoner at Aspromonte by the Royal troops. He was soon released, however, and returned to Caprera. In 1864 he received an enthusiastic welcome in Britain.

In 1866 he commanded a volunteer force against the Austrians in the Italian Tyrol, but failed to accomplish anything of consequence. Next year he attempted the liberation of Rome, but near Mentana was defeated by the French and Pontifical troops, and was again imprisoned by the Italian Government, but soon pardoned and released. In 1870 he gave his services to the French Republican Government against the Germans, and with his 20,000 men rendered valuable assistance in the south-east. At the end of the war he was elected a member of the French Assembly, but speedily resigned his seat and returned to Caprera.

Rome now became the capital of united Italy, and here in Jan., 1875, Garibaldi took his seat in the Italian Parliament. The latter part of his life was spent quietly at Caprera. His popularity with the British public led to the adoption by ladies of a species of blouse called a Garibaldi, more or less resembling the red shirt worn by the patriot. His autobiography was published in English in 1889.—BIBLIOGRAPHY: Bent, *The Life of Giuseppe Garibaldi*; R. Thurston, *Garibaldi and his Friends*; R. S. Holland, *Builders of Modern Italy*; G. M. Trevelyan, *Garibaldi and the Making of Italy*.

GARIGLIANO (gä-ril-yä-nō), a river of South Italy, formed by the junction of the Liri and Sacco near Pontecorvo. After a course of 40 miles it falls into the Gulf of Gaëta; but if the Liri is regarded as the same stream, its length is more than double.

GARLIC (*Allium sativum*), a hardy perennial allied to the onion, indigenous to the south of Europe, and forming a favourite condiment amongst several nations. The leaves are grass-like, and differ from those of the common onion in not being fistulous; the stem is about 2 feet high; the flowers are white; and the root is a compound bulb, consisting of several smaller bulbs, commonly denominated *cloves*, enveloped by a common membrane. It has a strong, penetrating odour, and a pungent acrid taste. Used as a medicine it is stimulant, tonic, and promotes digestion; it has also diuretic and sudorific qualities, and is a good expectorant.—*Oil of garlic* is a sulphide of allyl, $(C_3H_5)_2S$, a colourless, strongly-smelling oil, exceedingly irritant to the palate and the skin. It is contained also in the onion, leek, and asafœtida.

GARNET, a group of mineral silicates with a general formula of $R_3''R_2'''(SiO_4)_3$, R'' being iron, calcium, magnesium, or manganese, and R''' iron, aluminium, or chromium. Crystal form commonly the rhombic dodecahedron of the cubic system, often modified by other planes until it assumes almost a spherical form.

Almandine, iron aluminium garnet, is a red species very common in argillaceous rocks altered by contact with granite, and occurring over wide areas in metamorphic rocks. When translucent, it forms part of the *precious garnet* used as a gem. *Pyrope*, magnesium aluminium garnet, is also known as precious garnet, and has been obtained in large quantities from Bohemia. The 'cinnamon stone' of Ceylon is *grossularite*, a yellowish or red-brown calcium aluminium garnet. *Uvarovite*, calcium chromium garnet, is emerald-green. The high hardness of garnet makes it suitable for a gem-stone.

GARNETT, Richard, English writer, was born at Lichfield in 1835, died in 1906. He was the son of the Rev. Richard Garnett, Assistant Keeper of Printed Books in the British Museum. Entering the same department, he became Assistant Keeper of Printed Books in 1875, and Keeper in 1890, retiring in 1899. From 1875 to 1884 he was superintendent of the reading-room. He took an active interest in the library, and superintended the publication of the *General Catalogue of Printed Books*. In 1883 he received the honorary degree of LL.D. from Edinburgh University, and in 1895 he was made a C.B.

Besides many articles in periodicals and encyclopædias, Dr. Garnett published *Primula: a Book of Lyrics* (1858); *Io in Egypt, and other Poems* (1859); *Poems from the German*; *Relics of Shelley*; *Idylls and Epigrams*, republished as *A Chaplet from the Greek Anthology*; *Iphigenia in Delphi*; *Sonnets from Dante, Petrarch, and Camoens*; *The Queen, and other Poems*; in fiction, *The Twilight of the Gods, and other Tales* (1888); *Lives of Carlyle, Emerson, Milton, and E. G. Wakefield*; *The Age of Dryden* (1895); *William Blake, Painter and Poet*

(1895); *History of English Literature* (with Edmund Gosse); *History of Italian Literature*; *Essays in Librarianship and Bibliography* (1899); *Essays of an Ex-Librarian*, &c., besides numerous works which he edited.

GARNIERITE, a green mineral, a hydrous silicate of magnesium and nickel, forming an important ore of nickel in New Caledonia.

GARNISHMENT (O.Fr. *guarnir*, *warnir*; Eng. to warn). This is an order at the instance of a creditor inhibiting a third party who is known as 'the garnishee,' and who is in possession of goods belonging to the debtor, or is himself indebted to the debtor, from handing over the goods or making payment of the money pending a settlement of the creditor's claim.

Its purpose is to enable the goods or money to be made available for satisfaction of the debt in the event of the debtor's default. Should judgment have been obtained against the debtor, the order is known as a 'garnishee order.'

It is granted by the court upon an *ex parte* application supported by an affidavit setting forth the fact that judgment has been obtained against the debtor and has not been satisfied. The garnishee may show cause why the order should not be implemented, but failing due cause shown he must make payment into court, such payment operating as a discharge *pro tanto* by the debtor in favour of the *garnishee*.

Any debt in which the debtor has a beneficial interest and for which he may competently sue may be thus attached, including debts due to a corporation and money in bank other than money on deposit in the Post Office Savings Bank.

The following, however, are not attachable: (*a*) unliquidated damages; (*b*) dividends in a voluntary winding-up of a limited liability company or in a bankruptcy; (*c*) the half pay of naval and military officers; (*d*) the wages of seamen or sea-apprentices, servants, labourers, or workmen; and (*e*) future income of a tenant for life.

GAROF'ALO, Benvenuto (properly *Benvenuto Tisio da Garofalo*), an Italian historical painter, born at Ferrara, in 1481. He painted at Cremona, at Rome, where he became intimate with Raphael, and at Bologna, and finally returned to Ferrara, where he died blind in 1559. His work shows the influence of the Lombard school and still more of Raphael, though he was more than an imitator of the latter. Examples of his work are to be found in Ferrara, Florence, Rome, London, and Dresden.

GARO HILLS, a district of India, forming the south-western corner of Assam; area, 3,140 sq. miles. It is a mountainous and forest region intersected by tributaries of the Brahmaputra. The native Garos are a robust and active race. Among them the wife is regarded as the head of the family, and property descends through females. Pop. 180,000.

GARONNE' (Lat. *Garumna*), a river of S.W. France, rising in the Vale of Aran, in the Spanish Pyrenees; length, 430 miles. It enters France and flows north-west to the Atlantic, through Haute-Garonne, Tarn-et-Garonne, Lot-et-Garonne, and Gironde. Below Toulouse it receives, on the left, the Save, Ratz, Gers, and Baïse; on the right, the Tarn, the Lot, and the Dordogne, on joining which it changes its name to the Gironde. It is navigable on the descent from St. Martory, and both ways from Toulouse. The Canal du Midi, joining it at Toulouse, forms a communication between the Atlantic and the Mediterranean at Narbonne, and the Canal Latéral, from Toulouse to Castets-en-Dorthe (Gironde), supplements its direct navigation.

GARONNE, HAUTE, a department, south of France, one of the five separated by the Pyrenees from Spain. It is traversed from south to north by the higher reaches of the Garonne and for about 26 miles by the Canal du Midi. The valleys and the lower northern districts are often of great fertility, and cereals and wine are largely exported. Hemp, flax, oranges, and tobacco are also much grown. The principal mines are lead, copper, coal, antimony, iron, and zinc, and a fine marble is quarried. There is a large trade with Spain. Capital, Toulouse. Area, 2,457 sq. miles. Pop. (1931), 441,799.

GARRICK, David, actor, born at Hereford, 19th Feb., 1717, died 20th Jan., 1779. His grandfather was a French refugee, his father a captain in the army. He was educated at Lichfield Grammar School, spent a short time at Lisbon with an uncle, and, returning to Lichfield, was placed under Samuel Johnson, who was induced to accompany him to the metropolis (1737). Garrick then began to study for the law, but on the death of his father joined his brother Peter in the wine trade. He had, however, as a child, a strong passion for acting, and in 1741 he joined Giffard's company at Ipswich under the name of Lyddal.

At Giffard's theatre in Goodman's-fields he achieved a great success as Richard III, and in 1742 was not less successful at Drury Lane. In 1745 he became joint manager with Thomas Sheridan of a theatre in Dublin, and after a season at Covent Garden (1746) purchased Drury Lane in conjunction with Lacy, opening it 15th Sept., 1747, with the *Merchant of Venice*, to which Dr. Johnson furnished a prologue. From this period may be dated a comparative revival of Shakespeare, and a reform both in the conduct and licence of the drama.

In 1763 Garrick visited the Continent for a year and a half. He had already written his farces of *The Lying Valet*, *Lethe*, and *Miss in her Teens*; and in 1766 he composed, jointly with Colman, the excellent comedy of *The Clandestine Marriage*. After the death of Lacy, in 1773, the sole management of the theatre devolved upon Garrick, until 1776, when he sold his moiety of the theatre for £37,000, performed his last part, Don Felix in *The Wonder*, for the benefit of the theatrical fund, and bade an impressive farewell to the stage. He was buried with great pomp at the foot of Shakespeare's statue in Westminster Abbey.

Besides the pieces mentioned he wrote some epigrams, a number of prologues and epilogues, and a few dramatic interludes. As a man Garrick was highly respected, the chief defect of his character being vanity. As an actor he has probably never been excelled, and he was almost equally great both in tragedy and in comedy. He left a large fortune. The Garrick Club was founded in London in 1831 by Francis Mills. T. W. Robertson's well-known play *David Garrick* (1864) is of course mere fiction. It is based upon Mélesville's three-act comedy *Sull'van*, Robertson having with questionable taste substituted a real for an imaginary hero. — BIBLIOGRAPHY: *Lives* by P. Fitzgerald, J. Knight, and James Smyth; Boaden, *The Private Correspondence of David Garrick*; Mrs Parsons, *Garrick and his Circle*; F. A. Hedgcock, *A Cosmopolitan Actor: David Garrick and his French Friends.*

GAR'RISON, William Lloyd, American journalist and founder of the anti-slavery movement in the United States, born 1805, died at New York in 1879. He was apprenticed to a shoe-maker, but eventually became a compositor on the *Newburyport Herald*. In 1827 he became editor of the *National Philanthropist*, the first American temperance journal, and afterwards of a journal in support of the election of John Quincy Adams. With Mr. Lundy, a Quaker, he then started the paper called the *Genius of Universal Emancipation* (1829), his denunciations of slave-traders leading to his imprisonment for libel. On his release he commenced lecturing in Boston, and started the *Liberator* (1831), published weekly with the aid of one assistant and a negro boy.

In 1832 appeared his *Thoughts on African Colonization*, and in the same year he established the American Anti-Slavery Society. He subsequently visited England, where he was welcomed by Wilberforce, Brougham, Buxton, and others. In 1835 he was saved with difficulty from a Boston mob; but his principles made steady progress until 1865, when the Anti-Slavery Society was dissolved with its work accomplished. A volume of sonnets (1843) and one of selections (1852) bear his name. Some of his sonnets were pencilled on the walls of his Baltimore cell in 1830.— Cf. Goldwin Smith, *The Moral Crusader, W. L. Garrison.*

David Garrick

GARROT, the French name for ducks of the genus Clangula, having the bill shorter than the head, widely distributed over the temperate regions of Europe and America. The golden-eye (*C. glaucion*) is a common species in Britain, its general colour being white beneath, with head and sides of neck rich green, back and tail bluish or greyish-black, and the bill bluish-black. It has a round white spot before each eye, and two white bands on the wing; the female is ashy, with rufous head; length of male, about 19 inches. Related American species are the buffle-headed duck (*C. albeola*) and Barrow's duck (*C. islandica*), the latter ranging into Greenland and Iceland.

GARROTE (gär-rō'tā), a Spanish method of execution by strangulation, the victim being placed on a stool with a post or stake (Sp. *garrote*) behind, to which is affixed an iron collar with a screw. The collar is made to clasp the neck of the criminal, and is drawn tighter by means of the screw till life becomes extinct. This word, with the

French spelling and pronunciation *garrotte*, has become naturalized in Great Britain as a term for a species of robbery effected by throttling the victim and stripping him while insensible. In 1863 flogging was added to the usual penalty for the offence of garrotting.—Cf. W. Andrews, *Bygone punishments*.

GARRY, lake of Canada. In the North-West Territories, it is only just outside the Arctic regions, and covers nearly 1,000 sq. miles. The Great Fish River flows through it to take its waters to the Arctic Ocean. **Garry Island** is an island at the mouth of the

Insignia of the Garter

Mackenzie River in the Arctic Ocean. **Fort Garry** is the old name of Winnipeg.

GARRY, river of Inverness-shire, Scotland, having its source at Knoydart. It enters Loch Quoich, and emerging, passes through the beautiful Glengarry. After a course of 13 miles it flows into Loch Garry.

GARRYA, a genus of opposite-leaved evergreen shrubs, natives of California, Mexico, Cuba, and Jamaica. *G. elliptica* is a handsome garden plant with long drooping necklace-like catkins of pale-yellow flowers.

GARSHIN, Vsiévolod Mik-hailovitsh, Russian novelist, born 2nd Feb., 1855, in the government of Ekaterinoslav, died 24th March, 1888, at Petrograd (St. Petersburg). He entered the School for Mining Engineers but soon left it, and in 1877 enlisted as a volunteer in the army sent to Turkey during the Russo-Turkish War. Wounded and trans-

ferred to Kharkov, he completed his first story, *Four Days* (begun in Bulgaria), wherein he described the suffering and fancies of a wounded soldier left behind on the battlefield. This work was followed by *A Very Small Novel, An Accident, The Coward, The Meeting, The Artist, Attalea Princeps,* and *The Night*.

Garshin belonged to the school of Dostoievsky, and, like the latter, he was given to psychological analysis and excelled in the exposition of conflicting emotions. Inclined to melancholy from his early youth, he was insane for a time. He subsequently recovered, but his mind remained unbalanced until the end, when in a fit of insanity he killed himself. His other works include *The Red Flower* and *Nadejdna Nikolaevna*.

GARSTANG, an ancient English market town, North Lancashire, on the Wyre, 10½ miles south of Lancaster. Pop. (rural district, 1931), 11,562.

GARSTON, a port in Lancashire, now part of Liverpool city.

GARTER, ORDER OF THE, the highest and most ancient order of knighthood in Great Britain. The origin of the order, though sometimes assigned to Richard I, is generally attributed to Edward III, the legend being that the Countess of Salisbury having dropped her garter while dancing, the king restored it, after putting it round his own leg, with the words, which became the motto of the order, "*Honi soit qui mal y pense*"—"Shame be to him who thinks evil of it."

The date of the foundation or restoration by Edward III of the order, as given by Froissart, is 1344, while other authorities, founding on the statutes of the order, assign it to 1350. The statutes of the order have been repeatedly revised, more particularly in the reigns of Henry V, Henry VIII, Edward VI, and George III—the last in 1805. Ladies are said to have been admitted up till the reign of Edward IV. Until the reign of Edward VI the common title of the order was the Order of St. George, and it still bears this title, as well as that of the Garter.

The original number of knights was twenty-six, including the sovereign, who was its permanent head; and this number is still retained, except that by statutes passed in 1786, 1805, and subsequently, princes of the blood, sovereigns and princes of other realms, and extra knight companions may be admitted as supernumerary members.

The peculiar emblem of the order, the garter (5), made of dark-blue velvet edged with gold, bearing the motto and with a gold buckle and pendant is worn on the left leg below the knee. The mantle is of blue velvet, lined with white taffeta; the surcoat and hood of crimson velvet; the hat of black velvet, with plume of white ostrich feathers, having in the centre a tuft of black heron's feathers. The collar of gold (3) consists of knots alternating with garters enclosing roses, with the badge of the order, called the George (4), pendent from it. This consists of a figure of St. George on horseback fighting the dragon. The lesser George (2) is worn on a broad blue ribbon over the left shoulder, resting on the right hip. The star (1), formerly only a cross, is of silver, and consists of eight points, with the cross of St. George in the centre, encircled by the garter. A star is worn by the knights, on the left side, when not in the dress of the order.

The officers of the order are the Prelate, the Bishop of Winchester; the Chancellor, the Bishop of Oxford; the Registrar, Dean of Windsor; the Garter King of Arms, and the Usher of the Black Rod. There are a dean and twelve canons, and each knight has a knight-pensioner. The Sovereign of the order is always the King of England, and the number of members in 1933 was about forty.— Cf. Sir H. Nicolas, *History of British Orders of Knighthood*.

GARTER KING OF ARMS, the head of the heraldic establishment in England, consisting of three kings of arms—Garter, Clarencieux, and Norroy, and the herald of the Most Noble Order of the Garter. The office of Garter King of Arms was instituted by Henry V in 1417. The duties of the Garter King of Arms are principally to grant heraldic supporters, to arrange royal funerals, and to present the Order of the Garter to foreign princes.

GARTH, Sir Samuel, English physician and poet, born in 1661, educated at Peterhouse, Cambridge; M.D. in 1691, after studying at Leyden; made a Fellow of the College of Physicians, 1693. A division among the medical profession on the establishment of a dispensary for the metropolitan poor was the occasion of his successful mock-heroic poem *The Dispensary* (1699). He died in 1719. He wrote much in verse and prose, including translations.

GARTOK, the chief town of Western Tibet, and a trade mart.

GASCOYNE, a river of Western Australia, rising in the Carnarvon Range, and falling after a course of 300 miles into Shark's Bay.

GAS MANUFACTURE. The word 'gas' was coined by the Dutch chemist J. B. Van Helmont, but, as he himself states, it was suggested by the Greek *chaos*. Many gases of different kinds have now been discovered by the labours of the chemists, but the particular one with which we are now concerned is that which is obtained from coal. This is a colourless, pungent, and inflammable essence composed mainly of carbon and hydrogen, those elements taking the form, broadly speaking, of fats, oil, wax, and wood.

Fuel. There are two chief kinds of gas used for fuel. The first and most common is 'town's gas,' which is composed entirely of coal-gas, or partly of coal-gas and partly of water-gas, which may or may not be carburetted with oil-gas; and the second is natural gas, which is not known in England except in very small quantities. The first is made by man; the second, as the name implies, is produced by Nature herself. There are many large wells of natural gas in different parts of the United States and Canada, but these are already showing signs of exhaustion. 'Town's gas,' on the other hand, has, of course, the advantage over natural gas that the supply is not inconstant, but can, in normal times, and given an adequate supply of the raw material, be regulated to meet the demand.

It is necessary to give certain simple chemical facts in regard to coal-gas. It has a specific gravity of 0·44, and it is made up as follows:—

Hydrogen	48·49*
Marsh gas or methane	35·90*
Light-yielding hydrocarbons	3·83*
Carbon monoxide	6·61*
Carbon dioxide	0·12†
Nitrogen	5·05†

* Combustible and illuminant.
† Inert gases.

When mixed with air in the proportion of one part of gas to anything from five to fifteen parts of air, it becomes explosive. If there be less than five parts of air, the mixture will burn, not explode; while if it contain more than fifteen parts of air, it is too weak either to burn or explode.

As coal-gas is lighter than air it is found useful for inflating balloons in cases where hydrogen is too expensive. This characteristic of lightness, or volatility, accounts for the fact that all gas-works are built in the lowest-lying parts of a town.

Experiments and Discoveries. Van Helmont, who lived in the first quarter of the seventeenth century, was the first to apply the word 'gas' to the vapours known before his time by scientists under the generic term of *Spiritus Silvestris*. Later in the seven-to enth century Van Helmont's experiments were repeated in the United Kingdom by that great natural philosopher Robert Boyle. His chief work in this sphere of inquiry was to distinguish between the effect of combustion and distillation, and in 1680 he proved that 'air' could be produced by artificial means, and collected in a condition unmixed with ordinary atmospheric air.

Other earlier experimenters were Thomas Shirley, who discovered near Wigan a well of 'natural' gas, and the Rev. John Clayton, D.D., who was the first to discover that gas could be distilled from crude coal and afterwards stored in vessels. Dr. Clayton communicated the results of his experiment to Robert Boyle, but neither he nor his more famous philosophical correspondent seems to have suspected the industrial possibilities of this sun's essence, and they left the matter where they found it, in the realm of theory.

It remained for de Gensanne to describe, in the year 1770, the distillation of coal for industrial purposes, as applied at the ironworks belonging to the Prince of Nassau-Saarbrucken at Sulzbach. He supplied his own illustrations of the furnace employed for this purpose, and it is interesting to know that this was in reality a gasretort—probably the earliest one that was built on a practical, industrial scale, and closely akin to the present-day coke-recovery oven. The apparatus included 'an internal sealed firebrick chamber,' called by the author 'the retort.' But this furnace was used for coking only, and the fact that the more important commodity, gas, was formed at the same time was unnoticed by de Gensanne or any contemporary observer.

The latter half of the eighteenth century was marked by a great wave of chemical research, and the consequent discovery of many highly important substances and gases. Especially prominent among the discoveries to be attributed to this period were those of carbonic acid gas, the result of experiments by Dr. Joseph Black in 1754, and oxygen, of which the credit belongs to Dr. Priestley, though the year that saw the successful conclusion of his investigations, 1774, was the approximate date of the same discovery on independent lines by Scheele.

Seven years later Henry Cavendish began his epoch-making experiments on the nature of hydrogen, proving that the sole product of its combustion was water. At about the same period Lavoisier's researches into aeriform substances yielded him the honour of being the first to make 'water' gas. He was also the inventor of the gasometer.

In 1781 the results of experiments on the distillation of coal were issued to the public by the Rev. Dr. Watson, who afterwards became Bishop of Llandaff. But Dr. Watson's purpose was to discover the quantity of liquid, or tar, that was yielded by various substances in the process of distillation. Although he collected some of the resulting gas in bladders, and even burnt it, he did not realize the prospects which lay before his eyes. The same remark must apply to the tar-making activities of the ninth Earl of Dundonald, father of the famous admiral. He, too, entirely missed the significance of the gas which was one of his inevitable by-products.

Gas as an Illuminant. It was reserved for a Scotsman to carry out the epoch-making discovery of coal-gas as an illuminant, and also to put it to the great purpose of serving the needs of the public. William Murdock, who was born in 1754 in the parish of Auchinleck, Ayrshire, came to Birmingham in 1777 and obtained employment from his fellow-countryman James Watt (q.v.), the inventor of the steam-engine, in the firm of Boulton & Watt. He was sent to Cornwall to take charge of the firm's pumping machinery for the tin-mines, and it was here that he conducted and perfected his experiments to such purpose that in the year 1792 he lit up his house in Redruth by means of gas. Later he erected a gas apparatus on a large scale in the firm's Soho foundry at Birmingham, which in 1802, on the occasion of the Peace of Amiens, was illuminated for the public benefit.

At the same time a contemporary French inventor, Philippe Lebon, was experimenting with gas distilled from wood. In 1802 Lebon successfully lit his house in Paris by gas, and made plans to supply a large part of the city. In 1804, however, Lebon was murdered by an unknown assassin.

Both Lebon and Murdock aimed merely at a system of lighting for individual houses, and the application of gas to the general illumination of the community's streets and highways was reserved for an early admirer and follower of Lebon named Winsor. Winsor was a man of a totally different character from either Murdock or Lebon. He was of the company promoter rather than the inventor type. He came to London, and it was largely due to his enterprise that in 1812 a Royal Charter was granted to a company for the lighting of certain streets in Westminster. The resulting company, originally known as the Chartered Gas Company, was ultimately called the Gas Light and Coke Company. It has developed into a great organization. and is the largest, as well as the oldest, gas undertaking in the world.

By the middle of the century the position of gas as an illuminant was duly established in all the large towns in the kingdom. The gas-meter, invented in 1815 by Samuel Clegg and put into practical use ten years later, solved the initial difficulty of supply, and overcame the problem of checking the consumption of individual users.

Gas as a Heating Agent. During its earlier years gas was regarded as an illuminant solely; it was not until the middle of last century that the first serious efforts were made to use it

Von Welsbach's system consists briefly in constructing a mantle of textile fabric, and saturating it in a solution of the rare metallic salts thorium nitrate (99 parts) and cerium nitrate (1 part). The fabric is then burnt away so as to leave the oxides of the metals as a skeleton, which can be raised to brilliant incandescence by the heat of burning gas. About 1900 an improved form of incandescent mantle, the inverted mantle, was introduced. For all practical purposes the old flat-flame type of burner may be considered entirely obsolete.

The introduction of the incan-

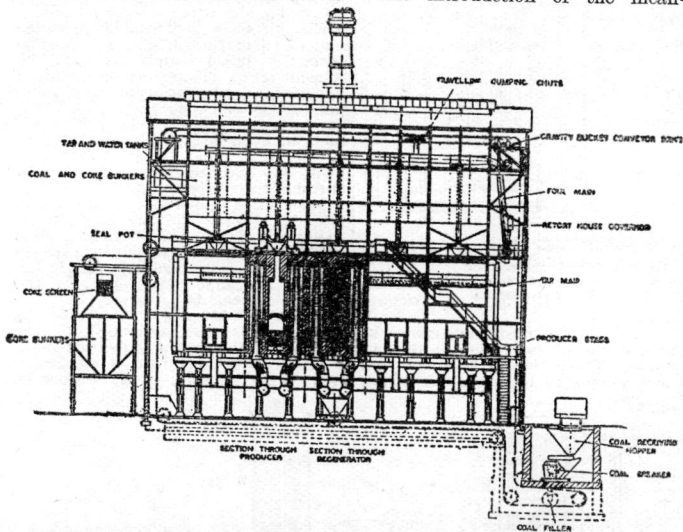

Installation of Five Settings of Four 5-ton Vertical Retorts. Longitudinal Section (*see* next page).
By permission of the Woodall-Duckham Vertical Retort Company, Limited

for heating purposes. During the last fifty years, however, both the popularity and the efficiency of gas as a heating agent have grown by leaps and bounds. Drawbacks have been gradually and continually eliminated, until the gas-fire of to-day from the point of view of hygiene, efficiency, and economy need fear no criticism. The gas-cooker has become no less popular, and for similar reasons. Domestically it has done much to help to solve the servant problem.

Incandescent Gas-mantle. As far as illumination is concerned, a revolution in the whole theory and practice of gas-lighting has been brought about by the invention of the incandescent gas-mantle in 1885 by the Austrian, von Welsbach.

descent mantle was of particular importance, because it meant that the illuminating quality of gas was now a matter of minor importance. For the light given by the incandescent mantle is due entirely to the *heating* of the mantle. Thus the heating or calorific value of the gas had become the essential factor, not only, of course, for cooking and heating, but actually for lighting also. This was recognized by the passage of the Gas Regulation Act 1920, which substituted a thermal or calorific standard for the illuminating power standard which had hitherto been insisted on.

Gas Manufacture. Gas manufacture in its present form is a highly complicated process, involving very different apparatus from the crude appliances that were designed by the original inventors and their immediate successors. It would be well to explain at the outset that the process

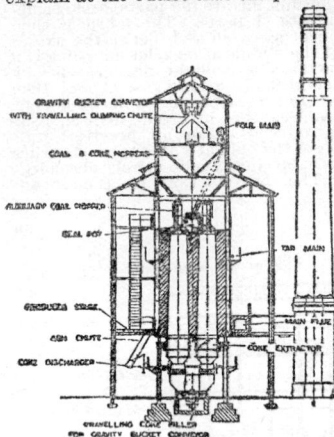

Cross-section of the Installation on previous page

of gas manufacture is known as 'destructive distillation' or 'carbonization.'

In a thoroughly up-to-date gasworks the crude coal is placed in fireclay retorts. These retorts have internal dimensions of 21 inches by 15 inches,

one large furnace placed in a central position. In the largest gasworks they are built in benches which contain upwards of 150 'through retorts.' These retorts are charged almost full with coal, and are charged and discharged about twice every twenty-four hours.

Retorts are generally horizontal, but they are sometimes inclined at an angle of 30° or so, and in some of the most modern systems of carbonizing the retort is vertical. The latter two systems have the great advantage of allowing the coal to enter the retort by gravity, and the coke to leave the retort by the same agency, thereby becoming in a large measure automatic. Horizontal retorts are, however, the more widely used at the present time. They can be operated by machinery using either hydraulic, pneumatic, or electric power. This is specially the case where the retorts are open at both ends, 'through retorts,' as they are called, the coal being fed in at one end and the coke removed through the other end.

Now let us follow the gas on its way from the retort. The gaseous matter is in its early progress laden with aqueous and tarry vapours, which it is necessary to remove in order to purify the gas in the first place, and, in the second place, to recover the by-products. Passing from the retort up what is called the ascension-pipe, the gas passes through a hydraulic main (B in illustration) into a condenser (D). This consists of a number of

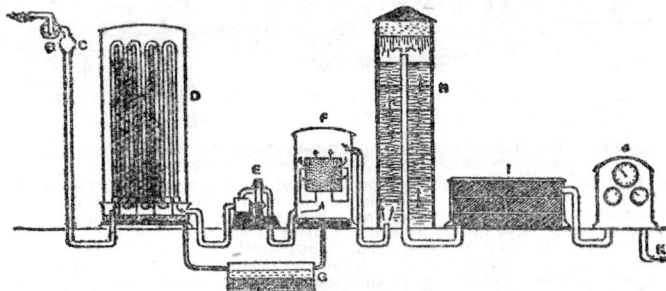

Diagram of a Gas-making Plant

A, From retorts. B, Hydraulic main. C, Foul main. D, Condenser. E, Exhaust pump. F, Washer, G, Tar well. H, Scrubber. I, Purifier. J, Meter. K, To gas-holder

and are generally 10 feet in length for the single-ended type, and 20 feet when open at both ends, although other sizes are sometimes used. They are fixed together in settings of two to ten, which are heated sometimes by one furnace and sometimes by two. In some of the larger works several sets of retorts are heated from

vertical or horizontal pipes of considerable diameter, for the purpose of cooling the gas. The pipes are kept cool by the surrounding air, supplemented, if necessary, by water-sprays. In passing through the condenser the gas is slowly reduced to a lower temperature, and thus the aqueous vapour condenses into water, heavily charged with ammonia, and this water proceeds to absorb sulphuretted hydrogen and carbonic acid from the gas, the heavier tarry vapours condensing at the same time into tar. The ammoniacal liquor is at one point drained off into an underground tank, while the tar, which separates from the liquor by gravity, is drained off into another tank.

The next stage is the passage through the exhauster E (a pump for drawing off the gas from the retorts and so reducing the pressure on them), and then into the washer F, the object of which is to absorb the ammonia and partly further to condense what tarry vapours are still left in its composition. In the following stage the gas undergoes a scrubbing process, where the last traces of ammonia are extracted. From the scrubber (H) the gas passes into the purifier (I), where the greater part of the carbonic acid and the sulphur compounds are removed, and then finally it is conveyed by a pipe (K) into the gas-holder, whence it passes through the large gasworks meters and governors, and thence to the consumers through the street mains.

By-Products. Of the by-products there is a very large number, and their value is very considerable. The most important of them is coke, which is the solid residue of the distilled coal, and is a most valuable smokeless fuel both in industry and for domestic use.

The second main by-product is tar, from the distillation of which an enormous number of subsidiary products, used for an enormous variety of different purposes, is produced. Dyes, acids, disinfectants, fuel oil for naval purposes, benzene, motor spirit, and high explosives (such as T.N.T.) are all produced from tar.

A third by-product is ammoniacal liquor, which by the application of sulphuric acid produces the well-known and invaluable artificial manure and fertilizer sulphate of ammonia. Another by-product is cyanogen liquor, from which prussic acid is derived, as well as the valuable pigment known as Prussian blue.

When coal is burned in the raw state, whether in domestic fire or industrial furnace, all these valuable products are, of course, lost to mankind. Instead they are poured forth, imperfectly consumed, into the air in the shape of smoke and soot, which cut off the health-giving rays of the sun, and are thus of great detriment to the health of urban communities. Not only so, but the actual buildings of a city are destroyed by the acids and tarry matter of the smoke, and the expenses of city life are considerably increased (e.g. in excessive expendi-

ture on laundry-work), while its amenities are correspondingly reduced.

BIBLIOGRAPHY: Walter Hole, *The Distribution of Gas*; Thomas Newbigging, *Handbook for Gas Engineers and Managers*; Charles Hunt, *A History of the Introduction of Gas Lighting*; W. H. Y. Webber, *Town Gas and Its Uses*; *Gas, Manufacture, Distribution, and Use*; *Notes for Lessons* (British Commercial Gas Association); L. G. Chiozza Money, *The Nation's Wealth*.

GASCOIGNE (-koin'), **George**, English poet, born 1535, educated at Cambridge, admitted to Gray's Inn in 1555. Being disinherited by his father, he served with distinction in Holland and was made prisoner by the Spaniards, but returned safely to

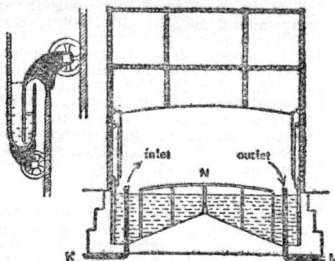

Section of Gas-holder (nearly empty)

N, Bridge to support dome. K, From meter. M, To consumer. On left is shown one of the grips that lift up telescopic divisions of gas-holder. Water forming a seal is picked up in grip from well

England, and died at Stamford in 1577. He is chiefly remembered for his blank-verse satire *The Steele Glas* (1576), and the *Complaynt of Philomene*, a rhyming elegy (1576), but he wrote two or three comedies and tragedies. Gascoigne's complete poems were edited by W. C. Hazlitt in 1868 for the Roxburgh Library. A new edition appeared in the Cambridge English Classics.

GASCOIGNE, Sir William, an English judge of the Court of King's Bench, born about 1350, died in 1419. He is chiefly famous for directing the imprisonment of the Prince of Wales (afterwards Henry V), who had struck him in open court for condemning one of his dissolute friends. He also declined to obey the king and sentence Archbishop Scroop to death, alleging that the law gave him no power over the life of an ecclesiastic. In each case the king ultimately approved his action.

GAS'CONY, an old division of France, between the Garonne, the sea, and the Pyrenees. The Gascons, who are of mixed Basque and Gothic descent, used to have the character of being brave, faithful, and tenacious of purpose, but much given to boasting, whence the word *gasconnade*.

GAS ENGINE. See INTERNAL-COM-BUSTION ENGINES.

GASES, PROPERTIES OF. The characteristic features which distinguish a gas from a liquid or a solid have been stated under FLUID. The term **Vapour** is used somewhat loosely to denote a gas under such conditions of temperature and pressure that it can be readily condensed into a liquid (*see* VAPORIZATION). For every substance there is a certain temperature, called its *critical* temperature, above which the substance cannot exist as a liquid or a solid, no matter how great a pressure is applied to it.

Certain gases used to be called the **Permanent** gases, the chief being oxygen, air, carbon monoxide, nitrogen, and hydrogen. The critical temperature of these is so low that they were never found occurring except in the gaseous state. Now, however, with improved means of obtaining very low temperatures, these gases (and others discovered recently, such as argon and helium) have all been liquefied and many solidified (*see* LIQUEFACTION OF GASES).

A **Perfect** gas is an ideal substance with properties of a specially simple type. These properties are expressed in 'laws' which no actual gas obeys perfectly, but only more or less approximately, the approximation becoming closer the further removed the gas is from the liquid phase. These laws of gases are:

(1) **Boyle's** (or **Mariotte's**) **Law.** The product of the pressure and volume of a gas is constant when the gas, its mass, and its temperature are given.

(2) **Charles's** (or **Gay-Lussac's**) **Law.** Every gas expands for a rise of temperature of $1°$ C. by the same fraction of its volume at $0°$ C., the pressure being constant. The fraction is $1/273$ nearly. If v_t is the volume at $t°$ C., the law gives $v_t = v_0(1 + t/273)$. If further we write T for $t + 273$, then T is the absolute temperature in degrees centigrade, and the equation becomes $v_t/T = v_0/273$; or, in words, the volume at constant pressure is proportional to the absolute temperature.

If p is the pressure, the laws (1) and (2) may be combined in the single statement $pv = RT$, R being a constant. When the mass of the gas is one gramme-molecule, i.e. a number of grammes equal to the molecular weight of the gas, then R has the same value for all gases.

(3) **Avogadro's Law.** At given temperature and pressure, equal volumes of all gases contain the same number of molecules. At $0°$ C. and 76 cm. pressure (*see* HYDROSTATICS), 1 c.c. of any gas contains $2·7 \times 10^{19}$ molecules. The **Avogadro constant** is the number of molecules in one gramme-molecule of any gas, or $6·06 \times 10^{23}$ (*see* ELECTRON).

(4) **Joule's Law.** The internal energy of a given mass of a gas is a function of its temperature only.

The deviations from these laws shown by actual gases have been the subjects of a great deal of important experimental work. Amagat, working with pressures up to 300 atmospheres, showed that hydrogen is less compressible than if it obeyed Boyle's Law; nitrogen and carbon dioxide behave like hydrogen at high pressures and temperatures, but in the opposite sense (i.e. they are too compressible for Boyle's Law) at low pressures. The deviation of a gas from Joule's Law—the Thomson-Joule effect—has an important practical application in the liquefaction of gases (q.v.). For the application of the properties of gases to the measurement of temperature, *see* THERMOMETRY. *See also* HEAT; TEMPERATURE; THERMO-DYNAMICS; DIFFUSION; SOLUTION; IONIZATION.

GASKELL Elizabeth Cleghorn, novelist, daughter of William Stevenson, editor of *The Scots Magazine*, born at Chelsea in 1810, died at Alton, Hampshire, in 1865. She was brought up by an aunt at Knutsford in Cheshire (the original of the village in her story of *Cranford*), and married in 1832 the Rev. William Gaskell, a Unitarian minister at Manchester.

Her first work of importance, *Mary Barton*, appeared in 1848, based upon the struggles then rife in Lancashire between workmen and employers. The *Moorland Cottage*, a Christmas story, appeared in 1850; and in 1853 her next regular novel, *Ruth*, which aims a distinct blow at the common moral judgments of society. *Lizzie Leigh, Cranford*, and other minor tales appeared at various times in *Household Words*, in which also she wrote her next novel, *North and South*, a Yorkshire tale. In 1857 appeared her admirable *Life of Charlotte Brontë*, and in 1860 *Sylvia's Lovers*. *Wives and Daughters* appeared posthumously in 1866. An edition of her works (The Knutsford Edition) appeared in 1906.

GASPÉ, a district of Canada, province of Quebec, on the south of the St. Lawrence estuary, washed by the Gulf of St. Lawrence, of which Gaspé Bay is an inlet. The fisheries are valuable; Gaspé Basin is a port on Gaspé Bay.

GASSEN'DI (properly GASSEND), Pierre, French philosopher and mathematician, born in 1592, died in 1655. At nineteen he was appointed to the chair of philosophy at Aix. His *Exercitationes Paradoxicæ adversus Aristotleos* (1624), while they gave great offence to the Aristotelians, obtained him a canonry in the cathedral of Digne; but a second book of *Exercitationes* excited so much enmity that he ceased all direct attacks on Aristotle, contenting himself with the exaltation of Epicurus. He strenuously maintained the atomic theory, in opposition to the views of the Cartesians, and, in particular, asserted the doctrine of a vacuum.

He was appointed lecturer on mathematics in the Collège-Royal at Paris in 1645, but was compelled to return to Digne, where he lived from 1647 to 1653, in which interval he published his *De Vita, Moribus et Doctrina Epicuri* (1647), and *Syntagma philosophicæ Epicuri* (1649). In 1653 he went again to Paris, where he published the lives of Tycho Brahe, Copernicus, Peiresc, and Regiomontanus (John Muller).—Cf. G. S. Brett, *Philosophy of Gassendi*.

GASTEIN, or WILDBAD GASTEIN, a watering-place in Austria, 3,000 feet above the sea, 48 miles south of Salzburg, with thermal springs (64° to 100°) containing salt and carbonates of magnesia and lime. It gives its name to a treaty, the Convention of Gastein, signed here on 14th of Aug., 1865, by the Emperor of Austria and the King of Prussia, the non-observance of which led to the German War of 1866.

GASTER, Moses, Rumanian philologist, Hebrew scholar, and folklorist, born at Bucharest in 1856. Educated in his native town, and at the universities of Leipzig and Breslau, he was for some time lecturer at the university of Bucharest, but was expelled from Rumania in 1885 for agitating on behalf of the persecuted Rumanian Jews. He proceeded to England, where he settled, and in 1886 was Ilchester lecturer at Oxford. In 1887 he was appointed Haham, or Chief-Rabbi of the Portuguese (Sephardi) Jewish Communities in the United Kingdom. A man of a vast erudition, a linguist and a scholar, he wrote on Rumanian philology, Biblical questions and folk-lore. His works include: *Chrestomathie Roumanie, Sephardi Prayer Book, The Samaritan Book of Joshua, The Hebrew Divorce,* and *Roumanian Bird and Beast Stories*.

GAS'TEROPODS (Gasteropoda), a class of molluscs, consisting of animals inhabiting a univalve shell, although some of the group are wholly destitute of a shell. The shell is either a small internal plate, as in slugs; or cone-shaped and spiral, as in the majority; or multivalve, the pieces following each other along the middle line, as in the chitons (coat-of-mail shells). The distinguishing characteristic is the foot, which is a broad, muscular expansion of the ventral surface.

The class is divided into four subclasses. (1) Amphineura: chitons, and some other primitive forms. (2) Prosobranchia: sea-snails with gills in front of the heart, as whelks, periwinkles, top-shells, cowries, &c. (3) Opisthobranchia: sea-snails and sea-slugs with gills—when present—behind the heart, as bubble-shells (Bulla), sea-hare (Aplysia), and the pelagic sea-butterflies (Pteropoda). (4) Pulmonata: land and fresh-water snails, and land-slugs, breathing by lung-like organs.

GASTON DE FOIX (fwä), Duke of Nemours, French soldier, born 1489, son of John de Foix, Comte d'Estampes, and Mary of Orleans, sister of Louis XII, whose favourite he became. At the age of twenty-three he routed a Swiss army, rapidly crossed four rivers, drove the Pope from Bologna, and won the celebrated battle of Ravenna (1512), but was killed while attempting to cut off a body of retreating Spaniards.

GASTOR'NIS, a large fossil bird, imperfectly known, remains of which have been discovered in the Lower Eocene deposits of Meudon, near Paris, and in the London Clay of England. The bones indicate a bird with poorly developed wings, as tall as the ostrich, and allied to the wading-birds.

GASTRIC JUICE is the chief agent of digestion in the stomach, and is secreted by the cells in its wall. It is a clear, strongly acid, odourless fluid in its pure state, and contains hydrochloric acid, a ferment called pepsin, and small quantities of various salts in solution, chiefly chlorides and phosphates.

The chief digestive function of the gastric juice is due to pepsin, which acts on proteins, converting them into peptones, the first step in breaking down the complex proteins into simpler substances. It also curdles milk, converts cane-sugar into simpler bodies, and begins the process of splitting up the fats.

Pepsin can only act effectively in an acid medium, hence the necessity of having hydrochloric acid present for efficient digestion. The presence of the hydrochloric acid further causes the gastric juice to be antiseptic, and thus leads to the destruction of many of the organisms swallowed with the food, and prevents putrefactive changes taking place in the stomach. Disease may cause a diminution, or even complete absence, of one or other of the ingredients of the gastric juice, and thus lead to serious disturbances of digestion and metabolism, with resulting malnutrition and emaciation.

GASTROLO'BIUM, a large genus of leguminous plants occurring in South-Western Australia. Several of the species often prove fatal to cattle which eat of their foliage, and they are hence known as poison-plants.

GASTROMY'CETES, the highest, class of Basidiomycetous Fungi, distinguished by the possession of elaborate and often curiously formed fruit-bodies, which remain closed until quite ripe; it includes, among other types, the puff-balls (Lycoperdon, Scleroderma), earth - stars (Geaster), bird's-nest fungi (Nidulariaceæ), and stinkhorns (Ithyphallus, Clathrus).

GASTROS'TEUS, the genus comprising the fresh-water three-spined and two-spined sticklebacks (*G. aculeatus* and *G. pungitius*).

GASTROSTOMY is the operation for the formation of a permanent artificial opening into the stomach through which the patient can be fed. It is performed in cases of malignant disease, or intractable obstruction, of the gullet when the patient is exposed to the risk of starvation from his inability to take nourishment.

GASTROTOMY is the operation of opening the stomach. It is performed for the removal of foreign bodies, for exploratory purposes, or as a means of dilating strictures at either of the orifices of the stomach.

GAS'TRULA, in embryology, that stage in the development of multicellular animals in which the embryo has the form of a two-layered sac enclosing a central cavity which communicates with the outside by means of an opening called a *blastopore*. The gastrula stage follows the *blastula* stage, which is either a hollow sphere (*blastosphere*) or a solid mass of cells (*morula*), smaller at one pole. It is developed from the blastosphere by a process of invagination, or infolding of the *hypoblast*, the inner layer of the cavity referred to, into the inside of the *epiblast* or outer layer. In the case of a morula the small cells increase and grow over the larger ones, a central cavity being formed by separation of the inner cells. The cavity, in either case known as an *archenteron*, is a primitive digestive cavity, and the blastopore is a primitive mouth.

GATCHINA, or **TROTSK**, a town, Russia, government of and 35 miles s.s.w. of Leningrad, on a small lake. It is regularly built, and contains one of the finest of the palaces of the former Emperors of Russia. Pop. 14,880.

GATES, Horatio, an American officer during the Revolutionary War, born in England in 1728, died in 1806. He rose to the rank of major by merit alone. At the capture of Martinique he was aide-de-camp to General Monkton, and he was with Braddock when the latter was defeated in 1755. On the conclusion of peace he purchased an estate in Virginia, on which he resided until the Revolutionary War in 1775, when he was appointed adjutant-general by Congress, with the rank of brigadier.

At the head of the American army of the north he compelled the British general, Burgoyne, to surrender his whole army at Saratoga (1777). In 1780, after the capture of General Lincoln, Gates received the chief command of the southern districts, but was defeated two months later by Cornwallis at Camden. He was then superseded by General Greene and tried by court-martial, but was finally acquitted, and reinstated in his command in 1782 after the capture of Cornwallis. He then retired to Virginia, and in 1790, having emancipated all his slaves, he removed to New York, where he died.

GATESHEAD, a municipal, county, and parliamentary borough, England, county Durham, on the right bank of the Tyne, opposite Newcastle, of which it is practically part, being connected with it by three bridges. Its industries are much the same as those of Newcastle, including large engineering and ironworks, the making of glass and chemicals, and ship-building. In the vicinity are quarries from which the celebrated 'Newcastle grindstones' are obtained, and numerous collieries. The town sends one member to Parliament. Pop. (1931), 122,379.

GATH (Heb., 'wine-press'), one of the five royal cities of the Philistines, which, from its situation on the borders of Judah, was of much importance in the wars of the Jews and Philistines. It was the native town of Goliath, and was captured successively by David, Hazael, and Uzziah, who dismantled it. The site cannot be determined with certainty, but it is sometimes identified with Tell-es-Sâfieh, between Ekron and Ashdod.

GATINEAU (gat-i-nō'), a river of Canada, Quebec Province, the largest affluent of the Ottawa, rising in some lakes, and flowing almost due south to enter the Ottawa nearly opposite Ottawa City. It is not navigable more than 5 miles above Ottawa except by canoes, but its rapid waters are well stocked with fish, and available as water-power.

GATLING-GUN, one of the original forms of machine-gun, i.e. a mechanical fire-arm controlled by one man, and capable of firing a great number of rounds in a given space of time.

The Gatling-gun was invented in the United States about 1862, and proved itself much superior to the earlier mitrailleuse which had been evolved by the French, and used in the Franco-German War. The Gatling had ten barrels fixed round an axis, and this axis was constructed to revolve by the simple method of turning a handle. The sheaf of barrels was connected by various arrangements of carriers and locks, with a drum or cartridge-container placed over the breech end of the barrels, and the action of the mechanism—controlled by the handle—caused the barrels, carrier, and locks to revolve, and the cartridges to be forced into the barrels, fired, and afterwards extracted. The rate of fire was limited by the speed at which the handle could be turned and by the capacity of the drum, which, when empty, had to be replaced by hand; 1,000 rounds a minute has been reached with this weapon. The whole gun was mounted on a wheeled carriage. The Gatling-gun was at one time in use in the British army, but has now been superseded by more modern weapons.

GAU (gou), a German word of doubtful origin, meaning in general, district, but in a special sense a district as a political unit, and its inhabitants as a political association. It formed a sort of middle division between the highest unit, the state, and the lowest, the village, corresponding in some respects to the 'hundred.' The freemen of the Gau met at certain periods, under an elected head, to settle matters relating to the public weal; and in the same way the head men of the Gauen met to settle matters relating to the state at large.

In the Frankish Empire the character of the Gau was altered, each Gau there having as its head one or more royal officers called Grafs or Counts. These countships became hereditary, and about the twelfth century the Gau ceased to exist as a political division, though the name has survived, e.g. in Aargau and Thurgau.

GAUCHOS (gä'ụ-chŏs), natives of the pampas of the La Plata countries in South America, of Spanish descent with only slight Indian admixture. The race is noted for its spirit of wild independence, for horsemanship, and the use of the lasso. Their mode of life is rude and uncivilized, and they depend for subsistence chiefly on cattle-rearing. The Gauchos, it seems, do not eat salt.

GAUGE, a standard of measurement. As applied to railways, gauge is the distance between the two lines of rails forming the way; the ordinary or British gauge being 4 feet 8½ inches. The 'broad gauge' of the Great Western Railway of England was 7 feet. The Irish gauge is 5 feet 3 inches, the Indian and Spanish gauge 5 feet 6 inches. Narrow gauges have often been adopted for cheapness, e.g. a 3-feet-6-inch gauge. A 'break of gauge,' where lines of different gauge meet, is a great hindrance to traffic. Gauge is also the name applied to contrivances for measuring any special dimensions, such as the wire-gauge, an oblong plate of steel, with notches of different widths cut on the edge and numbered, the size of the wire being determined by trying it in the different notches until one is found which it exactly fits.

GAUGE, STEAM, an instrument for indicating the pressure of the steam in a boiler or other vessel. The Bourdon instrument consists of a flat, spirally-coiled metal tube with a sealed end. When the pressure inside this tube exceeds the pressure outside, it tends to uncoil slightly, and to rotate a pointer on the front of the instrument. The amount of rotation depends on the pressure inside the coiled tube. If the pressure inside is *less* than that outside, the rotation is in the opposite sense, so the instrument can be used as a *vacuum* gauge. —BIBLIOGRAPHY: W. Inchley, *Steam Boilers and Accessories*; *Modern Mechanical Engineering* (The Gresham Publishing Company).

GAUGE, WATER, or **GAUGE-GLASS**, is a gauge for indicating the level of the water in a boiler. It consists of a glass tube which is attached by a brass or gun-metal fitting at each end to the boiler. One end of the glass tube communicates with the steam-space, and the other end with the water-space of the boiler, so that the water in the glass tube is at the same level as the water in the boiler. Also, in physics, any U gauge in which water is used, so that the difference of pressure registered is that due to the measured 'head' of water.

GAUGUIN, Paul, French painter, born 1848, died 1903, was originally in the merchant service and then in a financial house, and did not entirely devote himself to art until 1883. For a time he worked under Impressionist influences until he went to Martinique, and then in 1889 to Brittany, where he became the chief figure of the Pont-Aven group, and developed a highly individual and characteristic art.

In 1891 he went to Tahiti, where, except for a short return to France, he spent the rest of his life, living and working among the natives. He justified this course on the ground that only the primitive and uncivilized could sufficiently stir his imagination. His work is marked by a bold simplification of natural forms, decorative design, and the use of brilliant, arbitrary colour. He is represented by two small pictures in the Tate Gallery.

GAUL, or **GALLIA,** in ancient geography, the country of the Gauls, the chief branch of the great original stock of Celts. It extended at one time from the Pyrenees to the Rhine, and included also a part of Italy. Hence it was divided into Gaul on this side (the Roman side) of the Alps, or Gallia Cisalpina, and Gaul beyond the Alps, or Gallia Transalpina. Eventually the former was regarded quite as part of Italy, and the name Gallia was restricted to Transalpine Gaul, or the country nearly corresponding to modern France.

Julius Cæsar, about the middle of the first century B.C., found Transalpine Gaul divided into three parts: (1) Aquitania, extending from the Pyrenees to the Garonne, chiefly occupied by Iberian tribes; (2) Gallia Celtica, Celtic Gaul, from the Garonne to the Seine and Marne; (3) Gallia Belgica, Belgic Gaul, in the north, extending to the Rhine.

Migrations among the Gauls about 397 B.C., and their passage of the Alps, first bring the Gallic nation into the region of history. Having crossed the Alps, they fell upon the Etruscans, defeated the Romans at Allia (390 B.C.), and sacked and burned Rome, the Capitol however, being saved by Camillus.

More than a century after the burning of Rome, the Eastern Gauls, between 280 and 278 B.C., made three destructive irruptions into Macedonia and Greece. Several tribes pursued their course into Asia Minor, where, under the name of *Galatians,* they long retained their national peculiarities. After these migrations the Gauls along the banks of the Danube and in the south of Germany disappear. Tribes of German origin occupy the whole country as far as the Rhine, and even beyond that river. The Belgæ, who were partly German, occupied the northern part of Gaul, from the Seine and Marne to the

English Channel and the Rhine, from whence colonists passed over into Britain, and settled on the coast districts.

The Celts in Gaul had attained some degree of cultivation by intercourse with the Greeks and Carthaginians, before they came in contact with the Romans. Those of Cisalpine Gaul continued formidable to Rome until after the first Punic War, when the nation was compelled, after a war of six years duration, to submit to the Romans (220 B.C.). When Hannibal marched on Rome, they attempted to shake off the yoke; but the Romans, victorious over the Carthaginians, again reduced them to submission. Thirty-one years later (189 B.C.) their kindred tribe in Asia, the Galatians, met with the same fate; they also were vanquished, and their princes (tetrarchs) became tributary.

Between 128 and 122 B.C. the Romans conquered the southern part of Gaul along the sea from the Alps to the Pyrenees, and here established their dominion in what was called the Province (Provincia), a name that still exists as Provence. Not long after, Gaulish tribes shared in the destructive incursions of the Cimbri and Teutones on the Roman territory, which were ended by Marius in the battles of Aquæ Sextiæ (Aix) in 102, and Vercelli in 101 B.C.

On the appointment of Julius Cæsar to the proconsulship over the countries bordering on Gaul, he resolved to subject all Gaul, and executed his purpose, in less than nine years (58–50 B.C.), in eight bloody campaigns. The dominion of the Romans in Gaul was confirmed by colonies, and the liberal grant of the Roman citizenship to several Gallic tribes. The religion of the Druids, being suppressed in Gaul by Tiberius and Claudius, gradually retreated into Britain, soon also conquered by the Romans.

After the extinction of the Cæsars, the Gauls once more attempted to recover their liberty by aid of the Germans, but after this last effort became entirely Romanized, even their ancient language, the Celtic, being supplanted by a corrupt Latin dialect. About the year 486 the Franks subdued the greater part of Gaul, and put a period to the dominion of the Romans in that country. *See* FRANCE. — BIBLIOGRAPHY: Martin de Syr, *La France avant César;* Fustel de Coulanges, *Histoire des institutions politiques de l'ancienne France.*

GAULT, in geology, a series of stiff, but sometimes calcareous, clays, varying in colour from a light grey to a dark blue, occurring between the

Upper and Lower Greensands of the Cretaceous system of England. The gault is well developed at Folkestone, and forms a band of clay-land, with good brickworks, at the foot of the North and South Downs.

GAUNTLET, or **GANTLET** (O.Fr. *gantelet*, dim. of *gant*, glove), a glove made originally of chain-mail, later of plate, and jointed at the fingers, used as part of the armour of a warrior in former times. The gauntlet was introduced in the thirteenth century. The throwing down of the gauntlet was an accepted method of challenging to combat.

GAUR, or **GOUR**, a ruined city in Hindustan, 60 miles north by west of Murshedabad. From 1212 to 1574 it was the capital of Bengal, extending about 7 miles along the old Ganges. Its decay proceeded from the change in the course of the river, about two centuries since. The principal ruins are a magnificent mosque, faced with black porphyry, two gates, a large edifice faced with bricks of various colours, and a lofty obelisk or tower. Several villages now stand on the site of the city.

GAUR, or **GOUR**, one of the largest of all the ox tribe (*Bos gaurus*), ranging through India, Burma, and the Malay Peninsula, remarkable for the extraordinary elevation of its spinal ridge, the absence of a dewlap, and its white 'stockings,' which reach above the knee. It is so fierce when roused that neither tiger, rhinoceros, nor elephant dare attack it. The hide on the shoulders and hind-quarters is sometimes nearly 2 inches in thickness even after being dried, and is therefore much valued for the purpose of being made into shields. The animal is not domesticated to any great extent.

GAUSS (gous), **Karl Friedrich**, a German mathematician, born 1777, died in 1855. In 1801 he published his *Disquisitiones Arithmeticæ*, treating of indeterminate analysis or transcendental arithmetic, and containing, in addition to many new theorems, a demonstration of the theorem of Fermat concerning triangular numbers. He also calculated, by a new method, the orbit of the planets Ceres and Pallas. In 1807 he became professor of mathematics and director of the observatory at Göttingen, a position which he held till his death. He was pronounced by Laplace to be the greatest mathematician in Europe.

His chief works were the *Theoria Motus Corporum Cœlestium* (1809), *Intensitas Vis Magneticæ Terrestris* (1833), *Dioptrische Untersuchungen* (1841), and *Untersuchungen über Gegenstande der höheren Geodesie* (1844).

GAUTIER (gō-ti-ā), **Judith**, French poet and novelist, born at Paris 1850, died in 1917. A daughter of Théophile Gautier and Carlotta Grisi, the famous Italian singer, she married first Catulle Mendès, from whom she soon separated, and afterwards Pierre Loti. A distinguished Oriental scholar, her works deal mostly with Chinese and Japanese subjects. *The Book of the Jade*, her first work, appeared in 1867 under the name of Judith Walther. It was followed in 1869 by *The Imperial Dragon*, a Chinese romance, signed Judith Mendès. *The Usurper*, a Japanese romance, appeared in 1875, and was crowned by the Academy. Her other works include: *Lucienne* (1877), *The Cruelties of Love* (1878), *Potiphar's Wife* (1884), and *The Merchant of Smiles* (1888).

GAUTIER, Théophile, French poet and critic, born 1811 at Tarbes

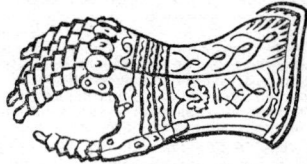

Gauntlet

(Hautes-Pyrénées), died in 1872. He studied painting under Rioult for two years, but gave up the brush for the pen, threw himself vigorously into the Romanticist movement, published a volume of poems in 1830, and for several years worked at general literary criticism.

In 1832 appeared his poem *Albertus*; but his first great success was the romance *Mademoiselle de Maupin*, which led to his engagement by Balzac as secretary. He was afterwards engaged as theatrical and art critic on the *Revue de Paris*, the *Artiste*, the *Moniteur*, and the *Journal Officiel*. Owing to his connection with the *Journal Officiel* his fortunes became linked in some measure with those of the Bonaparte family, and he was appointed librarian to the Princess Mathilde. In 1872 he was sent by the Republican Government on a literary mission to Italy, and died in the same year.

Among the most interesting of his productions may be ranked his *Voyages en Espagne* (1843), his *Italia* (1852), *Caprices et Zigzags* (1845), and *Constantinople* (1854), narratives of his travels; his *Roman de la Momie*

(1856), *Le Capitaine Fracasse* (1863), *Belle Jenny* (1865), *Spirite* (1866), novels, together with the brilliant short stories, *Fortunio, Une Nuit de Cléopâtre, Jean et Jeanette*, and *Le Roi Candaule* ; and his *Histoire de l'art dramatique en France depuis vingtcinq ans* (1849), and *Les Beaux Arts en Europe* (1852).—Cf. F. Brunetière, *Évolution de la poésie lyrique.*

GAVAR'NI, the assumed name of Hippolyte Guillaume Sulpice Chevalier, French caricaturist, born at Paris in 1801, died in 1866. Originally a mechanical draughtsman, he began his artistic career in 1835 by designing costumes for theatres and journals of fashion. He then established *Les Gens du Monde*; but the journal was a failure, and the artist spent some time in the debtor's prison of Clichy. On his release he was employed upon the *Charivari*, the success of which was due in great part to his genius.

In 1848 he visited England, and the sketches which he sent from St. Giles, London, to *L'Illustration* created an immense sensation. His best-known works are: *Les Enfants Terribles, Les Rêves, Les Fourberies de Femmes*, and *Impressions de Ménage*. He afterwards illustrated Eugène Sue's *Wandering Jew*, Balzac's novels, and other works.—Cf. E. and J. de Goncourt, *Gavarni, l'homme et l'œuvre.*

GAVAZZI (gä-vät'sē), Alessandro, popular Italian preacher and religious reformer, born at Bologna 1809, died at Rome 1889. At the age of fifteen he became a monk of the Barnabite order, at twenty he was professor of rhetoric in the College of Naples, and soon after made his mark as a pulpit orator. In 1846 he was chaplain-general of the Roman Patriotic League. Subsequently he threw off his Papal allegiance and joined the agitation which ended in the short-lived republic.

The French occupation of Rome drove him into exile, when he travelled through Britain and America lecturing against the Church of Rome, his power as an orator evoking much enthusiasm. He was with Garibaldi in 1860, and made subsequent visits to Britain gathering funds for the Free Italian Church, in the interests of which he lectured, preached, and travelled on deputation work till his death.

GAVELKIND (from *gabhail*, tenure, and *cine*, family), an old English tenure, by which the land of the father was, in the event of his intestacy at his death, equally divided among his sons, or in default of sons, among the daughters. The issue of a deceased son inherited the father's part. Collaterally, also, when one brother died without issue all the other brothers inherited from him. Gavelkind, before the Norman Conquest, was the general custom of the realm; it was then superseded by the feudal law of primogeniture, and only retained in Wales and Kent. The custom continued in Wales till the time of Henry VIII; in Kent all land is still held in gavelkind unless specially disgavelled by Act of Parliament.

GA'VIAL, or GHARIAL (*Gavialis gangeticus*), the Indian crocodile, characterized by the narrow almost cylindrical jaws which form an exceedingly elongated muzzle. The teeth (about 120 in number) are of equal length, and the feet are completely webbed. The males can be distinguished from the females by the shape of the muzzle, which is much smaller at the extremity. The only extant species occurs in South and Eastern Asia, especially in the Ganges, and attains a length of 20 feet. It feeds solely on fishes.

GAVOTTE', an air for a dance with two strains, each of four or eight bars, in $\frac{2}{4}$ or $\frac{4}{4}$ time, the starting notes occupying half a bar. Like the minuet, it has been introduced for free treatment into suites and sonatas. The name is said to be derived from the Gavots, the inhabitants of the Pays-de-Gap, in Dauphiné.

GAWAIN (W. *Gwalchmei*), one of the Knights of the Round Table, a nephew of King Arthur, and son of Loth, King of Norway and the Orkneys. Gawain tried in vain to pull the magic sword from the magic stone, and failed in his quest of the Holy Grail. He has been identified by some writers with the Irish hero Cuchullin (q.v.).—Cf. J. L. Weston, *The Legend of Sir Gawain.*

GAY, John, English poet, born near Barnstaple in 1688, died in 1732. He was apprenticed to a silk mercer in London, but in 1712 became secretary to Anne Duchess of Monmouth. In 1713 he published his *Rural Sports*, which he dedicated to Pope, with whom he formed a close friendship. In 1714 his caricature of Ambrose Philips's pastoral poetry was published, under the title of *The Shepherd's Week*, and dedicated to Lord Bolingbroke, by whose interest he was appointed secretary to the Earl of Clarendon, in his embassy to the court of Hanover. His mock-heroic poem, *Trivia, or the Art of Walking the Streets of London*, appeared in 1715, and in that year also was acted his burlesque drama of *What d'ye Call It?* but his next piece, the farce *Three Hours after Marriage*, altogether failed.

In 1720 he published his poems by

subscription, in 1724 his tragedy *The Captives*, and in 1727 his well-known *Fables*. His *Beggar's Opera*, the idea of which seems to have been originated by Swift, was first acted in 1728 at Lincoln's Inn Fields, where it ran for sixty-three nights, but the Lord Chamberlain refused to license for performance a second part entitled *Polly*. The *Beggar's Opera* was successfully revived at the Lyric Theatre, Hammersmith, in 1920. Gay also wrote the pastoral *Acis and Galatea* and the opera *Achilles*. The closing years of his life were mostly spent in the house of the Duke of Queensberry.—BIBLIOGRAPHY: Dr. Johnson, *Lives of the Poets*; Thackeray, *English Humorists*; Lewis Melville, *Life and Letters of John Gay*.

GAY, Marie - Françoise - Sophie, French authoress, born at Paris 1776, died at Paris in 1852. Her maiden name was Nichault de la Valette, and she was first married to a financier, M. Liottier, from whom after six years she was divorced to marry M. Gay, a Receiver-General under the Empire. Her salon was a famous resort for the men of letters and artists of the time. Her chief works are: *Laure d'Estell* (1802), *Léonie de Montbreuse* (1813), *Anatole* (1815), *Scènes de jeunes dyes* (1833), *La Duchesse de Châteauroux* (1834), *Les Salons célèbres* (1837), and *Le Mari confident* (1849). For her

John Gay

daughter, Delphine Gay, *see* GIRARDIN (MADAME DE).

GAYÁ, the chief town of a district of the same name in Bengal, on the right bank of the Phalgu, a tributary of the Ganges, 260 miles. N.W. of Calcutta. It consists of an old and a new town. The former occupies a rocky height, is inhabited chiefly by Brahmans, and, being regarded as a place of great sanctity, is annually visited by vast crowds of pilgrims. The latter, called Sahibganj, is the trading-quarter, and the seat of administration, where the European

Gayal or Gyal (*Bos frontalis*)

residents dwell. The place abounds with objects of Hindu worship, and almost every height in the vicinity is the subject of a legend. Pop. 67,562. The district has an area of 4,712 sq. miles, and a pop. of 2,225,000.

GAYAL', or GYAL, a species of ox (*Bos frontalis*) native to the mountains of Northern Burma and Assam, and long domesticated in these countries and in the eastern parts of Bengal. Its occurrence in the wild state is doubtful. The head is very broad and flat in the upper part, and contracts suddenly towards the nose; the horns are short and slightly curved. The animal has no proper hump, but on the shoulders and fore-part of the back there is a sharp ridge. The colour is chiefly a dark brown. Its milk is exceedingly rich, though not abundant.

GAY-LUSSAC (gā-lüs-ák), **Louis Joseph**, French chemist and physicist, born at St Léonard (Haute-Vienne) 1778, died at Paris 1850. He was educated in the École Polytechnique from 1797 to 1800, and afterwards in the École des Ponts et Chaussées, but preferring chemistry, he entered Berthollet's École Laboratoire at Arcueil. In 1802 he returned to the Polytechnique as demonstrator of chemistry, and in 1804 performed his two balloon ascents for scientific purposes, the first with Biot, the second by himself, an account of which appeared in the *Journal de Physique*. In 1806 he was elected to the Academy of Sciences. In 1808 he was appointed to the professorship of physics at the Sorbonne, a post he held for twenty-four years; in 1809 he was made professor of chemistry in the École Polytechnique, and then succeeded Fourcroy as professor of general chemistry in the Jardin des

Plantes. In 1831 he entered the Chamber of Deputies, and in 1839 he was made a peer of France, but he never took an active part in politics.

He was especially celebrated for his researches into the chemical and physical properties of gases and vapours. For many years he edited, in conjunction with Arago, the *Annales de chimie et de physique*; and many of his numerous memoirs were published in this or in the *Comptes Rendus*. He also published, along with Thénard, *Recherches physico-chimiques*, in which some of their most important discoveries are described. Other works are his *Cours de physique* and *Leçons de chimie*.

GAZA, Theodore, Renaissance scholar, born at Thessalonica about 1400, died in Calabria in 1475 or 1478. He came to Italy about 1430; became

Gazelles (Gazella dorcas)

teacher of Greek at Ferrara; and was patronized by Pope Nicholas V, Cardinal Bessarion, and King Alfonso of Naples. Gaza laboured for the diffusion of Greek literature, not only by teaching, but also by his writings, and especially by Latin translations of the Greek classics. His chief work is a translation of the writings of Aristotle on natural history.

GAZA, an ancient town of Palestine, the modern Ghuzzeh, originally a city of the Philistines, near the Mediterranean, 50 miles S.S.W. of Jerusalem. It is one of the most important ports of Palestine, manufactures pottery, is a centre of trade, and exports barley. The town was taken by Napoleon in 1799. During the European War the battles of Gaza were fought between the Turks and the British in March and in April, 1917. The town was captured by the British under Allenby in Nov., 1917. In 1930 Sir Flinders Petrie unearthed the remains of an early and great city here. Many re-

markable finds were reported. Pop. 17,480.

GAZELLE' (*Gazella dorcas*), the type of a sub-family of antelopes (Gazellinæ), which includes some twenty-five species of small, mostly desert-loving forms. Its colour is a light fawn upon the back, deepening into dark-brown in a wide band which edges the flanks and forms a line of demarcation between the colour of the upper portions of the body and the pure white of the abdomen. The eye of the gazelle is large, soft, and lustrous. Both sexes are provided with horns, round, black, and lyrated, about 13 inches long. It seems to be confined to the north side of the Atlas Mountains, Egypt, Abyssinia, Syria, Arabia, and South Persia.

GAZETTE' (from *gazzetta*, a small Venetian coin, which was the price of the first newspaper), a newspaper, especially an official newspaper. The first gazette in England was published at Oxford in 1665. On the removal of the court to London the title of *London Gazette* was adopted. It is now the official newspaper, and published on Tuesdays and Fridays. It is the organ by means of which all State intelligence, proclamations, and appointments are promulgated, and in which declarations of insolvency are published. A similar official newspaper is published also in Edinburgh and Dublin. *See* NEWSPAPER.

GAZETTEER', a geographical dictionary; a book containing descriptions of natural and political divisions, countries, cities, towns, rivers, and mountains alphabetically arranged. Among the more important general works of this kind are: M'Culloch's *Geographical Dictionary*, Longmans' *Gazetteer of the World*, Blackie's *Imperial Gazetteer*, Lippincott's *Pronouncing Gazetteer* (based upon Blackie's), Chambers's *Gazetteer of the World*, Vivien de Saint-Martin's *Nouveau dictionnaire de géographie universelle*, and Ritter's *Geographisch-Statistisches Lexikon*. There are also various gazetteers confined to particular countries.

GEAN (gēn), a kind of wild cherry tree (*Prunus Avium*), common in Britain. The name 'gean' is mainly confined to Scotland and the north of England. The fruit is smaller than that of the common cherry, of a red colour when unripe, and a deep purple or black when it arrives at maturity. The flavour is superior to that of most cherries. The wood is used for furniture and other purposes.

GEARING, in engineering, sets of toothed wheels working together. The object of gearing is to transform a rotational motion at one speed into a similar motion at another speed. From the 'Principle of Work' it follows that the turning moments (or torques) on each wheel are altered in the inverse ratio to the speeds of the wheels. The simplest set of gearing consists of two toothed wheels working on parallel axes, the teeth being parallel to the axes.

To reduce noise and friction as much as possible, it is important to shape the teeth so that as one tooth meshes into and leaves its mate, the teeth roll upon each other and do not slide relative to each other, i.e. the teeth must have a 'rolling' contact. When rolling contact exists, clearly no wasteful work is done against friction. The teeth can be shaped so as to have rolling contact. Two profiles are permissible, an involute profile or a cycloidal profile. The teeth are called involute and cycloidal teeth respectively. The gear-wheels are replaced for purposes of calculation by two circles which roll on each other without slipping. These circles are called *pitch circles*. The ratio of the speeds of rotation is clearly inversely proportional to the ratio of the diameters of the pitch circles. This ratio is called the *gear ratio*. The names given to some of the parts of teeth are shown in the figure below.

The *circumferential pitch* of the teeth is the distance from a point on one tooth to the corresponding point on the next, measured along the circumference of the pitch circle. This measurement is also called the *circular pitch*. The *diametral pitch* is the diameter of the pitch circle divided by the number of teeth. The ordinary proportions for cast-iron teeth are as follows: thickness at the pitch circle = $0.47p$; height of tooth = $0.7p$; height of pitch circle above root =

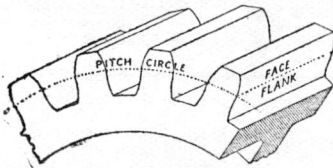

Fig. 1.—Names of parts of wheel tooth

$0.4p$; width = $2p$ to $3p$, sometimes in mill gears $5p$, where p is the circumferential pitch.

When two simple gears work in series so that the motion a is transformed by one gear into a motion b, and the motion b is transformed by a second gear into a motion c, the compound train is called a *double-re-*

duction gear. Similarly, we can have *treble-reduction* gears, and so on.

When the two axles are at right angles, the teeth lie on a conical surface, and the ends of the teeth are

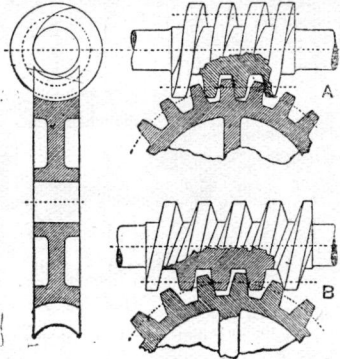

Fig. 2.—Worm Gear. A, Cycloidal teeth. B, Involute teeth

roughly at 45° to the plane of the wheels. Such trains are called *bevel-wheels*.

Sometimes a much higher gear ratio is required than can be conveniently provided with bevel-wheels. A *worm gear* is then employed, which is illustrated in fig. 2. Where great strength, high peripheral speeds, and freedom from vibration are required, *helical gears* are used for transforming motion between parallel axes. In helical gears the teeth are not parallel to the axis, but wind round the cylinder on which they are formed in the shape of a spiral or helix (*see* figure on p. 78). The cutting of such gears is a very difficult mechanical operation, and the process was perfected by Sir Charles Parsons about 1910. The perfecting of the methods for making these gears was a very great step in high-power mechanical engineering.

The special points of these gears are: (1) a very small pinion-wheel can be used with a large gear-wheel. The pinion-wheel need not be of very much larger diameter than the shaft fitting it. In this way very large gear ratios can be used—as much as 20 to 1. (2) The whole gearing can be run in oil, which is specially water-cooled. (3) Two pinions can be fitted on to the driving-shaft, each of which gears into a corresponding gear-wheel. The helical teeth on these two wheels are arranged to point in opposite senses, so that the axial reaction of the one exactly balances that of the other. (4) From the combination of these points a very high rotational speed of the pinion can be associated with a comparatively low rotational speed of the gear-wheel, and at the same time a powerful torque can be transmitted by

with the frame F. In rotating they drive B. A relative motion between A and B is thus made possible. Differential gearing is also used with governors, and in valve gears. See VALVES AND

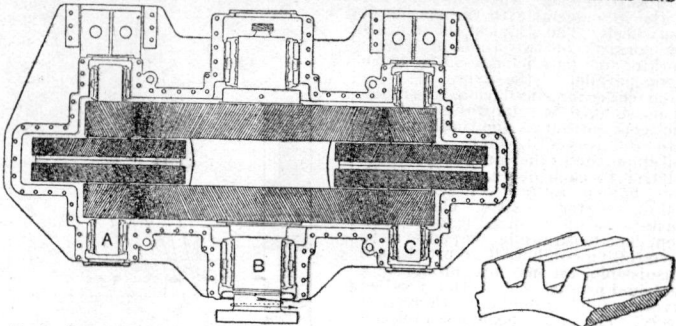

Fig. 3.—Parsons' Turbines for a single-screw Cargo Boat; plan view of double reduction helical gearing A, C, Turbine shafts (425 revolutions per minute). B, Propeller shaft (80 revolutions per minute)

the pinion owing to the oblique setting of the teeth.

It is not too much to say that the invention of this gearing has revolutionized naval engineering. The great difficulty in employing the turbine in naval work was this: to be efficient, the turbine must be run at a very high speed, and a propeller at a moderate speed. Consequently, so long as a transformation of speeds was inadmissible, the turbine could only be used in naval engineering by sacrificing either turbine or propeller efficiency. With the introduction of single-reduction gearing with gear ratios up to about 20 to 1, both the turbine and the propeller shafts can be run at economical speeds.

Gearing, Differential, any mechanism which depends for its action on *differences* in the motions of its component parts. A familiar example occurs in the motor-car. In going round a curve, one of the back wheels must move at a different speed from the other, if slipping is to be avoided. The back axle cannot therefore be made in one piece with a worm gear in the middle to drive it. It is made in two parts, coupled by an epicyclic train of wheels, the *differential gear*. One design is shown in fig. 4. The wheel EF, carrying the so-called *idle wheels* G, is driven direct by the engine. When the car is going along a straight road, the idle wheels do not rotate about the spindles J, but, of course, revolve with the wheel BF which holds them. They therefore drive the bevel wheels A and B, and these rotate the car wheels. But if A is fixed, the idle wheels rotate about the spindles J, and also

VALVE GEAR.—BIBLIOGRAPHY: D. A. Low, *Applied Mechanics*; *Modern Mechanical Engineering* (The Gresham Publishing Company); R. J. Walker, *The Application of Geared Turbines*

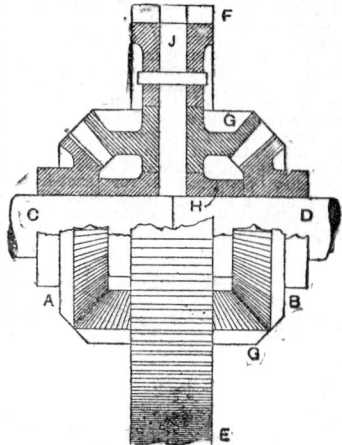

Fig. 4.—Differential Gear

to *Merchant Ships* (North-East Coast Institute of Engineers and Shipbuilders).

GEBANG PALM, the *Corypha gebanga*, a fan-leaved palm of South-Eastern Asia. Its pith furnishes a sort of sago; its leaves are used for thatch, and made into hats, baskets, and bags; the fibres of its leaf-stalks are made into ropes, nets, and cloth, and the root is highly medicinal.

GEBER (gē'bĕr), Arabian chemist or alchemist, often designated the father of chemistry, flourished during the eighth century. He was acquainted with nearly all the chemical processes in use down to the eighteenth century. Roger Bacon called him *Magister Magistrorum*. His writings describe various kinds of furnaces and other apparatus, and cupellation, distillation, and other chemical processes; the purification, composition, and properties of the metals then known —gold, silver, copper, lead, tin, and iron—and the functions of mercury, sulphur, and arsenic. He is the reputed author of an immense number of works on metaphysics, language, and astronomy, as well as on chemistry.

GEBWEILER (geb-vī'lĕr), a town of France, in Alsace, on the Lauch. It has two fine Roman Catholic churches, and works for cotton-spinning and weaving, woollen manufactures, bleaching, dyeing, calico-printing and machinery. Pop. 13,380.

GECKO, a name common to the members of a cosmopolitan family of nocturnal lizards (*Geckotidœ*), characterized by the general flatness of their form, especially of the head, which is somewhat of a triangular shape; the body is covered on the upper part with numerous round prominences or warts; the feet are rather short, and the toes of nearly equal length and furnished with flattened sucking-pads by means of which the animals can run up a perpendicular wall, or even across a ceiling. The greater number feed on insects and their larvæ and pupæ. Several of the species infest houses, where, although they are perfectly innocuous, their appearance makes them unwelcome tenants. One species (*Tarentola mauritanica*) is common in Northern Africa and Southern Europe.

GED (ged), William, inventor of stereotyping, born in Edinburgh about the beginning of the eighteenth century, died in poor circumstances in 1749. He first practised his great improvement in the art of printing in 1725; and some years later he entered into a partnership in London, the result of which was the production of two prayer-books only. He returned to Scotland in 1733, and published a stereotype edition of Sallust in 1744.

GEDDES (ged'es), Alexander, a Roman Catholic priest, poet, and miscellaneous writer, was born in the county of Banff, Scotland, in 1737, died in London 1802. At the age of twenty-one he was sent to the Scottish college at Paris, and, returning to Scotland in 1769, he took charge of a Roman Catholic congregation at Auchinhalrig, in Banffshire, where he became known for his scholarship. In 1779 the University of Aberdeen granted him the degree of LL.D., and the next year he repaired to London with a view to obtaining facilities for his scheme of a new English translation of the Old and New Testaments. Two volumes of his translation and a volume of critical remarks were published, but the rationalistic views promulgated met with much censure, and his own immediate superiors suspended him. He was in the midst of a translation of the *Psalms* when he died. His other works include numerous pamphlets, translations, and macaronic poems.—Cf. T. K. Cheyne, *Founders of Old Testament Criticism*.

GEDDES, Sir Auckland Campbell, G.C.M.G., politician, born in 1879. Educated at Edinburgh, he became a doctor, and was in succession assistant professor of anatomy at Edinburgh, and professor at the M'Gill University, Montreal, and at the Royal College of Surgeons, Dublin.

During the European War he first served at the front, where he rose to the rank of brigadier-general. In 1916 he was appointed Director of Recruiting, and in Aug., 1917, became Minister of National Service. President of the Local Government Board in 1918, and Minister of Reconstruction in Jan., 1919, he was appointed President of the Board of Trade in May of the same year. From 1920-24 he was ambassador to the United States and left this public service to become chairman of the Rio Tinto Company. In 1922 he was made G.C.M.G.

GEDDES, Sir Eric Campbell, British politician, born 26th Sep., 1875, in India. Educated at Edinburgh, he entered the service of a railway company in America, but returned to Britain, where he became deputy manager of the North Eastern Railway Company. In 1915 he entered the Ministry of Munitions, and was sent to France as director of military railways. Controller of the Navy in 1917, he became First Lord of the Admiralty, and in 1919 first Minister of Transport, resigning in 1921. He was knighted in 1916, made a Privy Councillor, a K.C.B. (military), and a Knight Grand Cross of the Order of the British Empire in 1917, and in 1919 a K.C.B. (civil). Returning to a business career in 1922, he became chairman of Imperial Airways, Ltd., and other companies.

GEDDES, Jenny, the name tradition gives to a street fruit-seller who, during the tumult in St. Giles Church, Edinburgh, on Sunday, 23rd July, 1637, when the dean attempted to introduce the Episcopalian service-book, threw her stool at his head exclaiming, 'Villain! dost thou say mass at my lug?' This tumult led to events which annulled Episcopacy and restored Presbyterianism. The honour of the exploit has been claimed for a Barbara Hamilton, wife of John Mein, merchant in Edinburgh, but Jenny Geddes the street fruit-seller's claim has always been the popular one, and a memorial brass has been placed in St. Giles to her memory.

GEEFS (gāfs), **Guillaume,** Belgian sculptor, born at Antwerp 1806, died 1883. Among his most important works are the monuments to the victims of the Revolution of 1830 at Brussels; a statue of Rubens in front of Antwerp Cathedral; and statues of King Leopold. His brothers Joseph (died 1860) and Aloys (died 1841) were also sculptors of reputation, the latter also producing some historical paintings.

GEELONG (jē-long'), an Australian seaport town, colony of Victoria, near the head of the west arm of Port Philip Bay, 45 miles south-west of Melbourne. The town is well laid out on ground sloping to the bay, and its streets abound with fine shops, business premises, and public buildings. There is an extensive and well-laid-out botanical garden and several public parks belonging to the town. There are three jetties in the bay, alongside of which ships of the largest tonnage can load and discharge. There are wool-mills, tanneries, and rope-works, and a considerable trade is done in wool. The country surrounding Geelong is essentially agricultural, and is taken up by farms and orchards. Pop. (1931), 42,760.

GEESTEMÜNDE or **WESER-MÜNDE** (gäs-tė-mùn-dė), a seaport town of Germany in the Prussian province of Hanover, at the mouth of the Weser, separated from Bremerhaven by the Geeste. Extensive docks were constructed here between 1857 and 1863. The port is strongly fortified, and the trade is considerable. The industries include shipbuilding, iron-founding, and engineering. Since 1889 Geestemünde has included the adjoining Geestendorf; total pop. 72,100.

GEFLE (yef'le), a seaport, Sweden, near the mouth of a river of the same name in the Gulf of Bothnia, 50 miles N. of Upsala. It stands on both sides of the river and two islands formed by it, and has an excellent harbour.

It has manufactures of linen, leather, tobacco, and sail-cloth; shipbuilding yards; and an extensive trade in deals, tar, pitch, and iron. Pop. (1932), 38,992.

GEGENBAUR (gä'gen-bour), **Karl,** German comparative anatomist, and advocate of the evolution theory, was born in 1826 at Würzburg, and died in 1903. He studied medicine, and became assistant physician in the Julius Hospital in his native town. In 1852 he gave up this post to undertake zoological researches in the Mediterranean and in 1855 went to Jena as professor. While there he abandoned zoology and devoted himself entirely to comparative anatomy. He was transferred in 1873 to Heidelberg, and retired in 1901, dying two years later.

In 1859 (the same year in which Darwin published his *Origin of Species*) Gegenbaur published an important work on comparative anatomy on evolutionary lines, which was followed by other works of a like kind, besides *Erlebtes und Erstrebtes* (1901), an autobiographical sketch.

GEHEN'NA a term used in the New Testament as equivalent to a place of fire or torment, and rendered in the Authorized (and the Revised) Version by *hell* and *hell-fire*. It is a form of the Hebrew *Ge-hinnom,* the valley of Hinnom, in which was Tophet, where the Israelites sometimes sacrificed their children to Moloch (2 *Kings* xxiii, 10). On this account the place was afterwards regarded as a place of abomination, and became the receptacle for the refuse of the city, perpetual fires being kept up in order to prevent pestilential effluvia.

GEIBEL (gī'bl), **Emanuel,** German poet, born at Lübeck 1815, died 1884. He studied at the Universities of Bonn and Berlin, and resided a year or two in Greece. He published his first collection of poems in 1840, which reached its hundredth edition in 1884. In 1843 he published a tragedy, *King Roderick*; in 1846 the epic *König Sigurd's Brautfahrt.* Collections of his poems appeared in 1848, 1857, and 1864. From 1851 to 1869 he was professor of æsthetics and poetry at Munich. He wrote also *Brunhild,* a tragedy; *The Loreley,* an opera; and other plays; but his fame rests on his lyrics, which were immensely popular.

GEIGER, Abraham, Jewish theologian and scholar, one of the foremost advocates and initiators of religious reform in Germany, born at Frankfurt-on-the-Main in 1810, died in 1874. He studied at the Universities of Heidelberg and Bonn, became Rabbi at Wiesbaden, and subsequently at Breslau, Frankfort, and Berlin. From 1862 till his death he edited the

Jüdische Zeitschrift, and stood for the reform of Judaism and liberality in the observance of the traditional law. His works include: *Urschrift und Uebersetzungen der Bibel, Sadducäer und Pharisäer, Das Judentum und seine Geschichte*, and *Salomon Gabirol und seine Dichtungen*.

GEIJER, Erik Gustaf, Swedish historian, born at Ransäter, Värmland, 12th Jan., 1783, died 23rd April, 1847. Educated at the University of Upsala, he began to lecture there in 1810, and in 1817 became professor of history. He was also a poet and a musician, and during the last ten years of his life he took an active part in politics. He exercised a considerable influence upon the historical literature of his native country.

Among his works are: *Svea Rikes Häfder* (Records of Sweden), in which he intended to relate the history of Sweden from mythical ages to the present time, but of which he only finished the introductory volume (1825); *Svenska Folkets Historia* (History of Sweden down to the death of Queen Christina), (1832–6). His collected works, with a biographical sketch, were published by his son (1873–7).

GEIKIE (gē′ki), **Sir Archibald,** K.C.B., O.M., geologist, born at Edinburgh 1835. Appointed to the geological survey, he became director of the Scottish branch in 1867; was professor of geology at Edinburgh from 1871 to 1882; director-general of the United Kingdom survey and head of the Museum of Practical Geology, London, from 1882 to 1901. He was awarded the Order of Merit in 1914. He is the author of *Text-book of Geology, Class-book of Geology, Field Geology, The Scenery of Scotland in connection with its Physical Geology, Ancient Volcanoes of Britain, Life of Sir R. I. Murchison, Memoir of Sir A. C. Ramsay, Scottish Reminiscences, Love of Nature among the Romans, The Birds of Shakespeare,* and *Annals of the Royal Society Club.* He died in 1924.

GEIKIE, James, geologist, brother of Sir Archibald Geikie, born at Edinburgh 1839, died in 1915. He was engaged on the Scottish survey from 1861 until he succeeded his brother in the geological professorship at Edinburgh in 1882. He was the author of *The Great Ice Age; Prehistoric Europe; Outlines of Geology; Mountains: their Origin, Growth, and Decay;* and *The Antiquity of Man in Europe.*

GEISHA, a term applied to a class of Japanese women, endowed with personal attractions and accomplished in the arts of music and danc-

ing. They entertain guests at social parties, dinners, and receptions, and customers in tea-houses. The meaning of the word is 'one with pleasing accomplishments.' The geishas are not only clever singers and dancers, but also amusing conversationalists. They are trained from the age of seven, and they correspond to the almehs of Egypt.

GEISSLER TUBES, vacuum tubes first made by Geissler of Bonn. They are made of glass, and contain a highly rarefied gas at a pressure of less than ½ mm. of mercury. When an electrical discharge is passed through a tube from an induction coil, it is accompanied by beautiful luminous effects, the colours of which depend on the nature of the gas. The tubes

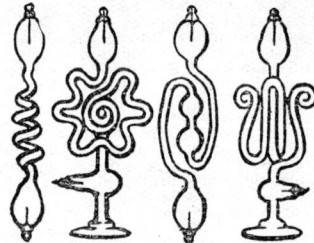

Geissler tubes

are useful for the spectroscopic examination of the luminous gas. *See* IONIZATION.

GELA (jē′la), one of the most important ancient Greek cities of Sicily, situated on the south coast of the island between Agrigentum and Camarina; founded in 690 B.C. by a colony of Cretans and Rhodians. The colony was remarkably prosperous, and in 582 B.C. sent out a portion of its inhabitants, who founded Agrigentum. In 280 Phintias, the tyrant of Agrigentum, utterly destroyed Gela. Its site has been the subject of much controversy.

GELADA (gel′a-da), a singular Abyssinian baboon, remarkable for the heavy mane which hangs over the shoulders, and which only grows when the animal is adult.

GELASIUS (je-), the name of two Popes—**Gelasius I** and **II**. The former, who held the see from 492 to 496, founding on the alleged primacy of Peter, was one of the first who openly maintained that the Roman bishop alone was entitled to regulate matters of faith and discipline, though in practice he had not then attained any such superiority. **Gelasius II,** Pope for only one year (1118–9), and originally called John of Gaeta, was elected by the party hostile to Henry V, but was obliged to give way to Gregory VIII, supported by the emperor, and shortly after died in the monastery of Clugny.

GELATINE is a nitrogenous substance derived from the cartilage and skins of young animals, and differs only from glue (q.v.) and size in the care with which the raw material is selected and treated. The purest form of gelatine is prepared from the head and leg portions of calves, which are useless for leather purposes. The raw material must be perfectly fresh, and all decomposition avoided during subsequent manufacture. It is first carefully cleaned from traces of blood and flesh by washing, and then treated with steam or boiling water. The solution of gelatine thus obtained is allowed to settle, and decolorized by treatment with sulphurous acid. After filtration, the hot solution is poured into moulds and allowed to set to a firm jelly, which is cut into slices and dried on nets; this imparts the crossmarkings always seen on sheet gelatine. The drying process must be very carefully watched, as the moist gelatine readily undergoes decomposition. Gelatine is also produced in the form of threads and as powder.

It is largely used in cookery for the preparation of soups and jellies, and in confectionery for making pastilles and jujubes. The gelatine capsules used in medicine are made from a more flexible mixture of gelatine and glycerine. Very large quantities are used in photography for the coating of films and plates; the introduction of gelatine for this purpose, in place of albumen and collodion, has revolutionized photography. It is essential that the gelatine should be absolutely pure, since the smallest amount of putrefaction would cause the formation of substances which would destroy the silver salts present in the film.

Chemically, gelatine is a substance closely related to, but not identical with, the proteins. It contains the elements carbon, hydrogen, nitrogen, oxygen, and sulphur. When pure, it forms a colourless, transparent, and flexible substance which is absolutely tasteless and odourless. Gelatine is insoluble in alcohol or ether, but caustic soda and potash dissolve it readily, even in cold weak solutions. It swells in cold and dissolves readily in hot water. A 1 per cent solution should set to a jelly on cooling. Gelatine, heated too often or too long, loses this property of setting, which is the main source of its value.

A solution of gelatine gives with tannic acid a flocculent precipitate which is insoluble in water; this reaction is practically identical with that which takes place during the tanning of hides for the manufacture of leather. Both as a jelly and in solution, gelatine gives a slight Tyndall effect, reflecting a beam of light sideways; but the ultramicroscope does not show definite particles. Gelatine is rendered absolutely insoluble in water by treatment with formaldehyde. In this form it is used, when dyed, for making spangles for dresses and for other purposes. Isinglass (q.v.) is a very pure form of gelatine derived from the swimbladder of the sturgeon.

Within recent years the importance of the chemistry of colloids (q.v.) for many industries and manufactures has become generally recognized, and much important research work in this field has been carried out by chemists. The colloid which has been most fully investigated is gelatine.

GELDERLAND, GUELDERLAND (gel'), or **GUELDERS**, a province of the Netherlands; area, 1,941 English sq. miles. It is generally flat, and has much alluvial soil, well fitted both for arable and grass husbandry. The manufactures, principally woollen, cotton, and linen goods, soap, salt, and glass, are carried on extensively in various quarters. The principal towns are Arnheim, Nijmegen, Thiel, and Zutphen. Pop. (1931), 843,233.

GELDERN (gel'dern), a town of Rhenish Prussia, 27 miles north-west of Düsseldorf. Pop. 6,501.

GELÉE (zhé-lä), Claude. See CLAUDE LORRAINE.

GELLERT (gel'èrt), Christian Furchtegott, German poet, born 1715, died 1769. He was appointed extraordinary professor of philosophy at Leipzig in 1751, where his lectures were received with great applause. His hymns, tales, fables, and essays enjoyed much popularity in their day.

GELLIUS, Aulus, a Roman author of the second century. His *Noctes Atticæ*, a sort of common-place book, is now of great value, as many of the works from which he drew his materials are lost.

GELLIVARA (gel-i-vä'rà), a mountain and town in Northern Sweden, within the Arctic Circle, in a locality exceedingly rich in iron ore. The town is connected by railway with Luleä, on the Gulf of Bothnia, and with the growing Norwegian port of Narvik on the Ofoten Fiord, in Norway, where quays and other works have been constructed for the shipment of the ore. Pop. 12,000.

GELNHAUSEN (geln'hoŭ-zn), an old walled town of Prussia, province of Hesse-Nassau, 16 miles E.N.E. of Hanau, on the Kinzig. Its principal buildings are a large Gothic church of the thirteenth century, and, on an island in the Kinzig, a palace in which Frederick Barbarossa and several of his successors used to reside. Pop. 4,859.

GELON (gē'lon), an ancient Greek ruler, tyrant of Gela, and afterwards of Syracuse. After the death of Hippocrates, tyrant of Gela, he seized the sovereign power (491 B.C.), and about 485 B.C. gained possession of Syracuse. From this time he bent all his energies to the aggrandizement of his new capital, the power and importance of which he greatly increased by his conquests and good government. His aid was sought by the Greeks against Xerxes, but a formidable invasion of Carthaginians under Hamilcar engaged him in Sicily. The result was the total defeat of the Carthaginians in the great battle of Himera (480 B.C.). It is celebrated in an ode by Pindar. Gelon died in 478 B.C., and was succeeded by his brother Hieron.

GELSE'MIUM (It. *gelsomino*, jasmine), a genus of plants belonging to the nat. ord. Loganiaceæ, the best known, *G. sempervirens* or Carolina jasmine, being an evergreen climbing shrub of the Southern States of America, with twigs producing a milky juice, opposite lance-shaped shining leaves, and sweet-scented yellow flowers. The root has valuable medicinal properties, being used for controlling certain forms of nervous irritability.

GELSENKIRCHEN (gel'zn-kirḥen), a town of Germany in the Prussian province of Westphalia, on the border of the Rhine Province, a few miles north-east of Essen and north-west of Bochum. It owes its rapid rise (from 844 inhabitants in 1852) to the development of the coal and iron industries, which it shares with neighbouring towns. The extension of its limits in 1903 greatly increased the population, which in 1932 was 330,186.

GEMARA (ge-mä'ra), in Jewish literature, the second part of the *Talmud* or commentary on the *Mishna. See* TALMUD.

GEMINI (gem'i-nī), the Twins (II), the third sign of the Zodiac. The constellation Gemini was supposed to represent Castor and Pollux, the twins of ancient mythology. The two brightest stars of the constellation are named Castor and Pollux. Castor, which is a double star, is of 1½ magnitude, Pollux just a little under normal first magnitude. The sun is in the sign Gemini from about 21st May till 21st June, but is now in the constellation Gemini during a period about one month later.

GEMMATION, in zoology, a mode of reproduction among certain animals of low type, which consists in the production of a bud or buds, generally from the exterior, but sometimes from the interior, of the body of the animal, which buds are developed into independent beings that may or may not remain attached to the parent organism. This mode of reproduction is typical of hydroid zoophytes, polyzoa, and some ascidians.

GEMS, or precious stones, are sometimes found crystalized in regular shapes and with a natural

Gems: Mediaeval Jewelled Pendant

polish, more commonly of irregular shapes and with a rough coat. The term gem often denotes more particularly a stone that is cut, polished, or engraved, and it also includes pearls and various artificial productions.

The first and most valuable class of gems includes diamonds, emeralds, rubies, sapphires, and a few others; the second class includes the amethyst, topaz, garnet, &c.; while agate, lapis-lazuli, cornelian, &c., though much used for ornament, can scarcely be called gems. The various precious stones are described under their proper heads.

The fabrication of artificial gems is now prosecuted with skill and capital, and has become an important industrial art. The base of one class of imitations is a peculiar kind of glass of considerable hardness, brilliancy, and refractive power called *paste* or *strass*, which consists of a complex borosilicate of lead and potassium, and is distinguished from ordinary glass by the presence of 50 per cent. of oxide of lead. When the strass is obtained very pure, it is melted and mixed with substances having a metallic base, generally oxides, which communicate to the mass the most varied colours. Another class, called semistones or doublets, are made by affixing thin slices of real gem to an under part of strass by means of an invisible cement. In some cases an imitation is made by setting uncoloured strass or quartz in jewellery with some coloured 'foil' at the back of it.

Attempts have within recent years been made with a fair measure of success to manufacture true gems by artificial processes. The French chemists Becquerel, Ebelman, Gaudin, Despretz, and others have done much in this direction. In 1858 MM. Deville and Caron communicated to the Academy of Sciences, Paris, a process for the production of a number of gems of the corundum class, as rubies, sapphires, &c. The process essentially consisted in exposing the fluoride of aluminium, together with a little charcoal and boracic acid, in a plumbago crucible protected from the action of the air, to a white heat for about an hour. Many experiments with a view to producing diamonds artificially have also been made. From hydrocarbons, subjected to a very intense heat and enormous pressure, minute crystals, differing from natural diamonds in no respect save brilliancy and size, have been produced. In this way Henri Moissan has prepared artificial diamonds by dissolving carbon (sugar charcoal) in molten iron, and Parsons has done much work in the same direction.

In art and archæology the term gem is usually applied to a precious stone cut or engraved in ornamental designs, or with inscriptions. Stones on which the design is raised above the general surface are called *cameos*; those having the design sunk below the surface are called *intaglios*. Early specimens of cut gems are seen in the scarabæi or beetle-shaped signets worn in rings by the ancient Egyptians. Among the Greeks, Etruscans, and Romans gemsculpture held a high place, reaching its highest point under Augustus.

Modern gem-engraving dates from the beginning of the fifteenth century, the chief seats of the art being Italy and Germany. Rome is now the headquarters of the seal-engraving art. The tools of the engraver consist of a lathe, and a series of little rods with heads of different shapes, all of which can be adjusted to the lathe. The axis of the lathe is pierced at the centre with an orifice, into which the tools for cutting the stone are firmly fixed by means of a screw. The en-

graver wets the extremity of the mounted rod with diamond-dust made into a paste with olive-oil, and as the wheel is in motion he applies the stone, firmly cemented to a piece of reed, to the revolving tool. The diamond-dust enables the tool to cut into the stone with ease. As the design is frequently very elaborate and of the greatest delicacy, the tools are necessarily multi-form. The stones used for cameo-cutting often exhibit layers of different colours, so that the raised design has a tint distinct from the ground. Intaglios are very often executed in transparent stones, and the subjects treated in this manner are more limited in number. They are chiefly such as seals, devices, and coats of arms.—BIBLIOGRAPHY: C. W. King, *Antique Gems*; J. H. Middleton, *The Engraved Gems of Classical Times*; L. Claremont, *The Gem Cutter's Craft*; G. F. Kunz, *Curious Lore of Precious Stones.*

GEMSBOK (gemz'bok), the *Oryx gazella*, a large powerful member of the antelope family, inhabiting the plains of South Africa. It equals the domestic ass in size, has a short erect mane, a long sweeping black tail, and long sharp-pointed heavy horns, nearly straight from base to tip, and obscurely ringed throughout the lower half. By the aid of these natural bayonets it can easily defend itself from the smaller Carnivora, and it has been known to drive off, and even kill, the lion himself.

GENDARMES (zhȧn'dȧrm), the name originally given in France to the whole body of armed men, but after the introduction of standing armies, to a body of heavy-armed cavalry, which composed the chief strength of the forces. Gendarmes are now the French armed police. They are all picked men; they are usually taken from the regular forces, and are of tried courage or approved conduct. There are *horse gendarmes* and *foot gendarmes*. They are formed into small units called *brigades*; and the union of a number of these forms a *departmental company.*

GENDER (Fr. *genre*, Lat. *genus*), in grammar, one of those classes or categories into which words are divided according to the sex, natural or metaphorical, of the beings or things they denote. It may be exhibited by a class of words marked by similarity in termination, the termination having attached to it a distinction in sex, as seen in nouns, adjectives, and participles.

There are three genders in all: *masculine, feminine,* and *neuter,* but these three distinctions only exist in some languages. In Sanskrit, Greek, and Latin all three are present, as also in German and English. English words expressing males are said to be of the *masculine* gender; those expressing females, of the *feminine* gender; and words expressing things having no sex are of the *neuter*, or *neither* gender. Gender is thus coincident with sex in English, and is a very simple matter. But in other languages sex and gender have little or no necessary relation, the majority of the names applied to inanimate objects being either masculine or feminine, and the grounds for such distinction being quite obscure.

In the languages derived from the Latin—Italian, French, Spanish, and Portuguese—a neuter gender is not recognized. In the highly inflected languages there are certain terminations distinctive of the different genders, but English gender only to a slight extent depends on the form of the word—*ess*, for instance, is a feminine termination. In English the gender of a noun only affects the pronoun substituted for it.

GENEAL'OGY, the systematical investigation and exhibition of the origin, descent, and relations of families (or their *pedigree*). Persons descended from a common father constitute a family. Under the idea of *degree* of relationship is denoted the nearness or remoteness of relationship in which one person stands with respect to another. A series of several persons, descended from a common progenitor, is called a *line*. A line is either *direct* or *collateral*. The collateral lines comprehend the several lines which unite in a common progenitor.

For illustrating descent and relationship genealogical tables are constructed, the order of which depends on the end in view. The common form of genealogical tables places the common stock at the head, and shows the degree of each descendant by lines. Some tables, however, have been constructed in the form of a tree, in which the progenitor (Ger. *Stammvater*) is placed beneath, as if for a root.—Cf. W. Rye, *Records and Record Searching*.

GENERAL, the military officer in whom is vested the command of a considerable body or formation of troops. Generically the two words 'general officer' are more properly used. In the British service there are three grades of general officer, the word general without prefix signifying the highest of these grades. Next below comes lieutenant-general, which again is followed by major-general. In conversation, and in all ordinary matters, the single word general is used for all three grades, while in formal official matters the full title

is given. The title of brigadier-general formerly in use in the service was abolished in 1921. This was merely a temporary rank given to officers holding certain appointments, such, for instance, as brigade commander. On relinquishing such appointment the officer reverted to his substantive or permanent rank. Officers holding such appointments, formerly colonels-commandant, have, since 1928, been known as brigadiers.

The badges of rank by which the various grades of general officers are distinguished are as follows: general, crossed sword and baton with star and crown; lieutenant-general, crossed sword and baton with crown only; major-general, crossed sword and baton with star only; while a brigadier wears three stars and a crown, the two lower stars being side by side. All these are worn on the shoulder-straps.

GENERAL ASSEMBLY, name given to the governing body of the Church of Scotland and other Presbyterian churches in Ireland, Canada, Australia and elsewhere.

The Scottish general assembly meets every year in Edinburgh in May, and consists of ministers and laymen sent as representatives by the presbyteries in the Church. The king is represented by a High Commissioner appointed each year. The assembly is presided over by a minister elected to the office, called the moderator. Until the union of the free churches with the established church, each had its own general assembly, which also met in Edinburgh in May.

Recent Lord High Commissioners were the Duke of York, Rt. Hon. James Brown, P.C., M.P., and, in 1933, Mr. John Buchan, the well-known author.

GENERAL LIEN, in law, the right to retain possession of a chattel until payment be made, not only of any debt due in respect of that particular chattel, but of any balance that may be due on general account in the same line of business.

A general lien exists (1) by virtue of the course of dealing between the parties in a particular case, (2) as a common law right arising from continuous and well-recognized usage, (3) by express agreement.

GENERAL SHIP, in maritime law, a ship which is announced by the owners to take goods from a particular port at a specified time, and which is not under special contract.

GENERAL STAFF, speaking generally, the staff consists of specially-trained officers who are appointed to assist commanders in carrying out their duties. A staff-officer as such has no military command, though in his rôle of confidential trained assistant he has considerable responsibility in working out details, sifting information, issuing the commander's considered orders, affording help to the troops when required, and attending to matters of routine.

The staff is divided into three main branches, the general staff, the adjutant-general's and the quartermaster-general's branches. The Staff Colleges at Camberley and Quetta are institutions where regimental officers are trained for war generally, and for service in all branches of the staff. The normal period of this course is two years, and, after each tour of service in a staff appointment, it is usual for an officer under the rank of substantive lieutenant-colonel to return to his unit for a further period of regimental service.

The **general staff branch** is charged with all matters affecting military operations and military training, such, for instance, as war organization, selection of lines of operation, plans for concentration of troops, information, and secret service. It is also the duty of this branch to appreciate the course of action in the event of war, and arrange it in accordance with the capabilities of the forces likely to be available. It also prepares in advance a plan of campaign.

The general staff, as the senior branch, and as being directly concerned with the collection of information, is responsible for the dissemination of any necessary information to the adjutant-general's and quartermaster-general's branches in sufficient time and in the necessary detail to enable these branches to carry on their work. Co-operation between the three branches is essential, and in general the chief staff-officer with a formation co-ordinates the work of the representatives of the various branches, though he does not interfere in the working out of details.

The **adjutant-general's branch** is responsible, among others, for the following questions: discipline and military law, supply of personnel, honours and rewards, sanitation, casualties, and routine duties.

The **quartermaster-general's branch** deals with questions relating to supplies, i.e. food, forage, &c., equipment and ammunition, transport, quarters, remounts, and veterinary affairs.

It has been suggested that in the future it may be found possible to abolish the dividing lines between the three branches, and to have one staff dealing with questions of every kind, but at present the three-branch system is in vogue. The chief of the imperial general staff is the official adviser of the Government on military matters.

The red gorget patches, formerly worn by all staff-officers of whatever grade, have now been abolished for all below the rank of general officer in favour of distinctive coloured armlets. The colour of these armlets varies according to whether the officer is serving on the War Office staff, or that of a command, division, or brigade, that for the War Office being French grey with the letter G, A, or Q; for a command, red, black, red; a division, red; and a brigade, blue, in each case with the appropriate letters denoting branch or appointment.

Officers of the G branch hold appointments such as general staff-officer, grade 1, 2, or 3; those of the adjutant-general's or quartermaster-general's branches as deputy, assistant, or deputy-assistant adjutant or quartermaster-general.

GENERATION, a single succession of human beings (or animals) who are born, grow up, and reproduce their kind; hence, an age or period of time between one succession and the next, as the third, the fourth, or the tenth generation. The length of a human generation is usually estimated at about thirty years.

GENERATION, SPONTANEOUS, or **ABIOGENESIS** the doctrine that living matter may originate spontaneously, 'that under certain circumstances dead matter may build itself up into living matter without the intervention of already existing protoplasm.' In the seventeenth century this was the dominant view, sanctioned alike by antiquity and authority, and was first assailed by Redi, an Italian philosopher, who proved that flies are not thus generated.

Buffon held the doctrine in a very modified degree. He was of opinion that life is the indefeasible property of certain indestructible molecules of matter which exist in all living things, and have inherent activities by which they are distinguished from not-living matter, each individual living organism being formed by their temporary combination. Since the time of Redi it is only animals or plants of very low type and minute size that have been supposed thus to be produced spontaneously from dead matter; and the readiness with which such appear, in circumstances in which one might suppose no germs of them could be present, gives some countenance to the belief. But there is every reason to believe that, whatever may have been the case with the first beginnings of life, living matter is now invariably derived from pre-existent living matter.

GENERATIONS, ALTERNATION OF. (a) **In Plants.** This phenomenon, rare among the lower forms (Thallophytes), becomes a constant and important feature in the higher groups (Cormophytes). It is seen in its most obvious form in the Ferns (q.v.), where the life-history comprises two distinct phases, the familiar fern-plant being the neutral or asexual generation or *sporophyte*, which ends with the production of asexual *spores*. When sown, these spores give rise *not* to a new fern-plant but to the prothallus or *gametophyte*, a small cellular structure which, as its name implies, produces *gametes*, viz. *spermatozoids* from antheridia and *egg-cells* in archegonia. An egg-cell, when fertilized, grows into a young fern-plant, which is at first (the embryo stage) parasitic on the prothallus, but soon becomes independent. In this case the different generations are easily distinguished, the sporophyte being a large, long-lived vascular plant, whereas the gametophyte is small, cellular, and transient.

Conversely, in Mosses and Liverworts the 'plant' is the gametophyte, and the sporophyte or *sporogonium* never becomes independent, but serves only for the production and dispersal of the spores. In other cases the two phases are not so distinct, e.g. in the Red Seaweed (Polysiphonia), where the sexual and neutral plants are externally indistinguishable except by their reproductive organs, or in the Angiosperms, where the gametophyte phase is practically suppressed.

The 'nuclear cycle,' which goes hand in hand with alternation of generations, furnishes a reliable means of distinguishing between the two phases, though it is not easy of application. At each fusion of gametes, the number of chromosomes is doubled, and if there is a sporophyte phase, this double (*diploid*) number persists up to the formation of spores, when reduction to the single (*haploid*) number characteristic of the gametophyte takes place.

(b) **In Animals.** The phrase 'alternation of generations' is applied to the life-histories of animals when these consist of two or more distinct stages which reproduce in a different way, and might be mistaken for distinct species. Among some of the hydroid zoophytes (Cœlenterata), for example, a fixed branching colony of polypes gives rise by budding to little free-swimming sexual jelly-fishes (medusæ), the fertilized eggs of which, instead of producing other jelly-fishes, develop into branching colonies. Such an alternation of an asexual with a sexual form is known as *metagenesis*. A well-

known jelly-fish (Aurelia) of larger size is the sexual stage of a similar life-history, derived from a single fixed polype by transverse division. Each such polype produces a number of medusæ in this way, which are at first placed on top of one another, like a pile of saucers, afterwards breaking away and growing to full size. Another well-known case is that of the transparent salps, marine creatures which are among the lowly relatives of the back-boned animals. Here a solitary asexual form gives rise by budding to a chain of sexual individuals.

Alternation of generations also included what is known as *heterogeny*, where the life-history not only includes a sexual stage in which the eggs are fertilized, but also a series of females of which the eggs develop without being fertilized, i.e. by *parthenogenesis*. This is illustrated by the common aphides popularly known as 'green fly,' in which during the summer a large number of generations of females are produced parthenogenetically, these being born alive (viviparously). In the autumn, however, the last generation of such females lays eggs from which both males and females hatch out. Examples of heterogeny are common among some of the parasitic worms, e.g. the liver-flukes, but here the life-history is still more complex.

GENERATOR, *electric generators*, or dynamo-electric machines, may be divided into two classes, each of which may be again divided into two groups: *Class 1*, generators of direct-current electricity, or *dynamos*; and *Class 2*, generators of alternating-current electricity, or *alternators*. Each of these classes is divided into *Group A*, high-speed machinery; *Group B*, medium- and low-speed machinery.

High-speed alternators are usually driven by steam-turbines, and the whole set is called a *turbo-alternator*. Medium- and low-speed alternators are used with water-wheels in hydro-electric installations. High-speed dynamos are comparatively rare nowadays. When steam-turbines are used to drive them, a single reduction gearing is often used, so that the turbine can run at a high speed and the dynamo at a medium speed. Medium- and low-speed dynamos are very common, and are driven by steam-turbines—through gearing—reciprocating engines, water-wheels, gas-engines, &c.

Speeds, speeds from 75–400 r.p.m. may be regarded as low speeds; from 400–1,000 r.p.m., say, as medium speeds, and above 1,000 r.p.m. as high speeds. For a generator of a given output there is a certain 'best' speed at which the weight and therefore the cost of the machine is a minimum.

Principles, the leading principles underlying the action of all dynamo-electric machinery are the same. Faraday discovered in 1831 that when

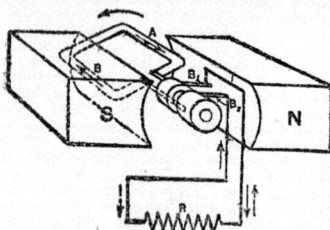

Simple Loop Dynamo

the magnetic flux through a coil of wire changes, an electro-motive force is set up in the coil. This e.m.f. is proportional to the rate of change of the flux. A powerful magnetic field is created by means of a large electro-magnet, between the poles of which an 'armature' revolves. This armature consists of a core of soft iron carrying coils embedded in the periphery of it through which the magnetic field passes. The armature is caused to revolve and the coils revolve with it, hence the magnetic field—the 'flux' as it is called—which passes through them, changes. An electro-motive force is therefore induced in the armature coils, and if these coils are closed by connecting the terminals of the machine to an outside circuit, an alternating current of electricity will flow (see ELECTRICITY).

Aim in Design, the general aim of the designer is to produce the machine required with the minimum amount of material. This will naturally lead to the cheapest machine. To this end the designer will use the highest current-densities he can in the armature conductors, and the highest magnetic flux-densities in the iron parts of the magnetic circuit. These quantities are limited by the heating of the machine.

Temperature Rise, the insulation of the armature conductor is very sensitive to temperature and temperature changes, and its temperature must not be allowed to exceed a certain limit. This limit depends on the kind of insulation used, and rarely exceeds about 80° C. If, then, the normal atmospheric temperature is 20° C., we have a permissible rise of temperature of 60° C.

Heating of Machine. the heating of the machine arises from two main causes: (1) the losses arising from the circulation of the current in the armature coils—the I^2R loss as it is called; and (2) the changes in the magnetic state of the iron of which the armature core is composed—the 'iron' or 'core' losses. The former depends upon the current density, the latter on the magnetic flux density; and these quantities must be limited to such values that the temperature of the machine does not exceed the prescribed limit.

Ventilation, the great importance of ventilation will now be evident. The harder we blow the machine with cold air the greater will be the heat we can get rid of without exceeding the temperature rise permitted, and hence the higher the current and flux densities we can use. All medium, turbo-alternators are ventilated by special fans, and the air used amounts to about ⅓ lb. per minute per kw. These heating limitations apply to all dynamo-electro machinery.

Dynamos, the special problem of dynamo design, as distinct from alternator design, is the design of the 'commutator.' If the ends of the coil AB were brought out to a pair of *slip rings,* as shown in the figure above, the e.m.f. between B_1 and B_2 would be an alternating one, and this pressure would give rise to an alternating current in the external circuit R. In a dynamo we want a constant pressure, and so a device called a 'commutator' is introduced. In the figure below a very simple commutator in two portions is shown. The two ends of the loop AB are connected, not to slip rings, but to a split metal ring (the commutator), the two halves of which s_1 and s_2, are insulated from each other. Two brushes, B_1 and B_2, are so placed as to press on diametrically opposite parts of the commutator. In

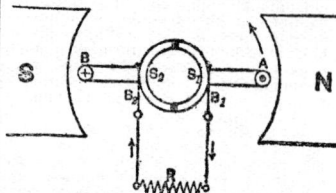

Simple Loop with Commutator

the figure, the current is flowing from wire A to segment s_1, then through brush B_1, the external circuit, brush B_2, segment s_2, to wire B, and so returns to A; but it will be seen that when A passes just out of the influence of pole N and begins to come into the influence of pole S, the spring B passes from one segment of the commutator to the other. The result is that the current in R is always in one direction; it is very fluctuating, as the pressure varies between nothing and the maximum value, but it is never reversed. By making the commutator in a great many segments, the pressure can be kept practically constant.

The design of the commutator offers both mechanical and electrical difficulties. The former arise from the fact that it is a complex structure of comparatively thin bars of copper held at the ends only, and the latter from the sparking which may occur at the brushes. Both difficulties increase with the speed of the machine, and they become almost insurmountable at the speeds of steam-turbines. Hence dynamos driven by steam-turbines are now usually driven through a single reduction gearing.

Alternators. The alternator has no commutator, and herein lies its superiority over the dynamo as a generator of electricity. There is no *a priori* reason why the armature should revolve at all; all that is necessary is that the armature shall revolve *relative to* the magnets. This can be secured by keeping the armature fixed and revolving the magnets, and, as there is no commutator to be considered, there is distinct advantage in so doing as the magnets are the simpler mechanical structure of the two. In all large alternators the field magnets revolve. There is no commutator to limit the speed, and so the alternator rotor is usually coupled direct to the engine, be it a slow-speed one or a steam-turbine.

Turbo-alternators. Special mechanical difficulties arise in the design of turbo-alternators from the high speeds used.

Stresses. A very common speed for a turbo-alternator, is 3,000 r.p.m. The force on a piece of matter on the outside of a cylindrical rotor, of 1 foot radius, rotating at this speed, is about 3,000 times its weight. Thus the force on 1 lb. becomes roughly 1½ tons weight. This is due to centrifugal action. The stresses set up by centrifugal action thus become very great, and require the best material and the highest skill in design to be successfully and safely used.

Vibration. The different parts of an alternator, such as any bolts in it, its rotor, &c., can vibrate, and each part has a set of definite frequencies at which it can be made to vibrate very easily. The lowest of these is usually called the *fundamental* frequency. The fundamental frequencies, for certain parts, are often fairly low, say about 40 cycles per second, because the stiffness of these parts is relatively small compared to their mass. For instance, a long,

relatively thin bolt passing through the alternator from end to end may have a fundamental frequency of 40 cycles per second, say. Low-speed machines are distinguished by a relatively large ratio of diameter to length, hence the parts are relatively much stiffer and have much higher fundamental frequencies. Now the long bolt mentioned above, having a fundamental frequency of 40 cycles per second, would synchronize with any disturbing alternating forces that might arise in an alternator giving current at the same frequency, 40 cycles per second. Resonance would not be likely to happen in the low-speed machine, because the fundamental frequency of the bar would be much higher.

This possibility of resonance is one of the evils of turbo-alternators. It may be a counsel of perfection, but the only way to avoid resonance is to design every part of the machine so that its fundamental frequency is higher than that corresponding to the running speed of the machine.—BIBLIOGRAPHY: *Modern Electrical Engineering* (The Gresham Publishing Company); Miles Walker, *Design and Specification of Dynamo-Electric Machinery*; A. Gray, *Electrical Machine Design*.

GENERIC NAME, in natural history, the denomination which comprehends all the species of a genus: thus Canis is the *generic* name of animals of the dog kind; Felis, of the cat kind; Cervus, of the deer kind. *See* GENUS.

GENESEE (jen-e-sē'), a river of the United States, which rises in Pennsylvania, flows north through New York, and falls into Lake Ontario 6 miles below Rochester, after a course of 145 miles. It is notable for its varied and romantic scenery, and its extraordinary falls. These falls are five in number; three of them occur about 90 miles from the mouth of the river, and are respectively 60, 90, and 110 feet high. The other two are near Rochester, and are both about 100 feet high.

GENESIS (Gr., creation, birth, origin), the first book of the Bible and of the Pentateuch; named in the Hebrew canon *B'reshith* (in the beginning), from the term with which it commences. From the Greek translators it received the name by which it is now commonly known.

Genesis consists of two great but closely-connected divisions: (1) The history of the creation, the fall of man, the flood, the dispersion of the human race, chap. i.–xi. (2) The history of the fathers of the Jewish race, chap. xii.–l. A certain apparent difference of style and language, the occurrence of what seem gaps on the one hand, and repetitions and contradictions on the other, and the different use of the term for the divine name (*Jehovah*, Everlasting; and *Elohim*, Almighty) led very early to the question of the

Genet (*Genetta vulgaris*)

integrity of the book, and various critics have assumed larger or smaller interpolations. *See* BIBLE.—BIBLIOGRAPHY: W. H. Green, *Unity of Genesis*; A. R. Gordon, *Early Traditions of Genesis*.

GENET (jen'et), a digitigrade carnivorous mammal of the family Viverridæ. The genus Genetta contains five species, the best known of which is the *G. vulgāris*, the common genet, whose range extends all around the Mediterranean, including Western Asia, Northern Africa, and Southern Europe. It is about the size of a small cat, but of a longer form, with a sharp-pointed snout, upright ears, and a long tail. It has a beautiful soft fur. The habits of the genet are like those of the weasel tribe; it is easily tamed, and is sometimes employed in Constantinople and elsewhere to catch rats and mice.

GENETIC PSYCHOLOGY (Gr. *genesis*, origin), the science of the mind as concerned with mental evolution, development, and growth of consciousness. It deals with the growth of ideas in the minds of children and adult human beings, and with the development of intelligence from the lowest species of animals to the most perfect races of man.

Genetic psychology is a branch of experimental psychology inaugurated by Lotze, and is psychology as viewed from a particular standpoint. It covers the departments of child-psychology (the development of the individual mind), of race-psychology (mental evolution in the animals and man), and of folk-psychology (differential forms in the human species). Thus genetic psychology is concerned with the developments of minds from simple beginnings into complex forms. —Cf. E. A. Kirkpatrick, *Genetic Psychology*.

GENEVA (from Fr. *genièvre*, Lat. *juniperus*, juniper), a spirit distilled from grain or malt, flavoured with juniper berries. The word is now usually in the form *gin*. Also called *Hollands*. *See* GIN.

GENEVA (je-nē'va; Ger. *Genf*, Fr. *Genève*), a town of Switzerland, capital of the canton of the same name, situated at the western extremity of the Lake of Geneva where the Rhône issues, here crossed by several bridges, and dividing the town into two portions, the larger and more important of which is on the left or south bank. The environs are covered with handsome villas, and the town itself, when approached either by land or water, has a very attractive appearance. It was formerly surrounded by walls and regular fortifications, but since 1850 these have been removed.

The town is divided into two parts, an upper and a lower. The upper town, occupied chiefly by the wealthier citizens, consists of well-built houses and handsome hotels; the lower town, the seat of trade and residence of the poorer classes, consists largely of houses remarkable for their height, and forming narrow, irregular streets.

The more important public buildings are the cathedral or church of St. Pierre, a Gothic structure of the tenth, eleventh, and twelfth centuries, which, somewhat defaced externally

Geneva. Cathedral of St. Pierre.

by a very incongruous Greek peristyle, occupies the highest site in the town, and with its three towers forms the most conspicuous object within it; the town house in the Florentine style; the Musée Rath, containing a collection of pictures and other works of art; the university building, nearly opposite the botanic garden, rebuilt between 1867 and 1871, and containing the public library, founded by Bonivard, the prisoner of Chillon, in 1551, and now numbering 150,000 volumes; and the Museum of Natural History.

The only important manufactures of Geneva are those of watches, musical-boxes, and jewellery, for all of which the town is justly famed. Geneva has ample railway communication, and is one of the principal entrances for tourists and travellers into Switzerland.

In literature and science Geneva has long occupied a distinguished place, and it has been the birthplace or the residence of many eminent men, including Calvin, Beza, Knox, Le Sage, Necker, De Candolle, Rousseau, and Sismondi. Geneva early adopted the principles of the Reformation, and chiefly through the teaching of Calvin the town acquired an important influence over the spiritual life of Europe, and became the centre of education for the Protestant youth of Britain, France, and Germany. In 1920 Geneva was selected as the official seat of the Council of the League of Nations, and the first assembly opened on 15th Nov. Pop. (1930), 142,812.—Cf. G. Fatio and F. Boissonnas, *Genève à travers les siècles.*

GENEVA, CANTON OF, is bounded by the canton of Vaud and the Lake of Geneva, and by France. Area, 108 sq. miles. It belongs to the basin of the Rhône, and the only streams of importance are that river and the Arve, which joins it a little below the town of Geneva. The soil has been so much improved by skilful and persevering culture that abundant crops of all kinds suitable to the climate are raised, and the whole territory wears the appearance of a garden.

Manufactures consist chiefly of clocks and watches, musical-boxes, mathematical instruments, gold, silver, and other metal wares, woollen cloths, and silk goods of various descriptions, hats, leather, and articles in leather; and there are numerous cotton-mills, calico-printing works, and dyeworks.

The territory of Geneva having, by the arrangements of the Congress of Vienna, obtained an accession of fifteen communes, detached from France and Savoy, was admitted a member of the Swiss Confederation in 1814, and ranks as the twenty-second canton. Its Constitution of 1848 is the most democratic in the Federation. All religious denominations are declared to have perfect freedom, but two of them are paid by the State— the Roman Catholics, amounting to rather more than a third of the population, and the Protestant National Church. The language spoken is French. Pop. (1930), 171,366.

GENEVA, LAKE OF, or LAKE LEMAN (Lat. *Lacus Lemanus*), the largest of the Swiss lakes, extending in the form of a crescent, with its horns pointing southward, between France on the south, and the cantons of Geneva, Vaud, and Valais: length, measured on its north shore, 55 miles, and on its south shore 40 miles; central breadth, about 6 miles; area, 223 sq. miles; greatest depth, 900 feet. It is 1,150 feet above the sea. On the north the shore is low, and the ground behind ascends gradually in beautiful slopes. On the south, and particularly at the east end, the shore is rocky and abrupt, and lofty precipices often rise sheer from the water's edge. It contains various species of fish, and its water is remarkably pure and of a beautiful blue colour. The Rhône, which enters its eastern extremity a muddy turbid stream, issues from its western extremity perfectly pellucid, and of the finest blue.

GENEVA BIBLE, a copy of the Bible in English, printed at Geneva, first in 1560. This copy was in common use in England till the version made by order of James I was introduced, and it was laid aside by the Calvinists with reluctance.

GENEVA CONVENTION, an agreement concluded at an international conference held in Geneva in 1864, for the succour of the sick and wounded in time of actual warfare. The neutrality of hospitals, ambulances, and the persons attending on them was provided for; and the use of the red cross on a white ground as a sign of neutrality has received the adhesion of all civilized powers.

GENEVIÈVE (jen'e-vēv or zhěn-vi-āv), the name of two women, well-known in legend.—(1) St. Geneviève, the patron saint of Paris, born at Nanterre, about 5 miles from Paris, in the year A.D. 423, died at Paris about the beginning of the sixth century. She devoted herself while yet a child to the conventual life. Her prayers and fastings are credited with having saved Paris from the threatened destruction by Attila in 451. Many legends are told respecting her, and several churches have been dedicated to her. Her festival is held on the 3rd Jan.

(2) Geneviève, by birth Duchess of Brabant, wife of Siegfried, Count Palatine in the reign of Charles Martel (about A.D. 750). According to the legend, which is the subject of several tales and dramas, she was accused of adultery during her husband's absence and condemned to death; but

was allowed to escape, and lived six years in a cavern upon nothing but herbs. She was finally found, and carried home by her husband, who in the meantime had become convinced of her innocence.

GENGHIS KHAN, or JENGHIS KHAN (jen'gis), Mongol conqueror,

Genghis Khan

born about 1160, died 1227. His father was chief over thirty or forty clans, but paid tribute to the Tartar Khan. He succeeded his father when only fourteen years of age, and made himself master of the neighbouring tribes. A great number of tribes, however, combined their forces against him, and a war of several years was the result. Genghis Khan was compelled to retire to Karakorum, where he found a powerful protector in the Great Khan of the Karaite Mongols, Oung, or Ung, who gave him his daughter in marriage.

After much intestine warfare with various Tartar tribes, Genghis was proclaimed Khan of the United Mongol and Tartar tribes. He now professed to have a divine call to conquer the world, and the idea so animated the spirit of his soldiers that they were easily led on to new wars. The country of the Uigurs, in the centre of Tartary, had long excited his ambition. This nation was easily subdued, and Genghis Khan became master of the greater part of Tartary. Soon after, several Tartar tribes put themselves under his dominion, and in 1209 he passed the great wall of China.

The conquest of China occupied the Mongols more than six years. The capital, then called *Yenking*, now *Peiping*, was taken by storm in 1215 and plundered. The murder of the ambassadors whom Genghis Khan had sent to the King of Kharism (now Khiva) occasioned the invasion of Turkestan in 1218 with an army of 700,000 men; and the two cities of Bokhara and Samarkand were stormed, pillaged, and burned. Seven years in succession was the conqueror busy in the work of destruction, pillage, and subjugation, and he extended his ravages to the banks of the Dnieper.

In 1225, though more than sixty years old, he marched in person at the head of his whole army against the King of Tangut (South-Western China), who had given shelter to two of his enemies, and had refused to give them up. A great battle was fought, in which the King of Tangut was totally defeated with the loss of 300,000 men. The victor remained some time in his newly subdued provinces, from which he sent two of his sons to complete the conquest of Northern China. At his death his immense dominions were divided among his four sons.—Cf. R. K. Douglas, *Life of Genghis Khan.*

GENII, tutelary deities; the ruling and protecting powers of men, places, or things; good or evil spirits supposed to be attached to a person and influence his actions. The Genii of the Romans were the same as the *Dai-*

An Evil Genie of Arabian Mythology

mŏnes (Demons) of the Greeks. According to the belief of the Romans which was common to almost all nations every person had his own Genius, that is, a spiritual being, which introduced him into life, accompanied him during the course of it, and again conducted him out of the world at the close of his career. The Genii of women were called *Junones.*

The Genii were wholly distinct from the *Manes*, *Lares*, and *Penates*, though they were allied in one important feature—the protection of mortals.

The term *genii* (with the singular *genie*) is also used as equivalent to the *jinn* (singular *jinnee*) of Arabic tales. These are supposed to be a class of intermediate beings between angels and men. *See* JINN; DEMONOLOGY.

GEN'IPAP (*Genipapo*, the Guiana name), the fruit of a South American and West Indian tree, the *Genipa americana*, nat. ord. Rubiaceæ. It is about the size of an orange, and of a pleasant vinous flour.

GENIS'TA, a genus of leguminous plants, comprising about 100 species, one of which is the *Planta genisla*, the *Plante genêt*, from which the Plantagenets took their name. The *Genista tinctoria*, or dyer's broom, so called, as it was formerly much employed by dyers, who obtained a good fixed yellow or orange colour from it, is frequent in England and the Lowlands of Scotland.

GENIUS. The term is applied not only to the highest and most unusual degree of mental superiority, but also, in a concrete sense, to the person endowed with such superiority. Men endowed with superior faculties are, as a rule, one-sided, i.e. they are mediocre, and even limited, in spheres lying outside their own particular domain and in which they excel. We speak of a political, philosophical, mathematical, literary, or scientific genius. History knows only a very few men who were universal geniuses.

Genius is to be distinguished from talent. The former implies innate individuality and originality. It manifests itself and creates *spontaneously*, involuntarily, and, so to say, unconsciously. Ideas and conceptions spring ready-made—Minerva-like—from the brain of the individual who is a genius, his spontaneity being like that of an explosive. Again, no amount of work, education, and methodical training will develop genius, whilst talent can be fostered, developed, and strengthened by these means. Talent, unlike genius, works methodically and consciously. It may be defined as conscious, teleological activity, whilst genius is spontaneous, inspirational, and highly original.

Genius creates, while talent avails itself of the creations of genius, is inspired by them, interprets, modifies, and applies. Genius is unconventional, knows no laws, and is not influenced by the rules and regulations of others; it is self-sufficient. It creates new values, and solves problems hitherto considered as insoluble. Talent, on the other hand, is conventional, moves and lives and has its being within the boundaries traced by others.

Genius has been defined in many various ways. Carlyle defined it as "the transcendent capacity of taking trouble first of all," whilst scientists define the man of genius as "one born with potential energy." Others describe genius as the "capability of grasping what is essential in all things." According to Schopenhauer, genius is "the completest objectivity," whilst Goethe said that "the first and last thing which is demanded of genius is the love of truth."

The problems of the origin and characteristics of genius, the hereditary character of mental superiority, and the relations between genius and insanity have been frequently discussed in the light of science. Sir Francis Galton, in his *Hereditary Genius* (1874), has shown the hereditary nature of greatness, and the transmission of mental endowment, whilst the relation between genius and insanity has been studied by Moreau de Tours, as well as by C. Lombroso and Max Nordau.

The relation of genius and of great men to historical movements and environment, and the question whether the great man is the cause or effect of social evolution, is another interesting problem which is being frequently discussed.—BIBLIOGRAPHY: Sir F. Galton, *Hereditary Genius*; C. Lombroso, *The Man of Genius*; J. F. Nisbet, *The Insanity of Genius*; Max Nordau, *Degeneration*; H. Türck, *The Man of Genius*; O. L. Schwarz, *General Types of Superior Men.*

GENLIS (zhän'lēs), **Stéphanie Félicité Ducrest de St. Aubin, Comtesse de,** French authoress, born near Autun 1746, died at Paris 1830. At four years of age she was admitted as a canoness into the noble chapter at Aix, and at seventeen married the Comte de Genlis. By this marriage she became niece to Madame de Montesson (who had been privately married to the Duc d'Orléans), and obtained through her the place of lady-in-waiting to the Duchesse de Chartres. In 1782 the Duc de Chartres (Philippe Égalité) appointed her governess of his children. She obtained great influence over her employer, and was the object of no little scandal in her relations with him, which was strengthened by the mysterious appearance of an adopted daughter, afterwards known by the name of Pamela, who married Lord Edward Fitzgerald. At this time she published several works on education. On the breaking out of the Revolution she retired for a while to Switzerland, and then to Altona. In 1800 she returned to France, and gained the favour of Napoleon, who gave her a pension. From that time she resided constantly in Paris.

Her works, which embrace a wide variety of subjects, amount altogether to about ninety volumes, and include some of the standard novels in the French language. Her voluminous *Mémoires*, written when she was upwards of eighty years of age, abound in scandal, and are full of

Cathedral of San Lorenzo, Genoa.

malignant attacks upon her contemporaries.—Cf. Jean Harmond, *A Keeper of Royal Secrets.*

GENOA (jen'o-a; It. *Genŏva*, 'La *superba*'), a seaport of North Italy, the chief commercial city of the kingdom, on the coast of the Mediterranean, at the head of the gulf of the same name, 75 miles S.E. of Turin. It is beautifully situated at the foot and on the slope of the Ligurian Alps, the lower hills of which form a background to the city. It is enclosed by extensive fortifications, and the heights around are crowned with detached forts. It has a most imposing effect when approached either by land or sea. In the older parts of the town the streets are extremely narrow, with lofty buildings on either side. In the newer quarters many of them are spacious,

and are lined with palaces and other noble edifices.

Palaces. Some of the palaces are filled with works of art by the greatest masters. The principal are: the Ducal palace (the old residence of the Doges, remodelled in later times and now containing the law courts and various public offices); the Palazzo del Municipio or town hall; the Palazzo Brignole or Rosso (presented to the city by the Duchess Galliera in 1874, along with its contents, including the largest picture-gallery in Genoa, and a valuable library); Palazzo Bianco (bequeathed by the same lady with its art treasures and now the museum); the Palazzo Marcello-Durazzo or Durazzo-Pallavicini; the Palazzo Reale (Royal Palace), built in the seventeenth century for the Durazzo family, purchased in 1815 by the royal family, and restored in 1842; and the palaces of Doria, Spinola, Cambiaso, and Balbi-Senarega.

Churches. The most remarkable of the churches is the Duomo, or cathedral of St. Lorenzo, founded in the eleventh century, but not completed till the beginning of the twelfth, and greatly altered in subsequent centuries, so that it now exemplifies three distinct styles, Romanesque, French Gothic, and Italian Renaissance. Other churches are those of S. Maria in Carignano, built in imitation of the original plan of St. Peter's at Rome; S. Stefano, a Gothic church, the oldest parts of which date from the end of the twelfth century; S. Ambrogio, containing two paintings by Rubens, and the *Assumption* of Guido Reni.

Buildings and Institutions. The principal charitable institution is the Albergo de' Poveri, in which 1,600 individuals, orphans and old people, find shelter. Others are the Ospedale del Pammatone, founded in 1430; and a hospital built by the Galliera family. Among the theatres of the city may be mentioned the Teatro Carlo Felice, a graceful building, with a splendidly appointed interior. Besides the university, founded in 1243 and refounded in the eighteenth century (1,233 students), the chief educational institutions are the theological seminary, the school of fine arts, the royal marine school, the navigation school, various secondary schools, &c. The building of the Bank of St. George, one of the most ancient banks of circulation and deposit in Europe, now contains the archives.

In one of the open spaces there is a fine marble statue of Columbus, with accompanying allegorical figures. There are also statues of Victor Emmanuel, Garibaldi, Cavour, and

Mazzini. The Campo Santo, or cemetery, about 2½ miles from the city, is one of the most beautiful burial-grounds in Europe. It contains fine mortuary buildings and much statuary in white marble.

Industries. The manufactures of Genoa include cotton and silk goods, gold, silver, paper, and leather goods, sugar, and preserved fruits; there are also engineering, shipbuilding, and other industries. Its connections by rail with the St. Gothard Tunnel make Genoa one of the chief Mediterranean ports. The old harbour, which is of a semicircular form and about ¾ mile in diameter, is formed by two moles projecting into the sea from opposite sides; there are now also two outer additional harbours formed by moles recently constructed, and there are also graving-docks, a naval harbour, and marine arsenal.

Commerce. Genoa is an important outlet for goods sent by sea from North Italy and Switzerland, and is of still greater importance for goods entering by sea. The principal articles of export at present are silk, oils, wine, fruit, cheese, rags, and the products of its manufactures. Among the chief imports are cotton, wool, wheat, sugar, coffee, coal, hides, and iron. Great quantities of British coal are imported. In 1931 her ocean trade amounted to £101,707,000. Many emigrants embark there.

History. Under the Romans, Genoa was famous as a seaport. After the breaking up of the empire of Charlemagne, it constituted itself a republic, presided over by Doges. From 1119 it was almost constantly at war with Pisa down to 1284, when it inflicted a crushing defeat on the latter town. The Genoese obtained the supremacy over Corsica, and nominally over Sardinia, possessed settlements in the Levant, on the shores of the Black Sea, on the Spanish and Barbary coasts, and had a very flourishing commerce.

The rivalry between Genoa and Venice was a fruitful source of wars during the twelfth, thirteenth, and fourteenth centuries. Meanwhile the city was convulsed by civil discord and party spirit. The hostility of the democrats and aristocrats, and the different parties among the latter, occasioned continual disorder. From the contests of noble rivals, in which the names of Doria, Spinola, Grimaldi, and Fieschi are prominent, Genoa was drawn into the Guelph and Ghibelline contest. The city sometimes submitted to a foreign yoke in order to get rid of anarchy. In the midst of this confusion St. George's Bank was founded. It owed its origin to the loans furnished by the wealthy

citizens to the State, and was conscientiously supported by the alternately dominant parties. In 1528 the disturbed state regained tranquililty and order, which lasted till the end of the eighteenth century.

The form of government established was a strict aristocracy. The nobility were divided into two classes—the old and new. To the old belonged, besides the families of Grimaldi, Fieschi, Doria, and Spinola, twenty-four others, who stood nearest them in age, wealth, and consequence. The new nobility comprised 437 families.

Gradually, however, Genoa lost all her foreign possessions. Corsica, the last of all, revolted in 1730, and was ceded in 1768 to France. After the battle of Marengo (1800) Genoa was taken possession of by the French. In 1805 it was formally annexed to the Empire of France, and in 1815 the Congress of Vienna awarded the town to the Kingdom of Sardinia, with which it became a portion of the Kingdom of Italy. Pop. (1931), 608,096. The province of Genoa has an area of 682 sq. miles, and a pop. (1931), 831,651.—Cf. Bent, *Genoa: how the Republic Rose and Fell.*

GENOA, GULF OF, a large indentation of the Mediterranean, in North Italy, at the head of which lies the city and port of Genoa. No precise points can be named as marking its entrance; but it may, perhaps, be generally said to comprise the entire space north of lat. 43° 40′ N.

GENRE-PAINTING (zhän-r), that branch of painting in which are depicted scenes of every-day life, in contrast, for instance, to historical painting, in which historical or mythological events are portrayed, or to landscape. Genre-painting was practised by the Greek artists, especially by the Alexandrian school, and in the fifteenth and sixteenth centuries by Ghirlandaio, Giorgione, and Peeter Brueghel. Watteau, Boucher, and Fragonard in France, and Hogarth in England, were famous genre-painters.

GENS, in Roman history, a clan or stock, embracing several families united together by a common name and certain religious rites; as, the Fabian *gens*, all having *Fabius* as part of their personal name; and the Julian *gens*, all named Julius.—Cf. article in Smith's *Dictionary of Greek and Roman Antiquities.*

GENSERIC (jen′), or **GAISERIC,** a king of the Vandals, who, having obtained joint possession of the throne of Spain with his brother Gonderic, crossed the Straits of Gibraltar with 50,000 men, A.D. 429, on the invitation of Bonifacius, the Roman governor of Africa, to assist him against the Moors. He, however, soon declared his independence, and, having completely defeated Bonifacius, founded a kingdom, which in 439 had its seat at Carthage. He collected a powerful fleet, ravaged the coasts of Sicily and Italy, and in 455 took and sacked Rome. Two unsuccessful attempts were made by the Eastern and Western emperors to overthrow his power, but Genseric secured all his conquests, and, notwithstanding all his cruelties, was permitted to die in peace A.D. 477.

GENTIAN, the name given to the members of the genus Gentiāna (ord. Gentianaceæ), a large genus of bitter herbaceous plants, having opposite, often strongly ribbed, leaves, and blue, yellow, or red, often showy flowers. The calyx consists of four or

Gentiane

five valvate segments, and the corolla is four or five parted; the fruit is a two-valved one-celled, manyseeded capsule. They are for the most part natives of hilly or mountainous districts in the northern hemisphere. The most important species is *Gentiāna lutea*, a native of Switzerland and the mountainous parts of Germany. The root has a yellowish-brown colour and a very bitter taste, and is imported into Britain in considerable quantities, where it is used medicinally, and also as an ingredient of cattle foods. In Switzerland and Bavaria a liqueur called *Enziangeist* or 'gentian-spirit' is made from it. Many of the blue-flowered species, as *G. acaulis*, *G. nivālis*, and *G. verna*, are among the most conspicuous and ornamental of European alpine plants. Five species are British.

GENTIANA'CEÆ, the gentians, an order of gamopetalous Dicotyledons, consisting mostly of annual or perennial herbaceous plants, with opposite often connate entire leaves, and yellow, red, blue, or white flowers, which are borne in dichotomous or trichotomous cymes or in globose terminal heads. All are characterized by their bitter principle. The order contains about 800 species, which are widely dispersed throughout the world, occurring most plentifully in temperate mountainous regions. Some very handsome species are tropical, while a few occur in Arctic latitudes.

GENTILE, in Scripture, anyone belonging to the non-Jewish nations and not a Christian; a heathen. The Hebrews included in the term *goyim*, or nations, all the tribes of men who had not received the true faith, and were not circumcised. The Christians translated *goyim* by the Lat. *gentes*, nations, and imitated the Jews in giving the name *gentiles* to all nations who were not Jews or Christians. In civil affairs the denomination was given to all nations who were not Romans.

GENTLEMAN, in English law, every man above the rank of yeomen, including noblemen; in a more limited sense, a man who without a title bears a coat of arms, or one who is 'a gentleman by reputation,' through belonging to some liberal profession or holding some office giving him this rank. The term is now by courtesy applied to almost every adult male. In a narrower sense the term gentleman is used as synonymous with the Fr. *gentilhomme*, denoting a man of noble blood and race. Chaucer's definition of a gentleman is a man who is virtuous and performs gentle deeds.

GENTLEMEN-AT-ARMS, a body of forty gentlemen, headed by a captain, lieutenant, and standardbearer, whose duties are to form a body-guard to the British sovereign on State occasions. The corps was established by Henry VIII in 1509, under the name of the Band of Gentlemen Pensioners. Appointments to the corps are made by the sovereign, from a special list of retired officers.

GENTZ (gents), **Friedrich von**, a German diplomatist and publicist, born 1764, died 1832. He was secretary to the Directory of Finances at Berlin when the French Revolution, of which he was an ardent opponent, broke out. He served alternately in the Prussian and Austrian civil service, and his pamphlets and manifestoes proved formidable obstacles to the invasions of Napoleon. He took part in the Congresses of Vienna and Paris, as well as in others. Among his various works was a *Life of Mary Queen of Scots*.

GENUFLEXION (from the Lat.

genu, knee, and *flectere*, to bend), the act of bending the knees in worship. There are frequent allusions to genuflexion in the Old and New Testaments, and it would appear that the use was continued among the early Christians. It is a modification of the Oriental custom of prostration. Genuflexion obtains, both by rule and prescription in various places in the offices of the Roman Catholic Church, and has been adopted to some extent by the Ritualistic wing of the Church of England.

GENUS, in biological classification, an assemblage of species possessing certain characters in common, by which they are distinguished from all others. It is subordinate to *family* in animals and *natural order* in plants. A single species, possessing certain peculiar characters which belong to no other species, may also constitute a genus, as the duck-billed platypus (Ornithorhyncus).

GEODES (jě'odz), round hollow nodules, containing sometimes earthy matters, sometimes a deposit of agate, sometimes quartz and other crystals. They are found more or less in all volcanic rocks, and have been formed by water depositing their materials in the hollows of those rocks.

GEODESY. The science of geodesy deals with the shape and dimensions of the earth, its density, and its attraction. It may be considered to have two sides, the experimental and the deductive. For the data from which its deductions are drawn it depends mainly upon the great trigonometrical surveys, and for this reason such surveys as, for example, the primary triangulation of the British Isles is commonly called geodetic. In considering the density and attraction of the earth, gravity and isostasy (*see* special articles on these subjects) are naturally included. Geodesy is largely a mathematical outcome of survey operations. No eminent surveyor can be ignorant of geodesy, nor can there be any eminent geodesist who does not partially understand the work of the surveyor.

That the shape of the earth was spherical was known in Egypt and Greece in the third century B.C. As early as 230 B.C., Eratosthenes actually calculated the dimensions in much the same way as we do to-day. It was not until the seventeenth century A.D., however, that substantial progress was made in the accurate measurement which should form the basis of such calculation. Perhaps the most memorable achievement in this progress was the conception of a measurement by triangulation due to Willebrord Snell in 1617.

If we assume the form of the earth to be spherical, we can calculate its dimensions in a variety of ways and arrive at a fair approximation. There is, however, only one exact method of arriving at both its form (which is not truly spherical) and its dimensions, and that is by actually measuring arcs on the earth (preferably along meridians), and by determining by astronomical observation the latitude of the ends of these arcs. Early in the eighteenth century a start was made in France in arc measurement. Towards the close of that century several national geodetic triangulations were developing, and to-day in Europe, Asia, North America, and Africa we have, through the continual extension of these triangulations, enough actual measurement to guarantee a very close approximation to the truth.

The linear geodetic measurements necessary for arc determination are given in terms of some standard of length. Thus distances in the geodetic triangulation of Great Britain are known in terms of a foot of the Ordnance Survey 10-foot standard bar. Of greater geodetic importance, however, are the standard yard and the international metre. Both are defined as the distance between two marks on a metal bar at a stated temperature. The most recent comparison between these two standards (in 1896) gives the following relationship: 1 yard = $\cdot 9143992$ metre.

The subsequent geodetic operations consist of a base measurement, a triangulation, and astronomical determinations of latitude and azimuth. Base measurement in the eighteenth and nineteenth centuries was carried out with copies of some national standard of length. As these copies were metallic and possessed marked co-efficients of expansion, the greatest care was necessary in order to gauge their exact length at the moment of measurement. Colby's compensating bars, designed to eliminate this factor, were used for the later English bases. Modern practice is to use tapes or wires of invar (36 per cent nickel steel), which has an extremely small coefficient of expansion (about $\cdot 0000003$ of its length per degree Fahrenheit), and the lengths of bases of from 10 to 15 miles are determined with probable error of measurement of one part in one or two million.

For the triangulation, theodolites of 10 inches to 12 inches diameter are used. As a general rule the length of a side of a principal triangle is of the order of 40 miles, and observations are made upon lamps by night, or upon heliostats by day. In modern geodetic triangulations the sum of the three observed angles of a triangle will be within 1 second of the truth. When the field-work has been completed, the whole network is subjected to a mathematical analysis or adjustment, so as to ensure that the length of any side, calculated through the triangulation, is the same from every base which may have been used in the adjustment, and by every possible path through the triangulation.

The astronomical observations for latitude are made with the theodolite, the zenith sector, or the *astrolabe à prismes*. It would be comparatively easy to determine the latitude within a few feet were it not for what is known as local attraction. Mountain masses and local variations in the density of the earth account for this local attraction, and the errors in latitude determination which result from its influence on the plumb-bob are generally in terms of several seconds of arc, or hundreds of feet. It is obvious, then, that latitude determinations must be made at as many of the stations of the triangulation as possible, in order to secure the best mean value.

The two most important, and most recent, determinations of the figure of the earth are as follows:—

Name.	Date.	Semi-axis Major in Metres.	$\frac{1}{\text{Compression.}}$
Helmert	1906	6,378,200	298·3
Hayford	1911	6,378,388	296·96

If the earth were a homogeneous sphere at rest, the force of gravity would be the same for all surface points. As it is, however, the earth's rotation and its spheroidal form cause an alteration in the force of gravity, the magnitude of which depends upon the latitude and the height above mean sea-level. This alteration in the force of gravity can be measured by counting the vibrations of a pendulum. In order to measure the force of gravity at any one place, it is a necessary preliminary to determine the length of the pendulum itself, and in practice it is not possible to do so with the necessary accuracy.

Accurate relative determinations may be made, however, by comparing the number of vibrations at any two places, and if the latitude of one and the ellipticity of the earth be known, the latitude of the other may be deduced; or the ellipticity may be deduced if both latitudes be known. Pendulum or gravity surveys give us, then, a second exact method of computing the form (though not the dimensions) of the earth. Clairaut's theorem, upon which such computations are based, is as follows:—

$$p = P[1 + (\frac{5m}{2} - e) \sin^2 \lambda],$$

where p is the length of a seconds pendulum at latitude λ;
P is the length of a seconds pendulum at the equator;
m is the ratio of centrifugal force at the equator to gravity;
e is the ellipticity of the earth.

The effect of local attraction, which has already been discussed, may be actually measured by determining the position of any point by triangulation, and by comparing the result with its astronomically determined latitude. If we now compute the resulting force, due to the attraction of topographical features, and tending to pull the plumb-bob out of the normal, and compare it with the attraction of the earth as a whole, we have a means of computing the earth's density. Unfortunately, there must always be an element of uncertainty in assessing the attraction exerted by any one feature. The torsion balance has also been used for comparing the attraction of the earth as a whole with that of lead weights. It must be admitted that there still remains a margin of doubt as to the mean density of the earth, but it may be taken as very closely equal to 5·5 times that of water.

In considering the figure of the earth, it is natural also to consider the size and importance of deviations from that figure. Under this heading come such questions as the relative movements of land and sea, and the determination of mean sea-level. These matters will be referred to under other headings, e.g. *Tides* but the operations of levelling (*see* LEVELLING) upon which such investigations largely rest are usually described as geodetic.

The initial step in such a levelling is to determine the datum to which it shall be referred. In cases where mean sea-level is to be datum, exact values must be obtained from tidal stations over a long period of years, in order to assess the effects of long-period fluctuations. The next step is to ensure by careful construction the stability of the controlling bench-marks.

The levelling itself is carried out with instruments and methods of special precision, but differing from those of ordinary engineering practice only in degree. They may be studied in C. Lallemand's book *Nivellement de Haute Précision*, and in vol. xix of the account of the G. T. Survey of India.

The International Geodetic Association has decided that levelling should not be regarded as geodetic (or of high precision), unless all the lines are levelled twice (once in each direction), and show probable accidental and systematic errors of less than 1 mm. and ·3 mm. respectively per kilometre.—BIBLIOGRAPHY: A. R. Clarke, *Geodesy*; G. L. Hosmer, *Geodesy*; M. Merriman, *Precise Surveying and Geodesy*; *Principal Triangulation of Great Britain and Ireland* (London, 1858); *Account of the Operations of the Great Trigonometrical Survey of India*; *Report on the Geodetic Survey of South Africa*; *Reports of the Superintendent of the Coast and Geodetic Survey* (Washington).

GEOFFREY OF MONMOUTH (called also **GEOFFREY AP ARTHUR**), an ecclesiastic and historian of the twelfth century. He sprang from the Norman settlers in Wales; became Archdeacon of Monmouth, whence he was, in 1152, raised to the bishopric of St. Asaph. He died in 1154.

His so-called *History of the Britons* (Historia Britonum), in circulation by 1139, is now known to consist mainly of fiction, but the writer professes that it was taken from an ancient book in the Breton tongue, discovered by Walter, Archdeacon of Oxford. It contains a spurious account of the Kings of Britain from the time of the fabulous Brutus, or Brute, the Trojan, to the death of Cadwallader, King of Wessex, in 688. It was soon translated into French, English, and Welsh, and became a great source of romance to the writers of successive generations.

GEOFFROY ST. HILAIRE (zhof-rwä san tē-lär), **Étienne**, French naturalist, born in 1772, died in 1844. He was educated at the colleges of Navarre and Lemoine, and became a favourite pupil of Haüy. At the age of twenty-one he obtained the chair of zoology in the Parisian Jardin des Plantes. As a member of the Egyptian expedition in 1798 he founded the Institute of Cairo, and returned about the end of 1801 with a rich collection of zoological specimens. In 1807 he was made a member of the Institute, and in 1809 professor of zoology at the Faculty of Sciences.

He devoted himself especially to the philosophy of natural history. The fundamental idea brought conspicuously forward in all his works is, that in the organization of animals there is only one general plan, one original type, which is modified in particular points so as to produce differences of genera. This view met with strong opposition from Cuvier. Among his principal works are: *Sur le principe de l'unité de composition organique*; *Philosophie anatomique*; *Histoire naturelle des mammifères*, written in conjunction with Cuvier; *Notions de philosophie naturelle* (1838).

GEOFFROY ST. HILAIRE, Isidore, physiologist and naturalist, son of the preceding, was born at Paris 1805, died 1861. He devoted himself to natural history, and in 1824 was appointed assistant to his father at the Jardin des Plantes. He was elected to the Academy of Sciences in 1833, and afterwards became successively inspector-general of the university, member of the Council of Public Instruction, and professor of zoology at the Academy of Sciences. One of his chief works, *Histoire générale et particulière des anomalies de l'organisation chez l'homme et les animaux*, added valuable confirmation to the theories of his father. He founded the Acclimatization Society of Paris.

GEOGLOSSUM, popularly known as earth-tongues, is the name given to a genus of ascomycetous fungi of the family Helvellaceæ.

GEOG'NOSY (Gr. *gē*, earth, and *gnōsis*, knowledge), a term which originated among the German mineralogists, and is nearly synonymous with *geology*. It is the science of the substances which compose the earth or its crust, their structure, position, relative situation, and properties.

GEOGRAPHICAL SOCIETIES are associations formed with the view of obtaining and disseminating geographical knowledge. In point of seniority the first of these associations is the Société de Géographie of Paris, founded in 1821, whose magazine, the *Bulletin de la Société de Géographie*, commenced in 1822. The Prussian Gesellschaft für Erdkunde held its first sittings in Berlin in 1828. The more important results of its investigations are published yearly in the *Zeitschrift der Gesellschaft für Erdkunde zu Berlin*.

The Royal Geographical Society, established in London in 1830, has a capital of over £47,000, and large sums are devoted annually to aid the cause of geographical research, or spent in recognition of services to geography. *The Geographical Journal* is published by it monthly. It has fine premises at Lowther Lodge, Kensington Gore, S.W.7. The Royal Scottish Geographical Society in Edinburgh, founded in 1884, also publishes a monthly magazine.

The Russian Geographical Society, founded at St. Petersburg (Leningrad) in 1845, has greatly extended our knowledge of Asia, and especially Asiatic Russia. The American Geographical Society was founded at New York in 1852, and publishes an interesting journal, *The National Geographic Magazine.* Italy has her Società Geografica, founded at Florence in 1867.

GEOGRAPHY. I. Introduction—Definition and Development of Geography. Geography is the description of the earth in its relation to man. It is based on knowledge of the surface of the earth as discovered by exploration, and interpreted by various sciences, such as meteorology for the weather, zoology and botany for animal- and plant-life, anthropology for the human race, and geology for the structure of the earth and the development of its surface features. Geography is dependent on astronomical methods for the determination of positions and the mathematical basis of maps, and is closely associated with history in the study of social conditions. Geography uses the results of each of these departments of knowledge for the advance of its own special subject—the relation of man to his environment.

Geography began in prehistoric times, when men were forced to wander far afield in quest of food and fuel, and to open trade routes to distant areas for other essential materials. Prehistoric traders from the Mediterranean crossed Central Europe to the Southern Baltic in quest of amber, sailed to the British Isles for tin, travelled overland to China for silk, and to East Africa, and probably also Southern India, for gold. The geographers of Egypt and Greece thereby acquired a general knowledge of remote parts of Europe, Asia, and Africa.

The Roman Empire advanced the development of the countries accessible by land from the Eastern Mediterranean, but did not greatly extend the area of the known world. The Vikings of North-Western Europe found their way to North America in the tenth century; but their discovery was forgotten, for Europe was unable to use it until the development of modern navigation in the fifteenth century. America was rediscovered in 1492, and its exploitation then begun. Spain acquired Central and Western South America; Brazil was developed by Portugal; France and Britain colonized North America; and the outlines of American geography were gradually traced as the two continents fell under European control.

Knowledge of the geography of Africa, with the exception of Egypt and of the Mediterranean lands, was delayed owing to the special difficulty of travel in the interior of the continent. The opening of the route to India around South Africa by Vasco da Gama in 1498 led to Portuguese settlements at the Cape and along both coasts. Early Portuguese missions penetrated the interior in all directions, but left there comparatively few permanent marks of their explorations.

Dutch, British, and Portuguese colonies were later used as bases for the investigation of Central Africa, in which the modern interest was inspired by Livingstone's great journey of 1853–6, and the mystery regarding the sources of the Nile. The partition of Africa among the European powers, and opportunity for detailed geographical study, resulted from Stanley's expedition across equatorial Africa and down the Congo (1874–7), and the consequent establishment of the Congo Free State (1885).

Australia and New Zealand, though known to early Malay sailors and South Sea Islanders, were revealed to Europe by the work of the Dutch seamen Hartog and Tasman. The colonization of Australia was undertaken largely owing to the faith in its future held by Sir Joseph Banks, after his voyage with Captain Cook along its eastern coast in 1770.

The exploration of the Arctic Regions was started in the effort to find northern routes to India. The search for a passage north of Asia led to the discovery of Spitzbergen, which was used as the base of the Arctic whale-fishery during the seventeenth century. The effort to force the north-west passage to the Pacific led to the exploration of Greenland and of the archipelago north of America, and to the development of methods of travel adapted to Polar Regions. The Antarctic continent was delimited by Captain Cook, and is still the least known of the great land areas of the earth; recent exploration has shown its unity as a great ice-clad land.

The scientific interpretation of geography began in Egypt and Greece from the study of the seasons, and the necessity of fixing boundaries between different districts and estates. The ancient Egyptians, in the time of Rameses II (1300 B.C.), made a careful land survey, which was used by Eratosthenes of Cyrene (276–196 B.C.) for the measurement of distance between Alexandria and Syene, and from that result he determined the size of the earth.

Astronomical geography was greatly advanced in Egypt by Ptolemy (A.D. 150), of whose famous map of the world the oldest-known copy dates from the twelfth or thirteenth century. The Arabs, inspired by Al Mamum, Caliph of Bagdad, in 827 measured an arc of the meridian and improved cartography; their charts of the Indian Ocean were superior to those of the Mediterranean, as was recognized by Vasco da Gama from those used by his Indian pilot. Modern cartography, based on scientific projections, was founded in the fifteenth century, and a century later, in 1569, Mercator prepared a map of the world on his useful projection.

Oceanography was established by the voyage of H.M.S. *Challenger* (1872–5), which by extensive systematic soundings, deep-sea temperature records and dredgings, analyses of sea-water, and collection of deep-sea organisms and deposits revealed the depths and general conditions of the ocean basins.

II. The Surface of the Earth. The surface of the earth consists of a rocky crust, of which the raised portions form the lands, while the intervening depressions are occupied by the seas. The earth as the home of man is dependent on the arrangement of these elevations and depressions. The major elevations are the continents; the major depressions are the ocean basins. Minor geographical features, including both hollows and ridges, have been largely excavated by various geographical agents. Rivers and glaciers wear out or enlarge valleys; the wind and the sea abrade the surface of the land into plains; the formation of beds of clay and sand over the floors of valleys, of lakes, or of the sea produces plains of deposition. Many hills and mountains are residual masses left between valleys excavated by erosion; others are piles of material discharged by volcanic eruptions. Some valleys, basins, and mountains are, however, due directly to earth movements, in areas that have been lowered or raised by fold or fracture.

Land-Forms. The variations in level of the earth's surface give rise to geographical structures known as the land-forms, of which there are two main categories. The positive land-forms are the solid features in the face of the earth, including plains, plateaus, and mountains; the negative land-forms are the spaces between the positive land-forms, and are classified into valleys and basins.

i. The Positive Land-forms. (a) *Plains* are wide-spread areas with an even surface and situated at a low level in relation to the surrounding country. There are four chief varieties of plains: coastal-plains, those due to the uplift of the sea-floor; river-plains, those formed by the deposition of material by rivers along their

course; planes of marine denudation, those due to the cutting back of the coast by the sea; and pene-planes, those due to the levelling of a country by rivers and wind.

(b) *Plateaus* are flat-topped areas which are well raised above the surrounding country. The surface of a plateau in countries with a moderate rainfall is gradually destroyed, for, as streams cut into it, the plateau is dissected into an irregular or old plateau; later, when the valleys have been deepened and widened, the plateau is converted into a tract of highlands, in which the essential structure is indicated only by the fact that the majority of the residual ridges and peaks reach the original surface and none rise above it.

(c) *Mountains* and *hills* are raised areas which culminate in well-marked summits or crests. Some of them are due to parts of the earth's crust having been crumpled into folded bands by lateral pressure, as a cloth is wrinkled into folds when pushed across a table. Fold-mountains occur as long, relatively narrow ridges, of which the unit is the mountain range. A series of ranges due to a common origin form a mountain chain, such as the Alps or Pyrenees. A connected series of chains formed about the same date and by a common cause forms a mountain system. Block-mountains are blocks or slabs of the earth's crust which have been uplifted, or which have been left upraised by the subsidence of adjacent areas. A mountain mass thus formed is known as a horst. Volcanic mountains are accumulations of lava or tuff discharged by volcanic eruptions. Residual mountains are those left upstanding owing to the removal of the adjacent land by denudation.

ii. Negative Land-forms. They include two classes—basins which are wide, and valleys which are narrow, in comparison to their length. The greatest of the basins are those occupied by the oceans. Some smaller but still extensive basins are occupied by the enclosed seas. Basins of which the floor consists of land are chief centres of population.

Valleys vary from great oceanic troughs, like that of the Atlantic, to wide old river valleys, and to the narrow young valleys known as gorges and canyons. The majority of the minor valleys and basins have been made by excavation. Basins are often due to a valley formed by excavation having been divided by the raising of a barrier across it by a 'warping' or rumpling of the surface. Some valleys and basins are due to the direct subsidence of their floors

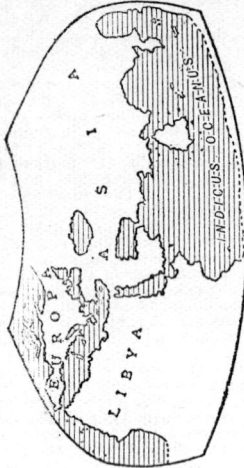

PTOLEMY, 2nd. Century B.C.

ANGLO-SAXON MAP, 9th Century A.D.

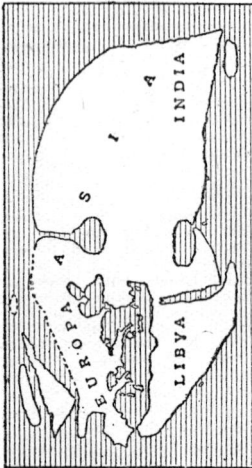

ERATOSTHENES, 3rd. Century B.C.

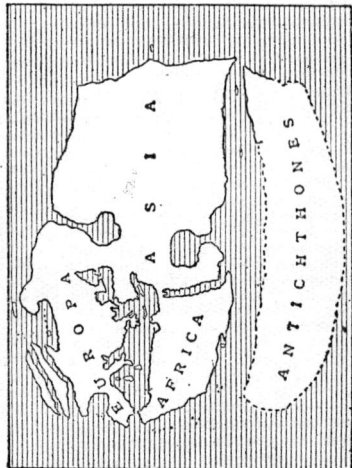

POMPONIUS MELA, 1st Century B.C.

forming sunk-lands in the case of basins, and rift-valleys in the case of valleys. Small basins due to the subsidence of their floors are known as caldrons.

The floor of the sea is diversified by variations in level, similar in kind to those on the surface of land. The negative forms on the sea-floor are the 'depression,' which includes basins, troughs, trenches (i.e. small troughs), and 'deeps' (i.e. the deepest part of a depression). The positive forms are the 'shelf,' a submerged coastal plain which slopes gradually from the level of low tide to the depth of from 300 to 600 feet; the 'rise,' a large, gently rising mound; the 'ridge,' which is long and narrow; the 'plateau,' which is about as long

THE HEREFORD MAP, circa 1280

MERCATOR, 1569

PARS CONTINENTIS AUSTRALIS

BEHAIM'S GLOBE, 1492

BLAEU, 1664

Emery Walker Ltd.sc

Series of Maps showing growth of Geographical knowledge

as it is broad; and the 'height,' a peak-like summit.

Coasts may be long and straight where the action of the tide has filled up the bays and cut back the headlands. Coasts are deeply indented where the land has sunk, so that the sea has flooded the former valleys. A drowned coast is characterized by having many irregular arms of the sea which run far inland, by projecting in long peninsulas and headlands with curved shores, and by a fringe or festoon of islands. Arms of the sea on drowned coasts are known as 'rias,' from those of North-Western Spain; the long bays, such as Bantry Bay, in South-Western Ireland are

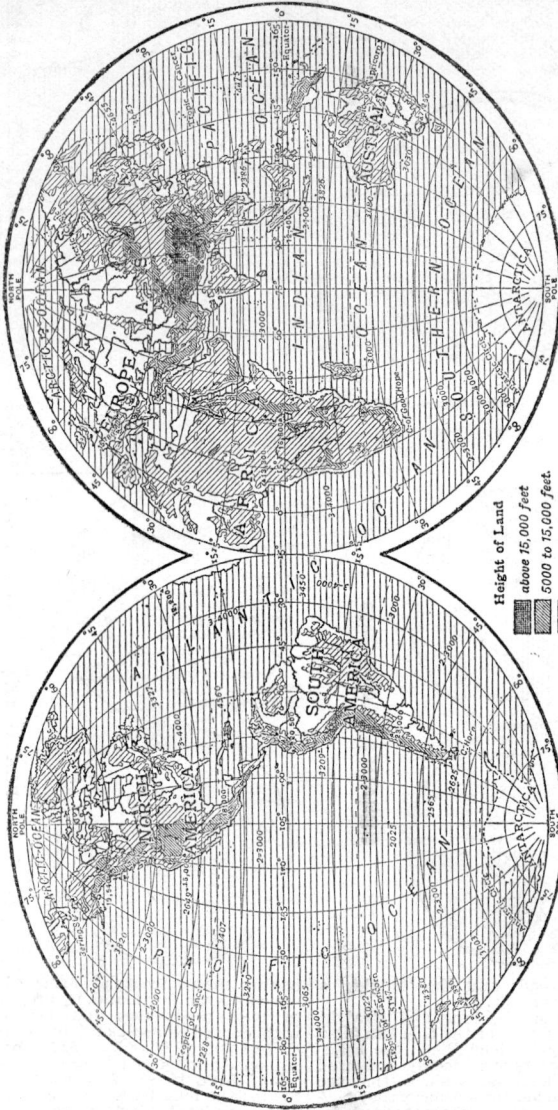

THE WORLD: OROGRAPHICAL

Height of Land

above 15,000 feet.
5000 to 15,000 feet.
1000 to 5000 feet.
Sea level to 1000 feet

Depths of Sea in fathoms, shown thus:-1200

typical rias. On a drowned fractured coast the sea extends inland in long, narrow, canal-like channels between high straight walls, with angular bends and branches; such arms of the sea are known as 'fiords.'

A. The Lands. 1. The Continent of Europe. Europe is the most complex of the continents. Its eastern and western divisions are strikingly different in structure and geographical character. Russia is an extension of the continental mass of Asia, while Western Europe consists of a series of peninsulas of which the axial peninsula includes France and Germany; secondary peninsulars project southward as the Balkans, Italy, Spain, and Portugal, and northward as Denmark. The peninsula of Scandinavia, which was formerly connected to Germany, is now united to the continent only to the north-east. The British Isles were a peninsula until isolated by the formation of the English Channel.

The Peninsular Axis of Europe lies along the mountains of the Alpine System, of which the central constituent is the Alps; extensions of these mountains continue westward as the Pyrenees, and eastward through the Carpathians to the Balkan Mountains and the Caucasus. This mountain axis of the continent includes its highest summits, Mt. Blanc (15,781 feet) in France, and Elburz, in the Caucasus (18,526 feet). The course of the mountain axis is sinuous owing to the resistance of old blocks of hard rocks, which form Brittany and the Central Plateau of France, the Black Forest, and other highlands of Southern Germany, Czechoslovakia, and the large area of ancient rocks known as the Russian Platform in South-Western Russia.

Southward from the Alps projects a series of mountain loops, which include the Sierra Nevada of Southern Spain, the Atlas Mountains of North-Western Africa, the Apennines of Italy, and the mountains of the Western Balkans, of Greece, and of Asia Minor.

North of the Alpine System and of the ancient plateaus beside it lies the European Plain, which extends from Eastern England across Holland, Denmark, and Germany, to the east of which it widens out to include most of Russia. South of the Alps sunklands have been formed by the subsidence of their floors; they include the Hungarian Plain within the loop of the Carpathians and the mountains of Transylvania, the basins of the Mediterranean, the Adriatic Sea, the Ægean Sea, the Black Sea, and the Caspian.

North of the European Plain are the remains of an ancient plateau which now includes Scandinavia, Finland, and Lapland; it was formerly continuous with the Scottish Highlands and North-Western Ireland, and doubtless once extended across the Atlantic to North America. The western coasts of Scandinavia and Scotland have been fractured, and are indented by numerous fiords.

As the main slopes of Europe have been determined by the east to west course of the Alpine System, most of the larger rivers flow northward or north-westward; this course holds from the Seine, which discharges into the English Channel, to the Dvina, which flows across Northern Russia into the White Sea. In Russia the main water-shed crosses the Valdai Hills, and lies farther north than in

Geography—River System of Europe

Western Europe; so its longest rivers flow southward, such as the Volga, Don, and the Dnieper.

The most important European river flowing from west to east is the Danube; it rises in Southern Germany; it cuts twice through the line of the Alpine System, firstly near Vienna, and secondly at the Iron Gates of the Danube in Western Rumania; and it discharges to the Black Sea.

The lakes of Europe mostly occupy narrow basins in the Alps, and in the highlands of Scandinavia and Scotland; the largest of the lakes lie in shallow depressions in the plains, such as Lakes Ladoga and Onega in Russia, Lake Balaton in Hungary, and Lough Neagh in Ireland.

The political division of Europe has been largely controlled by its physical structure. Holland, Denmark, North-ern Germany, and most of Russia belong to the great European Plain. To the north of it the peninsula of Scandinavia is a fragment of the ancient land of which the Scottish Highlands are an outlier; and the fact that Finland is structurally part of the same area explains the differences which kept it so aloof while it was part of the Russian Empire, and have led to its restoration as an independent state.

To the south of the European Plain Switzerland, Southern Germany, and Austria lie beside the Carpathian-Alpine Mountains, along which the Alpine people penetrated Central Europe. Hungary, consisting mainly of a great plain within the loop of the Carpathians and Alps of Transylvania, has maintained its political and ethnographic distinctness, as the country was especially attractive to the Magyars, who established there the most western permanent settlement of the Mongols in Europe.

France has the most advantageous commercial position in Europe, for its ports are open both through the Atlantic to America and through the Mediterranean to the East; it has also the advantage of a varied population, due to the advance of Alpine people from Switzerland, the spread of Celts along the western coast, and the settlement of Normans attracted by the superiority of the soils and climate of Normandy to those of their homeland in Scandinavia. These different races have been welded into a nation owing to the unity of the country between the Alps and Pyrenees to the south-east and south, the Atlantic and English Channel to the west and north, and the hills to the north-east, which formed a rampart against invaders advancing westward across the European Plain.

Italy, also a country inhabited by people belonging to several races, has achieved national unity owing to the physical unity given to the country by its mountain backbone, the Apennines. The Balkan Peninsula, on the other hand, has developed as the home of a series of small nationalities in accordance with its irregular structure; it is divided into the states of Rumania, Yugo-slavia, Albania, Greece, Bulgaria, and Turkey, which retains a footing in Europe, though it is given only nominal control of Constantinople.

Spain consists mainly of a high rugged plateau between the fold-mountains of the Pyrenees on the north and of the Sierra Nevada on the south. Its richest lands are on the marginal slopes to the sea.

Portugal has remained racially and politically distinct from Spain owing to the differences between the central plateau, which is held by Spain, and the western slope, which was occupied by Celts during their migration coastwise from the Mèditerranean to North-Western Europe.

2. The British Isles. The British Isles represent a former prolongation of North-Western Europe, from the mainland of which they have been detached in recent geological times. They consist of four chief geographical constituents, which give the islands their great variety in surface features and in agricultural and mineral resources.

The oldest geographical constituent forms the Scottish Highlands and the hilly country of Donegal in North-Western Ireland. It is composed of the oldest rocks present in any considerable extent in the British Isles; it was formerly part of the ancient land which comprised also Scandinavia and Finland, and doubtless extended westward across the Atlantic and included North-Eastern America.

The Scottish Highlands were upraised as a plateau, which has now been dissected into an irregular series of hills and valleys; their mountains included Ben Nevis, 4,406 feet high, the highest summit in the British Isles, and within their valleys are the longest and deepest of the British lakes. The western coast is deeply indented by a series of fiords known as 'lochs.'

Most of this country stands at a high level; the ground is rocky, the climate cold and wet, and no economic minerals occur in useful quantities. It is accordingly the most sparsely peopled part of the British Isles. The population in the highland counties is still declining, as they cannot provide such easy conditions of life as the industrial areas and the southern agricultural districts.

The Scottish Highlands are bounded to the south by a fracture known as the Highland Boundary Fault, which can be traced all across Scotland and into North Ireland. Between this fault and a parallel fault to the south, a strip of country about 50 miles wide has been lowered, and its beds of coal, oil-shade, iron-ore, and fire-clay have been thereby protected and preserved. They are now being worked by mines in the Midland Valley of Scotland. This valley, owing to its rich mineral resources and its commercial outlet through the Clyde, is the most densely populated and wealthiest part of Scotland.

South of the Midland Valley are the Southern Uplands, an area of downlike hills mostly occupied by sheep-farms, with arable land in the valleys; this type of country extends across the Scottish border to the Cheviot Hills in Northumberland, and along the Pennine Hills into Central England, and it has a western outlier in the mountains of the Lake District.

The lower country on either side of the Pennines contains four important coal-fields: that of Northumberland and Durham is along the eastern coast; that of Cumberland is beside and partly under the Irish Sea; farther south, to the west of the Pennines, is the coal-field of South Lancashire; and to the east is the coal-field of South Yorkshire, Derbyshire, and Nottingham.

The abundance of coal in these northern coal-fields has so greatly aided the industries which were founded.in the dales of Yorkshire and Lancashire on water-power, that the northern counties include some of the most active manufacturing districts and most densely populated parts of the British Isles.

South of the Pennines lies the Midland Plain, under which are the coal-fields that enabled Birmingham to become the manufacturing metropolis of the Midlands, and converted South Staffordshire into the Black Country. Great chemical industries have developed on the salt deposits of Cheshire.

To the east and south of the Midland Plain the country is traversed by an approximately parallel series of hills and valleys, with a general trend from south-west to north-east, along the geographical grain of the country. The hills are situated where the harder layers of rock have been left upstanding when the valleys were excavated, mainly by river action, along the softer bands.

Parts of the hill country, such as the Chalk Downs, are used for sheep, but South-Eastern England, owing to its moderate elevation and warm, dry, sunny climate, includes some of the richest agricultural areas in the British Isles. The Thames Valley and the hills to the south of it trend mainly east and west, owing to the structure of Southern England being determined by the course of a series of rocks which rise to the surface in Devon and Cornwall and there form extensive moorlands.

These rocks disappear eastward under younger rocks, which they underlie as a platform at a depth of more than 1,000 feet; they reappear at the surface in Belgium, and also outcrop in South-Western Ireland and Northern France. They are part of an ancient mountain chain, the Armorican Mountains, which can be traced from Central Germany to the hills of Cork and Kerry.

Their economic value depends partly on their coal-fields, including those of South Wales, the Forest of Dean, Bristol, and the coal-field of Eastern Kent. Wales lies mostly to the north of these hills, but the South Wales coal-field trends east and west in accordance with the grain of the Armorican System. This coal-field is especially important from its yield of smokeless anthracitic coal. The rest of Wales consists of hard rocks dissected into mountains and valleys, and mainly used as pastoral moorland.

Ireland consists in the main of a central plain of limestone, surrounded by a broken rim of hard rocks which resist denudation and remain as hills; they form the Mourne Mountains, the hills of Wexford and Wicklow, of Cork and Kerry, of Connaught and Donegal. The Antrim Plateau, in the north-eastern corner of Ireland, is built up of lava flows.

Within this mountain rim is the Central Plain of Ireland, mostly a tract of limestone. The chief river, the Shannon, flows across this plain, on the floor of which are many lakes, including Lough Neagh, the largest in the British Isles.

3. The Continent of Asia. Asia is the largest of the continents; its area, over 17 million sq. miles, contains one-third of the land and more than half the people of the world. It is traversed from east to west by a great mountain belt, the southern border of which encloses the highest mountains of the world, of which the traditional heights are Mt. Everest (29,002 feet) and Kunchinjunga (28,146 feet), though both are now regarded as somewhat higher than those figures. The Himalayan Chain was formed by earth movements at the same period, and due to the same cause, as those which made the Alpine System of Europe.

This mountain band separates the northern plains of Asia, which are continuous with the great European Plain, from a southern series of valleys and basins which are an extension of the Mediterranean. These valleys and basins are bounded to the south by plateaus of ancient rocks in positions corresponding to that of Africa to Europe.

The northern plains extend from the Ural Mountains and the Caspian across Turkestan and Siberia, gradually narrowing eastward to the peninsula beside Bering Strait. They sink 84 feet below sea-level beside the Caspian, and rise 1,700 feet above it in the Siberian Steppes. They have a long, gentle, northward slope, down which great rivers flow to the Arctic Ocean; the northern part of these plains, the tundras, are sparsely peopled, since they are frozen in winter and their soils are water logged in summer.

Southern Siberia includes vast areas of fertile land, has a good climate, and is already of great pastoral and agricultural value. The use that could be made of Siberia and of its extensive forests would be greatly increased if a route that would be practicable every summer could be found across the Arctic Ocean from the Siberian rivers to the markets of Western Europe. The older rocks in the southern part of the steppes are often rich in minerals, and especially gold.

The mountain backbone of Asia extends from the Caucasus to Bering Strait. Its greatest width consists of the plateaus of Turkestan, Mongolia, and Tibet. The southern margin of the plateau belt is formed of fold-mountains which are the continuation of the Alpine System of Europe; they extend from the Caucasus through the Elburz Mountains of Northern Persia, the Hindu Kush, and the Himalaya; their farther eastward continuation is uncertain.

According to one view, the north-eastward extension of the Himalayan line forms the mountain front that separates Tibet and Mongolia from China, and continues through the Great Kinghan Mountains of Northern China and the Yablonoi Mountains to Bering Strait. According to another view, these mountains are the dissected eastern margin of the central plateau of Asia, and the continuation of the Himalayan line is through the mountains of Western Burma and the Andaman Islands to Sumatra, and farther east its segments form the southern boundary of the Eastern Archipelago as far as New Guinea. The islands of that archipelago are the fragments of a disrupted ancient land which lay to the north of the fold-mountain belt.

The highlands of Tibet and Mongolia, the largest high plateau in the world, owing to their great elevation and distance from the sea, have a severe winter climate and low rainfall, and are one of the most extensive of the desert areas.

The fold-mountains of the Himalayan System are bounded to the south by a series of valleys and basins formed by subsidence. Asia Minor and Persia on the north are separated from Arabia by the long depression through which flow the Rivers Euphrates and Tigris. The north-western part of this depression forms the plains of Mesopotamia; the south-eastern part is occupied by the Persian Gulf.

A corresponding depression crosses India from Sind to Eastern Bengal; it is known as the Indo-Gangetic Plain, as its western portion includes the lower valley of the Indus, and most of the eastern belongs to the Ganges Valley. South of the Mesopotamian and Indo-Gangetic Valleys occur the plateaus of Arabia and of the peninsular portion of India, both of which consist of very ancient rocks with a high western front and a long eastward slope. In spite of these resemblances between Arabia and Southern India, their geographical development is fundamentally different, since the peninsula of India is well watered by the heavy rainfall of the monsoons, while Arabia has an arid climate, owing to its position on the desert belt that extends across the Old World from the Sahara into into Central Asia.

Arabia and India were delimited by the subsidences which formed the Arabian Sea and the Bay of Bengal. Corresponding subsidences formed the China Sea, which separates the plateau of ancient rocks in South-Eastern China from the Philippine Islands and the Eastern Archipelago; also the Sea of Japan, that lies between the mainland and the Japanese Archipelago, and the Sea of Okhotsk to the west of the peninsula of Kamchatka.

The arrangement of the main valleys and of the river system of Asia has been determined by the uplifts which formed its main mountain system. North of the mountain belt the Obi, Yenisei, and Lena Rivers flow across Siberia to the Arctic Ocean; others flow through Turkestan to the Sea of Aral, where their waters are lost by evaporation. In the valleys south of the mountain belt flow the Euphrates, Tigris, Indus, and Ganges; and owing to the tilt of the peninsula of India its rivers rise near the western coast and flow across the peninsula to the Bay of Bengal.

The plateau of Tibet and Mongolia gives rise to the Hoang-ho and Yangtse-kiang, which flow eastwards across China to the Pacific. South-Eastern Tibet is drained by four great rivers, the Tsing-po, the Salwin, Mekong, and upper part of the Yangtse-kiang. The Yangtse flows for some distance parallel and near to the Mekong and the Salwin; it suddenly turns eastward and reaches the Yellow Sea at Shanghai. The Mekong crosses French Indo-China and discharges into the China Sea in Cambodia; the Salwin reaches the Bay of Bengal through the Gulf of Martaban; the Tsing-po cuts abruptly across the eastern Himalaya and continues as the Brahmaputra to the Bay of Bengal.

Most of Asia is politically dependent on Europe. The plains of Siberia and of Turkestan fell under the dominion of Russia, which, by the Trans-Siberian Railway, opened the country and gave its agricultural and dairy produce access to the European markets. The hold of Turkey over South-Western Asia has been broken by the European War, and much of Asia Minor, Arabia, and Mesopotamia is now under French, Italian, Greek, and British control. Great Britain supplies expert advisers for the several departments of the Persian administration, and provides officers for a police and frontier force.

India, isolated from the rest of Asia by the Himalaya, by the barren mountains west of the Indus, and by the forest-clad mountains of Northern Burma, is one of the richest and most productive of Asiatic countries; its wealth has led to its repeated conquest. It is now the most populous dominion of the British Empire.

Most of South-Eastern Asia has been annexed by the European powers: Burma and part of the Malay Peninsula are British; Tonkin, Annam, and Cochin-China are French; most of the Eastern Archipelago, including Sumatra, Java, the larger part of Borneo, Celebes, and Western New Guinea, is Dutch. The independent countries are China, Japan, Afghanistan, Tibet, Angora, and Siam.

China, the oldest of existing states, was formerly one united monarchy, but since the revolution in 1911 it has lost part of its outlying provinces, and is now a series of semi-independent republics and provinces.

Japan, in addition to the Japanese Archipelago, rules Korea, Manchuria, and Formosa or Taiwan, most of Saghalien, and the Caroline and Pelew Isles. Owing to its efficient fleet and widening control over the islands of the Western Pacific, Japan has become the most powerful of Asiatic states.

Siam, including the northern part of the Malay Peninsula, is a kingdom of which the independence is guaranteed by an agreement between France and Britain. Tibet was formerly part of the Chinese Empire, but declared its independence after the Chinese revolution of 1911; it is still under Chinese suzerainty.

4. The Continent of Africa. Africa, the home of the negro race, is structurally the simplest of the continents. It consists mainly of an ancient plateau which has been affected by recent mountain folding along its north-western margin, where movements of the same date as those that formed the Alps raised the Atlas Mountains across Morocco, Algeria, and Tunis. Cape Colony is traversed by mountains trending east and west which were due to folds of a much earlier period than those of the Atlas. These South African folds thrust the southern part of Cape Colony against the African plateau.

Between these two remote lines of fold-mountains Africa stands as a vast block, the surface of which rises and falls in broad undulations due to sagging along the chief valleys. It has

been cut off to east and west by the subsidences that formed the Atlantic and Indian Oceans.

South of the Atlas Mountains lies a broad, low valley, which contains numerous shallow salt-lakes known as Shotts; it reaches the Mediterranean in the Gulf of Sirtis, east of which it continues to Egypt to the south of the plateau of Cyrenaica. South of this valley the country rises to the desert plateaus of the Sahara and Libya. Farther south the rainfall is heavier, and the plateau is covered in the equatorial zone by the dense forests of West Africa and the wide grassy steppes of East Africa.

Most of the mountains on the African plateau are residual, and are due to denudation throughout the geological

Geography—Water System of Africa

ages; but the highest individual peaks, those of Kilima Njaro (19,720 feet), Kenya (17,040 feet), and the Cameroons, are extinct volcanoes, or blocks of old rocks tilted by earth movements, such as Ruwenzori (16,815 feet). Many of the best known of African mountains are parts of the dissected front of the plateau.

The four chief rivers of Africa flow over the plateau. The Nile, the only great African river flowing in a meridional direction, has been formed by several distinct basins having been connected by a valley running north and south, roughly parallel to the earth movements which made the Red Sea and the East African coast. The lower Nile receives most of the water with which it irrigates Egypt from the rainfall on the mountains of Abyssinia, for the discharge from the equatorial lakes is mostly lost in the arid plains south of Khartoum. The Niger has an almost loop-shaped course, a series of rivers flowing east or west having been joined by valleys trending north or south, by the chief of which the river reaches the sea.

The Congo flows from east to west, and drains the largest basin of Equatorial Africa. It flows eastward over the plateau as a great navigable river until it reached the western front, down which it rushes in the wild cataracts between Stanley Pool and the sea. The Zambezi, on the other hand, rises behind the western coast and flows eastward; it descends from the plains over the Victoria Falls into the wide, deep valley through which it crosses Rhodesia and Portuguese East Africa to the Indian Ocean.

The lakes of Africa are of two kinds. The great rounded lakes occupy depressions in which the water accumulates until it is lost by evaporation as from Lake Chad, or overflows like the Nile from the Victoria Nyanza. The lakes of the other kind are long, narrow, and lie between high walls. They have often been described as fiord-like. They occupy depressions in the long trough known as the Great Rift Valley.

This valley was formed by the subsidence of its floor between parallel fractures. It extends from the Jordan Valley in Palestine through the Red Sea to East Africa, where it includes Lake Rudolf, the Albert Nyanza, Tanganyika, and Lake Nyassa, and ends south of the Zambezi. Tanganyika, the second deepest lake in the world, 4,708 feet deep, with its bed 2,172 feet below sea-level, is the largest of these lakes, and is one of the sources of the Congo.

Africa is almost entirely under foreign control; with the exception of Abyssinia and Liberia, the whole continent has been parcelled out amongst the European powers as colonies, protectorates, or dependencies. The political partition of Africa began in the fifteenth and sixteenth centuries with the establishment of settlements on the western coast and in South Africa as naval stations on the route to India. The stations in South Africa were originally Dutch and Portuguese.

After the British annexation of Cape Colony and Natal, many of the Dutch settlers migrated inland and founded the Boer republics of the Transvaal and Orange Free State. The Portuguese retain the colony of Mozambique on both sides of the lower Zambezi in East Africa, and also the colony of Angola from the Congo southward to the Cunene River in West Africa. The Portuguese claimed dominion over the whole intervening belt of the continent, but their possession lapsed through non-occupation.

The interior north of the British South African colonies was developed as the Protectorate of Rhodesia, which extends northward across the Zambezi to the southern end of Tanganyika. The European dominion over Northern Africa was begun by the French conquest of Algeria, which was followed by annexation of the Mediterranean coast states, from the Atlantic to the Gulf of Sirtis, including Morocco, Algeria, and Tunis. Italy holds the protectorate over Tripoli; Egypt has been an independent kingdom since March, 1922.

The partition of tropical Africa began after Stanley's journey across Africa revealed the conditions of the country and people along the Congo. His action led to the foundation of the Congo Free State (1885), and its ultimate success resulted in a scramble for tropical Africa by the European powers. Germany acquired extensive colonies which have, since 1919, been administered by other powers under mandates from the League of Nations. The former colony of German South-West Africa is attached to the Union of South Africa.

Most of the colony of German East Africa is administered by Britain as the Tanganyika Territory; north of it are the two British territories Kenya Colony and the Uganda Protectorate. Attached to Kenya Colony is the Protectorate of Zanzibar, which includes the clove-growing islands of Zanzibar and Pemba, and the East African coast from the Juba to the south of Mombasa. Kenya Colony and the Uganda Protectorate include the northern part of the basin of the Victoria Nyanza, whence they extend northward to the Anglo-Egyptian Sudan, which is conterminous with Egypt. The territories under British administration extend, therefore, from Cape Colony to the Mediterranean.

Opposite Aden, on 'the Eastern Horn of Africa,' is Somaliland, of which part is British and the rest Italian. North-west of Somaliland, along the shores of the Red Sea, the Italian colony of Eritrea and the French colony of Jibuti separate the highlands of Abyssinia from the sea. The mountains of Abyssinia form a fortress which is the only strong independent African state.

Most of North-Western Africa is under France; its dominion extends from the French Congo on the south across the Sahara to its Mediterranean colonies on the north, and through the Sahara westward to the Atlantic in Dahomey, Senegambia, and Morocco. The French hinterland forms the inland boundaries of the British colonies of the Gambia, Sierra Leone, the Gold Coast, and Nigeria.

5. The Continent of America. The two American continents are similar in general structure, which is different from that of the other continents. North and South America each consists of a great mountain belt to the west, of a series of ancient highlands to the east, and of a vast plain between the two mountainous bands. The story of the formation of each continent is that of how two originally independent lands have been united into a single continent by the gradual filling up of the sea which divided them. The sea was reduced to two gulfs, which were in time converted into land by the deposition of the sedimentary rocks that now form the great plains.

(a) **North America.** In North America the Western Mountain System extends from Alaska to the plateau of Mexico; its eastern front is known as the Rocky Mountains, while its western front consists in Canada of the Coast Ranges, and in the United States of the Sierra Nevada. Between the eastern and western marginal mountain chains are numerous mountain ranges, and also various basins; the most extensive is known as the Great Basin, and was once occupied by a great lake, of which the Salt Lake of Utah is now the remnant.

The highest peaks in the United States are in the Rocky Mountains (Gray's Peak, 14,341 feet); in Alaska are still higher mountains, including Mt. M'Kinley (20,300 feet), the highest in North America, Mt. Logan (19,850 feet), the highest in Canada, and the better-known peak Mt. St. Elias (18,008 feet).

From the eastern foot of the western mountains extend the Great Plains. They comprise in Northern Canada the barren Arctic tundras, farther south the wheat-fields of Central Canada, and in the United States vast areas of fertile prairies, corn-fields, and cotton-fields. The original northern extension of the plains has been dismembered into the islands of the Arctic Archipelago. On the mainland of Northern Canada the plains include the valley of the Mackenzie River, which discharges the overflow from depressions occupied by the Great Bear Lake, the Great Slave Lake, and Lake Athabasca; these northern plains disappear eastward beneath the still greater basin of Hudson Bay.

The plains in Canada rise southward to the 'height of land,' the broad divide near the Canadian-United States frontier, south of which they continue as the basin of the Mississippi, and through it descend to the Gulf of Mexico. The drainage of parts of South-Eastern Canada, and the adjacent areas in the North-Eastern United States, is through the greatest lake-group in the world, including

Lakes Superior, Michigan, and Erie, of which the waters are discharged over the Niagara Falls to Lake Ontario, and thence through the St. Lawrence to the Atlantic.

The eastern highlands of North America begin to the north with the ice-covered plateau of Greenland; they include the rocky peninsula of Labrador, the Island of Newfoundland, and the coastal provinces of Canada; they are continued in the United States by the Appalachian mountain belt, which separates the Great Plains from the Coastal Plain along the Atlantic.

The three separate divisions of North America yield such varied pro-

Geography—Water System of North America

ducts as to render the continent self-supporting: the Great Plains raise cotton, corn, and cattle; the Eastern Highlands yield coal, oil, timber, and iron ore; the Western Mountains are rich in copper, gold, lead, and silver; while the Pacific coastlands yield gold, timber, coal, oil, and the abundant fruits of California.

The political division of North America is simple, and has been determined by its physical structure and conditions. The climate of the continent is controlled mainly by the variations in temperature, which are dependent primarily on distance from the tropics. Central America and the low-lying coastal districts of Mexico have a tropical climate with a mean annual temperature of not less than 80° F. Southern Florida and Southern California have mean temperatures of 75° F.

The climate of most of the United States is temperate, in spite of the severity of the winter, during which the isotherm of 40° F. crosses the Canadian frontier near Vancouver, traverses the central states, where it passes close to Saint Louis, and reaches the Atlantic coast near Philadelphia.

Southern Canada is mostly in the colder Temperate Zone, with the mean annual temperature of only 45° at Ottawa in Eastern Canada, and also in British Columbia in the west. Northern Canada has an Arctic climate, the mean annual temperature falling on Boothia Peninsula to 5° F., or 27° below freezing-point.

The lines marking the distribution of temperature do not follow the parallels of latitude, but trend northward, as they cross the continent to the west, owing to the effect of winds and ocean currents. On the Pacific coast the mean annual temperature is higher than that of places at the same latitude on the Atlantic coast, hence the forests extend much farther north in Western than in Eastern Canada.

The European colonization of North America was begun in 1620 by British emigrants along the Atlantic coast, who were preceded by a French fur-trading station in Quebec established in 1608. The Dutch founded New York in 1623. After the War of Independence the British colonies became an independent republic as the United States. It was then a federation of thirteen states, with, in addition, the district of Columbia, the seat of the Federal Government.

The number of states has since grown to forty-eight. The area of the republic has been extended by the purchase of Florida from Spain, of the lower Mississippi Valley from France, and of Alaska from Russia. Texas was added by mutual agreement. New Mexico and California were acquired by conquest from Mexico. The development of the country was first restricted to the Atlantic coast, except for the isolated Spanish settlements in California.

The discovery of the Californian gold-fields in 1849 led to the development of the overland routes, and subsequently to the series of transcontinental railways, which have welded the country politically, and led to the settlement of the intervening country.

The development of the United States has been greatly aided by its rich mineral resources. Its output is greater than that of any other country in coal, iron, copper, and oil.

Canada was first settled by French colonists. It was conquered by the British in 1759. Its development was comparatively slow, being retarded by the cold climate. The large areas of wheat-growing country are separated from the coast by the rough forest-clad Eastern Highlands, and their utilization only became possible after the construction of railways to the eastern ports. West of the great wheat-fields of Manitoba and the surrounding provinces occur vast coalfields, and still farther west, in the Coast Ranges beside the Pacific, important mining-fields yield gold, copper, silver, and lead. Fields of oil and natural gas occur under the western part of the Great Plains.

(b) **Central America and the West Indies.** North and South America are joined by Central America; to the east of this great isthmus the Caribbean Sea and Gulf of Mexico occupy the site of a sunken land, of which the West Indian Islands are remnants. The structure of this land (Antillia) is very different from that of both North and South America, as its mountain ranges trend east and west, and in consequence the chief islands Cuba, Jamaica, and San Domingo, are aligned in that direction. The still-continued subsidence of the floor of the Caribbean Sea is indicated by the violent earthquakes and volcanic eruptions by which Central America and the West Indies have been so often devastated.

Central America consists politically of a series of independent republics. The country was originally all Spanish, but it has gained its independence with the exception of the colony of British Honduras (capital, Belize). Mexico is the largest and most powerful of the Central American states. It consists in the main of a high central plateau which has steep slopes down to each coast, and includes the long peninsula of Lower California. Mexico is very rich in minerals, especially oil in the coastlands of the Gulf of Mexico, and silver and lead in the plateau.

The other Central American states are: Guatemala, of which the capital is Guatemala City, and the commercial capital Quezaltenango; Honduras (capital, Tegucigalpa); Salvador (capital, San Salvador); Nicaragua (capital, Managua); and Costa Rica (capital, San José). In 1921 Guatemala, Honduras, and Salvador united as The Federal Republic of Central America.

Panama was separated from Colombia by a revolt in Nov. 1903. The establishment of that state enabled the United States to secure control over the zone containing the Panama Canal. This ship canal, between Colon on the Atlantic side and the Gulf of Panama on the Pacific, enables ships to pass from the eastern to the western parts of the United States without the long voyage around Cape Horn.

The West Indies include two main series of islands. The Greater Antilles include the four large islands Cuba, Jamaica, Haiti, and Porto Rico. They are arranged upon two convergent lines, and are fragments of the old mountain lines of the former land of Antillia. The second group, the Lesser Antilles, include the Bahamas, an archipelago of low islands north of Cuba and west of Florida, famous for their sponge fisheries; the Caribbean Chain between the Caribbean Sea and the Atlantic; the large island of Trinidad close to the coast of South America; and some islands in the Spanish Main off the coast of Venezuela.

The political allegiance of the West Indian Islands is very diverse. Haiti consists of two independent negro republics; Cuba and Porto Rico are under the protection of the United States; Jamaica and Trinidad, the Bahamas, and most of the Caribbean Chain are British; the Virgin Islands, including St. Thomas, formerly Danish, were sold to the United States in 1916; Curaçao, Aruba, and half of St. Martin are Dutch; the other half of that island, with Guadeloupe and Martinique, is French. The islands are therefore under very varied political influences; the cost of administration is high, and no general policy is practicable. Their chief industries are agriculture, the most important crops being tobacco (especially in Cuba), coffee, bananas, sugar, lime-juice, and other tropical products. Oil is found in Trinidad, and is known to occur in small quantities in some other islands. The inhabitants are mostly negroes, whose ancestors were introduced as slaves from Africa. The aboriginal people, the Caribs, are nearly extinct.

(c) South America. The Western Mountain System begins to the north in chains which trend approximately east and west across Northern Venezuela; in the north-western corner of South America the mountain lines bend round to a meridional direction, and continue as the Andes throughout the length of the continent; at its southern end the main mountain line bends again eastward through the Southern Argentine and Tierra del Fuego, and was probably continuous across Drake's Strait with the mountain chain of Graham Land.

At the eastern foot of the Andean Mountains lie the Great Plains, which extend from the valley of the Orinoco southward through the forests of the Amazon to the Parana and the grassy plains of the pastoral lands of Argentina. The Eastern Highlands in South America are much wider than the corresponding element in North America. They include the highlands of Guiana, north of the Amazon, and the wide plateau, known as the Brazilian Highlands, which extends from the Amazon to the La Plata. This plateau reaches the coast, and must formerly have been continuous across the Atlantic with the similar plateau of Equatorial Africa.

Most of the western coast is occupied by a narrow coastal belt with low ancient hills; but in Southern Chile and Patagonia this strip has been fractured and submerged to form the archipelago and fiords of Patagonia.

South America consists politically of ten independent republics and of

Geography—Water System of South America

three European colonies, British, French, and Dutch Guiana. The country was originally mainly occupied by Spain, attracted primarily by the mineral wealth along the Andes. The Portuguese settled on the coast of Brazil. A Bull of Pope Alexander VI separated the spheres of Spain and Portugal by the line of no magnetic variation, that is, the line on which the magnetic compass points due north. This line then crossed Brazil; but it is not fixed in position, and as it moved eastward into the Atlantic the frontier was resettled by the Treaty of Tordesillas (1494), which left Eastern Brazil to Portugal and its colonization and language are Portuguese. The rest of the continent was developed under Spanish influence, and its language is Spanish.

The South American states include

Venezuela (capital, Carácas), which lies along the southern coast of the Caribbean Sea, and includes most of the basin of the Orinoco. The Republic of Colombia (capital, Bogotá) extends along the north-western chains of the Andes and the valley of the Magdalena; it also includes the upper basin of the Orinoco and the north-western tributaries of the Amazon. Ecuador, established 1830 (capital, Quito), is the smallest of the western states. It lies along an important trade route over the Andes, from the Gulf of Guayaquil to the Upper Amazon.

Peru (capital, Lima) gained its complete independence in 1824; it lies along the parallel chains of the Andes, and includes a series of wide valleys and basins, of which the most important is that of Lake Titicaca (altitude, 12,800 feet).

Chile (capital, Santiago) won its freedom in 1818; it is a long, narrow state ranging for about 2,700 miles along the Pacific Coast, from Arica in the tropics to Cape Horn. It extends along the Andes, between the chief chains of which lies the Great Valley of Chile; this valley continues southward as a series of straits and channels, owing to the western chain of the Andes having been broken up into the fiord coast of Patagonia.

The Argentine, founded in 1810, the second largest of the South American states, extends from the Andes to the Atlantic; it includes vast grass-covered plains, now occupied as great sheep- and cattle-stations. Its capital, Buenos Aires, is one of the chief ports of South America.

Brazil, founded in 1822 (capital, Rio de Janeiro), is the largest of the South American states. It includes most of the valley of the Amazon, as well as the upper basin of the Rio de la Plata. Its eastern division consists of a high irregular plateau containing important gold-fields. The lowlands of the Amazon and along the coast have large rubber plantations.

Uruguay (capital, Montevideo) first obtained its independence in 1817, and had it guaranteed in 1828; the state lies along the Atlantic coast, north of the estuary of the La Plata.

Bolivia and Paraguay are the two inland states. Bolivia (nominal capital, Sucre; actual seat of Government, La Paz) is on the highlands of the water-shed between the Amazon and the western tributaries of the La Plata. Paraguay (capital, Asunción) lies between various tributaries of the Parana, by which it has water communication with Buenos Aires and the sea.

The first attraction of South America to European settlers was the wealth of its western mines. Their richness in gold and silver led to the conquest and development of the countries along the Andes; the mines of Chile at one time produced a larger output of copper than those of any other state in the world.

The tropical states are rich agriculturally, producing especially rubber, tobacco, and quinine. The southern plains are one of the great pastoral areas of the world. The development of the eastern and central areas is facilitated by the easy navigability of the great rivers. Ocean-going steamers, for example, ascend the Amazon to Iquitos, 2,000 miles from its mouth.

The three colonies of British Guiana (capital, Georgetown), Dutch Guiana (capital, Paramaribo), and French Guiana (capital, Cayenne) extend from the Atlantic coast east of the Orinoco southward to the water-shed of the Amazon, which forms their boundary from Northern Brazil.

The aboriginal inhabitants of South America were tribes of American Indians; their descendants are the basis of the native population, and their physiognomy shows marked Mongolian characteristics. For the cultivation of the plantations of Brazil and Guiana slaves were imported from Africa, and thus the negro is an important element in the existing population of the eastern parts of the continent.

6. The Continent of Australia. Australia is a southern extension of Asia through the Eastern Archipelago. It includes 2,974,581 sq. miles, and extends for 2,400 miles from east to west, and for 1,970 miles from north to south. Its western part consists of the ancient plateau of Western Australia, which has an arid climate, and is bounded to the west by the mountain front known as the Darling Range, and descends slowly eastward to the Great Plains. They extend from the Gulf of Carpentaria across New South Wales to South Australia, where, in Lake Eyre, their basin lies 39 feet below sea-level. These plains include large areas of valuable pastoral country and the basin of the greatest Australian rivers, the Murray and its long tributary the Darling.

The Great Plains are bounded to the east by the East Australian Highlands, which extend from the Cape York Peninsula in the north, throughout the length of Australia, to Bass Strait, to the south of which the mountainous island of Tasmania consists of a detached fragment of this highland belt. The East Australian Highlands include Mt. Kosciusko (7,328 feet), the highest summit on the continent.

The plateau structure of Australia

has greatly hampered its development. The coastal plains are narrow, and the ascent from them, especially along the eastern side of the continent, is so abrupt that it was long before explorers could find a way from the coast into the interior. The steepness of the ascent inland from all the capital cities has been a constant hindrance both in the construction and working of the Australian railways.

The abrupt rise of the highlands near the coast has another and still more prejudicial influence on the development of Australia by causing the unequal distribution of the rainfall, which is concentrated on a narrow marginal belt owing to the sudden uplift and chilling of the air.

The rainfall is therefore often excessive on the highland edge, and inadequate in the interior. These conditions have led to the popular misconception of Australia as a narrow ring of fertile country around a vast internal desert.

The minimum rainfall, less than 5 inches per annum, occurs around Lake Eyre in South Australia; thence westward is a wide tract with an arid climate and a rainfall of between 5 and 10 inches. Thanks, however, to the effect of the monsoons, large parts of North-Western Australia have a rainfall of from 10 to 20 inches, and cattle-stations now occupy areas formerly represented as impassable and useless desert.

The areas with a rainfall of over 40 inches are all coastal; they include the south-western corner of the continent around Cape Leeuwin, the Northern Territory, the Highlands of Victoria, Tasmania, and a belt behind the eastern coast, wherein the rainfall is especially heavy in the north at Innisfail in Queensland, amounting to 149½ inches as an average for twenty-five years.

The east Australian Highlands and the plains to the west of them, owing to the warm climate and rainfall from 15 to 30 inches, are covered with rich turf, and are well adapted to sheepfarming. Australia, therefore, made its first important progress by the pastoral settlement of these plains.

Melbourne, founded in 1835, was the first important centre of extensive pastoral development, owing to its easy access to the lava plains of Victoria. As the sheep-stations required but little labour, the population remained small, and in 1840 was only 190,000 in the whole continent, exclusive of aborigines. In 1851 the first important discoveries of gold led to an inrush of population and the rapid development of the continent. The population multiplied seven-fold in the next sixty years.

The most important of Australian minerals has been gold, especially from the mines in Victoria, Queensland, New South Wales, and Westralia; copper is mined in South Australia, Tasmania, and Queensland; lead, silver, and zinc at Broken Hill in New South Wales; and tin and copper in Tasmania.

One of the world's great coal-fields underlies the coastal regions of New South Wales between Sydney and Newcastle; coalfields also occur in South-Eastern Queensland. Large deposits of iron ore are known in Tasmania, South Australia, Queensland, and Westralia.

The rapid development of the continent after the mineral discoveries led to its existing political subdivision. The whole continent was originally

Geography—Water System of Australia

all included in the colony of New South Wales. Tasmania was separated in 1825. Western Australia, conveniently known as Westralia, was separated in 1829 after the establishment of the Swan River settlement around the present capital of Perth, owing to its remoteness from Sydney. South Australia was founded in 1836 as a political experiment, with its capital at Adelaide.

The discovery of the Victorian goldfields led to the conversion of the Port Phillip district into the colony of Victoria, with Melbourne as its capital, in 1851. Queensland was separated in 1859, with its capital at Brisbane. The Northern Territory remained at first part of New South Wales, from which it was completely isolated; so in 1863 it was placed under the administration of South Australia.

The Federal Government for Australia, established in 1901, has taken over some of the duties of government in all the states, and is solely responsible for the administration of the Northern Territory, of the Federal District, which includes the Federal capital,

Canberra; also of Papua, the British part of New Guinea, and some Pacific islands that formerly belonged to Germany.

With the decline of the predominance of metal-mining in Australia, the pastoral, agricultural, and dairy industries have become by far the most important source of Australian wealth. The value of the total production of Australia in 1918 was £300,000,000, of which various kinds of farming together yielded nearly two-thirds (or £190,000,000). Manufacturing yielded a quarter (£75,000,000), and mining under one-tenth (£26,000,000). In 1931 the value of the total production was £319,745,000, of which the various types of farming yielded £183,066,000; manufacturing £112,966,000, mining £15,400,000, and forestry and fisheries £8,313,000.

7. The Pacific Islands. When the Pacific was seen by the Spanish explorers from above Panama, as it lay to the south of that isthmus, they called it the 'South Sea,' a name now retained only in that of the South Sea Islands.

The distribution of these islands appears at first irregular; but, according to their geographical arrangement and geological structure, they may be divided into five well-defined groups. East of Australia lies a series of islands known as the Australian Festoon, of which the structure is continental; they range from New Guinea through Melanesia, Solomon Islands, and New Caledonia to their most important member, New Zealand.

Farther east lies the Micronesian Festoon; it is composed of volcanic and coral islands, and rises from a platform separated from the rest of the Pacific floor by a series of deep trenches, of which that south-east of the Tonga Islands is the most remarkable of known sub-oceanic valleys.

Beyond the trench, bounding Micronesia, occurs the South Pacific Chain; it extends from the Phœnix Island east-south-eastward through the Society Island (Tahiti) and the Paumotu or Low Archipelago to Easter Island, which is shown by its gigantic stone statues to have been occupied by a Polynesian race that came from the west.

The North Pacific Chain includes the Hawaiian Archipelago. In the far northern Pacific the Aleutian Festoon tends to connect Kamchatka and Alaska. In the west Pacific the chain of the Pelew and Ladrone Islands, to the north of New Guinea, lie along a ridge between the Challenger Trench to the east and a broad deep basin south of Japan.

8. Antarctica. Antarctica is the least known of the continents. Its existence was accepted by mediæval geographers from theoretical considerations. It was first circumnavigated by Captain Cook. Modern explorations have proved that it is a continent formed of a high ice-clad plateau. South Victoria Land and Wilkes Land continue southward the structure of Australia, while Graham Land, opposite South America, is traversed by a lofty mountain chain which appears to represent a structural continuation of the Andes.

B. The Oceans. The sea occupies five-sevenths of the earth's surface, and its chief divisions are the five oceans. The Atlantic forms the long sinuous trough between the Americas and the Old World. The Pacific, the largest geographical unit on earth, separates America from Asia and Australia, and ends southward against Antarctica. The Arctic Ocean around the North Pole occupies a deep basin connected by shallow broad outlets to the Atlantic, and by the narrow Behring Strait to the Pacific.

The Indian Ocean is comparatively small, and forms the basin between Southern Asia, Africa, and Australia, and ends to the south along about $35°$ s. lat. The Southern Ocean extends from South America and Graham Land eastward to New Zealand, and includes the long belt of sea to the south of the Atlantic and Indian Oceans and of Australia. The Southern Ocean and Southern Pacific together form a continuous ocean belt around the southern hemisphere.

III. Weather and Climate. The economic value of a land depends, as a rule, mainly upon its climate, which is the average of its weather. Climate depends mainly on the distribution of heat and moisture. The heat is received from the sun, and the moisture from the sea. The heat from the sun is very unevenly distributed upon the earth, as areas which are almost at right angles to the sun's rays receive more heat than those where the rays fall very obliquely upon the surface, so that the heat is more widespread, and more is absorbed by the atmosphere owing to the longer passage through it.

The irregularity in the distribution of heat is reduced by the earth's axis of rotation being inclined to the plane of its orbit. The sun accordingly passes sometimes north and sometimes south of the equator; the polar regions receive more heat than would reach them if the equator and ecliptic were coincident. If the amount of heat received by a place on the equator be taken as 100, a place at the latitude of $30°$ would receive 88 per cent; at lat. $45°$, 74 per cent; at lat. $60°$, 57 per cent; and at lat. $75°$, 45 per cent; and 41 per cent at the poles.

The earth is divided into five zones, distinguished by their position in respect to the sun. The Torrid Zone lies between the two tropics, and includes the belt over which the sun is sometimes directly overhead. The two Temperate Zones, between the parallels of about $23\frac{1}{2}°$ and $66\frac{1}{2}°$, are those in which the sun is never directly overhead, but rises above the horizon every day in the year.

In the two Frigid Zones, which include the areas north of $66\frac{1}{2}°$ N. and south of $66\frac{1}{2}°$ S., the sun during some days of the year does not appear above the horizon; the long winter night thus caused reaches its maximum of six months at the poles. The Polar Regions are the coldest, owing to the obliquity of the sun's rays there, and the darkness and severity of the winter is fatal to many forms both of animal and plant life.

The moisture that falls as rain and supplies the lands with fresh water is raised from the sea by evaporation, which is greatest within the tropics. The moisture is driven along by the winds until it is precipitated by an adequate fall in temperature. When the air is cooled to a degree at which it is 'super-saturated' with moisture, the excess is precipitated as dew, rain, snow, or hail.

The two main causes of precipitation are the uplift of air into a higher, colder level of the atmosphere, and the fall of temperature at night, which causes the deposit of dew. As the air is blown against rising land, it is forced upward and thus chilled, and part of its moisture is precipitated. Hence rainfall is, as a rule, greatest where air that has been carried inland from the oceans is uplifted against the mountains.

Thus the rainfall at Cherrapunji, the highest in the world, with an average of over 500 inches a year, is due to the moist air from the Bay of Bengal being uplifted over the mountains of Assam. Similarly, the highest rainfall in the British Isles occurs along the western mountains, where the air from the Atlantic is uplifted and cooled.

The circulation of air by the wind is the chief factor in the distribution of moisture and of rain. The main movements of the air are: (1) a general drift eastward, owing to its lagging behind the ground beneath it during the rotation of the earth. (2) The Trade Winds (so-called from the former use of the word 'trade' for a path or passage) are due to the air being drawn northward and southward in order to replace that which rises above heated tropical areas. These winds are deflected from their course due northward or southward owing to the rotation of the earth. In the northern hemisphere they blow from north-east to south-west, and in the southern hemisphere from south-east to north-west. (3) The Anti-Trades.

The air carried towards the equator by the Trade Winds is returned by a high-level current in the opposite direction. This air, becoming chilled, falls to the surface of the earth outside the Trade Wind belt, and there gives rise to strong, steady winds that blow in the opposite direction to the Trade Winds. They are known as the Anti-Trades or Counter-Trades. In the northern hemisphere they blow from the south-west; in the southern hemisphere they blow from the north-west, and as the sea extends uninterruptedly around the world in the zone of the southern Anti-Trades, the winds are of special power in the belt south of 40°, which is known as the 'Roaring Forties.'

(4) The Monsoons are a series of regular winds around the Indian Ocean which change their direction twice a year. The name is derived from the Arabic word for the seasons. They are due to the main ascending air-current shifting its position with the sun; it does not always rise above the equator, but above the 'thermal equator,' the line over which the sun passes in the daily rotation of the earth. This line moves northward and southward. During the northern summer it lies across Southern Asia, and causes a great ascending air-current over South-Central Asia. This air is replaced by a current from the Indian Ocean; so from April to October the monsoon blows from south-west to north-east. During the northern winter the sun travels across the earth south of the equator; the highlands of Central Asia are then cold, and a descending air-current upon them produces winds which blow outward to the Indian Ocean. Hence from October to April the monsoon blows from north-east to south-west.

In the Temperate Zones the air movements are irregular. They are due to circular wind systems around areas of low pressure known as cyclones, and around areas of high pressure known as anti-cyclones. As in cyclones the air is ascending, they are accompanied by rain. As the air in anti-cyclones is falling, the conditions under them are dry. The cyclones and anti-cyclones travel from west to east; but as the winds around them are circular, the regions crossed by them are subject to winds which are inconstant alike in strength and direction.

The air circulation, therefore, con-

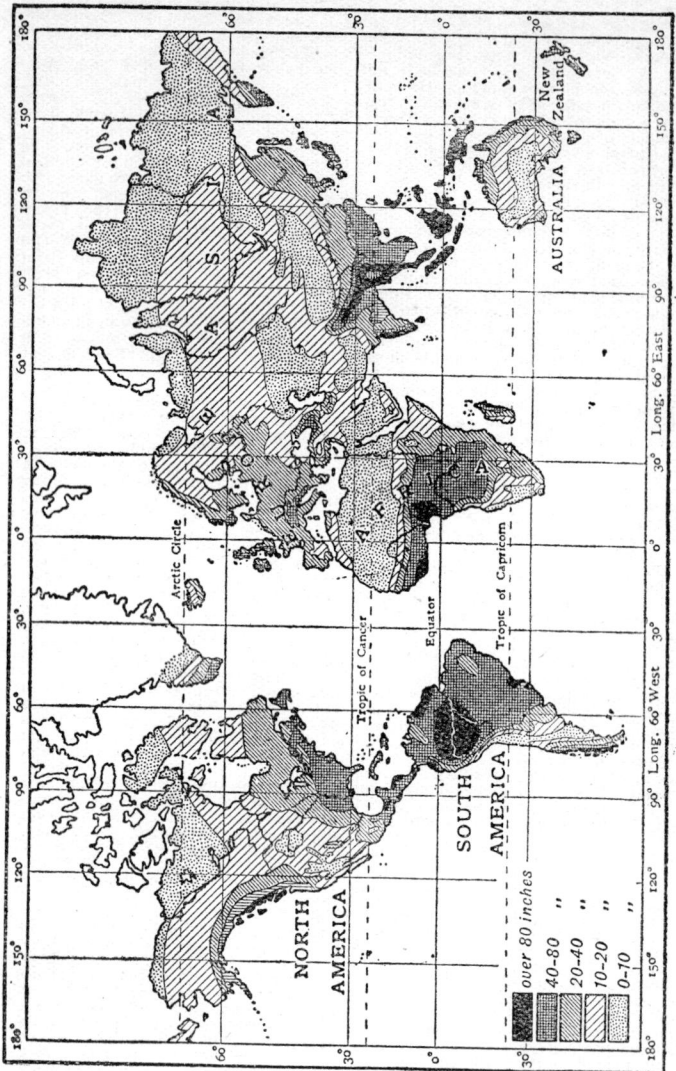

THE WORLD: MEAN ANNUAL RAINFALL

trols the rainfall, and mere proximity to the sea does not ensure a good supply of rain. Where the sea-water along a coast is cold, the air that blows ashore has its temperature raised and its capacity for carrying moisture increased by the greater heat of the land; hence this air does not drop its moisture as rain until it has been sufficiently uplifted to be cooled below its temperature on the sea. Parts of the coast of Chile and Peru, of South-Western Africa, and Somali-land, owing to these conditions, have arid climates.

The agricultural value of rain depends upon its distribution through the year and the period of its fall. In the monsoons, as the ascending air-currents over the land occur during the summer-time, the monsoonal regions have summer rains and dry winters.

In the Trade Wind belt, as the western coastlands have off-shore winds, they are usually dry; and as on the eastern side of the continents the Trade Winds blow in from the sea, the rainfall on them is heavy and mostly falls in the winter months. The Mediterranean type of climate is that in which the rainfall is mainly in the winter and the summers are dry; it occurs on the outer side of the Trade Wind belts, especially along the Mediterranean, along some of the western coasts of America, South-Western Africa, and Southern Australia.

The winds have a powerful effect upon climate by controlling the distribution of sea-water, and by drawing up to the surface some of the almost ice-cold deep-sea water, which has a chilling effect on the weather.

The ocean controls the environment of man on earth. From its surface is raised the water which maintains the rainfall and renews the rivers. It modifies the temperature of the winds which blow across them; it prevents injurious variations in the composition of the atmosphere by absorbing any excess of carbonic dioxide after volcanic eruptions, and by giving forth fresh supplies to replace the amount removed by absorption during the growth of vegetation or by the weathering of rocks. The deeper water of the oceans is almost ice-cold, having a temperature of about 39° F.

Its coldness is due mainly to the melting of the Antarctic ice, for the cold, heavy water thus produced sinks to a great depth and then drifts northward; this explanation is based on the fact that the deeper waters of the North Atlantic and North Pacific are slightly less cold than those of corresponding positions in the southern parts of the same oceans.

The temperature of the surface-waters of the ocean varies in accordance with the amount of heat received from the sun; it is warmest in the tropics, and the greater evaporation in that zone renders the surface-waters there salter than those in the Polar Regions, where the upper layers are diluted with fresh water from the melting ice. The salinity is also low off the mouths of large rivers, where the fresh water spreads out as a wide, shallow layer floating on the heavier sea-water.

The amount of salt in the sea-water is on an average about 35 parts in 1,000, but it rises to more than 42 parts in some tropical enclosed seas, as at the northern end of the Red Sea, and falls below 30 parts in the Baltic, where the long-continued inflow of fresh water from the rivers has rendered the water in the northern part little more than brackish.

The surface-waters of the ocean are pushed forward by the winds, thus giving rise to broad, slow movements known as drifts, and to narrow, swifter, and more constant streams known as ocean-currents. The equatorial parts of the oceans are mostly subject to a westward drift under the influence of the Trade Winds. In the mid-temperate zones the drift is mainly eastward under the pressure of the prevalent westerly winds. When the drift is obstructed by coming against a continent, the water is piled up, and the excess overflows as an ocean-current.

In the Atlantic the equatorial drift from east to west drives water into the Gulf of Mexico, thence it escapes as the Gulf Stream, which can be traced by the warmth and saltness of its water to Newfoundland. It is there dissipated, and the surface temperatures are lowered by the Labrador current, which flows southward from the Greenland seas.

In most of the North Atlantic there is a widespread drift, proved, for example, by parts of ships which have been wrecked in America being washed ashore on the coast of Europe. The water carried eastward by this drift is forced against the coast of Southern Europe, and is piled up there in a raised area, whence a regular outflow, the European Current, discharges northward past the British Isles and helps to warm the seas of North-Western Europe.

The Canaries Current from the same area discharges southward along the West African coast. In the South Atlantic some of the water that has drifted eastward across the Southern Ocean is driven against the western coast of South Africa, and thence flows north as the Benguella Current

The water of the western equatorial drift across the Atlantic impinges against the coast of Brazil, and then flows southward along the American coast as the Brazil Current.

The circulation in the Pacific is essentially similar to that in the Atlantic. A broad westward drift across the equatorial zone piles up water against the coast of China, whence a current known as the Kuro Sivo flows northward past Japan; it corresponds to the Gulf Stream. A current from Kamchatka flows southward to Japan, and corresponds to the Labrador Current that discharges into the North Atlantic from Greenland.

An eastward drift across the North Pacific banks water against the western coast of the United States; the overflow southward is the Californian Current, which corresponds to the Canaries Current in the Atlantic. In the South Pacific the eastward drift of the cold sub-Antarctic water is deflected northward by the obstruction of South America, and flows along the coasts of Chile as the Peruvian Current; this stream is dissipated near the equator, and its waters are returned westward across the tropical Pacific in the southern equatorial drift.

In the Southern Ocean a predominant easterly drift is maintained by the west winds, which give the belt east of Cape Colony its name of the 'Roaring Forties.' This drift feeds the Benguella and West Australian Currents.

The climatic effects of ocean-currents have been often over-estimated; to them have been attributed the greater warmth of the eastern as compared with the western coasts of the North Atlantic. The warm temperature of the British Isles is, however, due more to the warmth of the prevailing south-west wind and to the latent heat set free by the precipitation of its moisture than to ocean-currents.

IV. The Distribution of Plants. The distribution of plants is controlled by two series of factors—climatic and edaphic. The edaphic are those dependent on the soil, its textures, its properties as regards water, its supply of plant foods, and the presence or absence of poisonous constituents, some of which are fatal to special plants, and others to all plants. The climatic effects are due mainly to variations in heat, moisture, and light.

Heat has the broadest general effect on the distribution of plants, so that the character of the vegetation varies primarily with distance from the tropics. The secondary variations depend on distance from the coast, which affects the supply of moisture, and on height above sea-level, which largely controls the local temperature. For areas with similar positions and soils, distance from the equator is the dominant factor. The primary botanical divisions are therefore into seven parallel zones, the Tropical, North and South Subtropical, North and South Temperate, and the Frigid Zones, Arctic and Antarctic.

In the tropics, lowlands and mountain slopes which receive heavy rain are usually covered by dense forests with luxuriant foliage. These forests may have a jungly undergrowth through which passage may be difficult; or the ground may be open and the foliage form a high canopy, supported by a web of lianas or other twining plants which connect the crowns of the trees. Under such a roof dense undergrowth is impossible, owing to the lack of light; and most of the flowering plants live on the roof or attached to the tree trunks, up which they climb towards the light.

Muddy tropical coasts are often fringed with forests of mangroves, which are restricted to the tidal belt by their heavy dart-like seedling being fixed by falling from the parent tree into the mud. Sandy tropical shores and low islands, the soils of which are often saturated with salt water, support groves of coco-nut palms. The palms are characteristic of the tropics, and they grow isolated or in clusters, or as open forests, on the plains.

At some distance from the sea and in the drier areas forests give place to park-like grassy plains with scattered trees. In areas with a still more arid climate the conditions become those of the desert. The continuous turf breaks up into scattered tufts of dry grass; the herbs grow in cushion-like masses; shrubs have thick and fleshy leaves and stems like the aloe and cactus; the trees have needle-shaped instead of broad flat leaves, and their trunks may be succulent like the giant euphorbias, or may be huge masses of soft wood like the baobab. These modifications are adapted to reduce loss of water by evaporation.

The trees, moreover, in arid regions often have a growth of thorns to protect them from animals ravenous during drought; and they are often umbrella-shaped in order to lessen their resistance to the wind.

The Subtropical Zones have forests of hard-leaved evergreen trees, such as the cork-oak; they grow in areas with a Mediterranean rainfall, as along the Mediterranean, in California, South-Western Africa, and South-Western Australia. The structure

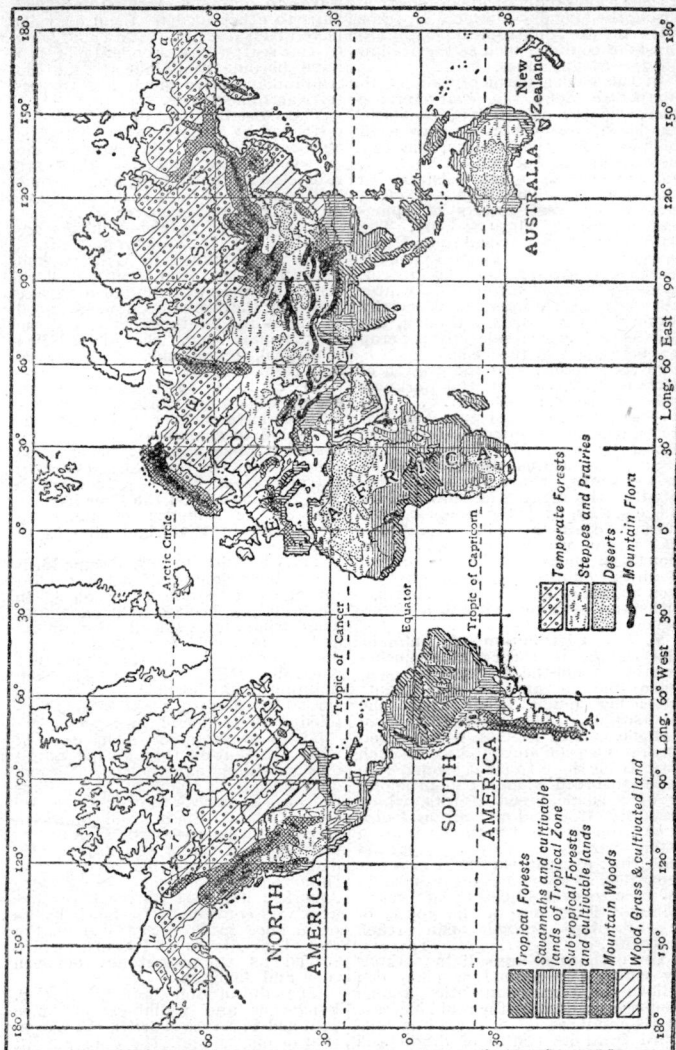

THE WORLD: VEGETATION

Temperate Forests

Steppes and Prairies

Deserts

Mountain Flora

Tropical Forests

Savannahs and cultivable lands of Tropical Zone

Subtropical Forests and cultivable lands

Mountain Woods

Wood, Grass & cultivated land

of their leaves reduces loss of moisture during the long dry summer. In other parts of the Subtropical Zone are forests of conifers, such as the Italian and the Aleppo pines.

In the colder parts of the North Temperate Zone the characteristic trees, e.g. the oak, beech, elm, ash, and birch, are deciduous; they shed their leaves in the autumn, whereby their foliage is not subject to frost, and the trees offer less resistance to winter gales. The hills are often covered by vast forests of spine-leaved trees, e.g. pines and firs. The plains and downs are clad in turf, and form the world's most extensive grazing-lands. The arable ground, owing to the moderate cold in winter and heat in summer, is especially favourable for cereals, although, unlike the tropics, as a rule only one crop can be reaped in the year.

In the Frigid Zones the growth of trees is prevented by the darkness and intense cold of winter. The vegetation consists of turf and low herbs, which are protected during the winter by a mantle of snow. The frigid plains are usually occupied by vast swamps, which are kept saturated by the melting of snow and ice in the spring, while the summer is too short to drain the soil. The Arctic plains are usually covered by a growth of moss and lichens and of swamp-dwelling plants (hydrophytes), such as rushes and sedges, which can withstand both cold air and a water-logged soil.

V. The Distribution of Animals. The Darwinian theory of evolution was based on the struggle for existence due to animals and plants increasing much faster than the food-supply. The descendants of a single pair of rabbits, which breed six times a year and produce in each litter from three to eight young, who begin to breed when six months old, or of a single breed of rats, which breed as often and as early and produce from four to ten young in each litter, would, if they all reached maturity, overrun the earth in a few centuries. A single pair of rats would increase to over 11,000 in two years. Comparatively few of the young of fast-breeding animals can reach maturity.

One of the most immediate methods by which any animal or plant can relieve the fierce competition among its species caused by the rapid increase in its numbers is by spreading outward from its centre of origin and occupying every accessible region which is suitable to it or to which it can adapt itself.

Animals, in the struggle to extend their geographical range, adapt themselves to different climates and perhaps to other media. Land animals have given rise to aquatic types such as the seal; the descendants of fish have become amphibious; and the Amphibians have given rise to terrestrial quadrupeds.

The distribution of animals is restricted by various factors, climatic and geographical. Some animals are so sensitive to cold that they are restricted to the tropics; and to some salt water is so fatal that they have no power of passage over sea.

Examples of restricted ranges are supplied by the anthropoid apes, which are confined to Western and Central Africa and South-Eastern Asia; the musk ox, limited to Arctic America; the elephants, now restricted to Africa and Southern Asia; and the monotremes (e.g. the duck-billed platypus), found only in Australia and New Guinea.

In contrast to these restricted groups others are world-wide. Some animals have such powers of accommodation to changes of temperature that they range across all the climatic zones. Thus the tern (*Sterna arctica*) extends from high Arctic to high Antarctic latitudes; the tiger lives in the tropical jungles of Southern India and in the frigid steppes of Siberia.

The wide distribution of some birds is due to their powers of flight. For example, a swallow hatched in England has been caught in Natal. The dog has been artificially distributed as the companion of early man, who doubtless introduced the dingo into Australia. Mice and rats have been unintentionally carried in boats and spread on floating trees, which supplied both food and transport.

There are, however, many cases of wide distribution that do not admit of such simple explanation. Normal distribution is 'continuous.' Thus the bird known as the dipper ranges from Ireland, Spain, and Morocco, across Europe and Central Asia, to the coasts of China and Japan. Its distribution across that area is continuous. It also occurs in Western America, but that its range to that area was continuous is shown by its occurrence in Southern Kamchatka and the Aleutian Islands, which served as stepping-stones between Asia and America.

The diprotodon Marsupials (e.g. kangaroos and wallabies) are now confined to Australia with the exception of one animal, the opossum rat (Cænolestes), which lives in the north-western corner of South America. The distribution of the Diprotodons is, therefore, discontinuous, and there are no intermediate colonies connecting Cænolestes and its Australian relatives.

The alligator is characteristic of tropical and sub-tropical America, but an isolated colony of it lives in the Yangtze-kiang in China. The chief home of the lizards, the Iguanas, is southern North America and South America; but isolated representatives live in Madagascar, and in the Fiji and Tonga islands in the South-Western Pacific. Such cases of 'discontinuous distribution' indicate either survival from a time when the arrangement of land and water on the globe was very different from the present plan, or the dispersal of eggs or larvæ by some agent that can cross wide tracts of sea.

The dispersal of plants is helped by the seeds being carried by wind and animals; larvæ or eggs may be carried across sea in mud on the legs of birds. Ocean-currents may carry small animals or larvæ on floating timber or in pumice. The occupants of islands lying near a continent are introduced by such agencies, for they are allied to those of the adjacent land, and are usually only such as may be thus carried. Remote small oceanic islands are inhabited by the few animals and plants that have been carried by wind or sea-drift, or been introduced by man.

The study of such islands shows that birds are of little importance in the distribution of other animals, and that though winds and currents may introduce insects and small animals, such cases are exceptional. These adventitious methods of distribution are inadequate to explain the range of some animals, such as the occurrence of the same mammals on both sides of the Atlantic, or the arrival in remote oceanic islands of mammals or animals dependent on a particular food to which salt water is as fatal as it is to slugs and worms.

Discontinuous distribution generally indicates former connections which have now been broken by bridges of land having sunk beneath the sea. Animals which appeared on the earth in early times, therefore, had better chances of securing a wider distribution than those developed more recently, and would have spread along different routes. The distribution of plants and animals varies with the date of their appearance on the earth.

The chief facts of the distribution of animals are summarized in the classifications of the world into different zoological regions. The classifications proposed vary according to the group of animals selected as their foundation. The earliest standard classification (proposed by P. L. Sclater in 1858) was based on the birds.

He divided the world into six zoological regions: The Palearctic Region, including Europe, some of the Mediterranean provinces of Africa, and nearly all Asia; the Ethiopian Region, including Africa south of the Sahara, and Southern Arabia; the Oriental Region for South-Eastern Asia, including India, Indo-China, Siam, and the western part of the Eastern Archipelago; the Australian Region, including Australia, New Guinea, the adjacent part of the Eastern Archipelago, and the islands of the South-Western Pacific; the Nearctic Region, North America as far south as the plateau of Mexico; the Neotropical Region, including Central America, the West Indies, and South America.

Lydekker (1896) pointed out that Sclater's divisions were of unequal value, and advanced a classification based mainly on the mammals, and having due regard to their geological history. He subdivided the world into three realms; of these Arctogea includes Sclater's Palearctic and Nearctic, owing to the striking resemblance of the fauna of Canada to that of the Old World; Canada and the Lake Region of the United States are included in the same subdivision, the Holarctic Region, as Europe and Asia.

The United States, having a fauna very different from that of Europe and Canada, belong to an independent region, the Sonoran. Africa south of the Sahara and Southern Arabia form the Ethiopian Region, from which Madagascar is separated as the Malagasy Region. South-Eastern Asia is the Oriental Region. Lydekker's second realm, Neogea, includes South and Central America. His third realm, Notogea, includes four regions—the Australian, Polynesian, Hawaiian, and Austro-Malayan (the eastern part of the Eastern Archipelago).

The inclusion of both the Nearctic and Palearctic in the Arctogea Realm is based on the occurrence on both sides of the North Atlantic of many animals, including the moles and beavers, bears, reindeer and elk, the grouse, and the salamander, and amongst freshwater fish, perches, sticklebacks, pike, and sturgeon. The characteristic animals of the Palearctic Region include the wolf, the hedgehog, fallow deer, the two-humped camel, yak, and in the far north the lemming.

Many of its mammals are the same as those of the Ethiopian and Oriental Regions; the porcupine, for example, ranges northward from Africa into Italy, the apes to Gibraltar, and the lion, which is characteristically Ethiopian, lived until recently in the Atlas Mountains of North Africa, during Old Testament times in Palestine, and still survives in Western India.

The Ethiopian Region is characterized by the African elephant, the hippopotamus, the two-horned rhinoceros, the giraffe, many species of antelopes, the earth-pig or Aardvark, the guinea-fowl, and the primitive lemur known as the Aye-Aye. The ostrich is typically Ethiopian, but ranges through Arabia as far north as Palestine.

The Oriental Region is characterized by the Indian elephant, the tapir, the orang-utan, the flying-lemurs, and many special species of antelope. Some antelopes occur in Northern Asia, and the tiger ranges from the jungles of India and Indo-China to Siberia. The Australian Region is specially characterized by including the few living representatives of the monotremes, and all the Marsupials except the American opossums and the South American opossum-rat (Cænolestes).

The Australian Region includes amongst birds the birds of Paradise, the bower birds, the lyre birds, the cassowaries, and emus. New Zealand, which has no indigenous mammals, includes the remarkable three-eyed lizard, the Tuatera or Hatteria, and the wingless birds, the kiwis; it is only in modern times that its great flightless birds, the moas, have become extinct.

The Neotropical Region is the special home of the sloths and the anteaters, while it is occupied by special families of monkeys (the Cebidæ), the opossum-rat (Cænolestes), many special families of birds, including the great walking birds, the rheas; the llamas, vicunas, and jaguars are its best known larger animals.

Many animals, doubtless of South American origin, such as the armadilloes, range northward into the Sonoran Region of North America, along with humming-birds, pumas, and alligators.

The faunas and floras of most of the continents and continental islands are composite, having been derived from various sources. This fact may be illustrated by reference to the British Isles. The oldest constituent in their fauna and flora is the Lusitanian element, which is found chiefly in the west of Ireland.

It includes such plants as the strawberry tree, the *Arbutus unedo*, which is found elsewhere in Europe only in Spain, Portugal, and along the Mediterranean; similar in range is a 'spotted slug' (Geomalacus) which lives in the south-west of Ireland and the north-west of Spain, or the saxifrage, well known as a garden plant under the name of London Pride, which occurs in the west of Ireland, in Spain, and the Pyrenees.

These organisms are all absent from England and France. The Irish members of the Lusitanian fauna and flora are, therefore, clearly survivals from a time when Ireland and Spain were directly connected by land. During the Great Ice Age most of the Lusitanian species were killed off; when the climate again became milder the severance of the former land connection prevented the entrance of new immigrants from Spain.

The British Isles were therefore mainly peopled from Germany across the site of the North Sea. Hence the predominant British element is the Teutonic. An earlier immigration along the same line introduced the Alpine flora, of which many plants are still found on the higher British mountains. They have often been regarded as due to migration from the north, but they appear to have come from Asia in pre-glacial times across Central Europe.

An American element in the British fauna and flora is represented in Ireland and Western Scotland by some American plants (e.g. the Pipewort Eriocaulon), the introduction of which has been attributed to seeds drifted by ocean-currents; but this explanation cannot be applied to some American freshwater sponges which are found in lakes in Western Ireland.

The presence of these American animals and plants in the British Isles is doubtless a result of the direct land communication across the Atlantic, which has caused the numerous affinities in their faunas and floras that has led to the inclusion of both Canada and Northern Europe in the same Holarctic Sub-region.

Oceanic Zoological Provinces. The ocean is more favourable than the land to a wide range of inhabitants, owing to the continuity of the sea and the uniformity of temperature below the surface layer. The distribution of marine organisms is mainly determined by depth, for the deep sea is of almost icy coldness, and apart from the light given by phosphorescence it is dark; in the consequent absence of plant-life all the dwellers in the deep sea are carnivorous.

The distribution of marine-life is into three divisions. The first is the Littoral Zone, which extends from high tide to the depth of about 40 fathoms; its water varies in temperature with the latitude and the seasons; and as it is illuminated from the surface, and constant movement keeps its waters well supplied with oxygen, it is usually rich in plant and animal life.

The second division is the Pelagic Zone, comprising the surface-waters of the oceans far from land; the dwellers in it always float; they are the Plankton, which merely drift, and the Nekton, which swim. The third division, the Abysmal Zone, is the deep sea, and the conditions of its inhabitants are controlled by the enormous pressure, the stillness of the water, and the absence of sunlight and plant life.

Owing to the free communication between the different oceans, biological marine provinces are less marked than those of the land. The classification by Ortmann is based mainly on climate and depth. It adopts three Pelagic Regions—the Arctic Pelagic Region, which includes the Arctic Circumpolar Sub-region, from which two projections, the Atlantic Boreal and Pacific Boreal Sub-regions, pass southward to about lat. 40°.

The Antarctic Pelagic Region consists of the Antarctic Sub-region, including the belt round the Antarctic continent, and the Notal Sub-region, which comprises the northern part of the Southern Ocean. The Atlantic Pelagic Region includes all the tropical and temperate parts of the Atlantic; the Indo-Pacific Pelagic Region includes the Indian Ocean and most of the Pacific.

The second division comprises the coastal regions; they bound the Arctic and Antarctic Pelagic Regions, and include the belts of sea along the Atlantic, Pacific, and Indian Oceans; these belts are reduced in size by long extensions of the Antarctic coastal regions along the western coasts of South America and South Africa, owing to cold Antarctic waters driven northward by the winds.

VI. Animals and Plants of Economic Importance.—A. Animals. The original distribution of domestic animals has been largely modified by man. He has taken with him in his wanderings those necessary for food, or as beasts of burden, or as companions. The chief animal foods, meat and milk, are supplied by cattle, which are now world-wide throughout the tropical and temperate zones. Sheep supply meat and wool, the most useful material for general clothing.

The most valuable wool is that of the merino sheep, of which the original home was North Africa. Spain long held a monopoly of this breed, and maintained it by prohibition of the export of the live sheep. During the Spanish occupation of the Netherlands the merino was introduced through Holland into Saxony, which thus gained for a time pre-eminence in high-class wool. From Holland some merino sheep were taken to the Cape, but there deteriorated.

The modern development of high-quality wool followed the introduction, after great difficulties only overcome by the Peninsular War, of some merino sheep into New South Wales, where by careful breeding the Australian sheep-farmers raised a wool combining the softness of the merino with the length of staple of the coarser British wools.

Goats' hair is used for clothing, as mohair, which is yielded by the Angora goats of Asia Minor, and as cashmere from those of North-Western India. Camels' hair is woven into carpets and strong textiles. The wool of the alpaca, which lives in South America, is especially soft and elastic.

Silk, a secretion from a caterpillar (Bombyx), was first cultivated in China, whence it spread to India, where the silk industry is partly maintained on the product of wild indigenous caterpillars, whose cocoons are collected in the woods. The silkworm was also carried across Southern Asia to Europe. Its range in climate is controlled by that of its chief food-plant, the mulberry. Silk cultivation is most important among European countries in Italy, while France is the greatest silk-manufacturing country.

Of furs, the most valuable are those of the animals of the colder regions, as the sable and various foxes in Siberia, Northern Russia, and Canada; the ermine in the north temperate parts of Eurasia; the fur-seal in the North Pacific Ocean near Bering Strait. The largest quantities of furs are obtained from the small animals of the north temperate zone, such as bear, squirrels, rabbits, hares, beavers, musquash, rats, cats, seals, &c. The southern forests of Australia yield the opossum.

Transport animals have been developed mainly in open grassy plains, where the rivers are not available for boats, and frequent migration is necessary in consequence of droughts and exhaustion of firewood. The steppes of Asia were probably the home of the horse and donkey, while the camel developed in the more arid regions of Asia and North Africa; oxen and buffalo are of most service for slow, heavy transport over bad roads, and yak among the mountains of Central Asia. In the Arctic regions the reindeer has been domesticated for transport, food, and fur.

The sea provides supplies of food-fish, which live at moderate depths mainly in the colder seas of the temperate zones. The chief fisheries are therefore in shallow seas or at banks which rise nearly to the surface, as around the British Isles, and especially in the North Sea, where the fishing-fleets of North-Western Europe compete for cod, herring, mackerel, and haddock, as well as for the scantier supplies of sole and turbot.

The largest Atlantic fisheries are on the banks of Newfoundland, and off the coasts of Canada and the northern parts of the United States, where the chief fish are cod, herring, and hake.

In the warmer parts of the temperate zone the chief sea-fish are the sardine and the anchovy. Of shell-fish the most important is the oyster, which grows in estuaries on temperate coasts. Fish are abundant in the tropical seas, but their flesh is usually coarser. The most important fresh water fisheries are for salmon in the rivers of both sides of the North Atlantic and of Western Canada.

B. Plants. In the tropics, owing to the heat and stimulus of the intense sunlight, plant growth, in the presence of ample moisture, is very rapid. Several harvests in the year may be reaped if the crops are supplied with water by irrigation, or by rain at suitable seasons.

Owing to the heat, numerous products are developed, such as spices, rubber, oil, sugar, and starch, which are not produced, or only in smaller quantities, by the vegetation of colder climes. Hence modern civilization is dependent on the tropics for several essential materials.

Cereals, on the other hand, which require slower growth and ripening, are characteristic of the temperate regions. The chief tropical and subtropical cereals are rice and dhurra.

The most valuable cereal is wheat, which thrives best under a cold wet spring and a hot dry summer; for when the plant is young, cold and wet increase the number of shoots, and therefore the yield in grain for each seed, while the maturing and ripening of the grain require warm dry weather before the harvest.

Hence countries with a Mediterranean distribution of rainfall are especially adapted for wheat cultivation. Southern Europe, owing to its hot summer, produces wheat of the best quality; Northern Europe, owing to the cold spring, produces heavier crops per acre, owing to the larger number of heads grown from a single seed.

Barley is of especial historical importance, as it was probably the first cereal cultivated by man, ears of it having been found in the ruins of the prehistoric pile-built lake villages of Switzerland. It has a wider range in climate than any other cereal, being grown in Norway as far north as 70° N. lat., while Northern Africa produces some of the most valuable, because

the hard dry grains grown in its hot summer are of special value for brewing.

Oats are of service because they are easily cultivated, and can be raised in a colder and wetter climate than wheat.

Rye was formerly the most widely cultivated of European cereals, and is still the chief crop of Eastern Europe. It grows on poor soil, and has therefore been replaced by wheat or barley in Western Europe with the adoption of improved methods of agriculture.

Maize, or Indian corn, is the chief grain native to America; it is there known as corn, and thus its flour is used in Europe under the name of corn-flour. Its growth requires a hot summer and repeated watering from frequent summer rains or irrigation. It is therefore unsuited for most of Europe, as the British climate is too cold and the Mediterranean summer too dry.

Rice is the cereal which is claimed to give a higher yield of food per acre than any other crop. It grows under special conditions in the subtropical climates—in China, India, Burma, and the Eastern Archipelago. The rapid growth of the young plant requires the flooding of the rice-fields; hence, with the exception of hill rice, it is cultivated in irrigated deltas and river plains.

Of the fruits, many of the most useful, including apples, pears, plums, peaches, oranges, and lemons, have been developed from trees native to the warmer temperate regions. Figs are grown especially in the Eastern Mediterranean, but are only largely cultivated where there is plenty of cheap labour at the right season for drying and packing.

The vine is most prolific where, as in Southern Europe, the summer is long and warm, and the soil is dry; it flourishes as far south as Palestine, but no farther unless artificially sheltered from the summer heat. Grapes are most largely used for wine, of which France is the greatest producing country. Raisins, sultanas, and currants are dried grapes grown from special varieties in South Europe, and particularly in the Grecian islands.

Sugar was primarily derived from sugar-cane, which was a native of South-Eastern Asia; it is now spread throughout the tropics and subtropical lowlands, and requires for its growth a high temperature and ample moisture. Its chief rival is beet, which produces large supplies of sugar in the temperate zone in France, Germany, and South-Western Russia.

The mangel, a near ally of beetroot, is grown for cattle fodder in the warmer and drier parts of Southern

England, where it is claimed that the beet may also be cultivated.

Spices, as a rule, require the heat of the tropics for the development of their aromatic constituents. Cloves and pepper come from islands like Zanzibar and Pemba, off Equatorial Africa; cinnamon from Ceylon; nutmegs, &c., from the Spice Islands of the Eastern Archipelago. Tobacco (Nicotiana) is a native of America, and has now spread throughout the subtropical countries; the United States is still the largest producer.

Opium, extracted from the poppy, appears to have had its home in the eastern Mediterranean, where until recently the juice extracted from it contained the highest proportion of morphine. The most extensive cultivation of opium was in India, in the Ganges Valley, whence the product was largely exported to China for use as a narcotic; but by improvements in culture the Indian poppy has been grown richer in morphine, and the opium-fields are now producing that most helpful drug morphia.

Tea (Camellia thea) was first used and cultivated in China, but its original home was probably in Assam, where a tea tree still grows wild. It thrives best with warm summers and frequent rain, and can withstand severe frost. Its cultivation requires abundant cheap labour at the right time, and so the chief tea plantations are in China, Northern India, and Ceylon.

Coffee appears to have come from South Abyssinia, whence it spread to Arabia; its growth requires a warm moist climate, for it can withstand neither severe frost nor excessive heat, and the young plants have to be protected from the sun under broad-leaved shelter plants. It is now most extensively grown in East Africa, Arabia, and Brazil. Cocoa (Theobroma) is the seed of an American tropical tree which supplies cocoa and chocolate, and is now largely cultivated in West Africa.

Of the vegetable fibres the most important for clothing is cotton (Gossypium), of which some species were indigenous to Europe and others to America. It is essentially a subtropical plant requiring a moderate amount of moisture, but frost is fatal to it. The American supply comes mostly from the plains beside the Mississippi. The Nile delta in Egypt produces varieties of especial value from the length of the fibre.

Cotton is largely grown on the lava plains of North-Western India, and although the quality produced is poor, its cultivation is cheap. Uganda, beside the Victoria Nyanza in Central Africa, is climatically well adapted for cotton, but is hampered by the limited transport available thence to the manufacturing districts of Lancashire and India.

Of the coarser fibre plants used for textiles, one of the most important is jute (Corchorus), of which the main cultivation is in North-Eastern Bengal on sandy plains flooded in the spring. It is mainly used for sacking and gunny bags, and for cheap carpets. As its fibre is lustrous, it is used to strengthen other fabrics, such as silk.

Flax (Linum) grows under a wide range of climate, but requires a stiff moist soil. It is cultivated in North-Eastern Ireland; the main supply came from Russia, and it is now being largely grown in the highlands of tropical Africa. The stems of the plant provide the flax for linen, and the seed (linseed) yields a valuable oil.

Of the fibres used for cordage and ropes, the most valuable grown in temperate regions is hemp. It is also woven into a strong fabric known, from the botanical name of the plant (Cannabis), as canvas. True hemp is mainly a temperate product, and the largest crops were grown in Russia and Italy. Manila hemp, which has a very long fibre, is obtained from the stem of a species of Musa, the banana.

Sisal hemp is a long-stapled fibre obtained from the leaves of an aloe native to Central America; it is now largely cultivated in East Africa, and is especially used for binder twine, its adoption for ropes being limited by the belief that it deteriorates when exposed to sea-water.

Fabrics are rendered waterproof by india-rubber, a secretion of many tropical trees native to South America, Africa, and the Eastern Archipelago. It was first known in America, where it was used by the Indians to render fabrics waterproof; as it was used to remove pencil marks, it was known as india-rubber. The American supply is derived from Hevea, a tree found in the forests of the Amazon; and from Manihot, which yields the Ceara rubber of the coastal provinces of Brazil. The native African rubber comes from Landolphia, a vine growing in the forests of Equatorial Africa.

Gutta-percha is derived from various trees, including Dichopsis, which live in South-Eastern Asia. Rubber as extracted is soft and elastic; it is hardened into vulcanite by combination with sulphur. Ebonite consists of about equal parts of sulphur and rubber.

Timber includes two chief sections: light woods, which are soft and easily worked, and hard woods, which are stronger, heavier, and often take a good polish. The light-wood trees are mainly coniferous, such as the pines and firs, which grow in vast forests, especially in the colder temperate regions. In the warmer temperate zones cedars and other conifers grow in forests mixed with other trees. The light woods provide planks and beams for building construction, props to support the roof in mines, and pulp for paper manufacture.

The hard woods grow in the temperate and tropical zones. The timber of the oak, elm, ash, beech, chestnut, and walnut provides strong durable woods suitable for building construction and shipping, toolhandles, furniture, &c. The tropical forests produce woods such as mahogany, which are especially prized owing to their beauty and hardness, while teak, from the forests of Burma and India, has the strength of oak, with the advantage that metals driven into it are less liable to rust.

The forests of Australia produce woods which are hard, beautiful in grain, and heavier than water, such as the iron bark, karri, and jarrah, which, owing to their exceptional strength and heaviness, and resistance to decay in water are used for piles and blocks for road-paving.

VII. The Distribution of Minerals.[1] Minerals are the inorganic constituents of the earth, and they constitute the whole of its crust. The minerals first used by man were such stones as flint, which could be easily chipped into cutting-tools; those of chief present service may be classified into five groups. (1) The ores of metals, which were first required for weapons, tools, and ornaments, and are now used also for constructional work and currency. (2) Fuels, which are essential for smelting metals, for domestic supplies in large cities, and for illuminants. (3) The commoner and more abundant earthy minerals used in building construction, such as clays and loams for bricks and tiles, rocks and marbles for building-stone, slates for roofing, limestone for cements, and tough rocks for road-metal. (4) Scarcer minerals, such as graphite, mica, and talc, used for various industrial purposes, and gems, used on account of their hardness, optical properties, or beauty. (5) Minerals required by the agriculturist to fertilize exhausted or barren soils.

The Metals. Of the metals, that most essential to modern civilization is iron (which is now mostly employed in the form of steel). Rocks containing iron are world-wide in distribu-

[1] The statistics quoted in this section are for the last pre-war year, 1913, as they probably indicate conditions to which there will be a tendency to recur, though doubtless some of the changes will be permanent, owing to movements which cannot be reversed, and to alterations in national boundaries.

tion, but only the richest are available as ores, since in the treatment of low-grade ores much of the labour and fuel spent in mining and smelting would be expended on useless material.

The present value of an ore depends upon its situation as well as upon its quality, for the possibility of its profitable use depends upon the proximity of the fuel and fluxes required in its smelting. Vast quantities of iron ores are known in places either so remote from markets or from fuel that they cannot be profitably worked at present. Sometimes, however, an ore with a low proportion of iron may be profitably used when its addition to a high-grade ore forms a suitable smelting-mixture.

Proximity of coal-fields and cheap transport largely determine the distribution of iron mining; the iron industry of the United Kingdom is mainly dependent on ores imported from the Mediterranean to ports on the British coal-fields. The use of the vast bodies of ore in Northern Scandinavia is restricted by their long distance from the coast, and by the presence in some of them of a considerable amount of titanium, the removal of which would be too costly in fuel. In 1913 the predominant iron- and steel-producing countries were the United States, with about 32 million tons; Germany, with 19 million tons; and the United Kingdom, with 9½ million tons.

The United States has the advantage of vast quantities of cheaply worked coal, and of the rich iron ores of Lake Superior. Germany had the rich coal-fields east of the Rhine, opposite the easily worked ironstone of Lorraine; in Great Britain the industry begun on native ores is maintained mainly on imported ores from Southern Europe.

Copper is of especial historical interest, for, being often found native and being easily wrought, it may have been the first metal used by man for tools and weapons. The subsequent discovery how to alloy it with tin into the more serviceable material bronze greatly increased its value. It is now chiefly used as the most convenient material for electric conductors, as wire, owing to its high ductility, and alloyed with zinc as brass, and with tin as bronze.

Copper was at first worked in many countries of which the supplies cannot now compete with those of the chief copper-fields. Of the total world's production in 1913 of a million tons, the United States supplied more than half, or about 550,000 tons. The outputs in that year of the other chief copper-producing countries were: Japan, 72,000 tons; Spain and Portugal, mainly from the ancient mines of Rio Tinto, 53,000 tons; Mexico, 52,000 tons; Australasia, 47,000 tons; Roumania, 43,000 tons; and Chile, which was once by far the leading copper-producing country, was seventh with 40,000 tons. The United Kingdom, in which the copper-mines were once important, yielded the negligible output of 300 tons.

Gold was one of the earliest metals used by man, for, though rare, it is conspicuous and attractive, and it is easily worked into ornaments of which the brilliant colour is not affected by rust or tarnish. The main use of gold is for money. In 1913, of a total output of 22 million ounces, the Transvaal supplied 40 per cent; the United States, 19 per cent; Australasia, 12 per cent; and Russia and Mexico each about 4 per cent; the other important contributions were from Canada, Rhodesia, and India. The British Empire, therefore, supplies by far the largest proportion of the gold output.

Silver is mainly worked as a by-product from ores of lead, and to a smaller extent from those of copper and gold. Its main uses are for ornaments, plate, jewellery, and currency. In 1913 Mexico was the largest producer with 82 million ounces; the United States was second with 67 million ounces; Canada third with nearly 32 million ounces; Australasia fourth with nearly 19 million ounces; and Germany fifth with 14 million ounces.

Lead is a useful metal, as it is easily melted, and is plastic when cold, so that it is convenient for small pipes which require to be bent; its weight renders it most suitable for shot; and it is the basis of some important alloys, as with tin in pewter and solder, and with antimony in type-metal. The world's output in 1913 was 1,130,000 tons, of which the United States supplied about one-third; Spain, one-fifth; Australasia, one-tenth; Mexico, one-twentieth; and the United Kingdom, one-thirtieth.

Tin, of the metals in common use, is the most sparse in distribution. It is indispensable as a constituent of bronze, for plating thin sheets of iron to save them from rust, and for lining cooking vessels to protect the food from being poisoned. The chief supply of tin from prehistoric times to the last century came from Cornwall, from which Britain gained its name of the Cassiterides, or Tin Islands.

The Cornish mines were worked by the Phœnicians, who obtained there the tin for the bronze used by the people of the Eastern Mediterranean. The chief supply now comes from

South-Eastern Asia. In 1913 the Straits Settlements yielded 36,000 tons; the Islands of Billiton and Banka, off Java, 18,000 tons; China, 3,800 tons; and Australia, 5,000 tons. The mines of England, Germany, and Bolivia yielded small supplies, but since then the Cornish mines have closed.

Aluminium is of increasing importance owing to its lightness and non-liability to rust. It is a constituent of ordinary clay, but it can only be extracted profitably from one or two pure earths, of which the chief is bauxite. This ore is smelted in electric furnaces which require cheap water-power. In 1913 the United States was the chief producer of aluminium with 29,000 tons; France produced 15,000 tons; Great Britain, 10,000 tons; and Switzerland, 10,000 tons. The British works use bauxite imported from the south of France. Large supplies of bauxite occur in the tropics, in India, West Africa, and tropical America, as in British Guiana.

Zinc is of value as an alloy of brass, and for protecting metals from rust, as in galvanized sheets and wire. It is widely distributed, but its extraction as metal (known as spelter) is mainly undertaken, owing to difficulties in the process, in industrial centres far from the mining-fields. The Australian mines at Broken Hill in 1913 produced 525,000 tons of concentrated ore, which was mostly exported to Europe for the separation of the zinc.

The United States is the largest producer. In 1913, of the world's output of about one million tons of zinc, the United States produced nearly one-third (323,000 tons); Germany, 285,000 tons; Belgium, 189,000 tons; and the United Kingdom, 59,000 tons. The zinc produced in the last three countries was mainly from imported ores.

Fuel. The supreme fuel is coal, of which the only serious competitors are wood and oil. Wood is too bulky except for local use; it is too dangerous for railways in dry climates, owing to the discharge of sparks; and the supplies are too soon exhausted in a populous country. Oil is in some ways an ideal fuel, as it is clean, concentrated, and easy to handle; but the supply is inadequate to serve as the world's primary fuel. In 1913 the total coal output of the world amounted to nearly 1,500 million tons; the total yield of oil is equivalent to about 100 million tons of coal, so that oil can replace coal only for special purposes.

Coal is the common fossil fuel, and has mostly been formed by accumulations of fossil vegetation in some places where it had grown on the sites of former forests or peat-bogs, and where it had drifted into swamps or lakes. The layer of the plant material is then covered by sand or clay, and is slowly altered into coal by the combined effect of pressure and of slow chemical and biological changes.

Coal is the main fuel under present conditions, as it is the most convenient and safest of concentrated fuels. It is indispensable in iron manufacture, not only as a source of heat, but as the reducing agent necessary in the smelting of the ores. Commercially, the coal-exporting countries enjoy the great benefit that the return steamers provide abundant freight for food and raw materials.

Industries which require large quantities of coal usually settle either on the coal-fields or in places easy of access to them, owing to its bulkiness and brittleness. Coal has, therefore, been the most powerful factor in the distribution of industrial centres.

Great Britain was for a long time the leading coal-producing country of the world. In 1800 its mines provided two-thirds of the total supply; in 1860 it still yielded 60 per cent of the world's output; and it was not until 1899 that the United States, which have 353,000 sq. miles of coal-field in contrast to the 12,000 sq. miles in the British Isles, produced a larger output than Britain.

The third great coal producer is Germany, which, with its pre-war boundaries, included larger reserves of coal than all the rest of Europe. In 1913 the United States produced 562 million tons, and Germany 278 million tons. The three countries, the United States, the United Kingdom, and Germany, together produced 87 per cent of the world's output.

The remainder was mainly contributed by Austria and Hungary, 44 millions tons; France, 42 million tons; Russia, 26 million tons; and India, 16 million tons. Australia has large coal-fields, but the demand on them is still relatively small.

China is believed to have larger reserves of coal than any other country; much of it is in areas still industrially undeveloped and far from the coast. China may, in centuries to come, be the world's great producer of coal.

In the British Isles the chief coal-fields are those of South Wales, with its outliers in Bristol and the Forest of Dean; Nottingham and South Yorkshire, with its recently proved great extension eastward; the Midland fields; Flintshire in North Wales; Northumberland and Durham; the Cumberland field, much of which is worked under the Irish Sea. The chief Scottish fields are in the Mid-

land Valley of Scotland, especially in Lanarkshire and Ayrshire; the largest Scottish reserves are in Eastern Scotland, largely under the Firth of Forth.

Mineral Oil. Petroleum (rock-oil) is the name given to a series of materials formed by the distillation of buried animal and vegetable matter under the influence of great pressure and long-continued moderate heat. This distillation produces four groups of materials: (1) natural gas and such volatile gases as petroleum-ether, which pass away as vapour at temperatures below 300° F.; (2) the illuminating oils such as kerosene and fuel oils, which are converted into vapour at temperatures of between 300° and 570° F.; (3) heavy oils used for lubricants; (4) the solid bitumens which occur in veins in rocks or as sheets on the surface, as in the Pitch Lake of Trinidad; they are the residues from which the more volatile constituents have escaped by evaporation. Asphalt is a limestone containing a sufficient amount of bitumen to serve as natural paving-stone.

The most important supplies of mineral oil come from porous beds in which the oil has been naturally collected. The pressure of its included gas tends to force it upward, and it accumulates in any accessible porous rock, which then acts as a reservoir or oil-pool. The natural gas collects in the upper part of this reservoir; the oil lies below it, and usually rests on beds charged with water. If a bore-hole be drilled into such a reservoir the gas escapes first, then the oil, and finally the well will discharge only water.

The chief supplies of mineral oil come from the United States, which in 1919 yielded 67·6 per cent of the total output; its fields are, however, believed to have reached or passed their maximum productiveness. Mexico is now yielding the second largest supply, and may for a time exceed the output from the United States. Other important oil-fields occur in Russia, Roumania, Burma, the Dutch East Indies, Persia, Egypt, and Trinidad.

In addition to oil which has been naturally distilled and can be obtained directly from wells, large supplies may be obtained from oil-shale. This material consists of clay charged with organic matters which, when heated in retorts, is distilled into oil. The most important producing oil-shale field is in the Midland Valley of Scotland, between Edinburgh and Glasgow.

Enormous reserves of oil-shale are known in other parts of the world, especially in the United States, Australia, the south-east of England, Canada, Burma, and Bulgaria: but their development has not hitherto been commercially possible in competition with the more cheaply produced native oil.

Cements and Fertilizers. Two series of minerals of primary importance, as they are indispensable for dwellings and for the production of food, are those that yield cements and fertilizers. Most permanent buildings are constructed either of bricks, which are made by baking mixtures of clay and sand, or of building stones, which are quarried from beds or masses of rock, especially granite, basalt, limestone, and sandstone. The cements used to bind the bricks or stones in buildings are made by burning a mixture of limestone with clay or sand, which produces a powder that after the addition of water sets as a hard cement.

The best known of the superior qualities is Portland cement, so called from its resemblance when set in mass to Portland stone. Its manufacture requires cheap fuel and local supplies of suitable limestone and silt. It was a British invention, but in 1913 (the pre-war year), of the world's production of 200 million barrels (usually 380 lb. each), the United States produced about 46 per cent; Germany, 18 per cent; and Great Britain, 7·5 per cent.

Fertilizers are used in agriculture to replace the plant-foods extracted by the crops. The most important are phosphate and potash. The former consists of phosphate of lime, and is made from various phosphatic limestones; they are deposited in warm temperate and tropical seas. Some of these phosphatic limestones are old coral reefs which have been altered into phosphate of lime by phosphoric acid washed out of overlying beds of guano; some of them are beds of earthy limestone containing layers of phosphatic grains, which are due to the alteration of shells by phosphoric acid in sea-water.

Guano (q.v.) is a fertilizer formed by the accumulation of dung from sea-birds, bats, &c.

Potash is a necessary constituent for many plants, and the supply in soils can be renewed by potash salts, of which the largest known supplies are in Central and Southern Germany; they were deposited by evaporation of the waters of a great inland sea, and the quantity there is so vast that Germany long enjoyed a monopoly of potash production.

VIII. The Races of Mankind. The use made of the different regions of the earth depends on the character of the people who inhabit them. It is inevitable that the physical influences which have produced the striking contrast between the fauna and flora of Greenland and those of India should also have profoundly affected man. The hard struggle against Arctic conditions has had an impoverishing effect on both the physical and mental qualities of man as compared with those developed by the generosity of nature in the tropical zone.

The main differences, however, between the inhabitants of different parts of the world are those based on race. South-Eastern Australia, Southern Europe, and subtropical America are generally alike in physical conditions; yet despite this similarity the Australian aborigines, the Europeans, and the American Indians have developed very different cultures.

The classification of mankind is difficult, owing to the prolonged intermixture of the different races and the lack of constant and reliable characteristics. Efforts have been made to classify mankind on the basis of language; but unwritten languages change rapidly, and nations often impose their own on aliens or adopt those of their conquerors.

Physical characters vary with change of climate and mode of life. Colour is the most conspicuous physical feature, but it is clearly inconstant; a race becomes fairer in complexion by dwelling higher above sea-level, and darker by exposure to the tropical sun. The skull, which affords the most precise basis for comparison, appears to be easily modified by a change in national food and mode of life. Probably the least variable and most reliable characteristic for the major divisions is the nature of the hair.

Mankind is divided into three primary sections: (1) the Caucasian, a name now used in a purely conventional sense for most of the people of Europe, Northern Africa, and South-Western Asia, and for the settlers of European race in America, Australia, and South Africa; (2) the Mongolian, including the people of Central and South-Eastern Asia, the aboriginal tribes of America, and some European immigrants, such as the Lapps and Hungarians; (3) the Negro, including the natives of most of Africa, the Papuans, and Melanesians of the Eastern Archipelago.

The Caucasians have long wavy to straight hair, which is oval in cross-section; the colour of the skin is fair in the Northern Caucasians, but varies through brown to black in some of the mixed races of the Sudan; the lower jaw is in general not protruding; the eyes are large and straight, and vary from blue to black.

The Mongolian is characterized by coarse, lank, straight, dull-black hair, which is circular in cross-section; the face is beardless; the characteristic colour is yellow, but is coppery in the 'Red Indian' of America; the jaw is of medium size; the cheek bones are high; the eyes are placed obliquely, are slit-like in form, and black in colour.

The negro is characterized by having short frizzly to woolly hair, which is flat in cross-section; the colour of the skin is from black to brown; the lower jaw is massive and strongly protruding; the nose is broad and flat, with widely-open nostrils; the eyes are large and black.

The skull in each of the divisions varies from long to broad.

The Caucasian section is the most varied of the three. Huxley subdivided it into two, the White Caucasian or Xanthochroi, and the Black Caucasian or Melanochroi. Of the White Caucasians the inhabitants of North-Western Europe are of especial importance, owing to their worldwide political and industrial influence; they include three chief races. Northern Europe was the home of the tall, flaxen-haired, blue-eyed Nordic race, of whom the purest representatives at the present time live in Scandinavia; other members of this race are the Teutons of Northern Germany, the ancient Caledonians of Northern Scotland, the Anglo-Saxons, and the Normans who migrated into the north of France from Scandinavia. From Southern Europe came the second race, the Mediterranean, which includes the Iberian or Celts who spread along the coasts of Western Europe in pre-historic times. They were short in stature, had long heads, and a dark complexion; they form the basis of the population of Portugal, Brittany, Cornwall, Wales, Ireland, and Western Scotland. Across Central Europe advanced the people of the Alpine race, who resembled those of the Mediterranean race in their short stature and dark complexion, but differed by being broad-headed. They entered from Asia, formed the basis of the Slav population of Eastern and Central Europe and of the East Prussians, and, spreading along the Alpine zone, occupied Switzerland, Southern Germany, Northern Italy, and Central France; and as the so-called Belgic tribes they formed the bulk of the population of England at the time of the Roman invasion.

The dark Caucasians, or Melanochroi, include the people of Southern Europe, the Semites of South-Western Asia, e.g. Jews and Arabs, the Hamites of North-Eastern Africa, such as the Egyptians, Somali, and Galla, and various mixed races due to intermarriage with negroes; most of the inhabitants of India; the Veddah of Ceylon; the Polynesian and Malay, and, therefore, also the people of Eastern Madagascar; also the aborigines of Australia, whose photographs, as has often been remarked, are strikingly similar to those of Europeans.

The typical Mongolians are the Chinese, Japanese, and Burmese; they include the Tartars, whose invasions as far west as Central Europe are marked by the occupation of part of the Danube basin by the Hungarians, and of parts of the Balkans by the Turks. A thousand years of European life has led to the Hungarian skull having become Europeanized, but the characteristic slit-like eye of the Mongolian is still conspicuous. Farther north, the westward advance of the Mongolians is represented by the presence of the Lapps, who have spread across Northern Russia into Northern Norway, and by the occupation of Finland by a Mongolo-Caucasian nation. Through North-Eastern Asia the Mongolians crossed to America, and the aboriginal people, or Indians, of both North and South America are a branch of the Mongolians.

The negro is the most distinct of the primary sections, and his distribution was the best defined. The original home of the negroes was probably in Africa, whence they spread to Western Madagascar, New Guinea or Papua, and the adjacent islands of Melanesia; thence in prehistoric times some members of this section spread southward to the east of Australia, and occupied Tasmania. The range of the negro has been extended in modern times by their introduction as slaves into America and South-Western Europe.

IX. The Centres of Population. Man doubtless at first lived in small family groups, which were widely scattered in order to draw on large areas for the scanty supplies of wild fruits and game. These families were in time forced to assemble in villages for protection against human enemies and wild animals. With the development of more civilized conditions, these village communities grew into towns in order to benefit by the specialized skill gained by workers in different industries, and for defence against robber gangs to whom the accumulated wealth was an attractive bait. As the towns increased in size, they and the land around them were organized into states, and towns especially favoured either by supplies of raw material or by position extended into cities.

As internal communications improved, still larger areas were politically united, and the increase of

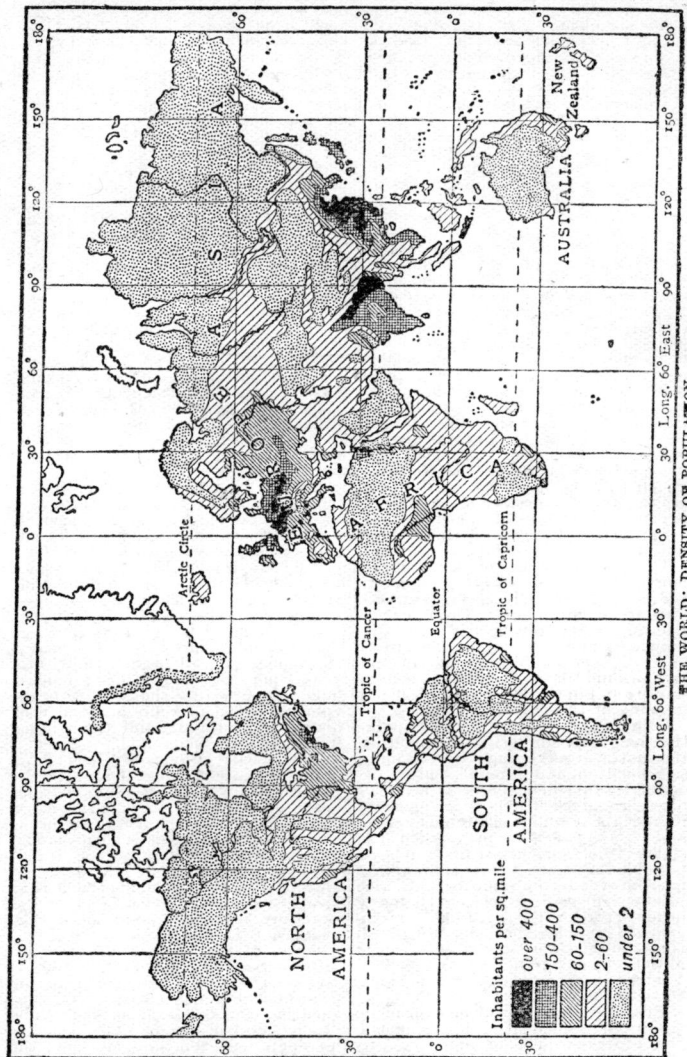

THE WORLD: DENSITY OF POPULATION

trade led to the development of some of the cities into large administrative capitals. For example, in England the original hamlets of hunters and fishermen developed into villages and small towns; with the Roman occupation the need for an administrative capital led to the growth of London, owing to its position at the first easy crossing of the Thames, and its accessibility by boat from the Continent and by road from all parts of England. London, therefore, became the most important political, commercial, and manufacturing centre.

Subsequently the transatlantic trade led to the growth of the western ports —Bristol for the south; Liverpool, which replaced Chester owing to the shallowness and shoaling of the Dee, for the Midlands; and Glasgow for Scotland. The abundant water-power in the Pennine valleys led to the settlement in western Yorkshire and Lancashire of the English textile industries, and subsequently the use of coal collected on or near the coal-fields all the chief iron-smelting and engineering works, the shipyards, and chemical and hardware factories. London continued to develop as the commercial capital, and as a great manufacturing city for the supply of the numerous requirements of a great administrative and world-trading centre.

The population of Great Britain is therefore densest around London and on the coal-fields. The concentration of the population near cheap coal and water transport is especially shown in Scotland, where the great bulk of the inhabitants live in the area around Glasgow, and each census shows a fall in the number of residents in some of the highland counties.

Throughout the world the population has been similarly controlled by the natural advantages of climate, soil, position, and mineral wealth. In countries in which man has retained his original conditions of nomad and hunter, the population remains sparse, and usually less than one to the square mile. Agriculture first rendered possible the aggregation of mankind into crowded communities. As rice produces more food per acre than any other crop, land suitable for its growth supports the densest agricultural populations, and vast areas of alluvial plains in China and North-Eastern India support over 400 people to the square mile.

Still denser segregations occur in the great industrial and administrative centres which are maintained by exchange of commodities or by commercial or political tribute from the scattered areas with which they trade or which they administer. Thus London, the greatest city in the world, derives its wealth and food from world-wide sources. New York, the second largest city, serves as the chief port and commercial centre of the United States. Chicago is another colossal city, due to the coming together of the routes from the central states to pass the southern projection of the great lakes, or to reach the southernmost great port on Lake Michigan.

A third type of concentration occurs on the coal-fields, which supply cheap power for the maintenance of many industries; they are usually distributed through numerous relatively small towns, which are maintained on the food received in exchange for their manufactures. Each of these three types of concentration has led to areas with populations of over 400 to the square mile. In areas of dense agricultural settlement the population is widespread, but they require markets and manufacturing centres.

The two countries with the densest industrial concentrations are England and Wales, with a population of 649 per square mile, and Belgium, which, owing to the wide distribution of its industries, has a population of 652 per square mile. In other states the population is most crowded in special areas, such as the Rhine Valley and Pennsylvania, owing to their prolific coal-fields; the north-western provinces of Italy, owing to the abundant water-power from the Alps; Bombay, where the cotton-mills are run by electricity generated by drainage from the adjacent mountains of the heavy monsoonal rainfall; and Java, with a dense population (675 per square mile) supported by the fertility of its volcanic soils, its abundant and well distributed rainfall, and the willing industry of its people.

The second grade of density of population, containing from 150 to 400 inhabitants to the square mile, is found chiefly in areas suitable for general agriculture, but for less intensive cultivation than the rice-lands. This grade covers most of India, Central China, and the Nile delta; in Europe it is found in Southern Germany and Austria, most of Italy, the north-west of Spain, Northern Portugal, and Eastern Ireland.

Areas of the third grade of population, that between 60 and 150 to the square mile, include most of the European Plain, exclusive of the industrial centres, such as the Rhine Valley, and of the capitals, such as Leningrad, Berlin, and Moscow; the agricultural districts of North Germany, of most of Central and Southern Russia, have populations of this grade, which is reached also by Southern

Sweden, owing to its sparse agricultural population being supplemented by those of the Baltic ports and of industrial towns maintained by the electric application of water-power. France, with the exception of the area around Paris, most of Spain, Hungary, and the Balkan Peninsula have the same density.

This division includes in America the Mississippi Valley and the country between it and the Atlantic coast; in Western America only California; in Central America, Southern Mexico and parts of some adjacent states, owing to the fertility of their well-watered soils; in South America some small areas near the capital cities, such as around Rio de Janeiro, the coastland along the estuary of the La Plata, parts of Chile, and of the Magdalena Valley in the Republic of Colombia.

In Africa this grade is represented by Natal, owing to the development of sugar and other plantations by coolie labour; by Abyssinia, which, owing to the numbers of its people and strength of their hill country, is the only strong independent state on the continent; also by the coastlands of the Gulf of Guinea, owing to the richness of their soil and the suitability of the crops produced there for development of the country by small holdings.

The areas which are least use to man and have less than two inhabitants to the square mile owe their sparse population to three chief causes. The severity of the winter in the northern plains restricts the population in Canada, Northern Europe, and Siberia. The opposite condition, the unmanageable exuberance of vegetation in the moist lowlands of the tropics, leads to the growth of impenetrable forest and jungle in which primitive people can live only as nomads and hunters, and thus causes the scanty population of the forests of the Amazon. The arid climate of the desert belt of the Old World, which extends across the Sahara, Arabia, and through Western Asia to Tibet and Mongolia, and the desert condition of some south central parts of South America restricts the population, owing to the scarcity and uncertainty of the rainfall and the consequently precarious condition of the food-supply. The term desert is often restricted to areas relatively unpeopled, owing to the arid climate; but the older use of the word applied it to areas with a population sparse due to excessive wetness or severe cold; thus Sir Walter Scott speaks of the deserts of the Grampians, and the Bible references to desert places are to sparsely populated country districts

in contrast to the villages and towns.

The great cities of the world include London, New York, and Chicago as the three greatest commercial centres; Paris and Berlin as the capitals of great European powers; Calcutta, Bombay, Canton, and Shanghai as the commercial centres of rich agricultural Asiatic areas; in the southern hemisphere the three greatest cities, Sydney, Melbourne, and Buenos Aires, are growing fast with the agricultural and pastoral development of Australia and the Argentine.

The rise of the great capital cities is primarily due to their natural advantages of situation; but they may be maintained after changed circumstances have removed their original advantages; for the obstinacy and ingenuity of man often override natural advantages and drawbacks, and from habit and sentiment maintain a great city after the conditions which nurtured it have passed away. Countries do not always develop along the natural lines of progress; for "that Nature proposes and the resolution of man disposes is a fundamental principle in the study of applied geography."—BIBLIOGRAPHY: H. R. Mill, *The International Geography*; Stanford, *Compendium of Geography*; H. J. Mackinder, *Britain and the British Seas*; J. W. Gregory, *Geography: Structural, Physical, and Comparative*; J. Murray and J. Hjort, *The Depths of the Ocean*; C. R. Beazley, *The Dawn of Modern Geography*; G. G. Chisholm, *Commercial Geography*; J. M'Farlane, *Economic Geography*; A. Stephens, *Applied Geography*; J. Bartholomew, *Atlas of Meteorology, Atlas of Zoogeography*.

GEOK TEPE, a town and fortress of Central Asia, oasis of the Akhal-Tekke-Turkomans, long. 58° E., lat. 38° N. In 1879 the Russians under General Lomakine were defeated here with heavy loss, but in Jan., 1881, it was stormed by General Skobelev after a three weeks' siege, when about 8,000 fugitives were massacred, no quarter being given.

GEOLOGY (Gr. *gē*, the earth, and *logos*, a reasoned description) is the science concerned with the investigation of the structure and the past history of the earth, and of the causes that have brought about its present surface-features. The relation of these features to the life of man may be left to the domain of geography, and the origin of the earth among other bodies in the universe to cosmogony, a subject that links geology with astronomy. The older geologists, in days when speculation went far beyond patient observation, were much at-

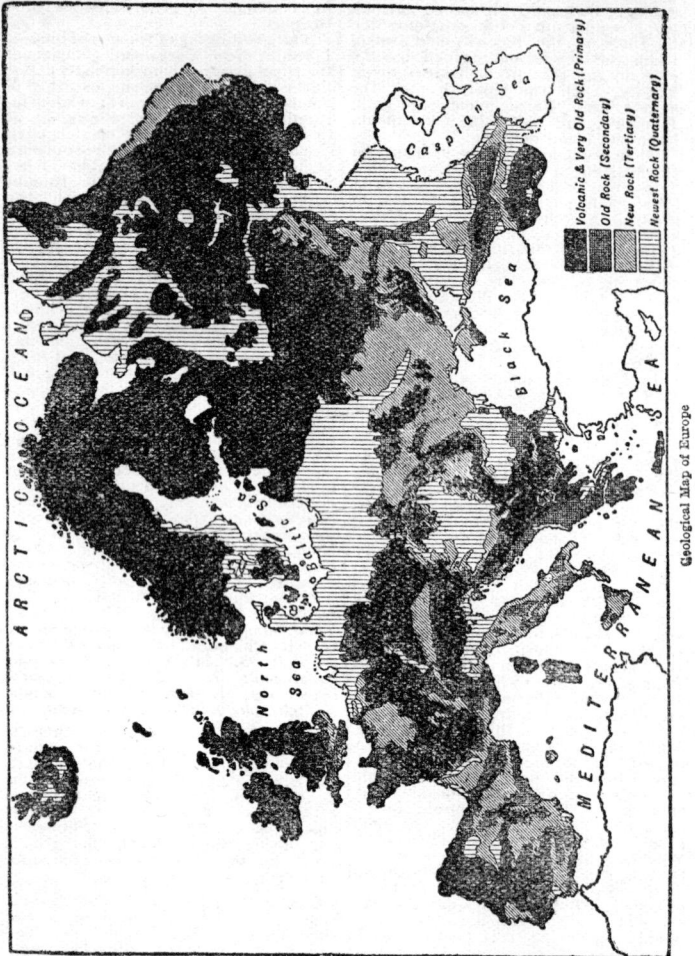

Geological Map of Europe

tracted by cosmogony; and there is no doubt that any sound theory of planetary growth must be based on a knowledge not only of dynamical laws, but also of the mineral constitution of the globe. So large a volume of the globe, however, lies beyond the sphere of direct observation that the modern geologist contents himself with the ample field afforded by its outer skin or 'crust.'

The crust of the earth may be defined as the region whose materials may be actually handled. Deep borings and mines provide vertical sections extending for little more than one mile of the four thousand that separate us from the centre of the earth; but the movements that have taken place in past times, and that are still in progress in the outer layers, have brought rocks from far greater depths within the reach of man. Some of the masses thus rendered accessible may at one time have lain fifteen or twenty miles below the surface.

The dawn of geological thought was no doubt stimulated by the activity of volcanoes, which were held to be a manifestation of internal fires fanned by subterranean wind. A wider field was opened by the observation of deposits containing marine shell far removed from the present margins of the sea. Xenophanes, a philosopher of the sixth century B.C., is credited by later writers with the assertion that these occurrences were due to an elevation of the ocean bed; and the fact that areas of sea and land had changed places was generally admitted by the naturalists of Græco-Roman schools.

The literal interpretation of the Hebrew book of *Genesis* led to more restricted views, and marine fossils came to be regarded either as proofs of the Noachian deluge or as imitations of organic forms by some inherent moulding force within the earth. The revival of scientific thought during the Renaissance in the sixteenth century encouraged observation of the rocks themselves, and in Italy the marbles of the Alpine foot-hills, and the unconsolidated but uplifted strata on the fringes of the Apennines, alike provided material for writers whose devoutness could not be called in question. For three more centuries, however, the changes in the relations of land and water were generally attributed, with Burnet, to violent convulsions, rather than, with Aristotle, to processes that went on slowly in comparison with the span of human life.

The spectacle of an Alpine valley, with the edges of similar strata revealed on its precipitous and opposing walls, the huge blocks flung down into the ravine from cliffs that lie two miles apart upon the sky-line, the insignificance of the torrent that strives to find a way between them, these features suggested a catastrophic rifting of the earth. The magnitude of modern landslides seemed to provide local illustrations of a time when destructive forces prevailed over those that mould and beautify the surface; the terrors of earthquakes in populous districts led to a belief in cataclysms that might have destroyed all life upon the globe. Abrupt obliteration and reconstruction seemed more in keeping with creative powers than an orderly process continued through immeasurable time; and when James Hutton, the Scottish philosopher, wrote his *Theory of the Earth* in 1785, his views were keenly contested even by his scientific colleagues.

Hutton urged the immense importance of the factor of time in allowing comparatively small forces to modify profoundly the surface-features of the earth. The swirl of a river may carve out a resonant ravine; the wash of rain may prevail against a range of crystalline rocks; the battery of the sea may work its way across a continent. The agents now in action tend to reduce the land areas to the level of the sea; but the products of decay accumulate in the ocean basins and form the substance of new continents. The planing down of one area is followed or accompanied by the upheaval of another, so that the balance of nature is preserved and homes are continuously provided for living things.

Hutton argued that subterranean heat, on which he laid somewhat undue stress, is the cause of the consolidation of the sediments that are washed down from the land, and also of their ultimate upheaval. Primitive masses, such as granite, are brought up in the rising region, and some of this granite is molten and penetrates rocks of younger origin. This cycle of decay and reconstruction is repeated in the long history of the earth, and Hutton in consequence led the geologist away from speculations on cosmogony. Geology by itself gave no evidence of a beginning and no prospect of an end.

Though for a time the exponents of creative methods felt a certain disappointment in being called back to the realms of observation, the arguments of Hutton formed the basis of the science of geology. They were expounded by his associate John Playfair, and expanded by Charles Lyell in his *Principles of Geology: being an attempt to explain the former changes of the earth's surface by reference to causes now in operation* (vol i, 1830). Contemporaneously, C. E. A. von Hoff, in Germany, maintained similar views in the face of considerable opposition.

Meanwhile, William Smith had made one of the most far-reaching advances in the realm of science by showing, in his *Strata Identified by Organized Fossils* (1816), that the types of organisms entombed in rocks had varied by a regular sequence in geological time. Each fauna and flora was still generally held to be a special creation, suited to the times when it arose; but the similarity of the later faunas to that now prevalent on the earth, and the absolute extinction of many of the older forms, soon impressed itself on those who took up the growing science of *palæontology*. An immensely wider interest was now attached to fossil organisms, and the way was open for the reception of a rational doctrine of descent.

Lyell, aided by the careful determinations of French and Italian colleagues, classified the more recent geological formations by the proportion of modern molluscan species that they contained. He was always ready to emphasize the imperfection of the record, and he pointed out the liability of the remains of mammals, birds, and land-animals in general to destruction; the rapid spread of *stratigraphical geology* in all parts of the earth confirmed the justice of his methods, and extended them to the whole history of living things. 'Geognostic' or mineral considerations no longer weighed with the stratigrapher. A study of the superposition of strata had revealed the true importance of their organic contents.

Petrology, the science of rock-constitution and rock-origins, became for a time dwarfed by what may

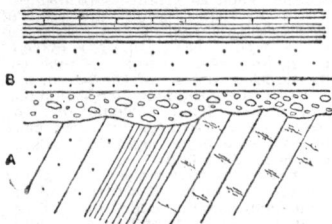

Unconformable Strata

be called 'historical geology, and the problems presented by the crystalline and highly-altered masses underlying the first fossiliferous strata were left for a future generation.

Stratigraphical Geology. Palæontologists soon observed that the change from the older to the newer faunas was more gradual than was at first supposed. Though breaks of great importance might occur in any one locality, yet these could be filled by the study of strata that had been deposited in some other region. The breaks were seen to be due to a local change of conditions, whereby land had been formed, its surface had been denuded, and a long period had elapsed before a new deposition could take place. Commonly in such cases the older series of strata are uptilted and folded, and the later series have been laid down across their denuded edges. Such a stratigraphical discordance is styled an *unconformity*. The time-interval represented by it may be enormous; but it does not record a general 'revolution of the globe.'

The publication of Charles Darwin's *Origin of Species* in 1859 gave a new meaning to palæontology, and a new incentive to the discovery of faunas and floras that might reduce the imperfection of the record. The establishment of a cause for the variation of species, though it did not pretend to explain the vital force behind the variation, destroyed the individual importance of specific forms, and directed attention to descent. The pursuit of fossils was turned in a vertical direction across the horizons so well traced by William Smith. The extinct mammals of the Paris basin, reconstructed by Georges Cuvier, the fishes so systematically studied by L. J. R. Agassiz, the shell-bearing cephalopods of L. von Buch, and the wealth of corals unfolded by Milne-Edwards and Haime, alike gained significance as parts of an impressive chain of animal forms. Though many of the variations, many of the by-ways, as it were, led ultimately to extinction, the minds of geologists were speedily captured by the sublimity of the sequence as a whole.

The search for the earliest forms of living things received a new stimulus; but it now seems that this search can never be rewarded. The preservation of animals or plants as fossils depends almost entirely on the possession of parts that can be mineralized or can resist decay. In exceptional circumstances moulds of soft-bodied creatures may remain, and casts of the digestive cavities of jelly-fish have been traced even in the earliest Cambrian strata; but beneath these strata very scanty relics, such as those found in Montana, fragments of crustacean carapaces, the tracks of worms, and a few traces of marine shells, alone testify to a fauna that already included a wide diversity of types. Beyond this, soft-bodied creatures, without protective covering, may have existed through æons of earth-history.

Eozoon canadense, described by J. Dawson in 1864 as a giant foraminifer from pre-Cambrian rocks, has proved to be a banded mineral structure, and palæontologists find no sure ground for study until the Olenellus-beds of the Cambrian system reveal a rich variety of invertebrate forms.

Following the principles of William Smith, geologists have divided the long range of fossiliferous rocks into *systems*, each system corresponding to a *period* of time bearing the same name. R. J. Murchison, by his work on *The Silurian System* (1839), familiarized this nomenclature at an early date. Adam Sedgwick was investigating contemporaneously what he styled Cambrian strata in North Wales, and these two names will serve as examples of the way in which the terminology of the systems grew.

The Silurian rocks are well revealed the earth; but the closing of the Cainozoic era with the Pliocene system, though dating back to Lyell, seems a matter of sentiment rather than of logic or convenience.

Details of the systems will be found under their separate names in this

Succession and General Arrangement of Strata in Wales and part of England
1, Cambrian and Ordovician. 2, Silurian. 3, Old Red Sandstone (Devonian). 4, Carboniferous Limestone (Carboniferous). 5, Coal Measures (Carboniferous). 6, Permian. 7, New Red Marl and Sandstone (Trias). 8, Lias. 9, Oolite. 10, Chalk, etc. (Cretaceous). 11, London Clay, etc. (Tertiary)

in the region once inhabited by the Silures; Cambria was the classic name for Wales. Other systems, such as the Carboniferous and the Cretaceous, were named less wisely from some prevalent type of rock. Charles Lyell found that he had a free hand with the later systems (*Principles of Geology*, vol iii, 1833), and he divided them according to the degree of resemblance of their molluscan species to those of recent seas. Hence each of the names terminates in 'cene,' anglicized from the Gr. *kainos*, recent. The group including these systems is, however, spelt more correctly 'Caino-zoic.'

The stratigraphical systems are marked by changes in the general fauna, and sometimes their establishment within certain limits has been influenced by the occurrence of an unconformity or a change in the type of deposit in the locality where the strata first received particular attention. The periods resemble those named in history after dynasties of kings, and by no means represent equal intervals of time. It has been convenient to bring them into five great 'eras,' each corresponding to a 'group' of systems, and named from the degree of approximation of the general fauna to that prevalent at the present day. The term Azoic, 'devoid of life,' has been used for the earliest rock-masses of the crust; but it is not safe to apply such a term to any stratified series. Archæan, implying high antiquity, has been used for rocks older than the Cambrian period, and has also been limited to the earlier section of these rocks.

Perhaps the name Proterozoic is that which is most applicable to fossiliferous or possibly-fossiliferous pre-Cambrian strata. Then follows the Palæozoic or 'old life' group; then Mesozoic or 'middle life'; then Cainozoic or 'recent life.' Many authors prefer to start a fifth era, the Quaternary (the Ger. *Quartär* is more correct), for the beds formed since reasoning man (*Homo sapiens*) appeared upon

Encyclopedia; but a general table may well be given here.

GROUP AND ERA.	SYSTEM AND PERIOD.
Quaternary.	Recent.
	Pleistocene.
Cainozoic or Tertiary.	Pliocene.
	Miocene.
	Oligocene.
	Eocene.
Mesozoic.	Cretaceous.
	Jurassic (sometimes divided in England into Oolitic and Liassic).
	Trias.
Palæozoic (newer sub-group).	Permian.
	Carboniferous.
	Devonian.
Palæozoic (older sub-group).	Gotlandian (or Silurian as now generally restricted).
	Ordovician (formerly Lower Silurian).
	Cambrian.
Proterozoic or pre-Cambrian.	(In the absence of satisfactory faunas, not divisible into systems.)

The subdivision of the systems and periods into *series* and *epochs*, and of these into *stages* (Fr. *étage*) and *ages*, can be effected locally, and it must be remembered that a marine stage in one country may be usefully represented by a freshwater or terrestrial in another.

Evidences as to changes of climate in past times are abundantly furnished by the study of strata. In this matter the rocks themselves are more convincing than the characters of the fauna, and the petrologist is here called to the aid of the stratigrapher. For instance, the gypsum and rock-salt beds of the British Trias indicate a region of desiccating lakes, and a granite surface etched by the sand-blasts of the desert has been unearthed at Charnwood Forest. The 'millet-seed' sands of Lancashire and Cheshire show how the grains were rounded by wind-action, that is, by more frequent contact than occurs in water on a shore. The red iron hydroxide that colours many strata suggests a lacustrine or terrestrial origin; and the 'lateritic' zone in the basaltic series of North-Eastern Ireland, where aluminium hydroxide takes the place of the ordinary hydrous silicate kaolin as a product of rock-weathering in Oligocene times, shows that this weathering took place under conditions now prevailing in the tropics.

During some epochs the fossil floras suggest that the climate over the whole earth was more uniform than now, and this point has often been raised in connection with the rapid spread and luxuriance of the Carboniferous forests. But it is probable that at all times the tilting of the earth's axis rendered the polar regions cooler than those nearer to the equator, and that the apparent uniformity of temperature was due to a general rise over the whole earth.

A general cooling, on the other hand, is evidenced by the occurrence of *glacial epochs*, the lacustrine and terrestrial strata of which are boulder-clays, or their ancient consolidated representatives 'tillites.' The stones in these show characteristically smoothed and scratched surfaces, owing to their inclusion in moving glacier-ice. The rock-floor beneath these beds, whether the quartzite under the post-Pliocene boulder-clays of Connemara, or the dolerite under the Permian 'tillite' of the Cape Province, is frequently scored and polished and mamillated by the passage of ice-sheets over what was then the surface of the land. The occurrence of such evidence in the Permian strata of the tropics, coupled with the great extension of Himalayan and Andean glaciers during the post-Pliocene ice-age, shows that the refrigeration was by no means confined to polar regions. Many causes have been suggested for these world-wide climatic changes, and they form one of the most interesting subjects placed before the stratigraphical geologist.

Petrology. The scientific description of rocks grew naturally out of the study of their mineral constituents, and this branch of geology, as its name suggests, has sometimes assumed the character of a separate science. It was largely developed by the treatises of mineralogists, notably by R. J. Haüy (1801 and 1822) and Alex. Brongniart (1813 and 1827). A. G. Werner, professor at the School of Mines in Freiberg, Saxony, from 1775 to 1817, was inspiring as a mineralogist, but exercised a retarding influence on geology by his views on the nature of what are now known as igneous rocks. His own pupil, however, L. von Buch, was one of those who, by travel and field-observation, acquired and spread sound views of rock-origins and rock-relations.

The discovery by James Hutton, in Glen Tilt in 1785, of the intrusive character of granite put an end to the idea that rocks formed of crystalline silicates were necessarily older than all others in the district where they happened to occur. It became clear that, while such rocks consolidate far down within the crust, they may represent material molten during any geological period.

Independently of the cycle traced by Hutton, it was obvious that rocks could be broadly divided into (1) those once molten (*igneous*); (2) those formed by the deposition of the products of rock-decay and denudation (*sedimentary*, with a subdivision called *aqueous*, for rocks deposited in water); and (3) those in which considerable changes in structure, and often in mineral character, have taken place under earth-heat or earth-stresses or both. This third class is styled *metamorphic*.

If the earth was once molten as a whole, the igneous rocks form a primary and fundamental series, from which all others have been derived. Their manifestations in upper regions of the crust are due to their ascent into cracks or domes formed respectively by crust-torsion or folding, and this ascent may be due to the expansion of the gases that they contain, as well as to pressures exerted on the liquid stratum of which they form a part. As they rise, saturated with gases in an intensely-heated state, they may melt up considerable masses of the covering rocks, 'stopping' off abundant blocks by intruding into the cracks between them, and absorbing them as they sink into the depths. The cauldron containing the molten matter thus enlarges; if cracks open from it to the surface, volcanoes may arise, and these are largely hydrothermal phenomena—the upwelling of *lava* and the explosive action that gives rise to *tuffs* and comminuted *volcanic dust* are mostly the result of the expansion and passage into steam of the water previously confined in the igneous mass. Much of the dust, however, arises from the friction of coarser material in the air. Igneous rocks, then, are, after all, hot silicate solutions; but they are not, as Werner taught, laid down as sediments from the sea.

The age of an igneous rock is that

of its last consolidation; it is clearly younger than the rocks into which it has intruded, forming in their cracks wall-like sheets or *dykes*; on the other hand, pebbles from it may be found in some overlying stratum. Maximum and minimum ages can be thus assigned to it. If it is obviously a lava-flow, its age is that of the beds associated with it. The material of the lava may represent primitive matter in the lower regions of the crust; but neither the lava nor intrusive granite can be called a primitive rock.

In a masterly treatise, T. C. Chamberlin (*The Origin of the Earth*, 1916) has viewed the earth as formed of 'planetesimal' bodies aggregated in a solid form from space, and subsequently melted locally by heat developed during the contraction of the sphere, and by the accumulation of radio-active bodies near the surface. The differentiation of the more highly siliceous crust from a core consisting largely of iron alloyed with nickel went on slowly, and the igneous stratum that appears to underlie the crust may be the product of melting at a comparatively late epoch in the consolidation of the earth.

R. A. Daly, on the other hand (*The Planetesimal Hypothesis*, in *Science Monthly*, 1920), maintains the general view that the earth was at one time molten as a whole, and that the igneous rocks rich in silica, such as granites, originated by gravitational separation towards the surface, while those less rich in silica, such as gabbros and basalts, now rise through them from considerable depths. None the less, remeltings must occur, and granites and highly crystalline rocks in general can no longer be regarded as necessarily very old.

In spite of artificial divisions that were at one time made on the continent of Europe between igneous rocks of Cainozoic and pre-Cainozoic age, we cannot trace any variation in the types of matter intruded or extruded since Proterozoic times. Any evolution that went on in the history of the molten mass of the earth occurred in the earliest ages. Within a deep-seated cauldron, however, various causes may bring about considerable mineral differentiation, and the tapping of the cauldron at one level or another may control the type of lava extruded at the surface.

Metamorphic rocks offer greater problems and present far wider variations. Some of the foliated masses known as *schists* are clearly sediments in which the minerals have developed along the bedding-planes under the influence of hot vapours streaming from some mass of igneous rock. In other cases, the intrusion of igneous matter along the bedding-planes, *lit par lit*, as French geologists have shown us, has produced a composite rock indistinguishable from the *banded gneisses* that were once regarded as a primordial type of sediment. Most schists, however, show signs of earth-pressure, and in some cases the essential structure, the foliation, whereby the minerals come to lie in planes parallel with one another, runs across indications of original bedding. Some of the felspathic and coarser metamorphic rocks, the *gneisses*, are clearly granitoid masses that have been partly crushed and caused to assume a solid flow.

Again and again, however, the pressure-schists may be traced into normal sedimentary series, or are associated with sedimentary bands that were incapable of assuming a schistose structure; while numerous areas of gneiss, once regarded as exposures of the primitive crust, have been found to display composite features. A. Lawson thus showed in 1887 that the 'Laurentian' granitoid rocks of Rainy Lake, in the pre-Cambrian region of Western Ontario, are intrusive in a schistose series, and the oldest rocks of Canada are now recognized, not in the Laurentian gneisses, but in the sedimentary Grenville beds.

In region after region, from N. America to Finland, S. Africa, or Mysore, the foliated gneisses, long deemed to be fundamental, have been found to result from injection of igneous matter into some still older series. The foundation-stones of the accessible crusts are sediments, and were formed by processes of denudation. Despite of all attempts to cast aside a rigid 'uniformitarian' dogma, the teaching of Hutton remains paramount—as far back as we can penetrate into the history of rocks, the processes that controlled their formation are those in operation at the present day.

Petrology, then, reveals no inspiring sequence corresponding to that of stratigraphical geology; but its study offers great attractions from the mineral and chemical point of view. P. L. A. Cordier in 1815, by examining the powdered rock with a microscope, proved that the apparently homogeneous ground of basalt was composed of minerals similar to those determinable in the rock-mass with the naked eye. C. G. Ehrenberg in 1839 prepared translucent sections of flints and limestones for his researches on minute organisms. A. Delesse applied the microscope with much success to the study of polished surfaces of igneous rocks. But it was not until H. C. Sorby in England in 1850 appreciated the value of thin sections that microscopical petrography began to enter on its ever-widening course.

Sorby's methods were adopted by F. Zirkel and H. Rosenbusch in Germany, and by F. Fouqué and Michel Lévy in France, and the observations of early workers in physics on the behaviour of minerals in polarized light were now utilized with great refinement for the determination of minute crystals in rocks. At the same time, the structures of rocks, and especially those due to various phases of cooling and to metamorphic deformation, became apparent with a delicacy that was regarded as almost finical by conservative workers in the field. Every geologist nowadays utilizes thin sections to fill in the details of his study of the ground itself, and microscopical observations go far in explaining the relative resistance of rocks to decay, and thus have a bearing even on large features of the landscape.

Micropetrology in itself is a fascinating pursuit, and has greatly extended our knowledge of the characters of mineral species. As examples of its applications to geological philosophy, three finely-illustrated and pioneer works may be cited: F. Zirkel, *Microscopical Petrography* (*United States Geological Survey of the 40th Parallel*, 1877); Fouqué and Lévy, *Minéralogie micrographique* (1879); and J. J. H. Teall, *British Petrography* (1888).

Petrology involves a study of some of the grandest geological processes. The description of an igneous rock means little unless we view it as giving off its long-imprisoned gases in the crater of a volcano; or moving slowly down some slope, already devastated by centuries of outpouring, until the mesh of microscopic crystals gathers, at an appointed temperature, from the glass; or, again, as a reminder of the mobile matter beneath the solid crust, softening the strata until they yield and crumple, corroding them in the triumph of its advance, and then by slow consolidation in some cauldron of the earth, fashioning the dominant masses of a future mountain-chain.

Sedimentary rocks are often looked on coldly, except from an economic point of view; but conglomerates suggest the rush of torrents, and the sudden floods that build up the plain with the detritus of parched and barren hills. Marine sediments mark ancient shore-lines, and their constituents provide a clue to the nature of the adjacent land. The irregular bedding of sandstones may suggest the wash of currents, and the nature of their cement may explain their jutting scarps along the hills. Lime-stones picture the sunlit surf on coral beaches, or the chill depths where white ooze gathers from a rain of protozoan shells. The soils, too long neglected, take their place as sedimentary rocks, and present all manner of physical and chemical problems, as we trace back the rich loams of the farm-lands to the crumbling surface of decay upon the moors.

Metamorphic rocks bring the geologist into near touch with the movements of underworld, and the ovoid forms of crystals in a gneiss, surrounded by aureoles of dust worn from them, connect a thin section occupying four square centimetres with immeasurable regions of unrest and reconstruction.

Structural Geology. The 'tectonics' of the earth have long appealed to miners, who are called on to trace valuable veins or deposits through a tangle of folds and across dislocating planes of fracture. The dislocations or *faults* probably drew early attention to the magnitude of earth-movements, and every gradation is now known, from those sometimes seen in slates, where the vertical shift of the beds may be a fraction of an inch, to those the 'throw' of which is measurable in miles.

The fracture of strata is connected with tension or compression; the latter produces an over-riding of a bed by others from a lower series. The tilting of beds was recognized as a sign of earth-movement by N. Steno in 1668. The instability of the crust has always been apparent through the occurrence of the tremors known as earthquakes; and in some cases these are accompanied by faulting visible at the surface. As C. Darwin noticed long ago, on the western coast of South America, large earth-movements may represent the sum of a number of successive steps. In 1899 the shore of Yakutat Bay in Alaska was raised by nearly 50 feet. Recent observations in the coral-reef region of the Pacific tend to show that an ocean-floor sinks by breakin into blocks rather than by sagging downwards as a whole, and E. Suess has invoked faulting to account for upstanding masses, or *horsts*, which, in his view, owe their pre-eminence to the falling in of areas round them.

Movements of the crust are commonly accompanied by compression in certain regions, and by considerable crumpling of the stratified rocks involved. Linear mountain-chains, even when they resemble long arches, are the sum of numerous and complicated folds. The bending of strata into ridges, known as *anticlines*, and downbent basins known as *synclines*, is frequently revealed in quarry-sections.

An anticline is an elongated dome; a syncline is a spoon-shaped downfold; and in a contorted region the sloping wall of an anticline is of course also that of the adjacent syncline. The tilted stratum is said to *dip* at such and such an angle to the horizon, and the direction of a horizontal line drawn on the surface of a bed is that of the general run or *strike* of the uptilted strata across the country. The strike of the gently-dipping Jurassic and Cretaceous systems in Central England is seen in the general direction of the escarpments of the Cotswold and the Chiltern Hills. In a crumpled district, dip and strike show marked variations in short distances; but even here the direction of the strike is a far more constant feature than the angle of the dip. There is a linear element in folded mountains that suggests a connection with potential lines of fracture in the crust.

A series of anticlines may become pushed from one side and overfolded, until their limbs come to dip in the same direction. Further movement may force them over on one another, so that they resemble almost horizontal sheets. In these *recumbent folds* the succession of strata of course becomes reversed in the lower limbs of the anticlines, which are also the upper limbs of the synclines; careful mapping, and the sections seen on great valley-walls, alone enable the geologist to realize the true relations. An overfold may part in the middle, and its upper limb may progress along a *thrust-plane*, a fault of low angle to the horizon, until rock-masses are imported into a district ten or twenty miles from their place of origin. By successive overfolding and thrust-movement one sheet may follow on another.

The study of the Alpine chains that were formed in Europe at the close of Miocene times has shown impressively how the final movements may be regarded as gravitational, the upthrust masses falling forward upon younger and more yielding strata like the front of a breaking wave. The noses of the over-folded anticlines thus come to rest in a synclinal attitude among series that they have penetrated and displaced. Schardt, Bertrand, Termier, and Uhlig are among those who have developed these newer views of mountain-structure.

A classic instance of the potency of thrust-planes occurs in northwestern Scotland, where the pre-Cambrian 'eastern gneiss' has been piled upon fossiliferous strata now known to be of Cambrian age. The correct reading of the district was given by James Nicol as far back as 1856; but it required the detailed mapping of C. Lapworth in 1883 to convince geologists that a reversal had taken place in what seemed to be an orderly succession.

The doctrine of *isostasy*, put forward by Pratt in India and by Hayford in the United States, implies a general maintenance of equilibrium from the time that continents and oceans were established in Proterozoic times. Determinations of gravity with the pendulum show a gravity-excess beneath the oceans and a gravity-defect beneath uplifted masses of the land. It is inferred that the roots of mountains are formed of relatively light material, like that which is common at the surface, while denser matter has gathered beneath the ocean-floors. Hence a continent is maintained above the general level by lateral pressure underground. It floats in denser matter which its root-region has displaced. Denudation, however, carries matter, both in suspension and solution, from the continent to the ocean, and the lightened continent rises until the isostatic balance is restored.

On this reasoning, elevated tracts are perpetuated; but we receive no help towards a rational theory of their origin. The movement of the outer crust has been generally ascribed to the contraction of the earth's interior and to the existence of a heated and mobile under-layer. It is probable, as O. Ampferer has urged, that weakenings of the crust by local meltings, and dragging movements in the under-layer, are responsible for ridging and overfolding at the surface.

Geosynclines, great downward saggings, in which for long ages marine deposits have accumulated, often seem to have preceded *geanticlines*, or great upward bulgings, and this fact has led to theories of expansion by heating and increase in bulk by the injection of lava into clefts. No general relation, however, can yet be traced between folded chains and the regions in which they now occur. We still await an answer from the underworld.

Structural geology, then, brings us into touch with the large and lasting problems of the inanimate yet restless earth. We realize them when a wave flows in across the denuded edges of upturned limestone on a shore, or when we trace in a worn and hummocked lowland the intrusions of granite into schists, the processes of absorption and reconstruction, that mark the unstable base of a long-lost mountain-chain. The waste of the continents, by rain and rivers, by frost and glacial scour, is but a step in the process by which new continents are reared.

Palæontology. The study of fossil remains is a branch of zoology and also of botany; but the biologist must bring to the work some knowledge of petrology, and of the fundamental facts by which we ascertain that one stratum is older than another. Despite the succession of faunas established by William Smith, the relative ages of stratified rocks cannot be proved by the arrangement of specimens in a supposed genetic sequence. As the literature of the Cambrian faunas in America shows, the hard facts of succession must be worked out in the field. But the palæontologist may justly claim that he has linked the strata one to another by a chain that

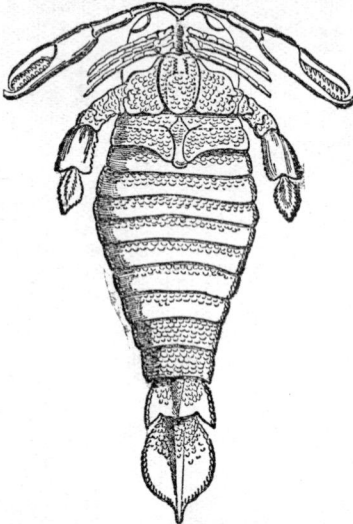

A Eurypterid (much reduced)

emerges from the unknown past and leads onward to the unknown future, the golden chain of life.

This chain, like a rosary, has beads on it recording great and salient things; but it is not closed, and its two ends can never meet. We look back to the Cambrian period, and see a world in which primitive crustacea already existed, in which corals, brachiopods, and even specialized molluscs inhabited the sea, but in which browsing trilobites were the dominant forms of life. Olenellus of the Lower Cambrian is about a decimetre long; Paradoxides of the Middle Cambrian measures at times 6 decimetres, say 2 feet. These were the largest animals of higher organization than the worms.

The trilobites show in Ordovician times a rich variety that indicates a corresponding natural enterprise and vitality; but in the succeeding Gotlandian (Silurian) period their supremacy was threatened by great arachnids, the eurypterida, marine allies of the scorpions, while scorpions and even beetles appear upon the land. The limbs of the eurypterida are specialized in certain genera, not only as strong swimming paddles, but as deadly claws for securing prey. Side by side with them fishes appear, the first recorded vertebrates, many of them so quaint in type that a separate class has been proposed for them. Others lead onward to the sharks, a type so strong and so well armed that, with all its primitive skeletal features, it persists as the tyrant group of fishes in the seas to-day.

The occurrence in the northern hemisphere during Devonian times of a continental (Old Red Sandstone) type of deposit as well as marine strata enables us to know something of the nature of life upon the land. The flora of primitive forest types, ancestors of many lines of vegetation that have since become specialized and divergent, indicates how plants as well as animals have moved onwards in a continuous chain of life. Fishes, in some cases protected by an armour of interlocked bony plates, in others bold and aggressive, and attaining a length of 30 feet, dominated the lakes and seas. Dipterus, a lung-fish, suggests the possibility of vertebrates taking to the land, and footprints in the Old Red Sandstone of Connecticut probably record the first amphibians.

The amphibia head the vertebrate series in the Carboniferous period, moving amid the swamps and forests that laid the foundations of so many industries throughout the world; but in the Permian of Texas, Russia, and South Africa reptiles of varied types appear. The 'theromorphs' among them, like the calamites among Carboniferous trees, bear in their structures the promise of far higher things. No modern reptile possesses the variety of teeth or the mammalian resemblances in skeletal details that occur in these transitional Permian forms. Both the amphibians and the reptiles adopted a bipedal attitude; they had no competitors, and could look out proudly on the world. The dinosaurs developed in the Trias, side by side with small mammals of humble and marsupial type. Tritylodon of South Africa seems to link the reptiles and the mammals. Throughout the whole Mesozoic era the mammals may have been cultivating craft and cunning, family devotion and the arts of self-preservation, but no prospect opened of their ever becoming the culminating race. The reptiles took to the ocean as swimming saurians 50 feet in length; they swept through the air on wings supported by an extended finger of the hand; in bulky and often well-armoured forms they tramped about the land, at times 100 feet long and in many genera standing erect, assisted by their massive tails. Light forms lived in the trees, perhaps for safety, and from these, in Upper Jurassic times, the feathered race of birds arose, toothed like the reptiles, their bodies naked, far as yet from the strength of the eagle, nesting amid crag and cloud, and farther still from the fairy gleam of the humming-birds that suck the flowers.

In Cretaceous times swimming birds existed; but the pterosaurs, the flying reptiles, still held the kingdom of the air, while the dinosaurs showed no diminution in variety and vigour on the land. Our modern type of flora, with familiar genera of flowering trees, arose in the middle of the period.

And then, probably swept by some wind-borne or insect-borne bacterial disease, the whole empire of the reptiles crumbled. The mammals, that had been so long kept under, became heirs of land and water, and even, as delicate bats, essayed the air. The unspecialized Phenacodus of the Eocene leads on to the tapir, the rhinoceros, and the horse. Eocene whales are known, and lemurs foreshadow the ingenious race of apes. Though remains are scanty, the line of the primates hereafter forms one of the main attractions of palæontology. Pliopithecus of the Miocene is a gibbon; Pithecanthropus of the Pliocene is either an erect gibbon or a man. The oldest fossil attributable with certainty to man is the chinless jaw found near Heidelberg, deeply covered by Glacial deposits with remains of extinct mammalia. It has an important rival in Eoanthropus of the Piltdown gravels in Sussex, found in 1911.

The spread of man was checked by the cold Glacial epoch of post-Pliocene times, and the climatic concentration of the human race may have led in some degree to social intercourse and to the more rapid development of the crowning acquisition, speech. Here the domain of palæontology closes, with brain-convolution dominant, and mere bulk vanquished in the fray. The future is yet for history to write, the history of this small upright mammal, now atavistically preying on his fellows like a rat, and now of so divine an apprehension that he would make the whole world round him a land of heart's desire. Geology, then, the science of the earth, links the growth and moulding of the globe with the great mystery of the origin and chain of life in time. It underlies all natural history, and leads from the strictly controlled field of mineral architecture to that of man's response to conscience, which is self-control.–BIBLIOGRAPHY: A. Geikie, *Text-book of Geology*, and *The Founders of Geology*; Professor Gregory, *Primer of Geology*; E. Haug,

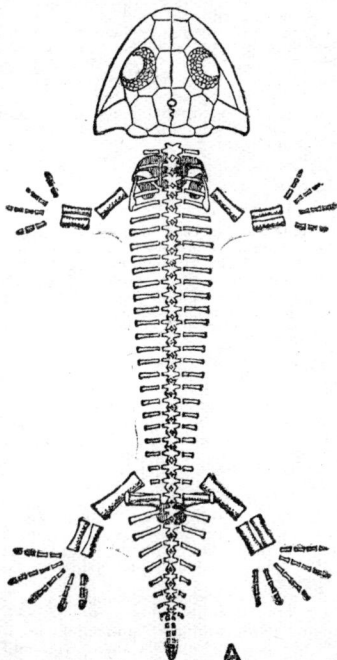

A Branchiosaur (restored). An amphibian of the Carboniferous period}

Traité de Géologie; C. Lyell, *Principles of Geology*; E. Suess, *Das Antlitz der Erde* (preferably in the annotated and illustrated French edition, *La Face de la Terre*); K. A. von Zittel, *History of Geology and Palæontology*, and *Handbuch der Palæontologie*; A. C. Seward, *Fossil Plants*.

GEOMETRICAL DECORATED, in architecture, applied to the earlier period of decorated Gothic, in which the tracery and other ornamentation consist entirely of distinct geometrical forms. *See* GOTHIC ARCHITECTURE.

GEOMETRICAL MEAN. Of any three successive terms of a geometrical progression the middle one is said to be the geometrical mean between the other two, and its value is equal to the square root of their product. It is the mean proportional between them. *See* next article.

GEOMETRICAL PROGRESSION, a series of numbers which increase or decrease by a common ratio: as 2, 6, 18, ... or 100, 50, 25, ... If a be the first term, r the common ratio, n any number of terms, then the nth term $= ar^n {}^{-1}$, and the sum of n terms $= a(1 - r^n) \div (1 - r)$. If r be less than unity, the sum approaches the limit $a \div (1 - r)$ as n is increased indefinitely. A recurring decimal is an example of an infinite geometrical progression:

$\dot{3} = \cdot 3333 \ldots = 3/10 + 3/10^2 + 3/10^3 \ldots$

Here $a = 3/10$, $r = 1/10$, so that $\dot{3} = a \div (1 - r) = \frac{1}{3}$.

GEOMETRY, the branch of mathematics which deals with the properties of space. The subject is a vast one, and its boundaries are continually being extended, but the foundations laid by the Greeks still stand, and the student of to-day, like his predecessor of 2,000 years ago, must begin with the facts which they discovered, and the problems which they solved. The science falls naturally into various divisions, according to the subjects treated and the methods employed. These divisions may be arranged in contrasted pairs, e.g. *plane* and *solid*; *plane* and *spherical*; *pure* or *synthetic* and *co-ordinate* or *analytical*; *metrical* and *projective*; *Euclidean* and *non-Euclidean*. Geometry is *plane, solid*, or *spherical*, according as it deals with figures in a plane, in space of three dimensions, or on the surface of a sphere.

Pure geometry proceeds by deductive reasoning, and never loses sight of the figure; **analytical geometry** makes use of co-ordinates, and tends to become a branch of algebra. **Metrical geometry** is concerned with measurements, such as those of length, area, and angle; **projective geometry** considers graphical properties not involving measurement, properties, e.g. relating to the intersection of lines, or the collinearity of points. **Descriptive geometry** deals with the representation of solid bodies by means of plane figures (*see* MECHANICAL DRAWING).

Differential geometry applies the methods and ideas of the calculus to such properties of curves and surfaces as tangency and curvature; the name is also used in a more restricted sense for a method of dealing with surfaces (or other continua) which starts from the expression for the differential element of length on the surface in terms of the variables and their differentials; by this method the geometry of the surface is made to depend on measurements made on the surface itself, without reference to any space outside the surface.

Line geometry deals with systems of straight lines in space. A line can be made to satisfy four conditions, passage through a given point counting for two. A system subject to one condition is called a *complex*; two conditions define a *congruence*, and three the lines of a *ruled surface*. The normals to a surface, e.g. form a congruence.

Elementary Geometry. The first six books of Euclid, with the eleventh book, contain the substance of what is usually called elementary geometry. Euclid starts from certain *definitions, axioms*, and *postulates*, and from these derives the properties of figures by a process of pure deductive reasoning. Of the *definitions*, perhaps the most important is that of a straight line. Euclid describes this as the shortest distance between two points, but the definition he really uses (in Book I, proposition 4) is that "two straight lines cannot enclose a space"; in other words, a straight line is that kind of line which is determined when two points of it are known. Most of the *axioms* are simple principles of general logic, such as, "things that are equal to the same are equal to another"; Euclid's enumeration of the principles of this type which he uses is by no means exhaustive.

The twelfth axiom is the famous axiom of parallels. This is now generally replaced by one equivalent to it, introduced by Playfair, viz. that "two intersecting straight lines cannot both be parallel to the same straight line." For centuries mathematicians, among them some of the most eminent, such as Gauss, tried to prove the axiom of parallels. It is now known that these attempts were bound to fail. We can, in fact, point to a case in which all the other definitions, axioms, and postulates hold good, but the axiom of parallels does not. Let a spherical surface be divided in two by a plane through the centre, and let figures be confined to one of the hemispheres. Then, if we suppose Euclid's phrase 'straight line' to denote an arc of a great circle, all his reasoning and results, up to the point where the axiom of parallels is introduced, will still be valid. Euclid's *postulates* amount in effect to a specification of the instruments the use of which is to be allowed, viz. ruler and compasses. Thus, when it is said that the problem of trisecting an angle cannot be solved by elementary geometry, what is meant is that in order to trisect an angle we need other instruments besides ruler and compasses. The *propositions* in the various books are of two classes, *problems* and *theorems*.

In Book I constructions are given for bisecting an angle or a line, and for drawing a perpendicular to a line from any point. Among the theorems of Book I those dealing with the congruence of triangles are very important. It is shown that a triangle is determined if we are given: (*a*) two sides and the angle between them, or (*b*) three sides, or (*c*) two angles and a side, the side being definitely placed with respect to the angles. Proposition 32 is the characteristic theorem of Euclidean geometry, that the sum of the angles of a triangle is two right angles. Proposition 47 is the *theorem of Pythagoras*, that the square on the longest side of a right-angled triangle is equal to the sum of the squares on the other two sides.

Book II deals with areas of squares and rectangles, the sides of which are connected by simple relations. The results are proved by actual construction and inspection of the rectangles and squares. From the modern point of view it is simpler to introduce the idea of the unit, so that lengths and areas can be represented by numbers; we can then prove the fundamental theorem of mensuration, that the area of a rectangle is the product of its length and breadth. The main theorems of Euclid's Book II are from this point of view equivalent to standard results in elementary algebra. A few of the theorems at the end of the book are more definitely geometrical. Propositions 12 and 13 are extensions of Pythagoras's Theorem, and are equivalent to the formula in trigonometry which gives the cosine of any angle of a triangle in terms of the sides. Proposition 14 solves the problem of constructing a square equal in area to a given rectilineal figure, this figure being first reduced to a rectangle by methods expounded in Book I.

Book III is taken up with the properties of circles. Theorems that may be noted are that angles in the same segment of a circle are equal, and that the opposite angles of a quadrilateral inscribed in a circle are supplementary. A tangent to a circle is defined as a line which meets the circle but does not cut it, and it is proved that a tangent is at right angles to the radius to its point of contact. This definition of a tangent would not serve for curves in general, but it is sufficient for conics, and allows us to dispense with the difficult idea of a limit (*see* TANGENT). Book III concludes with

important propositions about rectangles under segments of chords. The main result is that if through a fixed point in the plane of a circle any line be drawn, then the product of the two intercepts between the point and the circle has the same value for all directions of the line.

Book IV deals chiefly with the construction of regular polygons. With ruler and compasses an angle of 360° can be divided into 3, 4, or 5 equal parts. We can therefore find $\frac{1}{3}-\frac{1}{5}$ or $\frac{2}{15}$ of 360°, and, by halving this, divide 360° into 15 equal parts. Since, moreover, any angle can be bisected, it is possible to draw regular polygons of 3, 4, 5, 6, 8, 10, 12, or 15 sides, but not of 7, 9, 11, 13, or 14 sides. Gauss proved that a regular polygon can be constructed with Euclid's instruments when the number of sides is $2^n + 1$, where n is an integer, provided $2^n + 1$ is a prime. Taking $n = 4$, $n = 8$, we find that the construction is possible for 17 or 257 sides.

Book V is a treatise on ratio. The modern method of dealing with the ratio of two magnitudes, which must be of the same kind, is to express them both by numbers in terms of a unit; their ratio is then defined to be the fraction which the one number is of the other. This method presupposes that the magnitudes are commensurable, i.e. that a unit can be found which is contained in each of the magnitudes a whole number of times. That this is not always the case the Greeks knew very well; the familiar example of the side and diagonal of a square was probably first given by Pythagoras. Euclid's method, considered as a theoretical discussion, is admirable; it applies whether the magnitudes are commensurable or not. For practical applications, however, we need a numerical specification of a ratio; in modern theory this is attained by introducing the irrational number, which for purposes of calculation can be represented by an ordinary rational number to as high a degree of approximation as we wish (*see* NUMBER).

Book VI deals with the properties of similar figures, i.e. figures which are equiangular, and have the sides about the equal angles proportionals, so that the one figure is simply a copy of the other on a reduced scale. (It is only in Euclidean geometry that such figures are possible.) A fundamental theorem is that a line parallel to the base of a triangle divides the sides proportionally. Various conditions sufficient for the similarity of two triangles are proved, these being analogous to the conditions for congruence given in Book I. It is proved that the areas of similar figures are in the ratio of the squares on a pair of corresponding sides.

Books VII to IX deal with the properties of numbers, and Book X with incommensurable numbers; these books are not read now. Book XI,

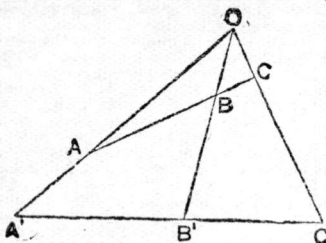

Fig. 1

XII, and XIII deal with solid geometry; Book XI, propositions 1 to 21, with sometimes a few propositions of Book XII, are still read. Much of Book XI hangs on the definitions of a plane and of a line perpendicular to a plane. A plane is defined to be a surface such that the straight line joining any two points in it lies wholly in the surface; a line is said to be perpendicular to a plane when it is perpendicular to every line which lies in the plane and which it meets. Euclid proves that a line perpendicular to two intersecting lines is perpendicular to the plane containing them; and shows how to draw a perpendicular to a plane from any given point.

Higher Geometry. There is a considerable body of geometry, both ancient and modern, which may be regarded as simply a continuation of the elements, the subject matter and the methods being the same as those of Euclid. The theories of harmonic section, of pole and polar for a circle, of coaxial circles, and of centres of similitude, are examples. The 'Apollonian problem,' to describe a circle to touch three given circles, with its many degenerate cases, was discussed by the Greek geometer Apollonius; a beautiful solution, which depends on the properties of radical axes, pole and polar, and centres of similitude, was given about 100 years ago by Gergonne.

Triangle Geometry is a special branch dealing with the properties of a triangle. It was much cultivated about the end of last century, and contains many pretty results. The Brocard points are the foci of the Brocard ellipse, an ellipse which is inscribed in the triangle, and has double contact with the circumcircle. The Tucker circles are circles having double contact with the Brocard

ellipse, and belonging to the same system as the circumcircle. Many properties of the triangle have long been known, such as those relating to the circumscribed and inscribed circles, the centre of medians, the orthocentre, and the nine-points circle. Feuerbach's Theorem states that the nine-points circle touches the inscribed and the escribed circles; this theorem has been extended to the sphere by Hart.

Geometrical Conics. The conic sections may be defined to be the plane sections of a circular cone, right or oblique. The treatise on conics by Apollonius, which is based on this definition, is an astonishing example of the power with which the Greek geometers could handle their method. Nowadays it is usual, for the sake of simplicity, to start from other definitions of the conic. The method followed in the branch of geometry conventionally called *geometrical conics* is to define the conic as the locus of a point which moves in a plane so that its distance from a fixed point, called the *focus*, is in a constant ratio to its distance from a fixed line, called the *directrix* (*see* CONIC SECTIONS). The properties are then deduced by Euclid's methods. It is usual to define the tangent as the limiting position of a secant when one of its points of intersection with the conic moves up to coincidence with the other. A good deal of the importance of the conic sections arises from the fact that the orbits of planets and comets are conics.

Projective Geometry. Take any figure in a plane P (the *original plane*). Let Q be another plane (the *plane of projection*), and let O (the

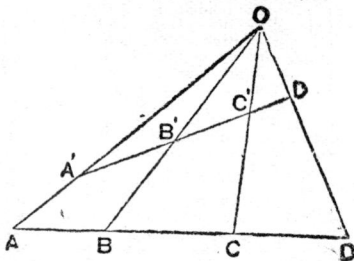

Fig. 2

centre of projection) be a fixed point outside those planes. Straight lines drawn from O to all the points of the figure in plane P will cut the plane Q in a new figure, which will be called the *projection* of the original figure. A straight line ABC in P will project into a straight line A'B'C' in Q (fig. 1), but lengths are altered; in general A'B' is not equal to AB, nor B'C' to BC; and the ratio A'B'/B'C' is not equal to AB/BC. Length of a line, and ratio of the segments of a line, are therefore said to be *non-projective* properties. If, however, we take *four* points A, B, C, D (fig. 2) in a line, and if A', B', C', D' are the projections of these, then there is a relation between the segments of ABCD and those of A'B'C'D'. This relation may be put in various equivalent ways; one way is to say that the ratio of the two ratios AC : CB and AD : DB is not altered by projection; or, otherwise, that (AC · BD)/(AD · BC) is not altered. This invariant fraction is called the *anharmonic ratio*, or the *cross-ratio* of the range of four points A, B, C, D. Points in a line form a *range*, and lines through a point form a *pencil* of lines. We have seen (fig. 2) that a pencil of four lines is cut by any *transversal* (crossing line) in a range of constant cross-ratio; this is called the cross-ratio of the pencil. The order of the letters in the name of a segment is to be attended to; thus DB = −BD. When the cross-ratio is −1, the points are said to form a harmonic range, of which A, B are one conjugate pair, and C, D the other. In this case C and D divide AB internally and externally in the same ratio. An important limiting case occurs when D goes to infinity. In this case AD : DB = −1, so that, if the range is harmonic, AC : CB = 1, or C is the middle point of AB. If A,B, C are three points in a line, we can find a fourth point D so as to make ABCD a harmonic range by the following construction (fig. 3). Take O any point outside ACB; join OA, OB, OC; in OC take any point G; let AG cut OB in E, and let BG cut OA in F. Then FE will cut AB in the required point D. It is remarkable that we get the same point D, however the points O and G are varied. This property of the figure, which can be deduced in a purely graphical way (without using the idea of distance at all) from solid geometry, or rather from the notions of plane, line, and point, has been used by von Staudt for the purpose of putting projective geometry on a basis quite independent of metrical considerations.

In the projection of one figure into another, relations connected with parallelism are of special importance. Suppose we are projecting a figure in the plane P into a figure in the plane Q, from the vertex O. The plane through O parallel to Q will cut P in a line; this is called the *vanishing line* in the plane P. Obviously the line from O to any point in this vanishing line does not cut the plane Q. A line from O to a point in P very near the vanish-

ing line would cut Q at a great distance; we are therefore led to say that a point in the vanishing line has its projection in Q at infinity. If we wish to retain, as quite generally true, the proposition that the projection of a line is a line, then we must say that the projection of the vanishing line is a line, or, in other words, that the points at infinity in the plane Q lie in a line. This line is called the *line at infinity* in the plane Q. By its introduction and systematic use, Euclidean geometry becomes more symmetrical, for we can now say that *any* pair of lines intersect in one point, parallel lines being lines intersecting at a point on the line at infinity. The introduction of the line infinity makes graphical Euclidean geometry projective, in the sense that *every* point projects into a point, and *every* line into a line.

The method of projection often enables us to replace a figure by a

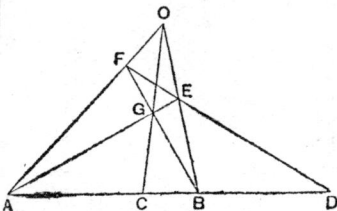
Fig. 3

simpler figure, and thus to give a simple proof of a proposed geometrical theorem. Take as an example the property that ABCD in fig. 3 is a harmonic range. (This is sometimes called the harmonic property of the complete quadrilateral, the quadrilateral being ABEF, completed by opposite pairs of sides being produced to meet at O and D.) Take OD for vanishing line, and any point V outside the plane ABO for centre of projection. In the projected figure O and D go to infinity, i.e. AFEB becomes a parallelogram and OC becomes a parallel to AF or BE through the centre of the parallelogram. Thus C', the projection of C, will be the mid point of A'B', the projection of AB. Hence A', C', B', with the point at infinity on A'B', form a harmonic range. Now project back to the original plane, keeping the same centre of projection. A', C', B', with the point at infinity on A'B', project into A, C, B, D; for the line at infinity in the plane of projection projects back into the line OD. But a harmonic range remains a harmonic range after projection; hence ABCD is a harmonic range.

Two lines which meet on the vanishing line project into parallel lines. With the right centre of projection we can therefore project any angle into an angle of assigned size α. By choosing centre and vanishing line properly, we can therefore project any line to infinity, and at the same time project any two angles into angles of given size. Any quadrilateral ABEF (fig. 3) may thus be projected into a square by projecting the line OD to infinity, and the angles BAF, AGF into right angles. A conic can be projected into a circle, and at the same time any line not intersecting it can be projected to infinity. Two conics intersecting in two real points, or in none, can be projected into circles. Projective methods are specially suitable for dealing with conics. The subject can be approached

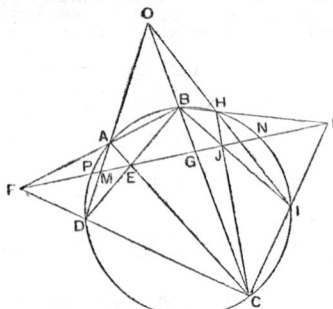

Fig. 4

in many different ways, and can be treated independently of Euclid's metrical geometry. It is easier, however, for one acquainted with Euclid, to begin with the circle, to develop its projective properties, and to pass these on to the conic, assuming the conic to be defined as any projection of a circle, i.e. as any section of an (oblique) cone.

One of the most important sections of the geometry of the circle from this point of view is the theory of *pole and polar*. If O is a fixed point in the plane of the circle, OAD any chord through O, and M the harmonic conjugate of O with respect to A and D (i.e. if OMAD is a harmonic range), then the locus of M is easily proved to be a straight line; this straight line is called the *polar* of O for the circle. If OBC is another chord through O, and if lines be drawn as in fig. 4, then the harmonic property of the quadrilateral (referred to above) shows that M and G lie on the polar of O, which is therefore the line FMEG. We have thus a purely graphical theorem which can be stated without any reference to har-

monic section, viz. if OAD, OBC are chords of a circle through a fixed point O, then AC, BD, as also AB, CD, intersect on a fixed line. If OHI is another chord, BI, CH, as well as BH, CI, also intersect on this line. If the polar EF of O meets the circle at P and N, then OP and ON are the tangents from O, so that these can be drawn with the ruler only, provided a drawing of the circle is actually given.

In fig. 4 the triangle OEF is *self-polar* for the circle, i.e. each side is the polar of the opposite vertex, or, the same thing, each vertex is the *pole* of the opposite side. We see that if the polar of E passes through F, then the polar of F passes through E; E and F are then said to be *conjugate points*. Similarly, EF and EO are said to be *conjugate lines*, the pole of each lying on the other. Since the theory of pole and polar is projective, it holds for any conic. The theory leads to an important method of transformation called the method of *reciprocal polars*, by which from any geometrical property we can deduce another, generally different, property. The transformation consists in replacing each straight line in the figure by its pole, with respect to a fixed conic, and each line by its polar. The two figures are *reciprocal*, for the same transformation applied to the second figure would restore the first.

Two very important reciprocal theorems are Pascal's and Brianchon's Theorems. Pascal's Theorem is: the three intersections of pairs of opposite sides of a hexagon inscribed in a conic lie in a line; and Brianchon's is: the lines joining opposite vertices of a hexagon described about a conic are concurrent. Pascal's Theorem leads to a very important method of defining, or generating, a conic as the locus of the intersections of corresponding lines (*rays*) of two homographic pencils; *homographic* pencils being such as have the cross-ratios or any four rays of the one pencil equal to the cross-ratio of a corresponding four in the other. The reciprocal theorem derives the conic as the envelope of (i.e. curve touching) the lines joining corresponding points of two homographic ranges. The derivation of all the properties of conics from these definitions is one of the most attractive chapters of geometrical theory.

Analytical, or Co-ordinate, Geometry. In this branch of geometry a point is defined by co-ordinates (q.v.), and a line or curve by an *equation*, i.e. by a relation between the co-ordinates of any point on it. The equation of a straight line is of the first degree, i.e. of the form $ax+by+c=0$, so that there are two *constants* involved, viz. the ratios $a:b:c$. Specially useful forms are: (1) $y = mx + b$, where m is the *gradient* of the line, or tangent of the angle the line makes with Ox; and b is the intercept the line makes on Oy. (2) $x \cos a + y \sin a = p$, where p is the perpendicular from the origin on the line, and a is the angle this perpendicular makes with Ox. Two lines are at right angles if the product of their gradients (mm') is -1. The equation of the line through the two points (x_1, y_1) and (x_2, y_2) is $(x - x_1)/(x_1 - x_2) = (y - y_1)/(y_1 - y_2)$. The square of the distance between those two points is $(x_1 - x_2)^2 + (y_1 - y_2)^2$. The length of the perpendicular from (x', y') to the line $ax + by + c = 0$ is $(ax' + by' + c)/\sqrt{(a^2 + b^2)}$. In proving these formulæ, the results of the ordinary Euclidean geometry are assumed.

To illustrate the method of applying them, take the equation of a circle. If (x, y) is any point P on the circle, and if C the centre is (a, b), the radius being c, then $PC^2 = c^2$, or $(x - a)^2 + (y - b)^2 = c^2$. This is a relation between the x and y of any point on the locus, and is therefore the equation of the locus. The equation is of the form $x^2 + y^2 + 2gx + 2fy + c = 0$. Comparing this with the most general equation of the second degree, viz. $ax^2 + 2hxy + by^2 + 2gx + 2fy + c = 0$, we see that (1) the term in xy is wanting, (2) the coefficients of x^2 and y^2 are equal.

Conversely, any equation with these features represents a circle, the centre and radius of which can easily be found when the equation is given. As an example, take the locus of a point P which moves so that PA:PB = a constant, m say, where A and B are fixed points. We may choose the axes, to simplify the work, so that A is $(a, 0)$, and B is $(-a, 0)$. If P is (x, y), we get $(x - a)^2 + y^2 = m^2\{(x + a)^2 + y^2\}$, or $(x^2 + y^2)(1 - m^2) - 2ax(1 + m^2) + a^2(1 - m^2) = 0$. From the form of this equation, the locus of P is a circle. The points of intersection of a line and curve are found by solving the equations of line and curve as simultaneous. The line $x \cos a + y \sin a = p$ will in general cut the circle $x^2 + y^2 = a^2$ in two points, for the simultaneous equations have two solutions. If $p = a$, the solutions coincide, and the line is a tangent; the common solution for $p = a$ being $(a \cos a, a \sin a)$, this is the point of contact. The line $xx' + yy' = a^2$ is therefore the tangent to $x^2 + y^2 = a^2$ at the point (x', y') on the circle. Suppose P (x', y') is outside the circle. We can find the equation of the chord joining the points of contact of the tangents from P. For let Q (x_1, y_1) and R (x_2, y_2) be the points of contact. The tangents there are $xx_1 + yy_1 = a^2$ and $xx_2 + yy_2 = a^2$. These pass through (x', y'). Hence $x'x_1 + y'y_1 = a^2$ and $x'x_2 + y'y_2 = a^2$; these equations show that the

line $x'x + y'y = a^2$ passes through Q and R; the equation of QR is therefore $x'x + y'y = a^2$. The properties of pole and polar can be deduced from this equation with great ease.

The discussion of the properties of a curve is often simplified by expressing the co-ordinates of a point on the curve in terms of a single parameter. In the circle $x^2 + y^2 = a^2$, we may write $x = a \cos\theta$, $y = a \sin\theta$; in the parabola $y^2 = 4ax$, we put $x = am^2$, $y = 2am$; in the ellipse $x^2/a^2 + y^2/b^2 = 1$, $x = a \cos\theta$, $y = b \sin\theta$; θ and m being parameters. Analytical geometry is a subject of immense extent; the above sketch ill give an idea of the nature of the processes followed. Other co-ordinates than Cartesian are often used, especially in more theoretical work.

Trilinear co-ordinates, which are the perpendiculars from a point on the sides of a triangle of reference, are specially useful, as all equations may be written in homogeneous form, i.e. with every term of the same degree.

Non-Euclidean Geometry. A great deal of geometry is independent of the idea of *distance*. Suppose that we think of a point simply as something represented by a combination of two numbers (x, y), or of the ratios of three numbers x, y, z; and that we define a line as the locus of points satisfying a homogeneous equation of the first degree in x, y, z; then the whole of projective geometry follows algebraically. How are we now to introduce the idea of distance into this scheme? It was shown by Cayley that the distance of two points may be regarded as a projective relationship of the two points to a fixed conic, which he called the *Absolute*. If we suppose the absolute to be a real conic, and if the line through P and Q cuts the absolute in E and F, then the distance PQ can be defined as a constant multiple of the logarithm of the cross-ratio (EQ/QF)/ (EP/PF). If, as a special case, we take for the absolute a circle with centre at a fixed point, and if we suppose the radius R of the circle to increase indefinitely, then it is easy to show that the limiting value of $\frac{1}{2}R$ multiplied by the logarithm of the above cross-ratio is the ordinary Euclidean distance. Angles are measured in a similar way by the logarithm of the cross-ratio of the pencil formed by the two lines and the two tangents to the absolute from their point of intersection. In the limiting case just mentioned, the two tangents would be the lines from the angular point to the circular points at infinity, i.e. the two imaginary points through which all circles pass, and at which every circle touches its asymptotes.

Euclidean geometry is thus a degenerate case of Cayley's non-Euclidean geometry, the absolute having degenerated to an infinite circle; from a slightly different point of view, to a conic which, regarded as a locus, consists of the line at infinity taken twice over; and, regarded as an envelope, is the envelope of all lines passing through the two circular points. Perpendicular lines are lines which are conjugate with respect to the absolute. In the Euclidean case, perpendicular lines therefore form a harmonic pencil with the lines from their intersection to the circular points. In Cayley's geometry, a circle, i.e. the locus of a point at a fixed distance from a given point, is a conic having double contact with the absolute; most of the properties of ordinary circles can be extended to this generalized case.

A non-Euclidean geometry of a different type was invented by Riemann, who founded his work on the methods applied by Gauss to the theory of surfaces. Instead of dealing with the distance of two points separated by any finite interval, he considered the distance of a point from points in its immediate neighbourhood. Every point in a continuum (e.g. curve, surface, solid space) is specified by co-ordinates; on a surface a point has two of these, in a solid space three. The co-ordinates are not defined geometrically; they are mere numbers chosen for the purpose of identifying points. On a surface, e.g. two systems of curves may be drawn; the curves of one system have numbers 1, 2, 3, 4, &c., attached to them; so have the curves of the other system; the point where the curve numbered p in the first system intersects the curve numbered q in the second is the point (p, q). Two points close to each other are supposed to be at a certain definite *distance*, which remains unaltered however its expression in terms of the co-ordinates may change. If dp, dq are the differentials of p and q, and ds the corresponding elementary distance, then we have a formula $ds^2 = A dp^2 + B dp dq + C dq^2$, where A, B, C are functions of p and q. The geometry of the surface is characterized by the functions A, B, C. All intrinsic relations in the surface, such as those connected with curvature, and with geodesics, or shortest lines, can be expressed in terms of these functions; we do not need to consider anything outside the surface. A certain function of A, B, C must vanish if it is possible to choose co-ordinates x, y such that ds^2 can be expressed in the form $dx^2 + dy^2$; the vanishing of this function is the condition that the geometry of the surface should be the same as that of a Euclidean plane surface. On a circular cylinder, e.g. if (a, ϖ, ϕ) are the cylindrical co-ordinates

of a point, we have $ds^2 = dz^2 + a^2 d\phi^2$; by putting $z = x$, $a\phi = y$, this becomes $ds^2 = dx^2 + dy^2$. The geometry is therefore Euclidean, as is otherwise obvious, since the surface may be developed into a plane, without rumpling or tearing, and therefore without altering differential distances; and without altering finite distances, if these be measured on the surface along a geodesic.

A question asked by Gauss and Riemann was: Is our space of three dimensions necessarily Euclidean? Riemann investigated the most general form for ds^2 consistent with the property that bodies can be moved about in space without change of size or shape, i.e. consistent with congruence relations being possible. He found the form $ds^2 = (dx^2 + dy^2 + dz^2)/N^2$, where $N = 1 + \frac{1}{4}a(x^2 + y^2 + z^2)$, a being a constant, which may be called the curvature of space. Euclidean space corresponds to $a = 0$. If a is negative, the geometry is called hyperbolic; this corresponds to the system invented for plane geometry by Lobatchewsky. If a is positive, space is finite, though unbounded, and every straight line is closed.

Gauss at one time thought of measuring the angles of the triangle formed by three mountain peaks, and testing whether their sum was greater than, equal to, or less than two right angles. Assuming that light travels along a geodesic in space, and that the experiment could be carried out with sufficient refinement, this would settle the matter; for Gauss has shown that, in a triangle ABC, formed by geodesic lines, the ratio of $A + B + C - \pi$ to the area of the triangle measures the curvature of space, i.e. the number a already mentioned. The relation between the geometries of Riemann and Cayley was worked out by Klein. If we discard free mobility, or the possibility of congruence, we can have a space of a much more general character such as that postulated by Einstein in his General Theory of Relativity.

BIBLIOGRAPHY: editions of Euclid's *Elements*, by J. S. Mackay, and by Hall and Stevens; J. Casey, *Sequel to Euclid*; J. W. Russell, *Pure Geometry*; L. B. Benny, *Plane Geometry* (a treatise on projective and analytical geometry, giving a full account of conics from various points of view); C. Smith, *Conic Sections* (analytical); G. Salmon, *Conic Sections* (analytical); R. Bell, *Co-ordinate Geometry of Three Dimensions*; J. L. Coolidge, *Non-Euclidean Geometry*; H. S. Carslaw, *Non-Euclidean Geometry*; A. N. Whitehead, *The Axioms of Projective Geometry*.

GEOMETRY, HISTORY OF. The origin of geometry is assigned by an ancient tradition to Egypt, but the history of the science, as far as it is known, commences in Greece with Thales (639–548 B.C.), who in conjunction with Anaximander founded the Ionic school. The most famous representative of this school was Pythagoras (582–500 B.C.), who with his associates, called Pythagoreans, made geometry a science by basing it on axioms, postulates, and definitions, and formulating methods of proof. They combined arithmetic with geometry, and investigated the properties of areas and volumes. The discovery of the relation between the squares on the sides of a right-angled triangle is attributed to Pythagoras, and he is also said to have been the first to prove that the circle contains a greater area than any plane figure having the same perimeter, and that the sphere contains the greatest volume bounded by a given surface.

Later Hippocrates of Chios, Theodosius of Cyrene, and Archytas of Tarentum made important discoveries, but the next great development of the science is due to the school of Plato. The Platonists added to the Pythagorean geometry the properties of the regular solids and of the cone, prism, and cylinder; they also developed the fundamental principles of geometrical loci. Euclid, who was born shortly after Plato, is probably the best known of all the ancient geometers. His *Elements* is the most famous treatise on geometry ever written. Although abandoned as a textbook on the Continent more than a hundred years ago, it continued to be the chief schoolbook on geometry used in the British Isles until the beginning of this century. In Euclid's *Elements* all the more important problems and theorems worked out by his predecessors are collected, systematized, and arranged in logical order. He wrote many other mathematical works—a book of data, a treatise of porisms, &c., most of which have been lost.

After Euclid came Archimedes (287–212 B.C.), the greatest scientist of ancient times, among whose works are treatises on spheres, conoids and spheroids, and spirals. He investigated the relations between the circumference, diameter, and area of a circle, found the surface and volume of a sphere and of a spherical segment, and proved that the area of a segment of a parabola cut off by a double ordinate is two-thirds of the parallelogram that encloses it. Apollonius (about 250 B.C.) wrote eight books on conics, considered as sections of the cone, and proved most of the properties which relate to their foci, tangents, asymptotes, and diameters. Apollonius was followed by Nicomedes, the inventor of the

conchoid; Diocles, who invented the cissoid; Hipparchus, who was one of the first to develop trigonometry; and Heron. In the early part of the Christian era Menelaus propounded his theorem on the segments of the sides of a triangle cut off by a straight line, a theorem which centuries afterwards led to the theory of transversals.

Ptolemy (A.D. 125) was responsible for many important researches; and the commentator Pappus (390), in addition to editing many of the researches of his predecessors, discovered an important case of Pascal's Theorem, and two well-known theorems on centres of inertia.

Diophantus, in the third century A.D., introduced methods of an algebraic kind, and may be said to be the connecting link between the ancient and modern geometers, the geometry of the Arabs, of Leonard of Pisa, Cardan, and, Vieta being based upon his methods. After the sack of Alexandria, scarcely any progress was made until the sixteenth century. The Romans had no liking for the subject, but the Hindus and Arabs gave it some attention. Vieta (1540–1603) used algebraic symbols for the solution of geometrical problems, and is said to have discovered many of the formulæ of trigonometry. Kepler (1571–1630) introduced the principle of geometrical continuity, and developed Archimedes' method of exhaustions on simpler lines than those of the Greeks.

Cavalieri (died 1647) discovered the method of quadratures; Descartes (1596–1650), by his invention of the method of co-ordinates, immensely extended the domain of geometrical science; Desargues and Pascal were the pioneers of modern geometry. About this time, however, attention was concentrated on fluxions and the infinitesimal calculus.

Fermat (1601–65) and Barrow (1630–77) with their methods of tangents and maxima, Huyghens (1629–95) with the theory of involutes, Roberval, Pascal, and Wallis with their processes of summation, were on the way to the calculus, which was finally established by the genius of Newton (1642–1727), although Leibnitz, who was working on different lines, disputed the claim of Newton to be the discoverer.

The study of geometry revived at the beginning of the nineteenth century under Monge (1746–1818) and Carnot (1753–1823). Monge invented the method of descriptive geometry, and established the theory of projections; Carnot contributed the theory of transversals. Poncelet introduced many new ideas, and is entitled to be called the founder of projective geometry. In Germany, Möbius, Plücker, and Steiner made notable advances. Chasles, in France, and Maccullagh, in Ireland, gave examples of the power and beauty of geometrical, as contrasted with analytical, methods. Projective geometry was placed on a basis independent of metrical considerations by von Staudt. Analytical geometry was enriched by applications of the method of invariants, developed especially by Cayley, Sylvester, Salmon, Aronhold, Hesse, and Clebsch. Sir William Rowan Hamilton invented quaternions, and Grassman applied to geometry a somewhat similar non-commutative algebra.

For centuries Euclid's axiom of parallels was the crux of geometry. The idea of dispensing with the axiom altogether is due to Bolyai and Lobatchewsky, who, with Gauss, Riemann, Clifford, Beltrami, Cayley, and Klein, have founded non-Euclidean geometry, interest in which has been greatly stimulated by the recent development of the theory of relativity. The logical foundations of the whole science of geometry have within recent years been searchingly criticized. Helmholtz and Lie analysed the idea of congruence, and investigated conditions for its possibility. Systems of axioms have been elaborated by Peano, Pieri, Hilbert, Whitehead, Veblen, and others, the object being to reach the irreducible minimum of assumption on which a geometry can be founded. One interesting effect of these various modern developments has been to emphasize the sharp distinction between abstract geometry, a purely ideal construction, and physical geometry, or the geometry of the world as it actually exists. Probably no philosopher would now maintain the view, at one time practically universal, that geometry is one of the subjects in which *a priori* knowledge is possible.

GEOPH'AGISM (Gr. *gē*, earth, and *phagein*, to eat), or EARTH-EATING, the practice of eating some kind of earthy matter, clay, chalk, &c., common amongst uncivilized peoples, such as the South American Ottamacs, the Indians of the Hudson Bay country, the West Indian blacks, the negroes in some of the United States of America, and others. In some cases it is probably done to allay hunger, but it is also practised where the supply of food is sufficient. Amongst chlorotic young women a similarly depraved appetite is not uncommon. Geophagism causes death by dropsy or dysentery.

GEOPONICI (Gr. *Geoponikoi*), a term employed to designate the Greek and Roman writers on agriculture, the Latin term being *Scriptores Rei Rusticæ*. The ancient Greeks devoted their attention to the scientific study of agriculture, and Geoponica, or books on this subject, existed already in the times of Socrates. Xenophon praised agriculture in his *Œconomicus* and in the *Memorabilia*. Among the Romans, Cato the Censor wrote a treatise entitled *De Agricultura*, M. Terentius Varro composed *De Re Rustica*, whilst Virgil glorified agriculture in his *Georgics*. Columella, a contemporary of Seneca, was the author of a work in twelve books (*De Re Rustica*), whilst the Alexandrian writers, too, compiled many treatises dealing with agriculture.

GEORGE I (George Louis), King of Great Britain and Elector of Hanover, was the son of the Elector Ernest Augustus, by Sophia, daughter of Frederick, Elector Palatine, and grand-daughter of James I. He was born 28th May, 1660, and died in 1727. In 1682 he was married to Sophia Dorothea of Zell, whom, in 1694, on account of a suspected intrigue with Count Königsmark, he caused to be imprisoned and kept in confinement for the rest of her life. In 1698 he succeeded his father as Elector. He commanded the imperial army in 1707 during the War of the Spanish Succession; and ascended the throne of Great Britain on the death of Queen Anne in 1714. Amongst the notable events of his reign were the risings of the Scottish Jacobites (1715–6); the Triple and Quadruple Alliances against Spain (1717 and 1718); the failure of the South Sea Company (1720). The private character of George I was bad, but he showed much good sense and prudence in government, especially of his German dominions. By Sophia Dorothea he had a son, George, afterwards George II of England, and a daughter, Sophia, the mother of Frederick the Great.—Cf. W. M. Thackeray, *The Four Georges*.

GEORGE II (George Augustus), King of Great Britain, son of George I, was born 30th Oct., 1683, died suddenly on 25th Oct., 1760. He married in 1705 Wilhelmina Caroline of Brandenburg-Anspach. In 1708, then only electoral prince of Hanover, he distinguished himself at Oudenarde under Marlborough. In 1727 he succeeded his father on the English throne, but inherited to the full the predilection of George I for Hanover. His reign is notable for the great events with which it is filled, and for the number of men great in art, letters, war, and diplomacy who then adorned England. The War of the Austrian Succession, in which George II himself took part at Dettingen, the Jacobite rebellion of 1745, the conquest of Canada, and the growth of the British Empire in India are amongst the chief events of his reign. He was a prince of very moderate abilities, and ignorant of science or literature; of obstinate temper and vicious habits; but honest and open in his disposition.—BIBLIOGRAPHY: Lord Hervey, *Memoirs of the Reign of George II*; J. McCarthy, *History of the Four Georges and William IV*.

GEORGE III, King of Great Britain, born in 1738, died 29th Jan., 1820. He was the eldest son of Frederick, Prince of Wales, by the Princess Augusta of Saxe-Gotha, and succeeded his grandfather, George II, in 1760. In the following year he married the Princess Charlotte Sophia of Mecklenburg-Strelitz. The sixty years of his reign are filled with great events, amongst which are the Wilkes controversy; the American Revolution, 1775–83, the result of which the king felt acutely; the French Revolution, 1789, and the Napoleonic wars which followed, comprising the long struggle that ended at Waterloo; and the Irish Rebellion, 1798. George III was a man of conscientious principles and of a plain, sound understanding, though his narrow patriotism and his obstinate prejudices were hurtful to British interests. His tastes and amusements were plain and practical, literature and the fine arts receiving but a small share of his attention. His private life was exemplary. In 1810 the king's mind, which had already given way several times, finally broke down, and from that time to his death his biography is a blank. Queen Charlotte bore him fifteen children—nine being sons. *See* BRITAIN.—Cf. W. E. H. Lecky, *History of England*.

GEORGE IV, King of Great Britain, son of George III and Queen Charlotte, born in 1762, died in 1830. His dissipated life, his extravagance, his supposed (and actual) marriage with a Catholic, Mrs. Fitzherbert, alienated from him the affection of his father and the esteem of the nation. In 1795 he married the Princess Caroline of Brunswick, from whom he soon separated, and who was afterwards tried for adultery in 1820. (*See* CAROLINE.) In 1811 George became regent, and, on the death of George III in 1820, king. The most important event of his reign was the passing of the Catholic Emancipation Act, by the Wellington ministry, in 1829. As his only daughter, Princess Charlotte, wife of Leopold of Saxe-Coburg (afterwards King of the Belgians), died childless in 1817, he was succeeded by his brother, William IV. *See* BRITAIN.— BIBLIOGRAPHY: L. Melville, *The First Gentleman of Europe*; W. H. Wilkins, *Mrs. Fitzherbert and George IV*.

GEORGE V, King of Great Britain and Ireland and of the oversea British dominions, Emperor of India, second son of Edward VII and Queen Alexandra, was born at Marlborough House on 3rd June, 1865. After being educated by a private tutor, he and his elder brother, Prince Albert Victor, became naval cadets, and as midshipmen visited many parts of the world. Prince George attained the rank of commander in 1891, but his brother's death in 1892, which placed him in direct succession to the crown, led to his practical withdrawal from a naval career. Created Duke of York in 1892, he next year married Princess Victoria Mary, daughter of the Duke of Teck. This union has produced five sons and

George II

one daughter, the eldest, Prince Edward, having been born on 23rd June, 1894. On the death of Queen Victoria and accession of Edward VII (22nd Jan., 1901) he became Duke of Cornwall, and later in the year was created Prince of Wales. He and the princess had just returned from a great colonial tour, one object of which was to open the first Parliament of the Australian Commonwealth at Melbourne. On their return they were entertained by the Lord Mayor of London at the Guildhall, when the Prince of Wales delivered a notable speech urging the old country to 'wake up' in order to maintain and strengthen her commercial position. The Prince and Princess of Wales spent the winter months of 1905–6 in India, visiting Calcutta and other cities. On the death of Edward VII, 6th May, 1910, the prince became king as George V, and on 22nd June, 1911, he and his consort, Queen Mary, were crowned in Westminster Abbey. Shortly before the outbreak of the

European War, King George summoned a conference of party leaders at Buckingham Palace for the purpose of solving the Irish question. No solution, however, was found. King George, who had become popular as the 'Sailor Prince,' increased his popularity by his conduct, efforts, and exertions during the European War. A serious illness which befell him in 1928–29 showed the extent of his popularity.

GEORGE I, 'King of the Hellenes,' was born at Copenhagen, 24th Dec., 1845, second son of the King of Denmark. In 1863 he was elected king by the Greek National Assembly, and in 1867 he married the Princess Olga, a niece of the Russian Tsar. His conduct as a constitutional monarch was always correct and regular, and he won the popular sympathies by the efforts he made on behalf of the expansion of Greek nationality. He was assassinated at Salonica on 18th March, 1913.

GEORGE II was a grandson of George I. He became king in Jan., 1922 on the death of his father, Constantine, but abdicated in 1923.

GEORGE, British prince. The fourth and youngest son of King George V., he was born at Sandringham, Dec. 20, 1902, his full name being George Edward Alexander Edmund. Having passed through Osborne and Dartmouth, he entered the navy and served with it for some years. This was followed by a spell in the Foreign Office, but much of his time has been taken up with public functions. In 1931 he went with the Prince of Wales to South America.

GEORGE, Duke of Saxony (the Bearded), born in 1471, died in 1539, was the son of Albert the Brave, the founder of the Albertine line of Saxony, and succeeded in 1500 to the hereditary dominions of the Albertine House. Later on he became involved in the turmoils of the Reformation period. He was not at first wholly hostile to reform, but thought that it could be better effected by means of Papal edicts than by the revolt of Luther. Accordingly he became embittered by the uncompromising tone of Luther's later writings, and endeavoured to suppress the Reformation in his dominions by violent measures. These, however, were unsuccessful, and in 1539, on the accession of his brother Henry, who was a Protestant, the Reformation was introduced into the dominions of the Albertine House of Saxony.

GEORGE, Henry, American writer on political economy and social reform, born in 1839, died in 1897. He became a journalist and editor of papers, and in 1879 published *Progress and Poverty*, a work that attained an enormous circulation. In it many of the older views of wealth, wages, and capital are attacked, and the conclusion is finally reached that all taxes should be replaced by a single tax levied on land values, thus practically making and recognizing the land as national property, whilst still leaving it in the occupation of individuals. He lectured in the United Kingdom on several occasions between 1881 and 1889. His other works include: *Our Land and Land Policy*; *Social Problems*; *Property and Land*; and *Protection and Free Trade*, a defence of the latter.

GEORGE, LAKE, a picturesque lake in New York State, among the Adirondacks, south of Lake Champlain, into which it discharges at Ticonderoga, 36 miles long and 4 miles in greatest width. It is surrounded by wooded hills, and dotted with islands.

GEORGE, ORDER OF ST. The following are the principal of the numerous orders which have been founded in honour of St. George: (1) A military order instituted in Russia in 1769 by the Empress Catherine II as a reward of military achievements. It consists of four classes, to which a fifth, intended for non-commissioned officers and privates, was added in 1807. (2) An order instituted in Bavaria by the Emperor Charles VII (Charles Albert) in 1729, and reorganized by King Ludwig II in 1871. Since the reorganization the order, which had previously been a mere decoration for the nobility, has devoted itself to such services as the care of the wounded on battlefields, &c. (3) An order instituted by Ernest Augustus of Hanover in 1839. (4) A Sicilian military order, instituted by Joseph Napoleon 24th Feb., 1808, and remodelled by King Ferdinand IV in 1819. (5) The name under which the Order of the Garter was first instituted in England. *See* GARTER, ORDER OF THE.

GEORGE, ST., a saint venerated both in the eastern and western Churches, and the patron saint of England. He is also the patron saint of Portugal. He was canonized in A.D. 494 or 496 by Pope Gelasius. His origin is very obscure, one of many legends representing him as a prince of Cappadocia martyred by Diocletian. Gibbon has sought to identify this legendary saint with the notorious and turbulent Arian heretic George of Cappadocia, who was slain in 361 in a rising of the populace, who had been infuriated by his oppression and his violence against pagans and orthodox. But the most eminent scholars, both Roman Catholic and Protestant, are of opinion that the veneration of St. George has been traced up to so early a period as to make it very improbable that a notorious Arian could have been foisted on the Catholic Church as a saint and martyr. The killing of a dragon that was about to swallow a maiden is a legendary feat attributed to him. The story first appeared in the Middle Ages in the *Legenda, Aurea*, of Jacobus de Voragine. It is plainly derived from the story of Andromeda and Perseus. St. George was adopted by the Genoese as their patron saint, and in 1222 the Council of Oxford ordered that his day (the 23rd of April) should be observed as a national holiday in England; in 1350 he was made the patron saint of the Order of the Garter by Edward III.—Cf. M. H. Bulley, *St. George for Merrie England.*

GEORGE, ST., one of the Bermudas. It is about 3 miles long and half a mile broad, is fortified, and contains a port of the same name, which is a British military station.

GEORGE-NOBLE, a gold coin of the time of Henry VIII of the value of 6s. 8d. sterling; so called from bearing on the reverse the figure of St. George killing the dragon.

GEORGE'S CHANNEL, ST., the arm of the sea which separates Ireland from Wales south of the Irish Sea. From Holyhead and Dublin on the north of St. David's Head and Carnsore Point it extends about 100 miles, with a breadth varying from 50 to 70 miles.

GEORGETOWN, or DEMERARA, the capital of British Guiana, at the mouth of the Demerara. It is neatly built, consisting of broad streets at right angles, with canals in the middle, and lofty wooden houses, often with luxuriant gardens, attached. There is a bar at the mouth of the river, and large ships have to discharge and load by means of lighters. The chief exports are sugar, rum, and coffee. It has a radio station. Pop. (1931), 62,690, about one-seventh being whites.

GEORGIA, a Socialist Soviet Republic, one of the constituent states of the Transcaucasian Socialist Federal Soviet Republic. It is bounded by the Black Sea, the Caucasus Mountains, Azerbaijan, and Armenia, and is composed of the former Russian provinces of Tiflis and Kutais, the Autonomous Socialist Soviet Republics of Abkhazia (part of the former province of Sukhum) and Adsharsk (formerly Batum province), and the Autonomous Region of Yugo-Osetie in the Caucasus Mountains. The total area is 26,380 sq. miles and the population (1931), 2,883,200. The capital is Tiflis, the chief seaports are Poti and Sukhum,

and, of course, Georgia has the right of using the free port of Batum, which is in Ajaria. There is a State University, a Trans-Caucasian Communist University, an Academy of Art, among other educational institutions.

Georgia is mainly a pastoral and an agricultural country, and offers great scope for development in these industries. Great irrigation schemes have been carried through. The principal crop is corn, and the country is rich in fruit trees, the wine industry being important. Silk production and beekeeping are extensively carried on. The minerals include naphtha, copper, coal, lead, manganese, iron, sulphur, zinc, and antimony. Of these the most important is manganese, which is mined at Tchiaturi. There are vast possibilities in the mineral wealth of Georgia, especially in petroleum. The Zemo-Avchal hydro-electric station, the most powerful in Transcaucasia, is in Georgia, on the River Kura. There are 570 miles of railway track in Georgia, and several extensions are under construction, e.g. the line from Akhal-Senaki to Tuapse.

Georgians. The Georgians are a fine-looking race, the women being renowned for their beauty. Their language, which is allied to those of other Caucasian races, is a member of a distinct linguistic family, and their literature, which commences with the introduction of Christianity into the country, is especially rich in lyric poetry. There is a Georgian Bible.

History. Georgia is known to have been subject to Alexander the Great, and to have become independent in 324 B.C. Christianity was introduced in the fourth century. After a period of subjection to the Arabian caliphs, the Georgians remained independent from the end of the tenth century till 1799, when their king ceded his dominions to the Russian Emperor Paul. In 1918 Georgia declared her absolute independence. The Act of Independence was formally approved in 1919 by the Constituent Assembly. In 1919 it was overrun by Bolshevist forces, subdued, and in 1922 formed with Armenia and Azerbaijan into the Transcaucasian federation (T.S.F.S.R.).—

BIBLIOGRAPHY: Foreign Office Handbooks, *Caucasia*; Karl Kautsky, *Georgia: a Social Democratic Peasant Republic*; M. Wardrop, *Georgian Fairy Tales*; O. Wardrop, *The Kingdom of Georgia*; Emmanuel Kuhne, *La Géorgie Libre*; W. Woytinsky, *La Démocratie Géorgienne.*

GEORGIA, one of the Southern United States, bounded north by Tennessee and North Carolina, east by South Carolina and the Atlantic, south by Florida, and west by Alabama; length, north to south, 320 miles;

breadth, 255 miles; area, 59,265 sq. miles, 540 sq. miles being water.

Physical Features. The coast is bordered by a chain of islands, separated from the mainland by narrow lagoons or sounds. On them the famous sea-island cotton is raised. The land is low towards the coast, beginning as a salt marsh, grown over with tall reeds, continuing next as swampy rice plantations and then as 'pine barrens' about 60 or 90 miles inland, gradually rising as a sandy district, interspersed with fertile tracts, till it reaches the lower falls of the Savannah, Ogechee, Oconee, and other rivers. Here the hilly and finally mountainous region called the Upper Country begins, a fertile and salubrious region extending north and west till it rises into the Appalachian mountain-chain. Of the rivers the Chattahoochee, which flows under the name of the Appalachicola into the Gulf of Mexico, is navigable for steamers for 300 miles; the Savannah is navigable for steamers part of the year for 250 miles; and the Altamaha and its affluents are navigable for small vessels 300 miles upwards.

Climate and Productions. The climate is mild, but unhealthy in the low country during July, August, and September. The soil in many parts is very rich. Cotton, rice, maize, and the sugar-cane are the staple productions; but tobacco, the sweet potato, and other crops are cultivated with success. The fruits, which include peaches, apples, melons, oranges, bananas, &c., are of the finest. Copper and iron, also gold in considerable quantities, are found in the northern parts.

Towns. Atlanta is the seat of the legislature and largest town; the other principal towns are Savannah (the chief seaport with 8 miles of river frontage), Augusta, Macon, and Columbus.

Education. Education is compulsory. Among the State institutions are the University of Georgia in Athens, the Georgia School of Technology, and the Emory University, both in Atlanta.

History. A charter for the foundation of a colony in the territory now called Georgia was obtained in 1732 by General Oglethorpe from George II, after whom the state was named. Georgia was one of the thirteen original states. In 1788 it adopted the Constitution of the United States by a unanimous vote. In Jan., 1861, Georgia seceded with the Confederates, took an active part in the Civil War, and was conquered by a Federal army under General Sherman (1864-5) and restored to the Union, since which, however, it has been twice occupied by United States troops on account of disagreements between Congress and the State Legislature regarding the Constitution. Pop. in 1900 2,216,329; in 1910, 2,609,121, in 1930, 2,908,506. The State sends two Senators and ten Representatives to Congress.— BIBLIOGRAPHY: C. C. Jones, *History of Georgia to* 1783; U. B. Phillips, *Georgia* (American Commonwealth Series); Brooks, *History of Georgia.*

GEORGIA, GULF OF, a large gulf of the North Pacific Ocean, between the continent of North America and Vancouver Island; about 120 miles in length from north to south; the breadth varies greatly in its different parts, from 6 to 20 miles. It communicates with the ocean on the north by Queen Charlotte's Sound, and on the south by the Straits of Juan de Fuca.

GEORGIA, SOUTH, an island in the South Atlantic, lat. at its north point, 53° 57′ S.; long. 38° 13′ W. It is 90 miles long, and has high and rocky coasts, inaccessible owing to ice during a great part of the year. It abounds with seals and sea-fowl.

GEORGIA BARK (*Pinckneya pubens*), a small tree of the Southern United States closely resembling the cinchona or Peruvian bark, and belonging to the nat. ord. Rubiaceæ. It has large white flowers, with longitudinal stripes of rose-colour, disposed in beautiful clusters at the extremities of the branches; each flower is accompanied by a floral leaf, bordered with rose-colour near the upper margin; the corolla is tubular; the stamens five, with a single style; and the capsule contains two cells and numerous seeds. The wood is soft and unfit for any practical use. The inner bark is extremely bitter, and is employed with success in intermittent fevers.

GEORGIAN BAY, formerly called **Lake Manitoulin,** the north-eastern part of Lake Huron, partly separated from the main body of the lake by the peninsula of Cabot's Head and the Island of Great Manitoulin. It is about 120 miles long and 50 miles broad. The Georgian Bay Canal, planned to connect the Georgian Bay with the St. Lawrence at Montreal, has not yet been constructed. Its cost has been estimated at £30,000,000.

GEORGICS, poem by Virgil. In Greek the word means husbandry, and the poem deals with pastoral life. It was written about 40 B.C., and is in four books. Scholars regard it as a perfect example of style and thought.

GEOTROPISM, the curvature of a plant-organ in response to the stimulus of gravity. If, for example, a seedling of bean, pumpkin, &c., be placed horizontally on damp sawdust for twenty-four hours, the root will be found to have curved downwards, and the stem upwards, thus returning to their normal vertical position. If, however, the seedling, while in the horizontal position, be slowly rotated around a horizontal axis, so as to equalize the effect of gravity on all sides of the stem and root, these organs, instead of curving, continue to grow in the horizontal plane, thus proving that the unequal growth which brought about the curvature in the first case was due to the one-sided action of gravity. Most primary roots behave like that of the bean, and are said to be *positively geotropic*; stems, on the other hand, are usually *negatively geotropic*. Leaves, as a rule, tend to take up a horizontal position, and are termed *transversely geotropic* or *diageotropic*. The twining of certain stems (e.g. scarlet runner, hop, convolvulus) is due to a special form of geotropic response called *lateral geotropism*.

GEOTRU'PIDÆ, a family of burrowing lamellicorn beetles. They inhabit temperate climates, and are useful in removing disgusting substances. When alarmed they feign death. The *Geotrüpes stercorarius*, or watchman-beetle of Britain, is the type of the family.

GERA (gā'rà), chief town of the former principality of Reuss-Schleiz, in Germany, on the right bank of the Elster, 35 miles S.S.W. of Leipzig. It has manufactures of woollen, linen, cotton, and other goods. Pop. 81,402.

GERANIA'CEÆ, a nat, ord. of Dicotyledons, the distinguishing characteristic of which is to have a fruit composed of five capsules or cases, connected with as many flat styles, consolidated round a long conical beak, giving some of the species the name of stork's-bill and crane's-bill. These plants are usually astringent and odoriferous, and many of them have beautiful flowers, especially those of the genus Pelargonium, natives of the Cape of Good Hope. The species are mostly herbaceous plants. A few of them have edible tubers.

GERANIUM, the typical genus of the ord. Geraniaceæ, popular name crane's-bill. They have usually palmately divided leaves and regular flowers, with ten stamens and five carpels. Some thirteen species are wild in Britain, of which the *G. robertianum* or herb-robert is the most common. An American species, *G. maculātum*, from its astringency called 'alum-root,' is used medicinally as a gargle and otherwise. The so-called geraniums of our gardens belong to the genus Pelargonium. Cultivation has produced many varieties, which from their beauty are great favourites.

GÉRARD (zhā'rär), François Pascal, Baron, a French historical and portrait painter, born at Rome in 1770, died in 1837. In 1786 he went to Paris, where he studied under David, and in 1795 he exhibited his first notable painting, *Belisarius* (now at Leningrad). He was much patronized by Napoleon, for whom he painted the *Battle of Austerlitz*, and was made a baron by Louis XVIII, after completing his large painting of the *Entrance of Henry IV into Paris* (in the Museum of Versailles). His portraits include: *Napoleon, Talleyrand, Louis XVIII, Murat*, and *Louis Philippe*.

GÉRARD, Hon. James Watson, American jurist and diplomatist, born at Genesco, New York, in 1867. Educated at Columbia University, he studied law and practised for some time. An associate justice of the Supreme Court from 1908 to 1913, he was appointed by President Wilson United States Ambassador to Germany, and remained in Berlin until 1917, when America entered the European War. During the first two years of the European War Gerard, as representative of a neutral state, looked after the interests of the British in Germany, and greatly interested himself in the welfare of war prisoners. He published *My Four Years in Germany* (1917), and *Face to Face with Kaiserism* (1918), wherein he severely indicted Germany and her war-aims. He was created a G.C.B. in 1917.

GÉRARD, Jean Ignace Isidore, a French caricaturist and book illustrator, generally known under the pseudonym of *Grandville*, was born at Nancy in 1803, died at Paris in 1847. He went to Paris in 1824, and after some minor works acquired great popularity in 1828 by his *Métamorphoses du jour*, a representation under the guise of animal heads of human foibles and weaknesses. Later on he became a contributor to *Le Charivari* and an illustrator of the works of Béranger and La Fontaine, and of *Gulliver's Travels* and *Robinson Crusoe*.

GÉRARD, Maurice Étienne, Count, Marshal, and Peer of France, born 1773, died at Paris in 1852. He served as a soldier during the republic and the empire, distinguishing himself at Austerlitz and other battles. In 1813 he was made a general of division and count, distinguished himself in the battle of Ligny, and at Waterloo acted under Grouchy. He took an active part in the revolution of 1830; became War Minister and Marshal; commanded the troops which reduced Antwerp in 1832; became Prime

Minister 1834, and commander of the National Guard in 1838.

GÉRARD de NERVAL, the pseudonym of **Gérard Labrunie**, French man of letters, born in Paris 1808. His earlier productions were poetic. *Élégies nationales* and *Poésies diverses*. As an adherent of the Romantic school he set himself to translate Goethe's *Faust*, and performed it in a manner which the old poet himself pronounced a marvel of style. Amongst his best works are his short tales and sketches, *Scènes de la vie orientale*, *Voyage en Orient*, *Contes et facéties*, *La Bohême galante*, &c. He became insane, and committed suicide in Paris in 1855.

GERASA (je-rä'sà), **GERASH**, or **DJERASH**, a ruined town in Palestine, among the mountains of Gilead. It was several times destroyed and rebuilt. The ruins, comprising ancient walls, gateways, a forum, baths, theatres, and temples, are very extensive.

GERBA, or **JERBA**, an island in the Gulf of Cabes, off the coast of

Gerbillus

Tunis. It is about 20 miles long and 14 miles broad. The surface is level and fertile, and occupied by a population of 35,000, mostly Berbers.

GERBIL'LUS, a genus of small burrowing rodents (the gerbils) of the family Muridæ (mice). They have a long tail, which is tufted at the end. There are numerous species, found in the sandy parts of Africa and Asia. The Egyptian gerbil (*G. œgyptiacus*), inhabiting Egypt around the pyramids, is the type. It is about the size of a mouse, and of a clear yellow colour.

GERHARDT (ger'hàrt), **Charles Frédéric**, French chemist, born 1816, died in 1856. He studied under Liebig at Giessen; went to Paris in 1838, was appointed professor of chemistry at Montpellier, but returned to Paris in 1842 to pursue his investigations. In 1855 he went to Strasbourg as professor of chemistry and pharmacy, but died soon after. Gerhardt is the author of several works, amongst which the most celebrated is his valuable *Traité de chimie organique*. He was the first to introduce the new combining weights, or rather to subject more completely combination by weight to combination by volume; to originate the theory of types; and to

furnish new ideas on classification, homology, and similar subjects. The methods he originated have had a great influence on modern chemistry.

GERHARDT, Paul, German hymn-writer, born in 1607, died in 1676. He studied theology, became pastor of Mittenwalde in 1651, and afterwards went to Berlin. A strict Lutheran, he opposed energetically all attempts to unite the Lutheran and Reformed Churches, and was removed from his church in 1666 in consequence of his refusal to subscribe to the edict of 16th Sept., 1664, prohibiting mutual insults or offensive language between the Churches. In 1668 he was made Archdeacon of Lübben, where he died. His excellent book of hymns appeared at Berlin in 1667 (*Geistliche Andachten*). Many particular hymns have found English translators, such as: *Commit thou all thy griefs*; and *Jesus, Thy boundless love to me*.—Cf. Kelly, *Gerhardt's Spiritual Songs*.

GÉRICAULT (zhã-rē-kō), **Jean Louis Théodore André**, a French painter, born at Rouen in 1791, came to Paris in 1806 and studied under Charles Vernet and Guérin. His first pictures (the *Chasseur Officer* and the *Wounded Cuirassier*) were exhibited in 1812 and 1814. In 1817 he visited Italy, returned to Paris in 1819, and painted the *Raft of the Medusa* (a well-known shipwreck of the time), a work of much power, which won great popularity. He took this work with him to England, where he exhibited it at a shilling admission and realized £800. During his stay in England he painted his *Race for the Derby at Epsom*. He died at Paris in 1824.

GERM, in physiology, the earliest form under which any organism appears, that is, the rudimentary or embryonic form. The name is also given to certain minute organisms which give rise to disease. See GERM THEORY OF DISEASE.

GERMAIN (zher-man), **ST.**, the name of a number of places in France, among which is St. Germain-en-Laye, a town in the department of Seine-et-Oise, about 6 miles north of Versailles and 11 miles w.n.w. of Paris, on the left bank of the Seine. The most remarkable building is the royal palace, commenced by Charles V in 1370, and embellished by several of his successors, especially Francis I and Louis XIV. It was used as a prison during the Revolution, afterwards as a school for cavalry officers, and was ultimately restored in 1862 by Napoleon III, who established in it a museum of Gallo-Roman antiquities. The Treaty with Austria was signed here on 10th Sept., 1919. The forest of St. Germain is one of the finest in

France, extending over 10,000 acres. Pop. 31,996.

GERMAN, Sir Edward, K.T., British composer, born at Whitchurch Shropshire, 17th Feb., 1862, and educated at Bridge House School, and the Royal Academy of Music, which he left in 1887. In 1888 he became musical director at the Globe Theatre, and while there produced incidental music to *Richard III*, which first brought him into prominence. His incidental music to *Henry VIII* (1892) and to *Nell Gwyn* (1900) is well known. He completed *The Emerald Isle*, an opera left unfinished by Sullivan (produced in 1901), and also composed the scores of the light operas *Merrie England* (1902), *A Princess of Kensington* (1903), and *Tom Jones* (1907). In 1909 he wrote the music for *Fallen Fairies*, Gilbert's operatic version of his early play *The Wicked World*. In 1919 he composed the *Theme and Six Diversions* for the Royal Philharmonic Society, and the *Willow Song* (Othello) for the R.A.M. Centenary, in 1922. He has also composed many orchestral symphonies and songs. His music is widely popular, and is distinguished by tunefulness. He was knighted in 1928.

GERMAN CATHOLICS, a religious sect which sprang up in Germany about the close of the year 1844. The immediate cause of its formation was the exhibition by Arnoldi, Bishop of Trèves, of the holy coat preserved in the cathedral of that city, accompanied by a promise of plenary indulgence to whoever should make a pilgrimage to Trèves to worship it. The announcement caused a general feeling of astonishment in Germany, and two priests, Johannes Ronge of Silesia and Johann Czerski of Posen, whose independent views had already caused the deposition of the one and the secession of the other, led a secession movement, appealing to the lower grades of clergy to unite in founding a National German Church independent of the Pope. Many congregations were formed, especially in Leipzig, under the celebrated Robert Blum, and in Magdeburg under the teacher Kote. Two creeds were drawn up for the new Church, the *Confession of Schneidemühl*, by Czerski, which, though substantially Roman Catholic, rejected indulgences, purgatory, and auricular confession, and the *Confession of Breslau*, drawn up by Ronge. The latter, which was much less orthodox, was substantially adopted by the Council which met at Leipzig on 22nd March, 1845.

Many Protestants joined the body, which in 1845 numbered nearly 300 congregations. Difficulties soon arose, however. The majority of the German Governments began to use repressive measures. More fatal were internal dissensions, one party, headed by Czerski, clinging to the traditions and doctrines of the Roman Catholic Church, the other, headed by Ronge, tending to mix up democratic and socialistic principles with their creed. The result, in spite of several attempts to re-establish unity, was disintegration and decay. The congregations rapidly dwindled, many being re-admitted to the State Church, and, especially after the rise of 'Old Catholicism,' the movement lost all importance.

GERMAN'DER, the common name of three British plants of the genus Teucrium, ord. Labiatæ, namely *T. Chamædrys*, wall-germander, *T. scordium*, water-germander, and *T. scorodonia*, wood-germander or wood-sage. They were all formerly used in medicine, and are still employed by country herbalists.

GERMAN EAST AFRICA. *See* TANGANYIKA TERRITORY.

GERMAN'ICUS, Cæsar, a distinguished Roman, son of Nero Claudius Drusus and the younger Antenia, a niece of Augustus, was born 15 B.C. He was adopted by Tiberius, his paternal uncle, and married Agrippina, the granddaughter of Augustus. When Augustus died, in A.D. 14, Germanicus was invited by the rebellious legions on the Rhine to assume the sovereignty, but refused, and quelled the revolt. He then crossed the Rhine, and surprised and defeated the Marsi with great slaughter. Next year (A.D. 15) a campaign against the Catti and the Germans, led by Arminius, resulted in a series of victories.

The following year he again made his way into Germany, defeated the Cherusci twice, and made an incursion into the country of the Marsi. Tiberius now became jealous of the glory of Germanicus, called him home under pretence of granting him a triumph, then, to get rid of him, sent him into the East to compose the disturbances in Armenia and Cappadocia. This he performed in A.D. 18, visited Egypt the following year, and died on his return to Syria (A.D. 19) under some suspicion of having been poisoned by Cn. Piso, the Governor of Syria.

GERMAN SILVER, NICKEL SILVER, or PACKFONG, is an alloy of copper, nickel, and zinc, containing 40 to 65 per cent copper, 15 to 30 of zinc, and 6 to 35 of nickel. The alloys containing most nickel are the most expensive, but they have the best colour and mechanical properties. Small quantities of lead are often added to assist the working of the metal. Alloys containing 30 per cent

V—F

of zinc, 6 to 12 nickel, the remainder being copper, are used for small mechanical parts. For castings, high-pressure steam-fittings, &c., 70 per cent copper, 10 zinc, 20 nickel is used; for tableware the alloy contains 55 to 60 per cent copper, 20 to 25 zinc, and 20 nickel. German silver has been used for coinage in Belgium and Chile.

GERMAN VOLGA REPUBLIC, Soviet Republic. One of eleven autonomous republics in the Russian

Germanicus

Socialist Federal Soviet Republics, it was created in 1924. It is enclosed by the Lower Volga Area, except in the south-east. The government is by Central Executive Committee and Council of Peoples' Commissaries, the capital being Pokrovsk, on the Volga, with a population of 34,352. There are railways running from Moscow to Astrakhan and Uralsk, with a junction at Urbakh. The chief crops are wheat, barley and rye, and there are agricultural and peasant industries.

GERMANY, a Central European federation of republics corresponding to the former German Empire. It is bounded by the North Sea, Denmark, the Baltic Sea, Poland, Czechoslovakia, Austria, Switzerland, France, Luxembourg, Belgium, and Holland. East Prussia, a Baltic district of Prussia (lying south of Lithuania), is separated from the rest of Germany by the Polish Corridor.

Area. The total area is 181,723 sq. miles (including the Saar district, which has an area of 738 sq. miles), and the total population by the 1925 census was 63,180,649 (770,030 of whom are in the Saar area); the estimated population in 1932 was 64,776,000, or, including the Saar, 65,594,000. The area is 27,252 sq. miles less than that of the Empire in 1914. This is accounted for by the cession (Treaty of Versailles, 1919) of Alsace-Lorraine to France, of Eupen and Malmédy to Belgium, of Memel (now part of Lithuania) and Danzig (now a free state) to the Allies, of part of Upper Silesia to Czechoslovakia, and of parts of West Prussia, Posen, Eastern Silesia, and East Prussia to Poland. As the result of a plebiscite in 1920, Northern Schleswig (now known as Slesvig) was transferred to Denmark.

Upper Silesia, which by a plebiscite in 1922 decided for annexation to Germany, was nevertheless transferred to Poland. The inhabitants of the Saar Basin (*see* SAAR), which is under League of Nations control, will decide the future of the territory by plebiscite in 1934. The Ruhr Valley was occupied by the French from 1923 till the signing of the London Agreement accepting the Dawes Plan in 1924 (*see* RUHR). The Cologne Zone of the Rhineland area in allied occupation (*see* map on p. 167) was evacuated subsequent to the signing of the Locarno Pact (*see* LOCARNO), in 1925.

Physical Features. Germany, as regards its surface, may be divided into three different regions. Farthest south is the Alpine region along the southern frontier, comprising parts of Bavaria, Württemberg, and Baden, lying next to Austria and Switzerland. North of this the Suabian-Bavarian plateau extends to the mountain region of Central Germany, where the chain known as the Fichtelgebirge is continued east by the Erzgebirge and the Riesengebirge, forming the boundary next Austria; west by the Thüringerwald, Rhöngebirge, and Spessart; farther north lie the Harz Mountains. The great plain in the north extends without interruption to the North Sea and the Baltic.

Rivers. Germany is remarkably well watered. Its central mountain region and plateau form part of the great water-shed of Europe. The Danube proceeds across it in an easterly direction, and the Rhine, though it neither rises nor terminates within Germany, flows within it for the greater part of its course. After these come the Elbe, Oder, Vistula, Weser, Main, Neckar, Mosel, Ems, and Eider—all of them navigable.

Minerals. Germany possesses much varied mineral riches, the most important minerals being coal and lignite, iron, zinc, lead, copper, and salt. Rich coal-mines are found in the Ruhr Valley, in the Saar Basin (occupied by

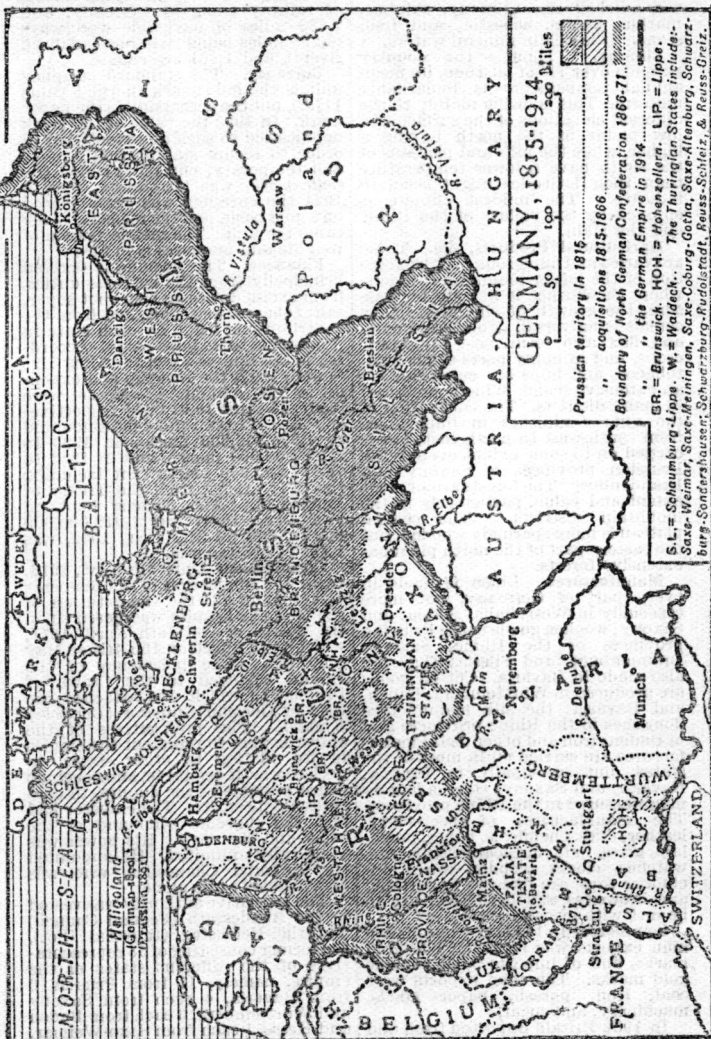

GERMANY, 1815-1914

0   50   100   200 Miles

Prussian territory in 1815.

„   acquisitions 1815-1866.

„   „   1866-71.

Boundary of North German Confederation 1866-71.

„   „   the German Empire in 1914.

BR. = Brunswick. HOH. = Hohenzollern. LIP. = Lippe.
S.L. = Schaumburg-Lippe. W. = Waldeck. The Thuringian States including: Saxe-Weimar, Saxe-Meiningen, Saxe-Coburg-Gotha, Saxe-Altenburg, Schwarz-
burg-Sondershausen, Schwarzburg-Rudolstadt, Reuss-Schleiz, & Reuss-Greiz.

The German Empire before the European War

France), and in Lower and Upper Silesia (the latter in the plebiscite area). Other minerals are tin, silver, quicksilver, antimony, sulphur, marble, kaolin, asbestos, and freestone. It is rich in mineral waters.

Climate. Though the country extends over $7\frac{1}{2}°$ of latitude, its mean annual temperature is remarkably uniform. This is owing mainly to the different elevations of the surface, the low plains of the north having a higher, while the hills and plateaus of the south have a lower temperature than their latitudes might seem to indicate. The mildest climate is enjoyed by the valleys of the Rhine and the Main.

Agricultural Products, &c. These are varied and numerous. With exception of the loftier mountain districts, where the surface is fit only for pasture, the growth of all the ordinary cereals is universal. Potatoes, hemp, and flax also form most important crops, and in many parts sugar-beet, tobacco, and hops are cultivated on an extensive scale. Wine is produced in many districts. The cultivation of the vine diminishes in importance from south-west to north-east, but is carried on to some extent even in the Prussian provinces of Saxony and Brandenburg. The forests are of great extent and value, particularly in the mountain districts. The central plateau is more sparingly wooded, but the eastern part of the north plain has extensive forests.

Manufactures. Linen is made in every part of Germany, but more especially in Westphalia, Silesia, and Saxony; woollen goods in the Prussian provinces of the Rhine, Saxony, Brandenburg, and Silesia; they are also made in Bavaria. Cotton goods are produced in Württemberg, Baden, and Bavaria; the silk manufacture flourishes in the Rhine provinces and in Baden; iron and other metal manufactures are carried on in most of the states, but principally in Prussia, Bavaria, and Saxony; steel is largely manufactured in the Rhine provinces. The manufactures of beet-sugar, leather, dyes, chemicals, paper, porcelain, glass, hats, musical instruments, watches, clocks, wooden wares, including toys, are likewise important; and breweries and distilleries are to be met with everywhere.

Commerce. In 1932 the value of German exports was 6,190,200,000 gold marks, and of imports 5,035,000,000 gold marks. The chief exports were coal, iron, potash, paper goods, machinery, and sugar.

In 1932 Britain imported from and exported to Germany goods valued at £30,410,492 and £14,580,763 respectively. The German Mercantile marine amounted in 1932 to 4,164,842 tons, compared with 5,459,296 tons in 1914. In 1931 there were 36,257 miles of railway track in Germany, and 7,689 miles of navigable waterways (6,228 miles being rivers or canalized rivers), and 1,461 are canals.

Currency. The standard currency unit is the gold mark (normal value $11\frac{3}{4}d.$), but the actual unit is the paper mark. In 1923 the value of the mark depreciated to such an extent that in order to secure stabilization a new, and temporary, currency, called the *rentenmark*, was introduced, but in 1924 the currency was again placed on a gold basis, and the reichsmark became the unit. The metric system of weights and measures is in force.

Finances. The revenue is derived principally from the customs duties, from excise duties on beet-root sugar, salt, tobacco, and malt, and from the contributions made by each state in proportion to its population. According to the Budget for year ending 31st March, 1932, the revenue and expenditure in millions of marks were 8,567,600 and 10,042,000 respectively. In 1913 the total debt amounted to 4,925,800,000 marks, in 1925 to 2,702,900,000 marks, and in 1932 to 12,137,300,000 marks (not including the debt arising from the Treaty of Versailles). The floating debt on 31st Dec., 1931, was 1,912,600,000 marks, and on 31st Dec., 1932, was 1,836,200,000 marks.

Constitution. Until 9th Nov., 1918, when the abdication of the emperor was announced, the Constitution of the German Empire was based upon the decree of the 16th April, 1871, which took effect on the 4th of May following. The presidency of the empire belonged to the Crown of Prussia, to which was attached the title of German Emperor (*Deutscher Kaiser*). The prerogatives of the emperor were to represent the empire in its relation to other states, to declare war, if defensive, and conclude peace in name of the empire, to contract alliances, &c. The emperor had also the supreme command of the army and the navy. His power was practically unlimited. He appointed the Imperial Chancellor, who was responsible to him alone.

The legislative authority was vested in the Bundesrath (Federal Council) and the Reichstag (Imperial Diet), the former consisting of 58 representatives of the different states of the empire, namely, 17 from Prussia, 6 from Bavaria, 4 each from Saxony and Württemberg, 3 each from Baden and Hesse, 1 each from Saxe-Weimar, and others. The Reichstag consisted of 397 Deputies, elected by ballot and universal suffrage in all the states of

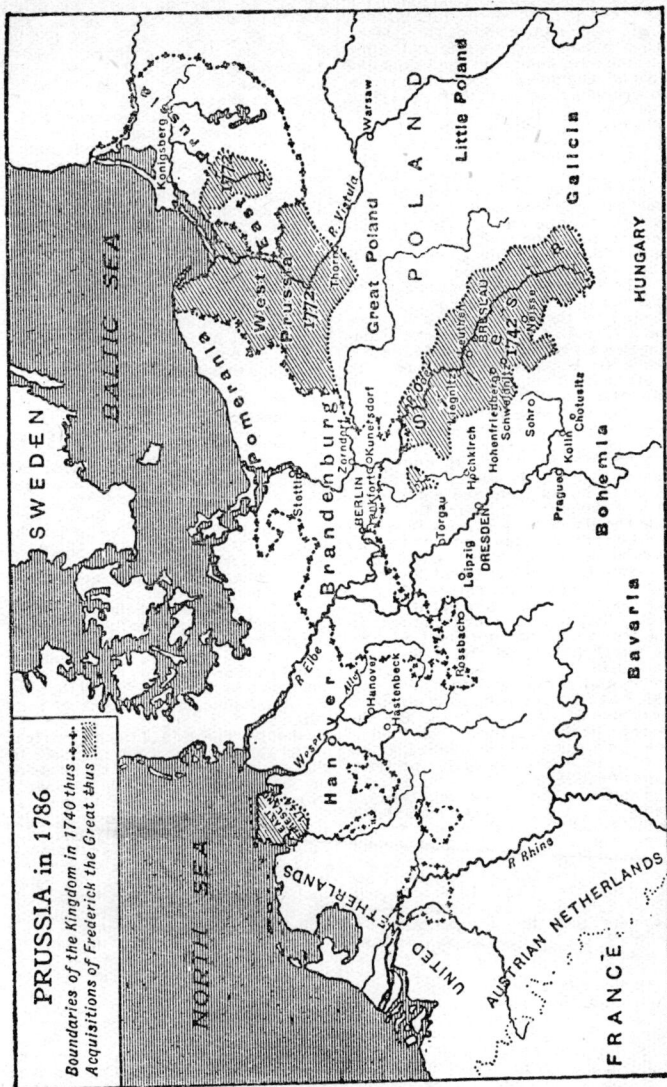

PRUSSIA in 1786

Boundaries of the Kingdom in 1740 thus ·—·—·—·
Acquisitions of Frederick the Great thus ▨▨▨

the empire. On the average one member was returned to the Reichstag for every 124,500 of the inhabitants.

After the abdication of the Kaiser, 9th Nov., 1918, the German Empire became a republic, and the Council of People's Commissioners took over the government. In Jan., 1919, elections were held for a National Assembly, which met at Weimar on 6th Feb., 1919. The first President of the Republic was elected on the 11th Feb., 1919, and the Constitution was adopted in July of the same year. In accordance with the new Republican Constitution, the power of the state is derived from the people. Suffrage is universal, equal, direct, and secret. The members of the legislative Reichstag are elected for four years, and the President of the Republic is elected by the whole German people for a period of seven years. Besides the Reichstag (or Parliament) there is also a Reichsrat (or Imperial Council), composed of representatives of all federated (republican) German states.

Defence. Before 1914 service in the German army or navy was obligatory on every man in Germany who was not morally or physically unfit, and no substitution was allowed. Liability to serve began from the completion of the seventeenth year, but as a rule the six years' service required in the standing army (seven in the cavalry and field artillery) was from the twentieth to the twenty-seventh year. Two of the six years (or three as the case might be) were spent on the active list, and the remaining four in the reserve. After quitting the army of reserve, the next five years were passed in the first class of the Landwehr, and seven in the second. All able-bodied men from seventeen to forty-five who were not in the line, the reserve, or the Landwehr, belonged to the Landsturm, which was called out only in case of invasion of the territory of the empire.

The peace strength of the German army before 1914 was about 584,000 men. During the European War Germany put in the field about 10,000,000 men; her strength decreased considerably, but the total strength of her army on 11th Nov., 1918, was still about 6,000,000 men. By the Treaty of Versailles the German army is reduced to 100,000 men, the total strength in 1932 being 4,500 officers and 96,000 men.

During 1919, however, various military organizations came into existence, under the pretext that they were required to maintain order. In 1920 these military associations were disbanded, except in East Prussia and Bavaria. Under the Treaty of Versailles the German navy ceased to exist. The German Government was allowed to maintain a navy recruited only on the voluntary system. The fleet may consist only of six battleships, six light cruisers, twelve destroyers, and twelve torpedo-boats. The scuttling of the German ships interned at Scapa (21st June, 1919) put an end to the German High Seas Fleet.

Religion and Education. The new Constitution of the German Republic provides for complete social and religious equality and for entire liberty of conscience. At the census of 1925 Germany contained 40,014,677 Protestants, 20,193,334 Catholics, 87,580 Christians of other denominations, and 564,379 Jews.

Education is compulsory throughout Germany. Every commune or parish must support at its own cost a primary school. Every town in addition must maintain one or more middle schools, which supply a higher education than the elementary schools. Above these are *real schools* (*Realschulen*) giving a still higher education, nearly corresponding to what is called the *modern side* in Great Britain; institutions of similar standing called *gymnasiums*, giving an education in which the ancient languages form a more important element; and, above all, the universities, of which there are twenty-three in the country, the chief being those of Berlin, Leipzig, and Munich. There are also numerous libraries, academies, and learned societies.

The Germans as a whole are perhaps the most systematically educated people in the world, although until the Revolution of 1918 the tendency of education was to lay stress on obedience to the State rather than on the development of a spirit of self-reliance.

History. The date of the first arrival of the Germanic or Teutonic races in Europe is unknown. At the close of the second century B.C. Germanic tribes called Cimbri and Teutones left their homes in the Danish peninsula, and descending upon Italy were defeated by Marius at Aquæ Sextiæ (Aix in Provence) and Vercellæ in Northern Italy. The Romans did not come again in contact with the Germans till Cæsar's invasion of Gaul brought on a contest with the Suevian prince Ariovistus (58 B.C.). At that time several German tribes had crossed the Rhine and settled in the district between that river and the Vosges Mountains, while others had pushed their way through what is now Belgium. The Germans on the left bank of the Rhine were soon subjugated, and two expeditions were made by Cæsar across the Rhine.

Under Augustus a systematic

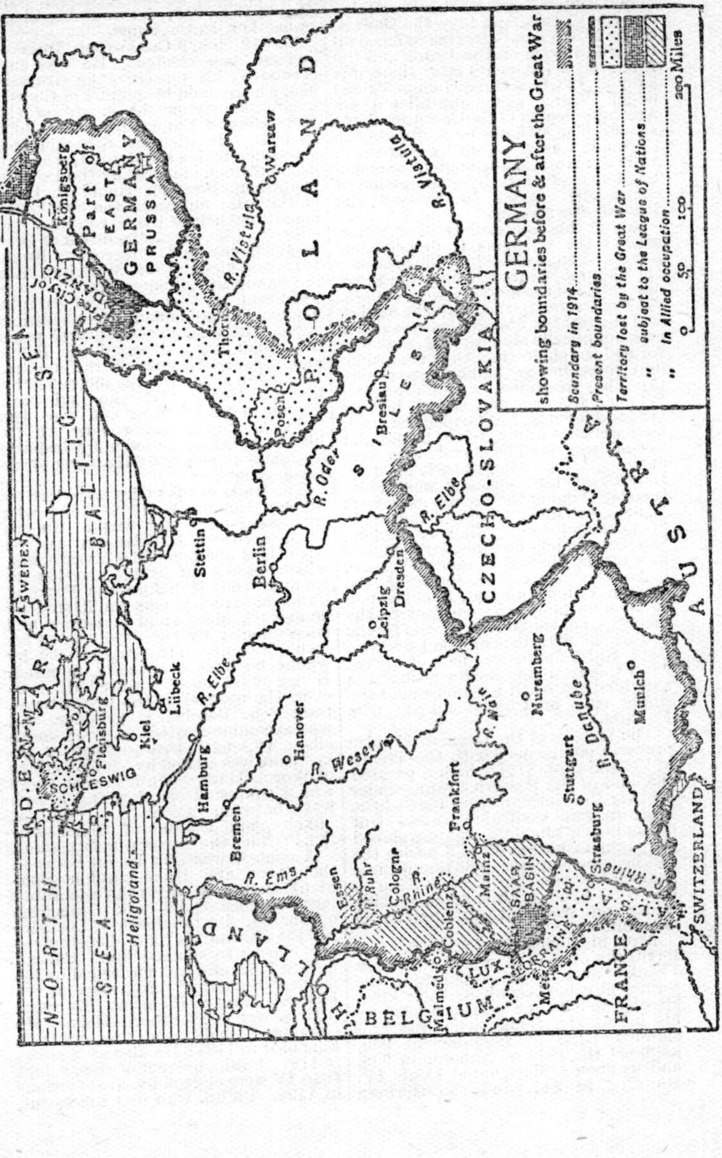

GERMANY
showing boundaries before & after the Great War
Boundary in 1914
Present boundaries
Territory lost by the Great War
" subject to the League of Nations
" In Allied occupation
0 50 100 200 Miles
Memel
Königsberg
Part of EAST PRUSSIA
GERMANY
Free City of DANZIG
Thorn
Warsaw
R. Vistula
POLAND
Posen
Breslau
SILESIA
R. Oder
BALTIC SEA
SWEDEN
DENMARK
SCHLESWIG
Flensburg
Kiel
Lübeck
Stettin
Berlin
Hamburg
R. Elbe
Bremen
Hanover
R. Weser
Leipzig
Dresden
CZECHO-SLOVAKIA
NORTH SEA
Heligoland
HOLLAND
R. Ems
Essen
R. Ruhr
Cologne
R. Rhine
Coblenz
Mainz
SAAR BASIN
Frankfort
R. Main
Nuremberg
Stuttgart
R. Danube
Munich
AUSTRIA
Strasburg
ALSACE
LORRAINE
Metz
LUX
Malmedy
BELGIUM
FRANCE
SWITZERLAND

attempt was made to subjugate the vast and little-known region Germania, extending between the Rhine and the Vistula, and from the Danube to the North Sea. Tiberius reduced all the tribes between the Rhine and the Elbe, but a few years later there was a revolt, in which three Roman legions under Varus were annihilated by Arminius, leader of the Cherusci, about A.D. 9. The attempt to subjugate the Germans was given up by Augustus; and Germanicus, although he avenged the defeat of Varus by a succession of campaigns, failed to recover the Roman ascendancy.

About this time each tribe or nation among the Germans is described as having been divided into four classes: (1) The nobles, from whom the kings and chiefs of the districts were chosen. (2) The freemen, who, with the nobles, had the right to choose their residence and hold heritable property, and who formed the chief strength of the armies and voted in the popular assemblies. (3) The freedmen, a middle class between freemen and slaves, had no landed property, but farmed the land; they were not admitted to the popular assemblies. (4) The slaves, who were entirely in the power of their masters. In religion the Germans were polytheists. Among their great gods were Weden (or Odin), Donar (Thor), Thiu (Tyr), and Frigga. They erected no temples and had no idols, but believed in a future life and in eternal justice.

As the aggressive force of the Roman Empire abated, it continued to be more and more subject to the incursions of the Germans, who by the end of the fifth century had overrun Gaul, Italy, Spain, and part of Africa. After this Germany itself continued in a divided state till it came under the single rule of Charlemagne. (See FRANCE.)

The history of the German Empire properly commences with the Treaty of Verdun (A.D. 843), which separated the land of the Eastern Franks under Ludwig the German from that of the Western and Central Franks. Out of Ludwig's kingdom was developed the German nationality. Charles the Fat became emperor in 881, and three years later was also elected King of the West Franks, thus again uniting under one sceptre the monarchy of Charlemagne.

After his deposition in 887 the two territories of the Eastern and Western Franks were again separated, the former electing Arnulf as their king. He died in 899, and was succeeded by his infant son Louis, who was proclaimed King of Lorraine in 900, assumed the title of emperor in 908, and as such is designated Louis IV. He died in 911, and the German

nations chose Conrad, Count or Duke of Franconia, as his successor. He died in Dec., 918, of a wound received in battle with the Huns.

In 919 Henry the Fowler, Duke of Saxony, was elected. He was succeeded by his son Otto the Great in 936, who revived the empire of Charlemagne, receiving the crown of the Holy Roman Empire from the Pope in 962. He died in 973, and was succeeded by his son Otto II, who had been crowned emperor by the Pope in his father's lifetime. Henry II, Duke of Bavaria, surnamed the Saint, the hereditary heir of the Saxon line, was elected at Mainz, on the death of Otto in 1002, crowned emperor in Rome 1014, and died in 1024. With him ends the Saxon line of emperors.

Conrad II, surnamed the Salic, a Franconian nobleman, was chosen to succeed him. He spent several years in Italian wars, defeated the Poles, and restored Lusatia to the empire. He died in 1039. He was succeeded by his son Henry III, who had been chosen in his lifetime, and who, the imperial power being now at its highest point, exercised more despotic authority in Germany than any of his predecessors.

The fruits of his policy were lost by his son Henry IV (1056–1106), who was passionate and weak. In his reign occurred the famous quarrel with the Pope regarding investitures, which ended in Henry having to humble himself before the Pope at Canossa. His life was embittered by contests against rival emperors, and subsequently by the defection of his own son Henry to the Papal party, by whom he was eventually deposed. Henry V (1106–25) inherited, however, the quarrel of the investitures, took Pope Paschal II prisoner, and was excommunicated by seven councils. At length the question of investiture was settled by the Concordat of Worms (1122). On his death there was a contested election and a civil war between Lothaire, Duke of Saxony, and Conrad of Hohenstaufen, in which the former was successful.

A contest was now begun between the Saxon and Hohenstaufen (Suabian) families, in which the celebrated party names Guelf and Ghibelline originated. On the death of Lothaire in 1138 Conrad III (of Hohenstaufen) was chosen to succeed him. Conrad died in 1152, and was succeeded by his nephew Frederick Barbarossa (q.v.). His son Henry VI began his reign with a war in Southern Italy. He conquered Sicily, and was crowned king of it in 1194. He died at Messina in 1197. Philip, brother of Henry, and Otto IV were elected by rival factions in 1198. Philip, who was successful, was assassinated in 1208. Otto IV, the son of Henry the Lion, was recognized by the Diet of Frankfort in 1208 as the successor of Philip. He attempted the conquest of the Two Sicilies without success, and died in 1218. Frederick II, King of the Sicilies, was elected emperor in 1212. His life passed in contentions with the Popes and the Lombard cities. He died in 1250.

Conrad IV, his son, had to contend against William of Holland. He died in 1254. He was the last emperor of the House of Hohenstaufen, which became extinct on the death of his son. His successor, William of Holland, was slain in Friesland in 1256. Richard, Earl of Cornwall, and Alfonso X, King of Castile, were chosen emperors in 1257; but the internal divisions of Germany had already deprived the office of all authority, and neither of them had any power. Until 1273 the German Empire had no real head.

Rudolph, Count of Habsburg and Cyburg, the most powerful prince in Helvetia, was chosen emperor (1272). He enriched his own family by his victories over the King of Bohemia, and acquired Austria, Styria, and Carinthia as imperial fiefs for his sons Albert and Rudolph. He died in 1291. Adolphus of Nassau, his successor, was deposed in 1298 by the Diet of Mainz. Albert I, son of Rudolph, was chosen emperor the same year. He is chiefly celebrated for his wars with the Swiss as Duke of Austria, which led to the independence of Switzerland. He died in 1308, and was succeeded by Henry VII of Luxembourg, nearly the whole of whose reign was passed in Italy, where he died in 1313. In 1314 a double election took place: Frederick, Duke of Austria, sometimes called Frederick III, was elected along with Louis of Bavaria. On the death of Frederick in 1330 the latter became sole emperor. He died excommunicated and deposed in 1347. Charles IV, King of Bohemia, was elected in 1346. His reign is chiefly distinguished for the Golden Bull (1356) regulating the electorate. (*See* GOLDEN BULL.) He died in 1378. Wenceslaus, his son, was deposed for his excesses in 1400. Rupert, Count Palatine, elected 1400, possessed little authority. Sigismund, King of Hungary and Bohemia, son of Charles IV, was elected by a party in 1410. His reign is distinguished by the commencement of the Reformation in Bohemia, by the Council of Constance, and the condemnation of Huss and Jerome. He died in 1437. Albert II (V of Austria) was elected in 1438, and died in 1439.

He was succeeded by Frederick III, Duke of Styria and Carinthia. He was

the last emperor who was crowned in Rome. Henceforth the German emperors were always of the House of Austria. He died in 1493. His son Maximilian I succeeded. During his reign the Diet of Cologne was held, which divided the estates of the empire into ten circles for the better maintenance of the public peace.

Since its rise the empire had undergone many changes. At the extinction of the Carlovingian dynasty Germany was divided into five nations or dukedoms—Franconia, Suabia, Bavaria, Saxony, and Lorraine. Henry the Fowler and the Ottos added the marches of Austria and Misnia; Henry the Lion and Albert of Brandenburg, Mecklenburg and Pomerania. The House of Austria added Styria, Carinthia, Carniola, and the Tyrol. But Switzerland had been lost, and the old Burgundian territories of the empire, Franche Comté, the Lyonnais, and Provence, had gone to consolidate the French monarchy under Louis XI.

Bohemia and Hungary, and many of the Italian cities, especially in the north, were also connected with the empire, but the connection was more formal than real, and the circles established by the Diet of Cologne (1512) represented at that time the estates of the empire, viz.: (1) Austria; (2) Bavaria; (3) Swabia; (4) Franconia; (5) the Upper Rhine (Lorraine, Hesse, &c.); (6) the Lower Rhine, or the Electorates (Mainz, Trier, Cologne); (7) Burgundy (Netherlands); (8) Westphalia; (9) Lower Saxony (Brunswick, Lüneburg, Lauenburg, Holstein); (10) Upper Saxony (Saxony, Brandenburg, Pomerania).

The chief political machinery of the empire was connected with the Diet. The exact constitution of the early German Diets is not known. In the twelfth century the counts of the empire became distinguished from the princes, and lost the right of voting in the Diets. The election of an emperor was at first undertaken by the whole Diet. In the thirteenth century the number of Electors was restricted to seven, to which two more were afterwards added. (*See* ELECTOR.)

The Diets were called by the emperor at his own pleasure, but as they had the power of granting supplies their meetings were frequent; and as their authority over the different states was partial, and their policy could only be carried out by the executive force of the emperor, they can hardly be regarded as an independent power in the state. Neither the time nor the place of meeting of the Diets was at first fixed. From an early period the cities of Germany were represented in the Diet. In early times they generally supported the authority of the emperor, as their interest was common with his in diminishing the power of the greater vassals.

Municipalities were at first established about the reign of Frederick I, and soon began to assert their independence. The predatory habits of the nobles, besides the claims of superiority over entire cities or particular citizens asserted by the princes, involved the cities in continual warfare with the feudal nobility, and often also with their ecclesiastical superiors. The necessity of defending their privileges compelled them to enter into leagues among themselves. Among the earliest of these combinations was the Hanseatic League,

Frederick the Great

formed to resist both the oppression of rulers and the depredations of land and sea robbers. A league was formed in 1255 by more than sixty cities of the Rhine, headed by the three ecclesiastical Electors, to resist the depredations of the lesser nobles. The Suabian League, formed in 1376, was of similar origin. These leagues were met by counter-associations of nobles and princes.

Maximilian, who succeeded to the empire in 1493, was succeeded in 1519 by his grandson Charles V. (See MAXIMILIAN I; CHARLES V.) The reign of Charles, the most important in the German annals and the most brilliant in the sixteenth century, was divided among three great conflicts— the continued struggle between France and Germany, the conflict with the encroaching Ottoman Empire, and that with the Reformation. In 1556

Charles resigned the empire to his brother Ferdinand. The Council of Trent was concluded in Ferdinand's reign. He died in 1564. Then followed Maximilian II, Rudolph II, Matthias, and Ferdinand II. By this time was begun a religious war, by which Germany was devastated for thirty years, hence called the Thirty Years' War.

The invasion of Germany by Christian IV of Denmark in 1625, the Peace of Lübeck (1629), the invasion of Gustavus Adolphus (1630), the battles of Leipzig in 1631, of the Lech and Lutzen in 1632, of Nördlingen in 1634, the war with France in 1635, belong to the history of the Thirty Years' War (q.v.). Ferdinand died in 1637, and was succeeded by his son Ferdinand III. Ferdinand III had gained a military reputation at the battle of Nördlingen, but Banér, Bernhard of Saxe-Weimar, Torstenson, Turenne, and the Great Condé gained repeated victories over his troops. He was at length induced to enter into negotiations; and the Thirty Years' War was concluded by the Peace of Westphalia (24th Oct., 1648), in which the policy of France and Sweden was triumphant. The principal conditions which concerned Germany were a general amnesty and restoration of rights. France received definitively the bishoprics of Metz, Toul, and Verdun, with Breisach, Upper and Lower Alsace, and ten imperial cities in Alsace. Sweden received Rügen, and Hither Pomerania and part of Farther Pomerania, with some other territories. Greater power was given to the Protestants; and the right of the princes and states to make war and alliances among themselves or with foreigners was recognized.

The emperor died in 1657. His son Leopold I was elected emperor in 1658. The success of Louis XIV in his invasion of Holland led to a coalition against him, in which the emperor joined (1673). The war was continued for some years, and terminated by the Peace of Nimeguen, 1679. The League of Augsburg, in which the emperor joined, led to a protracted war with France, which was concluded by the Peace of Ryswick. In 1692 the emperor erected Hanover into an electorate, and in 1700 he permitted the Elector of Brandenburg, Frederick III, to take the title of King of Prussia. The War of the Spanish Succession, in which Great Britain, Holland, and the empire were leagued against France, was begun in 1702. To it belong the victories of Marlborough and Eugene (Blenheim, Oudenarde, Malplaquet).

The Emperor Leopold died in 1705. He was succeeded by his son Joseph

I, who died in 1711. Joseph was succeeded by his brother Charles VI (q.v.). The alliance against France was dissolved by the Peace of Utrecht in 1713, to which the emperor refused to accede, and was left alone against France. After a brief campaign between Prince Eugene and Villars he acceded to the Treaty of Rastadt, negotiated between these commanders, 7th March, 1714. The Spanish Netherlands, and Naples, Milan, Sardinia, and other Italian conquests were left to the emperor. Having no male heirs, Charles had promulgated in 1713 the Pragmatic Sanction, regulating the succession to his hereditary dominions in favour of his daughters in preference to those of his brother Joseph I. He died in 1740. Charles Albert, Elector of Bavaria, son-in-law of Leopold I, got himself chosen emperor (as Charles VII) in 1742. He laid claim to the hereditary possessions of the House of Austria, and entered into an alliance with France, Spain, Prussia, &c., against Maria Theresa, daughter of Charles VI. But he died in 1745, and Francis I, Grand-Duke of Tuscany, the husband of Maria Theresa, was elected emperor; thus the House of Habsburg-Lorraine, which had succeeded to the hereditary possessions of Austria, was recognized as the head of the empire.

After a brief interval took place the Seven Years' War (1756–63), in which Austria, Russia, France, and Saxony combined against Prussia, then ruled by Frederick the Great. The Peace of Hubertsburg (15th Feb., 1763) concluded the war, Prussia retaining her acquisitions. In 1765 Joseph II succeeded to the imperial crown, becoming at the same time co-regent with his mother of the Austrian hereditary dominions. He joined with Russia and Prussia in the first partition of Poland (1772). He was succeeded by his brother Leopold, who, having died in 1792, was succeeded by his son Francis II. He joined in 1793 in the second partition of Poland. He took the command of his army against the French in 1794, concluded the Peace of Campo Formio with Bonaparte (17th Oct., 1797); joined the second coalition against France in 1799, and concluded the Treaty of Lunéville (3rd Feb., 1801); joined the third coalition in 1805, and concluded the Treaty of Pressburg (26th Dec., 1805). In 1804 Francis took the title of hereditary Emperor of Austria, renouncing two years later that of head of the German Empire, which, indeed, had ceased to exist, owing to the conquests of Napoleon.

The states of Germany were again united, by the Treaty of Vienna (1815), in a confederation called the German Confederation (der Deutsche Bund). In 1818 a general commercial league, called the Zollverein, was projected by Prussia, and was gradually joined by most of the German states, exclusive of Austria. Revolutionary outbreaks caused great disturbances in various German states in 1830 and 1848, particularly the latter. The German Diet was restored in 1851 by the efforts of Prussia and Austria, who were rivals for the supremacy in the Confederation. In 1866 the majority of the Diet supported Austria in her dispute with Prussia respecting the disposal of the duchies of Schleswig and Holstein, whereupon Prussia withdrew from the Confederation and declared it dissolved. The Seven Weeks' War between Austria and Prussia ended in the defeat of the former, the loss of her Italian possessions, and her exclusion from the German Confederation, which was reformed by Prussia under the title of the North German Confederation.

After the Franco-German War (q.v.), in which the South German States, as well as the North German Confederation, supported Prussia, the King of Prussia was proclaimed German Emperor (William I) at Versailles on 18th Jan., 1871. The Parliament of the new empire soon met at Berlin, and adopted the new Constitution. William I was succeeded by his son Frederick, who reigned only ninety-nine days, and was succeeded by his son, William II, in 1888. (See PRUSSIA.) The war gave Alsace-Lorraine to Germany, which afterwards acquired large areas in S.W. and E. Africa, with a portion of New Guinea, and the chief Samoan islands.

During the reign of Kaiser William II the progress of Germany wa very great. Her industries and trade developed considerably, and the military organization of the new empire was the most efficient in Europe. William II's ambition, however, was to make Germany a great naval power, and in this he succeeded, as the navy he had created was second only to that of Great Britain. But his ambition to found a world-empire, to bring about the downfall of the British Empire, and to establish German sway everywhere proved his misfortune.

In a European conflagration he saw an opportunity to realize his ambitions, and he was heartily supported by the entire German people. (See EUROPEAN WAR.) Germany fought well but lost, and in 1918 revolutions broke out all over the country, resulting in the abdication of the Kaiser and of all the other German rulers. The empire, which had lasted for nearly half a century, disappeared, and Germany became a Federation of

Republics. Ebert was elected first President of the new German Federated Republic, and Scheidemann became Chancellor. In March, 1920, a *coup d'état,* manœuvred by Dr. Kapp, momentarily succeeded, and the President was compelled to flee from Berlin to Stuttgart. Kapp became Chancellor, but his power lasted only a few days. The Ebert Government returned to Berlin. Germany became a member of the League of Nations in 1926.

In 1925 General von Hindenburg was elected President on the death of President Ebert. Hindenburg's desire was to reconcile the Royalists with the Republicans. Streseman the Foreign Minister, concluded the Locarno Treaties and also a Treaty with Soviet Russia. In 1925 the Ruhr district, which had been occupied by the French since 1923, was evacuated.

At the Reichstag elections of 1928 the Social Democrats proved the strongest party, Herman Müller becoming Chancellor. In 1929 the Dawes Plan, which had been drawn uo with regard to German reparations, was superseded by the Young Plan.

The death of Streseman in 1929 marked the beginning of a change for the worse. Like other countries, Germany was badly hit by the economic depression. She declared herself quite unable to make reparation payments, and there was much political unrest. Under Adolf Hitler a party called the Nazis became very strong and there was talk of a restoration of the monarchy. The Nazis came into conflict with the authorities about the wearing of their uniform and other matters, and Bavaria threatened to leave the federation.

In 1932 Hindenburg was re-elected President, but Brüning, who had proved a capable chancellor, was forced to resign. His successor, Von Papen, represented the country at Lausanne in July, 1932, when the question of reparations was settled, Germany undertaking in return for their abandonment to make a payment of £150,000,000 to a fund for European reconstruction. In the presidential election of 1932, Hitler, who had stood against Hindenburg, had polled several million votes and his party had won great successes at the elections in Bavaria and several other parts of Germany. From that time the Nazis gradually gained ascendancy until 1933 when Hitler became virtual dictator. One of his first measures was the expulsion of the Jews from key positions in Germany. He confiscated the funds of the Communist party, put down the Socialist party, and put a tax on the free port of Danzig. In foreign relations he demands that Germany be placed on an equal basis with other nations with regard to armaments.—BIBLIOGRAPHY: E. F. Henderson, *A Short History of Germany;* W. A. Holland, *Germany to the Present Day: a Short History;* Viscount Bryce, *The Holy Roman Empire;* B. E. Howard, *The German Empire;* J. W. Headlam, *The Foundations of the German Empire;* Price Collier, *Germany and the Germans;* J. E. Barker, *Modern Germany;* H. Lichtenberger, *Germany and its Evolution in Modern Times;* Prince von Bülow, *Imperial Germany;* F. Runkel, *Die Deutsche Revolution.*

German Language. German is one of the Teutonic family of languages, of the Aryan or Indo-European stock, and hence is a sister tongue to Gothic, Old English and English, Dutch, Danish, Swedish, and Icelandic. Of these the Gothic, now long extinct, presents us with the earliest specimens of any Teutonic speech that we possess in the fragments of a translation of the Bible made by Bishop Ulfilas about A.D. 360. Old English comes next; German follows somewhat later.

The German dialects spoken in the lower and more northern localities have long exhibited considerable differences from those spoken in the higher and more in and, thus giving rise to the distinction between High German and Low German. What is ordinarily called German (called *Deutsch* by the Germans) is High German. Low German includes Dutch, Frisian, &c. One of the earliest specimens of Old High German is the oath of Charles the Bald, sworn at Strasbourg in 842. Middle High German became literary in the twelfth century, its poetry giving it a predominance as far as Austria.

During the following century Suabian was the predominant dialect, and its influence is apparent in all the writings of the fourteenth and fifteenth centuries. Ultimately Upper Saxon became the language of literature and cultivated society in consequence of the translation of the Bible by Luther, which may be said to have fixed the New High German of modern times.

German Literature received its first impulse from the fondness of the early Germanic races for celebrating the deeds of their gods and heroes. According to Tacitus, the warriors would advance to attack chanting wild war-songs, with their shields held close to their mouths, which added to the discordant effect of the unknown and uncouth tongue. Of these early songs nothing even in a translated form has been handed down to us. The legends immediately connected with the Gothic, Frankish, and Burgundian warriors of the period of national migration—Dietrich (Theodoric), Siegfried, Hildebrand, &c.—have for the most part some historical foundation, and many of them were eventually incorporated in the *Nibelungenlied*, the most celebrated production of German mediæval poetry.

On the introduction of Christianity was opened another sphere of literary activity. Metrical translations of the Evangelists, the *Krist* and *Heliand*, appeared in the ninth century in the High and Low German dialects respectively. The *Ludwigslied*, a pæan in honour of the victory of Louis III, King of the Franks, over the Normans in 883, was composed in Old High German by a Frankish ecclesiastic. The preservation of the *Hildebrandlied* is also due to churchmen, who transmitted it partly in the High and partly in the Low dialect. The *Merseburger Gedichte*, two songs of enchantment written in the tenth century, throw light on the ancient religious beliefs of Germany; but in general the hostility of the clergy to the old pagan literature of heroic legends, beastfables, &c., was not favourable to its preservation.

In the twelfth and thirteenth centuries poetry passed from the monasteries and ecclesiastical schools to the palaces of princes and the castles of nobles. Under the cultured emperors of the House of Hohenstaufen, the first bloom of German literature came. Many of the poets of this period were nobles by birth, some of them even princes. Heinrich von Weldeke was the first to introduce into his heroic poem *Eneit* that spirit of devotion to women called by the old Germans *Minne* (love, hence the name *Minnesänger*, love-minstrel).

A still greater name is that of Wolfram von Eschenbach, the author of *Parzival*, a poem embodying the legends of King Arthur, the Knights of the Round Table, and the *San Graal* (Holy Grail). These traditions, together with the exploits of Charlemagne, of Alexander the Great, and the Trojan heroes, inspired also the lays of Gottfried of Strasbourg, Hartman von der Aue, and others. These subjects were all taken from the romances of the French *trouvères*, and treated in a style closely resembling theirs. But we have besides real national epics in the *Nibelungenlied* and *Gudrun* (q.v.).

The lyrics or minnesongs of this period are not less remarkable than its romances and epics. Perhaps the most gifted lyrist is the celebrated Walther von der Vogelweide. Next to him rank Heinrich von Otterdingen, Reinmar der Alte, the Austrian poets Nithard and Tannhäuser. Several hundreds of these poets were engaged in travelling from palace to palace and from castle to castle. Their songs were mostly in the Suabian dialect, and the poets constituted what is called the Suabian school. In the thirteenth century didactic poetry began to be cultivated with some success.

The dawn of historical literature is heralded by the *Limburg Chronicle* (1336–98) and the *Alsace Chronicle* (1386), but the age of chivalry, as Ulrich von Lichtenstein complained in his poem *Frauendienst*, was declining. During the troublous times of the Interregnum (1256–73) poetry passed to the homes of the private citizen and the workshops. These humbler poets formed themselves into guilds in the imperial cities—Nürnberg, Frankfurt, Strasbourg, Mainz, &c., and were called *Meistersänger*, in contradistinction to the knightly *Minnesänger*.

In the fourteenth century Germany produced several mystical theologians, disciples of Meister Eckhart, the most celebrated of whom were Tauler and Suso, whose sermons and writings paved the way, in some measure, for the Reformation. The only good poetry in the fourteenth, and up to the close of the fifteenth century, were the spirited lays of Halb Suter and Veit Weber, who celebrated the victories of Switzerland over Austria and Burgundy.

The invention of printing caused an increasing literary activity, and the works printed in Germany between 1470 and 1500 amounted to several thousand editions. In 1498 there was published the celebrated beast-epic *Reineke Vos* (Reynard the Fox). Other popular works were the *Narrenschiff* (Ship of Fools) of Sebastian Brandt, an allegorical poem in which the vices are satirized; *The Satires of Thomas Mürner*; and (in 1519) *Till Eulenspiegel*, a collection of humorous stories about a wandering mechanic.

In the sixteenth century a new era opens in literature with Luther's translation of the Bible. The writings of Luther, Zwingli (1484–1531), Sebastian Frank (1500–45 ?), Melanchthon (1497–1560), Ulrich von Hutten (1488–1523), one of the chief writers of the *Epistolæ Obscurorum Virorum*, constitute the principal theological literature of the Reformation. History was now written in a superior style, and with greater comprehensiveness, by Frank in the *Zeitbuch* and *Weltbuch*, and by Sebastian Münster (1489–1552) in his *Kosmographie*; also by Tschudi (1505–72) in *Chronicles of Switzerland*, and by Aventinus (1477 ?–1534), the Bavarian chronicler. The autobiography of Götz von Berlichingen also deserves mention as a sketch of the rude lives of the smaller nobility.

Amongst the poets of this period Hans Sachs (1494–1576), the cobbler of Nürnberg, the greatest of the Meistersänger, and Johann Fischart (died 1589), a great satirist, and author of *Das glückhafte Schiff*, stand much above their contemporaries. Many of the hymns and religious lyrics of the age are of high merit, particularly those of Luther, Eber, Waldis, and others. The drama also made considerable progress, Hans Sachs, before mentioned, and Jakob Ayrer (died 1605) being amongst the best writers in this department.

But it was in learned and scientific treatises that the age was most prolific. Amongst the chief learned

Hans Sachs

writers are Luther, Camerarius, Cornelius Agrippa, Paracelsus, Copernicus (astronomy), Leonhard Fuchs (botany and medicine), Conrad Gesner (zoology and classics), and Agricola (mineralogy).

By the beginning of the seventeenth century literature was on the decline. This century is known in German literature as the period of imitation. Most of the poets were graduates of universities; and learned societies were formed for the purpose of improving the language and literature.

A new school of poetry, known as the first Silesian school, was founded, of which Martin Opitz (1597–1639) was the leader. His works are more remarkable for smoothness of versification than for true poetic inspiration. As a critic his work *Die Deutsche Poeterie* became a kind of manual for verse makers. Amongst the chief

members of the Silesian school were Simon Dach (1605–69), von Zesen (1619–89), Johann Rist (1607–67), and, greatest of all, Paul Fleming (1609–40), whose lyrics are natural and cheerful as the songs of a lark. Of this school also was Andreas Gryphius (1616–64), who may be said to have founded the regular German drama. The second Silesian school, headed by Hoffmann von Hoffmannswaldau (1618–79), and Lohenstein (1635–83), carried affectation to its utmost. Both the Silesian schools were opposed by the 'court poets,' Canitz (1654–99), Besser (1654–1729), and many others who imitated the French school and took Boileau for their guide.

Germany's greatest hymn-writer, Gerhardt (1606–76), belongs to this period. Amongst the best satirists and epigrammatists were Logau (1604 –55) and Lauremberg (1591–1659). Amongst novelists Moscherosch with his *Geschichte Philanders von Sittewald*, and Grimmelshausen in his *Simplicissimus* give graphic pictures of life during the Thirty Years' War.

Among the scientific and philosophic writers of the period we may mention Kepler (1571–1631); Puffendorf (1632–94), the publicist; and Jakob Böhme (1575–1624), the great mystic, who stood almost alone in writing his books on philosophy in German. Leibnitz (1646–1716) was the first to lay a scientific basis for the study of philosophy, but his works were composed chiefly in French and Latin. Wolff (1679–1754), his disciple, shaped the views of his master into a comprehensive system, and published his works in the German language.

In the eighteenth century poetry revived with Haller (1708–77), remarkable as a descriptive poet, and Hagedorn (1708–54), a lyrist of considerable merit. The Saxon school, headed by Gottsched (1700–66) aimed at a reformation of German poetry, and modelled the drama as far as possible on the works of Corneille and Racine. These tendencies brought about a violent controversy with a group of writers in Zürich, known as the Swiss school, and headed by Bodmer and Breitinger, who took the English poets as their model, and laid stress on the function of imagination and feeling in poetry.

The result of the controversy was that most of the young writers at Leipzig shook off the authority of Gottsched, and even established a periodical (*Die Bremer Beiträge*) in which the principles of their former master were attacked. Among the contributors were Rabener (1712–91), a popular satirist with a correct and easy style; Zachariä (1726–77), a serio-comic epic poet; Gellert (1715–69), the author of numerous popular hymns, fables, and a few dramas now forgotten; Kästner (1719–1800), a witty epigrammatist and talented mathematician; Giseke, Cramer, Fuchs, Ebert, and many others of more or less note. To the school of Halle belonged Kleist (1715–59); Gleim (1719–1803), a celebrated fabulist; and others. Gessner of Zürich (1730–87) gained in his time a high reputation as a writer of idyls.

With the writings of Klopstock (1724–1803) and Wieland (1733–1813) the classical period of German literature (usually reckoned from 1760) may be said to begin. Though the epic poem of the first (*Messias*) is no longer counted a poem of the first rank, yet Klopstock's work, with its ardent feeling for the spiritual and sublime, is recognized to have had a beneficent effect on German literature. Wieland, a striking contrast to Klopstock, awakened with his light and brilliant verse a greater sense of gracefulness in style. But it was reserved for Gotthold Ephraim Lessing (1729–81) to give a new direction to German literature. He established a new school of criticism and dealt a fatal blow to French influence. His tragedy *Emilia Galotti*, his comedy of *Minna von Barnhelm*, and his philosophic drama *Nathan der Weise* were the best models of dramatic composition which German literature had yet produced, and his direction of the German mind towards Shakespeare and the English drama was not the least of the many impulses he contributed to the literary growth of his countrymen. Herder (1744–1803), with his universal knowledge and many-sided activity, followed Lessing as another great influence in the literary world.

The researches of Winckelmann (1717–68) in ancient sculpture led to a new understanding of art, as those of Heyne in ancient literature mark the development of modern German scholarship. A union of the students at Göttingen University, where Heyne taught, gave rise to the *Göttinger Dichterbund* or *Hainbund*, among the members of which were Gottfried Aug. Bürger (1748–94), author of *Lenore* and other wild and picturesque ballads and songs; Voss (1751–1826), the translator of Homer, and author of one of the finest German idyls, *Luise*; together with the two brothers Stolberg, Boie, Hölty, and Claudius.

This period was followed by a time of transition and excitement known in Germany as the *Sturm-und-Drang Periode* (Storm and Stress Period), which found its fullest expression in an early work of Goethe's (1749–1832), the *Sorrows of Werther*. The

literary excitement was raised to the highest pitch by the *Räuber* (Robbers) of Schiller (1759–1805), afterwards the friend and coadjutor of Goethe. By the joint exertions of these two great men German literature was brought to that classical perfection which, from a purely local, has since given it a universal influence. Of a highly individual character are the works of Jean Paul Richter (1763–1825), a writer of profound humour and pathos; and Jung Stilling (1740–1817), whose autobiography holds a peculiar place in German literature for the charming *naiveté* of its thought and style.

In the departments of science and philosophy, we have the names of Moses Mendelssohn (1729–86); A. G. Baumgarten (1714–62), the founder of the science of æsthetics; the historians Mosheim (1694–1755), Dohm, Möser, Spittler, Johannes Müller; Adelung the philologist; Basedow and Pestalozzi the educationists; Ernesti, Spalding, Rosenmüller, and Michaelis, theologians; Eichhorn in theology and universal and literary history; and the scientific writers Blumenbach, Euler, Vega, Herschel, and others. In the field of pure metaphysics Immanuel Kant was succeeded by Fichte (1762–1814), Hegel (1770–1831), and Schelling (1775–1854).

Partly produced by the influences of the *Sturm-und-Drang* period, and partly trained in the laws of art laid down and worked out by Goethe and Schiller, the so-called *Romantic school*, distinguished by its enthusiasm for mediæval subjects and its love of what is mysterious and transcendental in life or thought, gradually succeeded in gaining public attention about this epoch. Amongst the principal writers of this school are von Hardenberg, better known as Novalis (1772–1801), a pensée-writer of deep poetic insight; Ludwig Tieck (1773–1853), a writer of tales, dramas, and dramatic criticisms; La Motte Fouqué, Clemens Brentano, Hoffmann, Musæus, Werner, von Kleist, &c. The two Schlegels (August Wilhelm, 1767–1845, whose translation of Shakespeare is still celebrated, and Friedrich, 1772–1829, best known by his philosophy of history) also belong to this school.

The War of Liberation against Napoleon I introduced a strong manly enthusiasm for a time into the hitherto gloomy and melancholy productions of the romanticists. Amongst the patriotic poets of the time Ernst Moritz Arndt (1769–1860) and Theodor Körner (1791–1813) hold the first place. The ballads and metrical romances of Ludwig Uhland (1787–1872) have brought him a world-wide fame. Friedrich Rückert (1789–1866) also may be noticed as a lyric poet of merit.

During the excitement produced by the July Revolution in France (1830) a school of writers arose in whose works the social and political ideas of

Goethe

the time were strongly reflected. The most prominent names amongst this party are Ludwig Börne (1786–1837) and Heinrich Heine (1799–1856), whose writings combine the keenest satire and the finest pathos. Amongst the better-known members of the school is Karl Gutzkow (1811–78), a popular dramatist and novelist.

As in England and France, the novel, especially the novel of a social or political character, has since taken a prominent place in German literature. Most distinguished are Freytag, Spielhagen, Heyse, Auerbach, Fanny Lewald, Hackländer, Reuter, Jensen, Storm, Rosegger, &c.

Science and learning, just as literature and the arts, have produced also names of great eminence. Alexander von Humboldt (1769–1859) gave a great impulse to almost all branches of knowledge by his *Cosmos*, his *Travels*, and his *Views of Nature*, and by the general suggestiveness of his labours. In history, Niebuhr and Theod. Mommsen, the historians of Rome; Leopold Ranke, the historian of the Popes; Dahlmann, Gervinus, Sybel (*French Revolution*), Giesebrecht, Julian Schmidt, H. Kurz, and others may be mentioned. Biography has been well represented by Varnhagen von Ense, Pertz, David F. Strauss, and others.

German modern theology and Biblical criticism has had lately much influence in the religious world. Baur, Bleek, and Ewald are among the widely-known names. Histories of art have been written by Kugler, Burckhardt, Lübke, and others. The

brothers Grimm—Jakob (1785–1863), and Wilhelm (1786–1859)—were the founders of a new branch of philological and poetic investigation in ancient German literature. Eminent names in general philological science are those of Bopp, Pott, Schleicher, Steinthal, and Karl Brugmann. In natural sciences, Oken, Burmeister, Carus, Cotta, Liebig, Helmholtz, Virchow, Schleiden, Grisebach, Vogt, Bessel, Brehm, Häckel, Bastian, &c., are the eminent names; in philosophy, Schopenhauer, Feuerbach, Rosenkranz, Lotze, Kuno Fischer, von Hartmann, Nietzsche, &c.

Amongst poets Anastasius Grün (pen-name of Count von Auersberg) and Nikolas Lenau amongst Austrians, and Meissner and Hartmann, natives of Bohemia, have a considerable reputation. Hervegh, Hoffman von Fallersleben, Freiligrath, and Franz Dingelstedt infuse strong political sentiments into their poetry. Emmanuel Geibel, von Scheffel, Bodenstedt, and others represent a poetry more comprehensive in its aims and tendencies.

Among the prominent novel-writers belonging to the generation following the Franco-Prussian War are Ebers, Dahn, Gottschall, Wilbrandt, Paul Lindau, Baroness von Suttner, Anzengruber, Franzos, Sacher-Masoch, Clara Viebig, Thomas Mann, and

Sudermann

others. The greatest modern German dramatists are Sudermann, Hauptmann, Halbe, Fulda, and Schnitzler. Among lyrical poets the most prominent are Liliencron, Dehmel, Busse, and Agnes Miegel.

During the European War the literary activity of the German people, in spite of the stress of the war, was considerable. War books were published in great numbers, and there was quite a deluge of patriotic poetry.

Among war books Remarque's *All Quiet on the Western Front* and Fritz von Ulrich's *Opfergang* are notable, while the state of Germany at home during the war years is mirrored in the novels of Clara Viebig.

Noteworthy names associated with 'Expressionist' drama are Hesenclever, Werfel, and Toller. Ernst Toller's tragedy *Hinkermann* reflects life in post-war Germany.

In 1922 'Expressionism' subsided. Historical subjects became popular, and in this connexion the name of Lion Feuchtwanger, novelist and dramatist, is important. Among his works *Jew Süss* and *The Ugly Duchess* are pre-eminent.

Pre-war writers who are still important are the poets Stefan George and Rainer Maria Rilke and Thomas Mann, the novelist.

The novels (principally *Grand Hotel*) of Vicki Baum have attained a wide popularity.—BIBLIOGRAPHY: J. G. Robertson, *History of German Literature*; Kuno Francke, *German Literature as determined by Social Forces*; J. F. Coar, *Studies in German Literature in the Nineteenth Century*; G. M. Priest, *Brief History of German Literature*; M. Geissler, *Führer durch die Deutsche Literatur des Zwanzigsten Jahrhunderts*; T. Dresch, *Le Roman social en Allemagne*; B. Taylor, *Studies in German Literature*; G. Brandes, *Main Currents in Nineteenth Century Literature*; C. Thomas, *History of German Literature*.

GERMERSHEIM (ger'mèrz-hîm), a town and fortress in the Bavarian Palatinate, on the Rhine, 8 miles s.w. of Speier. In 1793 the French were defeated there by the Austrians. Pop. 5,838.

GERMINAL VESICLE, in biology the nucleus of the ovum or egg-cell. It contains within it a nucleolus called the *germinal spot*.

GERMINATION, the first act of growth by an embryo plant. The immediate causes of germination are the presence of moisture and atmospheric air and a certain elevation of temperature. Moisture softens the integuments of the seed and swells the tissue of the embryo; atmospheric air supplies oxygen; and a temperature which must be at least as high as 32° F., by exciting the vitality of the embryo, enables it to take advantage of the agents with which it is in contact. During germination various changes take place in the chemical constituents of the seed; they are usually accompanied by increase of temperature, as is seen in the process of malting. Along with these other changes commonly take place: for example, a root is produced.

GERMISTON, a town of the Transvaal, 9 miles from Johannesburg. It is a most important gold-mining centre. Pop. (1921), 42,355 (white, 15,697); white pop. (1931), 29,953.

GERM THEORY OF DISEASE. This phrase came into use between 1860–77, and implied that certain diseases may result from the growth of bacteria in the body. The discovery that bacteria are the cause of putrefaction, and the success attending Lister's efforts to prevent blood-poisoning by excluding bacteria from surgical wounds, form the historical setting of the theory. The first absolute proof of its reliability was furnished when, in 1877, Koch showed that the bacillus anthracis was the cause of anthrax in cattle. Koch held that three conditions must be fulfilled before an organism could be accepted as the cause of a disease: (1) the organism must be invariably demonstrable by the microscope in the body of the diseased animal; (2) it must be capable of being isolated in pure culture outside the body (*see* BACTERIOLOGY); (3) when a pure culture is introduced into a healthy animal of the same species, the disease must be reproduced.

All these conditions were fulfilled in the case of anthrax, and since 1877 evidence has been adduced for bacteria being the cause of the following diseases, each disease being associated with a special bacterium: inflammation and abscess formations (1881–4), erysipelas (1884), pneumonia (1886), epidemic cerebro-spinal meningitis (spotted fever) (1887), tuberculosis (1882), glanders (1882), typhoid fever (1880–4), bacillary dysentery (1898), diphtheria (1883–90), tetanus (1885–9), cholera (1884–93), plague (1894), and syphilis (1905).

While it is of course impossible in most cases of human disease to obtain absolute proof of the cause by injecting pure cultures of the suspected organism into man, there can be no reasonable doubt that the diseases cited are caused by the organisms associated with them. In other cases, e.g. rheumatic fever, whooping cough, and influenza, sufficient evidence is still wanting. The germ theory has thus been established on a firm basis, and probably the difficulties encountered in other infectious diseases (e.g. scarlet fever, measles, smallpox) will in time be overcome. In certain cases, although the infective agent is unknown, the means by which infection is carried has been proved: thus, in typhus fever the louse is the carrier, and in yellow fever a mosquito.

One of the hindrances to further advance probably is that the infective agent is often excessively small; this is known to be the case in infantile paralysis. Work on the germ theory has shed important light on the general phenomena of infectious disease. The causal organism usually gains access to man by the nose and mouth, more rarely through wounds (in bubonic plague infection is carried through the bites of fleas coming from infected rats, which also suffer from this disease); the former fact accentuates the significance of the sore throat which is so often the first symptom complained of.

Bacteria either multiply on some bodily surface and produce poisons which are absorbed (diphtheria), or they penetrate into the body and settle down in an organ for which they have a predilection (typhoid fever, pneumonia), from which they exercise their disease effects. The body resists their inroads; certain cells rush to the part and engulf and destroy the organisms, and a general mechanism throws substances into the blood which kill the bacteria or neutralize their effects (see ANTITOXIN).

Exposure to infection is not invariably followed by disease. This may be due to the dose of the infective agent being too small, which emphasizes the desirability of infectious cases being placed in large airy rooms. It may also be due to many individuals being insusceptible to the infection. This points to the part played by the constitution of the person exposed, and it explains how such not obviously infectious diseases as tuberculosis and pneumonia are in reality due to an agent introduced into the body from outside.

The failure of bacteriology to account for the cause of malaria led to an important development of the germ theory, whereby it was shown that the protozoa—a much more highly organized group than the bacteria—could act as the agents of infection. Malaria was proved to be due to such a cause. The parasite undergoes a complicated asexual cycle of development in man, with which the symptoms of a malarial attack are associated. Direct infection from man to man does not occur; if, however, a mosquito sucks the blood of an infected man, the parasite goes through a sexual cycle in the insect, and, when the mosquito bites a fresh human subject, the rejuvenated protozoon is injected and a fresh case of malaria originated.

Other protozoa cause sleeping sickness in man (the organism being carried by a biting fly), tropical dysentery, and the chronic ulcer known

as Oriental sore. See ANTITOXIN; BACTERIA; DISINFECTION; INOCULATION, &c.—BIBLIOGRAPHY: R. Muir and J. Ritchie, *Manual of Bacteriology*; R. T. Hewlett, *Manual of Bacteriology*; A. Besson, *Practical Bacteriology*.

GÉRÔME (zhā-rōm), **Jean Léon**, painter, born in 1824 at Vesoul, France, died in 1904. He studied in Paris under Paul Delaroche. In 1854 he travelled in the East, which provided subjects for some of his most popular pictures, such as *The Slave Market* (1867). In 1855 a large canvas, *The Age of Augustus and the Birth of Christ*, was purchased by the State, and was the first of a series of works on classical themes, including *Cæsar* (1859), *Phryne* (1861), *Le Roi Candaule* (1861), and *Socrates* (1861). The subject of these last three gave rise to much criticism.

Among his historical pictures is *Louis XIV and Molière*; and he was also a successful sculptor, his *Bellona* (1892, in ivory, metal, and precious stones) attracting much attention. In 1863 he was appointed a professor at the École des Beaux Arts. He received the Prussian Order of the Red Eagle, and was a Commander of the Legion of Honour.

GERONA (hā-rō′nä), a fortified town of N.E. Spain, capital of the province of Gerona, in Catalonia, at the confluence of the Oña and the Ter, 52 miles north-east of Barcelona. It consists of an old and new town, the former on the slope of a hill, with antiquated houses and a stately cathedral. There is spinning and weaving; also paper factories. Gerona was once the residence of the Kings of Arragon, and as a place of strategic importance has sustained many memorable sieges. Pop. 21,845.

GERONA, the province, area 2,264 sq. miles, abuts on the Mediterranean, is mountainous and mostly rugged, but with many fertile valleys, which produce olives, wine, wheat, rye, &c., and all kinds of fruits and vegetables. Pop. (1931), 325,545.

GEROPIGIA, or **JERUPIGIA** (je-ro-pi′ji-a, je-ru-pi′ji-a), a mixture composed of unfermented grape-juice, with sufficient brandy and sugar to prevent it from fermentation, and colouring-matter from rhatany root or log-wood, imported from Portugal, to give spurious strength and colour to port wines.

GERS (zhär), a department in the south-west of France, separated from the Bay of Biscay by the department of Landes; area, 2,428 sq. miles. The southern part is covered with ramifications of the Pyrenees separated by valleys, each of which is watered by its own stream. The chief of these are the Gers, Losse, and Save. More than half the land is under the plough, and about a seventh is in vineyards. Much of the wine is made into Armagnac brandy. Auch is the capital. Pop. (1931), 193,134.

GERSON (zhär-sŏn), Jean de, properly Jean Charlier, a celebrated French theologian, born at Gerson in 1363, died in 1429. He studied at the University of Paris, received the doctorate in 1392, and in 1395 became chancellor of the university. He was ardent and courageous in advocating improvements and reforms, but mostly only succeeded in making for himself powerful enemies.

He is mainly remembered in connection with his efforts to bring about a cessation of the great schism which had divided the Church since 1378. His proposal was to depose both the rival Popes and elect a third in their room—a step which was actually taken by the Council held at Pisa in 1409, of which Gerson was a member as deputy of the University of Paris. This proceeding, however, was a failure, the only result being that there were three rival Popes instead of two. When the Council of Constance (1414–8), in which also Gerson took a leading part, likewise proved unable to settle the differences existing in the Church, he at last gave up the struggle in despair, and not daring to return to France, where his enemies had then the upper hand, sought shelter for a time in Bavaria and Austria.

In 1419 he returned to his native country, and spent the last ten years of his life with his brother, the prior of a community of Celestine monks at Lyons, living an ascetic life, and devoting himself to religious meditation and the composition of theological and other treatises. The authorship of the *Imitation of Christ*, by Thomas-a-Kempis, was at one time erroneously ascribed to him.—Cf. M. Creighton, *History of the Papacy*.

GERSTÄCKER (ger'stek-ėr), Friedrich, a German traveller and novelist, born at Hamburg 1816, died in 1872. In 1837 he went to America, where he earned a living by the most various employments—as a sailor, stoker, innkeeper, wood-cutter, and trapper and hunter in the prairies of the west. He returned to Germany in 1843, and began his literary life by the publication of his experiences in America, *Streif- und Jagdzüge durch die Vereinigten Staaten Nordamerikas* (Dresden, 1844). This was followed by *Die Regulatoren in Arkansas, Die Flusspiraten des Mississippi*, and *Mississippibilder*.

In 1849 Gerstäcker was engaged on behalf of the German Government to collect information which might be useful to German emigrants. The results were published under the title of *Reisen* in 1853. He afterwards made voyages to South America, to Egypt, the West Indies, and other places, which are described in his *Neue Reisen* (1868). Amongst his many romances (most of which may be had in English) are: *Die beiden Sträflinge* (1856), *Im Busch* (1864), *General Franco* (1865), *Californische Skizzen* (1856), and others.

GERUND, the name given originally to a part of the Latin verb which possesses the same power of government as a verb, but also resembles a noun in being governed by prepositions. In early English or Anglo-Saxon a dative form of the infinitive is used to indicate purpose, and is often called the gerund. In modern English what seems to be a present participle governed by a preposition is sometimes called a gerund, in such phrases, for example, as 'fit for teaching'; but this is merely a verbal noun representing the old Anglo-Saxon noun in -*ung*.

GERVAISE, or **GERVASE**, a monk of Canterbury, born in 1150. Amongst his writings is an important chronicle, *Chronica de tempore regum Angliæ, Stephani, Henrici II et Ricardi I*. It is reprinted in Twysden's collection. He also wrote *Gesta Regum*, and *Mappa Mundi*, a survey of the counties of England. Gervaise died probably about 1200.

GERVAISE (or **GERVASE**) OF TILBURY, a chronicler of the twelfth and thirteenth centuries, born at Tilbury, in Essex, about the middle of the twelfth century. He appears to have spent most of his life on the Continent, living in France, Sicily, Italy, and elsewhere. He taught law at Bologna for a time, and was in the service of the Emperor Otto IV, by whom he was appointed to the post of Marshal of the Kingdom of Arles. He died, according to some, in 1218. His chief and only extant work is entitled *Otia Imperialia*. Its contents are of a very varied character, including facts pertaining to geography, natural history, and superstitions, besides an account of the history of Britain and of the English kings down to his own time.—Cf. W. Stubbs's edition of *Gervase of Canterbury* (Rolls Series, 1879–80).

GERVEX, Henri, French painter, born in Paris 10th Dec., 1852, died 1913. He studied under Fromentin, Cabanel, and Brisset, and first exhibited in 1873. Gervex started by painting mythological subjects and the nude. Devoting himself afterwards to representations of modern life, he achieved considerable success, and was entrusted with the execution of several official decorative paintings for public buildings.

Among his works are: *Satyr playing with Bacchante* (1874), *Diana and Endymion* (1875), *Return from the Ball* (1879), *Civil Marriage* (1881), *First Communion* (1884), *Meeting of the Jury on Painting* (1885), *The Coronation of Nicholas II* (1896), *The Mayors' Banquet* (1900), &c. He also painted the ceilings for the Salle des Fêtes at the Hôtel de Ville, Paris.

GERVI'NUS, Georg Gottfried, a German critic and historian, born at Darmstadt 20th May, 1805, died in 1871. He quitted commerce in 1825 to study at Heidelberg, was for some time a teacher, and qualified as a privat-docent. After a visit to Italy he published his *Geschichte der Poetischen Nationalliteratur der Deutschen* (History of the Poetic National Literature of the Germans, 1835–42). In 1835 he was appointed extraordinary professor at Heidelberg, and the following year ordinary professor of history and literature at Göttingen; but in 1837, being one of the seven professors who protested against King Ernst August's breach of the Constitution, he was banished from Hanover.

After another visit to Italy he returned to Heidelberg, where in 1844 he was appointed an honorary professor. He now began to take an active part in politics on the liberal side; became editor of the newly-founded *Deutsche Zeitung*, and was returned to the Federal Diet by the Hanse towns. Discontented with the tendency of affairs after 1848, he gave up politics and resumed his old studies. In 1849 he published the first part of his large work on Shakespeare, in 1853 his *History of German Poetry*, and in 1855 the first volume of his *History of the Nineteenth Century*, which, however, was never carried further than the French Revolution of 1830. Amongst his last writings was a critical essay, *Handel and Shakespeare*.

GESE'NIUS, Friedrich Heinrich Wilhelm, a German Orientalist and Biblical critic, born in 1786, died in 1842. He studied at Göttingen, and became professor of theology at Halle. Between 1810 and 1812 his *Hebrew and Chaldee Dictionary of the Old Testament* appeared. In 1820 he visited Paris and Oxford for the purpose of collecting materials regarding the Semitic languages. In 1829 he published his large *Thesaurus philologico-criticus Linguæ Hebraicæ et Chaldaicæ*, completed in 1858 by Rödiger. Besides the works mentioned, Gesenius

wrote a *Hebrew Grammar*, a *History of the Hebrew Language*, and notes to the German translation of Burckhardt's *Travels in Syria and Palestine*.

GESNER (ges'nèr), **Konrad von,** German scholar, born at Zürich in 1516, died in 1565. He studied at Strasbourg, Bourges, and Paris, and became schoolmaster in his native town. Hoping to raise himself from his needy condition, he went to Basel, and devoted himself particularly to the study of medicine. Afterwards he became successively professor of Greek at Lausanne, and of philosophy at Zürich, and did important work in the departments of history, zoology, and botany.

Gesner's *Historia Animalium* must be regarded as the foundation of zoology; and in botany he was the inventor of the method of classifying the vegetable kingdom according to the characters of the seeds and flowers. His *Bibliotheca Universalis* is a descriptive catalogue of all writers extant in Greek, Latin, and Hebrew. He died of the plague at Zürich.

GESNERA'CEÆ, an order of gamopetalous Dicotyledons, typical genus Gesnera, named in honour of Konrad von Gesner. There are many species, mostly natives of tropical and subtropical regions. They are shrubs or herbs, often with tuberous rhizomes, and scarlet, violet, or blue flowers. Some of the genera are frequent in our hothouses, such as Gloxinia, Achimenes, and Gesnera.

GESSNER (ges'ner), **Salomon,** a Swiss poet and artist, was born at Zürich in 1730, died there 1788. In 1749 he was sent by his father to learn the business of bookselling at Berlin, but, having taken a dislike to the business, he maintained himself by executing landscapes, mainly in water-colour. On his return to Zürich he published *Daphnis*, a small volume of idylls, and *Der Tod Abels* (The Death of Abel), a kind of pastoral idyll in prose, for which he etched several plates of ornaments. His *Idylls* appeared in English in 1798. These idylls acquired for him a great reputation amongst contemporaries. For some years afterwards he devoted himself to engraving, chiefly after pictures by Claude and Poussin.

GESTA ROMANO'RUM ('Deed of the Romans'), the usual title of a collection of short tales, legends, &c., in Latin, very popular during the Middle Ages. The book was probably written about the close of the thirteenth century by a certain monk Elinandus, an Englishman or a German. The separate tales making up the *Gesta* are of very various contents, and belong to different times and countries, the sources from which they are derived being partly classical, partly Oriental, and partly Western.

Whatever may have been the intention of the original compiler, they very soon were adapted to the moralizing tendencies of the time, and moral reflections and allegorical interpretations were added to them, it is said, by a Petrus Bercorius or Pierre Bercaire of Poitou, a Benedictine prior. The stories were very widely read and gave plots (directly or indirectly) to Gower, Chaucer, and Shakespeare. After the Reformation the book fell into oblivion. There is an edition by Oesterley (1894), and a translation by C. Swan.

GESTATION (Lat. *gestare*, to bear), in physiology, the name given to the interval which elapses between the impregnation of any of the mammalia and the period of birth. This period varies from 25 days in the case of the mouse, to 620 in that of the elephant.

GETÆ (Gr. *Getai*), an ancient people of Europe, dwelling at first in Thrace; afterwards a part of them moved west on the north bank of the Danube, where they were known to the Romans as the Daci. (*See* DACIA.) Another portion moved east into Asia.

GETHSEMANE (the Hebrew for ʻoil-press'), an olive garden or orchard in the neighbourhood of Jerusalem, memorable as the scene of the last sufferings of our Lord. The traditional site of this garden lies towards the east side of the city, a very little beyond the Kedron, near the base of Mt. Olivet. It contains some very old olive trees, piously regarded as having stood there in the time of our Lord. Excavations carried on in the garden of Gethsemane in 1920 led to the discovery of interesting remains dating back to the fourth century.—Cf. W. Sanday, *Sacred Sites of the Gospels*.

GETTYSBURG, borough and capital of Adams County, Pennsylvania. The

Garden of Gethsemane

Pennsylvanian College (Lutheran), founded in 1832, is there, as are the national cemetery for Union soldiers and a national homestead for the orphans of Union soldiers. At Gettysburg a battle was fought (1st, 2nd, and 3rd July, 1863) between the Union forces under General Meade and the Confederate forces under General Lee, in which the latter suffered a disastrous defeat. Pop. 4,500.

GEUM (jĕ'um), a genus of hardy herbaceous perennials, belonging to the nat. ord. Rosaceæ, chiefly natives of the northern parts of the world. Two of them are common British plants—*G. urbānum*, wood-avens or herb-bennet, and *G. rivāle*, water-avens (found also in Asia and North

America). *G. canadense*, chocolate-root, or blood-root, a North American species, has some reputation as a tonic.

GEYSERS, a slight alteration of the Icelandic name *geysir*, from *geysa*, to gush or rush forth, and applied to explosive springs of hot water of the kind that were first observed in Iceland. The geysers of Iceland, about a hundred in number, lie about 30 miles north-west of Mount Hecla, in a plain covered by hot springs and steaming apertures. The two most remarkable are the Great Geyser and the New Geyser, the former of which throws

GEZIRA IRRIGATION

up at times a column of hot water to the height of from 80 to 200 feet.

The geysers of Iceland, however, have been surpassed by those discovered in the Rocky Mountains in the Yellowstone Region of Wyoming, the largest of which throw up jets of water from 90 to 250 feet high. (See YELLOWSTONE.) The hot-lake district of Auckland, New Zealand, is also famous in possessing some of the most remarkable geyser scenery in the world. Ngahapu or Ohopia, a circular rocky basin, 40 feet in diameter, in which a violent geyser is constantly boiling up to the height of 10 or 12 feet, emitting dense clouds of steam, is one of the natural wonders of the southern hemisphere. Geysers frequently form cones and terraces of silica brought up in solution in their waters, and traces of gold and cinnabar occur in some of the deposits.—Cf. Malfroy, *On Geyser Action at Rotorua*.

A household geyser is a domestic apparatus for obtaining a quick supply of hot water. It consists of a cylinder containing a coil of copper or brass tubing connected with the water supply; and beneath the container is an arrangement of atmospheric gas jets by which the water stream through the coil is heated rapidly.

GEZIRA, a great plain in the Anglo-Egyptian Sudan, lying south of Khartoum and bounded by the White Nile and the Blue Nile. The area is approximately 10,000 000 acres, of which 3,000,000 are capable of growing cotton of high quality. In view of this, work was started in 1920 in connexion with an immense irrigation scheme which contemplated the bringing under cultivation of 300,000 acres stretching along the Blue Nile. The main parts of this scheme were the Sennar dam at Makwar, a main canal 62 miles long, and about 900 miles of subsidiary and field canals. The storage reservoir extends for 58 miles from Makwar to Singa, and has a capacity of 22,896,000 cubic feet. The actual dam (built of granite) is 2 miles long, and is one of the greatest engineering constructions in the world. It was opened in 1926.

The irrigation area was originally limited to 300,000 acres, because of the fixed but erroneous belief of the Egyptians that the irrigation of a wider district would prevent a sufficiency of water reaching the irrigated lands in Egypt. Provision was, however, made for future extension to 1,000,000 acres, and after the murder of the Sirdar (Sir Lee Stack) in 1924 the Egyptian authorities were informed that the Sudan Government would, if necessary, increase the Gezira irrigation area to an unlimited extent.

GHADAMES (ghä-dä′mes), a town of North Africa, in the south-west of Tripoli. It is about 300 miles south-west of the town of Tripoli, is situated in the midst of an oasis, and is the centre of caravan routes to Tunis, Tripoli, &c. Figs, dates, barley, and wheat are grown in the gardens, which are watered by a hot spring. Pop. 7,000.

GHARA, or **GARRA,** a river in the Punjab, being the name by which the united streams of the Bias and Sutlej are known, from their confluence at Endrisa to the junction with the Chenab, after which the united waters flow under the name of the Punjnad to the Indus. Length, about 300 miles.

GHÂTS (gäts), or **GHAUTS,** a Hindu term employed to designate landing-stairs on a river.

GHÂTS, or **GHAUTS, EASTERN** and **WESTERN,** two ranges of mountains in the peninsular portion of Hindustan the former running down the east side of India, but leaving broad tracts between their base and the coast; the latter running down the west side but leaving only a narrow strip between them and the shore. Both meet near Cape Comorin.

The general elevation of the Western Ghâts varies from 4,000 to 7,000 feet. Its best-known portion is the Neilgherries, with Dodabetta Peak, their highest point, 8,760 feet above the sea. The Western Ghâts form a watershed, and the rain collected on its eastern slopes makes its way right across India to the Bay of Bengal. They are covered with fine forests, and have most picturesque scenery. The Eastern Ghâts are of considerably less elevation, on the average about 1,500 feet, and have none of the beauty of the western range. They are, however, rich in metals.

GHAZIPUR, a town in Hindustan, headquarters of the Ghazipur District, in the United Provinces, about 44 miles north-east of the town of Benares. It stretches along the banks of the Ganges; has a trade in sugar, tobacco, rose-water, and otto of roses; and is a healthy place. The ruins of the Palace of the Forty Pillars, and a monument by Flaxman to Lord Cornwallis, who died there in 1805, are there. Pop. 24,708.—The district, one of the hottest and dampest in the north-west, has an area of 1,392 sq. miles and a pop. of 832,289.

GHAZNA, GHUZNEE, or **GHIZNI,** an ancient and celebrated city and fortress in Afghanistan, 84 miles S.S.W. of Kabul, on an eminence 7,280 feet above sea-level. The wall embraces the whole of the hill; the houses are of mud; the streets dark, narrow, and irregular. The country round Ghazna is very productive in grain, fruits, and tobacco. Three miles north-east are the ruins of the ancient city, which, under the celebrated Sultan Mahmud (999–1030) (see GHAZNAVIDES), was the capital of a great empire. It has been twice taken by British forces (1839 and 1842).

GHAZNAVIDES (-vĭdz), a dynasty of twenty-one rulers, founded in 961 by Alp-Tigin, originally a slave belonging to the Ameer of Bokhara. Ghazna was the seat of his power, and became, under his successors, the capital of an empire which reached from the Tigris to the Ganges, and from the Sihon to the Indian Ocean. The most brilliant period of the dynasty was that of Sultan Mahmud (999–1030). It became extinct towards the end of the twelfth century after having lost most of its possessions.

GHEE (gē), or **GHI**, a peculiar kind of butter in use among the Hindus. It is made from the milk of the buffalo or the cow. The milk is boiled for an hour or so, and cooled, after which a little curdled milk is added. Next morning the curdled mass is churned for half an hour; some hot water is then added, and the churning continued for another half-hour, when the butter forms. When, after a few days, it becomes rancid, it is boiled till all the water is expelled, and a little more curdled milk added with some salt or betel-leaves, after which it is put into pots. In this state it will keep for a long time. It is too strong for European taste, but is a favourite article of consumption amongst rich Hindus.

GHEEL (gāl), a village and commune in Belgium, 25 miles E.S.E. of the city of Antwerp and in the province of that name. It is situated in a fertile spot in the midst of a sandy waste, and is inhabited by a class of peasant farmers. It has manufactures of cloth, hats, wax and tallow candles; tanneries, dyeworks, ropeworks, and a considerable trade in butter.

The commune has been long remarkable for containing a colony of insane persons numbering at present about 1,300, who are lodged and boarded in the houses of the country people, who make use of their services, when available, in field and other labour. Little or no restraint is employed, and the results are satisfactory. Recently a hospital has been erected, with a medical staff, for the supervision of the relations between the insane and their custodians. Patients are sent hither from all parts of Belgium. Pop. 18,545.

GHENT (gent; Fr *Gand*; Fl. *Gend* or *Gent*), a city in Belgium, capital of the province of East Flanders, in a fertile plain at the confluence of the Lys with the Schelde. It is upwards of 6 miles in circumference, and is divided by canals into a number of islands connected with each other by bridges.

Buildings. Except in some of the older parts it is well built, and has a number of fine promenades and many notable buildings. Amongst the latter are the cathedral of St. Bavon, a vast and richly-decorated structure, dating from the thirteenth century; the church of St. Nicholas, the oldest in Ghent; the church of St. Michael, with a celebrated *Crucifixion* by Vandyck; the university, founded in 1816, a handsome modern structure, with a library of about 300,000 volumes and 2,500 MSS.; the Hôtel de Ville; the Belfry, a lofty square tower surmounted by a gilded dragon, and containing a fine set of chimes consisting of forty-four bells, one of which is the famous 'Roland of Ghent'; the new Palais de Justice; the Marché du Vendredi, an extensive square, interesting as the scene of many important historical events; and Les Béguinages, extensive nunneries founded in the thirteenth century, the principal occupation of whose members is lace-making.

Industries. Ghent has long been celebrated as a manufacturing town, especially for its cotton and linen goods and lace. Other industries of importance are sugar-refining, hosiery, thread, ribbons, instruments of steel, carriages, paper, hats, delft-ware, and tobacco. There are also machine-works, engine-factories, roperies, tanneries, breweries, and distilleries. Ghent is famous for its nurseries and flower traffic.

The general trade is large. A canal that admits large sea-going vessels connects the town with the Schelde at Terneuzen, but is less used than it might be on account of the heavy imposts levied by Holland on vessels passing through. Another canal con-

Ghent. 9th century Castle of Counts of Flanders

nects the Lys with the canal from Bruges to Ostend. Population (1931), 170,576.

History. Ghent is mentioned as a town in the seventh century. In the ninth century Baldwin, the first Count of Flanders, built a fortress there to check the Normans. Under the Counts of Flanders Ghent continued to increase, and in the fourteenth century could send 50,000 men into the field. The wealth and liberty of its citizens disposed them to a bold maintenance of their privileges against the encroachments of feudal lords like the Dukes of Burgundy and the Kings of Spain.

Two great revolts took place under the leadership of the van Arteveldes (1338 and 1369) against Burgundy, and again in the sixteenth century against Charles V. But by this time the great municipalities of the Middle Ages were decaying in power and vigour, and the citizens of Ghent, besides losing their privileges, had to pay for the erection of a citadel intended to keep them in bondage.

In 1792 the Netherlands fell under the power of France, and Ghent became the capital of the department of Escaut (Schelde). In 1814 it became, along with Flanders, part of the Netherlands, till the separation of Belgium and Holland. Ghent was the birth-place of Jacob van Artevelde and of John of Gaunt, or Ghent. The Treaty of Ghent between Great Britain and the United States was signed on 24th Dec., 1814. During the European War Ghent was occupied by the Germans in Oct. 1914, and remained in their possession until 11th Nov., 1918.

GHERARDESCA (gä-rár-des′kå), a family of Tuscan origin which plays an important part in the history of the Italian republics of the Middle Ages. Historically the most prominent member of the family is Ugolino, whose death, and that of his two sons and grandsons, by starvation in the 'Tower of Hunger,' is described in one of the celebrated passages of Dante's *Divina Commedia*. Ugolino had made himself master of Pisa, and had behaved in the most cruel and arbitrary manner for four years, when, in 1288, he was overthrown by a conspiracy.

GHETTO (get′to), a name used in different towns of Italy, Germany, and other countries to indicate the quarter set apart for the residence of Jews. The first Ghetto was that of Rome, in the time of Pope Paul IV, who compelled the Jews to dwell in a quarter set apart for them on the left bank of the Tiber.

GHIBELLINES (gib′el-līnz), the name of a political party in Italy which, in general, favoured the claims of the emperor against those of the Pope. The name is said to be derived from Waiblingen, a small estate belonging to the Hohenstaufen princes. *See* GUELFS AND GHIBELLINES.

GHIBERTI (gē-ber′tē), **Lorenzo,** Italian statuary, born about 1378 at Florence, died about 1455. From his stepfather Bartoluccio, an expert goldsmith, he learned the arts of drawing and modelling, and that of casting metals. He was engaged in painting frescoes at Rimini, in the palace of Pandolfo Malatesta, when the priori of the society of merchants at Florence invited artists to propose models for one of the bronze doors of the baptistery of San Giovanni. The judges selected the works of Donatello and Ghiberti as the best (according to Vasari, also that of Brunelleschi, who is not mentioned by Ghiberti himself as one of the competitors); but the former voluntarily withdrew his claims, giving the preference to Ghiberti. After twenty-one years' labour Ghiberti completed the door, and, at the request of the priori, executed a second, after almost as long a period. Michael Angelo said of these, that they were worthy of adorning the entrance to Paradise. During these forty years Ghiberti also completed other works, bas-reliefs, statues, and some excellent paintings on glass, most of which may be seen in the cathedral and the church of Or San Michele at Florence.—Cf. Vasari, *Lives of the Painters*.

GHILAN (gi-làn'), a province of Persia, on the south-west shore of the Caspian Sea; area, about 5,000 sq. miles. The lofty range of the Elburz Mountains forms its southern boundary. The whole province, except where cleared for cultivation and on the mountain summits, is covered with woods, and the excessive rain and dense vegetation render much of the level country a morass. The climate is consequently unhealthy. The province is rich in metals and very fertile. The capital is Resht (Pop. 80,000). Pop. about 150,000.

GHIRLANDAIO (gir-làn-dä'yō), or **CORRADI**.—(1) **Domenico**, Florentine painter, born at Florence in 1449, died 1494. He was the son of a goldsmith known as Il Ghirlandaio (the garland-maker) from his skill in making metal garlands. Important frescoes by him are in the Sistine Chapel at Rome and in S. Trinità and S. Maria Novella at Florence, where also he is well represented in the Uffizi and the Academy. He was fond of introducing contemporary portraits into his work. He was distinguished by fertility of invention, and by closer approximation in his work to normal external appearance than his predecessors, but lacks their power of giving his figures dignity and vitality, and is less of a colourist. (2) **Ridolfo** (1483–1560), son of Domenico, strongly influenced by Raphael, one of the most popular Florentine painters of the day, who, in addition to portraits and decorations for churches, produced many large scenic canvases for public festivals.

GHOST-MOTH, a nocturnal lepidopterous insect (*Hepialus humuli*), so called from the male being of a white colour, and from its habit of hovering with a pendulum-like motion in the twilight over one spot (often in churchyards), where the female, which has grey posterior wings and red-spotted anterior wings, is concealed.

GHUR, or **GHOR**, a mountainous district of Afghanistan, lying to the south of Herat, and of some importance in the history of the country. This district was the original seat of the second Mahommedan dynasty in Hindustan, the princes of Ghur, who, in the eleventh and twelfth centuries, included in their kingdom of Ghur, Afghanistan, Lahore, Sind, and Khurasan.

GIANIBELLI, or **GIAMBELLI** (jàn-i-bel'lé, jàm-bel'lé), **Federigo**, an Italian military engineer, born at Mantua about 1530. After having offered his services to Philip II of Spain, who received him coldly, he went to England, where Elizabeth gave him a pension and sent him to help the Netherlanders in their defence of Antwerp against the Spaniards (1585). Here he made himself famous by the damage which his inventions did to the enemy. After this he returned to England, where he fortified the coast-line against the Spanish invasion, and suggested the use of fire-ships, which was so disastrous to the Armada. He is supposed to have died in London, but the date of his death is unknown.

GIANNONE (jàn-ō'nä), **Pietro**, Italian author, born in 1676, died in 1748. He studied law in Naples, and after winning a high place as an advocate, retired to give himself up to the execution of his great work, the *Storia civile del regno di Napoli* (1723). The severity with which Giannone treated the Church and the attacks which he made on the temporal power of the Popes, drew upon him the persecutions of the court of Rome, and of the clergy in general. The offensive publication was burned, and the author excommunicated.

Giannone therefore quitted Naples, 1723, and took refuge in Vienna, where, for a time, he was protected by the influence of powerful friends, but had ultimately to leave and betake himself to Venice in 1734. Expelled from Venice by the suspicious republic, he finally took refuge in Geneva. Here he wrote his *Il Triregno*, a bitter attack on the Papal pretensions. In 1736, having been enticed by a Government emissary to enter the Sardinian States, he was seized and imprisoned in the citadel of Turin, where he died.

GIANTS (Fr. *géant*; Gr. *gigas*, giant), people of extraordinary stature. History, both sacred and profane, makes mention of giants, and even of races of giants, but this in general occurs only at an early stage of civilization, when the national mind is apt to exaggerate anything unusual. Hence the Cyclopes and Læstrygones of the ancients and the Cornish and Welsh giants of English folk-lore.

The first mention of giants in the Bible is in *Gen.* vi, 4, where the Hebrew word used is *nephilim*, a word which occurs in only one other passage, where it is applied to the sons of Anak, who dwelt about Hebron, and who were described by the terrified spies as of such size that compared with them they appeared in their own sight as grasshoppers. A race of giants called the Rephaim is frequently mentioned in the Bible, and in *Gen.* xiv and xv appear as a distinct tribe, of whom Og, King of Bashan, is said to have been the last. Other races of giants are mentioned, such as the Emim, the Zuzim, and the Zamzummim.

The giants of old Greek or of Norse mythology have, of course, merely a symbolic existence, representing benignant or adverse forces of nature on which man might count in his struggle to reduce the world around him into some kind of order. The gigantic stature attributed to these supernatural beings in mythology is merely a method of expressing their extraordinary power. The tales of old writers regarding gigantic human skeletons have now no importance, it being well established that these bones do not belong to giants, but to animals of the primitive world which, from ignorance of anatomy, were taken for human bones.

The ordinary height of men is between 5 and 6 feet; amongst the Patagonians of South America, however, the average seems to be considerably higher, though they are not a race of giants. Notable deviations from the medium heights are not at all uncommon, especially among the Teutonic peoples. The following are amongst recorded instances, ancient and modern, of persons who attained to the stature of giants: the Roman Emperor Maximin, a Thracian, nearly 9 feet high; Queen Elizabeth's Flemish porter, 7 feet 6 inches; C. Munster, a yeoman of the guard in Hanover, who died in 1676, 8 feet 6 inches high; Cajanus, a Swedish giant, about 9 feet high, exhibited in London in 1742; C. Byrne, who died in 1783, attained the height of 8 feet 4 inches; Patrick Cotter O'Brien, who lived about the same time, was 8 feet 7¾ inches; a Swede in the celebrated grenadier guard of Frederick William I of Prussia stood 8½ feet. In 1884 died Pauline Wedde (called Marian), over 8 feet 2 inches at the age of eighteen. The following were exhibited in more recent times: Anna Swan, a native of Nova Scotia, above 8 feet high; her husband, Captain Bates (died 12th Jan., 1919), a native of Kentucky, of the same height; Chang-wu-gon, the Chinese giant, 7 feet 9 inches high.

As a rule giants are comparatively feeble in body and mind, and are short-lived. Gigantic stature is generally accompanied by a want of proportion in parts, some parts growing too quickly for others, or continuing to grow after the others have ceased. The relation between the upper and lower half of the body is not dis-turbed; but the skull, brain, and forehead are relatively small, the jaws very large, the shoulders, breast, and haunches very broad, and the muscular system comparatively weak. Recent research in clinical medicine has revealed the fact that most of these cases of 'giantism' are pathological. Disease of a curious appendage of the base of the brain, known as the pituitary gland, causes an abnormal growth of the bones and connective tissues, especially of the hands and feet and of the face (especially the jaws), giving rise to a condition known as acromegaly.—BIBLIOGRAPHY: E. B. Tylor, *Early History of Mankind*; *Primitive Culture*; E. J. Wood, *Giants and Dwarfs*; Harvey Cushing, *The Pituitary Body*.

GIANT'S CAUSEWAY, a promontory of columnar basalt on the north coast of Ireland, in the county of Antrim, between Bengore Head and Portrush. The name is sometimes given to the whole range of basalt cliffs along the coast, some of which reach the height of 400 or 500 feet; but it is more properly restricted to a small portion of it where a platform of closely-arranged basalt columns from 15 to 36 feet in height runs down into the sea in three divisions, known as the Little, the Middle, and the Grand Causeway. The last is from 20 to 30 feet wide, and stretches some 900 feet into the sea. The Giant's Causeway derives its name from the legend that it was built by Finn MacCoul as a road which was to stretch across the sea to Scotland. There are similar formations on the west coast of Scotland, on the Island of Staffa.

GIAOUR (jour), a Turkish word from Persian *gawr*, an infidel, used by the Turks to designate the adherents of all religions except Mohammedan, more particularly Christians. The use of it is so common that it is often applied without intending an insult. *The Giaour* is the title of a narrative poem by Lord Byron (1813).

GIBBON, Edward, English historian, was born at Putney, in Surrey, 27th April, 1737, died 16th Jan., 1794. The son of a gentleman of an ancient Kentish family, he entered Magdalen College, Oxford, where he remained fourteen months. Having declared himself a Roman Catholic, his father placed him under the care of M. Pavilliard, a learned Calvinistic minister at Lausanne, by whom he was reconverted to the Protestant faith. His residence at Lausanne was highly favourable to his progress in knowledge and the formation of regular habits of study. The belles-lettres and the history of the human mind chiefly occupied his attention. In 1758 he returned to England, and immediately began to lay the foundation of a copious library; and soon after composed in the French language his *Essai sur l'étude de la littérature* (1761).

In 1763 he visited Paris and Lausanne, and during 1764 he journeyed in Italy. It was here that the idea of writing his great history occurred to him as he sat musing among the ruins of the capitol at Rome, while the barefooted friars were singing vespers in the Temple of Jupiter. In 1770 he published a pamphlet entitled *Critical Observations on the Sixth Book of the Æneid*. In 1774 he obtained a seat in Parliament for Liskeard, and was a silent supporter of the North administration and its American politics for eight years.

In 1776 the first quarto volume of his *Decline and Fall of the Roman Empire* was published, and at once made a public reputation for its author. In 1778 he drew up on behalf of the English Government a *Mémoire Justificatif* in answer to the manifesto of the French court, and for this service he was made one of the Lords of Trade. On the retirement of North he lost his appointment, and soon after withdrew to Lausanne (1783), where, in the course of four years, he completed the three remaining volumes of his history, which were published together in 1788. In 1793 he returned to England, where he died in the following year.

Gibbon's history though not without its defects, has great merits. Its style, if at times somewhat monotonous, has the energy and elevation required for so great a theme; his learning is vast and thorough, and his insight into human nature in every variety of circumstances is that of a great and philosophical historian. In 1796 his friend Lord Sheffield published two quarto volumes of his miscellaneous works, of which the most valuable part is the *Memoirs of his Life and Writings*. The best edition of the *Decline and Fall* is that of Bury (1909–12).—
BIBLIOGRAPHY: J. A. C. Morison, *Gibbon* (in English Men of Letters Series); Prothero (editor), *The Letters of Gibbon*.

GIBBON, a name common to the apes of the genus Hylobátes, but more particularly applied to the species *Hylobátes lar*, which inhabits the islands of the Indian Archipelago. It is distinguished from other man-like apes by the slenderness of its form, but more particularly by the extraordinary length of its arms, which, when the animal is standing, reach nearly to the ankles, and which enable it to swing itself from tree to tree with wonderful agility. Its colour is black, but its face

is commonly surrounded by a white or grey beard.

GIBBONS, Grinling, an English wood-carver and sculptor of Dutch origin, born 1648, died 1721, employed by royalty, and by most of the nobility of his time, to execute carvings in their houses and for churches. A ceiling at Petworth is among his most remarkable works.

GIBBONS, Orlando, English musical composer, born in 1583, died in 1625. At the age of twenty-one he was appointed organist of the Chapel Royal, and in 1622 he received the degree of Doctor of Music from the University of Oxford. Three years later he died

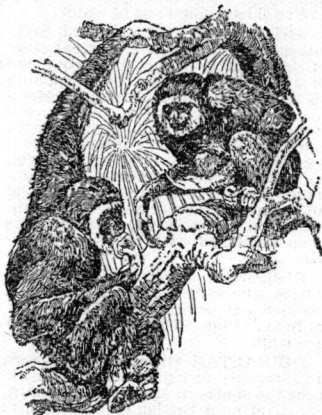

White-handed Gibbons (*Hylobátes lar*)

of smallpox at Canterbury, where he had gone to be present at the marriage of Charles I with Henrietta of France. He was buried in Canterbury Cathedral, where his wife caused a magnificent tomb to be erected to him. He is the author of madrigals and anthems (*Hosanna to the Son of David! Almighty and Everlasting God!*) and other works.

GIBBS, Sir Philip Hamilton, K.B.E., British novelist and war correspondent, born in 1877. Editor with Messrs. Cassell & Co. at the age of twenty-one, he entered journalism in 1902, and was successively on the staff of *The Daily Mail*, *The Tribune*, and *The Daily Chronicle*. He was war correspondent with the Bulgarian army in 1912, and with the French, Belgian, and British armies in France and Flanders during the European War. He was knighted in 1920, and in 1921 was appointed editor of the *Review of Reviews*.

His numerous novels and historical

works include: *The Individualist, The Street of Adventure, The Romance of Empire, Men and Women of the French Revolution, King's Favourite, The Soul of the War, Open Warfare, The Way to Victory, Realities of War, Darkened Rooms, The Hidden City* and (1931) *The Lion's Way.*

GIBEL (jib'e), a fish of the carp family, *Carassius gibelio*, generally known in England as the Prussian carp, and distinguished from the common carp (*Cyprinus carpio*) by having no barbules at the mouth. Probably only an elongated variety of the Crucian carp (*Carassius vulgāris*). It is a good table fish, but seldom weighs more than ½ lb. It is said to be able to live thirty hours out of water.

GIBEON, one of the ancient royal cities of the Canaanites, a 'great city' of the Hivites, who at an early stage of Joshua's conquests, by disguising themselves in old clothes and professing to come from a far country, obtained an alliance and covenant with the Israelites. When the stratagem was discovered, the Israelites resolved to observe the covenant, but condemned them to be "hewers of wood and drawers of water unto all the congregation" (*Jos.* ix, 21). Gibeon has been identified with the modern El-Jib.

GIBEON, a town of South West Africa, the centre of an agricultural district. It is near the Walvis Bay railway. Pop. 5,000, of whom 1,300 are white.

GIBRALTAR (jib-ṛạl'tȧr), a town and strongly-fortified rocky peninsula near the southern extremity of Spain, constituting a British Crown Colony. It is connected with the mainland by a low sandy isthmus, 1½ miles long and ¾ mile broad, known as the 'neutral ground,' and has Gibraltar Bay on the west, the open sea on the east and south. The highest point of the rock is about 1,400 feet above sea-level; its north face is almost perpendicular, while its east side exhibits tremendous precipices. On its south side it is almost inaccessible, making approach from seaward impossible; the west side, again, although very rugged and precipitous, slopes towards the sea; and here the rock is secured by extensive and powerful batteries, rendering it apparently impregnable.

Fortifications. Vast sums of money and an immense amount of labour have been spent in fortifying this celebrated stronghold, which, as a coaling-station, depot for war material, and a port of refuge in case of war, forms one of the most important points of support for British naval operations and British commerce eastwards. Numerous caverns and galleries, extending 2 to 3 miles in length, and of sufficient width for carriages, have been cut in the solid rock with port-holes at intervals of every 12 yards bearing upon the neutral ground and the bay, and mounted with more than 1,000 guns, some of them of the largest size. The garrison numbers about 5,000.

Town. The town of Gibraltar is situated on the west side of the peninsula, terminating in Europa Point, and thus fronts the bay. It consists chiefly of one spacious street about ½ mile in length, lined with shops, and paved and lighted. The principal buildings are the Governor's and Lieutenant-Governor's houses, the admiralty, naval hospital, victualling office, and barracks, and a handsome theatre. Its water-supply is derived from the rainfall. Gibraltar is a free port, but there is a duty on malt liquors, wine, spirits, and tobacco. It has a considerable shipping trade, being an entrepôt for the distribution of British manufactures. The chief export is wine.

The administration is vested in the Governor, who is also commander-in-chief of the troops. There is a harbour of 440 acres. In 1931 the civil population amounted to 17,613; military, 3,218; naval 541; total 21,372. In addition there were 1,480 aliens. The colony is self-supporting, its revenue and expenditure in 1931 amounting to £151,415 and £178,955 respectively.

History. Gibraltar, known to the Greeks as Calpe, was first fortified as a strategic point by the Saracen leader Tarik Ibn Zeiad in 711–12, from whom it was thenceforward called Gebel-al-Tarik, the rock of Tarik. It was ultimately taken by the Spaniards from the Moors in 1462, fortified in the European style, and so much strengthened that the engineers of the seventeenth century considered it impregnable. It was taken, however, after a vigorous bombardment in 1704 by a combined English and Dutch force under Sir George Rooke and Prince George of Darmstadt, and was secured to Britain by the Peace of Utrecht in 1713. Since then it has remained in British hands, notwithstanding some desperate efforts on the part of Spain and France to retake it.

During 1704–5 it was closely besieged; in 1727 it was hard pressed by a Spanish force when Admiral Wager, with eleven ships of the line, relieved it. In 1779, Britain being then engaged in a war with its revolted colonies and with France, a last grand effort was made by Spain to recover Gibraltar. The siege lasted for nearly four years, the fire being for the great part of that time very harassing, and rising on several occasions into a fierce and prolonged bombardment. It was heroically and successfully defended, however, by General Elliot (afterwards Lord Heathfield) and the garrison. Since that time, in the various British and Spanish, and also French wars, Gibraltar has only been blockaded on the landside.—BIBLIOGRAPHY:J.H.Mann, *Gibraltar and its Sieges*; Boyle, *Gibraltar* (British Empire Series); G. J. Gilbard, *Popular History of Gibraltar*; A. Macmillan, *Malta and Gibraltar*.

GIBRALTAR, STRAITS OF, the channel which forms an entrance from the Atlantic into the Mediterranean. The narrowest part is a little to the west of Gibraltar, and 8½ miles across. A strong and constant current flows into the Mediterranean from the Atlantic Ocean, in the middle of the Straits, but the undercurrent as well as two feeble lateral currents along the coast set towards the ocean.

GIBSON, Charles Dana, American artist. Born at Roxbury, Mass, 14th Sept.,1867, he studied in New York and Paris, and began his artistic career by contributing illustrations to various periodicals. His drawings of a type of American girl, the Gibson girl, secured him great popularity. Later he turned to portrait painting in oils. In 1920 he purchased the controlling interest in *Life*.

GIBSON, John, one of the most distinguished English sculptors of modern times, born near Conway, in Wales, in 1790, died at Rome in 1866. He was the son of a landscape-gardener, and was apprenticed to a wood-carver at Liverpool, and then to the proprietor of a marble-works, where he attracted attention by a figure of *Time*, modelled in wax, which he exhibited at the age of eighteen.

The patronage of William Roscoe, the historian, assisted him to go to Rome, where he was cordially received by Canova. On the death of Canova in 1822 Gibson entered the studio of Thorwaldsen. His reputation was now widely spread, and his works were eagerly sought after by his countrymen. In 1836 he was made a Royal Academician; but to the end of his life he continued to make Rome his chief place of residence. Most of Gibson's subjects are taken from classical mythology, and are executed with a noble severity and purity of style based upon close observation of nature. Amongst his best works are: *The Wounded Amazon, The Hunter and his Dog, Hylas surprised by Nymphs* (in the National Gallery), *Helen, Proserpine, Sappho*. He also executed portrait-statues; and in the bas-relief found a particularly congenial mode of expression. One of his peculiarities as an artist was the practice of colouring his statues.

GIBSON, Margaret Dunlop, *née* **Smith**, British Orientalist, born at Irvine, in Ayrshire, died 11th Jan., 1920. Educated privately, she visited Palestine several times, and in 1892 she and her sister, Mrs. Agnes Lewis, discovered and photographed the famous Syriac palimpsest of the Gospel. In 1897 she and her sister laid the foundation stone of Westminster Theological College, Cambridge, the site of which they had given. In 1915 she received the gold medal from the Royal Asiatic Society. Her works include: *How the Codex was Found* (1893), *Apocrypha Sinaitica* (1896), *Commentaries on Acts* (1913), and *Commentaries on St. Paul's Epistles* (1916).

GIDE,André Paul Guillaume,French novelist and critic. Born in Paris, 21st Nov., 1869, his first book was *Les Cahiers d'André Walter* (1889), and was followed by *Paludes* (1895) and *Les Nourritures Terrestres* (1897). His first novel, *L'Immoraliste*, was a masterpiece, and *La Porte Étroite* (1909) and *Isabelle* (1911) were characterized by the same sureness of touch. *Caves du Vatican* (1914) was less successful and *Les Faux Monnayeurs* (1927) and *Si le Grain ne Meurt* (1924) are unequal. *Le Retour du Tchad* was published in 1928. Gide insists on sincerity in life, without any fixed or moral beliefs.

GIDEON (Heb., meaning a destroyer), the son of Joash, of the tribe of Manasseh, divinely called to deliver the Israelites from the oppression of the Midianites. Having effected their deliverance, he was chosen judge of Israel. (*See* Judges vi–viii.)

GIERS (gĕrz), **Nicholas Carlovitsh de,** a Russian statesman descended from a Swedish family settled in Finland, was born in 1820, and died in 1895. After holding various posts, in 1875 he became assistant to Prince Gortschakov, the Minister of Foreign Affairs, whom he succeeded in 1882. His policy in general was of a peaceful tendency, and in particular opposed to Pan-slavistic ideas of development. In Central Asia, however, he continued the policy of advance, and in 1885 the Russian occupation of positions within the Afghan frontier nearly brought about a war with Britain.

GIESSEN (gē'sĕn), a town of Germany, capital of the province of Upper Hesse (Oberhessen), in the former Grand-Duchy of Hesse, on the Lahn. It was once fortified, and is still entered by four gates, but its ramparts have been converted into pleasant walks. It has a castle, now converted into Government offices, and a university founded in 1607, and possessing valuable apparatus, an observatory, and a botanical garden. Pop. (1925) 33,680.

GIFFEN (gif'ĕn), **Sir Robert**, British statistician and financial writer, born in Lanarkshire in 1837, died in 1910. After being in a solicitor's office, and studying at Glasgow University, he entered a Glasgow commercial house, and next became connected with the press, being successively on the staffs of *The Globe*, *Fortnightly Review*, *Economist*, and *The Daily News*.

In 1876 he was appointed chief of the Statistical Department of the Board of Trade. In subsequent extensions of the branch he became assistant-secretary to the Commercial Department (1886–92),and Controller-General of the Commercial, Labour, and Statistical Departments, retiring in 1897. He wrote numerous reports on financial matters, and gave evidence before many parliamentary committees and royal commissions. He became F.R.S. in 1892 and K.C.B. in 1895, and was a member of the Royal Commission on Agriculture, 1894–7. His publications include: *Stock Exchange Securities* (1878), *Essays on Finance* (1879 and 1886), *Trade Depression and Low Prices* (1885), *The Growth of Capital* (1890), *The Case against Bimetallism* (1892), and *Economic Enquiries and Studies* (1904).

GIFFORD, **William**, a critic and satirist, born at Ashburton, in Devonshire, in 1757, died in 1826. He was apprenticed to a shoemaker, but possessing a strong taste for study, he was enabled by the kindness of some friends to go to school and afterwards to Oxford University. After being some time tutor in Earl Grosvenor's family he published in 1794 *The Baviad*, a satire directed against the poetasters of the Della Crusca school; and in 1795 *The Mæviad*, a severe satire on the contemporary drama. In 1797 he became editor of the *Anti-Jacobin*; and he published a translation of Juvenal in 1802. On the foundation of the *Quarterly Review* in 1809 he became its editor, conducting it with much ability. He also edited the works of Massinger, Ford, Jonson, and Shirley. He was interred in Westminster Abbey.

GIFFORD LECTURES, lectureships endowed by Lord Gifford, one of the judges of the Court of Session, Edinburgh, from 1870 to 1881, who left £80,000 for the purpose. They were founded in connection with the Universities of St. Andrews, Glasgow, Aberdeen, and Edinburgh, and are for the exposition of natural religion in the widest sense of that term: the lecturers to be subjected to no test of any kind; to belong to any denomination whatever, or to no denomination.

The appointments are for two years, but may be held for six. The lecturers are to deliver a yearly course of about twenty original lectures open to all. The first lecturers were: Max Müller, Hutchison Stirling, Andrew Lang, and E. B. Tylor.

GIJON (hē-hōn'), a seaport in Spain, on the Bay of Biscay. It consists of an old and a new town, the former on the upper part of a slope and the latter below. It contains a cigar manufactory, employing about 1,400 persons, and has various other industries and a good trade. Pop. 57,573.

GILA (jē lä), **RIO**, a North American river, which rises in New Mexico and flows westward for 450 miles, and then unites with the Colorado. Curious ruins of stone-built houses occur all along its banks. In these are found fragments of pottery.

GILBERT, **John**. American film actor. Born at Logan,Utah, 30th July, 1897, he worked as a writer, director and editor of motion pictures. He achieved fame as an exponent of passion in *Big Parade*, *The Merry Widow*, *Flesh and the Devil*, and other pictures.

GILBERT, **Sir Alfred**. English sculptor. Born in London, 12th Aug, 1854, he studied in London, Paris and Rome, first exhibiting at the Royal Academy in 1882. In 1892 he was elected a Royal Academician, and 1900–09 was Professor of Sculpture at the Royal Academy. Gilbert is considered by many to be the greatest living English sculptor. Among his many works are the Eros Fountain in Piccadilly, the Kiss of Victory, and the statues of Queen Victoria at Winchester, of John Bright at Westminster, and of Queen Alexandria at Marlborough House. Gilbert was knighted by the King in June, 1932.

GILBERT, **Sir Humphrey**, English navigator of the reign of Queen Elizabeth, born in Devonshire about 1539. In 1578 he obtained from the queen a patent,empowering him to discover and colonize in North America any land then unsettled, and made an unsuccessful voyage to Newfoundland. in 1583 he sailed to it again, and took possession of the harbour of St. John's. Shortly after he embarked in a small sloop to explore the coast, and was lost in a storm.

GILBERT, **Sir John**, R.A., English painter, born in 1817, died in 1897. The first picture he exhibited (in 1836) was *The Arrest of Lord Hastings*, in water-colour, which medium he used constantly all his life. He also painted in oil, and among his more notable productions therein are, *Don Quixote giving Advice to Sancho Panza*, *The*

Education of Gil Blas, and a series of tableaux of the principal characters in Shakespeare. He was particularly successful in depicting scenes from old English life, and won a great reputation as an illustrator of books and periodicals, being a regular contributor to *Punch* and *The Illustrated London News.*

In 1871 he became president of the Royal Society of Water-Colour Painters. In the same year he was knighted, and in 1872 he became an A.R.A., becoming R.A. in 1876. In 1893 he presented a large collection of his pictures to various art galleries, including the Guildhall Gallery, London, and received the freedom of the city.

GILBERT, Sir William Schwenck, English dramatist, was born on 18th Nov., 1836, and died on 28th May, 1911. His father was William Gilbert (1804–90), who was an assistant surgeon in the navy, and a novelist of some note, his best-known books being *Shirley Hall Asylum* (1863), *Doctor Austin's Guests* (1866), and *The Wizard of the Mountain* (1867). Gilbert was educated at Boulogne, at the Western Grammar School, Brompton, and at the Great Ealing School. He entered King's College, London, in Oct., 1855, and graduated B.A. at London University in 1857. In 1855, when the Crimean War was at its height, he entertained the idea of competing for a commission in the Royal Artillery, but the declaration of peace put an end to this project. Gilbert, however, was interested in soldiering, and obtained a commission in the militia in the 3rd Battalion Gordon Highlanders in 1857, becoming a captain in 1867, and retiring with the rank of major in 1883. His military knowledge proved of some value to him subsequently when drilling the choruses of his operas.

In 1857 Gilbert entered the education department of the Privy Council office, where he spent four unhappy years. In 1861 a small legacy enabled him to leave this uncongenial work and read for the Bar. He was called in Nov., 1863, and joined the northern circuit, but only earned £75 in two years. Meanwhile he was supporting himself by means of journalism, writing for *Fun*, a comic paper then edited by H. J. Byron. To this paper he contributed the famous series of comic poems known as *The Bab Ballads.* Gilbert was a talented illustrator, and drew admirable illustrations for these ballads, as well as for some of his father's novels.

Gilbert commenced his career as a dramatist in 1866 with a burlesque on *L'Elixir d'Amore* entitled *Dulcamara, or The Little Duck and the Great Quack.* This was followed by several other burlesques, including *La Vivandière* and *Robert the Devil.* He then tried his hand at more serious plays, and wrote *The Palace of Truth* (1870), *The Wicked World* (1873), and *Pygmalion and Galatea* (1871). The last-named was highly successful, and brought Gilbert in £40,000. Assisted by Gilbert à Beckett, Gilbert wrote a burlesque on his own play *The Wicked World.* This burlesque was entitled *The Happy Land* (1873), and caused much sensation because three of the actors were made up to resemble Gladstone, Lowe, and Ayrton, members of the Government at that time. This feature of the performance was suppressed by order of the Lord Chamberlain. *Charity*, a serious play, was produced in 1874, and enjoyed only a moderate success. *Sweethearts*, a pleasantly sentimental dramatic contrast, appeared in the same year. *Dan'l Druce*, a serious play founded upon the story of *Silas Marner*, was produced in 1876, and *Engaged*, a cynical farce based upon the Scottish marriage laws, in 1877.

In 1871 Gilbert was introduced to Sullivan, and the immediate result was a comic opera, *Thespis, or The Gods Grown Old.* In 1875 they collaborated in *Trial by Jury*, a dramatic cantata of exquisite finish, satirizing the procedure in a breach-of-promise case. The great series of operas, however, may be said to have begun with *The Sorcerer* in 1877. The others are: *H.M.S. Pinafore, or The Lass that Loved a Sailor* (1878); *The Pirates of Penzance, or The Slave of Duty* (1880); *Patience, or Bunthorne's Bride* (1881); *Iolanthe, or The Peer and the Peri* (1882); *Princess Ida, or Castle Adamant* (1884); *The Mikado, or The Town of Titipu* (1885); *Ruddigore, or The Witch's Curse* (1887); *The Yeomen of the Guard, or The Merryman and His Maid* (1888); *The Gondoliers, or The King of Barataria* (1889); *Utopia Limited, or The Flowers of Progress* (1893); and *The Grand Duke, or The Statutory Duel* (1896).

A more perfect partnership than that of Gilbert and Sullivan never existed, and the Savoy operas are unique in every way. Indeed, they may all be said to be virtually flawless, and none of them has strong claims to pre-eminence over the others. For dainty whimsicality *Iolanthe* is hard to beat, and for deft construction and urbane satire *Patience* is unsurpassed. Gilbert had a marvellous mastery over comic metre, and, in point of fact, invented many new metrical forms. His words set themselves to music. His plots, though fantastic, are always coherent, and a curious strain of inverted logic runs through all his work. The operas brought Gilbert fame and wealth. *The Mikado*, perhaps the most popular of the series, brought him in £30,000, and *Ruddigore*, one of the least successful, £7,000.

Gilbert wrote one or two libretti for other composers. Alfred Cellier wrote the music of *The Mountebanks* (1892), and Dr. Osmond Carr that of *His Excellency* (1894). Edward German composed the score of *Fallen Fairies* (1909), an operatic version of *The Wicked World*. Gilbert's last play was a realistic sketch called *The Hooligan* (1911). He died in May, 1911, of heart failure while saving a lady from drowning in his swimming-lake. Gilbert was a J.P. and D.L. for Middlesex, and was knighted in 1907.

Gilbert had no predecessors in opera-writing; he invented his own methods and left no successor. He was a highly original genius, and left the mark of his originality on everything he wrote. He was a master of stage-craft, and thought no trouble too great to take to secure the effect he desired. Probably no dramatist ever had his own intentions so exactly carried out, as he was his own stage manager, and something of a martinet at rehearsals. In all his work there is literary grace and finish, and a logical absurdity to which the epithet 'Gilbertian' is applied. His works are full of quotations which have become part of the language, and are also full of sound common sense. Great as is the difference, in some ways, between the Athenian comic poet and the Victorian dramatist, in literary deftness, in whimsicality, and in lyric grace Gilbert stands nearer to Aristophanes than any other English author.—BIBLIOGRAPHY: E. A. Browne, *W. S. Gilbert*; P. Fitzgerald, *The Savoy Opera and the Savoyards*; W. Archer, *English Dramatists of To-day*.

GILBERTINES, an order of monks founded in England by Gilbert of Sempringham in the twelfth century. They followed the Augustinian rule.

GILBERT ISLANDS, or **KINGS-MILL GROUP,** a group of sixteen islands in the Pacific Ocean, cut by the equator. The area is 166 sq. miles, and the population 23,586(400 foreigners).—The **Gilbert and Ellice Islands Colony** comprises the Gilbert Islands, the Union (Tokelau) Group, and Fanning, Washington, Ocean, and Christmas Islands. Most of the islands in this group were proclaimed a British protectorate in 1892, and (at the request of the natives) annexed as a colony in 1915. Ocean Island is the administrative centre and the seat of the Resident Commissioner. They are of coral formation, low and not fertile. Their chief products are the coco-nut, pandanus, taro, and the bread-fruit tree.

GILBO'A (Heb., 'Bubbling Fountain'), a range of hills in Palestine, bounding the Plain of Esdraëlon on the north-east. One of them is identified with the ancient Gilboa, the scene of Saul's last fatal battle.

GILDAS (gil'das) **THE WISE** (*Sapiens*), a British ecclesiastic and historian of the sixth century, of whom little is known. There is extant a Latin treatise or diatribe ascribed to Gildas which bears the title of *Epistola de Excidio Britanniæ* (on the Destruction of Britain).

GILDING is the art of applying gold-leaf or gold in a finely-divided state to surfaces of wood, stone, or metals, an ancient art which was practised among the Egyptians, Greeks, Romans, and Ancient Persians. The processes employed at the present day are very varied. Metals are gilded either by what is called chemical gilding, mercurial gilding, by electro-gilding, or by the application of gold-leaf. Copper and brass, for instance, may be gilded by the process called *wash* or *water gilding*, with an amalgam of gold and mercury. The surface of the copper, freed from oxide, is covered with the amalgam, and afterwards exposed to heat till the mercury is driven off, leaving a thin coat of gold.

Iron or steel is often gilded by applying gold-leaf, after the surface has been well cleaned, and heated until it has acquired the blue colour which at a certain temperature it assumes. Several leaves of gold are thus applied in succession, and the last is burnished down cold. In one process of chemical gilding the article is dipped into a solution of gold, what is termed Elkington's solution being composed as follows: 5 oz. (troy) of fine gold; nitro-muriatic acid, 52 oz. (avoirdupois); dissolve by heat, and continue the heat until the cessation of red or yellow vapours; decant the clear liquid; add 4 gall. of distilled water, pure potassium bicarbonate 20 lb., and boil for two hours.

Gilding on wood, plaster, leather, parchment, or paper, is performed by different processes of mechanical gilding. The first of these is oil-gilding, in which gold-leaf is cemented to the work by means of oil-size. In the case of paper or vellum the parts to be gilt receive a coat of gum-water or fine size, and the gold-leaf is applied before the parts are dry. They are afterwards burnished with agate.

Lettering and other gilding on bound books is applied without size. The gold-leaf is laid on the leather and imprinted with hot brass types. Brass rollers with thin edges are employed in the same way for lines, and similar tools for other ornaments. When the edges of the leaves of books are to be gilt, they are first cut smooth in the press, after which a solution of isinglass in spirits is laid on, and the gold-leaf is applied when the edges are in a proper state of dryness.

Japanner's gilding is another kind of mechanical gilding, which is performed in the same way as oil-gilding, except that instead of gold-leaf a gold-dust or powder is employed. Frames of pictures and mirrors, mouldings, &c., are gilt by the application of gold-leaf, or by the cheaper process of 'German gilding,' that is, by tin-foil or silver-leaf, with a yellow varnish above.

Porcelain and other kinds of earthenware, as well as glass, may be gilt by fixing a layer of gold in a powdered state by the action of fire. The gold-dust or powder required in this operation may be obtained by precipitating it from a solution in aqua regia, by means of either sulphate of iron or proto-nitrate of mercury. In order that the gold-powder may be applied to the surface of the article to be gilt it must be well mixed with some viscous vehicle, such as strongly-gummed water. It is then laid on with a fine camel's-hair brush.—Cf. F Scott Mitchell, *Practical Gilding.*

GIL'EAD, a mountain region of Palestine, east of the Jordan, having Bashan on the north and Moab and Ammon on the south. It was noted for its balm, as well as for its pasturage.

GILES (jilz), **ST.** (*St. Ægidius*), a native of Greece, who, according to the legend, lived in the sixth century, and was descended from an illustrious family. He is said to have worked miracles, and founded a convent in France. He became patron saint of Edinburgh, and his festival falls on the 1st of September.

GILFIL'LAN, George, writer, born in 1813, died in 1878. He studied at Glasgow University, in 1835 he became a licentiate of the Secession (Presbyterian) Church, and in 1836 was ordained to the School Wynd Church, Dundee. His numerous writings, among which may be mentioned *A Gallery of Literary Portraits, The Bards of the Bible,* and *The Martyrs of the Covenant,* possess a vigorous style and great powers of fancy.

GILGHIT, or **GILGIT** (gil'git), a valley and district in Kashmir state, situated on the southern slopes of the Hindu Kúsh, and watered by the Gilgit, or Yasm, a tributary of the Indus.

GILL, Eric Rowland. English sculptor. Born at Brighton, Feb. 22, 1882, he was apprenticed to an architect, but preferred letter-carving, and in

1910 produced his first sculpture, "Madonna and Child." He became a Roman Catholic in 1913, and was commissioned to execute the Stations of the Cross for Westminster Cathedral. After the War he carved "Christ driving the Moneylenders from the Temple" for Leeds University War Memorial, and has done many other sculptures, including "S. Sebastian," "Torso," "Adam and Eve" (headless), and "Deposition." He published *Art Nonsense* (1929) and *Clothes* (1931).

GILL (gil), **Sir David,** astronomer, born in Aberdeenshire in 1843, died in 1914. He was educated at Aberdeen University, where he erected a private observatory for himself in 1868, and was associated with Lord Lindsay (Earl of Crawford) in the building of another at that nobleman's seat of Dunecht (Aberdeenshire), of which he was in charge from 1872 to 1876. He organized Lord Lindsay's Transit of Venus expedition to Mauritius in 1874, and subsequently measured the base line for the Geodetic Survey of Egypt. In 1877 he organized an expedition to the Island of Ascension to determine the solar parallax by observations of Mars, publishing an account in the *Memoirs of the Royal Astronomical Society.*

In 1879 he was appointed Astronomer Royal at the Cape of Good Hope, a post which he held till 1907. While holding this post he organized Transit of Venus expeditions, proved the value of photography for the complete cataloguing of stars, agitated for and set on foot the Geodetic Survey of South Africa, and directed the Boundary Survey between British Bechuanaland and German territory. He was created a K.C.B. in 1900, and received many other distinctions in recognition of his services to science. His numerous publications include works on *Heliometer Determinations of Solar and Stellar Parallax;* the *Cape Photographic Durchmusterung;* and *History and Description of the Royal Observatory, Cape of Good Hope.*

GILLIES (gil'iz), John, Scottish historian and scholar, born at Brechin in 1747, died at Clapham in 1836. He was educated at the University of Glasgow, and finally settled in London, where he applied himself to literature. He published *The Orations of Lysias and Isocrates, translated from the Greek; History of Ancient Greece;* a translation of Aristotle's *Ethics* and *Politics,* with other works upon Aristotle; and a *View of the Reign of Frederick II of Prussia.*

GILLINGHAM, a municipal borough of Kent, north-east of Chatham, on the Medway, which is navigable there. It has an interesting church, with

Norman font and fine fifteenth-century brasses, and there are some remains of a palace which used to belong to the Archbishops of Canterbury. A quantity of fruit is grown in the neighbourhood. Edmund Ironside conquered the Danes close by. Pop. (1931), 60,983.

GILLRAY', James, an English caricaturist, born in 1757, died in London in 1815. He studied at the Royal Academy schools, and some clever sketches, such as *Paddy on Horseback*, published about 1780, first attracted attention to him. From this time till about 1810 he achieved a European reputation by a succession of caricatures, numbering about 1,200 and marked by great technical mastery, in which the king (George III) and the members of the House of Lords, and afterwards the French and the French celebrities of the day, were the chief objects of ridicule. In his closing years he was attacked by a mental malady, largely due to intemperance, which continued till his death.

GILLS, the respiratory organs of animals which breathe by absorbing dissolved oxygen from water, as crustaceans, some insect larvæ, most aquatic molluscs, fishes, and amphibians. In fishes they consist of highly vascular folds or filaments, attached to cartilaginous or bony arches in the walls of the perforated pharynx. Water is taken in at the mouth and expelled through the gill-slits to the exterior, bathing the gills as it does so.

GILLYFLOWER (jil'i), a name bestowed on such cruciferous flowers as the wall-flower or carnation, &c. The clove-pink (*Dianthus Caryophyllus*) is termed clove gillyflower.

GILMOUR, Sir John. Scottish politician. Born May 27, 1876, the son of a baronet, he was educated at Trinity College, Glenalmond, and Trinity College, Cambridge. After serving in S. Africa, he entered politics and was elected Unionist member for East Renfrewshire. In 1918 he was elected for the Pollok division of Glasgow, and in 1919 became a Unionist whip. In 1921–22 he was a junior Lord of the Treasury, and from 1924–29 Secretary for Scotland. In 1931 he joined the National Government as Minister for Agriculture, and as such attended the Ottawa Conference in July, 1932. In October, 1932, he succeeded Sir Herbert Samuel as Home Secretary.

GILO'LO, JILOLO, or **HALMAHERA,** an island in the Indian Archipelago, the largest of the Moluccas; area, 6,950 sq. miles. It is of singular form, consisting of four peninsulas, radiating north, north-east, east-south-east, and south, from a common centre, and having large bays between. It is rugged and mountainous, the mountains being volcanic.

The principal productions are sago, coco-nuts, spices, fruits, edible birds'-nests, and timber; horses, cattle, and sheep abound. Deer, wild boars, and other game are likewise plentiful. The original inhabitants, called Alfuros, have been gradually pressed into the interior by the Malays. The island, included in the Residency of Ternate, belongs to the Netherlands; pop. 140,322.

GILTHEAD (*Chrysophrys aurātus*), a spiny-finned fish of the Sparidæ or sea-bream family common in the Mediterranean. It has strong grinding teeth for crushing the shells of the molluscs on which it feeds; a crescentic yellow band stretches from eye to eye (whence its generic name, signifying 'golden eye-brows'). Its colour is a mixture of silver and sky-blue, its dorsal and caudal fins are black, while brown lines pass along the sides. It sometimes reaches a weight of 18 to 20 lb. Giltheads were among the fishes fattened for the table by the ancient Romans.

GIMBALS (jim'balz; O.Fr. *gemeau*; Lat. *gemellus*, twin), the name of the pair of rings within which the mariner's compass is slung, or any pair of similar rings. The gimbals maintain the compass-bowl and the compass-card in a horizontal position, there being two concentric rings, the outer turning about a horizontal axis, and the inner turning about a similar axis at right angles to the other. Ship chronometers are often suspended the same way.

GIN, a spirit distilled from grain, and flavoured with juniper-berries, and sometimes with oil of turpentine and common salt, and other substances. The name is from *genièvre*, the French for 'juniper.' It is largely manufactured in Holland, particularly in Schiedam, and the gin thence imported is thus often called Schiedam as well as Hollands. In Great Britain gin is largely manufactured in London, where it often goes by the name of *Old Tom*, and to a less extent at Plymouth and Bristol. What is termed 'gin' in Great Britain differs materially from Hollands and even from the best English gin, as it is a plain corn spirit, which derives its flavour from oil of turpentine, with certain aromatics in small quantities.

GIN, the name of certain machines employed in raising weights. One form consists of three poles, 12 to 15 feet long, often tapering from the lower extremity to the top and united at their upper extremities, whence a block and tackle is suspended. A space of 8 or 9 feet separates the lower extremities planted in the ground, and a kind of windlass is attached to two of the legs. Another kind of gin is a sort of whim or windlass for raising coal, &c. It is worked by a horse, which turns a cylinder, and winds on it a rope, by which the weight is raised.

GINGER (*Zingiber officināle*), an East Indian plant of the ord. Zingiberaceæ. It grows in moist places in various parts of tropical Asia and the Asiatic islands, and has been introduced into the West Indies, particularly Jamaica, as also into South America and West Africa. The kind most esteemed is Jamaica ginger. The rhizome, or underground stem, is what is used, being employed in various ways. It has an aromatic, pungent taste, and when young is candied, and makes an excellent preserve. It is a favourite condiment, and is used medicinally as a carminative, and in debility of the stomach and the alimentary canal. It is often useful in cases of toothache, relaxation of the uvula, and paralytic affections of the tongue. It enters into the composition of a great number of confections, infusions, and pills. The special preparations are the *tincture* and the *essence* of ginger; and *syrup*, prepared by mixing twenty-five parts of syrup with one of the strong tincture. *Infusion* of ginger is a preparation useful for flatulence.

GINGER-BEER, a pleasant, non-alcoholic, effervescing beverage, made by mixing together ginger, cream of tartar, sugar, yeast, and water, and allowing the whole to ferment for a time, then bottling.

Ginger-beer may also be prepared thus: Add to each gallon of water 1 lb. of refined sugar, and ¼ oz. of ground ginger. Boil for an hour, add the white of two eggs, remove the scum. Strain into a vessel to cool, cask it up with the juice and peel of a lemon. Add a very small amount of brewer's yeast, and bung up tightly for a fortnight.

GINGHAM (ging'am), a cotton fabric distinguished from calico by having the colours woven with the fabric, not printed on it. The patterns are various; sometimes fancy designs, sometimes chequered, and sometimes striped. Umbrella ginghams are all of one colour.

GINKGO, a genus of Gymnosperms, comprising the single species *Ginkgo biloba*, the maidenhair tree, the sole living type of the ancient class Ginkgoales. It is a handsome, hardy, deciduous tree, reaching 100 feet in height. The leaves resemble those of a maiden-

hair fern, but are much larger and coarser; other fern-like characters are the forked venation of the leaf and the presence of motile spermatozoids (found also in Cycads, but not in Conifers). The seed is edible and the timber useful. The tree is a native of China and Japan, where it is held sacred and grown in temple gardens. In Tertiary times this or allied species flourished in Britain.

GINSBURG (gins'bụrh), **Christian David**, rabbinical scholar, born in 1831, died in 1914. He is the author of *Commentaries on the Song of Songs* (1857), *Ecclesiastes*, and *Leviticus*; *The Karaites: their History and Literature*; *The Essenes*; *The Kabbalah: its Doctrines, Development, and Literature*, and other works of similar character. His greatest work is, however, the

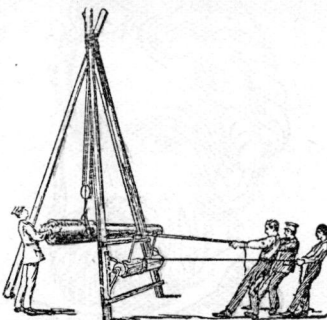

Gin

Massorah. He was one of the scholars engaged on the Revised Version of the Old Testament.

GINSENG (jin'seng), a plant of Northern Asia, *Panax ginseng*, ord. Araliaceæ, herbaceous, and about 1 foot high. Its root is regarded as a sort of panacea among the Chinese, and is largely imported, but it appears to be really of very little efficacy; the taste is sweet and mucilaginous, accompanied with some bitterness, and also slightly aromatic. Another species of ginseng, *Panax quinquefolium*, inhabits Canada and the northeastern parts of the United States. Quantities of its root are sent to China.

GIOBERTI (jō-ber'tē), Vincenzo, an Italian philosopher and statesman, born at Turin 1801, died at Paris 1852. Having been educated for the Church, he was appointed chaplain to Charles Albert, King of Sardinia, but having lost favour owing to his republican sentiments, he was first imprisoned, and, in 1833, banished. The first few years of his exile he spent at

Paris, and afterwards became a teacher of philosophy in a school at Brussels. There he published two works, one of which was an attempt to reconcile philosophy and Roman Catholicism.

In 1843 appeared his *Primato Morale e Civile degli Italiani*, a defence on liberal principles of the Papacy, a work which brought over the majority of the priests to the national party. In 1847 he published a work entitled *Il Gesuita Moderno* (The Modern Jesuit). When Charles Albert in 1848 granted a constitution to Sardinia, Gioberti returned to his native country, but he soon after withdrew to Paris.

GIOJA DEL COLLE (jŏ′yả del kol′lȧ), a town in Southern Italy, pro-

Giorgione

vince of Bari, on a slope of the Apennines. Pop. (commune), 21,837.

GIOLITTI, Giovanni, Italian statesman, born at Mondovi, in the province of Cuneo, 1842. He was educated at the University of Turin, where he studied law, but soon turned his attention to politics and entered the Chamber of Deputies. Minister of Finance in 1889 in the Crispi Cabinet, and Premier and Minister of the Interior in 1892, he had to resign on account of bank scandals. He was again Prime Minister from 1903 to 1905, from 1906 to 1909, and from 1911 to 1914, when he was succeeded by Salandra. At the outbreak of the European War Giolitti was in favour of Italian neutrality. At the fall of the Nitti ministry in 1920, Giolitti again became Prime Minister. In 1922 he published an autobiography. He died in 1928.

GIORDANO (jor-dä′nō), **Luca**, Italian painter, born at Naples about 1632, died there 1705. He was called 'Fa Presto,' his father having continually urged him on at his work with the words 'Luca, fa presto' (Luca, work quickly). He was a pupil of Ribera (Lo Spagnoletto), studied and copied the great Italian masters at Rome, and became the assistant of Peter of Cortona. Paul Veronese had afterwards great influence on his manner.

After working in Naples and Florence, in 1692 he was employed by Charles II to decorate the Escorial, and at the court of Spain he became a great favourite. His work there shows the immense but mechanical facility for which he was famous. He could imitate older masters, notably Bassano, so well as to impose upon connoisseurs. But his eclecticism killed his originality. After the death of Charles II he was retained in the service of Philip V, but eventually returned to his native country. His best-known work are his frescoes in the Escorial, and paintings at Madrid, Florence, and Rome. Among his best work are: *Venus and Mars* in the Louvre, and *The Judgment of Paris* in Berlin.

GIORGIONE (jor-jō′nả), properly *Giorgio Barbarelli*, born in 1477 at Castelfranco, and died 1511. One of the most celebrated painters of the Venetian school, he more completely expresses the spirit of pagan poesy which marks the Early Renaissance than any other painter, and combines in his work classical harmony with a romantic and lyrical spirit. He was among the first to study the effect of light and atmosphere in modifying colour. Titian was closely associated with Giorgione, who influenced his early work. In Venice he ornamented the façades of several large buildings with frescoes, which have mostly perished. His portraits are among the finest of the Italian school. His works are rare, but good examples may be seen at Milan, Castelfranco, and in the galleries at Florence, Venice, Vienna, and Dresden. He is also represented in the National Gallery (*Golden Age*) and at Hampton Court (*Shepherd*).

GIOTTO (jot′tō), properly *Ambrogiotto* or *Angiolotto Bondone*, a Florentine painter, born about 1266 at Vespignano, near Florence, died about 1337. In his boyhood he was a shepherd, and is said to have been seen by Cimabue, as he was drawing figures of his sheep upon a piece of slate, and to have been taken to Florence by that artist as a pupil.

The strong naturalism which marks his work was a complete break with older traditions, and definitely changed the whole course of European painting. Joined to a sense of the dramatic, a feeling for form (developed by the study of sculpture) and a power of dignified and rhythmic design make him one of the great figures of European art.

Among his most important work are frescoes at Rome, at Assisi, in the Arena Chapel at Padua, and in S. Croce at Florence. Some panel pictures are also attributed to him. He was also a remarkable architect, the campanile of the cathedral of Florence being his work.—Cf. Crowe and Cavalcaselle, *History of Painting in Italy*.

GIPPSLAND, the south-easternmost of the five districts into which the Australian colony or state of Victoria is divided; area, 13,898 sq. miles. Much of the north and east is covered by heavy timber, but the southern and western portions are fertile, and the mineral resources are enormous. The climate suits oranges, limes, hops, sugar-beet, tobacco, opium, &c. The mountain ranges rise to over 6,000 feet.

GIRAFFE (ji-raf'), or **CAMELOPARD** (Giraffa), a ruminant animal inhabiting Africa, and the type of a small family also including the Okapi (q.v.). It is the tallest of all animals, a full-grown male reaching the height of 18 or 20 feet. This great stature is mainly due to the extraordinary length of the neck, in which, however, there are but seven vertebræ, though these are extremely elongated. It has two bony excrescences on its head resembling horns, but permanently covered with skin. There is also a median prominence between the eyes commonly regarded as a third horn.

Its great height is admirably adapted to its habit of feeding on the leaves of trees, and in this the animal is further aided by its tongue, which is both prehensile and capable of being remarkably elongated or retracted at will. When it browses on the herbage on the ground, it stretches out its fore-legs as widely as possible till it can reach the ground by means of its long neck.

Its colour is usually light fawn, marked with darker spots. It is a mild and inoffensive animal, and in captivity is very gentle and playful. The giraffe is a native of a great part of Africa, from the latitude of Abyssinia southward to the Transvaal and the Kalahari Desert. There are two distinct species, one (*G. camelopardalis*) native to Somaliland, and the other (*G. australis*) to South Africa. The third horn is much better developed in the latter.

GIRAL'DUS CAMBREN'SIS, an early English historian, born about 1146. His proper name was Gerald de Barry, and he was the son of William

de Barry, a Norman noble of Pembrokeshire. He was educated under his uncle, the Bishop of St. David's, and afterwards at the University of Paris. He returned in 1172, and was appointed Archdeacon of St. David's. His uncle dying soon after, Gerald was elected to succeed him, but the king refused to confirm the appointment, and Gerald withdrew to Paris, where he was appointed professor of canon law.

In the following year (1180) he returned to England, where he was required to administer the bishopric of St. David's, the proper bishop having proved himself incompetent. Giraldus

Giraffe (*Giraffa australis*)

discharged this office for four years, and was then appointed a royal chaplain. As companion to the king's son, Prince John, he went to Ireland in 1185, where he collected the materials for his *Topographia Hibernica*. He afterwards drew up a similar work on Wales (*Itinerarium Cambriæ*).

After the departure of Richard Cœur de Lion for Palestine, Gerald remained to conduct the affairs of the Government, but in 1192 retired to Lincoln for purposes of study. He was again elected to the see of St. David's, but Richard prevented his installation. He now retired from the world, and refused the bishopric when again offered to him. The year of his death is unknown. He was a man of great vanity and ambition, and was also remarkable for his credulity. The *De Rebus a se Gestis*, which, with others of his minor works, is published in Wharton's *Anglia Sacra*, contains the most remarkable instances of the author's vanity and self-esteem.—Cf. H. Owen, *Gerald the Welshman*.

GIRARDIN (zhĕ-rär-dan), Émile de, French journalist and politician, born in Switzerland in 1802, died in 1881. Educated in Paris, he was connected as projector, editor, or otherwise with a number of newspapers and periodicals, the most successful being *La Presse*, a Conservative organ established in 1836. A controversy in its columns led to a duel between Girardin and Armand Carrel, in which the latter was killed.

In politics Girardin played many parts. He was fined 5,000 francs in 1867 for attacks on the imperial Government in *La Liberté*. He wrote numerous political pamphlets, and a few pieces for the stage.

His first wife, Delphine Gay, daughter of the novelist Madame Sophie Gay, was a well-known authoress; born 1804, died 1855. She wrote the novels: *Émile, Le Lorgnon, Le Marquis de Pontanges, La Canne de M. de Balzac, Il ne faut pas jouer avec la douleur,* and *Marguerite*; contributed to the *Presse* newspaper, and wrote for the stage *Lady Tartuffe, La Joie fait peur, Le Supplice d'une femme,* and other pieces.

GIRASOL (ji'ra-sōl), a precious opaline stone, which, under strong lights, reflects a brilliant reddish light. It is usually of a milk-white or bluish-white colour. The brightest are brought from Brazil and Siberia. The name is sometimes bestowed on the Asteria sapphire. One variety is known as the fire opal.

GIRDER, in structural engineering, a beam. The term 'girder' is usually reserved for a beam of iron or steel. A girder is designed to resist bending. The cross-section of the girder is, therefore, shaped so as to secure the maximum resistance to bending with the minimum weight of metal.

For a given working stress and depth of girder, the maximum resistance to bending is obtained when the moment of inertia of the cross-section about an axis parallel to the axis of the bending-moment is greatest. On the other hand, the area of the cross-section must be a minimum if the least amount of material is to be used. The best compromise is, therefore, to put as much of the area as possible at the maximum distance from the centre of the section.

Hence the I girder, consisting of a top and bottom flange, with a thin web connecting them, has come into being. The bulk of the area of the cross-section is the area of the flanges which are at the maximum distance from the centre of the cross-section. The formula for the working stress in a nearly straight girder is $p = \dfrac{My}{I}$, where p is the fibre stress on the out-

side layers of the flange in pounds per square inch, M is the bending-moment in pound inches, y is half the depth of the girder in inches, and I is the moment of inertia of the cross-section in inch units (in.⁴;), assuming the cross-section to be of unit density.

Girders may be supported at both ends, or they may be built into a wall at one end and unsupported at the other, when they are called *cantilevers*. Sometimes a very long girder is supported by three or four iron pillars. Such a girder is called a *continuous beam*.

In very large girders, such as those used for railway bridges, the shape of the girder is roughly the same as the bending-moment diagram. For instance, the bending-moment of a beam, supported at each end, is greatest at the middle of the span and least at the supports themselves, and a glance at any well-designed railway girder will show that its depth is greatest at the middle and least at the supports.

Continuous girders are apt to be dangerous, because the intermediate supports may sink a little and so entirely alter the distribution of the load.

In a design like the Forth Bridge each column supports its own load independently, and the intermediate connecting links between the columns are hinged and hung so that any slight movement in the foundations of any one of the columns would not materially alter the distribution of the loading. — BIBLIOGRAPHY: A. Morley, *Strength of Materials*; W. H. Warren, *Engineering Construction in Iron, Steel, and Timber.*

GIRDLE OF VENUS (*Cestum Veneris*), an animal belonging to the Ctenophora, found in the Mediterranean and Atlantic. In shape it resembles a ribbon, and may exceed a yard in length. It swims by gracefully undulating its body. It is iridescent by day, and brilliantly phosphorescent at night. Related species are found in the White Sea and Indian Ocean.

GIRGEH or **GIRGA** (jir'je), a town, formerly capital, of Upper Egypt, on the left bank of the Nile. It possesses a Roman Catholic convent, the oldest in Egypt. Pop. 19,893.

GIRGENTI (jir-jen'tē), or **AGRIGENTO** a town, in the south-west of Sicily, capital of the province of same name, 58 miles S.S.E. of Palermo, a few miles from the sea, on an elevated site, with a cathedral (dating from the fifteenth century), library (founded in 1765,) and museum. It exports wheat, oil, fruit, and sulphur, its port being Porto Empedocle. Near the town are the extensive and remarkable ruins of the ancient Agrigentum. Pop. (1930), 30,032.—The province has an area of 1,174 sq. miles, and is rather mountainous. Pop. (1931), 398,886.

GIRL GUIDES, THE (Incorporated), is the sister movement to that of the Boy Scouts, and was founded by Lord Baden-Powell shortly after the inception of his Boy Scout movement in 1908. The organization is identical in principle with that of the Boy Scouts, its aim being to inculcate upon girls of every class, self-development in the attributes of Character and Intelligence, Physical Health through Self-knowledge, Service for the Community, and Handicrafts.

Instruction is given in each of these four points by means of interesting games and hobbies, all encouraging friendly rivalry by means of interpatrol competitions. Proficiency badges are awarded to those who pass certain tests in such subjects as Ambulance, Child Nursing, Cookery, Dressmaking, Gardening, Housekeeping, Knitting, Laundry, Needlework, Sick Nursing, &c., all admirable womanly accomplishments which cannot fail to have a beneficial influence on the character of the girls. The Guide Promise and Law, on which the whole training is founded, corresponds with those of the Scout movement. Camps are held in the summer for the guides. The headquarters are in Buckingham Palace Road, London, S.W.1, where a new building was opened in 1931. The world membership is over 1,000,000. *See* BOY SCOUTS.

GIRODET-TRIOSON (zhĕ-ro-dā-trē-o-son), Anne Louis Girodet de Roussy, French historical painter, born in 1767, died 1824. A pupil and follower of Louis David, in 1810 he won the 'grand prix' (for his *Scene from the Deluge*) over his master's head. Like David he is a draughtsman rather than a colourist. Among his famous pictures are: *Endymion*, *Hippocrates*, *The Deluge*, *The Burial of Atala*, *Napoleon receiving the Keys of Vienna*, and *St. Louis in Egypt*.

GIRONDE (zhĕ-rŏnd), a department of France, on the Bay of Biscay, named from the Gironde estuary; area, 4,140 sq. miles. The surface is generally flat, and almost the whole department belongs to the basin of the Gironde, which is formed by the junction of the Dordogne and Garonne. The climate is generally mild and extremely moist. One-third of the surface is waste, and about one-fourth is arable land. The staple production is wine, Médoc, Graves Côtes and Entre-deux-Mers being the most celebrated growths. (*See* BORDELAIS WINES). The forests of oak and pine

are extensive. The minerals are unimportant, but much salt is obtained from lagoons. The manufactures are varied; the trade, which has its centre at Bordeaux, is very important. Bordeaux is the capital. Pop. (1931), 852,768.

GIRONDISTS (*Girondins*), one of the great political parties of the first French revolution. The Girondists were Republicans, but were more distinguished for visionary ideals than for a well-defined policy; hence they fell an easy prey to the party of the Mountain. Their leaders were three of the Deputies of the Gironde—Vergniaud, Guadet, and Gensonné—hence the name. Louis XVI was obliged, in 1792, to select a ministry from among the Girondists, but it was short-lived.

Ruins at Girgenti

In the Convention their struggles with the Montagnards forced them into extreme measures which they would otherwise have avoided. They wished to save the king, but many of them, from a mistaken policy, voted for his death. Their fall dates from their unsuccessful impeachment of Marat (1793), soon after which a large number of them were proscribed, and twenty-one of them were condemned and executed.—Cf. Mignet, *The French Revolution*.

GIRTIN, Thomas, English watercolour painter, born in Southwark in 1775, and died in 1802. He early made the acquaintance of Turner, and the two often went sketching together. He first exhibited at the Royal Academy in 1794, a water-colour drawing of Ely Cathedral; and he followed this up in subsequent years by showing, chiefly architectural subjects, whose romantic treatment marks an important development from the work of earlier topographical draughtsmen. His only oil-painting, *Bolton Bridge*, was hung in 1801, and a breakdown in health prevented further work.

Girtin was one of the first to use water-colour with the same power and freedom as oil-paint. Despite his early death, he has exercised great influence. He is well represented in the British Museum and in the Victoria and Albert Museum.

GIRTON COLLEGE. The institution now known as Girton College was founded in 1869 by a committee of eminent men and women, including Sir John Gorst, Miss Emily Davis, the Dowager Lady Stanley of Alderley, and Mr. Sedley Taylor. The college had its first home in a small house at Hitchin; but before long the dis-

GIRVAN (gir'van), a burgh and sea-port of Scotland, county of Ayr, situated at the head of a fine bay, on the Girvan. The winter herring fishery is the most important industry. Pop. (1931), 5,292.

GISBORNE, a town in New Zealand (North Island), capital of the Poverty Bay district and of Cook County, 85 miles north-east of Napier, on the Rivers Turanganui and Taruheru. It is the centre of a fine pastoral and agricultural district, which exports wool, frozen mutton, maize, and dairy produce. Petroleum has been discovered there, and there are hot springs in the neighbourhood. It was near the site of Gisborne that Captain

Girton College, Cambridge

tance between Hitchin and Cambridge became an inconvenience, and in 1872 the present building was opened at Girton village, near Cambridge.

Between 1872 and 1881 the students read for the Tripos examinations of Cambridge University, but the examiners retained the option of refusing to mark their papers. In 1881, however, the Senate reconsidered the whole matter of the women's colleges (Newnham College had by now been founded), and decided by a large majority formally to admit women to the Tripos examinations on an equal footing with men, and to grant them certificates.

Cambridge University was the first English university to grant these privileges to women. From the first the students of Girton have been required to pass an entrance examination. In 1921 this was replaced by the scholarship examination in the subject the candidate intends to read at college. The students generally read for the Honours examinations of the university—occasionally for the degree of Bachelor of Music.

Cook landed in 1769. Pop. (1932), 16,400.

GISH, name of two American actresses. Lillian was born at Springfield, Ohio, in 1896 and appeared on the stage at the age of five. In 1914, with her younger sister, Dorothy, she took up film work, appearing in *The Birth of a Nation, Broken Blossoms, Way Down East, The Scarlet Letter,* etc.

Dorothy was born at Dayton, Ohio, 11th March, 1898, and first appeared on the stage in 1903. Her chief screen successes have been *Nell Gwynne* and *Madame Pompadour.* Together the sisters appeared in *Hearts of the World,* and *Orphans of the Storm.*

GISORS (zhē-sŏr), a town of Northern France, department of Eure, with a well-preserved castle of the twelfth century. Pop. 5,508.

GISSING, George Robert, British novelist, born at Wakefield, 22nd Nov., 1857, died in the Pyrenees, 28th Dec., 1903. Educated at Owens College, Manchester, and at the University of

London, he went to America, and then to Jena, Germany, where he studied for some time. For years Gissing supported himself by teaching and writing under very adverse circumstances, continually suffering from poverty.

His first romance, *Workers in the Dawn*, appeared in 1878. Lower middle class life, the monotony of existence of the working men and of the shabby genteel, the suffering of souls in sordid environment, were the subjects which Gissing depicted in his subsequent novels, *Demos*, *Thyrza*, *The Unclassed*, *The Nether World*, *New Grub Street*, and *The Odd Women*, all gloomy and joyless, but all poignantly realistic and inspired by a moral ideal.

A brighter mood is revealed in his work, *By the Ionian Sea*, in the semi-autobiographical *Private Papers of Henry Ryecroft*, and in his monograph on Dickens. *Veranilda*, left incomplete at the author's death, appeared in 1904.—Cf. F. Swinnerton, *Gissing: A Critical Study*.

GITSCHIN (yit'shin), or **JICIN**, a walled town of North-Eastern Bohemia, in Czechoslovakia, in a fine valley, on the Cidlina. It has a castle built by Wallenstein, whose residence it was. Pop. 9,800.

GIULIO ROMANO (jō'lē-ō rō-mä'-nō), Giulio Pippi, or de' Giannuzzi, Italian painter, architect, and engineer, the most distinguished of Raphael's pupils, born at Rome about 1492, died at Mantua 1546. During the lifetime of Raphael he painted with him and under his direction, and imitated him in many of his productions.

After Raphael's death in 1520 he and his fellow-pupil, Gianfrancesco Penni, were entrusted with the completion of the frescoes in the Hall of Constantine in the Vatican at Rome. In 1524 he went to Mantua, where he executed a series of remarkable works in architecture, painting, and engineering.

The Palazzo del Te (palace of the T) was rebuilt and ornamented entirely by him, or under his direction. After the death of San Gallo in 1546 the building of St. Peter's was committed to him, but he died the same year.

His style is closely modelled on that of Raphael, but is bolder and coarser. His influence has been considerable, and he had many followers, among them being Primaticcio. He is well represented at Florence, Naples, Paris, Rome, and London (*The Infancy of Jupiter* in the National Gallery).

GIURGEVO (jụr-jä'vō), or **GIURGIU**, a town in Rumania, on the Danube, opposite Ruschuk, the most important shipping port on the Rumanian side of the river. The Russians were defeated there by the Turks, 1854. Pop. 30,348.

GIVENCHY (Givenchy-lez-la-Bassée), a French village in the department of Pas-de-Calais, 2 miles west of La Bassée. It was the scene of fierce fighting during the European War. The battle of Givenchy, between the British and the Germans, was fought in Dec., 1914. In April, 1918, during the German drive to the Channel Ports, Givenchy was defended by the 55th Division and later by the 1st Division.

Another Givenchy is **Givency-en-Gobelle**. This village, about 4 miles south of Lens, was also the scene of fighting during the Great War.

GIVET (zhē-vä), a town of North-Eastern France, in the Ardennes, with leather manufactories and other industries. It was formerly a place of great strategic importance, but the fortifications were dismantled in 1892, with the exception of the citadel of Charlemont. During the European War Givet was the scene of fierce fighting, Viscount French (then Sir John) stubbornly resisting here in Aug., 1914, against the Germans. Pop. 7,010.

GIVORS (zhē-vōr), a town of South-Eastern France, department of the Rhône, and on that river, a centre of the coal trade, with ironworks, glassworks, silk-weaving and dyeing-works. Pop. 12,784.

GIZA (gē'zä), a town of Egypt, on the left bank of the Nile, opposite Old Cairo. Some miles to the west, connected by an electric railway are the Sphinx and the celebrated pyramids, which have been named from it. In 1931 a fourth pyramid was discovered. The town has a palace built by one of the khedives. There is a British School of Archæology at Giza. Pop. (1927), 26,921.

GIZZARD, a strong muscular part of the alimentary canal of birds, which enables them to grind their food. A gizzard occurs also in crocodiles, many gasteropods, certain cephalopods and crustaceans, earthworms, and wheel animalcules (Rotifers). In birds it is lined by a thick muscular coat, and usually contains pieces of gravel, &c., to facilitate the grinding process.

GJELLERUP, Karl Adolf. Danish writer, born 1857, at Roholte, Zealand; died 1919. His earlier works include three novels, *En Idealist*, *Det Unge Denmark* and *Germænernes Læring*; also a volume of poems, Rödtjörn, published in 1882. Later novels were *Romulus* (1889) and *Minna* (1898). His plays were less successful. *Brynhild*, a Tragedy, appeared in 1884. Other tragedies were *Saint Just* (1886); *Thamigris* (1887); *En Arkadish Legende* (1887); *Hagbad og Signe* (1888); and *Herman Vandel* (1891). In addition he wrote many critical essays, reflections, &c. Extensive travel helped to develop his genius, and his best works are serious contributions to literature.

GLABRIO, Manius Acilius. A Roman statesman and general, grandson of the famous P. Mucius Scaevola. In 70 B.C. he became prætor urbanus, and as such presided at the trial *In Verrem*; in 67 B.C., he was consul with L. Calpurnius Piso and was responsible for the Lex Acilia Calpurnia against illegal canvassing. He was superseded by Pompey.

GLACE BAY, town and seaport of Nova Scotia, Canada, situated on Cape Breton Island, 14 miles from Sydney, with which it is connected by railway. It stands on the Cape Breton coalfield and its industries include railway workshops. Fishing is carried on. Pop. 17,000.

GLACIAL EPOCH. From time to time in geological history a cold epoch has set in, affecting the earth as a whole, and promoting falls of snow in place of rain. The conditions that favour the growth of glaciers have thus prevailed in low as well as high latitudes, and at low as well as high altitudes. Large areas have in consequence become covered by ice, while irregularities of precipitation have caused a slow movement outwards from certain centres, where the snow-domes rose sufficiently high to render the plastic ice-masses independent of the underlying land surface.

While pre-existing valleys at first guided the ice-tongues along their floors, the continuous precipitation of snow produced ice-sheets (*continental glaciers*) that moved across ridge and dale, collecting, like the massive glaciers of Greenland and Alaska, the soils and taluses formed by previous denudation, and carrying the materials into regions hundreds of miles from their place of origin.

Armed with these tools, the ice-sheets scoured the floor over which they moved, and plucked away blocks that projected, until a hummocked surface was imparted even to the hardest rocks. The characteristic forms named *roches moutonnées* (rocks like a sheep's fleece or a frizzled wig) by H. B. de Saussure, before their mode of origin was realized, and the smoothing and striation of their surfaces (*roches polies*), are the surest signs of the former passage of land-ice.

The huge *erratics*, blocks imported from a distance and stranded in striking positions on plateaus or on mountain sides, were formerly attributed to the Noachian deluge, or to some similar cataclysm affecting the whole globe.

In 1815 J. P. Perraudin, a chamois-hunter, called De Charpentier's attention to the evidence of the former extension of glaciers in the valley of the Rhône. In this he was the pioneer who opened up an entirely new range of observations; and when L. J. R. Agassiz some twenty years later invoked the agency of a general mantle of ice about the earth, he caught the attention of the catastrophists and laid the foundation for the recognition of a glacial epoch.

The exaggeration connected with his views led, however, to a reaction, the effects of which are still noticeable in certain English writings, and floating ice was regarded as responsible for much of the deposits of boulder-loam. None the less, the existence of a cold epoch following on the Pliocene period became generally accepted, and research has now shown that it affected regions far beyond the polar areas.

Ice-sheets are thus clearly traceable in the United States into the lowlands of Illinois, while in Russia the debris of Scandinavia was carried to the basin of the Don. G. de Geer's ingenious measurements of the annual deposits of sand and loam from the melting ice-front in the east of Sweden show that the passing of the latest ice-epoch from Europe occurred about 7000 B.C.

The spread of man in Europe was, indeed, for a long time limited by the presence of the ice, and early hunters fed their families in Southern France and Switzerland on animals now associated with Arctic climes. Though only one stage of ice-retreat, with a subsequent ice-extension, seems traceable in the British Isles, three interglacial stages have been proved by Penck and Brückner for the Alps (*Die Alpen im Eiszeitalter*, 1901–9), indicating fluctuations of climate that cannot be accounted for by movements of elevation or depression of the chain.

Attempts to connect the ice-extension generally with the prevalence of high land-masses at the close of Pliocene times have similarly failed, and attention has been directed to possible astronomical causes or to changes in the absorptive power of the atmosphere for solar rays. The simplest suggestion would seem to be that the radiation of heat from the sun varies at different stages of its evolution; but of this there is no proof, and the causes of world-wide cooling and world-wide warming remain obscure.

When a cold epoch has once set in, precipitation of moisture is likely to be checked through absence of adequate evaporation. But it must be remembered that all precipitation will be, over very wide areas, in the solid form. Five inches of 'rainfall' will perpetuate an ice-mantle, provided that this 'rainfall' occurs below freezing-point, and that all the moisture deposited is, therefore, in the form of ice-crystals.

The discovery of abundant evidence of a world-wide glacial epoch in early Permian times, affecting in a very marked degree what are now tropical regions of the earth, has added greatly to the interest of the problem. The Talchir Beds of India, long ago recognized as glacial, are now paralleled by the Dwyka conglomerates of South Africa, spreading from the Cape Province to Rhodesia, and by deposits of similar age in Australia, the Falkland Isles, and Brazil.

When the 'glacial period' is spoken of, it usually means the ice-age of Pleistocene times; but a succession of such epochs, not necessarily at rhythmic intervals, has undoubtedly affected the physiography and the life of our planet, and possibly of the other planets of our system.

James Geikie, in the three editions of his *Great Ice Age*, undoubtedly did most to bring the reality and magnitude of the Pleistocene glacial epoch before readers in the British Isles. W. B. Wright (*The Quaternary Ice Age*, 1914) has admirably discussed and summarized recent work upon the subject.

GLACIERS, ice-masses of great bulk, resulting from the compacting of snow as it accumulates on plateaus or in hollows above the snow-line, and becomes pressed outwards to lower levels. Glaciers may extend down valleys far below the snow-line, and may spread out in Arctic lowlands as confluent sheets which melt away along their fronts. The first stage in their formation is the production of a mixture of snow and compacter granular ice-crystals, called by French writers *névé*, by German authors *firn*. The ice of glaciers differs from that produced by the freezing of still water, being granular, a character that largely influences its downward flow.

Glaciers are continually moving downwards, and not infrequently reach the borders of cultivation. The rate at which a glacier moves generally varies from 12 to 24 inches in twenty-four hours. At its lower end it is usually terminated by a steep slope. In its middle course it resembles a frozen stream with an undulating surface, broken by fissures or crevasses. As it descends it experiences a gradual diminution from the action of the sun and rain, and from the heat of the underlying earth. Hence a phenomenon universally attendant on glaciers—the issue of a stream of ice-cold turbid water from their lower extremity.

The descent of glaciers is shown by changes in the position of detached masses of rock at their sides and on their surface. An important result of glacial action is the formation of *moraines*, which consist of accumulations of stones and detritus piled up on the sides of the glacier, or gathered within it, and deposited where it melts away. They are composed of fragments of rock detached by the action of frost, and also by the plucking action of the moving ice. The fissures or crevasses by which glaciers are traversed are sometimes more than 100 feet in depth, and from being often covered with snow are exceedingly dangerous to travellers.

One of the most famous glaciers of the Alps is the Mer de Glace, belonging to Mont Blanc, in the valley of Chamonix, about 5,700 feet above the level of the sea. Glaciers exist in all zones in which mountains rise above the snow-line. Those of Norway are well known, and still larger glaciers of the Alpine or 'valley' type may be studied in the Himalayas. Glaciers of the 'continental' type occur in Greenland and Alaska, containing in their lower levels enormous quantities of rock-detritus, and capable of concealing and over-riding the features of the land-surface on which they rest (*see* BOULDER-CLAY).

The problem of the descent of the glaciers is of extraordinary interest, and various theories have been put forward to account for it. It was shown by Professor J. D. Forbes, of Edinburgh, that a glacier progresses much like a river—the middle and upper parts moving faster than the sides and the bottom—and he showed that glacier motion was analogous to the way in which a mass of thick mortar or a quantity of pitch flows down in an inclined trough.

His theory is known as the *viscous theory* of glaciers, which presupposes that ice is a plastic body, and this plasticity has been satisfactorily explained by Professor James Thomson, of Glasgow, by the phenomenon of the melting and refreezing of ice. Water, he discovered, when subjected to pressure, freezes at a lower temperature than when the pressure is removed. Consequently, when ice is subjected to pressure it melts; if it is relieved from pressure, the water again solidifies. Therefore if two pieces of ice are pressed together, or even rest against one another, they tend to relieve themselves by melting at their points of contact, and the water thus produced immediately solidifies on its escape.

If ice is strained in any way, it

Glacier. The Mer de Glace, Chamonix

similarly relieves itself at the strained parts, and a similar *regelation* follows. This gives an explanation of the plasticity of glaciers. Pressed downwards by the vast superincumbent mass, the ice gradually yields. Melting and refreezing take place at some parts, at others the gradual yielding at strained points goes on. In the latter process there is no visible melting, but there is the gradual yielding from point to point to the pressure above, and there is the transference from ice-granule to ice-granule of the molecules that constitute the apparently continuous mass. If, however, at certain points the strain is intense, continuity is lost, and crevasses occur, as when a glacier rounds a corner in a valley or spreads out in a terminal 'fan.'

The plasticity of the individual ice-grains, each of which is a single crystal, also plays an important part in glacier motion.

GLACIER TABLES, large stones found on glaciers supported on pedestals of ice. The stones attain this peculiar position by the melting away of the ice around them, and the lowering of its general surface by the action of the sun and rain. The block, like an umbrella, protects the ice below it, and accordingly its elevation measures the level of the glacier at a former period. By and by the stone table becomes too heavy for the column of ice on which it rests, or its equilibrium becomes unstable, whereupon it topples over, and, falling on the surface of the glacier, defends a new space of ice, which in time becomes a pedestal.

GLACIS, in fortification, is the sloping surface of the outermost portion of a fortified line, descending from the parapet of the covered way to the level ground or open country in front. It must be so placed that the guns of the fort will rake it at every point.

GLADBACH (BERGISCH-) (berg'-ish-glâd-bâh), a town of Germany in Prussia, province of Rheinland, 8 miles north-east of Cologne. Pop. 18,200.

GLADBACH (MÖNCHEN-) (meun'-*hen*-glåd-*båh*), a town of Germany in Prussia, province of Rheinland, 16 miles west of Düsseldorf, with extensive manufactures of cotton and mixed cotton goods, &c. Pop. 193,529.

GLADIA'TORS, combatants who fought at the public games in Rome for the entertainment of the spectators. The first instance known of gladiators being exhibited was in 264 B.C., by Marcus and Decimus Brutus at the funeral of their father. They were at first prisoners, slaves, or condemned criminals; but afterwards freemen fought in the arena, either for hire or from choice; and eventually men of senatorial rank, and even women, fought.

The regular gladiators were instructed in schools (*ludi*), and the overseer (*lanista*) purchased the gladiators and maintained them. Men of position sometimes kept gladiatorial schools and *lanistæ* of their own. The gladiators fought in the schools with wooden swords.

In the public exhibitions (*spectacula*, or 'shows') the defeat of a gladiator was marked by a cry of 'Habet' from the spectators, who, if

Rt. Hon. William Ewart Gladstone

wards that he should be spared, some authorities maintain the opposite interpretation.

The victor received a branch of palm or a garland. The gladiators were classified according to their arms and mode of fighting; thus there were *retiarii*, who carried a trident and a net (Lat. *rete*) in which they tried to entangle their opponent; *Thracians*, who were armed with the round Thracian buckler and a short sword; and *secutores*, who were pitted against the *retiarii*.—Cf. L. Friedlaender, *Roman Life and Manners under the Early Empire*.

GLADI'OLUS, a genus of plants of the iris order, having a corm with a reticulated covering, natives of Europe and North Africa, but especially South Africa. The leaves are ensiform, the flowers brilliantly coloured. There are many species, some of them popular garden plants, others grown in hothouses.

GLADSTONE, Rt. Hon. William Ewart, British statesman, son of Sir John Gladstone, was born at Liverpool in 1809, and died at Hawarden in 1898. After some years at Eton, he entered Christ Church, Oxford, in 1828, and graduated in 1831 with high honours. After leaving Oxford he spent six months in Italy. In 1832 the first Reform Act was passed, and Gladstone's public career commenced by his being returned for Newark, and when Peel assumed office in 1834 he accepted the post of Junior Lord of the Treasury.

At this period he was a Tory, and as his party quickly went out it was not until 1841 that he again held any public office, in which year he became,

Glacier Table

the vanquished fighter was not slain in the combat, decided his fate by the position in which they held their thumbs. While the general opinion is that by pointing the thumb downwards the spectators expressed their wish that the defeated gladiator should be put to death, and by pointing it up-under Peel, Vice-President of the Board of Trade and Master of the Mint. In 1842 great fiscal reforms were inaugurated, some of which were understood to be due to Gladstone. Having become President of the Board of Trade, he carried, in 1843, a measure for the abolition of restrictions on the exportation of machinery, and in 1844 he carried a railway Bill, establishing railway travel on a less costly basis. He took part with Peel in the repeal of the Corn Laws, a course which cost him his seat for Newark.

In 1847 he was returned for Oxford University, and he then supported the Bill for the removal of Jewish disabilities, and that for the repeal of the Navigation Laws. He now began to develop remarkable ability as a financier, and fiercely attacked Disraeli's Budget of 1852. The same year he became Chancellor of the Exchequer under the Earl of Aberdeen, a post which he also held for a short time in 1855 under Lord Palmerston. In 1858 he became High Commissioner Extraordinary to the Ionian Islands, and his *Studies on Homer* appeared about the same time. In 1859 he again took office as Chancellor of the Exchequer under Lord Palmerston.

At the general election of 1865 Gladstone was returned for South Lancashire, and on the decease of Lord Palmerston he became the Liberal leader in the Commons in the Russell administration, still continuing to hold the Chancellorship of the Exchequer. The Government, being defeated on the Reform question, went out in 1866, and Lord Derby came into power. In 1867 a Reform Bill, establishing household suffrage in boroughs, was carried by the Conservatives, but to the final shape of it Gladstone and Bright materially contributed.

In 1868 Gladstone succeeded in abolishing compulsory Church rates, and he also carried his resolutions dealing with the Irish Church, but his Irish Church Suspensory Bill was rejected by the Lords. At the general election of 1868 he lost his seat for South Lancashire, but was returned by Greenwich. There being a great Liberal majority in the new Parliament, Disraeli was soon forced to resign, and Gladstone became Premier. Next year he carried his Bill for the Disestablishment of the Irish Church, and in 1870 his Irish Land Act, the English Education Act being also passed. In 1871 army purchase was abolished by royal warrant.

The Ballot Act and the Scottish Education Act were passed in 1872. Parliament was dissolved in 1874, and the Conservatives ousted Gladstone from office, as they had secured a good majority. During Lord Beaconsfield's tenure of office Gladstone denounced the Bulgarian atrocities, the Anglo-Turkish Treaty, and the Afghan War, and his speeches during his candidature for Midlothian greatly helped to render the Government unpopular.

In 1880 the general election reinstated Gladstone firmly in power (Midlothian being now his constituency), and his second Irish Land Bill became law in the following year. In 1882 a Prevention of Crimes and an Arrears Act for Ireland were passed, and in 1883 measures relating to bankruptcy were also carried. In 1884 the Bill extending household suffrage to the counties was carried, and the Gladstone ministry fell the next year. Lord Salisbury, who had formed an administration, got the Redistribution of Seats Bill passed, and under it took place the general election of 1885, Gladstone still continuing to represent Midlothian. Next year Lord Salisbury resigned after an adverse vote in the Commons, and Gladstone again came into power.

He now introduced a Home Rule Bill for Ireland (8th April, 1886). It failed to pass the Commons, and the result of the general election which followed was emphatically adverse to Gladstone's proposals. He had to make way for Lord Salisbury, but in 1892 he again became Premier. After passing a Home Rule Bill through the Commons he resigned office in 1894, and next year retired from political life.

His works include: *The State in its Relations with the Church* (1838), *Studies on Homer and the Homeric Age, Juventus Mundi, Homeric Synchronism, Landmarks of Homeric Study, The Impregnable Rock of Holy Scripture.* — BIBLIOGRAPHY: Lord Morley, *Life of William Ewart Gladstone*; G. W. E. Russell, *Biography of W. E. Gladstone*; J. McCarthy, *The Story of Gladstone's Life*; Williamson, *W. E. Gladstone, Statesman and Scholar*; H. Paul, *The Life of W. E. Gladstone*; Lord Eversley, *Gladstone and Ireland.*

GLADSTONE, Viscount, English politician. Born Jan. 7, 1854, Herbert John Gladstone was the youngest son of W. E. Gladstone. He was educated at Eton and Oxford, being in 1877 appointed history lecturer at Keble College. In 1880 he was elected M.P. for Leeds. He served in several minor offices before 1894, when he became Chief Commissioner of Works. From 1899–1905, he was chief whip of the Liberal Party, then in opposition, and was Home Secretary, 1905–09. In the latter year he was appointed Governor-General of S. Africa, holding that office for five years, and was made a viscount. On his death, May 6, 1930, the viscountcy became extinct. In 1928 he published *After Thirty Years*, a book dealing with his father's life.

GLAGOLITIC ALPHABET, an ancient Slavonic alphabet, based on the Greek, and used in many old religious works, while in others the Cyrillian letters (q.v.) are employed. Glagolitic is derived from the Old Church Slavonic word *glagolati*, to speak.

GLAISHER, James, born 1809, aeronaut and meteorologist, long connected with Greenwich Observatory, author of various books; died 1903. He made twenty-eight balloon ascents, in one of which he reached a height of 37,000 feet. He was the founder of the Royal Meteorological Society, and in 1849 he became a Fellow of the Royal Society. Among his works are: *Hygrometric Tables*, and *Travels in the Air*.

GLAMIS, village of Angus (Forfarshire), Scotland, 5¾ miles from Forfar. Near is Glamis Castle, the chief seat of the Earl of Strathmore. This is a 17th century building, but it contains fragments of a much older one. Many stories cling to it, one being that it was the residence of Macbeth. In the village there is an old sculptured cross, associated with the name of King Malcolm.

GLAMOR'GAN, or **GLAMORGAN-SHIRE,** a county in South Wales; area, 520,456 acres. The north and north-east parts of the county are extremely mountainous, and include scenery of the most romantic beauty. The southern portion is comparatively level and very fertile, particularly the vale of Glamorgan. The climate in this part is remarkably mild, as snow does not lie long on the ground, and tender shrubs thrive in the open air.

Glamorganshire belongs wholly to the basin of the Severn; and all its streams, of which the Taff is the largest, flow southward. The cattle are reckoned among the best in Wales. The mineral wealth of Glamorganshire is of incalculable value. Its coal-fields in particular are most extensive, and yield the best quality of steam-coal, and there are great ironworks (Dowlais, Cyfarthfa, &c.). The woollen manufacture is carried on to some extent. Principal towns: Cardiff (the capital), Merthyr-Tydfil, Swansea, and Neath. Since 1918 the county returns seven members to the House of Commons. Pop. (1931), 1,225,717.

>**GLANCE,** a name given to some minerals, generally sulphides, which possess a brilliant metallic lustre; as *antimony glance, bismuth glance, copper glance,* &c.

GLANDERS, one of the most formidable diseases to which horses are subject, indicated by a discharge of purulent matter from one or both nostrils, with a hard enlargement of the submaxillary glands. In acute glanders the discharge, by its copiousness, impedes respiration and ultimately produces suffocation. The disease is highly infectious, and may even be communicated to man by the purulent matter coming in contact with any part where the skin is broken. The disease is rarely, if ever, cured. *See* FARCY.

GLANDS, a certain class of structures in animals, some of them forming organs, which elaborate, from the material supplied by the blood, a fluid secretion which is conveyed by a duct into some hollow organ like the mouth, stomach, or intestine; or in other cases (ductless glands) is taken up again by the blood, to be distributed to the body as a *hormone*, a special chemical regulator of the growth and metabolism of different elements in the body.

In man there are two lachrymal glands, situated at the external angle of the eyes under the upper eyelid; six salivary, to pour fluid into the mouth, of which three are on each side, behind and under the lower jaw; two parotid, two submaxillary, two sublingual; two mammary glands to secrete milk (the breasts of women); the liver, the pancreas, the two kidneys, as well as a vast multitude of small glands in the skin (sweat and sebaceous) and in the lining membrane of the stomach, intestines, and, in fact, most of the hollow organs.

Of the ductless glands the most important are the thyroid, thymus, suprarenal, pituitary, in addition to a large number of smaller glands. The lymphatic glands, which filter the lymph, are somewhat different from these in character; and still more different are the blood-glands, such as the spleen. Botanists have given the name of glands to small bodies observed upon the surfaces of plants, many of which secrete certain fluids.

GLANVIL, or **GLANVILLE, Ranulph de,** English lawyer and warrior of the twelfth century. In the reign of Henry II he held the office of justiciary, and repelled the invasion of William the Lion, King of Scotland, who was taken prisoner as he was besieging the castle of Alnwick. Richard I is said to have imprisoned Glanvil, and obliged him to purchase his freedom with £15,000 towards a crusade to the Holy Land. He accompanied his master on this expedition, and perished at the siege of Acre in 1190.

To Glanvil is attributed a treatise on the laws and customs of England (*De Legibus et Consuetudinibus Angliæ*), written about 1181, and first printed in the year 1554 (at the instance of Sir W. Stanford), being the earliest treatise on English law. An English translation of the work, with an introduction by John Beames, appeared in 1812.

GLARUS (glä'rös), a Swiss canton, surrounded by St. Gall, the Grisons, Uri, and Schwyz; area, 264 sq. miles. On all sides, except towards the north, Glarus is walled in by lofty mountains; lakes are numerous, and the scenery in their neighbourhood is magnificent.

The inhabitants are chiefly engaged in the cotton manufacture and in agricultural pursuits, rearing sheep and cattle, and exporting cheese, butter, &c. The Constitution is a pure democracy. Pop. (1930), 35,653. The capital, Glarus, situated on the Linth amid grand scenery, is a well-built town, with a good trade. Pop. 5,000.

GLAS'GOW (Celt. *Cleschu*, subsequently *Glasghu*, from *glas*, green, and *ghu*, dear), the largest city in Scotland, and the second largest in the United Kingdom, is situated mainly in the county of Lanark, on both banks of the Clyde, the larger and more important part of it on the right or north bank. In 1893 Glasgow was made a county by itself, and the Lord Provost appoints the deputy-lieutenants and justices of the peace. The southern portion of Glasgow is built mainly on low-lying level ground, the northern portion to a great extent on a series of elevations. Since 1912 the city has included Govan and Partick, and it was further extended in 1925. The river is crossed by eleven bridges (including railway bridges) and by ferries; and there are also tunnels under it. The George V Bridge was opened in 1927. In 1933 it was proposed to build another cross-river bridge at Finnieston.

The streets run mostly at right angles east and west and north and south. Of the former the chief are Argyle and Sauchiehall Streets; of the latter Renfield and Buchanan Streets. The houses are built almost wholly of freestone, and as a whole Glasgow is now a city of considerable architectural beauty.

Buildings. Of the buildings the Cathedral, situated in the north-east of the city, is the most noteworthy. Certain parts of the present fabric date from the twelfth century, but most of it belongs to the three following centuries. It is a large Gothic edifice in the Early Pointed style, with tower and spire from the centre. It is especially distinguished for the beauty of its crypt or lower church, one of the most perfect in Britain.

The University buildings, erected after the designs of Sir George Gilbert Scott on the removal of the college to the west-end in 1870, cover about 4 acres of ground on a noble site. They form an oblong rectangular pile in the Collegiate Gothic style of the fourteenth century, divided into two quadrangles, united by a centre building, and with a high tower. To the south lie the Art Galleries and Museum, and the great Kelvin Hall. The Municipal Buildings, in George Square, completed in 1887, are built in the Renaissance style.

Among other noteworthy buildings are various churches, the Royal Infirmary near the cathedral, the Western Infirmary near the university; the Victoria Infirmary in the southern suburbs, Ruchill Hospital, Belvidere Hospital, the United Free Church College, Royal Exchange, Stock Exchange, County Buildings, Athenæum, General Post Office, the buildings of the Technical College, Christian Institute, the People's Palace, picture-houses, club-houses, banks, and insurance offices, some of the last new and noteworthy structures, and the large terminal stations (Central, St. Enoch, Queen Street). Most of the public monuments are collected in George Square.

In addition to the extensive open space called the Green, Glasgow has a number of fine public parks, while in 1906 Ardgoil, a large tract of mountain-land on the Firth of Clyde, was presented to the city, and in 1915 the Corporation purchased the magnificent stretch of country on the Braes of Balloch, since known as Loch Lomond Park. There are also Botanic Gardens with extensive hot-houses. There is a public museum, and a large and valuable collection of pictures belonging to the city.

Institutions. The principal libraries are the University Library; the Mitchell Library (for which a magnificent building was erected), the Stirling's and Glasgow Public Library, and the Baillie's Institution Library, all free reference libraries; the libraries of the Faculty of Medicine, the Faculty of Procurators, and other learned bodies; and also a large number of free district lending libraries. St. Andrew's Halls are the finest suite of public halls, and the City Hall is also a notable meeting-place. There are numerous theatres, music halls, and picture-houses.

The principal cemetery is the

Necropolis, on a rising ground near the cathedral, and there are many others. Among educational institutions, in addition to the university, are Anderson's College Medical School, the Royal Technical College, the United Free Church College, Queen Margaret College for Women, St. Mungo's College, the normal or training institutions for teachers in Glasgow district, the Glasgow School of Art, the Glasgow Athenæum, the West of Scotland Agricultural College, the Veterinary College, The High School of Glasgow, The Girls' High School, the Glasgow Academy (private school), Kelvinside Academy, Allan Glen's School, St. Aloysius' College(R.C.), and the Hutchesons' Grammar Schools.

In addition to the infirmaries and hospitals the benevolent and charitable institutions include the Eye Infirmary, Blind Asylum, Maternity Hospital, Hospital for Sick Children, Samaritan Hospital for Women, and lunatic asylum. There are also military barracks.

Industry and Commerce. The industries include cotton, linen, woollen, silk, and jute; calico-printing, dyeing, and bleaching; pig and malleable iron and steel; brass and copper; iron tubes and pipes, bolts and rivets, armourplates, bridges, roofs, and other forms of metal work; general mechanical engineering, boilermaking, locomotives, textile machines, sewing machines, machine tools; shipbuilding, which might perhaps be called the staple; chemical works, potteries, glassworks, brickworks, breweries, distilleries, tanneries, tobacco-works, sugar-refining works, and soapworks.

The commerce is also great and varied. The river itself, the chief highway of commerce, has been made navigable for large vessels up to the heart of the city, and there is extensive harbour accommodation, partly in the river and partly in the connected docks. The total value of seaborne trade at the port of Glasgow in 1931 was £70,388,000. The total net tonnage entered and cleared at Glasgow in 1931, including coastwise vessels, amounted to 9,017,000 tons.

The improvement of the navigation of the Clyde, which within the nineteenth century was fordable at and below the present harbour of Glasgow, has been of immense service to the city, though the cost has also been immense. The railways are, of course, the chief means of inland traffic, and the Forth and Clyde and Monkland Canals form auxiliaries. Electric tramways pass along the principal streets, and connect Glasgow with Paisley and other places. There is a cable subway in the city. The city is excellently supplied with water from

Loch Katrine, a distance of about 30 miles. The works are now capable of supplying 110,000,000 gallons daily.

History. The origin of Glasgow may be traced to the foundation of the cathedral by St. Kentigern (or Mungo) about 560. The bishopric was founded in 1115. Glasgow was erected into a burgh of barony about 1180, and for long the bishop had great powers over it. It became a free royal burgh in 1611. Glasgow Fair, now the chief holiday season of the city, was instituted about 1190. The Clyde was already crossed by a bridge in the thirteenth century, but the earliest stone bridge dates from the fourteenth. The Provost (now Lord Provost) is first mentioned in 1454.

A convent of Dominicans or Black Friars was founded in 1246, and a Franciscan house in 1476. Wallace is said to have defeated an English garrison in the city, and other battles or skirmishes have occurred within its present limits, notably Langside (1568). The General Assembly which abolished Episcopacy in Scotland met in Glasgow Cathedral in 1638.

Port-Glasgow was founded as the port of the city in 1668, but in the following century the deepening of the river up to the city was begun. In 1715 and 1745 Glasgow was conspicuously loyal to the reigning family. Up to the Union its trade was chiefly with the European continent. The Union opened up the trade with the American colonies, and tobacco became a source of wealth to the Glasgow merchants.

Afterwards commerce began to take other directions. The Monkland Canal was made in 1770, and the Forth and Clyde Canal was opened in 1790. The pioneer steamboat *Comet* began to ply on the Clyde in 1812. Gas-lighting was introduced in 1816, and electric lighting in 1890. Street tramways were started in 1872. Since 1894 they have been municipal, and in 1898 electric traction was introduced.

From the Union to 1832 Glasgow joined Rutherglen, Renfrew, and Dumbarton in sending a member to Parliament; from 1832 to 1868 it had two, from 1868 to 1885, three, from 1885 to 1918 it had seven members, and since 1918 it sends fifteen members to the House of Commons. Successful international exhibitions were held in 1888 and 1901. In 1920 Glasgow adopted the town of Vouziers in France. Pop. in 1610, 7,644; in 1712, 13,832; in 1801, 77,385; pop. of municipal borough in 1901, 775,561; in 1911, 784,455; in 1931, 1,088,417.—BIBLIOGRAPHY: A. Macgeorge, *Old Glasgow*; Sir J. D. Marwick, *Early Glasgow*; J. A. Kilpatrick, *Literary Landmarks of Glasgow*; G. Eyre-Todd, *The Story*

GLASGOW UNIVERSITY

of Glasgow; Renwick and Lindsay, History of Glasgow.

GLASGOW UNIVERSITY was founded by a bull of Pope Nicholas V, 1450–1, which conferred not only the power of creating masters and doctors, but privileges and immunities identical with those of the University of Bologna. In 1577 James VI prescribed rules for the government of the university, giving it a new charter. It has been reconstituted by the Scottish Universities Acts of 1858 and 1889, and its constitution is similar to that of the others. (*See* EDINBURGH UNIVERSITY.)

The old university buildings and ground were sold to the Glasgow Union Railway Company in 1864 for £100,000, a sum which, supplemented by university funds, Government grant, public subscriptions and donations, enabled upwards of £600,000 to be expended on fine new buildings in the west end of Glasgow. The university comprises six faculties, viz. arts, science, divinity, law, medicine, and music. With it is incorporated Queen Margaret College for women.

The exhibitions, scholarships, bursaries, &c., from funds administered by the university, have an annual value of about £8,000. The most valuable are the George A. Clark scholarships, four in number, tenable for four years, and each about £168 in annual value. The examinations for these are respectively in classics, mental philosophy, mathematics, and natural science. The Snell Exhibition (annual value £100) and the Newlands Scholarship (annual value £80) are held conjointly for four years at Balliol College, Oxford University.

There are also three Euing Fellowships, value £100 each, a Black Theological Fellowship, value £133; the Metcalfe Fellowship, value £100, besides others. The degrees conferred are almost the same as at Edinburgh. There were 303 professors and lecturers and 5,265 matriculated students in 1932. Since 1918 the University of Glasgow unites with the other Scottish universities (St. Andrews, Aberdeen, and Edinburgh) in returning three members to Parliament. The university library numbers over 250,000 volumes.

GLASS is a comparatively hard and brittle substance having no visible crystalline structure. It has a characteristic conchoidal fracture, and a surface that naturally reflects or refracts light regularly. Although it occurs in nature as obsidian, which has no commercial value, glass is essentially an artificial product, resulting most generally, but not invariably, from the fusion of silica with metallic oxides.

Transparency is the most valuable of its physical qualities, which may be varied through every degree of translucence and colour by suitable combinations of the ingredients. It is most extensively used as window glass. Special types of very transparent glass having particular refractive and dispersive powers are essential for the manufacture of optical instruments. It provides a suitable material for the construction of utensils such as bottles and chemical vessels, owing to its power of resisting the solvent or corrosive action of most liquids and acids. It is readily soluble in hydrofluoric acid.

Its decorative value is great, and to a small extent it is used as an electrical insulator. It is a bad conductor of heat, being about 120 times worse than iron, and six times worse than quartz. When glass is heated sufficiently, it can be cast, blown, drawn, or moulded to any desired form, or even spun into fine threads. The physical constants of an average type of crown glass are as follows:

Young's Modulus E = $700/10^5$ grammes/sq. cm.
Rigidity Modulus N = $240/10^6$ grammes/sq. cm.
Refractive Index N_D = $1·517$.

μ value, $\dfrac{N_D - 1}{F - C}$ = $60·5$.

History. Nothing is known of the origin of glass manufacture. That the art is extremely ancient is evident from certain pictures on tombs at Thebes, dating from about the year 1400 B.C., which represent processes closely resembling the hand methods of the present day. The art in a highly-developed state was practised by the Assyrians, Phœnicians, Greeks, and Etruscans.

When Egypt was subjugated by Cæsar Augustus about the year 26 B.C., glass formed part of the tribute imposed upon the conquered nation, and in the reign of Tiberius, about forty years later, the industry, according to Pliny, was already well established at Rome.

In the Middle Ages Venice was renowned for its artistic glass productions. To avoid the risk of fire, the industry, by an edict dated 8th Nov., 1291, was transferred from Venice to the adjacent Island of Murano, which is still renowned for its glass bead and decorative glassware manufactures.

Glass was certainly used for the glazing of windows towards the end of the third century. It was first generally used for this purpose in Italy. Although Abbot Benedict, in A.D. 764, caused the windows of the monastery of Weremouth, Durham, to be glazed by foreign artists, it was many years thereafter before its use for this purpose became general in Britain.

The development of optical glass is due to the work of many practical and scientific workers. Guinand, a Swiss watchmaker, discovered about the year 1790 a method of stirring optical glass, and in 1800 he was able to produce homogeneous discs of glass suitable for the construction of telescope objectives. Later, in association with Fraunhofer at Munich, the process was further developed.

About 1827 the son of Guinand became associated with Bontemps and Lerebours in the manufacture of optical glass in Paris. The work in France was continued later by Charles Feil, and still more recently by Messrs. Parra Mantois & Co. Under the auspices of the Royal Society,

for their own use, by the rangefinder manufacturers, Messrs. Barr & Stroud, Limited, of Glasgow. In Germany about the year 1880 the experimental work of Harcourt was revived under more favourable circumstances by Schott and Abbe, who with State aid established in Jena the factory of Schott und Genossen, which has produced many valuable types of optical and other special glasses.

Classification. Glass may conveniently be classified according to its use, as, for example: (1) *Window glass*, including: hand blown and flattened; mechanically blown and flattened; continuously mechanically drawn; rolled and polished plate glass; corrugated and figured. (2) *Bottle glass*,

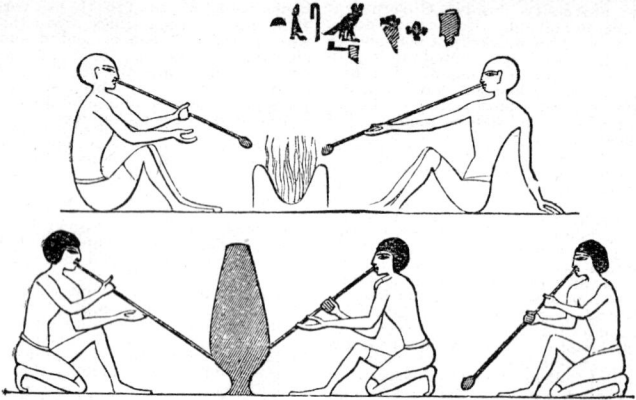

Glass-blowing in Ancient Egypt
From the wall-painting in the Tomb of Beni Hassan, Thebes (after Wilkinson)

Faraday in 1824 commenced his investigations, first at the Falcon Works of Messrs. Green & Pellatt, and later in the laboratories of the Royal Institution. Dolland was associated with Faraday in this work.

Between the years 1834 and 1871 Harcourt, an English parson, greatly increased the number of metals that could be utilized in the manufacture of optical glass and the knowledge of their physical properties. From the year 1862 he was assisted in this work by Stokes. Owing to political troubles in France, Bontemps left Paris in 1848, and became associated with Messrs. Chance Brothers of Birmingham, who until 1915 were the only manufacturers of optical glass in the British Empire.

Since that date optical glass has also been regularly produced by The Derby Crown Glass Company, and,

including: hand blown and automatic machine-made bottles. (3) *Pressed glass*. (4) *Blown glass*, including: chemical and temperature resistant glassware; hand blown and finished without moulds; hand blown in moulds; drawn tubing. (5) *Optical glass* of very many varieties.

With the exception of optical glass, which for most purposes must be as transparent as possible, any of the above types of glass may be clear or coloured.

Composition. Silica is the principal ingredient of practically all glass, although some types of optical glass contain no acid silica, its place being taken by phosphoric anhydride (P_2O_5) or boric oxide (B_2O_3). Silica itself is highly refractory. It can be softened under the oxyacetylene blow-pipe flame. Silica ware is now extensively used in the laboratory and the chemical industry, owing to its power of resisting rapid changes of temperature.

Many substances are available for fusion with silica to form glass, and such fusion may take place at the ordinary furnace temperature of about 1200° C. to 1400° C. Silica with an alkaline oxide produces a glass which is hygroscopic. If, however, an alkaline earth metal such as lime be added in the requisite proportion, the glass may be made durable, particularly as regards resistance to atmospheric corrosion. Addition of lime increases the temperature at which the glass is fluid.

The alkaline earth metal may be replaced by other materials, such as lead oxide, which is an important ingredient of flint glass. An excess of some constituent may, during slow cooling, result in opalescence of the glass or even devitrification of the mass, although at the higher temperatures or when cooled rapidly the glass may be quite transparent. Fluorides, phosphates, and arsenic produce opalescent glass, which is often used for decorative purposes.

The constituents of glass and their proportions within limits may be greatly varied, according to the type of glass required. Clear hard crown glass suitable for window glazing may consist of silica 72 per cent, lime 11 per cent, soda 17 per cent. Glass for blown ware may be either crown or flint. For the most brilliant cut-glass table ware, flint having a composition of silica 55 per cent, lead 10 per cent, and potash 35 per cent may be used. Chemical glassware may contain boric oxide, zinc oxide, and alumina.

Many varied and beautiful colours are obtained by the introduction of metals or metallic oxides, but to some extent the colours depend upon the composition or conditions of working. Thus a small quantity of iron will colour a heavy lead glass more intensely than a crown glass. Traces of cobalt produce a strong blue; copper may give the same colour; gold and copper colour glass ruby-red, and chromium green. Uranium produces a yellow-green glass, which is also fluorescent and is used for making X-ray screens. A minute proportion of iron colours glass green. Manganese imparts a reddish-violet colour.

To obtain sand entirely free from iron is extremely difficult; even Fontainebleau sand, used for optical glass, contains about 0·01 per cent Fe_2O_3. For purposes other than optical, a slight green coloration of the glass may be neutralized by the addition of manganese or special decolorizers. There is reason to believe that the coloration of glass is due to the presence of the colouring sub-

stance in an extremely fine state of division.

Manufacture. For the melting of comparatively small batches of glass, fire-clay pots are used. Tank furnaces are used for the large quantities required in the manufacture of window glass or the mass production of bottles. Fire-clay, free from iron impurities and having fire-resistant qualities combined with the necessary plasticity, such as is mined in the Stourbridge district, is commonly employed. After weathering, hand-picking, grinding, and mixing with the necessary water, its plasticity is considerably improved by working or pugging and natural maturing.

As the clay contracts excessively when drying, it is mixed with 25 to 30 per cent of well burnt and ground clay called grog, which has principally the effect of reducing the contraction and the liability to fracture during the firing process. Usually the pots are built by hand, the small pieces of clay being well combined to avoid the inclusion of air.

Wooden formers or moulds are sometimes used during the building operation to preserve the shape, which may be circular or oval. Most frequently the pot has a domed roof with a front port or opening just above the glass level through which the batch is inserted and the glass extracted, but for optical glass open pots are often used to facilitate the stirring operation.

To a smaller extent the casting of pots in plaster of Paris moulds is practised. The moist clay or slip is rendered liquid by the addition of an alkaline electrolyte. After the slip has set, the mould is opened and removed. The pots are allowed to dry naturally in dry air for a period of several months. Before use it is slowly heated during about seven days in a pot arch, the temperature of which can be gradually raised, as the pot under a rapid change of temperature might otherwise crack, especially if it contains much included moisture or air. It is then transferred as rapidly as possible to the furnace, within which it is enclosed.

One furnace often contains several pots grouped in a ring upon the floor or siege, with the port openings of the pots projecting through the furnace wall, thus giving access to them. The firing of the furnace is sometimes done by hand, but generally producer gas is employed, in which case the products of combustion are passed through regenerators or recuperators, which heat the air and gas before their combustion in the furnace around the pots, thus improving the thermal efficiency.

The constituents of the batch are well ground and mixed, and to the batch is added a proportion of glass chips termed cullet, which facilitates the fusion of the ingredients. Before the batch is inserted the interior walls of the pot are glazed, to protect them from the highly corrosive action of the unmelted batch. During the melting much gas is evolved through the reduction of the carbonates, nitrates, and other ingredients.

The separation of gas can be assisted by plunging a moist potato or new wood into the fluid glass. Large bubbles of steam thus formed in rising to the surface entrain minute gas bells, and also help to mix the glass more thoroughly. To plane or fine the glass, as the operation is called, the temperature is raised to an extent dependent upon its nature.

Of the several pots in the furnace, some are being filled or fined while the others are being worked, but in some installations the filling and fining operations are done during the night and the glass worked out during the day. Optical glass must be stirred as well as fined to destroy veins or striæ, which are threads of glass throughout the mixture of slightly different refractive index, most frequently due to solution of the pot, or the fire-clay stirrer.

From the pot the glass is gathered upon the end of a hollow blow-iron, and is then blown into the required shape, many beautiful results being obtained by skilful rotation and manipulation of the glass during the operation. For the production of incandescent globes and kindred articles, the gathered glass is blown within a mould which can be opened out to release the article. During the operation the tube is rotated, to prevent sticking and to produce a good surface. Blowing is done by the operator or by compressed air.

Glass can also be pressed solid in moulds into many shapes, such as pavement lights.

Window glass is hand-produced by gathering a large mass of glass on the blow-iron. It is formed into a cylindrical mass by rolling upon a smooth-shaped block called a marver. By careful blowing a hollow cylinder is formed. The mass of glass at the end of the cylinder is kept soft by frequent reheating, and, by swinging the mass and blowing, the cylinder is regularly extended, a uniform thickness of wall being obtained by skilful manipulation. After cutting off the cap and making a longitudinal cut, the cylinder is placed within a flattening furnace, upon the smooth floor of which it is opened out and flattened by means of a smoothing block. The plate is then removed and slowly cooled.

For the mass production of bottles and similar articles many ingenious automatic machines are employed, and the requisite glass is automatically gathered, siphoned, or drawn from the furnace. Tank furnaces are often used in conjunction with such machines, of which the O'Neill, the Owen, and the Westlake are typical examples.

Tank furnaces vary greatly in size. Some of the larger gas-fired ones are capable of holding nearly a thousand tons of molten glass. The batch is inserted at one end of the tank and the molten glass is extracted at the other. Thus the process is a continuous one. The tank which holds the glass is built of large refractory blocks accurately machined and closely fitted together without any cementing material.

Large sheets of window glass may be rolled or drawn in cylinder or sheet form. In the rolling process for plate glass a ladleful of glass extracted from the furnace is poured upon a long table, upon which the mass is evenly distributed by a heavy roller. The sheet is then transferred to an annealing furnace. For the production of thick plate glass the comparatively uneven plate is afterwards ground and polished.

Corrugated or figured glass is similarly produced by the use of a roller having a suitably corrugated surface. Long vertical cylinders, which are later cut longitudinally and opened out in a flattening furnace to form a sheet, are drawn mechanically from a special pot of molten glass extracted from the furnace. The diameter of the cylinder and the thickness of the wall are controlled by an automatic regulation of the internal air-pressure and the rate of drawing. In the still more recent Libby-Owens process a plane sheet is drawn.

Articles made of glass must be cooled slowly to avoid fracture, and still more slowly to anneal them, that is, to eliminate stresses that may ultimately cause them to break. If the thickness of the glass is very irregular, the thin parts may cool and set while the adjacent thicker parts are still hot and soft. As these thick parts cool they contract, and may severely strain the previously-cooled thinner portions. By slow uniform cooling these stresses can be greatly reduced.

Annealing of optical glass is a most important operation, which may last for three to five weeks or even more in the case of very large pieces. For hollow ware and window glass much shorter periods are required. The articles while hot are placed upon a conveyor which passes through a heated tunnel or lehr, the temperature of which throughout its length is suitably varied. Thus in their passage the articles are brought to the required annealing temperature, and then gradually reduced in temperature.

The variety of types of glass produced for special purposes is now very great. For spectacles a good hard type of crown glass is employed. There are also manufactured special types that are partially opaque to ultra-violet rays, though quite transparent to visual rays of light. Crooke's spectacle glass and certain anti-glare glasses have these properties, which are often realized by the use of cerium and didymium salts. Uranium glass, commonly used for X-ray screens, fluoresces also under the action of ultra-violet light. It is a hard crown or borosilicate glass containing about 4 per cent of uranium.

Ultra-violet glass, which has a dense violet colour, is opaque to most visual rays, but transparent to ultra-violet rays. It contains about 5 per cent of nickel oxide. Strass is a heavy lead glass having a high refractive index, coloured by the addition of various metallic oxides, and used for the production of imitation gems.

Flashed glass is often used for decorative ware. The article may be partially blown in white glass and then dipped into coloured glass and fully blown. The wall thus consists of a thin layer of coloured glass upon white glass. By grinding or cutting or etching through the coloured layer, highly decorative effects may be obtained. Tubing is still generally produced by a hand process of drawing. A large mass of glass is gathered upon a blow-iron, and marvered and blown to the form of a thick walled cylinder. A second operator holds the pontil over his shoulder with the hot mass of glass near his back which is protected by a leather guard. While the blow-pipe operator facing the mass walks backwards, the other walks forwards, and thus the mass of glass is drawn out between them into a tubular form, the size of which is controlled by the speed of separation and the skill of the blow-pipe operator. As the tube is formed it rests upon wooden straps laid ladderwise upon the floor of a passage, which may be two or three hundred feet long.

For the formation of heavy tubing quick cooling of the drawn glass by fanning is necessary. However small the tube may be drawn, it will always be found to be hollow. Rod or cane glass is produced in a similar manner by drawing a solid mass of glass which has no initial internal air-space. Tubes and canes of triangular, oval, or other special sections are produced by marvering the gathered glass to a corresponding shape. Many beautiful effects may be obtained by drawing.

Filigree work, for example, is produced by combining with the marvered cylinder rods of coloured and opal glass arranged in parallel or interlaced patterns which may also be superposed. When the mass is drawn, the original pattern is preserved in an extended form. Millefiore effects are obtained by combining numerous pieces of coloured glass upon the surface of the gathered block of glass, and then blowing or drawing as previously described.

Spun glass is an extremely fine form of cane, the necessary speed of drawing being attained by winding upon the periphery of a rotating wheel.

Aventurine, first produced and for many years secretly manufactured by the Venetians, has a peculiar spangled appearance, due to partial reduction to the metallic state of copper throughout the mass. Reduction of chromium produces a similar green effect.

Toughened blocks of glass are frequently used as guards for boiler glass gauge tubes subjected to high pressure. The highly-heated block of glass is plunged into hot oil, which chills the surface without fracturing it while the interior still remains soft. As the interior cools it contracts, and places the surface under great compression. Surface cracks are therefore closed, instead of being extended, and the toughened plate can resist the application of very considerable external force that would otherwise break it.

Sheet glass can be reinforced by rolling into its substance while plastic a wire mesh of suitable material. Sheets of celluloid are also sometimes combined by cementing with two surface layers of glass to form so-called unbreakable glass.

Table and fancy glassware can be very effectively decorated in a great variety of ways. The patterns may be cut into the glass by grinding and polishing wheels, rouge or putty powder being used as a polishing medium. They may be etched by means of hydrofluoric acid acting upon portions of the glass surface, the remaining portions being protected by a coating of beeswax or bitumistic compound, which is later dissolved away, or the pattern may be sand-blasted through the apertures of a stencil laid upon the glass surface.

The pattern may be transferred or hand-painted upon the surface with metallic vitreous paints, which, when heated, melt and combine with the surface layer, thus producing the desired coloured effects.—BIBLIOGRAPHY: *Journal of the Society of Glass Technology*; P. Marson, *Glass Manufacture*; W. Rosenhain, *Glass Manufacture*; W. A. Shenstone, *Glass Blowing*; A. B. Searle, *The Clay Workers' Handbook*; P. G. H. Boswell, *Sands for Glass-making*.

GLASS, in folk-lore. Beads of glass, variously coloured, and found in ancient British and Irish graves and at sites of habitations, are known as 'fairy beads,' 'Druid gems,' or 'Druid glass' (W. *Gleini na Droedh*, and Gael. *Glaine nan Druidhe*). Other names are 'adder stones,' 'snake stones,' 'serpent beads,' &c. It was believed that the beads had been produced by snakes hissing together, and that one of them wriggled through the hole of the bead.

In Cornwall the snakes were supposed to produce the blue bead, with a yellow figure of a snake (the spiral) on it, by breathing or spitting on a wand of hazel. Apparently the earliest glass beads used in Britain were imported as amulets and talismans. They had the virtues of the *ovum anguinum* of Pliny, protecting wearers against evil influences and assisting women at childbirth, &c. Glass objects were thus substitutes for 'luck stones,' amber and pearls. Apparently they were regarded as products of water, like other substances that could be reduced to liquid form by means of fire.

The Teutonic word 'glass' is derived from the same root as the Celtic *glas*, which originally meant 'water,' as in *Duglas* (dark stream) and *Finglas* (white stream), and especially the water of a sacred river or lake in which dwelt a goddess. The Celtic *glas* had the secondary meaning of 'vigour,' as in *Gaidheal glas* ('the vigorous Gael'). Vigour was promoted by charms worn by warriors, especially those of amber, pearls, and coral, as well as of gold and silver, and those of symbolic shape in other materials.

The goddess Freyja of Northern mythology wept tears that were transformed into pearls, amber, precious stones, and precious metals. Amber, being a product of water, and especially of the goddess who had, like Aphrodite, her origin in water, was impregnated with the influence of the deity. According to Tacitus, amber was called *glesse* by the Baltic people of Celtic speech, who collected it and traded in it. Pliny says that the Germans called amber *glessum*, and that one of the amber islands of the Baltic was known as *Glessaria*. The root *glas* is found in French in *glace*, which means 'ice' and 'yellow amber.'

In modern Gaelic and Welsh *glas* is a colour term signifying 'green' or 'grey' or 'greyish green.' In the Far East glass was, as in Western Europe, used for magic religious purposes. Objects of glass reached China from the west early in the Christian era. Glass rings were as 'precious' (sacred) as those of jade, or those of varieties of quartz. Thus the term *pi-liu-li* was applied in ancient texts to glass as well as to certain precious stones.

In modern Chinese glass is *po-li*. The Japanese *maga-tama* (or 'comma-shaped') beads, which were sacred objects, were made of jade, agate, chrysoprase, serpentine, chalcedony, steatite, quartz, crystal, and glass. A *tama* is an object containing the animating principle (soul substance), and the soul of a deity is called *mi-tama*, the *mi*, which originally meant a 'water-snake,' being used as a honorific prefix.

The glass beads found in Japanese prehistoric burial-mounds are coloured dark-blue as a rule, but some are green or amber coloured. It is believed that these glass beads were imported from or through China. The Chinese method of blowing glass was not introduced into Japan until the sixteenth century. It appears that the Chinese themselves became acquainted with glass as a result of contact with the Roman Orient. They did not begin to manufacture glass until the fifth century.

During the early Iron Age in Europe the trade in glass charms, including beads and armlets, was widespread. The ancient Egyptians produced glassy objects as far back as their Empire period (*c.* 1600 B.C.), but it was not until Roman times that glass was blown. Glassy beads were coloured and used as charms in ancient Egypt. They were substitutes for precious stones, &c., of religious value.

GLASSITES, a religious body founded in Scotland in the eighteenth century by John Glass (1695–1773), a minister of the Established Church. They maintained certain practices, such as weekly communions, love-feasts, washing each other's feet, and mutual exhortations. They disapproved of all games of chance, and of all use of the lot except for sacred purposes. They are now extinct; their last church in America was closed in 1890.

GLASS-PAINTING, the art of producing pictures upon glass with colours that are burned in, or by the use of pieces of coloured glass, in which the colour forms part of the composition of the glass itself. Originally there was but one method of making ornamental glass windows, which was by the latter process: the pieces of stained or coloured glass were cut to the desired shape, and let into the grooves of finely-made leaden frames which formed the pattern in outline, so that the pictures resembled mosaic work.

In the sixteenth century, the *enamel* colours having been discovered, a new process came into vogue, the designs being now painted on the glass and burned in. At the present day the two methods, or a combination of the two, are chiefly employed,

GLASS SNAKE, a lizard (*Ophisaurus apus*), in form resembling a serpent, and reaching a length of 3 feet. It is related to the *blind-worm* (q.v.). The joints of the tail are not connected by caudal muscles, hence it is extremely brittle, and one or more of the joints break off when the animal is even slightly irritated. It is native to the Balkans, South Russia, Morocco, and Asia Minor. Other species inhabit the Eastern Himalayas and North America, belonging to Tetrodon and allied genera.

Glastonbury—Remains of old Abbey

the *mosaic-enamel* method being the most common, and consisting of a combination of these two. The chief seats of the art in Britain are Birmingham and Edinburgh; in France, Paris and Sèvres; and in Germany, Munich and Nürnberg.—BIBLIOGRAPHY: P. Nelson, *Ancient Painted Glass in Europe*; M. Drake, *History of English Glass Painting*.

GLASS PAPER, or **CLOTH,** is made by strewing finely-pounded glass on a sheet of paper or cloth which has been besmeared with a coat of thin glue, the glue being still wet. It is much used for polishing metal and woodwork.

GLASS'WORT, a name given to the plants of the genus Salicornia, nat. ord. Chenopodiaceæ, succulent marine herbs growing abundantly on the coasts in the south of Europe and north of Africa, and yielding, by burning, ashes containing soda, formerly much employed in making both soap and glass. Two or three species are natives of Britain.

GLASTONBURY, a borough of England, county of Somerset. It was famous for a thorn tree supposed to have been planted there by Joseph of Arimathea. It is closely connected with Arthurian legend, and is identified with the Island of Avilion, Arthur's burial-place. It also derives interest from the ruins of its once magnificent Benedictine abbey, dating back to the twelfth century, and now consisting of some fragments of the church, the chapel of St. Joseph of Arimathea, and what is called the abbot's kitchen. Its abbots sat among the barons in Parliament. The last, Abbot Whiting, was hanged on a neighbouring eminence, the Tor, by order of Henry VIII for refusing to surrender the abbey. The fifteenth-century Pilgrims' Inn is now the 'George.' In 1892 remains of two lake villages were discovered in the neighbourhood of Glastonbury. Sharpham Park, the birth-place of Fielding, lies 2 miles to the south-west of the town. Pop. (municipal borough, 1931), 4,515.

GLATZ, a town of Germany, province of Silesia, on the Neisse, 51 miles s.s.w. of Breslau; manufactures of linen, cotton, and woollen goods, leather, carpets, &c. Pop. 16,563. •

GLAUBER, John Rudolph, a German chemist, born in 1603 or 1604. His life seems to have been somewhat unsettled—at least he resided in many different places—Vienna, Salzburg, Frankfort, Kitzingen, Cologne, and Basel, and finally in Amsterdam, where he died in 1668. He is chiefly remembered for his discovery of sulphate of soda or *Glauber's Salt*, which he termed *sal mirabile*, in consequence of his great faith in its medicinal qualities. Glauber's *Opera Omnia* were translated into English in 1689.

GLAUBER'S SALT, sulphate of sodium (Na_2SO_4, $10H_2O$), so called because of the importance attached to its chemical and medical properties by Glauber. It forms large colourless monoclinic prisms, which effloresce on exposure to the air. It is soluble in water, and when heated melts in its water of crystallization. It is found in many localities, dissolved in the water of mineral springs or of salt lakes, round which it effloresces.

GLAUCHAU (glou'hou), a manufacturing town of Germany in Saxony, on the Mulde, 54 miles w.s.w. of Dresden. It has manufactures of woollens, carpets, linens, leather, dye-works, print-fields, and worsted mills. Pop. 27,318.

GLAUCOMA, in medicine, an almost incurable disease of the eye, in which the eyeball becomes of stony hardness by the accumulation of fluid within, and the consequent increase of pressure causes disorganization of all the tissues. Loss of sight is sometimes very rapid. The progress of the disease may in some cases be arrested by pupil-contracting drugs or by surgical operation. Called also *Glaucosis*.

GLAUCONITE, a soft green mineral occurring as an infilling of foraminiferal shells, sponge-spicules, &c., on the sea-floor at depths of about 100 fathoms, and left behind as internal casts of these objects when the covering-matter is broken or dissolved away.

It is a hydrous silicate of iron and potassium, with some calcium, &c., and was formerly mistaken for chlorite. It is well known in the greensands (q.v.) of all ages, and its potash-content, some 3 to 8 per cent, adds to the fertility of soils formed on these rocks.

GLAZING is the covering of earthenware vessels with a vitreous coating in order to prevent their being penetrated by fluids. The materials of common glass would afford the most perfect glazing were it not that a glazing of this sort is liable to cracks when exposed to changes of temperature. A mixture of equal parts of oxide of lead and ground flint is found to be a durable glaze for the common cream-coloured ware, and is generally used for that purpose. *See* POTTERY.

GLEBE (Lat. *gleba*, a clod of earth), land attached to an Established church for the benefit of the incumbent in addition to his stipend. It may be let out and may be sold with the approval of the Land Commissioners.

GLEDITSCH'IA, a genus of plants, ord. Leguminosæ, to which *G. triacanthos*, the honey-locust, belongs.

GLEE (A.Sax. *gligg*, music), in music, a composition in three or more parts, generally consisting of more than one movement, the subject of which may vary greatly, from grave to gay. Instrumental accompaniment is illegitimate. Among glee composers were: Webbe, Stevens, Calcott, Horsley, Attwood, Lord Mornington, and others. In 1787 a Glee-club was founded in London, and existed until 1857.

GLEICHENIACEÆ, a small family of Leptosporangiate Ferns, largely tropical, mostly smallish plants, with creeping stems and dichotomously-branched leaves.

GLEIWITZ (glī'vits), a town of Germany, in the plebiscite area of Upper Silesia (q.v.). It is situated on the River Klodnitz not far from Beuthen, and near the mines. It has foundries, machine-works, glassworks, worsted and other mills. Pop. 95,572.

GLENCOE (glen-kō'), a valley in the county of Argyle, near the head of Loch Etive. It is bounded on both sides by almost perpendicular mountains over 3,000 feet high, and is traversed by a mountain stream, Ossian's "dark torrent of Cona." The valley was the scene of a tragedy known as the Massacre of Glencoe.

The state of the Highlands after 1690 was a subject of great anxiety to the Government. Although the Highlanders had ceased any important operations since the death of Dundee at Killiecrankie, they had not laid down their arms. In 1691 a proclamation was issued promising pardon to all who should swear allegiance on or before 31st Dec., 1691.

All the chiefs but the chief of the MacDonalds of Glencoe complied. The latter had unfortunately exceeded the prescribed period, and a certificate which he produced to prove that he had offered to take the oaths at Fort-William was suppressed, as is thought, by Stair. The king's signature was obtained to an order to extirpate the MacDonalds.

On the 1st of February a party of soldiers, 120 in number, commanded by Captain Campbell of Glenlyon, marched up the glen and took quarters as friends. The soldiers belonged mostly to the clan Campbell, enemies of the MacDonalds; but they were well treated, and all went merrily on for twelve days. At five in the morning of the 13th Glenlyon and his men suddenly fell on the MacDonalds. Thirty-eight men were murdered, but many who had escaped perished in the snow, sank into bogs, or died for lack of food. Much obloquy has been heaped upon King William on account of his share in the massacre, but the utmost of what he would seem to have been guilty was carelessness in signing without investigation the order mentioned above.—Cf. George Gilfillan, *The Massacre of Glencoe and the Campbells of Glenlyon*.

GLENDALOUGH (glen'da-loh), that is, 'glen of the two loughs,' a picturesque vale near the middle of County Wicklow, Ireland, containing two small lakes, and ruins known as 'the Seven Churches,' besides an old round tower; as an ecclesiastical centre it was associated with the name of St. Kevin as early as the sixth century.

GLENDOWER, Owen, last national leader of the Welsh people, born 1359. At an early age he was sent to London, and studied for the Bar, but he relinquished the profession on being appointed an esquire to Richard II, whom he supported to the last.

He carried on a contest with Lord Grey de Ruthyn respecting an estate, and the latter being charged with the delivery of a summons to Owen from Henry, to attend him on his Scottish expedition, purposely neglected to deliver it. Glendower was outlawed for disaffection, and his enemy seized upon his lands. Glendower dispossessed Grey of his lands, and, having raised a considerable force, caused himself to be proclaimed Prince of Wales on 20th Sept., 1400.

He defeated the king's troops, and, retiring to the mountains, foiled all subsequent attempts to bring him to action. He afterwards joined the coalition of the Percys, against Henry, and was crowned 'sovereign of Wales.' Glendower arrived with his force too late for the battle of Shrewsbury; and, seeing all was lost, retreated, and continued his marauding warfare. This he kept up with various success, occasionally assisted by Charles VI of France. Finding it impossible to subdue him, Henry V, in 1415, condescended to treat with him; but Owen died during the negotiation. —BIBLIOGRAPHY: Thomas, *Memoirs of Glendower*; A. G. Bradley, *Owen Glyndwr: the Last Struggle for Welsh Independence*.

GLENGAR'RY, Scottish parish and glen, Inverness, traversed by the Garry, which issues from Loch Quoich, forms Loch Garry in its course, and enters Loch Oich, one of the Caledonian Canal lochs. Glengarry was the home of the Macdonalds from the sixteenth to the beginning of the nineteenth century. The glengarry bonnet is named from this valley. There are also a river, loch, and glen of same name in Perthshire.

GLENLIV'ET, a valley or district of Scotland, in the county of Banff. Whisky of a particularly fine flavour has long been made in the district. In Glenlivet the Protestant army under the Earl of Argyle was defeated by a Roman Catholic force under the Earl of Huntly in 1594. Pop. 1,104.

GLEN ROY, a deep valley in the Highlands of Scotland, parallel to Glenmore (the Great Glen), in Lochaber, Inverness-shire. It is nearly 14 miles in length, and little more than ½ mile in breadth, and is celebrated for its so-called *Parallel Roads*, which are three parallel terraces running along either side of the glen. Not only do the lines on the same side run parallel to each other, but on both sides they respectively occupy the same horizontal level. These terraces project, at some parts only a few feet from the hill-side and at others widen out so as to be a number of yards in breadth.

The lowest terrace is 850 to 862 feet above the sea-level, the middle

1,062 to 1,077 feet, and the highest 1,144 to 1,155 feet. Their origin has been much disputed, but according to Macculloch, Agassiz, Buckland, and Geikie, the roads are shore-lines of freshwater lakes. As, however, no land-barrier is discoverable in the vicinity, they refer the lake or lakes to the Glacial period, holding that glaciers must have descended from Ben Nevis and dammed up the water in Glen Roy. As these glaciers did not disappear simultaneously, the surface of the lake had different elevations successively, and thus distinct shore-lines or beaches were formed at different times.

GLENTILT', a mountain valley in Scotland, Perthshire, traversed by the Tilt, having its southern extremity at Blair Castle, and there opening into the valley of the Garry. Marble of a pure white, of a light grey, and of a

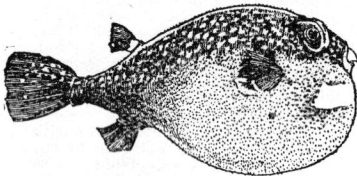

Globe-fish (*Tetrodon Fahaka*)

beautiful green has been quarried in its recesses.

GLIDER. Name given to a kind of air vessel. It is heavier than air and has no motor, being designed to descend gradually from a height to the ground. Experiments with gliders were of considerable help in developing the aeroplane. As a sport, gliding has been taken up a good deal in Germany since the Great War and to some extent in Great Britain. Gliding clubs have been established and there is a British Gliding Association at 44a, Dover Street, London, W.1. In 1931 an Austrian expert made a flight of over 70 miles in just over three hours, a record for England.

GLOBE, a sphere, a round solid body, which may be conceived to be generated by the revolution of a semi-circle about its diameter. An artificial globe, in geography and astronomy, is a globe of metal, plaster, paper, pasteboard, &c., on the surface of which is drawn a map, or representation of either the earth or the heavens, with the several circles which are conceived upon them, the former being called the *terrestrial globe*, and the latter the *celestial globe*.

Some celestial globes were made by Gerbert of Aurillac in the tenth century, and an Arabian celestial globe dating back to 1225 is in the museum at Florence. One of the oldest terrestrial globes is that of Behaim, constructed at Nürnberg in 1492. In the terrestrial globe the wire on which it turns represents the earth's axis, the extremities of it representing the poles. The *brazen meridian* is a vertical circle in which the artificial globe turns, divided into 360 degrees, each degree being divided into minutes and seconds. The brass meridian receives the ends of the axis on which the globe revolves. At right angles to this, and in a horizontal plane, is a broad ring of wood or brass representing the horizon; that is, the true horizon of the earth which lies in a plane containing the earth's centre. The horizon and brass meridian are connected with the stand on which the whole is supported.

On the surface of the globe, as on other maps, are marked parallels of latitude, meridians, &c. On a globe of some size the meridians are drawn through every 15° of the equator, each answering to an hour's difference of time between two places. Hence they are called the *hour circles*. A number of *problems* or questions, many of them more curious than useful, may be solved by means of a terrestrial globe. Among the most important are: to find the latitude and longitude of a place, the difference of time between two places, the time of the sun's rising and setting for a given day at a given place, &c.

GLOBE-FISH, the name given to several fishes, ord. Plectognathi, remarkable for possessing the power of suddenly assuming a globular form by swallowing air, which, passing into a ventral sac, inflates the whole animal like a balloon. They are common in tropical seas, and freshwater species are also known.

GLOBE-FLOWER, a popular name of *Trollius europæus* (nat. ord. Ranunculaceæ), a common European plant in mountainous regions, having five-lobed, deeply serrated leaves and round pale-yellow blossoms, the sepals of which are large and conspicuous, while the petals are very small. It is often cultivated in gardens, and is common in mountain pastures in the north of England, north of Ireland, Wales, and Scotland.

GLOBIGERI'NA, one of the perforate Foraminifera, a microscopic animal having a shell formed of several nearly globular chambers; found fossil in the Chalk and Tertiary formations, and still so abundant in our seas that its shells after death form vast calcareous deposits of mud or ooze known as 'globigerina ooze.'

GLOB'ULIN, a chemical compound belonging to the proteid class, found in the tissues of living organisms. The best-known forms occur in blood serum, in muscular tissue, and in the crystalline lens of the eye.

GLOCKNER, or GROSS GLOCKNER, a mountain belonging to the Noric Alps, on the frontiers of the Tyrol, Carinthia, and Salzburg. It is 12,461 feet in height, and takes its name from the resemblance of the principal summit to a large bell.

GLOGAU, or GROSS-GLOGAU, a German town and former fortress in Silesia, on the Oder, 54 miles N.W. of Breslau. It has a Lutheran and a Catholic gymnasium, some manufactories and a brisk inland trade. Its principal edifices are four churches, one of them formerly a cathedral. Pop. 26,098.

GLOMMEN, the largest river in Norway, issues from Lake Oresund, about 2,417 feet above the sea-level, in the south-east of South Trondhjem, flows generally south, and after a course of above 370 miles falls into the Skagerrak at Frederikstadt.

GLORIO'SA, a genus of tuberous-rooted climbing herbs of the nat. ord. Liliaceæ, so named from the splendid appearance of its flowers. They have branched stems and flowers mostly of a beautiful red and yellow colour, with six long lanceolate undulated segments, which are entirely reflexed. *G. superba,* a native of India and tropical Africa, is cultivated in hothouses.

GLORY PEA. *See* CLIANTHUS.

GLOSS, an explanation of some verbal difficulty in a literary work, written at the passage to which it refers. The earliest glosses, as those in Greek, Latin, and Hebrew MSS., were interlinear; they were afterwards placed in the margin, and extended finally in some instances to a sort of running commentary on an entire book.

GLOSSOP, a municipal borough of England, in Derbyshire, 30 miles from Sheffield. It is the principal seat of the Derbyshire cotton manufacture, and there are also woollen- and paper-mills, iron-foundries, dyeing and bleaching and printworks. Pop. (1931), 19,510.

GLOSSOPTERIS, a fossil plant with elongated leaves; allied to the ferns and also possibly to the cycads, characterizing widely distributed beds of Upper Carboniferous and Lower Permian Age. The 'Glossopteris flora' is associated with the Permian glacial deposits of the ancient southern continent of Gondwanaland, and has also been traced in the Permian of Russia.

GLOTTIS is the aperture between the vocal cords in front and the arytenoid cartilages behind at the upper part of the trachea (wind-pipe). Its shape and extent are altered by the movements of the vocal cord and larynx, thus causing modulations of the voice. *See* LARYNX.

GLOUCESTER (glŏs'tẽr), a city, county of itself, parliamentary borough, and river port, England, capital of the county of same name, on the left bank of the Severn, here divided into two channels enclosing the Isle of Alney and crossed by two fine bridges, 33 miles north by east of Bristol, and 95 miles west by north of London. It carries on a considerable shipping trade, the Gloucester and Berkeley Canal giving access to the docks.

The most remarkable public edifice is the cathedral; it was originally the church of a Benedictine abbey, dating from 1058, and was converted into a cathedral at the Reformation. It is cruciform, 444 feet in length, 154 feet in breadth, and 85½ feet in height, with a tower 230 feet high. It exhibits a great variety of styles, the choir, with its roof of fan-tracery, being a fine example of Perpendicular Gothic. Other buildings are several handsome old churches, the shire hall, the guildhall, the bishop's palace, and county schools of art and science.

The schools include the collegiate school founded by Henry VIII, the theological college, the blue-coat school founded in 1666 (and now known as Sir Thomas Rich's School), the grammar-school of St. Mary de Crypt, founded in the time of Henry VIII. The industries are varied. Gloucester, which formerly returned two, now sends one member to Parliament. Pop. (1931), 52,937.

GLOUCESTER, the county, is bounded by the Severn, Monmouth, Hereford, Worcester, Warwick, Oxford, Berks, Wilts, and Somerset; area, 804,638 acres, of which five-sixths are under crops and pasture. The county is naturally divided into three distinct districts, the Hill or Cotswold in the east; the Severn valley in the middle; and the Forest of Dean in the west.

The principal rivers are the Severn, with its affluents the Wye, the Leden, and Lower and Upper Avon; and the Isis or Thames, with its affluents the Colne, Churnet, and Windrush. Iron and coal are found in the Forest of Dean, and the collieries employ a large number of hands. Coal is also found and extensively worked in the south part of the county; and lead ore is found in various parts. Limestone and freestone are also met with.

Agriculture is in a flourishing state, especially in the vale districts of the county. Gloucester is, however, much more of a dairy than an agricultural county. The celebrated cheese known as double and single Gloucester is produced chiefly in the Vale of Berkeley.

Orchards are numerous, from the produce of which large quantities of cider are made. Gloucester is a considerable manufacturing county, and has been long famous for its fine broadcloths. For parliamentary purposes the county is divided into four

Gloucester Cathedral

divisions, one member to each. Pop. (1931), 785,656.—Cf. W. Page, *Victoria County History*.

GLOUCESTER, a town and port of Essex County, Massachusetts, near the extremity of Cape Ann, 28 miles N.N.E. of Boston. It is a popular summer resort; and fisheries and granite quarrying are the chief industries. About 2 miles distant is Norman's Woe, the scene of the wreck of the *Hesperus* celebrated by Longfellow. Pop. 24,204.

GLOUCESTER, Duke of. English title borne by several members of the royal family. Robert, an illegitimate son of Henry I., was Earl of Gloucester and the Clare family held the earldom for about 100 years before 1314, when the last earl was killed at Bannockburn.

Thomas of Woodstock, a son of Edward III., was Duke of Gloucester from 1385 to 1397. He was a leading figure during the reign of his nephew

Richard II., who had him arrested and executed in 1397. Humphrey, a son of Henry IV., was made duke in 1414. He is remembered as a benefactor to the University of Oxford. He died in 1447. The next duke was the prince who became Richard III.

There was no other Duke of Gloucester until Stuart times. Henry, son of Charles I., and William, son of Anne, were both given the title, but neither attained manhood. In 1764, William Henry, a son of Frederick, Prince of Wales, and a brother of George III., was made duke. He died in 1805 and the title became extinct when his son, William Frederick, died in 1834.

Henry, third son of King George V., became Duke of Gloucester in 1928. Born March 21, 1900, at Sandringham, he was educated at Broadstairs and then at Eton. In 1919 he entered the army, serving first with the King's Royal Rifles and later with a cavalry regiment. He is knight of the Garter and Privy Councillor, and in 1933 he was made a Knight of the Thistle.

GLOVER, Richard, an English poet, born 1712, died 1785. Though engaged in trade, he devoted much of his attention to literature, and acquired a high reputation as a scholar and a poet. In 1760 he entered Parliament, where his abilities gained him considerable influence. He was the author of two epics, *Leonidas* and the *Atheniad*; *London, or the Progress of Commerce*; and three tragedies, *Boadicea, Medea,* and *Jason*. His *Diary* was published in 1813.

GLOVER, Terrot Reaveley, English scholar, was born in 1869. He was educated at Bristol Grammar School, and at St. John's College, Cambridge, and was appointed Public Orator at Cambridge in 1920. In 1924 he was President of the Baptist Union. His works include *Studies in Virgil, The Jesus of History, Paul of Tarsus* and (1931) *The World of the New Testament*.

GLOVERSVILLE, a town, Fulton County, New York, 43 miles N.W. of Albany. Glove-making is the principal industry, hence the name of the place. Pop. 23,009.

GLOVES are coverings for the hand, or for the hand and wrist, with a separate sheath for each finger. They are made of leather, fur, cloth, silk, linen thread, cotton, or worsted. The chief leathers used in glove manufacture are doe, buck, and calf-skins; sheep-skin for military gloves; lamb-skin for many of the so-called kid gloves; true kid for the best and finest gloves; dog, rat, and kangaroo skins, &c.

The leather in all cases undergoes a

much lighter dressing than when used for boots and shoes. Leather gloves are usually cut out by means of dies, and sewed by a machine of peculiar construction. The best woollen, thread, and silk gloves are made by cutting and sewing, but commoner gloves are made by knitting and weaving.

In England leather gloves are manufactured at London, Worcester, Yeovil and elsewhere. Limerick was formerly celebrated for gloves of a peculiarly delicate kind. Gloversville, in New York, is the chief American seat of the manufacture. Italy, Belgium, Sweden, Denmark, and Germany all manufacture excellent gloves, but France supplies the world with most of the finer and more expensive kinds. Large quantities of cotton gloves are manufactured at Nottingham and Leicester; and the greater number of woollen gloves is made in Wales, Scotland, and the north of England.

Gloves are a very ancient article of dress, and many curious customs and usages are connected with them.

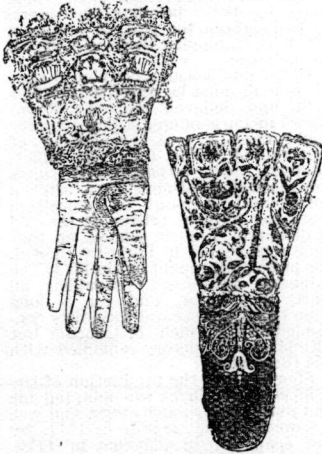

Gloves
Left, Leather embroidered with silk, gold, and seed pearls (temp. Henry VIII). Right, Crimson velvet embroidered with gold and silver (temp. Queen Elizabeth)

They were worn by the ancient Greeks and the Romans. During the early Middle Ages they were considered as a sign of rank, and taken off in token of respect in churches and before a superior. They were afterwards often worn in the hat as ladies' favours. Throwing the glove down before a person amounted to a challenge to single combat. The use of gloves was introduced into England only in the thirteenth century.

Queen Elizabeth set the fashion of richly-embroidered and bejewelled

Gloxinias

gloves. The judges in England used to be prohibited wearing gloves on the bench; and it was only in case of a maiden assize that the sheriffs were allowed to present a judge with a pair of gloves.—BIBLIOGRAPHY: S. W. Beck, *Gloves: their Annals and Associations*; W. M. Smith, *Gloves, Past and Present*; Côte, *L'Industrie gantière à Grenoble.*

GLOW-WORM, an insect of the genus Lampy̆ris (*L. noctilŭca*), of the ord. Coleoptera, or beetles, the name being strictly applicable only to the female, which is without wings, somewhat resembles a caterpillar, and emits a shining green light from the extremity of the abdomen. The male is winged, and flies about in the evening, when he is attracted by the light of the female, but is only faintly luminous himself, as also are eggs, larvæ, and pupæ.

Decapitated specimens retain their power of giving out light for a considerable time. In pure oxygen, in warm water, or when crushed, the light of the luminous organs is increased in intensity. The larvæ are very voracious, living on snails, which they attack and kill. Belonging to the same family are the firefly and the railway beetle.

GLOXIN'IA, a genus of plants, nat. ord. Gesneraceæ, distinguished by the corolla approaching to bell-shaped, the upper lip shortest and two-lobed, the lower three-lobed, with the middle lobe largest, and also by the summit of the style being rounded and hollowed. The species are natives of tropical America, whence they were introduced into Britain early in the eighteenth century. They are now among the greatest ornaments of European hothouses, owing to their richly-coloured leaves and their ample, graceful, delicately-tinted flowers. *See* SINNINGIA.

GLUCHOV, or **GLUKHOV** (glö'-hov), a town of the Ukraine, government of, and 148 miles east by north from Tchernigov. Pop. 14,856.

GLUCINUM, commonly known as beryllium, is a rare metal having a specific gravity lower than aluminium, viz. 1·9; it is silver-white in colour and resembles magnesium. It occurs in the minerals beryl, euclase, and gadolinite, and was named from its oxide, glucina, which was known long before the metal was isolated. The atomic weight is 9·1; it melts at 1800° F., and burns like magnesium when in the form of powder or ribbon.

GLUCK (glŭk), **Christoph Willibald, Ritter von,** German musical composer, born in Bavaria in 1714, died at Vienna 1787. When a boy he became a chorister, and acquired some skill on the harpsichord and organ. At eighteen years of age he went to Prague to enter the university, where he maintained himself by the exercise of his musical gifts. By degrees he attracted the attention of several Bohemian nobles, and Prince Lobkowitz assisted him when he went to Vienna to pursue his musical studies. The Lombardian Prince di Melzi then took him to Milan, where he studied under Giovanni Battista Sammartini, a famous organist and composer. In 1740 he was employed to compose an opera for the court theatre of Milan. The text chosen for him was the *Artaxerxes* of Metastasio, and the opera was a triumph, in spite of the innovations of style which the author introduced. In 1742 he wrote *Demofoonte* for Milan; *Demetrio* and *Ipermnestra* for Venice; in 1743 *Artamene* for Cremona, and *Siface* for Milan; in 1744 *Fedra* for the same theatre; and in 1745 *Allessandro nell' Indie* for Turin, all founded on classical subjects. Invited to London, he produced *La Caduta de' Giganti* (Fall of the Giants), which was not a success.

In London Gluck became deeply impressed with the majestic character of Handel's airs and choruses, and with the simple but natural dramatic style of Dr. Arne. This visit to London, and a short trip to Paris, helped to develop that lyric genius which was destined to create a new order of musical composition. After producing operas of the conventional type at Paris, Vienna, Rome, and Naples, he returned to Vienna. The *Trionfo di Clelia* (1762) was the last of his operas in his first style.

Pleased as the public was with his music, he was not satisfied. He felt himself continually cramped by the character of the libretti of Metastasio, who had hitherto furnished him with texts, which were rather lyrical dramatic poems than genuine dramas. The composer at last found a poet, in the person of Raniero Calzabigi, who sympathized with him in his ideas, and the result of their co-operation was the *Orfeo ed Euridice,* performed publicly for the first time in 1762.

This opera marked a new era. The fame it acquired at once it never lost. Various works of lighter character filled up the interval between this year and 1766, when his second great opera of *Alceste* was produced, which raised public feeling to the point of enthusiasm.

In his dedication of this work to the Grand-Duke Leopold of Tuscany he enunciates the principles of the new school, which shortly were that the opera should be a musical drama, not a concert in costume; that the text must be descriptive of real passion; that the music must voice fully the spirit of the text; that in accompaniments the instruments must be used to strengthen the expression of the vocal parts by their peculiar characters, or to heighten the general dramatic effect by employing them in contrast to the voice.

Gluck now became convinced that his system must be tested on a wider field, and believed that the Royal Opera in Paris offered all a composer could demand. A Frenchman of culture and genius, Bailly du Rollet, adapted Racine's *Iphigénie en Aulide* for musical treatment, and after a considerable amount of opposition from the musical critics of the old Italian and French school, at that time represented in Paris by Piccini, the piece was brought out in 1774. The intensest excitement prevailed; all Paris took sides, and for a long time the Gluckists and Piccinists contended with much bitterness, but ultimately the victory remained with the Gluckists.

Shortly after the production of the *Iphigénie,* the *Orfeo* was adapted for and put on the French stage, and was followed by the *Armide* in 1777, by the *Iphigénie en Tauride* in 1779, Gluck's last important work, and by many considered his greatest. It ends the series of works which gave a direction to the operatic genius of Méhul and Cherubini in France, and of Mozart and Beethoven in Germany.—BIBLIOGRAPHY: A. Reissmann, *Christoph Willibald von Gluck*; E. Newman, *Gluck and the Opera*; J. d'Udine, *Gluck, biographie critique.*

GLUCOSE, also known as dextrose or grape sugar, is a carbohydrate of the formula $CH_2(OH)\cdot(CHOH)_4\cdot CHO$, occurring naturally in honey, grapes, and other fruit. It is also present in the urine of persons suffering from *diabetes mellitus*; in chronic cases as much as 1 lb. of glucose may be excreted *per diem*.

Glucose has been synthetically prepared from its elements by a complicated series of reactions, but on a commercial scale it is manufactured by boiling starch with dilute sulphuric acid. As a source of starch, potatoes, maize, rice, or sago are used. The degree of concentration of the solutions is of great importance; in practice 1·5 parts of starch in the form of a thick solution are added with stirring about 2 parts of 2 per cent sulphuric acid, the mixture being kept boiling by means of steam.

The starch is converted firstly into dextrine (British gum) and maltose (malt sugar), and finally, on prolonged boiling, into glucose. The acid is then neutralized with chalk or limestone, the solution of glucose filtered from the precipitated matter and evaporated to a thin syrup. After decolorizing with bone charcoal the syrup is evaporated further in vacuo and allowed to crystallize. The process of solidification can be hastened by adding a small quantity of pure glucose, the mass being stirred continuously.

Pure glucose forms a colourless crystalline mass, less sweet than cane sugar, melting at 86° C., and losing its one molecule of water of crystallization at 110° C. It is very soluble in water but only sparingly so in alcohol. It is distinguished from cane sugar by the fact that it is not charred by warm sulphuric acid. Its solution rotates the plane of polarized light to the right (*dextro*-rotatory). It is readily fermented by yeast, giving alcohol and carbonic acid gas, and is consequently largely used in brewing.

Chemically it behaves as a polyhydric alcohol and also as an aldehyde, which accounts for its strong reducing properties. Thus a solution of glucose readily reduces a warm alkaline solution of cupric tartrate (Fehling's solution), red cuprous oxide being quantitatively precipitated. This test is employed in estimating the amount of glucose in solutions, notably in the case of diabetic urine.

Glucose is also formed, together with an equal quantity of fructose, when cane sugar is boiled with dilute acids. This mixture, known as invert sugar, forms a colourless syrup sweeter than cane sugar and is largely used in the manufacture of champagne, liqueurs, fruit preserves, and honey substitutes.

GLU'COSIDES, a group of carbon compounds (including amygdalin, salicin, &c.) occurring in the vegetable kingdom, and characterized by the fact that on hydrolysis or saponification with dilute acids a sugar, usually glucose, is formed along with other products.

GLUE (O.Fr. *glu*, bird-lime) consists of a sticky gelatinous material obtained from the cartilaginous substance of hides, bones, fish skins, &c.: from which it is prepared by prolonged boiling with water, a process which gradually dissolves the glue-forming tissue.

Leather Glue or Skin Glue. The best-quality brown glues are obtained from hides, but the skins of sheep and other animals are largely used in the preparation of good-quality light-coloured glues. The raw material, which is generally in the form of cuttings from tanneries and slaughterhouses must be quite fresh. After washing, it is soaked in milk of lime for two or three weeks. The swollen gelatinous substance is then treated with soft water or a dilute solution of sulphurous acid to remove the last trace of lime, as otherwise an inferior product would be obtained.

This substance is then 'melted' by boiling with a small quantity of water in an open vessel or by means of steam alone. The lower the temperature employed the better the resulting glue; for this reason vacuum apparatus is often used. The liquid obtained is purified by standing and filtering, and if necessary decolorized by animal charcoal. The purified glue solution is then run into moulds and allowed to cool to a firm jelly which is cut into pieces of a convenient size by a wire or wet knife, and dried in the open air on netting stretched over frames.

During the drying process the cakes must be carefully watched, as during warm moist weather the glue readily undergoes decomposition and is spoilt. The final drying is usually carried out in a warm well-ventilated room. To give the cakes a bright appearance they are dipped in water and again dried.

Bone Glue. This type of glue, though not such a strong adhesive as hide glue, is largely prepared in connection with the manufacture of bone meal and phosphorus. The raw bones are crushed, freed from oily matter, and decalcified by treatment with dilute hydrochloric or sulphurous acid; the remaining translucent cartilage is then treated with lime, well washed and finally boiled down to form glue as in the case of leather glue.

Fish Glue is prepared from the skins of fish, the heads and bones of cod, and also from whale blubber when freed from oil, by a method similar to that used for bone glue. If the boiling is carried out correctly, fish glue is a viscous liquid when cold, and forms a very tenacious adhesive. The best kind of fish glue is isinglass, which consists of the purified and dried inner skin of the swim-bladder of the sturgeon.

Marine Glue consists of a solution of india-rubber in turpentine, to which is added powdered asphalt or shellac. It is an extremely powerful adhesive and must be applied hot.

GLUME, in botany, the imbricate scale-like bract inserted on the axis of the spikelet in Gramineæ (grasses) and Cyperaceæ (sedges).

GLUTEN, a tough elastic substance of a greyish colour, which becomes brown and brittle by drying, found in the flour of wheat and other grain. Being a mixture of proteins, it contributes much to the nutritive quality

Glutton (*Gulo luscus*)

of flour, and gives tenacity to its paste. A similar substance is found in the juices of certain plants.

GLUTTON, the *Gulo luscus*, a carnivorous quadruped, about the size of a large badger, and belonging to the weasel family (Mustelidæ). It inhabits Northern Europe and America, and is known also by the name of *Wolverene* or *Wolverine*. The glutton is slow and deficient in agility, but persevering, cunning, fierce, and of great strength. It prefers putrid flesh, and has an extremely fetid odour. The fur is valuable, that from Siberia being preferred from its being a glossy black. The animal receives its name from its voracity, which, however, has been greatly exaggerated.

GLYCERINE, or **GLYCEROL** (*glycys* = sweet, *keros* = wax), is a trihydric alcohol which does not occur naturally in the free state, but always in combination with fatty acids as the essential constituent of fats and oils of animal or vegetable origin. It is obtained as a by-product in the manufacture of soap and candles from these fats. Chemically it is a

trihydroxy-propane of the formula $CH_2OH \cdot CHOH \cdot CH_2OH$. It was discovered by Scheele in 1779, and has been prepared synthetically from its elements. The principal sources of glycerine are stearin, the main constituent of mutton fat; palmitin, present in palm oil and other oils; and olein, which is found in the soft fats such as lard.

The hydrolysis ('saponification') of the fat is carried out by boiling with caustic soda solution; the soap (the sodium salt of the fatty acid) is then salted out. The residual lye contains practically all the glycerine present in the original fat. This lye is filtered, evaporated, and finally distilled with superheated steam.

The distilled glycerine solution is then decolorized with animal charcoal, and concentrated under reduced pressure. The purest form of glycerine is obtained in the preparation of fatty acids for candle-making by heating fats under pressure with water alone, or with the addition of a small quantity of lime, magnesia, or sulphuric acid. The liquor produced is distilled and finally concentrated in vacuo.

During the European War a new process for the manufacture of glycerine without the use of fats was carried out successfully in Germany. The process is based on the fact that when sugar is fermented by yeast, a large proportion of glycerine is formed if certain substances of an alkaline nature are present. Thus, if the fermentation is carried out with a quantity of sodium sulphite equal to that of the sugar used, about 30 per cent of glycerine is obtained, together with a quantity of alcohol and other products. After removing the yeast by filtration and the alcohol by distillation, the residual liquor is neutralized and finally distilled with superheated steam.

The yield of glycerine is said to be independent of the type of yeast, the nature of the sugar, and the temperature at which the fermentation is carried out. Raw sugar or even molasses may be used in the process.

Pure glycerine is a colourless viscid liquid with a sweet taste, having a specific gravity of 1·265. It absorbs moisture and when exposed to a low temperature crystallizes to a solid which melts at 20° C. It boils at 290° C. with partial decomposition, but may be distilled under reduced pressure without change. On rapid heating it loses water with the formation of acrolein vapours, which have a pungent odour.

Glycerine is used in enormous quantities for the manufacture of explosives such as dynamite and cordite, both of which contain nitroglycerine.

It is also largely used in dyeing, calico-printing, and in the manufacture of leather. Medicinally it is applied externally as a remedy for chapped hands, and internally as a demulcent, and in the form of a suppository as a means of relieving constipation. A mixture of glycerine and water is used as a filling for gas meters as it remains liquid at low temperatures.

GLY′COGEN, the principal carbohydrate in Fungi, where it takes the place of starch; also found in the Bacteria and in the liver of many animals.

GLY′COL, a generic name applied to all dihydric alcohols, that is, to alcohols which contain two hydroxyl groups in the molecule. These glycols are intermediate between ethyl alcohol and glycerine. The simplest representative is ethylene glycol, $C_2H_4(OH)_2$, usually known as glycol. It is liquid, inodorous, of a sweetish taste, and dissolves readily in water and alcohol.

GLYCYRRHIZA (gli-si-rī′za), a genus of leguminous plants, of which *G. glabra*, the liquorice plant, is the type.

GLYP′TODON (Gr. *glyptos*, engraved, and *odous*, tooth—so named from its fluted teeth), a gigantic fossil edentate animal, closely allied to the armadilloes, found in the Upper Tertiary and the Quaternary strata of South America. It was of the size of an ox, and was protected by a rigid coat of mail formed of polygonal osseous plates united by sutures.

GMÜND (gmünt), a town of Württemberg, on the Rems, 28 miles E.N.E. of Stuttgart, formerly an imperial free city. It has three churches of great antiquity, and an extensive museum of industrial products. The manufactures are chiefly woollen and cotton goods, jewellery, and trinkets. Pop. 20,406.

GMUNDEN (gmụn′den), an old town of Upper Austria, situated among magnificent scenery, on the Traun, where it issues from the northern extremity of the lake of that name, 35 miles south-west of Linz. Most of the inhabitants are employed in the neighbouring salt-mines. Gmunden is a favourite health-resort and summer residence. Pop. 7,190.

GNAPHA′LIUM, a genus of widely-spread composite plants having their foliage usually covered with a white woolly down, and their flower-heads of the 'everlasting' kind, some of them natives of Britain. *G. Leontopodium* (*Leontopodium alpīnum*) is the *edelweiss* of the Alps.

GNAT, the name applied to several species of insects belonging to Culex and related genera. The name is also given to the much smaller *midges* (q.v.). The common gnat (*C. pipiens*), type of the sub-family Culicidæ, is of wide geographical distribution, and is noted for its power of inflicting irritating wounds. The proboscis of the female is a tube containing four spiculæ of exquisite fineness, dentated or edged; these are modified mandibles and maxillæ. The males do not bite, and are further distinguished by their plume-like antennæ. These insects also feed on the juice of plants. The female deposits her eggs on the surface of stagnant water in a long mass. After having remained in the larval state for about twenty days, they are transformed into chrysalids, in which all the limbs of the perfect insect are distinguishable through the diaphanous robe with which they are then shrouded. After remaining three or four days wrapped up in this manner,

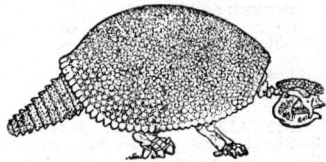

Glyptodon clavipes from the Pampa formation of Buenos Ayres

they become perfect insects. *Mosquitoes* (q.v.) are closely allied.

GNEISENAU (gnī′zn-ou), **August Wilhelm Anton, Count Neithardt von**, Prussian general, born 1760, died 1831. He served with the German auxiliaries of England in America; and as chief of Blücher's staff chiefly directed the strategy of the Prussian army at Waterloo. He was made a field-marshal in 1825.

GNEISS (nīs), a species of rock, composed of quartz, felspar, and mica, with a foliated or banded structure. The layers are often crumpled. Gneiss passes on one side into granite, from which it differs in its foliated structure, and on the other into mica-schist. It contains no fossil remains. Porphyritic gneiss presents large distinct crystals of felspar round which the foliated layers have flowed. Some gneisses have resulted from the crushing of crystalline rocks and the flow of the mass under pressure; others from flow in igneous masses; others from the intrusion of granite, in parallel sheets, along the foliation-planes of schists. Gneiss is the principal rock of very extensive districts; it predominates in Norway, and all the north of Europe. It abounds in the Southern Alps and the Pyrenees, and forms extensive areas in Central and Southern Africa. In Canada and the Northern United States gneiss is common, especially in the 'Laurentian Plateau' and the region of the Great Lakes.

GNEIST (gnīst), **Heinrich Rudolf Hermann Friedrich**, German jurist, born at Berlin 1816, died in 1895. He studied at the university of his native town, in which, in 1844, he became professor-extraordinary, and in 1858 ordinary professor. He took part in politics as a member of the Prussian House of Deputies, and of the Diet of the German Empire, ranging himself on the Liberal side.

He wrote extensively on law and constitutional history, and had a specially thorough knowledge of English constitutional history, his works on the *English Constitution* and the *English Parliament* having been translated and published in England in 1886.

GNESEN (gnā'zn), a town of Poland, formerly in Prussia, province of Posen, 45 miles south-west of Bromberg. It is an ancient place; is the see of an archbishop, and has a cathedral, in which the Kings of Poland used to be crowned. Pop. 26,000.

GNETALES, a small and peculiar family of Gymnosperms, approaching the Angiosperms in certain features. Genera: Ephedra, Gnetum, Welwitschia (q.v.).

GNETUM, the type-genus of Gnetales comprising tropical climbing or erect shrubs or small trees, with broad leathery, net-veined leaves. The fleshy 'fruits' of *G. Gnemon* and other species are edible.

GNOME (nōm; Gr. *gnōmē*), a short, pithy saying, often expressed in figurative language, containing a reflection, a practical observation, or a moral maxim. Among the Greeks Theognis, Phocylides, and others are called the *Gnomic poets*, from their sententious manner of writing.

GNOME (nōm), in the cabalistic and mediæval mythology, the name given to the spirits which dwell in the interior of the earth, where they watch over mines, quarries, and hidden treasures. They assume a variety of forms, but are generally grotesque dwarfs, ugliness being their appropriate quality. The term *gnome* has often been used as an equivalent of *fairy* or *elf*.

GNOMON (nō'mon), the style of a dial, or a structure erected perpendicularly to the horizon, for the purpose of determining the positions of heavenly bodies, particularly of the sun, by means of the direction and length of the shadow it casts. The gnomon often takes the form of a pillar, column, or pyramid erected upon level ground. It was much used by the ancient astronomers, and gnomons of great height, with meridian lines attached to them, are still common in France and Italy.

GNOSTICISM, a general term applied to the theories of certain early schools of speculators, which combined the fantastic notions of the Oriental systems of religion with the ideas of the Greek philosophers and the doctrines of Christianity. They nearly all agreed on the points that God is incomprehensible; that matter is eternal and antagonistic to God; that creation is the work of the *Demiurge*, an emanation from the Supreme Deity, subordinate or opposed to God; and that the human nature of Christ was a mere deceptive appearance. Gnosticism is the result of a fusion of diverse beliefs, and it covers a wide variety of religious thinking.

Certain forms of Gnosticism are mere adaptations of the Persian dualism to the solution of the problem of good and evil; while the pantheism of India seems to have been a pervading influence in others. Simon the magician (Simon Magus) of whom Luke speaks in the *Acts of the Apostles*, is generally looked on as the first of the Gnostics.

The Dogmas of the earliest Gnostics may be reduced to the following heads: God, the highest intelligence, dwells at an infinite distance from this world, in the Abyss, removed from all connection with every work of temporal creation. He is the source of all good; matter, the crude, chaotic mass of which all things were made, is, like God, eternal, and is the source of all evil.

From these two principles, before time commenced, emanated beings called *æons*, which are described as divine spirits, inhabiting the Plerōma, or plenitude of light, which surrounds the Abyss. The world and the human race were created out of matter by one æon, the Demiurge, or, according to the later systems of the Gnostics, by several æons and angels. The æons made the bodies and the sensual soul of man of this matter; hence the origin of evil in man. God gave man the rational soul; hence the constant struggle of reason with sense.

What are called gods by men (for instance, Jehovah, the God of the Jews) are merely such æons or creators, under whose dominion man became more and more wicked and miserable. To destroy the power of these creators, and to free man from the power of matter, God sent the most exalted of all æons, to which character Simon first made pretensions.

The Nicolaitans mentioned in the *Revelation of St. John*, so called from

Nicolas, a deacon of the Church at Jerusalem, were one of the earliest sects, and are described as forerunners of the Cerinthians. Cerinthus, a Jew, of whom John the Evangelist seems to have had some knowledge, combined such reveries with the doctrines of Christianity, and maintained that the most elevated æon sent by God for the salvation of man was Christ, who had descended upon Jesus, a Jew, in the form of a dove, and through him revealed the doctrines of Christianity, but before the crucifixion of Jesus separated from him, and at the resurrection of the dead will again be united with him, and lay the foundation of a kingdom of the most perfect earthly felicity, to continue 1,000 years.

Carpocrates and the sect of the Ophites (beginning of the second century), to whom the term Gnostic was first applied, saw in the Serpent a wise and good being, and carried to its extreme form the inversion of the Biblical story.

Syrian Gnostics. The later Gnostics have been divided into three schools. The first was the Syrian, founded by Menander, a pupil of Simon. This school emphasizes the conflict between Good and Evil—the Supreme Deity on the one hand, and the Demiurge and his angels or æons on the other.

Alexandrian Gnostics. The second was the school of Alexandria, represented by Basilides and Valentinus; the system of the latter being the most complete and ingenious of all. In that light or plenitude, which all the Gnostics speak of as surrounding the residence of the Supreme God, he has placed fifteen male and as many female æons.

The Supreme God, the Unbegotten, the Original Father, whom he also calls the *Deep* (Bathos), is the first of these æons; Thinking Silence was his wife, and Intelligence, a male, and Truth, a female, were their children. These produced The Word and Life, the latter a female, who gave birth to mankind and society. These eight constituted the first class of the thirty æons. The second class, of five couples, at the end of which stood the Only Begotten, and the third, of six couples, at the head of which stood the Comforter, were, in a similar manner, descended from Mankind and Society, and consisted, like the first, of personified ideas.

The officers of this heavenly state are four male æons—Horus, who guards the boundaries of the region of light; Christ and the Holy Ghost, who instruct the other æons in their duties; and Jesus, whom all the æons of the kingdom of light begat in common, and endowed with their gifts. Man

and the world were formed by a demiurge out of matter which was partly material, partly spiritual, partly soul-like. Christ, the Saviour of men, when he appeared on earth had a visible body made of the spiritual and the soul-like substance only. At his baptism the æon Jesus united itself with him, and instructed mankind.

Gnostics of Asia Minor. A third school of Gnosticism, whose centre was Asia Minor, was represented by Marcion of Pontus, the son of a Christian bishop, who flourished about the middle of the second century. Marcion assigned to Christianity, as the one absolutely independent religion, a complete isolation from the Old Testament revelation, the author of which was, in his opinion, merely a just but not a good thing. The true God begat many spirits, among which were the creator of the world, the righteous God, and the lawgiver of the Jews. The last, through the prophets, promised Christ; but Jesus, who actually appeared, and is the true Redeemer, was the Son of the truly good God, and not the Jewish Messiah.

Later Sects. Towards the end of the second century Tatian, a Syrian Christian, adopted Gnostic doctrines, and founded a sect. Bardesanes, a Syrian, and Hermogenes, an African, who, in the reign of the Emperor Commodus, apostatized from Christianity, and established sects, bordered, in their hypotheses concerning the origin of good and evil, upon Gnosticism. There have been no Gnostic sects since the fifth century; but many of the principles of their system of emanations reappear in later philosophical systems, drawn from the same sources as theirs.

BIBLIOGRAPHY: C. W. King, *The Gnostics and their Remains*; H. L. Mansel, *The Gnostic Heresies of the First and Second Centuries*; G. R. S. Mead, *Fragments of a Faith Forgotten*; F. Swiney, *Esoteric Teachings of the Gnostics*; E. de Faye, *Introduction à l'étude du gnosticisme*; J. Watson, *The Philosophical Basis of Religion*.

GNU, the *Wildebeeste* ('wild beast') of the colonists, the name given to three species of South African antelope (*Connochætes gnu, C. taurinus*, and *C. albogulatus*). The first, known as the common or white-tailed gnu, is now rarely found south of the Vaal; its form partakes of that of the antelope, ox, or horse. Both sexes have horns projecting slightly outwards and downwards, then forming an abrupt upward bend. They have bristly black hair about the face and muzzle, a white stiff mane, and horse-like tail. They attain a length of about 9 feet, and stand about 4 feet high at the shoulder.

They live in herds; are said to be

fierce when attacked, but when taken young have been found to be capable of domestication. The blue or brindled gnu (*C. taurinus*) is larger than the common gnu, has black stripes on the neck and shoulders, and a black tail.

Brindled Gnu

Gnus wheel in a circle once or twice before setting off when alarmed.

GOA, a city in India, on the Malabar coast, capital of the Portuguese colony of the same name. The name is applied to two distinct places, namely, Old Goa and New Goa or Pangin. The former was once the chief emporium of commerce between the East and West, and had a population of 260,000, but it is now nearly deserted, though some pains are taken to keep the ancient churches and convents in repair. Pop. 2,302.

New Goa or Pangin was chosen as the residence of the Portuguese viceroy in 1759; and in 1843 it was made the capital of Portuguese India. It is situated on the left bank of the Mandavi, about 3 miles from its mouth, contains many fine public buildings, a cathedral, and a viceregal palace. The trade of Goa, at one time the most extensive of any place in India, is now inconsiderable. Pop. 9,325.

The colony around Goa belonging to the Portuguese has an area of 1,460 sq. miles. It is well watered and fertile. About two-thirds of the total population numbering (1931), 569,187, are the descendants of Hindus converted to Christianity on the subjugation of the country by the Portuguese.

GOALPA'RA, a district of British India, in Assam; area, 3,897 sq. miles; pop. 462,000. It lies on both sides of the Brahmaputra, and is exposed to river floods. Rice is the staple crop; and brass and iron utensils, and gold and silver ornaments of an artistic character are manufactured. The town of Goalpara is the chief centre of trade. Pop. 5,500.

GOA POWDER, a powder used in the treatment of certain skin diseases, obtained from a leguminous tree of South America, the *Andira Araróba*, and called also Araroba Powder. *See* ANDIRA.

GOAT, a well-known horned ruminant quadruped of the genus Capra. The horns are hollow, erect, turned backward, annular on the surface, and scabrous. The male is generally bearded under the chin. Goats are nearly of the size of sheep, but stronger, less timid, and more agile. They frequent rocks and mountains, and subsist on scanty coarse food. Their milk is sweet, nourishing, and medicinal, and their flesh furnishes food.

There is a large number of varieties of goats, and it is not certainly known from which the domestic goat is descended, though opinion favours the *C. ægagrus*, or wild goat of Western Asia. Goats are generally subdivided into ibexes and goats proper.

They are found in all parts of the world, and many varieties are valued for their hair or wool. The skin is prepared for a variety of purposes, and yields the leather well known under the name of *morocco*. The Kashmir goat, as its name indicates, is a native of Kashmir; it is smaller than the common domestic goat, and has long, silky, fine hair. The Angora goat is also furnished with soft silky hair of a silver-white colour, hanging down in curling locks 8 or 9 inches long. Its horns are in a spiral form,

Angora Goat *(Capra hircus angorensis)*

and extend laterally. The Rocky Mountain goat is the *Haplocĕrus montānus*, or big-horn (q.v.).—BIBLIOGRAPHY: R. Lydekker, *Wild Oxen, Sheep, and Goats*; H. S. H. Pegler, *The Book of the Goat*.

GOATHLAND, village of Yorkshire (N.R.). It is 8 miles from Whitby, on the L.N.E. Rly. The place has a hydro, and a colony for disabled officers was founded here after the Great War. Near is Goathland Moor, on which are some waterfalls. Pop. 712.

GOAT ISLAND, a small island of 70 acres, which divides the current of the Niagara River at the Falls. It is connected with the American shore by a bridge.

GOAT-MOTH, a large British moth (*Cossus ligniperda*). The larvæ, which are about 3 inches in length, hollow out galleries in the wood of trees, which they first soften by a strong-smelling juice which they secrete. With the sawdust made in the operation they form cocoons, in which the chrysalids are developed. The larval condition lasts for three years. The fully-developed insect is ash-coloured, with numerous small black lines on the first pair of wings.

GOAT'S-BEARD, the general name of plants of the genus Trago-pōgon, ord. Compositæ, herbaceous perennials, chiefly natives of Europe. The fruits have feathery appendages; hence the name. The yellow goat's-beard (*T. pratensis*), greater goat's-beard (*T. major*), and purple goat's-beard (*T. porrifolius*) are found in Britain. The last species is commonly cultivated for its root as a culinary vegetable, under the title of *salsify*.

GOAT'S-RUE (*Galēga officinālis*), a leguminous plant indigenous to the south of Europe. It is used as forage, and is supposed to increase the milk of cows that feed upon it. It was formerly in repute as a cordial for fevers and convulsions.

GOAT'S-THORN, a name given to two hardy evergreen plants of the genus Astragălus, *A. Tragacantha* (great goat's-thorn), and *A. Poterium* (small goat's-thorn). The former, long cultivated in Great Britain, is a native of the south of Europe, the latter of the Levant.

GOATSUCKER, a name common to the birds of the genus Caprimulgus, also to all belonging to the same family —the Caprimulgidæ, given originally from the erroneous opinion that they suck goats. The European goatsucker or fern-owl (*C. europæus*) is one of our summer visitors, and ranges into Asia and Africa. It feeds upon nocturnal insects, as moths, gnats, beetles, &c., which it catches on the wing, flying with its mouth open.

Its mouth is comparatively large, and lined on the inside with a glutinous substance to prevent the escape of those insects which fly into it. As in all birds which catch flies when on the wing, the gape is surrounded by stiff bristles. When perched, it usually sits lengthwise on a bare twig, with its head lower than its tail, and in this attitude utters a jarring note, whence one of its common names—*nightjar* or *night-churr*. It is about 10 inches long, and has a light, soft plumage, minutely mottled with grey and brown, which renders it very inconspicuous when perching on a branch. The American chuckwill's widow, whip-poor-will, and night-hawk belong to the same family.

GOBELINS (gob-laŋ) **MANUFACTORY,** a tapestry manufactory at Paris, established by Colbert in 1667, on the site of a previously existing manufactory which had been set up by Jehan Gobelin, a celebrated dyer in the reign of Francis I. Colbert collected into it the ablest workmen in the divers arts and manufactures connected with house decoration and upholstery, and employed the artists Lebrun and Vouet as designers.

The Gobelins, closed during the Revolution, has continued since the

Goatsucker (*Caprimulgus europœus*)

restoration of the Bourbons to be the first manufactory of the kind in the world. Many celebrated paintings of the old Italian, French, and Spanish schools have, in the most ingenious manner, been transferred to tapestry. —Cf. J. J. Guiffrey, *Histoire de la tapisserie en France.*

GOBI, DESERT OF, the *Shamo* or 'sand-sea' of the Chinese, an immense tract of desert country, occupying the central part of the high tableland of Eastern Asia, and extending over a large portion of the Chinese territory of Mongolia. Its length is probably about 1,500 miles; mean breadth, between 350 and 400 miles; area, about 300,000 sq. miles. Its general elevation is over 4,000 feet above sea-level. The East Gobi is occupied by different tribes of the Mongolian race, who have numerous herds of camels, horses, and sheep. In the West Gobi are some nomadic tribes of the Tartar race. This tract is supposed at one time to have been a great inland sea.

GOBY, the general name of a family of spiny-finned fishes (Gobiidæ) characterized as follows: Two dorsal fins nearly united into one, the anterior fin having flexible rays, not spinous, as is usual in the group; ventral fins thoracic, and united more or less by their bases; body scaly, the head unarmed. Like the blennies they can live for some time out of water.

The family is very numerous, about 600 species being known, but does not include any important food-fishes. Several species of the type-genus Gobius are common on the British coast. The male constructs a sort of nest and jealously guards the developing eggs.

GOD'ALMING, a municipal borough of England, in Surrey, 4 miles s.s.w. of Guildford, on the River Wey, which is navigable from this point, in a most picturesque district. There are tanneries, paper-mills, &c. On an elevated plateau to the north stands the Charterhouse School, removed here from London in 1872. Pop. (1931), 10,400.

GODA'VARI, a large river of Central India, which rises about 50 miles from the shore of the Indian Ocean, flows across the Deccan from the Western to the Eastern Ghâts in a general south-easterly direction, and being joined by several affluents, falls by three principal mouths into the Bay of Bengal, after a course of 900 miles. Before the river divides there are three great obstacles to navigation, caused by three rocky barriers. The Godavari is one of the twelve sacred rivers of India, its rivals being the Ganges and the Narbadā. Bathing in its waters washes away all sins.—**Godavari** is also the name of a British district of the Madras Presidency; area, 5,634 sq. miles; pop. 1,500,000. Coringa and Coconada are its chief ports.

GODERICH, a port in Ontario, Canada, on Lake Huron, 55 miles N.N.W. of London; with manufactures of iron-castings and machinery, saltrefineries, fisheries, and large shipping trade. Pop. 4,491.

GODESBERG (go'des-ber*h*), a village and health-resort in the Rhineland, Germany, in a magnificent position on the left bank of the Rhine, 4 miles south-east of Bonn, nearly opposite 'the castled crag of Drachenfels.' It has its own ruined castle, dating from 1213, and has every year thousands of visitors, who go there to take the waters. Pop. 20,130.

GODETIA, a genus of Onagraceæ, natives of Western America. Several hardy species are grown for their showy flowers.

GODFREY, Sir Edmund Berry (Sir Edmundbury), the magistrate who received the depositions of Titus Oates with regard to the alleged Popish Plot, 28th Sept., 1678. He was soon after found dead, pierced with his own sword, though evidently not by his own hand. His death was imputed to the resentment of the Papists, and the excitement aroused was the actual cause of the Popish Plot agitation.—Cf. J. Pollock, *The Popish Plot.*

GODFREY OF BOUILLON, leader of the first Crusade, son of Eustace II, Count of Boulogne, born near Nivelles 1061, died in Jerusalem 1100. He distinguished himself while fighting for the Emperor Henry IV in Germany and Italy, and was made Duke of Bouillon. In order to expiate his sin of fighting against the Pope, he took the cross for the Holy Land in 1095, and led 80,000 men to the East by way of Constantinople.

On the 1st of May, 1097, they crossed the Bosporus, and began their march on Nice (Nicæa), which they took in June. In July the way to Syria was opened by the victory of Dorylæum (Eski Shehr), in Phrygia, and before the end of 1097 the Crusaders encamped before Antioch.

The town of Antioch fell into their hands in 1098, and in the following year Godfrey took Jerusalem itself, after a five weeks' siege. The leaders of the army elected him king of the city and the territory; but Godfrey would not wear a crown in the place where Christ was crowned with thorns; and contented himself with the title of *duke* and *guardian of the holy sepulchre.*

The defeat of the Egyptians at Ascalon placed him in possession of all the Holy Land, excepting two or three places. Godfrey now turned his attention to the organization of his newly-established Government, and promulgated a code of feudal laws called the *Assize of Jerusalem.* Godfrey was a favourite subject of mediæval poetry, and is the central figure of Tasso's *Jerusalem Delivered.*—Cf. Hagenmeyer, *Gesta Francorum.*

GODI'VA, the wife of Leofric, Earl of Mercia and Lord of Coventry in the reign of Edward the Confessor, heroine of a celebrated tradition. In 1040 Godiva appealed to her husband to relieve the inhabitants of Coventry of certain exactions imposed on them. Leofric, however, only laughed at her, and when she persisted in her entreaties at last said to her, half jocularly, that he would grant her request if she would ride naked through the town of Coventry.

Godiva took her husband at his word, proclaimed that on a certain day no one should leave his house before noon, that all windows and other apertures in the houses should be closed, and that no one should even look out until noon was past. She then mounted naked on her palfrey, rode through the town, and returned; and Leofric, in fulfilment of his promise, freed the inhabitants from the burdens he had imposed on them.

Only one person, 'Peeping Tom,' the story says, attempted to look out, and he was immediately struck blind. A yearly pageant, in which a young woman enacted the part of Godiva, was long kept up at Coventry, and still occasionally takes place. Tennyson's poem on *Godiva* is well known. —Cf. M. D. Harris, *Story of Coventry.*

GODLEY, Sir Alexander John. English soldier, born 4th Feb., 1867, and educated at Haileybury and Sandhurst, he entered the Royal Dublin Fusiliers and served in the South African War. In 1910, after experiences on the staff, he was sent to command the New Zealand defence force, and was there until 1914. During the Great War he commanded a division of Australians and New Zealanders in Egypt and Gallipoli, and was then in charge of an army corps on the Western Front. He was commander-in-chief of the British army on the Rhine, 1922–24. From 1924–28 he held the Southern command, and in 1929 he was made Governor of Gibraltar.

GODMANCHESTER, borough and market town of Huntingdonshire. It stands on the Ouse, just outside Huntingdon, 59 miles from London, by the L.N.E. Rly. There is a trade in agricultural produce. Pop. (1931) 1,991.

GODOL'PHIN, Sidney, Earl of Godolphin, English politician, was a native of Cornwall, date of birth unknown, probably 1645. Under Charles II, he was one of those who voted for the exclusion of the Duke of York from the throne in 1680. He nevertheless retained office under that monarch, as he did also under William III, with whom he had long been in correspondence. During the reign of Anne he was appointed Lord High Treasurer of England, and in this office did much to improve the public credit, and check corruption in the administration of the public funds.

In 1706 he was made Earl of Godolphin, and four years afterwards was obliged to retire from office. His death took place in 1712. He was a man of great business capacity, but his treasonable correspondence with James while he held an office of trust under William of Orange is a serious blot upon his character.—BIBLIOGRAPHY: Evelyn, *Diary*; H. Elliot, *Life of Sidney, Earl of Godolphin.*

GODOY, Manuel, Duke of El Alcudia, better known as the *Prince of the Peace*, was born at Badajoz 1767, died 1851. He entered the royal body-guard in 1787. His personal qualities soon made him a favourite at the Spanish court, and his promotion was rapid. In 1791 he became adjutant-general of the guards, in 1792 lieutenant-general, Duke of El Alcudia, grandee of Spain of the first class, and Prime Minister; and in 1795, as a reward for the part he had taken in concluding peace with France, he was presented with a large and valuable landed estate, and made a knight of the Golden Fleece. It was on this occasion also that he was named by the king Prince of the Peace.

As he used his vast power in the promotion of French more than Spanish interests, he became extremely unpopular, and the hatred of the people became so great in 1808 that he had to take refuge in France. Having lost everything, he lived for a long time only on the bounty of his royal friends. In 1847 he was permitted to return to Spain and resume his titles. The larger portion of his domains, however, was irrecoverably lost, and he ended his days in obscurity and poverty.—Cf. E. d'Auvergne, *Godoy, the Queen's Favourite.*

GOD SAVE THE KING (or QUEEN), the burden and common appellation of a well-known English national song. Concerning the author and the composer opinions differ. It has been attributed to Dr. John Bull (1562–1628), chamber musician to James I; his ode, dating from the Gunpowder Plot, beginning "God save great James our King." But the composition we now possess would seem to have been, both words and melody, the work of Henry Carey (died 1743).

It appears to have been first published, together with the air, in *Harmonia Anglicana* (1742), and in the *Gentleman's Magazine* in 1745, when the landing of the young Stuart called forth expressions of loyalty from the adherents of the reigning family. After Dr. Arne, the composer of another national song (*Rule, Britannia!*), had brought it on the stage, it soon became very popular. Since that time the harmony of the song has undoubtedly been improved, but the rhythm is the same as it was originally.—Cf. W. H. Cummings, *God Save the King.*

GODTHAAB, the oldest settlement in, and the capital of South Greenland. Pop. 1,000.

GODWIN, Earl of Wessex, an English statesman, born about 990; died 1052. In 1018 he was created an earl by Canute, and married the king's niece Gytha. During the reign of Edward the Confessor, who married Godwin's daughter, a quarrel arose between Godwin and the king, occasioned by the partiality of Edward for Norman favourites, and Godwin was compelled to quit the kingdom. In 1052, however, he returned with an army, forced Edward to enter into negotiations with him, re-established himself triumphantly in his old supremacy, and caused the expulsion from the kingdom of most of the Norman intruders. He was the father of King Harold, who was afterwards killed at Hastings (1066).

GODWIN, Mary, also well known by her maiden name of Wollstonecraft, born in or near London in 1759, died 1797. Her early training was very defective, but, fitting herself for a teacher, she set up a school, in conjunction with her sisters, at Islington in 1783. In 1786 she published *Thoughts on the Education of Daughters.* This was followed by an answer to Burke's *Reflections on the French Revolution,* the *Vindication of the Rights of Woman,* and other works.

She had peculiar ideas on marriage, and lived for a time with an American called Imlay, to whom she bore a daughter. Imlay subsequently deserted her, and in 1796 she met William Godwin, who married her in 1797. She died soon after giving birth to a daughter, who became the wife of Shelley the poet. Among her other works are a *Moral and Historical View of the French Revolution,* and *Letters from Sweden, Norway, and Denmark.*—BIBLIOGRAPHY: *A Defense of the Character and Conduct of the late M. W. Godwin* (anonymous); E. R. Pennell, *Life of Mary Wollstonecraft;* *Love Letters of Mary Wollstonecraft to Gilbert Imlay,* with preface memoir by Roger Ingpen; G. R. S. Taylor, *Mary Wollstonecraft.*

GODWIN, William, English novelist and political writer, son of a Dissenting minister, was born 1756, died 1836. In 1778 he became the minister of a Dissenting congregation near London, and continued in that capacity for five years, after which he removed to London, where he set himself to gaining his livelihood by literary labours. In 1793 appeared his *Inquiry concerning Political Justice,* the liberal tone of which exposed him to some danger of a Government prosecution.

The next year appeared his novel of *Caleb Williams, or Things as they Are,* which rapidly and deservedly attained an immense popularity. His *Cursory Strictures on the Charge of Chief-Justice Eyre* (to the jury, in the trial for high treason of Holcroft, Horne Tooke, and others) contributed materially to the acquittal of his friends. In 1797 he published *The Inquirer,* a collection of essays on moral and literary subjects; and in April of the same year he married Mary Wollstonecraft (*see* preceding article). A memoir of his wife was published by Godwin in 1798, along with her posthumous literary works.

In 1799 he published a new novel, *St. Leon.* Among his subsequent works are: *Faulkner,* a tragedy, published in 1807; an *Essay on Sepulchres,* in 1808; *Mandeville,* a novel, in 1817; *A Treatise on Population,* in reply to Malthus, in 1820; *History of the Commonwealth of England,* 1824–8; *Cloudesley,* a novel, in 1830; *Thoughts on Man,* in 1831; and *Lives of the Necromancers,* in 1834. In the latter years of his life Godwin held a clerkship in the Record Office.—BIBLIOGRAPHY: De Quincey, *Literary Reminiscences*; Sir L. Stephen, *English Thought in the 18th Century*; C. K. Paul, *William Godwin: his Friends and Contemporaries*; H. N. Brailsford, *Shelley, Godwin, and their Circle.*

GODWIN-AUSTEN, MOUNT, a great Himalayan peak, 28,250 feet high, next to Mount Everest, the highest on the globe. It received its name in 1888 after Lieutenant-Colonel H. H. Godwin-Austen.

GODWIT, the common name of the members of a genus of birds (Limōsa), belonging to the family Charadriidæ (plovers). There are several species, of which two are migrant visitors to Britain but do not breed there, viz. the bar-tailed godwit (*L. lapponica*), and the black-tailed godwit (*L. belgica*). Godwits are long-legged birds with elongated slightly-upcurved beaks. The male helps to incubate the eggs.

GOES (*hŏs*), or **TERGOES,** a fortified town and port in Holland, in the province of Zeeland, on the Island of South Beveland, 16 miles west of Bergen-op-Zoom. It has a Gothic church and a city town hall, both dating back to the fifteenth century. It has a considerable commerce, but unimportant manufactures. Pop. 7,620.

GOETHALS, George Washington, American soldier and engineer. Born at Brooklyn, 29th June, 1858; in 1898 was chief engineer of the First Army Corps in the Spanish-American War. In 1907 he was put in charge of the construction of Panama Canal, and on its completion in 1914, became first governor of the canal zone. On the entry of the U.S.A. into the Great War, he held various posts. He died 21st Jan., 1928.

GOETHE (*geu'tè*), **Johann Wolfgang von,** the greatest figure in German literature, was born on 28th Aug., 1749, at Frankfort-on-the-Main, died at Weimar, 22nd March, 1832. His father, who was a Doctor of Laws and Imperial Councillor, was a well-to-do citizen and an admirer of the fine arts. The Seven Years' War broke out when Goethe was eight years old, and Count de Thorane, *lieutenant du roi* of the French army in Germany, was quartered in the house of his father. The count, being an amateur and liberal patron of art, encouraged the boy's incipient taste for pictures.

At the same time young Goethe learned the French language practically; and a French theatrical company, then performing at Frankfort, awakened his taste for dramatic performances. Drawing, music, natural science, the elements of jurisprudence, and the languages occupied him alternately. After the breaking off of a youthful love affair, which gave a name to the heroine of his great work *Faust* and some features to his *Wilhelm Meister*, he was sent to the University of Leipzig to prepare himself for the legal profession, but he did not follow any regular course of studies.

It was during this period that Goethe developed the habit, which endured throughout his life, of embodying in a poem, or in a poetical form, whatever occupied his mind intensely, and no one, perhaps, was ever more in need of such a resource, as his nature continually hurried him from one extreme to another. In 1768 he left Leipzig, and, after an illness of some length, he went in 1770 to the University of Strasbourg to pursue the study of law, according to the wish of his father.

At Strasbourg he became acquainted with Herder—a decisive circumstance in his life. Herder made him more acquainted with the Italian school of the fine arts, and inspired his mind with views of poetry more congenial to his character than any which he had hitherto conceived. While here he fell in love with Frederica Brion, daughter of the pastor of Sesenheim, but the affair, though it made a more abiding impression on him than some others, resulted in nothing.

Goethe's numerous love affairs form one of the most curious studies in biography. His attachments were all fugitive; the love passion was continuous, but the object was ever changing. In 1771 he took the degree of Doctor of Jurisprudence, and wrote a dissertation on a legal subject.

He then went to Wetzlar to practise law, where he found, in his own love for a betrothed lady, and in the fate of a young man named Jerusalem, the subjects for his work *The Sorrows of Werther*, which formed an epoch in German literature. The attention of the public had already been attracted to him, however, by his drama *Götz*

von Berlichingen (published 1773). *Werther* appeared in 1774.

Not long after the publication of *Werther*, Charles Augustus, the hereditary Duke of Saxe-Weimar, made the acquaintance of Goethe on a journey, and when in 1775 he took the government into his own hands, he invited Goethe to his court. Goethe accepted the invitation, and on the 7th of Nov., 1775, arrived at Weimar. Wieland was already there, having been the duke's tutor; Herder was added to the band in 1776; Schiller was afterwards one of its members for a few years; and other poets and critics and novelists were gathered round these chiefs. Goethe was the leading spirit of the group even during the last quarter of the eighteenth century, when these men and others were constructing and guiding the literature of all Germany; and his supremacy became yet more absolute afterwards, when for another generation he stood alone.

In 1776 he was made Privy Councillor of Legation, with a seat and vote in the Privy Council. In 1782 he was made President of the Chamber, and ennobled. In 1786 he made a journey to Italy, where he remained two years, visited Sicily, and remained a long time in Rome. This residence in Italy had the effect of still further developing his artistic powers. Here his *Iphigenia* was matured, *Egmont* finished, and *Tasso* projected. The first of these was published in 1787, the second in 1788, and the third in 1790.

In the same year as *Tasso* was published the earliest form of the first part of *Faust*, with the title *Dr. Faust, ein Trauerspiel* (Dr. Faust, a Tragedy), a poem in a dramatic form, which belongs rather to Goethe's whole life than to any particular period of it. At the time that Goethe was engaged in the production of these works of imagination he had been pursuing various other studies of a scientific nature with as ardent an interest as if these had belonged to his peculiar province.

The result of his studies in botany was a work published also in 1790 *Versuch die Metamorphose der Pflanzen zu Erklären*, in which he gives expression to the view that the whole plant, and its different parts, may all be regarded as variously modified leaves. In the following year (1791) he began to apply himself to optics, and in 1791–2 he published a work on this subject called *Beiträge zur Optik*. On the 1st May, 1791, he became director of the court theatre at Weimar. In 1792 he followed his prince during the campaign of the Prussians against the revolutionary party in France, and was present at the battle of Valmy on the 20th of Sept.

At the Weimar theatre he brought out some of the dramatic *chefs-d'œuvre* of Schiller, and there, too, his own dramatic works first appeared, *Götz von Berlichingen*, *Faust*, *Iphigenia in Tauris*, *Tasso*, *Clavigo*, *Stella*, and *Count Egmont*. Between 1794 and 1796 Goethe published *Wilhelm Meisters Lehrjahre*, a novel which has become well known to English readers through the translation of Carlyle, and which had as a continuation *Wilhelm Meisters Wanderjahre* (that is, his travels as a journeyman; 1821). His next work of importance was *Hermann und Dorothea* (1797), a narrative poem in hexameter verse, the characters of which are taken from humble life.

In 1806 Goethe married Christiane Vulpius, with whom he had lived since 1788, and of whom he always spoke with warmth and gratitude for the degree in which she had contributed to his domestic happiness. In 1808 he published another edition of *Faust* in a considerably altered form. In 1809 was published *Wahlverwandtschaften*, another novel, and in 1810 the *Farbenlehre*, a work in which he had the boldness to oppose the Newtonian theory, and to which Goethe himself attached great importance, although the theory therein promulgated has met with no acceptance among men of science.

During 1811 and 1814 appeared Goethe's autobiography, with the title *Aus meinem Leben: Dichtung und Wahrheit*; in 1819 the *Westöstlicher Divan*, a remarkable collection of Oriental songs and poems. Goethe's last work was the second part of *Faust*, which was completed on the evening before the last anniversary of his birthday which he lived to see. Goethe's works taken altogether cover a wide range of subjects.

His greatest production is his *Faust*, emphatically a philosophical dramatic poem, and the best of Goethe's productions in a department for which he seems to have been born. Much light is thrown on Goethe's life and character by the published correspondence with his contemporaries, Herder, Frau von Stein, Lavater, Jacobi, Merck, and Countess Stolberg; by Eckermann's *Conversations*; and especially by his own *Autobiography*, which he himself describes as 'poetry and truth,' and in which probably the truth is sometimes clouded by the poetry. George Henry Lewes's *Life of Goethe* is a standard work both in Germany and Britain.—BIBLIOGRAPHY: K. Goedeke, *Grundriss zur Geschichte der Deutschen Dichtung* (complete bibliography); G. H. Lewes, *Life of Goethe*; H. G. Atkins, *Johann Wolfgang Goethe*; Houston Stewart Chamberlain, *Goethe*; H. Düntzer, *Life of Goethe*; J. R. Seeley, *Goethe, reviewed after Sixty Years*; J. G. Robertson, *Goethe and the Twentieth Century*.

GOG AND MAGOG. Ezekiel predicts the destruction of Gog and Magog (chap. xxxviii and xxxix) by the Jews, and mention is also made of them in *Revelation* (chap. xx). Interpreters generally understand them to be symbolical expressions for the heathen nations of Asia. Magog is mentioned as the second son of Japheth in *Genesis* (chap. x, 2).

Gog and Magog are also the names given to two reputed giants of early British history, whose statues are erected in the Guildhall in London. These statues are supposed to have been originally made for carrying about in pageants. The present figures of Gog and Magog, which are 14 feet high, were erected in 1708.

GOGH, Vincent Van, Dutch painter. Born in Holland in 1853, he early showed artistic genius. First influenced by Millet, then by the Impressionist School, he later became, with Cézanne and Gauguin, one of the leaders of the Post-Impressionists. A victim of sunstroke, he painted many of his best pictures in an asylum at Arles. In 1890 he died by his own hand.

GOGOL, Nikolai Vassiljevitsh, Russian author, born in the province of Poltava 1809, died 1852. He went to St. Petersburg in 1829 and tried the stage, but, failing, found his true vocation in literature. His works are extremely popular in Russia for their graphic and humorous delineation of everyday life and manners, and more especially Russian country life. Among his most notable works are: *Evenings at the Farm* (1832); *Mirgorod* (1834), a collection of tales; *Dead Souls* (1842), a satirical novel, depicting the public abuses and barbarism of manners prevalent in the provinces; and *Revisor*, a comedy. His later years were tinged with religious mysticism, and he wrote some curious *Confessions*. Gogol is the father of Russian realistic literature. The latest complete edition of his works appeared in 1911, and contains a biography by Dimitry Mereshkovsky.—Cf. M. Baring, *Landmarks in Russian Literature*.

GOGRA, the chief river of Oudh, forming an important water-way for that quarter of India. It is a tributary of the Ganges; length, 570 miles.

GOITRE (goi'tèr), or **BRONCHOCELE** (bron'ko-sēl), known also in Great Britain as 'Derbyshire neck,' a disease endemic in Derbyshire, Switzerland, some parts of France and South America, and in many other parts of the world, chiefly in valleys and elevated plains in mountainous districts. It is a morbid enlargement of the thyroid gland, forming a soft and more or less mobile tumour or swelling, without any sign of inflammation, on the anterior part of the neck.

It sometimes grows to such a size as to hang down over the breast, and respiration and swallowing may be impeded by it, though often it causes little inconvenience. It is regarded as the result of a combination of causes, among which malarial influences probably concur with those of the drinking-water in developing the disease.

GÖKCHA, or GÖKTSCHA, a lake in Armenia, occupying a triangular cavity 540 sq. miles in extent, at an elevation of 6,400 feet above the sea. It receives the water of several streams without having any considerable outlet.

GOLBORNE, an urban district in Lancashire, 5½ miles south by east of Wigan, with cotton manufactures, and a colliery. Pop. (1931), 7,322.

GOLCAR, a manufacturing town in the West Riding of Yorkshire, 3 miles west by south of Huddersfield, on the River Colne. There is a mineral spa, and a brisk manufacture of woollen goods. Pop. (1931), 9,812.

GOLCONDA, a fortress and ruined city of India in Hyderabad, 7 miles west of Hyderabad. The fort is now used as the Nizam's treasury, and also as a State prison. In former times Golconda was a large and powerful kingdom of the Deccan, but was subdued by Aurangzib in 1687, and annexed to the dominions of the Delhi Empire. It used to be famous for diamonds.

GOLD is a precious metal of a bright yellow colour, and the most ductile and malleable of all the metals; symbol, Au (Lat. *aurum*); atomic weight, 197·2. It is one of the heaviest of the metals, and, not being liable to be injured by exposure to the air, is well fitted for coins and jewellery.

Properties. Its ductility and malleability are very remarkable. It may be beaten into leaves so exceedingly thin that 1 grain in weight will cover 56 square inches, such leaves having the thickness of only $\frac{1}{282000}$th part of an inch.

It is also extremely ductile; a single grain may be drawn into a wire 500 feet long, and an ounce of gold covering a silver wire is capable of being extended upwards of 1,000 miles. It may also be melted and remelted without loss by oxidation. It is soluble in nitro-muriatic acid or *aqua regia*, and in a solution of chlorine. Its specific gravity is 19·3, or it is about nineteen times as heavy as water. The fineness of gold is estimated in carats, pure gold being 24 carats fine. (*See* CARAT.)

Gold is seldom used for any purpose in a state of perfect purity on account of its softness, but is alloyed with some other metal to render it harder. Standard gold, or the alloy used for the gold coinage of Britain, consists of twenty-two parts of gold and two of copper (being thus 22 carats fine). Articles of jewellery are made of varying degrees of fineness up to 22 carats, i.e. twenty-two parts of gold to two of alloy, the legal standards being 9, 12, 18, and 22.

The alloy of gold and silver is found in the native state. It is of a paler yellow than pure gold, while the copper alloy has a colour bordering upon reddish yellow. Palladium, rhodium, and tellurium are also met with as alloys of gold.

Processes. Gold has been found in smaller or larger quantities in nearly all parts of the world. It is commonly found in reefs or veins with quartz, and in alluvial deposits. Among the latter may be ranked the deposits in river beds, from which the gold is obtained by dredging. When gold is in rock, quarrying, crushing, washing, and treatment with mercury are employed. The rock is crushed by machinery, and the crushed material is treated with mercury, which dissolves the gold, forming a liquid amalgam, after which the mercury is volatilized, and the gold left behind.

Two other processes are also in use, viz. the chlorination and the cyanide. In the former the gold is transformed into soluble gold chloride, and the metal is obtained from this solution by means of ferrous sulphate, charcoal, or sulphuretted hydrogen. This process is rapidly being displaced by the cyanide process (*see* CYANIDING).

The cyanide process is the most important method of treatment, is suitable for ores in a fine state of division, and consists in dissolving the metal in dilute potassium cyanide solutions, from which it can be obtained by precipitation on zinc. The gold obtained by these methods always contains silver, from which it is separated by the process known as 'parting,' which consists in the solution of the silver in sulphuric or nitric acid, and washing and melting down the gold.

Electrolysis is also used for the parting of gold and silver, and when only small quantities of silver are present, chlorine is passed through the molten metal, thus forming silver chloride, which rises to the top and covers the pure gold left behind.

Washing. In alluvial (or *placer*) deposits it is extracted by washing, in the form of dust, grains, laminæ, or nuggets. After the gravel has been turned over and any nuggets have been taken out, the remainder is washed to recover the finer particles of gold. In washing in the pan— 'panning out'—a quantity of the 'dirt,' free from stones, is put into a shallow dish with a slight depression in the middle It is then mixed with water, and the dish held with one side lower than the other, while by a gentle motion the sand and other lighter bodies are washed over the edge of the pan, and the heavy matters containing the gold remain at the bottom.

The 'cradle' consists of a short box or trough 6 or 7 feet long, mounted on a kind of rockers, and slightly inclined to allow the mud to run off. A box, with a bottom of iron plate perforated with holes, is placed over the higher end of the trough. The 'pay dirt' (i.e. gravel or sand containing a sufficient amount of gold to be profitably worked) is thrown into this box, and water is run or poured upon it. The finer portion is thus carried through the holes, and directed by an inclined plate into the trough. The cradle is rocked from side to side, the light matters are carried away by the water, and the particles of gold and other heavy matters lodge behind the 'riffles,' or transverse bars of wood, with which the bottom of the trough is fitted, and are afterwards collected.

Sluicing. Where practicable, the method known as 'sluicing' is often adopted for treating alluvial deposits. The 'sluices' consist of troughs called 'flumes,' in sections about 12 feet long, inclined on trestles. The bottom of the sluice-box is crossed by 'riffle' bars of wood or iron. The smallest of the sluices consists of two such sections. Into the upper one the gravel is thrown, and the lower end is closed by an iron grid to keep back the pebbles and large stones, while the sand, &c, pass through to the lower trough. In this it deposits its gold and heavy matters behind the riffle bars.

In the longer sluices (say 250 feet long) the lower end of the upper section is not blocked, but near it the bottom consists of an iron grating— the 'grizzly.' The large stones are washed forward over the grating, but the sand and fine particles carried by the water fall through it on to the second section of the sluice. In some cases the fine sand, after passing through the first section of the sluice, falls on inclined tables covered with blankets, rough cloth, or hides with the hairy side up, over which it flows in a thin stream. These 'blanket-strakes' serve to arrest and recover the fine gold. In other cases amalga-

mated copper plates are employed for the same purpose.

Hydraulic Mining. Where water is plentiful, 'hydraulic mining' is the cheapest mode of working. Under this system 'deep leads' (which are alluvial deposits covered over with more recent matter in ancient river beds) and other alluvial deposits are worked by washing down the gravel by means of a powerful jet of water, a head of 200 to 250 feet being sometimes employed. In quartz mining—and the case is similar with the hard, solid 'banket' formation of South Africa that contains the gold—the ore to be crushed is first passed through a 'stone-breaker' or 'ore-crusher,' and is further crushed by the 'stamps' or other grinding-mill. The ordinary stamp-battery consists, in its lower part, of a cast-iron 'mortar-box,' fitted on one or both sides with a fine screen.

At the bottom of this box is a row of iron blocks called 'dies,' upon which the stamps, or heavy cylindrical cast-iron blocks, are made to rise and fall by means of cams, being thus kept pounding away at the ore in the mortar-box. A stream of water is admitted, and carries the crushed material through the screens. Mercury is fed into the mortar-boxes in small quantities, and much of the gold is retained there on amalgamated copper plates. Slightly inclined amalgamated plates, arranged in steps, are placed in front of the battery, and over these the crushed ore pulp passes slowly, the gold being retained by the amalgamated surfaces.

The remaining product, or 'tailings,' which may still contain some gold, is then treated either by 'concentration' and the concentrates smelted, cyanided, or chlorinated, whilst the remaining tailings are submitted to treatment by the cyanide process, or the whole is treated by the cyanide process. For the concentrating process 'vanners' are generally employed.

These consist of a slightly-sloping table, formed of an endless travelling belt of india-rubber, which is stretched over rollers and so mounted as to be capable of violent agitation (the vibrations numbering 200 a minute) while moving slowly in an upward direction. The pulp is led on at the higher end, and the flow of water carries the light matters down the slope, the separation being greatly assisted by the shaking movement. The heavy matters only are carried forward by the belt over the higher end, and pass into a box below, being then known as 'concentrates.'

Gold-Milling. In modern practice of gold-milling, that is, the extraction of the metal from vein material or rocks, there is a tendency to reduce the importance of extraction by means of mercury and to depend mostly on the dissolving power of cyanide solutions. In order to get efficient extraction, the material to be treated is crushed to an extremely fine state of division known as slime.

The most convenient method of carrying this out is by rock-breakers, then stamps, followed by treatment in tube-mills, which consist of horizontal revolving steel cylinders, about 5 feet in diameter and 14 to 22 feet long, charged with flint pebbles, the ore pulp being fed at one end, and the slime being discharged at the other end.

The tube-mill can do satisfactory work only with material that has been crushed medium fine, so that it is usual to take the material from the stamp-batteries, which may or may not have passed over amalgamated copper plates, to a classifier. This classifier is so arranged that the very fine material which does not need further crushing overflows at the top and the sandy material is separated and passed to the tube-mill for sliming.

The capacity and nature of product of the tube-mill are governed by the nature of the ore, the degree of preliminary crushing, the rate of feeding, the weight of pebbles, the revolutions per minute of the mill, and the amount of water used. The slimed material from the tube-mills is frequently passed over amalgamated copper plates for the purpose of collecting any free gold which may be present. The final slime is passed to thickeners for the removal of some of the water, and then to agitation-tanks, where cyanide of soda or potash is added and the whole agitated, either by mechanical means or by blowing air through a pipe situated in a central tube of larger diameter placed in the pulp.

In this latter method the specific gravity of the central column of pulp is decreased and circulation of the pulp set up. After sufficient agitation in the tanks, the pulp is removed and submitted to filtration, either in pressure or vacuum filters, the gold-bearing cyanide solution being removed for precipitation of the gold, either by passing it over zinc shavings or by agitation with zinc dust. The precipitate of gold thus obtained is refined by treatment with acid for the removal of the remainder of the zinc, and the resulting gold is melted down.

Output of Gold. Gold was probably the first metal to attract the attention of man, its presence in the native condition, its brilliant lustre, and its malleability rendering it an object of value from the earliest times. Although widely distributed in nature, it is only found in a few localities in sufficient quantities to repay the extraction costs. The chief producers of gold in the order of their importance are: Africa, United States, Australasia, Mexico, Russia, Canada, India, China, and South America. The total value of the gold produce of the world from 1493 to 1850 is estimated at £662,900,000.

An immense increase in the world's production was caused by the discovery of gold in California in 1848 and Australia in 1851, the world production between 1851 and 1885 being estimated at £890,500,000. Since 1884 the gold-fields of South Africa have become of increasing importance, and with the exception of war years have shown a constant increase in yield year by year. The Transvaal has been mainly responsible for this increase, and since 1902 has been the greatest gold-yielding country in the world.

Rhodesia and West Africa also yield much gold. In the United States the chief gold-producing states are Colorado, California, Nevada, and Alaska, although other states also yield gold. Considerable gold-fields exist in the western portion of the North American continent, reaching from Mexico up to British Columbia and the Klondyke district. In Russia gold is abundant in the Ural Mountains; in India the most important locality is that of the Kolar gold-fields in Mysore. In China gold has long been mined in the province of Shantung. In the United Kingdom gold has been found in Cornwall, Sutherlandshire, Perthshire, Wicklow, and has been worked to some extent in Wales. The world's output of gold remains fairly steady at about £90,000,000 a year. Of this the Transvaal mines produce about half. In 1930 the production of these mines reached the record figure of £45,558,980; in 1932 the output was 11,553,564 ozs. Other producing countries are the United States, Canada, which is rapidly increasing its output, Russia, Mexico, Australia, Rhodesia and India.—BIBLIOGRAPHY: G. Lock, *Gold: its Occurrence and Extraction*; T. K. Rose, *Metallurgy of Gold*; J. H. Curle, *Gold Mines of the World*; T. C. Earl, *Gold Dredging*; J. Park, *The Cyanide Process of Gold Extraction*; C. B. Horwood, *Gold Deposits in the Rand.*

The Gold Standard was devised to simplify trade between countries which all used a different currency. Its effect was to keep currencies, which had gold as a basis, virtually fixed in value in relation to each other and to prevent violent movements in the rates at which the currency of one country could be exchanged into that of another country. An English importer who bought goods in France,

Germany or the United States would know at any given time approximately how many francs, marks or dollars he would have to find to pay for the goods purchased from those countries and could plan his trade ahead in the knowledge that exchange would not vary to a great extent one way or the other. On occasions trade between two countries favoured one more than the other because one was selling more goods than the other. This caused a rise in the value of the currency of the exporting country which had a 'favourable trade balance.' Its currency became more expensive and the exchange rate moved to what was termed 'gold point.' It was then cheaper for the importing country to pay in gold for the goods purchased than to buy exchange or the currency of the exporting country.

Internally the amount of currency in a gold standard country is governed by the amount of gold held in its central bank.

GOLD-BEATING, the art or process of producing the extremely thin leaves of gold used in gilding. The gold is cast into ingots weighing about 2 ounces each, and measuring about ¾ of an inch broad. These ingots are passed between steel rollers till they form long ribbons of such thinness that a square inch will weigh 6½ grains. Each one of these is now cut into 150 pieces, each of which is heaten on an anvil till it is about an inch square.

These 150 plates are interlaid with pieces of fine vellum about 4 inches square, and beaten till the gold is extended nearly to the size of the vellum leaves. Each leaf is then divided into four, interlaid with goldbeater's skin, and beaten out to the dimensions of the skin. Another similar division and beating finishes the operation, after which the leaves are placed in paper books ready for use.

GOLD COAST, a British Crown Colony in West Africa, lying between the French Ivory Coast and French Togo, and including Ashanti (annexed 1901), the protected Northern Territories and part of Togoland (13,040 sq. miles mandated by the League of Nations); area, 78,802 sq. miles; pop. (1931), 3,121,214. The Gold Coast was settled first by Portugal and then by Dutch and English, but finally became British in 1871. The whole country, at one time a perfect deathtrap, has now no terrors for the white man if ordinary health precautions are observed.

The Gold Coast is the greatest cocoa-producing country in the world, exporting 244,097 tons in 1931. Other exports are manganese, timber, kola,

and gold. The value of exports for 1931 was £11,287,388. There are 500 (1932) miles of railway track, and 6,264 miles of motorable roads. Among the educational institutions is the Prince of Wales College at Achimota, opened in 1928.

With the pushing of the railways beyond Kumasi to the Northern Territory, and the extension of the road system, the enormous agricultural, forest, and mining resources of the country will become of great commercial importance. The chief towns and harbours are Accra (the capital), Cape Coast Castle, Keta, Koforidva, Winneba, Saltpond, Axim, Ada, and Sekondi. At Takoradi, near Sekondi, a deep-water port for large vessels has been constructed. *See* ASHANTI, &c. —Cf. J. Maxwell, *The Gold Coast Handbook.*

GOLDEN AGE, that early mythological period in the history of almost all races, fabled to have been one of primeval innocence and enjoyment, in which the earth was common property, and brought forth spontaneously all things necessary for happy existence, in which men did not engage in warfare, .while beasts of prey lived at peace with other animals. The Romans referred this time to the reign of Saturn.

The term 'golden age' is often applied to the finest period of Latin literature (Cicero to Ovid) in contradistinction to the 'silver age' (from the death of Augustus to that of Hadrian).

GOLDEN-BEETLE, the popular name of several beetles of the genus Chrysoméla. There are some British species, but most are tropical. Their most obvious characteristic is the great brilliancy of their colour. There are none of large size.

GOLDEN BULL (*bulla aurea*), an important document in the history of Germany issued by the Emperor Charles IV in 1356. Its immediate object was to regulate for all time coming the mode of procedure in the election and coronation of the emperors. Another document, also called Golden Bull, was issued in 1222 by Andrew II, King of Hungary, its object being to transform the government from an absolute to an aristocratic monarchy.

GOLDEN-CRESTED WREN, GOLD-CREST, GOLDEN-CRESTED REGULUS, or KINGLET (*Regŭlus cristǎtus*), a beautiful bird belonging to the sub-family Sylvinæ (warblers), distinguished by an orange crest. It is the smallest of British birds, being only about 3½ inches in length, is very agile, and almost continually in motion. The upper part of the body is yellowish olive-green, all the under parts pale reddish-white, tinged with green. The most usual haunts of the golden-crested wren are tall trees, particularly the oak, the yew, and the various species of pine and fir.

Its nest is most commonly open at the top, but sometimes it is covered with a dome, and has an opening on one side. It is always ingeniously suspended beneath the branch, being the only instance of the kind amongst the birds of Great Britain. The eggs are six to ten in number. Closely related, and very similar in appearance, is the fire-crest (*R. ignicapillus*).

GOLDEN DEITIES. The connection of gold with the sun ('the golden sun') and deities having solar attributes is of great antiquity. This precious (sacred) metal had originally a magico-religious significance. It was used in ancient Egypt to make models of cowries and snail shells, and the earliest gold jewellery found in the Nile Valley included a necklace of imitation shells (G. A. Reisner, *Early Dynastic Cemeteries of Naga-ed-Dêr*, vol. i, plates 6 and 7).

The gold was found on the trade-route between the Nile and the Red Sea, the special province of the goddess Hathor, one of whose names was 'Nubt.' A collar adorned with golden amulets was in Egyptian hieroglyphs the sign 'nub' (gold), and Nubia was 'gold-land.' It was apparently because Hathor had originally been in one of her phases a personification of the cowry that she became, as the goddess of the gold cowry, the 'Golden Hathor,' the prototype of the 'Golden Aphrodite' (Venus). Among the earliest gold ornaments found by Schliemann at Troy were models of cowries. As the shells were supposed to contain the animating principle ('soul substance'), the virtue of these appears to have passed to the precious metal.

In China gold was used with jade and pearls to stuff the mouths of dead emperors and other members of the royal household, so as to preserve the body from decay and assist the soul to rise to the celestial regions. The vital energy in gold was derived from *Yang* matter which was concentrated, according to Chinese belief, in the sun.

The golden deities of Greece were supposed to have acquired their golden hair by washing it in a river. Gold was in ancient times greatly favoured for ear-rings. It is of interest to note in this connection that ear-rings were connected with the sun, and that the human sons of the solar deity were fabled to have emerged from one of their mother's ears. Arjuna, the Aryo-Indian hero, son of Surya, the sun god, emerged from the

ear of his mother, the Princess Pritha. The gold ear-ring was reputed to strengthen the eyes of wearers. This belief may have arisen from the ancient belief that the sun and the moon were the eyes of the world-deity.

The Chinese dragon-gods were supposed to have had their origin from gold of various colours. The Egyptian alchemists produced gold of various tints by mixing metals. 'Green gold' was a mixture of 26 per cent silver and 75 per cent gold. In ancient Egypt electrum was found as a natural alloy, the proportion of silver being one-fifth. Electrum is found in Sutherland, Scotland, in small quantities.

GOLDEN FLEECE, in classical mythology, the fleece of gold of the ram Chrysomallus, in quest of which

Golden Crested Wren

Jason undertook the Argonautic expedition to Colchis. The fleece was suspended from an oak tree in the grove of Ares (Mars), and was guarded by a dragon. When the Argonauts came to Colchis for the fleece, Medea put the dragon to sleep and Jason carried the fleece away.

GOLDEN FLEECE, ORDER OF THE, the *Toison d'or*, a military order instituted by Philip the Good, Duke of Burgundy, in 1430, on the occasion of his marriage with the Portuguese princess, Isabella. The order used to belong both to Austria and Spain. The knights carried suspended from their collars the figure of a sheep or fleece in gold.

GOLDEN HORDE, originally the name of a powerful Mongol tribe, but afterwards extended to all the followers of Genghis Khan, and of Batu, the grandson of Genghis Khan, who invaded Europe in the thirteenth century. Under Batu the Golden Horde advanced westwards as far as the Plain of Mosi in Hungary, and Liegnitz in Silesia, at both of which bloody battles were fought in 1241.

They founded the empire of the Kiptshaks, or the Golden Horde, which extended from the banks of the Dniester to the Ural, and from the Black Sea and the Caspian to the mouth of the Kama and the sources of the Khoper. This empire lasted till towards the close of the fifteenth century, when it was overthrown by Tsar Ivan III.—Cf. S. Lane-Poole, *Mohammedan Dynasties.*

Goldfish: Some curious forms

GOLDEN LEGEND (*Aurea Legenda*), a collection of legends of the saints made in the thirteenth century by Jacobus de Voragine, or James of Viraggio, Archbishop of Genoa (died 1298). It consists of 182 sections, each of which is devoted to a particular saint or festival, arranged in the order of the calendar. Caxton printed a translation in 1483, and another edition was produced by Wynkyn de Worde in 1498. A modern edition of the work appeared in 1900. There is a poem entitled *The Golden Legend* by Longfellow.

GOLDEN NUMBER, in chronology, a number showing the year of the moon's cycle; so called from having formerly been written in the calendar in gold. To find the golden number add 1 to the given year, and divide the sum by 19, what remains will be the number required, unless 0 remain, in which case 19 is the golden number.

GOLDEN-ROD (Solidāgo) is a genus of plants, nat. ord. Compositæ, chiefly natives of North America. Most of the species have erect, rod-like, scarcely-branched stems, with alternate serrated leaves, and terminal spikes or racemes of small yellow flowers. *S. virgaurea*, often called Aaron's Rod, is the only British species, and is common in woods and heathy thickets.

GOLDEN ROSE, in the Roman Catholic Church an ornament of gold consecrated by the Pope on the fourth Sunday of Lent. It was originally a single flower of wrought gold, coloured red; afterwards the golden petals were decked with rubies and other gems; finally the form adopted was that of a thorny branch, with several flowers and leaves, and one principal flower at the top, all of pure gold. It is sent to some favoured Catholic prince or princess whom the Pope wishes to honour, to some eminent church, or distinguished personage. The custom is supposed to have originated in the thirteenth century. Henry VIII and Mary of England, James IV of Scotland, Mary Casimir, Queen of Poland, Isabella II of Spain, and Napoleon III were among the recipients of the golden rose.

GOLDEN-SAXIFRAGE, the popular name for plants of the genus Chrysosplenium, a small genus of Saxifragaceæ, consisting of annual or perennial rather succulent herbs, with alternate or opposite crenate leaves, and inconspicuous greenish axillary and terminal flowers. They are natives of Central and Northern Europe, the Himalayas, and parts of America. There are two British species.

GOLDFINCH, a common British bird, the *Carduelis elegans,* belonging to the Finch family. It is about 5 inches in entire length, black, scarlet, yellow, and white being beautifully mingled in its plumage. The colours of the female are duller than those of the male. Its brilliant plumage, soft and pleasant song, and docility make it a favourite cage-bird. The nest is an elegant cup-shaped structure. Goldfinches feed on various kinds of seeds, particularly those of the thistle, dandelion, and groundsel.

GOLDFISH, the popular name for a beautiful species of carp (*Carassius auratus*), found in the fresh waters of China and Japan. It is greenish in colour in the natural state, the golden-yellow colour being found only in domesticated specimens, and retained by artificial selection. These fishes are reared by the Chinese in small ponds, in basins, or porcelain vessels, and kept for ornament. By careful selection, many strange varieties and monstrosities have been propagated. They are now distributed over nearly all the civilized parts of the world, but in large ponds they readily revert to the colour of the original stock.

GOLD LACE, a fabric woven of silken threads which are either themselves gilt or are covered with fine gilt silver wire. In the former the gold-leaf is fixed directly on the threads by means of gum. In the latter and finer kind the fine gilt silver wire is twisted compactly round the silk-threads, which are then ready for being manufactured into lace.

GOLD OF PLEASURE, the *Camelīna satīva*, a cruciferous annual, ord. Cruoiferæ, with stem-clasping leaves, and terminal racemes of yellow flowers which produce pear-shaped pods containing numerous small seeds. It is found in Britain in cornfields, and is cultivated to a considerable extent on the continent of Europe for its seeds, which yield an oil used for burning, for dressing woollen goods, making soft soap, and in painting. The stems yield a fibre commonly used for making brooms.

GOLDO′NI, Carlo, the most celebrated Italian writer of comedies, born at Venice in 1707, died at Paris 1793. He early showed a taste for theatrical representations, and when scarcely eight years of age he ventured to sketch a comedy, which excited the wonder of his relatives.

His father, who was a physician, intended that his son should follow the medical profession, but Goldoni, dissatisfied with this study, obtained permission to study law in Venice. Soon after, however, a relative procured for him a place in the Papal college at the University of Pavia, from which he was expelled for writing scurrilous satires.

After his father's death he settled as an advocate in Venice, but soon took to a wandering life with strolling players, until in 1736 he married the daughter of a notary of Genoa, and settled down in Venice. Here he first began to cultivate that department of dramatic poetry in which he was to excel; namely, description of character and manners. In this he took Molière, whom he began to study about this time, for his model.

For five years he visited various cities of Italy, composing pieces for different theatrical companies, and for a time renewing his legal practice. In 1751 the Italian players invited him to Paris, where many of his pieces met with uncommon applause. He became reader and master of the Italian language to the daughters of Louis XV; and was granted a pension of 3,600 livres.

At the breaking out of the Revolution the poet lost his pension, and the decree of the National Convention of the 7th of Jan., 1793, restoring it and making up the arrears, found him already in the arms of death. His widow received the arrears and a pension for herself. Many of his numerous pieces still retain possession of the stage in his native country, and, in translations, of the stages of foreign countries. Among his best-known comedies (about 150) are: *La Donna di Garbo*, *Pamela Nubile*, *Todero Brontolon*, *La Casa Nova*, *Il Vecchio Bizarro*, and *L'Adulatore*.—Cf. Copping, *Alfieri and Goldoni: their Lives and Adventures*.

GOLDSCHMIDT, Madame. *See* LIND, JENNY.

GOLDSBOROUGH, village of Yorkshire (W.R.). It is 2½ miles from Knaresborough, on the L.N.E. Rly. It is noted for its hall, which is on the estate of the Earl of Harewood. This was the country home of the earl, then Viscount Lascelles, and Princess Mary from 1922 to 1929, when he became Earl of Harewood. In 1931 it was let.

GOLD-SINNY, or **CONNOR**, *Crenilabrus melops*, a small fish of the British seas; one of the wrasse family.

GOLDSMITH, Oliver, Irish poet, playwright, and novelist, was born at Pallas, County Longford, 10th Nov., 1728, and died 4th April, 1774. Goldsmith's father was a clergyman of the Established Church, with a large family and a small income.

Life. Goldsmith attended the village school, then kept by one 'Paddy' Byrne, a former soldier who had acted as quartermaster during Marlborough's campaigns. Byrne, who was an original character, seems to have had an important influence upon Goldsmith, and was blamed by the poet's family for imbuing him with a wandering and unsettled turn of mind. When aged about eight, Goldsmith had a severe attack of smallpox, which disfigured him greatly, and made him very sensitive.

After leaving the village school, he went to schools at Elphin, Athlone, and Edgeworthstown. On 11th June, 1744, he was admitted to Trinity College, Dublin, as a sizar. In those days sizars received free board and tuition in return for performing certain menial duties. The position entailed a good deal of humiliation, and Goldsmith was acutely sensitive about it.

Many stories and legends are still preserved of his scrapes and escapades at college. His tutor was a brutal and unsympathetic man and did not see any remarkable qualities in his pupil.

Goldsmith became a B.A. on 27th Feb., 1749. His name was last on the list.

He now coquetted with each of the learned professions in turn. He presented himself to the Bishop of Elphin for ordination, but as he appeared in brilliant scarlet breeches, he was turned down. He borrowed £50 from his uncle in order to study law, but was cheated of it before he got farther than Dublin. He then left Ireland—for ever, as it turned out—and went to Edinburgh to study medicine under Alexander Monro, the first of a dynasty of that name which reigned in the chair of anatomy at Edinburgh for over a hundred and twenty years.

Goldsmith remained two years in

Oliver Goldsmith

Edinburgh, and then in 1754 went to complete his studies on the Continent. A certain element of myth surrounds his adventures there. He studied at Leyden and Louvain, and went on foot through France, Germany, Switzerland, and Italy, supporting himself by playing on the flute, or by disputing with scholars at convents or universities, like the Admirable Crichton. He himself alleged that he took the M.B. degree somewhere; it has been thought it was either at Padua or Louvain; it has also been thought that he imagined the incident.

Anyhow, when he landed in England on 1st Feb., 1756, he was a distinguished graduate of the world's university. He had seen many sides of life, and was destined to see many more. He became an apothecary's

assistant, an usher, a reader to Richardson (the novelist and printer), and a poor physician. Finally he began to do hack-work for various publishers, commencing by writing many reviews and critiques.

Works. Goldsmith's literary works may be divided into two classes: those which were original, and those which were compilations. As an author he had almost a dual personality, like Dr. Jekyll and Mr. Hyde. Dr. Jekyll wrote the *Inquiry into the State of Polite Learning*, the *Essays*, the *Bee*, the *Citizen of the World*, the *Vicar of Wakefield*, and the poems and plays. Mr. Hyde, meanwhile, was busy at histories of Greece, Rome, and England, and at a work on natural history entitled *Animated Nature*, as well as writing various shorter works such as the *Life of Beau Nash*, *Memoir of Voltaire*, and *Life of Bolingbroke*.

It is not necessary to say much of Goldsmith's compilations. Even in them he displays his beautifully easy style, his own distinct way of writing. He was not a scholar by nature, and did not wish to undertake any laborious investigations, even had his slave-drivers given him time for them. Gibbon almost persuaded him to write an account of Alexander the Great's campaign against Montezuma.

In his *Animated Nature* he was sometimes indebted to his imagination for his facts. In his accounts of battles he takes the old-fashioned, not to say Homeric, view that it is only the leader on either side who really matters. Yet, in spite of some obvious absurdities, his compilation work is good, as he rendered attractive subjects which often become dry in more scholarly hands.

His original works are, however, on a different plane altogether. In them he expressed his unique personality. No one ever put so much of himself into his books as Goldsmith. His longer poems *The Traveller* and *The Deserted Village* are excellent poems of a didactic kind, exquisitely expressed. *The Traveller* made Goldsmith's reputation, and helped him into the best literary society in London. There has been much debate as to whether Auburn is the village of Lissoy in Ireland or an English village. It is really probably situated in Maritime Bohemia.

His lighter poems, *The Haunch of Venison* and *Retaliation* especially, are delightful. *Retaliation* is a masterpiece of urbane satire, which combines compliment and banter while describing the characters of some of his friends, such as Garrick, Burke, and Reynolds. Of the two plays, *She Stoops to Conquer* (1773) is a good deal better than *The Good Natur'd Man* (1768). The latter is a good comedy of manners, modelled upon Goldsmith's compatriot Farquhar; it has two well-drawn characters, Croaker and Lofty, but is not entirely successful.

She Stoops to Conquer is a splendid comedy of intrigue, introducing lively and farcical incidents and highly-drawn pictures of eccentric characters. The central incident, the mistaking of a house for an inn, is based upon a misadventure of the author's youth. This comedy still holds the stage, and is as amusing to-day as when it was first produced. It did much to kill the taste for sentimental or genteel comedies, such as those of Cumberland.

Some of the *Essays*, both those in the *Bee* and those not, are good, as is also the *Inquiry*. None of these are perhaps supremely good. *The Citizen of the World* (1762), in which a China-man describes English manners and customs, contains pieces more characteristic of Goldsmith, especially in the passages describing Beau Tibbs. These passages are as good as anything in Addison.

Goldsmith's great masterpiece, however, is *The Vicar of Wakefield*, which Johnson sold for £60 in 1762, but which did not appear until 1766. The plot is full of inconsistencies, and is less skilfully manipulated as the story progresses, and the book is made the right length by means of poems, tales, and a sermon; but in spite of these faults it is a real classic.

Dr. and Mrs. Primrose, Moses and his green spectacles, Olivia and Sophia, and the Misses Flamborough will live as long as any characters given us by Dickens, Thackeray, or Fielding. It is at once humorous and pathetic; unlike his contemporary Sterne, Goldsmith could be sentimental without being unmanly. By 1886 ninety-six different editions of it had been published.

Characteristics. Goldsmith was a friend of all the most notable literary men of his day: Johnson, Burke, Gibbon, Garrick, Boswell, and Reynolds. They seem to have regarded him with affectionate toleration, as one would regard a child. Indeed, like Peter Pan, he seems to have refused to grow up. He had many amiable weaknesses: a taste for gaudy clothes, a liking for gambling, and an ambition to shine in conversation.

Nature had made him an exquisite writer, but a poor talker. He was recklessly charitable when he had any money. He is said to have died £2,000 in debt, and his financial troubles hastened his end. He died in April, 1774, having unwisely prescribed a patent medicine, James's powder, for himself. He was buried in the burial-ground of the Temple Church. The cenotaph erected in Westminster Abbey has upon it a Latin epitaph by Johnson which contains the happiest verdict that can be given upon Goldsmith: "Nullum fere scribendi genus non tetigit; nullum quod tetigit non ornavit"—he touched almost every kind of writing, and touched none that he did not adorn.—BIBLIOGRAPHY: J. Forster, *Life and Adventures of Oliver Goldsmith*; Sir James Prior, *Life of Oliver Goldsmith*; Austin Dobson, *Life of Goldsmith* (Great Writers Series); W. Black, *Goldsmith* (English Men of Letters Series).

GOLD-STICK, a designation for the captain of the gentlemen-at-arms and the colonel of the Life Guards, from the gilt rod carried by them when attending on the sovereign on state occasions.

GOLD WORKINGS, ANCIENT. So far as is known, gold was first worked in Ancient Egypt where it acquired a magico-religious value (*see* GOLDEN DEITIES). Auriferous quartz veins are found in intrusive rocks among the large mountain masses of hornblendic granite in the Nile valley, especially between latitude 27° and 21°. Traces of extensive ancient mine workings indicate that a great amount of gold was obtained in the Eastern Desert. An ingot of gold was found in a pre-dynastic grave at El-Kab; there are in Cairo museum pre-dynastic flint knives with handles of gold.

The chief source of **Ancient Egyptian gold** was the Wadi Allagi, where the hills "have the appearance of having been ploughed. Quite 100 sq. miles of country," writes E. S. Thomas in *The Cairo Scientific Journal*, "have been worked to an average depth of 7 feet. So thoroughly has this been done that only the merest traces of gold remain."

Near old mine workings 5 miles north-east of Wadi Hammamat 2,000 old stone houses have been found. Wilkinson counted 1,320 huts near the old Fowachir workings which are close to Wadi Hammamat. In some mining areas the stone washing tables still remain. Ancient mine workings at Um Rus, 140 miles east of Luxor, were reopened in 1904 by a company. They were found "to extend 1,500 feet along the line of the reef and to a maximum depth of 292 feet."

This mine is believed to be the one referred to by Agatharchides (113 B.C.), who wrote: "Even in our time are found cutting hammers of brass and human bones in incredible numbers, crushed perhaps in these wide ill-propped galleries so vast and deep that they reach the sea."

A great deal of gold was exported from Ancient Egypt to Western Asia as the Tel-El-Amarna tablets bear evidence. Akhenaton, the heretical Pharaoh (1357–1358 B.C.) received frequent requests for gold from the kings of Cappadocia, Assyria, and Babylonia. Rameses III presented about £18,000 worth of gold to the gods. It is estimated that Ptolemy II derived about 4 millions sterling from the gold-mines. In the old mine workings on the Sudan border a great deal of Roman pottery has been found.

After the death of Cleopatra, such large quantities of gold and silver reached Rome that the loan rate of interest dropped from 12 to 4 per cent. It is believed that much of the gold came from the Egyptian mines.

The method of working gold in ancient times is described in a narrative transcribed by Diodorus Siculus. It is told that galleries were driven into the rock by strong young men who used hammers. Young lads carried out the fragments, which were taken by old men to the 'pounders' where middle-aged men broke the quartz in the mortars. The broken quartz was then ground in hand-mills by women. Three women worked each mill, and to those "who bear this lot," says the ancient writer, "death is better than life."

Men spread out the milled quartz on sloping tables, kneading it after it was drenched with water. Others used sponges to remove the lighter parts and separate the gold. The washing process was continued until the gold was fit to be placed in clay pots in which it was mixed with lead, salt, silver, and bran. The pots were sealed and set on fires for five days and five nights.

In Asia the demand for gold in ancient times caused prospectors to search for it far and wide. Gold was found on the Chota-Nagpur plateau and Malabar coast in India, and in Assam and in northern Burma, as well as in Tibet. The Altai mountains (gold mountains) yielded considerable supplies.

In Europe gold was found in Spain, Portugal, and France, in Cornwall and Devon and northern Wales, in various parts of Scotland, and in north-eastern and southern and south-western Ireland. Egyptian Empire period finds in Rhodesia indicate that the prospectors reached even that distant part of Africa. It is believed that the Phœnicians who circumnavigated Africa visited the Gold Coast and obtained the precious metal there.

GOLDWYN, Samuel. American film producer and business organizer. Born in Warsaw in 1882, his parents (named Goldfish) took him in 1896 to America, where he was naturalized in 1902. He was a pioneer in urging American authors to write directly for the screen. He organized the Jesse Lasky Photoplay Company and was associated for a time with the great Metro-Goldwyn combine at Los Angeles. He was the subject of a *Life* by John Drinkwater.

GOLF, a game played with clubs and balls over large commons, downs, or links. It is said to have originated in Holland, and the word golf itself is doubtfully derived from the Dutch *kolf*, a club.

History. It has been played in Scotland for centuries, and there are several references to the game in Scottish Acts of Parliament, as in one passed in 1491 under James IV, which classes football and 'gouff' with "uthir sic unproffitable sportis."

It was not till the middle of the nineteenth century that the game really began to take root in England, although the golf club with the oldest records is that at Blackheath, founded by James I, or his Scottish courtiers. Apart from this, the first English golf-club was started at Westward Ho, Devonshire, in 1864; and gradually this was followed by other clubs all over the country.

The Royal and Ancient Club of St. Andrews (founded in 1754) is now the recognized head-quarters of the game in the United Kingdom, and long laid down the law for the golfing community. Recently a Rules of Golf Committee has been formed; but all its members are members of the St. Andrews club, which thus practically maintains its supremacy. Other well-known golf-courses or links are at North Berwick, Prestwick (near Ayr), and Muirfield (Haddingtonshire), in Scotland; Westward Ho, Hoylake, and Sandwich, in England; and Portrush, in Ireland.

World-wide Popularity. A golf-club was founded at Calcutta in 1829, Bombay and Pau (in the south of France) coming next in order. The game spread to the United States, through Canada, about 1890, and has since become amazingly popular there.

It may be said that a golf-course will sooner or later always be laid down in any part of the world where Scotsmen congregate. The best courses are at sea-level, where sandy soil covered with short turf and provided with natural sandy 'bunkers' and with a fair supply of gorse, constitute ideal conditions. But often the worst natural disadvantages are either overcome by skilled artificial additions or overlooked by enthusiasts who will play whatever the circumstances, and one finds links in the most unexpected surroundings e.g. at the top of a high mountain, as in Switzerland.

The game is unique; it combines healthy exercise and recreation in good air with a maximum of variation and a minimum of fatigue; so that whilst the most vigorous devotees will be found among the young or early middle-aged, even the comparatively senile take advantage of the remarkable opportunities it offers. In modern times ladies have displayed equal keenness, and have developed such skill that the champion lady player is very little inferior to the greatest male exponents of the game.

The Clubs. The varying nature of the ground on a golf course, and the different obstacles to be surmounted, necessitate the use of a number of different clubs. The chief clubs are the *driver*, *brassy*, *spoon*, *irons* (numbered 1, 2, 3, 4, &c.), *mashie*, *mashie-niblick*, *niblick* and *putter*. Of these the first three have wooden heads, the rest iron, though the putter is often made of aluminium.

The heads of wooden clubs are made of beech, persimmon or logwood, weighted with lead behind. The shafts are of hickory or steel and are socketed into the heads. The *driver* is the club used for driving from the teeing-ground, but it may also be used for other strokes if the 'lie' of the ball is good. A good driver will send the ball, if accurately hit, some 200 to 300 yards.

The *brassy* is a wooden club shod with a brass plate. Its face is laid back somewhat, so as to loft the ball, and it is used in fairly good 'lies' on grass. The *irons* are iron-headed clubs, flat-faced, with a graded angle of inclination in the face. They are used variously for driving and lofting. The *mashie*, also an iron-headed club, is used for lofting the ball and for short 'approaches,' and accordingly has its face laid back. The *mashie-niblick* and *niblick* have each a very much lofted face, and serve to extricate the ball from deep sand, small holes, cart-ruts, &c.

The *putter* is used on the putting-green for coaxing the ball into the hole from short distances. A great many varieties of this club have from time to time been introduced by prominent players, whose success has induced enthusiastic novices to emulate their skill by adopting the same implement. The other clubs also are frequently duplicated (as *light* and *heavy irons*), while the number and varity of intermediate clubs used depend upon the individual player.

The Ball. The ball, which was originally of feathers covered with leather, was afterwards always made of gutta-percha, and now usually consists of a core round which india-rubber thread is wound, the whole being cased with gutta-percha. These balls have been found to be more springy, and can be driven farther than the older gutta-percha balls.

For a long time golf was the only ball game which did not require the use of a ball of standard size or weight. Attempts to introduce a standard ball were the subject of much controversy. On the whole the general opinion was an adverse one, the chief opposition being from the leading professionals, who thought they would thereby sacrifice some of their driving superiority. Now, however, no golf ball may be heavier than 1·62 oz. or smaller in diameter than 1·62 in. In the United Kingdom open and amateur championships are decided annually on the greens of St. Andrews, Prestwick, Muirfield, Hoylake, and Sandwich in rotation. Ladies' championships are also held.

The Course. A golf-course of full size is divided into eighteen sections by a series of small round holes, 4¼ inches in diameter, sunk in the turf at distances of from 100 to 500 yards from each other, so as to form a circuit or round; many courses have only nine holes. The ground between the holes must be varied in character, being diversified by obstacles, whether natural or artificial, such as sand or other bunkers, hillocks, ditches, streams &c. Round each hole a grass-grown space, known as the putting-green, is kept perfectly smooth.

The Play. The object of the game is, starting from the first teeing-ground (or place from which the balls are driven off towards each hole), to drive the ball into the next hole in as few strokes as possible, and so on with all the holes in succession, the side which 'holes out' on any occasion in the fewest strokes being said to win the hole.

The match is decided either by the greatest number of holes won, or by the aggregate number of strokes for the whole round. In medal play, and in some championships, the score is always reckoned by strokes. Often what are known as 'Bogey' competitions are held. 'Colonel Bogey,' who is a kind of 'Mrs. Harris' of golf, has a fixed score allotted to him for each hole, this score being approximately that of a good player who accomplishes the round without making any bad blunders. 'Bogey,' in fact, is a perfect player who always plays up to his best form whatever the conditions. The competitors contest each hole with this mythical opponent, and the winner is he who finishes the greatest number of holes 'up,' or more generally the least number 'down,' on 'Bogey.'

Ordinarily the ball may not be touched otherwise than with the club during the game, except to take it out of the hole and place it in position on the teeing-ground (the 'tee' being a little mound of sand, on which the ball is placed for the first drive to each hole). Sometimes, however, the local rules of a club recognize certain places on the course from which the ball is practically unplayable, and if a ball lodges in one of these places, the player

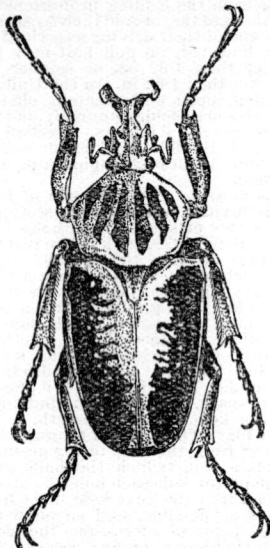

Goliath-beetle *(Goliathus druryi)* (Half natural size)

is allowed to take it out and drop it behind him under penalty of one stroke.

In 1932 the British Amateur Championship was held by J. de Forest, the British Open Championship by Gene Sarazen, the American, who also held the American Open Championship in the same year. The Walker Cup (America v. Great Britain —Amateurs) was won by America in 1932; the Ryder Cup (America v. Great Britain—Professionals), by America in 1931. The British Amateur Championship of 1933 was won by the Hon. John Michæl Scott.

Harry Vardon, James Braid and J. H. Taylor were known as "the great triumvirate" of British Golf, or with Robert T. ("Bobby") Jones, of America as "the Big Four."—

BIBLIOGRAPHY: H. G. Hutchinson, *Golf Greens and Green Keeping*; *The New Book of Golf*; G. W. Beldam, *Great Golfers*; H. Hilton and G. G. Smith, *The Ancient and Royal Game of Golf*. See also *The Golfer's Annual* and *The Golfer's Year-Book*.

GOLI'ATH, a Philistine giant of Gath slain by David (1 *Sam.*, xvii). His height was "six cubits and a span," which, taking the cubit at 21 inches, would make him a little over 11 feet. The *Septuagint* and Josephus make him only "*four* cubits and a span," or 7 feet 9 inches.

GOLIATH-BEETLE, the popular name of the beetles of the genus Goliäthus, natives of tropical Africa, remarkable for their large size, and on account of their beauty and rarity much prized by collectors. The largest species (*G. druryi*) attains the length of 4 inches.

GOLOSH'ES, a word introduced into our language from the French *galoche*, but originally derived from the Spanish *galocha*, meaning a wooden shoe or clog (cf. Gr. *kalopodion, kalon*, wood, and *pous*, foot). It was formerly applied by the English to a kind of wooden clogs. The name is now restricted to overshoes, now generally made of vulcanized india-rubber.

GOLTZ, Baron Colmar von der, German soldier and author, born at Bielkenfeld, East Prussia, 12th Aug., 1843, died 4th April, 1916. Entering the Prussian infantry in 1861, he fought in the Austrian campaign of 1866 and in the Franco-Prussian War, when he was attached to the head-quarters staff of Prince Frederick Charles.

He then served on the historical section of the general staff in Berlin, lectured on military history, and in 1883 went to Turkey for the purpose of reorganizing the Turkish army, and remained there until 1895. He received the title of Pasha, was made field-marshal, and in 1908 went again to Constantinople, where he was instrumental in furthering the Young Turk movement.

He revisited Constantinople in 1909 and in 1910. In 1913 he retired from the Prussian army, but at the outbreak of the European War he accompanied the German army, and was Governor of Brussels from Sept. to Oct., 1914, and afterwards Governor of Belgium. In 1915 von der Goltz again went to Turkey, where he supervised the defences of the Dardanelles and the Turkish operations against the Allies. He died, or, as some say, was assassinated, at his head-quarters in April, 1916. His works include: *Gambetta and his Armies* (1877), *The Nation in Arms* (1883), and *The War*

History of Germany in the Nineteenth Century.

GO'MARITES, or GOMARISTS, followers of *Francis Gomarus* (1563-1641), a Dutch disciple of Calvin in the seventeenth century. The sect, otherwise called Dutch Remonstrants, very strongly opposed the doctrines of Arminius, adhering rigidly to those of Calvin. *See* REFORMED CHURCH.

GOME'RA, one of the Canary Islands, about 140 sq. miles in extent; pop. 22,000. It has two towns, St. Sebastian and Villa Hermosa.

GOM'ERSAL, a town in the West Riding of Yorkshire, England, 6 miles S.S.E. of Bradford, with several collieries, worsted mills, and manufactures of blankets and cloth. Pop. 3,796.

G O M E Z, Sebastiano, Spanish painter, born at Seville about 1646, died about 1690. He was a mulatto, originally a slave of Murillo, but on account of his talent he was liberated by his master and became one of his pupils, after his death painting some pictures for churches and convents in Seville.

GOMPERS, Samuel, American labour leader, of Jewish extraction, born in London 27th Jan., 1850, where he was apprenticed to a cigarette-maker. He went to the United States in 1863, and as a boy already became a zealous worker in the cause of labour. One of the founders of the American Federation of Labour, he became its president in 1881. An active organizer of the labouring classes, he became an indefatigable champion of labour legislation, and through his efforts the American Labour Federation became a powerful organization.

When America entered the European War, Gompers used his influence in support of the Allied cause, opposing not only communist ideas as introduced into Russia by the Soviets, but also socialism. A labour leader, Gompers has nevertheless always remained a staunch supporter of the capitalistic régime. He visited Britain, France, and Italy in 1918, was president of the International Commission on Labour Legislation at the Paris Peace Conference, and president of the International Labour Conference at Washington in 1919. He was elected president of the American Federation of Labour in 1921. He died in 1924.

GOMPERZ, Theodor, Austrian philologist and classical scholar, born 29th March, 1832, at Brünn, died in 1912. He studied at the University of Vienna, where he became professor of classical philology. He occupied this post from 1873 to 1901, when he entered the House of Peers. Gomperz is well known for his decipherment of the papyri of Herculaneum. His works include: *Herculanische Studien* (1865-6); *Beiträge zur Kritik und Erklärung der Griechischen Schriftsteller* (7 vols., 1875-1900); *Platonische Aufsätze* (3 vols., 1887-1905); *Griechische Denker* (3 vols., 1893-1909; English translation by Magnus and Berry, 4 vols., 1905-12).

GOMUL PASS, a pass across the Sulaimán range, from the Punjab into Afghanistan. It follows the course of the Gomul River, and is an important trading highway.

GOMU'TI PALM, the sago-palm (*Arenga saccharifera*), which yields a bristly fibre, resembling black horsehair, known as gomuti. This fibre, which is also called *ejoo*, is manufactured into cordage, plaited into ornaments, employed for thatching, and put to various other similar uses. The sweet juice yielded by the palm is fermented, forming the 'toddy' of the natives. In Malacca the gomuti is cultivated chiefly for its saccharine juice, which is crystallized into the sugar named jaggery. It is also one of the sago-producing palms.

GONAÏVES, a town on the west coast of Haiti, on the bay of the same name, 65 miles N.N.W. of Port au Prince. It has an excellent harbour. The exports are cotton, coffee, salt, and mahogany. It was at Gonaïves that the independence of Haiti was proclaimed by Dessalines in 1804. Pop. 10,000.

GONCHAROV, Ivan Alexandrovitsh, one of the most eminent Russian novelists, born at Simbirsk, July 1812, died Sept., 1891. He studied at the University of Moscow, accepted a post in the Ministry of Finance, and was subsequently in the Censor's office. He went round the world as secretary to Admiral Putiatin in 1852. For a time he was editor of the *Northern Post*. His first novel, *A Common Story*, appeared in 1847, and his masterwork, *Oblomov*, in 1857. This novel is a personification of the apathy which has characterized and still continues to characterize the Russian nation. In a clear masterly way Goncharov depicted therein the intellectual and moral life of his nation its lack of will-power, and its chronic indolence as typified in his hero Oblomov.—Cf. P. Kropotkin, *Russian Literature.*

GONCOURT (goṇ-kör), **Edmond** and **Jules de,** French novelists and writers on social history, art, &c.; brothers, born respectively in 1822 and 1830, died 1896 and 1870. As novelists they belonged to the Realistic school, but they depicted life and character in a less coarse fashion than Zola. Their historical and biographical works dealt chiefly with the eighteenth century, and especially the period of the Revolution. Edmond left a fund for the establishment of an *académie* of men of letters. Their works include: *Portraits Intimes du XVIIIe Siècle, L'Art du XVIIIe Siècle.*—Cf. F. Brunetière, *Le Roman Naturaliste.*

GONDA, chief town of district of the same name, Oudh, India, 28 miles N.N.W. of Fyzábád. Pop. 17,400.— The district has an area of 2,881 sq, miles. Pop. about 1,500,000.

GONDAR, a chief town of Abyssinia, formerly the residence of the king, and still the ecclesiastical headquarters, is situated on a hill of considerable height, about 22 miles north of Lake Dembea. The town is divided into several quarters; contains many churches, and the ruins of a magnificent towered castle, built in the sixteenth century by Indian architects under the direction of Portuguese

Gondola

settlers. It was burned by King Theodore in 1868. Pop. about 3,000,

GONDO′KORO, a station and port on the Upper Nile (Bahr el Gebel), in Uganda, at the head of steamer navigation. At one time it was the chief seat of the Egyptian Government of the Upper Nile. In recent times it has again risen in importance.

GON′DOLA, a sort of barge, curiously ornamented, and navigated on the canals of Venice. The ordinary gondolas are upwards of 30 feet long and 4 feet broad; they always terminate at each end in a very sharp point, which is raised perpendicularly to the height of a man. Towards the centre there is a curtained chamber for passengers.

GONDS, a Dravidian people, the aboriginal inhabitants of the old territorial division of Hindustan called Gondwana, corresponding pretty nearly to what is now called the Central Provinces. The name Gond has been connected with *Telugu Konda*, a mountain, which would tend to prove that they are a hill tribe. After a long period of repression, the Gonds attained to a position of great prominence and power, and in the sixteenth, seventeenth, and eighteenth centuries three Gond dynasties simultaneously held almost the whole of Gondwana under their sway.

With the rise of the Mahrattas the power of the Gonds declined, and in 1781 the last of their dynasties was overthrown and the independence of the Gonds ceased. Their numbers have been variously estimated up to 2,000,000, partly under feudatory states and partly under the British Government, in the Central Provinces.

They used to offer human sacrifices to their deities, but now sacrifice instead an image of straw. They worship objects which are supposed to be the abode of spirits, and are reputed sorcerers. Less than a fortieth of Dravidian-speaking peoples speak the uncultivated dialect known as Gond.— BIBLIOGRAPHY: S. Hislop, *Papers relating to the Aboriginal Tribes of the Central Provinces*; J. Forsyth, *The Highlands of Central India.*

GON′FALON (O.Fr. *gonfanon*), an ensign or standard; especially an ensign having two or three streamers or tails, fixed on a frame made to turn like a ship's vane, or, as in the case of the Papal gonfalon, suspended from a pole like a sail from a mast. In many of the mediæval republican cities of Italy the bearer of the gonfalon was often the chief personage in the state, and was called a *gonfalonier*.

GONG, a Chinese musical instrument made of an alloy of copper (about seventy-eight parts) and tin (about twenty-two parts), in form like a round flat dish with a rim 2 to 3 inches in depth. It is struck by a kind of drumstick, the head of which is covered with leather, and is used for the purposes of making loud sonorous signals, of marking time, and of adding to the clangour of martial instruments.

GONGO′RA Y ARGO′TE, Luis de, a celebrated Spanish poet, was born at Cordova in 1561, died there in 1627. He was educated for the Church, and was made chaplain to the king, and a prebendary in the cathedral of Cordova. His works consist chiefly of lyrical poems, in which he excelled. He introduced a new poetic phraseology called the *estilo culto*, and founded a school of writers, the *Gongoristas*, who carried this depraved style to an absurd length. His poems were published at Madrid in 1627. *Gongorism* is a style somewhat resembling Euphuism in England or Marinism in France.

GONIATITES, an extinct group of shell-bearing cephalopods, now divided into many genera, such as Glyphioceras, Gastrioceras, &c., and ranging from the Ordovician to the Carboniferous system. The partitions in the shell are bent in an angular manner where they meet the wall, thus foreshadowing the complex suture-lines of the ammonites. The siphuncle connecting the chambers lies, as in the ammonites, against the outer side of the shell, that is, against the convex side in coiled forms; but the calcareous necks where it passes through the partitions are directed backwards, as in the nautiloids. Almost all the forms are closely coiled, and in marine Coal Measure beds they are familiar as small globose fossils.

GONIOM'ETER (Gr. *gōnia*, angle, and *metron*, measure), an instrument for measuring solid angles, particularly the angles formed by the faces of crystals. The reflecting goniometer is an instrument of this kind for measuring the angles of crystals by determining through what angular space the crystal must be turned so that a ray reflected from two faces successively shall have the same direction. The angle of rotation is the supplement of that between the faces.

GONORRHŒA is a specific contagious disease marked in its early stage by a profuse purulent discharge from the affected part—in the male, the urethra, and in the female, the vagina. It is due to an organism called the gonococcus, and the usual means of spread of the infection is sexual intercourse.

It is the more common of the two widespread venereal diseases, and though popularly supposed to be much less dangerous than syphilis, when treatment is neglected, the disease, especially in women, may have most far-reaching and devastating effects. After the acute stage, lasting from ten days to three weeks, the symptoms lessen, and it is frequently at this point that treatment is abandoned too early, with the result that the infection spreads inwards, leading in later years to bladder troubles and stricture in the male, and infection of the internal genital organs with resulting sterility in women.

GONSAL'VO, Hernandez y Aguilar, de Cordoba, Spanish soldier, called the *great captain* (*el gran capitan*), was born at Montilla, near Cordova, in 1453, died at Granada 1515. He distinguished himself in the Portuguese War which began in 1475, and in the great war with the Moors, which ended with the conquest of Granada in 1492. In 1495 he was sent to assist Ferdinand II, King of Naples, against the French, who occupied the whole of that kingdom.

In less than a year Gonsalvo drove the French over the Neapolitan frontiers, and returned to Spain, where he was engaged in subjecting the Moors

in the Alpujarras when Louis XII of France renewed the war against Naples. Gonsalvo again took the field, and by the victory near Seminara in 1502 obtained possession of both Calabrias. In 1503 he gained a still more important victory near Cerignola, in consequence of which Abruzzo and Apulia submitted, and Gonsalvo marched into Naples.

He then sat down before Gaëta. As the siege was protracted, he gave up the command to Don Pedro Navarro, and advanced to meet the enemy. He defeated the Marquis of Mantua; and on the Garigliano, with 8,000 men, obtained a complete victory over 30,000 French, the consequence of which was the fall of Gaëta. The possession of Naples was now secured. He was Viceroy in Italy until 1507, when, through the jealousy of the king and the calumnies of the courtiers, he was deprived of his office, and retired to Granada, where he died.—Cf. W. H. Prescott, *Ferdinand and Isabella.*

GONVILLE AND CAIUS (kēz) **COLLEGE**, Cambridge, was founded in 1358 by Edmund Gonville of Terrington, Norfolk. In 1558 Dr. Caius obtained the royal charter by which all the former foundations were confirmed and his own foundation was established. By this charter the college was thenceforth to be called Gonville and Caius College.

GONZAGA FAMILY, a famous Italian family who ruled over Mantua from 1328 to the beginning of the eighteenth century. Many illustrious soldiers, statesmen, churchmen, and promoters and cultivators of arts, science, and literature sprang from this stock. They became extinct in 1708.

GOOD, John Mason, English physician, author of various poems, translations, and professional treatises, was born 1764, died 1827. He was apprenticed to a surgeon at Gosport, and in 1784 engaged in practice at Sudbury, In 1793 he removed to London, where he carried on business for several years as a surgeon and apothecary. He obtained the diploma of M.D. from the University of Aberdeen in 1820, and from that date till his death practised exclusively as a physician.

His best-known work is a blank verse translation of Lucretius's Latin poem *De Rerum Natura.* Other translations by him are *The Song of Songs* and *The Book of Job.* He also wrote *The Study of Medicine* and *The Book of Nature*; and published in conjunction with his friend Olinthus Gregory a cyclopædia entitled *Pantologia* (in 12 vols.).

GOOD-FRIDAY, a fast of the Christian Church in memory of our Savour's crucifixion, kept on the Friday of Passion Week, that is, the Friday before Easter. It has been celebrated from a very early period. In the Roman Catholic Church the celebration of this fast includes prayers for all classes of people, including heretics, schismatics, pagans, and Jews, and the 'Adoration of the Cross,' but no mass is celebrated.

In Protestant Churches, with but a few exceptions, the day is observed with more or less solemnity. The practice of eating 'cross-buns' on this day has now no religious significance. In England and Ireland Good-Friday is a general holiday; in Scotland it is a bank holiday.

GOOD KING HENRY. *See* GOOSE-FOOT.

GOODRICH, Samuel Griswold, American author, born at Ridgefield, Connecticut, 1793, died 1860. He was a publisher in Hartford and afterwards in Boston. He is best known as 'Peter Parley,' a pseudonym which he assumed in writing, editing, and compiling upwards of 100 children's books. In 1851 he acted as American consul at Paris, and published there in French a treatise on *American Geography and History.*

He also wrote *Recollections of a Lifetime, Sketches from a Student's Window, A History of all Nations, The Outcast and other Poems,* and *An Illustrated History of the Animal Kingdom.*—His brother, Charles Augustus (1700–1862), was associated with him in some of the books published by him, and also wrote a *History of the United States, Geography of the Chief Places mentioned in the Bible,* and other works.

GOODRICH, village of Herefordshire. About 4 miles from Ross, it has an old and interesting church. Near are the ruins of a castle, which was built to protect England against the Welsh, probably in the 12th century.

GOOD TEMPLARS, a temperance brotherhood which combines the principles of teetotalism with certain mystic rites, imitated less or more from freemasonry, having secret signs, passwords, and insignia peculiar to itself. It originated in New York in 1851, and extended to Britain in 1868. The organization consists of local 'subordinate' lodges, county 'district' lodges, national 'grand' lodges, and an international 'right worthy' grand lodge. A 'juvenile order' is also attached; and the Templars have founded an orphanage at Sunbury, near London, at a cost of £10,000.

GOODWILL, a term applied to certain advantages which may attach

to and pass with a business. It has been variously defined as "the probability that the old customers will resort to the old place" (Lord Eldon); "the attractive force which brings in custom" (Lord Macnaghten); "the benefit arising from connection and reputation" (Lord Lindley); and "every affirmative advantage that has been acquired in carrying on the business, whether connected with the premises of the business or its name or style, and everything connected with or carrying with it the benefit of the business" (Wood, V.-C.).

Goodwill is an asset distinct from the physical assets such as buildings, stock, or cash. Not infrequently it is the most valuable asset of a business. It has, therefore, a monetary value, and is capable of sale or transfer. Such a disposal of goodwill carries with it (in the absence of contrary agreement) the exclusive use of the trade name and the sole right to canvass the former customers. The trademark is transmitted with it, and *Ad Valorem* stamp duty is leviable. Its value must also be ascertained for payment of death duties. Compensation is payable if injury is caused to goodwill by the exercise of statutory powers for the acquisition of land.

Goodwill may be real (heritable) or personal (moveable), or may partake partly of both qualities, according to circumstances. It is not usually regarded as attaching to a professional business, which is mainly dependent on individual skill, and where it can imply nothing more than the right to an introduction to the clientèle and an obligation, it may be, to refrain from competition.

GOODWIN SANDS, certain dangerous sand-banks, about 4 or 5 miles off the east coast of Kent, the intervening channel forming the well-known roadstead called the Downs. Their entire length, north to south, is about 10 miles; breadth, varying from 1½ miles to 3 miles; and in many places they are dry at low water.

This shoal has four lightships for the guidance of mariners. According to tradition, these sands formed at one time part of the Kentish land belonging to Earl Godwin, whence their name; and were submerged in the year 1037. In 1652 the Dutch won a naval victory over the English near the Goodwin Sands.

GOODWOOD, seat of the dukes of Richmond and Gordon. It is 3 miles from Chichester and is chiefly celebrated for its racecourse, where races take place at the end of July each year, as they have done since 1802.

GOOLE, a town and river-port, England, county of York (West

Riding), on the Ouse, 25 miles west by south of Hull. The Aire and Calder navigation system links it with the towns of Yorkshire and Lancashire. The town dates from 1829, when it became a bonding port, and it has a good shipping trade. Besides the tidal basin, a series of large and commodious docks has been constructed, and steamers go regularly from here to ports in Scandinavia and the Netherlands. The exports are mostly coal, machinery, and woollen goods. Ship- and boat-building, sail-making, iron-founding, artificial manure and agricultural machine-making, are carried on. Pop. (1931), 20,238.

GOORKHAS. *See* GURKHAS.

GOOSANDER (Mergus), the type genus of a subdivision (Merginæ) of the duck family, characterized by a beak thinner and more cylindrical than that of the ducks, and having each mandible armed at its margins with small pointed teeth, directed backward like a saw, the upper mandible being curved down at its extremity; there are about seven species.

The **Goosander** or **Merganser** proper (*M. merganser*) weighs about 4 lb. It is an Arctic bird, moving south in winter, and in severe seasons frequents the lakes and rivers of Britain. It feeds principally on fish, which it

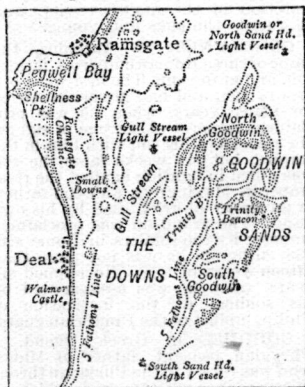

Map of the Downs, and Goodwin Sands

seizes by rapid diving. The **Red-breasted Goosander** (*M. serrātor*), a frequent visitor to Britain, measures about 21 inches in length and weighs about 2 lb. The **Smew** (*M. albellus*) ranges across the northern part of the Old World, and migrates southward in winter. Other species are native to America, Brazil, Central Asia, and the

Auckland Islands. The **Hooded Goosander** (*Lophodytes cucullatus*) is peculiar to North America.

GOOSE, the common name of the birds belonging to a subdivision (Anserinæ) of the duck family. The

Goosander

two sexes are similar in appearance. The domestic goose lives chiefly on land and feeds on grass; there are many varieties, but they do not differ widely from each other. It is valued for the table, and on account of its quills and fine soft feathers. The **Common Wild Goose**, or **Grey-lag** (*Anser cinereus*), which is migratory, possibly represents the original stock of the domestic goose.

The **Snow-goose** (*Chĕn hyperboreus*) of North America is 2 feet 8 inches in length, and its wings are 5 feet in extent. The bill of this bird is very curious, the edges having each twenty-three indentations or strong teeth on each side. The inside or concavity of the upper mandible has also seven rows of strong, projecting teeth, and the tongue, which is horny at the extremity, is armed on each side with thirteen long and sharp bony teeth. The flesh of this species is excellent.

The **Laughing** or **White-fronted Goose** (*Anser albifrons*) inhabits the northern parts of both continents, and migrates to the more temperate climates during the winter. The **Bean-goose** (*A. segĕtum*) is also common to both continents. The **Canada-goose** (*Bernicla Canadensis*) is the common wild goose of the United States, and is known in every part of North America. It is also found in Europe, and even breeds in Britain. Other species are the **Barnacle Goose** (*B. leucopsis*) and the **Brent-goose** (*B. brănta*); the **Red-breasted Goose** (*B. ruficollis*), that ranges southward from Western Siberia and figures in ancient Egyptian printings; and the **Pink-footed Goose** (*Anser brachyrhynchus*) of North Europe.

GOOSEBERRY (*Ribes grossularia*), a low, branching shrub, growing wild in Siberia and the north of Europe, other species being found in North America. Along with the currants it forms the ord. Grossulariaceæ, which is now usually combined with Saxifragaceæ. The brances are armed with numerous prickles, and bear three-to five-lobed leaves and inconspicuous flowers.

The fruit is a succulent berry, very wholesome and agreeable, of various colours—whitish, yellow, green, and red. Gooseberries are popular fruits for preserving, and are extensively cultivated, being of very easy culture. They may be raised from slips, which is the usual mode of perpetuating varieties; new varieties are raised from seed. The plant of four years old produces the largest and finest fruit; afterwards the fruit becomes smaller but increases in quantity. *R. niveum*, an American species, has fine white flowers, and is cultivated as an ornamental shrub.

GOOSEFOOT (Chenopodium) is a genus of plants, nat. ord. Chenopodiaceæ, indigenous to the temperate parts of the eastern continent. They are weedy plants common in waste places, and bear small greenish flowers, which are sessile in small clusters, collected in spiked panicles. Several species are found in Britain. *C. Bonus-Henricus*, English mercury, or Good King Henry, is a substitute for spinach. The seeds of *C. quinoa* of Peru are used as food.

GOOSSENS, Eugene, English conductor and composer. Born in London, May, 26th, 1893, he was a son of Eugene Goossens, at one time conductor of the Carl Rosa Opera Company. He was educated in Liverpool and at the Royal College of Music, London, and in 1915, after four years as a member of the orchestra at the Queen's Hall, London, became associated with the Beecham Opera Co. He founded an orchestra of his own and gave concerts of his own works in London and other centres.

GOPHER, the name of various burrowing animals, natives of North America. The *Geomys bursarius* or pouched rat has large cheek-pouches extending from the mouth to the shoulders, incisors protruding beyond the lips, and broad, mole-like forefeet. Several American forms (species of Spermophilus), intermediate between marmots and true squirrels, also get this name; as also a species of burrowing land-tortoise (*Testudo polyphemus*) of the Southern States, whose eggs are valued for the table.

GÖPPINGEN (geup'ing-en), a town of Württemberg, Germany, 22 miles E.S.E. of Stuttgart. It is regularly built; contains a handsome church, town house, old castle, and hospital; and has a mineral spring; manufactures of woollen and linen cloth, hats, and paper. Pop. 22,017.

GORAKHPUR, a town of India, United Provinces of Agra and Oudh, capital of the division and district of same name, on the left bank of the Rapti. It has a considerable trade in grain and timber, sent down the Rapti to the Gogra and the Ganges. Pop. (1931), 57, 985.—The division has an area of 9,543 sq. miles. It is generally flat, and traversed by numerous streams, of which the principal are the Rapti and larger Gandak. Pop. of division, 6,720,000.

GORAMY, or GOURAMI (gō-ra-mĭ', gŏ-ra-mĭ'), the Javanese name of a fish of the genus Osphromĕnus (*O. olfax*), family Osphromenidæ, a native of the Malay Archipelago, but introduced into the Mauritius, India, and Guiana (where it has multiplied rapidly) on account of the excellence of its flesh. It is deep in proportion to its length, and the dorsal and anal fins have numerous short spines, while the first ray of the ventral is protracted into a filament of extraordinary length. The male constructs a nest of air-bubbles, cemented together by a secretion of the mouth cavity, and he guards the eggs and young.

GORDIA'NUS, M. Antonius, the name of three Roman emperors, father, son, and grandson. The first was born in A.D. 158, and had governed Africa for many years, when he was proclaimed emperor at the age of eighty. He associated his son with him in the empire, but six weeks later the son was killed in fighting against the rival emperor, Maximinus, and the father, in an agony of grief, died by his own hand. The grandson was proclaimed emperor by the soldiers in Rome A.D. 238, although he was not more than fifteen years of age. He reigned six years, when he was assassinated by his soldiers at the instigation of Philip, prefect of the Prætorian guard.

GORDIUS, in Greek legend, a Phrygian peasant, father of Midas, who was raised to the Phrygian throne in accordance with an oracle which declared to its Phrygian consulters that their seditions would cease if they elected as king the first man they met, mounted on a chariot, going to the temple of Zeus. This was Gordius, who, to evince his gratitude, consecrated his chariot to Zeus, and fastened the pole with so ingenious a knot that the oracle promised the dominion o f the world to him who should untie it. Alexander the Great cut it with his sword, and to 'cut the Gordian knot' became a proverb.

GORDON, Adam Lindsay, Australian poet, was born in 1833 at Fayal, in the Azores, and died in 1870. Educated at Cheltenham, Woolwich, and Oxford, he left England when he was twenty for South Australia, and joined the mounted police.

He subsequently tried horse-breaking, entered the Colonial Assembly as member for Victoria district, and became noted as an adventurous steeplechaser. His first volume of poems, *Sea Spray and Smoke Drift* (1867), met with a very favourable reception, as did also *Bush Ballads and Galloping Rhymes* (1870), which depicted bush life with marvellous fidelity. He committed suicide the same year. He also wrote *Ashtaroth: a Dramatic Lyric.* His poems were edited by Marcus Clarke in 1880, and there have been various other editions, one by Douglas Sladen in 1912. *See* COLONIAL LITERATURE.

GORDON, Charles George, British soldier, known also as 'Chinese Gordon' and 'Gordon Pasha,' was born at Woolwich 1833, killed at Khartoum 1885. He entered the Royal Engineers in 1852, and served in the Crimea (1854–6). During the Taeping Rebellion in China Gordon succeeded in completely crushing the revolt by means of a specially-trained corps of Chinese, exhibiting marvellous feats of skilful soldiership.

On his return to England with the rank of colonel, he was appointed chief engineer officer at Gravesend, where his military talents and philanthropy were conspicuously displayed. From 1874 to 1879 he was Governor of the Sudan under the Khedive. For a few months in 1882 he held an appointment at the Cape, and he had just accepted a mission to the Congo from the King of the Belgians, when he was sent to withdraw the garrison shut up in the Sudan by the insurgent Mahdi. He was shut up in Khartoum by the rebels, and gallantly held that town for a whole year.

A British expeditionary force under Lord Wolseley was dispatched for his relief; an advance corps sighted Khartoum on 24th Jan., 1885, to find that the town had been treacherously betrayed into the hands of the Mahdi two days before, and Gordon murdered. Gordon's character was marked by strong religious feelings, which became so intensified as to make him somewhat of a religious enthusiast and fatalist.—BIBLIOGRAPHY: A. E. Hake, *The Story of Chinese Gordon*; A. Forbes, *Chinese Gordon*, Sir W. F. Butler, *Charles George Gordon*, D.

Boulger, *Life of Gordon*; W. S. Blunt, *Gordon at Khartoum*; Lytton Strachey, *Eminent Victorians.*

GORDON, FAMILY OF, a celebrated Scottish historical House, the origin of which is still wrapped up in a certain measure of obscurity. It is probable that the family came over to England with William the Conqueror, and at a subsequent period settled in Berwickshire, where a parish and village bear this name.

The adhesion of Sir Adam Gordon, Justiciar of Lothian, to the cause of Bruce gave him estates on Deeside and the Spey Valley. The direct male line

Lord George Gordon

died out in the person of Sir Adam of Gordon, who fell in the battle of Homildon (1402), but from his female and illegitimate descendants a number of branches sprang up.

His grandson was made Earl of Huntly (1445). The head of this branch was made marquess in 1599, and Duke of Gordon in 1684. The dukedom became extinct in 1836. The title Marquess of Huntly passed to a branch of the family which had acquired the title of Earl of Aboyne in 1660. The dukedom was revived in 1876, and given to the Duke of Richmond and Lennox, a nephew of the last duke. The Barons Lochinvar, the Viscounts Kenmure, and the Earls of Aberdeen are (or were) all branches of the Gordon family. Other members of the family became Earls of Sutherland. Lord Byron's mother was a Gordon.—Cf. J. M. Bulloch, *The House of Gordon.*

GORDON, George Stuart. British writer and savant, born 1881 and educated at Glasgow, Oxford and Paris. After a distinguished academic progress he became Professor of English Language and Literature at Leeds University (1913), and Dean of the Faculty of Arts in 1920. In 1922 he was appointed Merton Professor of English Literature at Oxford, and was at various times Warton Lecturer, Sir George Watson Lecturer, Rede Lecturer (Cambridge) and Gresham Professor of Rhetoric. From 1928 he was President of Magdalen College, Oxford.

Professor Gordon served in the European War, was wounded and mentioned in despatches, and subsequently appointed to the Staff of the Official Military History—His publications include many studies of English and classical literature, among them *Charles Lamb* (1921), *Shelly and the Oppressors of Mankind* (1923), *Andrew Lang* (1928) and the Warton Lecture on *Virgil* (1931).

GORDON, Lord George, son of Cosmo George, Duke of Gordon, born 1751, died 1793. He entered when young into the navy, but left the service during the American War. In 1774 he became a member of the House of Commons, and his parliamentary conduct was marked by a certain degree of eccentricity, and by his opposition to the Ministry.

A Bill having been introduced into the House for the relief of Roman Catholics from certain penalties and disabilities, in June, 1780, Lord George headed an excited mob of about 100,000 persons, who went in procession to the House of Commons to present a petition against the measure. The dreadful riots, known as the 'No Popery' Riots, which ensued led to his arrest and trial on the charge of high treason; but, no evidence being adduced of treasonable design, he was acquitted.

In the beginning of 1788, having been twice convicted of libelling the French Ambassador, Marie Antoinette, then Queen of France, and the criminal justice of his country, he retired to Holland, but he was arrested, sent home, and committed to Newgate, where he passed the remainder of his life. He was undoubtedly crackbrained. Dickens's *Barnaby Rudge* is in part a narrative of the Gordon Riots.—Cf. R. Watson, *The Life of Lord George Gordon.*

GORDON, Sir John Watson, Scottish painter, and president of the Royal Scottish Academy, was born in Edinburgh in 1788, died 1864. He applied himself almost exclusively to portrait-painting, in which he attained great excellence. He was employed to paint the portraits of many of the most eminent Scotsmen of the day. In 1879 his brother and sister endowed the Watson-Gordon Professorship of Fine Art, instituted in his memory in Edinburgh University.

GORDON, Patrick, a Scottish soldier, born 1635, died at Moscow 1699. In 1661 he entered the Russian service, became a general, and rose high in favour with Peter the Great. He kept a diary for the last forty years of his life, part of which was edited for the Spalding Club in 1859.

GORE, Catherine Grace, English novelist, born 1799, died 1861. In 1823 she was married to Charles Arthur Gore of the 1st Life Guards, and shortly afterwards appeared her first novel, *Theresa Marchmont, or the Maid of Honour.* She wrote altogether from sixty to seventy novels, clever pictures of fashionable life, among the best of which are *Preferment; The Courtier of the Days of Charles II; Cecil, or the Adventures of a Coxcomb; The Hamiltons; The Banker's Wife; Pin Money; Peers and Parvenues;* and *Temptation and Atonement.* She was also the author of a tragedy, *Lord Dacre of the South;* and two successful comedies, *A Quid pro Quo,* and *The School for Coquettes.*

GORE, Charles, English prelate and theologian. Born Jan. 20, 1853, he was made Bishop of Worcester in 1902. He was largely responsible for creating the new Diocese of Birmingham, and was bishop there from 1905 to 1911, when he became Bishop of Oxford, which post he resigned in 1919. He was one of the authors of *Lux Mundi,* and has written a number of theological works, being known also as a worker for social reform. He died Jan. 17, 1932.

GOREE', a small island, or rather rock, belonging to France, on the coast of Africa, in Senegal, a little more than a mile from the southern shore of the promontory that forms Cape Verde. Goree was amalgamated with Dakar in 1929. Pop. 998.

GORGET (Fr. *gorge,* throat), a piece of body armour, either scale work or plate, for the protection of the throat. The *camail,* or throat covering of chain mail, which is sometimes called the gorget of mail, belonged more to the helmet than to the body armour.

GORGIAS (gor'ji-as), Greek orator and sophist, born at Leontini, in Sicily, about 480 B.C. When about sixty years of age, he was sent as ambassador to Athens, where he spent the greater part of his remaining years. He was a popular teacher of rhetoric, had many distinguished pupils, and is protagonist in the *Gorgias* of Plato. Gorgias is said to have reached the extraordinary age

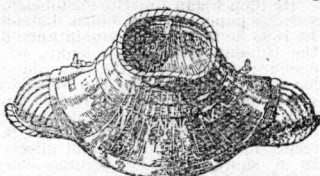

Gorget, 1535 (after Planché)

of 107 or 108 years. Two works attributed to him are extant, *The Apology of Palamedes*, and *The Encomium on Helena*, but their genuineness has been questioned. Cf. T. Gomperz, *Greek Thinkers*.

GORGONS (Gr. *Gorgŏnes*, terrible ones), in Greek mythology, three monsters whose names were Stheno, Euryăle, and Medusa, daughters of Phorcys and Ceto. They were all immortal, except Medusa.

Their hair was said to be entwined with serpents, their hands were of brass, their body was covered with impenetrable scales, their brazen teeth were as long as the tusks of a wild boar, and they turned to stones all those who looked upon them. Medusa was killed by Perseus (q.v.), and her head was afterwards placed on the Ægis of Athena. From her blood the

The Gorgon Medusa, from a marble at Munich

winged horse Pegasus is supposed to have sprung.—Cf. J. C. Lawson, *Modern Greek Folklore*.

GORGONZO'LA, a town and commune, Italy, 12 miles E.N.E. of Milan. It has a fine modern church, and a trade in a kind of ewe-milk cheese. Pop. 5,190.

v—I

GORIL'LA (*Gorilla gorilla*), the largest animal of the ape kind. It attains a height of about 5½ feet or more, is found chiefly in the woody equatorial regions of Western Africa, is possessed of great strength and fierceness, is a great frequenter of trees, and feeds chiefly on vegetable substances, as roots and fruits.

The erect position is more readily assumed by the gorilla than by most of the other anthropoid apes, owing to the shape of the sole of the foot, which is not inverted, and is shorter and broader; but the ordinary gait is on

Gorilla (*Gorilla gorilla*)

all fours. It has a ferocious and brutal cast of features, due to the prognathism of the jaws, the extremely prominent supra-orbital ridges, and retreating forehead.

Gorillas make a sleeping-place somewhat like a hammock, connecting the branches of a tree by means of the long, tough, slender stems of climbing plants, and lining it with dried fronds of palms or long grass. This abode is constructed at different heights from the ground, but there is never more than one such nest in a tree.

The gorilla, like the chimpanzee, has thirteen ribs, whereas man and the orang have twelve. The bones of the arm are much longer than in man, and the upper arm is longer than the forearm; the leg bones are shorter than in man. In the proportion of its molar teeth to the incisors and in the form of its pelvis it approaches somewhat closely the human form. It is less intelligent and docile than several other apes.

GORING, village of Oxfordshire. It stands on the Thames, 10 miles from Reading, opposite Streatley in Berkshire, on the G.W. Rly. It is much visited for boating, being one of the beauty spots of the Thames. **Goring Gap** is the depression in the chalk hills through which the Thames flows.

Another **Goring** is the seaside resort in Sussex, now part of the borough of Worthing.

GÖRIZIA, GÖRITZ or **GÖRZ** (geurts, geu'rits; It. *Gorizia*, Slov. *Gorica*), a town of Italy, capital of the former Austrian province of Görz and Gradisca, near the head of the Adriatic, 23 miles N.N.W. of Trieste. It occupies a very picturesque site on a mountain slope, and consists of the high town, surrounded by walls and defended by an old castle; the new town situated in the plain on the left bank of the River Isonzo; and several suburbs. Görizia is the seat of an archbishop, and manufactures silk, cotton, leather, and earthenware. Charles X of France died there in 1836. The town was captured from the Austrians in Aug., 1916, and retaken in Oct., 1917. Pop. (1931), 49,239.

GORKUM (properly *Gorinchem*), a fortified town of the Netherlands, on the Linge, at its junction with the Merwede, the name given for a short distance to the river formed by the union of the Waal and the Maas, 22 miles E.S.E. of Rotterdam. Pop. 12,053.

GORKY (pseudonym of *Alexei Maximovitsh Pyeshkov*), Russian author, born at Nijni-Novgorod, at the house of his maternal grandfather the painter Kashirine, in 1868. He chose the name of Gorky (meaning 'bitter' in Russian) on account of the hardships he had to endure in his early life.

Left an orphan at the age of five, he received a few months' schooling, and was apprenticed by his grandfather to a shoemaker when he was nine years old. He then worked for a draughtsman, and for an ikon painter, and subsequently tried his hand at many things and served in many employments, from that of a cook's assistant on a Volga steamer to that of a lawyer's clerk. At the age of sixteen he came to Kazan, but, unable to enter any educational institution, he continued to work, never remaining more than a few weeks in any occupation.

Of a roving disposition, he travelled over a large part of his native country as a tramp and mixed with the lowest of the population. The varied scenes and persons which he saw in this his vagabond life furnished him with the material for his literary work. Someone suggested to him the idea of writing, and he produced the story *Makar Tshudra*, which appeared at Tiflis in 1892 in the paper *Kavkaz*.

He then began to write sketches for various papers in the Volga district. In 1893 he made the acquaintance of the Russian author Korolenko, who encouraged him to write, and placed his story *Tshelkash* in the *Rousskoe Bogatstvo*. Henceforth Gorky continued his literary work, describing the outcasts and vagabonds, and interpreting their suffering and misery. In a short time he became very popular and looked upon as one of Russia's best authors. Gorky is a realist, and his realism is tinged with pessimism. His characters are all in conflict with society, and rebel against the existing order of things.

Since 1898 Gorky's works appeared exclusively in the Petrograd periodical *Zhizn* (Life). Among his other works are: *Foma Gordyeev* (1889); *Mushik* (1900); *Three of Them* (1902); *Malva, Mother* (1907); *The Spy* (1908); *A Confession* (1910); *In the World* (1917); *Bystander* (1930); *The Magnet* (1931). His play *The Lower Depths* was produced in London in 1903. A collection of his works was published by the publishing society Znanie.

A revolutionary since his early youth, Gorky was **imprisoned several** times under the autocratic régime. At the outbreak of the European War he enlisted and served with the Russian Red Cross. After the Russian Revolution of 1917 he joined the ranks of the Bolsheviks, and was a member of the Soviet of Petrograd, but in 1920 he definitely declared himself an opponent of the Bolshevik régime. —BIBLIOGRAPHY: P. Kropotkin, *Russian Literature*; E. J. Dillon, *Maxim Gorky: his Life and Writings*; A. S. Rappoport, *Gorky and Dostoievsky* (in *Twentieth Century Russia*, 1915); S. Persky, *Contemporary Russian Novelists*.

GORLESTON, watering place of Suffolk. It stands at the mouth of the Yare, 120½ miles from London, on the L.N.E. Rly. The sands are very good, and there are golf links. Gorleston is included in the Borough of Great Yarmouth. Pop. (1931), 20,391.

GÖRLITZ (geur'lits), a town of Germany in Prussia, province of Silesia, on the left bank of the Neisse. It is well built, having generally substantial houses, several large squares and spacious streets. Its industries include woollens, linens, and cottons, machinery, iron-founding, glass, porcelain, leather, and soap. The town was an important place for three centuries before the Reformation; it afterwards declined, but has rapidly increased in prosperity since the laying down of the railways; the population, which in 1831 was only 8,000, was, in 1925, 91,702. Founded about 1200, Görlitz passed to Saxony in 1635, and was annexed by Prussia in 1815.

GÖRRES (geur'res), **Jakob Joseph von**, a distinguished German publicist and author, born at Coblentz 1776, died at Munich 1848. He began life with very advanced ideas, but ultimately his republican views became much modified, and he ended as an uncompromising Ultramontane Roman Catholic.

He taught in a school at Coblenz, and having studied Persian, he produced a translation of part of the *Shahnameh*. In 1814 he started the *Rheinische Merkur*, the organ of the German national movement against Napoleon, but it was suppressed in 1816 as obnoxious to the Prussian Government. In 1826 he became professor of history at Munich. Among his chief works are: *Aphorisms on Art, Faith and Science, Mythological History of Asia*, and *Christian Mysticism*.

GORSEDD, name used in Wales and Cornwall for a national assembly. At these, bards contend for prizes, and they are almost identical with the eisteddfods. One was held near Penzance in 1931, this being a revival of a ceremony a thousand years old.

GORST, Sir John Eldon, British politician, born at Preston 24th May, 1835, died 1916. Educated at St. John's College, Cambridge, he was called to the Bar in 1865, and entered the House of Commons in 1866 for the borough of Cambridge. He afterwards sat for Chatham and for Cambridge University (1892–1906).

He was in succession Solicitor-General, Under-Secretary for India, Financial Secretary to the Treasury, and vice-president of the Committee of the Council on Education. An authority on social and labour questions, he was British plenipotentiary at the Labour Conference in Berlin in 1890.

GORTON, an urban district in Lancashire, and now included in Manchester, and giving name to one of its parliamentary divisions. One of the Manchester water-reservoirs is at Gorton.

GORTSCHAKOV, Alexander Michaelovitsh, Russian diplomatist, brother of Prince Michael, was born 1798, died 1883. He entered the diplomatic service in 1824 as secretary to the Russian embassy in London. His experience in diplomacy was extended in Vienna, Florence, and Stuttgart, and he showed considerable dexterity in securing the neutrality of Austria during the Crimean War. In 1856 he became Minister of Foreign Affairs, and in 1862 Chancellor of the Empire. He was a prominent member of the Berlin Congress, 1878.

GORTSCHAKOV, Prince Michael, Russian general, born in 1792, died 1861. He took part as an artillery officer in the battle of Borodino in 1812, and served in the subsequent campaigns of the Allies against the French. He took a prominent part in the Turkish War (1828–9); the Polish War (1831); the invasion of Hungary (1849); and in the war with Turkey and the Western Powers (1853–5). In the Crimea he held the command in Sebastopol during the siege. After the war he was made Governor of Poland.

GOSCHEN (gō'shen), **George Joachim, Viscount,** politician and financier, of German extraction, born in London 1831, died in 1907. Educated at Rugby and Oxford, he entered Parliament in 1863. In 1865 he was sworn of the Privy Council on becoming a member of the Russell ministry. In 1868 he became President of the Poor Law Board, and subsequently First Lord of the Admiralty.

On several occasions he found himself unable to move with the Liberal party; and when in 1886 Gladstone launched his Home Rule scheme for Ireland, Goschen became one of the leaders of the Liberal-Unionists. The same year he succeeded Lord R. Churchill as Chancellor of the Exchequer under Lord Salisbury, and in 1895 he again took office under the same leader as First Lord of the Admiralty. In 1900 he was raised to the peerage as Viscount Goschen. He was author of a well-known work on the *Theory of Foreign Exchanges*.

GOSFORTH, an urban district of England, in Northumberland, 3 miles north of Newcastle, with many residences of Newcastle merchants. In Gosforth Park race meetings are held. Pop. (1931), 18,042.

Another **Gosforth** is a village of Cumberland, 12 miles from Whitehaven.

GOSHAWK, a diurnal bird of prey of the hawk kind, belonging to the genus Astur (*A. palumbarius*). The general colour of the plumage is a deep brown, the breast and belly white. A full-grown female is 23 or 24 inches in length, the male a good deal smaller. It was formerly much used in falconry. This bird flies low, and pursues its prey in a line after it, or in the manner called 'raking' by falconers. The female was generally flown by falconers at rabbits, hares, &c., and the larger winged game, while the male was usually flown at the smaller birds, and principally at partridges.

GOSHEN, in ancient geography, a district of Egypt, which Joseph procured for his father and brethren. The land of Goshen was supposed to be between the eastern part of the ancient Delta and the western border of Palestine.

GOSLAR, an interesting old town of Germany in Hanover, 26 miles south-east of Hildesheim, on the north side of the Harz, at the foot of the Rammelsberg. It once ranked as a free imperial city, has remains of its old fortifications, and some old buildings, including part of a palace of the German Emperors, dating from the eleventh century, and containing an imperial throne dating from the twelfth century. There is also a town house of the fifteenth century. The inhabitants are chiefly engaged in the copper, silver, and other mines in the neighbourhood. Pop. 20,854.

GOSPEL, or **GOSPELS.** The Greek word for which *gospel* has been used as the equivalent is *evangelion*, or rather *euaggelion*, a good or joyful message. In the New Testament it denotes primarily the glad tidings respecting the Messiah and his kingdom—this was emphatically the *gospel* (O.E., *gôdspell*, good tidings). It was quite naturally employed as a common title for the historical accounts which record the facts that constitute the basis of Christianity.

It may be fairly said that the genuineness of the four narratives written by Matthew, Mark, Luke, and John rests upon better evidence than that of any other ancient writings. They were all composed in the latter half of the first century; those of Matthew and Mark some years before the destruction of Jerusalem; that of Luke about the year 64; and that of St. John about the close of the century.

Before the end of the second century we have abundant evidence that the four Gospels, as one collection, were generally used and accepted. While the early existence of these Gospels has been admitted, much discussion has taken place regarding their origin, and their relation one to another. They seem to have been viewed as so many original and independent sources, each one as much so as the others.

Successive Dependence Theory. The critical spirit of modern times has refused to halt at this point; it has sought to get at, so to speak, the genealogy of the several Gospels with their different degrees of relationship. Each of the four Gospels has in turn been assumed by different critics to be the first out of which the others arose. This view is known as the *Successive Dependence Theory.*

Another theory, known as the **Documentary Theory,** and propounded by Le Clerc (1716), Priestley (1777), and Lessing (1778), maintains that some prior, more strictly original document, no longer extant, formed the common basis of all the Gospels.

The supposition of an original document from which the three synoptical Gospels (those of Matthew, Mark, and Luke) were drawn, each with more or less modification, would naturally occur to those who rejected the notion that the evangelists copied from each other. The fourth Gospel, as the narrative coincides with that of the other three in a few passages only, is not drawn into the discussion, and the received explanation is the only satisfactory one with respect to it, namely, that John, writing last, had seen the other Gospels, and purposely abstained from writing anew what had been sufficiently recorded.

Oral Theory. Another conjecture is that the Gospels sprang out of a common oral tradition. This view is called the *Oral Theory*, and was suggested by Herder and Gieseler. According to this view of the origin of the Gospels, that of Mark, if not the oldest in composition, is yet probably the most direct and primitive in form; it is the testimony delivered by Peter, possibly with little alteration. The Gospels of Matthew and Luke, again, "represent the two great types of recension to which it may be supposed that the simple narrative was subjected. Luke represents the Hellenic, and Matthew the later Hebraic form of the tradition, and in its present shape the latter seems to give the last authentic record of the primitive Gospel." A comparison of the three synoptical Gospels yields some interesting results.

If we suppose the history they contain to be divided into sections, in forty-two of these all the three narratives coincide; twelve more are given by Matthew and Mark only, five by Mark and Luke only, and fourteen by Matthew and Luke. To these must be added five peculiar to Matthew, two to Mark, and nine to Luke. But this applies only to general coincidence as to the facts narrated; the number of passages either verbally the same, or coinciding in the use of many of the same words, is much smaller.

Summary. Briefly stated, the critical result is as follows: There is a singular coincidence in substance in the three synoptical Gospels. The verbal and material agreement is such as does not occur in any other authors who have written independently of one another. The agreement would be no difficulty without the differences; it would only mark the one divine source from which they were all derived. The difference of form and style, without the agreement, would offer no difficulty, since there may be a substantial harmony between accounts that differ greatly in mode of expression, and the very difference might be a guarantee of independence.

Apocrypha. Several biographies of Jesus and the holy family written by unknown authors of the second, third, and later centuries are known as *Apocryphal Gospels.* They have no historical nor doctrinal value whatever. The titles of the best known of these are: *The Gospel of James, The Gospel of Joseph the Carpenter, The Gospel of Thomas, The Gospel of Nicodemus, The Acts of Pilate,* and his *Letter to Tiberias.*—BIBLIOGRAPHY: B. F. Westcott, *Introduction to the Study of the Gospels;* A. Wright, *The Composition of the Four Gospels;* F. C. Burkitt, *The Gospel History and its Transmission;* J. Drummond, *The Character and Authorship of the Fourth Gospel;* B. W. Bacon, *The Beginnings of Gospel Story.*

GOSPORT (God's port), a municipal borough, fortified seaport, and urban district, England, county of Hants, on the west side of the entrance to Portsmouth harbour, and directly opposite the town of Portsmouth, with which it is connected by means of a ferry and floating bridge. Besides containing infantry barracks, it is an important naval depot, including the Royal Clarence victualling yard, large Government factories, and Haslar Hospital (1746), the chief establishment in Britain for invalided sailors. The urban district includes Alverstoke and Stokes Bay. Pop. (1931), 37,928.

GOSS, Sir John, English organist and composer. Born at Fareham, Hants., 27th Dec., 1800, in 1811 he became a chorister of the Chapel Royal, London. He was made organist of S. Luke's, Chelsea, 1824, and in 1838 succeeded his master, Attwood, as organist of S. Paul's, London, being knighted on his resignation in 1872. He died May 10, 1880. Goss was the composer of some fine anthems and other church music.

GOSSAMER (probably a corruption of 'goose-summer') is the name of a fine filmy substance, like cobweb, which is seen to float in the air in clear days in autumn, and to a less extent in spring, and is most observable in stubble-fields, and upon furze and other low bushes. This is formed by young spiders of many species as a means of migration.

GOSSE, Sir Edmund, author, son of Philip Henry Gosse, born in London 1849; became library assistant in the British Museum 1867, was translator to the Board of Trade from 1875 to 1904; librarian to the House of Lords from 1904 to 1914. He published *Northern Studies;* and wrote much in the way of criticism, biography, and the history of English literature; besides several volumes of poetry. He was Clark lecturer in English literature at Trinity College, Cambridge, from 1884 to 1890. His works include: *History of Eighteenth Century Literature, History of Modern English Literature, Collected Essays, The Life of Swinburne, Inter Arma, Diversions of a Man of Letters,* and *Malherbe.* He was made a Companion of the Bath in 1912, and knighted in 1925. He died in 1928.

GOSSE, Philip Henry, naturalist, born at Worcester 1810, died 1888. From 1827 to 1835 he was resident in Newfoundland, and afterwards travelled through Canada and the United States, making all the time large collections of insects. In 1844 he visited Jamaica. Among his many works are: *The Canadian Naturalist, The Birds of Jamaica, A Naturalist's Sojourn in Jamaica, The Aquarium, Marine Zoology, Life, Actinologia Britannica, Romance of Natural History,* besides many contributions to the publications of learned societies. His *Life* was written by his son, Edmund Gosse.

GOSSYPIUM. See COTTON.

GÖTEBORG. City and seaport of Sweden, formerly called Gothenburg, capital of the *län* of the same name. It stands near the mouth of the river Göta, on the s.w. coast of the country, and is its largest seaport. It is 285 miles from Stockholm, and is an important railway centre. Canals flow through the streets. It is the seat of a bishopric. The cathedral was rebuilt early in the 19th century. There is a university, also academies of commerce.

Göteborg has a fine harbour always free from ice, and does a very large trade in timber and other products. It has a good depth of water, is defended by forts; there is a dry dock cut in the solid rock. It has manufactures of sailcloth, cotton, and other goods, and possesses shipbuilding yards, tobacco factories, breweries, and sugar refineries; it is also a fishing centre. The completion of the Göta canal and railway facilities increased its importance. It has a broadcasting station (322 M., 10 kw.).

It was founded by Gustavus Adolphus in 1619. Pop. (1932), 247,911.

The **Gothenburg System** is one for the control of the liquor traffic. It was started in the city in 1871, and has been copied by other places. Under it, the liquor is sold in houses which are managed by a company under the control of the muncipality. This can only make a small profit on its capital, and those in charge of the houses have no interest in promoting the sales of drink. The system is practically the same as that of the Public House Trust in Great Britain. It has been widely adopted in Sweden, Norway and Finland, with variations.

The **Göta Canal** is a ship canal that goes from Göteborg to the Baltic at Mem. It is 240 miles long, but for much of its course uses the river Göta and the Lakes Wener and Wetter.

GOTHA (gŏ′tä), a town of Germany, capital of the former Duchy of Saxe-Coburg-Gotha, since Dec., 1919, in the Thuringian Republic. It is situated on the Leine, 14 miles w.s.w. of Erfurt, is well built, with fine environs and suburbs. The principal building is the palace, occupying the crown of the height on which the town is situated. It contains a museum, a picture-gallery a valuable cabinet of engravings, a library of 200,000 vols. and 7,000 MSS., of which 2,500 are Arabic and 400 Persian and Turkish; and a collection of over 80,000 coins and medals. The manufactures consist chiefly of woollen, linen, and cotton tissues, porcelain, musical instruments, and articles in gold and silver. Gotha is well known as a publishing centre, especially for maps, and the *Almanach deGotha* was long published here. Pop. (1925), 45,780. *See* SAXE-COBURG-GOTHA; THURINGIA.

The **Gotha** is the name of a German aeroplane. It is a small, swift biplane, many of which were built and used during the European War for raids on England.

GOTHAM, a parish and village in county and 6 miles s.w. of Nottingham. It has an old reputation for folly, similar to that of the people of Abdera in Thrace, but the stories told of the 'wise men of Gotham' are widespread. *The Merrie Tales of the Mad Men of Gotham* were first collected and printed in 1550, Washington Irving, in his *Salmagundi*, applied the name to New York. Pop. 1,066.

GOTHARD, ST., a mountain group, Switzerland on the confines of the cantons of Tessin and Uri, belonging to the Lepontine or Helvetian Alps, which it connects with the Bernese Alps. It forms a kind of central nucleus in the great water-shed of Europe. Its culminating point has a height of 10,600 feet. The Col of St. Gothard, at its summit level, where the Hospice stands, is 6,935 feet high. Over it an excellent carriage road was completed in 1832,

A railway tunnel has been pierced through this mountain group between Göschenen on the north and Airolo on the south, thus directly connecting the railway system of North Italy with those of Switzerland and Western and Central Germany This tunnel is the second longest in the world, its total length being 16,295 yards, or rather more than 9¼ miles. Its construction, begun in 1872, was completed in 1881, and it was opened for traffic early in 1882. Its total cost was about £2,400,000.

GOTHIC ARCHITECTURE, a term applied to the various styles of Pointed architecture prevalent in Western Europe from the middle of the twelfth century to the revival of classic architecture in the sixteenth. The term was originally applied in a depreciatory sense to all the styles which were introduced by the barbarians who overthrew the Roman Empire. But the invention or introduction of the pointed arch gave birth to a new style of architecture, to which the name Gothic is now properly restricted.

The chief characteristics of Gothic architecture are: the predominance of the pointed arch and the subserviency and subordination of all the other parts to this chief feature; the tendency through the whole composition to the predominance and prolongation of vertical lines; the absence of the column and entablature of classic architecture, of square edges and rectangular surfaces, and the substitution of clustered shafts, contrasted surfaces, and members multiplied in rich variety.

This style originated in France and spread very rapidly to England, Germany, Italy, Spain, and the Scandinavian countries. In England it was introduced by William of Sens, who built Canterbury Cathedral in 1174, and here followed an independent course of development.

The Gothic architecture of Britain has been divided into four principal epochs—the Early English, or general style of the thirteenth century; the Decorated, or style of the fourteenth century; the Perpendicular, practised during the fifteenth and early part of the sixteenth century (Flamboyant being the contemporary style in France); and the Tudor, or general style of the sixteenth century. From that time Gothic architecture declined in Britain, but a revival set in about 1825, and many fine specimens of Gothic have since been erected, chiefly ecclesiastical buildings.

GOTHIC ARCHITECTURE. SALISBURY CATHEDRAL

The several periods of Gothic architecture are clearly marked by the form and general treatment of the windows. Those of the Early English are of a simple lancet form of elongated proportions, or of two or more lancet forms combined by mouldings. Those of the Decorated are broader in proportion, and with the upper part highly enriched with tracery of various curves and combinations. Those of the Perpendicular are frequently of very large size and still broader in proportion, while the upper part is also highly enriched. The enrichments invariably consist of a series of forms in which vertical lines prevail. Between each of these styles there are transition periods in which the distinctions are less clearly marked. *See also* the separate terms.—BIBLIOGRAPHY: F. Bond, *Gothic Architecture in England*; A. Fairbairns, *Cathedrals of England and Wales*; Viollet-le-Duc, *Dictionnaire raisonné de l'architecture fran-*

of similar name is mentioned by Tacitus as dwelling south of the Baltic, and *Geats* or *Gauts* are known to us from the Old English poem, *Beowulf* as inhabitants of Southern Sweden; but there is no necessary connection between these and the Goths proper.

About the middle of the third century they began to encroach on the Roman Empire. Having seized the Roman province of Dacia, they were assailed by Decius, whom they twice defeated. In 253 they captured Trebizond, where a large fleet of ships fell into their hands. With this force they sailed down the Ægean and plundered the coasts of Greece and Illyria. They now began to threaten Italy, but in 269 they were defeated with great slaughter by the Emperor Claudius. His successor Aurelian was, notwithstanding, compelled to cede to them the large province of Dacia, after which there was comparative peace between them for many years.

Gothic Architecture

1, 2, Early English windows.   3, Later Early English window, introduction of plate tracery.   4, Geometrical. 5, Decorated.   6, Perpendicular.   7, Perpendicular tracery

caise; Lübke, *Ecclesiastical Art in Germany during the Middle Ages.*

GÖTHITE, a mineral iron hydroxide, FeO(OH), which may also be written as $Fe_2O_3 \cdot H_2O$, crystallizing in black lustrous prisms of the rhombic system. The colour of the powder is yellow-brown, like ordinary iron rust. Göthite seems to be the fundamental iron hydroxide in nature, other and more common types, such as limonite, being derived from it by adsorption of various amounts of water.

GOTHLAND, or GOTTLAND (Sw. *Götaland*), one of the large sections into which Sweden was originally divided, and including the portion south of lat. 59° 20′ N.

GOTHLANDIAN, or GOTLANDIAN, a term proposed by De Lapparent in place of Upper Silurian, or Silurian as now commonly restricted, for the system of strata between the Ordovician and the Devonian. From the Island of Gotland in the Baltic.

GOTHS, an ancient Germanic tribe occupying, when first known to history, the region adjacent to the Black Sea north of the Lower Danube. The historian Jordanes believes that they had a Scandinavian origin. A people

In the fourth century the great Gothic kingdom extended from the Don to the Theiss, and from the Black Sea to the Vistula and the Baltic. About the year 369 internal commotions produced the division of the Gothic kingdom into the kingdom of the Ostrogoths (eastern Goths) and the kingdom of the Visigoths (western Goths).

The Visigoths. In 395 Alaric, King of the Visigoths, made an irruption into Greece, laid waste the Peloponnesus, and became prefect of Illyria. He invaded Italy and sacked Rome in 409, and a second time in 410. After his death (in 410) the Visigoths succeeded in establishing a new kingdom in the southern parts of Gaul and Spain, of which, towards the end of the fifth century, Provence, Languedoc, and Catalonia were the principal provinces, and Toulouse the seat of government. The last king, Roderick, died in 711 in battle against the Moors, who had crossed from Africa, and subsequently conquered the Gothic kingdom.

The Ostrogoths. After the fall of the Western Roman Empire, by the invasion of Odoacer in 476, the Eastern emperor, Zeno, persuaded Theodoric,

King of the Ostrogoths, to invade Italy in 489. The Goth became King of Italy in 493, and laid the foundation of a new Ostrogothic kingdom, which, together with Italy, comprised Rhætia (a part of Switzerland and the Tyrol), Vindelicia (part of Bavaria and Swabia), Noricum (Salzburg, Styria, Carinthia, Austria), Dalmatia, Pannonia (Further Hungary, Slavonia), and Dacia beyond the Danube (Transylvania, Walachia). This kingdom came to an end in 554. Subsequently the Goths both here and in Spain entirely disappeared as a distinct people.

tunately only a small portion of this translation has come down to us; but this is quite sufficient to enable us to form an opinion of the language at that time, and is of the highest value from a philological point of view. Besides this translation there exist a few other monuments of the language, which are, however, of minor importance.

Gothic was one of the Teutonic tongues, being accordingly a sister of Old and Modern English, German, Dutch and Danish. Being committed to writing earlier than any other Teutonic language, Gothic exhibits pecu-

EUROPE
c. 410 A.D.
To illustrate the advance of the Goths on Rome

Boundary between the Eastern and Western Empire circa A.D. 400

Religion. Christianity appears to have early taken root among the Goths settled in Moesia, a Gothic bishop being mentioned as present at the Council of Nicæa (325). Their form of Christianity was Arianism, which was patronized by their protector, Valens, and certainly adopted by their bishop Ulfilas. The introduction of Christianity among the Goths, and the circumstances of their dwelling near, and even among, civilized subjects of the Roman Empire, greatly contributed to raising them in civilization above the other German tribes.

Language. Bishop Ulfilas, in the fourth century, translated, if not the whole, at least the greater part of the Bible into Moeso-Gothic, using an alphabet which he formed out of those of the Greeks and Romans. Unfor-

liarities entirely its own, and hence its value in the study of Teutonic philology in general. It is richer in inflections than any other of the Teutonic tongues.

Swedish is the least like the Gothic of all the Germanic dialects, and notwithstanding the name *Gothland* (q.v.), there is no evidence to show that the Goths ever formed part of the population of Scandinavia. See ULFILAS.— BIBLIOGRAPHY: E. Gibbon, *Decline and Fall*; T. Hodgkin, *Italy and her Invaders*; J. B. Bury, *History of the Later Roman Empire*; J. Wright, *Primer of the Gothic Language*; Prof. Skeat, *Moeso-Gothic Glossary*; Martroye, *L'Occident à l'Epoque Byzantine: Goths et Vandales.*

GOTLAND, or **GOTHLAND,** an island of the Baltic, belonging to and about 50 miles east of the coast of Sweden. It is of irregular shape, and has an area of 1,176 sq. miles. The coast is for the most part rocky and deeply indented. The interior consists of a limestone plateau, intersected near its centre by a range of heights from 200 to 300 feet above the sea. The soil is fertile, and agriculture flourishes. The chief town, Visby, was once a flourishing member of the Hanseatic League. Railways serve the island. Together with two adjacent islets, the Island of Gotland forms the Swedish *län* or government of the same name. Area of län, 1,220. Pop. (1931) 57,450.

GÖTTINGEN (geut'ing-en), a town of Germany in Prussia, province of Hanover, on the Leine, 59 miles S.S.E. of Hanover. It is a place of great antiquity, and is generally well built, having wide and spacious streets. Its chief attraction is the university, founded in 1734 by George II of England and Elector of Hanover, opened in 1737. In 1931 it had 235 professors and lecturers, and 3,880 students.

Connected with the university are a museum, an observatory, an anatomical theatre, botanical garden, and a library possessed of 500,000 printed volumes and 5,000 MSS. The manufactures comprise woollens, chemicals, and scientific instruments. It is also a publishing centre. Pop. 41,514.

GOTTSCHED (got'shet), **Johann Christoph**, German writer, born 1700, died 1766, he became professor of rhetoric and poetry, and afterwards of logic and metaphysics, at Leipzig; and for many years was dictator in Germany in matters of literary taste. In 1728 he published the first sketch of his *Rhetoric*, and in 1729 his *Kritische Dichtkunst* (Critical Art of Poetry). Both these works condemn the disfigurement of the language by the use of foreign words, and oppose the taste for bombast in poetry which then prevailed.

In 1730 he published his *Contributions towards a Critical History of the German Language, Poetry, and Eloquence*, and subsequently his *Erste Gründe der Weltweisheit* (First Principles of Philosophy). By advocating French taste in literature as opposed to English, he lost within his lifetime much of the influence he had acquired earlier in his career.—Cf. T. W. Danzel, *Gottsched und seine Zeit*.

GOUDA (gou'dä), a town of the Netherlands, in the province of South Holland, 10 miles north-east of Rotterdam, separated into two unequal parts by the Gouwe, which here unites with the Yssel. The town, founded in 1485, burned down and

rebuilt in 1552, is composed of neatly-built houses, and is intersected by numerous canals. The great market-place is the largest in Holland. The church of St. John (1485) is noted for its organ and its painted glass windows, said to be among the finest in Europe. There are pipe-works, potteries, and breweries, and manufactories of stearine candles, yarn, and cigars. Gouda is a great market for cheese, sold under the name of Gouda cheese. Pop. (1932), 29,832.

GOUDIMEL (gö-di-mel), **Claude**, French musical composer, born 1510; killed during the St. Bartholomew massacres at Lyons, 1572. Palestrina was one of his pupils at Rome. His most important work is a setting of the French version of the *Psalms* by Marot and Beza. Some of these tunes are still used by the French Protestant Church and by the German Lutherans.

GOUGH (gof), **Sir Hubert de la Poer**, British soldier, born 12th Aug., 1870. He was educated at Eton and Sandhurst, joined the 16th Lancers in 1889, and served in the Tirah Expedition and in the South African War. He commanded his regiment from 1907 to 1911. During the European War he held many responsible positions, being in command of the Fifth Army at the Third Battle of Ypres (July, 1917), and during the German advance at St. Quentin in March, 1918. He was created G.C.M.G. in 1919.

In the same year he was appointed chief of the Allied Mission to the Baltic States, and he retired from the army in 1922. He received his knighthood in 1916. In 1931 Gough wrote an account of the events of 1918.

GOUGH, Hugh, Viscount, British soldier, born at Woodstown, County Limerick, 1779, died 1869. He joined the army in 1794, and was present the year after at the capture of the Cape of Good Hope. He served in Spain from 1809 to 1813; was made major-general in 1830, and sent to India as commander of the Mysore division of the army in 1837. He commanded the land forces in the Chinese War of 1841; was made baronet, and returned to India as commander-in-chief. He suppressed the revolt of the Mahrattas in 1843, commanded in the Sikh Wars of 1845-8, but was superseded by Sir Charles Napier in 1849. He was made baron in 1846; created viscount and pensioned, 1849; became field-marshal, 1862.

GOULBURN (göl'bérn), a city of New South Wales, in Argyle County, 108 miles S.W. of Sydney, well laid out, with broad streets lined with substantial buildings. Among the more important of the public buildings are the Anglican and Roman Catholic cathedrals, several other churches, the court-house, and mechanics' institute.

The industries include jam-factories, flour-mills, breweries, tanneries, and boot and shoe factories. Being the centre of several important railways, it is the principal depot of the southern inland trade. There are no goldfields in the vicinity, but silver, copper and other metals, marble, slate and lime, are among the wealth of the quarter. Pop. (1931), 12,570.

There is a **river Goulburn** in Victoria. It is a tributary of the Murray, and is 280 miles long.

GOULD, Sir Francis Carruthers, English caricaturist. Born at Barnstaple, 2nd Dec., 1844, he was for some 20 years a member of the London Stock Exchange. In 1879 he first illustrated the Christmas number of *Truth*, and in 1887 he contributed cartoons to *The Pall Mall Gazette*. He later became assistant editor and cartoonist of *The Westminster Gazette*, for which he did some of his best work. His publications include: *Who Killed Cock Robin?* 1897; *Froissart's Modern Chronicles*, 1902–03; and *Picture Politics*, which were periodical collections of his *Westminster* cartoons. He was knighted in 1906, and died 1st Jan., 1925. Gould was the most popular caricaturist of his day. His pictures were clever, and without any trace of malice.

GOULD, Jay, American capitalist. Born at Roxbury, New York, 27th May, 1836, he left his father's farm in 1852 to work in an ironmongery store, learning surveying in his spare time. After a short period in the timber trade, he took advantage of the railway panic in 1857 to buy railroad shares, becoming president and manager of the Rutland and Washington line. He became a broker in New York in 1859. Acquiring interests in railway lines he obtained control of several, and so amassed a great fortune. In 1881 he formed the Western Union Telegraph system. He died 2nd Dec., 1892, his son, George Jay Gould (1864–1923), succeeding to his railway and other interests.

GOUNOD (gö-nō), **Charles François,** French operatic composer, born at Paris 1818, died in 1893. He studied at the Conservatoire under Halévy, Lesueur, and Pauer, and afterwards in Italy. His first important work was *Faust* (1859), which raised him to a high rank among composers. Other operas followed, among which are *Mireille* (1864), *Romeo et Juliette*, *Cinq-Mars*(1877),and *Polyeucte*(1878).

He wrote also a *Messe Solennelle*, a motet *Gallia*, and other choral works and songs; oratorios *Redemption*

(1882), *Mors et Vita* (1885), and a Mass for the Jeanne d'Arc festival (1887).—Cf. H. Imbert, *Charles Gounod*.

GOURAUD, Henri Joseph Eugène, French soldier. Born in Paris, 17th Nov., 1867, he entered the army in 1890 and saw service in the Sudan and Morocco. In May, 1915, having until then been at the head of a colonial army corps, he was given command of the French forces in Gallipoli, where he was severely wounded, losing his right arm. In Dec. 1915, and again, 1917–19, he commanded the 4th Army. In 1919 he was appointed

Gourd (*Cucurbita Pepo* or **Pumpkin**)

High Commissioner in Syria and Commander-in-Chief in the Levant; in 1922 he became a member of the Supreme Council of War, and in 1924 was appointed Military Governor of Paris.

GOURD (görd), the popular name for the species of Cucurbita, a genus of plants of the nat. ord. Cucurbitaceæ. The same name is given to the different kinds of fruit produced by the various plants of this genus. These are held in high estimation in hot countries; they attain a very large size, and most of them abound in wholesome, nutritious matter.

The *C. Pepo*, or pumpkin, acquires sometimes a diameter of 2 feet. The *C. Melopepo*, or squash, is cultivated in America as an article of food. The *C. Citrullus*, or water-melon, serves the

Egyptians for meat, drink, and physic. The *C. aurantia*, or orange-fruited gourd, is cultivated only as a curiosity, and is a native of the East Indies. The *Lagenaria vulgāris*, or bottle gourd, a native both of the East and West Indies, is edible, and is often 6 feet long and 18 inches in circumference. The outer coat or rind serves for bottles and water-cups.

GOUROCK (gö′rok), a burgh of Renfrewshire, Scotland, on the Firth of Clyde, 3¼ miles west of Greenock. It is a favourite watering-place and yachting station, and has a pier for steamers. The Gamble Institute is the chief building. Pop. (1931), 8,844.

GOUT, a form of arthritis, a constitutional disorder giving rise to paroxysms of acute pain with a specific form of inflammation, appearing after puberty chiefly in the male sex, and returning after intervals. It is very often preceded by, or alternates with, disorder of the digestive or other internal organs, and is generally characterized by affection of the first joint of the great toe, by nocturnal exacerbations and morning remissions, and by vascular plethora; various joints, organs, or parts becoming affected after repeated attacks without passing into suppuration.

It may be acquired or hereditary. In the former case it rarely appears before the age of thirty-five; in the latter, it is frequently observed earlier. It appears that the disease is due to an excess of uric acid in the blood, this either being formed in the body in too large quantity, or not being removed from the blood by the kidneys in the urine as it ought to be.

Indolence, inactivity, and too free use of tartareous wines, fermented liquors, and very high-seasoned and nitrogenous food are the principal causes which give rise to this disease. Gout is also called, according to the part it may affect, *Podagra* (in the feet), *Gonagra* (in the knees), *Chiragra* (in the hands), &c. It may be acute or chronic, and may give rise to concretions, which are chiefly composed of urate of soda. Strict regulation of the habits of life is one of the most important elements in the treatment of gout.

GOV'AN, a parish of Scotland, county of Lanark, on the left bank of the Clyde, to the west of Glasgow. It carries on shipbuilding and engineering. Elder Park is an open space. Since 1912 Govan is included within the municipal boundaries of Glasgow. It gives name to one of the fifteen parliamentary divisions of the city.

GOVERNMENT is a word used in common speech in various significations. It denotes the act of governing,

the persons who govern, and the mode or system according to which the sovereign powers of a nation, the legislative, executive, and judicial powers, are vested and exercised.

Aristotle divided the forms of government into three classes: first, Monarchy, or that form in which the sovereignty of the state is vested in one individual; second, Aristocracy, or that in which it is confided to a select portion of the community supposed to possess peculiar aptitude for its exercise; and third, Democracy, or that in which it is retained by the community itself, and exercised, either directly, as in the small republics of ancient Greece, or indirectly by means of representative institutions, as in the constitutional states of modern times.

Each of these forms, if brought into existence by the general will of the community, maintained by its consent, and employed for its benefit, is said to be a legitimate government. But each of these legitimate forms was considered by the ancients to be liable to a particular form of corrup-

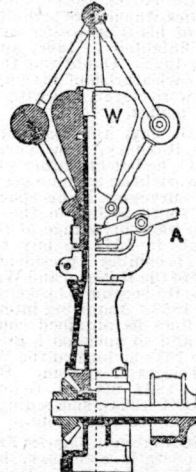

Porter Governor. A, Lever to steam-valve. W, Weight controlling mechanism

tion. Monarchy had a tendency to degenerate into tyranny, or a government for the special benefit of the single ruler; aristocracy became oligarchy; and democracy degenerated into ochlocracy or mob rule.

Through each of these various forms, each legitimate form being followed by its corresponding perverted form, government was supposed to run in a perpetual cycle; the last form, ochlocracy, being followed by anarchy.

As a means of avoiding these evils, a mixed government is supposed to have been devised. The best species of mixed government was believed by Aristotle to be a union of aristocracy and democracy. The most remarkable instance of this form is, however, supposed to be seen in that balance of powers which forms the essence of the British Constitution.

GOVERNOR, in engineering, a device for controlling the admission of steam to an engine or turbine. Most governors work on the principle of centrifugal force. If too much steam, say, is being admitted to a steam-engine, the speed of the engine rises, and the centrifugal forces in any rotating mechanism connected to it increase. The increased centrifugal forces are made to close the valve admitting the steam so that the speed falls.

A Porter governor is shown in the

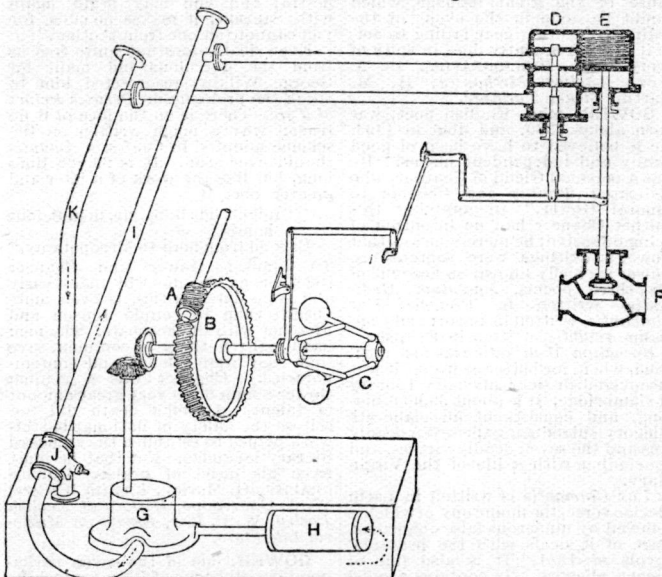

Oil-Operated Turbine Governor Gear

A, Worm-pinion on turbine shaft.　B, Governor worm-wheel.　C. Governor ball-gear.　D, Oil relay-cylinder. E, Oil-operated cylinder controlling steam-valve.　F, Steam-valve.　G, Oil-pump.　H, Oil-strainer. I, H.P. oil-main.　J, Relief-valve.　K, Oil-return pipe

See ARISTOCRACY; DEMOCRACY; MONARCHY; OLIGARCHY; REPUBLIC; LOCAL GOVERNMENT; SOVIETS; &c. —BIBLIOGRAPHY: Machiavelli, *The Prince*; Locke, *Civil Government*; Montesquieu, *The Spirit of Laws*; J. S. Mill, *Liberty and Spiritual Government*; W. Bagehot, *The English Constitution*; A. L. Lowell, *The Government of England*; Lord Bryce, *The American Commonwealth*; B. Bosanquet, *Philosophic Theory of the State*; J. S. Mackenzie, *Introduction to Social Philosophy*; J. A. Hobson, *Towards International Government*; F. A. Ogg, *The Governments of Europe*.

diagram on page 268. The balls are controlled by the conical cast-iron weight w. When the engine speed rises, the increased centrifugal force acting on the balls throws them outwards against the weight w. They therefore lift up the end of the rod A, which operates the admission-valve.

When the valves are too large to be operated directly in this way, they are operated hydraulically by oil. The hydraulic power is controlled by a relay-valve, which is itself controlled by centrifugal force. The diagram above shows the Continental design of oil-governor for a turbine plant.

Nearly all large turbine plants are fitted with a second main steam-valve, called the *emergency-valve*, which is held open against a powerful spring by means of a lever controlled by a trigger. At the end of the shaft a very simple centrifugal governor is provided, which consists of an eccentric weight controlled by a spring. If the speed of the machine exceeds a certain limit, this weight swings out far enough to trip the trigger and thereby close the emergency-valve. This is necessary for large power plants because of the great damage which would be done in the event of the ordinary governor gear failing to act, as it not infrequently does in spite of every care.—BIBLIOGRAPHY: D. A. Low, *Applied Mechanics*; H. M. Martin, *Steam Turbines*.

GOWER, John, English poet, was born about 1330, and died in 1408. He is believed to have been of good family and independent means. He was a personal friend of Chaucer, who dedicated *Troilus and Criseide* to "moral Gower." In applying this epithet Chaucer had no intention of being offensive; he merely meant that Gower's writings were sententious. Gower is chiefly known on account of his three poems, *Speculum Meditantis*, written in French; *Vox Clamantis*, written in Latin; and *Confessio Amantis*, written in English.

Speculum Meditantis was lost until 1895, when, for better or worse, it was discovered in the University Library at Cambridge. It is about 30,000 lines long, and consists of an elaborate allegory, introducing the seven deadly sins and the seven deadly virtues, and concluding with a life of the Virgin Mary.

Vox Clamantis is written in Latin elegiac verse, the monotony of which is relieved by numerous false quantities. Part of it deals with the peasants' revolt of 1381. It is also full of dreary allegory. It contains a good many passages borrowed from Ovid, Alexander Neckam, and Peter de Riga; these passages were for long believed to be Gower's own work.

The *Confessio Amantis* is Gower's masterpiece, and has the additional advantage of being written in English. It is highly allegorical also, but it contains a great many stories drawn from many sources. Gower, like Cerberus, was trilingual, but was unlike him in not being 'three gentlemen at once.' Gower is just the same whether he writes in French, Latin, or English; he can be tedious in all three languages.

J. R. Lowell, in his essay on Chaucer, speaks of Gower, and does not let mercy season justice. He says that he has positively raised tediousness to the precision of science, and speaks of his rhyme being regularly pertinacious as the tick of an eight-day clock.

"There is nothing beyond his power to disenchant, nothing out of which the tremendous hydraulic press of his allegory will not squeeze all feeling and freshness and leave it a juiceless pulp. Dip in at the middle or the end, dodge back to the beginning, the patient old man is there to take you by the button and go on with his imperturbable narrative. You may have left off with Clytemnestra, and you may begin again with Samson; it makes no odds, for you cannot tell one from t' other."

Even death does not quite free us from the garrulous old man, for George Wilkins resurrected him to speak the prologues in *Pericles Prince of Tyre*. There is on the face of it no reason why a poem written on the scheme adopted in *Confessio Amantis* should ever stop. It is 33,000 lines long, but like the work of a later and greater poet it

"might, ods bobs, sir, in judicious hands,
Extend from here to Mesopotamy."

To bracket Gower and Chaucer together, as was done by many early and some later critics, is even more absurd than to couple Jonson and Fletcher with Shakespeare. The men have really nothing in common, save that they were friends and contemporaries. Chaucer was a genius; Gower a man of no very great amount of talent. Gower's death did not eclipse the gaiety of nations; but his work helped to establish the standard literary language. For that he must have his meed of praise.—BIBLIOGRAPHY: H. Morley, *English Writers*; W. J. Courthope, *History of English Poetry*; W. P. Ker, *Essays on Medieval Literature*.

GOWER, one of the seven parliamentary divisions of Glamorganshire. It is peninsular, forming the west part of the county, and has Mumbles Head at one end and Worms Head at the other. Swansea and Oystermouth are the chief towns. Gower or Gwyr is famous for its romantic scenery, and its castles. These were built by the Normans who conquered the district in the 12th century. There are old old ruins and remains supposed to be Druidical. For long it had its own earl and sheriff, and was English rather than Welsh. In 1535 it was made part of Glamorganshire.

GOWRIE CONSPIRACY, one of the strangest episodes in Scottish history, took place in Aug., 1600. King James VI, while hunting in Falkland Park, Fifeshire, was asked by Alexander Ruthven (brother of the Earl of

Gowrie) to accompany him to Gowrie House, near Perth, on the pretext that they had caught a Jesuit with an urn of foreign golden pieces hidden under his cloak. On arriving at Gowrie House an attempt was made on the life or liberty of the king, but an alarm being raised, both the Ruthvens were slain, and James with difficulty escaped, as the Gowries were very popular with the inhabitants of Perth. —Cf. Andrew Lang, *James VI and the Gowrie Conspiracy.*

GOYA'NA, a city of Brazil, in the state of Pernambuco, 40 miles N.W. of the port of Recife or Pernambuco. Commerce in cotton, sugar, rum, hides, timber, castor-oil, &c. Pop. about 53,000.

GOYA Y LUCIENTES, Francisco José de, Spanish painter and etcher, born in Aragon 1746, died in Bordeaux 1828. He first worked in Saragossa under José Martinez, but as the result of a street brawl had to go to Madrid, whence he went to Rome. In 1774 he returned to Spain, and in 1789 became court painter to Charles IV. In 1824 he went to Paris, and finally settled at Bordeaux.

His work includes church decorations in Seville, Toledo, and Valencia; genre pictures of contemporary Spanish life; many portraits, notable among which are *The Duchess of Alba* and *Charles IV and his Family*; and a fine series of etchings. It is marked by great technical skill, a powerful and fantastic imagination, and a bitterly satirical outlook. Goya has exercised great influence on modern European art, especially in France. He is best seen in Madrid, but he is represented in the National Gallery, and the British Museum has a good collection of his etchings.

GOYAZ, an inland state of Brazil; area 288,462 sq. miles. Chief town, Goyaz. The chief occupation of the inhabitants is cattle-rearing and agriculture. Gold was formerly plentiful, and diamonds and other precious stones have been found. Pop. (1929), 712,210. The chief town, formerly called Villa Boa, has a cathedral and Government palace. Pop. 21,500.

GOZO, or GŌZZO, an island of the Mediterranean, belonging to Britain, about 4 miles N.W. of Malta; length, 9 miles; breadth, 4½ miles; area, about 26 sq. miles. A good deal of corn and fruit is raised; but the most important crop is cotton. Cattle of superior quality are reared. The chief town, Victoria (formerly Rabato), contains about 3,000, and the whole island about 22,500 inhabitants.

GOZZI (got'sē), Carlo, Italian dramatist, born at Venice 1722, died

1806. His principal work consists of a series of dramas based on fairy tales, which obtained much popularity.

GOZZOLI (got'so-lē) Benozzo, Italian painter, born at Florence 1420, died in 1498. He was a pupil of Fra Angelico, and worked at Florence, Rome, Orvieto, and Pisa. His name is specially identified with the great series of mural paintings in the Campo Santo, at Pisa, consisting of 24 subjects from the Old Testament, from *The Invention of Wine by Noah* to *The Visit of the Queen of Sheba to Solomon.* His *Virgin and Child Enthroned* is in the National Gallery, and

Portrait of Dona Isabel after Goya

The Glory of St. Thomas Aquinas in the Louvre.

GRAAFF-REINET (gräf-rī'net), a town, Cape Province, capital of a division of the same name, the oldest and largest town in the midland district of the province. There are churches and schools of the English Episcopalian and the Dutch Reformed denominations, a public library, and a college. The town is regularly laid out with streets at right angles, the intervening squares being filled up with vineyards and gardens. Pop. 9,222 (4,447 being Europeans).

GRAAFIAN VESICLES or FOLLICLES, in anatomy, numerous globular transparent follicles found in the ovaries of mammals. Each follicle contains one ovum, which is expelled when it reaches maturity. Small at first, and deeply imbedded in the ovary, they gradually approach the surface, and finally burst and discharge the ovum. They provide the mechanism for extruding ripe ova from the solid ovary; but the walls of the follicles are glands of internal secretion, forming hormones which determine the development of the secondary sexual characters and the secretion of milk.

GRACCHUS, a Roman family of the Sempronian gens, several members of which have become celebrated. *Tiberius Sempronius Gracchus*, a general of the Second Punic War, was consul 215 B.C., defeated Hanno 214 B.C., and was killed 212 B.C.

Another *Tiberius Sempronius Gracchus* became consul 178 B.C., and again 163 B.C. He married Cornelia, a daughter of Scipio Africanus, and was the father of the two most celebrated Gracchi, *Tiberius Sempronius* and *Gaius*, the former born about 169 B.C., killed 133 B.C.; the latter born 159 B.C., killed 121 B.C. The brothers, having lost their father early, received from their mother Cornelia a careful education. At a more advanced age their minds were formed and ennobled by the Greek philosophy.

Tiberius early made himself conspicuous by his military service. Under the command of his brother-in-law, the younger Scipio, he served at the siege of Carthage. While he was yet a mere youth he was received into the College of Augurs—an honour usually conferred only upon distinguished statesmen. He was subsequently quæstor to the Consul Mancinus, and was employed in the Numantian War, in which he greatly distinguished himself by the conclusion of a treaty by which he saved the lives of 20,000 men who were entirely at the mercy of the Numatines. This treaty was, however, repudiated by the Romans, but it increased his popularity immensely.

In 133 B.C. he offered himself as a candidate for the tribuneship, which office rendered his person inviolable so long as he was invested with it, and placed him in a situation to advance his great plans for the improvement of the condition of the people in a legal way.

His first efforts were directed to a reform of the Roman land system, by the restoration or enforcement of the old Licinian law, which enacted that no one should possess more than 500 acres of the public domains, and that the overplus should be equally divided among the plebeians. This law, which was now called, after Gracchus, the *Sempronian*, or the *Agrarian aw*, he revived, but with the introduction of several softening clauses.

He was violently opposed by the aristocracy and the tribune Marcus Octavius, whose veto retarded the passage of the Bill. Tiberius, however, by exerting all the prerogative of his office, managed to pass his bill, and three commissioners were appointed to carry it into execution, namely, Tiberius himself, his brother Gaius, and his father-in-law Appius Claudius.

Soon after this Attalus, King of Pergamus, died, bequeathing his treasures to the Roman people. Tiberius proposed that this bequest should be divided among the recipients of land under the new law, and to give the popular Assembly instead of the Senate the management of the State. But fortune turned against him; he was accused of having violated his office, and of aspiring to be king; and at the next election for the tribuneship he was slain, with 300 of his followers, at the entrance to the Temple of Fides.

Gaius. Ten years after the death of his brother Tiberius, the younger Gracchus obtained the tribuneship. In the discharge of his office he first of all renewed his brother's law, and avenged his memory by expelling many of his most violent enemies from the city. Several popular measures gained him great favour with the people, but the intrigues of the nobles ultimately caused his fall.

Livius Drusus, a tribune gained over to their interests, had the art to withdraw the affections of the populace from Gaius by making greater promises to them, and thus obtained a superior popularity for himself and the Senate. Hence it resulted that Gaius did not obtain a third tribuneship, and Opimius, one of his bitterest enemies, was chosen to the consulate.

A tumult, in which a lictor of Opimius was killed, gave the Senate a pretence for empowering the consuls to take strong measures. Opimius made an attack upon the supporters of Gracchus with a band of disciplined soldiers. Nearly 3,000 were slain, and Gracchus escaped to the grove of the Furies, where he was slain at his own request by a slave, who then killed himself.—BIBLIOGRAPHY: Beesly, *The Gracchi, Marius and Sulla*; Sir C. W. C. Oman, *Seven Roman Statesmen of the Later Republic*; A. H. J. Greenidge, *History of Rome*.

GRACE, in theology, the divine influence or the influence of the Holy Spirit in renewing the heart and restraining from sin; or, that supernatural gift to man whereby he is enabled to take to himself the salvation provided and offered through Christ (special or saving grace).

Before the fifth century little attention was paid to the dogmatic question of grace and its effects. Pelagius, a native of Britain, having used some free expressions, which seemed to attribute too little to the assistance of divine grace in the renovation of the heart of man, and too much to his own ability to do good, Augustine undertook an accurate investigation of this doctrine.

He came to the opinion, which has since been so much discussed, that God, of His own free will, has fore-ordained some to eternal felicity and others to irrevocable and eternal misery.

Doctrine of Predestination. In accordance with this view of Augustine is the doctrine of predestination. The majority of those who were considered Catholic or Orthodox coincided with Augustine, and, with him, pronounced the Pelagians heretics, for holding that human nature is still as pure as it was at its first creation, that all the corruption which prevails is the effect of the influence of bad example, and that, consequently, man, being sufficient for his own purification, has no need, at least, of preventing grace.

The Abbot Cassianus, of Marseilles, adopted a middle course, in order to reconcile the operations of grace and free-will in man's renovation, by a milder and more scriptural mode. He considered the predestination of God, in respect to man's salvation, as a conditional one, resting upon his own conduct. His followers were named *semi-* or *half-Pelagians*, though the Catholic Church did not immediately declare them heretics.

Protestant and Catholic Schisms. Subsequently a gradual change of sides was exhibited. During the Middle Ages the scholastic theologians so perverted the doctrines of Augustine as to make them easily reconcilable with those of the Pelagians. But at the Reformation Calvin and Beza, and the great body of their followers, returned to the fundamental principles of Augustine.

In the meantime, however, the Catholics had not come to a final agreement concerning this dogma. This appears from the quarrels of the Dominicans and Jesuits, and from the case of the Jesuit Luis Molina, in 1588, from whom the Molinistic disputes in the Netherlands received their name.

In the seventeenth century, also, two new parties, which had their origin in the dispute concerning the doctrine of predestination, sprang up in the Netherlands, namely, the Arminians or Remonstrants among the Protestants, and the Jansenists among the Catholics. (*See* ARMINIANS; JANSENISTS.) From that time the members of the Christian Church have continued to differ upon this subject. BIBLIOGRAPHY: A. Harnack, *History of Dogma*; H. W. Robinson, *Christian Doctrine of Man.*

GRACE, DAYS OF, in commerce, a certain number of days immediately following the day, specified on the face of a bill or note, on which it becomes due. Till the expiry of these days payment is not necessary. In Britain and America the days of grace are three. Austria (three days) and Russia (ten days) are the only other countries which allow days of grace. The number of days of grace depends on the law of the place where the bill is payable, not of that where it is drawn or indorsed.

GRACE, William Gilbert, famous cricketer, was born at Downend, Gloucestershire, in 1848, died 23rd Oct., 1915. Educated privately, he entered the medical profession and practised in Bristol for twenty years, 1879–99. He was a member of the Royal College of Surgeons of England and a licentiate of the Royal College of Physicians of Edinburgh.

In 1864 he made his first appearance in a leading cricket match at the Kennington Oval, Surrey's famous ground, and from 1870 to 1900 he played in the Gloucestershire county eleven. From 1899 he was secretary and general manager of the London County Cricket Club. His greatest achievements were accomplished with the bat, but he was a master of all departments of the game. His publications comprise: *Cricket* (1891), *Cricketing Reminiscences and Personal Recollections* (1899), and *W. G.'s Little Book* (1909).

GRACES (Gr. *Charites*, translated by the Romans *Gratiæ*), the goddesses of grace, from whom, according to Pindar, comes everything beautiful and agreeable. According to most poets and mythologists they were three in number, the daughters of Zeus and Eurynôme, and Hesiod gives them the names of *Aglaia* (brilliancy), *Thalia* (the blooming), and *Euphrosynê* (mirth).

Homer mentions them in the *Iliad* as handmaids of Hera (Juno), but in the *Odyssey* as those of Aphroditê (Venus), who is attended by them in the bath, &c. He conceived them as forming a numerous troop of goddesses, whose office it was to render happy the days of the immortals. The three graces are usually represented slightly draped or entirely nude, locked in each other's embrace or hand in hand.

GRACILARIA, a genus of Red Algæ. *G. lichenoïdes,* the 'Ceylon Moss' of the Indian Ocean, is one of the sources of the gelatinous substance called 'agar-agar,' largely used for preparing solid culture media in bacteriology, &c.

GRACIO'SA, one of the Azores· Chief town, Santa Cruz. Pop. 8,000.

GRA'DIENT, in mathematics· physics, engineering, and surveying, is a number measuring the slope of an inclined line relative to a horizontal plane. It may be measured either by the angle of inclination of the line to the plane, or by the sine or the tangent of the angle of inclination.

In surveying and engineering the gradient is usually measured by the tangent of the angle of inclination expressed in the form 1 in x; thus the gradient of 1 in 20 means that the sloping line makes an angle with the horizontal plane whose tangent is $\frac{1}{20}$. In America a gradient is expressed as a percentage; thus a gradient of 1 in 20 is described as a 5 per cent grade.

The heaviest gradients encountered in ordinary railway work are gradients of about 1 in 20. For steeper gradients, rack railways, or rope railways, are used. Some of the Alpine rack railways have gradients of 25 per cent.

GRADING, method of marking and arranging agricultural produce, so as to show its quality. In 1928 a national scheme of grading was introduced into Great Britain. It is used for apples, eggs, potatoes and other foodstuffs. At certain places there are stations for grading the fruits and vegetables.

GRADISCA, a town and district of Italy, formerly belonging to Austria-Hungary. The town of Gradisca is situated on the right bank of the Isonzo, about 30 miles north-west of Trieste. Captured by the Italians in 1915, but retaken by the Austrians, it was again captured by the Italians in 1918. Pop. of district, 34,155.

GRAD'UAL, the psalm, anthem, or hymn, said or sung in the service of the Roman Catholic Church between the Epistle and the Gospel; so named from being anciently chanted on the steps of the ambo or pulpit, or of the altar. By an easy transition the name was frequently applied to the *Antiphonary*, which was originally one of the three service books of the Church, but afterwards in the eleventh or twelfth century included in the missal.

GRADUATION, the art of dividing into the necessary spaces the scales of mathematical, astronomical, and other physical instruments. Original graduation is chiefly performed either by *stepping* or *bisection*.

Stepping consists in ascertaining by repeated trial with finely-pointed spring dividers the size of the divisions required, and then marking them.

In bisection an arc of radius nearly half the line is described from each end of the line by means of the beam compass, and the short distance between the arcs is bisected with the aid of a magnifier and fine pointer. This division is repeated for each of the two halves thus obtained until the required graduation is obtained. The original scale can henceforward be used as a pattern, and copies of it reproduced either by hand or machine.

If the copy be made by hand, the material which is to be divided must be placed parallel to the standard if the scale required is a linear one, or concentric with it if the scale be circular, and the divisions made by a dividing knife.

Linear and circular dividing engines have now replaced hand copying. These machines are constructed upon the principle of Ramsden's circular machine, invented in 1766. In this machine an accurately divided plate with notched edge is arranged to advance a certain amount (e.g. 10 feet of arc) for each revolution of a tangent screw. The screw is worked by a treadle, and the machine can be adjusted so that a movement of the treadle secures any desired part of a revolution of the screw. In Ramsden's linear machine a divided strip of metal, working in a slot, takes the place of the circular plate.

Ramsden's idea was improved and developed by Troughton and afterwards by Ross and Simms. Machines have also been constructed by Froment and others for dividing small spaces into a large number of intervals. The object to be graduated is slowly and intermittently pushed forward by a screw, while a fine steel or diamond point, working automatically, makes a cut at each cessation of the feeding motion. As many as 225,000 lines marking equal intervals have been cut in the space of 1 inch.

GRAFFI'TI, the rude designs and inscriptions of popular origin drawn or engraved with a style upon the walls of ancient towns and buildings, particularly of Rome and Pompeii. Those in Pompeii are in Latin, Greek, and Oscan, showing that the ancient language of Campania was still extant among a portion of the populace. The inscriptions are mostly amatory or humorous, sometimes malicious or obscene. In Rome graffiti occur frequently in the catacombs, some of them belonging to the fourth century having been discovered in 1915. Many of these are by Christians, some by Pagans in ridicule of Christianity.

GRAFTING, in horticulture, a method of artificial vegetative propagation, in which a twig bearing one or more buds, the scion, is inserted into a stem (or root) of a rooted plant, the stock. If the operation is successful, union between scion and stock takes place after a time, owing to the growing together of the cambial layers of the two.

There are many varieties of grafting, differing in the shape of the surfaces which are brought into mutual contact, or as regards the part of the stock in which the scion is inserted.

The objects of grafting are various, such as the perpetuation of a variety which does not set seed, the production of dwarf trees, the encouragement of early fruiting, &c. Budding and inarching (q.v.) are special forms of grafting.—Cf. L. H. Bailey, *The Nursery Book.*

GRAFTON, Augustus Henry, third Duke of, born 1735, died in 1811. He was Secretary of State under Rockingham, First Lord of Treasury under the elder Pitt, and Premier during the illness of the latter. He subsequently held the Privy Seal under Lord North, and again under Rockingham, but ultimately gave up politics. He is chiefly remembered as the subject of some of the most scathing of the letters of Junius.

GRAFTON, a town in New South Wales, on both sides of the River Clarence, here navigable, about 45 miles from the sea. It is a well-built place in a rich agricultural district, containing sugar-mills, and carries on a good trade with Sydney and other places; the see of an Anglican and a Roman Catholic bishop. Pop. 6,500.

GRAHAM, John, Viscount Dundee, commonly known as **Claverhouse,** eldest son of Sir William Graham of Claverhouse, was born about 1650, and educated at St. Andrews. He went abroad and entered the service of France and afterwards of Holland, but, failing to obtain the command of a Scottish regiment in the Dutch service, he returned to Scotland in 1677, where he was appointed captain of a troop of horse raised to enforce compliance with the establishment of Episcopacy.

He distinguished himself by an unscrupulous zeal in this service, especially after the murder of Archbishop Sharpe in May, 1679. The Covenanters were driven to resistance, and a body of them defeated Claverhouse at Drumclog on 1st June. On the 22nd, however, the Duke of Monmouth defeated the insurgents at Bothwell Brig, and Claverhouse was sent into the west with absolute power.

In 1682 he was appointed sheriff of Wigtownshire, and, assisted by his brother David, continued his persecutions. He was made a Privy Councillor, and received the estate of Dudhope, with other honours from the king, and although on the accession of James his name was withdrawn from the Privy Council it was soon restored.

In 1686 he was made brigadier-general, and afterwards major-general; and in 1688, after William had landed, he received from James in London the titles of Lord Graham of Claverhouse and Viscount Dundee.

When the king fled he returned to Edinburgh, but finding the Covenanters in possession he retired to the north, followed by General Mackay. After making an attempt on Dundee, Claverhouse finally encountered and defeated Mackay in the Pass of Killiecrankie (17th July, 1689), but was killed in the battle.

GRAHAM, Thomas, Master of the Mint, an eminent chemist, was born at Glasgow in 1805, died in 1869. Educated at Glasgow University, he commenced teaching private mathematical classes in Glasgow in 1827, and in 1829 succeeded to the lectureship of chemistry in the Mechanics' Institution.

In 1830 he was appointed professor of chemistry in the Andersonian University. In 1831 he established the law that gases diffuse at a rate inversely as the square root of their specific gravities. He afterwards made a series of investigations into the constitution of arseniates, phosphates, and phosphuretted hydrogen, and into the function of water in different salts.

In 1837 he was elected professor of chemistry in the University of London, and soon after settling in the metropolis he was appointed assayer to the Mint. In 1841 he was chosen first president of the Chemical Society, which he had assisted in founding; and in 1846 he helped to establish the Cavendish Society, over which he presided.

In 1849 and in 1854 he read the Bakerian lecture, the subject of both being the diffusion of liquids, which he further treated before the Royal Society in 1861. He distinguished the crystalloids and colloids in liquid solutions, and gave to their separation the name of *dialysis*. In a subsequent paper (*Philosophical Transactions,* 1866) he applied these discoveries to gases, under the name of *atmolysis*. The passage of gases through heated metal plates and the occlusion of gases were also ably investigated by him.

GRAHAM, Stephen, English writer. Born in 1884, he spent many of his early years in Russia, living among the peasants. He also travelled over a large part of Europe and Asia. As a writer he made his name with his books on Russia, notably *A Vagabond in the Caucasus* and *Changing Russia.* Having been also in America and Africa, Graham joined the Scots Guards, and served in France in 1917–18, recounting his experience in *A Private in the Guards.* After the war he returned to his wandering life, and as a result wrote, among other books, *Children of the Slaves, Russia in Division* and *The Gentle Art of Tramping.*

GRAHAM, William, British politician. Born at Peebles, 29th July, 1887, he was for a time in the civil service. In 1913 he was elected to the city Council of Edinburgh and, having become a figure in the Labour movement, he entered the House of Commons as M.P. for Central Edinburgh in 1918. Showing a grasp of financial matters, he was Financial Secretary to the Treasury in 1924, and from 1929 to 1931 was President of the Board of Trade. In Aug., 1931, he resigned office and was chosen deputy leader of the Labour Party in Parliament, but lost his seat at the general election in Oct. His writings include *The Wages of Labour.* He died 8th Jan., 1932.

GRAHAME (grăm or grā'am), **James,** Scottish poet, born in Glasgow in 1765, died there in 1811. He studied law in Edinburgh, and in 1791 became a Writer to the Signet. In 1795 he was admitted to the Faculty of Advocates, of which he continued a member until 1809, when he took orders as a clergyman of the Church of England.

Previous to this all his literary productions had been published. While at the university he printed and circulated a collection of poetical pieces. These appeared in an amended form in 1797. In 1801 he published a dramatic poem entitled *Mary, Queen of Scotland,* and in 1802 appeared, anonymously, *The Sabbath.* *The Birds of Scotland* and *British Georgics* are among his other publications.

GRAHAME-WHITE, Claude, British aviator and builder of aeroplanes, born 21st Aug., 1879. Educated at Bedford Grammar School, he engaged in the motor-engineering business, and in 1909 began to be interested in aeronautics, organizing an aviation school at Pau.

The first Englishman to be granted an aviator's certificate, he won the International Gordon-Bennet aeroplane race in America with a Gnome-Bleriot in 1910. The Grahame-White Aviation Company, which he formed, acquired the aerodrome at Hendon, where he started an aviation school. His works include: *The Story of the Aeroplane* (1911); *The Aeroplane, Past, Present, and Future* (1911); *Heroes of the Air: a Book for Boys* (1912); and *The First Airways* (1918). In 1930 he published *Flying, an Epitome and a Forecast.*

GRAHAM ISLAND, or FERDINANDEA, a volcanic island which in July, 1831, rose up in the Mediterranean, about 30 miles south-west of Sciacca, in Sicily. It attained a height of 200 feet, with a circuit of 3 miles, but disappeared in August. It reappeared for a short time in 1863. Jules Verne's story *Captain Antifer* hinges upon the appearance and disappearance of this island.

GRAHAM LAND, a tract of land in the Antarctic Ocean; discovered in 1832 by Biscoe, who took possession of it for Great Britain. It stretches between lat. 63° and 68° s., and lon. 61° and 68° w. There is a meteorological station on the west coast.

GRAHAMSTOWN, a town of Cape Province, the metropolis of the Eastern Provinces, on the slopes of the Zuurberg. It is a well-built thriving place, with a town hall, an Anglican and a Roman Catholic cathedral. Rhodes University College (founded in 1904), St. Andrew's College, schools, botanic garden, &c. Pop. 15,000 (including 7,592 whites in 1931).

GRAIL (variously spelt **Greal, Graal, Grazal, Grasal,** &c.), the legendary holy vessel, supposed to have been of emerald, from which Christ dispensed the wine at the Last Supper. It was said to have been brought to England by Joseph of Arimathea, but to have been taken back to heaven until the appearance of heroes worthy to be its guardians.

Titurel, a descendant of the Asiatic prince Perillus, whose descendants had allied themselves with the family of a Breton sovereign, was chosen as its keeper. He erected for it a temple on the model of that at Jerusalem, and organized a band of guardians. It was visible only to the baptized and pure of heart.

With this legend that of King Arthur became connected. Three of his knights, Galahad, Percival, and Bors, had sight of it, and on the death of Percival its last guardian, it was again taken to heaven. Popular in the Middle Ages, the romance of the Grail was revived by the poets of the nineteenth century (cf. Tennyson's *Idylls of the King).*—BIBLIOGRAPHY: A. Nutt, *Studies on the Legend of the Holy Grail;* E. Rhys, *Studies in the*

Arthurian Legend; J. L. Weston, *Legend of Sir Percival*.

GRAIN includes all those kinds of grass which are cultivated on account of their seeds for the production of meal or flour. All kinds of grain contain the following in varying quantities: water, albuminous substances (gluten, &c.), carbohydrates (starch), fat, and mineral compounds. In the husk are to be found small quantities of the complex substances known as vitamines, essential for the proper nutrition of the body.

GRAINING (*Leuciscus lancastriensis*), a fish of the dace kind, found chiefly in the Mersey and its tributaries, and in some of the Swiss lakes. The nose is more rounded than that of the dace, the eye larger, and the dorsal fin commences half-way between the point of the nose and the end of the fleshy portion of the tail. The most recent authorities, however, do not recognize it as a distinct species. It seldom weighs more than half a pound, in habit and food it resembles the trout.

GRAIN-MOTH, a minute moth of which two species are known, *Tinea granella* and *Butalis sitotroga cerealella*, whose larvæ or grubs devour grain in granaries. The moths have narrow, fringed wings, of a satiny lustre.

GRAINS OF PARADISE, Guinea grains or Meleguetta pepper, the pungent somewhat aromatic seeds of *Amōmum Meleguetta*, nat. ord. Zingiberaceæ, a plant of tropical Western Africa. They are chiefly used in cattle medicines and to give a fiery pungency to cordials. The 'Grain Coast' of Africa takes its name from the production of these seeds in that region.

GRAK'LE, or GRACKLE, a name applied to the Indian hill-starlings. One of these is the myna bird (*Eulabes religiosa*), which can be taught amusing tricks and can imitate the human voice. It is of a deep velvet-black, with a white spot on the wing, yellow bill and feet, and two yellow wattles on the back of the head. A number of other birds have also been called grakles, such as the purple grakle, or crow-blackbird of America. See CROW-BLACKBIRD.

GRALLATO'RES, the name, now obsolete for an artificial assemblage of wading and other birds, such as herons, flamingoes rails, and cranes. It was devised by Illiger in 1811 as an improvement on Linnæus's ord. Grallæ, which also included bustards and ostriches.

GRAMMAR, that branch of linguistic science which deals with and investigates the system of rules, principles, and facts which must be known in order to speak and write any language correctly.

Comparative grammar treats of the laws, customs, and forms which are shown by comparison to be common to various languages; general or universal grammar, of those laws which, by logical deduction, are demonstrated to be common to all. Historical grammar deals with the historical development of a given language, from the earliest traces of this language down to the present time.

The divisions of grammar vary with the class and also with the method of treatment. In common English grammars the division is generally fourfold: orthography, which treats of the proper spelling of words, and includes orthoepy, treating of the proper pronunciation; etymology, which treats of their derivations and inflections; syntax, of the laws and forms of construction common to compositions in prose and verse; prosody, of the laws peculiar to verse.

Although the systematization of grammar had begun in some sort in Plato's time, it was chiefly to the Alexandrian writers that it owed its development. The first Greek grammar for Roman students was that of Dionysius Thrax, in use about 80 B.C.

Comparative grammar can only be said to have existed from the beginning of the last century, when the critical study of Sanskrit established the affinities of the languages of the Indo-European group. The names of Bopp, Grimm, Pott, Schleicher, and Müller are especially associated with its development.—BIBLIOGRAPHY: H. Sweet, *A New English Grammar, Logical and Historical*; P. Giles, *Manual of Comparative Philology*; T. G. Tucker, *Introduction to the Natural History of Language*.

GRAMME. See WEIGHTS AND MEASURES.

GRAMMONT, a town of Belgium, East Flanders, 22 miles S.S.E. of Ghent, on both sides of the Dender. It was here that the Charter of Grammont was granted in 1068. Chief manufactures: linen, lace, thread, paper, and tobacco-pipes. Pop. 12,664.

GRAMMONT, ORDER OF (*Grandmontains*), a monastic order established by Stephen of Thiers in 1076 at Muret, but afterwards (1124) removed to Grandmont. The order became extinct at the Revolution.

GRAMONT, or GRAMMONT, Philibert, Comte de, son of Anthony, Duke of Grammont, born in 1621, died 1707. He served under the Prince of Condé and Turenne, went to England two years after the Restoration, and was highly distinguished by Charles II. A long career of gallantry was terminated by his compulsory marriage to Elizabeth Hamilton. His *Mémoires du Comte de Grammont* were dictated to his brother-in-law, Anthony, Count Hamilton, who followed James II, entered the French service, and died in 1720.

GRAMOPHONE, an instrument for recording and reproducing speech and music by purely mechanical means. Thomas A. Edison invented his first talking-machine in 1877, and called it a **phonograph;** and a later inventor introduced the word Gramophone, which was probably suggested by the word **phonogram.**

History. Edison's phonograph may be considered as a direct descendant

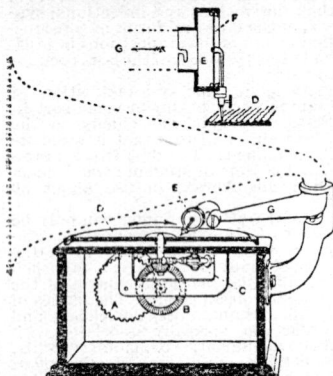

Section of a Gramophone

of the **phonautograph,** which had been invented in 1856 by Leon Scott. In this instrument there was a horn with a stretched membrane closing the narrower end, and to the outside of this membrane there was attached a bristle which acted as a stylus.

The free end of this stylus rested on a lamp-blackened paper which was wrapped around a cylinder capable of rotation by means of a crank-handle on the end of a long spindle, on part of which there was a screw-thread fitting into a similarly screwed bearing. Therefore, when the cylinder was rotated, it travelled along also in a horizontal direction, causing the stylus to trace a continuous spiral around the cylinder from the one end to the other. When words were spoken, the stylus traced the vibrations of the diaphragm upon the blackened paper; there was no suggestion of reproducing the sound.

Between this date (1856) and

Edison's phonograph (1877) there had been invented the electric telephone by Graham Bell, so that it was already known that a vibrating disc could reproduce speech. Edison's phonograph combined the ideas of the recording diaphragm of the phonautograph and the reproducing diaphragm of the telephone.

In the original instrument (1877) there was a brass cylinder having a deep spiral groove around it, and this cylinder moved exactly as in the phonautograph. As in Scott's machine, the horn with its diaphragm was fixed permanently. Attached to the centre of the vibrating diaphragm there was a steel point in contact with a sheet of tin-foil which was wrapped around the brass cylinder. When words were spoken into the mouthpiece, the diaphragm vibrated in sympathy with the air-waves produced by the voice, and the steel point made a succession of minute indentations on the tin-foil.

When this record was passed again under the steel point by the rotation of the cylinder, the diaphragm vibrated again exactly as it had done when under the influence of the voice. The air-waves thus generated impinged upon the ear, and caused the same sensation as would have been produced by the speaker's voice when acting directly.

In the early phonograph the tin-foil gave a very imperfect imitation of the human voice, and it made little advance for ten years, as Edison was engaged upon the problems of electric lighting, but in 1888 he brought out an improved phonograph. Others had introduced a wax cylinder, and Edison adopted this in place of his tin-foil record; this was a very great improvement.

As early as 1888 Berliner invented a phonograph with flat disc records in place of cylindrical ones, and he christened this machine a *gramophone,* but it should be noted that Edison had made records on flat discs before this date. In Berliner's early gramophone the record was made on a viscous-coated zinc plate. The stylus laid bare the zinc, which was then etched with acid; from this a copper matrix was made by an electroplating process. This matrix served to stamp out any number of records on a shellac-compound disc, made plastic when heated. Then followed a wax disc in place of a zinc one, and from this a copper matrix was made.

Principles of Construction. The principle of later forms of the gramophone is shown in the accompanying diagram. The driving energy was got from a large mainspring contained in the cylinder A, and the power was transmitted to the large bevel wheel

B by means of a ratchet wheel and pinion. A bevel pinion fitted into B, the pinion being carried on the lower end of a short upright shaft, to the top of which was fastened the turn-table on which the record D was placed. The rate of revolution was kept constant by means of the governor C, which consisted of three small weights, each fixed to a flat spring, and all three connected at one end to a stationary collar, while the other ends were fixed to a loose collar, which was capable of sliding on the spindle.

When the speed increased beyond the desired limit, the weights tended to fly outward under the influence of centrifugal force, and in moving outwards they pulled the loose collar along the spindle and applied a brake, thus retarding the motor until it reached the speed for which the governor was set.

The power was transmitted to the governor spindle by means of a worm and worm-wheel on the end of the spindle running through C. The sound-box E contained the diaphragm, which might be a disc of mica, and to this was attached the stylus, which moved with the vibrations of the diaphragm and cut the record on the disc of wax. In reproducing the sound the stylus was moved to and fro by the irregular grooves of the record, thus causing the diaphragm to vibrate just as it did under the direct influence of the voice or musical instrument. A large horn, acting as a megaphone, was attached to the tone-arm G, which was metal tube connecting the sound-box to the horn.

The smaller illustration is an enlargement of the sound-box E, showing the position of the mica diaphragm F, with its stylus, on the lower end of which was a socket and thumb-screw for holding the needle point in place. The grooves of the record D have been enlarged to show how the needle moved in the groove. The arrow indicates the direction of the propagation of the air-waves produced by the vibrating diaphragm F, and leading through the tone-arm G to the horn.

In recent models the sound box, tone arm and horn have been replaced by an electro-magnetic system of reproduction with valve amplification as in wireless.

The manufacture of gramophones and records is a large industry, the word "gramophone" itself being a protected trade name.

GRAMPIANS, THE, a range, or rather series of ranges and elevated masses, stretching across Scotland diagonally S.W. to N.E. for about 150 miles. It commences in Argyleshire, and at the boundaries of Perthshire and Aberdeenshire may be said to separate into two distinct branches —one on the north side of the Dee, terminating near Huntly; the other running on the south side of that river, and terminating near Stonehaven.

With the exception of Ben Nevis, the Grampians comprise all the highest mountains in Scotland, Ben Cruachan, Ben Lomond, Ben Lawers, Schiehallion, Ben Macdhui (4,296 feet), Cairngorm, and Cairntoul. The more remarkable passes are those of Leny, Aberfoyle, Glenshee, and Killiecrankie.

GRAMPUS, a popular name for several marine cetaceous mammals allied to the dolphins, especially *Orca gladiator* of the Atlantic and North Sea, which grows to the length of 30 feet, and is remarkably thick in proportion to its length. The spout-hole is on the top of the neck. The colour of the back is black; the belly is of a snowy whiteness, and on each shoulder is a large white spot. The grampus is carnivorous and remarkably voracious, even attacking the whale. The genus Grampus only includes Risso's dolphin (*G. griseus*) from the Mediterranean and Atlantic; and this is allied to the ca'ing whale (*Globicephalus melas*) of the North Atlantic; this attains the length of 20 feet.

GRAN, now **ESZTERGOM,** a town in Hungary, at the confluence of the Gran with the Danube, 25 miles north-west of Budapest. It was the residence of the Hungarian monarchs, and their finest city till ruined by the Turks about 1613. It is an archbishop's see and has a fine cathedral. Gran is the Etzelburg of the *Nibelungenlied*. Pop. 17,360.

GRANADA (grä-nä′dà), a city in the south of Spain, capital of the province of Granada. The streets rise picturesquely above each other, with a number of turrets and gilded cupolas, the whole being crowned by the Alhambra (q.v.), or palace of the ancient Moorish kings. In the background lies the Sierra de Nevada, covered with snow. The streets, however, are narrow and irregular, and the buildings inferior to those of many other towns in Spain. The town is partly built on two adjacent hills, between which the Darro flows, traversing the town and falling into the Genil, which flows outside the walls.

The cathedral is an irregular but splendid building, and the archbishop's palace and mansion of the captain-general are also noteworthy; but the special features of the town are the Alhambra, and another Moorish palace called the *Generalife*, built on an opposite hill. Granada has no manufactures of importance. Its university was founded about 1530.

History. The city was founded by the Moors before 800, and from 1036 to 1234 was included in the Kingdom of Cordova. In 1235 it became the capital of the Moorish kingdom of Granada, and attained almost matchless splendour. In 1491 it remained the last stronghold of the Moors in Spain, but was taken by the Spaniards under Ferdinand and Isabella in 1492, along with the kingdom, having then a population of perhaps 500,000. Its prosperity continued almost without diminution till 1610, when the decree expelling the Moors from all parts of Spain told severely upon it, and it has never recovered. Pop. (1931), 118,905.

The province, which is partly bounded by the Mediterranean, has an area of 4,928 sq. miles. Pop. 649,898.

A city of Nicaragua is called Granada. It stands on the Nicaragua, 28 miles from Managua, it has a university. The chief products are cocoa and coffee. Pop. 18,066.

GRANADA, formerly a Moorish kingdom in Spain, bordering on the Mediterranean, now represented by the three provinces Granada, Almeria, and Malaga; area, 11,100 sq. miles. The interior is mountainous, being traversed from east to west by several ranges, particularly the Sierra Nevada; but many of its valleys and low grounds are distinguished by beauty and fertility. The olive and vine are extensively cultivated, and fruit is very abundant. The sugar-cane thrives in some parts. After long forming part of the Kingdom of Cordova, Granada became a separate kingdom in 1235. In 1492 it passed into the possession of the Spaniards.

GRANADIL'LA, the West Indian name for the fruits of various species of Passiflóra, a genus of the passionflower family. Some species have been introduced into Europe, chiefly for their flowers, the chief being the purple-fruited, *P. edūlis*; the water-lemon, *P. laurifolia*; the flesh-coloured granadilla, and the *P. quadrangulāris*, the most valuable for cultivation in Great Britain.

GRANBY, John Manners, Marquess of, son of the Duke of Rutland, born 1721, died in 1770. He raised a foot regiment in 1745; became colonel of the Horse-Guards in 1758 and lieutenant-general in 1759; commanded the British troops in the Seven Years' War (1760–3); and was commander-in-chief of the British army from 1766 to 1770. He was elected to Parliament in 1754, 1761, and 1768.

Granby's immense popularity, which was, however, scarcely earned by his merits as a general, was in part attested by the frequent use of his name for public-houses. 'The Marquess of Granby' was the name of the inn at Dorking owned by the second Mrs. Weller (*Pickwick Papers*, ch. 27).

GRANBY, a town of Quebec, Canada, 56 miles from Montreal. It has saw-mills and manufactures leather goods. Pop. 10,587.

GRAN CHACO, EL, a territory of the Argentine Republic, lying mainly between the Vermejo, Paraná, and Salado; area, 52,740 sq. miles. In the west it is intersected by offsets of the Andes, and in the east forms extensive plains and marshes, while in the south are sandy tracts interspersed with salt pools. A large area, however, is covered with primeval forest. It is inhabited by Indian tribes, the Indian population being estimated at from 20,000 to 40,000.

Many parts seem well adapted for growing sugar-cane, tobacco, maize, rice, &c., if not for cereals generally. The name also embraces a much more extensive region extending into Bolivia.

GRAND, Sarah, English novelist, whose real name was Frances Elizabeth M'Fall. A daughter of a naval officer, Edward Clarke, she married, at the age of 16, an army surgeon named M'Fall, who became a colonel in the R.A.M.C. Her first novel was *Ideala*, but the most famous was *The Heavenly Twins*, 1893, which made somewhat of a sensation in its day. Later she wrote *The Beth Book*, *The Winged Victory*, *Adam's Orchard* and *Variety*. Madame Grand took some part in the movement for women's rights, and in the municipal affairs of Bath, of which city she was mayoress, 1923 and 1925–29.

GRAND COURONNÉ DE NANCY, a range of wooded hills in France, department of Meurthe-et-Moselle. It was the scene of fierce fighting during the European War (24th Aug. to 7th Sep., 1914).

GRAND COUSTUMIER OF NORMANDY, a collection of ancient laws or customs of the Duchy of Normandy, in use in England during the reigns of the early Norman sovereigns, and which still form the basis of the laws of the Channel Isles, which formerly belonged to that duchy. It is supposed to have been compiled subsequently to the reign of Richard I.

GRAND-DUKE, before the Revolution of 1918 the title of the sovereign of several of the states of Germany, who were considered to be of a rank between duke and king. The title was also applied until 1918 to members of the imperial family of Russia.

GRANDEE', in Spain a noble of the first rank, which consisted partly of the relatives of the royal House, and partly of such members of the high feudal nobility distinguished for their wealth as had, by the grant of a banner received from the king, the right to enlist soldiers under their own colours.

Besides the general prerogatives of the higher nobility, and the priority of claim to the highest offices of State, the grandees possessed the right of covering the head in the presence of the king, with his permission, on all public occasions. The king called each of them 'my cousin' (*mi primo*), while he addressed the other members of the high nobility only as 'my kinsman' or 'my relative' (*mi pariente*).

Under Ferdinand and Isabella and Charles V the independent feudal nobility became a dependent order of court nobles, and their privileges were curtailed, Entirely abolished after the accession of Joseph Bonaparte, the privileges of the grandees were partially re-established after the Restoration of 1814.

GRAND JURY, a body of jurors numbering not less than twelve nor more than twenty-three, summoned by the sheriff to hear the evidence for the prosecution in indictable offences, and upon such evidence to find whether there is sufficient cause for sending the prisoner to trial.

If the jury find no *prima facie* case, the indictment is 'ignored,' and the finding is that there is 'no true bill', but if otherwise, they bring in 'a true bill,' and the prisoner is then committed for trial before a judge and a common or petty jury. (This procedure is not applicable to Scotland.) By virtue of an Act passed in 1917 it was suspended for the period of the European War; it was, however, restored in 1922. *See* JURY.

GRAND NATIONAL, English steeplechase. It takes place in March or April at Aintree, near Liverpool, and is one of the sporting events of the year. The course is about 4½ miles long, and there are something like 30 jumps. The race has been run regularly, except in 1916–18, since 1839.

GRAND PENSIONARY, formerly an officer of the Dutch Republic, or rather of the Province of Holland. In the great towns of the Dutch Republic the first magistrate was called a pensionary, from the fact of his office being a paid one. The grand pensionary was the Secretary of State of the Province of Holland. He held office for five years, and was eligible for re-election. The office was abolished on the formation of the Kingdom of Holland in 1806.

GRAND PRIX, international horse-race, run in summer at Longchamps, France. The course is 1 mile, 7 furlongs in length, and the stakes are 250,000 francs, the largest in Europe. This race was won three years in succession by English owners from 1919–21, and again in 1928 by Lord Derby's horse, "Cri de Guerre."

GRAND RAPIDS, a city, United States, capital of Kent County, Michigan, situated on the rapids of the Grand River, 40 miles from its mouth. It is handsomely built, and has a pleasant and healthy situation. It is connected with the railway system of the United States and Canada, and is an important centre for the distribution of pine and hard-wood lumber. It has large manufactures of furniture, wooden ware, agricultural implements, brushes, and machinery. Pop. (1930), 168,592.

GRAND SERGEANTY, an ancient tenure of land similar to knight-service, but of superior dignity. Instead of serving the king generally in his wars, the holder by this tenure was bound to do him some specified honorary service, to carry his sword or banner, to be the marshal of his host, his high-steward, butler, champion, or other officer. It was practically abolished with other military tenures by Charles II.

GRANGE, or **GRANGE PARTY,** in the United States, a combination, society, or lodge of farmers for the purpose of promoting the interests of agriculture, more especially for abolishing the restraints and burdens imposed on it by the commercial classes and the railroad and canal companies, and for doing away with middlemen. Granges originated in the great agricultural regions of the Mississippi, and still prevail most generally there. The movement, which lost its influence after 1873, was revived in 1890.

GRANGE-OVER-SANDS, watering place and urban district of Lancashire. It is situated on Morecambe Bay, 245½ miles from London by the L.M.S. Rly. Pop. (1931) 2,648.

GRANGEMOUTH, a seaport and police burgh, Stirlingshire, Scotland, at the entrance of the Forth and Clyde Canal, 3 miles E.N.E. of Falkirk. The town was founded in 1777 in connection with the construction of the canal; it has docks opened respectively in 1843, 1859, and 1882. It has shipbuilding yards, sawmills, a rope and sail factory, and brickworks. An oil-pipe line runs to Dalmuir. Pop. (1931), 11,798.

GRANITE, a coarsely crystalline unstratified rock, composed generally of the minerals quartz, potassium-felspar, and mica, mingled without regular arrangement of the crystals. Granite is an igneous rock which has consolidated under pressure deep down in the earth.

It is one of the most abundant of the igneous rocks seen at or near the surface, and was formerly considered as the foundation rock of the globe, or that upon which all sedimentary rocks repose; but it is now known to belong to various ages from the Pre-Cambrian to the Cainozoic, the Alps of Europe and the hills of Skye containing granite of the latter age. It forms some of the most lofty mountain chains, and many parts of the principal ranges of Scandinavia, the Alps, the Pyrenees, and the Carpathian Mountains are of this rock.

Granite supplies the most durable materials for building, as many of the ancient Egyptian monuments testify. It varies much in hardness as well as in colour, in accordance with the nature and proportion of its constituent parts, so that there is much room for care and taste in its selection. The Aberdeen bluish-grey granite is celebrated for its great durability, and also for its beauty. The Peterhead red granite, the hue of which is due to its felspar being flesh-coloured, is highly esteemed for polished work, as columns, pillars, graveyard monuments, &c. In some granites, mica is replaced by hornblende; when both mica and hornblende are present, it is called **syenitic granite.**

The name of **graphic granite,** or **pegmatite,** is given to a variety composed mainly of felspar and quartz, so arranged as to produce an interlocked structure. The quartz and potassium-felspar have here crystallized simultaneously, and the name graphic granite arises from the resemblance of the irregularly developed quartz, as seen on a broken surface, to Hebrew characters. The term pegmatite has now been extended to any coarse granite found in veins. Granite contains many accessory minerals, such as beryl, garnet, and tourmaline. It is not rich in metallic ores.

GRAN'ITITE, a granite containing both dark and light mica in addition to the quartz and felspar.

GRANOPHYRE, a fine-grained granitic rock in which the groundwork has the structure of graphic granite (*see* GRANITE) on a small scale. The Cainozoic granite of the Inner Hebrides and the Mourne Mountains is now commonly styled granophyre.

GRAN SASSO D'ITALIA, or **MONTE CORNO,** a mountain of Naples, the culminating peak of the Apennines; height, 9,580 feet.

GRANT, in law, a gift in writing under seal of such a thing as cannot be passed or conveyed by word only;

also by the Law of Property Act, 1925, all lands and interests therein lie in grant; thus, a grant is the regular method by the common law of transferring the property in corporeal hereditaments, or such things whereof no actual delivery of possession can be had, e.g. a reversion. *See* DEED.

GRANT, Sir Alexander, Bart., born in 1826, died in 1884. He was educated at Harrow and Oxford, where he was public examiner in 1856. In 1858 he was appointed inspector of schools in the Madras Presidency; became professor of history and political economy in Elphinstone College, Madras, in 1860, and its principal in 1862; vice-chancellor of Bombay University in 1863; director of public instruction in Bombay Presidency in 1865; and vice-chancellor and principal of Edinburgh University in 1868.

He is best known by his annotated edition of Aristotle's *Ethics* (first published 1857), and his *Story of the University of Edinburgh during its First Three Hundred Years* (1884), published in connection with the University Tercentenary.

GRANT, Sir Francis, Scottish painter, born 1803, died 1878. The son of a landed proprietor, he was self-taught as a painter, but became noted for sporting scenes and portraits, afterwards painting many persons of note, including Queen Victoria, the Prince Consort, Lord John Russell, Disraeli (Beaconsfield), Lord Clyde, Palmerston, Macaulay, Landseer, Sir Hope Grant, J. G. Lockhart, &c. He became A.R.A. in 1842, R.A. in 1851, and president of the Academy in 1866, in which year he was knighted.

GRANT, George Munro, Canadian author and educationalist, born in Nova Scotia in 1835, died in 1902. He was educated at Pictou Academy, and at West River Seminary of the Presbyterian Church of Nova Scotia, gaining there a bursary which entitled him to continue his studies at Glasgow University. Here he studied with distinction both in arts and theology, and took the degree of M.A. Returning to Canada, he was for some time a missionary, then pastor of St. Matthew's Church, Halifax.

In 1877 he was appointed principal of Queen's University, Kingston, Ontario, a position which he filled with great ability. His works include: *Religions of the World in Relation to Christianity*; *Reformers of the Nineteenth Century.*

GRANT, James, novelist, born at Edinburgh 1822, died in 1887. He lived in America from 1832 to 1839, in which year he returned to England

and was gazetted ensign in the 62nd Foot. He resigned his commission in 1843; began to contribute to periodical literature, and in 1846 published his first book, *The Romance of War*.

A large number of work followed, most of them bearing marks of his military training, or based on historical events: *Adventures of an Aide-de-Camp* (1848), *Bothwell* (1851), *Jane Seton* (1853), *Philip Rollo* (1854), *Frank Hilton* (1855), *Yellow Frigate* (1855), *Harry Ogilvie* (1856), *Lucy Arden* (1859), *Mary of Lorraine* (1860), *Dick Rodney* (1861), *King's Own Borderers* (1865), *White Cockade* (1867), *British Battles on Land and Sea* (1873), and *Old and New Edinburgh* (1880–3).

GRANT, James Augustus, Scottish soldier and traveller, born 1827, died 1892; is chiefly noted as having accompanied Captain Speke in his search for the sources of the Nile (1860–3). The travellers explored the Victoria Nyanza, and discovered the river issuing from the lake, an expedition described in his work *A Walk Across Africa*. He also wrote *The Botany of the Grant and Speke Expeditions* (*Transactions of Linnean Society*, vol. xxix).

GRANT, Ulysses Simpson, general and eighteenth President of the United States, born in 1822 at Point Pleasant, in Clermont County, Ohio, died in 1885. His real name was Hiram Ulysses Grant, the name afterwards used by him having arisen out of an error in the registration of his cadetship.

After having studied in the military academy at West Point he served during the Mexican War, taking part in every battle except Buena Vista, and being brevetted captain for gallantry. In 1854 he resigned his commission and engaged first in farming near St. Louis, and then in the leather trade with his father at Galena, Illinois.

On the declaration of war in 1861 he was chosen captain of a company of volunteers, and was rapidly promoted to a brigadier-generalship of volunteers. He seized Paducah, commanding the Tennessee and Ohio navigation; checked the departure of reinforcements from Belmont, captured Fort Henry and Fort Donelson, and won the two days' battle of Shiloh. He then gained a new victory at Juka, and after repulsing the Confederates before Corinth commenced operations against Vicksburg.

After a siege of some months, in the course of which he took the town of Jackson and scattered an army under Johnson, the town surrendered. For this Grant was made major-general in the regular army, and placed in command of the Mississippi division.

The battles of Chickamauga and Chattanooga, which followed, opened the way into Georgia for the Federal troops. In Feb., 1864, he was appointed lieutenant-general, and assumed command of the armies of the United States. In a succession of hotly-contested battles at the Wilderness, Spottsylvania, North Anna, and Cold Harbour, he steadily advanced on Petersburg and Richmond. These speedily fell, and Lee, defeated at Five Forks and completely surrounded, surrendered to Grant on 9th of April, 1865. Grant returned to Washington, and in 1866 was made general of the armies of the United States.

After exercising an important influence during the presidency of Johnson, Lincoln's successor, he was himself elected President in 1868.

Ulysses S. Grant

His administration allayed the soreness which still survived from the great struggle between the states, and was also noteworthy for the reduction of the national debt and the settlement of the *Alabama* dispute with England. He was re-elected in 1872.

On his retirement he spent some time in travel. Afterwards he became involved in a bubble company which exploited his name and left him heavily in debt. He manfully endeavoured to repair his fortune by writing and publishing his *Memoirs*, and in this he was successful, though suffering greatly from the cancerous disease of which he died.—Cf. H. Garland, *Ulysses S. Grant: his Life and Character.*

GRANTCHESTER, village of Cambridgeshire. It stands on the Cam, once called the Granta, 2 miles from

Cambridge. Before its old mill was burned down in 1928, it was a very picturesque place. It owes some of its fame to Rupert Brooke's references to it.

GRANTHAM (grant'am), a municipal and until 1918 a parliamentary borough of England, in Lincolnshire, 24½ miles s.s.w. of Lincoln. It is well built, principally of brick, and has a fine Gothic church built in the thirteenth century, with a graceful tower and spire 273 feet high. The town hall has a handsome clock-tower. Among the notable buildings are the thirteenth-century Angel Inn, where Richard III signed Buckingham's death warrant, and the grammar school (founded in 1528), where Sir Isaac Newton was educated. The George Inn, rebuilt in 1780, is described in *Nicholas Nickleby*. The industries are mostly connected with agriculture. It is connected by canal with Nottingham and elsewhere. Pop. (1931), 19,709.

GRANTON, seaport of Midlothian. It is part of the city of Edinburgh, and is situated on the Firth of Forth. There is trade in coal, timber and grain. The harbour is used by the North Sea fishing fleet.

GRANTOWN-ON-SPEY, a burgh of Scotland, Elginshire; a favourite summer-resort. It is the chief town of the district called Strathspey. Near is Castle Grant, the seat of the Countess of Seafield. Pop. (1931), 1,577.

GRANULATION, the subdivision of a metal into small pieces or thin films, effected either by pouring the metal in a fine stream or through a sieve into water. It is employed in chemistry to increase the surface, so as to render the metal more susceptible to the action of reagents, and in metallurgy for the subdivision of a tough metal like copper. Furnace slags are also frequently granulated by causing the stream of molten slag to be met by a stream of water under pressure.

GRANULATION, in surgery, the formation of little grain-like fleshy bodies on the surfaces of ulcers and suppurating wounds, serving both for filling up the cavities and bringing nearer together and uniting their sides. The colour of healthy granulations is a deep florid red. When livid they are unhealthy, and have only a languid circulation.

GRANVELLA, or **GRANVELLE**, Antoine Perrenot, Cardinal de, Minister of State to Charles V and Philip II of Spain, was born in 1517 near Besançon, died at Madrid in 1586. He studied at Padua and at Louvain, in his twenty-third year was appointed Bishop of Arras, and was present at the Diets at Worms and Ratisbon.

In 1545 he was sent to the Council of Trent, and on the death of his father in 1550 was appointed by Charles V to succeed him in the office of Chancellor.

In 1552 he negotiated the Treaty of Passau, and in 1553 arranged the marriage of Don Philip with Mary, Queen of England. Under Philip II he remained chief minister, and in 1559 negotiated the Peace of Câteau-Cambrésis. Philip immediately after quitted the Netherlands, leaving Margaret of Parma as Governor, and Granvella as her minister. In 1560 he became Archbishop of Mechlin, and in 1561 was made a cardinal; but in 1564 he was obliged to yield to the growing discontent aroused by his tyranny in the Netherlands, resign his post, and retire to Besançon.

In 1570 Philip sent him to Rome to conclude an alliance with the Pope and the Venetians against the Turks, and afterwards to Naples as Viceroy. In 1575 he was recalled to Spain, and placed at the head of the Government with the title of President of the Supreme Council of Italy and Castile. In 1584 he was created Archbishop of Besançon, and died at Madrid.

He preserved all letters and dispatches addressed to him, nine volumes of which, published 1851–62, are of value in illustrating the history of the sixteenth century. Another edition of his correspondence appeared at Brussels between 1878 and 1896 (12 vols.).

GRANVILLE, Granville George Leveson-Gower, second Earl, English statesman, was born in London in 1815, died in 1891. Educated at Eton and Christ Church, Oxford, he entered Parliament in 1836 for Morpeth, afterwards for Lichfield, both in the Liberal interest.

In 1840 he became Under-Secretary for Foreign Affairs, in 1846 succeeded to the peerage, in 1848 was appointed Vice-President of the Board of Trade, and in 1851 succeeded Palmerston as Foreign Secretary. In 1855 he became Chancellor of the Duchy of Lancaster, President of the Council, and ministerial leader of the House of Lords (1855–8), and in 1856 represented the British Crown at the coronation of the Tsar Alexander.

From 1859 to 1866 he was again President of the Council. In 1868 he was Colonial Secretary under Gladstone, and on the death of Clarendon in 1870 succeeded to the Secretaryship for Foreign Affairs, which he held until 1874. During this period he negotiated the Treaty of 1870, guaranteeing the independence of Belgium, and 'protested' against the Russian repudiation of the Black Sea clause of the Treaty of Paris.

On the return of Gladstone to office

in 1880 Lord Granville again became Foreign Secretary, until Lord Salisbury came into power in 1885. The patched-up peace with the Boers, the protest against the French occupation of Tunis, the revolt of Arabi Pasha in Egypt, the appearance of the Mahdi, the occupation of Egypt, the Gordon mission, and Wolseley expedition belong to this period. In the short Gladstone ministry of 1886 he was Colonial Secretary.—Cf. Lord Fitzmaurice, *Life of Granville G. Leveson-Gower, Lord Granville.*

GRANVILLE (grán-vēl), a fortified seaport, France, department of Manche, at the mouth of the Boscq, in the English Channel. Pop. 11,347.

GRANVILLE, a town, New South Wales, Australia, within Greater Sydney. Pop. 16,000.

GRANVILLE-BARKER, Harley Granville, English dramatist. Born in London, 25th Nov., 1877, he took up the profession of actor, but turned to writing plays, his first, *The Marrying of Anne Leete,* being produced in 1901. This was followed by *The Voysey Inheritance,* 1905; *Waste,* 1907; and *The Madras House,* 1910, &c. He has also written plays in collaboration with other authors, *e.g.* Laurence Housman, Bert Thomas and Dion Clayton Calthrop. His non-dramatic works include *A National Theatre* (with William Archer), 1907, and *The Red Cross in France,* 1916. For a time in 1907 he was a successful manager of the Savoy Theatre, with J. E. Vedrenne, with whom he had earlier, in 1904, managed the Court Theatre. His wife, Helen Granville-Barker, was the author of novels and, in collaboration with her husband, wrote several plays and translated plays from the Spanish.

GRAPE- FRUIT, a fruit akin to the orange, but somewhat larger, grown in Jamaica and other West Indian islands, in Florida, and elsewhere, having a bitter-sweet flavour, and a juice considered wholesome and refreshing.

GRAPE-HYACINTH, the common name of plants of the lily family and genus Muscări, charming early spring-flowering bulbs, with flowers mostly of different shades of blue, on scapes 4 to 8 inches high; easily grown in borders and pots.

GRAPE-SHOT, a kind of shot generally consisting of three tiers of cast-iron balls arranged, three in a tier, between four parallel iron discs connected together by a central wrought-iron pin. Case-shot superseded grape-shot; both have long been superseded by shrapnel.

GRAPH, a line or curve which re-presents the relation between two variable quantities. We get the same kind of information from a graph as from a table of statistics or from a mathematical formula, and we get it usually at a smaller cost of time and mental exertion. As an example, take the following numbers giving the height of the barometer in inches at 9 a.m. on seven consecutive days:

Mon.	Tues.	Wed.	Thur.	Fri.	Sat.	Sun.
28·2	28·6	29·15	29·55	30·15	29·95	28·95

On a sheet of squared paper, take ten of the smallest divisions, measured vertically, to represent 24 hours; and ten of the same divisions, measured horizontally, to represent 1 inch of pressure.

Then, to indicate the reading 28·2 on Monday at 9 a.m., we mark, or *plot,* the point which lies on the horizontal line corresponding to Monday at 9 a.m., and also on the vertical line corresponding to 28·2 inches. Similarly, we plot the other points marked with a small circle in fig. 1.

The seven points marked on the squared paper exactly represent the seven facts recorded in the table. So long as we know nothing beyond these seven data, we cannot proceed further with any confidence in the construction of a graph. Between Monday at 9 a.m. and Tuesday at 9 a.m., e.g. the barometer may either have risen steadily, or have gone up and down several times. Sometimes, in a case like this, consecutive points are joined by straight lines, the understanding then being that no inference is to be drawn from any part of the graph except the plotted points.

If, however, we assume that the variation of pressure proceeded gradually and regularly, then we can draw a smooth curve through the plotted points, as in fig. 1, and take this curve to represent the pressure at any time between the first and the final readings. If the curve is traced continuously by some automatic recording apparatus, all uncertainty disappears, and the graph gives the height correctly for any value of the time. We learn from the curve the time for any given reading, and also the reading for any given time; examples are given on the figure. We can also read off the rate of rise or fall at any time, as well as the maximum height and the time when it occurred.

In fig. 2 two axes of co-ordinates (q.v.), OX and OY, are shown with the scales marked. In this figure the same length is taken for the unit of x as for the unit of y, but it is often

GRAPH   286   GRAPH

convenient to have different lengths for the two units. The oblique straight line shown is the graph of the equation $2x + 5y = 10$, or of the function $y = \frac{1}{5}(10 - 2x)$.

The graph of every function of the first degree is a straight line. Here, for example, the values $(2, 1\cdot2)$ for

The log of any intermediate number can now be read off the graph, and other problems can be solved. Thus, e.g., a value of x satisfying the equation $2x + 5 \log x = 10$ can be found. For this equation is the same as $\log x = \frac{1}{5}(10 - 2x)$, which is evidently true for the value of x at the point

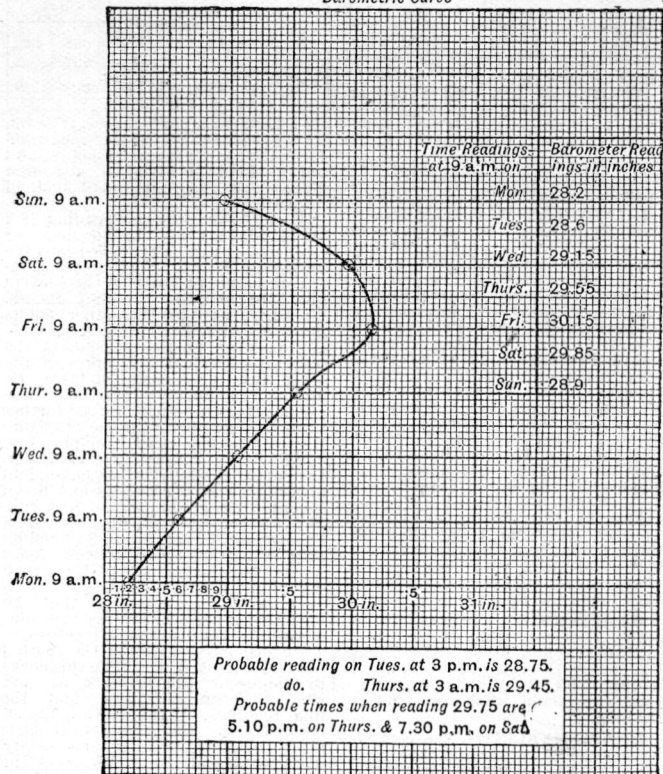

Barometric Curve

Time Readings at 9 a.m. on	Barometer Readings in inches
Mon.	28.2
Tues.	28.6
Wed.	29.15
Thurs.	29.55
Fri.	30.15
Sat.	29.85
Sun.	28.9

Probable reading on Tues. at 3 p.m. is 28.75.
do.   Thurs. at 3 a.m. is 29.45.
Probable times when reading 29.75 are
5.10 p.m. on Thurs. & 7.30 p.m. on Sat.

Fig. 1

(x, y) satisfy the equation, and the point $(x = 2, y = 1\cdot2)$, or $(2, 1\cdot2)$, lies on the line; the same happens with $(3, \cdot8)$ and $(4, \cdot4)$. The graph marked (i) represents the function $y = \log x$, the base being 10. To draw this graph, a number of logs are found from the tables, those used in the figure being the logs of $\cdot1, \cdot3, \cdot5, \cdot7, 1, 1\cdot5, 2\cdot5, 4, 5$. The corresponding points, such as $(2, \cdot30)$, $(3, \cdot48)$ are then plotted, and a smooth curve is drawn through them.

where the straight line and the log graph intersect, i.e. for $x = 3\cdot62$. The dotted graph (ii) represents $y = 10^x$, or $y = \text{antilog}\,x$; this graph can be plotted from the same numbers as before, for $y = 10^x$ implies $x = \log y$.

It often happens that an equation can be solved easily and with sufficient accuracy by means of a graph, when other methods would be tedious if not impracticable. Graphical methods for the representation of facts and the solution of problems are now much used in all departments of applied mathematics. *See* INDICATOR; VECTORS; RECORDING APPARATUS; STATICS; STATICS, GRAPHIC; THERMODYNAMICS.—BIBLIOGRAPHY: G. A. Gibson, *Treatise on Graphs*; E. H. Chapman, *Elementary Algebra*.

GRAPH'ITE, one of the forms under which carbon occurs in nature, also known under the names of **Plumbago,**

or other impressions of objects designed to be electrotyped, and for counteracting friction between the rubbing surfaces of wood or metal in machinery. Artificial graphite is produced by the treatment of anthracite in the electric furnace.

GRAPHOL'OGY, the judging of a person's character by means of his handwriting, a pursuit that has attained some vogue. The tendency to

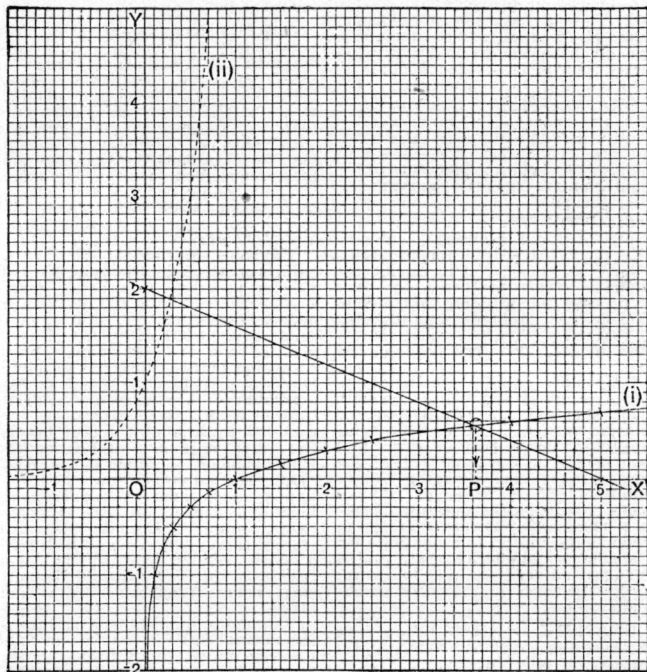

Fig. 2

Black-lead, and **Wad.** It occurs not infrequently as a mineral production, and is found at Borrowdale in Cumberland, and in large quantities in Canada, Ceylon, and Bohemia. Graphite may be heated to any extent in close vessels without change; it is exceedingly unchangeable in the air; it has an iron-grey colour, metallic lustre, and granular texture, and is soft and unctuous to the touch.

It is used chiefly in the manufacture of pencils, crucibles, and portable furnaces, in burnishing iron to protect it from rust, for giving a smooth surface to casting moulds, for coating wax

regard a certain style of writing as indicative of certain mental and moral characteristics appears to be natural, and is certainly not of modern origin; but the term graphology is modern, being attributed to the Abbé Michot in 1868, who also expounded a corresponding system, though other French writers, besides those of other nationalities, are said to have placed it on a more secure basis.

We are told that as gestures, movements of the features and the hands, and the sound of the voice help to reveal a person's character, so also handwriting can give us similar help, writing being the result of a series of small gestures, and the hands being influenced by the thoughts and feelings of the writer. But there is a good deal of scepticism regarding graphology, although it has been practised by, among others, Edgar Allan Poe, Goethe, Leibnitz Disraeli and St. Beuve.—Cf. Sauder, *The Psychology of Handwriting.*

GRAPNEL, a sort of small anchor, fitted with four or five flukes or claws, and commonly used to fasten boats or other small vessels. The name was also given to the grappling-iron formerly used in naval engagements to hold one ship to another.

GRAPPLE-PLANT, the Cape name of the *Harpagophytum procumbens,* a South African procumbent plant of the nat. ord. Pedaliaceæ. The fruits have many hooked thorns, and cling to the mouths of grazing cattle, causing considerable pain.

GRAPTOLITE, a member of a group of fossil hydrozoa, agreeing with the living sertularians in having a horny polypary, and in having the separate zooids protected by little horny cups, all springing from a common flesh or cœnosarc, but differing in that they were not fixed to any solid object, but were permanently free.

Graptolites usually present themselves as silvery impressions on hard black shales of the Ordovician and Silurian systems. The Ordovician graptolites have two or even four rows of cells on the same axis, or else two or more axes diverging from a common origin; those of Silurian times have typically one row of cells on a single axis. The axes are sometimes found united to a floating disc. The genera and species of graptolites have proved very useful as indicating successive zones in the early Palæozoic systems.

GRASLITZ, or **KRASLICE,** a town of Bohemia, Czechoslovakia, on the Zwoda, 89 miles w.n.w. of Prague. Pop. 10,000.

GRASMERE, a beautiful lake, England, county of Westmorland, of oval form, about 1 mile long by ½ mile broad.

The urban district of **Grasmere** stands on the Rothay, where it enters the lake and is 4 miles from Ambleside and 12 from Keswick. It is reached by road from either. The chief building is St. Oswald's Church, with the tomb of Wordsworth in the churchyard. Dove Cottage, where he lived, is near. A rush-gathering festival is held here every summer, and the sports in August attract many visitors. Pop. (1931), 988.

GRASS-CLOTH, the name of certain beautiful light fabrics made in the East from the fibre of *Bœhmeria nivea,* or China grass, *Bromelia pinguin,* &c. None of the plants yielding the fibre are grasses.

GRASSE (gràs), a town, France, department of Alpes Maritimes, 23 miles E.N.E. of Draguignan. It has extensive manufactures of perfumery. Grasse is a favourable winter-resort for invalids. Pop. 12,000.

GRASSES, a name equivalent to the botanical order Graminaceæ, a very extensive and important order of monocotyledons, comprising about 250 genera and 4,500 species, including many of the most valuable pasture plants, all those which yield corn, the sugar-cane, the tall and graceful bamboo, &c. The nutritious herbage and farinaceous seed furnished by many of them render them of incalculable importance, while the stems and leaves are useful for various textile and other purposes.

The roots are fibrous; the stem or culm is usually cylindrical and jointed, varying in length from a few inches to 80 or 90 feet, as in the bamboo (in maize, sugar-cane, &c., the stem is solid), and coated with silica; leaves, one to each node or joint, with a sheathing petiole; spikelets terminal, panicled, racemose, or spiked; flowers hermaphrodite or polygamous, destitute of true calyx or corolla, surrounded by a double set of bracts, the outer or *glumes* subtending the whole spikelet, the inner or *paleæ* enclosing the individual flower; stamens hypogynous, three or six; filaments long and flaccid; anthers versatile; ovary solitary, simple, with two (rarely three) styles, one-celled, with a single ovule; fruit known as a *caryopsis,* the seed-coat and the pericarp being inseparable from each other.

The more important divisions of the natural order of grasses are: the Paniceæ (millet, fundi, Guinea grass); the Andropogoneæ (sugar-cane, dhurra, lemon-grass); the Maydeæ (maize, Job's tears); the Phalarideæ (canary - grass, vernal grass); the Oryzeæ (rice); the Stipeæ (feather-grass, esparto); the Agrostidæ (bent-grass, foxtail grass, Timothy grass); the Aveneæ (oats, soft grass); the Festuceæ (fescue, meadow-grass, manna-grass, teff, cock's-foot grass, tussac grass, dog's-tail grass); the Bambuseæ (bamboo); the Hordeæ (wheat, barley, rye, spelt, rye-grass, lyme-grass).

In its popular use the term grasses is chiefly applied to the pasture grasses as distinct from the cereals, &c.; but it is also applied to some herbs, which are not in any strict sense grasses at all, e.g. rib-grass, scurvy and whitlow grass. After the culture of herbage and forage plants became an important branch of husbandry, it became customary to call the clovers, trefoils, sainfoin, and other flowering plants grown as fodder, *artificial grasses*, by way of distinction from the grasses proper, which were termed *natural grasses*.

Of the pasture grasses, some thrive in meadows, others in marshes, on upland fields, or on bleak hills, and they by no means grow indiscriminately. Indeed the species of grass will often indicate the quality of the soil; thus, *Holcus*, *Dactylis*, and *Bromus* are found on sterile land, *Festūca* and *Alopecūrus* on a better soil; *Poa* and *Cynosūrus* are only found in the best pasture land. *See* DOG'S-TAIL GRASS; FESCUE; FOXTAIL; TUSSAC; &c.

GRASS-FINCH, or GRASS-QUIT, names given to buntings of the genus Phonipara (Euethia), native to the West Indies and Florida.

GRASS'HOPPER, the name of various leaping insects of the ord. Orthoptĕra, included with locusts in the family Acrididæ. They are characterized by short antennæ, by very long and slender legs, the thighs of the hinder legs being large and adapted for leaping, by large and delicate wings, and by the wing-covers extending far beyond the extremity of the abdomen.

Grasshoppers are distinguished by the power which they possess of leaping to a considerable distance, and by the stridulous or chirping noise the males produce by rubbing the outer surfaces of their wing-cases against file-like ridges on the inner surfaces of their hind-legs There is an organ of hearing in the basal segment of the abdomen. They are often of a greenish colour.

Green grasshoppers, *par excellence*, belong to a different family (Locustidæ), and are more delicate in structure. They include a British species (*Locusta viridissima*) and the North American Katydid (*Microcentrum retinerve*). The antennæ are long and slender; the auditory organs are lodged in the front legs, below the knee; the chirping organs of the male are on the bases of the wing-covers; and the female usually possesses an ovipositor.

GRASS OF PARNASSUS, a genus of plants, ord. Saxifragaceæ, and found for the most part in boggy situations in the colder northern countries. The common grass of Parnassus (*Parnassia palustris*) is a beautiful autumnal plant with heart-shaped leaves and a single yellowish-white flower.

V—J

GRASS-OIL, OIL OF GERANIUM, or **OIL OF SPIKENARD,** a fragrant volatile oil, used chiefly in perfumery, and obtained from Indian grasses of the genus Andropogon.

GRASS-TREE, the popular name of a genus of Australian plants (Xanthorrhœa) of the nat. ord. Liliaceæ, having shrubby stems with tufts of long grass-like wiry foliage, from the centre of which arise the tall flower-stalks, which sometimes reach the height of 15 to 20 feet, and bear dense cylindrical spikes of blossom at their summit. The base of the leaves forms, when roasted, an agreeable article of diet, and the leaves themselves are used as fodder for all kinds of cattle. A resin, known in commerce as *akaroid resin*, is obtained from all the species, which are also popularly known as black-boys.

GRASS-WRACK, or SEA-GRASS (*Zostĕra marina*), a plant belonging to the Naiadaceæ, forming green beds at

Grasshopper (*Locusta viridissima*)

the bottom of the sea where it is of no great depth. It is common enough on the British and European coasts, and when dried is used for stuffing mattresses and packing goods. The ash contains soda.

GRATIAN, otherwise **FRANCISCUS GRATIANUS,** a Benedictine of the twelfth century, a native of Chiusi, and author of the *Decretum*, or, *Concordia discordantium Canonum*, a rich storehouse of the canon law of the Middle Ages.

GRATIAN, otherwise **GRATIANUS AUGUSTUS,** Roman Emperor, eldest son of the Emperor Valentinian I, was born A.D. 359, and when only eight years of age raised by his father to the rank of Augustus. On the death of Valentinian in 375 the Eastern Empire remained subject to Valens, and Gratian was obliged to share the western part with his half-brother, Valentinian II, then four years old. In 378 he succeeded to the Eastern Empire, which he bestowed on Theodosius I. He was deserted by his soldiers while leading them against

Maximus, and put to death at Lyons in the eighth year of his reign.

GRATI'OLA, a genus of plants, the hedge-hyssop genus, nat. ord. Scrophulariaceæ, containing about twenty species of herbs, widely dispersed through the extra-tropical regions of the globe. *G. officinalis* grows in meadows in Europe. It is extremely bittter, and acts violently both as a purgative and emetic, and in over-doses it is a violent poison.

GRATTAN, Henry, Irish orator and statesman, born at Dublin in 1746, died in 1820. Educated at Trinity College and Middle Temple, he was called to the Irish Bar in 1772, and in 1775 elected member for Charlton in the Parliament of Ireland. In 1780 he moved resolutions asserting the Crown to be the only link between Britain and Ireland, and in 1782 led the volunteer movement, which was instrumental in securing the concession of independence to Ireland. For these services the Irish Parliament voted him £50,000 and a house and lands.

The corruption of its members and the uncertain relations with England resulted in the failure of 'Grattan's Parliament.' Grattan himself became opposed to the popular feeling as represented by the United Irishmen, and in 1797 temporarily seceded from Parliament, and lived in retirement. In 1800 he came forward as member for Wicklow to oppose the Union, and on the passage of Pitt's measure was returned to the Imperial Parliament in 1805 for Malton in Yorkshire, and in 1806 for Dublin. He supported the war policy of the administration, but was afterwards chiefly occupied in promoting Catholic emancipation.—BIBLIOGRAPHY: A. E. Zimmern, *Henry Grattan*; W. E. H. Lecky, *Leaders of Public Opinion in Ireland.*

GRAUDENZ (grou'dents), or **GRUDZIADZ,** a town of Poland, formerly in Western Prussia, on the right bank of the Vistula, 18 miles s.s.w. of Marienwerder. The manufactures include machinery, castings, cigars, tobacco, brushes, &c. and there are several breweries and distilleries. The fortress of Graudenz, constructed by Frederick the Great (1722–6), was dismantled in 1874. During the European War Graudenz was seriously threatened by the first Russian advance in 1914. Pop. (1931), 50,405.

GRAVELINES (gráv-lēn), a small seaport and second-class fortress, France, department of Nord. It suffered from German air-raids in 1915. The battle of Gravelines, between the English and the Spaniards on one side, and the French on the other, was fought in July, 1558. Pop. 5,890.

GRAVELOTTE (gráv-lot), a village of France, in Alsace-Lorraine, 6½ miles west of Metz, the scene of one of the fiercest battles of the Franco-German War (18th Aug., 1870), resulting in the retreat of the French to Metz.

GRAVES, Alfred Perceval. Irish poet. Born in Dublin, 22nd July, 1846, son of Charles Graves, Bishop of Limerick, he was educated at Trinity College, Dublin. In 1869 he entered the civil service and was an inspector of schools from 1875 to 1910. He helped to found the Irish Literary Society, of which he was twice president, and did much to promote the revival of interest in folk songs and music. His many works include *Songs of Old Ireland, Irish Songs and Ballads, Songs of Irish Wit and Humour, Songs of Erin, Welsh Poetry Old and New* and *To Return to all That*, an autobiography. He wrote the popular song 'Father O'Flynn.' He died 26th Dec., 1931, two days after completing the MS. of a book for children on *The Lives of British and Irish Saints.*

Graves had four sons who were known as writers. **Philip Perceval Graves** became a member of the staff of the *Times*, which he represented at Constantinople. **Robert Ranke Graves** served in the Great War and became Professor of English in Cairo in 1926. He wrote several volumes of poems and an autobiography, *Good-bye to All That*, 1929. **Charles Graves** became a journalist and published *The Argentine and the Greek.* **John Graves** published *The Boys' Book of Football* in 1931.

Charles Larcom Graves, a brother of Alfred Graves, was assistant editor of *The Spectator*, 1899–1917. In 1902 he joined the staff of *Punch*, for which he wrote a great deal, including Punch's *History of Modern England.* He also wrote *Wisdom While You Wait, Hustled History*, and other books with E. V. Lucas, as well as the *Life of Sir Hubert Parry* and *New Times and Old Rhymes.*

GRAVESEND, a municipal borough, river port, and market town of England, in Kent, on the south bank of the Thames, 22 miles east of London. It is a great rendezvous for shipping, the boundary port of London, and troops and passengers frequently embark there to avoid the passage down the river. A ferry connects it with Tilbury, north of the river. The port is an important pilot centre; it is also a yachting centre. There is some trade in supplying ships' stores, and boat-building and iron-founding are carried on. A parliamentary borough until 1918. Gravesend now gives name to a parliamentary division. Pop. (1931), 35,490.

GRAVI'NA, a town of South Italy, province of Bari, on the Gravina. It has a cathedral and a college. Pop. 18,950.

GRAVITATION, the force by reason of which all the bodies and particles of matter in the universe tend towards one another. According to the law of gravitation discovered by Newton, every portion of matter attracts every other portion with a force directly proportional to the product of the two masses, and inversely proportional to the square of the distance between them.

Kepler had given the laws, deduced from observation, according to which the planets describe their orbits. From these Newton deduced the laws of the force in the case of the planets; and subsequently he generalized the statement of them, by showing the identity of the nature of the force that retains the moon in her orbit with that which attracts matter near to the surface of the earth.

The application of the grand law that he had discovered constituted a large part of Newton's mathematical work. Attacking the problem of *lunar inequalities,* he accounted for them by considering the perturbations due to the attraction of various bodies of the solar system; and, by accounting for all the observed perturbations by means of his newly-discovered law, he confirmed the truth of the law itself in such a way as to put it beyond all question.

The computation of these various attractions has reached such a degree of accuracy in the hands of mathematicians since Newton that the most complicated motions of the heavenly bodies can be predicted.

Theories of Gravitation. Many theories have been given to account for gravitation. The difficulty with any particular theory is to bring it to an experimental test. One theory is that gravitation is a residual effect of electro-static or electro-magnetic forces.

A remarkable theory was given by Le Sage of Geneva in 1818. He pictured the universe as filled with minute particles (*ultra-mundane corpuscles*) moving at great speeds in all directions. These particles can pass through dense matter, but not with perfect freedom, some being absorbed and giving up their momentum. A single body in free space is bombarded equally in all directions, and therefore not affected; but two bodies partially screen each other, and are attracted. Le Sage proved that Newton's law followed from this theory.

Lord Kelvin showed that gravitation could be explained by the hypothesis of an infinite fluid in which bodies are either all sources or else

all sinks, producing or absorbing the fluid at rates proportional to their masses. *See* GEODESY; GRAVITY; for Einstein's Theory, *see* RELATIVITY.

GRAVITY. Newton's law of gravitation tells us that any two masses attract each other with a force which acts in the line joining them, and which is directly proportional to their masses and inversely proportional to the square of the distance between them. We know further that the materials of which the masses are composed have no bearing on this law, and that the mass of any body is defined by its volume and its density. As an illustration of the magnitude of this force, two weights of, roughly, 23,300 tons, at a distance from each other of 100 yards, attract each other with a force of 1 pound.

Planetary System. Consider the effect of this law upon the planetary system. The sun and the planets are all roughly spherical, and their attractions act from their respective centres, where their masses may be considered to be concentrated. If M_s be the mass of the sun, M_p that of any planet, and d the distance between them, then the force acting on this planet is proportional, by Newton's law, to $M_s \times M_p \div d^2$. Astronomical observation confirms this law, for it shows that planets revolve round the sun in ellipses, with the sun in one focus, and at such speeds that the line joining the sun and planet sweeps out equal areas in equal times.

Naturally the movement of planets in space is affected also, and in due proportion, by the force of gravitation exerted upon them by other planets, or by their own satellites. Such irregularities are known as perturbations, and their observed magnitudes correspond sufficiently closely to those calculated by Newton's law.

Now the dimensions, movements, and relative positions of the planets are known from observation, and consequently their relative densities can be calculated. In order, then, to provide a common measure, we must find the density of the earth in terms of some known unit.

Density of the Earth. To find the density of the earth we must compare the attraction it exerts upon any body with the attraction exerted on this same body by some other body of known mass. This second body may be a mountain, as in Maskelyne's famous experiment of 1774 at Schiehallion in Perthshire, or it may be a leaden weight, as in the long list of laboratory experiments starting with Cavendish in 1797, and ending with Poynting's recent work.

In the former class of experiment

the mass and form of the mountain must be determined by careful survey and analysis of composition. Let M represent the mountain and its mass, E the earth's mass, A a point of observation near the mountain, O the centre of the earth, S distance AM, R the radius of the earth. Then the attractions of the mountain mass and of the earth upon the plumb-bob are as M/S^2 is to E/R^2. If the plumb-bob is attracted towards the mountain through an angle α, then $\tan \alpha = (M/S^2) \div (E/R^2)$. Now $E = \frac{4}{3}\pi R^3 \Delta$ where Δ is the density of the earth, and $M = V\delta$ where δ is the density of the mountain, and V its volume. If M, S, R, α are known, the value of Δ can be calculated.

Although Maskelyne's experiment, and a similar one carried out by Sir

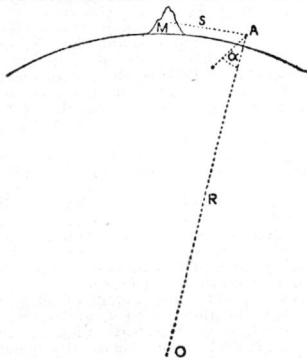

Fig. 1

Henry James, at Arthur's Seat, near Edinburgh, gave results for Δ which are singularly near the truth, this method is not a precise one, because it is difficult to assess the density and consequent mass of any topographical feature.

Another form of the same experiment is to swing a pendulum at the surface of a mine, and subsequently at some depth in that mine. We can think of the earth as having a layer skinned off to the depth of the lower point of observation, and if we then assess the density of the top layer, we can find the density of the remaining mass of the earth in much the same way as before. An interesting experiment on these lines was carried out by Airy in 1854, at Harton coal-pit, and later by Von Sterneck, in Saxony and Bohemia.

The second method of comparing the attraction of the earth with that of a known and small mass was due to Cavendish. His apparatus con-

sisted of two small leaden balls on the ends of a straight rod which was suspended by a fine wire. (In the most recent experiments on these lines a quartz fibre wire has been used.) Two larger leaden spheres were brought close to the lead balls on opposite sides of the rod, to attract them and cause the rod to rotate slightly. The large spheres were then turned round, acting upon the same respective sides of the rod, but attracting the opposite balls and causing the rod to swing back again. Now if we know the masses of balls and spheres, the torsion couple of the wire, and the length of the rod, we can find the force of attraction acting on either of the small balls. But we know the attraction of the earth for this ball, viz, the weight of the ball. We can therefore find Δ, the density of the earth, by the same kind of calculation as in the mountain experiment.

Many experiments have been made with this general idea, and the names of Baily, Reich, Cornu, Baille, Boys, and Braun are famous in this connection. Poynting's experiment is of a slightly different order, inasmuch as he uses a strong type of balance, instead of a torsion couple, and one leaden sphere on a turn-table below the pans of the balance, as his attracting mass.

These experiments have served to give us a number of values for the magnitude of the two factors, Δ the density of the earth, and G the gravitation coefficient (which is the constant in the expression: attraction$=MM'G \div d^2$). We may accept the following values as close approximations to the truth:

$\Delta = 5 \cdot 5$ times that of water.
$G = 6 \cdot 658 \times 10^{-8}$ c.g.s.

Centrifugal Force. We must now turn from gravitation to gravity, which is indeed but a special case of gravitation, and yet is perhaps of the greater importance. If the earth were a homogeneous sphere at rest, the attraction would be the same at all points on the surface. It rotates, however, upon its polar axis, and in so doing introduces the element of centrifugal force. The centrifugal force per unit mass at any spot is equal to $x\omega^2$, where x is the distance from the axis, and therefore$=R \cos\lambda$ (λ being the latitude), and ω is the angular velocity of rotation. The centrifugal force acts as diminishing the attraction of the earth, and varies as the cosine of the latitude, vanishing at the poles and reaching its maximum at the equator.

Now by virtue of the earth's attraction, any body at a height above the earth, and free to do so, will fall to the earth, and in doing so will, after a fall of 1 second in duration, acquire a certain velocity, which is commonly known as g. g is independent both of the mass and of the material of the body in question, but is dependent upon the attraction of the earth at that place, and is therefore a measure of gravitation—centrifugal force. Of these two, centrifugal force is always so much the smaller that whilst $g = 978\cdot024$ centimetres per second per second at the equator (its minimum) its maximum value at the poles is only 983.210 cm./sec.².

From the above it is clear that the weight of a body depends upon g, and that its actual value will change from a maximum at the pole to a minimum at the equator. It is still true that the masses of two or more bodies are proportional to their own weights at the same spot. In the above discussion on g it has been assumed that the earth is a perfect figure of revolution. In practice it is not so, however. We have inequalities of height, and, as we have already seen, the force of gravitation, and hence of gravity, is affected by the distance from the centre of the earth.

Pendulum Theory. The earliest experiments made with a view to determining the acceleration of a falling body were those of Galileo in the sixteenth century, but the most striking step in gravity experiment was the pendulum clock produced in 1657 by Huygens. The theory of the pendulum is briefly as follows: If a weight be hung by a thread and set vibrating, then if t be the time of one swing from rest to rest, and l be the length of the thread, then $t = \pi\sqrt{(l\,g)}$, or $g = \pi^2 l\, t^2$. The pendulum only obeys this theoretical law in a vacuum, for the actual weight of the air displaced by the pendulum, and its resistance to the vibration, introduce errors.

During the history of pendulum experiment from the seventeenth century to the present day, the design of the pendulum has been successively improved by Newton, Bouguer, Borda, Cassini, Kater, Bessel, Repsold, and others. The types now employed are used for relative determination rather than actual.

It is difficult to measure the length of the pendulum rod with sufficient accuracy to ensure a good determination of g. It is due to Clairaut, however, that we know how to use the pendulum relatively, and, from a series of observations, to arrive at the ellipticity of the earth. If L be the length of a seconds pendulum at the equator, and l its length at any latitude λ, m the ratio of centrifugal force at the equator to gravity, and e the ellipticity of the earth, then

$$l = L[1 + (\tfrac{5}{2}m - e)\sin^2\lambda].$$

Modern pendulums are generally of the half-seconds type, that is to say, of such a length that the time of one swing is approximately half a second. The support is made as rigid as possible to eliminate the error due to its flexure. The pendulum rod is supported on a knife-edge, which is generally an integral part of the rod, but is occasionally, as in the United States Coast and Geodetic Survey pattern, on the support.

The whole instrument is placed in a case from which the air can be exhausted. It is kept at a standard temperature, and the time of vibration is compared with chronometer signals. We secure then systems of comparative observation over large areas, which are gradually connected

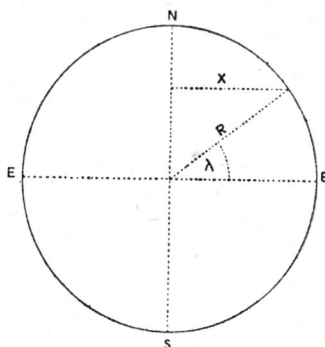

Fig. 2

up into a homogeneous whole, and we may say that the value of g is accurately known over wide areas. (Cf. *Physical and Chemical Constants*, Kaye and Laby.)

The best mean value of the ellipticity of the earth derived from recent pendulum experiments may be taken as 1/298·3 (Helmert). One matter of great importance in pendulum experiment has not yet been mentioned. Results must be reduced to the corresponding figure at mean sea-level in order to make comparison possible. Now this reduction has been made in various ways. In all cases the decreased distance from the centre of the earth has been allowed for. Bouguer allowed also for the additional attraction due to the mass above mean sea-level, as if this mass were independent of the general configuration and density of the earth.

In the 'free air' method this additional attraction is omitted altogether, and the use of the Isostatic method implies that the mass above mean sea-level is not a completely independent factor, but is compensated for by underlying portions of deficient density (*see* ISOSTASY), a conclusion which is now generally accepted.

Mention must also be made of Threlfall and Pollack's quartz-thread gravity balance and of the torsion balance used by Baron Eötvös in Hungary. Experiment indicates that considerable accuracy may be obtained by statical methods such as these, but we have as yet little observed result to go upon. Those interested in the subject will find details of Threlfall's balance in *Philosophical Transactions* for 1900.—BIBLIOGRAPHY: A. R. Clarke, *Geodesy*; F. R. Helmert, *Höhere Geodäsie*; Poynting and Thomson, *Physics: Properties of Matter*; the technical papers of the Survey of India, and of the United States Coast and Geodetic Survey.

GRAY, Asa, American botanist, born 1810, died in 1888. He was appointed Fisher professor of natural history in Harvard University in 1842, and held the chair till 1873, when he retired from its more active duties. His works include: *Elements of Botany* (1836), *A Manual of Botany* (1848), and other botanical text-books; also portions of works on the flora of North America and the *Genera Boreali-Americana*, a *Free Examination of Darwin's Treatise* (1861), and a volume entitled *Darwiniana* (1876).

GRAY, David, Scottish poet, born at Merkland, Dumbartonshire, in 1838; studied at Glasgow University, from which he went, with Robert Buchanan, to London in 1860 to try his fortune in literature. After a brief struggle consumption set in, and he died at Merkland in 1861. A small volume containing the poem entitled *The Luggie*, some lyrics, and a few sonnets, with the title *In the Shadows*, represents the whole of his work.

GRAY, Thomas, English poet, was born on the 26th Dec , 1716, and died on the 30th July, 1771. His mother had twelve children, of whom he alone grew up. His father was what we call on the Stock Exchange; he was a man of violent temper and a bad husband and father. Gray was sent to Eton in 1727; he was already of a studious disposition, and was shy and sensitive.

Education. In 1734 he entered Peterhouse, Cambridge, where his maternal uncle had been a fellow. He did not graduate at the normal time, and though he studied hard he seems to have followed no regular plan. He particularly disliked mathematics, but read Greek, Latin, French, and Italian voraciously, and had a passion for accurate knowledge in such subjects as entomology and botany.

He left Cambridge in 1738, and during the next year went a tour on the Continent with Horace Walpole, who had been his friend at Eton and Cambridge. It is typical of the scholarly bent of his mind that he studied the *De Bello Gallico* as he travelled through France, "Cæsaris visens monumenta magni." Livy and Silius Italicus accompanied him as he crossed the Alps. He eventually quarrelled with Walpole, and continued his travels alone. In 1741 he visited the Grande Chartreuse, and left behind him a beautiful poem in Latin alcaics, commencing "O tu severi religio loci."

Works. He returned to England in the same year, and spent some time in London. In 1742 he produced, for him, a considerable amount of poetry —some of it fragmentary, as the ambitious *De Principiis Cogitandi*, a poem which attempted to render Lock into Lucretian Latin, and *Agrippina*, a tragedy; but some of it completed, such as the *Ode on a Distant Prospect of Eton College*, and the *Hymn to Adversity*. In 1742, through lack of a more definite occupation, he returned to Peterhouse. He was destined to spend most of the rest of his life at Cambridge, although he never held a fellowship. In 1744 he proceeded to the degree of LL.B. The rest of Gray's life was uneventful.

In Feb., 1751, he published the famous *Elegy*; it had probably been begun some seven years previously, but the work of polishing it was very slow. He would not have published it even when he did had it not been impudently pirated. *The Progress of Poesy* and *The Bard* were published in 1757. In 1756 Gray migrated to Pembroke College, on account of a practical joke played upon him by some of the fellow-commoners of Peterhouse. The story of this joke, like the report of Mark Twain's death, would seem to be grossly exaggerated, but it is still a living legend at Cambridge.

During the last years of his life Gray became rather less sedentary in his habits, and went several long walking tours, visiting Scotland, Yorkshire, the English Lakes, Derbyshire, and the neighbourhood of Southampton. To his credit Gray had declined the offer of the Laureateship in 1757, so that the mantle of Colley Cibber fell upon William Whitehead. In 1768, however, he accepted the chair of modern history at Cambridge. The post was a sinecure, and although he intended to lecture he did not do so. He took ill in hall on 24th July, 1771, and died of gout in the stomach six days afterwards.

Analysis. Gray is perhaps the least

productive of all the greater English poets. No man has won so large a reputation with so small an amount of work. There are several causes to account for his sterility. He seldom enjoyed robust health, and seems to have lived in a state of gentle melancholy. He was not obliged to work for his living. One of his favourite maxims was "to be employed is to be happy," and he himself was never adequately employed. Moreover, Cambridge in those days was not an exhilarating place; many of the dons found their sole recreation in bickering with each other, and many were lacking not only in learning but in any desire to learn.

Perhaps, however, the main cause of Gray's sterility was the great load of learning which he bore. He was reputed to be the most learned man in Europe. He was probably the best Greek scholar at Cambridge between Bentley and Porson. He knew the literature and history of England, of France, and of Italy. He was interested in criticism, metaphysics, morals, and politics; he had a fine taste in painting, prints, architecture, and gardening. He excelled in his knowledge of botany, zoology, and entomology. He was also a good musician.

All this learning tended to make him over-fastidious in his writings. A brain which is continually receiving cannot create much. So Gray's poems occupy a few pages only in any collection, and yet they are among the best poems of their kind in English. They are, perhaps, too highly polished, and give an impression of cold perfection. It was not for nothing that he composed so much Latin verse; he would seem to have written English verse somewhat on the same principles, restlessly searching for exactly the right word.

The *Elegy* is popular because it contains much commonplace thought more exquisitely expressed than it had been before, or is ever likely to be. The two Pindaric odes are not unlike Pindar; preceding writers, in attempting this form of composition, had produced something that Pindar would have vehemently disowned.

Letters. No account of Gray would be complete without a mention of his delightful letters. In them we can read the whole story of his life. They are infinitely various. Were it not for them we should not know for certain that he possessed that gentle spirit of humour which is often complementary to a gentle spirit of melancholy. They are full of scholarship, wisdom, and wit in the best sense of the word. Gray's friend Dr. Wharton, writing of the poet a fortnight after he died, said of him: "He never spoke out."

These words exactly describe Gray's character, as a man and as a poet. His scanty writings, however, will live as long as English is spoken.—BIBLIOGRAPHY: E. Gosse, *Gray* (English Men of Letters Series); D. C. Tovey, *Gray and his Friends*; *Gray's Letters*, edited by D. C. Tovey.

GRAYLING, a genus of fishes of the family Salmonidæ. The common grayling (*Thymallus vulgāris*) is found in many English streams, and also in some in Scotland. It is scattered over Europe from Lapland to North Italy, and there are allied species in Asia and North America. It smells like thyme, hence the generic name. The grayling prefers rapid streams where the water is clear and cool, and the bottom sandy or pebbly, and it requires on the whole deeper water than the trout, to which it has a certain

Grayling

similarity in habit. The general colour is yellowish-brown, including the fins; several deeper brown lines run along the body; under the belly it is white. The colour often varies in different streams. It is a favourite fish of the angler.—Cf. T. E. Pritt, *The Book of the Grayling*.

GRAY'S THURROCK, a town of England, Essex, on the Thames, on the railway to Tilbury and Southend. Pop. (1931), 18,172.

GRAYWACKE (grä-wak'e), a strongly-cemented sandstone in which grains or fragments of various minerals, as quartz and felspar, or of rocks, as slate and siliceous clay rocks, are embedded in an indurated matrix, which may be siliceous or argillaceous. The colours are grey, red, blue, or some shade of these. The term, as used by the earlier writers, included all the conglomerates, sandstones, and shales of the older formations, when these had been subjected to considerable change. At first it was nearly synonymous with the Silurian strata, these, especially in Scotland, yielding the only geniuine graywacke.

GRAZ, or **GRATZ**, a town of Austria, capital of Styria, picturesquely situated on the Mur, 90 miles south-west of Vienna. The older town, on the left bank, is connected with the suburbs Lend and Gries on the right by several bridges, besides a railway bridge. The Schlossberg rises 400 feet above the river, but the fortifications of the town have given place to avenues and pleasure-grounds.

The cathedral of St. Œgidius, built in 1456, is a majestic Gothic structure with a fine altar and paintings; near it is the mausoleum of Ferdinand II. The university, founded in 1573, had in 1931, 2,258 students and a library of 80,000 vols. The Joanneum, for the promotion of agriculture and scien-

Thames, for the Eastern Steam Navigation Company, by Scott Russell, from plans by I. K. Brunel; length, 680 feet; breadth, 82½ feet, or, including paddle-boxes, 118 feet; height, 58 feet (70 to top of bulwarks). She had six masts, five of iron and one of wood, and could spread 7,000 sq. yards of sail, besides having eight engines, divided between her screws and paddles, and capable of working at 11,000 horse-power.

From the first her career was unfortunate, the launching process alone lasting three months and costing £60,000. After several unremunerative trips to New York she was employed first as a troopship, and then as a cable-laying ship, for which her size and steadiness specially qualified her. Various attempts were afterwards made to utilize her, but she at last came to be a mere holiday spec-

The *Great Eastern*

tific education, has a large library and museums.

The manufactures consist of woollen, cotton, and silk tissues, machinery, steel, rails, wagons, soap, leather, and ironware. Pop. 152,706.

GREAT CIRCLE SAILING, or **TANGENT SAILING**, a method of navigating a vessel according to which her course is always kept as nearly as possible on a great circle of the sphere, that is, a circle which has for its centre the centre of the sphere. An arc of such a circle joining two places gives the shortest distance between them, consequently the course of a vessel sailing on this arc will be the shortest possible. A simple instrument called a spherograph is employed for finding the great circle course between places, and this is accompanied by tables compiled for the same purpose.

GREAT EASTERN, an iron steamship, the largest vessel of her time, built (1854–8) at Millwall, on the

tacle, and was broken up in 1888, the materials being sold for about £60,000. An equal in size of the *Great Eastern* was not produced until 1901, when the *Celtic* was built.

GREAT FISH RIVER, a river of South-East Africa, near the eastern frontier of Cape Province. It rises in the Snowy Mountains, and falls into the sea after a course of 230 miles.

GREAT FISH or **BACK RIVER**, a river of Northern Canada, rising in Sussex Lake, and flowing, after a course of about 500 miles, into Cockburn Bay, an inlet of the Arctic Ocean.

GREAT LEBANON. *See* SYRIA AND LEBANON.

GREAT MARLOW, a town of England, county of Bucks, on the Thames, 5 miles N.N.W. of Maidenhead. Manufactures: chairs, lace, and paper. Pop. (1931), 5,087.

GREAT SALT LAKE, a lake, United States, state of Utah, 4,000 feet above sea-level, 70 miles in length north to south and 48 miles east to west. Five gallons of its water yield, by evaporation, 14 pints of salt. It has several islands, which, with its shores, are whitened by the salt; and it receives the Bear, the Utah, and several other streams. It contains no fish, but has several species of insects and a crustacean, and is frequented by immense flocks of gulls, ducks, geese, and swans.

GREBE, the common name of the birds of the genus Podiceps and allied genera, family Podicepididæ, characterized by a straight conical bill, no tail, tarsus short, toes flattened, separate, but broadly fringed at their edges by a firm membrane, and legs set so far back that on land the grebe assumes the upright position of the penguin. The geographical distribution of the genus is very wide, these birds haunting seas as well as ponds and rivers. They are excellent swimmers and divers; feed on small fishes, frogs, crustaceans, and insects; and their nests, formed of a large quantity of grass, &c., are generally placed among reeds and sedges, and rise and fall with the water.

Five species are British, the great crested grebe (*P. cristātus*), the little grebe or dabchick (*P. fluviatilis*), the Slavonian or horned grebe (*P. auritus*), the red-neck (*P. griseigena*), and the rare eared-grebe (*P. nigricollis*). The last three are winter visitors, but the first two remain all the year. A number of species are North American, some of these (crested grebe, horned grebe) being the same as those of Europe. The great crested grebe, which ranges across the Old World to New Zealand, is about 21 to 22 inches long, and has been called satin grebe from its beautiful silvery breast-plumage.

GRECO, El, the name usually given to Domenico Theotocopuli, Spanish painter, born in Crete about the middle of the sixteenth century, died at Toledo 1614. He studied and worked first in Venice, and his early work shows the influence of the Venetian school, especially Tintoretto and Bassano. He settled at Toledo some time before 1577, and shortly afterwards painted the *Disrobing of Christ*, now in the cathedral there.

Later appeared one of his masterpieces, *The Burial of the Count of Orgaz*, followed by a series of altarpieces, single figures of saints (including several versions of S. Francis), portraits, and a few landscapes. Soon after his arrival in Spain, El Greco threw off Italian influence and developed a very individual art, reflecting

J*

a singularly vehement and passionate temperament, and marked by the use of swinging rhythmic curves and arbitrary distortions of the human figure.

His colour in later years is remarkable for its use of cold, steely greys, combined with vivid and harsh, but very expressive colour. He is well represented in the National Gallery by the recently acquired *Agony in the Garden*.

GREECE, a republic of South-Eastern Europe, bounded by Albania, Yugo-Slavia, Bulgaria, Turkey, the

Great Crested Grebe (*Podiceps cristātus*)

Ægean Sea, and the Ionian Sea. Old Greece (territory acquired before 1912) comprises the southern part of the Balkan Peninsula and about 250 islands, including Eubœa, the Cyclades, (Syra, Andros, &c.) and the Northern Sporades in the Ægean, and Corfu, Zante, Cephalonia, &c., in the Ionian Sea. As a result of the war with Turkey in 1912-13, and of that with Bulgaria in 1913, Greece acquired Macedonia, Western Thrace, Epirus, Crete, and various Ægean islands.

By the Treaty of Sèvres after the European War, Greece obtained all the former territory of Turkey in Europe west of the Chatalja lines, Western Thrace (from Bulgaria), and the province of Aidin in Asia Minor.

Her defeat in the war with Turkey (1921–22), however, led to the loss of her Asiatic territory, and the Treaty of Lausanne (1923) declared the River Maritsa to be the Turco-Greek boundary.

The frontier with Bulgaria was fixed in 1919 by the Treaty of Neuilly. Crete, Samos, Mytilene, and Chios are now Greek. The area of the Republic is 50,257 sq. miles (including 23,799 sq. miles acquired since 1912), and the population is (1931), 6,480,000. On Mount Athos are 20 monasteries. The

Ancient Greece was divided into a number of independent states or territories, namely, in Northern Greece, Thessaly, Epirus, Locris, Phocis, Bœotia, Ætolia, Acarnania, Attica, Megaris; in the Peloponnesus, Corinth, Argolis, Achaia, Elis, Messenia, Laconia (Sparta), and Arcadia, the last entirely inland. These names are still kept up, but the country is now divided into nomes, some of which are formed of the Greek islands, namely, Eubœa, Corfu, Cephalonia, Zante, Leucadia, and the Cyclades.

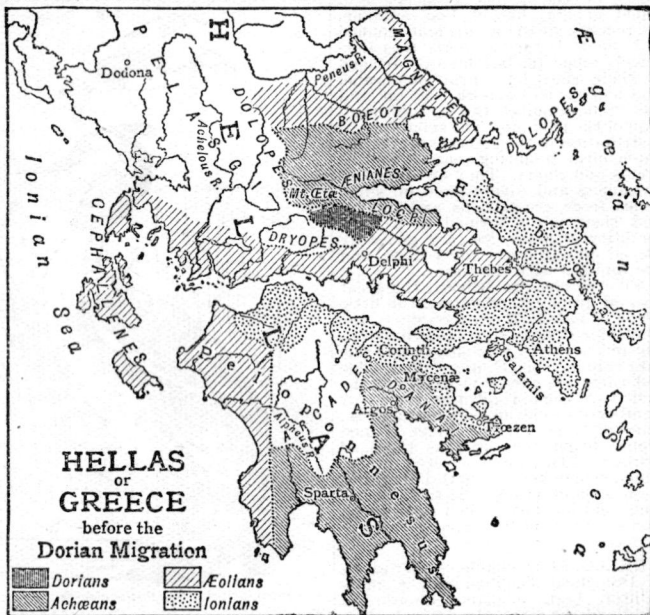

HELLAS
or
GREECE
before the
Dorian Migration

▓ Dorians   ▨ Æolians
▧ Achæans   ░ Ionians

monks (4,858 in 1928) form a community administered by a Council of 4 and a Representative Assembly of 20 members. In 1926 their autonomous government was recognised by the government. In the town of Salonika there has been a fiscal Free Zone since 1925; and in the port of Salonika a Yugoslav Free Zone since 1924.

The name Greece (Lat. *Græcia*) is of Roman origin, the native name for the country being **Hellas**, and the people calling themselves *Hellênes*. Anciently Hellas was used in a wider sense, so as to include both Greece itself and all countries that had become Greek by colonization.

Physical Features. Greece proper is remarkable for the extent of its coast line, formed by numerous gulfs which penetrate into it in all directions. The largest, the Corinthian Gulf, or Gulf of Lepanto, on the east, and the Saronic Gulf, or Gulf of Ægina, on the west, which nearly meet at the Isthmus of Corinth, separate Northern Greece from the Morea. Another striking feature is the mountainous character of the interior.

On the north are the Cambunian Mountains, with Mount Olympus (9,793 feet) at their eastern extremity. From this range a lofty chain, called Mount Pindus, runs southwards almost parallel to the eastern and western coasts of Greece. At a point in this chain called Mount Tymphrestus or Typhrestus (Mount Velukhi) two chains proceed in an easterly direction, the northern being called Mount Othrys, the southern terminating at Thermopylæ, Mount Œta (7,080 feet).

The Cambunian Mountains, Pindus and Othrys, enclose the fertile vale of Thessaly, forming the basin of the Peneus (Salambria), and the ranges of Othrys and Œta enclose the smaller basin of the Sperchius (Hellada). Another range, that of Parnassus (highest summit 8,068 feet), branches

ent directions. The highest range in the Peloponnesus, Mount Taygetus (7,904 feet), branches off from the circle round Arcadia, strikes southwards, and terminates in the promontory of Tænarum (Cape Matapan) The chief rivers in the Peloponnesus are the Eurotas (Basilipotamo), the Alpheus (Ruphia), draining Arcadia and Elis; and the Peneus, draining Elis.

The rock most largely developed in the mountains of Greece is limestone, which often assumes the form of the finest marble. Granite occurs in

GREECE
Distribution of Races
after their migration

Dorians   Æolians
Achæans   Ionians

off from Mount Œta and runs still more to the south.

The peaks of Cithæron, Parnes, Pentelicus and Hymettus lie in the same direction, and the range in which they are found is continued to the south-east point of continental Greece. This range on the south and that of Œta on the north enclose the basin of the Cephissus, with Lake Copais. The chief rivers on the west side of the Pindus chain are the Arachthus (Arta) and the Achelōus (Aspropotamo).

The chief feature in the mountain system of the Peloponnesus is a range or series of ranges forming a circle round the valley of Arcadia in the interior, having a number of branches proceeding outward from it in differ-

patches. Tertiary formations prevail in the north-east of the Peloponnesus; and in the north-west, along the shores of Elis, are considerable tracts of alluvium. Silver, lead, zinc, and copper are found and worked to some extent, the famous ancient silvermines of Laurium in Attica still yielding a little of the precious metal, but chiefly lead, iron ore, and zinc.

Climate. The climate is generally mild, in the parts exposed to the sea equable and genial, but in the mountainous regions of the interior sometimes very cold. None of the mountains attain the limit of perpetual snow; but several retain it far into the summer. In general the first snow falls in October and the last in April. During summer rain scarcely ever falls, and the channels of the minor streams become dry. Towards the end of harvest rain becomes frequent and copious; and intermittent fevers become common. In ancient times, when the country was more thickly peopled and better cultivated, the climate seems to have been better.

Vegetation, Agriculture, &c. Greece is mainly an agricultural country, and the economic life of the country depends on the products of the soil. The land is largely held by peasant proprietors. The principal crops are wheat, barley, and maize. The culti-

good breeds. Asses are almost the only beasts of burden employed; and dairy produce is obtained from the sheep and the goat.

Manufactures, Trade, &c. The manufactures are extremely limited, but with all other branches of industry in Greece are increasing. They include cottons, woollens, earthenware, and leather; and shipbuilding is carried on largely at various points of the coast, and at the Piræus. In 1932 the mercantile marine of Greece had an aggregate burden of about 1,470,064 tons. A large part of the shipping of

GREECE
at the time of the Persian Wars
Persia & Dependencies.................
Greek States in alliance with Persia.
Greek States at war with Persia.......
Neutral States..........................

vated land produces all the fruits of the latitude—figs, almonds, dates, oranges, citrons, and melons.

The vine also grows vigorously, as it did in ancient Greece. But a much more important product of Greece, especially on the coasts of the Peloponnesus and in the islands of Cephalonia, Zante, Ithaca, and Santa Maura, is the Corinthian grape or currant. The olive is also largely grown (as in ancient times), and the culture of the mulberry, for the rearing of silkworms, has been greatly extended.

The extensive forests contain among other trees a peculiar kind of oak (*Quercus Ægilops*), which yields the valonia of commerce. The domestic animals are neither numerous nor of

Greece is engaged in the carring trade between Britain, Germany, &c., and Greece, Turkey, and other Mediterranean countries. The chief ports are Corfu, Syra, Piræus (the port of Athens), and Patras.

The principal exports are currants and olive-oil; but valonia, emery, silk, dried figs, raisins, honey, wax, lead, tobacco, and other articles are also exported; the principal imports are cereals, and cotton, woollen, and silk goods, sugar, iron goods, and coffee.

Communications. The greatest hindrance to the development of Greece at the present time is the want of good roads, but that is being gradually remedied, there being now about 8611 miles of roads, with an additional

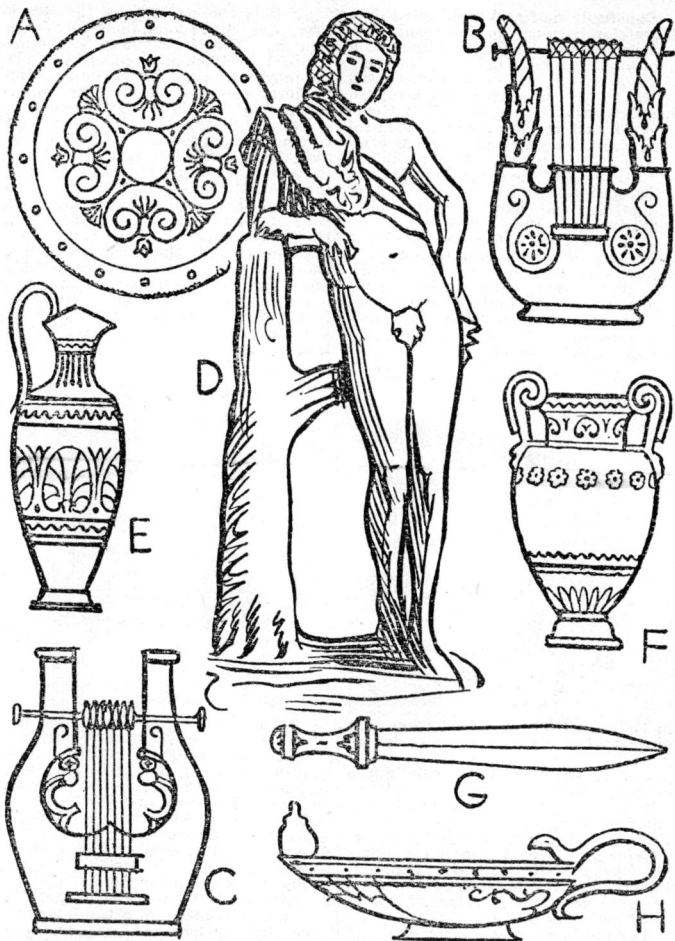

Greek Art

A, Greek Shield. B and C, Lyres. D, Faun, by Praxiteles. E, Wine Jug. F, Amphora. G, Greek Sword. H, Hand-lamp.

570 miles under construction. A canal across the Isthmus of Corinth was completed in 1893. In 1883 there were only 58 miles of railways open, but in 1929 there were 1,667 miles open, besides lines under construction; in addition the government has bought from England the Salonika-Angista-Stavros line (42 miles). The telegraph lines in 1931 were of a total length of 13,662 miles.

Currency &c. The money unit of Greece is the *drachma* of 100 *lepta*, which is nominally 1 franc, or 9¼d., but the stabilization has been suspended since April, 1932. The metric system is compulsory. The Gregorian Calendar was authorized in 1923.

Constitution, &c. A plebiscite taken throughout Greece in 1924 resulted in a majority for the establishment of a republic. Accordingly a National Assembly was elected and entrusted with the task of drawing up a republican constitution. When King Georgios II fled in Dec., 1923, Admiral Konduriotis became provisional head of the State, and then first president of the republic. He resigned in March, 1926, and was succeeded by General Pangalos, who had been virtually dictator since June, 1925.

In August 1926, General Kondylis overthrew Pangalos and Konduriotis again became president. The Constitution was revised in 1926; in 1927 the new constitution was published. Zaimis was elected President of the Republic in 1929 and will hold office till 1934. P. Tsaldaris became premier

In 1932 the strength of the Greek army was 64,622 men, including 5,010 officers. The Greek navy was reorganized in 1906, and consists of six submarines, ten destroyers, seven modern torpedo-boats, four mine-layers, and a number of other vessels.

People. The ancient Greeks were an Aryan race, probably most closely akin to the Italian peoples. They were noted for physical beauty and intellectual gifts. The present population contains a considerable intermixture of foreign stocks, among which the Albanese, or Arnauts, are the most numerous; but the great majority, though not without some taint in their blood, are of Greek extraction.

Education. Education in Greece is free and compulsory in theory (from the age of seven to twelve), but a large proportion of the people can

Greek Architecture (Doric order). The Temple of Poseidon, Pœstum

in 1933. In 1930 the right to vote at municipal elections was extended to women.

Justice, Religion. The Greek Church alone is established, but all forms of religion enjoy toleration. Justice is administered, on the basis of the French civil code, by a supreme court (*Areios Pagos*) at Athens; four courts (*Ephiteia*), at Athens, Nauplia, Patras, and Corfu; sixteen courts of primary resort (*Protodokeia*), one in each principal town.

The public revenue, derived chiefly from customs, land tax, tobacco and petroleum monopoly, state domains and national property, &c., amounted in 1932-3 to 8,676,294,740 drachmai, and the expenditure to 8,673,512,592 drachmai. All able-bodied males are liable to military service from the age of twenty-one, the periods being two years in the active army, ten in the reserve, eight in the national guard, and ten in the national guard reserve. The normal annual contingent of recruits for the army is about 60,000.

neither read nor write. There are three grades of schools, the primary national schools, the Hellenic or secondary grammar-schools, and the gymnasia, which are higher grammar-schools or colleges. In addition there are two universities at Athens, the National University, founded in 1836, and the Capodistria University; and one at Salonika, founded in 1925.

The national dress of the Greeks resembles the Albanian costume. In the men it consists of a tight jacket, generally scarlet, wide trousers descending as far as the knee, and embroidered gaiters; in the women it consists of a close-fitting vest, and a gown flowing loosely behind.

History. The earliest inhabitants of Greece were the Pelasgians, of whom little or nothing is known with certainty. To them are attributed certain remains of ancient buildings, especially the so-called Cyclopean works in the Peloponnesus. The Pelasgians were succeeded by the Hellênes, or Greeks proper, who may have been simply one of the Pelasgian tribes or races. To the early period of the Hellenic occupation of Greece belong the legends of the Trojan War, of Theseus, of Jason and the Argonauts, &c.

The Hellēnes were divided into four chief tribes—the Æolians, occupying the northern parts of Greece (Thessaly, Bœotia, &c.); the Dorians, occupying originally a small region in the neighbourhood of Mount Œta; the Achæans, occupying the greater part of the Peloponnesus; and the Ionians, occupying the northern strip of the Peloponnesus and Attica.

Of the four principal tribes the Ionians were most influential in the development of Greece, The distribution of the Hellenic tribes was greatly altered by the Dorian migration, sometimes called 'the return of the Heracleidæ' (descendants of Hercules), placed by Thucydides about eighty years after the fall of Troy, or about 1104 B.C., according to the ordinary chronology. Before the great migration several smaller ones had taken place, causing considerable disturbance; and at last the hardy Dorian inhabitants of the mountainous region about Mount Œta conquered a large part of Northern Greece, and then entered and subdued the greater part of the Peloponnesus, driving out or subjugating the Achæans, as the Achæans had the Pelasgians.

In the legend the Dorians are represented as having entered the Peloponnesus under Temenus, Cresphontes, and Aristodemus, three descendants of Heracles (Hercules), who had come to recover the territory taken from their ancestors by Eurystheus. Of the Achæan inhabitants of the Peloponnesus a large section occupied the territory formerly in possession of the Ionians, henceforward called Achaia.

The Ionians driven out of the Peloponnesus found at first a refuge among their kindred in Attica, but owing to its limited territory were soon compelled to leave it and found Ionic colonies on several of the islands of the Ægean Sea and on the middle part of the coast of Asia Minor, where they built twelve cities, afterwards forming an Ionic Confederacy. The principal of these were Ephesus and Miletus.

About the same time another body of Greeks, from Thessaly and Bœotia, are said to have founded the Æolian colonies on some of the northern islands of the Ægean, and on the northern part of the western coast of Asia Minor. The Æolic colonies of Asia Minor also formed a confederacy of twelve cities, afterwards reduced to eleven by the accession of Smyrna to the Ionic Confederacy. The southern

islands and the southern part of the west coast of Asia Minor were in like manner colonized by Dorian settlers. The six Doric towns in Asia Minor, along with the Island of Rhodes, formed a confederacy similar to the Ionic and Æolic ones.

In course of time many Greek settlements were made on the coasts of the Hellespont, the Propontis (Sea of Marmora), and the Black Sea, the most important being Byzantium (Istanbul), Sinope, Cerasus, and Trapezus (Trebizonde). There were also flourishing Greek colonies on the coasts of Thrace and Macedonia; for example, Abdera, Amphipolis, Olynthus, Potidæa, &c.; and the Greek colonies in Lower Italy were so numerous that the inhabitants

Greek Peasant Woman

of the interior spoke Greek, and the whole region received the name of Greater Greece (Magna Græcia).

The most famous of the Greek colonies in this quarter were Tarentum, Sybaris, Croton, Cumæ, and Neapolis (Naples). Sicily also came to a great extent into the hands of the Greeks, who founded on it or enlarged many towns, the largest, most powerful, and most highly cultured of the Greek colonies here being the Corinthian colony of Syracuse, founded in the eighth century B.C.

Other important colonies were Cyrene on the north coast of Africa, and Massilia (Marseilles) on the south coast of Gaul. All these colonies as a rule preserved the customs and institutions of the mother city, but were quite independent.

Although ancient Greece never formed a single state, the various Greek tribes always looked upon themselves as one people, and classed all other nations as *Barbaroi* (foreigners).

There were four chief bonds of union between the Greek tribes. First and chiefly, they had a common language, which, despite its dialectic peculiarities, was understood throughout all Hellas or the Greek world. Secondly, they had common religious ideas and institutions, and especially, in the oracle of Delphi, a common religious sanctuary.

Thirdly, there was a general assembly of the Greeks, the Amphictyonic League, in which the whole people was represented by tribes (not by states), and the chief functions of which were to guard the interests of the sanctuary of Delphi, and to see that the wars between the separate states of Greece were not too merciless. The fourth bond consisted in the four great national festivals or games, the Olympian, Isthmian, Nemean, and Pythian, on the first of which the whole of Greece based its calendar.

The various separate states of Greece may be divided, according to the form of their constitution, into the two great classes of aristocratic and democratic. Sparta, or Lacedæmon, the chief town of Laconia and of the Doric tribe, was the leading aristocratic state; and Athens, the capital of Attica and the chief town of the Ionic tribe, was the leading democratic state; and as a rule all the Doric states, and subsequently all those under the influence of Sparta, resembled that city in their constitution; and all the Ionic states, and those under the influence of Athens, resembled it. These two tribes or races are the only ones that come into prominence during the earlier part of Greek history subsequent to the Doric migration.

Sparta is said to have derived its form of government, and all its institutions, in the ninth century B.C., from Lycurgus, whose regulations developed a hardy and warlike spirit among the people, the results of which were seen in their conquests over surrounding states, especially over the Messenians in the eighth and seventh centuries B.C.

The constitution of Athens appears from the legends of Theseus and Codrus to have been at first monarchical, and afterwards aristocratic, and to have first received a more or less democratic character from Solon at the beginning of the sixth century B.C. This was followed about fifty years later by a monarchical usurpation under Pesistratus, and his sons Hippias and Hipparchus, the last survivor of whom, Hippias, reigned in Athens till 510 B.C.

After the expulsion of Hippias the Republic was restored, under the leadership of Cleisthenes, in a more purely democratic form than at first. A brief struggle with the Spartans, whose aid was invoked by some of the nobles, now took place, and Athens emerged from it well prepared for the new danger which threatened Greece.

The Greek colonies in Asia Minor and the adjacent islands, after being conquered by Crœsus, King of Lydia, fell with the fall of Crœsus into the power of Cyrus, King of Persia. In 500 B.C., however, the Ionians revolted with the assistance of the Athenians and Eretrians, and pillaged and burned Sardis. The rebellion was soon crushed by Darius, who destroyed Miletus, and prepared to invade Greece.

In 492 he sent an expedition against the Greeks under his son-in-law Mardonius, but the fleet which carried his army was destroyed in a storm off Mount Athos. A second army, under the command of Datis and Artaphernes, landed on Eubœa, and after destroying Eretria, crossed the Euripus into Attica; but it was totally defeated in 490 B.C. on the plain of Marathon by 10,000 Athenians and 1,000 Platæans, under Miltiades.

In the midst of preparations for a third expedition Darius died, leaving his plans to be carried out by his son Xerxes, who, with an army of 1,700,000 men, crossed the Hellespont in 481 by means of two bridges of boats, and marched through Thrace, Macedonia, and Thessaly, while his fleet followed the line of coast. In the pass of Thermopylæ he was held in check by Leonidas with 300 Spartans and 700 Thespians; but the small band was betrayed and annihilated (480 B.C.); and the way through Phocis and Bœotia being now open he advanced into Attica, and laid Athens in ruins.

The deliverance of Greece was chiefly due to the genius and courage of Themistocles. The united fleet of the Greeks had already contended with success against that of the Persians off Artemisium, and had then sailed into the Saronic Gulf, followed by the enemy. Themistocles succeeded in inducing the Persians to attack in the narrow strait between Attica and Salamis, and totally defeated them.

From a neighbouring height Xerxes himself witnessed the destruction of his fleet, and at once began a speedy retreat with his land army through Thessaly, Macedonia, and Thrace, leaving behind him 300,000 men in Thessaly. In the spring of the following year (479) these advanced into Attica and compelled the citizens once more to seek refuge in Salamis; but were so completely defeated at Platæa by the Greeks under Pausanias, that only 40,000 Persians reached the Hellespont. On the same day the remnant of the Persian fleet was defeated by the Greeks off Mount Mycale.

The brilliant part taken by the Athenians under Themistocles in repelling this invasion of Athens greatly increased her influence throughout Greece. From this date begins the period of the leadership or *hegemony* of Athens in Greece, which continued to the close of the Peloponnesian War, 404 B.C.

The first thing which Athens exerted her influence to effect was the formation of a confederacy, including the Greek islands and maritime towns, to supply means for the continuance of the war by payments into a common treasury established on the Island of Delos, and by furnishing ships. In this way Athens gradually increased her power so much that she was able to render tributary several of the islands and smaller maritime states.

In 469 B.C. the series of victories won by the Athenians over the Persians was crowned by the double victory of Cimon over the Persian fleet and army on the Eurymedon, in Asia Minor, followed by the Peace of Cimon, which secured the independence of all Greek towns and islands. Shortly after followed the brilliant administration of Pericles, during which Athens reached the height of her grandeur.

The position of Athens, however, and the arrogance and severity with which she treated the states that came under her power made her many enemies. In the course of time two hostile confederacies were formed in Greece, one consisting of Athens and the democratic states of Greece; the other of Sparta and the aristocratic states.

At last, in 431, war was declared by Sparta on the complaint of Corinth that Athens had furnished assistance to Corcyra in its war against the mother city; and on that of Megara, that the Megarean ships and merchandise were excluded from all the ports and markets of Attica; and thus began the Peloponnesian War, which for twenty-seven years devastated Greece.

In the first part of the war the Spartans, who invaded Attica in 431 B.C. and three times in the five years following, had considerable successes, which were aided by the pestilence that broke out at Athens and the death of Pericles. In 425, however, Pylos was captured by the Athenian general Demosthenes, and the Spartan garrison on the Island of Sphacteria was compelled to surrender to Cleon. Soon after Cythera fell into the hands of the Athenians, but they were defeated in Bœotia at Delium (424) and

at Amphipolis in Thrace by Brasidas in 422, when both Cleon and Brasidas were killed.

The Peace of Nicias (421 B.C.), which followed the death of Cleon, brought disaffection into the Spartan Confederacy, the Corinthians endeavouring with Argos and Elis to wrest from Sparta the hegemony of the Peloponnesus. In this design they were supported by Alcibiades; but Sparta was victorious at the battle of Mantinea in 418.

Soon after this the Athenians resumed hostilities, fitting out in 415 B.C. a magnificent army and fleet, under the command of Alcibiades, Nicias, and Lamachus, for the reduction of Syracuse. Alcibiades, however, being subsequently deprived of his command on a charge of impiety, betook himself to Sparta, and exhorted the city to renew the war with Athens. By his advice one Spartan army was dispatched to Attica, where it took up such a position as prevented the Athenians from obtaining supplies from Eubœa, while another was sent under Gylippus to assist their kindred in Sicily.

These steps were ruinous to Athens. The Athenian army and fleet at Syracuse were completely destroyed, and though the war was maintained with spirit the prestige of Athens was seriously diminished. Many of her allies joined Sparta, and a revolution and brief change of government tended still further to weaken her. Still she made not unsuccessful efforts to regain her position, conquered the revolted towns about the Bosporus, and defeated the Spartan admiral Callicratidas off the islands of Arginusœ in 406. Sparta, however, was now in receipt of Persian aid, and Lysander, having captured nearly the whole Athenian fleet at Ægospotami (405), retook the towns of Asia Minor, surrounded Athens, and blocked the Piræus.

In 404 B.C. the Athenians were starved into surrender, the fortifications were destroyed, and an aristocratic form of government established by Sparta, placing the supreme power in the hands of thirty individuals, commonly known as the Thirty Tyrants. Only a year later, however (403), Thrasybulus was able to re-establish the democracy.

The period which follows the fall of Athens is that of Sparta's leadership or hegemony in Greece, which lasted till the battle of Leuctra, in 371 B.C. The Spartan rule was not more liked than that of Athens, and the character of the Spartan state itself, with its increase of wealth and power, underwent great change.

To escape the stigma of having ceded

the cities of Asiatic Greece to Persia, Agesilaus was sent to retake them, but was defeated by the fleet of Pharnabazus under Conon the Athenian; and the states of Greece, the Spartans included, at last, in 387, agreed to the disgraceful Peace of Antalcidas, by which the whole west coast of Asia Minor was ceded to the Persians.

An act of violence committed by a Spartan general in garrisoning Thebes in 380 was the commencement of the downfall of Sparta. The Thebans revolted under Pelopidas and Epaminondas, and the Spartans on invading Bœotia, were so completely defeated at Leuctra in 371 B.C. that they never fully recovered from the blow.

With this victory Thebes won the leading place in Greece, which she maintained during the lifetime of Epaminondas, whose influence was paramount in the Peloponnesus. Epaminondas fell in defeating the Spartans and Arcadians near Mantinea in 362, and his death reduced once more the authority of Thebes in Greece.

Two years after the death of Epaminondas, Philip, the father of Alexander the Great, became King of Macedonia. An occasion for interference in the affairs of Greece was furnished him by the war known as the Sacred War (355–346), arising from the Phocians having taken possession of some of the land belonging to the sanctuary of Delphi. The Thebans besieged the Phocians, and called to their aid Philip of Macedon, who was accorded the place till then held by the Phocians in the Amphictyonic League.

It was not, however, till the Locrian War (339–338) that Philip acquired a firm hold in Greece. The Locrians had committed the same offence as the Phocians, and Philip, as one of the members of the league, received the charge of punishing them. The real designs of Philip soon became apparent, and the Athenians, on the advice of Demosthenes, hastily concluded an alliance with the Thebans, and sent an army to oppose him. The battle of Chæronea which ensued (338) turned out, however, disastrously for the allies, and Philip became master of Greece. He then collected an army for the invasion and conquest of the empire of Persia, and got himself declared commander-in-chief by the Amphictyonic League at Corinth in 337 B.C.; but before he was able to start he was assassinated, 336 B.C.

The design of Philip was taken up and carried out by his son Alexander the Great, during whose absence Antipater was left behind as Governor of Macedonia and Greece. Soon after the departure of Alexander, Agis III of Sparta headed a rising against Antipater, but was defeated at Megalopolis in 330 B.C., and no other attempt was made by the Greeks to recover their liberty, for nearly a hundred years. At the close of the wars which followed the death of Alexander, and which resulted in the division of his empire, Greece remained with Macedonia.

The last efforts of the Greeks to recover their independence proceeded from the Achæans, who had for the most part kept aloof from the quarrels of the other states, and did not even furnish assistance to repel the Persian invasion. They had taken part, though reluctantly, in the Peloponnesian War on the side of Sparta, and had shared in the defeat of Megalopolis in 330 B.C. In the course of the first half of the third century B.C. several of the Achæan towns expelled the Macedonians and revived an ancient confederacy, which was now known as the Achæan League.

Aratus of Sicyon became its leading spirit. It was joined also by Corinth, and even by Athens and Ægina. The Spartans, however, who had maintained their independence against Macedonia, naturally looked with jealousy on the efforts of Aratus, and during the reign of Cleomenes a war broke out between Sparta and the Achæan League.

The League was at first worsted, and was only finally successful when Aratus sacrificed the ultimate end of the League by calling in the aid of the Macedonians. In the battle of Sellasia (222 B.C.) Cleomenes was defeated, and the Macedonians became masters of Sparta. Aratus died in 213, and his place was taken by Philopœmen, 'the last of the Greeks,' who succeeded in making the League in some degree independent of Macedonia.

About this time the Romans, who had just come out victorious from a second war with Carthage, found occasion to interfere in the affairs of Greece. Philip V of Macedon having allied himself with Hannibal, the Romans sent over Flamininus to punish him, and in this war with Philip the Romans were joined by the Achæan League. Philip was defeated at Cynoscephalæ in 197 B.C., and was obliged to recognize the independence of Greece.

The Achæan League thus became supreme in Greece, having been joined by all the states of the Peloponnesus. But the League itself was in reality subject to Rome, which found constant ground for interference until 147 B.C., when the League openly resisted the demand of the Senate, that Sparta, Corinth, Argos, and other cities should be separated from it. In the war which ensued, which was concluded in 146 B.C. by the capture of Corinth by the

Roman consul Mummius, Greece completely lost its independence, and was subsequently formed into a Roman province.

On the division of the Roman Empire Greece fell of course to the eastern or Byzantine half. From 1204 to 1261 it formed a part of the Latin Empire of the East, and was divided into a number of feudal principalities. In the latter year it was reannexed to the Byzantine Empire, with which it remained till it was conquered by the Turks between 1460 and 1473.

In 1699 the Morea was ceded to the Venetians, but was recovered by the Turks in 1715. From 1715 till 1821 the Greeks were without intermission subject to the domination of the Turks. In 1770, and again in 1790, they made vain attempts at insurrection, but in 1821 Ali, the pasha of Janina, revolted against the Sultan Mahmoud II, and secured the aid of the Greeks by promising them their independence.

The rising of the Greeks took place on the 6th of March, under Alexander Ypsilanti, and on the 1st of Jan., 1822, they published a declaration of independence. In the same year Ali was assassinated by the Turks, but the Greeks, encouraged by most of the European nations, continued the struggle under various leaders, of whom the chief were Marcos Bozzaris, Capo d'Istria, Constantine Kanaris, Kolocotroni, &c.

In 1825 the Turks, with the aid of Ibrahim Pasha, took Tripolitza, the capital of the Morea, and Missolonghi, and though Lord Cochrane organized the Greek fleet, and the French colonel Fabvier their army, the Turks continued to triumph everywhere.

A treaty was then concluded at London (6th July, 1827) between Britain, France, and Russia for the pacification of Greece, and when the mediation of these three powers was declined by the Sultan, their united fleets, under Admiral Codrington annihilated the Turkish fleet off Navarino, 20th Oct., 1827. In the beginning of the following year (1828) Count Capo d'Istria became President of the state, and later on in the same year Ibrahim Pasha was forced to evacuate Greece.

At last, on the 3rd of Jan., 1830, a protocol of the allied powers declared the independence of Greece, which was recognized by the Porte on the 25th April of that year. The crown was offered to Leopold, Prince of Saxe-Coburg, and when he refused it, to Otto, a young prince of Bavaria, who was proclaimed King of the Hellenes at Nauplia in 1832. But his arbitrary measures, and the preponderance which he gave to Germans in the government, made him unpopular, and although after a rebellion in 1843 a Constitution was drawn up, he was compelled by another rebellion in 1862 to abdicate.

A Provisional Government was then set up at Athens, and the National Assembly offered the vacant throne in succession to Prince Alfred of England and Prince William George of Denmark. The latter accepted it, and on 30th March, 1863, was proclaimed as King George I. In 1864 the Ionian Islands, which had hitherto formed an independent republic under the protection of Britain, were annexed to Greece.

From the first Greece has sought an opportunity of extending its frontier northwards, so as to include the large Greek population in Thessaly and Epirus. In Jan., 1878, after the fall of Plevna, Greek troops were moved into Thessaly and Epirus, but were withdrawn on the remonstrance of Britain. The promises held out to Greece by the Berlin Congress were in danger of being withdrawn, but the persistence of Greece led in 1881 to the cession to her of Thessaly and part of Epirus. The union of Eastern Roumelia with Bulgaria, in 1885, gave rise to fresh demands, and war with Turkey was only prevented by the Great Powers.

In 1897 an insurrection in Crete led to the interference of the Greeks and to war with Turkey, the result being the speedy defeat of Greece, entailing the payment of a heavy war indemnity with some loss of territory on the Thessalian frontier. The European powers, however, compelled Turkey to withdraw her troops from Crete, which was thus liberated, and became an autonomous island (see CRETE).

In 1912 the Balkan War broke out, Greece joining Serbia and Bulgaria against Turkey. The result of this war was an acquisition of new territories by Greece. In March, 1913, King George was assassinated at Salonika, and was succeeded by his son Constantine.

During the European War Greece at first neutral, then, under King Constantine's influence more than sympathetic to the Central Empires, ultimately was prevailed upon by Venizelos to join the Allies. King Constantine was compelled to abdicate, being succeeded in June, 1917, by his son Alexander, who died in Oct., 1920. The Greek army, however, was not mobilized and re-equipped to assist the Allies before the spring of 1918, but it shared in the Macedonian offensive which brought about the capitulation of Bulgaria in September of that year. Venizelos was defeated at the 1920 election and Constantine was recalled, only to abdicate (1922) in favour of his son

Georgios II. He was forced to leave the country in 1923 and a republic was established in 1924, with Venizelos as Premier. In 1925 by a *coup d'état* Pangalos was made dictator. For a short time he was President after the resignation of Koundouriotes, who, however, returned.

After the setting up of a Coalition Government with Zaimes as premier, the Constitution was passed in 1926 after long discussion, and since that time the Republic has endured. Zaimes has been President of Greece since 1929, and Venizelos also returned to office. He became premier again in 1928, held it on this occasion for a longer term than any recorded in Greek history excepting the Premiership of Trikoupes in 1886–90, and Venizelos's own earlier period of office in 1910–15. In the 1932 elections the Venizelist party headed the poll with 100 seats (as decided by proportional Representation) out of 250, as against 178 in 1928. The Popular (or Royalist) party won 76 seats, bringing its strength to 95, and the remaining seats were divided between eight other small parties or groups. In this state of parties, a Coalition government was the only solution, and one was formed by Tsaldares, in November, 1932. (*See* CONSTITUTION above.)—BIBLIOGRAPHY: Sir C. W. C. Oman, *History of Greece*; G. Grote, *History of Greece*; J. B. Bury, *History of Greece to the Death of Alexander the Great*; *Cambridge Modern History*; L. M. Garnett, *Greece of the Hellenes*; P. F. Martin, *Greece of the Twentieth Century*; Sir J. P. Mahaffy, *Social Life in Greece*.

Religion of Ancient Greece. The religion of the ancient Greeks was polytheism, there being a great number of divinities, many of whom must be regarded as personifications of natural powers, or of phenomena of the external world, or personified sentiments. Thus there were gods corresponding to Earth and Heaven, the Ocean and Night.

The Romans, when they became acquainted with the literature and religion of the Greeks, identified the Greek deities with those of their own pantheon. In this way the Greek and Roman deities came to be confounded together, and the names of the latter even came to supersede those of the former.

The supreme ruler among the gods was Zeus (Roman Jupiter or Juppiter), the son of Kronos (Roman Saturn), who after the subjugation of the Titans and Giants ruled in Olympus, while his brother Pluto reigned over the lower world (Hades, Tartarus) and Poseidōn (Neptune) ruled in the sea. Like reverence was paid to Hēra

(Juno), the sister and wife of Zeus, and the queen of Heaven; to the virgin Pallas Athēnē (Minerva); to the two children of Lētō (Latona), namely, Apollo, the leader of the Muses, and his sister the huntress Artēmis (Diana), the goddess of love; to Arēs (Mars), the god of war, Hermēs (Mercury), the herald of the gods, and others besides.

In addition to these there was an innumerable host of inferior deities (Nymphs, Nereids, Tritons, Sirens, Dryads and Hamadryads, &c.) who presided over woods and mountains, fields and meadows, rivers and lakes. There was also a race of heroes or demigods (such as Heracles or Hercules and Perseus) tracing their origin from Zeus, and forming a connecting link between gods and men, while on the other hand the Satyrs formed a connecting link between the race of men and the lower animals.

Religious teachers were not a distinct class in Greece. The priests were in no sense preachers of doctrines, but merely hierophants, or exhibitors of sacred things, of rites, symbols, and images. They showed how a god was to be worshipped; but it was not their office to teach theological doctrine, or even as a rule to exhort to religious duty.

The true teachers of the Greek religion were the poets and other writers, and it is to the hymns, epics, dramas, and histories of the Greeks that we must turn in order to learn how they regarded the gods. No degree of consistency is to be found in them, however, the personality and local origin of the writers largely moulding their views.

A belief in the justice of the gods as manifested in the punishment of all offences against them was cardinal. The man himself might escape, but his children would suffer, or he might be punished in a future state—the latter view being less commonly held than the former of an entailed curse.

The gods are also represented by the Greeks as holy and truthful, although they are in innumerable other passages described as themselves guilty of the grossest vices, and likewise as prompting men to sin, and deceiving them to their own destruction. In their general attitude towards men the gods appear as inspired by a feeling of envy or jealousy. Hence they had constantly to be appeased, and their favour won by sacrifices and offerings. Certain classes were, however, under the peculiar protection and favour of the gods, especially strangers and suppliants.

The Greeks believed that the gods communicated their will to men in various ways, but above all by means of oracles, the chief of which were that of Apollo at Delphi, and that of Zeus at Dodona. Dreams ranked next in importance to oracles, and divination by birds, remarkable natural phenomena, sneezing, &c., was practised. The Greeks appear to have had at all times some belief in a future existence, but in the earliest times this belief was far from being clearly defined.—BIBLIOGRAPHY: Sir James G. Frazer, *The Golden Bough*; L. R. Farnell, *Cults of the Greek States*; L. Campbell, *Religion in Greek Literature*; J. E. Harrison, *Prolegomena to the Study of Greek Religion*; A. Fairbanks, *A Handbook of Greek Religion*; J. Adam, *The Religious Teachers of Greece*; G. Murray, *Four Stages of Greek Religion*.

Greek Language. The Greek language belongs to the Indo-European group, and is thus a sister of the Sanskrit, Latin, Teutonic, and Celtic tongues. It is customary to distinguish three leading dialects according to the three leading branches of the Greeks, the Æolic, the Doric, and the Ionic, to which was afterwards added the mixed Attic dialect; besides these there are several secondary dialects. Akin to the Ionic is the so-called Epic dialect, that in which the poems of Homer and Hesiod were written, and which was afterwards adopted by other Epic writers. The Doric was hard and harsh; the Ionic was the softest.

The Æolic was spoken on the north of the Isthmus of Corinth (except in Megara, Attica, and Doris), in the Æolian colonies of Asia Minor, and on some of the northern islands of the Ægean Sea. The Doric was spoken in the Peloponnesus, in Doris, in the Doric colonies of Asia Minor, of Lower Italy (Tarentum), of Sicily (Syracuse, Agrigentum); the Ionic in the Ionian colonies of Asia Minor, and on the islands of the Archipelago; and the Attic in Attica.

In each of these dialects there are celebrated authors. The Ionian dialect is found pure in Herodotus and Hippocrates. The Doric is used in the poems of Pindar, Theocritus, Bion, and Moschus. In Æolic we have fragments of Alcæus and Sappho.

After Athens had obtained the supremacy of Greece, and rendered itself the centre of all literary cultivation, the masterpieces of Æschylus, Sophocles, Euripides, Aristophanes, Thucydides, Xenophon, Plato, Aristotle, Isocrates, Demosthenes, &c., made the Attic the common dialect of literature.

Grammarians afterwards distinguished the genuine Attic, as it exists in those masters, from the Attic of common life, calling the latter the com-

mon *Greek* or *Hellenic* dialect. In this latter dialect wrote Theophrastus, Apollodorus, Polybius, Plutarch, and others. Many later writers, however, wrote genuine Attic, as Lucian, Ælian, and Arrian.

Except the dramatists, the poets by no means confined themselves to the Attic; the dramatists themselves assumed the Doric, to a certain degree, in their choruses, and the other poets retained the Homeric style, which was a congeries of forms occurring as peculiarities in the various dialects.

At what time this language first began to be expressed in writing has long been a subject of doubt. According to the usual account, Cadmus the Phœnician introduced the alphabet into Greece; and it is an undoubted fact that the most of the Greek letters are derived from the Phœnician ones. The Greek alphabet possesses the following twenty-four letters:—A, α (alpha), *a*; Β, β (beta), *b*; Γ, γ (gamma), *g*; Δ, δ (delta), *d*; Ε, ε (epsilon), *ĕ*; Ζ, ζ (zeta), *z*; Η, η (eta), *ē*; Θ, θ (theta), *th*; Ι, ι (iota), *i*; Κ, κ (kappa), *k*; Λ, λ (lamda), *l*; Μ, μ (mu), *m*; Ν, ν (nu), *n*; Ξ, ξ (xi), *x*; Ο, ο (omicron, i.e. small *o*), *ŏ*; Π, π (pi), *p*; Ρ, ρ (rho), *r*; Σ, σ, ς (sigma), *s*; Τ, τ (tau), *t*; Υ, υ (upsilon), *u*, commonly transliterated by *y*; Φ, φ (phi), *ph*; Χ, χ (chi), *ch* guttural (as in Scottish *loch*); Ψ, ψ (psi), *ps*; Ω, ω (omega, or great *o*), *ō*. The alphabet originally introduced into Greece is said to have consisted of but sixteen letters, Θ Ξ Φ Χ Ζ Η Ψ Ω being of later introduction.

Modern Greek, as spoken by the uneducated classes, is called Romaic, from the fact that those who speak it considered themselves before the descent of the Turks upon Europe as belonging to the Roman Empire, and hence called themselves *Romaioi*, or Romans. The Greek of the educated classes, Zakonian, that used in the newspapers and other literature of the present day, is distinguished from it by a greater resemblance to the Greek of antiquity, which renders it easy for anyone who has a satisfactory acquaintance with ancient Greek to read the modern literary Greek.

Besides the foreign words introduced into modern Greek, many words have changed their original signification. The grammar has also undergone considerable modification. For example the numbers have been reduced to two by the suppression of the dual; and the cases to four by the disappearance of the dative, which is now expressed by a preposition with the accusative. The first cardinal numeral is now used as an indefinite article. The degrees of comparison are sometimes expressed by the use of *pleon* (more).

The past and future tenses are formed by the aid of the verbs *echō* (I have), and *thelō* (I will). The infinitive mood has its place supplied by a periphrasis with the verb in the subjunctive, and the middle voice has disappeared.

The ancient orthography is still preserved, but the vowels η, ι, and υ, and the diphthongs ει, οι, υι, are all pronounced like *ee* in English *seen*; β is now pronounced as *v*, and the sound of *b* is expressed by μπ; Δ is pronounced like *th* in *thus*, and θ like *th* in *think*.—BIBLIOGRAPHY: J. Wright, *Comparative Grammar of the Greek Language*; A. T. Robertson, *A Grammar of New Testament Greek in the Light of Historical Research*; A. Thumb, *Handbuch der neugriechischen Volkssprache*.

Greek Literature. The commencement of extant Greek literature is to be found in the two epic poems attributed to Homer, the *Iliad* and the *Odyssey*, which it is commonly believed took shape on the Ionian coast or its islands somewhere between 950 and 850 B.C., and came thence to Greece proper (*see* HOMER). The former deals directly with the Trojan War; the latter describes the wanderings of Ulysses in returning from it.

Another poem, the *Batrachomyomachia* (Battle of the Frogs and Mice), a burlesque epic which is not remarkably entertaining, was originally attributed to Homer as a joke, and the joke was taken seriously by many generations of scholars. It was actually written by an unknown humorist of the time of Alexander the Great.

In European Greece there appeared about the middle of the ninth century, at Ascra in Bœotia, the poet Hesiod, who stood at the head of another epic school. Of the sixteen works attributed to him there have come down to us the *Theogony* (Origin of the Gods), the *Shield of Heracles* (a fragment of a larger poem of later authorship), and, most important of all, the *Works and Days*, a didactic work on agriculture.

The works of Homer and Hesiod were the principal schoolbooks in Greece, Homer in particular taking in Greek education the place once taken in English education by the Bible. The Homeric and Hesiodic schools begin to meet in the Homeric hymns composed by different hands between 750 and 500 B.C.

Next came the period of Elegiac and Iambic poetry (700–480), both Ionian, in which the poet's own feelings and personality became distinctly manifested, the chief names being those of Callinus of Ephesus (flourished about 690 B.C.), Tyrtæus, originally of Attica (675), Archilochus of Paros (670), Simonides of Amorgos (660), Mimnermus of Smyrna (620), Solon of Athens (594), Theognis of Megara (540), Phocylides of Miletus (540), Xenophanes of Colophon (510), Hipponax of Ephesus (540), Simonides of Ceos (480).

Greek lyric poetry was inseparably linked with music, the lyric period proper lasting from about 670 to 440 B.C. Two principal schools may be distinguished, the Æolian and the Dorian. To the former belong Alcæus (611–580), Sappho (610), and Anacreon (530), though the series of erotic poems long attributed to Anacreon is really Alexandrian.

To the Dorian school belong Alcman of Sparta (660 B.C.), credited with the invention of the strophe and antistrophe; Stesichorus (Tisias) of Himera (620), who added to these the epode; Arion (600), who gave shape to the dithyramb; and Ibycus of Rhegium (540). Simonides of Ceos (480) was even more famous as lyric poet than as elegist, his lyrics marking the commencement of a school of national lyric poetry. His nephew, Bacchylides, was also famous, but the chief was undoubtedly Pindar (522–443).

About this time began a new literary development, that of the drama, the earliest names in which are Thespis (536) and Phrynichus (512–476). The performance at first, however, was merely a sort of oratorio or choral entertainment, until Æschylus (525–456) introduced a second actor, and interspersed choral song with dialogue.

The tragedies of Æschylus are unsurpassed, and if equalled are equalled by Shakespeare alone. A third and (according to some authorities) even a fourth actor was added by Sophocles (495–405) B.C., who supplemented the heroic tragedy of Æschylus with the tragedy of human character and the fundamental passions. Euripides (480–406) brought new qualities of picturesqueness, homeliness, realism, and pathos with a less rigid artistic method, and formed a fitting third in the great tragic triad.

With this rapid growth of tragedy there was a corresponding development of comedy, which assumed an artistic form about 470 B.C. The names of Cratinus (448) and Eupolis (430) are overshadowed by that of Aristophanes (448–385), who for nearly forty years was the burlesque commentator upon the life of the period. His work, which alone has survived, but which probably follows the law of the survival of the fittest, may be regarded as closing the period of the old comedy; the middle comedy of from 390 to 320 (Antiphanes, Alexis, and others) was transitional from the great political comedy to the new comedy of manners, which was vigorous from 320 to 250 in the hands of Menander, Philemon, and Diphilus.

In the meantime a prose literature had arisen, commencing with the group of early Ionian writers (550–450), of which Pherecydes of Syros, Anaximenes, and Anaximander, philosophers, and the logographer or compiler Hecatæus of Miletus were chief.

Hellanicus of Mitylene (450) was one of the earliest critical historians, but Herodotus (484–428) was the first writer of great historic rank, as he was also the first great prose stylist. Thucydides (471–400?) was the founder of philosophic history, and Xenophon (431–354), who has left excellent historic narratives, was also the earliest Greek essayist.

The oldest piece of Attic prose is the essay on Athenian polity wrongly assigned to Xenophon. Other writers in history were Ctesias (415–398), Philistus (363), Theopompus (352), and Ephorus (340). From 360 onwards Attic history and archæology were preserved in works by various writers, of whom Philochorus (306–260) was chief.

The study which oratory and rhetoric received in Athens was an important factor in shaping Attic prose, the chief orators being Antiphon (480–411), Andocides (415–390), Lysias (403–381), Isocrates (436–338), Isæus (390–353), and, above all, Demosthenes (384–322) with his contemporaries Æschines, Lycurgus, and others, and Demetrius of Phalerum (318), the last of whom marks the beginning of decay in the art.

Philosophy shared the development of history and oratory, reaching a rare elevation in Plato (429–347), a rare comprehensiveness in Aristotle (384–322), the founders of the academic and peripatetic schools. Minor Socratic schools were the Cyrenaic, founded by Aristippus (370), the Megaric, founded by Euclid (399), and the Cynic, founded by Antisthenes. In the earlier part of the third century the rival schools of Epicurus (342–270) and of Zeno (344–260) became prominent.

From about the year 300 B.C. the literary decadence may be held to date; the period 300 to 146 being known as the Alexandrian. It comprises the learned poetry of Callimachus (who flourished at Alexandria 250 B.C.) and of Lycophron (260); the epic of Apollonius Rhodius (194); the didactic poetry of Aratus (270) and Nicander (150); the pastoral poetry of Theocritus, Bion, and Moschus; the satirical Silloi of Timon (280); the philology and criticism of Zenodotus (280), Aristophanes of Byzantium (200), Aristarchus (156),

and Apollodorus (140); the version of the *Septuagint*; and the scientific works of Eucleides (300), Archimedes and Eratosthenes (240).

From 146 B.C. dates the Græco-Roman period in Greek literature, to which belong the historians Polybius (145 B.C.), Diodorus Siculus (40 B.C.), Dionysius of Halicarnassus (25 B.C.), Josephus, Arrian (A.D. 100), Appian (A.D. 140), and Herodian (A.D. 240); the biographies of Plutarch (A.D. 90), of Diogenes Laertius and of Flavius Philostratus (A.D. 235); the geographies of Strabo (A.D. 18) and of Pausanias (A.D. 160); the astronomy and geography of Ptolemy; the informatory works of Athenæus (190), Ælian (220), and Stobæus (480); the rhetorical and literary works of Hermogenes (170), Aphthonius and Cassius Longinus (260); the medical works of Galen (160); the satirical works of Lucian (160) and of Julian (331–363); and the development of the Greek romance, best represented in Heliodorus (390), Achilles Tatius, and Chariton.

During this period philosophy is in the main divided between Stoicism and Neoplatonism, the former represented by Epictetus (A.D. 90) and Marcus Aurelius (170), the latter by Plotinus (240), Porphyry, and Iamblichus. The school of Athens had for chief exponent the eclectic Proclus (450). In verse the best names were the fabulist Babrius (40), Oppian (180), Nonnus, Quintus Smyrnæus (400–450), and Musæus (500).

The special feature of the later Græco-Roman period was the rise of a Christian Greek literature represented by the patristic epistles, homilies, &c., and ecclesiastical histories, such as those of Eusebius, Socrates, and Sozomen. Among the chief writers were Justin Martyr, Origen, and Clement of Alexandria, Eusebius, Gregory of Nazianzus, Basil, Gregory of Nyssa, and Chrysostom.

After 529 and until 1453 came the Byzantine period, of which the most important section was from about 850 to 1200. It was characterized by such writers as Eustathius, Photius, and Suidas, mainly occupied in the attempt to reduce to system a large, ill-ordered, and aimless erudition.

On the fall of Constantinople in 1453 the cultivated classes who still retained the pure Greek either perished or took to flight, or adopted the language of the conquerors. The popular Greek, however, survived, and despite its vulgarization and the modification of its grammatical forms and syntax, it cannot be said that Greek has been a dead language at any period since Homer.

By some, modern Greek literature

is dated from Theodore Prodromos (1143–80), a monk and writer of popular verse, but the only names of importance until the close of the eighteenth century are those of Maximus Margunius (1530–87), Anacreontic poet and letter writer; Leo Allatius (1586–1669), Sciote scholar and poet; George Chortakes (seventeenth century), Cretan poet; Franciscus Scuphos, Cretan writer on rhetoric (1681); Elias Meniates (1669–1714), a Cephalonian ecclesiastic; Vincentius Kornaros, Cretan poet, author of *Erotocritos* (1756); Kosmas, the Ætolian (1714–79), preacher and founder of schools; Rhegas Pherraios (latter half of eighteenth century), patriotic poet; Eugenios Bulgaris (1716–1806), writer of scientific and religious works; and Nicephorus Theotokes (1736–1800), writer on metaphysics and theology.

At this period the patriotic movement found one outlet in the purification of the language and the development of a new literary impulse. The most important figure was that of Adamantros Koraes or Coray (1748–1833), who did more than all his predecessors to found a literature. Anthimos Gazes (1764–1837) and Athanasius Christopulos (1772–1847) were eminent as grammarians and lexicographers, the latter also as a lyric poet. Neophytus Bambas (1770–1855), miscellaneous educational writer; Constantine Æconomos (1780–1857), theological writer; Theoclytus Pharmakides (1784–1862), ecclesiastic and journalist; Spiridion Zampelios, literary antiquary; and Trikoupis, orator of the struggle for independence, were also prominent.

The poetry of the people is represented chiefly in the songs of the Klephts and other songs dating from the war of independence. At this period the war-songs of Rhigas were sung by the whole nation, and at a later period the two Soutsos, Panagios and Alexander, Calvos, Dionysios Salomos (1798–1857), Julius Typaldos of Cephalonia (1814–83), Aristoteles Valaorites (1824–79), George Zalakostas (1805–58), and others, earned distinction in the same kind of poetry. The Soutsos were further distinguished as satirists, and Alexander Soutsos ranks also with the dramatists Rhisos, Neroulos, and Zampelios.

Among the most gifted of later writers are Rhisos Rangabé (1810–92), distinguished in lyric, dramatic, and epic poetry, also as a novelist and a scholar; Dimitrios Bikelas, George Soures, Angelos Vlakhos, and others. The early twentieth century was marked by the almost complete conquest of the literary field by the spoken language. Among poets may

be mentioned Kostis Palamas, whose fame is world-wide, Laurence Mavilis, Malakassis, Peter Vlastos, Angelos Sikelianos, Rigas Golphis, and others; among prose writers—Papadiamandis, C. Hatzopoulos, Madame Dendrinos, and G. Xenopoulos, who excels in the writing of novels and drama. Among younger writers Constantinides and Valsa are prominent.—BIBLIOGRAPHY: G. Murray, *History of Ancient Greek Literature*; W. C. Wright, *A Short History of Greek Literature*; Sir J. P. Mahaffy, *History of Classical Greek Literature*; J. A. Symonds, *Studies of the Greek Poets*; R. W. Livingstone, *The Greek Genius and its Meaning to Us*; L. M. J. Garnett, *Greek Folksongs from the Turkish Provinces of Greece*.

Ancient Greek Art. As in literature so in art the Greeks attained the highest pitch of excellence, and in architecture and sculpture furnished models for the rest of the world. In no other race has the artistic spirit been so generally diffused throughout the people, expressing itself in the minor arts of life, in the practical application of ornament in the forms of domestic furniture, pottery, metalwork, mosaics, and the like, not less perfectly than in the master-works of architecture and sculpture.

The earliest architectural remains in Greece are pre-Hellenic in origin and Asiatic in character, Greek architecture proper dating from about the close of the eighth century B.C. The earliest known example—the Doric temple at Corinth—belongs to about the middle of the seventh century B.C., and points to an Egyptian origin, the style being remotely derived from the so-called 'proto-Doric' temple of Beni Hassan in Lower Egypt.

Throughout the history of the art it is the public buildings, more particularly the temples, in which the genius of the Greeks displayed itself. The private houses remained simple and unfinished in appearance, rarely rising above a single story, and having no external decoration.

The temples were for the most part rectangular, though the circular form sometimes occurs in the later periods of Greek art. In the simplest form of the rectangular temple (the *apteral*) there were no columns; but, by an easy development from this, the side walls were carried out beyond those constituting the ends of the building, so as to form a porch. The extended walls terminated in pilasters (*antæ*) between which, in the front line of the porch, two columns were placed.

As a further development, four additional columns were placed in advance of the line connecting the *antæ*, sometimes in front only (pro-style), sometimes at both ends (amphiprostyle).

More complex forms were known as *peripteral*, where the columns were carried completely round the build-ing; as *dipteral*, where a double range of columns surrounded it; and as *pseudo-dipteral*, where a double range of columns was placed in front and rear, but only a single range at the sides. The dipteral and pseudo-dipteral styles were seldom employed, the chief example of the dipteral having been the temple of Diana at Ephesus, built by Ctesiphon in the sixth century B.C. Most of the famous temples in Greece were, however, peripteral.

Three orders are distinguished in Greek architecture, according to the treatment of the pillars and of the entablature — the Doric, Ionic, and Corinthian (q.v.). Of these the Doric is the most ancient, the most important examples in Greece, besides that already men-tioned, being the temple at Ægina (middle of the sixth century B.C.), the temple of Theseus at Athens, and the Parthenon, constructed about 448 B.C. by the architects Ictinus and Callicrates, and adorned with un-surpassed sculpture by Phidias and his pupils.

Next to these came the temple of Zeus at Olympia, the temple of Apollo at Bassæ, the frieze of which is in the British Museum, the temple of Athênê at Sunium, the great temple at Rhamnus, and those at Selinus in Sicily (middle of seventh century), Agrigentum, Segesta, and Pæstum.

The oldest Ionic temple in Greece was probably the temple of Ilissus (about 488 B.C.), but the oldest of which remains are still visible is that dedicated to Juno at Samos, and there are remains of a fine temple of this order at Teos. The most perfect example, however, is the Erechtheum at Athens. The Corinthian order, though Grecian in its origin, is repre-sented amongst the Greek temples by a single example only, that of the Zeus Olympius at Athens; and even this temple belongs to the Roman period. The Choragic monument of Lysicrates at Athens also belongs to this order.

The beauty of the Greek buildings was heightened in respect of form by a deviation from ordinary rectilinear construction, in the systematic sub-stitution of delicately-curved lines for straight lines in the columns and steps of their temples, and wherever the illusion attending the sight of straight lines in perspective was likely to prove an element of weakness.

Colour and gilding also played an important part in the total effect, the old tufa temples being coloured throughout, and even in the marble temples, though it is doubtful if the marble columns were ever coloured, the mouldings of cornices and ceilings, the capitals of the antæ, the mould-ings of the pediment and the triglyphs were all decorated with colour. The colonnades and porticoes, which were usually built round market-places and along quays in seaport towns, were similar in style to the temples. *See* ARCHITECTURE.

Greek Sculpture has been divided into five principal periods, namely: (1) the Dædalian or Early (–580 B.C.); (2) the Æginetan or Archaic (580–480 B.C.); (3) the Phidian or Grand (480–400 B.C.); (4) the Praxitelean or Beautiful (400–250 B.C.); (5) the De-cline (250 B.C. onwards).

The age of Dædalus marks an ad-vance from an earlier primitive sculpture in which blocks of wood and stone were roughly fashioned into the semblance of life, the imperfections of the art being concealed by real hair and adventitious draperies. During the Dædalian period the treat-ment was highly conventionalized, a single type serving for a variety of divinities and heroes, the hair being often entirely curled and gathered into a club behind, and the dresses of the female divinities being divided into a few perpendicular folds.

Many of these characteristics sur-vived in the Æginetan period, but a higher knowledge of anatomy and greater freedom and boldness of treat-ment are apparent. The sculptures of the Theseum form a connecting link between the Æginetan school and that of Phidias. To Phidias, besides his statues of Athena and Zeus, were due the designs for the sculptures of the Parthenon, the actual work of these, however, being probably done by his pupils Alcamenes, Agoracritus, and other artists of his time.

To this age belonged the sculptor and architect Polycleitus (about 452–412 B.C.), whose statue of a youth holding a spear obtained the name of *The Canon*, as being a standard of form. About the same time the Bœotian sculptor Myron flourished, the famous *Discobolus* being a reproduction in marble of one of his bronzes. The Praxitelean period is characterized by greater grace and elegance in choice of subject and treatment, together with more of the sensual element making for ultimate decline. Praxiteles ex-celled in female figures, his *Aphrodite* at Cnidus in Caria being his most famous work.

His rival, Scopas of Paros, was em-ployed on the bas-reliefs of the Mausoleum at Halicarnassus, and was the sculptor of the famous group representing the destruction of the children of Niobe. In Lysippus of Sicyon, in the time of Alexander the Great, the Praxitelean school found its last great figure prior to the decline of the art.

Painting in Greece is said to have had its origin in Sicyon, and to have existed as mere outline and monochrome until Cimon of Cleonæ introduced variety in colouring, foreshortening, and a less rigid art. The Greek artists worked in wax or resin or in *water-colour, brought to the required consistency by mixing with gum, glue, or white of egg; and they painted upon wood, clay, plaster, stone, parchment, and canvas.

Until a late period, however, they rarely painted upon walls, usually painting upon panels or tablets to be encased in walls. The earlier masters appear to have used only four colours —red, yellow, white, and black—but by the time of Apelles and Protogenes many other pigments were in use.

The earliest painters of renown were Micon of Athens (about 460 B.C.), and Polygnotus of Thasos and of Athens (about 463–430 B.C.); but a higher degree of illusion and realism appears to have been reached under Zeuxis and his rival Parrhasius, towards the close of the fifth century B.C.

A greater name than any of these is that of Apelles, the friend of Alexander the Great, contemporaneously with whom flourished Protogenes of Caria, painter and statuary, and Nicias of Athens, a distinguished encaustic painter. Of the work of these artists only a general conception can be formed from the mosaics and frescoes of Pompeii.—BIBLIOGRAPHY: E. A. Gardner, *Handbook of Greek Sculpture*; P. Gardner, *The Principles of Greek Art*; Perrot et Chipiez, *Histoire de l'art dans l'antiquité*; A. P. Laurie, *Greek and Roman Methods of Painting*; H. B. Walters, *The Art of the Greeks*.

GREEK CHURCH, or HOLY ORIENTAL ORTHODOX APOSTOLIC CHURCH, that section of the Christian Church dominant in Eastern Europe and Western Asia, especially n Turkey, Greece, Russia, and some parts of Austria.

In the first ages of Christianity numerous Churches were founded by the Apostles and their successors in Greek-speaking countries: in Greece itself, in Syria, Egypt, Mesopotamia, Asia Minor, Thrace, and Macedonia. These were subsequently called Greek, in contradistinction to the Churches in which the Latin tongue prevailed.

The removal of the seat of empire by Constantine to Constantinople.

and the subsequent separation of the Eastern and Western Empires, afforded the opportunity for diversities of language, modes of thinking, and customs to manifest themselves, and added political causes to the grounds of separation. During the earliest period the chief seats of influence in the Eastern Church were Jerusalem, Antioch, and Alexandria, the seat of that mystical philosophy by which the Oriental Church was distinguished.

In 341, soon after the Synod of Antioch, the rivalry between the Bishop of Rome and the Bishop of Constantinople began to assume importance, and before 400, differences of doctrines with respect to the procession of the Holy Spirit appeared. The Council of Chalcedon in 451 accorded to the eastern bishop the same honours and privileges in his own diocese as those of the Bishop of Rome, and in 484 each bishop excommunicated the other.

The title of *Œcumenical Patriarch* was assumed by John, Bishop of Constantinople, in 588, and in the following year the phrase *Filioque* ('and the Son') was added by the Latins to the Nicene creed (which now read 'proceeding from the Father and the Son'), an addition to which the Greek Church was opposed. In 648 Pope Theodore deposed Patriarch Paul II; but a reconciliation of the Churches was effected at the Council of Rome (680).

The doctrines of the Greek Church were defined by John Damascenus in 730. The disruption was hastened by the banishment of Ignatius by Michael the Drunken and the consecration of Photius (858). The Pope Nicholas I and Photius excommunicated each other in 867. The schism was temporarily healed after the death of Photius, but Michael Cerularius reopened it by charging the Latins with heterodoxy. He was excommunicated by Leo IX in 1054, and in turn excommunicated the Pope in the same year, since which the Greeks have been severed from the Roman communion, though the Russo-Greek Church was not separated until the twelfth century.

The presence of the Crusaders in the East aggravated the quarrel; Latin patriarchates were established in Antioch and Jerusalem, and, though on the capture of Constantinople by the Crusaders a Latin patriarchate was set up there (1204), the schism was revived there as soon as the Latin Empire fell (1262).

Reunion was proposed in 1273 by Patriarch Joseph, and effected, with the acknowledgment of the Pope as primate, at the Council of Lyons (1274). The union, however, was annulled in 1282 by Emperor Andronicus II, and in 1283 and 1285 by Synods of Constantinople. It was again effected under John Palæologus at Florence in 1439, but was repudiated in 1443 by the Patriarchs of Alexandria, Antioch, and Jerusalem. In 1453, when the patriarch fled from the Turks, a schismatic, Gregory Scholarius, was chosen in his place.

In 1575 unsuccessful negotiations were commenced with a view to union with the Lutherans, and in 1723 the English bishops even proposed that the Greek and Anglican Churches should unite, a proposal revived by the Archbishop of Moscow in 1866. The claims of the Tsar in 1853 to the protectorate of the Greek churches in Turkey was one of the causes of the Crimean War.

Doctrine. The Greek Church is the only Church which holds that the Holy Ghost proceeds from the Father only; the Roman Catholic and Protestant Churches deriving the Holy Ghost from the Father and the Son.

Like the Roman Catholic Church it has seven sacraments: Baptism, Communion, Confirmation, Penance, Orders, Matrimony, and Unction. But it is peculiar (1) in believing in baptism by threefold immersion, the chrism (confirmation) following immediately after it; (2) in adopting, as to the eucharist, the doctrine of the real presence and transubstantiation; but in ordering the bread to be leavened, the wine to be mixed with water, and both elements to be distributed to every one, even to children; (3) the parochial clergy are required to be married, but only once and to a virgin, and marriage must take place before ordination; widowed clergy are not permitted to retain their livings, but go into a cloister, where they are called *hieromonachi.*

The Greek Church grants divorce in case of proved adultery, but it does not allow even the laity a fourth marriage. It differs also from the Roman Catholic Church in anointing with the holy oil, not the dying but the sick, for the restoration of health, forgiveness, and sanctification. It rejects the doctrine of purgatory, works of supererogation, indulgences, and dispensations, but admits prayers for the dead, whose condition appears to be considered undetermined until the final judgment.

It recognizes no visible vicar of Christ on earth, but the spiritual authority of the patriarch is little inferior to that of the Pope. It allows no carved, sculptured, or molten image of holy persons or subjects; but the representations of Christ (except in the crucifix), of Mary, and the saints, must be merely painted, and

at most inlaid with precious stones. In the Russian churches, however, works of sculpture are found.

In the invocation of the saints, and especially of the Virgin, the Greeks resemble the Latins. They also hold relics, graves, and crosses sacred; and crossing in the name of Jesus they consider as having a wonderful and blessed influence.

Among the means of penance, fasts are particularly numerous with them. They fast Wednesday and Friday of every week, and besides observe four great annual fasts, namely, forty days before Easter; from Whitsuntide to the days of St. Peter and Paul; the fast of the Virgin Mary, from the 1st to the 15th of Aug.; and the apostle Philip's fast, from the 15th to the 26th of Nov.; besides the day of the beheading of John the Baptist, and of the elevation of the cross. The calendar of the Greek Church is in the old style, their New Year's Day falling on 14th Jan.

Constitution. The services of the Greek Church consist almost entirely in outward forms. Preaching and catechizing constitute the least part of it. Instrumental music is excluded altogether. The Mass is considered of the first importance. The convents conform, for the most part, to the strict rule of St. Basil. The Greek abbot is termed *higumenos,* the abbess *higumenē.* The abbot of a Greek convent which has several others under its inspection is termed *archimandrite,* and ranks next a bishop.

The lower clergy in the Greek Church consist of readers, singers, deacons, &c., and of priests or popes and protopopes or archpriests, who are the first clergy in the cathedrals and metropolitan churches. The lower clergy can rise no higher than protopopes, for the bishops are chosen from among the monks, and from the bishops are selected the archbishops, metropolitans, and patriarchs.

In Russia, before the Revolution of 1917, there were twenty-four dioceses. The seats of the four metropolitans of the country were Petrograd (now Leningrad),Kiev, Kasan, and Tobolsk. The dignities of Patriarch of Constantinople (Istanbul), Alexandria, Antioch, and Jerusalem still subsist. The Patriarch of Constantinople still possess the ancient authority of his see; the other three patriarchs exercise a very limited jurisdiction, and live for the most part on the aid afforded them by the Patriarch of Constantinople.

Repeated but fruitless efforts have been made to bring about a union between the Greek and Anglican Churches. The last proposition was made at Geneva in Aug., 1920.—

BIBLIOGRAPHY: J. M. Neale, *History of the Holy Eastern Church*; Dean Stanley, *History of the Eastern Church*; W. F. Adeney, *Greek and Eastern Churches.*

GREEK FIRE, an inflammable and destructive compound used in mediæval warfare, especially by the Byzantine Greeks. It was poured from cauldrons and ladles, squirted through long copper tubes, or flung in pots, phials, and barrels. The art of compounding it was concealed at Constantinople with the greatest care, but it appears that naphtha, sulphur, and nitre entered into its composition. The German *flammenwerfer* (see FLAME-THROWER), employed by the enemy during the European War, may be considered as a counterpart of Greek Fire.

GREEK WINES, though formerly well known in England under the names of Cyprus and Malmsey, are now less known than they deserve, several of them being strong, rich, full wines. Many different kinds of wines are produced both on the islands and the mainland, the former including those of Eubœa, Cephalonia, Corfu, Zante, Santorin, &c.; the latter those of Achaia, Corinth, and Attica. Both white and red wines are exported, and some of the fo mer resemble Hock and Chablis some of the latter Burgundy.

GREELEY, Horace, American journalist and politician, born in 1811, died in 1872. He worked first on a farm, then as compositor. In 1831 he went to New York, where, after an unsuccessful attempt to start *The Morning Post*, the first penny paper, he commenced in 1834 to issue *The Weekly New Yorker*, which ran for seven years. *The Log Cabin*, another weekly, established by him in 1840, reached a circulation of 80,000, and gave him a reputation which ensured the success of his *Daily Tribune*, founded in 1841, and edited by him till his death.

In 1848 he was elected to Congress, but failed to impress his constituents with the necessity of returning him a second time. In 1851 he visited Europe, and was one of the jurors in the Great Exhibition. He opposed the Civil War, but was a firm supporter of the Union and of President Lincoln, and at the close of the war advocated a general amnesty and universal suffrage. In 1872 he was nominated for the presidency in opposition to General Grant, but was defeated.

The strain of electioneering and the death of his wife brought on an illness, of which he died a few weeks later. Chief among his miscellaneous works are his *Hints towards Reforms* (1850), *Glances at Europe* (1851), *History of the Struggle for Slavery Extension* (1856), *The American Conflict* (1864), *Recollections of a Busy Life* (1869), and *What I Know of Farming* (1871).

GREEN, John Richard, historian, born in 1837, died in 1883. Ordained curate in 1860, he subsequently became vicar of St. Philips, Stepney, and librarian to the Archbishop of Canterbury at Lambeth. For some time he wrote constantly for *The Saturday Review*; but he was comparatively little known until the publication in 1874 of his *Short History of the English People*, which secured him immediate fame. It was followed by a larger edition of the same work entitled *A History of the English People* (1877-80), a volume of *Stray Studies from England and Italy*, and *The Making of England* (1882).

His work was afterwards carried on in distressing conflict with lung disease, which brought about his death. *The Conquest of England*, his last work, was published posthumously by his wife, being almost complete at his death.—Cf. Sir Leslie Stephen, *The Letters of J. R. Green.*

GREEN, Thomas Hill, English philosophical writer, born 1838; Fellow of Balliol College in 1862, and first lay tutor on that foundation in 1867. In 1877 he was appointed Whyte's professor of moral philosophy; but his work was abruptly closed by his death in 1882. Apart from his *Prolegomena to Ethics*, published posthumously in 1883, the bulk of his work was in the form of articles contributed to the *North British* and *Contemporary Reviews*. He was one of the strongest opponents of the English empirical school, leading the reaction against Hume's empiricism. The best edition of his works is that of R. L. Nettleship.—Cf. W. H. Fairbrother, *The Philosophy of T. H. Green.*

GREEN ALGÆ, or **CHLOROPHYCEÆ,** one of the principal subdivisions of the Algæ, including the great majority of the fresh-water forms together with a number of marine and a few terrestrial species. They are characterized by the pure green colour of their chromatophores and the relatively simple structure and small size (as compared with Brown and Red Algæ) of their thallus; the latter is most frequently filamentous, but unicellular types are common (e.g. Chlamydomonas, Protococcus), while on the other hand the green laver (Ulva) has a flattened leaf-like plant-body of considerable size.

The reproductive methods are varied. Motile asexual spores (zoöspores) are frequent (except in Conjugatæ). Isogamous sexual reproduction is the rule, but oögamous types are found in most of the families. The oöspore of Coleochæte divides up into a clump of resting-cells covered by a protective sheath; this 'oöspore fruit' was formerly regarded as a simple type of sporophyte, but recent research has shown this view to be erroneous, as reduction of chromosomes takes place at the first division of the oöspore-nucleus. No true case of alternating generations is, in fact, known among Green Algæ.

In spite of the evidently higher organization of the Brown and Red Algæ, it is customary to regard the Higher Plants (Cormophyta)—which always have pure green chromatophores—as derived from Green Algalike ancestors. The gap between the most complex Chlorophyceæ and the simplest Bryophytes is, however, serious, and the supposed immediate ancestors of the land-living plants must have been much more advanced than any known Green Alga.

On the other side, the simplest Green Algæ (such as Chlamydomonas and its allies) grade almost insensibly into the green Flagellates. A natural classification of Green Algæ cannot be attempted until much more is known about the minute characters of their cells.

The leading families, with representative genera, are as follows: (1) Volvocales. Permanently motile. Chlamydomonas (unicellular, isogamous), Volvox (multicellular, oögamous. (2) Conjugatæ (Akontæ). No motile cells. Isogamy by means of a conjugation tube. Spirogyra (filamentous), Desmids (unicellular). (3) Protococcales. Unicellular or forming loosely-connected cell-colonies. Never oögamous. Scenedesmus, Hydrodictyon. (4) Ulotrichales. Filamentous (plate-like thallus in Ulva). Zoöspores general. Isogamous or oögamous. Ulothrix, Ulva, Oedogonium, Cephaleuros, Coleochæte. (5) Siphonales. Filamentous; filaments non-septate or with occasional septa, often interwoven. Usually isogamous. Vaucheria, Codium, Caulerpa, Cladophora, Struvea, Acetabularia.

The Lower Fungi (Phycomycetes) show affinity with certain Siphonales and Protococcales. The economic value of Green Algæ is negligible. They occur in all parts of the world, many species having a very wide distribution.

GREEN'AWAY, Kate, English artist, born 1846, died 1901. Daughter of a wood-engraver, she was trained to art, and early became known by her charming designs for Christmas cards, children's books, &c., her quaint and pleasing figures of children dressed in old-fashioned costumes, and her flower designs, being specially noteworthy. As a book illustrator she soon made large sums of money, and became widely known. She was elected a member of the Institute of Painters in Water Colours, and exhibited in public galleries. Among her works are: *Under the Window, Mother Goose,* and *A Day in a Child's Life.*

GREENBACKS, the popular name given to the paper currency first issued by the United States Government in 1862 during the Civil War. It is sometimes used also to include United States bank-notes.

GREEN BAY, a city of Wisconsin, United States, on Fox River, near the head of Green Bay. It has a great trade in lumber and various flourishing industries. Pop. (1930), 37,415.

GREENE, Maurice, an English composer, born about 1696, died in 1755. He was in turn organist at St. Paul's, at the Chapel Royal, and held the chair of music at Cambridge. His works include a *Te Deum,* several oratorios, a masque, *The Judgment of Hercules,* an opera, *Phoebe* (1748), and various glees and catches. His collection of *Forty Select Anthems* is well known.

GREENE, Nathanael, a general of the American revolutionary army, born at Potowhommet, Rhode Island, in 1742, died in 1786. In 1770 he was elected to represent Coventry in the General Assembly of Rhode Island, and was soon after excommunicated by the Quakers for taking arms on the prospect of war with Britain. In 1774 he joined the Kentish Guards as a private, and in May, 1775, he was appointed brigadier-general and commander of the Rhode Island contingent in the army before Boston.

He gained at once the confidence of Washington, was made major-general, and appointed to the command in New Jersey. At Trenton (1776) and Princeton (1777) he led a division, and in the subsequent fighting he held important commands, and repeatedly distinguished himself. In 1778 he was quartermaster-general, and in 1780 presided at the trial of Major André. In the same year he was appointed to the command of the southern army, and succeeded, after repeated defeats, in wresting Georgia and the Carolinas from the British.

GREENE, Robert, English dramatist, born about 1560, died in 1592. He studied at St. John's College, Cambridge, and took his degree of B.A. in 1578, after which he travelled on the Continent. He graduated M.A. in 1583, lived a wild and profligate life, and died in poverty.

His works consist of plays, poems, tales, and tracts. His chief romances are: *Pandosto* (1588), *The History of Arbasto* (1617), *A Pair of Turtle Doves* (1606), *Menaphon* (1587). His plays include: *The Honourable Historie of Friar Bacon and Friar Bungay* (1594); *Orlando Furioso* (1594); *Alphonsus King of Arragon* (1597); and *James IV* (1598).

Amongst his miscellaneous works are: *The Myrrour of Modestie* (1584); *Morando* (1584); *Euphues, his censure to Philautus* (1587); *Perimedes* (1588); *Alcida* (1588); *Spanish Masquerado* (1589); and various pamphlets and autobiographical works, such as his *Never-too-late* (1590), *Greene's Vision* (1592), *The Repentance of Robert Greene* (1592), and *Farewell to Folly* (1591).

His *Groatsworth of Wit bought with a Million of Repentance* (1592) is remarkable for the allusion to Shakespeare, 'an upstart crow, beautified with our feathers.' His *Pandosto, or the Triumph of Time* (also known as *Dorastus and Fawnia*) furnished the basis for Shakespeare's *Winter's Tale*. An edition of his plays and poems by Prof. Churton Collins appeared in 1905; a more recent edition of his works is that of T. H. Dickinson (1909).

GREEN EARTH, an opaque, dull, olive-green, soft, earthy mass, generally met with in cavities in amygdaloidal rocks. It consists of silicate of iron and aluminium, with water. Some green earths are allied to glauconite and others to the chlorites.

GREEN-EBONY, an olive-green wood obtained from the South American tree *Jacaranda ovalifolia*, nat. ord. Bignoniaceæ, used for round rulers, turnery and marquetry work, and also much used for dyeing, yielding olive-green, brown, and yellow colours.

GREENFINCH, GREEN-LINNET, or **GREEN GROSBEAK** (*Ligurinus chloris*), a bird of the finch family, and one of the most common of British and European birds. It frequents hedges, gardens, and small plantations, and feeds on grain, seeds, or insects. It easily becomes tame, but its song is not melodious.

It builds in hedges, bushes, and low trees, the nest being of green moss and coarse fibrous roots, lined with finer roots, horsehair, and feathers. The eggs (four to six) are bluish white, spotted at the larger end with purplish grey and dark brown. The general colours of the male are green and yellow, those of the female inclining to brown.

GREENFORD. District of Middlesex, part of the borough of Ealing. It is 8 miles from London with a station on the G.W. Rly. Since the Great War, the district has been greatly developed, and various industries have been established here, including works owned by Messrs. J. Lyons & Co. The Grand Union Canal passes through the district.

GREENGAGE, a variety of the plum, the *reine claude* of the French, introduced into Britain by a family named Gage. It is large, of a green or yellowish colour, and has a juicy, greenish pulp of exquisite flavour.

GREENHEART (*Nectandra Rodiœi*), a tree of the nat. ord. Lauraceæ, a native of Guiana, called also the *bebeeru*. Its wood is hard and durable, and is used in shipbuilding, not being liable to attacks from the Teredo. The bark contains the alkaloid beheerine.

GREENHITHE. District of Kent. It stands on the Thames, 3 miles from Dartford, on the Southern Rly. The chief industry is shipping.

GREENLAND (Dan. and Ger. *Grönland*), an extensive island, the only colonial possession of Denmark, situated on the north-east of the continent of North America, from which it is separated by Davis Straits, Baffin Bay, and Smith Sound. It is more than 1,700 miles in length, and at its broadest part 700 miles in width. It extends north to lat. 83° 39' and south to lat. 59° 45'. It has an area of 46,740 sq. miles.

Climate, etc. Like the northern parts of North America generally, Greenland is colder than the corresponding latitudes on the east side of the Atlantic. In June and July the sun is constantly above the horizon, the ice on the coast is broken up and floats southward, and a few small lakes are opened; but the short summer is followed by a long and dreary winter.

The interior, which is lofty and has the appearance of one vast glacier, is uninhabitable, and all the villages are confined to the coasts, which are lined with numerous islands, and deeply penetrated by fiords. The Danish colony extends north, on the western coast, to the Bay of Disco, in lat. 69° N.

Production and Industry. Cultivation is confined to the low shores and valleys, where grassy meadows sometimes occur with stunted shrubs and dwarfed birch, alder, and pine trees. Attempts to raise oats and barley have failed, but potatoes have been grown towards the southern extremity. Turnips attain the size of a pigeon's egg, and cabbages grow very small. The radish is the only vegetable which grows unchecked. The inhabitants are largely dependent upon hunting and fishing. Whale blubber and seal oil are used as fuel. The trade is a State monopoly.

Flora and Fauna. Despite the proximity of America the flora and fauna are rather of a European character. The land animals are the Eskimo dog, the reindeer, the polar bear, the Arctic fox (blue and white), the ermine, the Arctic hare, and the musk-ox. Among the amphibia the walrus and several species of seal are common. The seas abound in fish, the whale and cod fisheries being of special importance. Sea-fowl are abundant in summer, and largely killed.

The chief mineral product is cryolite, but graphite and miocene lignitic coal are also found. Oil, cider down, furs, and cryolite are exported.

The population, which is chiefly Eskimo, numbers (1930), 16,630 (408 Danes). For administrative purposes Greenland, or rather its coast, is divided into two inspectorates of North and South Greenland. The capital is Godhaven, on Disco Island, but the largest settlement is Sydproven (pop. 789).

History of Exploration. Greenland was discovered by an Icelander named Gunnbjörn about 876 or 877. It was colonized from Iceland about the end of the tenth century, and other Scandinavians followed. In 1264 it was politically united with Norway, and about the middle of the fourteenth century possessed two flourishing colonies on the west coast, named West Bygd and East Bygd.

These settlements, however, gradually disappeared from history, and the expeditions sent by Denmark in 1585, 1606, 1636, 1654, and 1670 for the purpose of finding the colony were unsuccessful. Various relics and inscriptions have been found.

In the reign of Elizabeth Frobisher and Davis rediscovered the coast, but nothing was done to explore it until the Danish Government in 1721 assisted Hans Egede, a clergyman, to establish a European mission settlement, Good Hope (*Godhaab*), which was successfully carried on by him and his son.

Whale-fisheries were established on the coast by the English and Dutch about 1590. The interior of the country (in the south) was first crossed from east to west by Nansen in 1888. The American explorer Commander Peary (1892) did much to make the northern parts known.

Further explorations were undertaken by Nordenskiold (1883), von Drygalski (1892), Garde (1893), Mylius Erichsen (1906–8), and Mikkelsen (1909–12). Between 1916 and 1918 Knud Rasmussen explored the north-eastern and northern parts of Greenland. In June, 1930, some Norwegians hoisted their country's flag at a spot on the east coast of Greenland. The Danish Government raised objections to this and negotiations followed.

In 1929, 1930, and 1931 several expeditions set out to explore the interior of Greenland. One was the British Arctic Air Route expedition under H. G. Watkins. The aim of this was to find if an air route across Greenland to Canada from England was possible. A German expedition under Alfred Wegener went out, Wegener lost his life and a relief expedition was sent to search for him. Another expedition was organised by some Danes.—Cf. F. Nansen, *The First Crossing of Greenland.*

GREEN MOUNTAINS, a mountain range, United States, commencing near Newhaven, Connecticut, and extending north through Massachusetts and Vermont; highest summit, Mansfield Mountain (4,279 feet).

GREENOCK, a municipal and parliamentary burgh and seaport town of Scotland, county Renfrew, on the southern shore of the estuary of the Clyde, there between 3 and 4 miles wide, 22½ miles west by north of Glasgow. It stands partly on a narrow level tract of land stretching along the margin of the sea; and partly on some heights, which rise behind, and to the south and west of the lower parts of the town. The lower and older parts of the town are mean and crowded. The principal public buildings are the custom-house, the Tontine, the Watt monument, containing the Greenock library, and the Watt Museum and Lecture Hall, the municipal buildings, the sheriff court buildings, and post office. South-west of the town is a beautiful cemetery. There are several pieces of ground devoted to recreation, and the river esplanade, 100 feet wide and 6,200 feet long, forms a fine promenade.

The manufactures include numerous sugar-refineries, shipbuilding yards, iron-foundries and machine establishments; chemical works; worsted, woollen, and paper mills; grain, saw, and sundry other mills; jute and bagging factories, roperies, and sail-making establishments.

Greenock carries on a considerable coasting and foreign shipping trade, especially with East and West Indies, America, and Australia. The docks are spacious and possess every accommodation for shipping, including five graving docks and hydraulic and steam cranes. Large numbers of vessels unload at Greenock and ascend to Glasgow for cargoes. Unrefined sugar has long been the most valuable import, but has recently much declined; the exports to foreign parts are insignificant.

Greenock was an important fishing and shipping port in the end of the seventeenth century, after which it began rapidly to extend. It was the birth-place of James Watt. Greenock sends one member to Parliament. Pop. (1931), 78,948.

GREENORE, seaport and watering place of Co. Louth, Irish Free State. It is on the east side of Carlingford Lough and has a regular service of steamers with Holyhead.

GREEN PAINTS. See PIGMENTS.

GREEN RIVER, United States, Kentucky, flows generally west and north-west, and enters the Ohio 200 miles below Louisville. It is navigable for boats for about 200 miles.

GREENSAND, a sand rich in glauconite. The name is also used for two

Greenwich Observatory

series of strata, occurring in the southeast of England, the Isle of Wight, &c., the one (lower greensand) belonging to the Lower Cretaceous series, the other (upper greensand) to the Upper Cretaceous series : between them is the clay called the Gault. They consist chiefly of sands, with clays, limestones, and chert bands. They were named on account of the green colour, due to glauconitic granules. The fossil contents are marine, and both deposits represent shore accumulations.

GREENSHANK, a well-known species of sand-piper (*Totanus glottis*), often called the whistling snipe from the shrill note it utters when first flushed. It breeds pretty commonly in the Hebrides, and sometimes in the north of Scotland, and is found as a visitor in the coast districts, lakes, and marshes of Britain. The bird is about 12 inches long, rather prettily marked, and has the legs and toes olive-green.

GREENSTONE, an old and con-

veniently comprehensive term for igneous rocks of various grain, but mostly crystalline throughout, with about 60 per cent or less of silica. Used in contradistinction to granite, and covering diorite, dolerite, &c.

GREENWICH (grĕn'ich), a municipal and parliamentary borough of London, on the right bank of the Thames, about 5 miles s.E. of London Bridge. The Blackwall Tunnel for vehicular traffic, and a tunnel for foot passengers link it with the north side of the river. It is built partly on an acclivity, but chiefly on the level ground skirting the river. There are extensive iron-foundries and engineering works, barge and boat-building yards, boiler works, mast-, block-, and sail-works, telegraph cable works, roperies, chemical factories, &c. Near the river is an enormous power station for generating electricity.

The object of greatest interest is the magnificent hospital, the oldest portion of which was originally a palace of Charles II. It was converted to its charitable purpose in the reign of William and Mary. Three additional wings were built from designs by Sir Christopher Wren, who also completed the unfinished pile of Charles II. As a hospital for aged and disabled seaman of the navy, it was opened in 1705, and subsequently accommodated about 3,000. In 1865, however, it ceased to be an asylum for seamen; since 1873 it has been the seat of the Royal Naval College, for the education of naval officers. It also contains a naval museum and picture gallery. Adjoining it are the Royal Naval School for boys, and an infirmary for sick and disabled seamen. A new town hall overlooking the river is being planned.

Greenwich Park, an open, undulating piece of ground, area 180 acres, finely wooded and well stocked with deer, is a favourite resort of holiday-making Londoners during the summer. The celebrated observatory of Greenwich, erected by Charles II for Flamsteed, stands upon an eminence in the park.

The longitude of all British maps and charts, and also of those issued by the Government of the United States of America, as well as many of those published in other countries, is computed from this observatory, which is 2° 20′ 23″ w. from the observatory of Paris, and 18° E. from the meridian of Ferro.

Greenwich (including Deptford and Woolwich) was erected into a parliamentary borough in 1832, and returned two members to Parliament. Since 1918 Greenwich and Deptford send each one member, Woolwich returning two. Pop. (1931), 100,879.

GREENWOOD, Arthur, English politician. He studied at the University of Manchester and became a writer and lecturer on economic subjects. He held a post in the University of Leeds before 1917, when he was made Secretary to the Ministry of Reconstruction. Having joined the Labour Party, he became head of its information bureau and in 1922 was elected M.P. for the Nelson and Colne division of Lancashire. In 1924 he was Parliamentary Secretary to the Ministry of Health and in 1929 Minister of Health in the Labour Government. He resigned in Aug., 1931, and lost his seat in the following Oct. In 1932 he was elected for Wakefield.

GREGARIN'IDÆ, or **GREGAR-INES,** the old name for a large group of parasitic Protozoa. *See* STOROZOA.

GRÉGOIRE (grā-gwär), **Henri,** Compte, Bishop of Blois, a churchman and statesman of the French Revolution, born 1750, died at Paris in 1831. In 1789, while curé of Emberménil, in the district of Nancy, he was sent by the clergy of Lorraine as their representative to the States-General. As one of the secretaries of the Constituent Assembly he joined the extreme democratic section, and in the convention voted for the condemnation, though not for the death, of the king.

Although extreme in his democratic opinions, he was an unflinching Jansenist. He was a member of the Council of Five Hundred, of the Corps Législatif, and of the Senate (1801). On the conclusion of the Concordat he resigned his bishopric. He voted against the establishment of the Imperial Government, and alone in the Senate resisted the restoration of titles of nobility. He himself afterwards accepted the title of Comte, but in the Senate was always one of the small body who opposed Napoleon, and in 1814 was one of the first to vote for his deposition. He passed the latter part of his life in retirement.

He left numerous works, among them *Ruines de Port-Royal* (1801) *Essai historique sur les libertés de l'Église Gallicane, Histoire des sectes religieuses depuis le commencement de ce siècle* (1810 and 1828), *Annales de la religion* (1795–1803).

GREGORIAN CALENDAR, the calendar as reformed by Pope Gregory XIII in 1582 (*see* CALENDAR). The **Gregorian year** is the ordinary year, as reckoned according to the Gregorian calendar.

GREGORIAN TONES, in music, a tonal system introduced by Gregory the Great. In the early ages of church music the Greek system of tetrachords, or what was supposed to be the Greek system, was followed. There were in the time of Ambrose of Milan fifteen so-called Greek modes or scales in use. In order to simplify church music he selected four of these scales, the Dorian, Phrygian, Æolian and Mixo-Lydian, to which he attempted to reduce all the chants and melodies sung in church.

This selection of scales was soon found to be too limited. The church singers refused to be bound to it, and it failed to represent the melodies actually in use. In these circumstances Gregory the Great introduced a new reform and extension of church music. To each of the scales admitted by Ambrose he added a new scale or mode, commencing with the fourth below the key-note of the original scale. These new scales he called *plagal*, while to the four introduced by Ambrose he gave the name of *authentic*. He introduced the practice of naming the tones by the letters of the alphabet.

The following is the arrangement of his eight scales:

1st. Authentic		
	(Dorian)	D E F G A B C D
2nd. Plagal	..	A B C D E F G A
3rd. Authentic		
	(Phrygian)	E F G A B C D E
4th. Plagal		B C D E F G A B
5th. Authentic		
	(Æolian)	F G A B C D E F
6th. Plagal	..	C D E F G A B C
7th. Authentic,		
Hyper-Dorian or		G A B C D E F G
Mixo-Lydian	..	
8th. Plagal	..	D E F G A B C D

The scale of C, with the semitones between the 3rd and 4th, and the 7th and 8th, which in the modern system is called the natural scale, and is the pattern on which all the others are formed, was thus, it will be seen, one of the plagal scales introduced as an innovation by Gregory.

GREGOROVIUS, Ferdinand, German historian and poet, born at Neidenburg, 19th Jan., 1821, died at Munich, 1st May, 1891. Educated at Königsberg, where he studied theology and philosophy, he published several historical and literary works. In 1852 he went to Italy, where he remained until 1874. He also visited Greece, Egypt, Syria, and Constantinople.

His works include: *History of the Roman Emperor Hadrian* (1851); *The Death of Tiberius,* a tragedy (1851); *The Island of Capri* (1868); and *The Tombs of the Roman Popes* (1857). His principal work, however, is his *History of Rome in the Middle Ages* (1859–73, 8 vols.). This monumental

V—K

work is not only a history of Rome, but also of the Papacy and the Middle Ages.

GREGORY, Patriarch of Constantinople, born in 1739; studied at Mount Athos, lived as a hermit, was made archbishop of Smyrna, and, in 1795, Patriarch of Constantinople. He led an active, tolerant, and benevolent life, and promoted schools and the art of printing.

In 1798, however, and again in 1806, he was accused of intriguing for the freedom of Greece, and twice banished to Mount Athos, though each time restored to his post after a short interval. But in 1821, when the Greek insurrection broke out in the Morea, his native country, he became once more an object of suspicion to the

Gregory the Great

Porte, and when, shortly after, he allowed the family of Prince Morousi to escape from his guardianship, he was seized as he left the church on the first day of the Easter festival and hanged in his robes of office before the church gate.

GREGORY, the name of thirteen Popes, of whom we need notice only the following:—**Gregory I,** called also the **Great,** born at Rome, of noble family, about A.D. 540. He became a member of the Senate, and was made a prefect of Rome in 573. He expended his inheritance in the foundation of monasteries and charitable institutions, and then took monastic vows himself. Pope Pelagius II sent him on an embassy to Constantinople, and afterwards made him Papal secretary.

On the death of Pelagius in 590 he was chosen his successor. He displayed great zeal for the conversion of heretics, sending missionaries to Sicily, Sardinia, Lombardy, England, &c., as well as for the advancement of monachism, and the enforcement of clerical celibacy. He died in 604. The works ascribed to him are very numerous; his genuine writings consist of a treatise upon *Pastoral Duty, Letters, Scripture Commentaries,* &c.

Gregory VII (*Hildebrand*). Born about 1020 at Soana, in Tuscany; passed part of his early life in Rome, became a monk at Cluny, and then returned to Rome with Bruno on the election of the latter to the Papal chair. He exercised great influence over Leo IX (Bruno) and his successors, Victor II, Nicholas II, and Alexander II; and under Nicholas II he succeeded in depriving the clergy and people of Rome of a voice in the election to the Pontificate by giving the power of nomination to the cardinals alone. On the death of Alexander II (1073) he was raised to the Papal chair.

His chief aim was to found a theocracy in which the Pope should be the sovereign ruler, in political as well as ecclesiastical matters. He therefore prohibited simony and the marriage of priests (1074), and abolished lay investiture (1075), the only remaining source of the authority of princes over the clergy of their dominions.

The Emperor Henry IV refused to obey this decree, and Gregory, after deposing several German bishops who had bought their offices from the emperor, and excommunicating five imperial councillors concerned in this transaction, summoned the emperor before a council at Rome to defend himself against the charges brought against him.

Henry then caused a sentence of deposition to be passed against the Pope by a council assembled at Worms. The Pope, in return, excommunicated the emperor, and Henry, finding himself in difficulties, went to Italy and submitted at Canossa (1077) to a humiliating penance, and received absolution.

After defeating Rodolph of Suabia, however, Henry caused the Pope to be deposed by the Council of Brixen, and anti-pope Clement III, to be elected in 1080, after which he hastened to Rome and placed the new Pope on the throne. Gregory passed three years as a prisoner in the castle of St. Angelo, and though finally liberated by Robert Guiscard, he was obliged to retire under the protection of Guiscard to Salerno, where he died in 1085.

Gregory XIII (*Ugo Buoncompagno*). Born at Bologna in 1502; created cardinal in 1565; chosen successor of Pius V in the popedom in 1572. He permitted the Cardinal of

Lorraine to make a public thanksgiving for the massacre of St. Bartholomew, encouraged plots against Queen Elizabeth, and incited Philip II to attack her.

His foreign policy cost him much money for subsidies to excite enemies to the Turks and heretics, and his financial expedients to fill his exchequer ruined the trade and disturbed the peace of his own dominions. He did much to encourage education, his expenditure for this purpose exceeding two million Roman crowns, out of which many colleges at Rome were endowed. He reformed the Julian calendar (*see* CALENDAR). He died 10th April, 1585.—BIBLIOGRAPHY: H. K. Mann, *Lives of the Popes of the Middle Ages*; L. Pastor, *History of he Popes*.

GREGORY, Augusta, Lady. Irish dramatist. Born 5th Mar, 1852, in 1881 she married Sir William Gregory, an Irish M.P. who died in 1892. Deeply interested in the Irish literary revival, she became a director of the Abbey Theatre, Dublin, about which she wrote *Our Irish Theatre*, 1924. She translated three of Molière's plays for production there, but is better known by her own dramas. These include *The White Cockade, The Rising of the Moon, The Gaol Ga e, The Full Moon*, and many others. She died 22nd May, 1932.

GREGORY, James, mathematician and inventor of the reflecting telescope, was born at Drumoak, in Aberdeenshire, about 1638, and received his education at Marischal College. In 1663 he published *Optic Promota*, explaining the idea of the telescope which bears his name. He spent some years in Italy, and published at Padua in 1667 a treatise on the *Quadrature of the Circle and Hyperbola*. He became professor of mathematics at St. Andrews in 1668, and at Edinburgh in 1674, but died suddenly in 1675.

GREGORY, James, physician, eldest son of John Gregory, M.D., born at Aberdeen in 1753, died in 1821. He studied medicine at Edinburgh, and in 1776 was appointed professor of the institutes of medicine. In 1780–82 he published his *Conspectus Medicinæ Theoreticæ*, in 1790 became professor of the practice of physic, and in 1792 issued his *Philosophical and Literary Essays*.

GREGORY, John, physician, grandson of James Gregory, the inventor of the reflecting telescope, was born 1724, and died in 1773. He was successively professor of philosophy and medicine in King's College, Aberdeen, and of the practice of physic at Edinburgh. His works include: *Elements of the Practice of Physic, A*

Comparative View of the State and Faculties of Men and Animals, and *A Father's Legacy to his Daughters*.

GREGORY OF NAZIANZUS (*Gregorius Nazianzēnus*), a Father of the Greek Church, born near Nazianzus, in Cappadocia, between A.D. 318 and 329, died in 389 or 390. He studied at Athens, and in 355 and 356 taught rhetoric in that city. He afterwards retired for some time with Basil to the Desert of Pontus.

He began to preach in 362, and between 365 and 374 was associated with his father in the bishopric of Nazianzus. About 378 or 379 he went to Constantinople to oppose the Arians, and was appointed bishop of that see by Theodosius in 380, but in the following year retired to his former charge of Nazianzus.

His works consist of letters, sermons, and poetry. His eloquence is nearly on a level with that of Basil and Chrysostom. His festival is on 9th May.—Cf. Smith and Wall, *Dictionary of Christian Biography*.

GREGORY OF NYSSA, a Father of the Greek Church, brother of St. Basil, born at Sebaste, Pontus, about A.D. 332, died about 398. By his brother's influence he was made Bishop of Nyssa, in Cappadocia. Having opposed the Arians, he was banished by Valens at their instigation from 375 to 378. He took a prominent part in the Councils of Constantinople from 381 to 394. His festival is on 9th March. His works consist of dogmatic treatises, Scripture commentaries, sermons, and letters.

GREGORY OF TOURS (*Gregorius Florentius*), historian of Gaul, born in Auvergne in 539 or 544, died at Tours in 595. He became Bishop of Tours in 573. He had the courage to oppose Chiperic and Fredegonde in their violent courses, and acted the part of a peacemaker in the dynastic quarrels of the period. His *Historia Francorum* is a valuable chronicle of sixth-century events.

GREGORY'S MIXTURE, a popular stomachic and aperient medicine, consists of two parts of rhubarb, six of magnesia, and one of ginger. It may be used with benefit occasionally, but not systematically.

GREGORY THAUMATURGUS, Saint, born in Pontus about A.D. 210, became a Christian at an early age, and was a disciple of Origen; was Bishop of Neocæsarea from 244 till his death in 270. His life and miracles are narrated by Gregory of Nyssa.

GREGORY THE ILLUMINATOR, Saint, the apostle of Armenia, born about A.D. 258. From 302 to 331 he was patriarch of the Armenian Church, but the last years of his life were passed as a hermit. He died about 342.

GREIFFENHAGEN, Maurice, English artist. Born Dec. 15, 1862, he studied at the Royal Academy Schools, London. In 1906 he was made head of the Life Department at the Glasgow School of Art, but after a time settled in London. In 1916 he was elected A.R.A. and in 1922 R.A. His works include *The Judgment of Paris*, in Sydney, and *Dawn* and *Women by a Lake*, bought by the Chantrey trustees. He died 26th December, 1931.

GREIFSWALD (grīfs'vȧlt), a town of Germany in Prussia, province of Pomerania, on the navigable River Rick, about 3 miles above its entrance into the Baltic. It contains a university, founded in 1456, attended by (1931), 2,143 students, and possessed of a library (about 250,000 vols.) museum, observatory, &c. It has manufactures of machinery, oil, paper, and tobacco; and a considerable shipping trade.

Greifswald was one of the Hanse towns about 1270; was assigned to Sweden by the Peace of Westphalia, 1648; was occupied successively by various northern powers, and finally ceded to Prussia in 1815. Pop. 26,695.

GREIZ (grīts), a town of Thuringia, Germany, in the former principality of Reuss Greiz, in a valley on the right bank of the Elster, 16 miles south of Gera. It is the residence of the elder branch of the Reuss family; is walled, well built, and has a castle and palace. Pop. 37,490.

GRENADA, one of the British West Indian Islands, the most southerly of the Windward group. It lies 90 miles north of Trinidad, and has an area of 133 sq. miles. The island is traversed by forest-covered volcanic ranges, in the valleys of which are alluvial tracts of great fertility. In the centre of the island is the lake of Grand Etang, and numerous streams give a plentiful supply of excellent water.

The climate is extremely healthy, though it is often oppressively hot on the lowlands. The sugar-cane is now hardly grown in Grenada, the most important natural product being cocoa. The lime and other fruits, spices of all kinds, and rubber are also grown, and the chief exports are cocoa, spices, fruit, timber (mahogany, white cedar, locust), and turtle-shell. The total value of exports in 1931 was £281,260, and of imports £269,618. There are excellent roads in all parts of the island, and 1,354 miles of telephone line (1931). The capital is St. George's,

which has a wireless station communicating with Barbados.

Grenada, including some of the small Grenadines Islands, the largest of which is Carriacou (area 6,913 acres; pop. 7,104); has a Lieutenant-Governor and a legislative council of seven official and three unofficial members nominated by the crown and five elected members.

The island was discovered by Columbus in his third voyage in 1498, and colonized about the middle of the seventeenth century by the French, who exterminated the Caribs. In 1762 it was taken by the British, and though recaptured by the French in 1779 was restored to Britain in 1783. English and a French patois are spoken. Pop. (1931) 78,662.

GRENADE. This, in its original form, was a hollow sphere of metal of a convenient size for throwing, filled with powder and provided with a length of fuse. When required for use as a missile weapon, the fuse was lighted and the grenade thrown in the required direction (*see* GRENADIER).

Grenades were probably first used in the sixteenth century; but in the course of time, as fire-arms improved and the distance at which engagements were fought increased, the grenade as a means of offence went out of use. In the European War, in consequence of the hand-to-hand nature of the fighting which developed under the conditions prevailing in trench warfare, the grenade was resuscitated.

The modern grenade is of two main forms—one for use from a rifle, and one designed for throwing by hand. The hand-bomb or grenade is possibly the more usually known, and the one now in use in the British army is known as the Mills grenade or handbomb. In shape it is like a small barrel, some 4½ inches high, constructed of cast iron with a coarsely-granulated and deeply-furrowed surface designed to assist in the formation of splinters on explosion.

It is loaded with an explosive known as ammonal, which possesses the advantage of being very hard to explode by a mere concussion, and requires to be detonated by a proper detonating agent. At one end of the grenade case is a screw cap, at the other a firing-pin. The cap, on being removed, exposes a cavity into which the detonator is fixed; the firing-pin is prevented from falling by a collar engaging on a strip of metal attached to the outside of the case, and working with a spring fixed inside.

In the safety position the spring is prevented from acting on the metal strip retaining the striker by a split-pin arrangement, and in the firing position, after the pin has been removed, by the pressure of the hand grasping the bomb and holding down the metal strip. The split pin is not withdrawn till the very moment of throwing, and, as the grasp of the hand is relaxed as the grenade leaves the hand, the spring is allowed to work, the firing-pin falls, and the charge is detonated five seconds later. An expert can throw a Mills bomb about 45 yards, a fair average throw being 35 yards. The area of effect is some 25 yards.

GRENADIER, originally a soldier trained in the use of the hand grenade (q.v.). At the present time the word survives in the titles of the first regiment of foot guards (q.v.), and in two regiments of the Indian army, the 101st and 102nd Grenadiers. Formerly every regiment of infantry had its grenadier company, which took its place on the right of the line, and into which all the men of the finest physique were drafted. The method of fighting by means of the hand-grenade peculiar to the earlier grenadiers necessitated the slinging of the musket over the shoulder.

The customary head-dress in those days was a three-cornered hat; the shape of this was found to interfere with the proper performance of the necessary motions for slinging the musket, and this led to the introduction of the grenadier cap, in its original form a tall mitre-shaped head-dress with no protruding corners.

GREN'ADINES, a chain of small islands and rocks, West Indies, between the Islands of Grenada and St. Vincent; principal island, Carriacou. They produce coffee, indigo, cotton, and sugar. Pop. 7,500.

GRENFELL, George, British missionary and explorer, born near Penzance, Cornwall, 1849, died 1906. Educated at the Baptist College, Bristol, he was sent in 1874 by the Baptist Missionary Society to the Cameroons, reached the Congo, and rendered valuable services to science by his hydrographic survey of the Congo. In 1885 he explored the Mubangi, identifying it with the Welle Makua.

After Livingstone, Grenfell was one of the most intrepid travellers, who contributed considerably to the accurate scientific knowledge of the interior of Africa. In 1891 he was a member of the Commission appointed to delimit the boundary line between the Belgian and Portuguese possessions along the Lunda frontier.

GRENFELL, Sir Wilfred Thomason, English medical missionary. Born 28th Feb., 1865, and educated at Marlborough and Oxford, he became house surgeon of the London Hospital under Sir Frederick Treves. In 1889 he joined the Royal National Mission for Deep Sea Fishermen, and cruised the North Sea in the first hospital ship. In 1892 he went as medical missionary to Labrador, and established hospitals, missions, homes, &c., there and in Newfoundland. He was attached to the Harvard Surgical Unit in France early in the Great War. In 1927 he was knighted. He received the Livingstone Gold medal, Royal Scottish Geographical Society in 1930. His works include *The Harvest of the Sea*, 1905, and *A Labrador Doctor*, 1918, *Labrador Looks at the Orient*, 1928.

GRENO'BLE, a fortified town of Southern France, capital of the department of Isère, finely and strongly placed on the Isère, 60 miles S.E. of Lyons, on both sides of the river, which is crossed by three bridges and lined by fine quays. It has a cathedral, and a noteworthy church (Saint-André), formerly the chapel of the dauphins of the Viennois, with the monument of Bayard; a public library of over 400,000 volumes and 7,500 MSS.; a university founded in 1339, museum, bishop's palace, court-house, arsenal, and extensive public gardens.

The manufactures consist of gloves, linen goods, liqueurs, and leather. Grenoble existed in the time of Cæsar; and Gratian, who had improved it, changed its name from Cularo to Gratianopolis (whence Grenoble). There is a broadcasting station (566 M., 2kW.). Pop. (1931), 90,748.

GRENVILLE, George, a British minister, younger brother of Earl Temple, and father of William Wyndham, the first Lord Grenville; born in 1712, died in 1770. He became Treasurer of the Navy in 1754; Secretary of State and subsequently First Lord of the Admiralty in 1762; First Lord of the Treasury and Chancellor of the Exchequer in 1763. In 1763 he introduced a scheme of colonial taxation, and in 1764 proposed a stamp tax to be levied in the American colonies, which was one of the causes of the American War of Independence. In 1765 he was succeeded in office by Lord Rockingham. *The Grenville Papers* (1852–53) contain his most important political correspondence.

GRENVILLE, Sir Richard, British naval commander, a cousin of Sir Walter Raleigh, born about 1541, died in 1591. After performing such public duties as fell to a man of his position, and having distinguished himself in naval exploits against the Spaniards, in 1591 he was in command of the *Revenge* of 500 tons and 250 men, as vice-admiral under Lord Thomas Howard, who was sent to the Azores for the purpose of intercepting homeward-bound Spanish treasure ships.

Suddenly the Spaniards appeared with an overwhelming force of men-of-war, and Howard, seeing that resistance was useless, gave the enemy the slip. Sir Richard, however, was cut off from his countrymen, either by his own intention or accidentally, and instead of surrendering determined to fight to the last. For fifteen hours he kept up a desperate resistance, and when at last the *Revenge* was reduced to a helpless wreck the sorely wounded hero and the remnants of his gallant crew were overpowered and taken prisoners.

Sir Richard died within two or

The Old Smithy, Gretna Green

three days on board one of the Spanish vessels, and soon after the *Revenge* went down in a great storm. Tennyson's ballad of *The Revenge* commemorates the incident.—Cf. Hakluyt, *Voyages*, vols. ii and iii.

GRENVILLE, William Wyndham, Lord, third son of George Grenville, was born 1759, died in 1834. In 1783 he was appointed Paymaster-General of the Army; in 1789 became Speaker, and in the same year became Secretary of State for the Home Department. In 1790 he was created Baron Grenville, and from 1791 till Pitt's resignation in 1801 held the post of Foreign Secretary. On the return of Pitt to office in 1804 he declined to join him, and continued in opposition till Pitt's death, when he became the head of a coalition ministry, including Fox and Grey, 1806. This ministry resigned in 1807, after having passed

an Act for the abolition of the slave-trade. He did not again take office.

GRESHAM, Sir Thomas, a merchant of London, born in 1519, died in 1579. In 1552 he was sent as agent of Henry VIII's money affairs to Antwerp, where in two years he paid off a heavy loan, and raised the king's credit considerably. On the accession of Elizabeth he was deprived of his office, but it was soon restored to him, with that of queen's merchant, and he was also knighted.

In 1556 he planned and erected at his own expense an exchange (afterwards called by Elizabeth the Royal Exchange) for the merchants of London, in imitation of that of Antwerp. He founded in 1575 Gresham College, London (in which courses of lectures are given), and at his death set aside large sums for charitable institutions.

Gresham's law is the principle of economics that bad money drives out good. It was so named by Macleod in 1857, under the mistaken notion that the principle was first formulated by Sir Thomas Gresham in 1558. Earlier economic writers had stated the law clearly; and it was known at least as early as the time of Aristophanes.—Cf. *Frogs*, 720, sqq.

GRESSET (grä-sā), **Jean Baptiste Louis,** a French poet, born at Amiens, 1709, died in 1777. At the age of twenty-four he produced a small poem full of graceful badinage called *Vert Vert*, the subject being the adventures of a parroquet. It was followed by other pieces in a similar style.

GRETNA GREEN, a village of Scotland, in Dumfriesshire, on the Solway Firth, 9 miles north of Carlisle, for nearly a century notorious for the celebration of the marriages of fugitive lovers from England. To conclude a lawful (though irregular) marriage in Scotland it is only necessary for an unmarried couple to go and declare themselves man and wife before witnesses, and it was in this way that these runaway couples were married; but such marriages were put an end to, in 1856, by an Act declaring that no irregular marriage in Scotland shall be valid unless one of the parties has resided in Scotland for twenty-one days next preceding such marriage.

During the European War the largest British munition factory was established near Gretna. This was eventually closed after the Armistice, and in 1921 was abandoned by the Government and offered for sale.

GREUZE (greuz), **Jean Baptiste,** a famous French painter, born in Burgundy 1726, died in 1805. Although he devoted some time and attention to historical subjects, he afterwards confined himself to depicting scenes of the family life of the *bourgeois* or middle class. As a colourist he occupies a high place. Among his works the following may be mentioned: *The Village Marriage*, *The Wicked Son Punished*, *The Broken Pitcher* (all in the Louvre); *The Broken Mirror*, *Innocence* (in the Wallace Collection, London); *The Dead Canary* (National Gallery, Edinburgh).

GREV'ILLE, Fulke, Lord Brooke, English writer, born in 1544. Having studied at Cambridge and Oxford and made the tour of Europe, he became a courtier, and enjoyed the favour of Elizabeth, James I, and Charles I. In 1628 he was stabbed by an old servant, and immediately expired. He wrote the *Life of Sir Philip Sidney*; and a collection of verse entitled *Cælica*, containing CIX Sonnets.

GREVILLEA, a large genus of Australian shrubs and trees, ord. Proteaceæ. Some yield timber; young plants of *G. robusta* are often grown in pots for their ornamental fern-like foliage.

GREY, Charles, Earl, English statesman, eldest son of Charles, first Earl Grey, born in 1764, died in 1845. He was educated at Eton and at King's College, Cambridge. In 1786 he was returned to Parliament as member for Northumberland.

On the accession of the Grenville ministry in 1806, Grey, now Lord Howick, was made First Lord of the Admiralty, and on the death of Fox succeeded him as Secretary for Foreign Affairs and leader of the House of Commons. The death of his father in 1807 raised him to the House of Peers, and from this period up to 1830 he headed the opposition in the Lords, and especially opposed the proceedings against Queen Caroline.

On the accession of William IV and the retirement of the Wellington ministry, Earl Grey was summoned to office. The great event which marks his administration is the passing in 1832 of the First Reform Bill. In 1834 Earl Grey resigned, and was succeeded by Lord Melbourne. The remainder of his life was chiefly spent in retirement.—Cf. Charles Grey, *Life and Opinions of Charles, Second Earl Grey*.

GREY, Sir George, statesman and colonial governor, born at Lisbon 1812, died in London in 1898. He was for ten years in the army, carried on explorations in Australia during 1837–9 and in 1841 was appointed Governor of South Australia, becoming Governor of New Zealand in 1846, where he had Maori and other troubles to deal with.

From 1854 to 1861 he was Governor of Cape Colony, a post in which he was highly successful, his prompt dispatch of all available troops to aid in quelling the Indian Mutiny being a noteworthy incident. From 1861 to 1867 he was again Governor of New Zealand; had difficulties with the Maoris, gave offence to the Home Government, and was recalled. Subsequently (1877–80) he was Premier of New Zealand, and afterwards resided in England.

Besides writing an account of his Australian explorations, he published poems, traditions, and chaunts of the Maoris; *Polynesian Mythology*; and *Ancient Traditional History of the New Zealand Race*.

Jean Baptiste Greuze

GREY, Lady Jane, Queen of England for nine days, born in 1537, died in 1554. She was the daughter of Henry Grey, Marquess of Dorset, afterwards Duke of Suffolk, by Frances, daughter of Charles Brandon, Duke of Suffolk, and Mary, younger sister of Henry VIII. She displayed much precocity of talent; and under the tuition of Aylmer, afterwards Bishop of London, she acquired a knowledge of the learned languages, as well as French and Italian. She was married to Lord Guildford Dudley, fourth son of the Duke of Northumberland, in 1553.

Edward VI, who died in 1553, was induced on his death-bed to settle on her the succession to the crown. The Council endeavoured to keep his death secret, with a view to securing the persons of the princesses, Mary and Elizabeth, and when Mary discovered the design the Council proclaimed Lady Jane queen.

On the approach of Mary, however, the Council deserted Lady Jane, and Mary was proclaimed queen. Jane was now confined to the Tower. She and her husband were arraigned, and pleaded guilty of high treason; but their doom was suspended, and it was not until after the suppression of the rebellion of Sir Thomas Wyatt, in which the Duke of Suffolk, Lady Jane's father, had participated, that the sentence was executed. She was beheaded on Tower Hill, 12th Feb., 1554, her husband having previously suffered the same day.—Cf. R. Davey, *The Nine Days' Queen: Lady Jane Grey and her Times.*

GREYHOUND, a variety of dog, distinguished by a greater length of

Greyhound

muzzle than any other; very low forehead, short lips, thin and long legs, small muscles, contracted belly, and semipendent ears. There are several varieties, as the Irish greyhound, the Scottish, the Russian, the Italian, and the Turkish. The common greyhound is of a slender make of body, and is universally known as the swiftest of dogs.

A good hound has a fine, soft, flexible skin, with thin, silky hair, a great length of nose, contracting gradually from the eye to the nostril, a full, clear, and penetrating eye, small ears, erect head, long neck, chest capacious, deep, but not wide, shoulders deep and placed obliquely, ribs well arched, contracted belly and flank, a great depth from the hips to the hocks of the hind-legs, fore-legs straight, and shorter than the hinder. The name appears to have no reference to the colour, but is derived from the Icelandic *grey*, a dog.

They are chiefly used in the sport of coursing, a work for which their peculiar shape, strength, keenness of sight, and speed make them exceedingly well fitted. This sport is preferred by many to horse-racing, and large kennels of greyhounds are kept by several of the nobility and gentry, who also further the sport by preserving hares, and providing suitable coursing-grounds. (*See* COURSING.) The chief breeds are the Newmarket, the Lancashire, and the Scottish.

GREYHOUND RACING, outdoor sport. It is a form of coursing, the chief difference being that mechanical, not real, hares are used. It began in the United States and since about 1926 has become very popular in Great Britain. The hare is worked by electricity, and as soon as it is set in motion the dogs are released by opening a trap door. The sport affords ample opportunity for betting, and bookmakers attend the meetings, which are usually held in the evenings, and sometimes on Sundays.

The first track was opened in England in 1925. There are now some 50, controlled by the National Greyhound Racing Club. The Greyhound Racing Association has its headquarters at 70, Pall Mall, London, S.W.

GREYMOUTH, a seaport of New Zealand, on the west coast of South Island, province of Westland, in a district where coal is mined and gold obtained. It is connected by rail with both Christchurch and Westport. Pop. 6,100.

GREY OF FALLODON, Edward, first Viscount, British statesman, born 25th April, 1862. A grandson of Sir George Grey, for many years Secretary of State for Home Affairs, he was educated at Winchester and at Balliol College, Oxford. In 1885 he entered Parliament as a Liberal member for Berwick-on-Tweed, and continued to sit for this constituency till 1916.

Early in his career Gladstone is said to have predicted for the young member a great future. And, indeed, this prophecy became true, for Grey was destined to dominate the Councils of Europe more than any of his predecessors at the Foreign Office since 1854.

His first opportunity to show his capacity for parliamentary life, his comprehensive grasp of political problems, and his diplomatic skill came when he was appointed Under-Secretary for Foreign Affairs in 1892 in the Rosebery Cabinet. He enhanced his reputation during the time when the Liberal party was in opposition, and in 1905 he became Secretary of State for Foreign Affairs in the Campbell-

Bannerman ministry, retaining his office till 1916.

During his tenure of office the Triple Entente, uniting Great Britain, France, and Russia, was developed, an Anglo-Russian agreement was concluded in 1907, settling rivalries in Asia, and the Peace of London, putting an end to the Balkan War, was signed on 30th May, 1913. He failed, however, to bring about more cordial relations with Germany, and in 1911, during the quarrel between France and Germany over Morocco, he was on the side of France.

In spite of his earnest endeavours and continued efforts to preserve peace during the last twelve days preceding the outbreak of the European War, in spite of his appeals to Germany and Austria, he did not succeed, and when he saw that war was unavoidable, he did not hesitate to commit his country to the general struggle. In a famous historic speech, delivered on 1st Aug., 1914, he defined Britain's attitude, and the House of Commons decided to stand by the side of France against Germany.

A K.G. since 1912, he was created a viscount in July, 1916, and in December of the same year resigned with Asquith. He became one of the most ardent supporters of the idea of a League of Nations, and wrote a famous pamphlet on the subject in 1918. In spite of his impaired eyesight, he occasionally appeared on the public platform, and in Oct., 1919, he went on a special mission to the United States, returning in Jan., 1920. He was elected President of Armstrong College, Newcastle-on-Tyne, in 1918, and Chancellor of Oxford University in 1928.

On his two hobbies, fly-fishing and the observation of bird life, he wrote books, including *The Charm of Birds*, and in 1925 he issued his memoirs *Twenty-Five Years*. Later he edited *The Fallodon Papers*. In early life Grey was amateur tennis champion.

GREYTOWN, SAN JUAN DE NICARAGUA, or **SAN JUAN DEL NORTE,** the principal seaport of the Central American republic of Nicaragua, situated at the mouth of the San Juan. It is proposed to build a Nicaragua Canal and an immense breakwater has been built for the purpose. Pop. 2,500.

GRIEG, Eduard, Norwegian musical composer, born in 1843, died in 1907. He studied at Leipzig and at Copenhagen, and, after spending a few years in Christiania, received a government pension which enabled him to settle in Bergen and devote his whole time to composition. His most notable works are the music to

K*

Ibsen's play *Peer Gynt,* and his refined and lyrical renderings of Norwegian folk songs and dances

GRIFFIN, or **GRYPHON,** a fabulous monster of antiquity, commonly represented with the body, the feet, and claws of a lion, and the head and wings of an eagle. India, or Scythia, was anciently assigned as the native country of the griffins; and it was alleged that they guarded the gold in the mountains. The griffin is frequently used as a charge in heraldry. Hundreds of families in Great Britain, and particularly in Wales, adopted the griffin as the emblem on their family arms.

GRIFFITH, Arthur, Irish politician. Born in Dublin, 31st March, 1872, he became a printer and journalist. In

Eduard Grieg

1899 he founded *The United Irishman,* a weekly journal which he edited. In 1904 appeared his pamphlet *The Resurrection of Hungary.* He was one of the founders of the Sinn Fein movement, and in 1907 his paper took that name, although later it was changed to *Eire.* He supported the Irish volunteers, but took no part in the Easter Rising of 1916, though he was, nevertheless, interned. Imprisoned again in 1918, on his release he was elected Vice-President of the Irish Republic, and was again imprisoned for a short time. During De Valera's absence in America, 1919-20, he was head of the Republic and had a prominent share in the final settlement of the Irish question in 1921. He was then elected head of the Irish executive, but died suddenly, 12th Aug., 1922.

GRIFFITH, David Llewelyn Wark, American film producer. Born in Kentucky in 1880, in 1908 he was acting and directing the Biograph Film Company. Later, as an independent producer, he was responsible for *The Birth of a Nation, Intolerance, Way Down East,* &c. His films always expound some moral or propagandist principle.

GRILLPARZER (gril pär-tsér), **Franz,** a German poet and dramatist, born at Vienna 15th Jan:, 1791, died there in 1872. Having entered the service of the imperial court, he rose through various dignities, and at last was appointed member for life of the Imperial Council. He was the author of lyrical and other poems, a novel, and travels, and of the dramas *Sappho, Das Goldene Vliess,* and *Des Meeres und der Liebe Wellen.* Perhaps the finest of his productions is the historical drama of *König Ottokars Glück und Ende.*

GRILSE, or **PEAL,** a name given to the young of the salmon (smolts) after they return for the first time from the sea to fresh water. They then sometimes weigh from 5 to 8 or 9 lb.

GRIMAL'DI FAMILY, one of the four families of the high nobility in Genoa. The lordship of Monaco belonged, for more than 600 years (beginning with 980), to the Grimaldi, and the present ruler of the House of Goyon-Matignon still bears the name of Grimaldi. With the Fieschi they always played an important part in the history of Genoa, especially in the disputes between the Ghibellines and the Guelfs, to which latter party both families belonged.

GRIMALDI, Joseph, English clown. Born in London, 18th Dec., 1779, he came of a family of clowns and dancers, and began his theatrical career at Drury Lane, when an infant. Afterwards he played at Sadler's Wells and continued to amuse audiences in London and the provinces until 1828. He died 31st May, 1837.

GRIMALDI'S FRINGES, coloured diffraction bands first observed and described by Grimaldi in 1665.

GRIMM, Friedrich Melchior, Baron, German man of letters, born at Ratisbon in 1723, died at Gotha in 1807. He lived mostly in Paris and wrote in French. Having finished his studies, he went to Paris and there became acquainted with Jean Jacques Rousseau, Diderot, D'Alembert, D'Holbach, and other Parisian philosophers. He corresponded with Catherine II of Russia, Gustavus III of Sweden, and other great personages. Frederick the Great among others gave him marks of great esteem.

In 1776 he was appointed envoy from the Duke of Saxe-Gotha to the French court, and honoured with the title of baron. On the Revolution breaking out he retired to Gotha, where he died. His *Correspondance Littéraire* possesses great literary and historical value.

GRIMM, Jakob Ludwig, a German philologist, born at Hanau, in Hesse-Cassel, 1785, died at Berlin 1863. He was educated partly at Cassel, and finally at Marburg University. In 1806 he became librarian to Jerome Bonaparte, King of Westphalia, and from 1816 to 1829 he occupied the post of second librarian at Cassel. From 1830 to 1837 he resided at Göttingen as professor and librarian, lecturing on the German language, literature, and legal antiquities.

Having, along with six other professors, resisted the unconstitutional encroachments of the King of Hanover, he was banished, and after his retirement to Cassel he was, in 1841, called to Berlin as a professor and member of the Academy of Sciences. He sat in the National Assembly of 1848, and in that of Gotha in 1849. From that time till his death he occupied himself only with his various publications. He wrote on German mythology, German legal antiquities, the history of the German language, and published old German poems.

His two greatest works, both unfinished, are his *Deutsche Grammatik* (German Grammar, vols. i–iv, 1819–37), and his *Deutsches Wörterbuch* (German Dictionary), commenced in 1852, in conjunction with his brother Wilhelm, and being gradually completed by eminent scholars. He also published, in company with his brother, the *Kinder- und Hausmärchen,* one of the most popular collections of juvenile fairy tales.

GRIMM, Wilhelm Karl, brother of the preceding, born 1786, died in 1859. Educated at Cassel and Marburg, he followed his brother to Göttingen, and obtained a professorship. He joined in his brother's protest against the abrogation of the new Hanoverian Constitution, and was deprived of his office, but obtained an appointment in Berlin.

He devoted himself especially to the German mediæval poetry, and published a treatise, *Ueber die deutschen Runen,* a translation of *Altdänische Heldenlieder,* and *Balladen und Märchen,* all with valuable introductions and disquisitions.

GRIMMA, a town of Saxony, on the Mulde, 17 miles E.S.E. of Leipzig, charmingly situated, and with some interesting old buildings. Pop. 14,440.

GRIMM'S LAW, so called from its discoverer, Jakob Grimm, formulates the principle of the interchange of the mute consonants in the Aryan languages, in words derived from the same roots. For example: p, b, and f in Latin, Greek, and Sanskrit are in Gothic and English, Dutch, &c., respectively represented by f, p, and b, and in Old High German by b (v), f, and p. The subjoined table exhibits the principal mutations:

	Labials.	Dentals.	Gutturals.
Greek (Latin, Sanskrit)	p,b,f	t,d,th	k,g,ch
English (A.Sax.), Gothic, &c.	f,p,b	th,t,d	h,k,g
Old High German ..	b (v),f,p	d,g,t	g,ch,k

As examples: E. father = Lat. pater, Gr. patēr, Skr. pitri; E. brother = Lat. frater, Gr. phratēr, Skr. bhratar; E. kin = genus, Gr. genos; E. head, A. Sax. heafod = Lat. caput, Gr. keph (alē), &c.; E. thin = Lat. tenuis, Gr. tanaos. Certain exceptions to the law are explained by a law subsequently discovered, called Verner's law. See PHILOLOGY.

GRIMSBY, formerly **GREAT GRIMSBY,** a parliamentary, municipal, and county borough and thriving seaport, England, county of Lincoln, on the Humber. The docks which belong to the L.N.E. Railway, occupy an area of about 140 acres, and there is a large trade with Continental ports. Grimsby is the largest fishing-port in the world. It sends one member to Parliament. Pop. (1931), 92,463.

GRIMSEL (grim'zl), a pass in Switzerland, at the eastern extremity of the Bernese Alps, 7,103 feet in height and connecting the valleys of the Aar and the Rhône.

GRINDELWALD (grin'dl-vålt), one of the most beautiful of the upper Alpine valleys of Switzerland, about 36 miles south-east of Berne. The village of Grindelwald consists of picturesque cottages, and the inhabitants, about 3,500 in number, are chiefly employed in rearing cattle. It is a popular tourist centre, as near it are the Wetterhorn, Schreckhorn,

Grindelwald

Eiger, and other Alpine peaks, as well as two noted glaciers.

GRINDING, a general term for operations whereby materials are milled, crushed, pulverized, shaped, or reduced in size by the forces of attrition, abrasion, and impact. Rocks and minerals may be disintegrated between heavy steel jaws, one being slightly oscillated, as in the Blake stone-breaker. For fine grinding or milling gold-bearing quartz, batteries of stamps are used, the mineral being crushed by the fall of a heavy stamp shoe, alternately raised and released by a cam.

In the Griffin type of mill a heavy wheel, suspended pendulum fashion, swings around the periphery of a pan, and crushes the material as in a simple pestle and mortar. In edge-wheel or pan mills heavy broad-faced wheels roll over the floor of the pan containing the material. In 'ball-and-tube' mills the material is fed into rotating or tumbling steel barrels, sometimes lined with quartzite, containing loose flint or steel balls. Grinding may be done wet or dry, according to circumstances.

For softer materials, such as cereals, flat millstones, rotating one above the other, are employed. This arrangement is one of great antiquity. Cereals may be disintegrated to a very fine state of division by the impact of quickly-moving projections of rotating discs, between which the grain is passed. Paints, chocolate, and similar substances are ground and mixed between rollers rotating at slightly different speeds and reciprocating endwise.

Materials are reduced in size by grinding with loose abrasives or abrasive wheels, usually with water. At slow speeds the abrasive must be at least as hard as the material. Thus diamonds are ground on lead laps or rotating discs charged with diamond dust.

Brittle substances, such as glass, are ground as the result of a surface splintering action by means of loose abrasives, such as carborundum, corundum, emery, and sand, applied to the surface of rotating cast-iron discs; but abrasive wheels are sometimes employed. Metals are shaped or ground by abrasive wheels associated with many specialized machines—universal, cylindrical, internal, surface, tool, and drill.

The grains or grits of abrasive of various grades are held together by vitrified bonds of fused clay, silica bonds of clay and water-glass fused at a lower temperature, and elastic bonds containing shellac and gums.

Lapping is the operation of reducing sizes by very small amounts, or trueing, by grinding with fine loose abrasive mixed with oil or water. At high speeds a hard material can be ground with a softer; thus the ends of hardened armour plates are ground to size by quickly rotating blocks of sandstone or other substances. In *sandblasting*, material is removed by the impact of grains of sand or fine chilled shot impelled by a stream of compressed air.—BIBLIOGRAPHY: Sir E. Thorpe, *Dictionary of Applied Chemistry*; R. B. Hodgson, *Emery Grinding Machinery*.

GRINDSTONE, a cylindrical stone, on which sharpening, cutting, and abrasion are effected by the convex surface while the stone is revolving on its axis. They are made of sandstone, or sandstone grit of various degrees of fineness. Good stones are obtained in various parts of England, especially from the coal districts of Northumberland, Newcastle grindstones being especially famous. The Sheffield grindstone, used for grinding files and the like, is obtained from Hardsley, about 14 miles north of Sheffield. Artificial grindstones have been successfully tried.

GRINSTEAD, EAST, market town of Sussex. It is 29½ miles from London and is reached by the S. Rly. Here is Sackville College, an almshouse erected by an Earl of Dorset in the 17th century. Pop. (1931), 7,901. **West Grinstead** is a village 18 miles away. It also has a station on the S. Rly.

GRIQUALAND EAST, a district of Cape Province, South Africa, lying south of Natal between Pondoland and Basutoland; fertile and suited for stock-raising. It was incorporated with Cape Colony in 1874. Area, 6,602 sq. miles. Pop. 265,000 (including 7,643 whites).

GRIQUALAND WEST, a district of Cape Province north of the Orange River, and west of the Orange Free State; 180 miles from east to west, and 120 from north to south; area, about 15,197 sq. miles. The prevailing character of the surface is that of undulating grassy plains suitable for grazing.

Previous to the discovery of the diamond fields in the basin of the Vaal River, Griqualand was little known. In 1870 large finds of diamonds in that district began to attract wide notice, and in 1871 Waterboer, the Griqua chief, ceded all his rights to the British Government, and the territory was incorporated with Cape Colony.

The chief centre of the diamond-mining industry, and the seat of government, is Kimberley. The annual value of the diamonds produced usually reaches about £4,000,000. The Griquas are a mixed race sprung from the intercourse of the Boers with Hottentot women. Pop. 108,500 (including 32,570 whites).

GRISI (grē'sē), Giulia, a celebrated Italian vocalist, born at Milan 1811 or 1812. After having studied music at Bologna, and made her début in Rossini's *Zelmira*, she appeared at Milan as Norma. She acquired great celebrity at Paris, in England, and America, and was at the height of her fame between 1834 and 1849. In 1836 she married Mario, the great tenor singer. Her voice gave way in her later years, and she died at Berlin in 1869. Her principal character was Norma.

GRIS-NEZ (grĕ-nă), **CAPE**, a headland, north-west extremity of France, department of Pas-de-Calais, the nearest point of the French shore to that of Britain, the distance being barely 21 miles. It has a revolving light, 195 feet high.

GRISONS (grē-son; Ger. *Graubünden*), the largest and most easterly canton of Switzerland, bordering on Austria and Italy; area 2,746 sq. miles. Its boundaries and interior consist almost entirely of mountain chains, including more than twenty peaks above 9,000 feet.

The canton may be regarded as embracing three great valley districts, of which the Upper and Lower Engadine (Inn Valley) attain considerable breadth. The Inn, which flows to the Danube, and the Vorder and Hinter Rhine, are the principal rivers. The lakes are numerous, and many of them present scenery of the most magnificent description.

The climate varies greatly, ranging from the perpetual winter of the mountains to the almost Italian air of some of the valleys. The canton is in general pastoral, feeding large numbers of cattle and sheep. The mountain forests supply much timber. A considerable transit trade is carried on between Italy and Germany.

The canton was admitted into the Confederation as late as 1803. Both the Protestant and the Roman Catholic religions are established. The language of the public Acts is German, and the people speak German, Romansch, or Italian. Pop. 126,340.

GROAT (Du. *groot*, great, thick), an English silver coin, coined by Henry III in 1249, and by Edward III in 1351. It was equal to fourpence in value. A coin of this value, the *fourpenny-piece*, was revived in 1835, but

Groat—time of Edward III

none have been struck since 1856, and all are now withdrawn from circulation. The Scots groat was issued in 1358, and the Irish groat in 1460.

GRODNO, now **GARDINAS**, a town of Poland, formerly capital of a Russian government of the same name, on the Niemen, 160 miles north-east of Warsaw, a poorly-built place, the principal edifice being a palace erected by Alexander III. The manufactures consist of woollen, linen, and silk goods, and fire-arms. The fortress was taken by the Germans in Sept., 1915. The Bolshevist Government recognized Grodno as belonging to Lithuania, but the Council of Ambas-

Groin's GGG. Choir, Canterbury Cathedral

sadors fixed a boundary in 1923 which placed it in Poland. This has never been recognized by Lithuania. Pop. 61,600.

GROIN, the angular curve made by the intersection of two semi-cylinders or arches. It is either regular or irregular: *regular*, as when the intersecting arches are of the same diameters and heights; and *irregular*, when one of the arches is semi-circular, and the other semi-elliptical. In Gothic architecture groins are always ribbed.

GROMWELL, the name of plants of the genus Lithospermum, nat. ord. Boraginaceæ, containing a number of widely-distributed species, three of which are natives of Britain. The seeds of *L. officinale* are occasionally used as a diuretic.

GRONINGEN (grŏ'ning-en), a town of the Netherlands, capital of a province of the same name, situated on the River Hunse, here converted into a canal, 92 miles north-east of Amsterdam. It is a rich place, adorned with many excellent buildings, and has numerous canals crossed by bridges. The principal edifices are the cathedral, a fine exchange, and the university. It has manufactures of white lead and soap, oil, fulling, and sawmills, and an excellent harbour, with an active trade. It is also a printing centre. Pop. (1932), 107,158.

The province forms the north-eastern portion of Holland; area, 886 sq. miles. It is protected against the encroachments of the sea by dykes, is very level, and is intersected by innumerable canals. The inhabitants, 395,423 (1931), nearly all belong to the Calvinistic Church.

GRONO'VIUS (properly *Gronov*), the name of several Dutch classical scholars.

(1) Johann Friedrich, born at Hamburg in 1611, succeeded Daniel Heinsius as professor of belles-lettres at Leyden in 1658, and died there in 1671. His editions of Livy, Statius, Justin, Tacitus, Gellius, Phædrus, Seneca, Sallust, Pliny, and Plautus are valuable.

(2) His son Jakob, born at Deventer in 1645, studied there and at Leyden. He afterwards became professor of belles-lettres at that university, and died in 1716. He edited Tacitus, Polybius, Herodotus, Pomponius Mela, Cicero, and Ammianus Marcellinus, and compiled a *Thesaurus Antiquitatum Græcarum* (Leyden, 1697, 13 vols. fol.).

(3) His son Abraham, born at Leyden 1694, edited Justin, Pomponius Mela, Tacitus, and Ælian. He died at Leyden in 1775.

GROOTE EYLANDT (grō'te i'lant; 'great island'), the largest island in the Gulf of Carpentaria, north of Australia, belonging to the colony of South Australia; greatest length and breadth, 40 miles each.

GROS (grō), Antoine-Jean, Baron, French historical painter, born at Paris in 1771. He studied art under David, attracted the notice of Napoleon by his picture *The Victor of Arcola*, and became an honorary staff officer in the French army.

In 1804 he produced his *Plague at Jaffa*, showing Napoleon visiting the sick, a work crowned at the Louvre. He painted also battle scenes and a number of portraits; but his chief work is probably the cupola of St. Geneviève at Paris, exhibiting the saint protecting the throne of France, represented by Clovis, Charlemagne, St. Louis, and Louis XVIII. The artist received for it the sum of 100,000 francs.

His work shows more feeling for movement and a bolder use of colour than that of most of his contemporaries. The rise of the Romantic school and the criticism levelled at his work so affected his mind that he drowned himself in the Seine in 1835.

GROSBEAK (Fr. *grosbec*), a general popular name for several finches and other perching birds possessing unusually large beaks, e.g. the hawfinch (*Coccothraustes vulgāris*); other examples are the pine grosbeak (*Pyrrhula enucleātor*), scarlet grosbeak (*P. erythrina*), and the American cardinals (species of Cardinalis).

GROSCHEN (grō'shen), a name for German coins of which the oldest known were struck in Trèves in 1104. In 1525 the groschen was divided into twelve pfennige. Afterwards, in the currency system existing up till 1872, the groschen was a silver coin $=1\frac{1}{4}d.$ sterling, there being 30 to the *thaler* of about 3s. sterling.

GROSE, Francis, an English antiquary, born in 1731, died in 1791. Having dissipated the fortune inherited from his father, he turned his attention to the study of antiquities. In 1773 he commenced the publication in numbers of his *Views of Antiquities in England and Wales*. In 1789 he made a tour in Scotland for the purpose of illustrating the antiquities of that country. Before completing it, however, he proceeded to Ireland, with the view of collecting its antiquities, but was suddenly carried off by apoplexy.

His name is now perhaps chiefly remembered from his connection with Burns, who wrote his *Tam o' Shanter* for him. He was the original 'chield amang you taking notes.' Captain Grose also wrote a *Treatise on Ancient Armour and Weapons*, a *Classical Dictionary of the Vulgar Tongue*, and other works.

GROSS, in opposition to net, is applied to merchandize, including the weight of that in which it is packed. Thus we say, 'The bag of coffee weighs 9 cwt. *gross*,' that is, including the weight of the bag.

GROSSENHAIN (grōs'en-hīn), a town in Saxony, 20 miles N.W. of Dresden, on the left bank of the Röder. Woollen and cotton goods are manufactured. Pop. 12,893.

GROSSETESTE, Robert, an eminent English scholar and prelate, was born about the year 1175, died in 1253. He studied first at Oxford, and then went to Paris, where he mastered the Hebrew and Greek languages. On his return to England he became lecturer in the Franciscan school at Oxford, and acquired a great reputation for his linguistic abilities and his skill in logic.

In 1235 he was appointed Bishop of Lincoln, but soon came into collision with Pope Innocent IV on the question of the induction of foreigners into English benefices. He refused to institute the Pope's nephew, Frederick di Lavagna, to a canonry at Lincoln, and disregarded the Papal fulminations which he thus incurred. His writings, few of which have been published, are very voluminous.—Cf. F. S. Stevenson, *Robert Grosseteste, Bishop of Lincoln.*

GROSSE'TO, a province of Tuscany, Italy; area, 1,735 sq. miles; pop. (1931), 176,991. Being mountainous and marshy, it is little adapted for cultivation. Its capital, Grosseto, on the Ombrone, is the seat of a bishop, and has a beautiful cathedral. Pop. (commune) 23,997.

GROSSMITH, George, English actor and entertainer, born 9th Dec., 1847, he was a reporter at Bow Street, London, before he began his career as an entertainer in 1870. In 1877 he first appeared in Gilbert and Sullivan Opera, *The Sorcerer,* and later, at the Savoy, he took leading parts in eight others. In 1889 he returned to his old profession of entertainer. He died 1st March, 1912.

With his brother, **Weedon Grossmith** (1853–1919), who made a name both as an actor and an artist, he wrote *The Diary of a Nobody* for *Punch.*

His son, **George Grossmith** (born 1874), became an actor and played a large part in the popularizing of revues. From 1931 he was Managing Director of the Theatre Royal, Drury Lane. He was also Advisory Director of Programmes to the B.B.C. and Director of British Filmcraft Productions, Ltd., and himself played in films in Hollywood.

GROSSULA′CEÆ, or GROSSULA-RIACEÆ, a tribe of plants of the nat. ord. Saxifragaceæ, comprehending the gooseberry and currant of gardens, and consisting, in fact, of only one genus, Ribes; natives of most parts of the world except Africa and the tropics.

GROSSWARDEIN, now **ORADEA MARE,** a town in Rumania, formerly in Hungary, capital of the county Bihar, in a beautiful plain, on the Körös. It consists of the town proper, formerly fortified and surrounded by walls, and of extensive suburbs, is tolerably well built, and is a railway centre. The staple manufacture is earthenware. Pop. (1930), 82,355.

GROSVENOR GALLERY (grŏ′venor), a building erected in 1877 by Sir Coutts Lindsay in New Bond Street, London, for annual exhibitions of pictures. In these exhibitions, which began on 1st of May, preference was generally given to certain schools of art, represented by such names as Burne Jones, Rossetti, &c., and in

general to work appealing more to a peculiar æsthetic taste than to the popular mind; hence the allusion in *Patience*:—

A greenery-yallery, Grosvenor Gallery, Foot-in-the-grave young man.

GROTE, George, English historian and politician, was born in 1794, died in 1871. His grandfather, descended from German ancestors, was one of the original partners of the London banking-house of Prescott, Grote, & Co. Having been educated at Sevenoaks and at the Charterhouse, in 1810 he entered his father's banking establishment as a clerk. As early as 1823 he began to collect materials for his *History of Greece.* In 1832 he was elected a member of Parliament for the city of London, and his subsequent parliamentary career, until his retirement in 1841, was principally devoted to the advocacy of vote by ballot. He was also a leader of the 'Philosophic Radicals.'

In 1846 appeared the first two volumes of his *History of Greece.* The remaining ten volumes followed in rapid succession, the final volume being published in 1856. The work terminates with the death of Alexander the Great, and as a whole is a monument of erudition. It is, however, not strictly impartial, and some of it has been rendered obsolete by more recent discoveries, especially by the discovery of Aristotle's *Constitution of Athens.* In 1865 he published *Plato and the Other Companions of Sokrates,* and was engaged at the time of his death on an elaborate treatise on *Aristotle and the Peripatetics.*

In the latter part of his life he was concerned in the management of University College, the London University, and the British Museum. He refused a peerage in 1869, and was buried in Westminster Abbey. The fifth edition of his *History of Greece* appeared in 1888.—Cf. Mrs. Grote, *Personal Life of George Grote.*

GROTESQUE, in art, a capricious variety of arabesque ornamentation, which, as a whole, has no type in nature, the parts of animals, plants, and other incongruous elements being combined together; used by the Romans in decorative painting and revived by the artists of the Renaissance.

GROTIUS, or DE GROOT, Hugo, a Dutch scholar, born at Delft 1583, died at Rostock in 1645. He entered the University of Leyden when only eleven, was a pupil of J. J. Scaliger, under whose supervision he edited Marcianus Capella and *The Phenomena* of Aratus.

In his fifteenth year he graduated, and in the year after he accompanied the Dutch Ambassador to France. Having sided with the party of the Remonstrants, Grotius was condemned to perpetual imprisonment by the opposite and successful party, but he escaped. Louis XIII granted him a pension, subsequently withdrawn. After several vicissitudes he went to Stockholm, entered the service of Queen Christina, and was appointed Ambassador to France in 1635.

His greatest work is *De Jure Belli et Pacis* (1625), on the fundamental principles of international law. He also wrote *Annales et Historiæ de Rebus Belgicis*, and *Annotations on the Old and New Testaments.*—Cf. C. Butler, *Life of Hugo Grotius.*

GROUCHY (grö'shē), **Emmanuel,** Marquis de, a noted French general, born at Paris, 1766, died in 1847. He entered the Royal Life Guards at the age of fourteen, saw much service, and highly distinguished himself. In the war with Prussia in 1806, and Russia (1807), and at Wagram, he acquired increased renown. In 1815 he defeated Blücher at Ligny. Having been ordered to follow the Prussian retreat, he was unable to aid Napoleon at Waterloo. He was banished under the second Restoration, and lived for a few years at Philadelphia. In 1821 he returned to France, where he died.

GROUND, in painting, is used in several different senses. (1) The material on which the painting is carried out, such as plaster, wood, canvas, or paper. (2) The preparation applied to this material to facilitate application of the paint, often known as *priming.* (3) The first layer of colour given to (2).

The Italian school preceding and during the time of Raphael employed white grounds, but afterwards, when canvas had superseded panels, the Italian and Spanish schools frequently adopted an oil ground of a dull-red colour. Velasquez is said to have used a black or dark-grey ground.

The Dutch and Flemish masters used light grounds varying from white to grey, and their example has generally been followed by English painters and those of the modern European schools.

GROUND-ANNUAL, in Scottish law, the rent paid for a piece of ground that is built upon, to one who holds the ground in feu. It may thus be a perpetual annuity. A vendor often prefers a ground-annual to a lump sum. It is similar to the English term *Ground-rent.*

GROUND DOVE, or **GROUND PIGEON,** a name of various species of pigeons (family Peristeridæ), which resemble game-birds and fowls in living mainly on the ground, their feet being better suited for walking than perching. They include: American mourning doves (Zenaidinæ), white-winged doves (Melopelia), and others (species of Chamæpelia); the Old World turtle-doves (Turturinæ); the Cape dove (*Æna capensis*) and African ground dove (*Chalcopelia afra*); and the Australian bronzewings (Phaps, Histriophaps, Geophaps, Ocyphaps, Lophophaps, and Chalcoptēra).

GROUND IVY, *Glecōma hederācèa,* a common British plant of the ord. Labiātæ, with a creeping stem and purple flowers. Tea made from it is used by the poor for pectoral complaints. It was formerly employed to flavour ale.

GROUND-NUT, a term which denotes the seeds or pods of the *Arăchis hypogœa,* or the tubers of certain umbellifers (earth-nuts). The *Arăchis hypogœa* is a leguminous annual of diffuse habit, with hairy stem, and abruptly pinnate leaflets. The nut or pod is situated at the end of a stalk of some length, and is ripened underground, this stalk having the peculiarity after flowering of bending down and pushing the fruit into the earth. The plant is extensively cultivated in tropical countries. The nuts have a flavour similar to almonds, and yield an oil that may be used for olive-oil. *See* EARTH-NUT.

GROUND-PINE (*Ajŭga Chamœpitys*), a herbaceous labiate plant, so called from its resinous smell. Also a name given to some lycopods or club-mosses.

GROUND-RENT, in English law, is the rent paid to a landowner by a person for the use of ground on which buildings are erected. The usual arrangement is for a specified time, generally ninety-nine years. On the expiry of this period the whole of the buildings become the property of the ground-landlord.

GROUNDSEL (*Senecio vulgāris*), a European weed belonging to the nat. ord. Compositæ. The plant is emollient, has a slightly acid taste, but is rejected by almost every quadruped except the hog and goat; small birds, especially cage-birds, however, are very fond of the seeds.

GROUND SQUIRREL, the name of North American squirrels of the genus Tamias, somewhat resembling the marmot. They differ from the common squirrel in possessing cheekpouches, and in retreating into burrows. The name is also given to some African forms (species of Xerus).

GROUPS, THEORY OF. This branch of mathematics is a modern development which was started by

E. Galois (1811–32). A group of operations has the property that if one operation of the group is applied to any one of an appropriate set of objects, it produces another of the set.

A simple example of a group is that of the substitutions of three elements or letters a, b, c, taken in order. Denoting by S the operation of changing abc into bca, we may write S. abc = bca. Hence S(S . abc) =S (bca) = cab. This may be written S^2 . abc = cab. Similarly S^3 . abc = abc. The last result may be denoted by S^3 = 1, which implies that the operation S applied three times in succession will reproduce the original object abc.

In this contracted notation, it is obvious that S^{3n+r} = S^r, where n and r are positive integers; and that any succession of such operations is equivalent to 1, S, or S^2. The inverse operation S^{-1} is defined by the identity S(S^{-1}) = 1, so that S^{-1} . abc = cab = S^2 . abc, or S^{-1} = S^2. It follows that an operation consisting of any combination of successively applied operations of the set 1, S, S^2 will be equivalent to one of these three. These three operations form a group of the third order, since the number of distinct operations in the group is 3. If the inverse of any operation in the group is not included in the group, it is not a group in the full sense of the term, and is called a semi-group.

Let T, U, V be the operations which respectively change abc into acb, cba, and bac. Then T(T . abc) = T . acb = abc. Therefore T^2 = 1. Similarly U^2 = 1, V^2 = 1. Also U(V . abc) = U(bac) = cab = S^2(abc), so that UV = S^2. Note that while UV = S^2, VU = S.

The operations 1, T, U, V, S, S^2 form a group of order 6. It includes one sub-group 1, S, S^2 of order 3, and three sub-groups 1, T; 1, U; and 1, V, each of order 2. This is one of the class of permutation-groups. Every group of finite order can be represented, generally in several ways, by a permutation-group.

A **transformation of co-ordinates** in geometry is an operation coming under the theory of groups. If, for example, rectangular axes in a plane are rotated through 360°/n, where n is integral, the operation S which denotes such a transformation is one of the group 1, S, S^2 . . . S^{n-1}, a cyclic group of order n, which will have as many sub-groups as there are primes between 1 and n. If the rotation takes place through $k \times 360°$, where k is incommensurable, the order of the group will be infinite.

A more general problem, considered by S. Lic, who founded and developed the theory of **continuous groups**, is that of changing every point of space into another point. A very special class of continuous groups is associated with the displacements of a rigid body in space. A more general class deals with Contact Transformations, which are such that a surface transforms into a surface.

The theory of groups has shed new light on many branches of mathematics, such as Theory of Equations, Invariants, Geometry, and Kinematics.—BIBLIOGRAPHY: W. Burnside, *Theory of Groups of Finite Order*; H. Hilton, *Finite Groups*; Miller, Blichfeldt, and Dickson, *Theory and Applications of Finite Groups*; J. E. Campbell, *Theory of Continuous Groups*.

GROUSE, the general name of the game-birds of the sub-family Tetraoninæ, whose distinguishing

Grouse
1, Ptarmigan (*Lagōpus mutus*). 2, Red grouse (*Lagōpus scoticus*). 3, Black grouse or black cock (*Lyrurus tetrix*)

mark is a naked band, often of a red colour, in place of an eyebrow. They are wild, shy, and almost untamable. They live in families, in forests and barren regions, and feed on berries, buds, and leaves. They are polygamous, the male abandoning the female, and leaving to her the whole care of the progeny. The eggs number eight to fourteen.

The largest species is the **capercailzie** or **wood grouse** (*Tetrao urogallus*). (*See* CAPERCAILZIE.) Other British species are the black grouse, the red grouse, commonly called simply the grouse, and the white grouse or ptarmigan.

The **black grouse** (*Lyrurus tetrix*) is about the size of a common fowl. The male has the outer feathers of the tail curved outwards, so that the tail is lyre-shaped. It chiefly lives in high and wooded situations, feeding on various kinds of berries. The female is commonly called *grey hen*, and the male *black cock*.

The grouse with hairy feet, which undergo seasonal change of plumage form the genus Lagōpus. Of these the **red grouse** (*Lagōpus scoticus*) is the most important. This bird, also called *moorfowl*, is the only bird peculiar to Britain, and is found in large numbers in the Highlands of Scotland, also in Wales, the north of England, Ireland, and the Scottish islands. It pairs in the spring; the female lays eight or ten eggs. As soon as the young have attained their full size they unite in flocks of forty or fifty, and are extremely shy and wild. This bird attracts large numbers of sportsmen every August to the Scottish moors to take part in the grand sporting campaign which follows 'the twelfth.'

The **ptarmigan** or **white grouse** (*Lagōpus mutus*) is ash-coloured in summer, but its hue changes to a pure white in winter. It is found in Scotland and in most northern regions, inhabiting the tops of mountains.

Among North American grouse the most remarkable is the **prairie-hen** (*Tympanuchus americanus*), which inhabits open desert plains in particular districts of the Union. The male is furnished with wing-like appendages to his neck, covering two loose, orange sacs, capable of being inflated. Related species are the lesser prairie-hen (*T. pallidicinctus*) and the nearly extinct heath-hen (*T. cupido*), only found in the island of Martha's Vineyard.

The **pine-grouse** (*Dendragapus obscurus*, *D. fuliginosus*, and *D. richardsoni*) are Rocky Mountain forms. To these may be added the **cock of the plains** (q.v.) or **sage-cock** (*Centrocercus urophasianus*), the **prairie-chicken** (*Pediœcetes phasianellus*), and the **Canada grouse** or **spruce partridge** (*Canachites canadensis*). *See also* HAZEL GROUSE; RUFFED GROUSE; SAND GROUSE; WILLOW GROUSE.—BIBLIOGRAPHY: F. O. Morris, *A History of British Birds*; J. G. Millais, *The Natural History of British Game Birds*; G. Malcolm and A. Maxwell, *Grouse and Grouse Moors*.

GROUSE DISEASE, an epidemic causing, at certain seasons, great destruction to the grouse species in Britain. It is caused by various intestinal parasites, and also by microscopic forms (parasitic Protozoa) that infest the tissues.

GROVE, Sir George, English writer, born 1820, died in 1900. He was educated as a civil engineer, in which capacity he was connected with the Britannia Bridge and other important works. He was long secretary to the Crystal Palace Company, and did much for the popularizing of classical music in connection with its concerts. For some years he edited *Macmillan's Magazine*, and he was editor of, and a contributor to, the great *Dictionary of Music*, published between 1878 and 1889. He was also an extensive contributor to *Smith's Dictionary of the Bible*. He was knighted in 1883. A new edition of Grove's *Dictionary of Music*, by Fuller-Maitland, appeared between 1904 and 1910.

GROVES. Among various ancient nations groves have been, probably on account of the mental impressions their stillness is calculated to make, considered as suitable localities for religious rites. The Hebrew word *asherah*, translated 'grove' in the Authorized Version of the Old Testament, seems to signify some idol or idolatrous symbol. In the religion of the ancient Greeks and Romans groves played an important part. (*See* DODONA.)

GROWLER (*Micropterus nigricans*), a fresh-water fish of North America, called also black-bass. It emits a growling sound. *See* (DRUM-FISH.)

GROZNY, or **GROSNYI**, a town of Transcaucasia, U.S.S.R. It has large petroleum refineries. Pop. 148,900.

GRUB STREET, a London street near Moorfields, famous at one time for its literary hacks, and described by Dr. Johnson in his *Dictionary* as follows: "Originally the name of a street near Moorfields, much inhabited by writers of small histories, dictionaries, and temporary poems, whence any mean production is called Grub Street."

The street, called Milton Street since 1830 (whether in honour of the poet or of one Milton, a builder, it is doubtful), was inhabited by less fortunate writers, and hence the jest of the more favoured authors. The expression Grub Street was used in a contemptuous and disparaging way by Andrew Marvell, Pope, Swift, Goldsmith, and Carlyle.

GRUGRU, the larva of the *Calandra palmarum*, or palm weevil, found in the tropical parts of America. It is of the length and thickness of a man's thumb, burrows in cabbage-palms and canes, and is, when cooked, a great delicacy.

GRÜNBERG (grün'berh), a town in Silesia, Germany, surrounded by vineyards. Pop. 24,898.

GRUNDY, Sydney, English dramatist, born in Manchester 23rd March, 1848, died 4th July, 1914. Educated at Owens College, he was called to the Bar in 1869, and practised till 1876. He then began to write for the stage, and became known as a successful playwright.

Among his numerous plays are: *A Fool's Paradise* (1890), *A White Lie* (1893), *Sowing the Wind* (1893), *The New Woman* (1894), *The Degenerates* (1899), *The Musketeers* (1899), *Business is Business* (1905), *A Fearful Joy* (1908), &c. Many of his plays were clever adaptations from the French, such as *The Bells of Haslemere*, and *A Pair of Spectacles*.

GRUYÈRES (grü-yär), a village, Switzerland, canton and 16 miles south of Fribourg, on a hill crowned by a fine old feudal castle. It gives its name to the well-known cheese made from a mixture of goats' and ewes' milk, which is firm and dry, and contains numerous holes. Pop. 1,700.

GRYSBOK (grīs'bok, 'grey buck'), *Raphiceros melanotis*, a species of antelope found in Southern Africa. It attains about 3 feet in length, is 1½ feet high at the shoulder, and its colour is reddish-grey. It is hunted for the sake of its flesh.

GUACHARO (gwä-chä'rō), *Steatornis caripensis*, a bird related to the goatsuckers, but belonging to a special family (Steatornithidæ). It is of nocturnal habits, and found in great numbers in certain caves of Venezuela, Guiana, Trinidad, Colombia, Ecuador, and Peru. It is about the size of a common fowl, with a curved and toothed bill, wings long and pointed.

Its food is principally fruits, upon which it grows so fat that the Indians destroy great numbers for the sake of their oil or clarified fat, which is transparent, inodorous, and keeps long without becoming rancid. It is also called **oil-bird**.

GUADALAJARA (gwà-dà-là-hā-rà), a town, Spain, capital of the province of same name, on the Henares, 33 miles north-east of Madrid. It is substantially built, with manufactures of woollens, soap, and earthenware. Pop. 16,053.—The province—area, 4,676 sq. miles—is mountainous, or forms part of an elevated plateau. Pop. (1931), 204,253.

GUADALAJARA, a city of Mexico, capital of the state of Jalisco, in the fruitful valley of Atemajac, on the Rio de Santiago; a large and handsome city, with a fine cathedral (being an archbishop's see), and other good buildings; a university and a mint. Various manufactures are carried on, as those of silversmiths' and goldsmiths'wares, paper, leather, hats, pottery, and cloth. Pop. (1930),150,000.

GUADALQUIVIR (gwà-dàl-kē-vẽr;

Ar. *Wad-el-Kebir*, great river), a river, Spain, which rises in the frontiers of Murcia, traverses Andalusia from north-east to south-west, passing the towns of Cordova and Seville, and, thereafter flowing south-south-west, falls into the Atlantic. Its course is 360 miles, of which 70 miles are navigable. It abounds in fish.

GUADELOUPE (gwä-dè-löp), a French colony, one of the French West Indies, Lesser Antilles, composed of two portions, separated by a narrow arm of the sea called Rivière Salée (salt river). The western and larger portion is Basse-Terre, or Guadeloupe Proper, 27 miles long by about 15 miles broad. The eastern portion, called Grande-Terre, is nearly 30 miles long by 10 to 12 miles broad.

Guadeloupe Proper is of volcanic formation, the culminating point being La Soufrière, 4,900 feet. Grand-Terre, on the other hand, is generally flat, and of coral formation. Guadeloupe is watered by a number of small streams which become dry in summer. Grande-Terre has only a few springs of brackish, undrinkable water.

The climate is hot and unhealthy, with a remarkably humid atmosphere, and hurricanes are frequent and destructive. The soil is fertile. The chief exports (amounting annually to about 80,000,000 francs) are sugar, coffee, dye and cabinet woods, pepper, manioc, and tobacco. The chief town is Basse-Terre, (pop. 9,268), the chief port, Pointe-à-Pitre (pop. 30,465).

Discovered by Columbus in 1493 the island was alternately in the possession of France and Great Britain, transferred to Sweden in 1813, and restored to France in 1814. Area of Guadeloupe, 532 sq. miles; with dependencies, 688 sq. miles. Pop. (1932), 267,407.

GUADIANA (gwà-di-ā'nà), a river of Spain, which rises in New Castile, flows first north-west, then south-west into Estremadura, and on reaching Badajoz begins to form part of the boundary between Spain and Portugal. Entering that kingdom, it finally falls into the Atlantic after a course of 510 miles, of which only 35 miles are navigable.

GUADIX (gwà-ēdh'), a town of Southern Spain, Andalusia, in the province and 31 miles E.N.E. of Granada. Pop. 16,500.

GUAD'UAS, a town, Republic of Colombia, remarkable as being one of the most elevated places on the globe, being 3,300 feet above the sea-level. Pop. 9,000.

GUAIACUM (gwī'a-kum), a genus of plants, belonging to the nat. ord.

Zygophyllaceæ, and containing four or five arborescent species, natives of the West Indies and the tropical parts of America. *G. officināle* has wood that is exceedingly hard, of a pale-yellow colour near the exterior, and blackish-brown at the heart, heavier than water, and well known under the name of *lignum-vitæ*.

This tree yields the resin known as guaiacum. Its chief use is in medicine, the resin (as well as a decoction of the bark and wood) acting as a stimulant in chronic rheumatism, and being used also in gout, scrofula, syphilis, and other diseases.

GUAM, the largest of the Ladrones Islands in the Pacific Ocean. It formerly belonged to Spain, but was ceded to the U.S.A. in 1898 and was turned into a naval base. The area of the island is 206 sq. miles, and the total population including the military establishment (1932), 19,673 of whom 18,297 were natives, chiefly Chamorros. Guam is wooded, well-watered, and healthy, and exports copra, maize, fruit, and timber. Agaña is the capital, and the chief port is Apra, which has a magnificent but entirely undeveloped natural harbour. Piti is the port of entry. The harbours of Guam are closed to all foreign ships. (*See* LADRONES.)

GU'AN, a gallinaceous bird of the family Cracidæ or Curassows, genera Penelŏpē, Penelopina, Ortālis, Pipile, Aburria, and Chamæpetes. The sides of the head and front of the throat are naked and wattled, the wattles capable of inflation. The name Guan is more particularly applied to the *Penelŏpē cristāta*, the largest bird of the genus, measuring about 30 inches. The guans perch on trees, descending in search of grain and fruits, and range from Central America to the Argentine. They have been frequently carried to Europe, and with a little care would make a valuable addition to the farmer's stock of poultry in Britain.

GUANACO (gwăn-ă'kō), or **HUANACO**, *Llama huanacos*, a South American ruminant, of which the domesticated races are the llama and alpaca. It abounds most in Chile and Patagonia, attains a height of nearly 4 feet at the shoulders, and is extremely swift and sure-footed. When domesticated, its flesh, wool, and milk are prized by the natives. In domestication it is of uncertain temper, and ejects saliva on those who annoy it.

GUANAJUATO (gwä-nä-*h*wä'tō), a city of Mexico, capital of the state of the same name, 160 miles north-west of Mexico, is situated in a narrow defile, hemmed in by mountains, at the height of 6,800 feet above the sea,

with steep irregular streets but well-built houses. Pop. 35,682.

The state is situated in the centre of Mexico; area, 10,950 sq. miles; population, 981,963. Its mines, once the richest in the world, still yield a large amount of gold and silver. The surface is traversed by the cordillera of Anahuac 9,711 feet in height.

GUANCHES (gụ-ăn'chez), or **GUANCHOS**, the aborigines of the Canary Islands, long ago extinct as a separate nation, although Guanche blood probably flows in the veins of many of the present inhabitants. They possessed high moral and physical qualities. They practised the embalming of the dead. The few words of their language which remain seem cognate to the Berber tongue. Their culture reveals unmistakable evidence of Egyptian and Mediterranean inspiration.

GUAN'O (Peru. *huanu*, dung), a valuable manure, consisting of the partially decomposed and dry excrement of fish-eating sea-birds, which has in some places accumulated in great masses. The name has been also extended to accumulations of a similar kind from land-birds, and even from bats in caverns.

Owing to the fact that rain washes such deposits away, great accumulations of guano exist principally in hot and dry tropical regions. The most important of all were the deposits on the Chincha Islands off the coast of Peru, which yielded a considerable revenue to the country, but are now quite exhausted.

From 1853 to 1872, when the guano industry was at its height, about 8,000,000 tons were got from these islands. The guano which was found there was from 60 to 80 or 100 feet in thickness, and was entirely due to the droppings, accumulated for many ages, of the innumerable sea-birds which make these islands their resting-place and breeding-ground. Other deposits of less extent have from time to time been found, and Peru still remains the chief source of supply, its deposits being now, however, worked under the Peruvian Government.

Guano varies extremely in composition, but it may be roughly divided into nitrogenous and phosphatic. The first of these contains about 21 per cent of ammonia. This is the case with the Peruvian variety, which contains almost all the inorganic matter required by a plant, and that in a highly available form, so that it is looked upon as one of the best of all fertilizing agents for different crops.

Its use as a manure was known to the native Peruvians centuries ago, but no attention was paid to the accounts by modern travellers of its wonderful efficacy until A. von Humboldt brought some to Europe and had it analysed. It began to be brought to Europe about 1846.

It is used raw or in its natural state, but most of the phosphatic guanos (some of which hardly deserve the name of guano) require to be dissolved by sulphuric acid before using. There are very rich deposits of phosphatic guano on Christmas Island, south of Java.

There are also manures known as fish guano, prepared from fish or fish refuse, flesh guano, blood guano, &c. Large quantities of fish guano are made in the United States from the menhaden.

GUAPORE (gwä-pō′rä), or **ITENEZ**, a river of South America, which rises in the Brazilian province of Matto Grosso, and, after a varied course of about 800 miles, unites with the Mamore in forming the Madeira.

GUARANA BREAD (gwä-rä′nä), the seeds of the *Paullinia sorbilis*, ord. Sapindaceæ, a South American tree, pounded and made into cakes. It is extensively used in South America as a stimulant and restorative, and as a material for making a refreshing beverage. The active principle of guarana is said to be identical with theine or caffeine; and no known substance yields it so abundantly. the amount being 5·07 per cent, as against good black tea, which yields from 2 to 4 per cent, and coffee about 1·5 per cent.

GUARANTEE′ (O.Fr. *garantie*, warrantry), in law, an undertaking by which a person binds himself to answer for the failure of another. In England no person is liable on any special promise to answer for the debt, default, or miscarriage of another person, unless a written agreement, or some memorandum in writing for such purpose, shall be signed by the promiser or some other party lawfully authorized by him. It is a general rule that the surety shall not be bound beyond the express words of the engagement.

GUARDAFUI, CAPE, the most easterly part of Africa. It is in Italian Somaliland at the entrance to the Gulf of Aden.

GUARDIAN, in law, is one whose duty it is to support and educate either out of his own funds or otherwise infants, that is, persons under 21 years of age. In England they may be said to be of the following kinds: first, testamentary or appointed by will; second, customary by local usage; third, *ad litem* or appointed by a court in order to conduct legal proceedings; fourth, by appointment of the High Court, County Court, or to a limited extent a court of summary jurisdiction.

Guardianship lasts in the case of the young until the age of 21, but a parent acting as guardian is not obliged to maintain a child after it has reached the age of 16. *See* PARENT. If the father dies without appointing a guardian the mother becomes sole guardian, and even if a guardian has been appointed the mother is entitled to become a guardian conjointly. The Guardianship of Infants Act, 1925, is designed to give both parents equal rights in the appointment of guardians, &c.

GUARDIANS OF THE POOR, in England, persons elected to manage the affairs of the poor. The guardians had the management of the workhouse, and the maintenance, clothing, and relief of the poor. They were abolished in 1929 and their duties transferred to Public Assistance Committees appointed by the county and county borough councils.

GUARDS, BRIGADE OF, consists of the five regiments of foot guards. These are, in order of precedence, the Grenadier Guards of three battalions, the Coldstream Guards of three, the Scots Guards of two, and the Irish and Welsh Guards of one battalion each.

The **Grenadier Guards** date their official origin to 23rd Nov., 1660, when Charles II, on his return to England at the Restoration, issued a commission to Colonel John Russell to raise a regiment of foot guards under the name of the King's Regiment of Foot Guards. Four years previously, during his period of exile, Charles had in his service, while in Flanders, a regiment which was known as the Royal Regiment of Guards.

After the Restoration, this regiment continued to be stationed on the Continent at Dunkirk till, on the sale of that place in 1665, it was brought to England and incorporated with the later-raised King's Regiment of Foot Guards. The Grenadier Guards wear a white plume in their bearskins and have a red cap-band. They have the buttons of their tunics evenly spaced in the ordinary way.

The **Coldstream Guards** trace their official connection with the royal army of England to 14th Feb., 1661, though the actual origin of the regiment goes back to 1649, in which year a regiment was formed for General Monck by taking five companies from each of two existing new model regiments.

On 1st Jan., 1660, Monck, who was then stationed in Coldstream with his regiment, and who was dissatisfied with the state of affairs in London, set out on his march southwards. On arrival in London in February he took charge of affairs, and on the return of Charles II Monck offered his services, which were accepted.

An order had been given that all the Republican regiments were to be disbanded; but, in order to retain Monck's regiment in the royal service, its formal disbandment was left to the last, and even then was a mere matter of form, the men, drawn up on parade, simply laying down their arms as Republican soldiers and taking them up again as soldiers of the king. The Coldstreams wear a red plume and a white cap-band, and have the buttons of their tunics spaced in twos.

The Scots Guards were first raised in Scotland by Charles I in 1642 as Argyle's Regiment, becoming under Charles II the regiment of Scottish Foot Guards (on the Scottish establishment). In 1686 the regiment was brought on to the English establishment, one battalion serving at Windsor in 1695. In 1831 the regiment was known as the Scots Fusilier Guards, and received its present designation in 1877. The Scots Guards wear no plume and have a checked cap-band. They wear their buttons in threes.

The Irish Guards were formed in 1900 to commemorate the bravery of Irish regiments in the South African War. They wear a blue plume and green cap-band. Their tunic buttons are spread in two groups of four.

The Welsh Guards were raised by royal warrant on 26th Feb., 1915, a nucleus of some 300 men being found by other guards regiments.

All guards regiments have the distinction of company colours bearing separate royal badges, which are carried in turn on the regimental colours.

GUARD-SHIP, a vessel of war appointed to superintend the marine affairs in a harbour, and to visit every night the ships of war which are not commissioned; she also acts as a depot for seamen raised in the port until appropriated to other vessels.

GUARINI (gwà-rē'nē), **Giovanni Battista**, Italian poet, was born at Ferrara 1537, and died at Venice in 1612. After having studied at Ferrara, Pisa, and Padua, and lectured in his native city on Aristotle, he entered the service of Duke Alphonso II of Ferrara, who sent him on various important missions. Having lost the favour of the prince, he retired into private life, but was recalled in 1585 to the office of Secretary of State. Two years after he retired a second time.

In 1597 he entered the service of Ferdinand I, Grand-Duke of Tuscany, which he soon quitted. His propensity to litigiousness necessitated his residence at Venice, Padua, and Rome. In 1605 he went as an ambassador of his native city to the court of Rome, to congratulate Paul V on his elevation.

Guarini is one of the most famous authors of Italy, as is especially shown in his *Il Pastor Fido* (Faithful Shepherd), a pastoral drama. The work has gone through numerous editions, been translated into various European languages, and influenced Calderon and Shelley.

GUARNIERI (gwàr-nā'rē), the name of an Italian family belonging to Cremona, distinguished for its skill in violin-making. The most celebrated of the family was Giuseppe, whose best instruments belong to the years 1710-45.

GUASTALLA (gwàs-tàl'là), a small town of North Italy, near the Po, which in the sixteenth century gave its name to the dominion of the Gonzagas, Dukes of Mantua. Pop. 11,500.

GUATEMALA (gwà-te-mä'là), a republic of Central America; area estimated at 42,353 sq. miles; pop. 2,004,900.

Physical Features. It is in general exceedingly picturesque, and distinguished by a luxuriant and varied vegetation. It is wholly mountainous or elevated, the main chain of the Central American system traversing it south-east to north-west, and sending off numerous branches. Along the main chain are a considerable number of volcanoes, several of which are said to be active—as Fuego and Agua (12,139 feet high), which sends forth torrents of water.

The state is well watered by numerous streams, none of much importance. There are several lakes, the most important being Dulce, through which a great part of the foreign trade of the state is carried on; Amatitlan, Atitlan, and Peten. On the tableland, of which a considerable portion of the state is formed, the climate is mild; but in more elevated situations the cold is intense.

Production and Industry. There is much valuable timber. The soil generally is of great fertility, producing, according to altitude and soil, maize, wheat, rice, coffee, cotton, tobacco, sugar, cochineal, cacao, indigo, vegetables, and tropical fruits in great variety. Fibre plants are numerous, including ramie, henequen, and others.

The most important product is coffee, and the other chief exports are skins, caoutchouc, cochineal, and wool. Gold, silver, and lead are mined, and there are great but almost unexploited oil resources. The exports in 1931 were about 15,167,386 dollars in value (nine-tenths being coffee). The revenue in 1931 was 10,226,191 dollars, the expenditure 12,376,569 dollars; the total debt in 1932 was 17,481,149 dollars, including English debt amounting to £1,540,860.

In the *altos* or mountainous parts of the north-west considerable flocks of sheep are raised, the wool of which is manufactured into coarse fabrics. But the manufacturing industries are very insignificant, and trade is hindered by the want of roads and railways, the total length of the latter being only about 691 miles; in 1930 the first national electric railway in Central America was completed connecting Quezaltenango and San Felipe.

Only about a third of the population are of European or mixed descent, the rest being Indians of the Aztec, Toltec, or Maya races, mostly speaking their own native tongue. Numbers of the Indians are still quite uncivilized.

Education, &c. Great attention is now being paid to education, the children, even Indians, in small and remote villages being compelled to attend school. The University of Guatemala (Universidad Estrada Cabrera) was re-established in 1928. The chief port is San José on the Pacific; Champerico on the Pacific, and Livingston in the Bay of Honduras are the other ports.

Constitution and Government. The legislative power is vested in a National Assembly, elected for four years by universal suffrage, and a Council of State of seven members, three elected by the National Assembly and four appointed by the President. The executive is vested in a President, elected for six years, according to the Constitutional Charter of 1928.

New Guatemala, or Santiago de Guatemala, the capital, was situated about 5,000 feet above the sea, and 80 miles distant from the Pacific. Regularly built, with a fine cathedral, archbishop's palace, a university, and manufactures of textiles, cigars, pottery, saddlery, and embroidery, the city was completely destroyed by an earthquake on 3rd and 4th Jan., 1917. Pop. 165,928.—**Old Guatemala,** the former capital, is 10 miles southwest of New Guatemala. It was founded by the Spanish in 1542, and continued to be the capital till 1774, when it was destroyed by a volcanic outbreak. It has been rebuilt, however, and the population is now

about 10,000.—BIBLIOGRAPHY: N. O. Winter, *Guatemala and her People of To-day*; D Fife, *Guatemala and the States of Central America*.

GUAVA (gwä'va), the popular name for plants of the tropical genus Psidium of the nat. ord. Myrtaceæ: *P. Guaiava* (the guava tree) is a small tree, with square branches, egg-shaped leaves, and large white axillary flowers, which are succeeded by fleshy berries, which are either apple or pear shaped in the two principal varieties. The pulp is of an agreeable flavour, and of this fruit is made a delicious and well-known jelly. There is also a product called guava cheese.

GUAYAQUIL (gwī-ȧ-kēl'), a city and seaport in Ecuador, on the Guayaquil, here about 2 miles wide,

White Guava. Flowers, Foliage and Fruit

some 40 miles above its mouth in the Gulf of Guayaquil. Behind the town is an extensive marsh, which renders it unhealthy, causing fever. It is the seat of a bishop, and has a cathedral and a university. It is the chief port of Ecuador, and one of the best on the west coast of South America. Its principal exports are cacao (to the value sometimes of £1,000,000), coffee, and ivory-nuts. Pop. (1932), 120,000.

GUBBIO (gub'i-ō; ancient IGUVIUM), a town in Italy, in the province of Umbria. It is a bishop's see, and has manufactures of silk and woollen stuffs. Here were discovered the Eugubine Tables (q.v.) in 1444. Pop. 30,500.

GUBEN, a town in Prussia, province of Brandenburg. Brewing, dyeing, and tanning are carried on, and there are manufactures of woollen and linen cloth, and tobacco. Pop. 40,636.

GUBERNATIS, Count Angelo de, Italian Orientalist, man of letters, and critic, born at Turin 7th April, 1840, died 26th Feb., 1913. At the age of seventeen he contributed to several periodicals and wrote plays. In 1862 he went to Berlin, where he studied Sanskrit, and in 1863 he was appointed professor of Sanskrit at Florence. Drawn by Bakunin into the Republican party, he resigned his post and married a cousin of the Russian revolutionary. In 1867 he was re-elected to the professorship, and in 1891 he was called to the University of Rome. Gubernatis founded and carried on many periodicals, and through his efforts the Indian Museum at Florence was established. His numerous works include: *La Morte di Catone*, a drama (1863); *Il re Nala*, an Indian play (1869); *Gabriele*, a novel (1866). His fame, however, as a scholar he owes to the following works: *Zoological Mythology* (London 1872), *Mitologia Vedica* (1874), *Mythologie des Plantes* (1878–80), and *Storia Universale della Letteratura* (1882–5).

He also wrote: *Dictionnaire international des écrivains du jour* (1888–91), *Alessandro Manzoni* (1878), *La Donna Italiana* (1891), and *La Hongrie politique et sociale* (1885).

GUDGEON (*Gobio fluviatilis*), a freshwater fish, belonging to the carp family (Cyprinidæ). It has short dorsal and anal fins, without spines; on each side of the mouth there is a small barbel; neither jaw is furnished with teeth, but, at the entrance of the throat, there are two triangular bones that perform the office of grinders. These fish are taken in gentle streams, and measure only about 6 inches. They are common in England, Wales, and Ireland, and range through Europe to Siberia and Mongolia.

GUDRUN (gud'run), a celebrated German popular epic belonging to the end of the twelfth century, receiving its name from its heroine, Gudrun, daughter of King Hettel of Hegelingen. Hettel is defeated by Hartmut, son of King Louis of Normandy, who carries Gudrun off, and, on her steadfast refusal to marry him, has her subjected to various kinds of ill-treatment, and in particular lets his mother keep her for years engaged in the lowest kinds of drudgery. At last she is released and avenged by her brother and her betrothed, King Herwig of Seeland.

The poem also deals with the fortunes of Gudrun's father and mother, grandfather and grandmother, and the scene is partly in North Germany, Denmark, and Friesland, partly in Ireland and Normandy.—BIBLIOGRAPHY: F. E. Sandbach, *The Nibelungenlied and Gudrun in England and America*: A Fécamp, *Le Poème de Gudrun: ses origines, sa formation et son histoire*.

GUEBRES, or **GUEBERS** (gē'bĕrz), a name given to the fire-worshippers of Persia, represented in India by the Parsees. The original Guebres or followers of Zoroaster are now represented almost solely by those who inhabit the cities of Yezd and Kirman and the adjoining villages. At present they number only about 8,000 or 10,000.

As supreme deity they recognize Ahuramazda, or Ormuzd, the principle of light and source of all that is good; and his opposite and antagonist, the evil principle, the latter called Ahriman. They believe in the existence of heaven and hell, between which stretches the Bridge of the Gatherer or Judge; over this none but the righteous may pass.

Among their leading practices may be mentioned their refusal to contract marriages with those of other creeds; their objection to eating beef or pork, or to partake of anything cooked by one of another religion. They regard Ahuramazda as the source of light, and in their temples they feed the altars with perpetual fire, and hence their name fire-worshippers; but they do not revere it except as a symbol of the deity.

When, in A.D. 651, Yezdegird, the last of the Sassanides, was defeated by the Caliph Omar, the majority of the Persians embraced Islam. Those who continued Zoroastrians received the name of Guebres or infidels, and were subjected to persecutions so severe that the majority emigrated to India, where they became known as Parsees. —Cf. E. B. Tylor, *Primitive Culture*.

GUEDALLA, Philip, British author. Born March 12, 1889, he was educated at Rugby and Balliol College, Oxford, where he was President of the Union. He became a barrister and was legal adviser to certain government departments during the Great War. He won a reputation by his historical writings, notably the *Partition of Europe*, 1715–1815, 1914, and *The Second Empire*, 1922, and increased it by his sketches and essays, such as those in the volumes, *Supers and Supermen*, 1920, and *A Gallery*, 1924, and by his biography of Lord Palmerston, 1926. In 1931 his life of the Duke of Wellington appeared.

GUELDER ROSE, or **GUELDRES ROSE**, a name given to the cultivated variety of the *Viburnum Opulus*, or water elder, of the ord. Caprifoliaceæ. On account of the shape and colour of its flowers it is sometimes called the Snowball Tree. Its fruit is of a pretty red colour.

GUELFS, or **GUELPHS,** the name of a distinguished princely family which originated in Germany, but was also at one time connected with Italy, and which still flourishes in the two lines of the House of Brunswick, the royal (to which the four Georges and Victoria belonged) and the ducal. The first who bore the name is said to have been Welf, the son of Isenbrand, whose grandfather was a vassal of Charlemagne. *See* BRUNSWICK, FAMILY OF.

GUELFS (or **GUELPHS**) and **GHIBELLINES,** the names of two great Italian political parties in the thirteenth and fourteenth centuries. The names are derived from the Italian *Guelfi* and *Ghibellini*, which are corrupted from the German *Welfen* and *Waiblingen*. These latter words came to be used as party designations in Germany in the war between Henry the Proud and Conrad of Hohenstaufen, to whom belonged the estate of Waiblingen in Würtemberg.

About the year 1200 the designations Guelf and Ghibelline came to be employed to denote respectively the Italian patriotic and Papal party, and the party which supported the domination of the German emperors in Italy.

After the fall of the Hohenstaufen the Ghibellines became the partisans of aristocracy, and the Guelfs the partisans of democracy and liberty; but the designations ultimately denoted more communal and family feuds, and Dante, originally a Guelf, but subsequently a Ghibelline, asserted that the two parties were the cause of all the miseries of Italy.

The contest continued with bitterness for almost 300 years. Bologna, Florence, and Milan were Guelf, whilst Arezzo, Pisa, and Verona were Ghibelline. The poet Petrarch was a Guelf. Corresponding parties appeared in Italy under many different names, as the *bianchi* and *neri* (white and black) in Florence.—Cf. J. A. Symonds, *The Renaissance in Italy.*

GUELPH, a city of Canada, province of Ontario, in a rich farming district, 45 miles W. of Toronto by rail, with manufactures of machinery, agricultural implements, and pianos. It is the seat of the Ontario Agricultural College. Pop. 21,075.

GUENEVERE, or **GUINEVERE** (Guanhumara; W. *Gwenhwyfar*), daughter of King Leodograunce of Camelyard, and wife of King Arthur. She is a famous figure in the Arthurian romances, is supposed to have been the most beautiful of women, "surpassing in beauty all the women of the island," and to have fallen in love with Lancelot of the Lake, one of the Knights of the Round Table.

In Geoffrey of Monmouth's *History of Britain* she is a Roman lady of noble birth, and married Modred, King Arthur's nephew, during the king's absence. Arthur defeated Modred, and Guenevere fled from York to a nunnery. According to Layamon, she drowned herself. The story of Guenevere has also been treated by Malory, and by Tennyson in the *Idylls of the King.*—Cf. Professor Rhys, *Studies on the Arthurian Legend.*

GUEREZA, or **GUERZA** (ger'e-za, ger'za; Colŏbus), the popular name of about ten species of African monkeys,

Guereza (*Colobus guereza*)

remarkable for their beauty, and with a much reduced thumb. Short, glossy jet-black fur covers their limbs, back and head, while a long fringe of silky white hair depends from the flanks. They are arboreal in habit.

GUERICKE (ger'ik-e), **Otto von,** German physicist, born at Magdeburg (of which he became burgomaster or mayor) 1602, died at Hamburg 1686. About 1650 he invented the air-pump (q.v.), with which he made public experiments at the Diet at Ratisbon, before the Emperor Ferdinand III. His most important observations, collected by himself, appeared at Amsterdam in folio (in 1672) under the title *De Vacuo Spatio.*

GUÉRIN (gā-ran), **Pierre Narcisse, Baron,** French historical painter, born at Paris 1774, died at Rome 1833. He achieved great success with classical subjects such as *Death of Cato of Utica, Return of Marcus Sextus, Phædra and Hippolytus, Andromache, Clytemnestra.*

GUERNSEY (gẽrn'zi), the second largest and most westerly of the Channel Islands, lying off the north coast of France, 46 miles from Cherbourg, and about 68 miles from Start Point in Devonshire. It is of a triangular form, about 9 miles long, and 3 to 4 miles broad. The northern part is level, the southern more elevated, coast lofty and abrupt, the island being almost entirely of granite formation.

The climate is extremely healthy; snow is rare, and frosts light and of short continuance. The soil is fertile. The breeding of cattle and the dairy are the principal objects of attention; and the butter made is highly esteemed.

Horticulture and floriculture also receive much attention, and fruit, especially figs and grapes (the latter grown under glass), is very abundant. The grape-houses are further utilized for the raising of early vegetables and tomatoes, which are sent to the London market. The principal exports are cattle (the dairy cows being renowned), fruits, vegetables in the early spring, and granite for paving.

The dialect of the island is the pure Norman of some centuries ago; but a knowledge of English is general. The principal place of education is Elizabeth College, at St. Peter's Port, the capital, and only town in the island. Steamers ply regularly between Guernsey and London, Southampton, Plymouth, and Weymouth. The island is under a Lieutenant-Governor, who represents the sovereign in the Assembly of the States, a kind of local parliament. It is strongly fortified, and has a well-organized militia. Area (with Herm and Jethou), 16,018 acres; pop. (1931), 42,606.

GUERNSEY LILY (*Nerine Sarniensis*), a beautiful plant, with purplered flowers, native of South Africa, family Amaryllidaceæ, so called from some of its bulbs being cast up in Guernsey from a wrecked ship and there taking root. There are several other species also called Guernsey lilies.

GUERRERO (ger-rā'rō), a state of Mexico; area, 25,279 sq. miles. Its surface is finely diversified by mountain and valley, and partly covered by native forests; and it is rich in minerals, including gold, silver, copper, and iron. The capital is Chilpancingo, and the principal port Acapulco. Pop. (1930). 637,530, mostly Indians.

GUERRILLAS (ge-ril'az, in Spanish ge-ril-yàs) a name first given in Spain to light, irregular troops, consisting chiefly of peasants, who fought against the invading French in the early part of the last century. The name has now become quite a general term for such irregular troops, and has travelled far beyond Spain.

GUESDE, Jules Basile, French Socialist leader, born in Paris 11th Nov., 1845. A journalist by profession, he founded in 1870 a paper, *Les Droits de l'homme*, in which he defended the Commune, and was imprisoned and exiled like so many other Communards. He lived for some time in Germany, where he became an adherent of Karl Marx and an admirer of the Social Democratic party.

Guesde was always an opponent of opportunism, and maintained that no Socialist should take office in a capitalist or bourgeois Cabinet. Thanks to his efforts the United Socialist party in France was created, in consequence of which such Socialists as Millerand, Briand, and Viviani left the ranks of socialism.

In spite, however, of his stern, uncompromising Marxist tendencies, Guesde did not hesitate, when the European War broke out, to enter Viviani's Cabinet in 1914 as Minister without portfolio. He denounced Germany as the enemy of peace, and the German Socialists as traitors to the idea of socialism. He died in 1922. —Cf. S. P. Orth, *Socialism and Democracy in Europe.*

GUEST, Sir Josiah John, Welsh ironmaster. Born 2nd Feb., 1785, at Dowlais, Glamorganshire, he was the grandson of John Guest, founder of the Dowlais Iron Works. Of these works he became manager in 1815 and made them the largest of their kind in Great Britain. He was M.P. for Honiton, 1826–31 and for Merthyr Tydvil, 1832–52, and was made a baronet in 1838. He died 26th Nov., 1852. His eldest son was made Baron Wimborne, and one of his grandsons, **Frederick Edward Guest** (b. 1875), is a soldier and politician. The Dowlais Iron Works now belong to the firm of Guest, Keen and Nettlefolds.

Sir Josiah Guest married **Lady Charlotte,** daughter of the Earl of Lindsey. She published the collection of Welsh tales called *The Mabinogion*. She married a second time, and died 15th Jan., 1895.

GUEUX (geu; Fr. 'beggars'), a name given in derision to the allied nobles and other malcontents in the Netherlands who resisted the despotism of Philip II in 1566–7. The Count of Berlaymont having termed the malcontents *Gueux*, they adopted the name, and a suitable badge called the 'beggar's denier.' They were totally dispersed in 1567.

A branch of the Gueux, 'the beggars of the sea,' under the leadership of Count de la Marck, captured Brill in 1572, and initiated the great struggle for independence which resulted in the freedom of the Netherlands in 1648.

GUEVARA Y DUEÑAS (gā-vā′rä ē dų-en′yås), **Luis Velez de,** a Spanish dramatic poet, born in 1570, died 1644. His literary fame rests chiefly on his *Diablo Cojuelo* (Lame Devil), which suggested the famous *Diable Boiteux* of Le Sage.

GUGLIELMI (gųl-yel′mē), **Pietro,** Italian composer, born 1727, died 1804. He composed comic and heroic operas for the Italian theatre, visited Vienna, Madrid, and London, and afterwards returned to Naples, where he became the rival of Paesiello. In 1793 Pius VI named him chapel-master of St. Peter's. He left more than 200 pieces, remarkable for their simple and beautiful airs, their rich harmony, and their spirit and originality.

GUIANA (gī-an′a), **BRITISH,** a colony in the north of South America, about 560 miles long, and about 200 miles broad, having on the E. Dutch Guiana, W. Venezuela and Brazil, N. and N.E. the Atlantic, and S. Brazil; area, 89,480 sq. miles. It is divided into three settlements—Berbice, Demerara, and Essequibo.

Physical Features. The coast tract forms a dreary belt, 10 to 40 miles broad, of mud-banks and shallows, and when drained the surface sinks 1 foot below the sea-level, hence strict attention must be paid to dams and sluices. This alluvial deposit is succeeded by a range of low hills not exceeding 200 feet in height.

The interior is traversed in various directions by chains of hills or mountains. On the western boundary is the singular flat-topped and almost inaccessible mountain Roraima, rising to a height of 8,635, feet. The other principal ranges are the Sierra Imataca, in the north part of the country; the Cannucu or Conocou, and the Sierra Acarai—the last occuping the extreme S.E. corner of the territory, forming its boundary in this direction. They are densely wooded, but do not reach a greater elevation than 4,000 feet.

The geological composition of the mountains of British Guiana is various. Some of them consist of granite, gneiss, and trap rocks, and their different modifications; others are of sandstone; and others again appear to be of white quartz. Gold occurs in various places, and mining commenced in 1884, the output from 1884 to 1931 being valued at £9,849,083. There are also deposits of manganese ore and mica, and huge deposits of bauxite, which were examined in 1919. Diamonds are mined to the annual value of over £1,000,000. From 1901–31 the value of the diamonds amounted to £7,362,033; in 1931 £105,257; and white clay is found in the Essequibo. The flats along the shore are composed of alluvial soil and clays, resting upon granite. The chief rivers are the Essequibo, Demerara, Berbice, and Corentyn.

Flora and Fauna. The climate, though moist and warm, is not on the whole unhealthy. Cultivation is confined to the coast region; the soil is very fertile, and much of it well adapted for the sugar-cane, the cultivation of which is mostly carried on by Indian and Chinese coolies. Guiana also produces coffee, tobacco, and indigo. Vegetation is singularly luxuriant, and the forest trees are of the most magnificent description. Fruits, medicinal plants, fibrous vegetables, and dyeing woods abound. The flora includes the *Victoria Regia,* the largest of the water-lilies. Among the animals are the jaguar, tapir, armadillo, sloth, vampire bat, and alligator, and many species of birds, such as humming-birds and parrots. Snakes, some of them venomous, and troublesome insects are numerous.

Climate. Guiana has two dry and two wet seasons, each continuing for three months: December, January, February, June, July, and August constitute the wet season, the other months of the year the dry. The mean annual temperature is nearly 81° 2′. Violent thunderstorms occur at the change of the seasons; but the hurricanes so destructive in the West Indies are unknown. In the dry seasons the climate is agreeable, and in the interior more healthy than in many parts of the West Indies.

Trade. The trade is concentrated mainly in Georgetown, the capital. Sugar, rum, molasses, balata, drugs, bauxite, and gold are the principal exports. The value of exports in 1931 was £2,010,462, and the value of imports was £1,595,205. About half of the imports come from Britain.

Legislation. The Government consists of a Governor, an Executive Council, and a Legislative Council. The Legislative Council consists of the Governor as President, ten official members, and nineteen unofficial members. Executive and administrative functions are in the hands of the Governor and Executive Council.

Justice and Education. The Roman Dutch law is generally in force in civil cases, while the criminal law is based on that of Britain. There are a number of schools aided by Government, also estate schools for the instruction of children of immigrant labourers.

History. Guiana was first visited by the Spaniards about 1500, and settled by the Dutch about 1580. It was taken by the British in 1781, but restored to the Dutch in 1783. Similarly, it was taken again in 1796, restored by the Peace of Amiens in 1802, retaken by the British in 1803, and definitely given up to them in 1815. Boundary disputes with Venezuela and Brazil were settled by arbitration respectively in 1899 and 1904. Pop. (1911), 296,000; estimated pop. in 1931, 318,312, of whom 7,379 are of African race or coolies from India.—

Guido Reni

BIBLIOGRAPHY: G. D. Bayley, *Handbook of British Guiana*; J. Rodway, *Guiana, British, French, and Dutch*.

GUIANA, DUTCH, or SURINAM, a Dutch colony in South America, situated between British and French Guiana; area 54,291 sq. miles. The general aspect is the same as that of British Guiana—flat and swampy on the coast, and mountainous in the interior; well watered by numerous streams, of which the Surinam and its affluents are the chief. It has also a similarly warm, moist climate, and is very fertile. Only a small part of the colony is under cultivation.

On the Surinam River, about 10 miles from its mouth, is situated the capital, Paramaribo. The principal exports are sugar, coffee, molasses, and rum. There is a weekly air service between Paramaribo and the United States. Since 1930 Para-

maribo has been a regular stop on the United States to Buenos Aires route. The government is vested in the Governor-General and the Council, nominated by the Queen of the Netherlands. Pop. (1931), 155,888.

GUIANA, FRENCH, a French colony in South America, between Dutch Guiana and Brazil; area about 34,740 sq. miles. This territory resembles British Guiana in its physical features, climate, and vegetable productions, with the addition, among the last-named, of pepper, cloves, cinnamon, and nutmeg. The colony comprises the Island of Cayenne, celebrated for the pepper bearing that name. Gold has also been found in considerable quantities. Cayenne, the chief town, has a wireless station; also a penal settlement. The French are said to have first settled in Cayenne in 1604. Pop. (1931), 22,169.

GUICCIARDINI (gwē-chår-dē'nē), **Francesco,** Italian historian, born at Florence 1483, died 1540. He became professor of jurisprudence at Florence, and held various public appointments. He began in 1534 his famous history of Italy—*Dell' Istoria d'Italia*—which embraces the period 1490–1534. It has been translated into English.

GUIDO ARETINO (gwē'dō á-re-tē'no), or **GUIDO d' AREZZO,** an Italian monk, celebrated for his skill in music, flourished in the eleventh century. He was a native of Arezzo, became a Benedictine monk, and finally prior of Avellana, where he died (1050). He invented the musical staff of lines and spaces (or at least systematized their use), and he introduced the names of the first six notes of the scale, *ut, re, mi, fa, sol, la.* He has explained his musical doctrines in his works *Micrologus* and *Argumentum Novi Cantus Inveniendi.*

GUIDO RENI (gwē'dō rā'nē), Italian painter, born at Calvenzano in 1575, died at Bologna 1642. Being the son of a musician, he devoted some time to the study of music, but, as painting seemed his true vocation, he was placed under the tuition of Dionysius Calvaert, and subsequently joined, in his twentieth year, the school of the Caracci in Bologna. In 1602 he visited Rome, where he studied Raphael and the antique, and having seen the paintings of Caravaggio, he imitated his style.

At the request of Cardinal Borghese he painted *The Crucifixion of St. Peter* and the *Aurora.* He was also employed by Paul V to paint a chapel on Monte Cavallo, and one in Santa Maria Maggiore. Having quarrelled with Cardinal Spinola, the treasurer of Urban VIII, he left Rome and returned to Bologna, but was subsequently recalled. In 1622 he removed to Naples, but, after a brief stay, returned once more to Bologna, never to leave it again. He lived there in princely style, and died heavily in debt.

Guido's paintings fall into three groups. His earliest pictures, under the influence of Caravaggio and the Caracci, display powerful contrasts of light and shade. In his second manner bright colour plays a greater part. His third period is marked by careless haste

Among his best-known works may be mentioned *Aurora, S. Mary Magdalene, Michael vanquishing Satan, Lot and his Daughters, Fortune,* and *Ecce Homo.* Guido was also celebrated in his own day for his etchings, the style of which was freely imitated.

GUIENNE, or **GUYENNE** (gē-en'), an ancient province of France, now comprising the departments of Gironde, Lot, Lot-et-Garonne, Dordogne, and Aveyron, with part of Landes and of Tarn-et-Garonne. The capital was Bordeaux. It fell into the hands of the English in 1152, was nearly all conquered by Charles V in 1377, reconquered by Henry V and Henry VI, and finally annexed to France in 1453.

GUIGNET'S GREEN (gē-nyā), a pigment prepared by heating in a reverberatory furnace a mixture of three parts of boracic acid and one of bichromate of potassium, made into a thick paste with water. This colour is quite fixed—it does not alter by light or reagents—and it is quite harmless, so that it forms an excellent substitute for the greens which contain arsenic and copper.

GUILBERT, Yvette, French lyric artiste. Born in Paris in 1869, she worked for a dressmaker and on a newspaper. In 1893 she appeared on the stage in Paris, and was for many years the chief French actress in her own line. She appeared in London and other capitals, and passed some time in the United States. She has written two novels, volumes of autobiography and a book on how to sing a song, which has been translated into English. In private life she is the wife of Dr. M. Schiller.

GUILD, a society or association for carrying on commerce, a handicraft, or some other undertaking. Such associations are known from very early times in various countries. The societies of tradesmen exclusively authorized to practise their art, and governed by laws of their own, played a very important part in the Middle Ages. They often formed a bulwark against the oppression of the nobility, and were thus extremely conducive to the growth of municipal and civil liberty.

Traces of these trade societies are found in the tenth century. In Milan we find the mechanics united under the name *credentia.* At Florence the trades were federated into twenty-one guilds or *arti.* These originated in 1282, on the overthrow of the nobility, and every candidate for citizenship was obliged to enter some particular guild. Such a step became a necessity at a period in which individual rights, as such, failed to secure respect.

The purely Teutonic guilds, although connected with the constitution of the cities, possessed certain peculiarities. In the thirteenth century the German guilds of craftsmen obtained the right of defending by arms their own interests, and became so powerful that persons unconnected with a trade were often glad to attach themselves to them.

As illustrations of the manner in which associations originally instituted for defensive purposes became the mainstay of a tyrannical monopoly may be mentioned the frequent withholding of permission from more than a certain number of master mechanics to reside in one place, the restrictions placed upon particular branches of industry, and upon the free exercise, by each individual, of his trade except under the sanction of the guilds.

With the view of destroying the political influence which they had acquired, the Emperor Frederick II abolished them by a decree issued in 1240; but the decree remained without effect, as did also the clauses inserted with a similar view into the Golden Bull in 1356, and it was not until the last century that unrestricted freedom to practise any trade was established in the German states. In Austria this was done in 1860, and in 1868 it was done for all the states of the North German Confederation.

In Britain trade guilds long possessed an importance which was mainly political. As the right of voting was involved in the membership of a guild, many persons, not mechanics, acquired the rights of 'freemen' by connecting themselves with some body of this kind.

These guilds, in England, had no legal right to prevent any man from exercising what trade he pleased. The only restriction on the exercise of trades was the statute of Elizabeth, requiring seven years' apprenticeship. This the courts held to extend to such trades only as were in being at the time of the passing of that statute; but by an Act passed in 1835, every kind of restriction on artisans and trades was abolished.

The guilds or companies of the City of London (among the oldest of which are the weavers, founded in 1164; the parish clerks, in 1232; the saddlers, in 1280; the fishmongers, in 1284) are still very important corporations, which give relief to poor members, and also manage vast funds bequeathed for benevolent purposes.

Besides the secular guilds there were from a very early period, in Britain, religious guilds. From the time of Henry II all such guilds were required to have a charter from the Crown. In 1388 a return of these guilds was ordered to be made, and it was then found that that of Corpus Christi, York, numbered 14,800 members. The property of the religious guilds was sequestrated in the reign of Henry VIII.

In France guild-privileges were sold by the state from the tenth century till the revolution of 1789, but at that date guilds were entirely abolished. This was done also at a later period in Belgium, Holland, Italy, Sweden, and Denmark.—BIBLIOGRAPHY: Seligman, *Mediæval Guilds*; J. C. Thornley and W. L. Hastings, *Guilds of the City of London*; F. Armitage, *The Old Guilds of England.*

GUILDFORD, a municipal borough of England, the county town of Surrey, on the Wey, a well-built and thriving place. In 1928 it was made the seat of a bishop, and a new cathedral has been planned. It has an iron-foundry, corn-, paper-, and powder-mills, and an important grain market. The town has extensive caves which have been lit and opened to the public. It now gives name to one of the seven parliamentary divisions of the county. Pop. (1931), 30,753.

GUILDHALL, the city hall of London, Cheapside, first built in 1411, all but consumed in the great fire of 1666, and rebuilt in 1669. The front was not erected until 1789. The most remarkable room is the Great Hall, 153 feet long, 48 feet broad, and 55 feet high, used for city feasts. It contains the curious wooden statues of Gog and Magog. In the common council room is a collection of pictures (Guildhall Art Gallery, founded in 1885), some of them valuable. There is also a library in the Guildhall.

GUILD SOCIALISM, a theory for a Socialist reconstruction of society, based on communal ownership of the means of production, distribution, and exchange, the functions of administration and direction being vested in trade unions, which are to comprehend the whole of the workers in the industry concerned.

The theory is an attempt to reconcile the crude conception of worker's control (q.v.) of industry set out in syndicalism with the existence of some form of central state authority, but the numerous writers on guild socialism have had difficulty in describing the nature of the central economic authority in their new scheme of things, and of the way in which the relations between the different *guilds*, as the organized industries are to be called, will be regulated.

The intellectual origin of the movement was a strong reaction against state socialism, based on fear of the results of the concentration of the whole of the directive power of society in one authority, accompanied by a realization that the original theory of syndicalism, that each industry should simply be owned and directed by the workers in it, left room for great inequalities between the workers in different industries.

Accordingly, it is proposed that society shall be organized on a dual basis, the present state in a modified and limited form continuing as the representative of the interests of the inhabitants as 'consumers,' while the parallel industrial organization of guilds, centralized in a 'Guilds' Congress,' assumes responsibility for their interests as 'producers.'

The point at which the theory is incomplete, and on which there is much divergence of view among guild socialists, is the relation between these two authorities. The driving force of the movement is a desire to carry into industrial life the movement towards democratic control which was the feature of political life of the nineteenth century, and its

Guillemot (*Uria troile*)

importance lies in the fact that it is the most convincing expression that has so far appeared of the aspirations of the workers to control their own lives, not only as citizens of a political state, but also as units in industry.

It is to the credit of the movement that it has not been confined purely to theory and that a serious attempt is now being made to apply its principles in the building industry, in which a number of 'Building Guilds' have been formed in different localities, and have succeeded in building houses economically and efficiently.—BIBLIOGRAPHY: Cole, *Guild Socialism*; Orage, *National Guilds*.

GUILLEMOT (gil'e-mot), a name of several web-footed birds belonging to the family Alcidæ or auks. The guillemots have a straight, compressed, and pointed bill, covered with feathers as far as the nostrils, and have no hallux or hind-toe. The wings are pointed and very short, the legs also short, and placed far back. They live on fish, and build on precipitous rocks adjoining the sea.

The common guillemot (*Uria troile*), about 18 inches in length, is frequently found in Britain, and lays one egg; the black guillemot (*Cepphus grylle*) is smaller, and lays two or three eggs.

GUILLOTINE (gil-lo-tēn'), an engine for beheading persons at one stroke—an invention of the Middle Ages—adopted with improvements by the National Assembly of France during the first Revolution on the proposal of a Dr. Guillotine, after whom it is named. It was first used in Paris, at the Place de Grève, on 25th April, 1792.

In this apparatus decapitation is effected by means of a steel blade loaded with a mass of lead, and sliding between two upright posts, grooved on their inner sides, the person's neck being confined in a circular opening between two planks, the upper one of which also slides up or down.

The condemned is strapped to a board, which is able conveniently to rest horizontally on the table in front of the upright posts, but which is easily drawn forward and set upright when necessary, and again canted over upon the table and rapidly moved up so as to place the neck of the condemned within the semicircle of the lower plank, the other being raised for the purpose. On the right of the table is a large basket or trough of wicker-work for the reception of the body. Under the place where the head rests is an oblong trough for its reception.

The knife is fixed to the cap or lintel on the top of the posts by a claw in the form of an 8, the lower part of which opens as the upper part closes. This claw is acted upon by a lever to which a cord is attached. When the

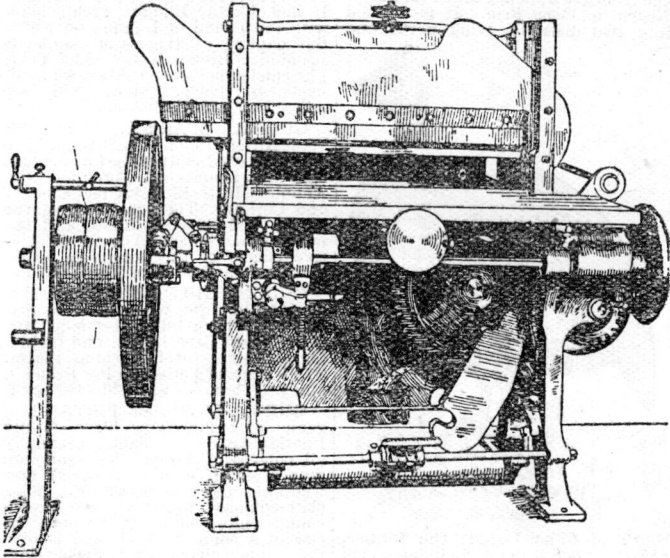

Guillotine for Cutting Paper

head of the condemned is in position, the cord is pulled, and by the action of the lever the knife is set at liberty, descending by the grooves in the upright posts and falling upon the neck of the condemned just behind the planks which keep the head in position. The scaffold, which is surrounded by an open railing, is raised 6 or 7 feet from the ground.

GUINEA (gin'ē), a geographical division of Western Africa, including the Atlantic coastline and an indefinite area of the interior between the frontiers of Senegambia and Cape Negro, or Cape Frio. It is divided into two districts, lying north and

Guinea-fowl

south of Cape Lopez: the former, called Upper Guinea, includes Sierra Leone, Liberia, the Grain, Ivory, Gold, and Slave coasts, and parts of Nigeria; the latter, called Lower Guinea, includes part of French Congo and Angola. See AFRICA, and the separate articles.

GUINEA, an English gold coin worth 21s. sterling. Guineas were first coined, in the reign of Charles II (1663), of gold from Guinea, and bore the figure of an elephant. Its value ranged at different times from 20s. up to 30s., until, in 1717, it was fixed at 21s. It was last coined in 1813, and in 1817 the coin was withdrawn from circulation.

GUINEA, FRENCH, a French colony in West Africa, lying between Portuguese Guinea and Sierra Leone. The area is 89,436 sq. miles and the

population (1931), 2,236,968, including 2,270 Europeans. The principal products are palm-oil and -nuts, rubber, rice, gum, earth-nuts, bananas, and gold. The capital (Conakry) is connected by a railway 366 miles long with Kourassa on the Niger. This line has been extended about 46 miles to Kankan. There is a wireless station at Conakry. See FRENCH WEST AFRICA.

GUINEA, PORTUGUESE, a Portuguese West African colony, on the coast of Senegambia. It is surrounded on the land side by French territory. It includes the Bijagoz Archipelago, with the Island of Bolama on which the capital of the same name is situated. Bissau is the chief port. The chief exports are rubber, wax, oil, seeds, and ivory. Area, 13,944 sq. miles; pop. (1930), 364,929.

GUINEA, SPANISH, a Spanish West African Colony consisting of Rio Muni, situated south of the Cameroons, and the Islands of Fernando Po, Annobon, Little Elobey, Great Elobey, and Corisco. The total area of the colony is 10,036 sq. miles, and the population 140,000. The administrative centre of the colony is Santa Isabel on the Island of Fernando Po.

GUINEA, GULF OF, that portion of the Atlantic which washes the shores of Upper Guinea, between Cape Palmas and Cape Lopez, and including the bights of Benin and Biafra. The islands of Fernando Po, Prince's, and St. Thomas are within this gulf.

GUINEA-FOWL, or PINTADO, a genus of gallinaceous birds, family Phasianidæ or pheasants, originally all natives of Africa. The common guinea-fowl (Numĭda meleagris), now well known as a domestic fowl, has a slate-coloured plumage varied with round white spots. It is about the size of a common fowl, and is of a noisy and quarrelsome disposition. Its eggs are good eating.

Among the other species of guinea-fowl may be mentioned the Numĭda vulturina (or Acryllium vulturinum) of Zanzibar, by far the most beautiful, with somewhat vulturine head and neck; the red-crowned Numĭda mitrāta, found in Madagascar; and the Numĭda cristāta of West Africa.

GUINEA-GRASS (Panĭcum maximum), a very tall species of grass, a native of Africa, of the same genus as the millet, often 6 feet, and sometimes even 10 feet in height. It has been naturalized in South America and the West Indies, and largely cultivated for fodder.

GUINEA PEPPER (Xylopia aromatica), a lofty tree of the same family as the custard apple. Its fruit, consisting of dry carpels, is used as pepper, 'Negro Pepper.' The term Guinea Pepper is often used as an equivalent for *Grains of Paradise*, or Malaguetta. It is also a common designation of *Capsicum frutescens*. See CAPSICUM.

GUINEA-PIG (*Cavia porcellus*), a well-known rodent mammal, family Caviidæ or Cavies. The name is probably a corruption of 'Guiana' pig. It is a native of South America (like the other cavies), and resembles the pig only in its grunting. It is a timid little animal, extremely prolific, and it feeds on vegetables (especially parsley), bread, and grain. It is not an intelligent animal.

GUINEA-WORM (*Filaria medinensis*), a parasitic worm of the ord. Nematoda, white, of the thickness of pack-thread, somewhat attenuated at the hook-shaped posterior extremity. It varies in length from 6 inches to several feet. It is frequently found in the tissue of the human body below the skin, and produces a painful ulcer.

GUIPUZCOA (gē-pụth′ko-à), one of the three Basque provinces, in the N.E. of Spain, bounded N. by the Bay of Biscay; N.E. by France; area, 728 sq. miles. The chief riches of the province are in its minerals, particularly iron, and its woods, which are used in smelting it. San Sebastian is the capital. Pop. (1931), 306,686.

GUISBOROUGH (giz′bu-rō), a town in England, in the county of York (North Riding), situated in a valley 9 miles S.E. of Middlesbrough. Cast-steel founding is carried on. The town has ruins of a priory. Pop. (1931), 6,306.

GUISCARD (gis-kär), Robert (that is, *Robert the Cunning*), Duke of Apulia and Calabria, a son of Tancred de Hauteville, born in 1015, died in

Guinea-pig

1085. His brothers having acquired large possessions in Italy, Robert followed them about 1053, and in the same year captured Pope Leo IX at Civitella. On the death of his brother Humphrey he was proclaimed Count of Apulia in 1057. He then conquered Calabria, and the Pope Nicholas II made him gonfalonier of the Church. Having become a tributary of the

Holy See, and suppressed the privileges of the Apulian nobility, he sent his youngest brother, Roger, to seize Sicily. Robert himself arrived in Sicily in 1061, and, in conjunction with his brother, defeated the Saracens at Enna. Returning to Italy, Robert

Charles of Guise, Cardinal of Lorraine

conquered the towns still remaining in the hands of the Saracens, being detained from 1068 to 1071 at the siege of Bari. In 1074 he was excommunicated by Gregory VII for refusing to become his vassal, but the ban was removed in 1080.

As his daughter Helen was betrothed to the son of the Byzantine emperor, Michael VII, Guiscard, on the latter's deposition, took up arms in his favour, and defeated Alexis Comnenus at Durazzo (1082). As Gregory VII had been meanwhile imprisoned by the invading forces of Henry IV of Germany, Guiscard delivered the Pontiff in 1084.

He then went again to Epirus, where he repeatedly defeated the Greeks, and, by means of his fleet, made himself master of many of the islands of the Archipelago. He was upon the point of advancing against Constantinople, when he died in the island of Cephalonia.

GUISE (gwēz), a distinguished ducal family of France, a branch of the House of Lorraine. The founder was Claude, a son of René II, Duke of Lorraine, who in 1506 became naturalized in France. In his favour the county of Guise was erected in 1528 by Francis I into a duchy. He died in 1550, leaving behind him five daughters (the eldest of whom, Marie, married James V of Scotland, and was the mother of Mary, Queen of Scots) and six sons—François, who succeeded him, Charles (Cardinal of Lorraine), Louis (Cardinal of Guise), Claude, François, and René.

The family acquired great political importance on the accession of Francis II, who was married to Mary, Queen of Scots. The direct line became extinct in 1675. In 1704 the title was revived for the House of Condé.

Two of the dukes require particular mention.—**François de Lorraine,** the second duke, born in 1519, early distinguished himself in war, especially at Metz, which he defended with success against Charles V, and at the battle of Renti, 1544. In his Italian expedition (1556–7) he failed to conquer the Kingdom of Naples. But he was successful in that which resulted

Guitars
Modern   French seventeenth century

in the final annexation of Calais to France. Under Henry II and Francis II he was the virtual ruler of France.

On the death of Francis II the factions of Condé and Guise arose, the Protestants (Huguenots) being on the side of the former, the Catholics on that of the latter. When civil war broke out, the Duke of Guise took Rouen and Bourges, and won the battle of Dreux in 1562. He was preparing for the siege of Orleans, the central point of the Protestant party, when he was assassinated by a Huguenot nobleman, Feb., 1563. He left *Memoirs* written by himself.—**Henry,** third duke, eldest son of the preceding, was born in 1550. He was a bitter opponent of the Huguenots, and fought against them at Jarnac and Moncontour, and advised the massacre of St. Bartholomew (1572).

To avenge himself he personally conducted the assassins to the house of Coligny.

In 1576 was formed the Catholic League, first projected by his uncle, the Cardinal of Lorraine. A period of civil war followed; the party of Guise proved too strong for his opponents, and having brought about a rising of the Catholics in Paris (May, 1588), he entered the city in triumph.

He might now have made himself master of the throne, but negotiations were set on foot, and the duke's displays of imprudent ambition led to his assassination in the king's Cabinet, 23rd Dec., 1588, at Blois, whither the estates-general had been summoned in order finally to ratify the treaty that had been arranged.—BIBLIOGRAPHY: H. Forneron, *Les Guise et leur époque*; R. de Bouillé, *Histoire des ducs de Guise.*

GUISE (gwēz), a town of France, department of Aisne, beautifully situated on the left bank of the Oise. It has manufactures of textiles, iron- and copper-foundries, &c., and a large work for making stoves, connected with which is an edifice in which live some 400 families of the working people. It is an ancient city, and its castle gave its title to the distinguished family of that name. Captured by the Germans in 1914, the town was recovered by the Allies in Oct., 1918. Pop. 7,370.

GUISELEY, urban district of Yorkshire (W.R.). It is 2 miles from Otley, on the L.M.S. Rly., and the woollen industry is the main occupation of the inhabitants. Pop. (1931), 5,607.

GUITAR (gi-tär′), a stringed instrument with a hollow body, and a neck somewhat similar to that of a violin, used especially to accompany the voice. The modern or Spanish guitar has six strings, the three highest of gut, the three lowest of silk covered with fine wire, tuned respectively to the E in the second space of the bass staff, A its fourth, and the treble D, C, B, and E. The intermediate intervals are produced by bringing the strings, by the pressure of the fingers of the left hand, into contact with the frets fixed on the keyboard, while those of the right pluck or twitch the strings. It is extremely popular in Spain. The Spaniards derived it from the Moors, who brought it from the East.

GUITRY, Lucien Germain, French actor. Born in Paris in 1860, he first appeared on the stage in *La Dame aux Camélias*, 1878. Then, after some years in S. Petersburg, he returned to Paris where he was a producer at the Comédie Française and manager of the Renaissance Theatre. He was the foremost French actor of his time. His wife was the actress Yvonné Printemps. He died June 1, 1925.

His son Sacha was born at S. Petersburg, Feb. 21, 1885, and made a name both as actor and as dramatist. Among his successful plays are *Le Page*, *Nono*, *La Clef*, *Deburau*, *Jacqueline* and *Mozart*.

GUIZOT (gē-zō), **François-Pierre-Guillaume**, French historian and statesman, born at Nîmes 1787, died 1874. His father, a lawyer, having been guillotined in 1794, his mother and her three sons retired to Geneva, where François was gratuitously educated at the gymnasium. In 1805 he commenced legal studies at Paris, but gradually drifted into the literary profession. In 1812 he married Mlle de Meulan, and in the same year became professor of history at the Sorbonne.

On the fall of the empire he obtained several public offices, such as Councillor of State, and director-general of the departmental and communal administration. In 1816 he published *Du Gouvernement représentatif et de l'état actuel de la France*, and *Essai sur l'instruction publique*. In 1820 the Duc de Berry was assassinated, and Guizot's party fell before an ultra-royalist reaction. In 1825 he was deprived of his chair on account of the political character of his lectures, but it was restored to him in 1828.

In 1829 he again became Councillor of State, and in 1830 was elected Deputy for the arrondissement of Lisieux. After the July revolution he was appointed Minister of the Interior, but resigned in 1831.

After the death of Périer, Guizot, along with Thiers and de Broglie, formed a coalition ministry, and he rendered great service as Minister of Public Instruction. He became Ambassador at the British court in 1840, and next year he became the real head of the Government of which Soult was the nominal chief. He retained the office of Minister of Foreign Affairs until 1848, and during that period opposed all measures of reform. After the fall of Louis Philippe, Guizot escaped and fled to England. Henceforth he practically retired from public life.

Born of a Calvinist family, Guizot always remained a stern Protestant of the orthodox type, although he zealously supported the temporal authority of the Pope.

Among his numerous works may be mentioned: *Histoire de la civilisation en France*, *Histoire générale de la civilisation en Europe*, *Histoire de la révolution d'Angleterre*, *Washington*, *Discours sur la révolution d'Angleterre*; *Méditations et études morales*, *Guillaume le Conquérant*, *Mémoires pour servir à l'histoire de mon temps* (1858–68), *Méditations sur l'état actuel de la réligion chrétienne*, *Mélanges biographiques et littéraires*, and *Histoire de France racontée à mes petits-enfants*. BIBLIOGRAPHY: Jules Simon, *Thiers*, *Guizot et Rémusat*; G. Bardoux, *Guizot* (in Les Grands Écrivains Français Series).

GUJARAT, GUJERAT, or GUZERAT, a maritime province in Western India, Presidency of Bombay; total area, 70,038 sq. miles; pop. 11,000,000. The south-west portion is an extensive peninsula, with the Gulf of Kach (Cutch) on the north-west side, and the Gulf of Cambay on the south-east. The central districts form an extensive plain, but the northern and eastern districts are mountainous, rugged, and jungly. The rivers include the Narbada, Myhe, and Sabarnati.

The climate is very hot in summer, and during the hot months the surface mostly appears sand or dust, and in the rainy season a thick mire; but it is extremely fertile.

Gujerat comprises a number of native states within its area, the chief being the scattered territories of the Gaekwar or Guicowar of Baroda. The population presents an extraordinary assemblage of sects and castes. It gives names to the vernacular language of Northern Bombay—Gujarati, spoken by about 10,682,000 persons.

The area of the British portion, comprising the districts of Surat, Broach, Kaira, Panch Mahals, and Ahmedabad, is 13,579 sq. miles, and the pop. 3,718,000. The battle of Gujarat, between the British and the Sikhs, was fought on 21st Feb., 1849.

GUJRANWÁLA, a town of India, in the Punjab, administrative headquarters of the district of the same name. It has inconsiderable manufactures of country wares, such as brass vessels. Pop. 37,887.—Area of district, 4,082 sq miles. Pop. 923,420.

GUJRÁT, a district of India in the lieutenant-governorship of the Punjab, in the Rawál Pindi division, between the Jehlam and the Chenab. Pop. 750,548.

Gujrat, the capital, 5 miles from the Chenab, is a commercial centre. Its manufactures are principally of cotton and of Gujrát ware, that is, inlaid work in gold and iron. Pop. 19,350.

GULBAR'GA, a town of India, in the state of Hyderabad. Pop. 35,820.

GULDBERG, Cato Maximilian, a Norwegian mathematician and physicist, born at Christiania, 1836, died 1902. He was the eldest son of Carl August Guldberg, a clergyman. He was educated in the Royal Norwegian

University at Christiania, and subsequently studied in France, Switzerland, and Germany. In 1869 he was appointed professor of applied mathematics in the Royal University, a position which he held until his death.

He devoted himself from his student days to the study of chemical dynamics. At the age of twenty-eight he contributed a paper (in association with Professor Waage), on the Law of Mass Action, to the Society of Science in Christiania. This was followed by a second paper in 1867 entitled *Etudes sur les affinités chimiques*, and by a third paper in 1879, in which the theory of Mass Action was given in its final form. He

Gulls.—Lesser black-backed gull (*Larus fuscus*). Black-headed gull (*Larus ridibundus*) flying

contributed many papers to learned societies on physical chemistry.

GULDEN, a silver coin of the Netherlands, having a par value of 1s. 8d. sterling. It is also called a **guilder** or **florin**.

GULEDGARH, or **GULEDGUD,** a town of India, in the Kaládji district, Bombay Presidency. Pop. 16,500.

GULF STREAM, one of the most celebrated of the oceanic currents, so called because it issues from the Gulf of Mexico. It owes its origin to the fact that the westward-moving waters of the tropical portion of the Atlantic, encountering the eastward projection of South America, become divided into two currents, one setting southwards along the Brazilian coast, and the other northward, past the mouths of the Amazon and Orinoco, into the

Caribbean Sea. It then enters the Gulf of Mexico, and thence emerges through the Channel of Florida as the Gulf Stream.

Its course is next to the north and eastwards, in a direction parallel to the coast of the United States, past Cape Hatteras (lat. 35° 13′), along the southern edge of the 'great banks' of Nantucket and Newfoundland (between the meridians of 48° and 60° west), after which its course as a distinct current cannot be traced.

In the earlier part of its course, especially when rounding the extremity of Florida, the Gulf Stream forms a well-defined current, distinguished by its high temperature and its deep blue or indigo colour. On account of the descent of the Polar or Baffin Bay current along the coast in a direction opposite to that of the Gulf Stream, the water on its inland side is colder than that to the eastward of it. The difference of temperature between the Gulf Stream and this cold current sometimes amount to 20° (or even 30°) F.

The velocity of the Gulf Stream varies with its course. Within the Florida Channel it attains a mean of 65 miles per day; this sinks to 56 miles off Charleston, becomes 36 miles to 46 miles off Nantucket, and 28 miles to the south of the Newfoundland Banks; 300 miles to the eastward of Newfoundland its movement is hardly perceptible. At the bottom of the Florida Channel the observed temperature is 34°, that of the surface from 80° to 84°.

Geographers have greatly exaggerated the influence of the Gulf Stream on the temperature of Europe. If it possesses any *direct* influence, such must be extremely small, as the current is both too narrow and too shallow, and its slight amount of superior heat probably vanishes after it has passed Cape Hatteras. The relatively high temperature of Western and North-Western Europe must rather be referred to the general set of the tropical waters to the north-east, and to the warm winds blowing in the same direction, and not to the Gulf Stream exclusively.—Cf. W. Ferrel, *Winds of the Globe*.

GULF-WEED (Sargassum), a genus of seaweeds (Algæ), sub-ord. Fucaceæ, of which one species, *S. Bacciférum*, grows on tropical coasts, and accumulates in great floating beds, but does not propagate when detached. It derives its ordinary name from the exploded idea that it is borne on the Gulf Stream from the Gulf of Mexico. Several areas of the ocean exhibit great quantities of this and other weeds floating on the surface. One such, the Sargasso Sea, is in the North Atlantic, lying south-west of the Azores, and north of the Tropic of Cancer.

GULL (W. *gwylan*, Bret. *goelann*, gull), the general name of a sub-family (Larinæ) of birds distinguished by their straight bill, bending downwards towards the point, and marked below the under mandible by a triangular prominence, by their large wings, slender legs, palmated feet, and small hind-toe.

Generally seen in large flocks, the larger species frequent the sea, the small lakes or rivers. They swim well, but are incapable of diving. Their flight is rapid and long sustained. They are extremely voracious, and feed on every kind of animal food, putrid or fresh. Their principal food is fish, which they catch with great agility, darting down like an arrow. They breed only once a year, laying two to four eggs.

The species are exceedingly numerous, and resemble each other greatly. Among the principal are the common gull (*Larus canus*), which breeds on the coast, or inland in moory districts; the lesser black-backed gull (*L. fascus*); the black-headed gull (*L. ridibundus*), of which the masked gull (*L. capistrātus*) is only a variety; the Iceland gull (*L. leucopterus*), distinguished by its white quill feathers from the herring gull (*L. argentatus*); the great black-backed gull (*L. marinus*; the little gull (*L. minutus*); Sabine's gull (*Xema sabinii*); the kittiwake (*Rissa tridactyla*); the ivory gull (*Pagophila eburnea*).

GULLANE, watering place of East Lothian, or Haddingtonshire. It stands on Gullane Bay, part of the Firth of Forth, and is 18¼ miles from Edinburgh, on the L.N.E. Rly. Gullane figures in R. L. Stevenson's *Catriona*. Pop. 1,441.

GUM, a substance of various properties which exudes spontaneously from the bark of certain trees, such as the plum or the peach; or from incisions made in the bark to facilitate the flow. Gums form non-crystalline rounded drops or tears, the purest varieties being transparent or translucent, of a pale-yellow but sometimes of a dark colour.

When dissolved in water, gum forms a thick, smooth fluid, with considerable viscosity. Some gums, such as gum-arabic, dissolve in water; others, like tragacanth, are only partially soluble; they are insoluble in alcohol. By being insoluble in alcohol gums are distinguished from resins. They have no odour, and only a very faint taste.

The different kinds of gum receive their names from the countries from which they are imported—such as gum-arabic, gum-senegal, Barbary gum, and East India gum, and from individual features, as cherry-tree gum and tragacanth. *Gum-resins* require water and alcohol to dissolve them. *See* GUM-RESINS.

GUM-ARABIC is the purest form of gum, and may be regarded as typical. It comes from various species of Acacia, such as the *Acacia vera*, *A. seyal*, and *A. arabica* or *nilotica* (see ACACIA). The gum exudes spontaneously, and its appearance is an indication of the tree being in an unhealthy condition; but in order to get it in sufficient quantity incisions are made in the bark.

Gum-arabic is very largely employed in the finishing and dressing of fabrics; for thickening the colours in calico-printing; in pharmacy; as a cement; in ink-making; for making crayons and water-colour cakes, and for many other purposes. The purest gum-arabic is in round tears, transparent, and almost colourless, faintly odorous, completely soluble in water, the solution being feebly acid.

GUMBIN'NEN, a German town, province of East Prussia, on the Pissa. It has brewing and distilling industries, and manufactures of woollen and linen cloth. During the European War severe fighting took place in the district of Gumbinnen, which was invaded by the Russians. Pop. 19,002.

GUMBOIL, an abscess in the gum, generally the result of toothache or of the presence of decayed teeth or stumps. The carious tooth or stump, if the inflammation proceeds from this cause, should be removed. The purulent matter should be evacuated by a free incision, and the mouth frequently washed with tincture of myrrh and water.

GUMMING, a disease of certain fruit-trees, as cherries, plums, apricots, and peaches, consisting in a morbid exudation of gum, and generally resulting in the death of the tree.

GUM-RESINS, solidified juices obtained from plants. They contain a gum, which is soluble in water, and a resin, which dissolves in spirit, so that the body usually is nearly quite soluble in dilute alcohol; but there are usually present in addition essential oil, and a variety of impurities. The gum-resins have frequently a strong and characteristic taste and smell. They are solid, opaque, and brittle. The common gum-resins are aloes, ammoniacum, asafœtida, bdellium, galbanum, gamboge, myrrh, olibanum, opoponax, sagapenum, and scammony.

GUMTI, or **GOOMTI,** a river of India, has its course in the United Provinces, and flowing south-east falls into the Ganges between Ghazipur and Benares. In its course it passes the cities of Lucknow and Jaunpur. Length about 500 miles.

GUN, a fire-arm from which projectiles are discharged by means of an explosion of gunpowder controlled by the firer. (*See also* CANNON for the use of the word in that connection; and MACHINE-GUN; PISTOL). The earliest form of portable fire-arm was known as a 'hand-gun,' and was merely a plain metal tube attached to a straight piece of wood; this wood or stock was passed under the arm-pit, where it was held in position by pressure, and the charge was ignited by the simple method of putting a match or taper to the powder by way of the touch-hole left for the purpose in the closed end of the tube or barrel.

Match-Lock. As in course of time, the quality of powder improved and mechanical knowledge increased, an adaptation of this very primitive method was invented by which the necessary match was affixed to a 'cock' or hammer, and, by the action of a trigger mechanism, was brought down to a pan containing powder (the priming pan) connected with the main charge through a small hole into the barrel. This contrivance was known as the 'match-lock,' and remained in general use till the seventeenth century.

Wheel-Lock. In the meanwhile experiments had been made with a view to the abolition of the match, which resulted in the production of the 'wheel-lock.' In this form of gun the priming pan was made of steel, and the cock took the form of a serrated wheel which was rotated against the priming pan by a mechanical device, and was supposed to produce sparks by which the priming powder would be fired.

Flint-Lock. The invention, however, proved unsatisfactory, and the match-lock retained its position till it was supplanted in the middle of the seventeenth century by the 'flint-lock.' In this gun the cock was provided with screw jaws into which a prepared flint was fitted. The cock or hammer was then released by a trigger-operated spring, and, falling with considerable force on the steel priming pan, ignited the powder therein, and so the charge.

Percussion Gun. For sporting purposes the flint-lock in its turn gave place to the percussion gun, in which the barrel was fitted with a small hollow nipple on which was placed a cap containing a fulminating material which, on being struck by the hammer, exploded the charge in the barrel.

All these guns were, of course, muzzle-loaders, and their form was practically the same, whether they were used for military or sporting purposes, or for shot or ball; sporting guns were generally known as fowling-pieces, and were rather more ornate and carefully made than were the muskets provided for military use.

Breech-Loaders. About the middle of the nineteenth century, assisted by the invention of the fulminating material referred to above, breech-loaders were beginning to come into use. For the sporting gun, or rifle, the method adopted (and still in use) was to have the barrel and stock in separate pieces. The barrel was attached to the forepart of the stock by a species of hinge, and, by the application of certain mechanism, could be broken or opened downwards; the stock was provided with a false breech—to close the open breech of the barrel—and contained the firing mechanism.

The first guns of this kind were known as pin-fire guns; that is to say, the cartridge containing the charge was provided with a pin which, when the cartridge was placed in the chamber or breech and the gun was closed and locked, fitted into a recess left for the purpose, and projected above the barrel. The hammer was then released, and, striking the pin, drove it downwards on to the cap of fulminating material contained in the base of the cartridge and exploded it.

This system was later improved by the elimination of the projecting pin on the cartridge, and the substitution of a firing-pin in the false breech on the stock, which was so arranged as to strike a cap in the centre of the cartridge base when operated on by the hammer. This form was known as the central-fire gun.

In modern guns the hammer disappears entirely, and all the firing mechanism is contained inside the false breech, only the triggers appearing outside. All such guns are fitted with a safety device by which the firing mechanism can be put out of gear till required. The action of closing the gun after loading cocks or makes the gun ready for firing without any further action, so some such safety device is very necessary. *See* RIFLE.—BIBLIOGRAPHY: F. Grose, *Military Antiquities*; T. F. Fremantle, *Book of the Rifle*; Lord Walsingham and Sir R. Payne-Gallwey, Bart., *Shooting* (Badminton Library); *Encyclopedia of Sport*.

GUNBOAT, a term applied to small war-vessels mounting often only a single heavy gun, and employed in coast defence or in attacking large and heavy-armoured vessels. Some gunboats have their one gun on the deck mounted so as to be turned in any direction by means of a pivot.

In others the single gun is placed on a platform, which can be raised to the deck or lowered to the hold. The gun in this case does not turn on a pivot, the manœuvring being effected entirely by the turning of the vessel.

Some of the gunboats of the present day are armed with several powerful breech-loading guns besides quick-firing and machine-guns; and they may also be fitted for discharging torpedoes. Many of them are very swift.

GUN-CARRIAGE, the structure on which an artillery weapon is mounted and on which it is fired. Ancient weapons were rigidly attached to the gun-carriage, with the result that on the shock of discharge the whole carriage ran back, and the weapon had to be relaid after each round fired.

A modern gun-carriage must stand steady on firing. The gun itself recoils through a cradle on the carriage, so that in the first place it requires no running up, and in the second place it maintains the direction and elevation of the gun, so that only a very slight correction, if any, is necessary after each round. Modern field-gun carriages are so steady that a full glass of water can remain on the wheel during firing without spilling a drop.

Provision must be made in modern gun-carriages for (1) checking the recoil; (2) running up the gun again to the firing position after recoil; (3) giving the necessary elevation to the gun; (4) traversing, i.e. giving the necessary direction to the gun. In the case of field mountings, the gun and carriage are mounted on two wheels, and are generally united for travelling with a two-wheeled fore-part called the *limber*, to which the horses are attached, so forming a four-wheeled vehicle. In the case of heavy field-pieces, the limber and horses may sometimes be replaced by some form of mechanical tractor.

In action the gun is unlimbered, and the weight of gun and carriage is taken on the axle between its pair of wheels, and on a strong support, called the *trail*, stretching backwards and downwards from the axle. The carriage is maintained in position by the friction of the brakes on the wheels, and by a *spade* which is fixed to the rear end of the trail, and which bites into the ground on firing.

The shock of discharge is taken up by one or more *buffers* interposed between the gun and the carriage. The gun is allowed to recoil several feet through a *cradle* fixed to the carriage, the buffer taking up much of the shock and communicating the rest gradually to the carriage, so that, instead of a violent jerk, there is a steady graduated pull.

The buffer consists of a cylinder and piston. The gun on recoil draws this piston through the cylinder, thereby further compressing compressed air or steel springs, and forcing oil in the cylinder to flow from one side of the piston head to the other through small regulated ports. After firing, the gun is run up through the cradle of the carriage to the firing position again by the compressed air or springs reasserting themselves as soon as the shock of discharge is over.

Elevation is generally given by means of a telescopic elevating screw under the breech end of the cradle, or by a toothed arc attached to the cradle, and gearing into a pinion on the carriage.

Traversing gear consists of an endless screw gearing into a toothed arc at the rear of the upper carriage. In field mountings the cradle and elevating gear may be mounted on an upper carriage pivoted vertically to the axle, or the whole carriage may be made to move along the axle-tree, moving about the spade as pivot.

Fixed carriages are those which are mounted on a solid base and not capable of being moved. *Disappearing carriages* are visible to the enemy only during the act of firing, the loading being effected under cover. A heavy counter-weight is used to bring the gun to the firing position, whilst the recoil brings it down into the loading position.

GUN-COTTON. *See* EXPLOSIVES.

GUN-LICENCE. No person may use or carry a gun (including rifles, pistols, and air-guns) without an excise licence, which must be produced on demand. The following are exempt from this law: (1) persons in the army, navy, volunteers, or police when on duty; (2) gun-smiths; (3) common carriers; (4) persons holding game licences (*see* GAME LAWS); (5) occupiers of lands using a gun to scare birds or vermin; (6) persons carrying the gun of a licence-holder. A licence is not necessary for a gun used or carried in the owner's house or curtilage. The penalty for breach of the Act is a fine of £10. Gun-licences in the United Kingdom expire on 31st July; they cost 10s. a year.

GUN-METAL, a variety of bronze containing approximately nine parts of copper and one part of tin. Originally used for ordnance, but now replaced by steel for this purpose. Commercial gun-metals are largely used for mechanical purposes when strong castings are required, the alloys containing from 88 to 92 per cent of copper. A small proportion of zinc is commonly added in order to increase the fluidity of the molten metal and thus assist in the production of sounder castings. This addition of zinc also softens the metal somewhat and facilitates machining. Small quantities of lead are added for the same purpose, but this is found to reduce the strength, especially when used at high temperatures.

GUNNEL, or **BUTTERFISH** (*Pholis gunnellus*), a small shore-fish which is the type of a family (Pholididæ) related to the blennies. The common gunnel resembles an eel, is about 6 inches in length, is brown in colour, and has black spots on the base of the dorsal fin. It is termed 'butterfish' on account of the mucous secretion of its skin. The female protects her eggs, sometimes assisted by the male.

GUNNER, in the navy, is a warrant-officer appointed to take charge of the ammunition and ordnance of a war-vessel, and to have a general supervision of the weapons. A *chief gunner* is a commissioned officer. In the army a gunner is simply an artilleryman, or one who has to work and attend to the guns. The term is colloquially applied to all ranks in the Royal Artillery.

GUN'NERA, a genus of plants, ord. Haloragidaceæ, one species of which (*G. scabra*), a native of South America, somewhat resembles the rhubarb, and is used as an ornamental plant. It has large rough leaves and astringent roots, while its leaf-stalks are a substitute for rhubarb.

GUNNERSBURY. District of Middlesex. It is 13 miles from London, on the L.M.S. and District Rlys. Gunnersbury House was the residence of Amelia, daughter of George II. Later the estate, on which a new house was built, became the property of the Rothschild family. After the Great War it was bought by the councils of Acton and Ealing, and made into a public park.

GUNNERY is the science of directing an artillery projectile so that it will strike a given target. The gun serves two purposes: first, to confine the propellant gases so as to allow them to act on the base of the projectile; and second, to give the projectile, called the *shell*, the proper direction.

As the powder charge burns it is converted into gas of greatly increased volume. This gas, in its endeavour to expand, presses upon the base of the shell and drives it up the bore. So long as it continues to exert a forward pressure upon the base of the shell it continues to accelerate the motion of the shell, and the velocity of the latter goes on increasing till it passes out of the muzzle.

Theoretical gunnery involves the study of both internal and external ballistics. The former is the study of the motion of the shell down the bore of the gun and the pressure generated by the expanding gases on the shell and the gun itself. This pressure can be measured by special crusher gauges and plugs invented by Major Mansell, R.A.

External ballistics concern the motion of the shell after leaving the bore, and the effects upon this motion of gravity, the resistance of the air, the shape and weight of the shell, atmospheric conditions, and wind. The velocity of the shell can be measured at any time during its flight by means of the Boulengé chronograph.

Sighting and Range-Finding. The path taken by a projectile in its flight through the air to the first point of impact is called the *trajectory*. This is always a curve, since, owing to the resistance of the air, the velocity of the shell is continually decreasing and the force of gravity is exerting a constant pull towards the ground. To allow for the fall of the projectile, it is necessary to point the axis of the bore as much above the mark aimed at as the projectile would have fallen below if the gun had been pointed straight. This angle of elevation is called the *range*.

In addition to the range it is necessary to give a second angle of either elevation or depression, according as the target is above or below the horizontal plane of the gun. This is called the *angle of sight*. When the target is visible from the gun, this angle is automatically put on by aligning the sights on the target. In *indirect laying*, when the target is not visible from the gun, this angle of sight must be calculated and given to the gun by means of a clinometer.

Direction or *line* is given to the gun by aligning the sights on the target when this is visible from the gun. When the target is not visible from the gun, the angle from some visible auxiliary mark is measured, and the gun laid for direction from this auxiliary mark.

GUNNY-BAGS are bags made of a coarse cloth or sacking manufactured in India of some native fibre, chiefly jute. They are extensively used in India in packing rice, sago, spices, &c., for export, and in America for bales of cotton.

GUNPOWDER. The early history of gunpowder is very obscure. According to some authorities it was known to the Chinese in very early times, while others attribute the invention of it to Roger Bacon or to Berthold Schwartz, a German monk. If Roger Bacon did not invent it, he at any rate was one of the earliest writers to allude to it, which he did in his *De mirabili potestate artis et naturæ* (1242). It seems likely, however, that Bacon only knew gunpowder as an explosive, not as a propellant.

Gunpowder seems to have been produced in England for the first time in the reign of Edward III (about A.D. 1345). It was not manufactured on a large scale until the reign of Elizabeth, when the works at Faversham were opened. It was still something of a novelty in Shakespeare's time, for he makes Hotspur speak of a certain lord denouncing "this villanous salt-petre" (1. *Henry IV*, i, 3, 60).

According to Thomas Carlyle the three great elements of modern civilization were gunpowder, printing, and the Protestant religion. For the composition and details of the manufacture of gunpowder *see* EXPLOSIVES.

GUNPOWDER PLOT, a conspiracy formed in England in 1604, the second year of the reign of James I, by some Roman Catholics, to blow up the king and Parliament in order to be revenged on the Government for its severities against their religion. The time ultimately fixed for the execution of the plot was the 5th of Nov., 1605, when Parliament was to be opened by the king in person.

The plot originated with Robert Catesby, Thomas Winter, and John Wright, and was at once made known to Guido Fawkes, a zealous Catholic, who had served in the Spanish army in Flanders, and to Thomas Percy, a relation of the Earl of Northumberland. These five were the original conspirators, but the plot was subsequently communicated to Sir Everard Digby, Ambrose Rookwood, Francis Tresham, Thomas Keyes, Christopher Wright (a brother of John), and to some Jesuit fathers and others.

The conspirators took a house next the Parliament House, and their original plan was by digging under this house to undermine the House of Parliament. They eventually discovered, however, that there was a cellar right under the chamber of Parliament, which was occupied by a coal-dealer. They at once hired this cellar, and filled it with powder, faggots, and billets.

The plot was discovered by means of a letter sent Lord Monteagle, a Catholic peer in favour with the court, who laid it before the Secretary of State, Cecil. It was a warning, couched in mysterious terms, not to be present at the approaching meeting of Parliament. Cecil showed it to some of the Council, and did nothing till the return of the king from a hunting party.

On hearing the letter James at once divined its meaning, and declared that it referred to gunpowder. This led to investigation and to the arrest of Fawkes in the cellar, where a hogshead and thirty-six barrels of powder were discovered.

It is now very generally thought that Tresham, the reputed author of the letter to Lord Monteagle, had previously informed his lordship of the plot, and that the sending and publication of the letter were merely intended as blinds. It seems also that Cecil, knowing the king's vanity, was desirous of making him the discoverer of the plot.

Catesby, Percy, and the two Wrights were killed in defending Holbeach House, in which they had taken refuge, against the sheriff. Sir Everard Digby was tried and executed at Northampton; Tresham died in prison. Fawkes, Rookwood, Winter, and others were tried at Westminster on 27th Jan., 1606 and executed on the 30th and 31st.—BIBLIOGRAPHY: John Gerard, *The Gunpowder Plot and the Gunpowder Plotters*; M. W. Jones, *The Gunpowder Plot.*

GUNTER, Edmund, an English mathematician and astronomer, who flourished in the reign of James I, and invented the instruments mentioned in the following articles. He was born in 1581, and died in 1626. Educated at Oxford, he became professor of astronomy in Gresham College, London, in 1619. He was the first to employ the terms *cosine, cotangent,* &c.

GUNTER'S CHAIN, the chain in common use for measuring land; so called from its inventor, Edmund Gunter. Its length is 66 feet, or 22 yards, or 4 poles of 5½ yards each; and it is divided into 100 links of 7·92 inches each. 100,000 square links make 1 acre.

GUNTER'S SCALE, a scale having various lines upon it, of great use in working problems in navigation. This scale is usually 2 feet long and about 1½ inches broad. On the one side are marked scales of equal parts, and of chords, sines tangents, &c.; on the other, scales of the logarithms of these.

GUNTUR, a town of India, Presidency of Madras, district of Kistna, 46 miles from Masulipatam, and 30 miles from the Coromandel coast. Pop. 48,184.

GURJUN, a thin balsam or oil, derived from trees of the genus Dipterocarpus, in Burmah and the Eastern Archipelago. It is used for mixing paints, preserving wood from the attacks of white ants, and also medicinally.

GURKHA. The name—pronounced Ghoorkha—by which the inhabitants of Nepal, on the north-east frontier of India, are generally known. The Gurkhas, from whom a large number of recruits for the Indian army are drawn, claim descent from Rajput immigrants from India who found their way into Nepal about the middle of the eighteenth century and established themselves in the district of Gurkha, from which point they overran the country and grafted themselves on the original indigenous inhabitants, a Mongoloid race.

The Gurkha nation is divided into tribes and clans, the four principal being known as Khas, Thakurs, Magars, and Gurungs; of these the Khas are predominant and highest in the social scale. By religion they are Hindus or Buddhists, Hinduism being

Red Gurnard (*Trigla cuculus*)

more prevalent, and they observe most of the Hindu caste rules, though they are not so particular as to ceremonial observances as are the more orthodox Hindus of India.

In build the Gurkha is a stout and sturdy little man, seldom over 5 feet 5 inches in height: as a soldier he has a considerable reputation, more especially in hill warfare, coming as he does from a country composed entirely of range upon range of steep and rocky hills. The national weapon of the Gurkha of all grades of society is the kukri, a short, curved, broad-bladed, and heavy knife about 20 inches long.

On one occasion only have Nepal and the Gurkha nation fallen foul of the British power. In 1814, owing to repeated incursions into British Indian territory, a campaign against Nepal became necessary; this, after some preliminary reverses, was finally

successful, and the peace and subsequent alliance entered into in 1816 continues to the present day on the basis of mutual non-interference.

In 1857 the Nepal Durbar (Government) sent a considerable number of its troops to assist in quelling the Mutiny; in 1914 the Durbar again provided troops to garrison Indian stations depleted for the requirements of the European War; and, in 1919—when unrest in India was very marked—the Prime Minister of Nepal wrote to the Viceroy offering "such help as it is possible for us to give, so that we may vindicate once again our century-old and honoured friendship."

In our Indian army there are ten regiments of Gurkha Rifles—numbered 1 to 10—of two battalions each, of which the first three regiments were raised in 1815 from Gurkha soldiers who had fought against us in the first stage of the Nepal War.

As soldiers Gurkhas are very amenable to discipline, and give little trouble; they do not, however, always get on particularly well with natives of India, on whom they are inclined to look down. They are very much addicted to sport of all kinds, and are fond of associating with the British soldier on terms of equality.

Examples of Gurkha names are: Amar Sing Thapa, Lalbir Limbu, Dhanbir Gurung, Harak Sing Gharti. Gurkhas do not wear the pagri or turban otherwise universal in the Indian army; instead, they wear a round forage-cap in full dress, and for ordinary and service purposes the slouch hat turned up on one side. They also wear short knickerbockers ending just above the knee, a most suitable kit for hill work.

GUR'NARD, or **GURNET**, the popular name of spiny-finned fishes belonging to Trigla and related genera. The head is angular and wholly covered with bony plates. The body is elongated, nearly round, and tapering; there are two dorsal fins; the pectoral fins are large, with finger-like appendages; the teeth are small and numerous.

The grey gurnard is the *Trigla gurnardus*, common on the British coast; the red gurnard is the *T. cuculus*, also common on the same coasts; other familiar species are the sapphirine gurnard (*T. hirundo*) and the piper (*T. lyra*). Flying gurnards (Dactylopterus), which can move short distances through the air, inhabit the Mediterranean, Atlantic, and Indian seas.

GUSTA'VUS I, commonly called **Gustavus Vasa**, was born in 1490, or, according to others, in 1496, died in 1560. He was the son of Eric Johansson, a Swedish noble, served under Svante Sture, the administrator of the kingdom, was treacherously carried off with other noble Swedes by the King of Denmark, and kept a prisoner in Jutland for more than a year, but at length escaped. After many dangers he reached Dalecarlia, where he roused the peasants to resist Danish oppression, defeated the Danes, took Upsala and other towns, and in 1523 was elected king.

In 1529 he procured the abolition of the Roman Catholic religion in Sweden, and established Protestantism. During his long reign Sweden made great progress in commerce and civilization.—Cf. R. N. Bain, *Scandinavia*.

GUSTAVUS II (*Gustavus Adolphus*), King of Sweden, a grandson of Gustavus Vasa, was born in 1594, and received a most careful education. He was trained to war under experienced generals, took his place in the State Councils at the age of sixteen, and was in command of the army in his seventeenth year during the war with Denmark, which was concluded in 1613, and by which Sweden recovered important possessions on the Baltic.

He then turned his arms against the Russians, drove them from Ingria, Karelia, and a part of Livonia, which were secured to him by the Peace of Stolbova in 1617. He was then engaged in a war with Poland, which lasted nine years, and was concluded on advantageous terms for Gustavus in Sept., 1629, he being allowed to retain important conquests in East Prussia.

His attention was now diverted from northern wars by the affairs of Germany. The oppression of the Protestants by Ferdinand II excited his sympathy, and the progress of Wallenstein alarmed him. Probably also he was moved by the ambition of foreign conquests He embarked for Germany in 1630 with about 20,000 men, landed near the mouth of the Oder, and in a short time had seized nearly all Pomerania. After taking many fortified towns, repeatedly defeating the imperial generals, at Leipzig (1631), Würzburg (1631), Passage of the Lech (1632) and conquering a great part of Germany, he was killed in the battle of Lützen, against Wallenstein, 16th Nov., 1632. (*See* THIRTY YEARS' WAR.)

Though a severe disciplinarian, he was beloved by his soldiers, and the prestige of success derived from his victories lasted long after his death.— BIBLIOGRAPHY: J. L. Stevens, *History of Gustavus Adolphus*; C. R. L. Fletcher, *Gustavus Adolphus*.

GUSTAVUS III, King of Sweden,

born in 1746, succeeded his father, Adolphus Frederick, in 1771, and died 29th March, 1792. Finding the country weary of the misrule of the nobles, he gained the good-will of the army, surrounded the Assembly of the States-General, and forced them to accept a new Constitution which much restricted their privileges.

In 1788 he took command of the army against Russia and Denmark, and stormed the defences of Frederickshall, destroying a great number of vessels. In 1789 he executed another *coup d'état*, arresting the opposition

Gustavus II

leaders, and passing a law extending the royal prerogative.

On the outbreak of the French Revolution he made strenuous exertions to form a coalition between Russia, Denmark, Sweden, and Spain, but while preparations were being made a conspiracy of the nobles was formed against him, and he was shot at a masquerade by Ankarstroem, a disbanded officer, on 16th March, 1792. He died thirteen days later.— Cf. R. N. Bain, *Gustavus III and his Contemporaries*.

GUSTAVUS IV (*Adolphus*), King of Sweden, was born on 1st Nov., 1778, and succeeded his father 29th March, 1792. On assuming power Gustavus showed that he had inherited his father's hatred of the principles of the French Revolution, which he carried to the extent of fanaticism.

After the Peace of Tilsit he exposed himself to a war with Russia while he was at war with France, by refusing to join the continental blockade and opening his ports to England; and in 1808 he quarrelled with England, his only ally. Finland was lost to Sweden, and in 1809 a revolution took place. Gustavus was dethroned, and his uncle, the Duke of Sudermania, proclaimed king under the title of Charles XIII. Gustavus died in poverty at St. Gall, 7th Feb., 1837. —Cf. Sophie Elkan, *An Exiled King, Gustaf Adolf IV of Sweden.*

GUSTAVUS V, King of Sweden. A son of Oscar II., he was born 16th July, 1858, and served for a time in the army. In 1907 he became king. Gustavus married in 1881 a daughter of the Grand Duke of Baden. Their family consists of two sons, the Crown Prince Gustavus Adolphus, and William, Duke of Södermanland. The former married, firstly, Margaret, daughter of the Duke of Connaught, and secondly, in 1923, Lady Louise Mountbatten. By his first wife he had five sons.

GÜSTROW (gŭs'trō), a town of Germany, in Mecklenburg-Schwerin, on the Nebel. It is well built, has a cathedral, a fine old castle, and an ancient and beautiful palace, once the seat of the Dukes of Mecklenburg-Güstrow. It served as an internment camp during the European War. Pop. 18,843.

GUTENBERG, Johann, the reputed inventor of printing with movable types, was born at Mayence or Mainz about the end of the fourteenth century. Little or nothing is known of his early life In 1434 he is said to have been living in Strasbourg, and in 1436 to have started or attempted to start a printing office there; but this seems false.

In 1448 we find him at Mainz, where he formed, two years after, a co-partnership with Johann Fust, and established, mainly with the money of the latter, a press, in which the *Mazarin Bible,* the *Letters of Indulgence,* and the *Appeal against the Turks* were printed. After five years this connection was dissolved, and Fust sued Gutenberg for large advances which he could not pay, and by a judgment at law obtained possession of most of the printing materials, with which, in company with his son-in-law Schöffer, he continued to print books.

After this, according to some, Gutenberg carried on a separate printing establishment; but this is doubtful, and there is no book or printed matter which can certainly be ascribed to Gutenberg after the date 1454. Gutenberg seems to have died at Mainz in 1468.—Cf. J. H. Hessels, *The So-called Gutenberg Documents.*

GUTHRIE, Thomas, a Scottish divine, born at Brechin, Forfarshire, in 1803, died 24th Feb., 1873. Educated at the University of Edinburgh, he was licensed as a preacher in connection with the Church of Scotland in 1825. He did not at once exert himself to procure a church, but assisted his father in the business of his banking office, and also spent a winter (1826–7) in Paris studying medicine. In 1830 he was presented to the parish of Arbirlot, and he accepted a call to Greyfriars, Edinburgh, in 1837, where he soon became very popular with all classes.

In 1843 the Disruption took place, and Guthrie took an active part along with Chalmers and Candlish in organizing the Free Church. He himself became minister of Free St. John's, Edinburgh. The work with which his name is chiefly identified out of Scotland was the introduction into Edinburgh of the ragged-school system, then recently originated in London and Aberdeen. Into this work he threw himself with characteristic energy, employing in it both his personal labours and his pen. His *Plea for Ragged Schools* (1847) remains one of the most celebrated of his productions. In 1849 he received the degree of D.D. from the University of Edinburgh.

In 1864 Dr. Guthrie was compelled in consequence of heart disease to resign the pastorship of St. John's. The remaining years of his life were spent in active promotion of philanthropic objects. He became editor of the *Sunday Magazine* in 1864, but never assumed full editorial responsibility. His chief works are: *The Gospel in Ezekiel* (1855), *A Plea for Drunkards* (1856), and *Christ and the Inheritance of the Saints* (1858). An *Autobiography and Memoir* has been published by his sons.

GUTTA-PERCHA (pĕr'cha; Malay name, meaning 'gum-tree'), a substance resembling caoutchouc in many of its properties, but stronger, more soluble, and less elastic. It is the inspissated milky juice of *Palaquium Gutta* and other kindred trees of the nat. ord. Sapotaceæ. It chiefly comes from Malacca, Borneo, and other islands of the Indian Archipelago.

Properties. When pure, gutta-percha is of a brownish-red colour. Below the temperature of 50° it is as hard as wood and excessively tough. By an increase of heat it becomes more flexible, until at a temperature of 115°F it becomes pasty, and between this and 140° or 150° it may be moulded into all varieties of forms with the greatest ease, retaining precisely the same form as it cools and hardens to its previous state of rigidity. It is insoluble in water, soluble with difficulty in ether and other caoutchouc solvents, but very readily in oil of turpentine and naphtha. It is not attacked by solutions of alkalies nor by hydrofluoric acid, but it is acted on by sulphuric, nitric, and hydrochloric acids.

Industrial Uses. Gutta-percha has been applied to a variety of purposes: as a substitute for leather, especially in the soles of shoes, &c.; as an insulating coating for the copper wires of submarine telegraph cables; as an ingredient in mastics and cements; for the manufacture of flexible hose-tubes and bottles. The amount of gutta-percha now produced yearly is declining considerably.

GUTTIF'ERÆ, a natural order of dicotyledonous trees or shrubs, which generally secrete an acrid, yellow, resinous juice, in some cases of considerable value, as the gamboge yielded by the *Garcinia Hanburyi* and allied species. They are found in the humid and hot places of tropical regions, chiefly South America. The fruit of some is highly esteemed, in particular the mangosteen and the mammee apple.

GUTZKOW (guts'kō), **Karl Ferdinand,** German writer, born at Berlin in 1811, died in 1878. After studying theology he took to journalism and politics, and became the leading spirit of a small body of reformers known as 'Young Germany.' In 1835 his novel *Wally, die Zweiflerin* appeared. It was at once suppressed by the Government as hostile to religion and society, and the author was imprisoned for three months.

In spite of Government prohibition Gutzkow managed to publish a number of works from Hamburg, where he had settled. Amongst these are: *Blasedow und seine Söhne* (1838), a satire, and *Börnes Leben* (1840). He was active, also, in dramatic literature, his tragedies *Richard Savage* (1840), *Patkul* (1841), and *Uriel Acosta* (1847), and his comedies *Zopf und Schwert* (1844), and *Das Urbild des Tartufe* (1847), having been very popular.

In 1842 he left Hamburg, and after a visit to Paris, described in *Briefe aus Paris*, settled at Frankfort till 1847, when he became director of the Dresden theatre. Here he devoted himself to novel-writing, producing the romances *Die Ritter vom Geist* (1850), *Der Zauberer von Rom* (1858), and *Hohenschwangau* (1868).—Cf. J. Dresch, *Gutzkow et la jeune Allemagne.*

GÜTZLAFF (guts'läf), **Karl,** a German missionary, born in 1803, died in 1851. He went out as a missionary to the Battas in Sumatra in Aug., 1826, but settled instead in Batavia, Singapore, and Siam. In 1831 he went to China, acted as British interpreter during the first Chinese War, visited Europe in 1849 and died at Victoria, Hong-Kong.

His principal works are: *Journal of Three Voyages along the Coast of China in 1831 1832, and 1833* (London, 1834): *China Opened, or a Display of the Topography, History, &c., of the Chinese Empire* (1838); *Geschichte des Chinesischen Reichs* (Stuttgart, 1847).

GUY (gī), **Thomas,** English philanthropist, the founder of Guy's Hospital, London, the son of a lighterman in Southwark, was born in 1645, and died in 1724. Brought up a bookseller, he dealt largely in the importation of Bibles from Holland, and afterwards contracted with Oxford for those printed at that university. His principal gains, however, arose from dealings in South Sea stock in 1720. He amassed a fortune of nearly half a million sterling, of which he spent upwards of £200,000 in building and endowing his hospital in Southwark, besides erecting almshouses at Tamworth and supporting various other charities. He was member of Parliament for Tamworth from 1694 to 1707. *See* GUY'S HOSPITAL.

GUYAU, Jean Marie, French philosopher, born at Laval 28th Oct., 1854, died 31st March, 1888, at Mentone. He was a son, by her first marriage, of Mme Fouillée, who wrote under the pseudonym of G. Bruno. At the age of nineteen he wrote a prize essay, *Mémoire sur la morale utilitaire, depuis Épicure jusqu'à l'école anglaise,* which was crowned by the Academy. Appointed tutor of philosophy at the Lycée Condorcet in 1874, he had to resign his post on account of ill-health, and lived until his death in the south of France.

Guyau's philosophy is a modified evolutionism, and life and art are the two fundamental ideas of his philosophy. According to him only two things defy criticism: life and beauty. The development of both life and art is only possible in society, and the sociological idea consequently becomes the third fundamental principle of Guyau's philosophy.

He has been rightly called 'un remueur des idées,' for he was a critic rather than a constructive scholar and philosopher. One of his theories was that altruism is instinctive and not artificial, and tends to be diminished or even destroyed when it becomes conscious.

His works include: *Vers d'un philosophe* (1881), *La Morale Anglaise contemporaine* (1885), *L'Irreligion de l'avenir* (1887), *La Genèse de l'idée du temps* (1890).—Cf. A. Fouillée, *La Morale, l'Art et la Religion d'après Guyau.*

GUYNEMER, Georges, French airman, born 1894, killed in 1917. Obtaining his pilot's certificate in 1915, he was promoted lieutenant and captain in 1917, having brought down numerous enemy aeroplanes. He became the champion 'ace' of the French air force, and had already brought down over fifty German aeroplanes when he was shot in an air-duel with Wissemann. He had received the Military Medal, been made an officer of the Legion of Honour, and his name was placed on the commemorative tablets of the Panthéon.

GUY OF WARWICK, an old English metrical romance, whose hero is an Anglo-Danish knight said to have been the son of Siward, Baron of Wallingford, to have become Earl of Warwick, and to have slain in single combat the Danish giant Colbrand, the Dun Cow of Dunsmore, and the dragon of Northumberland, and to have performed many other wonderful feats. He is said ultimately to have become a hermit in Warwick.

GUYON (gē-yŏn), **Jeanne-Marie Bouvier de la Motte, Madame,** a celebrated mystic, the introducer of the system of Quietism into France, was born at Montargis 13th April, 1648, died 9th June, 1717. At the age of sixteen she was married to Jacques Guyon, after whose death in 1676 the tendency to mystic enthusiasm which had characterized her younger years again acquired ascendancy, and she began the religious propagandism of her extreme views of self-abnegation, indifference to life and death, and even to future salvation or perdition.

She became associated with some enthusiastic priests, abandoned her children and her goods, reserving a moderate annuity, and moved from place to place, making numerous proselytes. She also published numerous works, such as *Le Cantique des Cantiques interprété selon le sens mystique* (1685), *Poésies spirituelles* (5 vols., 1685), and *Discours chrétiens et spirituels* (1716).

At last the Archbishop of Paris thought it necessary to take steps against the spread of Madame Guyon's mystical doctrines. Through his influence she was shut up in the convent of the Visitation, but afterwards released at the instigation of Madame de Maintenon, who herself became for a time a convert to the new doctrines, and allowed Madame Guyon to preach in the seminary of St. Cyr, where she made a convert and disciple of Fénelon.

A commission of ecclesiastics, chief amongst whom was Bossuet, now sat in judgment, and the doctrines of Madame Guyon were condemned (1695). This led to her being imprisoned for some years, afterwards in the Bastille, whence she was liberated in 1702. The rest of her life was spent in retirement and in works of charity. —BIBLIOGRAPHY: T. Upham, *Life, Religious Opinions, and Experiences of Mme Guyon*: L. Guerrier, *Mme Guyon, sa vie, sa doctrine, son influence.*

GUYOT, Yves, French politician and economist, born at Dinan, Côtes du Nord, 6th Sept., 1843. Educated at Rennes, he came to Paris, where he contributed to several papers. Editor of *Le Siècle* from 1892 to 1903, he advocated social and political reforms. Elected to the Chamber of Deputies in 1885, he was Minister of Public Works from 1889 to 1892.

Guyot became known as a champion of industrial freedom, an opponent of protection and socialism, and an authority on financial questions, and was appointed editor of the *Journal des Economistes* in 1909. His works include: *Études de physiologie sociale* (1882), *La Science économique* (1881), *L'Impôt sur le revenu* (1887), and *La Tyrannie socialiste* (1893). With A. Raffalovitsh he edited the *Dictionnaire du commerce, de l'industrie et de la banque* (1898-1901). He died in 1928.

GUY'S HOSPITAL, a London hospital, founded in 1723 by Thomas Guy (*see* GUY, THOMAS). The original building, completed in 1725 and endowed at a cost of over £200,000 (in addition to the cost of erection), contained accommodation for 400 sick or incurable persons. By an Act of Incorporation obtained shortly after Guy's death, the hospital property and management were vested in fifty gentlemen as perpetual governors. Part of the money was invested in landed property, and the estates now belonging to the hospital yield an annual income of £40,000.

The hospital buildings have been greatly improved and enlarged in modern times, more especially by means of a bequest in 1829 of £190,000 from William Hunt, one of the governors, and the hospital is now the largest in London, the beds amounting to 643.

Attached to the hospital is an extensive medical school, containing lecture-rooms, museums, and a medical library. There are usually about 350 students at the hospital medical school, with which many eminent names in the medical world are associated. A chapel forms part of the hospital buildings, with a fine statue of the founder, whose remains, along with those of Hunt and Sir Astley Cooper, rest in the vault beneath.—Cf. S. Wilkes and G. T. Bettany, *History of Guy's Hospital*.

GWAL'IOR, a city and fortress of India, capital of the state of Gwalior, situated about 65 miles south of Agra.

The fortress is the largest, the strongest, and the most magnificent of the native fortresses in India. It stands on an isolated rock about 340 feet high and nearly perpendicular in the upper part, being partly made so by art. The rocky mass has a length of 1½ miles, a greatest breadth of 300 yards. The fortress contains wells and reservoirs of water, and is inaccessible except by steps up the side of the rock. Notwithstanding its natural strength, it has been wrested from the natives by the British oftener than once.

Old Gwalior, the town at the eastern base of the rock, is built of stone, and has some remarkable ruins of temples and an interesting example of old Hindu palace architecture. One of the temples is now known as *Sāsbahū*, derived from *Sahasra-bahu*, an epithet of Siva, and meaning 'the thousand-armed.'

It is decaying, and a new town, known as **New Gwalior**, or Lashkar (the camp), the residence of the ruler, Maharajah Sindhia, has sprung up on the south-eastern skirt of the rock, and is a flourishing city with a large area and a population of (1931), 80,387 of whom the majority are Hindus. It possesses various educational and benevolent institutions, including Victoria College, founded in commemoration of Queen Victoria's diamond jubilee, high school, girls' school, hospital, museum, and palace.

The state of Gwalior, in political relationship with the Government of India, and connected with the Central India Agency, consists of several portions of territory, otherwise known as Sindhia's Dominions, the largest and most compact portion, usually known as Gwalior, being the one containing the above town and fortress.

The total area of Gwalior is 26,367 sq. miles. The drainage is chiefly taken by the Chambal, which forms part of the boundary on the north-west and north-east and finally joins the Jumna. The products are those which are generally produced in India: grains and pulse of various kinds, oil-seeds, considerable quantities of cotton, and in the south-west and south opium, that goes under the name of Malwa. Pop. 3,523,070.

GWYN, Eleanor, better known by the name of *Nell*, a celebrated mistress of King Charles II, was born of humble parentage in 1650; and died in 1687. She was at first an orange girl in Drury Lane Theatre, but took early to the stage, her first performance being in 1665 in *The Indian Emperor* of Dryden. She acted in many parts both in tragedy and comedy, though she was best in comic parts. About 1667 she became the mistress of Lord Buckhurst, who surrendered her about 1670 to the king. As mistress of the king she had an establishment, and was made lady of the privy chamber to Queen Catherine.

She was merry and open-hearted, is said to have been faithful to Charles, was mindful of old friends, and a liberal patroness of the poets Dryden, Lee, Otway, and Butler. From her are sprung the Dukes of St. Albans, but she herself received no title. She is repeatedly spoken of in Pepys's *Diary*.—Cf. C. Chesterton, *Nell Gwyn*.

GWYN'IAD, or **GWINIAD** (Welsh name, from *gwyn*, white), the *Coregōnus pennantii*, a fish of the salmon or trout kind found plentifully in Lake Bala. It is gregarious, and may be taken in great numbers at a draught. It is closely related to the *Houting*, *Pollan*, *Powan*, and *Vendace* (q.v.).

GYGES (gī'jēz), a king of Lydia who reigned, according to Herodotus, 716–678 B.C. He was the favourite of the Lydian king Candaules, who, to convince him of the beauty of his queen, showed her to him naked. The queen was so incensed that she ordered Gyges either to murder the king, ascend his vacant throne, and become her husband, or to atone for his curiosity by death. He chose the former.

GYMKHANA (jim-ka-na; Hind. *gend-khanah*, ball-house, or Eng. *gym*, short for gymnasium, and Pers. *khanah*, house), a term employed by Anglo-Indians, soldiers as well as civilians, to designate the grounds and buildings used for athletic recreation. The word is also applied to outdoor meetings arranged for sporting events and recreation purposes.

GYMNA'SIUM (jim-), the name given by the Greeks to the public building where the young men, quite without clothes (hence the name, from *gymnos*, naked), exercised themselves in leaping, running, throwing the discus and spear, wrestling, and pugilism. Its objects, however, were extended also to the exercise of the mind; for here philosophers, rhetoricians, and teachers of various branches of knowledge delivered their lectures.

Gymnasia were afterwards composed of a number of connected buildings, spacious enough to admit many thousands. The name is similarly used at the present day. See GYMNASTICS.

GYMNASIUM, a term applied in Germany to a class of schools corresponding pretty nearly to the grammar schools and secondary schools of Britain. Formerly in the gymnasia Latin and Greek were the chief subjects taught; but a more practical bent is given to the course of instruction in these institutions now, though the *real-schools*, as they are called, are the institutions specially established for high-class education in such branches as mathematics, physical science, and modern languages.

The gymnasia are the feeders of the universities. The last or exit-examination, to show whether the pupils are fit to enter the university, is very severe, and includes not only Latin and Greek, but also mathematics, physics, history, &c., and at least one foreign language (French or English).

GYMNASTICS (for derivation, *see* GYMNASIUM) is the technical term used to designate any system of exercises specially designed to promote the development of physical, and especially of muscular powers.

An excellent gymnastic training is given by cricket, football, rowing, and similar amusements, but the special value of formal gymnastic exercises is that they are capable of being scientifically arranged so as to secure not only a general development of muscular power, but also an accurate knowledge of the uses of the various muscles, and further that they are capable of being applied to each individual case, so as to meet, allow for, and as far as possible overcome defects in physical organization. For these purposes an elementary course of gymnastics is of great value to all, especially to the sedentary student.

In regard to gymnastic exercises two general rules may be laid down, which will form an efficient guide in self-imposed exercises. The first is the universal rule in mechanics that the strength of any machine is the strength of its weakest part; the second is the fundamental law of muscular exercise, that it is exercise within the extreme power of the muscle which develops and improves, while straining weakens and injures, and excessive exercise develops particular muscles abnormally at the expense of the general health.

Till the age of twelve the ordinary games and pastimes of childhood are generally quite sufficient exercise; after that some very light system of gymnastics may be adopted. After the age of thirty-five unusual mus-

cular efforts are apt to leave persistent strains, and moderate exercise becomes the safest means of developing and giving tone to the muscular system.

Places fitted up with special appliances for gymnastics are called gymnasiums, the appliances being such as horizontal and parallel bars, trapezes, vaulting-horses, ladders, climbing-poles and ropes, &c. Apparatus of various kinds is also made for being readily fitted up in private houses. In Swedish drill, or the Swedish system, from its origin in that country, little or no apparatus is needed, Eurhythmics is a form of gymnastics in which music plays a part.

GYMNEMA, a genus of Asclepiadaceæ. The leaves of *G. sylvestre*, when chewed, temporarily destroy the power of tasting sweet substances.

GYMNOS'OPHISTS (jim-; Gr. *gymnōs*, naked, and *sophistēs*, philosopher), a name given by the Greeks to certain Indian philosophers given to meditation and ascetic practices, corresponding in some respects with the yogis, modern fakirs or naked devotees.

GYMNOSPERM (jim'-), a plant with a naked seed, a term used in contrast to **Angiosperm**. The gymnosperms include pines and firs, yews and cycads. There is no ovary, the pollen coming into direct contact with the micropyle of the ovule without the intervention of a stigma.

GYMPIE (gimp'i), a municipal town of Australia, in Queensland, on the side of a range of hills overlooking the River Mary, 107 miles north of Brisbane. It owes its origin to the rich gold-reefs here, which are worked to a great depth. Its port is Maryborough, about 40 miles away. The town has some good public buildings, well-paved streets, and a public water-supply. Pop. 9,588.

GYNÆCEUM (ji-nē sē-um), in botany, the pistil taken in a collective sense, precisely as the stamens form the andrœcium, the petals the corolla, and the sepals the calyx.

GYÖNGYÖS (dyeun'dyeush), a town, Hungary, 44 miles north-east of Budapest; it has manufactures of woollen stuffs, and produces the celebrated Erlauer red wine. Pop. 21,281.

GYÖR. See RAAB.

GYPSIES (from *Egyptians*, the name by which they were called in the English statutes, possibly because they were supposed to have come from Epirus, known as Little Egypt) a wandering nation whose physical characteristics, language, and customs differ much from those of European nations. They are called by the French **Bohémiens**, from the belief that they were Hussites driven from Bohemia; in Germany the general name is **Zigeuner**, which is not unlike the Italian **Zingari**. They call themselves **Romany**, from *rom*, a word applied to the Byzantine Empire and still preserved in the name Rumania.

The race is slowly melting away and its total number in Turkey, Hungary, Transylvania, Spain, Germany, France, Italy, and Great Britain is about 500,000. The Gypsies are most numerous in the Balkan Peninsula, Rumania, and Russia. In Great Britain they number between 18,000 and 40,000. Only a small number of the race are tentgypsies, preserving the language and traditions of their race.

The gypsies are now considered to have come from India, the main body of their language, though mixed with a great number of borrowed words, having a close affinity with some of the Indian languages. They first appeared in Germany in 1417, and during the fifteenth century passed through the whole of Europe.

Gypsies are remarkable for the yellow-brown, or rather olive, colour of their skin, the jet-black of their hair and eyes, the extreme whiteness of their teeth, and generally for the symmetry of their limbs. The typical Gypsies rarely settle permanently anywhere, but live in tents, wandering about working in wood and iron, making domestic utensils, telling fortunes, and practising tricks.

Their talent for music is remarkable, and some of their melodies have become the much-valued property of other nations, or are incorporated in some of the best-known operas. They have no peculiar religion. Amongst the Turks they are Mohammedans; and in Spain at least, as well as in Transylvania, they follow the forms of the Christian religion, without, however, caring for instruction, or having any real interest in religion.

The marriage ceremony is of the simplest kind. If the husband becomes tired of his wife, he will turn her off without ceremony. When they first appeared in Europe, the Gypsies wandered about in hordes with a commander at their head. In the Austrian States, Maria Theresa formed the plan of converting them into orderly citizens. But her ordinances that they should dwell in settled habitations, practise some trade, and send their children to school remained to a large extent ineffectual.

In England the Gypsies first appeared about the beginning of the sixteenth century, and notwithstanding severely repressive enactments on the part of the Government continued to maintain themselves as tinkers and mat- and basket-makers. In Scotland they were more favourably received, and frequently inter-married with the natives. The town of Yetholm, in Roxburghshire, was once a sort of head-quarters for the race, and almost exclusively inhabited by Gypsies. Considerable numbers of the British Gypsies have emigrated to America, where they settle amongst the people and lose their distinctive characteristics.

With regard to their language, a large number of the words in all the different dialects are of Indian origin, as already mentioned. The grammar of the tongue is also Oriental, and corresponds with the Indian dialects. This similarity cannot be considered the work of chance, particularly as their persons and customs show much of the Hindu character.—BIBLIOGRAPHY: George Borrow, *The Zincali, or an Account of the Gipsies in Spain*, and *Romano Lavo-Lil*; C. G. Leland, *The English Gypsies and their Language*; B. G. Smart and H. J. Crofton, *The Dialect of the English Gypsies*; F. H. Groome, *Gypsy Folk Tales*, and *In Gypsy Tents*; D. MacRitchie, *Scottish Gypsies under the Stewarts*; G. F. Black, *A Gypsy Bibliography*.

GYPSOPHILA, a genus of Caryophyllaceæ, natives chiefly of the Mediterranean region. Several are cultivated for their flowers.

GYPSUM (jip'sum), a colourless or white monoclinic mineral, chemically a hydrated calcium sulphate ($CaSO_4$. $2H_2O$). Its crystallized varieties have been called **selenite**, and in a massive state it forms the rock **alabaster**. Gypsum can be scratched by the thumb-nail, which serves to distinguish alabaster from marble. At about 200° C. it gives off three-quarters of its water, and becomes a very fine white powder, extensively used under the name of plaster of Paris (q.v.). Gypsum is found in great masses near Paris, where it forms the hill of Montmartre, near Aix in Provence, and near Burgos in Spain.

Gypsum is mainly a product of desiccating lakes, and occurs abundantly as beds in the Triassic strata of Northern Europe. It is even now forming, either as a deposit from water holding it in solution, or from the decomposition of iron pyrites when the sulphuric acid combines with lime, or from the action of sulphurous vapours in volcanic regions on calcareous rocks. **Anhydrite**, $CaSO_4$, sometimes arises from the dehydration of gypsum.

Gypsum, pulverized by grinding or burning, has been used with good effect as a top-dressing for meadows, where it acts like powdered limestone or lime. As land-plaster, it is used for neutralizing the harmful sodium carbonates of 'alkali soils.'

GYPSY-WORT (*Lycŏpus europæus*), a labiate plant found in Britain in ditches and on river banks. It yields a dye said to be used by the Gypsies to render their skin darker.

GYRO-COMPASS. This instrument, sometimes called the gyrostatic compass, fulfils the same purpose as the mariner's or magnetic compass, but its principle is totally different. Its action has nothing to do with magnetism, but depends on the dynamical

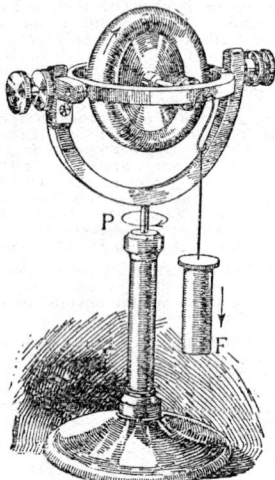

Fig. 1.—Gyro-compass

properties of bodies in rapid rotation. The leading navies of the world are now equipped with gyro-compasses— for use in submerged submarines they are indispensable.

At the British Association meetings of 1883 and 1884 Lord Kelvin suggested methods of making a gyrostatic compass, but the first practical instrument was constructed by Anschutz about 1910. Three forms of the instrument are in use: the Anschutz (German), the Sperry (American), and the Brown (British).

General Features. These three types have certain main features in common The pointer, which indicates direction by the transmission of its motion to a compass-card, is the axle of a gyrostat (*see* GYROSCOPE) electrically driven at very high speed. When the instru-

ment is to be used, it is set with its axle as nearly horizontal as possible, and left to itself.

The axle then begins to make slow spiral converging oscillations about a certain resting position. It may be a considerable time, perhaps two or three hours, before it comes to rest. The final direction of the axle is not true north; a correction has to be made for latitude, and, on board ship, for course and speed. To apply the correction, two dials are set by hand, one to the ship's speed, and the other to the latitude; the course is allowed for automatically, and the whole correction is transmitted to the ship's head lubber-line, which is moved to port or starboard by the amount of the combined errors. The compass-card then indicates true bearings.

Principles of Action. The main properties of a gyrostat are: (i) directional rigidity; (2) precession. If a gyrostat is not acted on by forces tending to turn it about its centroid, then as it is carried round by the earth's rotation the direction of its axle will remain fixed in space. The axle will therefore always point to the same fixed star, and so will sweep out a right circular cone relative to its surroundings in a period of twenty-four hours, the axis of the cone being parallel to the axis of the earth. If, for example, the axle is set so as to point to the pole star, it will continue to do so, and thus act as a compass.

At sea, however, the tilted axle is impracticable, and all gyro-compasses in actual use work on the principle of precession (*see* GYROSCOPE), a simple case of which is illustrated in fig 1. The weight F, hung to the end of the axle of the spinning wheel, causes the wheel with its horizontal and vertical supporting rings to turn round the vertical axis in the direction indicated at P, with constant angular speed.

The gyrostat has angular momentum round its axle, and the weight tends to generate angular momentum round an axis at right angles to the axle. The result is that the axle turns uniformly round towards the axis at right angles to it, while the angular velocity of the gyrostat round its axle remains unchanged.

On the same principle, in linear motion, a stone whirled round in a horizontal circle at the end of a string is acted on by a force tending to generate linear momentum in a direction at right angles to the direction of its actual momentum, and the result is that the direction of motion turns uniformly round, while the speed remains constant. An example of precession which everyone has noticed is the motion of the common spinning top. When the top is spun in the usual way, the axis sways round the vertical, that is, precesses.

Sperry Gyro-compass. A brief description of the more essential parts of an actual instrument may be useful. Fig. 2 shows diagrammatically some of the main features of the Sperry compass. The wheel s is 12 inches in diameter, and 45 lb. in weight. It is driven at 8,600 revolutions per minute. The wheel is mounted with its axle within a case C, which is supported at right angles to the axle upon the horizontal axis HK of a vertical ring V, which in turn is suspended vertically at L by means of a torsionless steel wire M of several strands, supported from the head of an outer frame P, called the 'phantom.' The phantom is electrically controlled to follow every movement in azimuth of the ring V. Suspended from the phantom is a vertical ring Q, which carries the 'bail' W, a weight which is shaped so as to swing between the vertical ring and the gyro-case, to which it is attached by a flexible pivot B, which can move in a slot in the case C, and is kept eccentrically displaced to the east of the vertical OA by means of an auxiliary gyrostat.

A fixed outer frame, not shown, supports the rotating parts and accessories, and is itself carried within

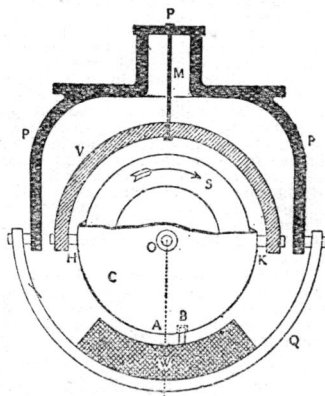

Fig. 2

a gimbal ring system enclosed within a binnacle similar to those used with ordinary magnetic compasses. Suppose, now, that we are in north latitude and looking along the axle, which passes through the paper at O, in a direction inclined, say, a little to the east of north. The wheel is rotating in the same direction as the

earth, which is essential. Owing to the earth's rotation, the north end of the axle begins to tilt upwards, so that the pivot B is displaced to a position where it is effective for causing precessional motion of the axle,

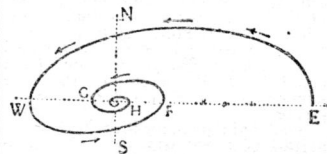

Fig. 3

which describes a spiral cone the trace of which, ENWSFGH on a vertical east-and-west plane, is represented in fig. 3.

It will be seen that the axle comes practically to a resting position after about three revolutions. For a given design of compass the period of revolution (the time from E to F, for example) is controlled by the gyro speed and the weight of the bail. These are adjusted so as to make the period about 85 minutes, as it is proved by calculation that with this period temporary oscillations due to sudden changes of speed or course are reduced to a minimum.

Mention should be made of a very troublesome fault common to all gyro-compasses, called the quadrantal error. This error does not arise if the ship is steaming north, south, east, or west, but on any other course, when the ship rolls, the rotating wheel tends to set itself with its rim in line with the roll. Unlike the errors depending on speed, course, and latitude, the quadrantal error cannot be dealt with as it occurs, and on this account has had more to do with the changes of design in the later forms of compass than any other factor.—BIBLIOGRAPHY: T. W. Chalmers, *The Gyroscopic Compass*; The Sperry Gyroscope Company, Ltd., Great West Road, Brentford, *Elementary Theory and Brief Description of the Sperry Gyro-compass*; S. G. Brown, *The Gyrostatic Compass* (articles in *Nature*, 11th and 18th March, 1920).

GYROSCOPE AND GYROSTAT, scientific forms of spinning top, by which the laws of rotational motion are illustrated or turned to practical use. In the gyroscope, the rotating wheel is exposed to view, and usually one point on the axis is fixed; in the gyrostat, as designed by Lord Kelvin, the wheel is concealed within a closed case. In practice, however, the two names are used almost indifferently.

The essential part of the instrument is the fly-wheel, which is generally a disc with a massive rim, and may be mounted in various ways. Fig. 1 of the article **Gyro-compass** shows one arrangement, in which the axis of the wheel is held by a ring resting on bearings, so that the ring can turn about an axis perpendicular to the axis of the wheel. These bearings are at the upper end of an upright fork, which with its stem (at P) is free to turn in a vertical socket. The wheel with its ring may be detached from the fork, and the end of the axle supported on a pivot, or by a string.

The main principles on which the action of a gyrostat depends have been briefly explained in the preceding article. Most people find it difficult to see why the weight F in fig. 1 should move to the side instead of down. In ordinary cases, when a force is applied to a body, the point of application moves in the direction of the force. In this case, it is not the direction of the applied force which counts, but the plane of the applied torque.

Before the weight F is attached, the gyrostat has an angular momentum $I\omega$ about its axis, I being its moment of inertia, and ω its angular velocity. The weight F produces a torque or couple C about the horizontal axis at right angles to the axis of rotation. This torque generates angular momentum Ct about the axis of the torque in the small time t. The resultant angular momentum after time t is found by the usual parallelogram construction. The axis of resultant angular momentum therefore turns through a small angle $Ct/I\omega$ in time t. This axis is very approximately simply the axis of rotation of the wheel, which therefore turns round in the horizontal plane with angular velocity ω', where $\omega' = C/I\omega$, or $I\omega\omega' = C$. It also follows that the direction of the precession is as indicated at P in fig. 1. The small increase of angular momentum, being $\sqrt{I^2\omega^2+C^2t^2}-I\omega$, is proportional to t^2; the angular momentum will therefore remain constant, its rate of increase being zero.

Most ordinary examples of gyrostatic action are readily understood by comparing them with the above simple case. It is easy to see, e.g., that pushing the weight F against the motion will raise F, but that pushing it so as to help the precession will bring it down: compare the method of steering a bicycle. When a motor-car turns a corner, the axles of the wheels are turned round in a horizontal plane; hence a torque in a vertical plane is required, which is supplied by the easing of the pressure of the inner wheels on the ground. The action of the **gyrostatic couple** (*see* CENTRIFUGAL FORCE), which is produced when a carriage turns a corner, tends therefore to turn the carriage over towards the outside of the-curve. In an aeroplane, the propeller and the rotor of the engine form a powerful gyrostat. When the aeroplane is turned in a horizontal plane, it tends to dive or to rear, according to the direction of turning.

The **Schlick controller** is a gyrostatic device for steadying a ship at sea. When the ship is on an even keel, the axis of the gyrostat is kept vertical by means of a heavy weight. Heeling makes the gyrostat precess, and couples resisting the rolling are brought to bear on the ship. In trials it was found that the angle of roll was under 1° in a cross-sea which produced a swing of 35° when the gyrostat was out of action.

A projectile shot from a rifled gun is a gyrostat which tends to preserve the direction of the axis of rotation. Torpedoes are kept in a straight course by the action of a gyrostat. In the mono-rail, a car balanced by gyrostats is carried on a single row of wheels, but no satisfactory method has so far been devized for enabling the car to turn a corner safely.—BIBLIOGRAPHY: Kelvin and Tait, *Natural Philosophy*; A. Gray, *A Treatise on Gyrostatics and Rotational Motion*; H. Crabtree, *Spinning Tops and Gyroscopic Motion*.

GYULA (dyö′lä), a market town of Hungary, on the Körös. It consists of two distinct villages, Magyar and Nemet (German) on opposite sides of the river. Pop. 25,221.

H

H, the eighth letter of the **English** alphabet, often called the *aspirate*, as being a mere aspiration or breathing, though not the only aspirated letter in English. The sound that distinctively belongs to it is that which it has at the beginning of a syllable before a vowel, as in *hard*, *heavy*. It is very commonly joined to other consonants to represent sounds for which there are no special letters in the alphabet, as in the digraphs *ch*, *sh*, *th* (*child*, *ship*, *thin*, *this*), or in other consonantal combinations of various origins and values, as in the words *enough* (*gh* = *f*), *plough* (*gh* silent), *philosophy* (*ph* = *f*), *rhetoric* (*h* silent), &c. *Ch* is common in words taken from the Greek, but in this case it generally has the *k* sound, as in *chemistry*, *chyle*, *logomachy*, &c. *See* GRIMM'S LAW.

HAAKON VII, King of Norway, born 3rd Aug., 1872. The second son of King Frederick VIII of Denmark, he was elected in 1905 King of Norway on the separation of this country from Sweden. In 1896 he married Princess Maud, youngest daughter of King Edward VII. He was baptized Charles, but on his election as King of Norway he assumed the name of Haakon, and gave to his son, born in 1903, the name of Olaf.

HAARLEM (här'lem), a town of the Netherlands, province of North Holland, 10 miles w. of Amsterdam, intersected by the Spaarne, which is joined by canals from Leyden and Amsterdam, and along which a considerable traffic is maintained. The town is well and regularly built; the streets exceedingly clean, planted with trees and laid out in promenades.

Amongst the notable buildings are the town hall, the church of St. Bavon with its celebrated organ, (built in 1735), the Prinsenhof, in which the Provincial Assembly meets. The manufactures of Haarlem, as well as its population, are less than what they were formerly; but it has still various industrial works, a celebrated type-foundry, the oldest and most famous printing-office in Holland, and its flower trade, especially in hyacinths and other bulbs, is very important.

On the south side of the town is the park of Haarlem, a plantation of fine old beeches surrounded by villas, cafés, and places of holiday resort. Haarlem was a prosperous place as far back as the twelfth century. During the revolt of the Netherlands it sustained a famous seven months' siege by the Spaniards. It is the birth-place of Laurence Coster, supposed inventor of movable types, and of a number of painters, Ostade, the Wouvermans, Ruysdael, and Van Loo. Pop. (1932), 122,386.

HAARLEM, LAKE OF, a former lake of the Netherlands, adjoining and communicating with the Y. between Haarlem and Amsterdam. Previously a swamp, it was formed in the fifteenth century by the overflow of the Rhine and the crumbling away of the banks of the Y, and imperilled by its growth the towns of Haarlem, Amsterdam, and Leyden. It was 18 miles long, 9 miles broad, and about 14 feet deep. The draining of it was commenced in 1840, and completed in 1853. The soil thus reclaimed, known as the Haarlemmer Polder, now forms a commune, which numbers about 20,000 inhabitants.

HAASE, Hugo, German Socialist leader, of Jewish extraction, born at Allenstein, Prussia, in 1863, died in 1919. He studied law at Königsberg, and in 1897 entered the Reichstag, where he became one of the leaders of the Socialist party and succeeded Bebel as president of the Social Democratic party.

In 1915 he formed an Independent Socialist party, which refused to vote the war credits. He took an active part in the revolution of Nov., 1918, was shot on 8th Oct., 1919, by an Austrian named Johann Voss, and died four weeks afterwards.

HABAK'KUK, the eighth of the twelve minor prophets. He flourished about 600 B.C. at the time of the invasion of Judah by the Chaldeans, against whom he prophesies God's retributive justice. He concludes with a kind of psalm (chap. iii) remarkable for the majesty of its language and the sublimity of its thought.

HABEAS CORPUS (Lat., 'that you have the body'), one of the most ancient and celebrated writs of English law. It has various forms, but that of paramount importance is the writ 'Habeas corpus ad subjiciendum.' This writ, issued by the High Court, is directed to any party unjustly detaining another in custody, and requires that 'the body' of the prisoner be produced and the cause of the detention stated. It is granted at the suit of the prisoner himself or other party. It is the great safeguard of personal liberty, and is as old as Magna Charta, but its constant evasion by weak and servile judges under the Stuart kings led to the strengthening of the law by the passing of the Habeas Corpus Act, 1679.—Cf. Hallam's *Constitutional History*.

HABIT AND REPUTE, in Scots law, an expression applied to denote something so notorious that it is taken without further proof to be true. Thus, marriage may be established by habit and repute, where the parties cohabit and are recognized by the neighbours as man and wife. Also if a person is by habit and repute a thief, that is, a notorious thief, the punishment inflicted is heavier.

HABITUAL CRIMINALS ACT, a British Act passed in 1869 (32 and 33 Vict. cap. xcix) to make further provision for the suppression of crimes. This statute was, however, repealed two years after by a more comprehensive Act known as the Prevention of Crimes Act. The Act of that title passed in 1908 applies the term 'habitual criminal' to one who has been at least three times convicted of crime since attaining sixteen years of age and who is leading a life of habitual dishonesty or crime. *See* PREVENTION OF CRIMES ACT.

HABSBURG (properly **HABICHTS-BURG**, the hawk's castle), a small place in the Swiss canton of Aargau, on the right bank of the Aar. The castle was built about 1027 by Bishop Werner of Strasbourg. Werner II, who died in 1096, is said to have been the first to assume the title of Count of Habsburg. After the death, about 1232, of Rudolph II, the family divided into two branches, the founder of one of which was Albert IV. In 1273 Rudolph, son of Albert IV, was chosen Emperor of Germany, and from him descended the series of Austrian monarchs, all of the Habsburg male line, down to Charles VI inclusive.

After that the dynasty, by the marriage of Maria Theresa to Francis Stephen of Lorraine, became the Habsburg-Lorraine. Francis II, the third of this line, was the last of the so-called 'Holy Roman Emperors,' this old title being changed by him for that of Emperor of Austria. From the Emperor Rudolph was also descended a Spanish dynasty which began with the Emperor Charles V (Charles I of Spain), and terminated with Charles II in 1700.

The Habsburgs ruled in Austria-Hungary until 1918, when, in consequence of the Revolution, Charles, a grand-nephew of Emperor Francis-Joseph, lost the throne. The castle of Habsburg is still to be seen on the Wülpelsberg.—BIBLIOGRAPHY: H. W. Stead, *The Habsburg Monarchy*; J. Gilbart-Smith, *The Cradle of the Habsburgs*.

HACKBERRY, the popular name of the North American varieties of the nettle-tree (*Celtis crassifolia*), also of the *Celtis occidentalis*, belonging to the nettle family Urticaceæ. *See* NETTLE-TREE.

HACKENSCHMIDT, Georges. Russian wrestler. He was born in 1878, and soon became famed for his strength and skill as a wrestler. After defeating many rivals in catch-as-catch-can contests on the Continent, he came to England in 1901 and on the music hall stage met some of the foremost wrestlers of the day. On 4th April, 1908, in a bout with Gotch at Chicago, after wrestling for two hours, Hackenschmidt refused to continue and forfeited the world's championship.

HACKLÄNDER (häk'len-dėr), **Friedrich Wilhelm von,** a German novelist and comedy writer, born in 1816, died in 1877. He engaged first in commerce, then entered the Prussian artillery, and commenced his literary career in 1841 with *Pictures from a Soldier's Life in Time of Peace*. He then became successively private secretary to Baron Taubenheim, whom he accompanied to the East, and to the Crown Prince of Würtemberg.

In 1849 he served with the Austrians during the war with Sardinia, and published his *Pictures from a Soldier's Life in Time of War*. He was ennobled by the Emperor Francis Joseph. Amongst his many writings distinguished by a mixture of pathos and humour we may mention *Daguerreotypen* (1842), *Handel und Wandel* (1850), *Der Neue Don Quixote* (1858), *Geschichten im Zickzack* (1871); of his comedies, *Der Geheime Agent* (1850) was the most successful.

HACKNEY, a municipal and parliamentary borough of London, 3 miles N.N.E. of St. Paul's. It includes Hackney proper, South Hackney, &c., and is still a favourite residence of wealthy merchants. It returns three members to Parliament. Pop. (1931), 215,380.

HACKNEY COACH, a coach let out for hire. Hackney coaches began first to ply under this name in London in 1625, when they were twenty in number. Hackney coachmen were generally put under police regulations, and a tariff of fares imposed upon them. Cabs were the common kind of hackney coaches until superseded by taxi-cabs.

HADDINGTON, a royal (formerly a parliamentary) burgh of Scotland, capital of the county of same name, 17 miles east by north of Edinburgh, on the Tyne. The town is neatly built, and has a town-house, a fine structure; handsome county buildings; a Gothic church of the eleventh or twelfth century, the nave of which forms the parish church; &c. John Knox, who was born near gives his name to the Knox Institute. Its grain-market is one of the largest in Scotland. Prior to 1885 it united with North Berwick, Dunbar, Lauder, and Jedburgh in sending a member to the House of Commons. Pop. (1931), 4,405.

HADDINGTON, the county, now called **EAST LOTHIAN,** is bounded by the Firth of Forth, the North Sea, Berwickshire, and Midlothian; area, 170,971 acres, of which fourth-fifths is arable or fit for cultivation. The surface rises gently from the coast towards the Lammermuir Hills, 500 to 1,700 feet high, which form its south boundary. It is divided into two nearly equal portions by the River Tyne. The minerals include coal, limestone, ironstone, and sandstone; the coal is worked.

Haddingtonshire has been long celebrated for the skill and success with which its husbandry has been conducted. The low lands of the north and the west are very fertile, while the high lands adjoining the Lammermuir Hills supply excellent pasturage for sheep. Fishing and fish-curing are carried on at Dunbar and other points. The county unites with Berwick in returning one member to Parliament. Pop. (1931), 47,369.

HADDOCK, a well-known fish of the cod family (Gadidæ), *Gadus æglefinus.* It is smaller than the cod, which it much resembles, but it has a dark spot on each side of the body just behind the head. This fish commonly weighs from 2 to 6 lb., though sometimes as much as 10 lb. It breeds in immense numbers in the northern seas, is caught by lines and trawl-nets, and is a valuable source of food. In Scotland haddocks are commonly cured by smoking over a wood fire.

HADERSLEV, a town of Denmark, in Slesvig, on the Haderslev Fiord, in the Little Belt. Pop. 14,487.

HADES (hā′dēz), originally the Greek name of the lord of the lower or invisible world, afterwards called Pluto; but in later times, as in the Greek Scriptures, it is applied to the region itself. According to the belief of the ancients, the departed spirits of good and bad alike went to the halls of Hades.

HADFIELD, town of Derbyshire, It is 187 miles from London by the L.N.E. Rly., and is 13 miles from Manchester. There are cotton manufactures. The Derwent rises near here. Pop. 6,371.

HADFIELD, Sir Robert Abbott. English scientist, Born at Sheffield, 29th Nov., 1859, he entered business

Hades (Pluto), from a Statue in the Vatican

there, and in the iron and steel industry he soon became a leading figure. He built up the business of Hadfields, Ltd., and was master cutler in 1899. He devoted much time to the technical side of the industry, and his inventions were of the highest importance. For those he was elected F.R.S., and received numerous other honours, both at home and abroad. In 1908 he was made a knight, and in 1917 a baronet. Hadfield has written a great deal on metallurgy.

HADHAM. Two villages of Hertfordshire, Great and Little. **Great or Much Hadham** is 3 miles from Bishop Stortford, and 26 from London, on the L.N.E. Rly. The Bishop of London had a palace here at one time. **Little Hadham,** which is quite near, possesses a 12th century church, Here is Hadham Hall, an Elizabethan building.

HADHRAMAUT, a district in the extreme south of Arabia, formerly stretching along the coast from Yemen to Oman, with the great desert as its northern limit. The name is now, however, usually applied by modern geographers to a much smaller area in the south-west. Some of the valleys are fertile, and there are numerous villages on the mountain slopes.

Dates, indigo, bananas, and grain are cultivated. Makallah, on the coast, is the chief commercial centre. It is under control and protection of Britain. The population is estimated at 150,000.

HADJ, the Mohammedan pilgrimage to Mecca, which every Mohammedan ought to perform once in his life, and after which he is entitled to prefix *Hadji* to his name. The pilgrimage has been made in disguise by Burckhardt in 1814, by

Roman Coin showing the Emperor Hadrian

Burton in 1853, by T. F. Keane in 1878, by Snouck-Hurgronje in 1884, and by A. J. B. Wavell in 1911.

HADJI KHALIFAH, the surname of Mustapha-Ben-Abdallah, a Turkish historian, born at Constantinople about 1605; became 'first secretary' to Sultan Mourad IV; and died at Constantinople in 1658. His most important work is *Kesshf-ul-tzunûn*, a kind of encyclopædia of Arabic, Turkish, and Persian literature. Among his other works are: *Chronological Tables, Mirror of the World,* and *History of the Maritime Wars of the Turks.* All the works mentioned have been translated into Latin or modern languages.

HADLEIGH, village of Essex. It is 5 miles from Southend and is notable because of the farm colony founded here by the Salvation Army in 1891.

HADLEIGH, an old market town of England, Suffolk, 9½ miles west of Ipswich, formerly one of the chief seats of the woollen manufacture introduced by the Flemings, and still possessing some interesting old houses.

There are flour-mills and malting works. Pop. (1931), 2,952.

HADLEY, John, English astronomer, born towards the end of the seventeenth century, died in 1744. He is the reputed inventor of the quadrant that goes by his name, though the honour is also claimed for Newton, from whom Hadley got a description of the instrument in 1727, and for Thomas Godfrey of Philadelphia, who produced his instrument about the same time as Hadley in 1731. The Royal Society decided that Godfrey and Hadley were both entitled to the honour of the invention. Hadley also invented the sextant.

HADLEY WOOD, district of Middlesex. It is 10 miles from London, on the L.N.E. Rly. It is part of the urban district of Barnet.

HA'DRIAN, in full, **PUBLIUS ÆLIUS HADRIANUS,** the fourteenth in the series of Roman emperors, born at Rome 24th Jan., A.D. 76. His father, who was cousin to the emperor Trajan, died when Hadrian was ten years old, and left him under the charge of his illustrious kinsman. He married Sabina, Trajan's grandniece, accompanied the emperor on his expeditions, filled the highest offices of State, and, on the death of Trajan, assumed the government as his adopted son (117).

He made peace with the Parthians, renouncing all conquests east of the Euphrates, and bought off a war with the Roxolani by payment of a sum of money. From the year 121 he spent most of his time visiting the various provinces of the empire. Hadrian's policy was a peaceful one, because he saw that the further extension of the empire only weakened it.

Although avoiding war as much as he could, he kept the armies in excellent condition, fortified the frontiers in Germany, and, crossing over into Britain, constructed the wall known as Hadrian's Wall (or that of Severus), which protected the Roman province from the barbarous tribes of the north. He next travelled into Asia and Africa, and lived in Athens for three years.

In 131 he promulgated the *Edictum Perpetuum,* a fixed code of laws, which forms an important epoch in the development of Roman law.

In 132 the Jews revolted, and for four years carried on a bloody war, the only notable one of his long reign. Hadrian died at Baiæ in 138.—BIBLIOGRAPHY: F. Gregorovius, *The Emperor Hadrian*; Aelius Spartianus, *The Life of the Emperor Hadrian*; J. B. Bury, *The Student's Roman Empire.*

HADRIAN'S WALL. *See* ROMAN ROADS AND WALLS.

HADROSAURUS (Gr. *hadros*, thick, and *sauros*, lizard), a genus of large extinct reptiles, remains of which have been found in the Upper Cretaceous strata of the United States, and in England. It appears to have resembled the gigantic iguanodon of Europe in its size, herbivorous habits, and anatomical structure.

HAECKEL (hek'l), **Ernst**, German scientist and natural philosopher, born at Potsdam in 1834, died in 1919. He studied medicine and science at Berlin, Würzburg, and Vienna; travelled in Norway and Italy; and became professor of zoology at Jena in 1865. Later he visited Syria, Egypt, Algeria, Ceylon, &c., to perfect his knowledge of natural forms. He was the most prominent exponent of the Darwinian theories in Germany.

Among his works are to be found: *The Radiolariæ* (1862), *The History of Creation* (1868), *Anthropology* (1874), *History of the Evolution of Man* (1875), *Collected Popular Discourses on the Development Theory* (1878–9), and *The Riddle of the Universe* (1900—very widely sold). Haeckel was one of the ninety-three German intellectuals who signed the famous manifesto at the beginning of the European War, wherein they defended Germany's action.

HÆMAL CAVITY, in anatomy, a term applied to the cavity which contains the great centres of circulation in the Vertebrata, together with the digestive and respiratory apparatus. The *Hæmal Arch* is the arch formed by the projections anteriorly of the ribs and the sternum from the vertebræ

HÆMANTHUS, the blood-flower, a genus of South African bulbous plants.

HÆ'MATIN, or **HEMATINE** is a brown pigment found in the hæmoglobin of the red blood corpuscles. Its composition has not been definitely made out, but it is one of the few substances in the body that contain iron.

HÆ'MATITE, RED AND BROWN. *See* HEMATITE: IRON.

HÆMAT'OPUS, a genus of plover-like birds, the best-known species of which is *H. ostralĕgus*, or common oyster-catcher, sea-pie, or mussel-picker. This has a wide range in the Old World. Related species inhabit America, Australia, and New Zealand.

HÆMATOX'YLIN ($C_{16}H_{14}O_6$), the colouring-matter of logwood, or *Hæmatoxylon campechianum.* This colouring-matter is a constituent part of all the colours prepared with logwood, and the changes which it undergoes by the action of acids and alkalies render it useful as a reagent to detect their presence.

HÆMATOZO'A (Gr. *haima*, blood, and *zōon*, an animal), a name given to the parasitic animals which, under certain conditions, exist in the blood of mammals, birds, reptiles, fishes, and many invertebrate animals. They are generally microscopic, and some of them are connected with various diseases.

HÆMATU'RIA (Gr. *haima*, blood, and *ouron*, urine) is blood in the urine, usually arising from disease of the kidneys or bladder. Endemic hæmaturia occurs in Egypt as a result of the action of a blood parasite in the disease known as bilharziosis

HÆMOG'LOBIN, or **HÆMOGLOB'-ULIN,** the semi-fluid or quite fluid matter of a red colour contained in the red corpuscles of the blood. It can be resolved into an albuminous substance called globulin and the colouring-matter hæmatin.

HÆMOP'TYSIS (Gr. *haima*, blood, and *ptysis*, a spitting), the coughing up of blood, sometimes produced by fullness of the blood-vessels of the lungs or throat, or by the rupture of blood-vessels as a consequence of ulceration. It is distinguished from blood coming from the stomach by the comparative smallness of its quantity, and by its usually florid colour. It may occur in heart disease, in pneumonia, and is one of the serious signs of progressive tubercular disease of the lungs (phthisis). In women it is sometimes a case of vicarious menstruation.

HÆMORRHAGE. *See* HEMORRHAGE.

HAFIZ, Mohammed Shems-ed-din, one of the most celebrated and most charming poets of Persia, was born at Shiraz in the beginning of the fourteenth century, died there about 1390. He studied theology and law, sciences which, in Mohammedan countries, are intimately connected with each other. He preferred independent poverty as a dervish to a life at court, whither he was often invited by Sultan Ahmed, who earnestly pressed him to visit Baghdad. His poems, known collectively as the *Divan*, are Anacreontic in sentiment, abounding in the praise of love and wine. An English translation of the *Divan*, by H. W. Clarke, appeared in 1891.

HAG, the name of the fish-like vertebrates of the genera Myxine and Bdellostoma, that, with the allied lampreys, constitute the class Cyclostomata, which are lower in the scale than fishes, though they are sometimes included in the latter as a distinct order (Marsipobranchii). They are of eel-like form, and have no eyes, limbs, or scales; the mouth is formed for suction, is without a lower jaw, and furnished with fleshy filaments or barbels. There is a single fang upon the palate and other horny teeth by which the hag cats its way into the interior of other fishes, such as the cod, ling, or haddock. *Myxine glutinōsa*, the common hag, is found in the British seas, and is about 12 or 15 inches long.

HAGEN, Walter, American golfer. Born at Rochester, New York; in 1893, he became a professional golfer. In 1914 and 1919 he won the open championship of the U.S.A., and in 1922 he won the open championship of Great Britain, as he did also in 1924, 1928 and 1929. One of the world's greatest golfers, he won many other trophies, including the open

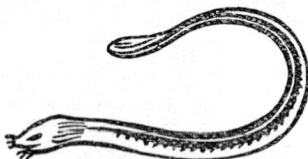

Hag Fish

championship of France in 1920, of Belgium in 1924, and of Canada in 1931. In U.S.A. Hagen won the open championship in 1921, and in four successive years, 1924, 1925, 1926, and 1927, and the professional championship in 1914 and 1919. He has played several times in international matches.

HAGEN (hä'gėn), a manufacturing town of Germany in the Prussian province of Westphalia, at the confluence of the Volme and Ennepe. It has iron- and steel-works, and manufactures of metal goods and textiles. Pop. 143,701.

HAGENAU (hä'gė-nou), a town of France, Alsace-Lorraine, 16 miles N. of Strasbourg, on the Moder. It has some manufactures, and is a centre of hop culture. Pop. 19,514.

HAGENBECK, Carl. German trainer of animals. He was born at Hamburg in 1844, the son of a man who did a little business in buying and selling wild animals. Carl took this up with avidity, travelled a good deal and showed in public animals he had trained. In 1897, at Stellingen, near Hamburg, he opened a zoological garden on new principles, keeping the animals, as far as possible, in the

open. Hagenbeck died in 1913, but the gardens still bear his name.

HAGERSTOWN, a town, United States, Maryland, 6 miles north of the Potomac River. Pop. 30,861.

HAGGAI (hag'ā-ī), the tenth in order of the minor prophets, and first of those who prophesied after the captivity. The book of Haggai consists of four distinct prophetical addresses—two in the first and two in the second chapter—intended to rouse his disheartened countrymen to the rebuilding of the temple.

HAGGARD, Sir Henry Rider, English novelist, born in 1856, son of a Norfolk landed proprietor, became secretary to Sir Henry Bulwer, Governor of Natal, in 1875, and held various other appointments in South Africa, including the mastership of the high court of the Transvaal; but since 1879 has mainly resided in England, being called to the Bar in 1884. He has made Africa the scene of some of his novels, and his pictures of life and fighting among Kaffirs and other South African peoples are often more highly coloured than artistic.

His first book was *Cetewayo and his White Neighbours* (1882), but he became much better known by his *King Solomon's Mines* (1886), and still more by his romantic *She* (1887), which have been followed by *Allan Quatermain*; *Jess*; *Maiwa's Revenge*; *Mr. Meeson's Will*; *Colonel Quaritch V.C.*; *Cleopatra*; *Eric Bright-eyes*; *Nada the Lily*; *Montezuma's Daughter*; *Joan Haste*; *Swallow: a Story of the Great Trek*; *Pearl-Maiden*; *Ayesha* (a continuation of *She*); *Red Eve*; *When the World Shook*; and *The Ancient Allan*.

His tales are strong in incident and adventure, but weak in character-drawing. Haggard greatly interested himself in the agriculture and rural industries of England, and made personal investigations by travel and otherwise, the results being the works *Rural England* (1902), *The Poor and the Land* (1905), and *Rural Denmark* (1911). He was knighted in 1912, and created K.B.E. in 1919.

An elder brother, Andrew Charles Parker (born 1854), entered the army, and rose to the rank of lieutenant-colonel, after a distinguished career, especially in Egypt. He has also written novels, as well as poetry, and articles on sport. He died in 1925.

HAGIOLOGY. *See* ACTA SANCTORUM; CANONIZATION; SAINT.

HAGLEY, village of Worcestershire. It is 13 miles from Wolverhampton, on the G.W. Rly. Hagley Hall has been for some centuries the seat of the Lytteltons.

HAGUE, THE (hāg; Du. *'S Graven-hage*—the Count's Hedge; Fr. *La Haye*), the third largest town in the Netherlands, practically, though not formally, the capital of the Netherlands, is in the province of South Holland, 33 miles south-west of Amsterdam, and within 3 miles of the sea. It is the residence of the sovereign and of the foreign ambassadors, and the seat of the States-General of the Netherlands and of the chief part of the central administration. It is pleasantly situated, and is distinguished for width and straightness of streets, and general stateliness of public buildings. Near the centre is a fine sheet of water—the Vijver—surrounded by important buildings.

There are some manufactures—furniture, pottery, gold and silver wares, hats, &c.—but the town mostly depends on the presence of the court and the number of strangers that come for sea-bathing to Scheveningen, about 3 miles distant. The Hague took its origin in a hunting-seat of the Counts of Holland in 1250, and became the political capital of the states in the sixteenth century, but it has grown to be a place of real importance chiefly since the beginning of the nineteenth century.

An international conference (the 'Hague Conference') was held here in 1899, at the suggestion of Tsar

The Hague, Peace Palace

Among the chief structures are the royal palace, the palace of the queen mother, the Binnenhof, a large irregular building, founded in 1249, and containing the hall of assembly of the States-General, and various Government offices; the provincial Government house, a large roomy edifice, the town hall, royal library (500,000 vols.), high court of justice; the Groote Kerk, or church of St. James, with hexagonal tower and finely vaulted interior; and the Mauritshuis, built by Prince John Maurice of Nassau, now converted into a picture gallery, containing some of the finest works of the Dutch masters. The Palace of Peace, built at the expense of Andrew Carnegie, was opened in Aug., 1913.

Nicholas II, and questions regarding the reduction of armaments, the use of inhuman practices in warfare, &c., were discussed, but the chief outcome was the establishment of a permanent court of arbitration, before which disputes among the different powers may be brought for peaceful settlement. Another conference was held at the Hague in 1907. In 1920 it was proposed to make The Hague the seat of the League of Nations, but Geneva was finally selected. Pop. (1932), 449,614.

HAGUENAU. *See* HAGENAU.

HAHNEMANN (hä'nė-män), **Samuel Christian Friedrich**, the founder of the homœopathic system, born at Meissen in 1755, died in Paris in 1843. He studied medicine **at**

Leipzig, Vienna, and Erlangen, taking his degree at the last-mentioned place in 1779. After practising in various places, he published in 1810 his *Organon der rationellen Heilkunde*, which fully explained his new system of curing any disorder by employing a medicine which produces a similar disorder. (*See* HOMŒOPATHY.)

Hahnemann was driven from Saxony by the Government prohibiting him from dispensing medicines, but found an asylum ultimately in Paris, where his system was authorized by the Government and acquired a certain popularity. Among his works are a *Dictionary of Materia Medica, Essay on Poisoning by Arsenic, On the Effects of Coffee*, and his treatise *On Chronic Affections*.

HAHN-HAHN, Ida, Countess of, German authoress, born in 1805, died

Earl Haig

in 1880. She was the daughter of Count Karl Friedrich of Hahn-Hahn, who squandered most of his means as an entrepreneur of dramatic companies. In 1826 she married a wealthy cousin, but three years later was divorced, after which she travelled extensively in Italy, Spain, and the Levant.

In 1835 she made her debut in literature with *Poems*, followed by *Venetian Nights* (1836), *Songs and Poems* (1837). But her popularity is chiefly founded on her novels, especially those of social life, amongst which *Aus der Gesellschaft* (1838), *Gräfin Faustine* (1841), and *Sigismund Forster* (1843) may be mentioned.

HAIDUCKS, or **HAIDUKS** (Hun. *Hajduk*, drovers), a term originally applied to certain herdsmen of Hungary who refused to submit to Turkish rule and found an asylum in the Eastern Hungarian mountains, where they were regarded as patriotic heroes. Afterwards the name was applied to the bands of Magyar foot soldiers who placed themselves at the service of any potentate who was willing and able to pay them.

Their fidelity to the cause of Bocskai, Prince of Hungary, in the War of Succession was rewarded by a grant from that prince, in 1605, of a separate district of the country for their residence, with privileges of nobility, &c., which they continued to enjoy till 1848. In Poland and Hungary the term Haiduks is also applied to servants of great houses.

HAIFA, a seaport of Palestine, on the south side of the Bay of Acre, at the foot of Mt. Carmel; starting-point of a railway to Damascus. Cotton is being grown locally, and trade is rapidly increasing. Pop. 24,634.

HAIG, Douglas Haig, first Earl, British soldier, Knight of the Thistle, Knight Grand Cross of the Bath, Order of Merit, Knight Grand Cross of the Victorian Order, Knight Commander of the Order of the Indian Empire, was born in Edinburgh on 19th June, 1861, and died in London on 29th Jan., 1928.

He was educated at Clifton and Brazenose College, Oxford, and in 1885 was gazetted to the 7th Hussars. In 1891 he was promoted captain, received a brevet majority in 1898, became a substantive major in the following year, received a brevet lieutenant-colonelcy in 1900, and was appointed to the command of the 17th Lancers with the substantive rank of lieutenant-colonel on the 16th July, 1901.

As a captain he went to the Staff College at Camberley, and in 1898 was serving with the Egyptian army in the Sudan. From Egypt he returned to England for a brief spell of duty as brigade major of the Aldershot Cavalry Brigade, from which, on the first hint of trouble in South Africa, he received promotion to the appointment of Deputy Assistant Adjutant-General in South Africa. From this time onward he never looked back, and, with the exception of a few years as regimental lieutenant-colonel (17th Lancers), his subsequent service has been on the Staff.

From Deputy Assistant Adjutant-General he became Assistant Adjutant-General in South Africa, and acted in other important positions till July, 1901, when he went to the 17th

Lancers. After the conclusion of peace with the Boers, Haig was sent to India as Inspector-General of Cavalry (1903-6), after which he returned to England and was employed at the War Office first as Director of Military Training and later as Director of Staff Duties, where he had much to do with the creation of the General Staff. In 1909 he accepted the appointment of Chief of the Staff, Army Head-quarters, India, which he held until Feb., 1912.

European War. In that year he was ordered to England to take up the important appointment of Commander-in-Chief, Aldershot Command, which he was still holding when the European War broke out. While Chief of Staff in India, Haig had been promoted lieutenant-general (31st Oct., 1910)—he had been a major-general since 1904—and in Aug., 1914, he stepped naturally into the position of Commander of the 1st Army Corps of the British Expeditionary Force.

In November of the same year he was promoted to full General, and when in Dec., 1915, Sir J. French resigned the Chief Command of the British armies in France, it was Sir Douglas Haig, a full General of only twenty-nine years' service and in his fifty-fifth year of age, who was selected by the Cabinet to succeed him in his difficult post.

By this time the army in France was growing daily both in personnel and material: fed in the one case by battalions and divisons of the New Army, and in the other by the war material provided by the Ministry of Munitions (formed in June, 1915). Vol. iii of the *Chronology of the War* gives some interesting figures showing how the supply of munitions increased after the formation of the Ministry, and from this we take the following as an example.

In the third quarter of 1915, i.e. just after the Ministry had been formed, the output of guns—light, medium and heavy—was 1,118, and of rounds of artillery ammunition, 2,083,000. In the third quarter of 1918 the output under the same headings was 3,064 guns and 15,780,000 rounds. In Dec., 1915, in spite of the fact that men and munitions were arriving in increasing numbers, Haig refused to be stampeded into an attack until he was ready and was quite certain that his new divisions had been sufficiently initiated into the practical part of modern soldiering to permit them to take part in a general attack. With this end in view he, so to speak marked time, during which period his battalions were being trained and his reserves of munitions were piling up.

A reference to p. 108 of vol. ii of the *Chronology of the War* will show that the British army in France took the initiative in no main events till 1st July, 1916, on which date began the great combined Franco-British offensive on the Somme.

These operations, though they did not perhaps produce the far-reaching effects expected, were nevertheless of great value, and, beyond the actual tangible gains, the experience obtained enabled General Head-quarters to make further improvements and adjustments in the still-growing British Expeditionary Force; and to such an extent were the lessons learnt and acted upon that towards the end of 1917 a writer in the *National Review* says: 'Profiting by the situation which Haig and his men have created, the French have been able to deal a tremendous blow near Verdun in that dramatic fashion of theirs. ... Vienna had to pray in vain for troops to meet Cadorna's devastating strokes. ... The great General Staff in Berlin had been unable to overwhelm the Rumanian army. . . . For four months Haig had been calling the tune ... and we are bound to acknowledge that it is in no small degree due to the grit and abilities of the Commander-in-Chief himself that the military resources of the empire occupy the centre of the stage at the beginning of the fourth year of the world-wide conflict.''

On 1st Jan., 1917, Sir Douglas Haig was promoted Field-Marshal, and on 14th July of the same year he was created a Knight of the Thistle. The great German attack of the early part of 1918 was the occasion on which the Field-Marshal issued his stirring Order of the Day (13th April) in which occur the very human words: ''Many of us are now tired. ... Victory belongs to the side which holds out longest. . . .'' On the 13th March, 1919, Haig was appointed to the Command of the Forces at Home, which he retained till General Head-quarters of Great Britain ceased to exist with the official end of the war in the following year. On 6th Aug., 1919, in recognition of his great services, he was created an Earl.

Work for Ex-Service Men. After the end of the war Earl Haig made the cause of the ex-service men his own, and spared neither time nor trouble in his endeavours to obtain fair treatment for them—both from the Government and from employers of labour. Earl Haig's principal Dispatches were published in London as follows: 1916 —30th May, 12th Dec.; 1918—1st Jan., 20th Feb., 16th April, 23rd April, 21st Oct.; 1919—1st Jan., 11th April.—Cf. Lieutenant-Colonel J. H.

Boraston (editor), *Despatches* 1915–1919.

HAIL, small masses of ice or frozen rain falling from the clouds in showers or storms, varying in their form, being either angular, pyramidal, or stellated, as well as in their consistency, being sometimes as hard as ice and sometimes as soft as snow. At the centre there is generally an opaque spongy mass, resembling sleet in its composition, and round this a semi-transparent congealed mass, consisting of a succession of layers or strata, is formed.

Properly there are two kinds of hail —the small grains which generally fall in winter and usually before snow; and the large hail which occurs chiefly in spring and summer, and is most severe in very hot climates. The small-grained hail is probably formed by the freezing of rain-drops as they pass in falling through colder air than that from which they started. The large or common hail is probably due to the meeting of two currents of air,

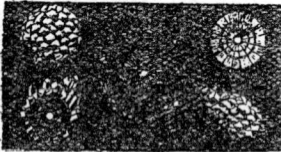

Hail. 1, Soft hail. 2, 3, Sections of hailstones. 4, 5, Remarkable types of crystalline form

of very unequal temperature and electric tension.

The usual size of hailstones is about ¼ inch in diameter, but they are frequently of much larger dimensions, sometimes even 3 or 4 inches in diameter. In hot climates they are very destructive to crops.

HAILES, LORD. *See* DALRYMPLE, SIR DAVID.

HAILEYBURY. English public school. It is just outside Hertford and originated as a college, opened in 1806 by the East India Co., for educating boys for its service. In 1862, the company having been dissolved, the buildings were acquired for a public school and have since been much enlarged. There is accommodation for over 500 boys.

HAILSHAM, market town of Sussex. It is 54 miles from London by the S. Rly., and 7 miles from Eastbourne. It is an agricultural centre. Pop. 4,907,

HAILSHAM, Viscount, English lawyer. Born in 1872, Douglas McGarel Hogg was the eldest son of the philanthropist, Quintin Hogg. He was educated at Eton and, after some years in business, became a barrister in 1902. In 1922 he was elected Conservative M.P. for Marylebone, was made Attorney-General and was knighted. He left office in 1923, but returned in 1924 and was Attorney-General until made Lord Chancellor and a peer in 1928. In 1929 he resigned with the other members of the Unionist Government and acted as one of the Opposition leaders in the House of Lords. In 1929 he was made a viscount and in 1931 he joined the National Government as Secretary for War, an office he still holds (1933). He is also leader of the House of Lords.

HAINAN, an island of China, belonging to the province of Kwangtung, between the China Sea and the Gulf of Tongking, and separated from the mainland by a channel of 15 miles, encumbered with shoals and coral reefs. It is almost oval in shape, and has an area of nearly 14,000 sq. miles.

The fertile lowlands on the northern and western coasts are occupied by immigrant Chinese, to the number of about 1,500,000, who cultivate rice, sugar, tobacco, &c. The fisheries are also productive. The interior, which is mountainous and covered with forests, is inhabited by a distinct race still in a very primitive stage. The capital is Kiung-chow, on the northern coast, a large seaport.

HAINAUT, or HAINAULT (ā-nō; Du. *Hennegowen*; Ger. *Hennegau*), province of Belgium, bounded on the south and west by France; area, 1,437 sq. miles. Though nowhere properly mountainous, it is very hilly in the south-east, where it is covered by the Western Ardennes. In other directions it is generally flat, though well diversified.

About three-fourths of the whole surface is arable, and scarcely a hundredth part is waste. The soil is generally fertile, and there are extensive coal-fields, coal, together with flax, linen, hemp, tobacco, and porcelain being the chief articles of export. Manufactures, chiefly cutlery, woollen and linen goods, &c., are carried on to a great extent. The capital is Mons. Estimated pop. in (1931), 1,274,375.

History. The old province of Hainault, in Cæsar's time the native district of the Nervii, was in the tenth century governed by a race of counts, the succession of which continued unbroken till 1436, when Jacqueline, heiress of William IV, was forced to cede her lands to Philip, Duke of Burgundy. With Mary of Burgundy, Hainault passed to the House of Austria, but in 1659 a part of it was ceded to France, and is now included in the department of Nord.

HAINBURG, or HAIMBURG (hīn'bụrh, hīm'bụrh), a town of Austria, beautifully situated on the Danube, 27 miles south-east of Vienna. It is walled; has an ancient town house, remains of a Roman aqueduct, and other antiquities. The old castle on the height is the Heimburg of the *Nibelungenlied*, the old frontier fortress of the Huns. Pop. (district), 15,200.

HAINICHEN (hī'nih-en), a town of Saxony, 41 miles south-east of Leipzig. It has manufactures of woollen, linen, and cotton cloth, and is the chief seat of the German flannel manufacture. Pop. 8,010.

HAIPHONG, chief port of the French colony of Tonking. It was opened to foreign residence and trade in 1876. Pop. about 18,500.

HAIR, the fine, thread-like, more or less elastic substance, of various form and colour, which constitutes the covering of the skin in the class of Mammalia. It has the same use as feathers in birds, and scales in fishes and reptiles.

No species of Mammalia is without hair in an adult state, not even the Cetacea. In quadrupeds it is of the most various conformation, from the finest wool to the quills of a porcupine or the bristles of the hog. The human body is naturally covered with long hair only on a few parts; yet the parts which we should generally describe as destitute of it produce a fine, short, colourless, sometimes hardly perceptible hair. The only places entirely free from it are the palms of the hands and the soles of the feet; but the body of the male often produces hair like that of the head on the breast, shoulders, arms, &c.

Each hair consists of a shaft and a root. The shaft or part outside the skin does not grow; but the root embedded in the skin expands at its lower end into a swelling or bulb which is composed of little cells and grows by forming new cells, the old ones being pressed forward and becoming part of the shaft. The colour is due to minute pigment granules in the cells of the hair.

The colour of the hair is a race character; and the shape of the shaft has likewise been used in this way, transverse sections showing circular, oval, flat, or reniform outlines. The human hair varies according to age, sex, country, and circumstances. At birth an infant generally has light hair. It always grows darker and stiffer with age. The same is the case with the eyelashes and eyebrows. At the age of puberty the hair grows in the armpits, &c., of both sexes, and on the chin of the male. The hair of men is stronger and stiffer; that of females longer (even in a state of nature), thicker, and not so liable to be shed.

Connected with the hairs are small glands which secrete an oily substance serving as a lubricant to the skin as well as the hair. These are called sebaceous glands. If the root is destroyed, there is no means of reproducing the hair; but if it falls out without the root being destroyed, as is often the case after nervous fevers, the hair grows out again of itself. Each hair, indeed, lasts only a certain time, after which it falls out and is replaced by another as long as the papilla is not weakened.

Greyness of hair is caused by a deficient amount of pigment granules in the hair cells. The deficiency arises at the hair bulb where the cells are produced. Any influences that affect the nutrition of the bulb may thus affect the colour as well as the growth of the hair.

Baldness is caused by atrophy of the papilla, generally due to lessened circulation of the blood in the scalp. For some diseases which have a close connection with the hair, *see* PLICA POLONICA, RINGWORM, SYCOSIS.

Under ordinary circumstances hair is a very stable substance. It is the last thing which decays, and it often grows after death and lasts for centuries. Hair is not acted on by water, but heated in it under pressure it decomposes, evolves sulphuretted hydrogen, and dissolves; it is also dissolved by alkalies and acids. When burned, it emits a disagreeable odour as of burning horn.

In Manufacture. Hair for manufacture is obtained chiefly from the horse, the ox, the hog, the goat, especially the Angora or Mohair goat, the camel, and the alpaca, also very widely to-day, from the rabbit (soft felt hats). That of the first three is most used for upholstery purposes, the short hair being manufactured into curled hair for stuffing, and the long straight hair manufactured into hair-cloth for seating. The long hair is also reserved for the manufacture of fishing-lines, brushes, &c. White hair is of the most value, being most adapted for dyeing and for the manufacture of fancy articles.

The horsehair used for weaving comes chiefly from Russia, Germany, Belgium, South America, and Australia. Before the European War Russia supplied the largest quantity of the bristles so largely used for brushes. The sable, the miniver, the marten, and the badger supply the finer brushes or hair-pencils of painters. The hair of the goat, the camel, and the alpaca is chiefly used in combination with or subordinated to wool and other fibres for spinning and weaving into dress fabrics.

Human hair is used chiefly for the manufacture of wigs, curls, beards, chignons, &c. Most of the supply comes from France, Germany, and Italy, where the peasant girls sell their hair to itinerant dealers. In every case, and for any purpose, hair is always best taken from the living subject, dead hair being much inferior. —BIBLIOGRAPHY: Walsh, *The Hair and its Diseases*; W. A. Kidd, *The Direction of Hair in Animals and Man.*

HAIR-DYES, substances for giving hair some particular colour desired. The numerous preparations sold for this purpose have generally a basis of lead or nitrate of silver. Bismuth, pyrogallic acid, sulphur, the juice of green walnut shells and other astringent vegetable juices, are also employed.

HAIR-GRASS (Aira), a genus of grasses belonging to that division of the order in which the spikelets have two or more florets, and the inflorescence is a loose panicle. It is of little use for cattle, which dislike it, but may serve where covert is wanted for game. *A. cæspitōsa*, or tufted hairgrass, the Scottish windlestrae, is used as thatch for ricks, and in some places for making mats.

HAIR-POWDER, a preparation of pulverized starch and some perfume, formerly much used to whiten the head. Sometimes the powder was coloured. The custom of wearing it was introduced from France into England in the reign of Charles II. To make the powder hold, the hair was usually greased with pomade. It is now scarcely to be seen except on the heads of footmen in attendance on people of rank or wealth.

HAIRS OF PLANTS, outgrowths from the superficial layer or *epidermis*, consisting of one to many cells, and varying greatly in form and use. The commonest function of a hairy covering on leaves is the reduction of transpiration; other hairs secrete essential oils, resins, &c. (glandular hairs of Primula or Hop), or serve to absorb water (many epiphytes), or afford protection by their harshness (Boraginaceæ) or stinging properties (nettle). The *root-hairs* are the principal absorbing structures of the Higher Plants.

HAIR-SPRING, in watches, the fine hair-like spring made of steel which is attached to the axle of the balance wheel, and serves by its resisting power to equalize the vibrations of the escapement-wheel.

HAITI, or SANTO DOMINGO, one of the West Indies, after Cuba the largest of these islands. It lies south-east of Cuba, from which it is separated by the Windward Passage, has a length of 400 miles, and is 29,536 sq. miles in area.

It is of irregular shape and is traversed from west to east by three chains of mountains with extensive plains between. In the central range is Loma Tina (10,200 feet), while the principal plain, the Vega Real, lies between the northern and the central ranges. There are extensive forests from which lignum vitæ, dye-woods, and mahogany are obtained. Rivers are numerous but small, and the climate is hot, humid, and generally unsuited to Europeans. Politically it is divided into two republics, Haiti and Santo Domingo (*both of which see*).

History. Haiti was discovered by Columbus in 1492. It was then inhabited by perhaps 2,000,000 natives, but so ruthlessly did the Spaniards deal with the aborigines that within a century they practically exterminated them, having introduced negro slaves in their place.

In 1630 the French settled in the western part of the island, which part was ceded to them in 1697, and which they retained till 1803 when they were driven out by Dessalines. In 1821 the Spanish portion declared itself independent of the mother country, and assumed the name of Spanish Haiti; but it was subjugated by Boyer, the President of the Haitian Republic, or French Haiti.

In 1844 the inhabitants of the Spanish portion rose, and formed themselves into a republic under the name of San Domingo (Republica Dominica). Spain evacuated the island in 1865. From that period its history has presented an almost uninterrupted scene of revolution and bloodshed. It now comprises the Republic of Haiti on the west side of the island, and the Dominican Republic, Santo Domingo, on the east.

HAITI, a republic comprising the western end of the Island of Haiti, West Indies. The area is 10,204 sq. miles, and the population of 2,300,200 is composed of negroes and mulattoes. The religion is Roman Catholicism (the clergymen being French). Education is free and compulsory, and there is a university at Port-au-Prince. French is the official language. The capital and chief port is Port-au-Prince, and other towns are Cape Haiti, Aux Cayes, and Jacmel.

Production and Industry. Agriculture is the main industry, coffee, cocoa, cotton, tobacco, and sugar being the chief products. Logwood is a valuable export. There is a large sugar central at Port-au-Prince, rum is made (but not exported), and pineapple packing and tobacco manufacture are increasing in importance. The mineral resources of the republic are neglected.

Trade, &c. In 1931 the exports and imports were valued at 8,963,419 dollars and 9,576,318 dollars respectively. The exports to and the imports from Great Britain were valued at £190,547 and £110,347 respectively; in 1932 they amounted to £257,871 and £189,005 respectively. The principal exports (in order of value) are coffee, cotton, sugar, log-wood, and cocoa. There were 158 miles of railway track in 1932, and 935 miles of good roads. There is an automatic telephone exchange at Port-au-Prince. The currency unit is the gourde (fixed value 5 gourdes = 1 U.S. dollar). The metric system is compulsory. For defence there is an armed constabulary, the officers of which are partly drawn from the U.S. Marine Corps and Navy, and will retire in 1936.

Legislation. Haiti, which became independent in 1804, is governed by a Constitution ratified in 1932. The legislative power is vested in a Senate (20 members) and a Chamber of Deputies (36 deputies) who elect the President and sit as a National Assembly for six years. The administration is carried on by the President and five Secretaries of State.

In 1915 a treaty was signed with the United States of America whereby that country established a virtual protectorate over Haiti. The American President now appoints a High Commissioner to Haiti. This has tended to stabilize the country, and the era of revolution and bloodshed has given way to a period of industrial and commercial development. This treaty expires in 1936. *See* HAITI (island).—BIBLIOGRAPHY: Sir Spenser St. John, *Haiti, or the Black Republic*; H. Pritchard, *Where Black Rules White*; J. N. Léger, *Haiti: her History and Detractors.*

HAJIPUR, a town of India, in the Muzaffarpur district, Bengal, on the Little Gandak, a short distance above its confluence with the Ganges. Its command of water traffic gives it considerable commercial importance. Pop. 22,000.

HAKE, the *Merluccius vulgāris* of Europe, and the *M. albĭdus* of North America, fishes belonging to that division of the cod family, or Gadĭdæ, which has the head much flattened, and two dorsal and one long anal fin. The European hake is known in some places as king of the herrings, on which it preys.

HAKIM, a Turkish word, originally signifying *sage, philosopher,* and then a *physician. Hakim bashi* is the physician of the Sultan, that is to say, the chief of the physicians, always a Turk; whilst the true physicians in the seraglio under him are western Europeans, Greeks, and Jews.

HAKLUYT, Richard, one of the earliest English collectors of voyages and maritime journals, was born in 1553, died in 1616. He entered Christ Church, Oxford, in 1575, and became so eminent for his acquaintance with cosmography that he was appointed public lecturer on that science. About 1584 he went to Paris as chaplain to the English Ambassador, and stayed there five years.

After his return home he prepared for the press his collection of *The Principal Navigations, Voyages, and Discoveries of the English Nation, made by Sea, or over Land, within the Compass of these* 1,500 *Years.* The first volume, in folio, was published in 1589, and the third and last in 1600. Besides narratives of nearly 220 voyages, these volumes comprise patents, letters, instructions, and other documents not readily to be found elsewhere. Hakluyt died a prebendary of Westminster and rector of Wetheringset in Suffolk, and was interred in Westminster Abbey.

The **Hakluyt Society,** named after Richard Hakluyt, was founded in 1846 for the purpose of printing rare and unprinted voyages and travels. More than 165 volumes have now been issued under its supervision. Hakluyt's *Voyages* were reprinted at Edinburgh (1889–90), and in London in 1904–6. —Cf. J. W. Jones, Introduction to the Hakluyt Society's edition of *Divers Voyages.*

HAKODA'TE, a city of Japan, near the south end of the Island of Yezo, at the foot of a hill on the shore of a beautiful and spacious bay, which forms one of the best harbours in the world. Hakodate is one of the ports opened to British commerce through Lord Elgin's treaty with the Japanese Government in 1858. Pop. (1930), 197,252.

HAL, or **HALLE,** a town of Belgium, province of South Brabant, on the Senne, about 10 miles from Brussels. It has a fine old Gothic church and town house; manufactures of beetroot sugar, soap, and leather. The town was occupied by the Germans from 1914 to 1918. Pop. 16,000.

HALACHA (hal'a-ka), or **HALAKA** (Heb., 'rule'), the Jewish oral or traditional law, as distinguished from the written law laid down in the Scriptures, and like it believed to be of divine origin. It was finally reduced

V—M

to a written code forming part of the *Talmud*.

HALBERD, or HALBERT (O.Fr. *haleberde*, Fr. *hallebarde*), an offensive weapon, consisting of a pole or shaft about 6 feet long, having its head

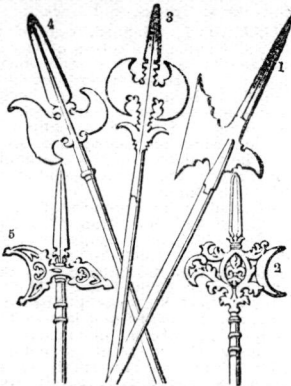

Halberts. 1, Halbert (time of Henry VIII). 2, Halbert with fleur-de-lis (Henry VII). 3, Double-axed Halbert (Charles I). 4, Halbert (Charles II). 5, Halbert (William III)

armed with a steel point edged on both sides. Near the head was a cross piece of steel somewhat in the form of an axe, with a spike or hook at the back. It was used by the Danes, Germans, and Swiss previous to the thirteenth century.

In the English army it was much used in the sixteenth century, and gave its name to troops called halberdiers, to whom was confided the defence of the colours, and other special duties. It is now used only on ceremonial occasions.

HALBERSTADT (hàl'bĕr-stàt), a town of Prussia, in the province of Saxony, 32 miles s.w. of Magdeburg, on the right bank of the Holzemme. It is an old town, with many timber-framed and curiously ornamented houses. Its principal buildings are the cathedral, the Liebfrauen church, an old Episcopal palace, and town house. It has considerable manufactures of carpets, soap, leather, oil, and gloves Pop. 48,184.

HAL'CYON, an old or poetical name for the kingfisher. It was fabled to lay its eggs in nests that floated on the sea, about the winter solstice, and to have the power of charming the winds and waves during the period of incubation, so that the weather was then calm. *See* KINGFISHER.

HALDANE, Professor John Burdon Sanderson, British scientist. Born 1892, the son of Professor John Scott Haldane, and educated at Eton and Oxford, he has been Sir William Dunn Reader in Biochemistry at Cambridge University since 1922, and head of the Genetical Department, John Innes Horticultural Institution since. In 1930 he was appointed Fullerian Professor of Physiology at the Royal Institution. During the European War he served with the Black Watch in France and Iraq, and was twice wounded. He is a prolific writer on scientific subjects, particularly on his own branch of chemical physiology and genetics, and his works have achieved wide popularity. They include *Dœdalus*, (1924); *Possible Worlds* (1927); *Science and Ethics* (1928); *Enzymes* (1930). *Animal Biology* (1927), was written in collaboration with Professor J. S. Huxley.

HALDANE, Rt. Hon. Richard Burdon, Viscount Haldane, K.T., O.M., F.R.S., philosophical writer and politician, born 1856, and studied with distinction at Edinburgh and Göttingen. He was called to the Bar in 1879; entered Parliament as Liberal member for Haddingtonshire in 1885, a constituency which he represented

Halcyon

till 1911. In 1890 he became Queen's Counsel, in 1902 a Privy Councillor, and in 1911 he was raised to the peerage.

From 1905 to 1911 he occupied the post of Secretary of State for War, and was able to carry into effect a new scheme of army organization. In 1912 he was made Lord Chancellor, and held this office till 1915, when he was not included in the Coalition ministry. He was made Lord Chancellor in the Labour Cabinet of 1924.

From 1902 to 1904 he was Gifford Lecturer in St. Andrews University. Among his publications are: *The Life of Adam Smith*; *Education and Empire*; *The Pathway to Reality*; *The Philosophy of Humanism*; *Human Experience: A Study of its Structure*. He died in 1928. Strenuous as was Haldane's political and professional life, it by no means occupied the whole of his versatile mind. He kept up the study of philosophy and ranked among the leading philosophers of the day. Education was another of his interests. He was chairman of the Royal Commission on the university of London and helped to found the newer English universities. In 1929 his *Autobiography* appeared; in his lifetime he had published *Before the War*, a defence of his activities.

HALE, George Ellery. American astronomer. Born in Chicago, 29th June, 1868, he was educated at Boston. His first experience of astronomical work was gained in the observatory at Harvard, and he soon became a director of an astrophysical observatory and professor of astrophysics. In 1895 he became director of the Yerkes Observatory, and in 1897 Professor of Astrophysics at Chicago. He invented the spectroheliograph and in 1904 was appointed director of the great observatory at Mount Wilson, California. He has edited *The Astrophysical Journal*, and written a good deal on his particular subject, astrophysics.

HALE, Sir Matthew, an eminent English judge, was born at Alderley, in Gloucestershire, in 1609, and died in 1676. He studied at Oxford, was called to the Bar, became a judge of the common bench in 1654, was knighted and made chief baron of the exchequer in 1660, and was raised to the chief-justiceship of the King's Bench in 1671. After his death appeared his *History of the Pleas of the Crown*, *The Jurisdiction of the Lords' House*, and *The History of the Common Law of England*; of which there have been repeated editions, with comments. He also wrote several religious works.

HALE, urban district of Lancashire. It is 10 miles from Manchester, on the Cheshire Lines. Rly., and is practically a residential suburb of that city. In the churchyard is the grave of John Middleton, who was said to be 9 ft. 3 ins. high. He died in 1623. Pop. (1931) 10,669.

HALES, Alexander de, surnamed the *Irrefragable Doctor*, an English theologian, born at Hales, in Glouces-

tershire, date unknown, celebrated among the controversialists of the thirteenth century. He studied at the Universities of Oxford and Paris, became, in 1230, a professor in the latter city, where he died in 1245. His *Summa Theologiæ* put the the *Sententiæ* of Peter Lombard into syllogistic form. He also commented on Aristotle, on the *Psalms*, and the *Apocalypse*.

HALESOWEN, an urban district and market town of England, Worcestershire, in a fertile valley watered by the Stour and its tributaries 7½ miles south-west of Birmingham and 10 miles from Birmingham on the joint line of the London, Midland and Scottish and Great Western Railways; with extensive manufactures of iron and steel goods, &c., Pop. (1931), 31,058. The Leasowes, where William Shenstone, the poet, was born and died, was in the parish of Halesowen. Near are the remains of a Premonstratensian abbey, founded in 1215.

HALÉVY. Name of a family of French scholars. Ludovic Halévy made his reputation as a dramatist. He died May 8, 1908, leaving a son, Elie Halévy. He was born at Etretat, 6th Sept., 1870 and became a professor in Paris. He is known as a student of English history and institutions and his works include *The Formation of Philosophic Radicalism* and *The History of the English People in the 19th Century*, to give them their English titles.

HALÉVY (à-lā-vè), **Jacques François Fromental Élie,** a French musical composer, born of Jewish parentage at Paris 1799, died at Nice in 1862. He studied at the Conservatory under Lambert and Cherubini, and was sent to Italy to finish his musical education. Here he wrote his first two operas *Les Bohémiennes* and *Pygmalion*. The first of his pieces performed was a little comic opera, *L'Artisan*, given at the Théâtre Feydeau, in Paris, in 1827.

His *chef-d'œuvre*, *La Juive*, appeared in 1835, and rapidly obtained a European celebrity. Among his other works are: *L'Éclair*, *Guido et Ginevra*, *La Reine de Chypre*, *Le Val d'Andorre*, *Le Fée aux roses*. He was a cultivated and scholarly composer but without much genius.

HALÉVY, Joseph, French Orientalist, born at Adrianople 15th Dec., 1827, died in 1917. He studied in his native town and at Bucharest, and in 1868 was commissioned to study the conditions of the Falashas in Abyssinia. In 1869–70 he travelled in Yemen in search of Sabæan inscriptions. He was a prominent Biblical critic and an Assyriologist. He contended that the Sumerian people never existed, and that their so-called writing was a cryptography invented by the Babylonian priests. He founded and edited the *Revue Sémitique*.

HALÉVY, Ludovic, son of Léon Halévy, born in 1834, died in 1908, was a dramatist, a popular author of vaudevilles, and wrote the librettos of most of Offenbach's operas. He collaborated with Henri Meilhac, and their first success was *La Belle Hélène* (1865). Halévy also wrote novels, among which *L'Abbé Constantin* (1882) is famous.

HALF-BLOOD, in law, relationship by being born of the same father, but not of the same mother (consanguinean relationship); or born of the same mother, but not of the same father (uterine relationship). In the succession to real or landed property in England, the half-blood relations by the father's side succeed after the

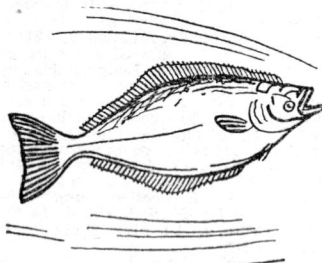

Halibut

full-blood relations; and next, the half-blood relations by the mother's side.

HALF-MOON, in fortification, an outwork composed of two faces forming a salient angle, whose gorge is in the form of a crescent or half-moon.

HALF-PAY, in effect a species of temporary pension. An officer may be placed on the half-pay list either compulsorily, according to certain regulations, or, as substantive lieutenant-colonels or colonels, voluntarily. The most usual reason for being placed on the half-pay list is medical unfitness contracted in the service. Officers on the active list elected to the House of Commons are also usually placed on the half-pay list. The rates of half-pay vary, for example, from £1,800 a year for a field-marshal, £3 5s. a day for a full general (q.v.), 18s. 6d. for a senior major, to 5s. 6d. for a 2nd lieutenant.

HALIAËTUS (hal-i-a'ē-tus), the genus of birds to which belong the white-tailed sea-eagle or erne (*H. albicillus*) of Britain, and the white-headed or bald eagle (*H. leucocephalus*) of America, the chosen symbol of the United States. *See* EAGLE.

HALIBURTON, Thomas Chandler, British humorous writer, born at Windsor, Nova Scotia, in 1796, died in 1865. He practised as a barrister in Halifax, wrote *An Historical and Statistical Account of Nova Scotia,* in 1829, and contributed a series of humorous letters to a Halifax newspaper under the pseudonym of 'Sam Slick.' These were published in book form and were augmented by others, forming *The Clockmaker, or Sayings and Doings of Samuel Slick.* In 1842 he became judge of the Supreme Court of Nova Scotia, but subsequently gave up his professional duties and came to reside in England. Here he published *The Attaché, or Sam Slick in England.* His hero again appears in *Sam Slick's Traits of American Humour* (1852). Another work of his of some importance is *Rule and Misrule of the English in America* (1851). In 1859 Judge Haliburton was elected member of Parliament for Launceston.

HALIBUT, or **HOLIBUT,** the *Hippoglossus vulgāris*, one of the largest of the Pleuronectidæ or flat-fish family, sometimes attaining a length of over 10 feet and weighing more than 300 lb. The fish has a compressed body, one side resembling the back and another the belly, and both eyes on the right side of the head. It is caught on both sides of the Atlantic, and is much prized for the table.

HALICARNAS'SUS, in ancient geography, the capital of Caria, in Asia Minor, once an important city. Queen Artemisia erected here, in honour of her husband, King Mausōlus, the celebrated tomb hence known as the *Mausoleum.* Halicarnassus was the native place of Herodotus.

HALICHONDRIA (-kon'-), a genus of sponges comprising the common siliceous sponges of the British coasts. The crumb-of-bread sponge (*H. panicea*) encrusts rocks between tide-marks, and a branching species *H. oculāta,* is popularly known as the 'mermaid's glove.'

HALICORE (ha-lik'o-rē). *See* DUGONG.

HALIDON HILL, an eminence about a mile to the north-west of Berwick, the scene of a disastrous defeat of the Scots by the English, 19th July, 1333. Edward III of England had laid siege to Berwick, the Governor of which promised to surrender on 20th of July if not previously relieved. On the 19th Archibald Douglas, Regent of Scotland, led a Scottish army to the relief of the town, and attacked the English at Halidon Hill, but was totally routed with the loss of 10,000 men.—Cf. A. Lang, *History of Scotland*.

HAL'IFAX, Charles Montague, Earl of, an English poet and statesman, born in 1661, died in 1715. Educated at Westminster School and Trinity College, Cambridge, he first attracted notice by his verses, and in 1687 wrote, in conjunction with Matthew Prior, *The Town and Country Mouse.* He entered the House of Commons as member for Malden during the Convention Parliament, became a Lord of the Treasury in 1692, and Chancellor of the Exchequer in 1694. His administration was distinguished by the adoption of the funded debt system, and by the establishment of the Bank of England.

In 1700 he was raised to the peerage as Baron Halifax, was twice impeached by the House of Commons, and remained out of office during the reign of Anne. Having taken an active part in securing the succession of the House of Brunswick, George I created him an earl, and bestowed on him the order of the Garter. In 1714 he became First Lord of the Treasury.

His character was a mixture of meanness and arrogance, but his taste in literature and the arts was good, and he had a great talent for finance.—Cf. Burnet, *History of his Own Times.*

HALIFAX, George Savile, Marquess of, son of Sir William Savile, English statesman and writer, born 1630, died 1695. Having exerted himself for the return of Charles II, he was created Viscount Halifax in 1667, in 1669 Earl, and in 1682 Marquess of Halifax, being also Keeper of the Privy Seal and President of the Council. He supported James II, but lost his favour by opposing the repeal of the Test and Habeas Corpus Acts. He was chosen Speaker of the House of Lords in the Convention Parliament, and largely contributed to the elevation of William III to the throne.

He wrote *Advice to a Daughter,* and various political tracts, such as the *Character of a Trimmer,* and *Maxims of State.* Halifax himself was a specimen of the trimmer, his conduct, however, being guided more by patriotic than personal reasons.

HALIFAX, a municipal and county borough of England, in the county of York (West Riding), on the Hebble, 36 miles w.s.w. of York. It is built on a rising slope, and has a very picturesque appearance. The more modern streets are spacious and well paved. Among the principal buildings are the parish church of St. John the Baptist (restored 1879), All Souls' Church, the Square Church, the town

hall, market hall, theatre, assembly rooms, infirmary, and the Crossley and Porter orphan home and school. There are excellent schools and four public parks.

Halifax commands abundant supplies of coal, and inland waterways connect it with Hull and Liverpool. It is one of the centres of the woollen and worsted manufactures in Yorkshire, a great variety of goods being produced. There are also iron-, chemical-, and machine-works. From 1832 to 1918 Halifax was also a parliamentary borough, sending two members to Parliament. Pop. (1931), 98,122.

HALIFAX, a Canadian city and naval station, capital of Nova Scotia, situated near the middle of the south coast, on the western side of Halifax harbour, one of the best and most spacious in North America, and easy of access for the largest ships at all seasons.

The length of the harbour is about 6 miles, and it terminates in a beautiful sheet of water called Bedford Basin, within which are 10 sq. miles of good anchorage. City and harbour are strongly fortified, and there is an extensive dockyard, with a great graving dock. The European War retarded the improvements begun in 1914–5.

Halifax is an important naval station, and the dockyard is now in Canada's hands. Being the Atlantic terminus of great railway systems, and a winter port, it has a steamship trade with Liverpool, New York, Boston, &c., and is also an important coaling-station.

The industries embrace cotton, sugar, iron, paint, machinery, cars, and paper. The city has spacious and regular streets, some handsome public buildings, and among its institutions is the Dalhousie University. The city was founded in 1749 and named in honour of the second Earl of Halifax. It has a broadcasting station (49. 59M.). Pop. (1931), 59,275.

HALIO'TIS, a genus of sea-snails, commonly called *ormers, ear-shells,* or *sea-ears,* found adhering to rocks on the shore, and remarkable for the pearly iridescence of the inner surface of the shell, which is perforated by a row of holes near the margin. They are esteemed as a delicacy in the Channel Islands. The name is derived from their likeness to an ear.

HALL, Basil, a naval officer and traveller, son of Sir James Hall of Dunglass, born at Edinburgh in 1788, entered the navy in 1802, and became post-captain in 1817. Amongst his principal works are: *A Voyage of Discovery to the west coast of Corea and the great Loo Choo Island* (1817);

Extracts from a Journal (written on the Pacific coast of America); *Travels in North America* (1829); *Fragments of Voyages and Travels*; *Schlos Heinfeld, or a Winter in Styria*; besides many papers contributed to journals and scientific societies. Ultimtely his mind gave way, and he died in Haslar Hospital, Gosport, in 1844.

HALL, Charles Francis, an Arctic explorer, born at Rochester, New Hampshire, United States, in 1821, died 8th Nov., 1871. He began life as a blacksmith; became a journalist in Cincinnati; in 1860 organized an Arctic expedition in search of Franklin, and remained amongst the Esqui-

Ear Shell

maux two years, acquiring their language and habits. In 1864 he undertook a second expedition to the same regions, where he remained till 1869.

In 1871, at the instigation of Hall, the United States Government fitted out the *Polaris* for an expedition to the North Pole, and placed Captain Hall in command. The *Polaris* sailed from New York 29th June, 1871, and on 30th Aug. reached lat. 82° 16′ N. and then turned back to winter in a sheltered bay, lat. 81°38′, where Hall died. The *Polaris* was ultimately abandoned by her crew, who reached home only after experiencing many privations and adventures. An account of his first expedition was given by Captain Hall in his *Arctic Researches and Life amongst the Esquimaux.*

HALL, Edward, an English chronicler, born in London about 1495, died in 1547. He was a lawyer by profession, and attained the rank of a serjeant, and the office of a judge in the sheriff's court. He had a seat

in the House of Commons, and was a zealous Catholic.

Hall's great work *The Union of the Noble and Illustre Famelies of Lancastre and York,* known as *Hall's Chronicle,* was first published in 1542. Other editions, containing a continuation compiled from Hall's notes by Richard Grafton, appeared in 1548 and 1550. It is a curious picture of the manners and customs of the age. An edition of the latter part of the *Chronicle,* by C. Whibley, appeared in 1904.

HALL, Joseph, an English prelate and writer, born 1574, died in 1656. He was educated at Emmanuel College, Cambridge, became successively Dean of Worcester, Bishop of Exeter (1627), and Bishop of Norwich (1641). He agreed with the Puritans in doctrine, but disapproved of their views of church government, and took a prominent part in defending the liturgy of the Church against the views published by the Nonconformists in the tract *Smectymnuus.*

In 1642 he was sent to the Tower along with twelve other prelates who had protested against their expulsion from the House of Peers. In 1643, when the destruction of the Establishment was finally resolved on by the Puritans, he was specially named in the ordinance passed for sequestering what were called notorious delinquents, and heartlessly robbed of all his property by inquisitors, who turned him houseless into the streets.

Ultimately he was allowed to take possession of a small estate which he possessed at Higham, in the vicinity of Norwich. Here he spent the remainder of his days unostentatiously, performing the duties of a faithful pastor. Amongst his writings are; *Virgidemiarum,* a series of poetical satires written in his earlier years; *A Century of Meditations*; and *Contemplations.*—Cf. G. Lewis, *Life of Joseph Hall.*

HALL, Oliver, English artist. Born in London in 1869, he studied art there. He became known by his etchings, and then by his landscape paintings, one of which, 'Shap Moors,' is in the Tate Gallery, London. In 1920 he was elected A.R.A., and in 1927 became an R.A.

HALL, Robert, English Baptist minister, was born at Arnesby, Leicestershire, 1764, and died in 1831. He studied at the Baptist College at Bristol, and afterwards at Aberdeen. In 1783 he became assistant pastor of Broadmead Church in Bristol, suffered for a time from mental alienation, recovered, and became pastor of the Baptist church at Cambridge, where he soon acquired a great reputation by his preaching and his writings, such as *Apology for the Freedom of the Press* (1793), *Modern Infidelity* (1800), and *Reflections on War* (1802).

He again became insane and re-signed his charge, but, recovering, married and settled at Leicester in 1808, till in 1826 he was again called to Bristol. Nearly all his life he suffered so intensely from calculus in the kidney that for twenty years he was never able to pass an entire night in bed, and could obtain rest only by a ruinous use of laudanum. An edition of his works by Dr. O. Gregory appeared in 1831–3.

HALL, an ancient town of Austria, in the Tirol, 6 miles east of Innsbruck, on the Inn, which is here navigable. It has salt-works connected with the Salzberg (2,000 ft.). Pop. 7,520.

HALL, a town of Württemberg. *See* SCHWÄBISCH-HALL.

HALLAM, Henry, English historian, a son of the Dean of Bristol, born at Windsor in 1777, died in 1859. He was educated at Eton and Oxford, and studied for the law, but abandoned it for literary pursuits. His contribu-tions to the *Edinburgh Review* brought him into notice, and his *View of the State of Europe during the Middle Ages,* which appeared in 1818, at once established his reputation.

His next work, the *Constitutional History of England,* published in 1827, showed like the first the solid learning, patient research, accuracy and im-partiality of statement, which are the characteristics of his work. Between 1837 and 1839 appeared his last great work, the *Introduction to the Litera-ture of Europe,* a useful survey of literary history, though wanting in the fineness of judgment necessary for such a work.

His eldest son, Arthur Henry, a youth of high promise, who died suddenly at the age of twenty-two, is the subject of Tennyson's poem *In Memoriam.*

HALLAMSHIRE, until 1918 one of the parliamentary divisions of the West Riding of Yorkshire, being that in which Sheffield is locally situated; one of the Sheffield parliamentary divisions is named Hallam.

HALLÉ, Sir Charles, English musi-cian. Born in Germany, 11th April, 1819, he studied music in Paris and elsewhere. In 1848 he settled in London and became a naturalized Englishman. Hallé won a reputation by the concerts he gave in London and by his work for music in Man-chester, where he founded the Royal College of Music and conducted a fine orchestra (the Hallé Orchestra). In 1888 he was knighted and he died, 25th Oct., 1895.

In 1888 Halle married Wilma Neruda, the widow of Ludwig Normann. She, too, was a German by birth, and having studied music, became one of the lead-ing violinists of the day. Lady Hallé died 5th April, 1911.

HALLE (häl'lĕ), usually called **HALLE AN DER SAALE** (Halle on the Saale), to distinguish it from other places of the same name, an important German town in the Prus-sian province of Saxony, about 20 miles north-west of Leipzig, on the River Saale. The older streets are narrow and crooked, but the appear-ance of the town has been much improved.

Among the principal buildings are the church of the Virgin and that of St. Maurice, the 'Red Tower' (a clock-tower) in the market-place, the mediæval town house, the ruined Moritzburg (originally the citadel), the university buildings, the Pro-testant cathedral, the theatre (com-paratively new), and Francke's In-stitution, founded by Pastor Francke in 1698, comprising an orphan asylum and schools.

The university, with which that of Wittenberg was incorporated in 1817, is a celebrated institution founded in 1694, and attended, before the Euro-pean War, by about 2,500 students.

The town has extensive trade and manufactures, including chemicals, oils, dyes, and agricultural and other machines, besides its old and cele-brated salt-works. Halle is mentioned as early as 1046. It was long a power-ful member of the Hanseatic League. Pop. (1925), 194,636.

HALLECK, Fitz Greene, an Ameri-can poet, born in 1790, died in 1867. He became a clerk in a New York banking-house, and for years was in the employment of John Jacob Astor. In 1809 poems by him and a friend (J. R. Drake) appeared in the *New York Evening Post* under the signa-ture of Croaker & Co., and attracted some attention. In 1820 he published *Fanny,* his longest poem, a satire on the follies and fashions of the day. In 1822 he visited Europe.

Amongst his best poems are: *Marco Bozzaris, To the Memory of Burns, Alnwick Castle,* and *Red Jacket.*

HALLECK, Henry Wager, an American general, born at Utica, near New York, in 1815, died in 1872. He was educated for the army at West Point, and entered the engineers in 1839. In 1846 he published *Elements of Military Art and Science,* and he was raised to the rank of captain for his services in the Mexican War. In 1854 he left the army and settled in San Francisco as a lawyer and director of a mining company.

On the outbreak of the Civil War in 1861 he was created major-general in the United States army. After the victories at Paducah, Fort Henry, Fort Donelson, and the capture of Corinth, he became in 1862 commander-in-chief, till superseded by General Grant in 1864. Ultimately he received the command of the South Division at Louisville, where he died. Amongst his writings are two works on *International Law*.

HALL EFFECT, an electrical effect observed by E. H. Hall in 1879. When a current is passed through a very thin rectangular metal sheet by means of conductors connected to the mid-points of the short edges, on connecting the mid-points of the long edges to a sensitive galvanometer no current is at first observed. If a strong magnetic field is set up at right angles to the metal sheet, a feeble current now flows through the galvanometer. The magnetic field, by disturbing the position of the lines of flow, causes a small portion of the main current to flow through the galvanometer.

The effect is positive in certain metals and negative in others; it appears to be related to the magnetic rotation of polarized light and to the change of resistance of metals in a magnetic field.

HALLELUIA, HALLELUJAH, or **ALLELUIA** (praise ye the Lord), a Hebrew formula of praise often occurring in the *Psalms*, and which is retained in the translations of the various Christian Churches, probably on account of its full and fine sound, so proper for public religious services. The *Great Hallel* is the name given by the Jews to *Psalms* cxx–cxxxvi, which are sung on the feasts of the Passover and Tabernacles.

HALLER, Albrecht von, Swiss physician and physiologist, born in Bern 1708, died in 1777. He studied medicine at Tübingen, and afterwards at Leyden under the famous Boerhaave. He became a public lecturer on anatomy at Bern, and afterwards physician to the hospital and principal librarian. In 1736 he was made professor of anatomy and surgery in the University of Göttingen.

In 1747 his *Primæ Lineæ Physiologiæ* appeared, and in 1757 his *Elementa Physiologiæ Corporis Humani*. Amongst his other works are: *Icones Anatomicæ* (1743), *Bibliothæca Botanica* (1771), *Bibliotheca Anatomica* (1774), *Bibliotheca Chirurgica* (1774), *Bibliotheca Medicinæ Practicæ* (1776).

He was ennobled by the Emperor Francis I, and became chief magistrate of Bern, to which he had retired in 1753. Haller had a considerable reputation as a poet, and he also wrote three philosophical romances, *Usong*, *Alfred the Great*, and *Fabius and Cato*.

HALLEY, Edmund, an English mathematician and astronomer, born in 1656, died in 1742. He was educated at Queen's College, Oxford, published before he was nineteen a method for finding aphelia and eccentricity of planets and stayed two years in St. Helena (1676–8) cataloguing the stars of the southern hemisphere and arranging them into constellations. In 1682 he discovered the comet which bears his name, and his prediction of its return in 1759 was the first of its kind that proved correct.

He surveyed the coast of Dalmatia at the request of the German Emperor, and, returning to England, was elected Savilian professor of geometry at Oxford (1703). In 1713 he was made secretary of the Royal Society, and Astronomer Royal in 1719.

HALLIWELL-PHILLIPPS, James Orchard, originally J. O. Halliwell, Shakespearean scholar, born 1820, died 1889. In 1839 he began his editorial labours with a reprint of *Mandeville's Travels*. He was a leading and active member of the Percy and Shakespeare societies; for the former he edited the *Minor Poems of Lydgate*, *Early Naval Ballads of England*, *Nursery Rhymes of England*, &c.; and for the latter, *The Coventry Mysteries*, *Tarleton's Jests*, *The Fairy Mythology of Shakespeare*, &c.

His chief Shakespearian publications are a *Life of Shakespeare* (1848), the *Works of Shakespeare* (in 16 folio volumes, only 150 copies printed), *Calendar of the Records of Stratford-on-Avon*, *History of New Place*, and *Outlines of the Life of Shakespeare*. He issued also 47 volumes of lithographed facsimiles of the quarto plays, and a great number of pamphlets on Shakespeare, Stratford, and kindred topics. He also published a valuable *Dictionary of Archaic and Provincial Words*.

HALL-MARKS, the marks stamped on plate and other gold and silver

London marks for the first year of the current cycle: lion passant to indicate standard quality; leopard's head, the London hall-mark; date letter; and maker's initials

goods, by means of which the quality (standard of precious metal contained), the maker, and the date of manufacture may be recognized. In the thirteenth century the London Guild of Goldsmiths and Silversmiths had attained great importance, a large monopoly, and numerous privileges.

In order to ensure a high standard, each piece of plate was assayed and marked.

The **King's mark**, so named in 1363, was introduced in 1300 as a leopard's head; really a lion's head, miscalled leopard's owing to the heraldic term *leopart* being applied to a *lion passant guardant*. This mark, the hall-mark proper, still remains in use on London plate; the form has often changed in detail, the present head being much less bold in style than the original.

The maker's mark, originally such a

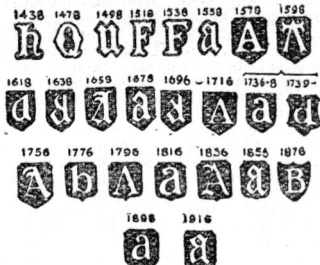

1438 1478 1498 1518 1538 1558 1578 1596

1618 1638 1659 1675 1696—1716 1736-8 1739—

1756 1776 1796 1816 1836 1856 1876

1896 1916

A characteristic London date mark from each cycle of 20 years, commencing in the year specified above the mark

symbol as a fish, bird, horse, or—frequently—a rose or other flower, dates from 1363. In 1696–7 it was changed to the first two letters of the maker's name and now consists of his initial.

The date mark, first used in the fifteenth century—the earliest known example being that on the Nettle-combe chalice of 1479–80—is a single letter of the alphabet from A to U, J being excluded. One of several different forms of alphabet is used for

1784-5 1786-1820 1821-1830 1831-6 1837-1890 1697-1718

Duty marks indicating the payment of duty, which was imposed only between 1784-1890. The two marks 1697-1718 on the right were used when the standard was raised to 11 oz. 10 dwt., and may still be used for that standard. The usual one of 11 oz. 2 dwt. was restored in 1720 with the leopard's head and lion passant

a cycle of twenty years and then changed, Lombardic giving place to court-hand, small or capital Roman, black letter, &c. The shape of the shield enclosing the letters also varies; and in this way, the sequence of the cycles being known, the date of a marked piece is readily identified.

Duty mark: this, the head of the reigning sovereign, was added in

M*

1784, but disappeared in 1890 with the abolition of the duty upon plate.

The **standard mark**, a lion for London, Birmingham, and Chester, denotes the standard proportion of 11 oz. 2 dwt. of silver to 18 dwt. of alloy; other marks denote various pro-

CHESTER   BIRMINGM   SHEFFIELD

1701-1778 1681-903 1779- 1773-   1773-

YORK   EXETER

1411-170G 1701-1856 1575-1698 1701-1875

NEWCASTLE

1248-   1701

Town marks and the periods during which they have been used. York, Exeter, and Newcastle are now closed

portions of silver, while yet others are employed for gold and by the provincial assay towns.

Nominally it was held that provincially-made plate must be sent to London, there to be assayed and marked; but difficulties of transit early led to the tacit recognition of provincial assays and marks, made either by the mayor, or, where a mint existed, by the master of the mint. York had in 1410 its own assay or 'touch'—so called from the primitive early method of rubbing the article

EDINBURGH   GLASGOW   DUBLIN

Scottish and Irish hall-marks and standard marks. The shape of the punch varies from time to time

upon a stone to test the quality; and in 1423 local assays were legalized for York, Newcastle Lincoln, Norwich, Bristol, Salisbury, and Coventry.

The marks of some of these towns, as also those of the present provincial assays (Birmingham, Chester, Sheffield, Edinburgh, Glasgow, Dublin), will be found in the accompanying plate. In 1483 the Edinburgh goldsmiths ranked with other metal-workers as 'hammermen,' and two years later articles of local manufacture were to bear the maker's mark, the mark of the deacon of the guild, and the town mark. Glasgow, with a circuit of 40 miles around the city, was long independent of the rest of Scotland with regard to marks. A duty on Scottish manufactured plate was imposed in

1720, abolished in 1758, and reimposed in 1784—Cf. C. J. Jackson, *English Goldsmiths and their Marks.*

HALLOW-EVEN, or HALLOW-E'EN, the evening of the 31st of Oct., so called as being the eve or vigil of All Hallows, or All Saints, which falls on the 1st of Nov. It is associated in the popular imagination with the prevalence of supernatural influences, and in Scotland is frequently celebrated by meetings of young people, with the performance of various mystical ceremonies humorously described by Burns in his poem *Hallowe'en.*—Cf. Sir J. G. Frazer, *The Golden Bough (Balder the Beautiful).*

HALLSTATT, village of Austria. It is on the lake of the same name, 32 miles from Salzburg. The chief industry is the working of the salt mines. Hallstatt owes its main interest to the prehistoric cemetery unearthed in 1846. No fewer than 3,000 graves were found and an examination of the articles therein, which were of gold, bronze, iron and amber, showed that their occupants were men and women who enjoyed a fairly high measure of civilization. They worked the salt mines, grew crops and possessed cattle. Their implements were of iron and the name has been given to the first part of the Iron Age. The early **Hallstattian Age** is from 850–600 B.C. and the later 600–400 B.C.

HALLUCINATIONS, according to Esquirol, are morbid conditions of mind in which the patient is conscious of a perception without any impression having been made on the external organs of sense. Hallucinations are to be distinguished from illusions, for in these there are real sensations, though they are erroneously interpreted.

Pinel was the first who connected hallucinations with a disturbance of the phenomena of sensation, and the investigation has been pursued further by Esquirol, Maury, Brière de Boismont, and others. All the senses are not equally subject to hallucinations; the most frequent are those of hearing; next, according to many, come those of sight, smell, touch, and taste; and hallucinations of several senses may exist simultaneously in the same individual, and also be complicated with certain delusions.

The simplest form of hallucinations of hearing is the tingling of the ears; but the striking of clocks, the sounds of musical instruments and of the human voice are often heard, and in these instances, as in those of the perturbations of the other senses, there must be a diseased sensorium, though there should be no structural derangement of the nerves.

Hallucinations are not confined to those whose mental faculties have been alienated, but occasionally assail and torment even the sane. Occasionally hallucinations supervene where the system is healthy, and the individual fully conscious of the unreality of the objects that address his senses. Sometimes this disorder is associated with much ability and wisdom in the conduct of life.

Amongst well-known and authenticated hallucinations are that of the second Earl Grey, who was haunted by a gory head, which, however, he could dismiss at will, and that of Bernadotte, King of Sweden, who was beset in his rides by a woman in a red cloak, although perfectly conscious of the hallucination under which he laboured.

Hallucinations may be caused by some experience which excited the emotions with such intensity that the patient represses the memory of the painful episode; in sleep, or at times when the repressive forces are relaxed, the memory of the experience is apt to force itself into consciousness in a more or less distorted form as a hallucination of vision, hearing, &c.— BIBLIOGRAPHY: J. E. D. Esquirol, *Mental Pathology;* W. James, *The Principles of Psychology;* H. Taine, *De l'Intelligence;* E. Parish, *Hallucinations and Illusions.*

HALLUIN (ál-ü-an), a town of France, department of Nord, on the right bank of the Lys 10 miles N.N.E. of Lille. It has considerable manufactures of cloths, linen, and calicoes, besides cotton- and oil-mills. It was occupied by the Germans during the European War. Pop. 16,000.

HALLUX, the innermost of the five digits which normally compose the hind-foot of a vertebrate animal; in man the great toe, in a bird the hind-toe.

HALMSTAD (hâlm'stät), a seaport of Sweden, on the Kattegat, at the mouth of the Nissa. It has cloth-making, brewing, salmon fisheries, and a trade in deals, lumber, and pitch. Pop. (1932), 24,197.

HA'LO. (1) **Halos proper** are due to refraction of light through minute crystals of ice. These crystals are mostly right hexagonal prisms. The angle between two adjacent sides is 60°, and that between a side and an end face 90°. From these different angles, and the different directions in which the axes may be oriented, various refractive effects can be produced. The halo most often seen has a radius of 22°; less frequently one of 46° radius is visible. The former is generally reddish on the inner border.

Occasionally a horizontal circle is seen, at an altitude equal to that of the sun, through which it passes. Parhelia or mock suns, and paraselenæ or mock moons, when seen, appear at about 22° to right or left of the actual luminary. Sometimes halos have small tangent arcs at top or bottom. (2) **Coronas** are much smaller rings surrounding sun or moon and produced by diffraction of light. They are variable in size, and often show prismatic colour strongly, violet on the inside, red on the outside. (3) **Aureolas** or **glories** are the circles seen surrounding the shadow of an observer's head, or surrounding the shadow of a balloon or aeroplane, projected upon a cloud or fog-bank. The term *halo* was originally applied to the luminous ring which surrounded the head in representations of saints. The halo originated from the small metal plates or discs which the Greeks used to fasten over the heads of their statues to protect them from the droppings of birds.—Cf. Aristophanes, *Birds*, 1114 *seqq.*

HALOGENS (salt producers), the name give to a group of chemically related elements. The group comprises four elements: fluorine, chlorine, bromine, and iodine. Of these fluorine is the most active chemically, and activity decreases, iodine being the least active. Fluorine and chlorine are greenish gases at ordinary temperature, bromine a brown liquid, and iodine a blackish solid.

The resemblance of these elements to one another is shown in the compounds. All four unite readily with hydrogen, yielding colourless gases soluble in water, the halogen acids hydrofluoric acid, hydrochloric acid, hydrobromic acid, and hydriodic acid. The halogens unite readily with the metals, forming salts, e.g. sodium fluoride, sodium chloride or common salt, sodium bromide, and sodium iodide; these again show marked resemblance. Fluorine is used industrially to etch glass. Chlorine is a disinfectant, and iodine an antiseptic.

HAL'OPHYTES, a class of plants which inhabit salt marshes and other saline ground, and by combustion yield barilla, as Salsola, Salicornia, and Chenopodium.

HALORAGIDACEÆ, a small and peculiar natural order of polypetalous Dicotyledons, consisting mainly of widely distributed water- or marsh-herbs such as Hippuris (Mare's Tail), Myriophyllum (water milfoil), and Gunnera.

HALS, Frans, Dutch painter, born in Antwerp soon after 1580, is first heard of in Haarlem in 1611, where he studied painting under Karel van Mander. In 1637 he made a stay in Amsterdam, and there came under the influence of Rembrandt, which affected all his work.

In earlier life a prolific and successful painter, he was subsequently deserted by his patrons, and his work takes on a more sombre, meditative character. In part owing to his dissolute habits, he was constantly in pecuniary embarrassment, and was finally supported by the municipality of Haarlem, where he died in 1666.

Among the most notable work of his earlier period are *The Laughing Cavalier*, in the Wallace Collection, and the groups of the Haarlem Guild of Archers, in Haarlem; while char-

Franz Hals—after the portrait by himself

acteristic of the later work are the groups *The Regents* and *The Regentesses*, at Haarlem.

Hals is chiefly notable for the vitality and vigour of his portraits, and his brilliant and direct handling. He has exercised great influence, numbering among his followers many modern portrait-painters.

A brother, Dirk, and several sons, notably Frans the Younger, were also painters of some note.

HALSBURY, Hardinge Stanley Giffard, first Earl of, born in London 3rd Sept., 1823. He was educated at Merton College, Oxford, where he graduated B.A. in 1852. He was called to the Bar at the Inner Temple in 1850, and became a Q.C. in 1865. He was Solicitor-General from 1875 to 1880, and sat as Conservative member of Parliament for Launceston from 1877 to 1885. He was Lord High

Chancellor of England from June, 1885, to Jan., 1886, from July, 1886, to Aug., 1892, and from June, 1895, to Dec., 1905. He was knighted in 1875, created Baron Halsbury in 1885, and Earl of Halsbury and Viscount Tiverton in 1898.

As a barrister Lord Halsbury was engaged in the celebrated Overend and Gurney and Tichborne cases. As Lord Chancellor he did much to adapt English common law to the changing conditions of the times. As a politician he was prominent among the wing of his party which unfalteringly opposed the passing of the Parliament Act through the House of Lords. He was editor of *The Laws of England,*

with coal-mines in the neighbourhood. Pop. (rural district, 1931), 8,909.

HAM, one of the three sons of Noah. He had four sons—Cush, Mizraim, Phut, and Canaan—from the first three of whom sprang the tribes that peopled the African continent, as Canaan became the father of the tribes that principally occupied the territory of Phœnicia and Palestine. *See* HAMITES.

HAM (âm), a town of France, department of Somme, on the Somme. It is an ancient place, and contains a church with fine bas-reliefs and a curious crypt; but is chiefly deserving of notice for its citadel, which served

Ham—Mediaeval Castle

and Senior Grand Warden of English Freemasons. He died in Dec., 1921.

HÄLSINGBORG. *See* HELSINGBORG.

HALSTEAD, a town of England, county of Essex, pleasantly situated on the Colne, 13 miles from Colchester. Pop. (1931), 5,878.

HALTON, village of Buckinghamshire. It is 4 miles from Aylesbury and is one of the centres of the Air Force. A camp was established here in 1917, and this became, as it now is, a training ground for those entering the air force.

Another **Halton** is a village of Cheshire. It is 11 miles from Chester, on the L.M.S. Rly. Here are the ruins of a castle. Pop. 1,250.

HALTWHISTLE, an old market town of England, in the south-west of Northumberland, on the South Tyne,

as a State Prison. Louis Napoleon (afterwards Napoleon III) was kept prisoner there from 1840 to 1846. During the European War the town was occupied by the Germans. Pop. 3,000.

HAM, urban district of Surrey. It is about 10 miles to the west of London, lying between Twickenham and Teddington. There is a common at Ham. Near are Richmond Park and Ham House, built early in the 17th century and a seat of the Earl of Dysart. It is famous for its art treasures and its meadows called Ham Walks. Pop. (1931) 2,206.

HAM, the inner angle of the joint which unites the thigh and the leg of an animal, but more generally understood to mean the cured and smoked thigh of the ox, sheep, or hog, especially the last. Usually the meat is first well rubbed with salt, and a few days after it is rubbed again with a mixture of salt, saltpetre, and sugar, though sometimes the saltpetre is omitted. After lying for eight or ten days it is ready for drying.

The smoking of hams consists in subjecting them to the smoke of a fire, wood being used in preference to coal in the process of smoking. A good ham should have the recently-cut fat hard and white, the lean fine-grained and of a lively red.

HAMADAN', a city of Persia, on the site of the ancient Ecbatana, in the province of 'Iraq-Ajemi, 260 miles north-west of Isfahan. It is agreeably situated near the base of a great range of mountains has narrow and dirty streets, and is surrounded by heaps of ruins as well as by beautiful orchards and gardens. It had extensive caravanserais and bazaars, a number of tanneries, and also considerable manufactures of carpets, woollens, and cotton stuffs.

It is an important centre of trade, especially for goods passing in or out of Persia by way of Baghdad, being on the route between this place and Teheran and other towns. Hamadan was occupied by British troops in 1918. Pop. about 30,000.

HA'MA, or **HA'MATH**, a city of Syria, on the banks of the Orontes or El-Azy, on the caravan route between Aleppo and Damascus, and on the railway that runs northwards towards Aleppo from the Beirut-Damascus line, in a well-watered and productive district. It is a flourishing place, with manufactures of cotton and silk, but is of chief importance as an agricultural centre.

The town is dirty and the streets narrow, the houses mostly built of sun-dried bricks and wood. The palace of the Governor and the mosques are the chief buildings, and there are also some fine private residences. Amongst the curiosities are huge Persian water-wheels, 70 or 80 feet in diameter, which are turned by the current of the river and supply the houses and gardens with water.

The famous Hamath Inscriptions were noticed by Burckhardt in 1812. They are cut in relief on four stones of black basalt. The characters are entirely different from any others known, and no key to their decipherment has yet been discovered. They are believed to be in the Hittite speech.

Hama is a very ancient town, being repeatedly mentioned in the Bible (as Hamath). In early times it was the capital of a small kingdom which seems to have been included in the dominions of Solomon, and after-

wards to have regained its independence, though subsequently taken by the Assyrians. It was known to the Greeks and Romans as Epiphaneia. In A.D. 639 it fell under the Mohammedan power. Pop. 39,960.—Cf. Burckhardt, *Travels in Syria and the Holy Land.*

HAMAMELIDA'CEÆ, the witch-hazels (or wych-hazels), a small natural order of dicotyledonous trees or shrubs, varying in height from 6 to 30 feet. *Hamamēlis virginica*, a native of North America, yields a useful drug. (*See* HAZEL.) Another species belongs to Japan. One of the most important of the genera is Liquidambar (q.v.).

HAM'-BEETLE, the name for several beetles whose larvæ injure hams, the bacon-beetle (*Dermestes lardarius*) being often included.

HAMBLE, river of Hampshire, much favoured for yachting. It falls into the sea near Southampton where it forms Hambledon Creek. At its mouth on Southampton Water, 5 miles south of Southampton, is a station for flying boats and seaplanes, also called Hamble. In 1931 a flying school was opened here.

HAMBLEDEN Viscount. English title borne by the family of Smith. The statesman, W. H. Smith, left a widow who in 1891 was created Viscountess Hambleden. This title was inherited on her death in 1913 by their son, William Frederick Danvers Smith. Born 12th Aug., 1868, he was educated at Eton and New College, Oxford. From 1891 to 1910 he was Unionist M.P. for the Strand division of London and until his death head of the firm of W. H. Smith and Son, the distributors of newspapers. He was known as an oarsman and a benefactor of King's College Hospital. He died 16th June, 1928, his title passing to his elder son.

Hambleden is the name of a village in Buckinghamshire.

HAMBLEDON. Village of Hampshire. It is 6 miles from Fareham and is famous as the early home of cricket in England. About 1750 the Hambledon Club was formed and this played the game on Windmill and Broad Halfpenny Downs. William Beldham, called Silver Billy, and other famous cricketers of that time were among the Hambledon men.

HAMBURG, a seaport and free city of Germany, the greatest commercial port on the continent of Europe, is situated about 80 miles from the North Sea, on the north branch of the Elbe, which is navigable for large vessels. The town of Altona adjoins it on the west. From the Elbe proceed canals which intersect the eastern and lower part of the city in all directions, and it is also intersected by the Alster, which here forms two fine lakes, the Binnenalster and Aussenalster, the former much smaller than the latter, which extends a considerable distance to the northwards. The quays and harbour accommodation are very extensive.

After the destructive fire of 1842 whole streets were rebuilt in a magnificent and expensive style. Hamburg is not, however, very rich in notable buildings. Amongst the most important are the church of St. Nicholas's, a noble Gothic structure with a lofty tower and spire, built between 1845 and 1874; St. Peter's, another lofty Gothic edifice; St. Michael's (destroyed by fire in July, 1906); St. Catherine's, an ancient edifice; St. James's, erected in 1354, but surmounted by a modern tower; a graceful Jewish temple; the new Rathaus (town house or guild-hall), a fine large building in the Renaissance style; the court-houses (civil and criminal law-courts); an exchange, a noble edifice, consisting chiefly of a magnificent hall, surrounded by a fine colonnade.

There are also the Johanneum Institution, containing an ancient college, museums, and the city library, with about 600,000 volumes; the new university; several well-endowed hospitals; zoological and botanic gardens; the Kunsthalle, a large collection of pictures and sculpture; and theatre.

Hamburg is of most importance on account of its great shipping trade and the business of banking, exchange, and marine assurance carried on in connection with that. Until the beginning of the European War Hamburg was one of the greatest ports of the world, and its trade, paralysed between 1914 and 1919, again revived in 1920. It is now making a large bid for shipping (the Bremen, Europa, &c., being built there).

Its manufactures and kindred industries, though large and varied, are less important, including shipbuilding (in several large establishments), the making of machinery, boilers, and many articles of metal, the smelting of ores of various kinds, tobacco- and cigar-making, sugar refining, spirit refining and distilling, brewing, &c.

The harbour accommodation and equipment are most complete and extensive in the way of quays, docks (floating and other), cranes, warehouses, and railways; and a considerable area is set apart as a 'free harbour,' being exempted from customs duties and restrictions. A great many emigrants embark there. It has a broadcasting station (372 m., 1.5 kw.).

The state of Hamburg, which with the free city forms a republic, embraces a territory of 160 sq. miles, and consists of two divisions, viz. (1) City of Hamburg, with a population of (1926) 1,143,079; (2) outlying towns and bailiwicks (Cuxhaven, Ritzebüttel, &c.), pop. 83,032.

The legislative power belongs to the House of Burgesses. The executive power is vested chiefly in the Senate, which is composed of twelve members. The members are elected for life. The House of Burgesses consists of 160 members. The present Constitution dates from 7th Jan., 1921. The budget for 1932 was balanced at 362,924,000 reichsmarks. The public debt was in 1932, 410,860,000 reichsmarks.

The city owes its foundation to the Emperor Charlemagne, who (808–811) built a citadel and a church on the heights between the Elbe and the eastern bank of the Alster, as a bulwark against the neighbouring pagans. It became important as a commerical city in the twelfth century, and in the thirteenth it combined with Lübeck in forming the Hanseatic League. In 1618 Hamburg was formally acknowledged a free city of the empire.

During the Thirty Years' War its population and prosperity continued to increase on account of the immunity of its position, and in the following century it obtained a large share of the trade with North America. In 1810 it was formally incorporated in the French Empire along with the north-western part of Germany. In 1815 it joined the Germanic Confederation as a free city. In 1888 the city was included in the Zollverein or German Customs Union.

After the revolution of 1918, when there was rioting in the city, Hamburg remained within the German Reich, or new republic.—Cf. W. King, *Three Free Cities.*

HAMEL, a French village department of Somme. Captured by the Germans during the European War, it was retaken on 4th July, 1918.

HAM'ELN, a town of Germany, in Hanover, on the Weser, which is here crossed by a suspension bridge. It has many picturesque old buildings and remains. Pop. 25,649.

HA'MERTON, Philip Gilbert, an English painter and art critic, born at Laneside, in Lancashire, in 1834, died in 1894. He studied landscape-painting, but deviated into literature, publishing a work on *Heraldry* in 1851, and in 1855 *The Isles of Loch Awe* and other poems, illustrated by himself. In 1859 Hamerton married a

French lady, and thereafter resided chiefly at Autun.

He made himself well known to the English public as a writer on art, acting as art critic for the *Saturday Review*, and editing the *Portfolio*. His writings largely contributed to the revival of etching in England. Amongst his works are: *Thoughts about Art* (1862); *Etching and Etchers* (1866); *Contemporary French Painters* (1867); *Wenderholme*, a novel (1869); *The Intellectual Life* (1873); *Round my House* (1876); *Marmorne*, a novel (1878); *Modern Frenchmen* (1878); *Landscape* (1885); and *French and English* (1889).

HAMIL'CAR, the name of several Carthaginian generals, of whom the most celebrated was Hamilcar, surnamed Barca (the lightning), the father of the great Hannibal. While quite a young man he was appointed to the command of the Carthaginian forces in Sicily, in the eighteenth year of the first Punic War, 247 B.C., when the Romans were masters of almost the whole island.

For two years he defied all the efforts of the Romans to dislodge him; but the Carthaginian admiral, Hanno, having been totally defeated off the Ægates, 241 B.C., he reluctantly consented to evacuate Sicily. A revolt of the returned troops, joined by the native Africans, was successfully repressed by Hamilcar.

He then entered on a series of campaigns in Spain, where he founded a new empire for Carthage. Here he passed nine years, and had brought the whole southern and eastern part of the country under Carthaginian rule when he was slain in battle against the Vettones, 229 B.C. His great design of making Spain a point of attack against Rome was ably carried out by his son Hannibal.

HAMILTON, Alexander, a distinguished American officer and legislator during the contest for independence, was born in 1757 in the Island of Nevis, West Indies, died 1804. At the age of sixteen he became a student of Columbia College, New York. On the outbreak of the war he received (1776) a commission as captain of artillery, and soon attracted the attention of Washington, who appointed him his aide-de-camp and employed him in the most delicate and difficult affairs.

In 1781 he left the service, studied law, became a delegate from the state of New York in 1782, and in 1787 was one of the delegates who revised the Articles of Confederation. He was a strong supporter of the Federal party, and by the letters which he wrote to the *Daily Advertiser* of New York,

afterwards published under the title of *The Federalist*, contributed greatly to the success of the party.

On the organization of the Federal Government in 1789, with Washington at its head, Hamilton was appointed Secretary of the Treasury. This office he held till 1795, when he resigned and retired into private life. In 1798 he was appointed second in command of the provisional army raised under the apprehension of a French invasion, and on the death of Washington, in 1799, he became commander-in-chief.

In 1804 he became involved in a political dispute with Aaron Burr, then candidate for the governorship of New York, accepted a challenge from that gentleman, and was shot by him, 11th July, 1804.—Cf. F. S. Oliver, *Alexander Hamilton*; F. T. Fox, *A Study in Alexander Hamilton*.

HAMILTON, Anthony, Count, a poet, courtier, and man of letters, was descended from a younger branch of the family of the Dukes of Hamilton in Scotland, but was born in Ireland about 1646. After the death of Charles I he went with his parents to France, but after the accession of Charles II made frequent visits to England, and was appointed Governor of Limerick by James II. Afterwards, on the ruin of the royal cause, he accompanied the king to France. His talents and agreeable manners made him a favourite in the best circles. He died at St. Germain in 1720.

Count Hamilton is chiefly known by his *Memoirs of Count Grammont* (his brother-in-law), a lively and skilful picture of the frivolous life at the French and English courts of the time. The count's other works are *Poems and Fairy Tales* (burlesque), which, as well as the *Memoirs*, are in French, and are also remarkable for their fine wit and elegance of style.

HAMILTON, Emma, Lady, wife of Sir William Hamilton (q.v.), was the daughter of people in humble circumstances. She was born about 1761, and died at Calais 1815. After being his mistress, at the age of thirty years she became the wife of Sir William Hamilton, British Ambassador at Naples.

It was while in this position that she made the acquaintance of Lord Nelson, who became devoted to her, although she was an ignorant woman, and set no bounds to her flatteries of Nelson. Nelson left her his house at Merton, and an annuity of £500, but she became hopelessly involved in debt, and died in distress after spending a year in a debtors' prison.—Cf. W. Sichel, *Emma, Lady Hamilton.*

HAMILTON, FAMILY OF, a family long connected with Scotland, though probably of English origin, the name being evidently territorial. The first person of the name in Scotland of whom we have reliable information was Walter Fitz-Gilbert of Hamilton, who, in 1296, swore fealty to Edward I of England for lands in Lanarkshire, and held Bothwell Castle for the English at the time of the battle of Bannockburn. For his early surrender of this fortress King Robert Bruce gave him important grants of land. He continued faithful to King David Bruce, and had a command at Halidon Hill under the Regent of Scotland.

In 1445 the family was ennobled in the person of Sir James Hamilton of Cadzow, who was created Lord

1st Duke of Hamilton

Hamilton of Cadzow. At first he adhered to the Douglases against the Crown; but, deserting them opportunely, he was rewarded by large grants of their forfeited lands, and at a later period by the hand of the Princess Mary, eldest daughter of King James II, and widow of Thomas Boyd, Earl of Arran. He died in 1479.

His only son was James, second Lord Hamilton and first Earl of Arran, who died in 1529, and was succeeded by his son James, whose nearness to the throne, and his great possessions and following, made him a person of such mark and consequence that Henry II of France gave him a grant of the duchy of Châtelhérault; and his eldest son was proposed at one time as the husband of Elizabeth of England, and at another as that of Mary of Scotland.

This son having become insane, the second son, Lord John Hamilton,

created Marquess of Hamilton in 1599, succeeded in 1575 to the family estates. Dying in 1604, he was succeeded by his son James, who was created Earl of Cambridge in 1619, and died in 1625. His son James, the third marquess, one of the ablest and most distinguished of the family, created Duke of Hamilton in 1643 by Charles I, was taken prisoner by the Parliamentary forces soon after the battle of Preston, and beheaded in March, 1649.

A successor was created Duke of Brandon in 1711, and was killed in a duel with Lord Mohun in 1712. James George, seventh duke, on the death of Archibald, Duke of Douglas, in 1761, became also the male representative and chief of the red or Angus branch of the House of Douglas, with the titles of Marquess of Douglas and Earl of Angus.

He died in 1769, and was succeeded by his brother, Douglas, eighth Duke of Hamilton, who, in 1799, was succeeded by his uncle Lord Archibald Hamilton. He died in 1819, and was succeeded by his eldest son Alexander, who, dying in 1852, was succeeded by his only son William Alexander Anthony Archibald. In 1843 he married the Princess Marie of Baden, and he died at Paris 15th July, 1863.

William Alexander Louis Stephen Douglas Hamilton, twelfth Duke of Hamilton, and ninth Duke of Brandon, premier peer of Scotland, and hereditary keeper of Holyrood House, died in 1895, and, leaving only a daughter, was succeeded by a distant kinsman.—BIBLIOGRAPHY: Sir R. Douglas, *Peerage of Scotland* (Sir J. B. Paul's edition); J. Anderson, *The House of Hamilton*; G. H. Johnston, *The Heraldry of the Hamiltons.*

HAMILTON, Sir Ian Standish Monteith, British soldier, born at Corfu 16th Jan., 1853. Educated at Wellington College, he entered the army (Gordon Highlanders) in 1873, and saw service in the Afghan War (1878–9), the Boer War of 1881, being wounded and taken prisoner at Majuba Hill, and in Burmah (1886–7). During the South African War he was at Ladysmith as chief of the staff to Sir George White. He was made a general in 1915, and commanded the forces which landed on the Gallipoli Peninsula. He retired from the army in 1920. His works include: *A Staff Officer's Scrap Book, Icarus, Fighting of the Future,* and *A Gallipoli Diary.*

HAMILTON, Patrick, usually considered as the first Scottish reformer, was the second son of Sir Patrick Hamilton of Kincavel and Stanehouse, and of Catherine, daughter of the Duke of Albany, second son of James II. He was born in Glasgow probably in 1504, and was educated partly at St. Andrews and partly at Paris, where he took his degree in 1520. While still a boy he had been appointed Abbot of Fearn, in Ross-shire, but never went into residence, settling instead at St. Andrews in 1523.

Here he began to announce his convictions in the principles of the Reformation, and was summoned in 1526 by Archbishop Beaton to stand his trial for heresy. He fled to Germany, where his education as a reformer was completed by an intimate acquaintance with Luther and Melanchthon.

After six months' absence he returned to Scotland, and began to preach the gospel openly at Linlithgow, but was allured by Beaton to St. Andrews under pretence of a friendly conference, put on his trial, convicted of various heresies, and burned at the stake, 1st March, 1527, in the twenty-third year of his age.

His death did perhaps more to extend the principles of the Reformation in Scotland than even his life could have done.—Cf. P. Lorimer, *Life of Patrick Hamilton.*

HAMILTON, Sir William, grandson of William, third Duke of Hamilton, was born in Scotland in 1730, died in 1803. In 1761 he was elected member of Parliament for Midhurst, and in 1764 he received the appointment of Ambassador to the court of Naples.

He devoted his leisure to science, making observations on Vesuvius, Ætna, and other volcanic mountains; and the results of his researches are detailed in the *Philosophical Transactions,* and in his *Campi Phlegræi or Observations on the Volcanoes of the Two Sicilies* (Naples, 1776–9, 3 vols. folio). He took an active part in the excavation of Herculaneum and Pompeii, and collected a cabinet of antiquities, of which an account was published by D'Hancarville in a splendid work with finely-coloured plates.

Sir William's second wife was the notorious Lady Hamilton (*see* HAMILTON, EMMA, LADY).

HAMILTON, Sir William, a prominent Scottish metaphysician, was born in 1788 at Glasgow, and died suddenly at Edinburgh in 1856. He studied with distinction in his native town, where his father and grandfather held in succession the chairs of anatomy and botany. In 1809 he entered Balliol College, Oxford, as a Snell exhibitioner, and gained a first-class in 'Greats.'

In 1813 he was admitted to the Scottish Bar, but never acquired a practice in his profession, his taste lying much more towards the study of

philosophy, in which he had already made extensive researches. In 1820 he became a candidate for the chair of moral philosophy in Edinburgh, rendered vacant by the death of Thomas Brown, but being defeated by Professor John Wilson he was obliged to content himself with the unimportant chair of universal history, to which he was appointed in 1821 by its patrons, the Faculty of Advocates.

In 1829 the publication in the *Edinburgh Review* of his celebrated critique of Cousin's system of philosophy gave him at once a first place amongst the philosophical writers of the time. This was followed in 1830 by his criticism of Brown, and in 1831 by his article on the authorship of the *Epistolæ Obscurorum Virorum.*

In 1836 he was appointed to the chair of logic and metaphysics in Edinburgh University. Here he gathered about him a number of ardent students, and re-established the fame of the Scottish school of metaphysicians, which had begun to wane. In 1846 he published an annotated edition of the works of Thomas Reid, and in 1854 the first volume of a similar edition of the works of Dugald Stewart. His lectures on logic and metaphysics were collected and edited by Dean Mansel and Professor Veitch.

Philosophy. Hamilton's most important contributions to philosophy are connected with his doctrine of the Quantification of the Predicate in his system of logic; his theory of the 'relativity of knowledge,' in the Kantian sense, held along with an apparently incompatible doctrine of immediate perception of the non-ego; and his definition of the infinite or unconditioned as a mere negation of thought.—BIBLIOGRAPHY: J. Veitch, *A Memoir of Sir W. Hamilton;* J. Seth, *English Philosophers and Schools of Philosophy.*

HAMILTON, Sir William Rowan, mathematician and astronomer, was born in Dublin in 1805. died in 1865. Before he had completed his fourteenth year he had made himself acquainted with thirteen languages, among which were Arabic, Persian, Hindustani, Sanskrit, and Syriac. At the age of seventeen he was pronounced by a competent authority the first mathematician of his age. At Trinity College, Dublin, he gained the highest honours, and he was appointed in 1827 professor of astronomy in Trinity College, as well as Astronomer Royal. He was knighted in 1835, and elected in 1837 president of the Royal Irish Academy.

He contributed numerous papers to the transactions of learned bodies, and made some valuable discoveries; but his fame is chiefly founded on his invention of the calculus of quaternions, a new method in the higher mathematics. Amongst his published works are: *General Method in Dynamics, Algebra as the Science of Pure Time*, and *Memoirs on Discontinuous Functions*.

HAM'ILTON, a royal burgh of Scotland, in Lanarkshire, on the Clyde, about 11½ miles south-east of Glasgow. Numerous villas and gardens give it a pleasant rural aspect. Coal, ironstone, and limestone are extensively worked in the vicinity. The county buildings, town hall, and extensive cavalry barracks are the most important public buildings.

Near the town was Hamilton Palace, seat of the Duke of Hamilton, a large building, built in 1700 and rebuilt in 1830, but found unsafe and, with the splendid mausoleum, dismantled (1921). The park in which it stood (1,500 acres) is now used as a race-course.

In the adjacent grounds are the ruins of Cadzow Castle and a few old oaks, the remains of Cadzow Forest. Here a herd of wild cattle is kept, white, with black ears and muzzles.

Hamilton gives name to a parliamentary division of the county, returning one member to Parliament. Pop. (1931), 37,863.

HAMILTON, the inland metropolis of the western district of Victoria, Australia, 224 miles w. of Melbourne, with which it is connected by railway. There are a hospital, town hall, mechanics' institute, a district college, the usual Government buildings, churches, and schools, and a number of hotels. The district is pastoral and agricultural. Races are held here. Pop. (1931), 5,300.

HAMILTON, a town in the state of New South Wales, 3 miles E. of Newcastle of which it is a suburb; with churches, schools, municipal buildings, &c.; collieries give employment to a number of hands. Pop. 7,900.

HAMILTON, the capital of the Bermudas, on the coast of the largest island, near the middle of the group. It has a landlocked harbour. Pop. 3,259.

HAMILTON, a city of Canada, the third largest in the province of Ontario, is beautifully situated on Burlington Bay, at the west end of Lake Ontario, and is overlooked by the eminence known as Hamilton Mountain, on which are many handsome residences. It is on the edge of the Niagara Peninsula, and thus belongs to the finest fruit-growing district in Canada, and is an important railway junction on the C.P. and C.N. Rail-

ways; from here electric railways radiate.

The city is well built, the streets are wide, well paved, and lined with trees, and there are many handsome public buildings and important institutions, including McMaster University. It is the seat of an active trade, and manufactures large quantities of iron goods, including machinery and stoves. There is also some shipping to other ports of the Great Lakes. Electrical energy is obtained from water power. Pop. (1931), 159,914.

Burlington Beach is a strip of land in front of the city, and is used as a pleasure resort. A canal passes through it.

HAMILTON, a town of North Island, New Zealand, 70 m. S.S.E. of Auckland. Pop. (1932), 18,250.

HAMILTON, a town, United States, Ohio, capital of Butler County, on the Miami River, 25 miles N. of Cincinnati. It is a prosperous manufacturing place. Pop. (1930), 52,176.

HAMIRPUR, a town of India, in the United Provinces, on the right bank of the Jumna. Pop. 7,452.

HAMITES (descendants of Ham), the name given to a number of peoples in North Africa, who are regarded as of kindred origin and speak allied tongues. They include the ancient Egyptians and their modern descendants, the Copts, the Berbers, Tuaregs, Kabyles, the Agaos, the Bejas, the Gallas, Somali, Dankali, &c. The Hamite race is closely akin to the early Mediterranean, so-called Iberic race, as well as to the Arabs (who belong to the so-called Semitic race).—Cf. A. H. Keane, *Man, Past and Present*.

HAMM, a town of Prussia, province of Westphalia, at the confluence of the Ahse with the Lippe. Its industries embrace iron-foundries and machine-works, rolling-mills and puddling-works, and wire-works. Pop. 50,040.

HAMMER-BEAM, a short beam attached to the foot of a principal rafter in a roof, in the place of the tie-beam. Hammer-beams are used in pairs, and project from the wall, extending less than half-way across the apartments. The hammer-beam is generally supported by a rib rising up from a corbel below; and in its turn forms the support of another rib, constituting with that springing from the opposite hammer-beam an arch.

HAMMERFEST, a maritime town in Norway, in Finmarken, on Hvalöe (Whale Island), a bare, treeless, barren spot, in lat. 70° 40′ N., being thus the most northerly town in the world. It is a fishing centre, and carries on a lively trade. Though within the Arctic circle, the winter is comparatively mild, and the surrounding waters seldom freeze. Pop. 2,709.

HAMMER-OYSTER, a bivalve shell-fish, *Malleus vulgāris*, inhabiting the Indian Archipelago, resembling the pearl-oyster when young, but becoming always more hammer-like as it advances in age, by the lengthening of its two ears. It belongs to the wing-shells (Aviculidæ).

HAMMERSMITH, a municipal and parliamentary borough of London, about 6 miles w.s.w. of the General Post Office. The Thames is here crossed by a fine suspension bridge. It adjoins Chiswick and Kensington, and part of it is now called West Kensington. The borough includes Wormwood Scrubs with the prison. Formerly celebrated for its nurseries and market-gardens, it is now a busy commercial district. In the borough are Olympia, a vast building used for exhibitions, &c., and the White City at Shepherd's Bush. Hammersmith returns two members to Parliament. Pop. (1931) 135,521.

HAMMOCK (Sp. *hamaca*), a rectangular piece of cloth or netting about 6 feet long and 4 feet wide, gathered together at the two ends and slung horizontally, forming a sort of bed. Hammocks are in common use on board ships of war. The word, probably derived from the hamack tree, is said to be of Caribbean origin, and the Caribs certainly make use of similar hanging beds.

HAMMOND, Walter Reginald. English cricketer, born at Dover, 3rd June, 1903. Having become a professional cricketer he played first for Gloucestershire. His performance in 1927, both as a batsman and bowler, made his reputation and he became one of the leading cricketers in England. He visited Australia in 1928–29 (when he made the highest aggregate of runs for England in any test match), and again in 1932–33, and in 1930 played in the test matches in England. In 1932 he had a high batting average (2,528 for 49 innings, his highest score 264 in a county match) and a good bowling average.

HAMMURA'BI, a king of ancient Babylonia, who flourished about 2250 B.C., and did much for the welfare of the country, encouraging agriculture and commerce by irrigation and otherwise, regulating the finances, and building temples.

To him is attributed a code of laws discovered in the end of 1901, in-scribed upon a block of stone found in the ruins of Susa, and extending to 282 paragraphs, being the oldest law-book known. The laws pertain to civil and criminal matters, are of an enlightened character, and long prevailed in Babylonia, as well as having an influence extending to the Persians and Jews.—Cf. S. A. Cook, *The Laws of Moses and the Code of Hammurabi*.

HAMOON, LAKE. See SEISTAN.

HAMPDEN, John, celebrated for his patriotic opposition to taxation by prerogative, was born in London

Hammurabi receiving the "Code of Laws" from the Sun God

in 1594, being cousin-german by the mother's side to Oliver Cromwell. In 1609 he was entered a gentleman commoner at Magdalen College, Oxford. He began the study of law in the Inner Temple, but, having inherited an ample fortune on his father's death, he lived the usual life of a country gentleman.

He entered Parliament in the beginning of Charles I's reign as member for Grampound, and continued to sit in the House of Commons three times in succession as member for Wendover, and finally as member for Bucks. Although for some years a uniform opposer of the arbitrary practices in Church and State, it was not till 1636 that his resistance to Charles's demand for ship-money made him the argument of all tongues. Although the decision in the Court of Exchequer was given against him by seven voices to five, the victory, as far as regarded public opinion, was his.

In the following year (1637) he was one of those who meditated emigration to America, which they were prevented from carrying out by an Order in Council detaining them. Henceforward he took a prominent part in the great contest between the Crown and the Parliament, and was one of the five members whom the king, in 1642, so imprudently attempted, in person, to seize in the House of Commons.

When the appeal was made to the sword, Hampden accepted the command of a regiment in the Parliamentary army under the Earl of Essex, and was fatally wounded on Chalgrove Field, 18th June, 1643, dying six days later.—Cf. Lord Nugent, *Memorials of John Hampden.*

HAMPDEN. Name of two villages in Buckinghamshire. Great and Little. **Great Hampden** is three miles from Missenden and in its church is a memorial to John Hampden who was buried here. Near is Hampden House, once his residence. This was rebuilt in 1754 and is now the seat of the Earl of Buckinghamshire.

The title of **Viscount Hampden** has been borne since 1884 by the family of Brand. Henry Bouverie William Brand was a Liberal M.P. from 1852 to 1884. From 1872 to 1884 he was Speaker of the House of Commons. He died 14th March, 1892.

HAMPSHIRE, HANTS, or **SOUTH-AMPTONSHIRE,** a maritime county, including the Isle of Wight, in the south of England; area, 961,665 acres. Its surface is pleasantly varied with gently rising hills, fruitful valleys, and extensive woodlands.

The coast-line is very irregular; the principal indentation, Southampton Water, is navigable almost to its head. The magnificent docks of Southampton (one of the finest ports in Britain) admit ships of 40,000 tons. The country is well watered by the Avon, Exe, Test, Itching, and Hamble. In the west is the New Forest; in the south-east are the Forests of Bere and Waltham Chase. Two ranges of chalk hills, the North and South Downs, traverse the county, running in direction nearly east and west. On the Downs large flocks of sheep known as the 'Hampshire Downs' are fed.

Hampshire is famous for its early association with the game of cricket, and is now a first class county. It is also famous for its wool, bacon, honey, and timber. The manufactures are unimportant, but the shipping is very extensive. For parliamentary purposes it is divided into six divisions, viz. Aldershot, Basingstoke, Fareham, New Forest and Christchurch, Petersfield, and Winchester, one member for each. Pop. (1931), 1,014,115.—BIBLIOGRAPHY: T. W. Shore, *History of Hampshire*; W. Page, *Victoria History of the Counties of England.*

HAMPSTEAD, a municipal and parliamentary borough of London. It is situated on the declivity of a hill on the north-western side of the city, and has long been celebrated for its fine air and the beauty of its surroundings. It returns one member to Parliament. **Hampstead Heath** crowns the summit of the hill, and is one of the most frequented of public recreation grounds. On the Heath and near it are the old inns The Bull and Bush and Jack Straw's Castle. To the north is the **Hampstead Garden Suburb.** This was laid out in 1907, and is one of the most successful enterprises of its kind. The land is owned by a trust. Pop. (1931), 88,914.

HAMPTON, a village of Middlesex, situated 11½ miles s.w. of London, on the left bank of the Thames. Pop. (1931), 13,053.

About a mile from the village are the palace and park of **Hampton Court,** originally built by Cardinal Wolsey in 1525. Hampton Court has been the residence of many sovereigns, from Henry VIII, to whom it was presented by Wolsey, down to George II. It contains a valuable collection of pictures by Holbein, Lely, Kneller, West, &c. Part of the palace is set apart for the residence of persons of rank in reduced circumstances. The gardens, which contain the Maze, the Grape Vine, and the Long Water, comprise about 44 acres.

HAMPTON COURT CONFERENCE, a conference which took place in 1604 at Hampton Court, under the presidency of James I, between the representatives of the Episcopalian and Puritan parties in the Church. The proceedings consisted largely of browbeating of the Puritan members and theological dogmatizing on the part of the king himself. A few slight alterations were made in the *Common Prayer Book,* and it was determined that a new version of the Bible should be undertaken. This, the Authorized Version, appeared in 1611.

HAMSTER (Cricĕtus), a genus of rodent animals belonging to the family of the Muridæ (mice), and closely allied to the rats, which they resemble in their dentition. They are distinguished, however, by their having short hairy tails, as well as cheek-pouches in which they convey grain, peas, &c., to their winter residence.

The common hamster (*C. frumentarius*) is from 10 to 12 inches without the tail, which is not more than 3 inches long. It is common in the north of Europe and Asia, but is not found in Britain nor to the south of the Alps. It is very destructive, sometimes storing as much as 60 lb. of corn in its burrow as winter provision. It is carnivorous as well as graminivorous, and hibernates during the colder months.

HAMSUN, Knut. Norwegian novelist. Born 4th Aug., 1859, he became a clerk and then tried various other occupations, farming and teaching among them. He went to the United States, but was equally unsuccessful. In 1888 his first novel, *Sult*, was published in a Danish magazine, and this made his reputation. He wrote other novels which have been translated into English and other languages. The English titles of some are, *Shallow Soil, Growth of the Soil, The Women at the Well, Mysteries* and *Vagabonds* (1931). In 1920 he received a Nobel Prize.

HAN, a Chinese dynasty (206 B.C. to A.D. 220) with which commences the modern history of China. It was founded by Liupang, 217 B.C. to 195 B.C.

HAN'APER, formerly an office in the Court of Chancery, so called because all writs regarding the public were once kept in a *hanaper* or hamper. The clerk of the hanaper received all fines due to the king for seals of charters, patents, commissions, and writs. The Act 5 and 6 Vict. cap. ciii transferred the duties of the hanaper office to other officials. The office was abolished in England, but survived in Ireland till 1921.

HANAU (hän'ou), a town of Germany in the Prussian province of Hesse-Nassau, at the confluence of the Kinzig with the Main, 13 miles E. of Frankfurt. It is the chief manufacturing town in the province. It contains an ancient castle and an electoral palace (Philippsruhe), and has manufactures of jewellery, carpets, tapestry, silk and woollen goods, and ironware.

During the Thirty Years' War, Ramsay, a Scotsman, held the town for nine months against the Imperialists (1653–6) till the siege was raised by the Swedes, an event still celebrated by the inhabitants; and in 1813 Napoleon there defeated the Bavarians under Wrede. Pop. 38,670.

HAND, the distal extremity of the arm, connected with the rest of the arm at the wrist; the principal organ of touch and prehension, and the instrument whereby man performs a great variety of highly-skilled actions which are his exclusive prerogative.

Structure. The skeleton of the human hand is composed of twenty-seven bones, namely eight bones of the carpus or wrist arranged in two rows of four each, the row next the fore-arm containing the scaphoid, the semilunar, the cuneiform, and the pisiform, and that next the meta-carpus, the trapezium, the trapezoid, the os magnum, and the unciform. The metacarpus consists of the five bones which form the palm, the first being that of the thumb, the others that of the fingers in succession.

Lastly, the fingers proper contain fourteen bones called phalanges, of which the thumb has but two, all the other digits having three each. These bones are jointed so as to admit of a variety of movements, the more peculiar being those by which the hand is flexed backwards, forwards, and sideways, and by which the thumb and fingers are moved in different ways.

Action. The chief muscles which determine these movements, the *flexors*, which pass down the forearm, are attached by tendons to the phalanges of the fingers, and serve to flex or bend the fingers; and the *extensors* for extending the fingers. There are two muscles which flex all the fingers except the thumb. The thumb has a separate long and short flexor.

There is a common extensor for the fingers which passes down the back of the forearm and divides at the wrist into four tendons, one for each finger, each being attached to all three phalanges. The forefinger and little finger have, in addition, each an extensor of their own, and the thumb has both a short and a long extensor.

The tendons of the muscles of the hand are interlaced and bound together by bands and aponeurotic fibres, and from this results a more or less complete unity of action. It is sometimes difficult to make a movement with a single finger without the others taking part in it, as in executing instrumental music, for instance; but practice gives to these movements perfect independence.

Of all the properties of the hand the opposition of the thumb to the other fingers, alone or united, especially characterizes the human hand. This action of the thumb results from its length, from the first metacarpal bone not being placed on the same plane as the other four, as is the case in the monkey, and from the action of a muscle—the long flexor of the thumb—peculiar to the human hand. This muscle completes the action of the other motor of the thumb, and permits man to hold a pen, a graver, or a needle; it gives to his hand the dexterity necessary in the execution of the most delicate work.

Functions. In man the hand has attained a remarkable delicacy of perception, and powers of complicated skilled movements far transcending those of the apes and all other creatures. As a tactile instrument and a means of discriminating form, size, weight, and texture the human hand is one of the essential elements in man's intellectual supremacy.

It cannot be considered, as in the ape, a normal organ of locomotion. It is essentially the organ of touch and prehension. It moulds itself to a body to ascertain its form; it comes to the aid of the eye in completing or rectifying its impressions.

George Frederick Handel

The functions of touch devolve principally upon its anterior or palmar face, the nervous papillæ abounding specially at the ends of the fingers. A layer of adipose tissue, very close in texture, protects, without lessening its power or its delicacy, the network of muscles, vessels, and nerves with which this remarkable organ is equipped.

HANDEL (properly **HÄNDEL**), George Frederick, a great German composer, born at Halle, on the Saale, 23rd Feb., 1685, died 13th April, 1759.

Training. The strong passion which he early showed for the art overcame his father's opposition to training him as a musician, and at the age of seven he was placed under the tuition of Zachau, organist of Halle Cathedral, and was soon so far advanced in the practical part of the science as to be able to officiate occasionally as deputy to his instructor.

In 1696 he was sent to Berlin, where he heard the music of Buononcini and Ariosti, then at the head of the Berlin Opera House. He returned to Halle, was appointed organist of the cathedral in 1702, but soon left to visit Hanover and Hamburg, where Steffani and Reinhard Keiser, the latter the greatest German operatic composer of his day, resided.

Operas. At Hamburg he played second violin in the orchestra, and brought out in 1704 his first work, an oratorio on the *Passion*, and his first opera, *Almira*, followed in February by his *Nero*, and subsequently by his *Florinda and Daphne*. In 1706 he went to Italy, visiting Florence, Venice, Naples, and Rome. On his return to Germany he entered the service of the Elector of Hanover, afterwards George I of England, as musical director. He visited England twice, and ultimately, having received a pension from Queen Anne, settled down there. He was for a time organist at Canons Park, Edgware.

For some years his popularity was very great. He was placed at the head of the newly-founded Royal Academy of Music, and accumulated a large fortune in spite of the heavy losses which he incurred by setting up an opera company in opposition to that supported by the leading nobility and the principal Italian singers. Amongst the operas which he had composed up to this date (1735) are: *Radamisto, Ottone, Giulio Cesare, Flavio, Tamerlano, Scipio, Ricardo I, Orlando,* and *Ariadne.* His last opera was performed in 1740.

Oratorios. By this time he had begun to devote himself chiefly to music of a serious nature, especially the oratorio. The approval which his first works of this kind (*Esther*, 1731; *Deborah*, 1732; *Athalia,* 1733) had met with encouraged him to new efforts; and he produced in succession *Israel in Egypt, L' Allegro and Il Fenseroso, Saul,* and *The Messiah.* The last mentioned, which is his chief work, was brought out in 1741, for the benefit of the Foundling Hospital. It was not much appreciated at the first representation, but increased in reputation every year.

In 1742 the *Samson* appeared, in 1746 the *Judas Maccabæus,* in 1748 the *Solomon,* and in 1752 the *Jephthah.* In 1752 he became blind, but did not lose his spirits, continuing to perform in public and even to compose. He died at London, and was buried in Westminster Abbey.

Handel was of large and ungainly

person. His manners were rough and his temper violent, but his disposition was humane and liberal. As a musician his characteristics are boldness and strength of style and combination of vigour, spirit, and invention in his instrumental compositions.—BIBLIOGRAPHY: W. H. Cummings, *Handel*; J. A. F. Maitland, *Age of Bach and Handel*; P. Robinson, *Handel and his Orbit*; R. A. Streatfeild, *Handel*.

HANDICAPPING is a system of equalizing the chances of victory in a contest by allowing certain advantages to an inferior competitor. Such a system is witnessed in the large majority of games and sports. Thus in horse-racing the best horses are compelled to carry heavier weights proportional to their capabilities. In athletic sports the principle of giving a start is in vogue, the best performer being on the 'scratch mark,' the others starting a selected number of yards in front of him, a distance based on their estimated form.

Occasionally in a high-jumping contest the system is adopted of allowing a certain number of inches to be added to the athlete's actual performance, a system analogous to the time allowance sometimes seen in long-distance races when the men engage in what is known as a 'sealed handicap,' the time allowance of each being previously allotted, and deducted at the finish from the actual time taken.

In lawn tennis, allowance is made either by making the best players owe points, or granting points to the inferior players; these two alternatives are often used conjointly. In golf, the handicap is based upon the number of strokes which a player generally requires to complete a course, and in a contest his handicap is deducted from the number of strokes he plays in his round. In cricket handicapping rarely occurs, but it is seen occasionally when a strong team handicaps itself by playing a bigger side of 14, 18, or even 24 players.

In chess, as is well known, a strong player may be handicapped by giving up one or more of his men at the beginning of his game. Perhaps football is the only game in which the system of handicapping is never seen.

HAND-PLANT, the *Cheirostëmon platanoides*, a Mexican tree of the ord. Sterculiaceæ. It grows about 30 feet or more in height, and has flowers the stamens of which present an appearance somewhat like that of the human hand.

HANDS, LAYING ON OF. The rite, as a token of blessing, or the communication of spiritual gifts, or of something else which could not be literally delivered into the hands of another, has been in use from the earliest times.

It occurs in Scripture as a patriarchal usage, appropriate and becoming perhaps rather than strictly religious, but later assumes more of the character of a formal rite, as in the ritual of animal sacrifice amongst the Jews, when the officer was required to lay his hands on the victim while still alive, except in the case of the paschal lamb.

In the early Church this rite was used in benediction, absolution, the unction of the sick, and the reconciliation of penitents, as well as in ordination and confirmation. The rite is still retained by most Western Churches in the ceremony of ordination, and in the Roman Catholic, Anglican, and Lutheran Churches both in confirmation and ordination.

HANDSWORTH, a parliamentary division of Birmingham, England, and a north-western suburb of the city. Handsworth College is a centre for training Wesleyan ministers. In 1931 the population of the division was 72,622.

Another **Handsworth** is in the West Riding of Yorkshire, forming an urban district 3 miles south-east of Sheffield, with collieries, quarries, &c. Pop. 15,889.

HANGCHOW, or **HANG-CHOO,** a Chinese treaty port, capital of the province of Chekiang, on the estuary of the Tsien-tang-kiang. It is one of the handsomest cities of China, with many magnificent temples, monuments, and triumphal arches.

It has extensive manufactures in silks, furs, gold and silver ornaments, tapestries, lacquered ware, fans, &c., and a large trade. The larger portion of the inhabitants live outside the walls in the handsome suburbs and in boats on the river. It is also a great centre of literary and ecclesiastical life. Pop. (1931), 506,930.

HANGING-BUTTRESS, in architecture, a buttress not standing solid on a foundation, but supported on a corbel. It is applied chiefly as a decoration.

HANKEY, Sir Maurice Pascal Alers. English administrator. Born 1st April, 1877, he was educated at Rugby and entered the marines. In 1902 he became an official in the Naval Intelligence Department at the Admiralty and was soon associated with the Committee of Imperial Defence. In 1912 he became its secretary, and in 1916 Secretary to the War Cabinet. In 1919, when a secretariat for the cabinet was formally established, he was placed at its head. In 1916 he was knighted and in 1919 he was awarded £25,000 for his work at the Peace

Conference. He was Secretary-General to the Hague Conference in 1929–30, and in 1930 to the London Naval Conference.

HANKOW ('Mouth of the Han'), a town and river-port in China, in the

Hanging-buttress, St. Helen's, York

province of Hupeh, at the junction of the Han with the Yang-tze-kiang; Hanyang being on the opposite bank of the Han, and Wuchang on the other side of the Yang-tze.

The port was opened to foreign trade in 1862, and has become the chief emporium for the great tea districts in the central provinces. In 1857 Hankow fell into the hands of the Taiping rebels, and was almost completely demolished by them. In 1911 the town was attacked by the revolutionaries and partly burned. Pop. of Hankow, Hanyang, and Wuchang (1931), 777,993.

HAN'LEY, a district, formerly a town, of North Staffordshire, England, pleasantly situated on rising ground near the Trent, 18 miles north by west of the county town of Stafford. It is quite a modern town, owing its growth entirely to the vast manufactures of china and earthenware in which the inhabitants are mostly

employed; there are also iron-furnaces, foundries, brick-works, and collieries. Formerly a parliamentary borough, Hanley now gives name to a parliamentary division of Stoke-on-Trent, in which it is now included. Pop. (1931), 67,891.

HANNAY, Canon James Owen, better known under his pen-name of **George A. Birmingham,** was born in Belfast in 1865, and educated at Haileybury and Trinity College, Dublin, where he graduated B.A. in 1887 and M.A. in 1895. He was rector of Westport, County Mayo, from 1892 to 1913.

His novels include: *Spanish Gold, The Seething Pot, The Red Hand of Ulster,* and *The Lost Tribes.* They deal for the most part with the lighter side of Irish life. His play *General John Regan* (1913), which was highly successful in London, was strongly disapproved of in Ireland. Among his later publications are *The Major's Candlesticks* (1929); *Wild Justice* (1930); and *Fed Up* (1931).

HAN'NIBAL, one of the greatest generals of antiquity, born 247 B.C., was the son of Hamilcar Barca, also a

Hannibal

general and leader of the popular party amongst the Carthaginians. He was but nine years of age when his father made him swear at the altar eternal hatred to the Romans. He grew up in his father's camp in Spain (*see* HAMILCAR), but returned to Carthage when his father fell in battle, in 229 B.C.

At the age of twenty-two he returned to the army in Spain, then commanded by his brother-in-law Hasdrubal, and three years after, on the murder of Hasdrubal, received the chief command by acclamation.

Hannibal now prepared to carry out his great designs against Rome. His siege and capture of Saguntum, a city in alliance with Rome, led to a declaration of war from the Romans, who made preparations to carry on the war in Spain.

But Hannibal, judging that Rome could be overthrown only in Italy, undertook his great march on Rome across the Pyrenees, the Rhône, and the Alps. He set out with 90,000 foot-soldiers, 40 elephants, and 12,000 horsemen. When he reached the northern foot of the Alps he had still 50,000 foot-soldiers, 9,000 horse, and 37 elephants. When he arrived at the southern foot, after 15 days of incredible toils, his force had diminished to 20,000 foot-soldiers and 6,000 horse. The point at which he crossed is generally believed to have been the Little St. Bernard.

On the banks of the Ticino he first encountered a Roman army under Publius Scipio, and defeated it mainly by the superiority of his Numidian cavalry, 218 B.C. Shortly after, another Roman army, under Sempronius, was totally routed on the Trebia. After wintering in Cisalpine Gaul, Hannibal opened next year's campaign (217) by defeating the Roman general Flaminius, whom he enticed into an ambush at Lake Thrasymenus. In this battle half the Roman army perished, and the rest were taken prisoners.

Hannibal now marched into Apulia, spreading terror wherever he approached. Rome, in consternation, proclaimed Fabius Maximus dictator, who sagaciously resolved to hazard no more open battles, but exhaust the strength of the Carthaginians by delay. But for some time the wisdom of this policy was not understood by his countrymen, who, dissatisfied with his inactivity, appointed Minutius Felix his colleague. The result was that the latter was drawn into a battle by Hannibal, and would have perished but for the aid of Fabius.

After this the Roman generals avoided engagements, and Hannibal at this critical period saw his army wasting away in inactivity. Next year (216), however, the rashness of the new consul Terentius Varro gave Hannibal the last of his great victories. The battle was fought at Cannæ, the Romans under L. Æmilius Paulus and Varro numbering more than 80,000 men, the Carthaginians about 50,000, and ended in a total defeat of the Romans, 40,000 or 50,000 of whom were slain and the rest scattered.

Instead of marching on Rome, Hannibal now sought quarters in Capua, where luxurious living undermined the discipline and health of his troops. The campaigns of 215, 214 and 213 were comparatively unimportant. While Hannibal was seizing Tarentum (212), Capua was invested by two Roman armies. To relieve Capua Hannibal marched on Rome, and actually appeared before its gates (211), but the diversion remained fruitless, and Capua fell.

In 207 a reinforcement tardily sent by the Carthaginians to Hannibal, under command of his brother Hasdrubal, was intercepted by the Romans and destroyed at the Metaurus. Hannibal now retired to Bruttium (the toe of Italy), where he still maintained the contest against overwhelming odds, till, in 203, he was recalled to defend his country, invaded by Scipio. In Africa he was defeated by the Romans at Zama (202 B.C.), and the second Punic War ended, after a bloody contest of eighteen years, in Carthage having to accept the most humiliating conditions of peace.

Hannibal now devoted himself as civil magistrate to restoring the resources of Carthage, and was working at reforms of administration and finance when the jealous Romans sent ambassadors to demand his surrender. He fled to the court of Antiochus of Syria, and offered his services for the war then commencing against the Romans. They were accepted, but Hannibal's advice for the conduct of the war was not followed, and he himself as commander of the Syrian fleet failed in an expedition against the Rhodians.

In 190 B.C. Antiochus was forced to conclude a disgraceful peace with the Romans, one of the terms of which was that Hannibal should be delivered up.

Hannibal, again obliged to flee, took refuge with Prusias, King of Bithynia, and is said to have gained several victories for Prusias against Eumenes, King of Pergamus, an ally of the Romans. But the Roman Senate once more sent to demand the surrender of their inveterate enemy, and Hannibal, finding that Prusias could not protect him, took poison rather than fall into the hands of the Romans. He died in 183 B.C.—BIBLIOGRAPHY: F. A. Dodge, *Hannibal* (Great Captains Series); W. How, *Hannibal and the Great War between Rome and Carthage*; E. Hennebert, *Histoire d'Annibal* (3 vols.).

HANNIBAL, a town in the United States, in Marion county, Missouri, on the right bank of the Mississippi, 150 miles above St. Louis. It has tobacco factories, machine-shops, foundries, pork-packing establishments, saw- and flour-mills, and an extensive trade in lumber. Pop. (1930), 22,761.

HANNO, a Carthaginian navigator of the fifth and sixth centuries B.C., who made a voyage on the western coast of Africa for the purpose of discovery and of settling colonies. He wrote an account of his voyage, which still survives in a Greek translation known as the *Periplus of Hanno.* From this account Hanno would appear to have gone as far as the coast of Guinea.

HANOI', or **KESH'O,** capital of Tonking, and of Indo-China since 1902, on the River Song-ka, in a fruitful plain. The river is here crossed by a bridge a mile long. Gold and silver filigree, lacquered wares, silks, mat- and basket-weaving are its principal industries. Although the river is navigable only for small vessels the trade of Hanoi is considerable, chiefly with the southern provinces of China. There is a school of medicine for natives, opened in 1902, which since 1917 belongs to the University of Indo-China. Pop. (1932), 123,210.

HANOTAUX, Albert Auguste Gabriel, French politician and historian, born at Beaurevoir, Aisne, in 1853. After being sub-chief of the Cabinet of Gambetta and chief of that of Jules Ferry, he entered the Chamber of Deputies in 1886 as member for the Aisne, opposed General Boulanger, and was Minister of Foreign Affairs from 1894 to 1895, and again from 1896 to 1898. He was an ardent supporter of the Franco-Russian Alliance, which was strengthened during his tenure of office. To a certain extent he was responsible for the Fashoda incident (1898).

In 1907 he was elected a member of the Academie Française, and his works include: *Henri Martin* (1885); *Histoire du Cardinal Richelieu* (1893–1903), crowned by the Académie (Gobert prize); *L'Affaire de Madagascar* (1896); *La France et la Royauté avant Richelieu* (1898); *Histoire de la France contemporaine* (1903–8); and *Histoire de la Guerre* (1914–20).

HAN'OVER (Ger. *Hannover*), formerly a kingdom in the north-west of Germany, now a province of Prussia. It is of very irregular shape, and is divided by intervening territories into three distinct portions, besides some small territories to the south, and a range of sandy islands lining the coast. The total area is 14,897 sq. miles. For administrative purposes it is divided into six districts —Hanover, Hildesheim, Lüneburg, Stade, Osnabrück, Aurich.

The surface in the south is covered by the Harz Mountains, but the rest of the country is a low, monotonous flat, with a gentle slope to the North Sea. The Ems, the Weser (with its tributaries the Leine and Aller), and the Elbe flow through fertile districts industriously cultivated for corn and flax. Near the coast the land is marshy, but feeds large numbers of very superior cattle. In Central Hanover the soil is of a barren, sandy nature. The Harz Mountains are rich in minerals, the working of which is an important industry.

History. Hanover was long connected with the Brunswick family, and subsequently more especially with the line of Brunswick-Lüneburg. Ernest Augustus, a prince of the latter line, became in 1692 the first Elector of Hanover, married a granddaughter of James I of England, and was succeeded in 1698 by his son, George Louis, who in 1714 became George I of England. Henceforth it was ruled in connection with England.

In 1814 the Congress of Vienna raised Hanover to the rank of a kingdom, the crown of which was worn by George IV and William IV, but on the accession of Queen Victoria passed by Salic law to Ernest Augustus, Duke of Cumberland. In 1851 he was succeeded by his son, George V, but in 1866, Hanover having become involved in the Austro-Prussian contest, the kingdom was occupied by Prussian troops, and absorbed into the dominions of Prussia. Pop. of the province (1925), 3,190,439.

HANOVER, capital of the Prussian province of Hanover, situated in an extensive plain on the Leine, which here receives the Ihme and becomes navigable. It is an important railway junction, also an airport, and is connected with the Rhine by a canal. The old town, irregularly built and with many antiquated buildings, is surrounded by the handsome new quarters which have arisen to the north, east, and south-east. There are fine promenades, and a large wood with beautiful walks, the Eilenriede, lies on the eastern side of the city. The suburbs include Calenberg and Linden.

Buildings. Amongst the principal buildings are the market church, the old town house, the theatre (one of the finest in Germany), the royal palace, the Museum of Art and Science, the Royal Library (containing over 200,000 volumes), the Central Railway Station, and the Waterloo Monument. About a mile to the northwest is Schloss Herrenhausen the favourite residence of George I, George II, and George V. Nearer the town is the colossal Welfenschloss, or palace of the Guelphs, now fitted up as a polytechnic school of high rank.

Manufactures. Hanover is a manufacturing town of importance, producing machinery, iron-work, metallic goods of various kinds, chemicals, carpets, pianos, and stationery. It is first mentioned in 1163, and joined the Hanseatic League in 1481. It became the residence of the Dukes of Brunswick-Lüneburg, and capital of the principality in 1636. It has a broadcasting station (566 m., 0·25 k.w.). Pop. (1925), 425,274.

HAN'SARD, a firm of printers in London, which long printed the parliamentary debates and papers. The founder of the business was Luke Hansard (1752–1828), who, in 1800, became printer to the House of Commons. The reports of speeches printed were extracted from the London newspapers, but were generally sent to the speakers for revision. The name is still retained for the reports furnished by the *Times* staff from 1895 to 1908, and since that date by a Government staff.

HANSE TOWNS, certain German and other commercial cities of Northern Europe associated for the protection of commerce and united by what was called the *Hanseatic League.* In the middle of the thirteenth century the sea and land swarmed with pirates and robbers. In particular the thriving ports of the Baltic and the North Sea were infested, and in 1219 a compact was made between Hamburg, Ditmarsh, and Hadeln to protect the adjacent waters.

This was followed in 1241 by an alliance between Hamburg and Lübeck to keep open the road across Holstein, connecting the North Sea with the Baltic. In 1247 this league was joined by Brunswick, and out of this grew the Hansa or league, which at its most flourishing period embraced eighty-five towns, maritime and inland, from Reval and Narva to Amsterdam and Middelburg, and from Cologne to Breslau and Cracow. Amongst these the town of Lübeck was recognized as the chief town of the League. Here assembled the Deputies of the other Hanse towns to deliberate on the affairs of the confederacy; but the decrees of the Diet had no effect unless they received the sanction of the separate towns.

The chief trading centres of the League were the factories of Novgorod in Russia, Bergen in Norway, Bruges, and London (the so-called Steelyard). These factories were subject to an almost monastic discipline, which even required their officers to be celibates and live at a common table. During the latter half of the fourteenth century the power of the League was at its height. It had armies and navies, gained victories in war over the Kings of Norway and Denmark, and deposed a King of Sweden. It made thorough provision for the security of commerce on the Baltic and North Seas, constructed canals, introduced a uniform system of weights and measures, and developed the principles of mercantile law. But as its power and ambition increased it was felt to be an oppressive monopoly established mainly in the interests of the great seaport towns. It became less needful also for commercial security, as the princes learned the advantages of trade, formed naval forces of their own, and encouraged navigation. Most of the inland members of the confederation withdrew, and during the fifteenth and sixteenth centuries the cities of Hamburg, Lüneburg, and Lübeck were almost alone in their active efforts to maintain the power of the Hansa and secure for it the command of the Baltic.

About the middle of the sixteenth century the Dutch became predominant in the Baltic trade. In 1597 England revoked all special privileges of the Hanseatic merchants, and in 1614 Lübeck, Stettin, Danzig, Brunswick, Lüneburg, Hamburg, Bremen, and Cologne, with a few smaller towns, were the only places that contributed to the support of the Hansa. The League still made desperate efforts to retain its monopolies, but the cost of doing so now became a heavy tax on the remaining allies. At the last General Assembly, held in 1630 at Lübeck, many of the members sent representatives only to renounce their allegiance.

The name still remained attached to the free cities of Lübeck, Bremen, and Hamburg, under whose protection the surviving factories continued to exist, that of Bergen being still managed in the old way till 1763. In 1813 Frankfort-on-the-Main was included in the number of the Hanse towns, and in the German Confederation these four cities had together one vote in the Diet. Frankfort was incorporated in Prussia in 1866, but the three other towns are still separate constituents of Germany, with new Constitutions adopted in 1919.— BIBLIOGRAPHY: W. King, *Three Free Cities*; H. Zimmern, *The Hansa Towns*; G. F. Sartorius, *Geschichte des hanseatischen Bundes* (3 vols.).

HANSI, a town of Hissar district, Punjab, on a branch of the Western Jumna Canal. Pop. 15,425.

HANSOM-CAB, a two-wheeled hackney-carriage or cabriolet formerly used in large cities. It holds two persons besides the driver, who sits on an elevated seat behind the body of the carriage, the reins being brought over the top. The hansom was so named after its inventor, Joseph Aloysius Hansom, an English architect (1803–82).

HANUMĀN', in Indian mythology, the name of a fabulous monkey-god, who plays a prominent part in the epic *Râmâyana.* He was the son of a nymph by the god of the wind, Indra, envious of his prowess, tried to kill him by the thunderbolt, but only succeeded in breaking his jaw. From this circumstance he received the name *Hanūmān,* i.e. he of the (broken) jaw. As the monkey-general who aided Rama (the seventh incarnation of Vishnu) in his war against the giant Ravana, he is worshipped as a demi-god, and on his account the whole tribe of monkeys, to which he is fabled to belong, is treated as sacred and allowed to multiply indefinitely —Cf. A. C. Wilson, *Hindu Mythology.*

HAN'WAY, Jonas, English traveller and philanthropist, born in 1712, died in 1786. At an early age he was apprenticed to a merchant at Lisbon, and in 1743 became a partner in a British house at St. Petersburg (Petrograd). He travelled in Persia, and published *An Historical Account of the British Trade over the Caspian Sea.* Afterwards he settled in London, where he became widely known as an active philanthropist. He is popularly known as one of the first Englishmen who regularly used an umbrella.

HANWELL, a former urban district on the west of London, now in Ealing; near it is the London County Lunatic Asylum. The Brent and The Grand Union Canal flow through the district which includes Ellhorne.

HANWORTH, district of Middlesex It is 16 miles from London, and its station is Feltham on the S. Rly. Here is the London Air Park.

HANYANG. *See* HANKOW.

HAPTOTROPISM, curvature of a plant-organ in response to the stimulus of touch; the most familiar illustrations are provided by the tendrils of climbing plants.

HAPUR, a town of India, in the Meerut district, United Provinces. It has a considerable trade in sugar, grain, cotton, and timber. Pop. 19,140.

HAR'AKIRI, or **SEP'PUKU,** a mode of inflicting death upon themselves allowed in Japan to criminals of the Samurai or two-sworded class

as more honourable than public execution. It consists in cutting open the body so as to disembowel it by means of a wound made with one sword perpendicularly down the front and another with the other sword horizontally. It is frequently resorted to to save dishonour or exposure. In 1912 General Nogi and his wife, out of loyalty to the dead emperor committed Harakiri on the eve of the funeral of their sovereign. During the Russo-Japanese War, 1904–5, Japanese officers captured by the Russians also resorted to this mode of suicide. —BIBLIOGRAPHY: B. H. Chamberlain, *Things Japanese*; J. H. Longford, *The Evolution of New Japan.*

HARAR, a town of North-Eastern Africa, included in the Abyssinian territories, about 150 miles from the coast of the Gulf of Aden, now reached by a railway from the French port of Jibouti. The inhabitants are strict Mahommedans. Pop. estimated at 40 000.

HARBIN, or **KHARBIN,** a town of China, in Manchuria, province of Kirin, about 330 miles north-east of Mukden, near the right bank of the Sungari, a tributary of the Amur, and close to the Mongolian frontier. It is the place where the Siberian railway forks, one branch going to Mukden and Port Arthur, the other to Vladivostok. Pop. 252,988.

HARBOUR, any sheltered area of water on a sea coast which ships can enter, and in which they can safely anchor during stormy weather.

In ancient times, about 3000 B.C., the Phœnicians of Tyre had two harbours, one on each side of a peninsula, extending to about 14 acres and joined together by a ship canal. At a later date the Carthaginians and Romans made extensive harbours, and the latter constructed Civita Vecchia, Ostia, and many others; that at Ostia, built at the mouth of the Tiber, enclosed about 140 acres, and was provided with a lighthouse, 1½ miles of quays, grain warehouses, &c.

Harbours are either 'natural' or 'artificial.' Natural harbours occur on deeply-indented coasts, and may be riverine estuaries or mouths of rivers, or simply a deep indentation with a comparatively narrow entrance. The estuaries of the Thames, Forth, and Clyde are entirely natural harbours, requiring no engineering works in their lower reaches, and, owing to their bell-mouth shape and ample depth of water, are of easy access. Milford Haven, Sydney Harbour, and many others represent deeply-embayed indentations which form excellent shelters.

On the other hand, there are many stretches of coast where the art of the engineer has to be employed, either to improve the shelter of areas of water already partially protected by the contour of the coast-line, as at Plymouth, or to construct an entirely new harbour completely enclosed by breakwaters, as at Madras. The latter is a notable instance of a harbour constructed on a long, straight stretch of coast, and consists of breakwaters in the form of three sides of a square projected out into the sea, having an entrance at the outer northern corner.

Navigable rivers with narrow mouths also require protective breakwaters projected out in a horn shape and converging to a narrow entrance, ranging sometimes from 400 to 600 feet. The distance of the entrance to the river mouth should be such that ships on entering the smoother water can lose way sufficiently to be under control when negotiating the narrow river mouth.

The tides play a very important part. Where there are no tides, as in the Mediterranean, river estuaries are blocked with deltas, and the river is split up into many mouths, generally only navigable in the natural condition for small craft. In the case of large rivers so situated, it is frequently possible to select one of the mouths and make it navigable for large vessels, as in the Mississippi and the Danube. Captain Eads, United States, by constructing parallel jetties in the former case, made one of the mouths navigable for ships of almost 30 feet draught, but at a cost of over £1,000,000. It is only possible to make very large rivers navigable under such conditions because of the large volume of fresh water available to prevent silting by keeping the channel scoured. It is a consequence that, except in similar cases to those mentioned, all ports in tideless seas are on or near the coast.

If this state of things is compared with that obtaining in tidal waters, it will be noted that large ports are frequently many miles up rivers. The tide, in fact, acts as the scouring agent, clearing out deltas and conserving the depth of navigation channels in estuarine harbours. It enables comparatively small rivers, such as the Thames, Forth, and Clyde, to act as harbours in the outer reaches and conveyers of ships to far inland ports. Hamburg is 75 miles from the sea, and had there been no tides, neither that port nor the ports of London and Glasgow would be in existence.

In riverine estuaries and narrow river mouths one of the chief diffi-culties is the tendency to silt up at the point where they join the open water, forming an incipient delta termed a 'bar': the water shoals suddenly, forming a more or less pronounced mound, and this is due partly to littoral drift and partly to detritus carried down by the river current and deposited where the current is checked. The method of removing this is either to form training walls to concentrate tidal scour, and so to sweep out a navigable passage through the bar, or simply to dredge it out.

Harbours are of three categories, according to their uses: (a) refuge harbours, (b) commercial harbours, and (c) fishery harbours. Class (a) are constructed on dangerous coasts where there are no natural harbours. They must be easy to reach, and must provide good shelter. Peterhead breakwater is an example of a national harbour of refuge constructed to save ships caught in a nor'-easter from having to run back to the Forth. Class (b) are those which from the entrances or vestibules to ports, and they may at the same time be excellent harbours of refuge. Class (c) are generally of small extent, but the entrances must be easily taken in rough weather. Such harbours are not always easy to design efficiently and the works may be costly. The Government frequently assists by loans or grants.—BIBLIOGRAPHY: W. Shield, *Harbour Construction*; B. Cunningham, *Harbour Engineering*.

HARBOUR GRACE, a seaport of Newfoundland, on the west side of Conception Bay. It is the seat of a Roman Catholic bishop, has a handsome cathedral, and an active trade. Pop. 3,825.

HARBURG, a town in Prussia, in the province of Hanover, on the left bank of the South Elbe, opposite to Hamburg. It has varied manufactures and an important trade. Pop. (with suburbs), 105,765.

HARCOURT, Sir William George Granville Venables Vernon, lawyer and politician, son of Rev. William Vernon Harcourt, was born in 1827, died in 1904. He was educated at Trinity College, Cambridge; was called to the Bar in 1854, became Queen's Counsel in 1866; contributed frequently to the Press, in particular the letters to the *Times* signed 'Historicus'; was returned for Oxford city in 1869 in the Liberal interest; distinguished himself by his powers of satire and ridicule in debate; was made Solicitor-General in Gladstone's ministry, Nov., 1873; Home Secretary in 1880, when he lost his seat for Oxford but was returned for Derby. He introduced the Arms Bill (Ireland),

1881; Prevention of Crimes Bill, 1882; and Explosives Bill, 1883. In 1886 he was Chancellor of the Exchequer under Gladstone, as he was under the same leader and under Lord Rosebery in 1892–5, when he remodelled the death duties.

HARCOURT, Viscount. Title held by the family of Harcourt. The first viscount was **Simon Harcourt,** who was made Lord Keeper of the Great Seal in 1710. He was made a baron in 1711 and a viscount in 1721. He died 23rd July, 1727. His son, Simon, the 2nd viscount, was made an earl in 1749, and was Lord Lieutenant of Ireland, 1772–77. When he died in 1777 the titles passed in turn to his two sons. When, in 1830, William, the 3rd earl, who was a distinguished soldier, died, the Harcourt titles became extinct

In 1916 the title of Viscount Harcourt was revived for **Lewis Vernon Harcourt.** Born 1st Feb., 1863, he was the elder son of Sir William Harcourt who had inherited the family estates, including the manor house of Stanton Harcourt and Nuneham Park, both in Oxfordshire. The former had been a family residence for 600 years. Lewis Harcourt was an M.P. from 1904 to 1916. From 1905–10 he was First Commissioner of Works, and from 1910–15 Secretary for the Colonies. He died 24th Feb., 1922, leaving an only son to inherit his title.

HARDANGER, fjord or inlet of the coast of Norway. It extends for about 70 miles inland, Vik being at its head, and has a branch which goes to Odde. The fjord is much visited by tourists who are attracted by the wonderful mountain and other scenery. Near is the waterfall called the Võringfos.

HARDEN, Maximilian, German journalist and author, born in Berlin 1861. His real name was Witkowski, and he first wrote essays on political and social questions under the pseudonym of *Apostata.* A satirical writer of considerable talent, Harden frequently criticized the Government, especially that of Caprivi. In 1900 he was prosecuted for *lèse-majesté* and condemned to six months' imprisonment.

In 1892 he founded the famous weekly paper the *Zukunft* (The Future), wherein he published numerous sensational articles. His famous campaign of 1907 against the friends of the ex-Kaiser, Philip zu Eulenburg and Wilhelm von Hohenhau, created a stir. During the European War Harden frequently criticized the German Government, which retaliated by suppressing his paper more than once. His works include: *Apostata*

(1892), *Kampfgenosse Sudermann* (1903), *Word Portraits* and *Monarchs and Men.* He died in 1927.

HARDENBERG, Friedrich von, German writer, better known under the name of Novalis, born 1772, died 1801. He studied at Jena, Leipzig, and Wittenberg, was the friend of Tieck and the Schlegels, and spent his brief life in study and literary production. He was one of the leaders of the 'Romantic School,' and his writings are a strange mixture of imagination, profundity, and mysticism. Amongst his works are an unfinished novel, *Heinrich von Ofterdingen,* and *Spiritual Songs.*

HARDENBERG, Karl August, Prince von, Prussian Chancellor of State, was born at Essenrode, in Hanover, in 1750, died in 1822. He entered the civil service of his country, but left it for that of Brunswick, and next became Prussian Minister of State, and in 1804 First Minister of Prussia. His conduct was vacillating, now favouring an alliance with Napoleon and again hostile to him.

After the Peace of Tilsit, he was banished from the Prussian court by command of Napoleon, was recalled to office as Chancellor in 1810, and after the French disaster at Moscow was amongst the first to declare that the time had now come for a general effort against Napoleon. Hardenberg signed the Peace of Paris, and was created prince. He was one of the most prominent actors at the Congress of Vienna; became President of the Prussian Council of State; was present in 1818 at the Congress of Aix-la-Chapelle; in 1819 at Carlsbad; in 1820 at Troppau; in 1820–1 at Laibach; and in 1822 at Verona. He abolished feudal privileges in Prussia, and was a munificent patron of the sciences.

HARDERWIJK (hâr-dér-vīk), a town of the Netherlands, in the province of Gelderland, on the Zuider Zee, 30 miles east of Amsterdam. From 1648 to 1811 Harderwijk had a university, and it was also a Hanse town. Pop. 7,415.

HARD-FERN, the popular name for *Lomaria spicant,* which is also known as *Blechnum boreale.* It is a very common fern, being found everywhere in Britain growing on heaths, in glens, on old roadside walls, and other places.

HARDICANUTE, or **HARTHACNUT,** King of England and Denmark, was the only legitimate son of Canute. At the time of his father's death, in 1036 he was in Denmark, where he was immediately recognized as king. His half-brother Harold, however, who happened to be in England at the time, laid claim to the throne of that part of their father's dominions, and succeeded in getting possession of Mercia, Northumbria, and Wessex, but died in 1042, when Hardicanute succeeded him unopposed. He reigned till 1042, leaving the government almost entirely in the hands of his mother and the powerful Earl Godwin, while he gave himself up to feasts and carousals.—Cf. Sir C. W. Oman, *A History of England before the Norman Conquest.*

HARDIE, James Keir, British politician and labour leader, born in Scotland 15th Aug., 1856, died 26th Sept., 1915. From the age of seven to twenty-four he worked first as a messenger, and then, at the age of ten, in the coal-mines, and in 1880 was elected secretary of the Lanarkshire Miners' Union. Later he became secretary of the Ayrshire Miners' Union and a contributor to the *Cumnock News* from 1882 till 1886. He afterwards founded and edited the *Labour Leader,* originally the *Miner* (1887–1903). He entered Parliament in 1892, and sat for West Ham from 1892 till 1895, and for Merthyr Tydfil from 1900 till his death.

Hardie was the real founder of the Independent Labour Party which came into existence in 1893; he was its first chairman, as he was also of the Labour Party which the I.L.P. helped to create in 1900. As the most popular and widely known leader of the I.L.P. he had a wide reputation as a Socialist and anti-militarist, and a woman's suffragist. His works include: *Labour Politics* (1903), *India* (1909), and *After Twenty Years; all about the Independent Labour Party* (1913).—Cf. W. Stewart, *James Keir Hardie.*

HARDING, Warren Gamaliel, President of the United States, born near the village of Blooming Grove, Morrow County, Ohio, on 2nd Nov. 1865. Educated at the school of Blooming Grove and at a college in Caledonia, he was a schoolmaster for some time, but in 1884 he acquired *The Marion Star,* a local newspaper, and subsequently became president of the Harding Publishing Company. Member of the Ohio Senate from 1899 to 1903, Lieutenant-Governor of the state of Ohio from 1904 to 1906, he was elected to the United States Senate in 1914. A political opponent of President Wilson, he supported the candidacy of C. E. Hughes for the presidency in 1916.

When the European War broke out, Harding backed up Roosevelt when the latter tried to urge President Wilson to join the Allies and to send troops to Europe. Nominated for the presidency in June, 1920, Harding was elected, by a vast majority, against Cox, the Democratic candidate, on 2nd Nov., 1920. Although he had opposed President Wilson's scheme of the League of Nations, he was nevertheless indefatigable in his endeavour to bring about a new Union, or Association, enabling his country to work hand in hand with the European Powers and to establish a permanent peace. In 1921 he convened a conference of European and American Statesmen at Washington for the purpose of discussing and settling the question of disarmament. His administration was marred by several serious scandals concerning the transfer of public property in oil lands (Teapot Dome) to private interests; and after his death rumour was busy with both his public and private reputation: the truth, however, appears to be that he was a weak, well-meaning man in the hands of far more unscrupulous and able men than himself. He died in August, 1923.

HARDINGE (här'ding), **Henry,** Viscount, English commander, was born in 1785, and died in 1856. He was a son of the Rev. Henry Hardinge, rector of Stanhope, Durham. In 1799 he was gazetted ensign, and was present at all the great battles and sieges in the Peninsula. He lost his left hand at the battle of Ligny, became member of Parliament for Durham in 1820, was made Secretary-at-War, Secretary for Ireland, and in 1844 succeeded Lord Ellenborough as Governor-General of India. Being forced into war by an invasion of Sikhs, he took a command under Lord Gough, and, after the great battles of Mudki, Ferozeshah, and Sobraon, dictated a peace in the Sikh capital of Lahore. As a reward for his services he was created Viscount Hardinge and received a pension of £3,000. In 1852, on the death of the Duke of Wellington, he succeeded to the post of commander-in-chief. In 1855 he was made a field-marshal.

Charles Hardinge, a younger son of the 2nd viscount, entered the diplomatic service in 1880. In 1904-06 he was ambassador at St. Petersburg and 1906–10 was Under-Secretary at the Foreign Office. From 1910 to 1916 he was Viceroy of India, and in 1910 was made Baron Hardinge of Penshurst. When he left India he resumed his former position at the Foreign Office, remaining there until 1920, when he became ambassador in Paris, a post he vacated in 1922.

A railway bridge across the Ganges at Sara, opened in 1917, is named the **Hardinge Bridge.**

HARD LABOUR, particular kind of imprisonment. In Great Britain, under certain conditions, judges can sentence those convicted of crime to a term of imprisonment with hard labour. This means solitary confinement and the discharge of some heavy task, making sacks or picking oakum. This lasts for the first 28 days of the term of imprisonment; after that time, unless they are unruly, the prisoners are given easier tasks, similar to those given to prisoners who are not sentenced to hard labour.

HARDOI, a town of India, administrative headquarters of Hardoi district, Oudh, 63 miles from Lucknow. Pop. 14,412.

Thomas Hardy

HARDWAR (*Haridwara*, gate of Hari), a town of India, in Saharanpur district, in the United Provinces. It is situated on the Ganges, and is one of the principal places of Hindu pilgrimage, and of the ceremonial bathing in the sacred river. The town, originally known as Kapila, is of great antiquity and has interesting ruins. Pop. 30,744.

HARDWICK HALL, seat of the Duke of Devonshire. It is in Derbyshire, 6 miles from Chesterfield, and is reached from Rowtharn station on the L.M.S. Rly. It was built by Elizabeth, Countess of Shrewsbury, about 1600, and from her it passed to the Cavendish family who have since retained it. The long gallery is a fine apartment, but the house is chiefly famous for its windows (whence the saying, "Hardwick Hall more glass than wall") and its tapestries. Near are the ruins of an earlier hall.

HARDWICKE, Cedric Webster. English actor. Born in 1893 at Lye in Worcestershire, he was educated at Bridgnorth. He made his first appearance on the stage in London, and in 1914 was touring in South Africa with F. R. Benson's Shakespearean Company. In 1924 he settled in London and during the next few years made a great reputation. His successes included parts in *Back to Methuselah*, *The Apple Cart* and others of G. B. Shaw's plays, as well as in *The Farmer's Wife*, *Yellow Sands* and *The Barretts of Wimpole Street*. He has also acted for the films in the characters of Nelson and Dreyfus. In 1932 he published an autobiography, *Let's Pretend*.

HARDY, Thomas, O.M., LL.D. (Aberdeen), Litt.D.(Cambridge), and D. Litt. (Oxford), novelist, born at Upper Bockhampton, near Dorchester, Dorset, 2nd June, 1840, he was educated at the grammar school there. He went to London to study architecture, winning prizes from the professional associations and working under Sir Arthur Blomfield. Hardy's real interest, however, was in literature, and he soon began to write. His first novel, *Desperate Remedies*, appeared in 1871 and *Under the Greenwood Tree* in 1872, and he has since written a series of famous novels.

Among his best-known works are: *Far from the Madding Crowd*, *The Hand of Ethelberta*, *The Trumpet Major*, *The Woodlanders*, *The Return of the Native*, *The Mayor of Casterbridge*, *Tess of the D'Urbervilles*, *Jude the Obscure*, *The Pursuit of the Well-Beloved*. *The Dynasts*, *Time's Laughing-stocks*, *A Changed Man*, *Satires of Circumstance*, *Moments of Vision*, *Late Lyrics and Earlier*, and *Human Shows*. *Tess* is perhaps the greatest as it is the most popular of his prose works. His poetic play *The Famous Tragedy of the Queen of Cornwall at Tintagel in Lyonesse* was produced in 1923.

Hardy also published several volumes of verse. His last great work was a dramatic poem of the Napoleonic wars. *The Dynasts*, regarded by some as the supreme achievement of his genius. His last poem, written shortly before his death, was *Christmas in the Elgin Room*. In 1910 he was given the Order of Merit. He died at his residence, Max Gate, Dorchester, 12th Jan., 1928. He was twice married, but left no children. His *Life* was written by his widow. In 1931 a statue to him was erected in Dorchester.

To Hardy recognition came slowly, but for many years before his death he was regarded as one of the great English writers. His style is remarkably lucid and his powers of description, especially of scenes of rural life, have rarely, if ever, been excelled. Two other qualities help to assure him a place amongst the immortals. One is his philosophy of life and the other the intense local colour which permeates his works. His philosophy is that of fate, indifferent to suffering, caring nothing for either good or evil, playing with the lives of men and women as it will. His books are full of the history and folklore of the country which he knew and about which he wrote with such detail. He calls it Wessex, but to many it is the Hardy country, and its towns and villages can be easily recognized beneath the pseudonyms which he has given them.

HARE, Sir John, British actor-manager, was born in 1844, and educated at Giggleswick Grammar School, Yorkshire. He first appeared on the stage in Liverpool in 1864, and began his acting career in London in the following year. He acted for ten years with the Bancrofts, and soon made his mark, especially in the plays of T. W. Robertson, though he also acted in the plays of Sheridan and Goldsmith.

In 1875 he became manager of the Court Theatre, and joint-manager (along with Kendal) of St. James's Theatre in 1879. The Garrick Theatre was built by Sir W. S. Gilbert for Hare in 1889, and opened with Pinero's *Profligate.* Here he also produced *The Notorious Mrs. Ebbsmith,* and in 1890 had a remarkable personal success in Sydney Grundy's *A Pair of Spectacles,* where he took the part of Benjamin Goldfinch. He enjoyed another triumph when playing the title rôle of Pinero's *Gay Lord Quex* in 1899. He toured in America with great success. He was knighted in 1907. He died 28th Dec., 1921.

HARE, Julius Charles, an English writer on theological and social subjects, born in 1796, died 1855. He was educated at the Charterhouse, and Trinity College, Cambridge. In concert with his brother, Augustus William Hare, he published a well-known work entitled *Guesses at Truth by Two Brothers.* His other writings include several volumes of sermons, *A Memoir of John Sterling,* and a *Vindication of Luther against his Recent English Assailants.*

HARE, the common name of rodent mammals of the genus Lepus, with long ears, long hind-limbs, a short tail, soft hair, and a divided upper lip; its dental formula is:

$$I. \frac{2-2}{1-1}, C. \frac{0-0}{0-0}, P.M. \frac{3-3}{2-2}, M. \frac{3-3}{3-3} = 28;$$

the two fore-feet have five and the hinder four toes. The soles of the feet

are hairy, and there is a patch of hair on the inner surface of each cheek. They run by a kind of leaping pace. The female produce litters of three to six about four times a year. The young leverets have their eyes open at birth.

Species. The common hare (*L. europæus*) is found throughout Europe and some parts of Asia. It is tawny red on the back and white on the belly, and is about 2 feet long. The mountain hare or variable hare (*L. variabilis*), confined to Northern Europe and the mountainous regions of the south, is smaller than the common hare, and becomes white in winter. *L. cuniculus* is the rabbit, properly so called, distinguished by its smaller size and burrowing habits. (*See* RABBIT.) The American hare (*L. americanus*), not much larger than a rabbit, is found in most parts of North America. In North America there are also the polar hare, a variety

Mountain Hare (*Lepus variabilis*) in winter

of the variable hare (*L. variabilis*), but of superior size and purer colour; and the prairie hare (*L. campestris*), one of the species known as jackass hares or jack-rabbits, from their size and length of limb.

The hare, which has no courage and little cunning, is protected from its enemies mainly by the acuteness of its sight and hearing and its extraordinary swiftness of foot. Its voice is never heard except when seized or wounded, when it utters a sharp loud cry, not very unlike that of a child. Its flesh is rather dry, but is much prized for its characteristic flavour.

HAREBELL, or **HAIRBELL,** the Scottish Bluebell (*Campanula rotundifolia*), a plant of the nat. ord. Campanulaceæ, common on dry and hilly pastures, by roadsides, &c., in most districts of Europe, with a bell-shaped, blue (sometimes white) flower. The radical leaves are cordate or reniform, the stem-leaves partly ovate or lanceolate, partly linear. Its slender stem is from 4 to 6 inches high, and bears sometimes a single flower, but more commonly more than one, in a panicle.

HAREFIELD, village of Middlesex. It stands on the Colne, 5 miles from Uxbridge. The village is famous because here, at Harefield Place, now pulled down, Alice Spenser, Dowager Countess of Derby (born 1637), with her second husband, Lord Egerton, lived. She was the Amaryllis of Spenser and for her Milton wrote *Arcades.* Some almshouses founded by the Countess still stand. Pop. 3,000

HAR'ELD (*Harelda glacialis*), the long-tailed duck, an oceanic duck having a short thick bill, a high forehead, and two very long feathers in the tail of the male, whilst the females have the tail short and rounded. It inhabits the northern seas, and is frequent in Orkney and Shetland, where it is known as the calloo. During the winter it ranges to the Mediterranean, Central Asia, China, Japan, and the Central United States.

HARE-LIP, a malformation consisting in a fissure or vertical division of the upper lip, on one or both sides of the middle line of the lip, sometimes extending also to the palate. Children are frequently born with this malformation, and the cleft is occasionally double. It is due to the fact that in the embryo the upper lip is formed of three segments, a median and two lateral, which normally fuse to form a continuous band; but if anything interferes with this normal process, one or both of the lateral pieces may remain separated by a cleft from the central process. The name is given from the imagined resemblance which the part has to the upper lip of a hare. The cure of hare-lip is performed by cutting off quite smoothly the opposite edges of the fissure, and then bringing them together and maintaining them in accurate apposition till they have firmly united.

HA'REM, or **HAREEM'** (Ar., the prohibited), is used by Mohammedans to signify the women's apartments in a household establishment, forbidden to every man except the husband and near relations.

The custom of setting aside a special apartment for women is an Oriental idea much older than Islam. It existed in Babylonia, where woman was also called *kharimtu*, and in Persia. But it was Islam which raised the harem to an institution rigidly maintained in the East. In Turkey and in India the women of the harem enjoy more liberty than in other Mohammedan countries.

The women of the harem may consist simply of a wife and her attendants, or there may be several wives and an indefinite number of concubines or female slaves, with black eunuchs, &c. The greatest harem was that of the Sultan of Turkey. The women of the imperial harem were all slaves, generally Circassians or Georgians. Their life was spent in bathing, dressing, walking in the gardens, and witnessing the voluptuous dances performed by their slaves. The women of other Turks enjoy the society of their friends at the baths or in each other's houses, and appear in public accompanied by slaves and eunuchs; but the women of the Sultan's harem had none of these privileges. It is, of course, only the richer Moslems who can maintain harems; the poorer classes have generally but one wife. The harem, however, is no longer what it used to be, and under the influence of Western civilization it is gradually becoming modified.—BIBLIOGRAPHY: E. W. Lane, *Manners and Customs of the Modern Egyptians*; A. van Sommer and Zwemer, *Our Moslem Sisters*; W. M. Ramsay, *Everyday Life in Turkey*; P. Loti, *Les Désenchantées.*

HARE'S EAR (Bupleurum), a plant of the nat. ord. Umbelliferæ. The most common British species (*B. rotundifolium*) flourishes best on a chalky soil. Under the name of *thorough-wax* it was at one time used as a vulnerary.

HARESFIELD, hill or beacon of Gloucestershire. It is one of the Cotswold Hills and is near Gloucester. It commands a magnificent view, and on it the Romans had a watch station. In 1931 260 acres of the beacon became the property of the National Trust.

HAREWOOD, Earl of, English title held by the family of Lascelles. In 1796 Edward Lascelles, the head of a Yorkshire family, residing at Harewood House near Leeds, was made a baron, and in 1812 an earl. The title passed from one descendant to another until it came in 1929 to Henry George Charles Lascelles as the 6th earl. He was born 9th Sept., 1882, and educated at Eton and Sandhurst. During the Great War he served with the Grenadier Guards, winning the D.S.O. On 28th Feb., 1922, being then Viscount Lascelles, he married Princess Mary. Their family consists of two sons, the elder bearing the courtesy title of Viscount Lascelles. The earl inherited a large fortune from his uncle, the Marquess of Clanricarde, who died in 1916.

Harewood House, about 12 miles from Leeds, is a fine building dating from the 18th century. The church has some interesting monuments.

HARFLEUR (àr-fleur), a town, France, department of Seine-Inférieure, on the Lézarde near its entrance into the Seine, 6 miles east of Havre, once the chief port at the mouth of the Seine. Pop. about 3,320.

HARGREAVES (här'grĕvz), **James**, English inventor, author of two important improvements in the art of cotton-spinning, was born near Blackburn about 1720, died 1778. In 1760 he invented a machine for carding, and some years after the spinning-jenny, by which he was able to spin with several spindles at once. Suspecting that he employed machinery, his neighbours broke into his dwelling and destroyed his machine; and on the repetition of this kind of persecution Hargreaves removed in 1768 to Nottingham. In 1770 he obtained a patent for his invention, but it was after all declared invalid on the ground that he had sold several of the machines before taking out the patent. For the rest of his life he carried on business as a manufacturer.

HAR'ICOT. See BEAN.

HARINGTON, Sir John, English writer, born 1561, died 1612. At his baptism Queen Elizabeth stood sponsor. In 1596 he was excluded from court on account of his book *The Metamorphosis of Ajax* (written in the manner of Rabelais), but was soon allowed to return. His best-known performance is, perhaps, his translation of *Orlando Furioso* in heroic verse.

HARÎRI, Abu Mohammed el Kasim Ben Ali, surnamed El Harîri, or the silk merchant (his father's occupation), a celebrated Arabic scholar and poet, who lived chiefly at Bassorah in the time of the Abbasside caliphs, born A.D. 1054, died 1121 or 1123. He is best known by his *Makâmmât*, a collection of tales narrated as incidents in the life of the hero Abu Zeid, a clever impostor who adopts every career in life; and succeeds in all to admiration. There are many editions and translations of the *Makâmmât*. English translations appeared in 1850 (by T. Preston), in 1867, and in 1898 (by T. Chenery and F. Steingass).

HARLEBEKE, or HAERLEBEKE (här'le-bä-ke), a town in Belgium, in West Flanders, on the Lys. It is said to be the oldest town in Flanders, and has a beautiful parish church, and a pulpit regarded as a masterpiece of carving. Pop. 7,450.

HARLECH, town of Merionethshire. It is 10½ miles from Barmouth, on the G.W. Rly. At one time it was a borough and the county town, but now it is a small pleasure resort with golf links and sands. The chief object of interest is the ruined castle built in the time of Edward I. With it is asso-

ciated the popular song, "March of the men of Harlech." Pop. 1,000.

HARLEIAN LIBRARY. See HARLEY.

HARLEQUIN (Fr. *arlequin*; It. *arlecchino*), a conventional personage in pantomime. On the Italian stage he is a comic character full of drolleries, tricks and knaveries, and somewhat resembles the English clown. The harlequin of British pantomimes is quite different. He is supposed to be the lover of the columbine, and possesses a wonder-working wand, with which he protects his mistress against the clown and pantaloon, who pursue and endeavour to capture her, until the pursuit is brought to a termination by a good fairy. The harlequin wears a tight dress of bright colours, and glittering with spangles—hence a name for brightly and differently coloured sets of similar articles—e.g.

Harlequin Duck

harlequin tea-set. See PANTOMIME.—BIBLIOGRAPHY: R. J. Broadbent, *A History of Pantomime*; M. Sand, *History of the Harlequinade.*

HARLEQUIN DUCK (*Cosmonetta histrionica*), a species of duck, so called on account of its part-coloured plumage of white, grey, and black. It inhabits the Arctic regions, and during the winter ranges south to Japan and the United States, more rarely to Britain. In length it is about 17 inches.

HARLESDEN, district of northwest London. It is part of the urban district of Willesden and is 4 miles from the city.

HARLEY, name of the family that once held the earldom of Oxford. Robert, the 1st earl, and his son, Edward, the 2nd earl, made a valuable collection of books and manuscripts. In 1753 this enormous collection, the Harleian Manuscripts, was bought for the nation and it is now in the British Museum. The Harleian

Society at 4 Trafalgar Square, London, W.C., was founded in 1869.

The London thoroughfare called Harley St. is named after this family. It runs from Cavendish Square to Marylebone Road, and is famous for its association with the medical profession. In or near Harley St. nearly all the leading physicians have their consulting rooms.

HARLEY, Robert, Earl of Oxford, English statesman, born 1661, died 1724, the son of Sir Edward Harley. After the accession of Anne he and his colleague St. John, afterwards Lord Bolingbroke, became leaders of the Tories. Harley was chosen Speaker of the House of Commons in 1702 under Rochester, and in 1704 was appointed Chief Secretary of State, but resigned in 1708. After the fall of Marlborough Harley became Chancellor of the Exchequer in 1710, and next year was created Earl of Oxford. He and Bolingbroke secured the Treaty of Utrecht (1713), but afterwards quarrelled.

Early in the reign of George I he was impeached of high treason on the ground of his alleged Jacobite intrigues. He was kept in the Tower for two years, but, owing to the inability of the Peers and the Commons to agree about the mode of procedure, he was acquitted. His patronage was extended to Swift, Pope, and other literary men, and he made a valuable collection of books and MSS., which latter are preserved in the British Museum, where they form the Bibliotheca Harleiana. Those which have been printed constitute the *Harleian Miscellany.*—Cf. Burnet, *History of his Own Times.*

HARLINGEN (hår'ling-en), a seaport of Holland, province of Friesland, intersected by numerous canals. It has great trade with England in corn, cattle, and butter. Pop. 10,443.

HARLINGTON, an industrial area of Middlesex. It is 13 miles from London. Henry Bennet, Earl of Arlington, a member of the Cabal, took his title from here. Harlington is now part of the urban district of Hayes and Harlington. Pop. (district), 23,646.

HARLOW, town of Essex. It is 23 miles from London, on the L.N.E. Rly. At one time Harlow was a market town and had manufactures of cloth and pottery. In 1928 Roman remains, including those of a temple, were unearthed here. Pop. 2,962.

HARMAT'TAN, a hot and dry wind, which, coming from the interior of Africa, prevails at times on the coast of Guinea in December, January, and February. Under its influence vegetation withers, and the grass becomes like hay. It is similar to the simoom of Egypt and the sirocco of Italy and Malta.

HARMO'DIUS. (*See* ARISTOGEITON and HIPPIAS.)

HARMON'ICA, Benjamin Franklin's name for a musical instrument constructed with glasses of different sizes, revolving by means of mechanism worked by the foot, and played upon by touching the rim of the glasses with the moistened finger. It constituted the 'musical glasses' of Goldsmith's era. The instrument, known in the seventeenth century, was improved by an Irishman, Richard Pockrich, and still more developed by Franklin. The name is now usually applied to an instrument consisting of a series of glass keys played by two small hammers.

HARMONICAL PROGRESSION, in algebra, a series of numbers the reciprocals of which are in arithmetical progression. The simplest A.P. is the series of natural numbers, 1, 2, 3, 4, . . .; and the simplest H.P. the series of reciprocals of these $1, \frac{1}{2}, \frac{1}{3}, \frac{1}{4}, \ldots$ (*see* HARMONICS). An arithmetical progression can be *summed*, i.e. a formula can be given for the sum of n terms. To sum the first n natural numbers, e.g., write the series in reverse order and add the result to the original series term by term. We get $(1+n)+\{2+(n-1)\}+\{3+(n-2)\}+\ldots$ i.e. $(n+1)+(n+1)+(n+1)+\ldots$ to n terms or $n(n+1)$. Hence the sum $1+2+\ldots+n$ is $\frac{1}{2}n(n+1)$. There is no simple formula, however, for the sum of n terms of an H.P. *See* HARMONIC RANGE.

HARMONIC ANALYSIS, a mathematical method much used in the solution of advanced physical problems. In these problems the data are not often expressed in a form immediately amenable to mathematical treatment. The given functions have first to be resolved by analysis into their harmonic components, somewhat after the manner in which a complex sound is resolved by the ear *see* FOURIER SERIES. The suitable harmonic components are by no means always sines and cosines of multiples of a variable; these sines and cosines are sometimes called *simple* harmonic functions. For harmonic functions of other types *see* LAPLACE'S EQUATION. For an arithmetical method of resolving a function given graphically into its simple harmonic components, *see* VIBRATIONS; WAVES.—Cf. G. A. Gibson, *Introduction to the Calculus.*

HARMONIC MOTION, any oscillatory or reciprocating motion. The phrase is also used as equivalent to *simple harmonic motion*, which is the motion of a point M in a straight line A'OA, when OM = OAcos$(pt + e)$; t being the time and p, e, constants. Draw the circle on A'A as diameter (fig.). Suppose a point P to move counter-clockwise round the circumference so that the angular velocity of the radius OP is uniform, and equal to p radians per second. If we count time in seconds from the moment when P is at E, where angle AOE is e radians, then angle EOP is pt radians. Draw PM perpendicular to A'A; then OM = OPcosMOP = OAcos$(pt + e)$; the motion of M is therefore simple harmonic. If OM = x, OA = a, then $x = a\cos(pt + e)$. In this equation x is called the *displacement*, a the *amplitude*, e the *epoch*, and $pt + e$ the *phase*. The *period* T is the time taken to describe 2π radians at angular speed p, or T = $2\pi/p$. Here T is the time taken for the point M to move from one end of its range to the other and back; so that it is the time of a *complete oscillation* or *double vibration*, or *swing-swang*. The period of a pendulum which beats seconds is thus two seconds.

The *velocity* of M is the horizontal component of the velocity of P, i.e. $-v\cos$OTP or $-pa\sin(pt + e)$. The *acceleration* of M is the horizontal component of the acceleration of P, i.e. $a\cos$MOP, or $p^2a\cos(pt + e)$, towards O. These expressions for the velocity and acceleration of M can also be found at once by differentiating the equation $x = a\cos(pt + e)$. From the value found for the acceleration of M, there follows the characteristic property of S.H.M. viz. that the *ratio of acceleration to displacement is constant*, its value being p^2 or $4\pi^2/T^2$. It follows conversely that motion of a material particle in a straight line under a force which is directed towards a fixed point in that line, and the magnitude of which is in a constant ratio to the distance of the particle from that point, is simple harmonic; also, if μ is the value of the constant ratio, then $\mu = 4\pi^2/T^2$, or T = $2\pi/\sqrt{\mu}$. We have thus the remarkable property that the period, for a given ratio μ, is independent of the amplitude. This is the principle of the *isochronism of vibrations*. For examples see KINETICS; PENDULUM.

Two S.H.M.'s of the same period, and in the same line, can be compounded into a single S.H.M. of that period; for $a\cos(pt + e) + a'\cos(pt + e')$ can be expressed in the form A$\cos(pt + E)$. Two S.H.M.'s of the same period, but in different lines, give a resultant motion which may be rectilinear, circular, or elliptic. The case of a circular resultant motion is important in physical optics (circular polarization of light), and in electrical engineering (rotating magnetic field). It arises when the rectangular components of a plane vector are $x = a\cos(pt + e)$, $y = a\sin(pt + e)$, so that the phases of the components differ by 90°. A figure shows at once that the vector is of constant magnitude a, and that its direction makes an angle $pt + e$ with the axis of x, so that the vector rotates with constant angular velocity p.

Any oscillatory rectilinear motion of period T can be analysed into simple harmonic components of periods T, $\frac{1}{2}$T, $\frac{1}{3}$T, &c. In other

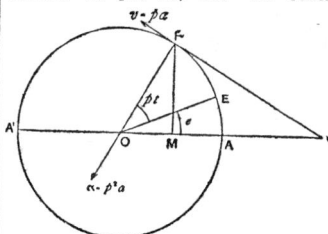

words, any function x of the time, of period T, can be expressed in the form

$$x = a_0 + a_1\cos(2\pi t/T + e_1) + a_2\cos(4\pi t/T + e_2) + a_3\cos(6\pi t/T + e_3) + \ldots$$

(see FOURIER SERIES). Cf. Kelvin and Tait, *Natural Philosophy*.

HARMONIC RANGE, in geometry. If a line AB is divided internally and externally in the same ratio at C and D, the four points are said to form a harmonic range. AB is cut in *harmonic section* at C and D; and CD is cut in harmonic section at A and B. If the four points are joined to any point O not in line with them, the four lines, or *rays*, OA, OB, OC, OD are said to form a *harmonic pencil* (see GEOMETRY). When AB is divided harmonically at C and D, the distances (taken with proper sign and in proper order) of any one of the points A, B, C, D from the other three are in harmonical progression (q.v.). Thus, e.g., we have AC : CB = AD : BD; from which it is easy to deduce that $1/AC - 1/AB = 1/AB - 1/AD$.

HARMONICS, the system of simple tones given out by a vibrating body; or these tones with the exception of the gravest, which is called the fundamental. The vibrator may be any elastic solid or fluid; but, for the production of musical sound, it is usually either a stretched string, as in the violin and piano, or an enclosed volume of air, as in the organ and other wind instruments. When a string fixed at its two ends is vibrating in its fundamental mode, there is no fixed point, or node, between the ends. In the harmonic modes certain points of the string do not move during the vibration—the mid-point in the first harmonic mode, the two points of trisection of the string in the second mode, and so on. If the period of the fundamental be taken as 1, then the periods of the harmonics are $\frac{1}{2}$, $\frac{1}{3}$, $\frac{1}{4}$, &c. This relation is the origin of the name *harmonical progression* (q.v.) in algebra.

A relation of exactly this form holds for the *longitudinal* and for the *torsional* vibrations of a rod. In an organ pipe, also, the law of succession of the harmonics is practically of this type, but two cases have to be considered separately. When both ends are open, the frequencies of fundamental and overtones are, as in the case of the string, in the ratios of the natural numbers 1, 2, 3, 4, &c.; but when one end is open and the other closed, the frequencies are as the *odd* numbers 1, 3, 5, &c.

For the *flexural* vibrations of a rod or bar, the law of periods is more complicated; for a bar free at both ends, the frequencies are (approximately) as $3^2:5^2:7^2$, &c.; for a bar clamped at one end and free at the other, the first three frequencies are nearly as $1:6\cdot25:17\cdot5$—a tuning-fork may be regarded as an example of this type. For a few bodies of more complex shape (e.g. a thin plate and a solid sphere) the law of periods can be found theoretically. For bodies in general the chief harmonics can be found by experiment (*see* RESONANCE).

Well-made bells give out three prominent notes—the fundamental, the 'nominal' (an octave higher), and the 'hum-note' (an octave lower). The best form for bells has been found by trial, not by theory. A body taken at random is much more likely to give out a discordant than a harmonious sound. Two simple tones only concord with one another if their frequencies are in the ratio of two small whole numbers. For an interval of an octave the frequencies are as 2:1; for a fifth, 3:2; fourth, 4:3; major third, 5:4; minor third 6:5. Hence, in a vibrating string or organ-pipe, the lower harmonics, which are the strong ones, satisfy the condition for harmony. *See* SCALE; MUSIC; ACOUSTICS; RESONANCE; WAVES.

HAR'MONISTS, or **HARMONY SOCIETY,** a religious sect founded at Würtemberg about the year 1788 by two brothers called George and Frederick Rapp. They endeavoured to re-establish the social practices of the early Christian Church, encouraged celibacy, held all their goods in common, and taught the second advent. Persecuted by their countrymen, the followers of Rapp emigrated to America, and established themselves (1805) successfully at Harmony, in Pennsylvania. They afterwards migrated to Indiana, but this venture not proving successful, they sold their land at New Harmony to Robert Owen, the Socialist, and finally settled at a place which they named Economy, 17 miles from Pittsburg. George Rapp died in 1847, but the Society continued to exist until 1906, when it was formally dissolved.

HARMO'NIUM, a musical instrument of modern invention, producing sounds somewhat resembling those of the organ, resulting from the pressure of wind on a series of vibrating metallic reeds. By the action of bellows, to which the feet communicate a more or less rapid movement, the air is made to impinge against thin tongues of metal (here termed *reeds*), and to set them vibrating. These metal tongues are fitted into a slit in the top of a small box or sonorous cavity, called a wind-box, and are enabled to vibrate by being fixed only at one end. The discovery that the form of the wind-boxes determines the quality of the sound produced by the vibration of these metallic tongues contributed very much to the development of the harmonium, as it enabled the maker to provide stops for the oboe, flute, &c.

The instrument has a key-board like that of a piano, and when one of the keys is pressed down a valve is opened, which allows the wind from the bellows to rush through one of the wind-boxes and act on the vibrator. There are several stops, by means of which the performer can direct the stream of wind into the wind-boxes which produce a flute, clarionet, or any other sound. There is also a knee action, which either serves as an expression stop, or brings all the stops of the instrument into play at once, and what is called the percussion action, which consists in the application of a small hammer, which strikes the vibrator as soon as the key is pressed down, and thus aids the action of the wind. The better makes of harmoniums have now usually two or more extra rows of vibrators, which, acted upon by separate stops, add so many octaves to the compass.

HARMONY. *See* MUSIC; COUNTERPOINT.

HARMONY, EVANGELICAL, or **HARMONY OF THE GOSPELS,** the title of works written with a view to prove the substantial agreement of the four Evangelists. The heretic

Tatian composed in the second century the *Diatessaron*, the first work of this kind, a continuous narrative of the events written in the Gospels. From this harmony all passages were omitted which favoured the doctrine of the real humanity of Christ, and hence told against the peculiar doctrines of Tatian.

Theophilus of Antioch is said to have composed a book of a similar kind, and Ammonius Saccas (died A.D. 243) executed another *Diatessaron*, with the corresponding passages arranged in parallel columns. The *Ten Indexes* of Eusebius probably appeared in the first half of the fourth century, and was more complete than its predecessors.

HARMONY OF THE SPHERES, an hypothesis of Pythagoras and his school, according to which the motions of the heavenly bodies produced a music imperceptible by the ears of mortals. He supposed these motions to conform to certain fixed laws, which could be expressed in numbers corresponding to the numbers which give the harmony of sounds.—Cf. *Merchant of Venice*, v, 1, 60.

HAR'MOTOME, or **CROSS-STONE,** a mineral hydrous silicate of potassium, barium, and aluminium. It crystallizes in the monoclinic system, usually in quadruplets formed by the interpenetration of two twin crystals at right angles to one another, so that the cross-section is cruciform. Its colour is usually white, but may be yellow, red, or brown; it is translucent or semi-transparent, with a somewhat pearly lustre, and is nearly as hard as glass. Harmotome is a member of the zeolite group.

HARMSWORTH, name of a family famous in journalism. Alfred Harmsworth, a barrister, left seven sons. Two became respectively Viscount Northcliffe and Viscount Rothermere. Of the others two became baronets, Robert Leicester in 1918, and Hildebrand in 1922, Sir Robert was Liberal M.P. for Caithness, 1900–18.

Cecil Bisshopp Harmsworth, another brother, was a Liberal M.P. from 1906–10 and again, 1911–22. He was Under Secretary to the Home Office, 1915, and to the Foreign Office, 1918–22. Viscount Rothermere's only surviving son, Esmond, was Unionist M.P. for the Thanet division, 1919–29. All the members of the family are interested in newspaper companies.

HARNACK, Adolf, German theologian, son of a Lutheran theological professor, born in 1851 at Dorpat. He became extraordinary professor in Leipzig in 1876, ordinary professor in Giessen (1879), Marburg (1886), and Berlin (1889). Harnack is the most prominent leader of a notable neo-Ritschlian movement in German theological thought, and has exercised great influence outside his own country.

His principal works, many of them available in English translations, are: *Martin Luther; Lehrbuch der Dogmengeschichte; Das Mönchtum, seine Ideal und seine Geschichte; Grundriss der Dogmengeschichte; Das apostolische Glaubensbekenntnis; Texte und Untersuchungen zur Geschichte der altchristlichen Litteratur; Das Wesen des Christentums;* and *Essays and Addresses.* His works, notably those on the *Apostles' Creed* and the *Essence of Christianity,* have called forth violent opposition from Prussian orthodoxy. Other works are: *Die Mission und Ausbreitung des Christentums in den ersten drei Jahrhunderten, Beiträge zur Einleitung in das neue Testament,* &c. In 1905 he gave up his Berlin chair in order to become director of the Royal Library. He died in 1930.

HARNESS, the various articles which are required to yoke a horse or another animal to any vehicle, or to control and suit them for any kind of work. *See* BIT; BRIDLE; SADDLE; &c.

HAROLD (or **HARALD**) **I,** *Haarfager* (Beautiful-haired), King of Norway, one of the greatest monarchs of that country, succeeded his father in A.D. 863. He brought all the Norwegian jarls under his power, and completely subjected the country, allowing his hair to remain uncut for twenty years until he attained this object (885).

Of the conquered jarls, Hrolf, or Rollo, emigrated to Neustria (France); others established themselves in Iceland, the Shetland Isles, the Faroes, and the Orkneys. In consequence of their incursions into his dominions, Harold embarked with a naval force to subdue them, and having conquered the Orkneys, &c., returned home. He fixed his residence at Trondhjem, and died there in 933.

HAROLD I, surnamed *Harefoot,* Danish King of England, succeeded his father Canute in 1035 as king of the provinces north of the Thames, and became king of all England in 1037. His countrymen, the Danes, maintained him upon the throne against the efforts of Earl Godwin in favour of Hardicanute; and Harold eventually gained the earl over. After a reign of four years Harold died in 1040.—Cf. Sir C. W. Oman, *History of England before the Norman Conquest.*

HAROLD II, King of England, born about 1022, was the second son of Godwin, Earl of Kent. On the death of Edward the Confessor, 5th Jan.,

1066, he stepped without opposition into the vacant throne, without attending to the claim of Edgar Atheling, or the alleged bequest of Edward in favour of the Duke of Normandy. The latter immediately called upon

Egyptian Harps

him to resign the crown, and upon his refusal prepared for invasion. He also instigated Harold's brother, Tostig, to invest the northern coasts of England in conjunction with the King of Norway. (See HAROLD III.) The united fleet of these chiefs sailed up the Humber, and landed a numerous body of men, but at Stamford Bridge, in Yorkshire, were totally routed by Harold, whose brother Tostig fell in the battle. Immediately after he heard of the landing of the Duke of Normandy at Pevensey, in Sussex. Hastening thither with all the troops he could muster, a general engagement ensued at Senlac, near Hastings, 14th Oct., 1066, in which Harold was slain, and the crown of England passed to William.—Cf. E. A. Freeman, *The Norman Conquest*.

HAROLD III (*Hardrada*, the Hardy), King of Norway, the son of Sigurd, a descendant of Harold Haarfager. In his youth he went to Constantinople, joined the Varangian Guard, and took part in the expedition to Italy and Sicily against the African pirates. He was ultimately appointed commander of the imperial body-guard, and defeated the Saracens. About 1042 he returned to Norway, after having, on his way through Russia, married the daughter of the Grand-Duke Jaroslav. In 1047 he succeeded his nephew, Magnus the Good, as sole King of Norway. In 1066 he joined Tostig, the brother of Harold II of England, in an invasion of that country, but was defeated and slain at the battle of Stamford Bridge. See HAROLD II.

HAROUN AL RASCHID. *See* HARUN AL RASHID.

HARP (A. Sax. *hearpe*, Lat. *harpa*, Fr. *harpe*), a stringed instrument of great antiquity, found among the Assyrians, Egyptians, Hebrews, Greeks, Irish, Welsh, and other nations. Its variety of form and construction was only equalled by its universality. The modern instrument is well known: its form is nearly triangular, and the strings distended from the upper part to one of the sides. It stands erect, and is played with both hands, the strings being struck or pulled with both fingers and thumbs.

The instrument in its ancient forms was very defective. Egyptian harps are represented with four, seven, ten, twenty, or more strings, but we have little idea of the scale to which they were tuned. The frames are depicted as being curved in various forms, and the front pillars are wanting. The harps of the Hebrews were probably similar to the Egyptian instruments. It is probable that the various Celtic harps were derived from some Oriental pattern. Among the Anglo-Saxons the harp was a favourite instrument. The harp was held in great honour among the Celtic bards. It is still in use in Wales, although it has disappeared in the Highlands of Scotland.

Irish Harp

The modern harp was by no means an efficient instrument, until pedals were invented, an invention finally perfected by Sebastian Erard, whose patent was taken out in 1795. In 1810 he patented a double-action harp with seven pedals, each effecting two changes in the pitch of the strings. The harp thus constructed contains forty-three strings tuned according to the diatonic scale, every eighth string being a replicate in another octave of the one counted from.—BIBLIOGRAPHY: article in Grove's *Dictionary of Music and Musicians*; W. H. Grattan-Flood, *The Story of the Harp*.

HARPE. See LA HARPE.

HARPENDEN, an urban district of England, Herts, 5 miles south-east of Luton, the seat of laboratories, experimental fields, &c., established by Sir John Bennet Lawes for the furtherance of agriculture, and made over for public use. Here also is St. George's co-educational school, and nearby is Rothamstead. Pop. (1931), 8,349.

HARPER'S FERRY, a village, United States, West Virginia, on the Potomac, at its junction with the Shenandoah, and formerly a United States depot of military stores. It is famous as the scene of the unsuccessful rising headed by John Brown with a view to destroying slavery (16th Oct., 1859). The rising was suppressed, and Brown was executed. Harper's Ferry is the seat of Stover College for coloured students. Pop. 706.

HARPIES, the ancient Greek goddesses of storms. Their parentage, ages, appearance, names, and number are very differently given by the poets. In the Homeric poems they are ministers of untimely death, 'snatchers,' and personifications of the angry winds. Hesiod represents them as two young virgins of great beauty called Aëllo and Ocypete, daughters of Thaumas and Electra, and sisters of Iris. The later poets and artists vied with each other in depicting them under the most hideous forms, covered with filth and polluting everything in contact with them. They are often represented as having female faces.

HARP-SHELL, the shell of a genus (Harpa) of sea-snails constituting a special family (Harpidæ). The species are found more especially at the Mauritius. The shells are very beautiful, but exposure to light causes their colours to fade.

HARP'SICHORD (O. Fr. *harpechorde*, Fr. *clavecin*), a keyed, stringed instrument formerly in use, in appearance and construction similar to a grand pianoforte. In the front the keys were disposed, the long ones being the naturals, and the short ones the sharps and flats. These keys being pressed by the fingers, their enclosed extremities raised little, upright, oblong slips of wood called *jacks*, furnished with crow-quill plectrums which struck the wires, instead of the hammers of the modern pianoforte. It is uncertain when the harpsichord was invented, probably in the fifteenth

century. It was introduced into England in the seventeenth century.

HARPY-EAGLE (*Thrasaëtus harpyia*), a diurnal bird of prey which inhabits tropical America from Southern Mexico to Southern Brazil. It is extremely powerful, and in total length slightly in excess of the golden eagle. It has, however, a somewhat shorter expanse of wing. Its shoulder muscles possess enormous strength. Its bill is powerful and crooked, and its claws are extremely strong and sharp. The harpy-eagle feeds on birds, sloths, fawns, raccoons, &c., as well as on fish, water-snakes, and the eggs of the tortoise.

HARQUEBUSE. See ARQUEBUS.

HARRIER, a kind of dog employed to hunt the hare. It closely resembles the foxhound, but is smaller in size.

Harpsichord

HARRIER, the name of several hawks of the genus Circus, allied to the buzzards. They strike their prey upon the ground and generally fly very low. The marsh-harrier, the hen-harrier, and Montagu's harrier are found in Great Britain.

The marsh-harrier (*C. æruginōsus*) is from 21 inches to 23 inches long. The hen-harrier (*C. cyanĕus*) is 18 inches to 20 inches long; the adult male is of an almost uniform grey, the female brown. It is very destructive to poultry-yards, whence the name. Montagu's harrier (*C. cinerĕaceus*) is smaller and darker than the last species, but with longer wings. Harriers are found in most parts of the world, and there are over a dozen species besides those mentioned above.

HARRINGAY, district of London. It lies about 4 miles to the north of the city, in the borough of Hornsey, and is reached by the L.N.E. and

L.M.S. Rlys. There is a track for greyhound racing and speedway racing here.

HARRINGTON, urban district of Cumberland. It stands on the coast, 5 miles from Whitehaven, and the chief industry is coal mining. Pop. (1931) 4,125.

HARRINGTON, Earl of, English title borne since 1742 by the family of Stanhope. **William Stanhope,** a leading politician in the time of George II., was the first earl. A son of John Stanhope of Elvaston, Derbyshire, he served as a soldier and a diplomat, chiefly in Spain, and in 1730 was made a baron. From 1730 to 1746 he was a Secretary of State, and from 1747 to 1751 Lord Lieutenant of Ireland. In 1742 he was made an earl, and died, 8th Dec., 1756.

William, the 2nd earl, and **Charles,** the 3rd earl, were both soldiers of note. **Charles,** the 4th earl, was the eccentric being who married the actress, Mary Foote, and **Leicester,** the 5th earl, was a noted sportsman, being perhaps the most prominent master of the foxhounds in his day. He died in 1917. The earl's seat is Elvaston Castle, near Derby, and his eldest son is called Viscount Petersham.

HARRINGTON, James, a celebrated political writer, born 1611, died 1677. Having studied under Chillingworth at Oxford, and travelled on the Continent, he was, on the outbreak of the Civil War, desirous of procuring a reconciliation between the king and Parliament, but his efforts were futile. During the Protectorate he wrote his *Oceana,* which describes an ideal republic, and which was published in 1656. In the reign of Charles II he was imprisoned on a charge of conspiracy. It was not long before he was released.

HARRIS Baron, English title. **George Harris,** born at Brasted, Kent, 18th March, 1746, was the son of a clergyman and became a soldier. After service in America he went to India, where he made his reputation by his successes against Tippoo Sahib. He led the force that stormed Seringapatam and was instrumental in the acquisition of Mysore by Great Britain. In 1875 he was made Baron Harris. He died, May, 1829.

In 1872 the title came to **George Robert Canning Harris,** as 4th baron. Born 3rd Feb., 1851, he went to Eton and Oxford, where he was famous as a cricketer. From 1875 to 1899 he was captain of Kent, and in 1930, when 80 years old, he played in a match at Eton. He had played also for England against Australia. He was Under Secretary for India and then for War, 1885–89, and from

1890-93 was Governor of Bombay. He is also known for his connection with the mining industry of South Africa. He died, 24th March, 1932.

HARRIS, James, an English philologist, born in 1709, died 1780. In 1744 he published a volume containing three treatises—*On Art, On Music and Painting,* and *On Happiness.* His most celebrated work is *Hermes, or a Philosophical Inquiry concerning Universal Grammar* (1751). He was afterwards a member of Parliament, and held important Government offices. In 1775 he published *Philosophical Arrangements,* a work on Aristotle's logic. His concluding work *Philological Inquiries,* was completed in 1780, but was not published till after his death.

HARRIS, James Rendel, a distinguished Biblical scholar belonging to the Society of Friends. Educated at Clare College, Cambridge, of which he became a Fellow, he has held professorships at Johns Hopkins University, Baltimore, and Haverford College, Pennsylvania. He was for a time university lecturer in palæography at Cambridge, and from 1903 to 1904 professor of theology in the University of Leyden. From 1903 to 1918 he was director of studies at the Friends' Settlement for Social and Religious Study at Woodbrooke, near Birmingham, and from 1918 to 1925 Curator of MSS. at the John Rylands' Library, Manchester. He travelled extensively in the East, and was in Armenia at the time of the massacres in 1896, engaged in the distribution of relief.

His published works include: *The Teaching of the Apostles* (1887), *The Diatessaron* (1890), *A Study of Codex Bezæ* (1890), *The Apology of Aristides* (1891), *The Newly Recovered Gospel of St. Peter* (1892), *Lectures on the Western Text of the New Testament* (1894), *Union with God* (1895), *Letters from Armenia* (1897), *The Gospel of the Twelve Apostles* (1900), *The Dioscuri in Christian Legend* (1903), *The Guiding Hand of God* (1905), *The Odes and Psalms of Solomon* (1910), *Boanerges* (1913), *The Sufferings and the Glory* (1914), *Origin of the Cult of Apollo* (1915), *Origin of the Cult of Aphrodite* (1916), *Origin of the Doctrine of the Trinity* (1919), *The Last of the Mayflower, The Finding of the Mayflower* (1920), *A New Christian Apology* (1923), *The Stature of our Lord* (1926), *Traces of Egypt in the Mediterranean* (1927), *Jesus and Osiris* (1927), *St. Paul and Greek Literature* (1927), *Egypt and the Atlantic Seaboard* (1928), *St. Bees* (1928), *Origin of the Cult of Hermes* (1929), *Fomors and Firbolgs* (1930), *Maeldune* (1931).

HARRIS. See LEWIS-WITH-HARRIS.

HARRISBURG, a city of the United States, capital of Pennsylvania, 110 miles north of Washington, on the Susquehanna, over which there are three railway bridges besides a bridge for ordinary traffic. It occupies a commanding site, and has important industries connected with iron and steel, various other industries, and an active trade. Pop. (1930), 80,339.

HARRISON, Frederic, English writer on philosophical and miscellaneous subjects, born in London 1831, educated there and at Oxford, was called to the Bar and practised as a conveyancing and equity lawyer, held the professorship of jurisprudence and international law at the Inns of Court (1877–89), was several years an alderman of the London County Council, and had been a parliamentary candidate. He was the chief representative in England of positivism and the religion of humanity.

His writings include: *The Meaning of History* (1862, and again 1894); *Order and Progress; Social Statics* (a translation from Comte); *Science and Humanity; The Present and the Future; The Choice of Books, &c.; Oliver Cromwell; Studies in Early Victorian Literature; William the Silent; Tennyson, Ruskin, and Mill; Byzantine History in the Early Middle Ages; Life of Ruskin; Theophano* (a historical romance); *The Creed of a Layman; The Positive Evolution of Religion; The German Peril; Obiter Scripta;* and *Novissima Verba.* He died in January, 1923.

HARRISON, John, English horologist and inventor, famous as 'Longitude Harrison,' was born in Yorkshire in 1693, and died 1776. He was the son of a carpenter, and became an assistant to his father, who was occasionally employed in repairing clocks.

An Act of Parliament had been passed in 1714 offering rewards of £10,000, £15,000, or £20,000 for a method of ascertaining longitude within 60, 40, or 30 miles. This Harrison set himself to accomplish, but it was not till 1765 that he was fully successful, the highest award being then allotted him for the invention of his chronometer. He also applied the principle of the different expansibility of metals in his gridiron pendulum, and invented a fusee by which a watch could be wound up without interrupting its movements. Among his writings is *A Description concerning such Mechanism as will afford a Nice and True Mensuration of Time.*

HARRISON, a town of the United States, New Jersey, on the Passaic, practically a suburb of Newark. Pop. 15,601.

HAR'ROGATE, a municipal borough of England, county of York, noted for its magnesia, sulphur, and chalybeate springs. The waters are especially recommended for patients with deranged digestive organs, chronic gout, and some cutaneous diseases. The sulphureous springs possess laxative and diuretic properties. The chalybeate are tonic. The bathing season lasts from May to September. In the vicinity is some of the finest Yorkshire scenery, with Fountains Abbey, Bolton Abbey, and other beauty spots. The chief buildings are the Royal Hall, the opera house, and the winter gardens, as well as the various pump rooms, baths and hotels. Harlow Moor and The Stray are open spaces. Since 1897 the town has been extended in area and greatly improved. Pop. (1931), 39,785.

HARROW, an agricultural implement, employed for pulverizing soil, covering in seed, &c. It consists of a frame of woodwork, or of iron, in which are fixed rows of iron teeth. There are several varieties of this implement, or implements serving similar purposes, such as the 'brake' for breaking down rough land; the 'drill harrow' for pulverizing between furrows of green crops; the 'grubber' for breaking up and pulverizing soil before the deposition of seed. Flexible chain-harrows are useful for dragging out couch grass, and for employment on grass-land.

HARROW (or HARROW-ON THE-HILL), a town of England, county of Middlesex, on a hill of peculiar form. The grammar-school of Harrow, the rival of Eton, was founded by John Lyon, in 1571, for the education of poor children of the parish, certain fees being charged for strangers; but it is now almost entirely a school for the wealthy. The school numbers about 600 boys, and there are eleven houses. The education originally given was exclusively classical, but mathematics, science, English history and literature, modern languages, music, and drawing are now among the subjects taught. A memorial hall was erected in honour of 619 Harrovians who fell in the Great War. The headmasters of Harrow have included Christopher Wordsworth, C. J. Vaughan and H. M. Butler. Among its pupils were Byron, Peel, Palmerston and, more recently, Baldwin, Churchill and Galsworthy. For many years the school has been famous for its music. A new hospital was opened at Harrow in 1931. Pop. 26,378.

HARROWBY, EARL OF. English title borne by the family of Ryder.

Sir Dudley Ryder, who was Lord Chief Justice, 1754–56, had a son, **Nathaniel,** who in 1776, was made a baron. His son, **Dudley,** entered the House of Commons and took office under Pitt in 1789. In 1804–05 he was Secretary of State for Foreign Affairs, and from 1812–27 he was Lord President of the Council. In 1827, when he was made an earl, he refused the office of Prime Minister. In 1831–32 he had a good deal to do with the negotiations that led to the passing of the Reform Bill. Although a Tory, he was in favour of religious liberty and other reforms. He died 26th Dec., 1847, the last survivor of Pitt's colleagues.

His son, **Dudley,** the 2nd earl (1798–1882), and his grandson, **Dudley,** the 3rd earl (1831–1900), were both active politicians, the latter being Vice-President of the Council, 1874–78, and President of the Board of Trade, 1878–80. The present earl inherited from his brother who became the 4th earl. The earl's seat is Sandon Hall, Staffordshire, and his eldest son is called Viscount Sandon.

Harrowby is a village of Lincolnshire, just outside Grantham.

HART, Sir Robert, inspector-general of Chinese customs, born in County Armagh in 1835, died in 1911. Educated at Taunton, Dublin, and Belfast, he entered the British consular service in China in 1854, and in 1859 he accepted an appointment in the Chinese Imperial Maritime Customs of which he became inspector-general in 1863. He discharged the important and responsible duties of this post with conspicuous ability during a critical period, and his services were recognized by the grant of honorary distinctions from all European countries and from China. He was created K.C.M.G. in 1882, G.C.M.G. in 1889, and was made a baronet in 1893. He retired in 1908. He wrote *These from the Land of Sinim* (1901).

HARTE, Francis Bret, American novelist and poet, born at Albany, New York, 1839, died in 1902. He went to California in 1854, and worked successively as a teacher, a miner, and a type-setter on *The Golden Era,* in which appeared some of his earliest literary efforts. He afterwards joined the staff of *The Californian,* to which he contributed the humorous burlesques afterwards published as *Sensation Novels Condensed* (1870). From 1864 to 1870 he was secretary of the United States branch mint in San Francisco, and in 1870–1 held the post of professor of recent literature in the University of California.

In 1868 he became editor of *The Overland Monthly,* in which appeared *The Luck of Roaring Camp* (1868), *The Outcasts of Poker Flat* (1869), two of his best short stories, and *The Idyl of Red Gulch,* also the humorous poem of *The Heathen Chinee.* In 1878 he became United States Consul at Crefeld, whence he was transferred to Glasgow in 1880, and remained there until 1885, afterwards making London his residence.

His short stories, mostly dealing with the rough western life of former days, include *Stories of the Sierras* (1872), *Tales of the Argonauts* (1875), *The Twins of Table Mountain* (1879), *An Heiress of Red Dog* (1879), *Jeff Briggs's Love-Story* (1880), *Flip* (1882), *A Drift from Redwood Camp* (1888), *From Sand Hill to Pine* (1900).

He was less successful in his novels, among the chief being *Gabriel Conroy* (1876), *In the Carquinez Woods* (1883), *Maruja* (1885), *Snowbound at Eagle's* (1886), *A Waif of the Plains* (1890), and *Three Partners* (1897). He also wrote much verse, comprised in volumes entitled *Poems* (1871), *East and West Poems* (1871), *Echoes of the Foot-Hills* (1874), *Some Later Verses* (1898), and *Under the Redwoods* (1901).

HARTEBEEST, or **CAAMA** (här′tê-bäst, kä′má; *Alcelaphus* or *Bubalis caama*), a South African antelope, which measures about 5 feet high at the shoulders, has a long head, horns projecting outwards and backwards, black marks on the face and legs, a white mark on the rump, and a bushy tail. It is generally to be found in small herds.

HARTFORD, a city of the United States, capital of Connecticut, on the Connecticut River, 50 miles above its mouth. It is pleasantly situated, is built with great regularity, and has among its edifices the handsome white marble capitol, city hall, Trinity College (Episcopal), Roman Catholic Cathedral, the Wadsworth Athenæum, and various asylums. Both manufactures and trade are of large extent, the former embracing motor cars, typewriters, cycles, steam-engines, small-arms and foundry and machine-shop products. It is a great centre of the insurance business. Hartford was settled in 1635 by colonists from Massachusetts. The Hartford Convention of 1814–5 was a meeting of delegates of the New England states occasioned by the war with Britain. Pop. (1930), 164,072.

HARTLAND, village of Devonshire. In the north of the county, it is 5 miles from Clovelly. Four miles farther is Hartland Point, a cape on which a lighthouse stands. Pop. 1,483.

HARTLEBURY, village of Worcestershire. It is 6 miles from Bewdley on the G.W. Rly. It is chiefly famous for its castle, the residence of the Bishops of Worcester since the 13th century. The present building dates from the 18th century.

HARTLEPOOL, borough and seaport of Durham. It stands on the coast, 18 miles from Durham and 247 from London, on the L.N.E. Rly. The principal industries are shipping, shipbuilding and fishing. There is a good harbour. The Sandwell Gate is a relic of the city's past. With West Hartlepool it was bombarded by the Germans, 16th Dec., 1914. A good deal of damage was done to property and 113 persons were killed, a further 300 being wounded.   Pop (1931), 20,545.

HARTLEPOOL WEST, county borough and market town of Durham. It is 245 miles from London and 2 miles to the south of Hartlepool, being served by the L.N.E. Rly. The industries are shipping and shipbuilding, much coal being exported from here and timber imported. There are also engineering works and flour mills. The extensive docks cover some 400 acres. The town which is quite modern includes the watering place of Seaton Carew, to the south, and Stranton with an old church. Pop. 68,134.

HARTLEY, David, an English physician, principally celebrated as a writer on metaphysics and morals, born 1705, died 1757. He became a Fellow of Jesus College, Cambridge, and finally practised medicine at Newark, Bury St. Edmund's, and in London, and ended his days at Bath. In his *Observations on Man* (1749, 2 vols.) he formulates his hypothesis of nervous vibration and of the association of ideas.

HARTMANNSWEILERKOPF, called by the French Vieil Armand, a summit in the Vosges, near Mulhouse. It was the scene of fierce fighting between the French and the Germans during the European War (Jan. to Dec., 1915).

HARTSHORN, in pharmacy, the horn of the common stag, from which substances deemed of high medical value were formerly prepared by distillation, such as spirits of hartshorn, oil of hartshorn, and salt of hartshorn. The active ingredient of these was ammonia, which is now obtained from gas-liquor and other sources. It was the principal remedy used by the heroines of Fielding's and Richardson's novels in their fainting fits.

HART'S-TONGUE (Scolopendrium, a genus of ferns. Their fronds are simple and undivided. There are about a dozen species known, the *S. vulgāre* being British.

HARTY, Sir Herbert Hamilton, British conductor and composer. Born at Hillsborough, Co. Down, 4th Dec., 1879, he studied music in London and elsewhere. He made a reputation with his piece, *An Irish Symphony,* which was followed by others. In 1920 he was appointed conductor of the Hallé Orchestra in Manchester, a post which he resigned in 1933 to come to London to take over the London Sympnony Orchestra. In 1925 he was knighted. In 1931 he was prominent as a critic of the B.B.C. programmes. He married in 1904 Agnes Nicholls, well known as an opera and oratorio singer. In July, 1933, he received the honorary degree of Doctor of Law, from Queen's University, Belfast.

HARUN AL RASHID (hä-rön' äl-ra-shĕd'; Harun the Orthodox), a celebrated caliph of the Saracens, 786–809, the fifth of the Abbasside caliphs (q.v.). The popular fame of this caliph is evinced by the *Arabian Nights' Entertainments,* in which Harun, his wife Zobeide, his vizier Giaffer, and his chief eunuch Mesrur are conspicuous characters.—Cf. Sir W. Muir, *The Caliphate.*

HARVARD, John, founder of Harvard University. The son of a butcher, he was born in Southwark in 1607. He went from school at Southwark to Emmanuel College, Cambridge. In 1637 he went to America and was chosen minister of a church at Charlestown, now part of Boston, but in the next year, 14th Sept., 1638, he died. Memorials to Harvard in England are a chapel in the cathedral at Southwark and Harvard House at Stratford-on-Avon, which was built by his maternal grandfather.

HARVARD UNIVERSITY, the oldest university in the United States, situated in Cambridge, Massachusetts. The nucleus of it was formed in 1636 by the voting of a sum of £400 by the general court of Massachusetts. In 1638 the Rev. John Harvard bequeathed half of his property and his entire library to the projected institution. The college was immediately opened, and received the name of its benefactor, and the first graduation occurred in 1642. Its endowments have greatly increased since that time, and its property and funds now amount to over 40,000,000 dollars. The principal college buildings number twenty-five, and include several halls, such as University Hall, Harvard Hall, &c. The libraries contain about 1,940,000 volumes (1919). There are 1,807 (1932) members of the teaching staff, and the number of students is 8,536.

An entrance examination is required in one of two sets of subjects, of which classics predominate in the one, mathematics and science in the other. After the first year's course, which embraces a prescribed series of studies, the student has a large number of different courses to select from in order to qualify for the degree of Bachelor of Arts, the course of study extending to four years.

Among the departments connected with the university are: (1) The Law

Harvest Mouse and Nest

School; (2) The Lawrence Scientific School; (3) The Divinity School; (4) The Medical School; (5) The Dental School; (6) The Bussey Institution of Agriculture; (7) The Veterinary School. We may also mention the Museum of Zoology (the Agassiz Museum), Botanical Garden, Peabody Museum of American Archæology and ethnology, Fogg Art Museum, Semitic Museum, and Radcliffe College for Women.—BIBLIOGRAPHY: W. R. Thayer, *History and Customs of Harvard University*; J. H. Gardiner, *Harvard.*

HARVEST-BUG (Trombidium), the six-legged larvæ of certain mites. They are of a bright red colour, so small as scarcely to be visible, and resemble a grain of cayenne pepper. They appear in June or July, and attack the skin of domestic animals, as horses, dogs, and sheep under which they burrow, causing red pustules to arise. It attacks the legs, thighs, and lower part of the abdomen of human beings.

HARVESTER, HARVESTMAN, or **HARVEST-SPIDER** (species of Phalangium, Oligolophus, &c.), the popular name of active long-legged arachnids of the ord. Phalangidea. They differ from true spiders by fusion of the abdomen with the cephalothorax.

HARVEST-MOON, the name given to the moon during that lunation whose full moon is the nearest to the autumnal equinox (23rd Sept. in northern latitudes). For some days before and after her full the moon then rises nearly at the same hour on successive evenings, at about the time of sunset. There is thus a continuity of natural light, and as this facilitated harvest operations, the name 'harvest-moon' was applied. The cause of the phenomenon is that this full moon is situated near the First Point of Aries, and travelling towards the more northern constellations of the zodiac. Her northward motion in declination nearly or quite counter balances, in higher latitudes, the daily retardation which would else result from her eastward motion in right ascension.

HARVEST-MOUSE (*Mus messorius*), the smallest British mammal, except the lesser shrew, first made known to science by White of Selborne. The body is about $2\frac{1}{4}$ inches long, and the prehensile tail a little shorter. It builds a globular nest usually suspended among stalks of wheat

HARVEY, Sir George, a Scottish painter, born 1806, died 1876. He was a native of St. Ninians, near Stirling, and in his eighteenth year entered the Trustees' Academy, Edinburgh. In 1826 he became an Associate of the Royal Scottish Academy, and in 1829 an Academician. He chiefly painted scenes connected with the religious history of Scotland, such as *The Covenanters Preaching, The Battle of Drumclog, Quitting the Manse,* and others, but he was also prominent as a landscape-painter, especially in later life. In 1864 he was president of the Royal Scottish Academy, and was knighted in 1867.

HARVEY, Sir John Martin, British

actor-manager, was born at Wyvenhoe, Essex, in 1867, and educated at King's College School, London. He originally intended to become a naval architect, but abandoned this idea and studied elocution under John Ryder with a view to going on the stage. He began his career with Clayton and Wyndham, but subsequently joined Sir Henry Irving, and remained many years with him.

He has managed the Lyceum, Prince of Wales's, the Court, the Royalty, and the Apollo Theatres. Among his productions are: *The Only Way, Ib and Little Christina, The Breed of the Treshams, The Corsican Brothers, The Faun, Armageddon, The Burgomaster of Stilemonde, Via Crucis,* and *The Showing up of Blanco Posnet;* and also many plays of Shakespeare. He was knighted at the New Year, 1921.

HARVEY, William, an English physician, the discoverer of the true theory of the circulation of the blood, was born at Folkestone 1578, died 1657. He entered Caius College, Cambridge, in 1593, and about 1599 proceeded to Padua, then the most celebrated school of medicine in Europe, and attended lectures on anatomy, surgery, and other branches of medical science. He took the degree of M.D., and returned to England in 1602. He settled in London, was admitted Fellow of the College of Physicians, elected physician of St. Bartholomew's Hospital, and in 1615 was chosen Lumleian lecturer.

His views on the circulation of the blood were formally given to the world in his *Exercitatio Anatromica de Motu Cordis et Sanguinis in Animalibus* (On the Movement of the Heart and Blood in Animals), published at Amsterdam in 1628, in which he claims to have expounded and demonstrated them for upwards of nine years. Harvey's theory was attacked by several foreign physicians; but from the commencement his views were widely received.

In 1623 he was appointed physician extraordinary to James I, and in 1632 he became physician in ordinary to Charles I. He was present at the battle of Edgehill, and afterwards accompanied Charles to Oxford. Here he received the degree of M.D., and was elected Warden of Merton College, an office which he lost on the surrender of Oxford to the Parliament. He returned to London in 1646, and spent the remainder of his life in retirement. Of Harvey's works, the next in importance to the *De Motu* is his *Exercitationes de Generatione Animalium* (On the Generation of Animals, 1651).—Cf. R. Willis, *Life of Harvey.*

HARVEYELLA, a genus of Red Algæ, family Gigartinaceæ. The only species, *H. mirabilis,* is a small colourless parasite growing on another red seaweed, Rhodomela.

HARWICH (har'ich), a borough and seaport of England, Essex, 71¾ miles E.N.E. of London. The harbour is spacious, and has been improved by the construction of two breakwaters. From Parkestone Quay the L.N.E. Railway runs a regular service of boats to Amsterdam, the Hook of Holland, Hamburg and elsewhere. It is also the terminus of the ferry service to Zeebrugge. Shipbuilding and other maritime employments are carried on, and cement is dredged up outside the harbour. Harwich (with Dovercourt) is much frequented by sea-bathers, and is a famous yachting centre. An important naval base during the European War, Harwich was raided by German air-craft in 1917. Pop (1931), 12,700.

HARWOOD, GREAT, a town (urban district) of England, Lancashire, 4½ miles north-east of Blackburn, with cotton manufactures, coalmines, &c. Pop (1931), 12,787.

HARZ, or **HARTZ** (härts; Ger. *Harzgebirge*), the *Hercynia Silva* of the Romans, the most northerly mountain chain of Germany, from which an extensive plain stretches to the North Sea and the Baltic. It extends from south-east to north-west, and comprises an extent of about 60 miles in length and nearly 20 miles in breadth, embracing the towns of Klausthal, Goslar, Blankenburg, and Wernigerode. The Brocken, its highest summit, is 3,745 feet high. (*See* BROCKEN.)

That part of the Harz which includes the Brocken, with the neighbouring high summits, is called the Upper Harz, and consists entirely of granite. The south-east portion is called the Lower Harz. The Harz abounds in woods and fine pastures; and is rich in minerals, including silver, iron, lead, copper, zinc, arsenic, manganese, granite, porphyry, slate, marble, and alabaster.

HAS'DRUBAL (more correctly Asdrubal, 'Baal is his help'), the name of several Carthaginian leaders, particularly the brother of Hannibal, the hero of the second Punic War. On the departure of Hannibal for Italy, 218 B.C., he was left in command of the army in Spain, in which capacity he carried on a long series of military operations against the Roman troops, which were commanded by Cnæus and Publius Scipio. His brother Hannibal requiring his assistance in Italy, Hasdrubal led an army from Spain into that country (207 B.C.), but before he could join forces with his brother he was defeated on the right bank of the Metaurus by Claudius Nero and M. Livius. Nero is said to have thrown Hasdrubal's head into Hannibal's camp, by way of announcing the defeat and death of his brother.

HASH'ISH (Ar. *hashish*, herbage, hay, from *hashsha*, to cut grass), an intoxicating preparation made in Eastern countries from common hemp (*Cannábis sativa*), or rather from the Indian variety of it (*Cannábis indica*); also a name for this plant itself or for its tender shoots. The juice of the plant has powerful narcotic properties, and is variously made use of. A resin which the plant gives out is often gathered and kneaded and formed into small balls called **churrus,** and from this a narcotic is prepared. It has the appearance of a tenacious ointment of a greenish-yellow colour, with an acrid savour and a nauseous smell.

Hashish produces a kind of intoxication, accompanied with ecstasies and hallucinations. When dried and smoked as tobacco, the plant is called **bhang;** or this name is given to a drink prepared from the leaves and shoots. Ganja or Gunja is the dried shoots of the female plant with the resin on them. Hashish in several forms is employed in medicine. The English 'assassin' is derived from the Ar. *hashishin*, or hemp-eaters.

HASLAR, district of Gosport. Here is a naval hospital, the largest in the country. Opened in 1753 it has since been enlarged. It accommodates over 2,000 patients and the grounds cover 60 acres. On Haslar Point, at the entrance to Portsmouth Harbour, the Navy has a submarine depot.

HASLEMERE, borough and market town of Surrey. It is 40¾ miles from London, on the S. Rly. Near by are Hindhead and other beauty spots; also Aldworth, once the residence of Lord Tennyson. Pop. (1931) 4,340.

HASLINGDEN, a municipal borough, England, county of Lancaster, 16 miles north of Manchester, with manufactures of cottons and woollens; coal-mines, quarries, &c. Pop. (1931), 16,637.

HASSELT, a town, Belgium, capital of Limburg, on the Demer, with manufactures of tobacco, lace, linen; distilleries, &c. Pop. 22,602.

HASTINGS, Francis Rawdon, Marquess of, Governor-General of India, born 1754, died 1825. Having studied at Oxford, he entered (1771) the 15th Foot, and from 1776 to 1782 he served with distinction in the American War.

In 1793 he became Earl of Moira, and in 1795 commanded the expedition to Quiberon. From 1813 to 1823 he was Governor-General of India, and was successful in the Nepaulese and Mahratta Wars. In his latter years he was Governor of Malta.

HASTINGS, Rev. James, Scottish Biblical scholar, born 1855 at Huntly, Aberdeenshire, and educated at Old Aberdeen grammar-school and the University of Aberdeen, where he graduated M.A. in 1876. He entered the ministry of the Free Church, and was ordained minister at Kinneff, Kincardineshire, in 1884. From 1901 to 1911 he was minister of St. Cyrus United Free Church, in the same county. He edited *The Expository Times* from its foundation by himself in 1889, but he is better known as editor of a *Dictionary of the Bible* (4 vols. and supplementary vol., 1898–1904), a *Dictionary of Christ and the Gospels* (2 vols., 1906–7), a *Dictionary of the Bible* (in one vol., 1908), and the *Encyclopædia of Religion and Ethics.* He died 15th Oct., 1922.

HASTINGS, Sir Patrick, English lawyer. Born in 1880, he was educated at Charterhouse School and became a mining engineer. Soon he turned to the law, became a barrister and in a few years had a large practice. In 1919 he was made a K.C., and in 1922 he entered the House of Commons as Labour M.P. for the Wallsend division. In the Labour Ministry of 1923 he was Attorney-General, but in 1926 he resigned and left political life. He received a knighthood in 1924. Sir Patrick has written two plays.

HASTINGS, Warren, English statesman and first Governor-General of India, was born at Daylesford, in Worcestershire, 1732, and died there 1818.

A grandson of the rector of Daylesford, he was educated at Westminster School, and in 1750 he set out for Bengal in the capacity of a writer in the service of the East India Company. When stationed at Cossimbazar, he was taken prisoner by Surajah Dowlah on the capture of the place (1756). Having made his escape, he served as a volunteer under Clive in 1757. He was representative of the Company at Moorshedabad from 1758 to 1761. In the latter year he removed to Calcutta, having obtained a seat in the Bengal Council, but returned to England in 1764. As he lost the bulk of his means by unfortunate Indian investments, he again entered the Company's service, and sailed for India in 1769.

In consequence of the misgovernment of the Nawab of Bengal the Company had deprived him of all real power, and now wished to have the country more directly under their control. Warren Hastings was its chief instrument in this undertaking, and in 1772 became president of the Supreme Council of Calcutta. Mohammed Reza Khan the administrator of the revenues of Bengal, was now accused, by an unprincipled character named Nuncomar, of corruption and abuses of power. In this prosecution Hastings acted as the tool of the Company. Mohammed and Shitab Roy, Dewan of Behar (who had been similarly accused), were afterwards honourably acquitted, but meantime the reorganization desired by the Company had been carried out.

In 1773 the Company's powers were considerably modified by an Act of Parliament, and Hastings now received the title of Governor-General of India. As the majority of the Council disapproved of Hastings's past policy, Nuncomar, his old ally, took advantage of the circumstance to accuse him of peculation (1776). The accusations were favourably received by the Council, when Nuncomar was suddenly accused by a Calcutta merchant of forgery, was tried, and executed—a fate which he undoubtedly deserved.

In 1776 the directors of the Company petitioned Government for his removal from the Council, but Hastings resigned, and a successor to him was appointed. In 1777 one of the members of the Council died, and Hastings, having thus procured a casting vote, withdrew his resignation and returned to office. He now displayed extraordinary resource in meeting dangerous movements on the part of the Mahrattas, the Nizam of the Deccan, and Hyder Ali of Mysore, and to procure the needful money was less than scrupulous in his treatment of the rulers of Benares and Oudh. He thus gave good grounds for censure, and a motion for his recall was passed in the House of Commons. Fox's India Bill was thrown out in 1783, but next year Pitt's Bill, establishing the board of control, passed, and Hastings resigned.

He left India in 1785, and was impeached by Burke in 1786, being charged with acts of injustice and oppression, with maladministration, receiving of bribes, &c. This celebrated trial, in which Burke, Fox, and Sheridan thundered against him, began in 1788, and terminated in 1795 with his acquittal, but cost him his fortune. The Company in 1796 settled on him an annuity of £4,000 a year, and lent him £50,000 for eighteen years free of interest. He passed the remainder of his life in retirement at Daylesford, which he purchased.— BIBLIOGRAPHY: Lord Macaulay, *Essay*

on *Warren Hastings*; L. J. Trotter, *Warren Hastings*; Sir G. W. Forrest, *The Administration of Warren Hastings*; Sir A. Lyall, *Warren Hastings*; F. M. Holmes, *Four Heroes of India*; G. W. Hastings, *A Vindication of Warren Hastings*.

HASTINGS (hās′tingz), a parliamentary, county, and municipal borough, and market town of England, county of Sussex, one of the Cinque Ports, pleasantly situated on the seacoast, and including the suburb of St. Leonards-on-Sea. In front of the town is an esplanade, an older and a newer pier, large baths, and an outdoor bathing pool, while there are public gardens and pleasure-grounds, sheltering hills, and cliffs.

Fishing and boat-building are carried on, but the principal support of the town is derived from the numerous visitors who frequent it during the bathing and winter seasons. There are here the ruins of an ancient castle, and of a church and conventual buildings, supposed to have been founded in the reign of Henry I. William of Normandy defeated Harold near here, 14th Oct., 1066. Pop. (1931), 65,199.

HASTINGS, a town New Zealand, North Island. It is the business centre of a district where sheep are reared, and has refrigerating works and other industries. The town was seriously damaged by the great earthquake of 1931. Pop. (1932), 16,750.

HASWALL, market town of Durham. It is 252 miles from London, on the L.N.E. Rly. The chief industry is coal mining. Pop. 5,860.

HAT (A. Sax. *hœt*), an outdoor covering for the head of various shapes and materials (as felt, silk, wool, straw), but having a *brim* as its most distinctive and general feature.

Hats are of ancient origin. Among the Greeks, for instance, the *petasos* was worn, which had a brim, and was similar to the round felt now worn. The shape of the hat has varied extremely in Europe at different periods. The first modern hat, as we now know this article, was made in Paris at the beginning of the fifteenth century, but it was adopted only half a century later by the French. The *dress hat* or *silk hat* with a smooth nap outside is still an important article of attire, though felt hats are in more general wear. (*See* FELT.)

The silk hat was invented at Florence about 1760. The manufacture, however, did not make much progress till 1828. Up to and even after this time beaver fur was the chief material for hats. A silk hat is composed of a skeleton, to which the silk

HATS
1, Eleventh century. 2, Twelfth. 3, Thirteenth. 4, 5, Fourteenth. 6, Fifteenth. 7, 8, Sixteenth.
9, 10, 11, Seventeenth. 12, 13, 14, 15, Eighteenth. 16, 17, Nineteenth

plush is glued. The skeleton, consisting of three parts, the cylindrical part or body, the crown, and the brim, is usually made of linen, covered with gum-lac, and to the cylindrical part the crown is gummed. The cylindrical part is made by gumming together the edges of a piece of cloth shaped on a cylinder. The brim is composed of superposed layers of stiffer cloth, and made with a flat projecting surface round its inner edge, which is gummed to the skeleton. For covering the hat a sort of hood of silk plush is made, cut across in an oblique line. This cover is drawn over the skeleton on the block, and fitted exactly to it by the application of a hot iron. The heat of the iron melts the gum-lac, which on cooling cements the covering to the skeleton. The edges of the oblique cut are also coated with gum-lac. The hat is finally shaped on the block or form, and the plush damped and polished while the hat revolves on a turning-lathe.

In the manufacture of straw hats the straw commonly used is that of wheat or barley. The best comes from Italy, and particularly from Tuscany, but straw hats are also largely made in England. Palm-leaf hats are imported from China and elsewhere, and are also machine-made in the United States.

Felt hats are made of fur, wool, or a mixture of the two. When fur is used, it is fed from a rapidly revolving cylinder to the perforated surface of a more slowly revolving metal cone. By means of a fan, a strong current of air is drawn through the perforations, so that the fibres of fur cling closely to the cone. When the proper amount for a hat has been collected, the mass is treated with hot water and made to cohere firmly by pressure. It is then roughly shaped, dyed, and stiffened. Soft felt hats are stiffened with water paste, hard felt hats with a solution of shellac. Lastly, the hat is shaped on a block, polished with emery paper, bound and lined. Opera hats have collapsible metal frames, and are covered with silk or merino.— Cf. G. W. Rhead, *Chats on Costume.*

HATCHMENT (corrupted from *achievement*, Fr. *achèvement*), in heraldry, the coat of arms of a person dead, usually placed on the front of a house, in a church, or on a hearse at funerals, by which the fact of the death and the rank of the deceased may be known; the whole being distinguished in such a manner as to indicate whether the person was man or woman, married or single.

HAT'FIELD, or BISHOP'S HAT-FIELD, a town of England, in the county of Hertford. Near it is Hat-field House, built by Sir Robert Cecil, the residence of the Marquess of Salisbury. It was under an oak tree in the park here that Elizabeth is supposed to have been seated when she was informed of her accession to the throne. The church of St. Etheldreda, dating from Norman times, was restored in 1872. Pop. (1931) (Rural district), 10,999.

HATFIELD PEVEREL, town of Essex. It is 6 miles from Chelmsford on the L.N.E. Rly. Pop. 1,300.

HATHERSAGE, village of Derbyshire. It is 34 miles from Manchester and 161 from London, on the L.M.S. Rly. Around the village is some of the finest of the Derbyshire scenery. Little John is said to have been buried in the churchyard. Pins and needles are made here. Pop. 2,025.

HÁTHRAS, a town of India, United Provinces, Aligarh district, formerly one of the strongest fortresses in India, now a great commercial centre. Pop. 38,763.

HATRY, Clarence Charles. English financier. Born in 1890, he went into business in London, and became a successful company promoter. He founded the Commercial Bank of London, and, until this failed in 1920, controlled a number of associated undertakings. In 1929, with his associates, he raised money by pledging securities with the banks. It was soon discovered that some of the stock was forged, and the shares of his companies fell heavily. On 19th Sept., he made a full confession and steps were taken to deal with the situation. In Jan., 1930, he and his associates were tried and found guilty. All were sentenced to penal servitude, his sentence being for 14 years. The amount of money involved in this failure was over £13,000,000, but the net loss was a much smaller sum.

HATTO, the name of two Archbishops of Mainz, of which the second, who died in A.D. 969 or 970, is the best known. He was Abbot of Fulda until 968, when he was appointed Archbishop of Mainz. Of his subsequent life very opposite accounts exist; some represent him as an upright prelate and reformer of abuses; others in the blackest colours. The legend of his being devoured by rats (the fable of the 'Mäusethurm'), popularized by Southey, is well known.—Cf. S. Baring-Gould, *Curious Myths of the Middle Ages.*

HATTON, Sir Christopher, Lord Chancellor of England, a favourite of Queen Elizabeth, born about 1540, died 1591. He was introduced at court in 1564. He entered Parliament in 1571, became captain of the queen's guard in 1572, Vice-Chamberlain and a Privy Councillor in 1577, and Lord Chancellor in 1587. He was one of the Commissioners for the trial of Mary, Queen of Scots, in 1586.

HAUFF (houf), **Wilhelm**, German novelist and writer of humorous and fantastic stories, born 1802, died 1827. His first publication was his *Almanack of Tales for the Year* 1826, which was followed by similar collections for the next two years, the whole forming a collection that has been highly popular. Extracts from the *Memoirs of Satan* appeared in 1827, but remained uncompleted.

Lichtenstein, a novel written under the inspiration of Sir Walter Scott, appeared in 1826, and is one of the best German novels of its class. In 1827 was issued *The Man in the Moon*, and the same year *Fantasies in the Wine Cellar of Bremen Council*, a piece of excellent humour. Among the best of his works are two novelettes, *The Picture of the Emperor* and *The Beggar-woman of the Pont-des-Arts*.

HAUPTMANN, Gerhart, German dramatist, born at Salzbrunn, 15th Nov., 1862, the son of an hotel-keeper and grandson of a weaver. After studying art at Breslau and Rome, he returned to Germany in 1885, where he married a lady of wealth and settled to literary work, especially play-writing. His first dramas, *Vor Sonnenaufgang* (1889), *Das Friedensfest* (1890), *Einsame Menschen* (1891), and *Die Weber* (1892), breathe a spirit of revolt against social conditions and artistic ideals. The author's naturalism is distinctly pessimistic, and one feels the influence of Zola and Tolstoy.

His plays produced after 1892 are of a more varied nature, more humorous, and less pessimistic. Among these are: *Kollege Crampton* (1892), *Der Biberpelz* (1893), *Hannele's Himmelfahrt* (1894), *Fuhrmann Henschel* (1898), *Griselda* (1909), and *The Island of the Great Mother* (1926). Some of his later plays have been translated into English. He was made an honorary D.C.L. of Oxford in 1905, and received the Nobel prize of literature in 1912. *Anna*, an epic poem, appeared in 1921.—Cf. Paul Fechter, *Gerhart Hauptmann*.

HAURAN, a district of Syria, east of the Jordan and south of Damascus. It contains the ruins of many ancient towns, with numerous Greek inscriptions, both Christian and pagan. In the Roman period it was one of the four provinces of Bashan. It is fertile but thinly inhabited. A railway reaches it from Damascus.

HAUSTO'RIUM, in botany, a special organ for the absorption of food, such as the suckers of dodder and other parasites. Most parasitic Fungi (e.g. and mildews) live in the intercellular spaces of their hosts, whence they tap the living cells by means of haustoria. In monocotyledonous plants the tip of the cotyledon remains inside the seed at germination, and digests and absorbs the food stored in the endosperm; this is well seen in the date-palm, where the haustorial part of the cotyledon grows enormously during germination, gradually eating its way through the entire stone.

HAÜY (á-ü-ē), **René Just**, a French mineralogist, born 1743, died 1822. He studied theology, became an abbé, and during twenty-one years occupied the place of a professor, at first in the College of Navarre, and afterwards in that of the Cardinal Le Moine. He studied botany, and subsequently mineralogy, and introduced a once celebrated system of crystallography. On the outbreak of the Revolution Haüy was imprisoned for refusing to subscribe to the new Constitution, but his life was saved by the exertions of Geoffroi de St. Hilaire.

In 1793 he was appointed a member of the Commission of Measures and Weights, in 1794 conservator of the Cabinet des Mines, and in 1795 teacher of physics in the École Normale. In 1802 Napoleon made him professor of mineralogy in the Musée d'Histoire Naturelle, and also shortly after in the Faculté des Sciences. Haüy was remarkable for the extreme modesty of his disposition. His principal writings are his *Essai sur la théorie et la structure des cristaux* (1784), his *Traité de minéralogie* (1802), his *Traité élémentaire de physique* (1803), and his *Traité de cristallographie* (1817), &c.

His brother Valentin, born 1745, died 1822, started the first institution for the instruction of the blind.

HAVAN'A (Sp. *La Habana*, 'the haven'), an important maritime city, capital of Cuba, on the north-west side of the island, with an extensive and excellent natural harbour. The town in the older parts has narrow, badly-paved streets, but there are also wide and handsome promenades and avenues. The houses, which are low and with flat roofs, resemble those of Southern Spain. Havana is the see of a bishop, and the seat of the Governor.

The cathedral long contained the ashes of Columbus, which were brought hither from San Domingo in 1796. Among the other buildings are the Governor's house, the admiralty, the university, the exchange, and the opera-house.

The staple manufacture is that of its celebrated cigars. The other manufactures, consisting chiefly of chocolate, straw hats, and woollen fabrics, are not of much consequence. The trade is extensive, the most important articles of export being sugar and tobacco, unmanufactured or in the form of cigars and cigarettes; other exports are molasses, coffee, wax, honey, and rum. The United States have the principal share of the trade, and Spain and England rank next. Several railways start from Havana.

The town was founded in 1511, but was only fairly begun in 1519. For a long time Spain derived the chief part of her fleet from the building-yards of Havana, which still have some shipbuilding. It has a broadcasting station (49·5 M.). Pop. (1930), 589,079.

HAVANT, urban district and market town of Hampshire. It is 8 miles from Portsmouth and 65 from London on the S. Rly. It stands on Langstone Harbour, and was at one time a prosperous port. The industries are tanning, brewing and malting. Pop. (1931) 4,264.

HAV'EL, a navigable river of Germany, with extensive canal connections, rises in Mecklenberg-Schwerin, enters Prussia, flows past Spandau, receives the Spree, and joins the Elbe after a course of 221 miles

HAVELBERG, a town in Prussia, province of Brandenburg, on the Havel, engaged in brewing, sugar-refining, and shipbuilding. Pop. 6,170.

HAVELOCK (hav'lok), **Sir Henry,** British soldier, born at Bishop-Wearmouth, near Sunderland, on 5th April, 1795, died 24th Nov., 1857. Having entered the army, he served with distinction in the Burmese War (1824–6). In 1829 he married a daughter of Marshman, the celebrated missionary, became a Baptist, and was distinguished during the remainder of his life by his earnest religious zeal.

He attained his captaincy in 1838, participated in the Afghanistan War, was present at the storming of Ghazni and the capture of Kabul, and in Sale's march to Jelalabad, and assisted in the defence of that city, and in the defeat of Mohammed Akbar, 1843. He was made a Companion of the Bath, and brevet-major, took part in the Mahratta War, and distinguished himself in the Sikh War of 1845, being present at Mudki, Ferozeshah, and Sobraon. In 1851 he was promoted to the adjutant-generalship of the queen's forces in India, and he commanded a division in the Persian War (1856–7).

On the outbreak of the Indian Mutiny he was dispatched to Allaha-

bad in order to support Sir H. Lawrence at Lucknow and Sir H. Wheeler at Cawnpore. On his march to Cawnpore he defeated the rebels at Fattihpur, Aong, Pandunadi, and Maharajpur. On arriving at Cawnpore he found that Nana Sahib had massacred the prisoners. Pursuing his march to Lucknow, he defeated the rebels at Bithoor, and finally, with the aid of Outram, won the battle of Alumbagh. Having captured Lucknow, Havelock and Outram were shut up there until relieved by Sir Colin Campbell, 17th Nov., 1857. A week later he died of dysentery at Dilkusha. He was raised to the rank of major-general, made a K.C.B., and (before his death was known) created a baronet.—BIBLIOGRAPHY: A. Forbes, *Havelock*; F. M. Holmes, *Four Heroes of India.*

HAVERFORDWEST, a borough of Wales, county town of Pembroke,

Morro Castle, Havana

and one of the Pembroke district of parliamentary boroughs, on the West Cleddaw River. The old town is on one side of the river and the suburbs of Prendergast and Cartlet on the other, two bridges connecting them. It manufactures paper, and has a small shipping trade. Pop. (1931), 6,113.

HAVERGAL, Frances Ridley, English hymn writer. Born at Astley, Worcestershire, 14th Dec., 1836, the daughter of a clergyman, she wrote an enormous quantity of verse of a religious character, including many hymns. She died 3rd June, 1879.

HAV'ERHILL, a market town of England, in the south-west corner of Suffolk, with manufactures of horsehair cloth, silk, boots, clothing, &c. Pop. (1931), 3,827.

HAVERHILL, a town of the United States, in Massachusetts, on the Merrimac, with extensive manufactures of boots and shoes. Pop. (1930), 48,710.

HAVILDAR', the highest non-commissioned rank in the infantry of the Indian army. It corresponds with the rank of sergeant in the British service, but does not give authority over British soldiers. In the cavalry the corresponding rank is that of duffadar. The rank is also used in the Indian police force.

HAVRE (ä-vr), **LE** (formerly **Le Havre-de-Grâce**), a seaport of Northern France, department of Seine-Inférieure, on the north side of the estuary of the Seine, 108 miles north-west of Paris, built of brick or stone in straight, wide streets. The public buildings possess little interest. The town has a number of industrial

Hawfinch (*Coccothraustes vulgāris*)

establishments, sugar-refineries, breweries, and shipbuilding-yards. But the chief dependence of Havre is on its commerce, which is the greatest of any French port next to Marseilles. It has a large trade with England and Germany, and especially with America, importing great quantities of cotton and other produce; and exporting numerous articles of French manufacture. In 1932, 2,696 vessels with a tonnage of 8,543,321 entered the port, and 2,061 vessels with a tonnage of 7,733,223 cleared it. There is a regular steamer service with Southampton.

The importance of Havre dates from the early part of the sixteenth century. Havre was a base of the British Expeditionary Force during the European War, and the seat of the Belgian Government from Oct., 1914, to Nov., 1918. Pop. (1931), 165,076.

HAWAII (hä-wī'ē). *See* SAND-WICH ISLANDS.

HAWARDEN (har'den; Welsh name *Penarlag*), a town in Flintshire, Wales, lying in a coal district, and having valuable clay beds in the vicinity. In the neighbourhood is Hawarden Castle (built in 1752), the residence for years of W. E. Gladstone. In Broadlands House is the Gladstone Museum. Pop. (rural district) (1931), 26,570.

HAWES, Stephen, an English poet, born about 1474, died about 1523, but the exact date of his birth and death is unknown. His principal work is *The Historie of Graunde Amour and la Bell Pucell, or The Pastime of Pleasure.*

HAWES, market town of Yorkshire (N.R.). It is 16 miles from Leyburn, on the L.N.E. Rly. It is chiefly a market for agricultural produce and is also a good centre for tourists. Pop. 1,430.

Hawes Junction, an important junction on the L.M.S. system, is 6 miles from the town. A terrible accident took place here on Christmas Eve, 1910.

HAWESWATER. Lake of Westmorland. It is 14 miles from Penrith and 9 from Shap, in the E. of the Lake District. It is 2½ miles long and is surrounded by somewhat desolate scenery.

Like Thirlmere the lake is used to supply Manchester with water, and in 1930 it was decided to enlarge it for this purpose. The scheme includes raising the level of the lake by 90 ft., and the destruction of a church, a vicarage, an inn and three farm houses at Mardale.

HAWFINCH *Coccothraustes vulgāris*), one of the largest of the finches. It resembles the chaffinch in colour, but is distinguished from it by its enormous beak, larger size, and bill-hook formation of some of its wing-feathers. It feeds on all kinds of berries. It is found in some parts of Britain.

HAWICK (ha'ik), a municipal burgh of Scotland, in Roxburghshire, on the Teviot, 50½ miles s.w. of Edinburgh. The staple industries of the town are the manufacture of hosiery and tweeds, but tanning, skin-dressing, oil-making, dyeing, and iron-founding, are also carried on. The common riding is a festival held here every year. Until 1918 the Border or Hawick Burghs, of which Hawick was one, returned one member to Parliament. They are now merged in the county of Roxburgh. Pop. (1931), 17,059.

HAWK, a name often applied to all birds of prey except the eagles, vultures, and owls. In this broader sense it includes falcons, buzzards, harriers, and kites, as well as the hawks proper. These last are long-legged birds with short wings which do not reach the extremity of the tail, and have the fourth quill longest and the first short; their beaks are comparatively weak, and never notched. Of the hawks proper the chief British species are the goshawk and the sparrowhawk. (q.v.). *See* FALCON.

HAWKE, Edward, Lord, a celebrated naval commander,born in 1705, died 1781. Entering the navy as a midshipman, he received the command of the *Wolfe* in 1734, and in 1747 he became commander of a squadron, and defeated the French fleet at Belleisle. Hawke was in consequence made a K.B., and Vice-Admiral of the Blue. In 1759 he defeated the French at Quiberon, and in 1765 he was appointed Vice-Admiral of Britain, and was elevated to the peerage in 1776.

HAWKE'S BAY, a district of New Zealand, on the east coast of North Island; area 4,260 sq. miles, containing much fertile soil, well adapted for agricultural and pastoral purposes. The capital is Napier, other ports are Hastings and Gisborne. All three

Sparrow Hawk

were severely damaged by an earthquake in 1931. Pop. (1932), 70,600.

HAWKHURST, town of Kent. It is 48 miles from London, on the S. Rly. At one time Hawkhurst was a market town and a centre of the cloth manufacture. Pop. 3,120.

HAWKINS, Sir John, English sea commander, born at Plymouth 1532, died 1595. He made several voyages in his youth, and in 1562 and 1564 he went on expeditions to Africa in order to procure negroes for the West Indies. A third expedition, in 1567, was dis-

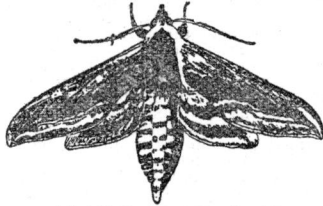

Privet Hawk-moth (*Sphinx ligustri*)

astrous, as his fleet was defeated by the Spaniards.

He became Treasurer of the Navy in 1573, and in 1588 was appointed vice-admiral in the expedition against the Armada, and received a knighthood for his services. In 1590 he and Frobisher unsuccessfully attempted to intercept the Spanish plate fleet, and in 1595 he and Drake led an unsuccessful expedition against the Spaniards in the West Indies, in the midst of which Hawkins died.— Cf. W. H. D. Adams, *English Heroes in the Reign of Elizabeth.*

HAWK-MOTH, one of the sphinx moths, so called from its hovering motion, which resembles that of a hawk looking for its prey. The smooth caterpillars usually possess a hornlike projection on the eleventh segment, are strikingly coloured, and often assume remarkable attitudes. Well-known species are: death's-head hawk-moth (*Acherontia atrŏpos*), privet hawk-moth (*Sphinx ligustri*), and humming-bird hawk-moth (*Macroglossa stellatarum*).

HAWKSHEAD, village of Lancashire. It is situated in the Lake District, being about a mile from Bowness, and is chiefly interesting because Wordsworth was educated at the grammar school. This was closed in 1910.

HAWKSTONE, village of Shropshire. It is 4 miles from Wem and is famed for its hall, long the seat of the Hill family. It dates from the early 18th century and stands in a fine park. The hills near are called the Hawkstone Hills.

HAWKWEED (Hieracium), a genus of composite plants, sub-ord. Cichoraceæ, consisting of numerous species with yellow flowers, common weeds in Britain and other parts of Europe. The pappus is brown and brittle, and in many species the leaves, involucres, and stems are hairy. *H. Pilosella* is the best known in Britain. Its brilliant yellow flower often appears in heaths and pastures.

HAWKWOOD, Sir John, an English soldier of fortune, date of birth unknown, died 1394. His name is spelt by contemporaries as Aguto, Aucud, and Haccoude. On the invasion of France by Edward III Hawkwood was knighted on account of his courage and ability. He is said to have fought at Crécy and Poitiers. In 1360 he occupied a prominent place in the marauding companies which harassed France. He next took regular service under the Pisan Republic for twenty-three years, but in 1387 he entered that of the

Nathaniel Hawthorne

Florentines. He founded the English hospital at Rome, and died at Florence.

HAWORTH, a parish and town (urban district) in the West Riding of Yorkshire, 8 miles north-west of Bradford. The Rev. Patrick Brontë, father of the famous sisters Brontë, was long incumbent, and the graves of Charlotte and Emily are there. Pop. (1931), 5,912.

HAWTHORN, or **WHITETHORN** (*Cratægus Oxyacantha*), a small spiny European tree, belonging to the subord. Pomeæ of the ord. Rosaceæ, rising sometimes to the height of 20 to 25 feet. The leaves are alternate, obovate, 3- to 5-lobed; the flowers are white, sometimes with a reddish tinge, disposed in corymbs, and possess and agreeable perfume; the fruit is a drupe of a red colour, and is edible.

The species are about fifty in number, all shrubs or small trees. A number of them belong to the United States. When young, the hawthorn springs up rapidly, and, if pruned, grows into a thick hedge. When it arrives at the height of a tree, however, it makes wood very slowly. The timber is hard and durable, and fit for many purposes of utility. The double-flower kind is one of the most ornamental for shrubberies.

HAWTHORN, a residential suburb of Melbourne, Australia. Pop. 27,795.

HAWTHORNDEN, village of Midlothian. It is 6 miles from Edinburgh, on the L.N.E. Rly. The glen through which the Esk flows is a noted beauty spot, and the place is also famous as the home of William Drummond, the poet.

HAWTHORNDEN PRIZE. In Drummond's memory the Hawthornden Prize was founded by Miss Alice Warrender. This is a sum of £100 given each year to the author of an imaginative work. The author selected must be under 41 years of age. It has been won by Siegfried Sassoon with *Memoirs of a Fox Hunting Man*, and Lord David Cecil with *The Stricken Deer*.

HAWTHORNE, Nathaniel, American author, born at Salem, Massachusetts, 1804, died 1864. He studied at Bowdoin College, where he took his degree in 1825 along with the poet Longfellow. For a number of years after this he led a retired and studious life in Salem, writing tales, some of which appeared in newspapers and magazines. In 1837 appeared his *Twice-told Tales*, a collection of stories which he had contributed to various American periodicals. In 1838 he was appointed a weigher in the Boston custom-house, a post which he held for a few years. In 1846 he published his *Mosses from an Old Manse*, in 1850 *The Scarlet Letter*, in 1851 *The House of the Seven Gables*, and in 1852 *The Life of Franklin Pierce*, and *The Blithedale Romance*. In 1853 he became American Consul at Liverpool, a post which he held until 1857. He died at Plymouth, New Hampshire. Other works are his *Transformation* (1860), and *Our Old Home* (1863).—BIBLIOGRAPHY: Henry James, *Hawthorne* (English Men of Letters Series); Moncure D. Conway, *Life of Nathaniel Hawthorne* (Great Writers Series).

HAWTREY, Sir Charles Henry, English actor manager. Born 21st Sept., 1858, he was a son of Rev. John Hawtrey, a master at Eton and a grandson of Rev. Edward Craven Hawtrey, who was headmaster of that school, 1834–52. He went to Rugby and Oxford and became an actor, first appearing on the London stage in 1881. In 1883 he adapted a German play, and calling it *The Private Secretary*, produced it in London. A conspicuous success, it made Hawtrey's reputation, and for the next 30 years he was one of the most popular comedians on the stage, numerous successes standing to his credit. As a manager he controlled Her Majesty's Theatre, and then The Comedy. He was knighted in 1922 and died 30th July, 1923.

HAXEY, village of Lincolnshire. It is in the Isle of Axholme, 9 miles from Gainsborough and has a station on the L.N.E. Rly. It is famed for the game called **Haxey Hood** that has been played there for over 600 years. It is a kind of football and in it hundreds of players take part.

HAY, town of Brecknockshire. It is on the Wye, 20 miles from Hereford on the G.W. Rly. It is a good centre for the Black Mountains. There are remains of a castle. Pop. 1,509.

Hay is the name of a town of New South Wales. In the Riverina district, it stands on the Murrumbidgee, 460 miles from Sydney. Pop. 2,500.

A river of Canada is called the **Hay.** It rises on the borders of Alberta and British Columbia and flows for 350 miles to the Great Slave Lake.

HAY, Ian. *See* BEITH, JOHN HAY.

HAY (A.Sax. *hieg,* Goth. *hawi*), the stems and leaves of grasses and other leaves of grasses and other plants cut for fodder, dried in the sun, and stored usually in stacks. The time most suitable for mowing grass intended for hay is that in which the saccharine matter is most abundant in the plants, viz. when the grass is in full flower. For the operation of mowing, dry weather, and, if possible, that in which sunshine prevails, is chosen.

The making of the grass into hay generally takes three or four days to get it ready for stacking. This period is principally occupied in alternately *tedding* (i.e. shaking out the grass loosely) and gathering it up into cocks or small heaps, previous to stacking. Care must be taken to avoid haymaking either under a scorching sun or during the prevalence of rain, and the cocks should never be opened in the morning until the disappearance of the dew. In stacking, the great object is to preserve the freshness of the herbage, and to induce a slight degree of fermentation. If the weather has been wet, a few layers of straw may be inserted at intervals. Salting is also recommended.

HAYASHI, Count Tadasu, Japanese diplomatist, born at Sakura 22nd Jan., 1850, died 10th July, 1913. Educated in England, he was employed in the Japanese Foreign Office from 1891 to 1895, when he was sent as Minister to China till 1897, and to Russia till 1899. He represented Japan at the Hague Peace Conference in 1900, and in the same year became Ambassador in London. During his tenure of office treaties were concluded between Japan and Great Britain (in 1902 and 1905). He returned to Japan in 1905, and was Foreign Minister from 1906 to 1908, and Minister of Commerce from 1911 to 1913.—His namesake, **Baron Gonsuke Hayashi,** born in 1860, was Japanese Ambassador in London in 1920–1925.

HAYDN (hī dn), **Franz Joseph,** a celebrated Austrian musical composer, born at Rohrau, near Vienna, 1732, died 1809. At the age of six he was sent to school at Hainburg, where he learned, among other things, singing and playing by rote. On account of the excellence of his voice he was appointed a choir-boy at St. Stephen's Church, Vienna. At the age of sixteen his voice began to break, and he lost his situation as a chorister Having made the acquaintance of Metastasio, Porpora, and Gluck, Haydn gradually attracted public attention, was appointed organist to two churches, and obtained many pupils. From 1761 to 1790 he was musical director to Prince Esterhazy, and composed during this period a great number of works, including some 120 symphonies for the orchestra, 12 operas, &c. In 1791 and 1794 he visited England, staying there nearly three years altogether, and writing his opera *Orpheus and Eurydice.* In 1798 he published his oratorio of *The Creation,* and in 1800 that of *The Seasons.* His old age was exempt from pecuniary troubles, and he was surrounded by appreciative friends. His last public appearance was at a performance of his *Creation* in 1808.

Haydn's principal merit consists in his opening up a new development of instrumental composition, of which his 125 orchestral symphonies furnish abundant proof. He may be said to have been the originator of the symphony and of the stringed quartette.—BIBLIOGRAPHY: C. F. Pohl, *Joseph Haydn*; P. D. Townsend, *Joseph Haydn*; J. C. Hadden, *Joseph Haydn* (Great Musicians Series); article in Grove's *Dictionary of Music and Musicians.*

HAYDOCK, a town (urban district) of south-west Lancashire, 3 miles north-east of St. Helens, with large collieries. **Here is Haydock** Park race course. Pop. (1931), 10,352.

HAY'DON, Benjamin Robert, an English historical painter, born in 1786, died by his own hand in 1846. In 1804 he became a student of the Royal Academy, and in 1807 exhibited his first work, *Joseph and Mary Resting* (in Egypt), and his *Dentatus* in 1809. His *Judgment of Solomon* appeared in 1814. In 1815 he established a school in opposition to the Academy, an undertaking which ended in pecuniary failure in 1823. He was several times in prison for debt, was always complaining of injustice and neglect, and finally became deranged when he failed to be employed in decorating the new Houses of Parliament.

He was the chief English historical painter of his time, and a man of great intellectual ability generally, but self-willed, perverse, and devoid of tact. Of his pictures the principal are: *Christ's Entry into Jerusalem, The Raising of Lazarus, The Mock Election, Chairing the Member, Pharaoh Dismissing Moses, The Burning of Rome, The Banishment of Aristides,* and *Quintus Curtius Leaping into the Gulf.* He left an interesting autobiography.—Cf. F. W. Haydon (editor), *Haydon's Correspondence and Table-Talk.*

HAYES, urban district of Middlesex. It is 13 miles from London, and the Grand Union Canal passes through it. Of late Hayes has become an industrial centre, and here are works for making printing machines, gramophones, &c. Harlington forms part of the district. Pop. of district (1931), 23,646.

HAYES, village of Kent. **It is** 12 miles from London, on the S. Rly. Hayes Common is a fine open space covering over 200 acres. At Hayes Place the Earl of Chatham lived and died, and his son, William Pitt, was born. In 1930 the house was pulled down.

HAY-FEVER, HAY-ASTHMA, or **SUMMER CATARRH** is a disease affecting the upper air-passages, often associated with asthmatic attacks, and due to the action of the pollen of certain grasses and plants. It is more common in America and Great Britain than on the Continent. Women are more subject to it than men, and there is a definite hereditary disposition. City dwellers are chiefly affected, and of those the educated and highly nervous are most susceptible.

The symptoms are those of a severe coryza, but there may be more headache and distress. There is often severe itching of the eyes, and sneezing-bouts of from twenty to fifty sneezes are not uncommon. Treatment consists of tonics for the nervous system, change to mountain air, local treatment of the nose, and antitoxin treatment; the particular infecting pollen should be discovered and the equivalent antitoxin used.

HAYLE, urban district and seaport of Cornwall. It is 7 miles from Penzance on the G.W. Rly. It has a harbour and fishing is the chief industry. Pop. (1931) 915.

Hayle is the name of a river 10 miles long that flows into St. Ives Bay.

HAYLING, island of Hampshire. It is situated between the harbours of Langstone and Chichester and covers about 10 square miles, being about 4 miles long. The island is a popular seaside resort, and on it are golf links. Havant is the nearest town.

HAYNAU, (hī'nou), **Julius Jakob,** an Austrian general, born in 1786, died 1853. He took part in the battles of Austerlitz and Wagram, and was wounded in both. He also distinguished himself in the campaigns of 1813–5. In 1848 and 1849 he rendered valuable services to Austria against the Italians, took Brescia by storm, and visited it with unrelenting severity. He was afterwards carrying on the siege of Venice, when recalled by the emperor to Hungary.

The storming of Raab, the advance southwards in the face of almost insurmountable difficulties, the siege of Szegedin, the battle on the Theiss, followed by the capture of Temesvar, were all effected by Haynau. He incurred extreme odium, however, on account of his severities and arbitrary measures, and in 1850 he was deprived of his powers, and retired into private life. He had an evil reputation for brutality, and had ordered women to be flogged on various occasions. When visiting London in 1850, he was flogged himself by some of the draymen of Barclay & Perkins's brewery.

HAZ'ARD (O.Fr. *hazard*; Sp. *azar*, unlucky throw; Ar. *al*, and *zār*, dice), a game at dice played for money. The player is called the *caster*, and his opponent, who bets with him, is called the *setter.* The former calls a *main*, i.e. any number from 5 to 9 inclusive. He then throws with two dice, and wins if he 'nicks'. 5 is a nick to 5; 6 and 12 are nicks to 6; 7 and 11 to 7, &c. The caster loses or 'throws out' if he throws aces, or deuce ace (called *crabs*). Hazard is a game involving nice calculations.

HAZARIBAGH (ha-zär-i-bäg'), chief town of the district of the same name, in Chota Nagpur, Bengal. Pop. 17,500. The district contains 7,021 sq. miles. Pop. 1,276,946.

HAZEBROUCK (ăz'brŭk), a town of France, department of Nord, having a fine church with an open spire 240 feet high. It has linen manufactures, breweries, tanneries, dyeworks, &c. During the European War Hazebrouck was shelled by the German long-range gun in 1917, and in April, 1918, it was seriously threatened by the German advance, but never captured. Pop. 13,390.

HAZEL (Corўlus), a genus of shrubs or small trees of the ord. Corylaceæ or Cupuliferæ. It belongs to Europe, North Africa, Asia, and North America. The leaves are roundish-cordate, alternate, and shortly petiolate. The European hazel (*C. Avellāna*) produces the nuts called filberts, and grows best in a tolerably dry soil. It bears male and female flowers, the former composing cylindrical catkins. The hazel-nut oil is little inferior in flavour to that of almonds. Hazel branches form excellent walking-sticks, fishing-rods, &c., and the wood produces good charcoal, often employed by painters.

The American hazel (*C. americāna*) very much resembles the European. The roots are used by cabinet-makers for veneering; and in Italy the chips are sometimes put into turbid wine for the purpose of fining it.—The *witch* (or *wych*) *hazel, Hamamēlis virginica,* is a shrub or small tree of a different natural order, the Hamamelidaceæ. It is a native of the United States, and healing properties have long been ascribed to it both by the Indians and the whites. A liquid prepared from it is said to be useful as an application to wounds, stanching the bleeding and promoting healing, being applied also to bruises, sprains, bleeding piles, in internal bleeding, &c. There are several officinal preparations of the witch-hazel, especially a fluid extract and a tincture.

HAZEL-GROUSE (*Bonāsa sylvestris*), a species of grouse inhabiting elevated forests in the continent of Europe and great part of Asia. It feeds on berries, buds, insects, and worms; and is very good eating.

HAZEL GROVE, with Bramhall, an urban district of England, Cheshire, 2 miles S.S.E. of Stockport. It is a centre of the cotton industry. Pop. (1931), 13,300.

HAZLITT, William, British essayist and critic, was born 10th April, 1778, and died 18th Sept., 1830. Hazlitt was educated at a school at Wem, in Shropshire, where his father was living, and in 1793 went to Hackney Theological College, with the intention of becoming a Unitarian minister. He abandoned this idea, and in 1802 decided to become a portrait-painter. He was not successful in this career. He became friendly with Lamb and Coleridge, however, and they increased his natural inclination towards literature as a profession. He married a Miss Stoddart in 1808; his domestic life was extremely unhappy, and he finally dissolved his marriage in 1822. After indulging in an infatuation for one Sarah Walker, he married a rich widow, and parted from her a year afterwards.

Towards the end of his life he became involved in money difficulties owing to the failure of his publishers. He was bitterly attacked by his political opponents, foremost amongst whom was the redoubtable Gifford. Both his attempts at marriage were failures. All these misfortunes soured his temper and shortened his life, and he died in his fifty-third year.

Hazlitt's chief works are: *An Essay on the Principles of Human Action* (1805), *A Reply to Malthus* (1806), *View of the English Stage* (1818), *Lectures on the English Comic Writers* (1819), *Characters of Shakespeare's Plays* (1817), *The Spirit of the Age* (1825), and the *Life of Napoleon Buonaparte* (1828–30).

Hazlitt was a great essayist, and possessed a beautiful and lucid style. As a critic of Shakespeare he stands extremely high. He had not Coleridge's flashes of inspiration, but he is far more reliable than Coleridge. He is nearly always sound and sensible. Some of his criticisms, which seem commonplace and orthodox to-day, were daring and original when they were first uttered. He was one of the first to emphasize what Ben Jonson had said in the poem prefixed to the First Folio:

Yet must I not give Nature all; thy Art,
My gentle Shakespeare, must enjoy a part.

His lectures on the English Comic Writers are less good; in many cases he seems to have got up his subject for the occasion and not to have meditated upon it sufficiently. *The Spirit of the Age* is one of Hazlitt's best books. It is written with great animation, and is in a beautiful style. In his *Letter to William Gifford* Hazlitt gave that malignant and ungentlemanly critic a lesson and a knock-down blow. Hazlitt's *Life of Napoleon* was a very large piece of work intended to be a counterblast to the biography by Scott. It was not a success. Hazlitt was an enthusiastic Liberal all his life, or rather he considered himself to be one. Actually he retained unchanged all the opinions he had formed as a young man, and did not move with the times. All those who did progress he considered as dishonest and traitorous. As he was also of a very sensitive disposition, it is not to be wondered at that he quarrelled with many of his friends.

In his literary tastes Hazlitt was a confirmed Tory. He liked the old writers—Shakespeare, Milton, and Fielding were among his favourites—and he only admitted Scott grudgingly to a place in his affections. He read little after he was thirty, and was always unwilling to break new ground. In his younger days he was a keen fives player and an enthusiastic supporter of the ring; he was also an ardent theatre-goer. In spite of his many misfortunes, and their warping effect on his nature, his last words were: "Well, I've had a happy life."—BIBLIOGRAPHY: A. Birrell, *William Hazlitt* (English Men of Letters Series); P. G. Patmore, *My Friends and Acquaintances*; Sir L. Stephen, *Hours in a Library*; H. Crabb Robinson, *Diary*.

HEAD, the term applied to the anterior part of the body of an animal when differentiated from the rest of the body. A gradual increase of complexity in the structure of the head is observable as we ascend from the lowest to the highest forms of life.

In the Protozoa, Infusoria, and Cœlenterates nothing that can be regarded as a head is found, and it is not till we ascend to the worms proper, the articulated animals (crustaceans, myriapods, spiders, and insects), the land and freshwater gasteropods (snails and whelks), and the cuttlefishes that a head proper is found. The cuttle-fishes have a remarkable cartilaginous box, which, like a skull, protects their anterior nervous ganglia and gives support to the muscles.

The head of the vertebrated animals presents a regular series of increasing complexity, from the lancelet upwards, and as the anterior nervous mass enlarges, and its ganglia increase in complexity, so do the anterior vertebræ change their character; as the brain becomes specialized, so does the brain-case or skull, attaining its highest development in man.

In man, and in the higher vertebrates, the head consists of an upper chamber, lodging the brain, with special compartments for the organs of smell, vision, and hearing, and a lower, lodging the first portion of the alimentary canal. In proportion as the vertebrates become developed, the brain increases in size, and its position advances anteriorly, until, in man, it comes to overhang the face. The head is the seat of intelligence and of consciousness, as it contains the brain and the organs of sense, touch being the only sense not limited to it. *See* SKULL.

HEAD, Sir Francis Bond, English colonial Governor and miscellaneous writer, born 1793, died 1875. He was present at the battle of Waterloo, being in the Royal Engineers; in 1825 he undertook the working of gold- and silver-mines in Rio de la Plata; in 1835 he became Governor of Upper Canada; and in 1838 he suppressed the Canadian insurrection, and was made a baronet. He was the author of *Bubbles from the Brunnen of Nassau*, *Rough Notes of Rapid Journeys across the Pampas*, *A Faggot of French Sticks*, and *The Horse and his Rider*.

HEADACHE is a symptom of a great number of diseases, and it may be due to any of a very wide range of causes, such as the onset of most fevers and constitutional diseases, local injuries to the head, disease of the bones of the skull, tumours and abscesses of the brain. One of the commonest causes of severe and persistent headaches is eye-strain due to some uncorrected error of refraction in the eyes. Another remarkable type of headache is migraine, in which the trouble is confined to one side of the head, and may be associated with dizziness and visual disturbances. But perhaps the commonest cause of all is disturbance of the digestive organs and especially constipation. Headache is thus a symptom of an almost unlimited series of ailments, and its rational treatment depends upon the discovery of the cause.

HEAGE, urban district of Derbyshire. It is 2½ miles from Belper and is an industrial centre. Pop. (1931). 4,054.

HEADLAM, Arthur Cayley, English prelate. Born at Whorlton, Durham, 2nd Aug., 1862, the son of a clergyman, he was educated at Winchester and Oxford. He was ordained and for some years remained in Oxford as a lecturer. In 1896 he was made rector of Welwyn, and in 1903 Principal of King's College, London, where he remained until 1918, when he was appointed Regius Professor of Divinity at Oxford. In 1923 he was made Bishop of Gloucester, having been for 20 years (1901–21) editor of *The Church Quarterly Review*. He has written extensively on theology and Church history.

HEALY, Timothy Michael, Irish politician. Born in Bantry, 17th May, 1855, he was educated by the Christian Brothers. In 1871 he went to England, and in London he worked as a clerk and then as a journalist. In 1880 he was elected M.P. for Wexford, in 1883 for Monaghan, in 1885 for Londonderry, South, in 1887 for Longford, North, in 1892 for Louth, North, and in 1910 for Cork, North-East, a seat he retained until 1918.

Healy threw himself keenly into political work, and was soon one of the most prominent members of the Nationalist Party and one of the few real orators in the House of Commons. Strongly attached to the Roman Catholic Faith, he was one of the small group who actively opposed Parnell in 1890, and in 1900, when the party was united again, he was expelled from it for his opposition to the United Irish League.

In 1922 Healy was selected as the first Governor-General of the Irish Free State, a post he held for five years. He died 26th March, 1931. Both an Irish and English barrister, Healy wrote *Letters and Leaders of My Day.*

HEALTH ACTS, PUBLIC, Acts passed in order to secure the good sanitary condition of any country or district. The first British Public Health Act was passed in 1848, and was followed by others, a comprehensive general Act being the Public Health Act (1875), which has been amended and extended since. The Acts contain provisions respecting sewers, water-supply, unsound food, contagious diseases, &c.

By the Act of 1848, the Board of Health was established, which existed until 1858, when its work was transferred to the Home Office. In 1871 the duties were taken over by the Local Government Board, which remained the principal authority for all matters concerning health until 1919. In this year an Act was passed, establishing the Ministry of Health for England and Wales, and the Board of Health for Scotland. These departments have taken over all the work and duties which were hitherto performed by the Local Government Board and the National Health Insurance Commission.

HEANOR (hē′nor), a town (urban district) of England, Derbyshire, 3½ miles north-west of Ilkeston, with ironworks, hosiery manufactures, and collieries. The mansion, Heanor Hall, is now the technical college. Pop. (1931), 22,386.

HEARNE (hērn), Thomas, an English antiquary, born 1678, died 1735. Hearne studied at Oxford, and was in 1701 appointed assistant-keeper of the Bodleian Library, and he held the post of second librarian from 1712 to 1715, but had to resign as his Jacobite principles precluded him from taking the oaths to the Government. Among his works may be mentioned: *Ductor Historicus, Reliquiæ Bodleianæ, History and Antiquities of Glastonbury,* editions of Leland, of Spelman's *Life of Alfred,* and of Fordun's *Scotichronicon.*

HEARST, William Randolph, American journalist. Born in California in 1863, his father was a rich mine owner and a senator. In 1886 young Hearst took over *The San Francisco Examiner,* which he developed on the lines of the so-called yellow press, everything sacrificed to sensation. In 1895 he obtained a paper in New York, which he called *The New York American,* and round these two he gathered others until he was the owner of a powerful group, all showing the same features. He also secured weekly and monthly papers, including several in London.

HEART, a hollow muscular organ, the function of which is to maintain the circulation of the blood, the organs of circulation being the heart, the arteries, the veins, and the capillary vessels.

The heart in men, quadrupeds, birds, and some reptiles is composed of four cavities, two *auricles* and two *ventricles.* It is enveloped in a membrane called the *pericardium,* and is situated near the centre of the cavity of the chest, between the lungs. With each beat the apex of the heart strikes against the wall of the chest in the space between the fifth and sixth ribs, a little below and to the right of the left nipple. The right auricle is the chamber that receives the blood returned from the body by the *vena cava superior* (from the head, arms, and chest), and the *vena cava inferior* (from the legs and abdomen), and from the substance of the heart itself by the *coronary vein* (or *sinus*). The blood is then passed into the right ventricle. The communication between this auricle and ventricle is closed by a valve when the ventricle contracts. The right ventricle communicates with the pulmonary artery which transmits the blood to the two lungs to be oxygenated and to get rid of its superfluous carbonic acid gas. The opening into the artery is guarded by a valve formed of three flaps. When these are brought together they interrupt the communication between the ventricle and the artery.

The blood is brought from the lungs by the pulmonary veins and poured into the left auricle. The left auricle communicates through a valved opening with the left ventricle. The left ventricle distributes the oxygenated blood to the body by means of the aorta, also provided with a valve similar to that of the pulmonary artery. The auricles and ventricle of one side are separated from those of the other by a complete muscular partition, the *septum cordis.* The valves at the openings of the arteries are called *semilunar,* that at the orifice of the right auricle *tricuspid,* that at the orifice of the left auricle *mitral*, and that at the orifice of the vena cava inferior the *Eustachian* valve.

The heart is formed of a firm thick muscular tissue, composed of interlacing fibres. The aorta gives off branches that carry the blood from the heart to all parts of the body. These arteries terminate in the capillary vessels, a series of extremely minute tubes which pass over into the veins. The veins are the channels by which the blood is brought back from the body to the right auricle of the heart. The blood which is returned from the veins is bluish in colour from excess of carbonic acid gas and deficiency in oxygen, and is called *venous*; that which leaves the left ventricle is bright red, being oxygenated, and is called *arterial*. The venous blood parts with its excess of carbonic acid and receives new supplies of oxygen in the capillary system of the lungs, flows into the pulmonary veins, thence into the left cavities of the heart, thence it passes into the aorta, and is transmitted to all parts of the body, returning to the veins by the capillary system. It is now become venous, passes through the veins from the extremities towards the heart, receiving the chyle and the lymph, and is emptied into the right cavities of that organ, which returns it through the pulmonary artery to the capillary vessels of the lungs, where it is subjected to the influence of the air, resumes the qualities of red or arterial blood, and is ready for a new course.

Circulation. The mechanism of the circulation is as follows: The blood contained in the two venæ cavæ is poured into the right auricle, which contracts, and thus forces the fluid to escape; but the venæ cavæ oppose to its backward passage the column of blood which they contain, and it must therefore pass into the right ventricle. The ventricle then contracts, and the tricuspid valve closing the passage through which the liquid entered, it is forced into the pulmonary artery, along which it must flow (return to the ventricle being prevented by the semi-lunar valve) into the capillary system of the lungs, whence it passes into the pulmonary veins, which pour it into the left auricle by four orifices. The contraction of the auricle impels it into the left ventricle, by which it is driven forward into the aorta (the mitral valve preventing its return into the auricle), and thence into the general circulation. The two auricles contract and relax simultaneously with each other, as do also the two ventricles. The relaxation is called *dia-*

stole; the contraction *systole*. The quantity of blood projected at each systole is generally estimated at 6 ounces. The causes of the alternate contraction and relaxation are entirely involuntary; but events happening elsewhere in the body can influence the heart's action either by restraining or by quickening its action. This is effected partly by the vagus nerves and the sympathetic system. The systole of the ventricles is the cause of the motion of the blood in the arteries, which dilate with each wave driven into them.

Diseases. The heart may be the seat of various and generally dangerous diseases. One of these is *pericarditis* or inflammation of the pericardium, the double lining membrane or bag enveloping the heart. The cause of this disease may be some direct infection, exposure to cold, or an injury, or it may be complicated with other diseases.

Inflammation of the inner lining is termed *endocarditis*. *Valvular* disease is a common after-result of such a disease, which is often caused by rheumatic fever, the valves becoming thickened, contracted, rigid, or otherwise affected, so that they cannot properly perform their duty. The mitral valve, for instance, may become too narrow and contracted, and the result is that all the blood does not pass into the aorta. In other cases of valvular disease, the same result follows, viz. imperfect depletion of the ventricles and auricles, the return of blood being termed *regurgitation*. The heart consequently becomes over-grown or hypertrophied as the result of the extra work thrown upon it to compensate for this defective action. In otherwise healthy subjects this compensation may be complete and satisfactory for a time, but when it fails, *dilatation* may occur, and a variety of evil effects manifest themselves in different systems of the body. In such cases the avoidance of violent exercises and emotions is necessary. The use of *digitalis* is often successful in strengthening and soothing the heart.

Certain diseases produce atrophy, in which the heart becomes feeble in action, while *fatty degeneration* occurs, when the muscular fibres are replaced by oleaginous particles. This renders the heart peculiarly liable to rupture under any strain or violent emotion, hence such should be carefully avoided by patients.

Among other organic diseases of the heart are *angina pectoris*, distinguished by a sense of strangling or suffocation in the breast. A very common symptom is *palpitation*, often caused by indigestion, and the excessive use of tea and tobacco. *Syncope* or *fainting* results from the sudden cessation of the heart's action, and may be caused by excitement, emotion, or shock of some kind. Some of the above forms of heart disease can be discovered only by auscultation or percussion; others are very evident to non-professional observers.—BIBLIOGRAPHY: R. O. Moon, *Diseases of the Heart*; J. Cowan, *Diseases of the Heart*.

HEART-WOOD, or DURA'MEN, the older central wood in the trunks of trees, distinguished from the younger or *sap-wood* by its darker colour and harder consistency. It is quite dead, and serves only to give support to the stem. Joiners prefer it on account of its greater strength and durability. It is not formed by all trees.

HEAT, a form of energy possessed by all bodies, and consisting of vibrations of the molecules, atoms, and electrons of these bodies. The most obvious physical effects produced by heat on matter are rise of temperature, change of dimensions and change of state; heat also causes changes in the elastic and magnetic properties of bodies, thermo-electric effects, change in the electrical resistance of conductors, and change of solubility of salts in their solvents.

When heat is supplied to a body, the temperature of the body will, as a rule, rise, the rise of temperature caused by a given quantity of heat depending on the thermal capacity of the body. Thus it requires about thirty times as much heat to raise the temperature of 1 lb. of water 1° as to raise the temperature of 1 lb. of mercury by the same amount.

Temperature is measured by means of thermometers constructed on various principles according to the particular heat effect which is employed. The common thermometer is that of mercury in glass, which employs the expansion of mercury to measure temperatures on the Centigrade and Fahrenheit scales (*see* THERMOMETER; PYROMETER).

Heat changes the dimensions of bodies. Increase of volume is the normal effect, although the reverse is observed in water between 0° C. and 4° C., in Iceland spar crystals in a direction perpendicular to the axis, and in certain makes of invar, a steel alloy containing 36 per cent of nickel. The expansion of articles made from fused silica is extremely small. Liquids expand more than solids, and gases show the greatest amount of expansion (*see* EXPANSION).

When heat is continuously supplied to a solid body, rise of temperature goes on until the solid reaches its melting-point, and the body gradually changes from the solid to the liquid state. During this change the temperature becomes stationary in crystalline bodies like ice; in other bodies, such as paraffin wax, the temperature rises more slowly than at first. Heat which is absorbed, during a change of state, without causing increase of temperature, is called latent heat. If the liquid continues to receive heat, its temperature rises until the boiling-point is reached. The temperature then becomes stationary, and the liquid boils until it has all been turned into vapour, latent heat being absorbed during the change from the liquid to the gaseous state.

Calorimetry. Calorimetry deals with the measurement of quantities of heat, the unit employed being the amount of heat required to raise unit mass of water through 1°. By the aid of this unit may be measured the quantities of heat which are gained or given out by a body during a change of temperature or a change of state. This leads to a knowledge of the relative capacities of different substances of heat.

The thermal capacity of a body is measured by the amount of heat required to raise the temperature of the body 1°. If we take the thermal capacity per unit of mass, i.e. per gramme, we obtain the specific heat of the substance of which the body is composed. The specific heat, or quantity of heat, required to raise unit mass through 1°, varies for different substances, having the value 1 for water at 15° C., and, in general, smaller values for other substances. For elementary substances, the product of the specific heat and the atomic weight is nearly constant, this product being called the atomic heat of the element (*see* CALORIE; CALORIMETRY).

Transmission of Heat. Heat may pass from one body to another by one or other of the processes of conduction, convection, and radiation. In the process of conduction, heat is transferred from particle to particle of a body, or from one body to another in contact with it. When heat is applied to one end of a bar of iron, it is propagated through the substance of the bar, producing a rise of temperature which is first perceptible at points near the source of heat, and afterwards at remote parts of the bar. This transmission of heat is called conduction.

Substances vary in regard to their powers of conducting heat; metals have the highest conductivity, and of these silver is the best conductor; next follow, in order of their conductivity, copper, gold, brass, zinc, tin, steel, iron, lead. Liquids, with the exception of mercury and other melted metals, are poor conductors of heat. Gases have the lowest conductivity of all bodies; this property is employed to prevent or diminish the loss of heat, as in the use of clothes and of the tea-cosy, and in the wrapping of straw round a pump in winter.

Convection of heat is brought about by the actual motion of the hot body. This is the usual process by means of which heat is distributed within liquids and gases. When heat is applied to the lower layers of a fluid, some of the particles become warmer than their neighbours, and expanding become relatively lighter and rise through the fluid, carrying heat with them. They are replaced by other colder particles, which in their turn become warm and rise through the fluid. Convection currents are thus set up within the fluid and a process of circulation is established. It is by means of convection that hot water is circulated in large buldings for heating and other purposes. All winds are due to convection currents in the atmosphere; convection is utilized in the ordinary methods of ventilation, and in the boiling of a kettle of water.

Radiation of heat. Radiation of heat consists in the propagation of heat from a hotter body to a colder one through an intervening medium which is not heated during the process. The heat is transmitted by the same medium that transmits light from a luminous body, and it is propagated at the same speed as light. Radiant heat and light are both vibrations of an elastic medium—the æther—and they obey the same laws of reflection, refraction, interference, and polarization. They also obey the general laws of wave motion.

The rays which are given out from a luminous body are in part visible and in part invisible. Those rays which are not perceptible to the eye are partly heat rays (infra-red) and partly ultra-violet. Heat rays are further distinguished from the visible and ultra-violet rays by their greater wave-length, which ranges from about a fifty-thousandth of an inch to about a three-hundredth of an inch.

The general tendency of radiation is to equalize the temperature of any system of bodies so placed as to be capable of radiating one to the other. Every body of the system is constantly sending out heat rays in all directions, and receiving the heat radiated from the other bodies. The hotter bodies emit more than they receive, whilst the colder bodies receive more than they emit, and the temperature of the system is thus gradually equalized.

The rate at which heat is emitted from the surface of a body depends on the size and nature of the surface and on its temperature. Surfaces that are good radiators are also good absorbers, and surfaces which are good reflectors are bad absorbers. The best radiating surface is one which is dull black. Some substances allow rays of heat in great part to pass through them, and are said to be diathermanous. Glass allows heat rays to pass through it to a small extent, but rock salt and sylvine (chloride of potassium) transmit about 90 per cent of the incident heat rays. A solution of iodine in bisulphide of carbon and a thin plate of ebonite are opaque to light, but are capable of transmitting heat rays.

Theories of the nature of heat. A materialistic theory of the nature of heat was held by scientists up to the beginning of the nineteenth century, the most distinguished supporters of this view being Lavoisier and Black.

The experiments of Rumford and Davy demolished this theory and substituted a dynamical theory, and between 1840 and 1843 Joule conclusively established the dynamical theory of heat by measuring the amount of energy required to produce a definite heating effect. The conclusions arrived at by him were: that the quantity of heat produced by the friction of bodies, whether solid or liquid, is always proportional to the quantity of work expended; and that the quantity of heat capable of increasing the temperature of 1 lb. of water by 1° F. requires for its evolution the expenditure of mechanical energy represented by the fall of 772 lb. through 1 foot. This amount of energy or work is called the dynamical equivalent of heat, or Joule's equivalent. Determinations made by investigators by various methods in recent times show that Joule's value is too small, and the value 778 is now taken for Joule's equivalent.

After Rumford and Davy, Fourier and Carnot acquired fame by their inquiries into the mathematical theory of heat. Fourier investigated the theory of conduction and radiation, whilst on the investigations of Carnot has been founded the science of thermodynamics (q.v.) which treats of the conversion of heat into mechanical energy and vice versa. The researches of Joule led to the enunciation of the principle of the conservation of energy (q.v.).—BIBLIOGRAPHY: C. H. Draper, *Heat and the Principles of Thermodynamics*; J. Clerk Maxwell, *Theory of Heat*; T. Preston, *Theory of Heat*; E. Edser, *Heat for Advanced Students*.

HEATH, the common name of many plants of the nat. ord. Ericaceæ. Those that belong to the genus Erica have their leaves simple and entire; their flowers oval, cylindrical, or even swollen at the base; the corolla is four-cleft; the stamens eight, terminated by anthers which are usually notched or two-awned at the summit; and the fruit dry, four or eight-celled. From 400 to 500 species are known, twelve or fifteen of which inhabit Europe, and have small flowers, whilst all the remainder are natives of South Africa (the vicinity of the Cape of Good Hope). Many of them bear brilliantly-coloured flowers. In Britain six species are enumerated, of which *E. tetralix* (cross-leaved heath) and *E. cinerea* (fine-leaved heath) are the most common, both with beautiful bell-shaped flowers.

HEATHCOAT, John, English inventor. Born at Duffield, Derbyshire, 7th Aug., 1783, he finished his apprenticeship to a blacksmith and went to Nottingham. After a short spell in business in that town he began to manufacture lace in Loughborough, and there in 1808 he invented a machine for making lace, hitherto made by hand. In 1816 his factory was destroyed by the Luddites so he transferred his business to Tiverton. From 1832 to 1859 Heathcote was M.P. for Tiverton. He died 18th Jan., 1861. His descendants, the family of Heathcoat-Amory, still carry on the business he founded.

HEATHER, or **LING** (*Calluna vulgāris*), a low shrub, ord. Ericaceæ, which covers extensive tracts of otherwise barren moorland in Western Europe, especially in the British Islands.

HEATHFIELD, George Augustus Eliott, Lord, British general, born in Roxburghshire in 1717, died 1790. He studied at the University of Leyden, and at the French military school at La Fère, and served for some time in the Prussian army. He entered the British army in 1735, was wounded at Dettingen in 1743, and in 1762 took part in the capture of Havana. In 1775 he became commander-in-chief of the forces in Ireland, and soon after Governor of Gibraltar. Spain and France having sided with America against Britain, Gibraltar was besieged by the two former powers, and successfully defended by Eliott from 1779 to 1783, the siege and defence being among the most memorable in history. The king sent Eliott the Order of the Bath, and shortly after he returned to England, and was created Baron Heathfield in 1787. There is a portrait of him by Reynolds in the National Gallery.

HEATHFIELD, village of Sussex. It is on the Cuckmere, 15 miles from Tunbridge Wells and 52½ from London, on the S. Rly. Near is Cade Street, where, in 1450 Jack Cade was killed. Pop. 3,658.

HEATING. The ancient and common method of warming houses was by the open fire built centrally on the floor. In course of time, when economical use of fuel was desired, the fire was enclosed in a brick furnace, and the hot gases of combustion were conducted in a brick flue, generally under stone flags forming the floor, which was thus warmed, and so heated the room more equally. The smoke finally escaped to the outside air, or to an upright vent. An improved form of this method, with a meandering hot-air duct and larger furnace, was the Roman hypocaust.

In the east of Europe it was the custom to have large furnaces, well built and finished with porcelain or fancy tiles. In cold weather families slept on the top of the stove. In Russia a vapour bath was obtained by heating stones in a fire, and dropping them into a vessel of water, the vapour thus generated giving a pleasing and cleansing heat. Development continued, and a furnace was devised around which was an enclosed air space, the heated air from which was conducted by tubes or ducts to various parts of the house. This cheap and simple method is not yet obsolete. A serious objection to it is that the furnace is apt to fracture, allowing carbonic acid gas to escape and make the air poisonous. Occasionally, moreover, sparks of fire get into the air ducts and through some open joint and set fire to the house. In America the fire was confined to an iron stove and the iron smoke-pipe taken up through the house to the roof—an economical but dangerous system.

In Britain heating was accomplished by open fire-places, with the smoke escaping through a slanting hole in the adjacent wall. If the wind was unfavourable, the smoke circulated and hung about the room of the Norman castle where the ladies sat at their tapestry, for ventilation as a science was not considered.

In England chimneys were first built about the time of Henry VII, the idea coming from Italy. As a novelty the architects made a feature of them in their buildings, hence the tall, ornamental, twisted spirals of chimneys seen in Elizabethan and early Jacobean architecture. In Renaissance architecture the fire-places became a prominent feature in the houses of the rich, setting a fashion which still exists for decoration about a fire-place. It is interesting to note how architecture has been affected by heating arrangements. The walls of the palaces in Rome were of fine white marble, but as smoke and vapours arose from the open joints of the floor, under which were the hot-air ducts already described, they marked the walls with streaks of black, so that architects came to adopt a scheme of dark marbles.

In the eighteenth century the fashion was introduced in this country of warming greenhouses, attached to noblemen's mansions, by means of hot air warmed by a furnace and led into a stone duct built beside the greenhouse. The escaping gases were injurious to the plants, so that the Marquis de Chabannes, a French refugee, about 1800 introduced a system of heating by large hot-water pipes, the water being heated in an iron boiler, with a supply tank open to the air connected to the pipe which joined the top of the boiler. The water circulated because the heated water, becoming expanded, was lighter than the cold water and moved upwards, cold water from the supply taking its place.

One of the first buildings to be heated in this way was the Drury Lane Theatre, where the pipe rose from the boiler to an open tank, from which a pipe dropped to a large coil on each side of the stalls, and then returned to the boiler. A coil of pipes was set above the large candelabra in the gallery to assist in rarefying the air and causing an upward current through a ventilator placed in the roof. This was an immense improvement, and shows that ventilation was now being considered.

In the seventeenth century the air of the House of Commons was allowed to escape through the flat ceiling into the upper space, and thence outside as best it could. Consequently there was no ventilation, and the atmosphere soon became foul. As a remedy an ingenious Frenchman hit on the idea of building two fire-places with chimneys, one at each end of the space above the ceiling, the heat from the fires in which induced an upward current which escaped by the chimneys and made room for fresh air from outside. The atmosphere was so much improved that he received a handsome reward.

Heating by hot water, on what is known as the low-pressure system, has now superseded the hot-air method. About 1845 A. M. Perkins, of London, had a system of using strong malleable iron pipes of about one inch bore, some of which, formed into a coil, were set in a furnace and connected to pipes of the same size distributed along the rooms to be heated. A larger tube was connected to these circulating pipes. Water was pumped in and air forced out, only a small space being

left in the expansion tube. A plug was then screwed into the end of this tube and heat applied. A rapid circulation of water ensued, and the pipes were raised to a high temperature. The system heated well, but as the high temperature of the pipes gave an unpleasant quality of heat, and the coils in the furnaces were apt to give way and cause accidents, it has become obsolete. One form of the system, however, is still used for heating bakers' ovens, a very high temperature being obtained.

Hot water with a maximum temperature of 200° F. gives the most suitable heat for dwellings and offices.

Steam heat is used for warming large spaces of factories and workshops. As the temperature in this system is higher, the air is more speedily warmed.

In heating buildings, pipes of suitable diameter are used, of cast iron or malleable iron, 3 inches or 4 inches being standard diameters. These sizes distribute the heat very evenly, but sometimes it is not desirable to use such large sizes, and small diameters are used, the heating surfaces being obtained by using radiators, which are cast-iron tubes formed to hold a minimum amount of water and give a maximum of radiation.

The water is heated in boilers made of malleable iron, formed in a saddle shape over the fire, and encased with brick-built flues. The modern type of boiler is made of cast iron, with waterway, and in sections connected by coned iron nipples. Each section is bolted to its neighbour, and when the sections are pulled tightly together, the boiler is watertight and any section can readily be replaced. As the sections each have cross tubes, a considerable part of the furnace heat is absorbed before the gases leave at the outlet. In some types the heated gases descend to an outlet at the base of the boiler. This is economical but requires a good draught in the vent or chimney.

There are several methods in use for hot-water and for steam heating. To anyone proposing to install a heating system some words of practical advice may be useful. Do not overheat the house, and, if fire-places are disused, see that ventilation by window and vent is maintained. In heating a house place a large radiator in the hall near the front door, so that its heat may diffuse through the house generally. It is also usual to warm the sitting-room, other public rooms, and certain bedrooms, but to leave the fire-places in public rooms for social gathering round the hearth at a small fire, and to warm the cold air at the windows by the radiator. This gives equable heating and ventilation.

When it is desired to heat below boiler-level or to have overhead flow and return pipes, dropping to radiators, this may be accomplished by using a small rotary pump worked by motor, and fitted on return pipe; or by the Hyflo-Gould system, which requires no pump, but has a cylinder in which the water movement of the system is accelerated by the expansion of boiling water from the boiler through a siphon and sieve, inside the cylinder, from which the flow-pipe is connected to the system. The cylinder has a vent-pipe. The system is ingenious, is not complicated, and works well.

Steam heating is used in large factories and works, in modern practice in this country. The steam is often the exhaust from the engine, and is either directed through pipes branching into the various rooms and under valve control, and finally exhausting to the air, or it may be diverted into coils of pipes with an iron casing and a centrifugal fan fitted preferably at its base: the pipes being arranged so that air forced by the fan will have the maximum heat contact with them. This air is drawn from a pure source to the fan, and a valve arrangement made so that this supply may be shut off, and the air of workshop used. The warmed air is forced from the top outlet of the casing, and circulates to a considerable radius. The waste water from the steam coil goes to a drain. Live steam up to 80 or 90 lb. per square inch may be used, and in this case the waste is returned by lifting traps to the feed tank of boiler for use. In some variations the coils form large 'batteries' of heating surface, and the air warmed by these is directed by iron ducts, fan propelled, throughout the factory. These systems are excellent, because they combine warmth and ventilation, and in summer the ducts are the means of sending cool, fresh air into the sultry workshop atmosphere. It requires proper consideration and practical experience to select the best method.

In heating by steam-pipes or radiators, it is now usual to work with a low pressure, 5 lb. or even less, because an air-pump is applied, causing a partial vacuum in the pipes, so that steam at very low pressure rapidly circulates. The waste or condensed steam is pumped back to the feed-well of boiler.

When public buildings, such as poorhouses and hospitals, are in separate blocks, it is usual to have a central source of power for heat and light, consisting of steam boilers, Cornish or Lancashire type. For heating and hot-water supply, steam from the boilers is sent through copper coils

fitted inside cylinders connected to these systems, and thereby warms the water which is pumped and circulated to the various buildings. The pipes are fitted in spacious ducts and insulated to conserve heat. Another practice is to take the steam supply in pipes via the ducts and to calorifiers, which are forms of the cylinders already described, and which are placed in the basement of each block and directly connected to the apparatus. The waste steam passes through

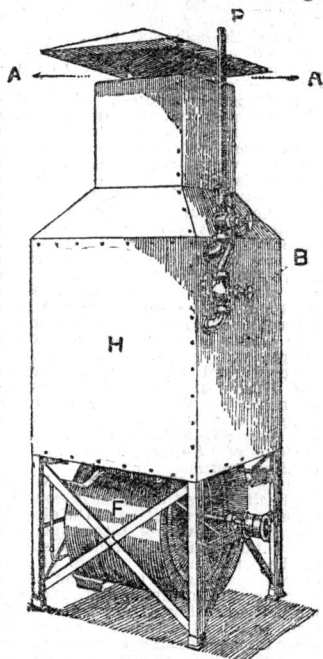

By courtesy of Messrs. J. Combe & Son, Ltd., Glasgow.
Steam Heater. High-pressure Belt-driven Type.
P, Steam inlet. B, Control valve. H, Heater casing.
F, Fan and casing. A, Hot air

steam traps, and is thence returned to the feed tank of the boilers. Some of the large housing schemes have similar systems from a central source. Each house has radiators for heating, with valve control, and also a supply of hot water. This saves fitting a separate system in each house and is economical in fuel consumption. Gas is used for cooking purposes.

In large towns central heating will help to keep the atmosphere pure, especially when the fuel in use is a proper type of coal, which has been coked. Where open fires are desired, they should be of the low-hearth type, with sides properly bevelled, so that a bright cheerful warm fire is evident.

Oil and Gas Fired Furnaces. Gas or oil can be used instead of coal or other solid fuel for heating the boiler. The use of either of these fuels has obvious advantages over coal in that storage is easier and there are no ashes to handle. If oil is used, the fuel is usually injected into the furnace through an atomizer, by means of air under pressure. Gas or oil also lends itself readily to thermostatic control.

Thermostatic Control. Many devices are now available which are so arranged that when the temperature of the room exceeds a pre-determined figure a valve controlling the heat supply is closed, whereas, if the temperature falls below this figure, more heat is supplied. These devices usually use a volatile liquid which evaporates and sets up sufficient pressure when the temperature is above the pre-determined figure. On the other hand it condenses when the temperature falls below the pre-determined figure. The excess pressure which is set up at the excess temperature provides the motive force wanted to work the valve. *See* HEATING, ELECTRIC.—BIBLIOGRAPHY: F. W. Dye, *Hot Water Supply*, and *Warming Buildings by Hot Water*; J. W. Hart, *The Principles of Hot Water Supply*; F. W. Raynes, *Heating Systems.*

HEATING, ELECTRIC. When electricity flows through any conductor a certain proportion of the electric energy is converted into heat, the amount depending upon the resistance of the wire and the square of the current passing. This action takes place in the ordinary incandescent lamp, the heating action being sufficient to raise the temperature of the lamp filament until it becomes incandescent. The proportion of energy converted into light is very small; the major portion of the energy is converted into heat, and electric heaters are manufactured employing large electric lamps of substantial proportions fitted in a frame with a reflecting back. The carbon-filament type of lamp is the most suitable for this purpose as the light efficiency is lowest. Since radiant heat can be felt directly the lamps are switched on, radiators of the luminous type are useful in all cases—such as dressing-rooms, bathrooms — where heat is desired temporarily and quickly.

Another type of electric heater employs resistance wires in sections, or elements held on thin plates or tubes of quartz or other refractory material. The wires are raised to a red-heat, and in some cases parabolic reflectors are provided, so that the heat can be directed in any desired path.

Non-luminous types of heaters employ fine wire or metal-strip elements, either bare or covered with fireproof material mounted in an ornamental case or frame. In this type the wires attain a much lower temperature than in the radiator type, and the heat is given to the cold air in the neighbourhood of the wires, raising its temperature, causing it to rise in the cold atmosphere and be replaced by cold air entering at the foot of the heater. In this way convection-currents are set up in the air and its average temperature gradually raised.

In large units the convector type of heater is provided with a fan to increase the air velocity over the heated coils. The cleanliness and ease of control are the main factors that have determined the use of electric heating, for on a question of cost it cannot compare with coal or gas.

Although electricity cannot compete with fuel for heating water in bulk, yet its convenience when dealing with small quantities has led to extensive developments in its use in such appliances as kettles, urns, and geysers, where cost of power is not the main consideration. Electric kettles are constructed with a heating element as part of the base, but an ordinary kettle of suitable make can be employed on a small heater unit, such as is used for simple cooking operations.

Electric ovens are constructed with a number of heater elements connected in sections with separate switches, so that the temperature can be regulated to suit the operations in progress. Electric irons are, perhaps, the most used of all domestic electrical appliances; in this case the heater element is fitted in a space in the base of the iron.

Electric Thermal Storage. In countries where electricity is available at very cheap rates, electric heating can be used in conjunction with what is called a "thermal storage system." In this arrangement, electric current is passed through water between electrodes in what amounts to a steel boiler. The electricity generates large quantities of heat in this boiler and sets up a considerable pressure. This heat is then available when required. The advantage of this system is that the daily variations in the requirements of heat in a large building are met by the reserves which are stored up in the thermal storage tanks, so that the power house is called upon to supply a much more steady load. Often these electric thermal accumulators are worked with 3-phase current at a considerable pressure—sometimes as much as 30,000 volts—so that transformer plant is not required. The system has been much developed in Sweden.

Ceiling Panel Warming. A system of heating usually described as "Ceiling Panel Warming" has come into use comparatively recently. In this system the room to be warmed is warmed by means of heating devices covering patches of the ceiling or walls. The heat is supplied either by means of hot water or steam or electricity. When electricity is used as the heating medium the panels, which are quite thin, are put up as part of the ceiling and covered over with a lining paper and a coat of paint or distemper. It is usually not necessary to cover the entire ceiling with warm panels. The surface required depends upon the size of the room, the amount of window space and the favourable or unfavourable situation of the room. On an average, some 20 sq. feet of panel surface are required per thousand cubic feet of space, but this figure necessarily varies a good deal depending on the actual conditions. The panels themselves are kept between 80° and 100° F. by means of electricity (or hot water or steam). This system can be used in conjunction with the thermostatic control already described so that a room heated in this way can be maintained all the year round within a degree or two of any desired temperature.

HEATON NORRIS, an urban district of England, Lancashire, forming a suburb of Stockport, with which it is connected by bridges spanning the Mersey. Near are the districts of Heaton Mersey, Heaton Chapel and Heaton Moor, in the Stockport area. Pop. 10,846.

HEB'BURN, a town (urban district) of England, North Durham, on the Tyne, above Jarrow, carrying on shipbuilding, and the manufacture of chemicals. Near is Hardcastle Crags, a pleasure resort. Pop. (1931),24,125.

HEBDEN BRIDGE, a town (urban district) of England, West Riding of Yorkshire, 7½ miles north-west of Halifax, with cotton manufactures, dyeworks, and foundries. Pop. (1931), 6,312.

HÉBÉ, in Greek mythology, the goddess of youth, and the cup-bearer to the gods, until replaced by Ganymede, a daughter of Zeus and Hera, who gave her as a wife to Heracles. In the arts she is represented with the cup in which she presents the nectar, under the figure of a charming young girl, her dress adorned with roses, and wearing a wreath of flowers. In Rome she was worshipped as Juventas, personifying the eternal youth of the city. She is represented in art as caressing an eagle.

HEBER, Reginald, English hymnwriter and bishop, was born 21st April, 1783, died 1st April, 1826. In 1800 he entered Brasenose College, Oxford, and in 1803 wrote his Newdigate prize poem on *Palestine*. After travelling on the Continent, he became, in 1807, rector of Hodnet, and having married Amelia, daughter of the Dean of St. Asaph, was appointed prebend of the cathedral.

On the death of Bishop Middleton, Heber was consecrated Bishop of Calcutta in 1823: but he had only occupied the position for about two years, when he died of apoplexy at Trichinopoli in 1826. In addition to his hymns (*Brightest and best of the sons of the morning, From Greenland's icy mountains,* &c.), the best-known productions are *Palestine,* an edition of the works of Jeremy Taylor (with Life), and *Poems and Translations.*

HÉBERT (ā-bār), **Jacques René,** notorious during the French Revolution, was born at Alençon in 1757, executed 1794. Hébert first attracted notice as editor of the violent Jacobin organ *Le Père Duchesne.* In 1792 he became a member of the municipality of Paris which contributed to the massacres of September, and he was named Attorney-General under the Commune. In 1793 the Girondists procured his arrest, but he was released by the Convention. He was one of those who established the worship of reason, and he was always on the side of savage measures. Having denounced Danton, the latter, in conjunction with Robespierre, secured his destruction by the guillotine in 1794.

HEBREW LANGUAGE AND LITERATURE, the language and literature of the Jews, Israelites, or Hebrews, especially at that period when they formed a compact nation inhabiting Canaan or Palestine. (For a sketch of the history of the people, *see* JEWS.) The Hebrew language forms a branch of the Semitic family of languages, being akin to the Aramaic (Chaldee and Syriac), Arabic, Ethiopic, and Assyrian. In the antiquity of its extant literary remains Hebrew far surpasses the other Semitic idioms, and in richness and development is only inferior to the Arabic.

The language is deficient in grammatical technicalities, especially in moods and tenses of the verb, in the absence of the neuter gender, &c. Its

Form.		Name.	Pronunciation.
	Final.		
א		Aleph	' (smooth breathing).
ב		Beth	b (bh).
ג		Gimel	g (gh).
ד		Daleth	d (dh).
ה		He	h.
ו		Waw	w, v.
ז		Zayin	z.
ח		Heth	h.
ט		Teth	t (emphatic).
י		Yod	y.
כ	ך	Kaph	k (kh).
ל		Lamed	l.
מ	ם	Mem	m.
נ	ן	Nun	n.
ס		Samekh	s.
ע		'Ayin	' (rough breathing).
פ	ף	Pe	p (ph).
צ	ץ	Sade	s (emphatic).
ק		Qoph	q (guttural k).
ר		Resh	r.
שׁשׂ		Sin, Shin	s, sh.
ת		Taw	t (th).

Form, Name, and Pronunciation of the Letters of the Hebrew Alphabet roots are triliteral (consisting of three consonants), and words are derived from them by the reduplication of the letters of the root, and by the addition of formative elements before and after the roots. The alphabet is composed of twenty-two consonants, the vowels being expressed by marks above or below these letters. The accents and marks of punctuation amount to about forty. The writing is from right to left.

There are three kinds of Hebrew alphabet now in use—the square or Assyrian (properly called the Babylonian), the most common; the rabbinical, or mediæval; and the cursive, or alphabet used in ordinary writing.

The extant classical Hebrew writings embrace a period of more than 1,000 years from the era of Moses to the date of the composition of the books of *Chronicles*, which stand last in the Hebrew Bible. During this period the written language underwent surprisingly little change. In passing from the book of *Genesis* to the books of *Samuel* we do not recognize any very striking difference in the language. Even those who assert that the *Pentateuch* as a whole is of a comparatively late era admit the great antiquity of some of its contents, which do not differ in language from the rest.

There is, indeed, to be observed a very decided difference in style and language between the earliest and the very latest Hebrew writings; but this change was sudden, hence Hebrew literature is distinguished into Pre-exilian and Post-exilian, the Babylonish captivity forming the break between the two. The writings which belong to the age subsequent to the Babylonish captivity differ very considerably from those which belong to the preceding age; the influence of the Aramaic or Chaldee language, acquired by the Jews in the land of their exile, having greatly corrupted the tongue. The historical books belonging to this age are the books of *Chronicles, Ezra, Nehemiah,* and *Esther.*

In the prophets who prophesied during and after the captivity, with the exception of Daniel, the Aramaic impress is by no means so strong as we might anticipate, they having evidently formed their style on that of the older prophets. At what time Aramaic became the dominant element in the national language it is impossible to determine, but it entirely took the place of the old Hebrew as a spoken tongue. The fragments of the popular language in the New Testament are all Aramaic; and ever since the Hebrew proper has been preserved and cultivated only as the language of the learned and of books and not of common life.

After the return from the captivity, the Jewish literature was carefully cultivated. Under Ezra the Scriptures were collected, and arranged into a canon. The *Pentateuch* was publicly read, taught in schools, and translated into Aramaic. The legal or religious traditions explanatory or complementary to the law of Moses were collected and established as the oral law. These labours resulted in the *Midrash,* a general exposition of the Old Testament, divided into the *Halacha* and the *Haggada.*

To the Maccabean era belong the *Apocrypha* (in Greek), various Greek versions of the Bible, and several collections of prayers, poems, and proverbs. To the succeeding epoch belong some celebrated doctors of the law—Hillel, Shammai, Gamaliel, and others; while the age following the destruction of Jerusalem (A.D. 70) witnessed the completion of the New Testament and the works of Josephus, written, however, in the Greek language.

On being driven from their capital by the Romans, numerous schools were established by the Jews in which their language and literature were taught. Of these schools the most celebrated were those of Babylon and Tiberias.

The *Mishna,* which contains the traditions of the Jews and interpretations of the Scriptures, is supposed to have been compiled in the latter part of the second or in the earlier part of the third century; and the rabbis of Tiberias and Babylon wrote numerous commentaries on it. These commentaries were at length collected into two separate works, the *Jerusalem* and the *Babylonian Talmuds.* The *Jerusalem Talmud* seems to have been completed about the end of the fourth century, and the *Babylonian Talmud* about a century later, under the care of Rabbi Ashe. What are called the *Targums*—that is Aramaic translations of portions of the Old Testament—belong partly to times somewhat anterior, partly to times subsequent to this period. The Jews adopted the languages of the various peoples among whom they happened to dwell, though they also wrote in classical Hebrew as well as in the less pure form of the *Rabbinical* Hebrew.

The most brilliant epoch of mediæval Hebrew literature is that of the domination of the Moors in Spain. Numerous scholars, however, continued to write in Hebrew from the thirteenth century down to the present day. Towards the end of last century, with the rise of Zionism, a new patriotic effort was made to encourage the use of Hebrew both for speaking and writing, and in Palestine

Hebrew has practically become a living language. Among living authors writing in Hebrew may be mentioned, among others, Asher Ginzburg (Akhad Haam) and the poet Bialik.—BIBLIOGRAPHY: Davidson, *Introductory Hebrew Grammar*; Wright, *Lectures on the Comparative Grammar of the Semitic Languages*; I. Abrahams, *Short History of Jewish Literature*; Graetz, *History of the Jews*; see also article in *Jewish Encyclopædia*.

HEBREWS, EPISTLE TO THE, one of the canonical books of the New Testament, the canonicity and authorship of which have been much discussed. The immediate successors of the Apostles (Clement of Rome, Justin Martyr, &c.) seem to have considered it as of canonical authority. Its canonicity was also maintained by St. Jerome, by the almost universal consent of the Latin and Greek Churches, and by Ambrose of Milan; while in A.D. 416 a decretal of Innocent III was issued in favour of this view.

Authorship. As to the authorship, the early Roman Church denied its Pauline origin. In Carthage it was (in the second century) ascribed to Barnabas, while at the same time in Alexandria it was ascribed to Paul. This view was supported by Clement of Alexandria, and Origen, the former believing that it was written by St. Paul in Hebrew, and translated into Greek by Luke. The Pauline authorship became generally accepted throughout Christendom, but in modern times the prevalent opinion is that St. Paul was not the author. The epistle was probably addressed to a Jewish section of the Roman Church, although some maintain that it was addressed to Jews of Alexandria. If the latter view be correct, Apollos, as suggested by Luther, may be the author, although tradition seems to favour the claim of Barnabas.—Cf. J. Moffatt, *Introduction to the Literature of the New Testament*.

HEB'RIDES, or WESTERN ISLANDS (the *Heboudai* of Ptolemy, and *Hebudes* of Pliny, the *r* being an erroneous insertion), a group of islands and islets off the west coast of Scotland, usually divided into the Outer Hebrides (popularly called the Long Island), of which the principal are Lewis and Harris, North Uist, Benbecula, South Uist, and Barra; and the Inner Hebrides—Skye, Mull, Islay, Jura, Coll, Rum, Tiree, Colonsay, &c. The islands within the Firth of Clyde (Arran, Bute, the Cumbraes, &c.) are not now considered as part of the Hebrides.

The Outer are separated from the Inner, and from the mainland, by a strait called the Minch, 12 miles broad. The Outer Hebrides consist of a continuous series of islands and islets, running south-west and north-east through a space of 130 miles, having Barra Head at the south extremity, and the Butt of Lewis at the north extremity. The Inner Hebrides are more widely scattered and more irregularly disposed. The Hebrides are divided between the shires of Ross, Inverness, and Argyle. They number about 520 in all, but only about 120 are inhabited; area, about 2,850 sq. miles. Pop. about 75,000.

The islands are, on the whole, mountainous, and abound in moss and moor. Although humid, the climate is mild. The soil is mostly poor, and agriculture, except in certain localities, especially Islay, is very backward. Oats and barley, with potatoes and turnips, constitute almost the entire produce of the soil. Cattle-rearing and fishing are staple industries. The land is mainly occupied by sheep-farmers, and by great numbers of crofters occupying small pieces of arable land and having often the right in common with others to a tract of rough pasture. There are also many cottars or sub-tenants, and excess of population has arisen in various localities from the minute subdivision of land. The condition of the inhabitants generally is very depressed, their dwellings miserable—the older being without chimneys or windows—and their living poor. Gaelic is the universal language, although English is tolerably well known.

History. The Hebrides were early colonized by Norwegians, and belonged to Norway from the ninth to the thirteenth century, being annexed to Scotland in 1265. In 1346 a chief of the Macdonald clan assumed the title of 'Lord of the Isles,' and he and his successors affected a sort of semi-independence, but the Hebrides were finally annexed by James V in 1540. —BIBLIOGRAPHY: R. Buchanan, *The Hebrid Isles*; C. F. Gordon-Cumming, *In the Hebrides*; W. C. Mackenzie, *History of the Outer Hebrides*.

HE'BRON (anciently **KIRJATH-ARBA** or **MAMRE,** now **EL-KHALIL**), a town in Palestine, 18 miles south by west of Jerusalem, 2,835 feet above sea-level. It lies in the narrow valley of Mamre, and was one of the three cities of refuge west of the Jordan. Its streets are narrow and dirty. A mosque, called *El-Haram*, formerly a church, erected by the Crusaders between 1167 and 1187, contains the alleged tombs of Abraham, Isaac, Jacob, Sarah, &c. Hebron is one of the oldest of existing towns. It was the residence of Abraham and the patriarchs, and at one time of David.

During the European War Hebron was occupied by British troops, under General Allenby, on 7th Dec., 1917. Pop. 16,577.

HECATÆ'US OF MILETUS, an eminent ancient Greek historian and geographer, born (probably) about 550 B.C., died about 476 B.C. He visited Egypt, Thrace, Greece, the coasts of the Euxine, Italy, Spain, and Africa. His two great works were his *Tour of the World* (the authenticity of which is, however, questioned) and his *Genealogies* or *Histories.* Only fragments of his writings are extant.

HEC'ATÊ, an ancient Greek goddess, whose powers were various. She could bestow wealth, victory, and wisdom; good luck on sailors and hunters; prosperity on youth and on the flocks. She was afterwards confounded with other divinities, such as Demêter, Artêmis, and Persephônê (Proserpine), and finally became especially an infernal goddess, and was invoked by magicians and witches. Dogs, honey, and black female lambs were offered to her at places where three roads met. She was often represented with three bodies or three heads, with serpents round her neck. Her festivals were celebrated annually at Ægina.—Cf. L. R. Farnell, *Cults of the Greek States.*

HEC'ATOMB (Gr. *hecaton,* a hundred, *bous,* an ox), in ancient Greek worship literally a sacrifice of a hundred oxen, but applied generally to the sacrifice of any large number. It was necessary that the victims should be without blemish. Only parts such as the thighs, legs, or hide were burned, the rest furnishing the festive meal at the close of the sacrifice.

HECKMONDWIKE, a town of England, county of York (West Riding), with extensive blanket, carpet, woollen cloth, and woollen yarn manufactories. Pop. (1931) 8,991.

HECLA, or **HEKLA,** a volcano of Iceland, about 20 miles from its southwest coast, about 5,095 feet in height, and having several craters. It is composed chiefly of basalt and lava, and is always covered with snow. Many eruptions are on record. One of the most tremendous occurred in 1783, after which the volcano remained quiescent till Sept., 1845, when it again became active, and continued with little intermission till Nov., 1846, to discharge ashes, some masses of pumice-stone, and a torrent of lava. The last outbreak was in 1878.

HECTOR, the son of Priam and Hecuba, the bravest of the Trojans, whose forces he commanded. His wife was Andromache. His exploits

v—o*

are celebrated in the *Iliad.* Having slain Patroclus, the friend of Achilles, the latter sought revenge, and Hector was slain by him. The body of Hector was dragged at the chariot wheels of the conqueror; but afterwards it was delivered to Priam for a ransom, who gave it a solemn burial. Hector is the most attractive warrior in Homer's *Iliad,* in which one of the finest episodes is his parting from Andromache before his last combat.

HEC'UBA, of Phrygia, in Greek legend the second wife of Priam, King of Troy, to whom she bore Hector, Paris, Cassandra, Troilus, and other children. After the fall of Troy she was given as a slave to Odysseus, and,

Hecatê, from an ancient statue

according to one form of the legend, in despair leaped into the Hellespont. There is a tragedy by Euripides entitled *Hecuba,* where a different fate is assigned to her.

HEDGE, a fence formed of living trees or shrubs. Hedges are often composed of one or more of the following: hawthorn, crab, blackthorn, holly, privet, beech, hornbeam, maple, barberry, furze, broom, alder, poplar, willow, yew, box, arborvitæ, sweet-briar, &c. Although superior to dry-stone walls, they take up much room, and exhaust the soil to some extent; but they are economical, and, if properly kept, improve from year to year in efficiency and appearance. Hedges are probably more common in England than in any other country. It has been calculated that judicious trimming of hedges would increase the cultivated land in England and Wales by 490,000 acres, an effect similar to the addition of a new county of moderate size. They were not very common in England till the close of the seventeenth century. *See* BARBED WIRE, WIRE.

HEDGEHOG (*Erinacēus europæus*), an insectivorous mammal partly

Hedgehog (*Erinacēus euræopus*)

covered with spines. By means of a special muscle it is able to roll itself up into a ball, and in this form can defy most of its enemies. It has a rudimentary tail, elongated snout, short ears, with a cranium comparatively broad. The hind-feet have five toes, and strong coarse hair covers some parts of the body. The teeth are numerous. Including the tail it attains a length of 11 inches. It usually resides in small thickets, and feeds on fruits, roots, and insects. It is fond of raw or roasted flesh, and devours cockroaches in large numbers when kept in houses. It hibernates in winter. The female bears four to six young at a birth, the young soon becoming covered with prickles. It is found in Britain and in most parts of Europe. Other species are found in Asia and Africa.

HEDGELEY MOOR, district in Northumberland. It is 8 miles from Alnwick and is famed for the battle fought there during the Wars of the Roses. On 25th April, 1464, a Lancastrian force was beaten by the Yorkists and one of their leaders, Sir Ralph Percy, was killed.

HEDGE-WARBLER, or HEDGE-SPARROW (*Accentor modulāris*), a bird of the sub-family Sylviinæ, common in Britain and all the temperate parts of Europe. It feeds on insects, worms, and seeds; its nest is generally finished early in March. The eggs, four or five in number, are bluish-green. The cuckoo often deposits her egg in its nest. The plumage is of a reddish-brown, streaked with dark-brown. The song of the male is short and plaintive. The length of the bird is about 5½ inches.

HED'IN, Sven, Swedish traveller and explorer, born in 1865. He studied at Stockholm and Upsala, also at Berlin and Halle, making himself well acquainted with natural science, especially geology. In 1885–6 he travelled in Persia and Central Asia, and in 1890–1, having been appointed secretary to the Swedish mission to the Shah of Persia, he took the opportunity of climbing and measuring the height of Demavend, and made an excursion to Kashgar.

Supported by King Oscar II, he began in 1893 a series of exploratory journeys in Central and Eastern Asia, traversing the Pamir Plateau, the region around the Lob-Nor Lake, Northern Tibet, and after many hardships finally reaching Peking, from which he returned to Europe across North China and Siberia (1897). In 1899 he entered on a similar extended course of travel, further investigating the Lob-Nor region and the connected deserts, and attempting to reach Lhasa in the guise of a pilgrim, but being turned back by the Tibetans. On his return in 1902, he was ennobled by the King of Sweden, and received various other distinctions. In 1908 he made important discoveries in the mountainous region north of the Himalayas, the 'Transhimalayan Range.' In 1931 while he was exploring in Central Asia his camp was plundered by robbers and his scientific instruments stolen.

He has produced a number of works on his travels, some translated into several languages. They include: *Through Asia* (1898); *Central Asia and Tibet* (1903); *Overland to India* (1910); *The War against Russia* (1915); *My*

Hedge-warbler, or Hedge-sparrow

Life as an Explorer (1926); *Jehol, City of Emperors* (1931); and *Lob-nov, the Wandering Lake* (1931). During the European War Sven Hedin repeatedly attacked the British in his writings, and expressed his admiration of Germany. At the request of the Kaiser he visited Belgium in 1917 to investigate the destruction caused there by the war. He abandoned the honour of K.C.I.E., which he had received in 1909, in order to anticipate his expulsion.

HEDINGHAM, name of two villages in Essex, Castle Hedingham and Sible Hedingham. Castle Hedingham is famed for its castle, the seat of the great family of De Vere. The keep remains. Pop. 900.

Sible Hedingham, 60 miles from London, has also a fine old church. It dates from the 14th century and has associations with the family of Hawkwood. Pop. 1,750.

HEDNESFORD, market town of Staffordshire. It is 123½ miles from London by the L.M.S. Rly., and is 10 miles from Walsall. There are tile works and collieries. Pop. 5,768.

HEDON, borough of Yorkshire (E.R.). It stands near the Humber, 5¼ miles from Hull, and is served by the L.N.E. Rly. At one time Hedon was a flourishing port. It is still a chartered town. Pop. (1931) 1,509.

HEDONISM (Gr. *hēdonē*, pleasure) is the philosophical theory that pleasure is the highest human good, and that every man's goal is his own happiness and pleasure. This is called ethical hedonism to be distinguished from psychological hedonism, according to which theory pleasure is the only end that can be pursued. The Cyrenaics, Epicurus, and even Hobbes and Locke, were hedonists, teaching that pleasure was the supreme end for the individual. Universalistic hedonism is the theory that not the individual's greatest pleasure, but the good of the community, is the supreme end of moral action. *See* UTILITARIANISM.—Cf. J. Watson, *Hedonistic Theories from Aristippus to Spencer.*

HEEM (hām), **Jan Davidsz de,** Dutch painter of fruits, flowers, and still life, born in Utrecht in 1600, died in Antwerp in 1683 or 1684. He studied under his father, David de Heem, also well known as a painter of still life, and soon obtained large sums for his pictures, which are characterized by great delicacy and attention to detail and richness of colour. He is the chief master, and in some respects the inventor, of a highly-elaborate phase of still-life painting in the Netherlands, well represented in the Wallace Collection. His son, *Cornelius de Heem* (born 1630) imitated him, but is inferior to him.

HEEMSKERK (hāmz'kerk), **Martin,** or **Van Veen,** Dutch painter, born in 1498, studied in Haarlem and Rome, and settled in Haarlem, where he died in 1574. His earlier paintings are marked by the realism of the earlier Dutch painters; his later show an increasing amount of mannerism due to imitation of Michael Angelo and the antique. He was a popular painter, producing a number of pictures for public buildings, and was also an etcher and designer for wood-carving and glass-painting.

Among his works are: *St. Luke Painting the Madonna,* an *Ecce Homo, The Crown of Thorns,* and *The Criticism of Momus.* His *Last Judgment* is in the palace of Hampton Court.

HEGEL (hā'gl), **Georg Wilhelm Friedrich,** a celebrated German metaphysician, born at Stuttgart 1770, died 1831. He studied at the theological institute of Tübingen from 1788 to 1793, and was next a private tutor at Berne (1793–6), and subsequently at Frankfort-on-the-Main (1797–1800). Having removed to Jena, and contracted an intimacy with Schelling, he devoted himself to metaphysical study. After the battle of Jena, Hegel was employed on a newspaper at Bamberg until 1808, when he became successively rector of Nürnberg Gymnasium, professor of philosophy at Heidelberg (1816), and at Berlin from 1818 to his decease in 1831.

Works. Among his works the most important are his *Phänomenologie des Geistes* (1807), *Wissenschaft der Logik* (1812–6), *Encyclopädie der philosophischen Wissenschaften* (1817), and *Grundlinien der Philosophie des Rechts oder Naturrecht und Staatswissenschaft* (1821).

Philosophy. The philosophy of Hegel followed that of Schelling, in adopting as a presupposition the identity of Knowing and Being, of Thought and Reality, of Subjective and Objective. But he differs from Schelling, who contemplates this identity with its inner opposites through the medium of a purely intellectual intuition, for Hegel seems rather to revert to Kant's Transcendental Logic. He thus asserts that if the order and connection of our thoughts are involved in the order and connection of things, the universal form in the course of objective action must exactly agree with the form of the development of our thoughts, and vice versa. As there are, according to him, three stages in the process of thought and existence, his system has necessarily a threefold division: logic, the philosophy of nature, and mental philosophy. Hegelianism is divided into three camps, representing respectively the supernatural, the rational, and the mystical.

Hegel's philosophy has influenced British and American thought. In England the Hegelian system was expounded by E. Caird and T. H. Green. In Prussia and Germany, however, Hegelianism was influential in the domains of politics and sociology more than in any other department. The theory of might is right, as explained in Hegel's *Philosophy of Right*, found many adherents among the philosopher's own countrymen.—BIBLIOGRAPHY: R. R. Haym, *Hegel und seine Zeit*; Kuno Fischer, *Hegels Leben und Werke*; E. Caird, *Hegel*; Millicent Mackenzie, *Hegel's Educational Theory and Practice*; J. H. Stirling, *The Secret of Hegel*; A. Seth Pringle-Pattison, *Hegelianism and Personality*.

HEIBERG (hī'berh), **Peter Andreas**, Danish satirist and dramatist, born 1758, died 1841. His satiric attacks were so severe and general that he had to leave his native country, and spent great part of his life in Paris.

Heidelburg.—The bridge over the Neckar

He aimed at giving Denmark a truly national comic drama, a task which was attempted with more success by his son, Johan Ludvig (1791–1860), who was a prolific and successful dramatist, and wrote also on philosophy and æsthetics. Among his works are: *The Theatre for Marionettes, A Soul After Death*, and *The Newly Wedded*.

HEIDELBERG (hī'dl-berh), a town of Baden, beautifully situated on the left bank of the Neckar, here crossed by two bridges, in one of the loveliest districts of Germany. It stands on a narrow strip between the river and the Castle-rock and Geisberg, spurs of the Königstuhl (1,850 feet); and chiefly consists of one main street and less important cross and parallel streets.

The principal buildings are: the church of St. Peter, the church of the Holy Ghost; the town house; the castle, anciently the residence of the Electors Palatine; the university, founded in 1386, and now possessed of a library of 500,000 volumes, and an observatory. It was attended in 1931 by 3,701 students. One block, the gift of some Americans, was opened in 1931. The castle, begun in the end of the thirteenth century, and exhibiting elaborate examples of early and late Renaissance architecture, is the most remarkable edifice in Heidelberg. Is is now an ivy-clad ruin, but is carefully preserved from further decay.

The principal industry is brewing. One of the greatest curiosities of the place is the Heidelberg tun, kept in a cellar under the castle. It is 36 feet in length, 26 feet in diameter, and capable of holding 800 hogsheads. Heidelberg is rich in public walks and fine views, that from the Königstuhl being of surpassing beauty. It was long the capital of the Palatinate, but was superseded by Mannheim in 1720. In 1622 Tilly captured and sacked the city. A similar fate overtook it in 1689 and 1693 at the hands of the French. Pop. (1925), 78,196.

HEIDELBERG CATECHISM, a catechism of the Reformation, drawn up by Zacharias Ursinus, in 1563, at the bidding of Frederick III, Elector of the Palatinate. Approved by the Synod of Dort in 1619, it served as the model on which the Westminster Assembly framed the *Shorter Catechism.*

HEIDELBERG JAW, a jawbone of an early type of man. It was found near Heidelberg in 1907.

HEIDENHEIM (hī'dīn-hīm, a town of Württemberg, 46 miles E.S.E. of Stuttgart. It has manufactures of woollen and linen cloth. Pop. (1925), 19,363.

HEIGHTS, MEASUREMENT OF, or HYPSOMETRY, is that department of geodesy which treats of the measurement of the absolute or relative heights of various points on the earth's surface. Trigonometrical methods may be employed, or the result may be obtained by levelling, by the use of the barometer, or by the boiling-point of water as given by the thermometer.

The trigonometrical method is often the only one available, as the height to be measured may be quite inaccessible.

The barometric method is based on the fact that as the mercurial column is supported by the atmospheric pressure, it must fall when conveyed from a lower to a higher level, as in the latter case the pressure is diminished. Were the atmosphere uniform in density throughout, nothing could be simpler than the measurement of heights by the barometer, but gases being very compressible, the lower strata of the atmosphere are denser than the upper strata, being exposed to greater pressure. Thus a column of air 100 feet high has far greater weight at the sea-level than a similar column at the top of a mountain 4,000 feet high; and the effect on the barometric column of rising 100 feet from sea-level is correspondingly greater than the effect of rising 100 feet from a height of 4,000 feet above the level of the sea. Moreover, increase of temperature affects the density of the mercury in the barometer, and also that of the air, and further complicates the problem. A rule which serves for rough purposes is to multiply the difference of the logs of the barometric heights by 60,000; this gives the difference of levels of the two stations, in feet.

With the help of tables of vapour pressure the barometric pressure can be deduced from observation of the boiling-point of water; the height of the station can then be calculated. For moderate heights, the boiling-point is lowered $1°$ F. for about every 600 feet of ascent. These barometric and boiling-point methods are not used now in accurate work, the uncertainties due to weather changes being too great. For modern methods, see LEVELLING ; SURVEYING.

HEILBRONN, a town of Württemberg, beautifully situated on the Neckar, quite a mediæval place in the older parts, but having modern suburbs. Its finest edifice is the old Gothic church of St. Kilian. It has flourishing industries. Heilbronn was long an imperial free town, and came into the possession of Württemberg in 1802. Pop. (1925) 45,520.

HEILUNGCHIANG, a province of Manchuria; area, 203,000 sq. miles; pop. 2,500,000.

HEIMDALL, a divinity in the Scandinavian mythology, who keeps watch on the bridge Bifröst, which connects the domain of the Æsir or Gods with that of men.

HEINE (hī'nĕ), **Heinrich**, a German poet and author, was born of Jewish parents at Düsseldorf 13th Dec., 1797, and died at Paris 17th Feb., 1856. He studied law at Bonn, Berlin, and Göttingen; took his degree at the last-mentioned place, and in 1825 embraced Christianity. He afterwards lived at Hamburg, Berlin, and Munich, but in 1830 he settled in Paris, supported himself by his literary labours, and dwelt there until his death. From 1837 to the overthrow of Louis Philippe in 1848 he enjoyed a pension of 4,800 francs from the French Government. **Works.** Of the numerous literary works of Heine may be mentioned in particular: *Gedichte* (Poems), *Reise-bilder* (Pictures of Travel), *Buch der Lieder* (Book of Songs), *Deutschland*, *Ein Wintermärchen* (Germany, a Winter Tale), *Shakespeares Mädchen und Frauen* (Maidens and Wives), *Die Romantische Schule*, *Letzte Gedichte und Gedanken* (Last Poems and Thoughts), *Atta Troll*, and *Romanzero*. —BIBLIOGRAPHY: M. Arnold, *Essays in Criticism*; G. Brandes, *H. Heine*; G. Karpeles, *Heine und seine Zeitgenossen*; H. Lichtenberger, *H. Heine*, *penseur*; W. Stigand, *Life, Works, and Opinions of Heinrich Heine*; W. Sharp, *Life of H. Heine*.

HEINEC'CIUS, **Johann Gottlieb**, a German writer on logic, jurisprudence, and ethics, born 1681, died 1741. His works on Roman law were once highly valued.

HEINSIUS, Daniel, Dutch scholar, poet, and critic, born 1580, died 1655. He studied at Franeker and Leyden, at the latter under Joseph Scaliger; became professor of history and politics at Leyden in 1605, and librarian and secretary in 1607. He published editions of Hesiod, Horace, Virgil, and other classical writings, and wrote Latin and Greek poems (*Iambi, Elegiæ, Poemata*, &c.).

HEIRLOOM, in English law, means some personal chattel which descends by special custom with land. The term is often loosely applied to the case where certain chattels, such as pictures, &c., are directed by will or settled upon trusts to follow along with some mansion or estate. By the Settled Land Act, 1925, a tenant for life of settled land may sell such chattels on certain conditions despite the trusts.

HEJAZ, a kingdom of Arabia, stretching along the Red Sea from south of 'Aqaba to Hali Point. All the inland boundaries are uncertain, but it borders on Syria in the north, Nejd and the Arabian Desert in the east, and Asir in the south. The area is estimated at 1,150,000 sq. miles, and the population at 500,000. The whole country is barren or semi-barren, though a little wheat and barley and a considerable amount of dates are produced in the south. Dates are the chief product but are all consumed locally, and the exports, which are of little value, are hides, wools, and gum. The country, by virtue of its possession of Mecca and Medina, the Holy Places of Islam, is the most important in Arabia. Mecca (pop. 130,000) is the capital, Taif the summer capital, and Jedda (pop. 40,000) the principal seaport.

It was formerly a Turkish vilayet, and the Hejaz Railway (completed in 1908), connecting Aleppo and Damascus to Medina, enabled the Turks to maintain garrisons throughout the country. In spite of this, however, the Grand Sherif or Emir of Mecca wielded great influence throughout the whole Moslem world, and thus, when the European War broke out and the Turks joined Germany, the Sherif Husein Ibn Ali, who had been promised autonomy by Britain in the event of a successful revolt, declared the independence of his country in 1916. He was then proclaimed King of the Hejaz, and by the Treaties of Sèvres and Lausanne the Hejaz was recognized as an independent state.

In 1917 Husein assumed the title of King of Arabia, though this was deeply resented by the other Arabian states and was not recognized by Britain. For several years Britain paid Husein a monthly subsidy, but this was ultimately discontinued.

In 1924 the Wahabis, a tribe inhabiting the neighbouring Emirate of Nejd and Hasa, invaded the Hejaz and overran the country. Husein, owing to the inability of his Government to protect the Holy Places, was forced to abdicate, and his eldest son the Sherif Ali, Emir of Medina, succeeded him. Before negotiations for peace could be arranged, Mecca fell and Jedda was invested. To understand the situation it is necessary to note that the people of Hejaz are Hashimites, the descendants of the prophet's own tribe, while the Wahabis are a wild, war-like race, who hold the rigorous, austere creeds of early Islam, deprecating luxuries and pilgrimages to Holy Places. In Dec., 1925, Ali abdicated and fled to Baghdad. On the same day the Wahabis under Ibn Sa'ud entered Jedda, and in Jan., 1926, Ibn Sa'ud was proclaimed King of the Hejaz. (See NEJD.) Ibn Sa'ud's independence was recognized by Britain in a treaty signed in May, 1927. Ma'an vilayet was added to Transjordan in 1925. In 1932 the kingdom of Hejaz and Nejd changed its name to the kingdom of Savdi Arabia or Savdieh.— Cf. H. St. J. B. Philby, *The Heart of Arabia.*

HEJRA, HEJIRA, or **HEGIRA** (Ar. *Hijra*), a word signifying emigration, flight, from *hajara*, to go away. The Mahommedans designate by it the flight of Mahommed their prophet from Mecca to Medina. From this flight, which happened on the 13th of Sept., A.D. 622, but which they fix on the 16th of July of the same year, they begin their computation of time.

HELDER, THE, a fortified seaport of the Netherlands, in the most northern part of the province of North Holland, opposite the Island of Texel, and commanding the entrance to the Zuider-Zee. From a fishing-town Napoleon converted it, in 1811, to a fortress and naval station of the first rank, and called it his Northern Gibraltar. Being much exposed, the port and coasts are protected by gigantic dikes, one 6 miles long and built entirely of Norwegian granite. Pop. (1932), 31,112.

HELEN, or **HEL'ENA,** in ancient Greek legend, the most beautiful woman of her age, daughter of Zeus by Leda. By advice of Ulysses her numerous suitors were bound by oath to respect her choice of a husband, and to maintain it even by arms. She chose Menelaus, but was afterwards carried off to Troy by Paris, the Trojan War arising from the claim made by Menelaus for the fulfilment of the oath.

HEL'ENA, the name of several saints, of whom the chief was the mother of the Emperor Constantine the Great, a woman of humble origin, and a native either of Bithynia or of Britain. She became the wife of Constantius Chlorus, who, however, was compelled to repudiate her when made Cæsar by Diocletian in A.D. 292. At the same time he made her son his sole heir, and Constantine, on his accession, took her to reside with him at the palace, and gave her the title of Augusta. She did much for the advancement of religion, and is said to have discovered the *true cross,* in honour of which she founded the Church of the Holy Sepulchre at Jerusalem. She died shortly after at the age of eighty, in A.D. 328 or 326.

HELENA, the capital of Montana, United States, on the west side of the valley of Prickly Pear and Ten Mile Creeks, at the foot of the Rocky Mountains, 15 miles w. of Missouri River, and 110 miles N. of Virginia City. It is chiefly supported by the rich quartz and (placer) gold-mines. In the vicinity are hot medicinal springs. Pop. (1930), 11,803.

HELENSBURGH, a town of Scotland, in Dumbartonshire, prettily situated at the entrance of the Gare Loch, on the north shore of the Firth of Clyde, opposite Greenock, from which it is distant about 4 miles. It is chiefly a residential town and summer resort for Glasgow and neighbouring towns. It takes its name from Helen, wife of Sir James Colquhoun, by whom it was founded in 1777. Henry Bell, the pioneer of steam navigation, died at Helensburgh in 1830, and there is a monument to him on the esplanade. Pop. (1931), 8,893.

HEL'ENUS, a Trojan soothsayer, son of Priam and Hecuba, twin-brother of Cassandra, and husband of Andromache after Hector's death. He foretold the destiny of Æneas, and welcomed the latter in Epirus, where he ruled after the death of Neoptolemus.

HELI'ACAL rising and setting, in astronomy, terms used with reference to the beginning and ending of the period during which a star (or planet) is lost to view by reason of the sun's proximity in right ascension. The heliacal setting occurs when the sun approaches so near as to terminate the season of the star's visibility in the evenings. The heliacal rising is when the star just re-emerges into view, and can be seen in the morning sky before the sun rises.

HELIAN'THUS, a genus of Compositæ, chiefly North American annual or perennial herbs, with rough leaves and large yellow flowers, of which the common sunflower (*H. annuus*) and the *H. tuberōsus* (the Jerusalem artichoke) are examples.

HEL'ICON (now **SAGARA**), a mountain range of Greece, in the west of Bœotia, in some sense a continuation of the range of Parnassus. It was the favourite seat of the Muses, who, with Apollo, had temples here. In it also were the fountains of Aganippe and Hippocrene. The highest summit, now called *Paleovuni*, is barely 5,000 feet high.

HELIGOLAND (Ger. *Helgoland*, Holy Land), an island belonging to Germany, in the North Sea, about 40 miles from the mouth of the Elbe; 1¼ miles long and ½ mile broad; highest point, 200 feet. Its rocks, of reddish sandstone, present a perpendicular face to the sea, and are protected against erosion by sea-walls. Before fortification it produced some cereals and vegetables, but oysters and lobsters were the staple products, and it had a town of some 400 houses (Pop. 3,400) celebrated for its sea-bathing. On account of the small amount of vegetation, Heligoland was visited in summer by many sufferers from hay fever. The inhabitants were of Frisian descent, and mainly fishers, pilots, and boarding-house keepers.

Heligoland was captured by Britain from Denmark in 1807, and ceded to Germany in 1890, in return for Germany's recognition of the supremacy of British interests in Zanzibar. It became an important strategic point and was strongly fortified by Germany, but in accordance with the Treaty of Versailles (1919) the fortress was dismantled. The naval battle of Heligoland between the Germans and the British, under Admiral Beatty, was fought on 28th Aug., 1914.

HELIODO'RUS, of Emesa in Syria, a Greek romance writer. According to his own account, his father was named Theodosius, and was an hereditary priest of the sun. He himself was probably a sophist of the latter half of the third century A.D. According to the ecclesiastical historian Socrates, however, he is to be identified with a certain Bishop of Tricca, in Thessaly (*c*. A.D. 300). There is a legend that he was told by his metropolitan that he must either resign his bishopric or destroy his novel, and that he chose the former alternative. This is probably too good to be true.

The romance of Heliodorus is known as the *Æthiopica*, because its opening and closing scenes are laid in Æthiopia; it is also called *The Loves of Theagenes and Chariclea*. It is written in ten books, in a poetical kind of prose. It is by far the best extant Greek romance, and offends less against good taste and decency than the works of Achilles Tatius and Longus. It had a considerable influence upon the writings of later authors, such as Tasso and Cervantes. Its plot is well managed, its characters are well drawn, and it abounds in pleasant descriptions of scenery, and vivid portrayal of manners and customs. There is a famous Elizabethan translation of the *Æthiopica*, by T. Underdowne, published in 1587. It has been reprinted in the 'Tudor' series, with an introduction by C. Whibley (1895).

HELIOGAB'ALUS, or **ELAGABALUS**, a Roman emperor, son of Sextus Varius Marcellus, born about A.D. 205, and originally called *Varius Avitus Bassianus*. He received his name from having been, while still a child, priest of Elagabalus, the Syro-Phœnician sun-god. After the death of Macrinus he was invested, at the age of fourteen, with the imperial purple, but his licentiousness soon displeased the populace, and he was slain in an insurrection of the prætorians, A.D. 222, after a reign of less than four years.

HE'LIOGRAPH, a name given to various contrivances for reflecting the sun's light either temporarily or continuously to an observer at a distance. The simplest heliograph is a mirror hung up at a distant station so as to reflect a flash to the observer, whose station may be many miles from it. This mirror is generally so adjusted that the flash occurs exactly at some pre-arranged hour, and by being in readiness the observer can get an observation with precision as regards time. Some heliographs are visible for 80 miles. By being fitted with an adjustment of clock-work, the mirror can be made to revolve with the sun, and so to reflect a beam of sunlight steadily in one direction, being then called also *heliotrope*. The principal use of the heliograph is for signalling in war.

HELIOM'ETER, an instrument for measuring small distances on the sky. It was originally used for measurements on the sun's disc, hence the name. It was invented by Bouguer in 1747, and improved by Dollond and Fraunhofer. In the common modern form the object-glass of the telescope is cut into two halves, relatively movable by a screw. Each half forms a perfect image in the focus of the eyepiece, and by varying the distance between the half-lenses the images may be made to diverge from, or approach, each other. If, in contemplating a celestial body which presents a real disc of circular form, the object-glasses are placed so as to bring the images to touch each other externally, the distance of the centres of the object-glasses forms a measure of the angular diameter of the image.

HELIOP'OLIS (City of the Sun), the On, Rameses, or Beth-shemesh of the Hebrew Scriptures; now called Matarieh; situated a little north of Memphis. It was a centre of sun-worship at an early period in Egyptian history. The chief symbol of Ra, the sun-god, was a pyramidal stone in his temple. During the Fourth Dynasty the priesthood was of increasing influence. The Fifth Dynasty begins with the Ra high priest as Pharaoh, the first of a solar line of kings, and the Ptah priest of Memphis as Vizier. The legend was thereafter, until the time of Alexander the Great and later, insisted on that the Pharaoh was the physical son of the sun-god.

Although Heliopolis suffered decline as a political centre after the rise of Thebes, it continued to be a centre of learning; both Eudoxus and Plato visited its famous schools. Moses was educated at On. Here Joseph and Mary are said to have rested with the infant Christ. Near the village stands the Pillar of On, 67½ feet high, and 6 feet broad at its base. Cleopatra's Needle on the Thames Embankment, London, stood in front of the great Ra temple of the ancient city before being removed in Greek times to Alexandria. The Turks were defeated here by the French in 1800.

HELIOPOLIS, in Cœlesyria. *See* BAALBEK.

HE'LIOS, the god of the sun (Lat. *Sol*) in the Greek mythology; son of the Titan Hyperion and Theia, or Euryphæssa, and brother of Eos (Aurora, the dawn) and Selēnē (Luna, the moon). He dwells with Eos in the ocean behind Colchis, from which he issues in the morning, and to which he returns at night. His worship was extensively diffused, and he had temples in Corinth, Argos, Trœzene, Elis, but particularly in Rhodes, the Colossus of which was a representation of Helios.

HE'LIOSTAT, a contrivance used in solar observation, whereby the telescope through which the observer looks can be kept fixed in one position, while the light from the sun is fed into it by apparatus arranged to move in such a manner as to follow the sun in the course of its diurnal motion due to the earth's rotation. In one form of the instrument a mirror is connected to an axis directed to the pole of the heavens, and caused to revolve from east to west at the rate of 360° in twenty-four hours. The mirror is so placed that a normal to its surface bisects the angle between the pole and the sun; thus it reflects a ray from the sun's centre in a constant direction, parallel to the earth's axis. By an additional mirror the ray may be reflected in a horizontal or any desired direction. The heliostat is largely used in connection with spectroscopic work, for eclipse observations, or with the great horizontal telescopes.

HE'LIOTROPE, a genus of plants (Heliotropium), nat. ord. Boraginaceæ. The species are herbs or undershrubs, mostly natives of the warmer parts of the world, and have alternate leaves and small flowers usually disposed in scorpioid cymes. *H. europæum*, the common heliotrope, is indigenous in the south and west of Europe, and has small white or pale-red flowers with a fruit of four drupes under a thin fleshy covering. The *H. peruvianum* is a very fragrant garden plant, growing to about 2 feet in height and bearing small lilac-blue flowers.

HELIOTROPE, the bloodstone, a variety of quartz, partaking of the character of jasper or of chalcedony. It is of a deep-green colour, and covered with red spots. It is hard, and is used for burnishers; the more finely-marked stones are prized for seals, and signet-rings.

It is found in Tartary, Persia, Siberia; in the Island of Rum, Scotland, and elsewhere. It received the name heliotrope, or elitropia, because it was said that if the mineral were put into water in a basin rubbed with the juice of the plant heliotrope, and were exposed to the sun, the water would appear red and the sun blood-like, as if it was eclipsed. The stone rubbed with the juice of the plant was said to render its wearer invisible.

HELIOTROPISM, or PHOTOTRO-PISM, the curvature of a growing plant-organ in response to the stimulus of light. Most stems bend towards the brightest light (*positive* *heliotropism*), whereas leaves generally place themselves at right angles to the most intense illumination (*transverse heliotropism* or *diaheliotropism*); this behaviour on the part of stems and leaves tends to bring the foliage into the position most favourable for photosynthesis and transpiration. Similarly, primary roots, being *negatively heliotropic* as well as positively geotropic, push straight down into the soil, which is their proper medium. *See* GEOTROPISM; IRRITABILITY OF PLANTS.

HELIUM (from Gr. *Hēlios*, the sun), a chemical element, symbol He, originally discovered by Rayleigh and Ramsay in the chromosphere of the sun by means of the spectroscope. Ramsay afterwards discovered the element in the gases given off when certain minerals such as cleveite, monazite, pitch-blende, &c., are heated. It is contained in minute quantity in the atmosphere, and in larger quantity in American natural gas. From this source Ramsay, in 1915, showed it possible to isolate considerable quantities. Helium is a colourless gas which liquefies at $-268 \cdot 8°$ C.; it is non-inflammable, and next to hydrogen is the lightest gas known. The $\propto$ -particles expelled from radium are atoms of helium which have lost two electrons.

After it was found possible to isolate the gas in quantity, Ramsay proposed its use in air-craft, as its lifting power is almost as great as that of hydrogen, and it has the advantage over the latter in being non-inflammable. It was produced in considerable quantities in Canada during the European War, for this purpose. Helium is very valuable as a thermometric substance in high-class gas thermometry, for it has practically no chemical affinity, it is monatomic, and possesses an extremely low liquefaction point. It is now coming into general use for work at low temperatures, but at high temperatures it, like hydrogen, readily diffuses through quartz and glass.

HELIX, (1) a spiral line shaped like a spiral spring with a straight axis. The line is formed by the edge of an inclined plane, which is wrapped round a circular cylinder so that the base of the inclined plane lies always in the end plane of the cylinder.

(2) In architecture, a small volute or twist under the abacus of the Corinthian capital, of which in every perfect capital there are sixteen, two at each angle, and two meeting under the middle of each face of the abacus.

HELL. *See* IMMORTALITY.

HELLADOTHE′RIUM, an extinct genus of ungulate quadrupeds allied to the existing giraffe. Fossil remains occur in the Upper Miocene rocks of Attica and Northern India.

HELLAS, or HELLENES. *See* GREECE.

HEL′LEBORE (Hellebŏrus), a genus of plants, nat. ord. Ranunculaceæ, consisting of perennial low-growing plants with palmate or pedate leathery leaves, yellowish, greenish, or white flowers, having five conspicuous persistent sepals, eight to ten small tubular petals, and several many-seeded carpels. *H. orientālis* is the species which produced the black hellebore of the ancients, considered by them to be the best of all cures for madness (Horace, *Satires*, ii, 3, 80, *Ars Poetica*, 300). Anticyra in Phocis was famous for its hellebore, hence *naviga Anticyram* (sail to Anticyra) was a polite way of indicating mental alienation in the person addressed.

H. niger, the Christmas-rose common in gardens, is a native of South and East Europe. and is the source of the black hellebore of modern pharmacopœias. *H. viridis* and *H. fœtidus* are herbaceous plants with green flowers, and grow in Britain; their leaves are emetic and purgative. The whole of these plants are accounted purgative, and in large doses act as a narcotic acrid poison; but they are now little used in medicine. *Veratrum album*, ord. Liliaceæ, a very different plant, is known as white hellebore. It is extremely acrid, and in the form of powder is used to destroy caterpillars and household vermin.

HELLEN, in Greek mythology, son of Deucalion and Pyrrha, and founder by his three sons, Dorus, Æolus, and Xuthus, of the four great branches of the Greek people or Hellenes.

HELLENISTS, a name for those Jews who, especially in Egypt after the time of Alexander the Great, became imbued with Greek culture and civilization, and spoke and wrote in Greek. To them was due the formation of the peculiar dialect termed the *Hellenistic* dialect of Greek, the special feature of which was its use of foreign, and more particularly of Hebrew and Aramaic words and idioms. The most noted of the Jewish Hellenistic philosophers was Philo of Alexandria, and the chief of the learned labours of the Alexandrian Jews was the *Septuagint* version of the Old Testament.

HELLESPONT. *See* DARDANELLES.

HELLEVOETSLUIS (hel′vụt-slois), a fortified seaport of the Netherlands, province of South Holland, 18 miles south-west of Rotterdam, on the Haringvliet, the largest mouth of the Rhine. William III embarked here for England in 1688. Pop. 4,355.

HELMET, an article of armour for the protection of the head, composed of leather or of metals. Some of Homer's heroes are represented as wearing brazen helmets, with towering crests. Among the Romans the *cassis* was a metallic helmet; the *galea*, a leathern one. The earlier Greek and Roman helmets did not protect the face.

During the Middle Ages helmets were made of steel, frequently inlaid with gold, and provided with bars and flaps to cover the face in battle and to allow of being opened at other times. The full-barred helmet entirely covered the head, face, and neck, having in front perforations for the admission of air, and slits through which the wearer might see the objects around him. The open helmet covered only the head, ears, and neck, leaving the face

Gas Helmets, worn by combatants in the European War as a protection against gas attacks, were fabric helmets or facepieces (masks) with attached respirators, through which filtered air was breathed. Charcoal mixed with other substances was the usual filtering medium. For protection against a particular irritant "gas" (really a very finely divided solid) pads of cellulose were sometimes added. In the British type the respirator was carried in a haversack and attached to the mask by a rubber tube.

HELMET-SHELL, the common name of sea-snails belonging to the genus, Cassis, the type of a special family (Cassididæ). Most of the species are inhabitants of tropical shores, but a few are found on the coast of the

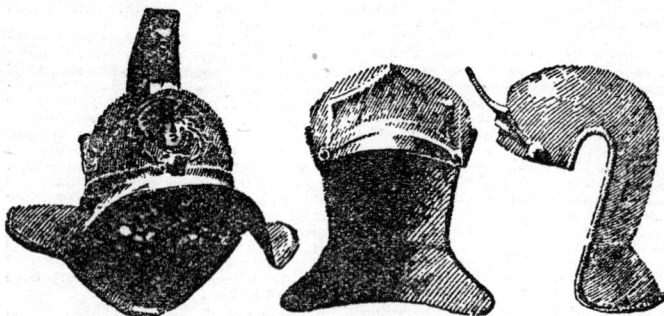

Roman Helmets. The helmet on the left has a perforated visor and ridge on the top to which a crest or plume of horse-hair was fastened

unguarded. Some open helmets had a bar or bars from the forehead to the chin, to guard against the transverse cut of a broadsword.

The modern military helmets worn in full-dress afford no protection for the face. Firemen wear a heavy headpiece of leather and brass, or other materials, to protect them as far as possible from falling ruins at conflagrations. Helmets of white felt, with folds of linen wrapped round them, are worn in India and other hot climates as a protection against the sun. The name helmet is also given to a kind of hat worn by policemen. In *heraldry* the helmet is borne over a coat of arms, and the form and position of it vary according to the quality or dignity of the bearer. (*See* HERALDRY.)

In 1916 the **steel shrapnel helmet,** colloquially known as a 'tin hat,' was introduced into the British army. A similar helmet was eventually worn by all the combatant armies; it saved a large number of casualties.

Mediterranean. Some of the shells attain a large size. Those of *C. rufa*, *C. cornuta*, *C. tuberosa*, and other species, are the material on which shell cameos are usually sculptured.

HELMHOLTZ, Hermann-Ludwig Ferdinand von, German physiologist and physicist, born 1821 at Potsdam, died in 1894. Educated at Berlin, he became professor of anatomy at the Academy of Fine Arts in 1848, and in 1849 he obtained the chair of physiology at Königsberg, from which he was successively transferred to the same post at Bonn (1855) and at Heidelberg (1858). In 1871 he was appointed professor of physics at Berlin.

His work was chiefly in those departments of physics which are in closest relation with physiology, notably in acoustics and optics. Of his many publications the best known are: *The Conservation of Force* (1847), *Manual of Optics* (1856–66), *Popular Lectures on Scientific Subjects* (London 1873 and 1881), and *Sensations of*

Tone as a Physiological Basis for the Theory of Music (1862, London 1875). He was ennobled by the German Emperor in 1883.—Cf. J. G. McKendrick, *H. L. F. von Helmholtz.*

HELMINTHOSPO'RIUM, a genus of Fungi Imperfecti, section Hyphomycetes. Several species are troublesome parasites, notably *H. turcicum*, which often proves destructive to Indian corn, and *H. gramineum*, the cause of 'leaf-stripe' and 'blind ears' in barley.

HELMOND, a town of the Netherlands, province of North Brabant, on the Aa, with industries of several kinds. There is an old château dating from 1403. Pop. (1932), 25,857.

HELMSLEY, market town of Yorkshire. It is 23½ miles from York, on the L.N.E. Rly. Near is a ruined castle, and also Duncombe Park, once the seat of the Earl of Feversham, whose eldest son is called Viscount Helmsley; it is now a school for girls. Pop. 1,303.

HELMSTEDT, or HELMSTÄDT (helm'stet), a town in Brunswick, 20 miles E.S.E. of Brunswick; formerly a member of the Hanseatic League. There are a fine church of the twelfth century, and buildings in the Romanesque style, formerly accommodating a university, founded in 1576 and closed in 1809. Pop. 17,166.

HELMUND, a river in Afghanistan, which it traverses diagonally northeast to south-west, and ultimately falls into the extensive Lake Hamoon, after a course of about 600 miles. Its source is 11,500 feet above sea-level.

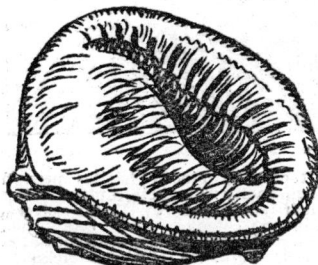

Helmet Shell

HELOISE, or ELOISE (el-o-ēz), celebrated for her beauty and wit, but still more on account of her love for Abelard, was born in Paris in 1101, and died in 1164. After the mutilation of her lover she was persuaded by him to take the veil at Argenteuil, and ultimately became prioress of the convent there until 1129, when she

entered, with some of her nuns, the oratory of the Paraclete, built by Abelard at Nogent-sur-Seine, where she lived in exemplary piety. Contemporary writers speak in high terms of her genius. She understood Latin, Greek, and Hebrew, was familiar with the ancients, and well read in philosophy and theology.

HE'LOTS, slaves in ancient Sparta, the lowest of the four classes into which the population of the city was divided. They were the property of the State, which alone had the disposal of their life and freedom, and which assigned them to certain citizens, by whom they were employed in private labours. Agriculture and all mechanical arts at Sparta were in their hands, and they were also obliged to bear arms for the State in case of necessity. They behaved with great bravery in the Peloponnesian War, and were rewarded with liberty (431 B.C.), but 2,000 appear to have been subsequently massacred. They several times rose against their masters, but were always unsuccessful and finally reduced.

HELPS, Sir Arthur, English essayist and historian, born 1813, died in 1875. He graduated at Cambridge in 1835, and from 1859 until his death was clerk of the Privy Council. His works, which are for the most part of a pleasant moralizing type with many indications of a fine, if not of a robust personality, comprise an early volume of essays; *Thoughts in the Cloister and the Crowd* (1835); *Catherine Douglas, a Tragedy* (1839); *Essays written during the Intervals of Business* (1841); *Claims of Labour* (1844); the series entitled *Friends in Council* (1847–59); *Companions of my Solitude* (1851); *Brevia* (1871); *Conversations on War* (1871); *Thoughts on Government* (1872); *Animals and Their Masters* (1873); *Social Pressure* (1875); *The Spanish Conquest of America* (1855 –61); *Life of Pizarro* (1869); *Life of Cortes* (1871); *Realmah, a Romance* (1868); and *Ivan de Biron, a Russian story* (1874). He also edited the Prince Consort's *Speeches* (1862), and the Queen's *Leaves from a Journal* (1868), receiving knighthood (K.C.B.) in 1872.

HELSINGBORG, a seaport in Sweden, at the narrowest part of the Sound, opposite Elsinore. It has manufactures of leather, dyeworks, tileworks, saltworks, and a spacious harbour. Pop. (1932), 56,620.

HELSINGFORS. *See* HELSINKI.

HELSINGÖR.—*See* ELSINORE.

HELSINKI, a seaport, capital of the Republic of Finland, on a peninsula in the gulf of that name, 180 miles W.N.W. of Petrograd. It is the seat of important courts and public offices, and contains a university, removed from Åbo in 1827. It has manufactures of linen, sail-cloth, and tobacco, an important trade in timber, corn, and fish, and one of the best harbours in the Baltic. Pop. (1930), 243,560.

HELST, Bartholomew van der, Dutch portrait-painter, born at Haarlem in 1611 or 1612, died at Amsterdam 1670, where and at Rotterdam and the Hague he worked. His single portraits, such as the *Paul Potter* at the Hague, are his best works; though his picture of a banquet of a company of the civic guard in the Stadthouse at Amsterdam was called by Sir Joshua Reynolds "perhaps the first picture of portraits in the world."

HELSTON, a municipal, and until 1885 parliamentary borough of England, county of Cornwall, on an acclivity on the left bank of the Cober, 12 miles s.w. of Falmouth. Principal industries: mining and shoemaking; and there is some shipping trade from Port Leven, 3 miles distant. Helston is famous for its celebrations on 8th May, known as Furry Day. The principal art of the ceremony consists in dancing through the houses. Pop. (1931), 2,544.

HELVEL'LYN, one of the highest mountains of England, county of Cumberland, between Keswick and Ambleside; height, 3,118 feet.

HELVE'TII, anciently a Gallic or Celtic people dwelling in the country now nearly corresponding with Switzerland. They were not much known to the Romans until the time of Julius Cæsar, who, as Governor of Gaul, prevented their intended emigration, and after many bloody battles pressed them back within their frontiers. After their subjection by Cæsar several Roman colonies were established amongst them. On the death of Galba the Helvetii, for refusing to acknowledge Vitellius as emperor, were mercilessly punished by Cæcina, one of his generals.

HELVÉTIUS (el-vā-si-ūs), Claude Adrien, French philosophical writer, born in 1715, died in Paris in 1771. Having made a fortune as a farmergeneral, he devoted himself to philosophic work. In 1758 he published his one important book, *De l'Esprit* (On the Mind), the materialism of which

Helvellyn

drew upon him many attacks. It was condemned by the Sorbonne, and publicly burned by decree of the Parliament of Paris. In 1764 he went to England, and the year afterwards to Germany, where Frederick the Great and other German princes received him with many proofs of esteem. He also wrote a work, *De l'Homme*, and an allegorical poem, *Le Bonheur*. As a philosopher Helvetius belonged to the Utilitarian school.— Cf. A. Keim, *Helvétius, sa vie et son œuvre*.

HELWĀN', a health-resort in Egypt, about 14 miles south-east of Cairo, with warm sulphur, saline, and chalybeate springs, which now attract many visitors. There are a well-equipped bathhouse, hotels, lodging-houses, &c. The place is an artificial oasis, to which water is conveyed from the Nile, 3 miles to the west. It is highly suitable as a winter residence.

HE'MANS, Felicia Dorothea, maiden name Browne, English poet, born at Liverpool in 1793, died in 1835. She first appeared as an author in 1808, with a volume entitled *Early Blossoms*, which was followed in 1812 by her more successful volume *The Domestic Affections*. In the same year she married Captain Hemans, who, however, left her six years later, shortly before the birth of her fifth son. She then devoted herself to literature, winning public notice by her poems entitled *The Restoration of the Works of Art to Italy*, *The Sceptic*, *Modern Greece*, and *Dartmoor*, the last, in 1821, gaining the prize of the Royal Society of Literature.

In 1825 she took up her residence at Rhyllon, near St. Asaph, where she wrote her *Lays of Many Lands*, *Forest Sanctuary*, and *Records of Woman*. In 1828 she changed her residence to Wavertree, near Liverpool, where, in 1830, she published one of her most popular volumes, entitled *The Songs of the Affections*. In 1831 she removed to Dublin, where she published her *Hymns for Childhood*, *National Lyrics and Songs for Music*, and *Scenes and Hymns of Life*. Her poetry is essentially lyrical and descriptive, and is always sweet, natural, and pleasing. In her earlier pieces she was imitative, but she ultimately asserted her independence, and produced many short poems of some beauty and pathos.

HEM'ATINE, or **HÆMATINE,** the red colouring-matter of the blood occurring in solution in the interior of the blood corpuscles or cells. It is the only structure of the body, except hair, which contains iron.

HEM'ATITE, or, more correctly, **HÆMATITE,** an important ore of iron, taking its name from its dull blood-red streak. Its composition is Fe_2O_3, and its crystals are trigonal, with a brilliant metallic lustre; they appear black, but the characteristic colour is revealed on powdering. *Specular iron ore* is a name for crystallized varieties. Commonly the ore is concretionary and mammillated, showing fibrous structure and a deep purple-red colour. *Limonite* (q.v.) is often called brown hematite, but contains only some 56 per cent of iron as

Mrs. Hemans

against 70 per cent in true hematite. The hematite crystals of Elba are especially famous.

HEMEL HEMPSTEAD, a market town and municipal borough of England, Herts, 6½ miles west of St. Albans, carrying on paper-making, iron-founding, straw-plaiting, &c. The name is due to the fact that hemp was once grown in the neighbourhood. Pop. (1931), 15,122.

HEMERALO'PIA is a term at one time used for night-blindness, a defect of vision whereby the person loses his sight at night. As it was also used for the reverse condition, day-blindness, its use has been largely discontinued.

HEMEROBI'IDÆ, the ant-lions, lace-wing flies, &c., a family of neuropterous insects, noted for their predaceous larvæ. Those of ant-lions (species of Myrmeleon, &c.) dig conical pitfalls in sandy soil for catching ants and flies. The lace-wing flies (species of Chrysopa), small fragile forms with eyes shining like metal, are common in Britain, and their larvæ prey upon Aphides.

HEMILEIA, a genus of Fungi, family Uredineæ (rusts), closely allied to Uromyces. *H. vastatrix*, the coffee-leaf disease or coffee-rust, is a terrible scourge in coffee plantations. It is difficult to check, and in Ceylon, where it first spread to coffee from certain wild host-plants, has been responsible for damage estimated at many millions of pounds sterling.

HEMIP'TERA, bugs, an ord. of four-winged insects, having a suctorial proboscis, the outer wings, or wing-covers, either entirely formed of a substance intermediate between the elytra of beetles and the ordinary membranous wings of most insects, or leathery at the base and transparent towards the tips. In one group (Aphides) all the wings when present are membranous. The true wings are straight and unplaited. Some feed on vegetable and some on animal juices.

Those having the upper wings of a uniform substance throughout (whether leathery or transparent) have been constituted into a section, and by some naturalists into an order named Homoptera; those having them partly leathery and partly transparent constitute the section or ord. Heteroptera. To the Hemiptera belong the plant-lice, boat-fly, cochineal and other scale-insects, bed-bug, lantern fly, &c.

HEM'ISPHERE, half a sphere, especially one of the halves into which the earth may be supposed to be divided. It is common to speak of the Eastern Hemisphere and the Western Hemisphere, the former, also called the Old World, comprising Europe, Asia, Africa, Australia, &c.; the latter, North and South America, &c. The boundary between the two is quite arbitrary, and a more natural division of the earth is into the northern and the southern hemisphere, the equator forming the dividing line.

HEMLOCK, a poisonous plant, *Conium maculatum*, nat. ord. Umbelliferæ, supposed to be identical with the plant *kôneion* of the Greeks. It is a tall, erect, branching biennial, with a smooth, shining, hollow stem, usually marked with purplish spots, elegant, much-divided leaves, which when bruised emit a nauseous odour, and white flowers in compound umbels of ten or more rays, surrounded by a general involucre of three to seven leaflets.

It is found in Britain and throughout Europe and temperate Asia in waste places, banks, and under walls. It is said to be fatal to cows when they eat it, whereas horses, goats, and sheep may feed upon it without danger. In the human subject it causes paralysis, convulsions, and death. The poison administered to Socrates is supposed to have been a decoction of it, though others are of opinion that the potion was obtained from water-hemlock (*Cicūta virōsa*).

Hemlock is a powerful sedative and is used medicinally. The extract is considered the best preparation. It is often serviceable as a substitute for, or an accompaniment to opium. It has been found very useful in chronic rheumatism and in whooping-cough, and in allaying the pain of irritable sores and cancerous ulcers. The virtues of hemlock are due to the alkaloid coniine.

HEM'ORRHAGE is a flow of blood from the blood-vessels from any cause. Hemorrhage from different parts and organs of the body is given special names, hemoptysis, hematemesis, hematuria, epistaxis, while the terms accidental, postpartum, and unavoidable hemorrhage are used with reference to the separation of the placenta in pregnancy and parturition. The treatment varies with the cause and situation of the hemorrhage. *See* HÆMATURIA *and* HÆMOPTYSIS.

HEM'ORRHOIDS, or PILES, are a varicose condition of the veins surrounding the anus and lower part of the rectum. In the mild form the condition is very common, and when more severe causes much pain and discomfort, requiring an operation for relief. The predisposing causes are sedentary occupation, alcoholic excess, and chronic constipation. The mild form may be present for a long time without producing much discomfort, but severe symptoms may be brought on by the use of drastic purgatives, sudden exposure to cold or damp, congestion of the liver, or a chill.

The hemorrhoids may be either external or internal, or both conditions may be present together. When the internal variety is alone present, hemorrhage from the rectum is often the first sign, and this hemorrhage becomes gradually more frequent and severe. Treatment consists of avoidance, as far as possible, of the predisposing causes, especially chronic constipation, and when the condition is well established operation for removal of the hemorrhoids is the only satisfactory course. There is a modern treatment by injection that is proving highly successful.

HEMP (*Cannăbis sativa*), a plant, the only known species of the genus Cannăbis, nat. ord. Moraceæ. It is an annual herbaceous plant; the leaves are divided into five lanceolate and coarsely-serrate leaflets; the male flowers, which are on separate stems, are green, resembling those of the hop; the female flowers are inconspicuous, and the fruit is a little hard capsule containing a single seed.

It is a native of Western and Central Asia, but has long been naturalized in Brazil and tropical Africa, and is extensively cultivated in Italy and many other European countries, particularly Russia and Poland. The Indian variety, often known as *Cannăbis indica*, is the source of the narcotic drug variously known as *hashish*, *bhang*, or *gunjah*. The hemp fibre is tough and strong, and peculiarly adapted for weaving into coarse fabrics such as sail-cloth, and for twisting into ropes and cables. The finer sorts are used for shirtings, sheetings, &c., which, though coarser than those made from flax, are very much stronger and equally susceptible of being bleached. The hemp of England is much superior, but the plant does not pay the farmer, and very little of it is grown. In some of the United States it is a crop of considerable inportance.

The seed must be sown thin, not more than 1 to 2 bushels to an acre. Small paths are often left open along the field lengthwise, about 7 feet distant from each other, to allow the plucking of the male plants first, as the female require to remain standing a month longer to admit of the seed becoming ripe. But in some parts the whole crop is cut at once, plants for seed being separately cultivated.

The plant being stripped of its leaves, and dried in the open air, may be stored, but when steeped green it turns out of a better colour. The steeping takes from four to eleven days, and the operation is known to be completed by the inner *reed* or woody fibre separating easily from the fibres of the outer bark. When thoroughly steeped, it is taken out of the water and spread out in rows on the grass to bleach. This takes three weeks or more, during which period it requires constant turning with a light, long pole. After drying it is scutched or broken by breaks and scutching-stocks, resembling those employed for flax. Beating is the next operation, which separates the 'boon' from the fibre. The hemp is now ready for being heckled, after which it may be spun. Hemp-seed is much used as food for cage-birds, and also yields an oil. Sisal hemp or 'henequen' and Manila hemp are not true hemps.

HEMS, or HOMS (Rom. *Emesa*), a town of Syria, on the railway running northwards from the Beyrout-Damascus line. It has manufactures of cotton, silk, &c., and an active trade. In this locality Zenobia was defeated by Aurelian in A.D. 272; and the Turkish forces by Ibrahim Pasha in 1832. Pop. 52,792.

HEMSWORTH, urban district of Yorkshire (W.R.). It is 8 miles from Wakefield and 168 from London, by the L.N.E. Rly. It is a coal mining centre. Pop. (1931) 13,001.

HENBANE, a plant of the genus Hyoscyămus, nat. ord. Solanaceæ. The only British species is *H. niger*, a native of Europe and Northern Asia. It is a coarse erect biennial herb, found in waste ground and loose dry soil, having soft, clammy, hairy foliage of disagreeable odour, pale yellowish-brown flowers streaked with purple veins, and a five-toothed calyx. The expressed juice of the leaves and seeds contains several alkaloids, and is often used as a sedative, anti-spasmodic, and narcotic, having in many cases the great advantage over laudanum of not producing constipation. When taken in considerable quantity, it proves quickly fatal to man and most animals, particularly to domestic fowls, whence the name. Called also **Stinking Nightshade**.

HENDERSON, Arthur. British politician. Born in Glasgow, 15th Sept., 1863, he was apprenticed to an engineering firm in Newcastle-on-Tyne and worked for some years as a moulder. He soon became a leading trade unionist and a member of the city council and in 1895 was suggested as a candidate for parliament. Soon he moved to Darlington where he was equally active, being mayor in 1903. He was one of the first three members of the Labour Party in Parliament. In that year he was elected M.P. for the Barnard Castle Division, a seat which he retained until 1918. In 1919 he was elected for Widnes; in 1923 for Newcastle East, and in 1924 for Burnley, where he was defeated in 1931. He held many offices in his trade union and was officially connected with the Labour Party from its inception, first as treasurer and since 1911 as secretary. He has been actively connected also with the Labour and Socialist International.

Henderson began his career as a minister when in 1915 he was made President of the Board of Education in the first coalition ministry, formed by Mr. Asquith; subsequently he became Paymaster-General, a position involving no departmental duties which left him free for his real work of advising his fellow ministers on labour matters. In Dec. 1916, he became minister without portfolio in the War Cabinet formed by Mr. Lloyd George, but in Aug. 1917, after a visit to Russia, he resigned. In 1924 he was Home Secretary in the first Labour Ministry and in 1929 he became Foreign Minister, a post he filled with marked success. He was Chairman of the Parliamentary Labour Party, 1908–10 and 1914–17 and its chief whip, 1921–24 and 1925–27. In 1931 he resigned with the other members of the ministry and became leader of the Labour Party in its opposition to the National Government under Mr. Ramsay Mac-Donald, retaining also control of the party machine. He was president of the disarmament conference at Geneva, 1932–33. He resigned the leadership of the Labour Party in the autumn of of 1932 on the ground that his work at Geneva kept him temporarily out of domestic politics. In April 1933 he was awarded the Peace Prize of the Carnegie Foundation. In 1923–24 two of his sons sat in parliament: Arthur for Cardiff South, and William Watson for Enfield. They were re-elected in 1929, but lost their seats in 1931. A third son was killed in the Great War.

HENDON, an urban district of Middlesex, forming a suburb of London, north-west of Hampstead. It gives name to a parliamentary division of the county. Mill Hill Grammar School and a Roman Catholic Missionary College are here. Hendon is now an aviation centre, and there are flying-schools and aeroplane-works. An annual air pageant is held in June. Pop. (1931) 115,682.

HENGEST, a prince of the Jutes, founder of the Kingdom of Kent in Great Britain, in conjunction with his brother Horsa. In A.D. 449 the Britons sued for aid from the Saxons against the inroads of the Scots and Picts. The Saxons under Hengest and Horsa accordingly landed at the mouth of the Thames, and defeated the northern tribes near Stamford in A.D. 450. Being reinforced from home, they afterwards united with the Scots and Picts against the Britons, whom they ultimately dispossessed.

Hengest, who had lost his brother in the battle near Eglesford (now Ailsford) in A.D. 445, founded the Kingdom of Kent, established his residence in Canterbury, and died about the year 488. By some writers the brothers are, with insufficient reason, regarded as mythical personages.

HENGISTBURY HEAD, headland on the coast of Hampshire. It is about 2 miles to the south of Christchurch and from it magnificent views

are obtained. In 1930 it became the property of the Borough of Bournemouth.

HENGOED, district of Glamorganshire. It is 31 miles from Neath and 160 from London, on the G.W. Rly. It is a populous coal mining district.

HENGSTENBERG, Ernst Wilhelm, German divine and commentator, born in 1802, died in 1869. He was long professor of Old Testament exegesis at the University of Berlin. His influence as leader of the orthodox party was established by the publication of the *Evangelische Kirchenzeitung* (1827), of which he was editor, and which had for contributors Otto and Ludwig von Gerlach, Neander, Tholuck, Lange, Huber, Stahl, Vilmar and Leo.

His works include a translation of Aristotle's *Metaphysics*; a *Christology of the Old Testament*, and *Introduction to the Old Testament*; a *Commentary on the Psalms*; *The Revelation of St. John*; a *History of the Kingdom of God in the Old Testament*; &c.—Cf. F. Lichtenberger, *History of German Theology in the 19th Century.*

HENLEY, William Ernest, English poet, critic, and journalist, born 1849, died 1903. He took up journalism, and edited the magazines *London, Magazine of Art, Scots Observer* (later *National Observer*), and lastly the *New Review* (1893–7). His first publication, *In Hospital : Rhymes and Rhythms* (1888), was inspired by his own experiences as a patient in Edinburgh Infirmary, in which city he met and became a friend of Robert Louis Stevenson, his collaborator in several plays.

A Book of Verses appeared in 1890, *The Song of the Sword and other Poems* in 1892, and a collected edition of his poems in 1898, followed by a fresh volume of verse, *For England's Sake*, in 1900. He did much editorial work in connection with both prose and poetry, including that done for *The Centenary Burns* in conjunction with T. F. Henderson, the most important outcome of which was an elaborate and illuminating estimate of Burns as a poet and as a man. He also edited *Lyra Heroica*, an anthology of verse.

HENLEY-ON-THAMES, a municipal borough of England, in Oxfordshire, on the left bank of the Thames, here crossed by a handsome bridge, 35 miles W. of London, giving its name to a parliamentary division of the county. Brewing is an industry. Pop. (1931), 6,618.

Henley Regatta. Principal rowing event in England. It is held every July and attracts the best oarsmen from all over the world. The first meeting was held in 1839. The chief races are the Grand Challenge Cup, the Ladies' Challenge Plate and the Thames Challenge Cup for crews of eight. For crews of four there are the Stewards' and the Visitors' Challenge Cups. The Silver Goblets are for the best pair of oarsmen and the Diamond Sculls for single scullers. The Amateur Rowing Association controls the meeting.

HENNA, a shrub (*Lawsonia inermis*), nat. ord. Lythraceæ, bearing opposite entire leaves and numerous small white fragrant flowers disposed in terminal panicles. Externally it bears considerable resemblance to the European privet. It grows in moist situations throughout North Africa, Arabia, Persia, and the East Indies, and has acquired celebrity from being used by the inhabitants of those countries to dye yellow the nails of their fingers and the manes, hoofs, &c., of their horses. It is cultivated extensively in Egypt, and the powdered leaves form a large article of export to Persia and the Turkish possessions. It may be used for dyeing woollens, not only yellow, but brown, when alum and sulphate of iron are employed.

HENNEBONT (en-boṇ), an ancient seaport, France, department of Morbihan, on the Blavet, 27 miles W.N.W. of Vannes. Pop. 8,682.

HENRIETTA MARIA, queen of Charles I of England; youngest child of Henry IV of France by his second wife, Maria de' Medici; born in Paris 1609, died at Colombes, near Paris, in 1669. The proposed marriage between Charles, Prince of Wales, and the Infanta of Spain having failed, a matrimonial negotiation was opened with Henrietta, whom he had met at a ball in Paris while on his way to Spain. The marriage was celebrated by proxy at Paris in 1625, but her popularity in England was soon destroyed by her bigotry, hauteur, and despotic ideas as to divine right. Much of the subsequent procedure which brought Charles to the block may be traced indirectly to her influence. On the breaking out of civil war she proceeded to Holland, procured money and troops, and afterwards joined Charles at Oxford. She again went to the Continent in 1644, and resided in France till the Restoration. On that occasion she visited England, but soon returned to France, where she died.—Cf. I. A. Taylor, *The Life of Queen Henrietta Maria*.

HENRY I of Germany, surnamed *The Fowler*, according to tradition because his election to the German Empire was announced to him while fowling. He was the son of Otho the Illustrious, Duke of Saxony, was born

in A.D. 876, and died in 936. On the death of his father he became Duke of Saxony and Thuringia, was elected Emperor of Germany in 919, and was the true founder of the empire. By his prudence and activity Suabia and Bavaria were forced to tender allegiance, and Lorraine was reunited to the German Empire in 925.

He was defeated, however, by the Hungarians, and forced to pay a yearly tribute to obtain a truce for nine years. He spent this period in developing a sound military organization, and turning his arms against various Slavonic tribes in the south, was everywhere victorious. At the end of the truce with the Hungarians he refused the tribute, and completely

Henrietta Maria

routed them in 933. Besides his military reforms he diminished the feudal privileges, and granted to the cities of the empire their first municipal charters.—Cf. G. Waitz, *Jahrbücher des deutschen Reichs*.

HENRY II, *The Saint*, Emperor of Germany, born 972, died in 1024. A son of Henry the Quarreller of Bavaria, and great-grandson of the Emperor Henry I, he inherited Bavaria in 995, and on the death of Otho III in 1002 laid claim and was elected to the empire. He had to proceed to Italy to assert his sovereignty there, the Lombard cities having chosen Harduin of Ivrea as their king.

During his absence Boleslas of Poland extended his sway over the whole of Bohemia, but after repeated campaigns Henry succeeded in recovering Bohemia, and in 1018, in the Peace of Budissin (Bautzen), reduced him to complete subjection. In the midst of these campaigns against Boleslas he made another expedition into Italy (1013) against Harduin. On this occasion Henry was crowned emperor by Pope Benedict VIII. He made a third expedition into Italy in 1022 to aid Benedict against the Greeks.

HENRY III, Emperor of Germany, the second belonging to the House of the Salian Franks, son of the Emperor Conrad II, born in 1017, died in 1055. He was chosen king in 1026, and succeeded his father in the imperial dignity in 1039. He weakened the power of the great feudal lords, and forced the Duke of Bohemia in 1042, and the King of Hungary in 1044, and again in 1047, to accept their dominions as imperial fiefs. His influence was also paramount in Italy, especially in Milan, and in the south, where the Normans in Apulia and Calabria paid him homage.

In 1046 he deposed the rival Popes Benedict IX, Sylvester III, and Gregory IV, and caused Suitger, Bishop of Bamberg, to be elected in their stead as Clement II. His efforts to secure the permanence of the influence of the empire over the See of Rome were thwarted by Cardinal Hildebrand (Gregory VII). His first wife was a daughter of Canute the Great of England.

HENRY IV, Emperor of Germany, son of Henry III, was born in 1050, died in 1106. At the death of his father he was only five years old, and his whole life was a series of troubles, partly of his own causing. His severe treatment of the Saxons led to a rising which was cruelly punished. His treatment of the conquered people was such that they complained to the Pope, and Gregory VII (Hildebrand) accordingly summoned Henry, in 1076, to appear before him at Rome and answer the charges, at the same time forbidding the sale of ecclesiastical dignities. Henry not only disregarded the threat, but instigated the bishops, assembled by his order at Worms, to renounce their obedience to the Pope. Gregory, however, pronounced sentence of excommunication against him, and Henry, finding himself deserted, was obliged to go to Italy and make his submission to the Pope (1077).

The insolence with which the Pope used his victory produced a reaction; the Italian princes, who had long been dissatisfied with Gregory, offered Henry their assistance. The German princes, however, at the instigation of the Pope, elected Rudolph, Duke

of Suabia, king. Henry hastened back to Germany and overcame his rival, who lost his life in 1080. Gregory again excommunicated Henry; but at the Council of Brixen, in 1080, he was deposed by the German and Italian bishops as a heretic and a sorcerer, and Guibert, Archbishop of Ravenna (Clement III) set up in his place. In 1084 Henry succeeded in establishing Clement at Rome, but was obliged to return to Germany to maintain his ground against two rivals who successively arose.

In 1085 Henry was again obliged to cross the Alps in aid of his protégé Clement III. But the dissatisfaction against him in Germany had not subsided, and though he succeeded in crushing the rebellion of his eldest son, Conrad, who died deserted at Florence in 1101, his second son, Henry, made himself master of his father's person in 1105 by stratagem, and compelled him to abdicate the throne at Ingelheim. Henry IV ended his life and his sorrows in neglect at Liége.—Cf. H. Floto, *Kaiser Heinrich IV und sein Zeitalter.*

HENRY V, Emperor of Germany, the son and successor of Henry IV, was born in 1081, and died at Utrecht in 1125. On his ascension the question of investiture distracted the empire anew. Pope Pascal would only confer the imperial crown upon condition that rights claimed by Gregory should be formally conceded. Henry therefore seized the Pope at the altar, and imprisoned him until he yielded two months later, and crowned Henry in April, 1111. Disturbances, however, arose in Germany, especially with Lothaire of Saxony, and the Pope, declaring that his peace with the emperor had been compulsory, fomented the strife. The war continued two years, and devastated Germany, and after a second expedition to Italy, and excommunication by successive Popes, Henry was compelled to yield in the matter of investiture, and in 1122 subscribed the Concordat of Worms. He was the last of the Salic or Frankish family of emperors, which was succeeded by the Suabian House. He married Matilda, a daughter of Henry I of England.

HENRY VI, Emperor of Germany, son of Frederick I and Beatrice of Burgundy, the third emperor of the House of Hohenstaufen, born in 1165, crowned king in 1169, and succeeded his father as emperor in 1190. He kept Richard Cœur de Lion in prison, and obtained a large ransom for him. He died in 1197.

HENRY VII, Emperor of Germany, born in 1262, was chosen emperor in

1308. Among the first acts of his reign were recognition of the independence of the Swiss cantons of Schwyz, Uri, and Unterwalden, and the granting of the Kingdom of Bohemia to his son John. He compelled the Milanese to give him the iron crown of Lombardy, suppressed by force the revolt which then broke out in Upper Italy, captured part of Rome, which was in the hands of Neapolitan troops, and was crowned Roman Emperor by two cardinals. He died suddenly in 1313.

HENRY II, King of France, born in 1519, succeeded his father, Francis I, in 1547, and died in 1559. Throughout his reign his mistress, Diana of Poitiers, exercised an important influence over king and court. After a brief war with England for the recovery of Boulogne, a war of longer duration and more serious results originated in 1551 in disputes between Henry and the Pope as to the duchies of Parma and Placentia, and continued to devastate Europe till the general peace of Câteau-Cambrésis, 1559. To confirm the peace, Philip II, who was a widower since the death of Mary of England, was to marry Elizabeth, Henry's eldest daughter by Catherine de' Medici. In the course of a tourney held to celebrate the event, Henry was mortally wounded by a splinter from the lance of Lord Montgomery, captain of the Scottish guard. He was succeeded in 1559 by his eldest son, Francis II.—BIBLIOGRAPHY: H. N. Williams, *Henri II, his Court and Times*; H. Lemonnier, *La France sous Henri II* (in Lavisse's *Histoire de France*).

HENRY III, King of France, third son of Henry II and Catherine de' Medici, born in 1551, succeeded his brother, Charles IX, in 1574, and died in 1589. In 1573 he was chosen King of Poland, which he was obliged to quit secretly when called to the throne of France. In 1576, after a civil war, he granted to the Protestants the favourable Edict of Beaulieu, but the concession led to the formation of the League, and Henry, to re-establish his authority, declared himself its head. Civil war, however, again broke out, and though hostilities were again put an end to by the Peace of Bergerac in 1577, they were renewed in 1580 until the Peace of Fleix (Nov., 1580).

The death of his brother the Duc d'Anjou in 1584, which left Henry of Navarre, a Calvinist, heir-apparent to the throne, brought on another war, called the War of the Three Henrys, the leading persons engaged in it besides the king being Henry of Guise, the real head of the League, and Henry of Navarre. In 1588 Henry of Guise expelled the king from his capital. An apparent reconciliation at Blois was followed by the assassination of the Guises, and Henry, finding himself everywhere opposed by the Catholic party, was compelled to ally himself with Henry of Navarre. The two princes advanced on Paris, but in 1589 Henry III was stabbed by Jacques Clement, a Dominican, and died next day. He was the last of the branch of Orléans-Angoulême of the stock of the Valois, and was succeeded by Henry of Navarre, the first of the House of Bourbon. — Cf. J. H. Mariéjol, *La Réforme et la Ligue* (in Lavisse's *Histoire de France*); Jackson, *The Last of the Valois*.

HENRY IV of France was the son of Anthony of Bourbon, Duke of Vendôme, and of Jeanne d'Albret, daughter of Henry, King of Navarre, and herself afterwards Queen of Navarre. He was born in Dec., 1553, at Pau, and died in 1610. Educated by his mother in the Calvinistic faith, he early joined, at her wish, the Protestant army of France, and served under Admiral Coligny. In 1572 he married Margaret of Valois, sister of Charles IX, and after the massacre of St. Bartholomew, which took place during the marriage festivities, was forced to adopt the Catholic creed.

In 1576 he escaped from Paris, retracted at Tours his enforced abjuration of Calvinism, put himself at the head of the Hugenots, and took a leading part in all the subsequent religious wars. On becoming presumptive heir to the crown in 1584, he was obliged to resort to arms to assert his claims. In 1587 he defeated the army of the League at Coutras, and after the death of Henry III gained the battles of Arques (1589) and Ivry (1590). He was obliged, however, to raise the siege of Paris; and convinced that a peaceful occupation of the throne was impossible without his professing the Catholic faith, he became nominally a Catholic in 1593.

After his formal coronation in 1594 only three provinces held out against him—Burgundy, reduced by the victory of Fontaine-Française in 1595; Picardy, reduced by the capture of Amiens in 1596; and Brittany, which came into his hands by the submission of the Duke of Mercœur in the spring of 1598. The war against Spain was concluded in 1598 by the Peace of Vervins to the advantage of France. The same year was signalized by the granting of the Edict of Nantes, which secured to the Protestants entire religious liberty.

He made use of the tranquility which followed to restore the internal prosperity of his kingdom, and particularly the wasted finances, in which he was successful with the aid of his Prime Minister, Sully. At the instance of Sully Henry divorced Margaret of Valois, and in 1600 married Maria de' Medici, niece of the Grand-Duke of Tuscany, mother of Louis XIII. She was crowned at St. Denis in 1610, but on the following day Henry was stabbed by a fanatic named Ravaillac, while examining the preparations for the queen's entry into Paris. The great benefits which Henry IV bestowed upon France entitle him to the designation which he himself assumed at an assembly of the Notables at Rouen in 1596, the Regenerator of France (*Restaurateur de la France*).—BIBLIOGRAPHY: G. P. R. James, *Life of Henry IV, King of France and Navarre*; A. Poirson, *Histoire du Règne de Henri IV*; C. C. Jackson, *The First of the Bourbons*.

HENRY I, King of England, surnamed *Beauclerc* ('fine scholar'), youngest son of William the Conqueror, was born at Selby, in Yorkshire, in 1068, died at Rouen in 1135. He was hunting with William Rufus when that prince was killed, in 1100, and, instantly riding to London, caused himself to be proclaimed king, to the prejudice of his elder brother Robert, then absent as a Crusader. He re-established by charter the laws of Edward the Confessor, recalled Anselm to the primacy, and married Matilda, daughter of Malcolm III of Scotland, thus conciliating in turn the people, the Church, and the Scots. Robert landed an army, but was pacified with a pension, and the promise of succession in event of his brother's decease. Soon after, however, Henry invaded Normandy, took Robert prisoner in 1106, and reduced the duchy. He was successful also in the struggle with France.

The last years of his reign were very troubled. In 1120 his only son William was drowned in returning from Normandy, where, three years later, a revolt occurred in favour of Robert's son. The Welsh also were a source of disturbance. Henry appointed as his heir his daughter Matilda or Maud, whom he had married first to the Emperor Henry V, and then to Geoffrey Plantagenet of Anjou. Henry was succeeded by Stephen.—BIBLIOGRAPHY: Sir James Ramsay, *Foundations of England*; E. A. Freeman, *History of the Norman Conquest*.

HENRY II, King of England, first of the Plantagenet line, born in Normandy in 1133, died at Chinon in 1189. He was the son of Geoffrey, Count of Anjou, and Matilda, daughter of Henry I. Invested with the Duchy of Normandy, by the consent of his mother, in 1150, he succeeded to Anjou and Maine in 1151, and by a marriage with Eleanor of Guienne gained Guienne and Poitou. In 1152 he invaded England, but a compromise was effected, by which Stephen was to retain the crown, and Henry to succeed at his death, which took place in 1154.

The commencement of his reign was marked by the dismissal of the foreign mercenaries: and although involved with his brother Geoffrey, who attempted to seize Anjou and Maine, and in a temporary dispute with France, he reigned prosperously till the contest with Thomas Becket regarding the Constitutions of Clarendon. Although sufficiently submissive after Becket's death in the way of penance and expiation, Henry only gave up the article in the Constitutions of Clarendon which forbade appeals to the court of Rome in ecclesiastical cases. Before this matter was terminated, Henry, in 1171, completed the conquest of Ireland, a great part of which had been reduced by Richard de Clare, Earl of Pembroke, commonly known as Strongbow.

Henry's last years were embittered by his sons, to whom he had assigned various territories. The eldest son, Henry, who had been not only declared heir to England, Normandy, Anjou, Maine, and Touraine, but actually crowned in his father's lifetime, was induced by the French monarch to demand of his father the immediate resignation either of the Kingdom of England or of the dukedom of Normandy. Queen Eleanor excited her other sons, Richard and Geoffrey, to make similar claims; Louis and William of Scotland gave them support; and a general invasion of Henry's dominions was begun in 1173 by an attack on the frontiers of Normandy, and an invasion of England by the Scots, attended by considerable disturbance in England.

Conciliating the Church by his penance, Henry took prompt action; William of Scotland was captured, and an accommodation arrived at with Henry's sons. These, however, once more became turbulent, and though the deaths of Henry and Geoffrey reduced the number of centres of disturbance, the king was forced to accept humiliating terms from Richard and Philip of France.

He ranks among the greatest English kings both in soldiership and state-craft. He partitioned England into four judiciary districts, and appointed itinerant justices to make regular excursions through them; revived trial by jury, discouraged that by combat, and demolished all the newly-erected castles as 'dens of thieves.'—BIBLIOGRAPHY: L. F. Salzmann, *Life of Henry II*; Mrs. J. R. Green, *Henry II*; Sir J. H. Ramsay, *The Angevin Empire*.

HENRY III, King of England, son of John by Isabel of Angoulême, born at Winchester in 1207, succeeded his father in 1216, and died in 1272. At the time of accession the Dauphin of France, Louis, at the head of a foreign army, supported by a faction of English nobles, had assumed the reins of government; but was compelled to quit the country by the Earl of Pembroke, who was guardian of the young king until 1219.

As Henry approached to manhood he displayed a character wholly unfit for his station. He discarded his most able minister, Hubert de Burgh, and after 1230, when he received homage in Poitou and Gascony, began to bestow his chief favours upon foreigners. His marriage in 1236 with Eleanor of Provence increased the dislike to him felt by his subjects, and although he received frequent grants of money from Parliament, on condition of confirming the Great Charter, yet his conduct after each ratification was as arbitrary as before.

At length the nobles rose in rebellion under Simon de Montfort, Earl of Leicester and husband of the king's sister; and in 1258, at a Parliament held at Oxford, known in history as the Mad Parliament, obliged the king to sign the body of resolutions known as the Provisions of Oxford. A feud arose, however, between Montfort and Gloucester, and Henry recovered some of his power. War again broke out, and Louis was called in as arbitrator, but his award being favourable to the king, Leicester refused to submit to it. A battle was fought near Lewes, in which Henry was taken prisoner. A convention, called *the Mise of Lewes*, provided for the future settlement of the kingdom; and in 1265 the first genuine House of Commons was summoned. Leicester, however, was defeated and slain in the battle of Evesham (1265), and Henry was replaced upon the throne. His son, Edward I, succeeded him.—Cf. K. Norgate, *The Minority of Henry III*.

HENRY IV, King of England, first king of the House of Lancaster, born in 1366, and died in 1413. He was the eldest son of John of Gaunt, Duke of Lancaster, fourth son of Edward III, by the daughter of Henry, Duke of Lancaster, great-grandson of Henry III. In the reign of Richard II he was made Earl of Derby and Duke of Hereford, but having in 1398 preferred a charge of treason against Mowbray, Duke of Norfolk, he was banished with his adversary.

On the death of John of Gaunt in 1399 Richard withheld Henry's inheritance, and Henry, landing in England, gained possession of Richard's person. The deposition of Richard by Parliament, and the election of Henry, was followed by the murder of the late king. A plot against the king in 1400 was discovered in time to prevent its success, and many executions of men of rank followed; but an insurrection in Wales under Owen Glendower proved more formidable.

The Scots were decisively defeated by the Percies at Homildon, and their leader, the Earl of Douglas, was captured (1402). An order from Henry not to permit the ransom of that nobleman and other Scottish prisoners was regarded as an indignity by the Percies, who set Douglas free, made an alliance with him, and joined Glendower. The king met the insurgents at Shrewsbury (1403), the battle ending in the defeat and death of Percy. The Earl of Northumberland was pardoned, and but few victims were executed. A new insurrection, headed by the Earl of Nottingham and Scrope or Scroop, Archbishop of York, broke out in 1405, but was suppressed.

The rest of this king's reign was comparatively untroubled. In 1405 James, son and heir to King Robert of Scotland, was captured at sea on his way to France, and was detained a prisoner in England. Henry was succeeded by Henry V.—Cf. J. H. Wylie, *History of England under Henry IV*.

HENRY V, King of England, born at Monmouth in 1387, died in August, 1422. On succeeding his father, Henry IV, in 1413, he showed a wisdom in marked contrast to a somewhat reckless youth. He restored their estates to the Percies, and liberated the Earl of March, but in other respects based his internal administration upon that of his father. The persecution of the Lollards is the chief blot upon the early part of his reign.

The struggle in France between the factions of the Dukes of Orleans and Burgundy afforded Henry a tempting opportunity for reviving the claims of his predecessors to the French crown. He accordingly landed near Harfleur in Aug., 1415, and though its capture cost him more than half his army, he decided to return to England by way of Calais. A large French army endeavoured to intercept him at the plain of Agincourt, but was completely routed (Oct., 1415). A year later the French were defeated at sea by the Duke of Bedford.

In 1417 the liberal grants of the Commons enabled Henry once more to invade Normandy with 25,000 men. The assassination of the Duke of Bur-

HENRY

A. Henry II of France. B.—Henry III of Germany, 1039-56. C.—Henry V of England. D.—Henry VI of Germany, 1190-97. E.—Henry IV of France

gundy, which induced his son and successor to join Henry, greatly added to his power, and the alliance was soon followed by the famous Treaty of Troyes (21st May, 1420), by which Henry engaged to marry the Princess Catherine, and to leave Charles VI in possession of the crown, on condition that it should go to Henry and his heirs at his decease.

He returned in triumph to England, but on the defeat of his brother, the Duke of Clarence, in Normandy by the Earl of Buchan, he again set out for France, drove back the army of the dauphin, and entered Paris. A son was at this time born to him, and all his great projects seemed about to be realized, when he died of fever at Vincennes, at the age of thirty-five, and in the tenth year of his reign. He was succeeded by his son, Henry VI.—Cf. C. L. Kingsford, *Henry V, the Typical Mediæval Hero.*

HENRY VI, King of England, born at Windsor in 1421, was crowned at Westminster in 1429, at Paris in 1430, and died in 1471. As he was an infant not nine months old at the death of his father Henry V, his uncle John, Duke of Bedford, was appointed Regent of France; and his uncle Humphrey, Duke of Gloucester, made Protector of the Realm of England.

A few weeks after Henry's succession Charles VI of France died, when, in accordance with the Treaty of Troyes, Henry was proclaimed King of France. The war which followed at first proved favourable to the English, but in the end, by the heroism of Joan of Arc, the death of the Duke of Bedford and the defection of the Duke of Burgundy, resulted in the loss to the English of all their possessions in France except Calais.

In April, 1445, Henry married Margaret of Anjou, daughter of René of Provence. Two years later Humphrey of Gloucester died. When the Earl of Suffolk acquired the chief power in the kingdom, but his government was very unpopular. The insurrection of Cade followed, and the Duke of York returning from Ireland, a great party was formed in his favour, and he was declared by Parliament Protector of the Kingdom, the imbecile Henry being by this time unable even to personate majesty. The appointment was annulled in the following year, the king having recovered his faculties. York retired to the north, and being joined by his adherents, marched upon London. He encountered and defeated the king's army at St. Albans (1455), the first battle of the thirty years' wars of the Roses. The king again becoming deranged, York was once more made Protector.

Four years of peace followed, but

the struggle was soon renewed. The king's forces were beaten at Blore Heath and Northampton, and though they gained the battle of Wakefield, at which York was killed, they were again defeated by his son Edward at Towton and Hexham. Henry was restored for a few months in 1471 by Warwick, 'the king-maker,' but the battles of Barnet and Tewkesbury proved the hopelessness of his cause, and he died, some say was murdered, a few days after the last battle. He was a gentle, pious, well-intentioned, hopelessly incompetent king, whose principal claim to remembrance is that he founded Eton College and King's College, Cambridge.—Cf. Sir C. W. C. Oman, *Political History of England,* 1377–1485.

HENRY VII, King of England, first sovereign of the race of Tudor, born in 1456, died at Richmond in 1509. He was the son of Edmund, Earl of Richmond, son of Owen Tudor and Catherine of France, widow of Henry V. His mother, Margaret, was the only child of John, Duke of Somerset, grandson of John of Gaunt. After the battle of Tewkesbury he was carried by his uncle, the Earl of Pembroke, to Brittany, and on the usurpation of Richard III was naturally turned to as the representative of the House of Lancaster.

In 1485 he assembled a small body of troops in Brittany, and, having landed at Milford Haven, defeated Richard at Bosworth, and was proclaimed king on the field of battle, his right being subsequently recognized by Parliament. In 1486 he married Elizabeth, daughter of Edward IV and heiress of the House of York, and thus united the claims of the rival Houses of York and Lancaster.

The reign of Henry VII was troubled by repeated insurrections, of which the chief were that headed by Lord Lovel and the Staffords (1486), and the impostures of Lambert Simnel (1487) and Perkin Warbeck (1496–9). He brought about a match between the Infanta Catherine, daughter of Ferdinand of Aragon and of Isabella of Castile, and his eldest son Arthur; and on the death of the latter, in order to retain the dowry of this princess, he caused his remaining son Henry to marry the widow by Papal dispensation, an event which, in the sequel, led to a separation from the See of Rome. He married his eldest daughter to James IV, King of Scotland, from which marriage there ultimately resulted the union of the two crowns.

In his latter years his avarice became increasingly marked, two exchequer judges, Empson and Dudley, being employed in all sorts of extortion and chicanery in order to gratify this passion. His reign, however, was in the main beneficent. Its freedom from wars permitted the development of the internal resources of the country. His policy of depressing the feudal nobility, which proportionably exalted the middle ranks, was highly salutary. For a time, however, the power lost by the aristocracy gave an undue preponderance to that of the crown.—Cf. A. F. Pollard, *The Reign of Henry VII.*

HENRY VIII, King of England, son of the preceding, born in 1491, succeeded his father in 1509, and died 28th Jan., 1547. He was soon prevailed upon to join in a league formed against Louis XII of France. Some campaigns in France followed, but the success of the English at the Battle of the Spurs (1513) was succeeded by no adequate result, the taking of Tournay being the only fruit of this expensive expedition.

Meantime, more splendid success attended the English arms at home, James IV of Scotland being completely defeated and slain at Flodden Field (1513). Henry, however, granted peace to the Queen of Scotland, his sister, and established an influence which rendered his kingdom long secure on that side. Finding himself deluded by his allies, he soon after made peace with France, retaining Tournay and receiving a large sum of money.

From 1515 until 1529 the government was practically in the hands of Wolsey, no Parliament being summoned in that period until 1523. After the election of Charles V to the German Empire, both Charles and the French king, Francis I, sought the alliance of England. A friendly meeting took place between Henry and Francis at the Field of the Cloth of Gold (1520), but the interest of Charles preponderated, and Henry declared war against France, though with no important results.

Now came the determination of the king to divorce his wife Catherine, who was older than he, had borne him no male heir, and had, moreover, been in the first place the wife of his elder brother. The last of these points was the alleged ground for seeking divorce, though Henry was probably influenced largely by his attachment to Anne Boleyn, one of the queen's maids of honour. Wolsey, for his own ends, had at first been active in promoting the divorce, but drew back and procrastinated when it became apparent that Anne Boleyn would be Catherine's successor. This delay cost Wolsey his power and the papacy its authority in England. Henry in disgust eagerly caught at the advice of Thomas Cranmer, afterwards Archbishop of Canterbury, to refer the case to the Universi-

ties, from which he soon got the decision that he desired. In 1533 his marriage with Catherine was declared null and an anticipatory private marriage with Anne Boleyn declared lawful; and as these decisions were not recognized by the Pope, two Acts of Parliament were obtained, one in 1534 setting aside the authority of the chief pontiff in England, the other in 1535 declaring Henry the supreme head of the Church.

But although Henry discarded the authority of the Roman Church, he adhered to its theological tenets; and while, on the one hand, he executed Bishop Fisher and Sir Thomas More for refusing the oath of supremacy, he brought many of the reformers to the stake. Finding that the monks and friars in England were the most direct advocates of the Papal authority, and a constant source of disaffection, he suppressed the monasteries by Act of Parliament.

The fall of Anne Boleyn was, however, unfavourable for a time to the reformers. Henry then married Jane Seymour, and the birth of Prince Edward in 1537 fulfilled his wish for a male heir. The death of the queen was followed in 1540 by Henry's marriage with Anne of Cleves, the negotiations of which were conducted by Cromwell. The king's dislike to his wife, which resulted in another divorce, became extended to the minister who had proposed the union, and Cromwell's disgrace and death soon followed. A marriage with Catherine Howard in 1541 proved no happier, and in 1542 she was executed on a charge of infidelity. In 1543 he married his sixth wife, Catherine Parr, a lady secretly inclined to the Reformation, who survived the king.

In the meantime Scotland and France had renewed their alliance, and England became again involved in war. James V ravaged the borders, but was defeated at Solway Moss in 1542, and in 1544 Boulogne was captured, Henry having again allied himself with Charles V. Charles, however, soon withdrew, and Henry maintained the war alone until 1546. Disease now so much aggravated the natural violence of Henry that his oldest friends fell victims to his tyranny. The Duke of Norfolk was committed to the Tower, and his son, the Earl of Surrey, was executed. Henry was succeeded by his son, Edward VI.—BIBLIOGRAPHY; J. S. Brewer, *Reign of Henry VIII*; A. F. Pollard, *Henry VIII*; M. A. S. Hume, *The Wives of Henry VIII and the Parts they played in History*; F. Mumby, *The Youth of Henry VIII.*

HENRY OF HUNTINGDON, an English historian, born towards the end of the eleventh century; Archdeacon of Huntingdon. He composed in Latin a general history of England (*Historia Anglorum*, published in the Rolls Series in 1879) from the earliest times down to his own day, the latter part being of considerable value. A letter of his, *De Contemptu Mundi* (On Contempt of the World), contains curious contemporary anecdotes of kings, nobles, and prelates. The time of his death is not known, but he must have been alive in 1154.

HENRY, O., pseudonym of **William Sydney Porter**, an American writer whose short stories are accounted among the greatest in the language. Born at Greensboro, North Carolina, on 11th Sept., 1862, he had a varied career, and saw much of the life with which his stories pulsate. His first post was that of clerk in a drug store. Two years were spent on a ranch in Texas, and then he was in turn bookkeeper, clerk in the General Land Office and teller in the First National Bank of Austin, Texas.

Meanwhile he had spent his leisure in writing articles and skits for the local press, and in 1894 he acquired a weekly humorous journal, *The Rolling Stone*, which, however, did not prosper in his hands. He next appears on the staff of the *Houston Post*.

In 1896 the tragedy of his life occurred. He was charged with the embezzlement of the funds of the Austin bank, and in 1898 was sentenced to 5 years (the actual term was 3¼ years) in Ohio penitentiary.

Here his literary genius asserted itself. Already he had had some stories accepted, and while he was in prison he wrote diligently and to such good effect that by the time he was free again his reputation was fully established. In 1903 an important commission from a New York journal brought him $100 a week. In 1904 he issued his first book, *Cabbages and Kings*, followed by *The Four Million*, *Heart of the West*, *The Trimmed Lamp*, *The Gentle Grafter* and (in 1908) *The Voice of the City*. He died on 5th June, 1910.

O. Henry's books have had an enormous circulation. They are marked by a fine narrative quality, sparkling and kindly humour, keen sympathies and an endless ingenuity. On these and on the breadth and clarity of the author's vision, his wide experience and his power to use it rests his title to fame as a master of the short story.

HENRYSON, **Robert**, a Scottish poet of the fifteenth century, born about 1425, died about 1506. He spent most of his life at Dunfermline, where he was schoolmaster. The *Testament of Cresseid*, his most important work,
V--P

is a continuation of Chaucer's *Troilus and Creseide*. He was probably the author of the early Scottish pastoral *Robin and Makyne*. Amongst his other works were a *Tale of Orpheus*, *The Moral Fables of Æsop in Scottish Metre*, and an allegorical ballad, *The Bludy Serk*. The earliest extant edition of his *Fables* is that of 1570, and a new edition by Gregory Smith (Scottish Text Society) appeared in 1906.

HENRY THE LION, Duke of Saxony, the most remarkable prince of Germany in the twelfth century, was born in 1129, and died at Brunswick in 1195. He succeeded his father, Henry the Proud, in 1139, assuming the government of Saxony himself in 1146. At the Diet of princes in Frankfort (1147) he demanded restitution of Bavaria, taken from his father by Conrad VII; but was worsted in the war which followed. It was restored to him, however, in 1154, after the death of Conrad, by the Emperor Frederick, Henry's cousin. His possessions then extended from the Baltic and the North Sea to the Adriatic, and he was successful in opposing the league formed against him at Merseburg in 1166.

About two years afterwards he separated from his wife and married Matilda, daughter of Henry II of England. He then went on an expedition to the Holy Land, and during his absence his enemies, and even the emperor, made encroachments on his dominions. In 1174 he followed Frederick I on his fifth expedition to Italy, but left him at the siege of Alessandria. He was then put under the ban of the empire, and his dominions were given to other princes. Henry defended himself for a time successfully, but was at last obliged to take refuge in England.

In 1182 he asked pardon of the emperor on his knees, and Frederick promised him his hereditary possessions, Brunswick and Lüneburg, on condition of his undergoing exile for three years. He therefore again went to England, but returned to Brunswick in 1184. In 1188 he was once more compelled to leave the country, and it was only in 1190, at the close of a year's fighting, that a reconciliation was finally effected. He was much in advance of his age in fostering industry, science, commerce, and the arts.

HENRY THE NAVIGATOR (*Don Henrique el Navegador*), fourth son of King John I of Portugal, born in 1394, died at Sagres 13th Nov., 1458. In his youth he gave brilliant proofs of courage. When the Portuguese conquered Ceuta in 1415, Henry distinguished himself by his bravery, and was knighted by his father, after whose death he chose for his residence the city of Sagres, in Algarve, near Cape St. Vincent, and vigorously prosecuted the war against the Moors in Africa. He erected at Sagres an observatory and a school of navigation.

From time to time he sent vessels on voyages to the coasts of Barbary and Guinea, resulting in the discovery of the islands of Puerto Santo and Madeira, and some years later of the Azores. In 1433 Gilianez, one of his navigators, safely doubled Cape Bojador, and other adventurers, pushing still farther south, discovered Cape Blanco in 1441 and Cape Verd in 1445. A profitable commerce with the natives of West Africa was soon developed, and the Senegal and Gambia partially explored. In 1458 he acted as general against the Moors. His efforts not only laid the foundations of the commerce and colonial possessions of Portugal, but gave a new direction to navigation and commercial enterprise.—Cf. J. P. Oliveira Martins, *The Golden Age of Prince Henry the Navigator*.

HENSON, Herbert Hensley. English prelate. Born in London, 8th Nov., 1863, he was educated at Oxford, where he won a fellowship at All Souls College. He was ordained in the Church of England and in 1887–88 was head of Oxford House, Bethnal Green. From 1888 to 1895 he was vicar of Barking; from 1895–1900, incumbent of St. Mary's Hospital, Ilford; and from 1900 to 1912, canon of Westminster and rector of St. Margaret's. In 1912 he was made Dean of Durham; in 1918, Bishop of Hereford; and in 1920, Bishop of Durham.

A broad Churchman, deeply read in church history, a fearless thinker and a powerful controversialist, the bishop occupies a unique position in the Church of England. He has written a great deal, both books and articles, and has set forward clearly and incisively his ideas of the creeds in modern life, the relations between church and state and other matters. His powers were seen at their best during the debates on the revised prayer-book in 1926–27. After its rejection by the House of Commons he came forward as an advocate of disestablishment. Among his latest books are Disestablishment (1929) and Sibbes and Simson (1932).

HENTY, George Alfred, writer of novels and boys' stories, born 1832, died 1902. He was for a time connected with the army, and was a war correspondent in several campaigns, but is most widely known as the author of a large number of stimulating stories of adventure, many of them based on famous historical events. His stories are not merely readable and exciting, but are designed to interest boys in history.

Among his works are: *All but Lost, Gabriel Allen, In the Irish Brigade, With Buller in Natal, Malcolm the Water-Boy, With Roberts to Pretoria, With the British Legion,* and *With Kitchener in the Soudan.*

HEPAR SULPHURIS (literally 'liver of sulphur,' so called from its brownish-green and liver-like appearance), a mixture of polysulphides of potassium with sulphate or thiosulphate of potash. It is a common homœopathic medicine.

HEPHÆS'TION, a noble Macedonian of Pella, the friend of Alexander the Great. He accompanied the king in his Asiatic campaigns, and died at Ecbatana (325 or 324 B.C.). Alexander had his body conveyed to Babylon, and erected a monument to him costing 10,000 talents.

HEPHÆS'TUS, a god of the ancient Greeks, identified by the Romans with their Vulcanus. He presided over fire, and was the patron of all those who worked in iron and metals. He fixed his residence in Lemnos, where he built himself a palace, and raised forges to work metals. The Cyclopes of Sicily were his workmen and attendants; and with him they fabricated not only the thunderbolts of Zeus, but also arms for the gods and the most celebrated heroes. His forges were supposed to be under Mount Ætna. Aphroditê (Venus) was the wife of Hephæstus, although according to the *Iliad*, he was married to Charis, one of the Graces.

HEP'TARCHY (Gr. *hepta*, seven, and *archê*, rule), a term used during the sixteenth century to designate the period of English history from 449 to 828, and the seven principal kingdoms into which England was divided in Anglo-Saxon times. The kingdoms were founded at different times, and at no one time were they all independent monarchies together. In 827 King Egbert of Wessex united the other kingdoms into one, and assumed the title of King of England. *See* ENGLAND.

HERA, an ancient Greek goddess, identified by the Romans with their Juno, the sister and wife of Zeus (Jupiter), and daughter of Kronos (Saturn) and Rhea. The poets represent Zeus as an unfaithful husband, and Hera as an obstinate and jealous wife, the result of which was frequent strife between them. She was worshipped in all Greece, but her principal seats were at Argos and at Samos.

The companions of Hera were the

Nymphs, Graces, and Hours. Iris was her particular servant. Among animals, the peacock, the goose, and the cuckoo were sacred to her. Her usual attribute is a royal diadem on her head. The festivals in her honour were called Heræa. The principal were those celebrated every fifth year at Argos, which city was considered to be especially under her protection.—Cf. L. R. Farnell, *Cults of the Greek States.*

HER'ACLES, called by the Romans *Hercules*, the most celebrated hero or semi-divine personage of Greek mythology, was the son of Zeus (Jupiter) by Alcmena, the wife of Amphitryon. The name of Hercules is explained as 'renowned through Hera' (*Hera*, and *cleos*, glory). He was brought up at Thebes, and before he had completed his eighth month strangled two snakes sent by the jealous Hera (Juno) to devour him. His tutor was the Centaur Cheiron.

Early in life he had, at the command of Zeus, to subject himself for twelve years to the will of Eurystheus, on the understanding that after he had ac-

Hercules, from a Roman Lamp

confined for many years; (6) to kill the birds which ravaged the country near the Lake Stymphalus, in Arcadia, and ate human flesh; (7) to bring alive into Peloponnesus a prodigious wild bull, which laid waste the Island of Crete; (8) to obtain the mares of Diomedes, which fed upon human flesh; (9) to obtain from the queen of the Amazons a girdle which she had received from Ares (Mars); (10) to kill the monster Geryon, King of Gades, and bring to Argos his numerous flocks, which fed upon human flesh; (11) to obtain apples from the garden of the Hesperides; (12) the last and most dangerous of all, to bring from the infernal regions the three-headed dog Cerberus. Besides these labours, he also achieved of his own accord others equally celebrated. Thus, he assisted the gods in their wars against the giants, and it was through him alone that Zeus obtained the victory.

Having attempted to plunder the temple at Delphi, he became engaged in conflict with Apollo, and was punished by being sold to Omphâlê, Queen of Lydia, as a slave, who restored him to liberty and married him. On his return to Greece, he became the husband of Deïanira, who unwittingly brought about his death by giving him a tunic poisoned with the blood of the Centaur Nessus, which she innocently believed would retain for her Heracles's love. The poison took effect whenever the garment was put on, and as the distemper was incurable, Heracles placed himself on a burning pile on the top of Mount Œta, was received

Hera

quitted himself of this duty he should be reckoned in the number of the gods. He therefore went to Mycenæ, and performed at the bidding of Eurystheus the tasks known as the *twelve labours of Heracles.* These were: (1) to kill a lion which ravaged the country near Mycenæ; (2) to destroy the Lernæan hydra; (3) to capture, alive and un-up into heaven, and being there reconciled to Hera, received her daughter Hebe in marriage.

In ancient works of art Heracles is generally represented naked, with strong and well-proportioned limbs; he is sometimes covered with the skin of the Nemæan lion, and holds a knotted club in his hand, on which he often leans. The principal ancient statue of him which remains is the Farnese Hercules at Naples, a work of the Athenian Glycon. The myth of Heracles is believed by many writers to represent the course of the sun through the twelve signs of the zodiac. His marriage with Hebe was explained even by the ancients as symbolic of the renewing of the sun's course after its completion.—BIBLIOGRAPHY: Ch. Daremberg and E. Saglio, *Diction-naire des Antiquités Grecques et Romaines*; Gayley, *The Classic Myths in English Literature and in Art*; J. G. Winter, *Myth of Hercules at Rome*.

HERACLE'UM, a genus of large umbelliferous herbs, the cow-parsnips, of which *H. Sphondylium* (common cow-parsnip or hog-weed) is very common in Britain in damp meadow ground and pastures. *H. giganteum* (the Siberian cow-parsnip) is often grown in shrubberies, reaching the height of 10 feet.

HERACLI'DÆ, the descendants of Heracles, but more particularly those who, assisted by the Dorians, successfully asserted by arms their claim to the Peloponnesus, whence their ancestors had been driven by usurpers. *See* GREECE (HISTORY).

HERACLI'TUS, a Greek philosopher, born at Ephesus about 540 B.C. He travelled in different countries, particularly in Africa. On his return to Ephesus he was offered the chief magistracy, but refused it. He is said to have subsequently repaired to solitary mountains to live on roots and herbs; but, being attacked by a fatal disease, was obliged to return to the city, where he died soon afterwards, it is said in his sixtieth year. He left a work *On Nature*, in which he treats also of religion and politics. About 130 genuine fragments of this work remain.

He is considered as belonging generally to the Ionic school of philosophers, though he differed from it in important particulars. He considered fire as the first principle of all things, describing it as an ethereal substance ' self kindled and self-extinguished,' from which the world is evolved (not made) by a natural operation. It is also a rational principle, and the source of the human soul. Phenomena exist in a constant state of flux, always tend-ing to assume new forms, and finally returning again to their source. Heraclitus is the profoundest thinker before Plato and the founder of Idealism. In modern times Hegel and Nietzsche have been influenced by his philosophy. —Cf. T. Gomperz, *Greek Thinkers*.

HERACLI'US, Roman emperor of the East, born in Cappadocia about A.D. 575, the son of Heraclius, exarch of Africa. At the head of a fleet from Carthage, in 610, he assisted in de-throning Phocas, the murderer and successor of the Emperor Mauritius, and himself ascended the throne. In a succession of splendid victories he crushed the Persians under Chosroes; but the energy of his earlier years seems to have worn itself out, and he made no effort to check the victorious progress of Mohammed. Before his death Syria, Palestine, Mesopotamia, and Egypt had fallen under the dominion of the caliphs.

His last years were devoted to ecclesiastical reforms and theological speculations. Whilst endeavouring to reconcile the Christian sects, his enthusiasm made him oppress his Jewish subjects. He died in 641, and was succeeded by his son, Constantine III.— Cf. J. B. Bury, *The Later Roman Empire*.

HER'ALD (O.Fr. *herault, heraut*), an officer whose functions primarily were to carry messages of courtesy or defiance between sovereigns or persons of knightly rank, to superintend and register the results of trial by battle, tournaments, and other chivalric exercises, to record the valiant deeds of combatants, proclaim war or peace, marshal processions and public ceremonials, and especially, in later times, to regulate and determine all matters connected with the use of armorial bearings.

Heralds began to appear about the twelfth century, and assumed the functions which ultimately belonged to their office gradually. The first use of the word in English documents occurs in 1337. The herald, after the office was fully constituted, was created with many ceremonies, and had to pass through various grades of protracted service before reaching the full dignity of a herald.

The office is now shorn of much of its importance. Heralds are appointed in England by the Earl Marshal, whose office is hereditary. The Heralds' College, or College of Arms, founded by charter of Richard III in 1483, consists of the three chief heralds (*see* GARTER KING-OF-ARMS), the six subordinate or provincial heralds of York, Lancaster, Chester, Windsor, Richmond, and Somerset; two heralds appointed on the accession of George I, called

Hanover herald and Gloucester king-of-arms, together with the Earl Marshal and secretary, in all thirteen persons.

There are four marshals or pursuivants, called blue-mantle, rouge-croix, rouge-dragon, and portcullis, who usually succeed to vacancies in the Heralds' College. Among the duties of the Heralds' College are the banners, &c., naturally occurred in the earliest times, and the symbols were sometimes hereditary.

Origin. The origin of heraldic arms, properly so called, is, however, to be attributed to the necessity which arose during the Crusades of distinguishing the leaders of the numerous and motley bands of warriors which constituted the Christian armies. One

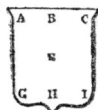     

Points of the Shield   Or   Argent   Azure   Gules   Sable

Vert   Ermine   Vair   Chief   Pale   Bend

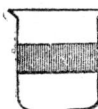     

Fesse   Bar   Chevron   Cross   Saltire   Paly

Bendlet   Party per pale   Rampant   Trippant   Volant   Naiant

Displayed   King   Noble   Knight   Esquire

Heraldry

recording of pedigrees and the granting of coats of arms to persons who wish to assume them. The Heralds' College, or Lyon Court, in Scotland, consists of Lyon king-of-arms, and six heralds, with six pursuivants.

HER'ALDRY, the whole science of a herald's duties, or more commonly the knowledge of the forms, terms, and laws which pertain to the use of armorial bearings or coats of arms. Badges and emblems on shields, helms of the oldest specimens of heraldic bearings extant is the shield at Mans of Geoffrey Plantagenet, who died in 1150. Rolls of arms in England are extant from the reigns of Henry III, Edward I, and Edward II. The use of arms on the Great Seal of England was introduced by Richard I. The bearing of coat armour by private persons was prohibited by proclamation in the reign of Henry V.

Courts of Jurisdiction. The chief

courts of jurisdiction in questions of heraldry are the Heralds' College in England, and the Lyon Court in Scotland. (*See* HERALD.) The rules of heraldry now practised at the Heralds' College are comparatively modern, and differ in some respects from those of other European courts.

Coat of Arms. A coat of arms consists of the figure of a shield marked and coloured in a vast variety of ways, so as to be distinctive of an individual, a family, or a community. The shield or *escutcheon* represents the original shield used in war, and on which arms were anciently borne. The surface of the escutcheon is termed the *field*, and the several parts or *points* of it have particular names, so that the figures which the field contains may be precisely located. In the accompanying illustration A B C marks the part of the shield called *the chief*, which is the highest and most honourable part of the shield. A is the *dexter chief* or upper *right-hand* side of the shield; B, the *middle chief*; and C, the *sinister chief* or upper *left-hand* side of the shield; E, the *centre* or *fesse point*; G H I, the *base*, that is, G, the *dexter* or right-hand *base*; H, the *middle base*; and I, the *sinister* or left hand *base*.

Colour. Colour is given in the coat of arms by means of *tinctures*, two of which are *metals*—*or* and *argent*, that is, gold and silver—the rest *colours* proper. These colours are, in heraldic terminology: *azure*, blue; *gules*, red; *sable*, black; *vert*, green: *purpure*, purple; *tenney*, orange; *sanguine*, blood-colour. The two last are comparatively uncommon. An object represented in its natural colours is said to be *proper*. When not given in colours or by actual gilding, the tinctures are represented by points and lines in black and white. *Or* is distinguished by small dots covering the part; *argent* is represented by leaving the space blank; *azure* is shown by horizontal lines; *gules*, by perpendicular lines; *sable*, by perpendicular and horizontal lines crossing each other; *vert*, by diagonal lines running from the dexter chief to the sinister base; *purpure*, by diagonal lines running from the sinister chief to the dexter base. Another class of tincture are the *furs*, of which the two principal are *ermine* and *vair*, which have also their special method or representation.

Figures. The figures borne on the shield may be either purely artificial and conventional, or may represent real objects, animals, plants, &c. Of the former the most common are known as *ordinaries*, and have the following names: Chief, Pale, Bend, Fesse, Bar, Chevron, Cross, and Saltire. The *chief* is a portion of the shield at the top marked off by a horizontal line, and covers the upper third part of the field. The *pale* occupies the middle third part of the field perpendicularly. The *bend* is drawn diagonally from the dexter chief to the sinister base in the form of a belt, and also occupies the third of the field. A diminutive of the bend is the *bendlet*. The *fesse* occupies the middle third of the field horizontally. The *bar* is formed after the manner of a fesse, but occupies only a fifth of the field, and is not confined to any particular part of it, except when there is only one bar, when it is put in the place of a fesse. Bars are mostly two in a field, sometimes three or more. A diminutive is the *barrulet*. The *chevron* may be regarded as made of a bend dexter and sinister issuing from the right and left base points of the escutcheon and meeting like two rafters. The *cross* is the ordinary cross of St. George. The *saltire* is the equally well-known cross of St. Andrew.

The shield is often divided by lines running similarly to the ordinaries; hence when divided by a perpendicular line it is said to be *party per pale*; when by a horizontal line, *party per fesse*; when by a diagonal line, *party per bend*. Similarly, when it seems to bear several pales or bends or bars, it is said to be *paly, bendy, or barry* of so many pieces, 'paly of six argent and gules' for instance, as in illustration.

Charges are the figures of natural and artificial things, and include animals and plants, implements and objects of all sorts and various imaginary monsters, being drawn either on the field or on one of the ordinaries. It is a rule in heraldry that metal must not be put on metal nor colour on colour; hence, if the field, say, is *argent*, it cannot have a charge or an ordinary tinctured *or* directly upon it.

Various technical terms describe the position of animals; thus, a lion is *rampant* when he is erect standing on one of his hind legs; *sejant*, when sitting; *couchant*, when lying at rest, with the head erect; *passant*, in a walking position; *gardant*, looking full-faced; *rampant gardant*, erect and looking full-faced; *salient*, in a leaping posture. So *trippant* is said of the stag when trotting; *lodged*, of the stag when at rest on the ground; *volant*, of birds in general in a flying posture; *rising*, of a bird that is preparing to fly; *displayed*, of birds seen frontwise with outspread wings: *naiant*, of fishes when swimming; and so on. The teeth and claws of lions and other ravenous beasts are called their *arms*; and when these have a special tincture, the animal is said to be *armed* of such a tincture; similarly, if their tongue be of a special tincture, they are said to be *langued* of this tincture.

Marshalling. Often two or more coats of arms are united together on one shield, so that the whole may be a very complicated affair. The art of arranging arms in this way is known as *marshalling*, and when the shield is divided up into squares for the reception of different coats, it is said to be *quartered*.

There are also certain exterior ornaments of the shield or escutcheon, namely, the helmet, mantling, crest, wreath, motto, and supporters. The helmet, which is placed on the top of the escutcheon, varies both in form and materials. Those of sovereign princes are of gold, those of the nobility of silver, and those of gentlemen of polished steel. The *full-faced helmet*, with six bars, is for the king and princes of the blood; the *sidelong helmet*, with five bars, is for dukes and marquesses, &c.; the *full-faced helmet of steel*, with its beaver or vizor open, is for knights; and the *sidelong helmet*, with the vizor shut, for the esquire. The mantling or mantle was anciently fixed to the helmet, to which it served as a covering. Mantlings are now used like cloaks, to cover the whole achievement. The crest is placed above the helmet, with the wreath serving as a kind of support: the latter is composed of two colours wreathed or twisted together. The motto consists of the word or phrase carried in a scroll under or above the arms. Supporters were originally only ancient devices or badges, which by custom came to embellish armorial ensigns. They are called *supporters* because they hold the shield, as the lion and the unicorn in the well-known royal arms of England.

The present royal arms of Britain exhibit the arms of England, Scotland and Ireland in the four quarters of the shield; that is: Quarterly, 1 and 4, England; 2, Scotland; 3, Ireland. The arms of England are; Gules, three lions passant gardant in pale or; Scotland, Or, a lion rampant within a double tressure flory counter-flory gules; Ireland, Azure, a harp or, stringed argent.—BIBLIOGRAPHY J. W. Papworth, *Dictionary of Coats of Arms*; J. Edmonson, *Complete Body of Heraldry*; Woodward and Burnet, *A Treatise on Heraldry, British and Foreign*; P. Allen, *Peeps at Heraldry*; G. C. Rothery, *A.B.C. of Heraldry*; J. H. Stevenson, *Heraldry in Scotland*.

HERAT', a city in the north-west of Afghanistan, in a beautiful and fertile plain, about 370 miles west of Kabul. It is enclosed by a broad deep moat, and an earthen mound surmounted by a lofty wall of unburned brick, and defended by a strong citadel. From each of four of the five gates a long street of bazaars (one vaulted throughout its entire length) leads towards a square in the centre of the town. The remaining streets are narrow and dirty.

The most important manufactures are carpets, sword-blades, shoes, cloaks, and sheepskin caps. The trade, is almost entirely in the hands of Hindus, is greatly favoured by the situation of the town on the great thoroughfare from India westward. Herat was long the capital of the empire founded by Tamerlane. Pop. about 30,000.

HÉRAULT (ā-rō), a department of France, on the Mediterranean coast; area, 2,402 sq. miles. In the north-west it is covered by the Cevennes, but it descends rapidly towards the coast, which is lined by lagoons. The chief rivers, the Hérault, Orb, and Lez, are partly navigable; but the most important water communication is the Canal du Midi. The arable land, about one-sixth of the whole, is generally fertile. The vine and mulberry are extensively, the olive more partially cultivated; fruit is abundant; and aromatic, medicinal, and dye plants are largely grown. Salt is obtained in large quantities. Capital Montpellier. Pop. (1926), 514,819.

HERBA'CEOUS PLANTS, plants of which the stem is not woody, and perishes annually; in herbaceous perennials, the underground parts remain permanent, and send forth a new aerial shoot in the following season.

HERBA'RIUM, or HORTUS SIC-CUS, a collection of dried plants systematically arranged. The specimens should be collected in dry weather, and carried home in a japanned tin box or vasculum; a small pocket box being desirable, however, for mosses and small plants; in the tropics a wicker basket is the best receptacle. Very delicate specimens should be at once placed in a small field-book of unsized blotting-paper carried tightly strapped between suitable boards.

At home they are carefully arranged upon bibulous paper, and pressed between smoothly planed deal boards either by putting weights upon the boards or by using a screw-press. The paper is changed every day or two, as the specimens are found to part with their moisture more or less freely. In moist climates it may be necessary to change the papers several times a day. Succulent plants (such as stone-crops) should be killed by immersion in boiling water, and left for some time to drain, before pressing. If the stem be thick and woody, or if the flower be thick and globular, as in the thistle, one half may be cut away without depriving it of its character.

When the process of desiccation has been completed, specimens are fastened upon stiff paper (16½ by 10½ inches) with a mixture of gum-tragacanth and gum-arabic, or thin glue, or with slips of gummed paper, or a needle and thread. The finished specimens must be painted with an antiseptic solution such as the following: carbolic acid, 2 oz.; bichloride of mercury, 2 oz.; methylated spirit, 1 gall. As an additional precaution naphthalene should be placed in the cabinet and frequently renewed.— BIBLIOGRAPHY: J. C. Willis, *Flowering Plants and Ferns*; *Kew Bulletin*, 1914.

HERBERT, Alan Patrick. English author. Born 24th Sept., 1890, the son of a civil servant, he was educated at Winchester and New College, Oxford, and became a barrister. He served during the Great War in Gallipoli and France with the Royal Naval Division, and when it was over made a name by his contributions to *Punch*. In 1924 he joined the regular staff of that paper. Herbert's books include *Sea Shanties*, *Plain Jane*, *Misleading Cases*, *The Trials of Topsy* and *The Water Gipsies*. In 1931, with T. F. Dunhill, he produced a successful musical comedy, *Tantivy Towers* and also an operetta *Derby Day*. He is a strong advocate of "water buses"—a service of passenger boats on the Thames in London.

HERBERT, Edward, Lord Herbert of Cherbury, in Shropshire, an English writer, born 1581, and died in London 1648. Educated at University College, Oxford, he distinguished himself at the siege of Juliers under the Prince of Orange in 1609, and in 1614 served again in the Low Countries under the same leader. In 1618 he was sent as Ambassador to the court of France, but was recalled in consequence of a quarrel with Constable Luynes, the favourite of Louis XIII. On the death of Luynes, however, he was sent back to France as resident Ambassador.

At Paris, in 1624, he printed his famous book *De Veritate*, with the object of asserting the sufficiency, universality, and perfection of natural religion. In 1625 he returned from France and was created an Irish peer, and in 1631 an English baron. He joined the Parliamentary party, but subsequently quitted it, and suffered in fortune in consequence. The character of Lord Herbert, as shown in his memoirs, was vain, punctilious, and quixotic, but open, generous, and brave. Another work of his was *De Religione Gentilium*. Soon after his death was published his *Life and Reign of Henry VIII*, and a collection of his poems was published in 1665.

HERBERT, George, poet and divine, brother of Lord Herbert of Cherbury, born 1593, died in 1633. He was educated at Westminster and at Trinity College, Cambridge, of which he became a Fellow in 1615. From 1619 till 1627 he was university orator. The death of James I in 1625 put an end to his prospects of civil promotion, and in the same year he took orders, and became a prebendary in the diocese of Lincoln. In 1630 he took priest's orders, and was presented to the rectory of Bemerton, near Salisbury, in Wiltshire.

His collection of religious poems, *The Temple*, was published in 1631, and the *Jacula Prudentum*, a collection of proverbs, in 1640. His poems bear the marks of an exceptionally fine nature, if not of genius, but they are marred by conceits and mannerisms. His chief prose work was *The Country Parson* (1652).—Cf. A. G. Hyde, *G. Herbert and his Times*.

HERBERT, Sidney, Lord Herbert of Lea, English statesman, son of the eleventh Earl of Pembroke, was born in 1810, died in 1861. He was educated at Harrow and Oxford, and was Conservative member for South Wilts from 1832 till shortly before his death. He was Secretary to the Admiralty under Peel in 1841, and in 1845 was made Secretary for War, but became a convert to free-trade, and quitted office with Peel in 1846.

In 1852 he became War Secretary in the Aberdeen Cabinet, and retained it till the dissolution of the ministry in 1855. For a short time he was Colonial Secretary under Palmerston, and in 1859, became once more Secretary for War. In 1861 he was transferred to the House of Lords, but died in the same year.—Cf. Lord Stanmore, *Sidney Herbert, Lord Herbert of Lea*.

HERCEGOVINA.—*See* HERZEGOVINA.

HERCULA'NEUM, an ancient city about 5 miles S.E. of Naples, completely buried, with Pompeii, Stabiæ, &c., by lava and ashes during an eruption of Vesuvius in the reign of Titus, A.D. 79. The modern villages of Resina and Portici are situated on the present surface.

The site had been long sought in vain, when in 1713 three statues were found in digging a well at the village of Portici. In 1738 the well was dug deeper, and traces of buildings were found. The theatre was then discovered, but though the excavations were continued for many years it is now the only building to be seen underground, as the successive excavations were immediately filled up with rubbish from a new digging. A number of public buildings and private dwellings were laid bare, and many objects of great value discovered, such as statues, busts, beautiful mosaics, wall paintings, charred papyrus manuscripts, &c. One of the houses discovered contained a quantity of provisions, consisting of fruits, corn, oil, peas, lentils, pies, and hams. It would appear from the human remains found that fewer people escaped from Herculaneum than from Pompeii.

Among the most interesting objects discovered here were the papyri, over 1,750 of which are now in the Naples Museum. The knowledge of ancient art has, however, gained more by the discoveries made than has literature. Excavations undertaken in 1906 had to be abandoned, owing to the attitude of the Italian Government, and financial difficulties with property-holders in Resina.—Cf. Sir C. Walston and L. Shoobridge, *Herculaneum, Past, Present, and Future.*

HERCULES.—*See* HERACLES.

HERCULES, one of Ptolemy's northern constellations, between Lyra and Corona Borealis. The point to which the sun, with its accompanying system of planets, is travelling at present is situated in Hercules. The constellation contains a magnificent globular star cluster.

HERCULES, PILLARS OF, the ancient name of the two promontories,

The House of Argo, Herculaneum

Calpe (Gibraltar) and Abyla (Ceuta), at the entrance to the Mediterranean.

HERCULES BEETLE, a very large lamellicorn beetle, *Dynastes hercules,* native to tropical America. An enormous horn projects from the head and a smaller one from the thorax, and the beetle attains a length of 5 inches.

HERDER, Johann Gottfried von, German author, born in poor circumstances in 1744, died 1803. In 1762 he went to Königsberg, procured an appointment in Frederick's College, and was permitted by Kant to hear

Hercules-beetle

all his lectures gratis. From 1764 to 1769 he was an assistant teacher at the cathedral school of Riga, with which office that of a preacher was connected, and it was during this period that he published his *Fragments on German Literature.* In 1769 he resigned his post in order to travel, and became travelling tutor to the Prince of Holstein-Oldenburg. But in Strasbourg he was prevented from proceeding by a disease of the eyes; and here he became acquainted with Goethe, on whom he had a very decided influence.

Besides his *Fragments,* his *Kritische Wälder* (Critical Woods) and other productions had gained him a considerable reputation, and he was appointed in 1771 court preacher, superintendent, and consistorial counsellor at Bückeburg, and in 1776 to the same offices at Weimar. In 1801 he was made president of the high consistory, a place before only given to noblemen. He was subsequently made a noble by the Elector of Bavaria.

For some time Herder was interested in the poetry of the North, particularly in the poems of Ossian and the works of Shakespeare. As a result he broke with Classicism, and became one of the leaders of the 'Sturm und Drang' movement. A still greater influence on his mind was his friendship with Hamann, which stimulated his appreciation of poetry and national literature.

As a theologian Herder contributed to a better understanding of the historical and antiquarian part of the Old Testament. His *Geist der Hebräischen Poesie* (Spirit of Hebrew Poetry) is highly valued. He did much also for the better appreciation of the classical authors. His greatest work is his *Ideen zur Philosophie der Ger-*

chichte der Menschheit (Ideas on the Philosophy of the History of Man; 1785 *et seq.*). He is the author of some graceful songs, and of an epic entitled *The Cid*.

HEREDIT'AMENTS is property which under the old law would have descended to the heir and is often synonymous with 'land.' 'Corporeal hereditament' is an interest in land in possession, that is, a present right to enjoy the possession of land. 'Incorporeal hereditament' is a right over land in the possession of another, such as a future right to possession, i.e. a reversion, or a right to use land in the possession of another, such as a right of way, &c.

HERED'ITY, the transmission from parents to offspring of the physical characters and intellectual aptitudes of themselves and their ancestors. Ever since man began to domesticate and breed animals and cultivate plants he has been aware of the general facts of the hereditary transmission of qualities from one generation of living beings to another, even if he had not observed among his fellows the effects of inheritance in their family likenesses.

How fully the ancients realized these essential facts is shown in many references to the subject in Greek and Latin literature, and nowhere more clearly than in *The Nature of Things* by Lucretius. But it was not until about forty years ago that the attempt was seriously made to elicit the real meaning of these well-established data by rigid scientific methods. Lucretius called attention to the observation that the offspring may present features distinctive of either the father or the mother or a mixture of the peculiarities of both parents; moreover, he also recognized that a child may reveal traits of its grandparents or even more distant ancestors that were not apparent in its parents. Within recent years the principles underlying these observed facts have been investigated, and the suggested explanations have been submitted to the test of scientific experiment.

At the present time no branch of biology is more active than the investigation of these problems, which are still the subject of vigorous controversy, and are exciting a vast amount of attention both in popular and technical journals and books. Many scientific journals are exclusively devoted to the discussion of the problems of heredity, and the mere enumeration of the titles of recent books dealing with the subject would fill many pages of such a volume as this.

In man and all those animals that reproduce their kind by means of the congress of the sexes, a new organism originates by the union of a male cell or spermatozoon with a female cell or ovum. Each of these cells contains a number of exceedingly minute bodies which are known as *chromosomes,* from the fact that they display a special avidity for many of the dyes used in staining sections of the tissues for microscopical examination. The material of which the chromosomes are formed is for the same reason called *chromatin.* When an ovum is fertilized, the paternal chromosomes of the spermatozoon are added to the maternal chromosomes of the ovum, so that the body of the offspring that develops contains a mixture of these minute particles which determine the development of traits of both parental stocks.

Mendelian laws. But before it was recognized how this mosaic of biparental characters was conveyed from one generation of living beings to another, the laws regulating the process of admixture had been elucidated by the observations and experiments of the Abbé Mendel, which were published in 1866, but were totally neglected until 1900, when their far-reaching significance was first recognized. Since then a vast amount of experimental breeding of plants and animals has been done by many biologists to confirm and extend the application of the principles laid down by Mendel and to elucidate the mechanism of inheritance. In particular the attempt has been made to bring these results of breeding experiments into correlation with the information independently collected with reference to chromosomes and the part played by them as the bearers of the hereditary qualities. The information relating to these two lines of research will be found in Bateson's *Mendel's Principles of Heredity* and Wilson's *The Cell;* but the reader who merely wants a concise and reliable summary of a very extensive and complex subject will find in Professor Goodrich's *The Evolution of Living Organisms.*

The Mendelian laws of inheritance have been determined by crossing allied races of plants and animals which differ one from the other by some character that is easily recognized, and recording what happens (and especially the numerical results) in the succeeding generations. For example, Mendel crossed two races of the common pea (*Pisum sativum*), a tall and a short. The first generation consisted entirely of tall offspring. But on breeding from these one-quarter of the next generation was short and three-quarters tall; and of the latter one-third bred true (i.e. produced exclusively tall offspring), but the other two-thirds a mixture of tall and short in the same proportions as the second generation.

In this case tallness is said to be dominant and shortness recessive; and by this is meant that when the embryo is formed by an admixture of long and short factors, the result is determined by the former, which overcomes the influence of the latter. There is no real blending of the effects resulting in a generation intermediate in height between the long and the short; it is an all-or-none effect—either long or short. Recognizing this fact, what happens in the mingling of the long and short elements is expressed in the simple arithmetical statement that by mixing the hereditary factors tall and short, one-quarter of the progeny will be purely tall, one-quarter purely short, and the rest an admixture of tall and short; and as tallness is dominant this half will be tall and, being added to the other quarter, will make three-quarters tall; but as the half that contains the admixture of tall and short elements will segregate when bred from, they will give rise to three talls to one short.

In the interpretation of inheritance these facts suggest the absence of any real blending of characters in the offspring in the sense that a particular feature is intermediate between those of its two parents or two ancestral stocks, but rather that every individual is a mosaic of ancestral units built up into a new pattern, each element of which influences the rest in a manner sensibly different from that of any of its ancestors, and thus gives rise to a personality that is individual and distinctive.

In the process of development of an embryo from a fertilized ovum certain of the cells become specialized in structure and built up into skin, muscle, bone, nerves, glands, &c., of the new being; but some of them retain their primitive characters unaltered and become lodged as guests in the body formed from the other cells. These are the germs of the next generation, the potential ova or spermatozoa from which the children of the hosts of these cells will eventually be formed. Hence the saying that a child is the offspring of its grandparents, seeing that the ovum and spermatozoon from which it was developed were not formed from the tissues of its parents, but merely harboured and protected by them after being formed like the cells of the body itself from the ovum and spermatozoon of a preceding generation.

Weismann's theory. This contrast between body-cells (soma) and germ-cells was emphasized by Weismann, who gave expression to the theory of the continuity of the germ-plasm. By this he claimed that the special protoplasm of the ova and spermatozoa handed on from generation to generation in unbroken sequence, which gave rise to new individuals, was in a sense independent of the soma which, from the point of view of inheritance, was little more than the vehicle of the germ-cells. This was taken to imply that no change in the structure of the body acquired during the life of a parent could be transmitted to the offspring; but it is now recognized that the problem is much more complicated than this crude statement of Weismann's suggests. A great many factors in the animal's environment, as well as in the process of development in its own body, exert a far-reaching influence on the inheritance of characters, and only those traits are brought out and regularly developed which are evoked by the circumstances of the individual's environment and the development of special biochemical stimuli in its own body.

The trend of recent research in heredity is to discredit both Weismann's absolute denial of the inheritance of acquired characters and the no less crude interpretation of Lamarck as to the direct influence of environment. Once it is admitted that a special stimulus, either in the environment or in the growth-processes of the individual's own body, is required to call forth the distinctive features of every organism, the way is opened for the recognition of a multitude of factors other than mere continuity of germ-plasm that play a part in moulding the structure of the body and in determining its functional capabilities.

During the last thirty years, largely as the effect of Weismann's teaching, an altogether undue importance has been attached to the influence of heredity in the causation of certain disorders of body and mind, such as tuberculosis and insanity, and the effect of this tendency is nowhere revealed more clearly than the reliance put upon such evidence, especially of insanity, in courts of law. It cannot be too strongly emphasized that, far reaching as are the effects of heredity in fashioning the body and determining the mental and moral aptitudes of every individual, environment and individual experience are factors of at least as much importance in the causation of such disorders as have been mentioned. One of the factors in increasing the incidence of tuberculosis or insanity in homes where some member of the family is subject to these affections is environmental: the constant subjection of other members of the family respectively to the risk of infection or to the domestic worries and social anxieties that are caused by an insane or neurasthenic person in the house. The realization of this truth is a factor of tremendous importance in medicine and sociology, for it affords hope for the prevention of these grave ills to the individual, and the social amelioration that follows in the train of such hope and its realization.

Applied statistics. During the last quarter of a century a new line of attack on the problems of inheritance has been developed, especially by Professor Karl Pearson and his school of applied statistics at University

Hereford Cathedral, West Front

College, London (see EUGENICS). By the use of statistical methods the procedures and results of investigators using other methods have been subjected to drastic criticism; but a great deal of constructive work has been done in analysing the data relating to the inheritance of such conditions as albinism and interpreting their significance. Such questions as the hereditary transmission of insanity and the tendency to tuberculosis and the possible effects of alcohol on the descendants of intemperate parents have been made the subject of prolonged research, the results of which have been published in a series of Draper's Company Research Memoirs by the Cambridge University Press, and especially in the journal *Biometrika*.—BIBLIOGRAPHY: E. B. Wilson, *The Cell in Development and Inheritance*; A. Weismann, *The Germ Plasm: a Theory of Heredity*; R. H. Lock, *Variation, Heredity, and Evolution*.

HEREFORD (he're-ford), a city and municipal borough of England, capital of county of same name, on the left bank of the Wye. The principal streets are broad and straight; houses mostly of brick, and the public buildings of stone. The beautiful cathedral near the Wye was rebuilt, in the reign of William the Conqueror, on the site of an earlier edifice, and restored in 1863 under the direction of Sir G. G. Scott. There is a map of the world made in 1313 (*Mappa Mundi*) preserved in the south choir aisle. Other public buildings are the college adjoining the cathedral, the shire hall, the county jail, Coningsby Hospital and St. Ethelbert's Hospital, museum and free library re-opened in 1931, corn exchange, market hall, and post office. Every three years a musical festival is held here. It is given by the choirs of Hereford, Gloucester and Worcester.

The manufactures, which are inconsiderable, consist of gloves, leather, turnery, and nails. Hereford was long an important garrison town on the Welsh border, and was the last city to surrender to the Parliamentarians. David Garrick was born at Hereford in 1716. Hereford was a parliamentary borough until 1918, returning two members till 1885, and only one from that date till 1918. Pop. (1931), 24,159.

HEREFORDSHIRE is an inland county which borders on Wales, and has an area of 538,924 acres, of which about 500,000 are arable, meadow, and pasture. The county belongs wholly to the basin of the Severn, towards which river it has a general slope north to south, as indicated by the course of its rivers, the Dye and its affluents.

The soil is in general fertile. Wheat is the principal crop, but barley, oats, beans, pease, hops, and turnips are also extensively cultivated. Orchards are numerous, and a large quantity of excellent cider is made. The Herefordshire cattle are held in high estimation for meat, though not good milkers. Horses are bred in considerable numbers. Oak timber is abundant, and forms, with oak-bark, an article of export. For parliamentary purposes Herefordshire forms two divisions, each returning one member. Pop. (1931), 111,755.—Cf. *Victoria County History, Herefordshire.*

HERESY (Gr. *hairesis*, choice), a religious opinion declared by ecclesiastical authority to be erroneous. Heretics are those who embrace a heresy, that is, those who hold some theological doctrine which conflicts with the beliefs of the Catholic or

Universal Church, but who, at the same time, call themselves Christians.

Many of the early Christians preserved their Jewish or Greek philosophical notions, and mingled them with the doctrines of Christianity. Even in the time of the Apostles we find traces of the Gnostics, and subsequently a great variety of heretical sects or sectaries arose. Among the chief may be mentioned the Manichæans, Sabellians, Arians, Apollinarians, Nestorians, Monophysites, Pelagians, Monothelites, Paulicians, &c. Among religionists stigmatized as heretics in later times by the Roman Catholic Church were the Waldenses, the Wycliffites, Hussites, Lutherans, and all Protestant sects and Churches.

Before Christianity was made the religion of the Roman State, nothing but excommunication was inflicted upon the heretic; but severe laws were passed soon after the conversion of the emperors. The Code of Justinian contains many ordinances against heretics, and the canon law made it a duty to denounce them, under pain of excommunication. As early as A.D. 385 Priscillian was condemned to death as a heretic by the Spanish bishops at the Council of Trèves; but the persecutions of heretics, properly so called, began in the pontificate of Gregory VII, in the eleventh century. Spain, Italy, and France, from the thirteenth to the sixteenth century, suffered much from these persecutions, but the states of Germany showed greater moderation. In England the burning of heretics was practised before 1200, and long continued. Heresy is now left entirely to the cognizance of the ecclesiastical courts.—BIBLIOGRAPHY: Burton, *Heresies of the Apostolic Age*; A. Harnack, *History of Dogma*.

HERFORD, a town of Germany, in the Prussian province of Westphalia, 16 miles south-west of Minden. It has manufactures of linen and cotton goods, leather, basket-work, and tobacco, and oil-mills. Once a free city, Herford passed to Prussia in 1815. Pop. 35,940.

HERGESHEIMER, Joseph, American novelist. He was born in Philadelphia, 15th Feb., 1880, and for a time studied art. In 1915 he made a name with his novel, *Mountain Blood*, and rose to the front rank with *The Three Black Pennys*, 1917; *The Bright Shawl*, 1922; *The Presbyterian Child*, 1923, and *Tampico*, 1926. Later books are *Quiet Cities*, 1928; *Swords and Roses*, 1929; *The Limestone Tree*, 1931; *Sheridan*, 1931; and *Berlin*, 1932.

HERIOT (O.Eng., *here*, army, and *geatu*, equipment), in English law, a tribute or fine, as the best beast or other chattel, payable to the lord of the fee on the decease of the owner, landholder, or vassal.

HER'IOT, George, founder of the hospital in Edinburgh which bears his name, and jeweller to King James VI, was born in 1563, and died in 1624. He followed his father's profession, and was admitted a member of the Incorporation of Goldsmiths in 1588. In 1597 he was appointed goldsmith to the queen by James VI, and on the accession of the latter to the English crown followed the court to England. From his settlement in London little is known of his history.

He left nearly the whole of his fortune to found a school in Edinburgh, styled in the bequest as a "hospital for the maintenance and education of poor fatherless boys, freemen's sons, of the town." The present building known as Heriot's Hospital was built between 1628 and 1659, and renovated in 1828. *See* EDINBURGH.

HERISAU, a town of Switzerland, in the canton and 4 miles north-west of Appenzell. It has manufactures of muslin and other kinds of cotton goods. Pop. (1930), 13,599.

HER'KOMER, Sir Hubert von, painter, born in Bavaria 1849, died 1914; lived mostly in England, where he received his art training. He first exhibited at the Royal Academy in 1869, and gained great reputation by his picture *The Last Muster—Sunday at the Royal Hospital, Chelsea*; and increased his reputation by paintings such as *Eventide: a Scene in Westminster Union*; *Life, Light, and Melody*; *Missing: a Scene at the Portsmouth Dockyard Gate*; *Hard Times*; *Found*; *The Chapel of the Charterhouse*; and *On Strike*. His works include many portraits, among them Wagner, Ruskin, Tennyson, and a large group, *The Council of the Royal Academy*, now in the Tate Gallery.

He was elected A.R.A. in 1879, R.A. in 1890, and from 1885 till 1895 was Slade professor of fine art at Oxford. He founded and superintended for a number of years an art school at Bushey, Herts. His work includes water-colours, etchings, and mezzotints, and he published lectures on these subjects. He was knighted in 1907.

HERLIES, a village in France, department of Nord, 5 miles north-east of Neuve Chapelle. It was the scene of fierce fighting during the European War (battles of Ypres).

HERM, one of the Channel Islands, 3 miles east of Guernsey, from which it can be visited. After the Great War it was bought by an English Company for development as a holiday resort. Pop. 40.

HERMADA, a mountain in Italy, south of the Carso Plateau, and the scene of fighting between the Austrians and the Italians during the European War (Carso battles).

HER'MANN, Johann Gottfried Jakob, a German scholar, born in 1772, died in 1848. He began to lecture on ancient literature at Leipzig in 1794, and with this university he was connected till his

Hermes. From a bronze statue

death. Hermann originated valuable reforms in the method of Greek grammatical instruction; and he is especially known for his editions of Æschylus, Euripides, Aristophanes, Bion, and Moschus, and for the controversies in which his theories involved him with Voss, Creuzer, Böckh, and other scholars.

HER'MANNSTADT, now **SIBIU,** a town of Transylvania, Rumania, on the Sibiu, 54 miles s.s.e. of Klausenburg. It consists of a high and a low town, connected by steep stone stairs, and of three suburbs. It was strongly fortified up to quite recent times. The manufactures are varied, and there is an important transit trade, chiefly to and from Istanbul. The battle of Hermannstadt, between the Rumanians and Austro-Germans, was fought in Sept. and Oct., 1916. Pop. (1930), 48,013.

HERMAPH'RODITE, a biological term for an animal in which the characteristics of both sexes are either really or apparently combined, especially an animal having the parts of generation both of male and female. Hermaphrodites are divided into true and spurious, the first exhibiting a real combination of the characteristics of the two sexes; while in the second the combination is only apparent. The animals in which the organs of the two sexes are normally combined in the same individual are mostly confined to the invertebrate division of the animal kingdom, as, for example, certain groups of the inferior worms, molluscs, barnacles, &c. There are no real hermaphrodites in the human species.

HERMAPHRODI'TUS, in Greek mythology, the son of Hermes and Aphrodite, born on Mount Ida, and brought up by naiads. He rejected the love of the nymph Salmacis, but the latter, embracing him, prayed to the gods to unite her to her lover for ever. The two finally formed a being half male and half female.

HERMAS, one of the so-called Apostolic Fathers, generally supposed to be the person mentioned by that name in *Rom.* xvi, 14, though others maintain that he lived much later and was a brother of the Pope Pius I (140–155). He is known as the author of a work entitled *The Shepherd,* circulated at Rome early in the second century, and for which a place in the canon was even claimed. Only a few fragments exist of the Greek original, but the Latin translation, probably made in the second century, and printed in 1513, appears to be complete. The book is an ethical not a theological work, treating of Christian virtues and their exercise.

HERMĒS, called by the Romans *Mercurius* (*see* MERCURY), in Greek mythology the son of Zeus and Maia, the daughter of Atlas. He was born in Arcadia, and soon after his birth left his cradle and invented the lyre by stringing the shell of a tortoise with three or seven strings. The lyre, however, he resigned to Apollo, with whom it was ever after identified. Hermēs also invented the Pandean pipe.

The ancients represent Hermēs as the herald and messenger of the gods. He conducted the souls of the departed to the lower world. He was the ideal embodiment of grace, dignity, and persuasiveness, but also of prudence, cunning, fraud, perjury, theft, and robbery. His cunning was frequently of service both to the gods and the heroes, and even to Zeus himself. Later writers ascribe to him the invention of dice, music, geometry, letters, &c. He was worshipped in all the cities of Greece, but Arcadia was the chief place of his worship, his festivals being called *Hermœa*. In the monuments he is represented as in the flower of youth, or in the full power of early manhood. He often appears with small wings attached to his head and to his ankles. Among his symbols are the cock, the tortoise, a purse, &c., and especially his winged rod, the *caduceus*.—Cf. A. Lang, *Myth, Ritual, and Religion*.

HERMES, Georg, a German theologian, born 1775, died in 1831. He studied theology at the University of Münster; became teacher in the gymnasium of that city, and in 1807 professor of dogmatic theology in the university.

When the Prussian Government established the University of Bonn, Hermes was appointed to the chair of Catholic theology (1820). Here he distinguished himself by an ingenious effort to base the doctrines of the Church on Kant's system of philosophy. His theological system, known as Hermesianism, was rationalistic in its character, endeavouring as it did to defend the Catholic faith by pure intellectualism. His system aroused powerful opposition, being condemned as heretical by a Papal letter of 1835, four years after the death of its originator. Among his works are: *Untersuchungen über die innere Wahrheit des Christenthums* (1805), and *Einleitung in die Christliche Theologie* (1819–29).

HERMES TRISMEGIS'TUS, a mythical personage, the reputed author of a great variety of works, probably written by Egyptian Neo-Platonists, who ascribed the authorship of the highest attainments of the human mind to Thoth, the Egyptian Hermes; regarding him as the source of all knowledge and inventions, the *Logos* incarnate, thrice greatest (Gr. *tris megistos*). Clement of Alexandria mentions the contents of forty-two books of Hermes which were extant in his time. Of those which now remain, the most important is *The Poimandrēs* or *Poimander* (consisting of fourteen or fifteen chapters), a dialogue on nature, the creation, the deity, the soul, knowledge, and similar topics. Of the extant works none belongs, in all probability, to an earlier date than the fourth or perhaps the third century of our era. Like the name of Homer, that of Hermes Trismegistus stands for a whole literature, religious and philosophical. Indeed, during the third and following centuries the name of Hermes was usually adopted by all authors of philosophical writings.—Cf. G. R. S. Mead, *Thrice Greatest Hermes*.

HERMIT-CRAB, a name common to a family (Paguridæ) of well-known decapod crustaceans. These crabs take possession of and occupy the cast-off univalve shells of various molluscs, carrying this habitation about with them, and changing it for a larger one as they increase in size. The most common British species is the *Pagurus Bernhardus*, popularly known as the soldier-crab. Anemones, sponges, and zoophytes are asso-

Hermit Crab (*Pagurus Bernhardus*)

ciated with hermit-crabs as messmates.

HERMON, a mountain of Syria, belonging to the Anti-Lebanon, about 9,400 feet high. The primitive name was Siryon, and it also occurs in the plural form *Hermonim*.

HERMOSILLO (-sil'yō), capital of the state of Sonora, Mexico, on the River Sonora, 110 miles north from the port of Guaymas, with which it has a large traffic. It has a mint, distilleries, and flour-mills. Pop. 25,000.

HERNE BAY, an English watering-place on the north coast of Kent, 8 miles north-east of Canterbury, with fine sands, marine parade, iron pier and pavilion, and baths. Pop. (urban district), 11,244. Herne is a village one mile inland.

HERNIA, in surgery, a tumour formed by the displacement of a soft part, which protrudes by a natural or accidental opening from the cavity in which it is contained.

The brain, the heart, the lungs, and most of the abdominal viscera may become totally or partially displaced, and thus give rise to the formation of hernial tumours. But the term is ordinarily applied to abdominal hernia. Any part of the abdomen may become the seat of hernia, but it most commonly appears in the anterior and inferior region, which, being destitute in a great measure of muscular fibres, and containing the natural openings, offers less resistance to the displacement of the viscera. Most of the viscera, when displaced, push the but generally occurs at the margins of the opening through which the hernia protrudes.

As soon as a patient perceives that he is affected with a hernia he should have recourse to medical advice, for the disease is then in its most favourable state for treatment. The hernia, when it is reduced, must be prevented from recurring by the constant pressure of a pad or truss. An irreducible hernia must be supported with great care. All violent exercises, and excess in diet, must be avoided. The strangulated hernia requires prompt relief, and may necessitate an operation.

Mount Hermon

peritoneum forward before them: this membrane thus forms an envelope of the hernia, which is called the *hernial sac*. The hernia itself is usually a loop of the small bowel, and though it has been pushed through the wall of the abdomen, forming a tumour under the skin, the fæces still pass along it. If the hernia can be returned to the abdomen, it is said to be reducible; if, from its size or other cause, it cannot be replaced, it is irreducible. A hernia is said to be strangulated when it is not only irreducible, but also subjected to a continual constriction, which interferes with the circulation through the blood-vessels of the part and the passage of the fæces. It may be rapidly fatal. Constriction may be produced by different causes,

HERNÖSAND (her'neu-sán), a seaport and cathedral town of Sweden, capital of Västernorrland, on the Island of Hernö, in the Gulf of Bothnia, with a considerable shipping trade. Pop. (1932), 11,769.

HERO, a Greek priestess of Aphrodite at Sestos, on the coast of Thrace, for love of whom Leander, a youth of Abydos, swam every night across the Hellespont, guided by a torch from her tower. One stormy night the torch was blown out, Leander drowned, and his body washed ashore, when Hero, overcome with anguish, threw herself from the tower on the corpse of her lover, and perished. There is a Greek poem by Musæus on this subject, and the story was beautifully retold by Marlowe, who left it incomplete at his death. Chapman completed it, besides making a more literal translation of the poem of Musæus.

HERO (of Alexandria), one of the most distinguished Greek mathematicians and mechanists of ancient times, who flourished about 150–100 B.C. According to a modern theory, however, he is supposed to have lived during the second half of the first century A.D. A common pneumatic toy, called Hero's fountain, is attributed to him, and he also invented the æolipile, and a heliostat.

HER'OD, called *the Great*, King of the Jews, was a native of Ascalon, in Judea, where he was born about 74 B.C. He was the second son of Antipater the Idumean, who, being made Procurator of Judea by Julius Cæsar, appointed Herod to the government of Galilee. He at first embraced the party of Brutus and Cassius, but after their death reconciled himself to Antony, by whose interest he was first named Tetrarch, and afterwards King of Judea.

After the battle of Actium he successfully paid court to Augustus, who confirmed him in his kingdom. On all occasions his abilities as a politician and commander were conspicuous; but his passions were fierce and ungovernable, and his wife Mariamne, her brother, grandfather, and mother, and his own sons by her, were all put to death by him. He rebuilt the temple at Jerusalem with great magnificence, and erected a stately theatre and amphitheatre in that city. He also rebuilt Samaria, which he called Sebaste, and constructed many strong fortresses throughout Judea, the principal termed Cæsarea, after the emperor. The birth of Jesus Christ is said to have taken place in the last year of the reign of Herod, viz. 4 B.C., the year also signalized by the massacre of the children of Bethlehem.

Herod's policy and influence gave a great temporary splendour to the Jewish nation, but he was also the first to shake the foundation of the Jewish Government, by dissolving the National Council, and appointing the high priests and removing them at pleasure, without regard to the laws of succession.—BIBLIOGRAPHY: W. Willett, *Life and Times of Herod the Great*; J. Vickers, *The History of Herod*.

HEROD AGRIPPA I, son of Aristobulus by Berenice, daughter of Herod the Great. Owing to his attachment to Caligula he was imprisoned by Tiberius, but on the accession of Caligula (A.D. 37) he received the government of part of Palestine, and afterwards all the dominions of Herod the Great. To please the Jews, with whom his rule was very popular, he caused St. James to be put to death, and imprisoned St. Peter. He died in the circumstances related in *Acts*, xii, in A.D. 44.

HEROD AGRIPPA II, son of the preceding, and last of the Herodian line. Being too young to govern, Judea was, on his father's death, reduced to a Roman province. He subsequently received the Kingdom of Chalcis, and obtained the superintendency of the temple at Jerusalem, where, with his sister Berenice, he heard the defence of Paul before Festus. Being driven from Jerusalem by the revolt of the Jews, he joined Cestius, and later on Vespasian, and during the siege of Jerusalem was very serviceable to Titus. After its reduction (A.D. 70) he and Berenice (with whom he was suspected to have an incestuous intercourse) returned to Rome. He is supposed to have died there, A.D. 94.

HEROD AN'TIPAS, son of Herod the Great by the Samaritan Malthace, was appointed Tetrarch of Galilee on his father's death (4 B.C.). This was the Herod who put to death St. John the Baptist, in compliment to his wife Herodias and in revenge for his reproaches of their incestuous union. Having visited Rome, he was accused of having been concerned in the conspiracy of Sejanus, was stripped of his dominions, and sent (A.D. 39) with his wife into exile at Lugdunum (Lyons), or, as some say, to Spain, where he died.

HERODAS, or **HERONDAS**, Greek writer of mimes, lived in the third century B.C., probably at Cos. Very little was known about Herodas (even the exact form of his name is uncertain) until 1890, when Sir F. G. Kenyon found at Fayum, in Egypt, a papyrus containing seven mimes in a practically perfect condition, and some fragments. These mimes are written in the old Ionic dialect, though the structure of the sentences is Attic. The metre is the curious *scazon* or limping iambic metre, with a spondee instead of an iambus in the last foot. A mime is a short dialogue in verse describing some scene of actual life.

Herodas is an unqualified realist, and gives us much information about the manners and customs of his time. The first mime is a conversation between a matchmaker and a grasswidow, who rejects some of the matchmaker's proposals, but consoles her with a drink of wine. The second is a law-court scene, where a pandar is prosecuting a sailor who has broken into his place of business. It is an immensely clever skit upon the Attic orators, especially Hyperides. The pandar boasts of his family traditions in true rhetorical style: "I am a pandar, and Sisymbras was my grand-father, and Sisymbriskos my father —pandars all." In the third mime a distracted mother gets her incor-rigible boy soundly but ineffectually flogged by his schoolmaster. In the fourth two ladies are sacrificing to Asclepios, with an accompaniment of small-talk. In the fifth a jealous woman orders a favourite slave to be flogged, and then countermands the order. The sixth is a conversation, mainly about a new belt, between two women; and the seventh is a scene depicting some customers in a shoe-maker's shop. The eighth, which is fragmentary, is about a dream.

Herodas is not a great writer, but he is extremely clever and amusing. The mimes are full of delicate touches of humour—humour which is none the worse for being unobtrusive. They bear close study and re-reading. In general tone they are not unlike Mr. F. Anstey's *Voces Populi*.—BIBLIO-GRAPHY: editions by Sir F. G. Kenyon and by J. A. Nairn; H. Sharpley, *A Realist of the Ægean*; R. T. Clark, *Theophrastos, Herodas, and Kebes*.

HEROD'OTUS, the oldest Greek historian whose works have come down to us, the 'father of history,' born at Halicarnassus, in Asia Minor, about 484 B.C. Before writing his history he travelled extensively, visiting the shores of the Hellespont and the Euxine, Scythia, Syria, Pales-tine, Babylon and Ecbatana, Egypt as far as Elephantine and other parts of Northern Africa, everywhere in-vestigating the manners, customs, and religion of the people, the history of the country, and the productions of the soil.

On returning home he found that Lygdamis had usurped the supreme authority in Halicarnassus, and put to death the noblest citizens, among others his uncle, the epic poet Panyasis, and Herodotus was forced to seek an asylum in the Island of Samos. Having formed a conspiracy with several exiles, he returned to Halicarnassus and drove out the usurper, but the nobles who had acted with him immediately formed an aristocracy more oppressive than the government of the banished tyrant, and Herodotus withdrew to the recently founded colony of Thurii, in Italy, where he seems to have spent most of his remaining life. Here, at an advanced age, we are told by Pliny, he wrote his immortal work, a statement strengthened by

the fact that events are noticed in the body of the book which occurred so late as 409 B.C., while its abrupt ending proves almost beyond ques-tion that he was prevented by death from completing it.

The history is divided into nine books, each bearing the name of a muse, and is written in the Ionic dialect. The object of the historian is to narrate the conflict between the Greeks and Persians, and he traces the enmity of the two races back to mythical times. Rapidly passing over the mythical period, he comes to Crœsus, King of Lydia, of whom and of his kingdom he gives a compara-tively full history. The conquest of Lydia by Cyrus induces him to relate the rise of the Persian monarchy and the subjugation of Asia Minor and Babylon. The history of Cambyses and his Egyptian expedition leads him to introduce the valuable details of the history, geography, and manners and customs of Egypt, which occupy the second book. The Scythian expedition of Darius causes the historian to treat of the Scythians and the north of Europe; and the subse-quent extension of the Persian king-dom affords him the opportunity for giving an account of Cyrene and Libya. In the meantime the revolt of the Ionians breaks out, which eventually brings on the conflict between Greece and Persia. An account of this outbreak and of the rise of Athens, after the expulsion of the Peisistratidæ, is followed by what properly constitutes the principal part of the work, and the history of the Persian War now runs on in an uninterrupted stream until the taking of Sestos.

In his history Herodotus merely relates what he saw and heard. He knows nothing of either historical criticism or the philosophy of history. He never traces the causes under-lying political changes, or the ulti-mate forces behind historical pheno-mena. There are English translations of his history by Littlebury, Beloe, Cary, G. C. Macaulay, and Rawlin-son, the last being accompanied by important notes and dissertations.—BIBLIOGRAPHY: W. C. Wright, *A Short History of Greek Literature*; J. B. Bury, *Ancient Greek Historians*; Sir J. P. Mahaffy, *History of Greek Classical Literature*.

HÉROLD, Louis Joseph Ferdinand, a French musical composer, born 1791, died 1833. He entered the Conserva-toire at Paris, afterwards studied at Rome, and became musical tutor to the daughters of Murat, King of Naples. His first successful opera was *Les Rosières*, produced in 1817. This was followed by, among other minor compositions, *Le Muletier* (1823) and *Marie* (1826). His chief works, however, are the famous *Zampa* (1821) and *Le Pré aux Clercs* (1832).

HERON, the common name of birds of the genus Ardĕa, constituting with the bitterns and shoebills the family Ardeidæ. The herons are very numerous, and almost universally spread over the globe. They are distinguished by having a long bill cleft beneath the eyes, a compressed body, long slender legs naked above the tarsal joint, three toes in front, the two outer united by a membrane, and by moderate wings. The tail is short, rounded, and composed of ten or twelve feathers.

Species. The common heron (*Ardĕa cinerĕa*) is about 3 feet in length from the point of the bill to the end of the tail, builds its nest in high trees, many being sometimes on one tree. Its food consists of fish, frogs, molluscs, mice, moles, and similar small animals. It has an insatiable voracity, and digests its food with great rapidity. It haunts freshwater streams, marshes, ponds, and lakes, as also the seashore. It was formerly in high esteem for the table, and, being remarkable for its directly ascending flight, was the special quarry pursued in falconry by the larger hawks. The great heron (*A. herodias*) is an inhabitant of America, and is called also great blue heron; the great white heron or egret (*A*, or *Herodias alba*) belongs to Europe; and the green heron (*A virescens*), the flesh of which is considered a delicacy, is a native of North America.

HERPES is a skin disease and takes the form of an acute eruption of vesicles occurring on the lips, nostrils or other parts of the face, and in these situations is known as *Herpes simplex*. It also occurs on the genital regions, buttocks, nipples, and mucous surfaces, but is rarely seen in other regions.

Herpes Simplex is frequently seen in pneumonia, cerebro-spinal meningitis, influenza, and catarrhal affections, but on the other hand a person may be affected with recurring attacks on the same part for no obvious cause.

Herpes'zoster (shingles) is an acute infection characterized by an eruption of grouped vesicles occupying a nerve area on one side of the body. There may be considerable general disturbance with fever, and there is much pain and discomfort in the affected region. It is most common on the chest, back, and neck, but may affect any nerve area in the body.

HERRE'RA, Francisco de, one of the leading painters of the Seville school, was born there about 1576, died at Madrid 1656. His design and handling are spirited and vigorous, and he may be regarded as to some extent the founder of a new national school. Among his pupils was Velasquez. He painted several pictures for churches in Seville, including an important *Last Judgment*, and four historical pictures for the Archiepiscopal Palace there. His frescoes have mostly disappeared. —His youngest son, Francisco, surnamed *El Mozo*, born 1622, died 1685, studied in Rome, and became court painter to Philip IV. He became Master of the Royal Works under Charles II.

HERRICK, Robert, English poet, was born in Aug., 1591, and died in Oct., 1674. His father, a goldsmith in Cheapside, died when Herrick was little more than a year old, and was believed to have purposely thrown himself from an upper window of his house. Herrick was probably educated at Westminster; he was for a time bound apprentice to his rich uncle, also a goldsmith, but in 1613 he entered St. John's College, Cambridge. After being there three years he migrated to Trinity Hall, with the idea of spending less money and of getting better value for what he did spend. He intended to study law, and Trinity Hall then, as now, was famous for its teaching of law. He took his B.A. degree in 1617 and his M.A. in 1620.

For some years we lose sight of him; he may have been studying for the Church at Cambridge, or may have been engaged in less reputable pursuits in London. In 1629 he was presented to the living of Dean Prior, a lonely place in Devonshire. He bemoaned his fate in leaving behind the gaieties of the capital, and the society of Ben Jonson, whose literary 'son' he had long been. But he seems soon to have settled down to a quiet and happy life in the country, and it is certainly to his country life that we owe the most exquisite of his poems. He never married, but lived a contented life surrounded by pets of various kinds, and faithfully cared for by his maid Prudence Baldwin. He delighted in the quaint rural customs which he saw all around him, and some of his most charming poems celebrate such things as May Day festivities, harvest home, and Christmas mumming.

Herrick was a sturdy Royalist, and accordingly was evicted in 1648 to make way for one Dr. John Syms, a Puritan. In 1648 he published his only volume of poems, entitled *Hesperides, or the Works both Human and Divine of Robert Herrick*. He had the satisfaction of ousting Dr. Syms from Dean Prior in 1662. Little is known of the last twelve years of his life, but he was buried on 15th Oct., 1674. A monument was erected in Dean Prior church in 1857.

Appreciation. There are few poets more charming than Herrick, and few who lend themselves less to critical disquisitions. His work is all self-explanatory, and beautifully lucid. He was an enthusiastic admirer of the Greeks and Romans, and imitated their manner as well as their matter. He frequently imitated Martial, but he is daintier and more spontaneous than the Roman poet. At times he is like the better contributors to the Greek anthology; and some of his work is not unlike that of the pseudo-Anacreon. Some of his poems do not merely remind us of Horace; they place him within a measurable distance of Catullus.

He was a perfect master of metre, and experimented with many new forms of it, nearly always successfully. In his poems of country life he shows himself a true lover of nature, and though born in Cheapside, as much a Devon man as Blackmore. In his love poems he is charming and dainty, though he never is more than the equal of Horace. His ladies were probably not really loved by him, so that he lacks the poignancy of Catullus. In his fairy poems he shows himself the poet-laureate of the court of Oberon and Titania. In his *Noble Numbers* he shows that he could write songs of good life as well as love-songs. They sustain his reputation as a clergyman more than his reputation as a poet. They help us to understand his strong personality, and are full of manly and practical piety.

In personal appearance Herrick was more like a buccaneer than a clerk in holy orders. In his nature he was a curious mixture of pagan and Christian, the pagan element predominating. The essence of his philosophy is to be found in Horace's famous phrase "Carpe diem" or his own "Gather ye rose-buds while ye may." Among all the Cavalier lyrists Herrick reigns as king by the indefeasible right of his daintiness and charm.—BIBLIOGRAPHY: Floris Delattre, *Robert Herrick*; F. W. Moorman, *Robert Herrick: a Biographical and Critical Study*; E. Gosse, *Seventeenth Century Studies*.

HERRING, the general name of fishes of the genus Clupĕa, the most important of which is the *Clupĕa harengus*, or common herring. It is of wide distribution in the North Atlantic, 45° N. lat. being about the southern limit. It measures from 10 to 12 inches in length, with blue-green back and brilliant silvery white under parts. It has small teeth in both jaws, and is of an elegant shape, the body being much compressed.

It was formerly supposed that the herrings migrated in two great shoals every summer from the Polar Seas to the coasts of Britain and France, returning in the winter, but the migration is probably only from a deeper part of the ocean to a shallower. The feeding-ground of the herring is probably the mud deposits found in the deeper parts of the sea, and it seems to be a fact that during their visits to the shallower waters of the coast for the purpose of spawning they do not feed, or feed very little. They are generally followed by multitudes of hakes, dog-fishes, &c., and gulls and other sea-birds hover over the shoals. They swim near the surface, and are therefore easily taken by net. So great is their fecundity that the enormous number taken appears to produce no diminution of their abundance, as many as 68,000 eggs having been counted in the roe of one female, though this is exceptional.

Herrings are taken throughout the year, but in the greatest quantities in summer. There are in fact two races, winter and summer, named from the spawning season. Contrary to the general rule in marine fishes the spawn is heavy, and sticks to various objects on the seafloor. Winter herring are taken in the Firth of Forth, on the Ballantrae Banks, and off Plymouth. In Scotland the summer or sea-herring fishery is one of the most important industries. The regular fishing begins in May at the Hebrides, in July on the northern coasts, and during August, September, and October along the east coasts of Scotland and England.

The mode of fishing most common to Scotland is with the drift-net. A series of nets with meshes about an inch square are joined together on a long rope, the nets being marked by floating corks or bladders, and the united nets are sunk by leaden weights, They thus stand across the path of the fish, which are enmeshed by their gills. Trawling or seine-net fishing is also practised.

In Scotland the catch of herrings is generally measured by the 'cran' = 45 gallons; a large proportion are cured or pickled, but great quantities are also disposed of fresh. There are upwards of 7,000 boats engaged in the Scottish fishery, with an aggregate of 230,000,000 sq. yards of netting. The annual value of herrings cured in Scotland is usually over £1,000,000. Herrings may be dried and smoked as bloaters (chief centre, Yarmouth) or split open and smoked as kippers.

Other prominent members of the herring family (Clupeidæ) are the sprat or garvie (*Clupĕa sprattus*); the pilchard or gypsy herring (*C. pilchardus*), of which the young are the true sardine; the anchovy (*Engraulis enchrasicholous*). Whitebait chiefly consists of the fry of herrings and sprats.

HERRIOT, Edouard. French statesman. Born July 5, 1872, at Troyes, he became a brilliant classical scholar. In 1897 he wrote *Philon le Juif*, which was crowned by the Academy, and later *Madame Recamier et Ses Amis* and other books showing scholarship of a high order.

In 1912 Herriot entered public life as a member of the Senate. He was later chosen leader of the Socialist-Radical party. He was Minister of Public Works in the Briand Government of 1916–17; Prime Minister in 1924–25, and again for one day in 1926; and Minister of Public Instruction in Poincaré's Cabinet, 1926–28. He again became Premier in June, 1932, and in July signed the Lausanne agreement for France. He was in office when the question of War Debt payment to the United States entered upon its present acute phase; he was himself opposed to the proposal to withhold payment of the annual instalment and refused to become responsible for France's defaults. Accordingly he left office in 1932 and was succeeded by M. Daladier. In the spring of 1933 he visited the U.S. to discuss with the new President (Mr. Roosevelt) the general question of economic and financial policy on the agenda of the World Conference for which preparations were then being made.

HERRNHUT, a village of Saxony, 50 miles E. of Dresden. It was founded by Count Zinzendorf, in 1722, for the Moravian Brethren (q.v.), and it afterwards became the metropolis and centre of that sect of Christians, who, from this town, are often called *Herrnhuters*.

HERSCHEL, Caroline Lucretia, sister of the astronomer Sir William Herschel, born at Hanover 1750, died 1848. She joined her brother at Bath in 1771, and acted during his life as his astronomical assistant. She also found time to conduct a series of observations for her own. In 1828 she received the gold medal of the Royal Astronomical Society, of which she was made an honorary member. On her brother's death she returned to Hanover.

HERSCHEL, Sir John Frederick William, only son of Sir William Herschel, was born in 1792 at Slough, near Windsor, died in 1871. In 1813 he graduated B.A. at Cambridge, and was Senior Wrangler and Smith's Prizeman. After his father's death he spent eight years reviewing the nebulæ and clusters of stars discovered by his father. The results were given in 1833 to the Royal Society in the form of a catalogue of stars. The catalogue contained observations on 525 nebulæ and clusters of stars not noticed by his father, and on a great number of double stars, between 3,000 and 4,000 in all.

In 1830 he produced his excellent *Preliminary Discourse on the Study of Natural Philosophy*, and about the same time published several treatises in the *Encyclopædia Metropolitana*, *Lardner's Cyclopædia*, &c. In 1834 he established, at his own expense, an observatory at Feldhuysen, near Cape Town, his object being to discover whether the distribution of the stars in the southern hemisphere corresponded with the results of his father's labours in the north.

He returned to England in 1838, and in 1847 was published *Results of Astronomical Observations made during 1834–38 at the Cape of Good Hope, being the Completion of a Telescopic Survey of the Whole Surface of the Visible Heavens*. He was one of the earliest pioneers in photography; was made a D.C.L. of Oxford; and was created a baronet. In 1848 he was president of the Royal Astronomical Society, and in 1850 was appointed Master of the Mint, an office which he resigned in 1855. Among Sir John's other works are: *Outlines of Astronomy, Familar Lectures on Scientific Subjects*, and a translation of the *Iliad* in verse.—Cf. A. M. Clerke. *The Herschels and Modern Astronomy*.

HERSCHEL, Sir William, astronomer, son of a musician of Hanover, born 1738, died 1822. He came to England in 1757, and was employed in the formation of a military band, and in conducting, while organist at Bath, several concerts and oratorios. Although enthusiastically fond of music, he had for some time devoted his leisure hours to the study of mathematics and astronomy; and being dissatisfied with the only telescopes within his reach, he set about constructing instruments for himself.

Late in 1779 he began a regular survey of the heavens, star by star, with a 7-foot reflector, and discovered, 13th March, 1781, a new primary planet, named by him the *Georgium Sidus*, but now known as *Uranus*. This discovery extended his fame throughout the world, and brought him a pension of £400 a year, with the title of Private Astronomer to the King. Assiduously continuing his observations, he measured the rotation of Saturn, discovered two of its satellites, and observed the phenomena of its rings. He also discovered the satellites of Uranus, and observed the volcanic structure of the lunar mountains. At Slough, near Windsor, he erected a telescope of 40 feet length, and completed it in 1787.

Herschel received much assistance in making and recording observations from his sister Caroline; and afterwards his brother, a skilful optical-instrument maker, lent him valuable aid. In 1802 he laid before the Royal Society a catalogue of 5,000 nebulæ and clusters of stars which he had discovered. He was made D.C.L. by the University of Oxford, and in 1816 was knighted.—Cf. J. L. E. Dreyer, *A Short Account of Sir William Herschel's Life and Works.*

HERSTAL, or HERISTAL, a town of Belgium, on the Meuse, 3 miles north-east of Liége. It was the residence of Pepin le Gros, and afterwards of several French kings of the second race; and has a church founded by Charlemagne. Pop. 24,283.

HERTFORD, a town and municipal borough of England, capital of the county of same name, on the Lea, 21¾ miles north of London. It consists of three principal streets, meeting in a central square. There are breweries and oil and flour-mills. Hertford now gives name to a parliamentary division of the county. The castle, which was built by Edward the Elder about A.D. 905, was occupied by John of Gaunt, and by the queens of Henry IV, V, and VI; and Elizabeth also resided in it occasionally. John II, King of France, and David, King of Scotland, were both in captivity here. Pop. (1931), 11,376.

HERTFORDSHIRE(contracted HERTS), English county, is bounded by Cambridgeshire, Essex, Middlesex, Buckingham, and Bedford; area, 404,520 acres, of which about five-sixths are arable, meadow, and pasture. The general aspect of the county is pleasing, being diversified by hill and valley, pasture lands, arable farms, and picturesque parks and woods. The principal rivers are the Lea and Colne, both of which have numerous tributaries. Agriculture employs a large number of the inhabitants; there are manufactures of paper, silk, and straw. For parliamentary purposes it forms five divisions, each returning a member to the House of Commons. Pop. (1931), 401,206.

HERTLING, Georg Friedrich von, German writer and statesman, born at Darmstadt 31st Aug., 1843, died 4th Jan., 1919. Educated at the Universities of Munich and Berlin and in Italy, he was professor at Bonn and afterwards at Munich. In 1875 he entered the Reichstag, where he became the leader of the Catholic party. During the Kulturkampf, Bis-

marck employed him to secure concessions from Rome. Bavarian Minister of State in 1891, Hertling became President of the Council and Minister of Foreign Affairs in Bavaria in 1911, but laboured for the supremacy of Prussia. His attitude was appreciated by William II, who appointed him Imperial Chancellor in Nov., 1917, in succession to Michaelis. Although in favour of peace without annexations, Hertling lacked the strength and courage to fight against the Pan-Germanists. He resigned on 30th Sept., 1918.

's HERTOGENBOSCH, town of the Netherlands, capital of North Brabant, 39 miles S.S.E. of Utrecht. Pop. (1932), 43,090.

HERTZ, Heinrich Rudolf, German physicist, born at Hamburg 1857, died 1894. He was assistant to Helmholtz, and afterwards professor at Karlsruhe. His work in Dynamics is important, but his great achievement was the discovery of Hertzian Waves (q.v.).

HERTZ, Henrik, Danish dramatic poet, was born at Copenhagen, of Jewish parents, 1798, died 1870. He wrote a great number of poems and novels, but his best works are his plays. Among his best known are: *Sparekassen*; *Ninon*; *Svend Dyring's Hus*, a tragedy founded on an old saga; and *King René's Daughter*, which has been translated and performed in France, Germany, and Britain.

HERTZIAN WAVES, ether waves predicted by Clerk Maxwell in 1864 and demonstrated by Hertz in 1888. Using the spark caused by an induction coil in an 'oscillator,' he received and observed the waves by means of a 'resonator,' the latter a simple circuit of wire with a narrow gap across which sparks passed when the circuit was placed in the path of the waves. Hertz showed that these waves could be reflected from metal surfaces, bent out of their course by means of a prism made of pitch, and he found that the waves could pass through stone walls and wooden floors. The waves are propagated through the same medium, and with the same velocity, as light waves, but have a much greater wavelength than the latter. See WIRELESS TELEGRAPHY.—BIBLIOGRAPHY: H. Hertz, *Electric Waves,* translated by D. E. Jones; S. P. Thompson, *Light, Visible and Invisible.*

HERTZOG, James Barry Munnik, South African politician, born April 3, 1866, of Boer parents. In the war of 1899–1902 he held an important command, and after the annexation of the republic appeared as a champion of the Boer cause. In 1915 he was elected leader of the Nationalist party, and as such repeatedly claimed independence for South Africa. In 1924 he became premier and was still in office in 1933.

HER'ULI, an ancient Germanic people, originally found on the northern shores of the Black Sea. Under the leadership of Odoacer they helped in the overthrow of the Western Empire. About the end of the sixth century they ceased to have a separate existence as a people.

HERVEY ISLANDS, group of islands in the Pacific Ocean, lat. 20° S., long. 160° W., consisting of two coralline islands, annexed to New Zealand (1901), and belonging to the Cook Group. (Area of Cook Group about 280 sq. miles; pop. 13,877.) The natives have legends of their migration from Samoa. Pop. 23 (1926).

HERZEGOVINA (hert-se-go-vē'nä), a province of Yugo-Slavia area, 3,568 sq. miles. The surface is generally mountainous, but contains many fertile valleys. Pop. about 200,000. An insurrection which broke out in July, 1875, formed the beginning of a train of events resulting in war between Russia and Turkey. In accordance with the Treaty of Berlin (1878) the province was occupied by Austrian troops, and was ruled by an Austrian military governor until 1918. After the fall of the Austrian Empire Herzegovina became part of Yugo-Slavia (q.v.).

HERZL, Theodor, Jewish politician, founder and leader of political Zionism (q.v.), born at Budapest 2nd May, 1860, died at Edlach, Austria, 3rd July, 1904. Educated in Vienna, where he studied law, he almost exclusively devoted himself to journalism and literature, and to the writing of comedies and dramas. Paris correspondent of the *Neue Freie Presse,* he afterwards became its literary editor.

He was in Paris from 1891–5, and moved, no doubt, by the Dreyfus affair, he published his *Judenstaat* (The Jewish State), wherein he advocated the restoration of the Jewish national home as the only remedy against the suffering of the Jews, and the only way of liberating the Jewish nationality as such. Henceforth he devoted his energy and activities to the propaganda of Zionism.

In 1897 he founded *Die Welt,* a Zionist organ, and convened the first International Zionist Congress at Basel, of which, as well as of the following six Congresses, he was elected president. Recognized leader of the Zionist movement, he was indefatigable in his efforts, although he encountered only ridicule and hostility among the Jewish opponents of Zion-

ism, and later on had to fight against the intrigues of a faction of Zionists whose ringleaders, envious of Herzl's authority and aspiring themselves to the leadership, did their best to bring about his overthrow.

Herzl was received in audience by Kaiser William II, and by the Sultan Abdul Hamid, and in 1901–2 was called to give evidence before the British Royal Commission on Alien Immigration. Abdul Hamid demanded £10,000,000 for a concession in Palestine, but the Jewish millionaires, who could have easily provided the sum, were intransigent in 1903, although the majority of them were to be converted to Zionism less than two decades later. Finding Palestine out of reach for the time being, Herzl therefore negotiated with the British Government and secured the offer of Uganda. The sixth Zionist Congress decided to appoint a Commission to study the fitness of Uganda for colonization, but the minority of the delegates, led by Herzl's personal enemies and political opponents, left the Congress hall in a body. This was a terrible blow to the leader, whose health was already giving way under the strain and stress of his labours. He died of heart failure less than a year afterwards. Besides his *Judenstaat,* Herzl's works include: *Das neue Ghetto, Prinzen aus Genieland,* and *Altneuland. See* ZIONISM.

HERZOG (här'zōh), **Johann Jakob,** German Protestant theologian, born at Basel 1805, died at Erlangen 1882. He was successively professor of historical theology at Lausanne, church history at Halle, and afterwards at Erlangen. His chief works are: *Calvin and Zwingli, Life of Œcolampadius,* and *The Reformation in Basel;* and his great *Real-Encyklopädie für Protestantische Theologie und Kirche,* a vast collection of German learning and speculation, of which he was the editor, and to which he contributed over 500 articles.

HE'SIOD, the father of Greek didactic poetry, lived probably in the eighth century B.C. Little is known of his life beyond what he tells us himself. His father emigrated from Asia Minor to Bœotia, and Hesiod was born at Ascra, near the foot of Mount Helicon. Here he lived the life of a shepherd and farmer. After his father's death the poet is said to have been involved in a lawsuit with his lazy brother Perses, and on losing his case to have migrated to Naupactus. Here he was said to have been murdered by the sons of his host.

Bœotian School of Poetry. The poems of Hesiod belong to the Bœotian school of poetry. This school arose partly in opposition to Homer, though the influence of Homer is apparent in all the Hesiodic poems. Homer wrote to please the imagination, Hesiod wrote to instruct. He is strictly utilitarian in all his writings. By far the most important and interesting of them, and the only one which the Bœotians acknowledged as genuine, is the *Works and Days* (Erga kai Hemerai). It is addressed to his brother Perses, and is in the main an exhortation to work. It may be divided into three parts: the first is a glorification of labour; the second contains maxims for farmers; and the third is a sort of calendar, not unlike Ovid's *Fasti*, telling which days are lucky and which unlucky for agricultural employments and for sailing. The poem contains many well-known passages, such as the story of Pandora and her jar, the account of the five ages of the world, the fable of the hawk and the nightingale, and the descriptions of winter and summer. Hesiod lets us see that he was a conservative farmer, an unenterprising stay-at-home man, and a woman-hater.

The Theogony is a much less interesting poem. It is an attempt to systematize mythology, and might be called a sort of Olympian Peerage. It gives an account of the creation, a history of Zeus and Cronos, and a list of women who married gods. Its best passages are those which deal with the war between the gods and Titans. In these passages, and in the lines describing the creation, it is more sublime than the *Works and Days*, but it is not all up to this standard. *The Shield of Heracles* is, in the main, simply a description of that article; it is an imitation of Homer's description of the shield of Achilles (*Iliad*, xviii, 479). It is not a valuable poem.

Appreciation.—Hesiod is not a great poet; he rarely attains to anything that could be called sublimity, but he is none the less an interesting and important figure in Greek literary history. He is full of quaint sayings; thus a snail is a "house-carrier," a burglar is a "day-sleeper," a serpent "the hairless one," and to cut one's nails is "to sever the withered from the quick upon that which has five branches." He takes a naïve and childlike interest in everything that happens in nature, particularly when it concerns himself.

His chief poem embodies much of the proverbial philosophy of early Greece. Much of it is probably founded upon traditional peasant poetry of Bœotia, maxims simply put into verse for the sake of convenience in remembering, and no more intrinsically poetry than "Thirty days hath September." From this material it was scarcely possible to make great poetry, but Hesiod has done his best.

The *Works and Days* gives us a most valuable picture of life in the village-communities of the eighth century B.C. *The Theogony* preserves some interesting myths, and attempts to throw some light upon the matrimonial affairs of the Olympians. Last, but not least, Hesiod helped to inspire Virgil to write the most finished and delightful of all didactic poems—the *Georgics*. — BIBLIOGRAPHY: translations by A. W. Mair (Oxford Library of Translations) and by H. G. Evelyn-White (Loeb Library); M. Croiset, *Histoire de la Littérature Grecque*; J. Adam, *Religious Teachers of Greece*.

HESPER'IDES (-dēz), in Greek mythology, certain nymphs who lived in gardens, of rather uncertain locality, as guardians of the golden apples that grew there, being assisted in the charge by a dragon. Hesiod places the gardens in an island of the ocean far to the west. It was the eleventh labour of Heracles to kill the dragon and bring the golden apples of the Hesperides to Eurystheus.

HESPEROR'NIS, a fossil bird found in the cretaceous of Kansas, about 6 feet long, without wings, and having its jaws armed with teeth, which are not set in sockets, but in a common groove. It has been described as "a kind of swimming, loon-like, raptorial ostrich, without fore-limbs, with the gape armed with formidable rows of strong teeth like a gigantic lizard, and with a large, broad, and flattened tail like a beaver."

HESSE (hes), or HESSEN, anciently a territory of Germany, situated mainly between the Rivers Neckar, Rhine, Main, Lahn, and Fulda. After various changes it was ruled by the landgrave Philip I, who succeeded in 1509, and at his death in 1567 divided his dominions among his four sons. The death of two of these, however, reunited the territories in part, so that there remained only the two main divisions of Hesse-Cassel and Hesse-Darmstadt, the latter known since 1866 simply as Hesse. *See* following articles.

HESSE, or HESSEN, a state of the German Republic, until 1918 a grand-duchy. It was formerly known as *Hesse-Darmstadt*, an independent state of South Germany, consisting of sundry distinct portions. Of the two main portions, one (forming the provinces of Rheinhessen on the left, and Starkenburg on the right bank of the Rhine) lies immediately to the north of Baden; the other, Oberhessen (Upper Hesse), is entirely enclosed by the Prussian province of Hessen-Nassau; area of the whole state, 2,968 sq. miles.

Oberhessen is generally mountainous; the provinces Starkenburg and Rheinhessen are also mountainous towards their frontiers, more especially in the south-east, but there are also extensive plains belonging to the valleys of the Main and the Rhine. The climate is greatly diversified, being cold and bleak in the mountainous districts, and mild and pleasant in the valleys of the Rhine and the Main. Much of the soil, particularly in the provinces of Starkenburg and Rheinhessen, is remarkably fertile. The vine forms a most important object of culture, and fruit is very abundant. The principal towns are Darmstadt, the capital (pop. 89,465), Mayence or Mainz (pop. 130,915), Giessen (33,600), Offenbach (79,362), and Worms (47,015). About two-thirds of the inhabitants are Protestants. Pop. 1,347,279.

History. The former Grand-Duchy of Hesse originated in the division of the Landgraviate of Hesse in 1567. (See previous article.) In 1806 the Landgraviate was erected into a grand-duchy with an enlarged territory by Napoleon. It was reduced to its present limits in 1866, when it had to cede to Prussia some districts in the north, besides Hesse-Homburg, which, after being separated from it since 1596, had been reunited to it in the beginning of the year in which it was ceded. The grand-duke, Ludwig (Louis, 1837–92), was married to Princess Alice of Great Britain. Hesse was proclaimed a republic in Nov., 1918, and the new Constitution was adopted in Jan., 1919.

HESSE-CASSEL, or KURHESSEN ('Electoral Hessen'), a district of Germany, formerly an independent Electorate, containing 4,430 sq. miles, but now, with the exception of several small strips of territory, forming part of the Prussian province of Hesse-Nassau.

It was founded in 1567. (See HESSE.) The last twenty years of its independent history is simply a narrative of conflicts between the people for political freedom and the Elector for absolute rule. At last, on the outbreak of the German War of 1866, the Elector declared himself on the side of Austria, and his territory was occupied by Prussian troops. On the conclusion of the war Hesse-Cassel was annexed to the Prussian territories.

HESSE - DARMSTADT. See HESSE.

HESSE-HOMBURG, before its absorption by Prussia after the German War of 1866, a Landgraviate of Germany, consisting of two parts, the lordship of Homburg, situated N.N.W of Frankfort, and the lordship of Meissenheim. It had an area of about 100 sq. miles, and a population of 27,000 inhabitants. The greater part of the public revenue was obtained from the gaming-tables of the watering-place, Homburg, the capital.

HESSE-NASSAU, or HESSEN-NASSAU, a province of Prussia, formed out of the former Principality of Hesse-Cassel, the Duchy of Nassau, the Landgraviate of Hesse-Homburg, the territory and town of Frankfort, &c. Waldeck was included in 1929. It borders on the Prussian provinces of Westphalia, Hanover, Saxony, and the Rhineland, the Republic of Bavaria, &c., and encloses Upper Hesse. (See HESSE.). The boundary is partly formed by the Rhine, Main,

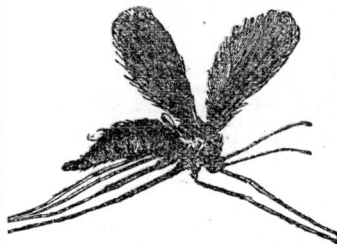

Hessian Fly (*Cecidomyia destructor*) (magnified)

Weser, and Werra. Other rivers are the Lahn and Fulda.

The greater part of this province belongs to the Central German Plateau, and has a rugged surface, partly covered by branches of the Harz. Still, about 40 per cent of the whole is arable, while about the same is under wood. The chief mineral is iron. Mineral springs are numerous. The manufactures consist chiefly of woollens, cottons, and linen. The principal towns are Cassel, the capital, Wiesbaden, and Frankfort. Its area is 6,471 sq. miles, and its pop. 2,452,748.

HESSIAN, known in America as *burlap*, is the name of a jute fabric originally made from flax and tow. The standard width is 40 inches. It is used extensively for packing dry-goods and for bag-making, and, when specially prepared, for cheap clothing and stage decoration. In the manufacture of linoleum and the upholstery of furniture large quantities of Hessian are used. The main centres of its manufacture are Dundee and Calcutta; in the former town every variety of the cloth is made.

HESSIAN FLY (*Cecidomyia destructor*), a fly of the family Tipulidæ, of the ord. Diptera (two-winged flies), the larva of which is very destructive to wheat, barley, and rye crops (it does not attack oats). It is so named from the unfounded belief, prevalent in America, where it is specially destructive, that it was brought over to that country in the baggage of the Hessian mercenaries employed against the Americans in the War of Independence.

The female fly is about an eighth of an inch in length, with a wing expanse of about a quarter of an inch. Its body is brown, with the upper parts, the thorax, and the head of a darker shade, approaching to black. The wings are of a dusky grey, and are surrounded by fringes. The male is somewhat smaller than the female and has longer antennæ. The female flies usually lay their eggs on the young plants twice in the year, in May and September, out of which eggs the maggots hatch in from four to fourteen days. These work themselves in between the leaf-sheath and the stem, and fix themselves near the lowest joints, often near the root, and suck the juices of the stem, so that the ear falls down at a sharp angle. These maggots turn to pupæ, from which the flies develop in about ten days. It did not appear in Britain till the summer of 1886.

HESTON AND ISLEWORTH. *See* HOUNSLOW.

HESSLE, market town and urban district of Yorkshire (E.R.). It is on the Humber, 4 miles from Hull and 192 miles from London. It has industries similar to those of Hull. Pop. (1931), 6,430.

HETEROCER'CAL, a term applied to the tails of fishes, when these are externally asymmetrical, the vertebral column running to a point in the upper lobe, as in the sharks and sturgeons, causing this lobe to be much larger than the other.

HETERŒCIOUS FUNGI, those parasitic species which divide their life-history between two hosts; the most familiar example is the wheat-rust, *Puccinia graminis,* which lives alternately on wheat (in summer and autumn) and on barberry (in spring).

HETEROG'AMOUS PLANTS, those in which the male and female gametes differ from one another, sometimes only in size, but more often also in structure. *See* ISOGAMOUS PLANTS; OOGAMOUS PLANTS; BROWN ALGÆ.

HETEROOUSIANS (het-e-ro-ou'zi-anz), in ecclesiastical history a branch of the Arians who held that the Son was of a different substance from the Father. *See* HOMOOUSIANS.

HETEROP'ODA, a group of marine sea-snails, the most highly organized of the Gasteropoda. The foot is compressed into a vertical muscular lamina, serving for a fin, and the gills, when present, are collected into a mass on the hinder part of the back. They swim in an upside-down position. Typical genera are Atlanta (spiral shell), Carinaria (cap-shaped shell), and Pterotrachma (no shell).

HETEROP'TERA (Gr. *hetĕros,* different, and *pteron,* a wing), a section of hemipterous insects comprising those in which the two pairs of wings are of different consistence, the anterior pair being horny or leathery, but generally tipped with membrane. They comprise the land and water bugs. By some naturalists the Heteroptera are separated from the Homoptera (the other section of the Hemiptera), and raised into a distinct order.

HETEROS'PORY, the condition of such plants as Selaginella, in which the sporophyte bears two kinds of spores, viz. small *microspores,* produced in large numbers in *microsporangia,* and giving rise to purely male gametophytes, and larger *megaspores,* produced in small numbers (typically four in Selaginella) in *megasporangia,* and giving rise to purely female gametophytes. In Selaginella the two types of sporangia are indistinguishable up to a fairly advanced stage of growth; after that, all the spore mother-cells of a microsporangium develop equally, and give rise to microspores; in the megasporangium, on the other hand, one spore mother-cell develops at the expense of all the rest, which are digested and absorbed by it. In this case, therefore, the heterosporous condition is partly a matter of nutrition, but its actual origin is obscure.

Heterospory is an ancient development, being found in living or extinct members of all the great groups of Pteridophyta. The seed-habit found in all Angiosperms and Gymnosperms, as well as in the extinct Pteridosperms, and in a partial form in some fossil Lycopods, is a secondary consequence of heterospory, which, therefore, ranks as one of the most important evolutionary advances made by land-living plants.

HETEROTRO'PHIC PLANTS, those which depend entirely on organic food-materials, i.e. on food obtained at second-hand; they may be *saprophytes* feeding on dead organic material, or *parasites* nourishing themselves at the expense of a living host. Opposed to Prototrophic Plants.

HETMAN, or **ATAMAN,** the title of the head (general) of the Cossacks. This dignity was abolished among the Cossacks of the Ukraine by Catherine the Great. Until the Russian revolution of 1917 the title of chief hetman was held by the Russian heir apparent to the crown. *See* COSSACKS.

HETROSTY'LY, or HETEROSTY'-LISM, in flowers a condition seen in its typical form in the primrose and other species of Primula. Two kinds of flowers are found, each on a separate plant, distinguished by the relative lengths of stamens and styles. One type, the 'long-styled' or 'pin-eyed,' has a style reaching to the eye of the flower, with the anthers half-way down the tube of the corolla; in the 'short-styled' or 'thrum-eyed' type the anthers are in the eye of the flower, whereas the style extends only half-way up the tube. In other words, the stigma of the long-styled flower is at the same level as the anthers of the short-styled flower, and vice versa.

Evidently the pollinating insect-visitors will tend to bring about cross-pollination between flowers of opposite types, and, as Darwin has shown, it is precisely this 'legitimate' pollination which results in a full yield of fertile seed. Heterostylism is thus one of the devices favouring cross-pollination. Similar dimorphism of flowers occurs in many other plants, such as water-violet, bog-bean, sea-lavender, and buckwheat; purple loosestrife has trimorphic flowers (long-, short-, and medium-styled), and Epigæa tetramorphic flowers.—Cf. C. Darwin, *Forms of Flowers*.

HETTON, urban district of Durham, 256 miles from London, and 8 miles from Sunderland. Coal mining is the chief industry. Pop. (1931), 17,672.

HEUCHERA, a genus of perennial herbs, ord. Saxifragaceæ, natives of North America and Siberia. Several species, with panicles of pink or white flowers rising from a rosette of graceful lobed and toothed leaves, are favourites of the rock-garden and herbaceous border.

HEUDICOURT, French village, department of Somme. It was the scene of fighting during the European War, and was captured by the British in April, 1917, and again in Aug., 1918.

HEVEA, a genus of tropical American trees, ord. Euphorbiaceæ. Para rubber is obtained from *H. elastua, H. brasiliensis*, and other species. *See* RUBBER.

HEVER, village of Kent, on the Eden, near Edenbridge, 27 miles from London. Its castle, where Anne Boleyn lived, was restored by the 1st Viscount Astor. Pop. 700.

HEWART, Lord, English lawyer. Gordon Hewart was born at Bury, 7th Jan., 1870, and was called to the Bar in 1902. In 1913 he was elected M.P. for Leicester as a Liberal; in 1916 he became Solicitor-General, and in 1919 Attorney-General in the coalition ministry. In 1922 he was made Lord Chief Justice and a baron. His book *The New Despotism* attracted a good deal of attention when published in 1929. *Essays and Observations* appeared in 1930.

HEXAM'ETER (Gr. *hex*, six, and *metron*, measure), a verse of six feet, the heroic or epic measure of the Greeks and Romans. The sixth foot is always a spondee (two long syllables), or a trochee (a long and a short). The first five may be all dactyls (one long syllable and two short), or all spondees, or a mixture of both. The scheme of this verse then is:

$$-\smile\smile \mid -\smile\smile \mid -\smile\smile \mid -\smile\smile \mid -\smile\smile \mid -\smile$$
$$\text{or,} --- \mid --- \mid --- \mid --- \mid --- \mid -\smile$$

with all the varieties which the mingling of the two kinds of feet affords. In modern poetry the hexameter has been frequently used. In English hexameters accent is almost entirely substituted for quantity, and trochees generally take the place of spondees. Longfellow in his *Evangeline*, Kingsley in his *Andromeda*, and Clough in his *Bothie* have adopted this form of verse. The following lines are specimens of Clough's English hexameters:

O let us | try, he | answered, the | waters them | selves
    will sup | port us, |
Yea very | ripples and | waves will | form to a | boat
    under | neath us.

The hexameter is not well suited to the genius of the English language; the least unsuccessful English hexameters are valuable in spite of their metre rather than because of it.

HEXHAM, a town of England, in Northumberland, on the Tyne, 21 miles west of Newcastle. There are here ruins of an abbey church, originally a cruciform structure, built about A.D. 674, destroyed two centuries later by the Danes, renovated in 1113, and demolished by the Scots in 1296. Hats, gloves, and leather are manufactured, but the industries are chiefly agricultural. Hexham gives name to a parliamentary division of the county. Pop. (1931), 8,888.—**The Battle of Hexham**, fought 15th May, 1464, was one of those belonging to the Wars of the Roses. The Lancastrians under Somerset were defeated by Montague, the former being slain.

HEYLIN, Peter, English theologian, born 1600, died 1662. He published his *Microcosmos, or Description of the Globe*, in 1625. In 1629 he became chaplain to Charles I, and obtained several benefices, from which he was ejected during the Civil War. At the Restoration he was made sub-dean of Westminster. He wrote a *Life of Laud*, a *Defence of the Church of England*, and several theological works.

HEYNE (hī-né), **Christian Gottlob**, German scholar, born 1729, died 1812. He was educated at Chemnitz and at Leipzig University, and after a long struggle with poverty he received, in 1763, an invitation to become pro-fessor of rhetoric and poetry at Göttingen. He was soon after (1764) appointed first librarian, and remained there till his death. He particularly applied himself to classical criticism and the illustration of the writings of the ancients, and published valuable editions of Homer, Pindar, Diodorus Siculus, Epictetus, Virgil, and Tibul-lus, all with full commentaries.

HEYSE (hī-zé), **Paul Johann Lud-wig**, German novelist and dramatist, born at Berlin 1830, and died in 1914. He wrote many plays, and short stories for newspapers and magazines; but his fame rests on his great novels *Die Kinder der Welt* (1872), and *Im Paradiese* (1875), and his tale entitled *L'Arrabbiata* (1853).

HEYSHAM, a seaport and water-ing-place of Lancashire on Morecambe Bay, 5 miles from Lancaster. There are regular sailings from Heysham to Ireland and the Isle of Man. It is within the borough of Morecambe and Heysham. Pop. 3,350.

HEYWOOD, **John**, an early English dramatist, born in the end of the fifteenth century, died at Mechlin sometime about 1580. Sir Thomas More introduced him at the court of Henry VIII, with whom he became a favourite. His zealous attachment to the Roman Church recommended him to Queen Mary; but this very circum-stance rendered him an object of sus-picion during the two succeeding reigns, and he found it expedient to retire to the Continent. Heywood's dramatic works are known as *Inter-ludes*, and they stand between the miracle-plays and the drama proper. Among them are: *A mery Play between the Pardoner and the Frere*, *the Curate and Neybour Pratte*; *The Play of Love*; *The Four P's*; &c. He also wrote epigrams and ballads.

HEYWOOD, **Thomas**, dramatist, lived in the reigns of Elizabeth, James I, and Charles I. He was born in Lincolnshire, and educated at Cambridge. He composed wholly or in part 220 different plays. Of these only about twenty-four remain, of which the one most admired is *A Woman Killed with Kindness*, published in *Dodsley's Collection*. He

was also the author of *Great Britain's Troy*, *An Apology for Actors*, and a number of other works.—Cf. A. W. Verity (editor), *The Best Plays of Thomas Heywood*.

HEYWOOD, a municipal borough of England, in Lancashire, about 8 miles north-west of Manchester. The making of power-looms, iron- and brass-founding, boiler-making, and all branches of cotton-spinning and manufacturing, with other industries, are extensively carried on. Heywood and Radcliffe give name to a parlia-mentary division. Pop. (1931), 25,967.

HEZEKI'AH (*Hizkiyah*, generally *Hizkiyahu*, strength of Jehovah), the twelfth, and one of the best of the Kings of Judah. He succeeded Ahaz about 717 B.C., and died about 698 B.C. He repressed idolatry, fought successfully against the Philistines, and hoped to become entirely inde-pendent of Assyria, but had his fenced cities captured, and was mulcted in a large tribute.

About this time Hezekiah had a serious illness from which he miracu-lously recovered, and celebrated his fresh lease of life in a thanksgiving, preserved in *Is.* xxxviii. Among the ambassadors who came with letters and gifts to congratulate him on his recovery was the Viceroy of Babylon, to whom he displayed the royal treasures. For this he received a terrible rebuke, and he was told by Isaiah that from Babylon would come the ruin and captivity of Judah. The greater part of the Scripture records bearing on the reign of Hezekiah is occupied by the two invasions of Sennacherib, and the sudden destruc-tion of the Assyrian army. Hezekiah did not long survive this deliverance.

HIBBERT LECTURES, a course of lectures founded by Robert Hibbert, in 1847, for the promotion of compre-hensive learning and thorough re-search in relation to religion wholly apart from the interest of any parti-cular Church or system. The first course was given at Westminster in 1878 by Professor Max Müller, *On the Origin and Growth of Religion, as Illustrated by the Religions of India*. Subsequent lecturers have been M. Renouf, M. Ernest Renan, Rhys Davids, Kuenen, Pfleiderer, Sayce, Montefiore, Drummond, and Farnell.

HIBERNATION.—*See* DORMANT STATE.

HIBIS'CUS, an extensive genus of plants, nat. ord. Malvaceæ (mallows), chiefly natives of tropical climates. They have large showy flowers, borne singly upon stalks towards the ends of the branches, these flowers having an outer calyx (called the epicalyx) of numerous leaves in addition to the true five-lobed persistent calyx. They are chiefly shrubs, one or two being herbs, and a few attaining the dimension of trees. The species are remarkable for abounding in mucilage and for the tenacity of the fibre of their bark, whence several are employed for many economical purposes in the different countries where they are indigenous.

The petals of *H. rosa sinensis*, a plant with large, handsome, usually red flowers, frequent in green-houses, are astringent and used in China as a black dye for the hair and eyes. The handsome flowering shrub known in gardens as *Althœa frutex* is a species of hibiscus (*H. syriacus*). The root of *H. Manihot* yields a mucilage used in Japan as size and to give a proper consistence to paper. The leaves of *H. cannabinus* are eatable, and an oil is extracted from its seeds, while it is cultivated in India for its fibre, and hence known as Indian hemp.

HICCUP, or HICCOUGH, is a convulsive catch of the respiratory muscles, with sonorous inspiration, repeated at short intervals. Though generally a trivial and transient inconvenience, its occurrence in the last stages of acute disease is a grave, and often a fatal symptom. The frequent swallowing of small pieces of ice, or small doses of anti-spasmodic medicines, usually relieves a severe fit.

HICKES, George, English divine, philologist, and antiquary, was born 1642, died 1715. He became Dean of Worcester in 1683, but he was deprived of his deanery in 1690 for refusing to take the oaths to William III after the Revolution. He followed the fortunes of James II, and was consecrated Suffragan Bishop of Thetford in 1694 by the non-juring Archbishop Sancroft. Of his numerous works the most important are: *Institutiones Grammaticœ Anglo-Saxonicœ et Mœso-Gothicœ,* &c. (Oxon, 1689), and *Linguarum veterum septentrionalium Thesaurus Grammatico-Criticus et Archœologicus* (Oxon, 1705).

HICK'ORY, the name given to several species of timber trees of the genus Carya, belonging to the nat. ord. Juglandaceæ (walnut). They are natives of North America, and are remarkable for stateliness and general beauty. The wood is heavy, strong, and tenacious, and is used for making carriage-shafts, screws, whip-handles, cogged wheels, &c.

The shag-bark (*C. alba*) yields the hickory-nut of commerce, and its wood is very valuable. *C. olivæformis* yields the pecan-nut. The pig-nut or brown hickory is the *C. glabra*, and the swamp hickory is *C. amara*, so called from the bitterness of its nut.

HICKS, Edward Seymour, English actor. Born at St. Helier, 31st Jan., 1871, he first appeared on the stage in 1887 and in 1905 opened his own theatre, The Aldwych. Hicks has written many plays, including *The Man in Dress Clothes* and *The Beauty of Bath,* also several books, among them *Twenty-four Years of an Actor's Life*; *If I were your Father, Chestnuts Re-roasted, Hullo Australians, Between Ourselves* (1930). and *Acting: a Book for Amateurs* (1931). He married, in 1902, the actress, Ellaline Terriss.

HIDALGO, a Spanish nobleman of the lower class. There were *hidalgos de naturaleza,* of noble birth, and *hidalgos de privilegio,* that is, those on whom the king had conferred nobility, and those who purchased nobility. The title is now obsolete.

HIERAP'OLIS, a ruined city of Asia Minor, near the right bank of the Lycus, 121 miles east by south of Smyrna. It was famous for its thermal springs, was the birthplace of Epictetus, and is mentioned by St. Paul in his *Epistle to the Colossians* (iv. 13).—Another **Hierapolis,** called Bambyce, is in Syria.

HI'ERARCHY (from Gr. *hieros,* sacred, and *archē,* government), sacred government, sometimes the Church, sometimes the rule which the ecclesiastical governing body exercised as at once priests and civil magistrates. In the former sense the hierarchy arose with the establishment of the Christian Church as an independent society. In the Middle Ages the Papal hierarchy gathered great strength, and the Pope became a spiritual monarch, ruling western Christendom with power but feebly limited by princes and councils. A reactionary movement began in the fourteenth century, and the general tendency of subsequent events has always been to make the civil and hierarchical power more and more independent of each other.

The term *hierarchy* as used to denote the governing and ministering body in the Church, according to its several gradations, can strictly be applied only to those Churches which are ruled by bishops, such as the Roman Catholic Church and the Anglican Church, which also holds the theory of a hierarchical gradation of rank and authority. Both these Churches acknowledge the three orders of bishops, priests, and deacons.

HI'ERO I, ancient Greek ruler or 'Tyrant' (that is, absolute monarch) of Syracuse, in Sicily, brother of Gelon, whom he succeeded in 478 B.C.

He was an enlightened ruler, and a patron of genius and learning. His court became the rendezvous of the most distinguished writers of his time, including Pindar, Æschylus, Bacchylides, Epicharmus, and Simonides. The *Hiero* of Xenophon contains the finest eulogium of this monarch. He was several times victor in the Grecian games. Pindar has celebrated his victories: several odes of this poet are filled with his praises. Hiero died at Catana, 467 B.C.

HIERO II, King or Tyrant of Syracuse (269–214 B.C.), son of Hierocles, a noble Syracusan, who claimed a descent from the family of Gelon. He was chosen by the soldiers as general in 275 B.C., and recognized as king about 270. In 264 he made an alliance with the Carthaginians against Rome, and thus began the first Punic War. Being defeated by the Romans, he made peace by the payment of tribute, and was ever after a faithful and useful ally to them. His subjects enjoyed great prosperity during his reign. Hiero devoted himself to the construction of military machines of all kinds, and ships of great size, under the direction of Archimedes, who lived in Syracuse during this reign.

HIEROGLYPH'ICS (from Gr. *hieros*, sacred, and *glypho*, I engrave), a term originally applied to the inscriptions sculptured on buildings in Egypt, in the belief that the writing was confined to sacred subjects, and legible only to the priests. The term has also been applied to picture-writing in general, such as that of the Hittites and of the Mexicans and the still ruder pictures of the North American Indians.

Three different modes of writing were used by the ancient Egyptians, the *Hieroglyphic*, the *Hieratic*, and the *Demotic*. Pure hieroglyphic writing is the earliest, and consists of figures of natural objects from every sphere of nature and art, with certain mathematical and arbitrary symbols. Next was developed the hieratic or priestly writing, the form in which most Egyptian literature is written, and in which the symbols almost cease to be recognizable as figures of objects. Hieratic writings of the third millennium B.C. are extant. In the demotic or *enchorial* writing, a very cursive form (the ancient 'running hand'), derived directly from the hieratic, the symbols are still more obscured. The demotic was first used in the ninth century B.C., and was chiefly employed in social and commercial intercourse.

Down to the end of the eighteenth century scholars failed to find a clue to the hieroglyphic writings. In 1799, however, M. Bouchard, a French captain of engineers, discovered at Rosetta the celebrated stone which afforded European scholars a key to the language and writing of the ancient Egyptians. It contained a trilingual inscription in hieroglyphics, demotic characters, and Greek, which turned out to be a decree of the priests in honour of Ptolemy V, issued in 195 B.C. The last paragraph of the Greek inscription stated that two translations, one in the sacred and the other in the popular Egyptian language, would be found adjacent to it.

The discovery of an alphabet was the first task. The demotic part of the inscription was first examined by de Sacy and Akerblad, and the signification of a number of the symbols ascertained. The hieroglyphic part was next carefully examined and compared with the demotic and Greek. At last, after much study, Champollion and Dr. Thomas Young, independently of each other, discovered the method of reading the characters (1822), and thus provided a clue to the decipherment of the ancient Egyptian writing.

Hieroglyphic characters are either *ideographic*, i.e. using well-known objects as symbols of conceptions, or *phonetic*, i.e. representing words by symbols standing for their sounds. The phonetic signs are again divided into alphabetical signs and syllabic signs. Many of the ideographic characters are simple enough; thus the figure of a man, a woman, a calf, indicate simply those objects. Others, however, are less simple, and convey their meaning figuratively or symbolically. Water was expressed by three zigzag lines, one above the other, to represent waves or ripples of running water; milk by a milk-jar; oil by an oil-jar; fishing by a pelican seizing a fish, i.e. fishing; seeing and sight by an eye; and so on. The nature of the phonetic hieroglyphs, which represent simply sound, will be understood from an explanation of the accompanying cuts.

1. The first hieroglyph in the name of Kleopatra is a knee, which is *kne* or *kle* in Coptic, and represents the K of Kleopatra. K does not occur in the name of Ptolemaios. 2. The second hieroglyph in Kleopatra is a lion couchant, which is *laboi* in Coptic and *labu* in the old Egyptian, and represents the L of both names. In Kleopatra it occupies the second place, and in Ptolemaios the fourth. 3. The third hieroglyph in Kleopatra is a reed, which is *aké* in Coptic, and *aak* in the old Egyptian, and represents the E of Kleopatra. The reed is doubled in Ptolemaios and occupies the sixth and

 A

 F

 Á

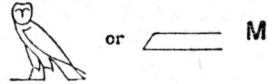 or M

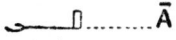 Ā

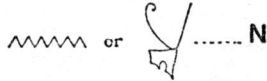 or N

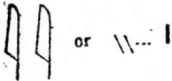 or I

 R and L

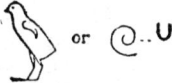 or U

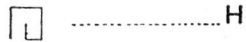 H

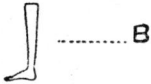 B

 H

 P

 K H

S

 Ķ

 S

 T

 SH (Ś)

 T

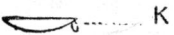 K

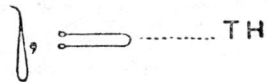 TH

 Q

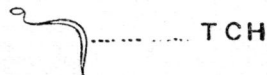 T CH

Hieroglyphics: The Egyptian Alphabet
(By permission of Sir E. A. Wallis Budge.)

seventh places, where it represents the diphthong ai of Ptolemaios. 4. The fourth hieroglyph in Kleopatra is a noose, which represents the O of both names, and occurs in the third place of Ptolemaios. 5. The fifth hieroglyph of Kleopatra is a mat, which represents the P of both names, and is the initial of Ptolemaios. 6. The sixth hieroglyph in Kleopatra is an eagle, which is akhoom in Coptic, and represents the A, which is found twice in the name Kleopatra, but does not occur in the name Ptolemaios, although the diphthong ai occurs as described above, No. 3. 7. The seventh hieroglyph in Kleopatra is a hand, which is toot in Coptic, and represents the T of Kleopatra, but does not occur in Ptolemaios, where it might be expected to occupy the second place. The second place of Ptolemaios is occupied by a semicircle, which is found at the end of feminine proper names, and is the Coptic feminine article T. The researches of Champollion satisfied him of the existence of homophones, or characters which have the same phonetic value and which might be interchanged in writing proper names. 8. The eighth hieroglyph in Kleopatra is a mouth, which is ro in Coptic, and represents the R of Kleopatra. 9. The ninth hieroglyphic in Kleopatra is the eagle, which is explained in No. 6 above. 10. The semicircle is the T of Ptolemaios, which with 11, the egg found at the end of proper names of women, is a feminine affix. In the name of Ptolemaios there is still the M and the S to account for. The fifth hieroglyph in the cartouche of Ptolemaios is a geometrical figure, consisting of three sizes of (probably ?) a parallelogram, but now called a hole, because the Coptic mu has that signification, and represents the M. The hook represents the S. of the word Ptolemaios. Vowels were only regarded by the Egyptians as they were needed to avoid ambiguous writing.

There are groups of hieroglyphs of which one element is an ideographic sign, to which a phonetic complement is added to indicate the pronunciation of the ideographic sign. The words of a text could be written in hieroglyphs in three ways: (1) by phonetic hieroglyphs; (2) by ideographic hieroglyphs; and (3) by a combination of both. According to Ebers, in the perfected system of hieroglyphics the symbols for sounds and syllables are to be regarded as the foundation of the writing, while symbols for ideas are interspersed with them, partly to render the meaning more intelligible, and partly for ornamental purposes, or with a view to keep up the mystic character of the hieroglyphics.—BIBLIOGRAPHY: E. A. T. W. Budge, The

Literature of the Ancient Egyptians; E. Revillout, Chrestomathie démotique; A. Erman, Life in Ancient Egypt; M. A. Murray, Elementary Egyptian Grammar; A. H. Gardiner, Egyptian Hieratic Tests.

HIEROGLYPHIC WRITING.—See HIEROGLYPHICS.

HIERON'YMITES, or **JERONYMITES,** hermits of St. Jerome (Hieronymus), an order of religious persons established in 1374, who wear a white habit with a black scapulary. They possessed the convent of St. Lawrence in the Escurial, and still have convents in Sicily, the West Indies, and South America.

HIGGINS, Edward John, English preacher. Born at Highbridge and educated at Bridgewater, he joined the Salvation Army in 1882. He was chosen, in 1929, general in succession to W. Bramwell Booth.

HIGHAM FERRERS, borough of Northamptonshire, on the Nen, 62 miles from London and 5½ miles from Wellingborough. The staple industry is the making of boots and shoes. Pop. (1931), 2,928.

HIGHBRIDGE, urban district of Somerset. It is 137½ miles from London and 25½ miles from Bristol, and is on the little River Brue. The G.W. Rly. has works here. Pop. (1931), 2,584.

HIGHBURY, district of London, about 4 miles N. of the city, in the borough of Islington. Highbury Park is a pleasant residential district. Highbury Fields is an open space. At Highbury is the ground of the Arsenal Football Club.

HIGH CHURCH, a term applied to a party in the Church of England. It was applied first to a party among the younger clergy, during the latter part of the reign of Elizabeth, who asserted that Calvinism was inconsistent with the ancient doctrine and constitution of the primitive Church, and who claimed a divine right for episcopacy. Bishop Andrewes was the chief writer of this party, and Laud became its most active leader. The term now generally refers to those who exalt the authority and jurisdiction of the Church, and attach great value to ecclesiastical dignities and ordinances, being more or less identified with the ritualistic party. See RITUALISM.

HIGH COMMISSION, COURT OF, an ecclesiastical court created by 1 Eliz. c. i. 1559, by which all spiritual jurisdiction was vested in the Crown. Under Charles I and Laud it assumed illegal powers, and was abolished in 1641.

HIGHGATE, a suburb of North London, partly situated on a hill and commanding fine views of the surrounding country. It is 5½ miles from St. Paul's.

HIGH GERMAN, originally the Teutonic dialect spoken in the southern and elevated parts of Germany, as distinguished from Platt Deutsch or Low German, spoken in the northern and more lowland portions of Germany. *See* GERMANY.

HIGHLAND REGIMENTS are regiments originally raised and recruited in the Highlands of Scotland, and wearing the tartan either in the shape of kilts or trews. These regiments are, in order of seniority, the Black Watch (42nd and 73rd), the Highland Light Infantry (71st and 74th), the Seaforth Highlanders (Ross-shire Buffs, the Duke of Albany's, 72nd and 78th), the Gordon Highlanders (75th and 92nd), the Queen's Own Cameron Highlanders (79th), Princess Louise's (Argyll and Sutherland Highlanders, 91st and 93rd).

The majority of these regiments were first raised in the latter part of the eighteenth century in order to deal with the situation arising out of the French Revolution, but the 42nd dates from the earlier part, and was originally raised in 1730 as independent companies of a sort of *gendarmerie* whose duty it was to keep a semblance of order in their respective districts. After an existence of some eight years in this form, these companies, of which there were six, were brought together and formed into a regiment of ten companies under the Earl of Crawford. The 73rd, the present 2nd battalion of the Black Watch, was raised in 1779 as the 2nd battalion 42nd, became the 73rd Regiment in 1786, and again became connected with the Black Watch on the introduction of the two-battalion system in 1881.

The **Highland Light Infantry** dates from 1777, when a regiment was raised by Lord Macleod and numbered the 73rd. In the reshuffling of numbers in 1786 it became the 71st, and in 1881 was joined with the 74th to form a two-battalion regiment.

The **Seaforths** take their name from the present 2nd battalion, which was raised as the 78th by Lord Seaforth in 1793. The 'letter of service' authorizing the raising of the 78th was dated 7th March, 1793, and the regiment was at full strength by 10th July the same year.

Of the **Gordon Highlanders,** the 1st battalion—the old 75th—was raised in 1787, and the present 2nd—the 92nd—in 1794. The latter was the fourth of a series raised by the Duke of Gordon, of which the three first had been raised for special purposes, and,

as was the custom in those days, disbanded when no longer required.

The **Cameron Highlanders** date their origin from 1793, when a regiment of Cameronian volunteers was raised by Alan Cameron. In the following year the title was changed to the 79th Cameron Highlanders. At the reorganization of 1881 this regiment remained a single battalion till the early days of this century, when a second battalion was added.

The **91st**—the 1st battalion of the Argyll and Sutherland Highlanders—was raised by the Duke of Argyll in 1794 as the Argyll Regiment, and was first numbered the 98th. Four years later the number was changed to the

Bridge over the Forth

91st, and in 1881, when the two-battalion system became universal, the 91st was joined with the 93rd to form the Argyll and Sutherland Highlanders.

All these regiments, with the exception of the Highland Light Infantry, wear the kilt.

HIGHLANDS OF SCOTLAND, a somewhat vague and indefinite geographical division of Scotland, north and west of a line running north-east from Dumbarton on the Clyde through the counties of Dumbarton, Stirling, Perth, Forfar, Kincardine; then northwest through Aberdeen, Banff, Moray, and Nairn to the shores of the Moray Firth.

The Highlands are generally subdivided into two parts, the West Highlands and the North Highlands; the former of which contain the shires of Argyll and Bute, the Southern Hebrides, and part of Perth and Dumbarton; and the latter comprehend the counties of Inverness, Ross, Sutherland, the districts of Athol, Rannoch, and the Isles of Skye, Lewis, and others belonging to Inverness and Ross. The mountainous parts of Banff, Moray, Aberdeen, and Kincardine are also recognized as forming part of the Highlands; while Caithness (partly) and the Orkney and Shetland Isles are excluded, because their inhabitants are of Scandinavian origin.

The whole of the district, which embraces the Celtic-speaking part of Scotland, is wild, rugged, and mountainous, with much grand and picturesque scenery. The western coast is indented by many narrow arms of the sea, and is flanked by numerous islands. Forming, by their natural characteristics, a region distinct from the Lowlands of Scotland, the Highlands were long in a state of political semi-independence, and socially and otherwise—and particularly in retaining the use of the Gaelic tongue—the people have still certain characteristics peculiar to themselves. What especially separated this region from the rest of Scotland was not only the Celtic language and blood, but also the clan system and all connected with it. *See* CLAN.

History. In the earliest times the Highland chiefs gave allegiance to higher chiefs or princes, by whom the Scottish kings were acknowledged as sovereigns merely in name. Among these native princes were the powerful Lords of the Isles, who flourished from very ancient times to the reign of James V. They ruled over all the Western Islands (the Hebrides) from Islay north, and over the western part of the county of Inverness, and as powerful allies exerted an influence over the greater part of the Highlands.

In the early part of the fifteenth century the Highlanders threatened to overrun great part of the Lowlands, but they received a check in the defeat of Donald of the Isles at Harlaw in 1411. From this time onward their incursions on the Lowland parts of Scotland were confined chiefly to occasional plundering raids.

In the wars of the seventeenth century the Highlanders were largely engaged on the side of the Stuarts, and great numbers fought under both Montrose and Dundee. After the suppression of the rising of 1715 a strenuous attempt was made to break up the tribal organization of the Highlanders. An Act was passed in 1724 for their disarmament; between 1726 and 1737 great military roads were formed under the direction of General Wade, and a chain of fortified military posts constructed, to overawe the people. The chieftains made every effort to maintain their threatened power, and to destroy the effect of the innovations with which the Government sought to weaken the bonds of the clans, but the weakening went on.

The rebellion of 1745 gave the Government an opportunity of hastening the process, by the abolition of heritable jurisdictions, and of the ancient privileges of the chiefs. A stringent law for disarming the people was passed, and they were even prohibited from wearing their national dress, a prohibition not formally removed till 1782.

The great extension of sheep-breeding and the appropriation of large tracts to game have tended much to depopulate some parts of the Highlands. In other parts, notably in some of the Western Islands, the population has increased beyond a point where their circumscribed condition could support them, and much discontent, agitation, and trouble has been the result. *See* CROFTERS.

The Highland dress, so well known at the present day, is modern in a good many of its features, and especially so in the great variety of tartans that have been invented, and of which each clan now appears to claim one. *See also* HIGHLAND REGIMENTS.—Cf. Browne, *History of the Highlands and the Highland Clans.*

HIGH PLACES, in Scripture, eminences or mounds on which sacrifices were offered. Altars and places of worship were erected from early times on high places, for the worship of Jehovah. Afterwards such a practice, as leading to idolatrous observances, was strictly forbidden among the Jews. High places are frequently mentioned in conjunction with *groves.*

HIGH-PRIEST, the head of the Jewish priesthood. In the books of Moses the holder of this dignity is simply designated the priest; the epithet *high* occurs on one or two occasions, but as a distinctive epithet it appears to have been added subsequently. The formal consecration of Aaron, the brother of Moses, together with his sons, to an hereditary priesthood, is recorded in *Exod.* xxviii. The high-priesthood continued in the line of Aaron, sometimes in one, and sometimes in another branch of it, until the coming of Christ. From 153 B.C. till the time of Herod the Great the regal and priestly authority were united in members of the Asmonæan family (the Maccabees). After the subjugation of the Jews it was often arbitrarily conferred. In the time of our

Saviour it appears to have been held by several priests alternately.

HIGH RIVER, a town of Alberta, Canada, 40 miles S. of Calgary. Pop. 1,198.

HIGH-SEAS, the open sea or ocean, 'High-seas' includes the whole of the sea below low-water mark and outside the body of a country. Nevertheless the soil of the sea between the low-water mark and so far out to sea as is decided by international law to be within the territorial sovereignty of the Crown is claimed as the property of the Crown although outside the realm. The jurisdiction of maritime states extends only for three miles. Inland seas and estuaries, of course, are excepted.

HIGH-SPEED MACHINERY, the general name given to rotating machinery which runs at speeds exceeding say, 500 r.p.m. The earliest commercially successful high-speed prime movers were the reciprocating engines designed by Willans, Ferranti, and Bellis & Morcom. They are compound two- or three-cylinder vertical engines running at about 600 r.p.m.

The next step in speed was taken with the impulse and reaction turbine of Parsons, Rateau, Curtis, and Zoelly. These machines run at speeds ranging from, say, 750 r.p.m. to 5,000 r.p.m. High speeds of rotation are essential in turbines because the blades are attached to the periphery of the rotating member, and, to be efficient, the blades must run at speeds comparable with the speed of steam in the jets used. The steam speeds are often very high, some 1,000 to 3,000 feet per second.

The next step in speed is a very long one, namely, to about 20,000 to 30,000 r.p.m. Speeds of this magnitude are used in the De Laval turbine. The design of such a machine is a very special problem, and the machine possesses many curious features, which the engineer is apt to look upon with suspicion. For instance, the De Laval machine for 10 horse-power has a flexible shaft about the thickness of a thick knitting-needle.

So far we have spoken of prime movers. High speeds are also used with centrifugal pumps, fans, electric motors, &c. The advantage of the high speed is that the weight of the machine for a given output is very roughly inversely proportional to the speed, unless the machine is a very small one, so that by using a high speed we get a light and cheap machine.

In the design of high-speed machinery special attention must be given to two points, apart from the ordinary details of design which apply to all machinery. These special points are (a) the balancing of all forces which are due to centrifugal force; (b) the examination of the structure from the point of view of vibration. The bugbear of high-speed machinery is not so much the stresses set up by the high speed as the vibration it is apt to produce. The vibration can only be kept within permissible limits (1) if the disturbing forces are eliminated as far as possible, and (2) if the parts of the machine itself are very stiff against vibration.—BIBLIOGRAPHY: H. M. Hobart and A. G. Ellis, *High-speed Dynamo-electric Machinery*; H. M. Martin, *The Design and Construction of Steam Turbines.*

HIGH WYCOMBE, borough and market town of Buckinghamshire, also

St. Hilary

known as Chipping Wycombe, 28¾ miles from London. The making of furniture, especially chairs, is the chief industry, and there is an agricultural trade Pop. 27,987.

Near is the beautiful village of West Wycombe, which it is proposed to preserve to show what an English village was like.

HIL'ARY, or **HILARIUS, St.,** one of the early Fathers of the Church, born at Poitiers, of which city, after his conversion from heathenism, he became the bishop about A.D. 350. His contests with the Arians, which won him the epithet Athanasius of the West, caused his banishment to Phrygia, whence he returned after some years, and continued to distinguish himself as an active diocesan till his death in 367 or 368. He wrote *De Trinitate, libri xii.*

HILARY TERM, one of the four English law terms. It begins on the

11th, and ends on the 31st of Jan.; named from the festival of St. Hilary, 13th Jan. In 1873 the name Hilary Sittings was substituted for Hilary Term. Hilary Term at Oxford University begins on 14th Jan., and ends on the Saturday before Palm Sunday.

HILDA, Saint, a grand-niece of Edwin, King of Northumbria, born about 614, died at Whitby in A.D. 680. At the age of fourteen she was baptized along with her royal kinsman by Paulinus. She was consecrated by Bishop Aidan, and was successively head of the abbey of Hartlepool and for twenty-two years of the famous monastery at Whitby. Cædmon, the

Rowland Hill, Viscount. (British General)

Old English poet, was attached to the monastery during her rule.

HILDBURGHAUSEN (hilt′burh-hou-zn), a town of Germany, in Saxe-Meiningen. From 1683 to 1826 it was the capital of the Duchy of Saxe-Hildburghausen. Pop. 8,500.

HILDEBRAND. See GREGORY VII.

HILDEN, a town of Prussia, Rheinland, on the Itterbach, 8 miles E.S.E. of Düsseldorf, with thriving woollen and linen manufactures. Pop. 20,024.

HILDESHEIM (hil′des-hīm), a city of Prussia, province of and 20 miles from Hanover, the see of a bishopric, founded by Louis le Debonnaire in A.D. 818. It possesses a considerable trade and various industries. It was a free city till 1803. Pop. 58,522.

HILL, Sir Rowland, English postal reformer and originator of the penny postal system, born at Kidderminster 1795, died 1879. He was engaged as a schoolmaster till 1833, shortly after which he was appointed secretary to the Commissioners for the Colonization of South Australia.

In 1837 he published a pamphlet recommending the adoption of a low and uniform rate of postage throughout the United Kingdom. The scheme was approved by a committee of the House of Commons, which examined it in detail in 1838, and in Jan., 1840, the penny postage system, which seems to have been originally proposed by James Chalmers, of Dundee, was carried into effect with the assistance of Hill, who, for this purpose, received an appointment in the Treasury. In 1846 he received a public testimonial of the value of upwards of £13,000. In 1846 he was made Secretary to the Postmaster-General, and in 1854 Chief Secretary to the Post Office. In 1860 he became K.C.B. He also invented a rotary press for printing newspapers, and the adhesive stamp. He retired from the Post Office in 1864 with a pension of £2,000, besides a grant of £20,000 voted by Parliament.—Cf. E. C. H. Smyth, *Sir Rowland Hill; the Story of a Great Reform.*

HILL, Rev. Rowland, popular preacher, notable for his humour and eccentricities, son of Sir Rowland Hill, Bart., of Hawkstone in Shropshire, born 1744, died 1833. He was ordained in the Anglican Church, but embracing the views of the Calvinistic Methodists, he soon began to preach in barns and meeting-houses, and when they were too small or too distant, or not to be procured, in streets, fields, and highways.

In 1783 he laid the foundation of Surrey Chapel in the Blackfriars Road, London, where he preached with great success every winter for about fifty years, making summer excursions to the provinces, where his preaching attracted immense crowds. He was one of the founders of the Religious Tract Society and the British and Foreign Bible Society. He published sermons and other theological works, of which the best known are his *Village Dialogues,* which passed through thirty-four editions in thirty years.

HILL, Rowland (Viscount Hill), British general, nephew of the above, born 1772, died 1842. He entered the army in his sixteenth year, was promoted captain in 1793, and became colonel of the 90th Regiment in 1800. He took part in the Egyptian campaign, and in 1806 was made major-general. He served with great distinction during the campaigns of

Moore and Wellington in the Peninsula. In 1809 he became lieutenant-general; in 1812 he was made a G.C.B.; and in 1814, on being made a peer by the title of Baron of Almaraz and of Hawkstone, Parliament voted him a perpetual pension of £2,000.

At Waterloo he commanded the right wing of the British, and was personally thanked by Wellington for his services. In 1828 he was appointed general commanding-in-chief, the British army, a post which he held till 1842, when he retired and was created viscount. Viscount Hill was often styled 'the right hand of Wellington,' and was also known as 'the soldier's friend,' as he was greatly beloved by the troops.—Cf. A. E. Shand, *Wellington's Lieutenants*.

HILLA, or **HELLA**, a town of Iraq, 60 miles south by west of Baghdad, on the Euphrates, among the ruins of ancient Babylon. It has good bazaars, and manufactures of silk and leather. The Euphrates is here crossed by a floating bridge. Pop. about 30,000.

HILLEL, Jewish rabbi, born at Babylon about 80 or 60 B.C., died about 10 B.C., and according to others A.D. 10. He is known as 'the Babylonian' and also as 'the elder,' to distinguish him from later teachers of the same name. He came to Jerusalem, it is said, at about forty years of age, became president of the Sanhedrin and founder of the school of Hillel. Shammai, another member of the Sanhedrin, became the head of a rival and hostile school. Hillel's party was the more liberal of the two, and became the dominant one. Hillel himself was greatly distinguished as a teacher of ethics. Among his numerous sayings is the following: "What is hateful unto thee do not unto others; this is the whole law, the remainder is only commentary."

HILLSBOROUGH, town of Co. Down, Northern Ireland, 12 miles from Belfast. Hillsborough Castle is the seat of the Marquess of Downshire, the head of the family of Hill. Pop. 544.

HILL TIPPERA, a native state, India, adjoining the British district of Tippera, Eastern Bengal. The state is hilly, several ranges of hills running parallel from north to south, with broad intervening valleys. Wild elephants and other large game abound in the forests. The principal crop is rice, and tea is indigenous in some parts of the hills. The government is despotic and patriarchal, and a resident political agent protects British interests. Area, 4,116 sq. miles. Pop. 304,437.

HILTON, Harold Horsfall, English golfer. Born 12th Jan., 1869, in 1892 he won the English open championship, a feat he repeated in 1897. He was amateur champion 1900, 1901, 1911 and 1913, and he also won the Irish championship on four occasions. In 1911 he won the Amateur Championship of the United States. Since 1913 Hilton has been editor of *Golf Illustrated*.

HILVERSUM, town and watering-place of the Netherlands. It is on the coast, 18 miles from Amsterdam, and is a railway junction. There are various attractions for visitors, including a kursaal. There is also a powerful broadcasting station (296·1 M.; 20 (7) kW). Pop. (1932), 59,632.

HIMALAYAS (Skt. *Himálaya*, the abode of snow), a chain of snowy

Himalayas

mountains in Asia, the most elevated on the earth, which separates the Indian peninsula from the plateau of Tibet, between the 72nd and 96th degrees of E. long., or between the Indus on the west and the Brahmaputra on the east; length, about 1,500 miles; average breadth, about 150 miles. The direction of the Himalaya range from the Indus is for great part of its length from north-west to south-east, after which it curves gradually to the east, or slightly to the north-east.

The great plain of India, south of the Himalaya, has a general elevation of 1,000 feet above the sea. The transition from this plain to the ascent of the range is marked in the north-west by a belt of dry porous ground broken up into numerous ravines. East of this the *Tarai*, a belt of sloping marsh land, occupies the same position. The *Tarai* is covered with forest and jungle, is crowded with wild animals, and is very malarial. Beyond this lies the *Bhabar*, a belt of a gravelly and sandy nature covered with forests of valuable timber trees. The *dúns*, *maris*, or *dwars*, longitudinal valleys partly cultivated and partly yielding forest growth, occupy the space between the *Bhabar* and the slope of the Himalaya themselves.

The general height of the Himalaya is double that of the Alps; the passes over the former ordinarily exceed, often by half a mile, the elevation of Mont Blanc. The Ibi-Gamin Pass in Garhwal, the highest of all, is 20,457 feet, the Mustagh 19,019 feet, the Parangla 18,500 feet, the Kronbrung 18,313 feet, and the Dura Ghát 17,750 feet high.

There are several summits in the Himalaya which approach closely to double the absolute elevation of the highest of the Alps, and 120 of them are stated to be above 20,000 feet. The rivers of the Punjab ('Five Waters') spring from a portion of the great chain which may be considered a distinct group under the title of the North-Western Himalaya. Some of the peaks here rise to a height of 24,000 to 25,000 feet; or to 28,278 feet if the Karakorum is regarded as part of the Himalaya.

In the Central or Middle Himalaya rise the sources of the Ganges and Jumna, in a region regarded by the Hindus as holy ground. Farther eastward, in Nepal, is the highest part of the Himalaya, as far as it is known and measured. Dhawalagiri has an elevation of 26,826 feet, the Gauri-sankar or Mount Everest (q.v.), the highest known mountain in the world, is 29,002 feet; the Yassa group rises to the height of 26,680 feet, the Ibjibia group to 26,306 feet. Going farther east, in Sikkim, or on its borders, we find Kanchenjunga, the western peak of which is 28,156 feet high, the eastern 27,815 feet, while the Kábru ridge rises to 24,015 feet. Sikkim forms a comparatively narrow but interesting territory, walled in on three sides by stupendous mountains from 17,000 to 28,000 feet high. Here terminates the region of the Middle Himalaya, most of the streams from which unite in the Ganges.

The Eastern Himalaya, which extends from Sikkim east to the Brahmaputra and completes the chain, sends all its waters to the last-named river, and is all comprised in Bhutan. A little to the east of Sikkim, Chamalari attains the height of 23,944 feet. About 250 miles farther east a conspicuous group has been observed with two peaks, named the Gemini or Twins, 21,500 feet high. Thence towards the east the mountains sink rapidly, but the range may be traced

beyond the right bank of the Brahmaputra. This stream, as well as the Indus, rises on the little-known north side of the Himalaya, their sources not being far apart.

The snowy ridge of the Himalaya, as far as examined, consists everywhere of granite, with which are immediately associated gneiss and mica-slate, followed, in descending, by metamorphic and secondary rocks till we arrive at the more recent alluvial deposits. Earthquakes are still frequent within this region; and hot springs gush forth in abundance, even from beneath the snow. The limit of perpetual snow in the middle division (long. 78° E.) is stated to be about 15,500 feet on the south side and 18,500 feet on the northern. In Sikkim the snow-line decends on the south side to 14,500 feet, while on the north it rises to a level of 19,600 feet. Immense glaciers exist at various parts.

The vegetation of the Himalaya is very rich, there being forests of pine, spruce, silver-fir, and deodar cedar at suitable elevations, with rhododendrons in rich profusion. Among the more characteristic animals are the yak, musk-deer, and wild sheep.— BIBLIOGRAPHY: F. B. Workman, *In the Ice-World of Himalaya*; *Ice-bound Heights of Mustagh*; C. G. Bruce, *Twenty Years in the Himalaya*.

HIMANTHA′LIA, a genus of brown Algæ, family Fucaceæ. *H. lorea*, the sea-thong, is plentiful on some parts of our coast. The thallus proper is a small top-shaped disc and is perennial; from it grows up each year a long, repeatedly-forked fertile shoot or *receptacle*, each branch of which somewhat resembles a leather strap in appearance and texture; hence the scientific and popular names.

HIM′ERA, an ancient Greek town on the north coast of Sicily, the site of which is near the modern Termini. Here Gelon and Theron annihilated the army of Hamilcar the Carthaginian (480 B.C.). In 409 B.C. Hannibal, grandson of Hamilcar, razed the town to the ground, and in 407 B.C. the Carthaginians built Thermæ Himerenses on the opposite bank of the River Himera.

HIMYARITES, the Homerites of Ptolemy, a group of peoples in Arabia, regarded as descendants of Himyar, one of the mythical ancestors of the Arabs. According to tradition they became the dominant race in Yemen about 3,000 years before Mahomet, and spread to the Euphrates on one hand and Abyssinia on the other. Their most flourishing period appears to have been from about 100 B.C. till A.D. 629, when they succumbed to

Mahommedanism. The Mahrah tribes of Southern Arabia are the direct descendants of the ancient Himyarites.

HIMYARITIC LANGUAGE, The, not now spoken, formed, with the Arabic and Ethiopic, the southern branch of the Semitic family of tongues. During the last hundred years several hundreds of Himyaritic inscriptions have been collected, and deciphered by means of alphabets with the corresponding Arabic letters which had been preserved.

HINCHINGBROOKE, village of Huntingdonshire. It adjoins Huntingdon, and here is Hinchingbrooke House, the seat of the Earl of Sandwich. At one time the residence of Oliver Cromwell, it is a fine house dating from the 16th century.

Hinchingbrooke is also the name of an island off the coast of Queensland.

HINCKLEY, a town and rural district of England, in the county of Leicester. It lies 13 miles south-west of Leicester, and contains an ancient church. The staple trade is hosiery, but there are also large boot and shoe factories. Pop. (1931) 16,030.

HINCMAR, Archbishop of Rheims, ecclesiastic and statesman, was born about A.D. 806, died at Epernay 882. He was at first a monk in the Abbey of St. Denis. In 845 he was elected Archbishop of Rheims, where he exercised extensive political as well as ecclesiastical authority. He was a man of enlightenment, one of the best scholars of his age, and was distinguished as a defender of the liberties of the Church. He was an opponent of predestinarianism, and wrote two treatises on it, and numerous other works.—Cf. J. C. Prichard, *Life and Times of Hincmar.*

HINDENBURG, a town of Upper Silesia, Germany, formerly called Zabrze, the centre of a coking-coal region in the Upper Silesian coalfield. It has iron-works and foundries, rolling-mills, a glass-furnace, and large chemical-works, and is a railway junction. Pop. 122,671.

HINDENBURG, Paul von, German soldier, born at Posen 1st Oct., 1847. Educated at the Military College, he entered the Prussian army in 1865, and served both in the Austro-Prussian and Franco-Prussian Wars. He distinguished himself at Königgratz, St. Privất, and at the battle of Sedan. He became major-general in 1900, rose to the rank of general of infantry, and retired from the army in 1911. When the European War broke out, Hindenburg was living in retirement in Hanover, but was recalled and appointed commander of the German forces in East Prussia. He defeated the Russians at the battle of Tannenberg, and pursued them to the Niemen. Appointed commander-in-chief of the Austro-German forces in Poland, he attacked Warsaw in Oct., 1914, and again in November of the same year, when he defeated the Russians at Kutno (15th–16th Nov.).

Hindenburg became the idol of Germany, and it was considered a pious act to drive nails of homage into his wooden effigy in Berlin. Commander-in-chief of the Austro-German forces on the Eastern front in 1915 and 1916, he became German generalissimo on 30th Aug., 1916, but accomplished little in the West. He re-

Von Hindenburg

tained this position till 11th Nov., 1918, when the Armistice was signed. He was decorated with the Iron Cross and made a Field-Marshal in 1914. In July, 1919, he wrote to Marshal Foch and offered himself as a sacrifice for the ex-Kaiser, and in November, 1919, he gave evidence as to the responsibility for the European War before the Reichstag Committee. He became President of the German Republic in 1925, and was re-elected on 10th April, 1932, after a second ballot. In 1933, however, Adolf Hitler (q.v.), leader of the National Socialist party, became Chancellor and virtual dictator of Germany.

In 1920 Hindenburg published a volume of reminiscences which has been translated into English (*Out of my Life*).

HINDHEAD, district of Surrey, 3 miles from Haslemere and 40½ from London. Its common is a famous beauty spot and near it many literary men, including Tennyson, have lived. The Devil's Punch Bowl, a glen below the Portsmouth Road, is notable. Near is Gibbet Hill. The common belongs to the National Trust. Pop. 2,200.

HINDI, one of the languages of India, being that form of Hindustani which employs the Devanágari or Sanskrit character. There are many varieties of it. Hindustani, the *lingua franca* of India, developed out of one of its dialects.

HINDLEY, a town of England, in Lancashire, giving name to one of the parliamentary districts of S.W. Lancashire. Cotton manufacture is the chief industry. Pop. (1931), 21,629.

HINDLIP, village of Worcestershire, 4 miles from Droitwich. The chief building is Hindlip Hall, the seat of Lord Hindlip. In 1886 Sir Henry Allsopp, head of a firm of brewers, was made Baron Hindlip.

HINDUISM is a general term covering a vast number of various and often very discrepant cults and socioreligious systems of Hindustan, which have in some cases developed out of the religion of the Aryan tribes who made their way into the north-west of India at least 1000 B.C. (perhaps considerably earlier), and in other cases represent the religious ideas of certain races settled before the Aryans in Hindustan—Dravidians, Kolarians, &c., who have in greater or lesser measure accepted certain fundamental ideas from the Aryans.

The earliest document of the religion of the Aryans is the *Rig-véda*, a collection, in ten books, of 1017 hymns by various priestly poets, which reveal the Aryans as dwelling at the time in the north-west of Hindustan, probably for the most part in the Eastern Punjab, in a state of civilization very much like that of the Homeric Greeks. These hymns are mostly addressed to the chief gods of the Aryan pantheon, who are in some cases nature-powers with a thin veil of anthropomorphic personality, such as Dyaushpitā the Sky-father (phonetically equal to Ζεὺς πατήρ, but in character very shadowy and impersonal), Prithivi the Earth-mother, Ushas the Dawn-goddess, Parjanya the god of the Rain-storm, Sūrya the Sun-god, Vāyu the Wind-god; in other cases they are essentially personal deities of uncertain origin, such as Indra, the most popular of the gods, typifying the hard-fighting and hard-drinking Aryan, whose chief exploit, however, the destruction of the Dragon Vritra and the liberation of the Cows or Waters seems to suggest an origin in nature-myth, and Varuṇa, whose chief function is to guard the moral order of the world; others again frankly physical in origin, have developed special features in religious practice, such as Agni the Fire-god, who, as conveying to the gods the oblations cast into the sacred fire, has become the divine Priest, and Sôma, the spirit of an unknown plant of which the fermented juice was drunk in various rites to inspire mystic ecstasy. Among other gods worshipped were Vishṇu, a kindly deity of obscure origin, and Rudra (later more commonly styled Siva, 'The Gracious,' on the principle of *lucus a non lucendo*) a spirit inclined to malignity.

The Brahmans. The rites connected with these cults were in earlier times fairly simple, but gradually they became more and more elaborate. The numbers of priests employed, the Brahmans, grew to large proportions, and their functions came to be subdivided; details of ceremony were intricately elaborated in a spirit of ritualistic professionalism, which considered the sacrifice as an end in itself, capable of controlling the order of nature at the will of the sacrificant, and which regarded the accompanying Vedic hymns merely as catch-words or spells for the mechanical purposes of the rites. To expound these ideas there arose a voluminous literature (at first oral, as was the Vēda), known as the *Brāhmaṇas*.

During this period the Aryan division of society into the four castes or *varnas* (literally 'colours'), viz. Brahmans or spiritual leaders, Kshatriyas or warriors, Vaiśyas or traders, and Śūdras or serfs, came to be fixed as a part of the social and religious order; and also the first steps were taken towards the establishment of a doctrine which has become universal in Hinduism, viz. the doctrine that the moral quality of every act inevitably and mechanically causes the agent to suffer corresponding happiness or sorrow in time to come (*karma*), and that the soul transmigrates and passes from birth to birth, higher or lower, in strict accordance with the merit of its previous works (*samsāra*).

The ritualism of the Brahmans developed in two directions. On the one hand, orthodoxy carried on its principles through the ages with little change, except that the loss of patronage compelled it to curtail and ultimately to abandon most of the expensive and complicated public rites. The principles of these schools are summed up in the *Pūrvamīmāmsā*, aphorisms ascribed to the sage Jaimini, with their commentaries by various scholars. To this day there exist, especially in Southern India, numerous Brahman families who preserve this tradition and maintain on a modest scale the ancient rites of domestic sacrifice.

The Upanishads. On the other hand, many Brahmans (possibly influenced by thinkers of the Kshatriya caste) advanced through divers allegorical interpretations of the rites of sacrifice to idealistic conceptions of the universe, expressed in the *Upanishads* (*Vedānta*). The Upanishads were later summarized in the *Brahmasūtra*, which with its commentaries forms the *Uttaramimāmsā*. Their ultimate teaching is that the individual soul, the Self (*ātman*), is in essence one with the universe and the World-spirit Brahma, and that by the mystic intuition in which the soul realizes this unity it attains salvation, viz. immunity from future births and certainty of coming after death to the Infinite Brahma. The loose and often poetical style in which the Upanishads express this thought has led to great divergence between different schools of commentators, of whom some, headed by Śaṇkara (born *c.* A.D. 788), maintain a thorough monism or *Advaita*, explaining away the phenomenal world as illusion or *māyā*, while others, under the leadership of Rāmānuja (died A.D. 1137), preach a theism in which the absolute unity of the Supreme Being is qualified by the admission of a relatively real world of individual souls and matter (Viśishtâdvaita).

Other interpreters hold other views; there is even a system of dualism, taught by Madhva or Ánanda-tirtha (A.D. 1199–1278), who asserts an eternal and essential distinction between God, spirit, and matter. Though thus variously interpreted, the Upanishads have come to be recognized as the prime source of authority for all the higher religious systems of India. Many thinkers have accepted them without further religious admixture as guides in life and death; others have combined them with the theistic worship of *Siva*, *Vishṇu*, *Rāma*, *Krishṇa*, and other gods.

These theistic cults seem for the most part to have arisen outside the Established Church of the Brahmans, but were adopted by the latter and recognized as orthodox as soon as they had become formidable rivals. They have practically ousted the old cults and rites of the Vēda and Brāhmanas, except in limited circles.

Siva. The worship of Śiva (the Vedic Rudra) is founded upon terror: white or yellow of hue, with a blue throat, smeared with ashes, wearing a garland of skulls, accompanied by bands of hideous goblins, he dwells in the wilds of the Himálaya, and his wife is Umā (Durgā or Pārvatī) the daughter of the god of these mountains. He has thus become the ideal Yōgī or ascetic saint, and he is commonly regarded as the power that brings about the dissolution of the universe in each æon of its beginningless and endless course. His worship is widely spread, being found with its phallic symbols (the *liṇga* and *yōni*, representing respectively the male and the female organs of generation) in almost all parts; it is especially strong in the extreme north and in the Dravidian regions of the south, except the Telugu country.

Vishnu on the other hand developed early into a god of gracious and beautiful attributes. His chief consort is the goddess Śri or Lakshmi (Fortune), and he is generally regarded as representing the forces of order in the cosmos. Of his incarnations or *avatāras* for the preservation and regeneration of the world the most important are those in which he appeared as Rāma and Krishṇa. Originally the cults of Rāma and Krishṇa were quite distinct from that of Vishnu. Rāma is a local hero of Aydōhyā (near the modern Ajodhya, in Fyzabad District); the famous epic *Rāmāyaṇa* narrates his exploits—his exile in company with his faithful wife Sitā and his brother Lakshmana in consequence of his father's Daśaratha's rash vow, the rape of Sitā by the demon king Rāvaṇa of Laṇkā, and Rāma's successful expedition to recover her, in which he was aided by a host of apes led by Hanumān—and in the portions of this poem which were composed later than the main body of the narrative he is represented as an incarnation of Vishnu.

Krishna. The cult of Krishna is composite. Possibly he was a real person, a prince of the Satvat clan, who, on account of his religious and moral teaching (or perhaps for other reasons) was worshipped after death, under the title of Bhagavān, 'The Lord,' by sects called Bhāgavatas, Sātvatas, Pāñcharātras, &c., and in course of time was identified with Nārāyana and Vishnu. The great document for this apotheosis is the *Bhagavad-gitā*, which has been inserted into the great epic *Mahābhārata*. With these traditions has been combined a cycle of Arcadian and erotic stories describing the childhood and youth of Krishna among the herdsfolk of Vraja (*Bhāgavatapurāṇa*, &c.).

With these gods is associated a vast mass of legend and ritual, mostly recorded in Purāṇas and other religious works. But they do not by any means exhaust the resources of Hinduism. It has a crowd of other deities, ranging from important personalities such as

Brahman the Creator, Sarasvatī the goddess of learning, Ganēsa or Gaṇapati the remover of obstacles, and the war-god Skanda (Kumāra or Kārttikēya, the son of Siva), down to insignificant and nameless local godlings, each with rituals and legends of his own, but all more or less definitely recognizing and recognized by the laws of the Greater Gods' pantheon.[1]
—BIBLIOGRAPHY: Monier Williams, *Religious Thought and Life in India*; J. C. Oman, *Cults, Customs, and Superstitions of India*; J. Murray Mitchell, *Hinduism, Past and Present*; J. N. Farquhar, *Primer of Hinduism*; R. W. Frazer, *Indian Thought, Past and Present*; E. O. Martin, *The Gods of India.*

HINDU KUSH, or INDIAN CAUCASUS, a mountain system of Central Asia. It is generally considered as a continuation of the Himalaya, which it adjoins at the Indus, and then stretches west till it unites with the Ghur Mountains in North Afghanistan. Its culminating point, in the range of Hindu-Koh, to the north

Hindu Kush

of Kabul, is far beyond the limit of perpetual snow, but is not supposed to exceed 20,000 feet. In many features the Hindu Kush resembles the Himalaya proper, though it is lower and destitute of forests.

HINDU LAW is in the main based upon the *dharma* or social-religious order prescribed by the Brahmans for Aryan society, and the books in which it is laid down arose at a time when the Aryans, settled in North India, and in some degree mixed with the darker races who inhabited the land before their coming, were developing the peculiar Indian social system denoted by the word *caste*, while preserving the patriarchal character of the household.

The textbooks are of various ages: the oldest were probably composed several centuries B.C. The 'Laws of Manu' (*Mānava-dharma-śāstra*) may perhaps be of the second or third cen-

[1] In the above survey we have omitted mention of Buddhism and Jainism. Though both these systems are developed from certain currents of early Hindu thought, their attitude towards official Hinduism in nearly all its forms has been one of nonconformity. Space forbids more than passing mention of the modern reformd theistic churches (Brāhma Samāj, Ārya Samāj, &c.).

tury A.D.; the *Yājñavalkyasmṛiti* is possibly of the fourth century A.D. But the administration of law has always had to take account of local usage, both Aryan and non-Aryan, and particularly Dravidian; an example of the latter is the law of succession in parts of the South, which follows the female line, in accordance with the ancient rule of Dravidian society, and in defiance of the Hindu law-books.

The unit of Aryan society was the joint household or family, comprising the patriarch with his wives, his unmarried daughters, and his sons with their wives and descendants; but in the course of time the patriarchal authority and the unity of the household have undergone some limitations. Women theoretically were always in tutelage, but had certain rights of inheritance and personal property. Widows as a rule were not expected to marry again; the custom of widows burning themselves on their husbands' pyre (*sati*), though without Vedic authority, became common in aristocratic circles, but was forbidden when the woman was pregnant or had a young son to educate. Polyandry was contrary to usual Brahmanic law, but was not unknown in some quarters. Infant marriage, though not practised in the earliest times, later became and is now very common, the bride remaining until puberty with her parents.

Legal, moral and religious responsibilities were graduated according to the degrees of caste. The theory of caste, based upon one of the later hymns of the Rig-vēda (X, 90), is that Aryan society consists of the Brahmans as its spiritual and intellectual leaders, the Kshatriyas (warriors) as its defenders, the Vaisyas (farmers and traders) as its 'middle class,' and the Sūdras (serfs and villeins, mostly of non-Aryan blood) as its lowest class of workers. Some general division of this kind seems to have existed already in the early days of Aryan settlement in India; but centuries passed before it established itself as an imperative law with a divine sanction. The system is fissiparous; each caste, following its own peculiar rules of endogamy and its social-religious constitution, tends to subdivide itself into equally exclusive minor societies based mainly upon the vocation of their members, or upon the issue of cross-marriages for which the existing order has made no provision, or upon the result of new political, religious, or social conditions. There are now more than 400 castes in India, and the number tends to grow.

HINDUSTAN' (country of the Hindus), the name at one time given to the whole Indian Empire, but which properly applies only to the Punjab and the valley of the Ganges. *See* INDIA.

HINDUSTA'NI, the *lingua franca* of India, one of the chief languages of the country. It is analytic in structure, and is divided into nearly sixty sub-dialects. Hindustani is the vernacular of about 100 million people. When written in the Persian character, and containing many Persian words and phrases, it is known as Urdu; another form of it is Hindi.

HINKLER, Chick Bert. Australian airman, born at Bundaberg in Queensland in 1894. He entered the flying service, and after the Great War made several notable flights. The longest was his flight from Croydon to Port Darwin, 10,340 miles in 15½ days, in Feb., 1927. In Nov., 1931, he crossed the Atlantic from Brazil to Africa. In January, 1933, he set out from Britain on a flight to Australia. He disappeared, and it was not until April that his body was found in the mountain wilds of Tuscany where his machine had crashed.

HINNY, a hybrid, the produce of a stallion-horse and a she-ass. It is more docile but smaller and weaker than the mule produced by a jackass and a mare, and it is also much less common.

HIO'GO (modern: **HYOGO**), suburb of Kōbe, Japan. Hiogo was the Japanese capital in the twelfth century, and was a flourishing place before Kōbe was in existence. As in the case of Yokohama, on the decision to erect Kōbe as a Treaty Port, Hiogo was absorbed (1887). *See* KŌBE.

HIP-JOINT, a ball-and-socket joint formed by the reception of the globular head of the femur or thigh-bone into the socket or acetabulum of the os innominatum. For flexion, extension, rotation, and strength combined it is the most perfect joint in the body.

HIPPAR'CHUS. *See* HIPPIAS.

HIPPARCHUS, ancient Greek mathematician and founder of scientific astronomy, was born at Nicæa in Bithynia, and lived about 160–125 B.C. He resided for some time at Rhodes, but afterwards went to Alexandria, then the great school of science. *A Commentary on the Phænomena of Aratus* is the only work of his extant. He first ascertained the true length of the year, discovered the precession of the equinoxes, determined the revolutions and mean motions of the planets, and prepared a catalogue of the fixed stars.—Cf. Sir G. C. Lewis, *Historical Survey of the Astronomy of the Ancients*.

HIPPA'RION, a fossil genus of the horse family, of the Upper Miocene and Pliocene periods. The members are distinguished by the fact that each foot possesses a single fully-developed toe, bordered by two functionless toes which do not touch the ground, but simply dangle on each side of the central toe. The hipparion was between the size of an ass and that of a zebra.

HIP'PIAS, ruler of Athens, son of Pisistratus, after whose death (527 B.C.) he assumed the government, in conjunction with his brother Hipparchus. The latter being assassinated while conducting a solemn procession to the temple of Minerva, Hippias seized the reins of the government alone, and revenged the death of his brother by imposing taxes on the people, selling offices, and putting to death all of whom he entertained the least suspicion. His tyranny became at last unbearable, and he was expelled from the city 510 B.C.

HIPPO, sometimes called **HIPPO REGIUS** to distinguish it from another town of the same name on the Carthaginian coast; an ancient Numidian city, the ruins of which still exist a short distance south of Bona, in Algeria. It was the episcopal see of St. Augustine, and was destroyed by the Vandals in 430, and by the Moslems in the seventh century.

HIPPOBOS'CIDÆ, or **PUPIPARA**, a family of dipterous insects, parasitic on birds and quadrupeds; also on bees. The eggs develop internally and come into the world as nearly mature larvæ (puparia). The type is *Hippobosca equina*, the horse forest-fly. Here also belong the fowl-fly (*Ornithomyia avicularia*), with the wingless ked or sheep 'tick' (*Melophagus ovinus*) and bee-louse (*Braula cæca*).

HIPPOCAM'PUS, a genus of fishes closely allied to the pipe-fishes, of singular construction and peculiar habits; the upper parts have some resemblance to the head and neck of a horse in miniature, which has suggested the name. When swimming, they maintain a vertical position and progress by rapid lateral movements of the dorsal fin; their general length is from 6 to 10 inches, and they occur in the Mediterranean and Atlantic.

HIPPOC'RATES, the most famous among the Greek physicians, called the father of medicine, born in the Island of Cos 460 B.C. Besides practising and teaching his profession at home he travelled on the continent of Greece, and died at an advanced age, 357 B.C., at Larissa, in Thessaly.

His writings, which were early celebrated, as they are quoted by Plato, became the nucleus of a collection of medical treatises by a number of authors of different places and periods, which were long attributed to him, and still bear his name. These works, seventy-two in number, include treatises by his sons Thessalus and Draco, by Polybus, and others. The best edition is that of Littré (in 10 vols. 8vo, Paris, 1839-61). An English

Hippocampus, or Sea-horse. *Phyllopteryx eques* above *Hippocampus brevirostris* below

translation of *The Genuine Works of Hippocrates* was published by Adams in 1849. Among his genuine writings are the first and third books on epidemics; the aphorisms; on diet in acute diseases; on air, waters, and localities; on prognostics; on wounds of the head. Hippocrates was one of the first to insist on the importance of diet and regimen in disease. He had remarkable skill in diagnosis, practised auscultation, and taught the doctrine of 'critical days.'

HIPPOCRAT'IC OATH, an oath taken in olden times by students on entering upon the practice of medicine. It commenced with the words: "I swear by Apollo, the physician, by Æsculapius, by Hygieia, Panacea, and all the gods and goddesses, that according to my ability and judgment I will keep this oath, and stipulation." The would-be practitioner promised to pass his life in purity and holiness, to practise his art honestly and to the advantage of his patients, in accordance with the principles of honour and humanity. He furthermore pledged himself never to divulge the secrets of his profession. The oath is said to have been administered by Hippocrates himself to his disciples, and hence the name.

HIPPOCRENE (-krē'nē; 'The Horse's Fountain'), a spring on Mount Helicon, a mountain in Bœotia,

consecrated to the Muses, the waters of which possessed the power of poetic inspiration. It is said to have risen from the ground when struck by the hoofs of Pegasus.

HIP'PODROME (Gr. *hippos*, horse, and *dromos*, race-course), the Greek name for the public place where the horse- and chariot-races were held. In Byzantine times the hippodrome at Constantinople acquired great renown, and factions originating in the hippodrome caused perpetual confusion in all departments of the public service. The name is sometimes applied to a modern circus, and also to a theatre of variety entertainments, such as the London Hippodrome (opened in 1900).—Cf. E. N. Gardiner, *Greek Athletic Sports and Festivals*.

HIPPOL'YTUS, in Greek mythology, son of Theseus and Antiope or Hippolyte, queen of the Amazons. His stepmother, Phædra, fell in love with him, and accused him to his father in order to revenge herself for his indifference. He was put to death, but his innocence being afterwards established. Phædra destroyed herself. According to a tradition of Epidaurus, Hippolytus was restored to life by Æsculapius. The story is told by Euripides in his drama *Hippoly-*

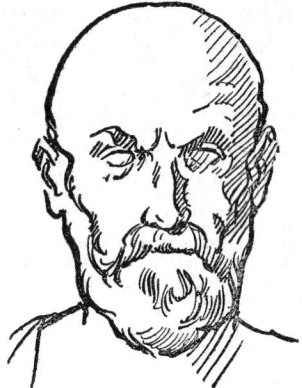

Hippocrates

tus, and by Racine in *Phèdre*. See PHÆDRA.

HIPPOLYTUS, an early Christian bishop and writer, the details of whose history are involved in obscurity. He appears to have lived about the beginning of the third century, and is supposed to have suffered martyrdom under Alexander Severus. The most important of his writings is the *Philo-*

sophumena, a refutation of heresies, discovered at Mount Athos in 1842, and published in 1852. He also wrote *Christ and Antichrist.*

HIPPO'NAX, a Greek satirist, lived probably about 540 B.C. He is supposed to have been undersized and ugly, and, like many men of small dimensions, endowed with a caustic wit. The sculptor Bupalus was the chief butt of his satire. Bupalus had made a statue of him in which he had intensified his already remarkable ugliness; Hipponax retaliated in satirical verses full of withering scorn. According to some authorities, Bupalus was so overwhelmed by this attack that he committed suicide; this feature of the story is, however, probably derived from the tale of Archilochus and Lycambes.

Hipponax is chiefly celebrated for introducing or inventing a new metre, that curious variant of the iambic senarius which is obtained by substituting a spondee or a trochee for an iambus in the last foot, and which is known as the choliambic, scazon, or limping iambic. This metre is extremely suitable for playful satire, and was used to the exclusion of other metres by Babrius in his *Fables*, and Herodas in his *Mimes*, and by Catullus in some of his poems (e.g. *Carmen VIII, Carmen XXII*, and the beautiful poem on Sirmio, *Carmen XXXI*).

Hipponax was notorious for the bitterness of his satire, although in a well-known epigram Theocritus warns the wicked to beware of his tomb, but says that good men may even sleep there without fear. With unerring taste Theocritus wrote this epigram in scazons, even as Wordsworth wrote his three poems on Burns in one of Burns's favourite stanzas. The fragments of Hipponax which have been preserved amount in all to about a hundred lines.

HIPPOPH'AGY (Gr. *hippophagos*, horse-eating), the practice of feeding on horse flesh. Hippophagi was the name given by old geographers to certain nomadic Scythian tribes on the north of the Caspian Sea, who fed on horse flesh. Horse flesh has been eaten for a considerable time in Germany, and in Paris, where Geoffroy St. Hilaire founded a society of hippophagists, it has been regularly sold since 1866.

HIPPOPOT'AMUS, the typical genus of a family of non-ruminating artiodactyle Ungulates, of which two living species are known. One species, *H. amphibius*, is of large size, and is common throughout the greater part of Africa, but has become extinct in Madagascar; the other, *H. liberiensis*, is not only smaller, but has other important differences, and is found only in the African west coast rivers, and those flowing into Lake Tchad. The former species has a thick and square head, a very large muzzle, small eyes and ears, thick and heavy body, short legs terminated by four toes, a short tail, two ventral teats, skin about 2 inches thick on the back and sides, and without hair, except at the extremity of the tail. The incisors and canines of the lower jaw are of great strength and size, the canines or tusks being long and curved forward. These tusks sometimes reach the length of 2 feet and more, and weigh upwards of 6 lb. The animal is killed by the natives partly as food, but also on

Hippopotamus

account of the tusks and teeth, their hardness being superior to that of elephant ivory, and less liable to turn yellow.

The hippopotamus attains the length of 14 feet, or possibly more. It delights in water, living in lakes, rivers, and estuaries, and feeding on water-plants or on the herbage growing near the water. It is an excellent swimmer and diver, and can remain under water a considerable time. The *behemoth* of Job is considered by commentators to be the hippopotamus, as the description of its size, manners, food, and haunts is not unlike those of the latter animal. Among the ancient Egyptians it was revered as a divinity, as it is among the negroes in some localities.

The oldest extinct species occur in the Lower Pliocene of India and Burma, while during the Late Pliocene and Pleistocene periods *H. amphibius* (or a closely-related form) lived in Western, Central, and Southern Europe. The remains of extinct dwarf species are found in the Pleistocene of Sicily, Malta, and Madagascar.

HIPPURIS.—*See* MARE'S-TAIL.

HIPPURITES (-ī'tĕz), a genus of fossil bivalve molluscs, often of massive dimensions, having the under shell of great depth, and of a conical form, with a flat lid or operculum. They are of the Upper Cretaceous age. They are allied to the living Chama, or gaping cockle. The *Hippurite limestone* is an important representative of the Cretaceous rocks in the south of France, the Austrian Alps (Gosau beds), &c., characterized by an abundance of shells of the family Hippuritidæ.

HIRING (known in the law of England as bailment for hire, and in the law of Scotland as location) is a contract whereby the possession of a subject is ceded by its owner (the locator or lessor or letter) to another person (the conductor or lessee or hirer) for a specified period for his use and enjoyment (*locatio rei*), or whereby services are rendered as by a clerk or workman (*locatio conductio operarum*), or a particular piece of work done as by a shoemaker employed to mend shoes (*locatio conductio operis faciendi*) in return for a hire or price.

Locatio rei is distinguished from sale in that there is no transfer of the ownership of the subject, and from borrowing in that there is a consideration for the use. The subject may be land or houses (*see* LANDLORD AND TENANT; LEASE) or any moveable subject or chattel capable of being returned. It cannot, therefore, strictly be anything which is consumed by use, as corn, wine, money, &c., though it may be something which suffers depreciation by tear and wear, as furniture. The use must not be for an illegal or immoral purpose.

The obligations of the parties are generally as follows. The letter undertakes to do nothing inconsistent with the hirer's use and possession for the agreed-on period of the let, warrants the subject as fit for the use for which he has let it, and must keep it in adequate repair; whilst the hirer must return the subject at the expiry of the period in the like condition in which he received it (excepting always ordinary tear and wear), is liable in damages if, by putting it to any other use than that stipulated for, it is injured or destroyed, and in his use of it must exercise the care of a prudent man for his own property.

A special form of the contract is known as hire-purchase. Under this system the goods become the property of the hirer when he has paid the hire for a specified number of terms. Should he fall into arrears, the goods are recoverable by the letter, and all payments already made are forfeitable. Until the final payment has been made, the hirer is not owner and cannot sell or pledge the goods. They are, however, subject to distraint for rent. The system is much resorted to by persons of restricted means who wish to obtain immediate possession of expensive articles such as pianos, sewing-machines, &c., without immediate payment. *See* MASTER AND SERVANT; CARRIER; INNKEEPER.

Hiring of custody occurs when goods are delivered to a wharfinger, warehouseman, livery stabler, &c., for safe custody in return for payment. The custodier must show ordinary care and diligence, and is liable for loss caused by his negligence.

HIROHITO, Emperor of Japan. Son of the Emperor Taisho, he was born 29th April, 1901. He succeeded his father in 1926, but had been virtual ruler since 1921, when his father retired from public life owing to ill-health. His great aim is peace and prosperity at home and abroad.

HIROSHIMA, a city of Japan, Island of Honshiu, 175 miles w.s.w. of Kobe, to which it ranks next in commercial importance. It is a large cotton-spinning centre and a depôt for artistic wares. Multitudes flock to the bay annually to visit the ancient Shinto temple, one of Japan's three chief wonders, on the Itskushima or Island of Light. Pop. (1930), 270,417.

HIRSCHBERG, (hirsh'berh), a town of Germany, in Silesia, 26 miles southwest of Liegnitz. Pop. (with suburbs), 28,673.

HIRST, George Herbert, English cricketer. Born at Kirkheaton, Yorkshire, 7th Sept., 1871, he became a professional cricketer and first played for his county in 1892. For nearly 30 years he was one of the mainstays of the team, both as a batsman and a bowler, and on many occasions played for England against Australia. As an all-round cricketer Hirst has probably only been surpassed by Grace and equalled by another Yorkshireman, Rhodes. From 1920 to 1930 he was cricket coach at Eton College.

HISPANIA, the name by which the Spanish Peninsula was known to the Romans. The Greeks called it Iberia, and the Roman poets sometimes applied to it the name of Hesperia.

HISSAR', a town of India, in the Punjab, administrative head quarters of the district of the same name, on the Western Jumna Canal, 102 miles w. of Delhi. Pop. 21,415. The district has an area of 5,213 sq. miles. Pop. 816,810.

Hissar is also the name of a district and town in Turkestan, in E. Bokhara, Soviet Central Asia, having the Hissar chain on the north and intersected by tributaries of the Oxus. Pop. of town, 10,000.

HISTOL'OGY, in biology, the study of the cell aggregates or *tissues* composing the bodies of higher organisms, and specialized for diverse functions in accordance with the principle of division of physiological labour. The lowest plants and animals consist of single cells, which are sometimes complex, while in multicellular organisms there is gradual differentiation of cell-groups, which reaches its climax in seed-plants and vertebrate animals.

Plant Histology. Typical plant cells are invested by firm membranes or *cell-walls*, which vary in thickness and chemical composition in the different tissues. In some cases the protoplasmic contents entirely disappear, being used up in formation of the thickened cell-walls, which play a passive part in the economy.

The following tissues are those of most importance. A. *Meristem*. Actively dividing tissue composed of small cells with thin cellulose walls and abundant protoplasm. The products of their division become modified in various ways, and add to the bulk of the plant by becoming permanent tissue.

(1) *Primary meristem* entirely composes the bodies of very young embryos and organs, and also the growing points of root and stem, enabling these to increase in length.

(2) *Secondary meristem*, existing as layers or masses intercalated among permanent tissues. *Cambium*, for example, is found in the roots and stems of Gymnosperms and Dicotyledons, between wood and bast, to both of which it makes successive additions that bring about growth in thickness among perennial forms. *Cork cambium* (phellogen) comes into existence in the periphery of thickening roots and stems, developing layers of cork which replace the epidermis when this is ruptured and shed as the result of expansion. Pollen grains and embryo-sacs are also the products of minute masses of secondary meristem situated, respectively within anthers and ovules.

B. *Permanent Tissues*. (1) *Piliferous layer* and *epidermis*. The former is a delicate membrane, composed of a single layer of flattened cells, that invests young roots. A little way behind the apex of the root there is a zone where these cells are drawn out into delicate *root-hairs*, which absorb water from the soil. Leaves and young stems are covered by a somewhat similar investment of *epidermis*, typically made up of a single layer of flattened cells, the outer walls of which are more or less thickened and *cuticularized*, i.e. converted into *cutin*, a modification of cellulose which is practically waterproof and serves to prevent undue evaporation. Epidermis is transparent, so that light can reach the underlying green tissue. Microscopic holes, *stomata*, are present in the epidermis of the stem and under side of the leaf, less frequently in the upper epidermis of the latter. Through these pores gaseous exchanges can take place between the interior of the plant and the external air. Each stoma is bounded by two kidney-shaped *guard-cells*, which contain chlorophyll granules, and by alterations in shape regulate the size of the cleft between them. *Hairs* of different shape and nature are often present as outgrowths of the epidermis.

(2) *Vessels and tracheides*. Wood largely consists of microscopic tubes, *wood vessels*, developed from longitudinal rows of cylindrical cells by thickening and lignification of their walls, absorption of the cross partitions, and disappearance of the protoplasm. Thin places, *pits*, are left in the thickened walls, or the thickened part may be in the form of rings or a spiral (pitted, annular, and spiral vessels). *Tracheides* are dead, elongated cells, that take the place of vessels in the wood of Gymnosperms, but are not limited to this group of plants. *Bast vessels*, or *sieve tubes*, are conducting elements typical of bast, and are developed, like wood vessels, from longitudinal rows of cells. Their thickened walls, however, are composed of cellulose, and they contain protoplasm. The cross partitions are not absorbed, but perforated by numerous holes, owing to the presence of which they have received the name of *sieve plates*. The holes are traversed by threads of protoplasm.

(3) *Parenchyma* is made up of cells which, in the most typical cases, are fairly equal in length, breadth, and thickness. They are characteristic of cortex, medullary rays, and pith, where their walls are usually of cellulose, and protoplasmic contents are generally present, though these may disappear in old pith. Small-celled parenchyma also occurs in wood and bast, its walls being lignified in the former. The green external tissue containing chlorophyll is of parenchymatous nature. In the leaf there is a compact upper layer of *palisade parenchyma*, with cells elongated at right angles to the surface, and lower *spongy parenchyma*, where numerous

air-spaces are present between the irregular constituent cells.

(4) *Collenchyma* is a supporting tissue found in the superficial parts of herbaceous structures, and may be described as a modification of parenchyma composed of prismatic cells, with thickened edges to the prisms.

(5) *Fibrous tissue*, of supporting nature, consists of elongated spindle-shaped dead cells, with lignified walls, most abundantly found in wood and bast. Tissue of this kind belongs to what is commonly known as *sclerenchyma*, shorter-celled varieties of which often make up strengthening layers in the cortex of the stem, and also invest the vascular bundles of leaves, connecting them with upper and lower epidermis, and thus preventing collapse of the delicate green parenchyma.

Animal Histology. The vast majority of animal cells are devoid of definite external walls, and when these do occur, they are not composed of cellulose. *Intercellular substance* is present between the component cells of a tissue, and the term *matrix* is applied to this when it is relatively abundant. In some tissues, cells are associated with fibres and other cell products. As might be expected from their relative complexity, animals are possessed of certain tissues which are either absent from higher plants, or at most faintly represented, as in the case of muscular, nervous, and sensory structures.

The following summary account sets forth a selection of the more important facts. A. *Embryonic tissue.* The embryo of a vertebrate animal is made up of three actively dividing *germinal layers*, very broadly comparable to the primary meristem of a higher plant. The external layer, *epiblast* (ectoderm), gives rise to the epidermis, lining of the mouth cavity, nervous system, retina and lens of the eye. From the innermost layer, *hypoblast* (endoderm), are produced the cells lining the greater part of the digestive tube and its outgrowths, and also the *notochord*, an elastic longitudinal rod situated below the central nervous system, and commonly partly or entirely replaced by the backbone. From the middle layer, *mesoblast* (mesoderm), arise all the other parts of the body.

B. *Permanent tissues.* (1) *Blood and lymph.* These are tissues in which the constituent cells, *corpuscles*, float freely in a liquid matrix. These corpuscles are either white or red. The former are typical cells, of irregular shape and capable of executing creeping movements; also of engulfing and digesting intruding bacteria and other noxious germs. Their average diameter, in man, is $\frac{1}{2500}$ inch. The *red corpuscles*

of mammals are non-nucleated biconcave discs, nearly always circular in shape. Those of man are about $\frac{1}{3200}$ inch in diameter. The red corpuscles of other vertebrates are oval, nucleated, and of larger size, especially in Amphibia. *Lymph* resembles blood, except in the absence of red corpuscles.

(2) *Epithelium*, layers of cells covering the exterior of the body and lining the internal cavities. It is *simple* when only one cell thick, *stratified* when consisting of several layers of cells. The constituent cells may be flattened (*squamous*), or elongated at right angles to the surface (*columnar*). *Simple squamous epithelium* lines the heart and blood-vessels, and *simple columnar epithelium* lines the greater part of the digestive tube. *Stratified squamous epithelium* lines the mouth cavity and constitutes the *epidermis*, or outer layer of the skin. *Glandular epithelium* makes up the essential parts of the tubules composing glands, such as liver, pancreas, salivary glands, and kidneys. Its cells are granular and cubical or polyhedral. In the case of certain internal tubes, the epithelial lining is *ciliated*, i.e. the cells adjoining the cavity are provided with innumerable short protoplasmic threads, *cilia*, which alternately bend and straighten in rhythmic fashion, independently of nervous control. The stratified epithelium of the windpipe, for example, has a surface layer of columnar ciliated cells, of which the cilia work in such a way as to move particles of dust, bacteria, &c., towards the exterior. Slender *sense cells* are the most important part of the epithelium of sense organs, and they differ in character according to the stimuli by which they are affected. *Germinal epithelium*, producing sexual cells (ova and spermatozoa), makes up the essential parts of the generative glands (ovary and testis).

(3) *Supporting tissues* include connective tissue, cartilage, bone; dentine and enamel. (*a*) *Connective tissue* is made up of branching cells and delicate fibres. In *white connective tissue* these fibres are exceedingly narrow, unbranched, inelastic, and arranged in wavy bundles, as, for example, in tendons. *Yellow connective tissue* contains branching, elastic fibres of rather larger size, and is found in parts of the body where elasticity is necessary, e.g. the lungs and arteries. *Areolar connective tissue* contains both white and yellow fibres. It occurs below the skin, between bundles of muscle, &c. (*b*) *Cartilage* or *gristle* consists of cells embedded in a tough translucent matrix, which may be traversed by fibres (fibro-cartilage). (*c*) *Bone* contains branching cells embedded in an organic matrix which is strengthened by

the deposit of salts of lime (carbonate and phosphate). It may be spongy or compact, as in the ends and shaft, respectively, of a long bone. In compact bone, blood-vessels and nerves are contained in narrow tubes (Haversian canals), round which the bone cells are disposed in concentric *Haversian systems*. Each cell occupies a corresponding chink (lacuna) in the hard matrix, and its processes are contained in exceedingly small passages (canaliculi) which radiate from this. (d) *Dentine* and *enamel* are hard substances making up the greater part of teeth. The former, also known as *ivory*, surrounds the pulp cavity, and consists of wavy tubules. Still harder *enamel*, composed of microscopic prisms, covers the projecting crown. The fangs of the tooth are invested by a thin layer of *cement*, which is to be regarded as bone.

(4) *Muscle* is of three kinds. (a) *Unstriated*, composed of spindle-shaped cells, which are not marked by transverse striations. It is found in the walls of arteries, veins, and hollow internal organs. (b) *Cardiac muscle* makes up the wall of the heart. It consists of cylindrical cells united together into a complex network, and marked by transverse striations. (c) *Striated muscle* constitutes the flesh, by which voluntary movements are effected. Its constituent fibres are formed by the fusion and specialization of rows of cells. Each fibre is transversely and longitudinally striated, and invested by a delicate sheath (sarcolemma), under which are nuclei, which indicate the origin of the fibre as a cell fusion. Various theories have been advanced to explain transverse striation, but none are entirely satisfactory. It is associated, however, with the power of rapid and vigorous contraction, i.e. shortening and broadening without change in volume.

(5) *Nerve.* The nervous system is essentially composed of greatly specialized cells known as *neurons*, which are not connected together as formerly supposed. A typical neuron consists of a nucleated swelling, *cyton* (often called a nerve-cell), with one or more branching processes, *dendrons*, and a single rather larger process, *axon*, continued to form the central conducting thread (axis cylinder) of a nerve fibre. Nerve impulses pass inwards along the dendrons, and outwards along the axon. The so-called *grey matter* of brain and spinal cord chiefly consists of cytons, which are also present in outlying nervous centres known as *ganglia*. The *white matter* of the organs named is mostly made up of axons. Nerve fibres are of two kinds, non-medullated and medullated. The former consist of

an axis cylinder covered by a delicate membrane, the *neurilemma* (primitive sheath), beneath which nuclei are present at intervals. Such fibres are characteristic of the sympathetic nervous systems, and also make up the olfactory nerve. In medullated nerve-fibres there is a layer of fat (medullary sheath) between the axis cylinder and neurilemma, and each fibre is divided into a number of segments, between which the neurilemma dips inwards to touch the axis cylinder. All the spinal and cranial nerves (except the olfactory) are made up of such fibres.
—BIBLIOGRAPHY:(1) Plant Histology: F. Cavers, *Practical Botany*; Flatters, *Vegetable Histology*; Chamberlain, *Methods in Plant Histology*. (2) Animal Histology: Sir E. A. Schäfer, *Essentials of Histology*; C. Hill, *Manual of Normal Histology*; Jordan and Ferguson, *Text-book of Histology*; R. Krause, *Course in Normal Histology*; Arey, *Laboratory Guide in Histology*; A. Bolles Lee, *Microtomist's Vade Mecum.*

HISTON, village of Cambridge-shire, 5 miles from Cambridge, on the L.N.E. Rly. The village is a centre for jam-making. Pop. 1,400.

HISTORY in its widest sense relates to the whole past of mankind and to the natural and physical conditions which have influenced human life. Thus geology may be regarded as a part of history, because it deals with the development of the physical construction of the globe, i.e. with conditions which have determined much of the action of mankind. Such an extension of its meaning would obviously deprive the study of any distinctive significance, and history proper is concerned primarily with the acts and the thoughts of human beings.

It has been urged that "History is, above everything else, geography," but such a view gives undue emphasis to the admitted importance of geography in relation to historical investigation. Geography is the term employed to indicate one series of conditions with which mankind has had to deal; it explains many human activities, but these activities themselves are the interests of the historian. Part of the story of mankind is the record of the triumph of human invention over geographical obstacles, and it may be said that the development of methods of communication and transport constitutes a practical modification of geography. Freeman's saying, "History is past politics, and politics is present history," is valuable because of the stress it lays upon the essential element of human action in relation to the physical and other conditions which influence the life of mankind, but it is insufficient as a definition.

The province of history, in the ordinary sense in which the term is used, is restricted not only by the circumstance that its main topic is the record of human action, but also by the nature of the materials which provide that record. It has to be distinguished from anthropology, which is mainly concerned with the customs of savage life and their survival in ancient or modern civilized societies. The border-line between anthropology and history cannot be drawn very accurately, but, as a rough indication, we may take the existence of written documents as a test of historical material. The historian is mainly occupied with written records (whether on stone, parchment, or paper), and his business is to discover from written records the facts about the past of mankind, to interpret and explain them, and to present them in literary form.

There has been, in recent years, considerable controversy about the methods and aim of history, and about its connection alike with ethics and with literature. The older tradition of historical writing involved great care about literary form, and the mode of presentation was regarded as the test of the author's achievement, while the older writers also were given to moralizing upon the characters they drew and the events they narrated. The task of producing a graceful narrative has been rendered much more difficult by the opening up of national and family archives, and the consequent multiplication of historical sources.

The ascertainment of fact and the examination of conflicting evidence has become the primary duty of the historian, and it is very difficult to present the process and the results of an elaborate investigation in a form which deserves the term 'literary.' Hence there has arisen a school of historians who hold that history is a science and not an art; that it is not a branch of literature, but a branch of science, dealing with man under political and social and economic conditions, in the same manner as other sciences deal with man under biological or physiological conditions. On this theory, the business of the historian is to collect and classify facts and to explain their meaning, and he is not called upon to attempt the work of a literary artist, to excite the imagination or the emotions. There is, however, a reaction against the scientific school, and other authorities argue that the historian must not merely accumulate and interpret facts, but must also provide "the exposition of these facts in their full emotional and intellectual value to a wide public by the difficult art of literature."

The choice between these different points of view depends, in part, upon the qualifications of the writer and upon the nature of his subject, for not every historical investigation is capable of being made attractive to a wide public in literary form, but there can be little question about the ideal at which the historian should aim. The prejudice against the literary and artistic presentation of the results of historical investigation is ceasing to exist, and the older models are exercising a growing influence.

On the other hand, there is no such reaction against the divorce of history from ethics. It is admitted that history cannot formulate general laws or establish universal relationships of cause and effect, because history never repeats itself, and no two historical 'events' are precisely similar; each is a set of circumstances, and there are numberless variations in the circumstances. This fact not only militates against the conception of history as a science; it also restricts the tendency to treat the subject as a storehouse of moral lessons. The late Lord Acton, indeed, exhorted his Cambridge students "never to debase the moral currency or to lower the standard of rectitude, but to try others by the final maxim that governs your own lives, and to suffer no man and no cause to escape the undying penalty which history has the power to inflict on wrong."

But the general tendency of modern writers is to leave the reader to form his own moral judgment, and, except in the clearest cases, to refrain from pronouncing sentence. Indeed, the ideal of impartiality has been carried so far that it has been argued that modern historiography encourages "the idea that all sides in the quarrels of the past were equally right and equally wrong." This is an exaggeration of the reaction against the use of history as a political or ecclesiastical pamphlet, and it may be carried too far.

It is the duty of an historian to state his facts accurately and in their proper proportion; if he does so, a statement of his individual opinion, clearly expressed as opinion and not disguised as historical doctrine, will be helpful to the reader whether he differs from the author or not. The real test of impartiality lies rather in the selection of the facts presented to the reader and in the discrimination between what is definitely ascertained and what is conjectural, than in the employment of adjectives or the expression of personal opinions.

History, it may be said, is, in the first place, the discovery and the examination of sources of evidence, and the determination of the value of conflicting records, and, in the second place, the presentation of the results of this investigation in literary form in a manner which will arouse both the emotional and intellectual interest of the reader and lead him to apply his information to the problems of his own time. No such problem can be solved by mere reference to historical parallels or precedents, but a knowledge of the past "can mould the mind into the capability of understanding great affairs;" it can help to remove current prejudices and to place the essential features of modern difficulties in a new perspective, to widen the outlook, and to create new ideals and enthusiasms.

History is usually divided into three compartments, ancient, mediæval, and modern. Such distinctions are useful as a convenient method of arrangement, and as emphasizing the effects of certain very great events, though the very existence of dividing lines is apt to create a misapprehension and to obscure the continuity of human history.

Ancient history covers the history of the world up to the fall of the Roman Empire. It includes the records of the Hebrew, Arabian, Phœnician, Egyptian, and other races, as well as the history of Greece and Rome, but for the ordinary reader, who has no knowledge of Eastern languages, the subject tends to mean Greek and Roman history and the history of the Jews.

The two earliest centres of recorded human civilization were Babylonia and Egypt, and for the long period of over 2,000 years (c. 5000–2500 B.C.) ancient history is the story of the independent development of these two countries, each of which produced a remarkable civilization. The next stage is the expansion of Babylonia, which, under the rule of Hammurabi (c. 2250 B.C.), founded an Empire that lasted until about 1600 B.C., when it fell, largely owing to the growth of the new Assyrian power in the North. For about 500 years after that date, the Egyptian Empire was the great World Power, and it exercised dominion over Syria.

From about 1100 to 900 B.C., when the power of Egypt had declined, we have the rise of independent kingdoms in Syria—Tyre in the north, the Philistines in the south, and the Israelites in the south-east. The Kingdom of Israel reached the height of its greatness in the reign of Solomon (c. 1015–977 B.C.). Then for nearly three hundred years (c. 900–600 B.C.) the As-

syrian Empire was the ruler of the world, its greatest period being the reign of Sennacherib (705–681 B.C.). It collapsed from internal weakness and from the attack of the Medes, and the very site of its great capital, Nineveh, was long unknown. Its place was taken by two powers, the Chaldeans or Babylonians under Nebuchadnezzar, and the Medes, who, about 550 B.C., were conquered by the Persians under Cyrus. He subsequently reduced the Babylonians to subjection and formed the Persian World-Empire, which lasted for half a century, under Cyrus, Cambyses, and Darius.

The Persian Empire came into conflict with the Greeks, and the victory of the Greeks shifted the centre of civilization from the East into Europe. Greek history begins not later than 1000 B.C.; but it is not until about 700 B.C. that much is known about it, and its greatness followed the Persian Wars and the battles of Marathon and Salamis (490 and 480 B.C.). The result was the development of a series of Greek Empires—Athenian, Spartan, Theban, and Macedonian, which occupy the historical stage until the death of Alexander the Great in 323 B.C. The division of his Empire after his death prepared the way for the emergence of the Roman power.

The early centuries of Roman history are occupied with the rise of the city and the extension of its authority over the Italian Peninsula. When this task was accomplished, in the end of the third century B.C., Rome became involved in a struggle with the African power which had arisen at Carthage, and its victory was followed by the establishment of a Roman Empire in the East (200 B.C.–44 B.C.), and by the creation of a World-Empire, which coincides with the end of the Roman Republic and the institution of the Principate or Empire under Augustus and his successors.

Mediæval history begins with the fall of the Roman Empire. A more suitable date has been suggested in the reign of Constantine (A.D. 324–337), which marks the transference of the seat of Empire from Rome to Byzantium or Constantinople, and the reconciliation of the Empire with the growing power of the Christian religion, but the general usage is to place the end of ancient history about the year 476, which marks the end of the existence of the Roman Empire in the West. It had been revived after the death of the Emperor Theodosius in 395, when there was a permanent division into the Eastern and Western Empires, and for nearly a century had carried on an ineffectual resistance against the hordes of barbarians, Goths and Vandals, who swept down upon Western

Europe and destroyed the civilization of the Empire. It is this destruction of the institutions which had been built up by the political genius of the Romans that creates a definite dividing-line between the ancient and the mediæval world. The process was gradual, and in many ways the year 476 has no special significance, for there are later traces in Italy of the recognition of the Imperial power as represented by the Eastern Empire, but it affords a convenient label for the end of Roman, and the rise of German, influence in Europe.

The centuries which are called 'mediæval' are subdivided into the 'Dark Ages' and the 'Middle Ages' proper. The name of the Dark Ages is given to the confused history of the sixth, seventh, eighth, and ninth centuries, in the course of which the barbarian tribes made their settlements in Western Europe, were converted to Christianity, and developed into the great European countries of mediæval and modern times. The most important event of the period was the restoration of the Roman Empire by Charlemagne, King of the Franks, in 800 A.D., but after his death the territories which he had united were partitioned under his successors. The history of the Dark Ages also includes the rise of the Papal power in Italy and throughout the greater part of Europe, the origin and development of the great religious system of Mahomet, and the external and internal conflicts of the Eastern Empire which maintained its existence at Constantinople.

The Middle Ages (q.v.) proper may be said to begin with the second restoration of the Roman Empire by Otto the Great in 962, and a large portion of their history relates the struggle between the revived Empire and the Papacy, which distracted Italy and Germany for about two centuries, and culminated in the fall of the Imperial House of Hohenstaufen and an interregnum in the Empire (1250–1273). This struggle was succeeded, in the fourteenth century, by the Great Schism in the Papacy and by the period of the great Church Councils at Pisa (1409), Constance (1414), and Basel (1431), which attempted to bring peace and unity into the Church and the Empire.

In England, the Middle Ages witnessed the consolidation of the kingdom under the strong dynasty founded by William the Conqueror; the origin and growth of a parliamentary system; the attempts at the expansion of English power in Ireland, Wales, Scotland, and France; and the civil war between the Houses of Lancaster and York which followed the expulsion of the English from France. The history of France is the story of the gradual growth of the power of the monarchy, which was interrupted by the English invasion, but ultimately received a great impetus from its failure.

All over Europe, society in the Middle Ages was deeply affected by the long series of Crusades in the Holy Land, and by the intellectual and religious movements which led to the foundation of universities and the establishment of the various orders of Friars. The Eastern Empire maintained until 1453 an unequal struggle against the growing power of the Turks, who, in that year, captured Constantinople.

Modern History. The capture of Constantinople is sometimes taken as the beginning of modern, as distinguished from mediæval, history. The transition is marked by the rise of new intellectual interests, known as the Renaissance or Revival of Learning, by the revolutions in geographical conceptions and in trade routes brought about by the discovery of the New World, and by the inauguration of a new era of national conflicts, inspired by dynastic ambitions. The year 1453 marks only the early stages of this transition, and other dates are also employed.

In England, 1485, the year of the battle of Bosworth, is usually taken as the end of one era and the beginning of another, and for Europe generally, historians often regard the expedition of Charles VIII of France into Italy in 1494 as the beginning of modern history. Just at the close of the mediæval period, a new Great Power had been created by the union of Spain under Ferdinand and Isabella in 1479, and the first years of the modern period were marked by the rivalry of France and Spain, the power of which was greatly increased by a marriage alliance with the Imperial House of Habsburg.

National rivalries were interrupted by the Reformation, which caused internal divisions in every European country, and brought about the Wars of Religion in which the combatants were influenced rather by religious than by national sympathies. This period ended with the close of the Thirty Years' War in Germany and of the great Civil War in Britain in the middle of the seventeenth century, and a fresh series of conflicts was brought about by commercial jealousies, by the attempt of France to attain supremacy in Europe, and by the rivalry of Great Britain and France in India and North America.

A marked dividing-line in modern history is given by the French Revolution of 1789, and it may be argued that we should cease to describe the period from 1494 to 1789 as 'modern,' and reserve that name for the era inaugurated by the Revolution, to which and to the wars which followed it may be traced the origins of the great events of the nineteenth century—the national developments in Italy and Germany, the disruption of the Ottoman Empire, and the causes of the great European War of 1914–8.

Until the year 1783, the history of the New World can be studied only in relation to the Old, but from the establishment of the United States the American continent has its own independent history. The history of Africa, of many parts of Asia, and of Australia cannot be separated from the history of the European Powers, although China has its own independent story, and the rise of Japan is one of the most important aspects of world-history in recent years.

Apart from this chronological division, history is also distinguished according to topics. The history, for example, of the Christian Church, of law and institutions, of war, of trade and commerce are all part of the general matter of history, but are capable of independent treatment throughout the whole range of our knowledge. Biography is also closely allied with history, and one of the best methods of understanding a period is to study the lives of its most illustrious men. In recent years, the study of local history has formed an excellent avenue to the wider study of general history, to which it has also made valuable contributions. Among the great historical publications in recent years are: Lavisse and Rambaud's *Histoire générale*; *The Cambridge Modern History*; Dr. William's *Historian's History of the World*; Oncken's *Allgemeine Geschichte*; &c.—BIBLIOGRAPHY: Langlois, *Manuel de bibliographie historique*; Lord Acton, *Lecture on the Study of History*; F. Harrison, *The Meaning of History*; Langlois and Seignobos, *Introduction aux études historiques*; C. W. Smith, *Lectures on the Study of History*; E. A. Freeman, *Methods of Historical Study*.

HITCHCOCK, Edward, American geologist, born 1793, died 1864. In 1825 he became professor of chemistry and natural history at Amherst College, and in 1845 president of the same college, and professor of natural theology and geology. He was author of various works, including: *Geology of the Connecticut Valley*; a highly popular work on *Elementary Geology*; *Illustrations of Surface Geology*; *Religion of Geology and its Connected Sciences*; and *Reminiscences*, published shortly before his death.

HITCHIN, a market town of England, Hertfordshire. The parish church contains some fine old brasses and a fine altar-piece by Rubens, and there is a grammar-school. The chief industries are malting and dealing in agricultural produce. Straw-plaiting is carried on, and lavender and peppermint are grown and distilled. Girton College was originally established at Hitchin in 1869, but removed to Cambridge in 1872. Pop. (1931), 14,382.

HITHER GREEN, district of S.E. London in the Borough of Lewisham, on the S. Rly. Here is Mountfield Park, a pleasure ground, and a large fever hospital.

HITLER, Adolf. Leader of the National-Socialist ("Nazi") move-

Adolf Hitler

ment in Germany and now (1933) dictator throughout the Reich; was born in Austria in 1890. By trade a house painter, he rose to power with astonishing rapidity, mainly by the organization of a semi-militarized Fascist movement, the "Brown Shirts," which concentrated all the nationalistic elements of post-war Germany against Communism (q.v.) and Social Democracy. In the Reichstag elections of March, 1933, the Nazis gained 52 seats over their total in the previous elections in the summer of 1932 and became the strongest single party in the Reichstag. Hitler thereupon formed an alliance with the Nationalists, the party of the big industrialists and landowners, led by Herr Hugenberg and Von Papen, and wrung from the aged President Hindenburg (q.v.) his assent to Hitler becoming Chancellor.

Extraordinary measures were taken by Hitler, as soon as he obtained power, to consolidate the supremacy of the Nazis and to destroy their opponents. On 23rd March, 1933, the Reichstag passed, by 441 votes to 94, an Enabling Bill giving the Hitler Government autocratic authority throughout the Reich. The 81 Communists, who had won seats in the elections, were in prison and could not vote, and the minority of 94 against the Bill represented the full strength of the Social Democrats in the Reichstag. Measures were immediately taken, in May, to suppress the Social Democratic Party and the

Hittites. Relief from Carchemish (Chimæra)

free Trade Unions which were in alliance with them: their leaders were driven out of office and many of them into exile, their offices were raided and occupied by Nazis, their funds seized, their journals suppressed, and their membership and organization throughout the country placed under the orders of Nazi functionaries responsible only to Hitler himself. Simultaneously the Nazis overthrew every State Government in the Reich and established themselves in power. A policy of terrorism and persecution directed against the Jews roused world-wide protest.

Hitler's Nationalist allies were soon driven out of the Government; Hugenberg resigned, and his party was 'voluntarily' dissolved. The Junker elements represented by Von Papen alone remain in the Government; every other organized political party or group, including the Catholic 'Centre', has been wound up and abolished. The 'nazification' of

Germany is thus complete and Hitler rules Germany with absolute power, free from any Parliamentary interference or from the constraints which an organized Opposition can impose. Social Democracy has sought by removing the party headquarters to Prague to keep the struggle against the Hitler dictatorship going from outside, but within the Reich there is no party or organization capable of withstanding Hitler.

HITOPADESA (hit-ō-pa-dā'sha; Skt., goodly instruction), an ancient Sanskrit work by an author named Narayana. It is similar to and mostly taken from an older work called the *Panchatantra* or the five books, the source also of the collection known as the *Fables of Bidpai or Pilpay*. The book consists of fables, one story growing out of another after the Eastern fashion, with verses cited from ancient writers by the interlocutors, and was designed for the instruction of princes. It has been translated into many Asiatic and European languages.

HITTITES, the Biblical name given to the people (called Kheta on the ancient Egyptian monuments, and Hatti by the Assyrians) whose powerful empire extended from Northern Asia Minor (east of the Halys River) south as far as Hamath in Syria, or even Hebron in South Palestine, where Abraham is reported to have bought from them the cave of Machpelah as a burial-place for Sarah (*Gen.* xxiii). The first reference to them is in *Gen.* x, 15, where we are told that Canaan begat Sidon, his first-born, and Heth. This suggests that the sons of Heth were in Syria in 2100 B.C.; but we know that they were a powerful empire, able to stand up against the mighty Mesopotamian and Egyptian powers for many centuries. It was not until 717 B.C., when the Assyrians took Carchemish, the southern capital of the Hittites, that their empire was broken. Their chief capital was in the north at Boghazkeui in Cappadocia.

Little progress has yet been made in the interpretation of the hieroglyphic writings of the Hittites, but at present the language is supposed to belong neither to the Indo-European nor to the Semitic groups. Recent research, especially excavations in Carchemish and Boghaz-keui, has revealed something of the great part played by the Hittites in the early history of civilization. — BIBLIO-GRAPHY: A. H. Sayce, *The Hittites: the Story of a Forgotten Empire*; J. Garstang, *The Land of the Hittites*; A. E. Cowley, *The Hittites* (Schweich Lectures, 1920).

HITU'. *See* ITU.

HIVAOA. *See* MARQUESAS.

HI'VITES ('snake clan,' or 'dwellers in encampments'), a Canaanitish tribe first noticed in *Gen.* xxxiv. At the conquest of Canaan the main body occupied the northern confines of Western Palestine. Gibeon and Shechem were their chief cities.

HOADLY, Benjamin, English prelate, born 1676, died 1761. He was educated at Cambridge; took orders in 1700, and, after being settled in London, distinguished himself in controversy with Bishop Atterbury and others. A staunch Low-Churchman, he was appointed Bishop of Bangor in 1715. A sermon, on 'The Kingdom of Christ,' preached before the king in 1717, gave rise to the 'Bangorian Controversy' (q.v.) regarding the divine the body, on which it is accustomed to rest. The precocious young climb actively about with the aid of two claws on each wing; they can also swim and dive.

HOBART, up to 1881 **HOBART TOWN,** the capital of Tasmania, situated at the foot of Mount Wellington (4,166 feet), on the River Derwent, about 12 miles from its mouth. The city, founded in 1804, is built in the form of a square, the streets crossing each other at right angles. Among the public buildings are the Government house, the Government offices, the Houses of Parliament, town hall, university, museum, Episcopal and Roman Catholic cathedrals, and several other places ot worship, many public and private schools, and the general hospital.

There are several jam manufac-

Sailing Craft at Hobart

authority of the king and the Church. He was translated to the see of Hereford in 1721, to Salisbury in 1723, and Winchester in 1734.—Cf. Sir L. Stephen, *History of English Thought in the Eighteenth Century.*

HOAR CROSS, village of Staffordshire, 4 miles from Abbots Bromley. It has a hall, long the seat of the Meynell family. The church of the Holy Angels, built by Mrs. Meynell-Ingram, is one of the finest modern churches in the country.

HOATZIN, or **HOACTZIN,** *Opisthocŏmus cristătus,* a singular gregarious South American bird, is the sole representative of a distinct sub-order (Opisthocomi) of gallinaceous birds. The plumage is brown streaked with white, and the head has a movable crest. It is of the size of a pheasant, and has an enormous crop with a very small gizzard. The powers of flight are limited, and there is an area of hardened skin on the under side ᵥf tories, breweries, flour-mills, tanneries, and a woollen factory; and in connection with the shipping interest first-class patent slips. The harbour is easy of access, and has ample depth, capacity, wharf and dock accommodation. Hobart is connected by rail with Launceston. Pop. (1932), 58,270.

HOB'BEMA, Meindert or **Minderhout,** after Ruysdael the greatest Dutch landscape-painter, born at Amsterdam in 1638, died 1709. He died in poverty, but few facts of his life are known. His paintings consist chiefly of forest scenes, ruins, villages, or water-mills. With Jacob van Ruysdael he stands at the head of the seventeenth century Dutch landscape school. Less imaginative than Ruysdael's, his work shows the same intimate knowledge of nature and feeling for space and atmosphere. His colour is apt to be heavy and sombre: and at times he loses breadth by over-emphasis of detail. He considerably influenced the English landscape painters, notably Crome and Constable. *The Avenue of Middelharnis, Showery Weather, Ruins of Breberode Castle,* &c., are in the National Gallery. There are also paintings by him in the Wallace Collection, in Buckingham Palace, and in the Fitzwilliam Museum, Cambridge.

HOBBES, John Oliver. Pen name of the English novelist, Pearl Mary Teresa Craigie. The daughter of John Morgan Richards, an American business man who settled in London, she was born in Boston, Nov. 3, 1867. She made a reputation with *Some Emotions and a Moral,* 1891, and other novels. *The School for Saints,* 1897, and *Robert Orange,* 1900, are her best books. Her plays include *The Ambassador.* She died Aug. 13, 1906.

HOBBES, Thomas, English moral and political philosopher, born 1588 at Malmesbury, died 1679. Educated at Magdalen Hall, Oxford, he afterwards travelled on the Continent as tutor in the Earl of Devonshire's family, becoming acquainted with Gassendi, Descartes, and Galileo. He was also intimate with Bacon (some of whose works he translated into Latin), Lord Herbert of Cherbury, and Ben Jonson. From 1637 to 1641 he resided much at Chatsworth, but becoming alarmed at the likelihood of an outbreak of civil war, he went to Paris. He stayed abroad some years, and during that time published most of his works. Hobbes also taught mathematics to the Prince of Wales (Charles II), then in Paris, who after the Restoration gave him a pension of £100. He spent his latter days with the Devonshire family.

Works. The most remarkable of his works is his *Leviathan, or the Matter, Form, and Power of a Commonwealth* (1651). Other works are: *De Cive* (1642); *De Corpore Politico* (1650); *De Libertate, Necessitate, et Casu* (1654); and *Behemoth,* a history of the Civil War, published after his death. He also published a metrical version of the *Iliad* and *Odyssey.*

Philosophy. In the history of the development of free-thought in Europe Hobbes holds an important place, and he was one of the first great English writers on government. Hobbes was above all a political philosopher, and would have the State supreme in all matters affecting the mutual relations of men. He conceived the state of nature to be one in which all are at war with one another, and government as the result of a compact, suggested by selfishness, for the sake of peace and protection. Absolute rule was the best form of government, but this is qualified by the assertion that

obedience to a ruler is only due so long as he can afford protection to the subject.

A sensationalist and at times a materialist in philosophy and psychology, Hobbes was hedonistic in his ethics. It was man's desire for pleasure that made him, according to Hobbes, first establish civil authority. Hobbes made religion also a political matter, and defined it as fear of power invisible, feigned by the mind or imagined from tales publicly allowed. The philosophy of Hobbes, so depreciated among his contemporaries, has been more or less adopted by Locke, Hartley, Hume, and Priestley, and his ideas on government have formed the foundation of the utilitarianism of the Benthamites.— BIBLIOGRAPHY: Sir Leslie Stephen, *Hobbes*; G. Croom Robertson, *Hobbes*; E.H. Sneath, *The Ethics of Hobbes*; M. W. Calkins, *The Metaphysical System of Hobbes.*

HOBBS, John Berry. English cricketer. Born in Cambridge, 16th Dec., 1882, Hobbs became a professional cricketer and played first for his native shire. In 1905 he joined the Surrey county eleven, for which he played for over 25 years. In 1925 he beat W. G. Grace's record of 126 centuries. Hobbs was for years one of the opening batsmen in all test matches and the captain of the Players against the Gentlemen. He played in the test matches for the last time in 1930. Hobbs has written several books on cricket, including *Playing for England,* 1931.

HO'BOKEN, a city, New Jersey, United States, on the Hudson River, and close to Jersey City, which stretches immediately to the south. It lies opposite New York, with which it is connected by tunnels and ferries. It has various manufactories, and among the public institutions are the Stevens' Institute of Technology and the public library. Shipping is an important industry. (1930), Pop 59,261.

HOBSON, Thomas, carrier at Cambridge. He kept a livery stable and attained notoriety by his stubborn refusal to let out his horses except in their proper order, hence the phrase "Hobson's choice," which means no choice at all.

HOCHE (ōsh), **Lazare,** general in the French revolutionary war, born 1768, died suddenly in Sept., 1797. At the age of sixteen he took service in the French guards, and at the Revolution joined the popular party. He greatly distinguished himself at the siege of Thionville and the defence of Dunkirk, and shortly afterwards, when scarcely twenty-five years of age, received the command of the Army of the Moselle. In 1793 he drove the Austrians out of Alsace, and soon after was arrested by the Jacobins and imprisoned at Paris. In 1794 he was released, and appointed commander of the army detailed to quell the rising in the west, and afterwards to that in La Vendée.

In 1796 he conceived the plan of attacking Britain, by making a descent on Ireland. He accordingly set sail in December from Brest, but the expedition failed utterly, and he was obliged to return without having even effected a landing. After his return he received the command of the Army of the Sambre and Meuse. He opened the campaign of 1797 by a bold passage over the Rhine, and had defeated the Austrians in several engagements, when he was stopped in the path of victory by the news of the armistice concluded in Italy. He died shortly afterwards.—Cf. A. Griffith, *French Revolutionary Generals.*

HOCHHEIM (hōh'hīm), a town of Prussia, in the province of Hesse-Nassau, 4 miles E.N.E. of Mayence. It is famous for its wine, called in Germany *Hochheimer*, English *Hock.* Pop. 4,082.

HOCHKIRCH (hōh'kirh), or **HOCH-KIRCHEN** (hōh'kirh), a village in Saxony, 6 miles E.S.E. of Bautzen, the scene of the surprise and defeat of Frederick the Great, in 1758, by the Austrians under Marshal Daun, in which Marshal Keith was killed; and also of a defeat of the Russians and Prussians by the French in 1813. Pop. 500.

HÖCHSTÄDT (heuh'stet), a town, Bavaria, left bank of the Danube, 23 miles N.W. of Augsburg, the scene of several great battles, of which the most celebrated is that of Blenheim in 1704. (*See* BLENHEIM.) Pop. 2,156.

HOCK. *See* WINES; HOCHHEIM.

HOCKEY, a ball game, the name of which is probably derived from the hooked stick employed. It is cognate with the Scottish *shinty*, and the Irish *hurley*, and is known in certain circles as *bandy.* It is of considerable antiquity, and appears to have been played by the Romans.

Whilst in general popularity it cannot rival either code of football in this country, hockey possesses certain advantages which make a very strong appeal. Deprived of many of the dangers inseparably associated with football, it is still sufficiently strenuous to appeal to the most athletic, and yet afford opportunities to the less vigorous who still desire to participate in match play. It is popular in girls' schools, and mixed hockey matches are also arranged, although not as a serious competition. On the whole it is not popular with the authorities of public schools, probably because of the desire to preserve a more wholehearted allegiance to football as the winter game *par excellence.* Nor have the Continental nations taken to it with enthusiasm, although international matches between France and England have been occasionally played.

Rules and Constitution of Teams. In its rules and in the constitution of teams hockey bears a very close resemblance to Association football. Eleven a side comprise a goalkeeper, two backs, three half-backs, and five forwards. The ball employed is of leather, white or painted white; usually a painted cricket-ball is used.

The sticks must not exceed 28 oz. in weight, and must be of such size as to pass through a 2-inch ring. They are slightly curved at one extremity, and flattened on the left-hand surface.

The ground for play is rectangular, 100 yards long and 60 yards in width, with boundaries marked by chalklines, and flags at the corners. The boundaries are known as goal-lines and side-lines. The goals (in the centre of each goal-line) are two posts 4 yards apart joined by a crossbar 7 feet from the ground. In front of the goal is drawn 'the striking circle'—a semicircle, having the goal-line as a diameter and with a radius of 15 yards.

The game is started by the 'bully off,' as it is called. The centre-forwards of the respective teams face each another with the ball between them, and each strikes the ground with his stick on his own side of the ball and his opponent's stick three times alternately, after which the ball itself may be struck.

A goal is scored by the ball being hit through the goal by a player whilst within the striking circle. The offside rule applies exactly as in Association football, viz. a player is 'off-side' if he is nearest the opponent's goal at the moment when the ball is hit or rolled in from touch (the side-lines) unless there are at least three of his opponents nearer their own goal than he is.

The ball may be caught by the hand, but must be immediately dropped, that is to say, it may not be picked up, carried, or thrown, nor may the ball be actually kicked, although it may be stopped by the foot. Only the flat side of the stick may be used for striking the ball; using the other side constitutes a foul with a penalty attaching thereto. An opponent's progress may be stayed by hooking his stick, but only if the stick is within striking distance of the ball. Further, if a player strikes at the ball, no part of the stick must rise above his shoulders throughout the stroke. Disregard of this rule is penalized (as in the case of other fouls) by the award of a free hit to the other side.

As has been stated, the general principles of the game are exactly those of Association football, with a roll in from touch whenever the ball crosses the side-lines, and a corner hit allowed to a side if an opposing player hits the ball behind his own goal-line. Play is usually for two periods of thirty-five minutes, with a short interval during which ends are changed.

Hockey is an exceedingly popular game in the London suburbs, and prominent teams which may be mentioned are Surbiton, Finchley, Hampstead, Wimbledon, Southgate, and Beckenham. Most of the London hospitals have teams, and the same applies to the colleges at Oxford and Cambridge. So high is the standard of hockey regarded that Cambridge has since 1907 awarded a full Blue to the representatives selected to meet the Oxford eleven, thus classing the game with rowing, football, cricket, track athletics, and tennis (not lawn tennis). The members of the Oxford team are awarded half Blues.

County matches lead by gradual selection to the international matches, the first of which was played in 1895 (Oxford had competed with Cambridge first in 1890). Ladies' intercounty and international contests also take place. The Hockey Association, which is responsible for the rules and organization of the game, was founded in 1875.

The skill and combination of firstclass players are remarkable. In dribbling the ball and dodging opponents the necessity arises for rapidly changing the position of the stick in order to keep the flat surface in contact with the ball, and a first-class player exhibits greater superiority in this than perhaps in any other game. It is no exaggeration to say that five really good players could with ease beat an eleven of mediocre capability, a claim which would hardly apply to any other game.

Ice-hockey is a game rarely seen in this country owing to the infrequent occasions when skating can be enjoyed. The game requires exceptional experience of skating, and when teams representing Oxford and Cambridge meet at Mürren in December, the majority of the players are Canadians who have had many years' experience before coming to study in this country, with a minority of English players who have had exceptional opportunities. The 'ball' is a flat piece of wood, and the boundaries of the field of play are raised platforms of wood about a foot in height, so that the 'ball' rebounds into play. Much skill is possible in utilizing this platform during a dribble. Ice-hockey is probably the fastest and in some respects the most skilful of all games.—Cf. A. Farrel, *How to Play Hockey* (Spalding's Athletic Library).

HOCKING, Joseph, English author. Born in 1855, he became a minister of the United Methodist Free Church and, like his brother, Silas Hocking, made a name as a novelist. His first book was *Jabez Easterbrook*, 1891, after which others followed in quick succession. Recent publications are *The Eternal Challenge* (1929); *Out of the Depths* (1930); *The Man Who Was Sure* (1931); and *The Eternal Choice* (1932).

HOCKING, Silas Kitto, British novelist, born 24th March, 1850, at St. Stephen's in Cornwall. Educated privately, he entered the Wesleyan ministry in 1870, and held several pastorates until 1896, when he retired. His attempts to get into Parliament in 1906 and 1910 failed. His works include: *Alec Green* (1878), *Her Benny* (1879), *Sea Waif* (1882), *Real Grit* (1887), *Where Duty Lies* (1891), *God's Outcast* (1898), *Pioneers* (1905), *The Silent Man* (1906), *Who Shall Judge?* (1910), *The Third Man* (1911), *The Beautiful Alien* (1916), *His Own Accuser* (1917), *Nancy* (1919), *Watchers in the Dawn* (1920), *My Book of Memory* (1923), and *The Mystery Man* (1930).

HODEIDA, a seaport of Yemen, Arabia, on the Red Sea, with an extensive trade in coffee. It was occupied by the British during the European War, and they evacuated the town early in 1921. Pop. 40,000. *See* YEMEN.

HODOGRAPH. If from a fixed point O as origin a vector OQ is drawn to represent in magnitude and direction the velocity of a moving point P at any instant, the locus of Q will be a curve which is called the *hodograph* of the motion of P. Here the term curve is to include a straight line as a special case. It is to be noted that the hodograph is not merely a curve, but a curve described by a moving point Q which itself has a velocity at every instant. It is easily proved that the *acceleration* of the moving point P is fully represented by the velocity of Q at the same instant.

Simple Examples of the Hodograph. (1) If a particle P is projected vertically upwards or downwards, under gravity, in a vacuum, it is known to have a constant downward acceleration. Hence the hodograph is a vertical straight line, described by the point Q with a uniform downward velocity equal to g, the acceleration of

P, and Q is at the origin O at the instant when P is at its highest point, i.e. when its velocity is zero.

(2) An unresisted projectile P under gravity describes a parabolic path. Since in this case also the acceleration of P is constant and vertically downward, the hodograph is exactly the same as in case (1), except that the origin O is no longer in the hodograph, but at a horizontal distance from it which represents the velocity of P when at its highest point.

(3) The hodograph of a point P moving with uniform speed V in a circle of radius R is another circle whose radius measures V, the origin being at the centre. The speed of the point Q which describes the hodograph being V^2/R, this is the measure of the acceleration of P.

(4) The hodograph of a point on the rim of a circle which rolls uniformly on a straight line is also a circle uniformly described, but having the origin on its circumference.

(5) The hodograph of the motion of a planet or comet is a circle, which, however, is not uniformly described. The origin in this case is at a distance e x raidus from the centre of hodograph, when e is the eccentricity of the orbit.

The conception of the hodograph and the name are due to Sir William Rowan Hamilton.

HÓDMEZÖVÁSÁRHELY, a town of Hungary, on Lake Hodos. It is the centre of an important agricultural and vine-growing district. Pop. (1930), 60,342.

HOE, an instrument for cutting up weeds and loosening the earth in fields and gardens, in shape something like an adze, being a plate of iron, with an eye for a handle, which is set at a convenient angle with the plate. The Dutch hoe differs from the common hand-hoe in having the cutting-blade set like the blade of a spade.

A *horse-hoe* is a frame wheel-mounted, and furnished with ranges of shares spaced so as to work in the intervals between the rows of turnips, potatoes, &c. It is used on farms for the same purpose as the hand-hoe.

HOF (höf), a town in Bavaria Upper Franconia, on the left bank of the Saale, 30 miles N.N.E. of Baireuth. It has woollen, linen, cotton, leather, and paper manufactures. Marble and ironstone are worked in the vicinity. Pop. 41,377.—There is also a town called Hof in Norway, north of Oslo.

HOFER, Andreas, Tyrolese peasant-leader and patriot, born in 1767. In 1796 he led a company of sharp-shooters against the French, and after the Peace of Lunéville took a prominent part in the organization of the Tyrol militia. In 1809 he took the lead in an insurrection of the Tyrolese for shaking off the yoke of Bavaria, to which their country had been transferred by the Treaty of Pressburg. In a short time, with intermittent assistance from the Austrians, he defeated the French and Bavarian troops, and nearly the whole country was liberated.

Hofer then carried on the military and civil administration, under the most singular circumstances, till the Peace of Vienna was proclaimed. Misled by false reports, he commenced hostilities anew, and thus forfeited the protection of the amnesty. He remained concealed for some time, but was at last betrayed to the French, and carried to Mantua, where he was tried by a court-martial and shot, 20th Feb., 1810. His family was indemnified for the loss of their property by the Emperor of Austria in 1819, and

Horse Hoe

his son ennobled. There are numerous patriotic songs about Hofer, and he is the hero of tragedies by Auerbach and Immermann.—Cf. K. T. Heigel, *Andreas Hofer.*

HOFFMANN, August Heinrich, called also Hoffmann von Fallersleben, German lyric poet and philologist, born at Fallersleben, in Hanover, 1798, died at Corvey 1874. Under the influence of the brothers Grimm he took to investigating old German literature, and became professor of German literature at Breslau in 1835. He also made special studies of Dutch and Silesian literature. Dismissed in 1842 for the supposed revolutionary tendencies of his songs (*Unpolitische Lieder*), he led a wandering life for some years. In 1860 he became librarian to the Duke of Ratibor. He wrote *Horæ Belgicæ*, but he is best known by his songs. One of his most popular songs is his patriotic *Deutschland, Deutschland über Alles*, which he composed on the Island of Heligoland in 1841.

HOFFMANN, Ernst Theodor Amadeus, or, properly, **Ernst Theodor Wilhelm,** German novelist, born at Königsberg 1776, died in 1822. He studied law in his native town, and afterwards held several minor judicial appointments under Government, but intemperate habits ruined his health.

He cultivated music and art, especially caricature, with success.

Among his works of fiction are the *Phantasiestücke in Callots Manier* (1814), the *Elixiere des Teufels* (1816), the *Nachtstücke* (1817), the *Serapionsbrüder* (twenty-three tales, 1819 *et seq.*), *Lebensansichten des Katers Murr* (1820-2), and many others. In his longer novels he has a strong tendency to make use of supernatural machinery; but his masterpieces are his short stories.

HOFMANN, Josef Casimir, Polish musician. Born at Cracow, 20th Jan., 1876, the son of a professor of music, he studied at Warsaw and appeared in public as a pianist when a boy. He gave recitals in London, New York and other capitals, composed concertos and sonatas and wrote on piano playing. In 1927 Hofmann was made director of the Curtis Institute of Music in Philadelphia.

Hog Fish

HOFWYL (hof'vil), a village of Switzerland, 6 miles north of Bern, noted as the seat of the educational institution founded by Fellenberg and Pestalozzi in 1802.

HOG. *See* PIG.

HO'GARTH, William, painter and satirical artist, born in London 1697, died 1764. He was apprenticed to a silversmith, who employed him in engraving spoons. In 1720 he began business for himself as a designer, and produced designs and book-plates for the booksellers. Among these was a series of illustrations to *Hudibras*. He also painted a number of small genre pieces in oil.

In 1729 he married the daughter of Sir James Thornhill, the painter, against her father's wishes, who is said, however, to have been mollified when Hogarth produced his celebrated series of pictures called *The Harlot's Progress*, a work which brought his great powers fairly before the public. The engravings of these, which became exceedingly popular, were published in 1734. This was followed by *The Rake's Progress* and *Marriage à la Mode*, two similar series of paintings and engravings; *Industry and Idleness,*

Beer Street and Gin Lane, The Election, The Enraged Musician, The Country-Inn Yard, The March to Finchley, Strolling Actresses Dressing in a Barn, Four Stages of Cruelty, and many other engravings which all evinced his extraordinary powers of satire, wit, and imagination. He also painted a number of masterly and strongly characterized portraits, notably those of himself, Garrick, Lovat, and Wilkes. He was also ambitious of shining as an historical painter, but in this line he was not so successful.

In 1753 his work on the *Analysis of Beauty* appeared, a treatise which brought him little fame, and which was severely ridiculed by his enemies and professional rivals. In originality of imagination and invention, and for vigour of realism and dramatic power, Hogarth stands in the highest rank, and his genius was always enlisted on the side of virtue and morality. He is the first and among the greatest of a distinctively English school of painting, marked by literary tendencies, realism, and feeling for colour. He is well represented in the National Gallery, Tate Gallery, and Sir John Soane's Museum. The best edition of his engravings is that published by Boydell (London, 1790), the plates of which, retouched by Heath and others, have been repeatedly published since. —BIBLIOGRAPHY: Samuel Ireland, *Hogarth Illustrated*; W. C. Monkhouse, *Works of William Hogarth*; Austin Dobson, *Hogarth*; Nichols and Steevens, *The Genuine Works of Hogarth*; *see also* HIND'S GREAT ENGRAVERS SERIES.

HOG-FISH, the popular name given to teleostean fishes of the genus Scorpæna, family Scorpænidæ. The best-known species is the *S. scrofa*, common in the Mediterranean, having a spiny laterally-flattened head adorned with membranous lobes or filaments. It is of a large size and a red colour.

HOGG, James, more familiarly known by the name of the *Ettrick Shepherd*, was born in Selkirkshire in 1770, died at Altrive, on the Yarrow, in 1835. After a very scanty education, he began life as a shepherd. His early rhymings, *Donald Macdonald*, in imitation of Burns, and his *Scottish Pastorals*, brought him under the notice of Sir Walter Scott, by whose advice he published a volume of ballads under the title of *The Mountain Bard*.

The failure of an ill-judged agricultural scheme brought him to Edinburgh, where he published *The Forest Minstrel* (1810), and started a weekly periodical entitled *The Spy*, which after a short time became defunct. The appearance of *The Queen's Wake* in 1813, with its charming ballad of *Kilmeny*, established Hogg's reputation as a poet.

In 1815 he published his *Pilgrims of the Sun*, which was followed by *Mador of the Moor*, *The Poetic Mirror* (a collection of imitations of living poets), *Queen Hynde*, and *Dramatic Tales*, as well as by *The Brownie of Bodsbeck*, and other prose tales; *The Jacobite Relics* (partly written by Hogg), &c. From 1817 he had held the farm of Altrive from the Duke of Buccleuch at a merely nominal rent; but his farming schemes never thrived, and he was generally in narrow circumstances.—Cf. Mrs. M. G. Garden (Hogg's daughter), *Memorials of James Hogg*.

HOGMANAY is used in Northern England and Scotland for the last day of the year and for the New Year's Day gift. The French form is *aguillanneuf*, but the Norman form *hoguinané* is more like the Scottish. Brittany boys used to visit houses at Christmas and knock at doors. When asked who knocked, they answered 'the hoguihanneu.' They were given lard. Another Brittany Christmas custom was for children to cry out '*au guyane.*' They were given lard or beef. The children in Guernsey went round on New Year's Day chanting,

Oguinâni! Oguinâno!
Ouvre ta pouque, et pis la recelios.

In Scotland the children on New Year's Eve, or New Year's Morning, attired grotesquely and with faces darkened, went round from house to house to receive their 'hogmanay' (gift), and were called 'guisers' or 'guisarts.' They sang:

Get up, good wife, and shake your feathers,
And dinna think that we are beggars;
For we are bairns come oot to play,
Get up and gie us oor hogmanay.

Another form of the rhyme is:

Rise up, good wife, and be no swier
To deal your bread as long's you're here:
The time will come when you'll be dead
And neither want nor meal nor bread.

HOG-PLUM, the popular name of the plants belonging to the genus Spondias, nat. ord. Anacardiaceæ. Some of the species yield pleasant fruits, as *S. purpurea* and *S. lutea* of the West Indies, the species generally called hog-plum, because their fruit is a common food for hogs.

HOG-RAT, a genus (Capromys) of rodent animals, family Octodontidæ, including four species inhabiting Cuba and Jamaica, and related to the cavies. Best known is the hutia (*C.*

melanurus), which is rather smaller than a rabbit, and of dark-brown colour with a blackish tail.

HOG'S BACK, elevation in Surrey, part of the North Downs. It is about 10 miles long and 505 feet high, and stretches from Guildford to Farnham with a road along the top.

HOGSHEAD. See WEIGHTS AND MEASURES.

HOHENLIN'DEN (hō-en-), a village of Bavaria, 20 miles east of Munich, celebrated for the victory gained by the French under Moreau over the Austrians under the Archduke John, 3rd Dec., 1800.

HOHENLOHE (hō'en-lō-e), formerly a principality of Germany, containing 680 sq. miles, now chiefly under Württemberg.

Hog Plum

HOHENLOHE-SCHILLINGS-FÜRST, Chlodwig Karl Victor, Prince, of Hohenlohe-Schillingsfürst, German statesman, born 31st March, 1819, died at Ragatz, Switzerland, 6th July, 1901. He studied political science at the Universities of Heidelberg, Göttingen, and Bonn, entered the diplomatic service, was Bavarian Minister for Foreign Affairs and President of the Council of Ministers, and from 1866–70 assisted Bismarck in bringing about the union of South and North Germany.

German Ambassador in Paris in 1874, he represented Germany at the Berlin Congress in 1878. Governor of Alsace-Lorraine from 1885 to 1894, he succeeded Caprivi as Imperial Chancellor, retaining his office till 1900. During his tenure of office he promoted Germany's colonial policy, and did much for the creation of a German navy. Dissatisfied with the ex-Kaiser's aggressive policy, he resigned in Oct., 1900, and was succeeded by Count von Bülow. His *Memoirs*, which caused an international sensation, and incurred the condemnation of the ex-Kaiser, were published in 1906.

HOHENSTAUFEN (hō'en-stou-fn), a German princely family, several members of which filled the imperial throne. The founder of the family was Frederick, lord of Hohenstaufen, a castle in the Suabian Alps, who for his services to the Emperor Henry IV received the Duchy of Suabia, and the hand of his daughter Agnes. His son Conrad was elected emperor in 1138. After the death of Conrad (1152) the confidence which was felt in the Hohenstaufen family caused the choice to fall on his nephew, Frederick III of Suabia, who was followed by Henry VI. (1190), who added by his wife the Kingdom of Sicily and Naples to the hereditary dominions of

Hans Holbein

the family; and he again by Otto IV (1197) and Frederick II (1215-50), all belonging to the same House.

After the death of Frederick II his son Conrad was acknowledged as his successor, with the title of Conrad IV, by most of the states of the empire; but Innocent IV laid him under an interdict, declared him to be deprived of all his lands, and persecuted him with relentless hatred till his death in 1254. The possessions of the family ultimately fell to Bavaria, Baden, and Württemberg.—Cf. F. von Raumer, *Geschichte der Hohenstaufen.*

HOHENSTEIN (hō'en-stīn), a town of Germany, in Saxony, 10 miles north-east of Zwickau. Pop. 16,754.

HOHENZOLLERN (hō-en-tsol'èrn), a small territory of Germany. It consists of a long, narrow, irregular strip of country, entirely surrounded by Württemberg and Baden. Area, 441 sq. miles. Pop. 71,840. Hohenzollern was the family name of the ruling house of Imperial Germany.

HOKUSAI, Japanese painter, born at Yeddo in 1760, died there in 1849. At the age of thirteen he left home and apprenticed himself to an engraver, but five years afterwards he gave up engraving and studied under Shunsho. He created the popular Japanese style, and produced pictures free from the conventionalities of either his contemporaries or predecessors. His pictures are known as the *Ukiyo-ye* (pictures of this passing world), and are highly appreciated in Western Europe.

HOLBACH (hol'bàh), **Paul Heinrich Dietrich, Baron von,** philosopher, born at Heidelsheim, in the Palatinate, in 1723, died in 1789 in Paris. Educated in Paris, where he passed the greater part of his life, he became the patron and associate of the Encyclopædists, and contributed many papers on natural history, politics, and philosophy to the *Encyclopédie.* The Abbé Galiani called him the *maître d'hôtel* of philosophy. In 1767 Holbach published *Christianisme dévoilé.* The principal work attributed to him, which appeared under the name of M. Mirabaud, is the *Système de la Nature.* This work, which has been called 'the Bible of Naturalism or Atheism,' is said to have offended both Voltaire and Frederick II.

He afterwards published *Système social, ou Principes naturels de la morale et de la politique; Bons Sens, ou Idées naturelles opposées aux idées surnaturelles*—a sort of atheist's catechism; and *Éléments de la morale universelle.* According to Holbach, matter is the only form of existence, and everything is the effect of a blind necessity. Wolmar, in Rousseau's *Nouvelle Héloïse,* is a portrait of Holbach.

HOLBEACH, market town and urban district of Lincolnshire, 8 miles from Spalding and 108 from London. Near the town is a stretch of reclaimed land known as Holbeach Marsh. Pop. (1931), 6,111.

HOLBEIN (hol'bīn), **Hans,** an eminent German painter, born at Augsburg in 1497, died of the plague at Whitehall in 1543. He studied under his father, Hans Holbein the elder, a painter of considerable merit (1460-1524), and at an early age settled at Basel, where he exercised his art till about 1526, producing some religious pictures, mural decorations (now destroyed), and some notable portraits, including several of his friend Erasmus. He then came to England, where letters from his friend Erasmus, whose *Praise of Folly* he had illustrated by a series of drawings, procured him the patronage of the Chancellor, Sir Thomas More. Here he painted a series of portraits mainly of More and his friends.

In 1528 he returned to Basel, but in 1531 finally settled in England. He was appointed court painter by Henry VIII; and in the Windsor collection has left portraits of all the eminent Englishmen of the time. In 1538 he was sent to Belgium to paint the portrait of Christina of Denmark (now in the National Gallery), and in 1539 painted the portrait of Anne of Cleves. He also executed some important mural decorations, now destroyed.

A good many of his pictures are supposed to have been destroyed by the Great Fire in 1666. The most celebrated of his pictures are the *Madonna* at Darmstadt (better known through the replica at Dresden), representing the Burgomaster Meyer and his family kneeling to the Virgin; and the Solothurn *Madonna*. His famous *Dance of Death* has only been preserved in the engravings of Lützelburger. There are a considerable number of engravings on wood and copper from Holbein's designs.—BIBLIOGRAPHY: H. Knackfuss, *Holbein*; A. B. Chamberlain, *Hans Holbein the Younger*; R. N. Wornum, *Some Account of the Life and Works of Hans Holbein*.

HOLBERG, Ludwig, Baron, Norwegian-Danish novelist, poet, dramatist, and historian, the father of modern Danish literature, was born at Bergen, in Norway, then part of the Danish dominions, in 1684, died at Copenhagen, 27th Jan., 1754. He studied at the University of Copenhagen, and afterwards travelled through a good part of Europe, spending some time in Oxford, where he taught music and modern languages, and studied modern history and philosophy. In 1718 he was appointed to an ordinary professorship in the University of Copenhagen, where after this date he chiefly resided till his death. In 1735 he was elected rector, and in 1737 treasurer of the university in which he held his professorship, and in 1747 he was raised to the rank of baron.

Works. His works may be divided into four classes—poems, stage pieces, philosophical treatises, and historical works. His poems are chiefly of a satirical nature. The most celebrated is *Peder Paars*, a comic heroic poem in fourteen cantos, which is still regarded throughout the Scandinavian countries as a masterpiece. This work was published by him in 1719 under the pseudonym of Hans Mikkelsen, citizen of Kallundberg. Almost equally famous is his *Nicolas Klimm's Subterraneous Travels*, a satirical romance in prose. His stage pieces are all either comedies or farces, and are nearly all characterized by true comic power.

Among his philosophical writings the most important is his *Moral Reflections* (1744). His historical works include: *The Political, Ecclesiastical, and Geographical Condition of the Danish Monarchy*; *A General History of the Jews*; and *A History of Famous Men and Famous Women* (1739–46). Holberg made Danish a literary language, and for two centuries his influence was paramount.—Cf. Georg Brandes, *Holberg and his Contemporaries*.

HOLBORN, borough of the county of London. Covering only 400 acres, it lies between the city and Westminster. The district includes Bloomsbury, Lincoln's Inn and Gray's Inn. Holborn Viaduct was built in 1867-69 to carry the road over the valley where the River Holbourne once flowed. It is 1,400 ft. long, and on it is the City Temple. Pop. (1931), 38,816.

HOLBROOKE, Joseph Charles, English musician. Born at Croydon, 6th July, 1878, the son of a musician, he was a pianist and conductor, but his reputation rests mainly upon his compositions. In 1901 he produced *The Raven*, his first orchestral work. A number of others include *Queen Mab*, *The Bells*, *Auld Lang Syne*. He also wrote operas and ballets, as well as a comic opera, *The Snob*, and gave concerts of modern English chamber music in London and in the provinces. Holbrooke has also written a great number of songs.

HOLCUS, a genus of grasses (nat. ord. Gramineæ), extremely common in some pastures, where they are called soft grasses. Whether because of their innutritious quality, or of the soft hairs with which they are covered, they are neglected by cattle. *H. saccharatus* contains a large quantity of sugar, and *H. odorātus* is celebrated for its fragrance.

There are only two species native to Britain, woolly soft grass or Yorkshire fog (*H. lanātus*), and creeping-rooted soft grass (*H. mollis*), which are both perennial, growing about 2 feet high when in flower, and equally covered with soft dry hairs.

HOLDEN, Sir Edward Hopkinson, English banker. Born in Manchester, 11th May, 1848, he became a clerk in the Manchester County Bank in 1866. He moved to Birmingham, where he became manager of the Birmingham and Midland Bank. About this time the era of banking amalgamations began, and in this he took a leading part. In 1898, his bank, having taken over others, became the London, City and Midland Bank, and of this he was managing director. In 1918 it took over the London Joint Stock Bank and later became known as the Midland Bank. Of this, the largest in the country, Holden was chairman and managing director until his death, 23rd July, 1919. From 1906–10 he was a Liberal M.P., and in 1909 he was made a baronet.

HOLDEN, Sir Isaac, English manufacturer. Born at Hurlet, near Paisley, 7th May, 1807, the son of a Cumberland miner, he became a teacher in Paisley, but soon moved to Leeds, and from there to Reading. In 1830 he gave up teaching and took a position as a bookkeeper to a firm in the woollen industry at Cullingworth. Holden invented a wool-combing machine that proved a success and started in business with Samuel C. Lister, afterwards Lord Masham. A little later he opened mills at Bradford, with his sons, and this concern became very prosperous. He was a Liberal M.P., 1865–68 and 1880–85, and in 1893 was made a baronet. As a Liberal Unionist he represented the Keighley division, 1885–95. He died 13th Aug., 1897. His son Angus was made a baron in 1908.

HOLDING OVER. If a tenant in England disregards written notice to quit at the expiry of his tenancy, and retains possession, he is said to 'hold over,' and is liable to pay to the landlord as compensation (*a*) double the annual value of the premises should the notice have come from the landlord (except in weekly lets), and (*b*) double the rent should it have come from the tenant himself.

HOLDERNESS, district of Yorkshire, E.R., formerly called a wapentake, extending from the Humber to Spurn Head.

The title **Earl of Holderness** was held by the old Yorkshire family of Darcy from 1682 to 1778. Robert, the 4th earl, was Secretary of State from 1751 to 1761. His estates passed to his son-in-law, the Duke of Leeds.

HOLFORD, Sir George Lindsay, English collector. Born 2nd June, 1860, he was the son of Robert S. Holford, who built Dorchester House, Park Lane, London, and was a great collector of works of art. His collections were left to his son, Sir George, who in 1923, sold some of his possessions. After his death on 11th Sept., 1926, the pictures and books were all sold, the pictures fetching over £530,000 and the books £200,000. Dorchester House (q.v.) was pulled down, and a hotel erected on its site.

HOLIDAY (a corruption of Holy Day), any day set apart as a religious or national festival; in a general sense,

a day or a number of days during which a person is released from his everyday labours. In Britain certain days were fixed as bank-holidays by Parliament in 1871, and it was enacted that all business transactions which would have been valid on any such holiday shall be held as valid if performed on the day following. In England the bank-holidays are Good Friday, Easter Monday, Whit-Monday, the first Monday of August, Christmas Day, and the 26th of Dec. (or the 27th should the 26th be a Sunday).

The days fixed as bank-holidays for Scotland are New Year's Day, Good Friday, the first Monday of May, the first Monday of August, and Christmas Day; and if either New Year's Day or Christmas Day falls on a Sunday, the Monday after is held as a holiday. These holidays are observed also by Custom Houses, Inland Revenue, and other public offices.

HOL'INSHED, Raphael (Ralph), an English chronicler of whom nothing more is known than that he was descended from a family originally belonging to Cheshire, that he lived in the age of Queen Elizabeth, and that he died about 1580. He is only known by his *Chronicles of Englande, Scotlande, and Irelande,* the first edition of which, known as the 'Shakespeare edition,' because it is the one which is supposed to have been used by him in collecting material for his historical plays, was published in London in 1577. In the preparation of this work Holinshed was assisted by several of the most learned men of the day.— Cf. W. G. Boswell Stone, *Shakspere's Holinshed.*

HOLL, Frank, R.A., portrait and genre painter, son of Francis Holl, an eminent engraver, was born in London 1845, died 1888. He was a very successful student at the Royal Academy, and exhibited constantly from his student days. Among his best-known pictures are *Faces in the Fire, Fern-Gatherers, No Tidings from the Sea, Leaving Home,* and *The Gifts of the Fairies.* Towards the end of his life he devoted himself to portraiture, in which he greatly excelled, and painted many of the celebrities of the day, including the Prince of Wales, W. E. Gladstone, and Joseph Chamberlain.

HOLLAND, Sir Henry, an English physician, born at Knutsford, Cheshire, in 1788, died in London 1873. He was educated at the University of Edinburgh, where he took the degree of M.D. in 1811. In 1816 he established himself in London as a physician, and he rapidly acquired a great reputation. In 1840 he was appointed physician in ordinary to the Prince Consort, in 1852 physician in ordinary to the Queen, and in 1853 was created a baronet. He published *Travels in the Ionian Isles, Albania, and Greece; Medical Notes and Reflections; Mental Physiology;* and *Recollections of Past Life.*

HOLLAND, Henry Richard Vassall Fox, third Lord, born 1773, died 1840. He succeeded to the peerage by the death of his father when less than one year old. In 1798 he took his place in the House of Lords, and as the nephew of Charles James Fox was at once acknowledged as a Whig leader. In 1806 he was Commissioner for settling disputes with the United States; Lord Privy Seal in 1806-7; and Chancellor of the Duchy of Lancaster. He and his wife made Holland House the resort of the wit, talent, and beauty of his day. He wrote a *Life of Lope de Vega* (1806), *Three Comedies from the Spanish* (1807), *Foreign Reminiscences* (1850), and *Memoirs of the Whig Party* (1852).

HOLLAND, Philemon, physician, teacher, and 'translator-general in his age,' born at Chelmsford 1552, died 1637. He became master of the free grammar-school of Coventry, and also practised as a physician. His translations include Livy, Pliny, Plutarch's *Morals,* Suetonius, Xenophon, &c., and he published an edition, with additions, of Camden's *Britannia* (1610).

HOLLAND, Sir Thomas Henry, English scientist. He was born, 22nd Nov., 1868, of Canadian parentage. He was Director of Geological Survey in India, 1903-1909; Professor of Geology in Manchester University, 1909-1918; and Rector of the Imperial College of Science, 1922-1929. In 1929 he was president of the British Association, and he has done a great deal of work on commissions and committees appointed to report on scientific matters. In 1929 he became Principal of Edinburgh University. Since 1927 he has been chairman of the Empire Council, mining and metallurgical Institution.

HOLLAND, KINGDOM OF. *See* NETHERLANDS.

HOLLAND, NORTH(*Noordholland*), and **HOLLAND, SOUTH**(*Suidholland*), two provinces of the Netherlands. The greater part of the former consists of a peninsula, bounded by the North Sea on the west and the Zuider Zee on the east. Area, 1,059 sq. miles. It lies very low, some portions of it being at least partially below the level of the sea, and is generally fertile. A broad margin of downs or sand-hills protects it from the sea on the west. Besides rivers (Vecht, V—R

Amstel, Zaan, &c.), it is intersected by the Great North Holland Canal. The chief towns are Amsterdam, Alkmaar, Haarlem, Helder, and Zaandam. Pop. (1931), 1,537,580.

South Holland, the most populous province of the Netherlands, is bounded on the north by North Holland, on the west by the North Sea. The southern part of the province is broken up into several islands. Area, 1,130 sq. miles. Like North Holland, it is a flat and depressed tract, and it also is protected from the sea on the west by a margin of downs or sand-hills. The chief river is the Rhine, with its numerous branches. The lakes were formerly numerous, but most of them are now drained. The soil is fertile and well cultivated. The principal towns are Delft, Dort, Gorkum, Gouda, Leiden, Rotterdam, Schiedam, The Hague. Pop. (1931), 1,989,946.

HOLLAND HOUSE, a famous mansion in London, on a hill at the west end of Kensington Gardens. It was built in 1607 in the Tudor style, and derived its name from one of its early owners, Henry Rich, Earl of Holland. When Lord Holland was executed for treason, the mansion passed into the possession of the Parliamentary generals, Fairfax and Lambert. It was restored to Lady Holland after the Restoration (1665), but was purchased in 1762 by Henry Fox, afterwards Baron Holland, the father of Charles James Fox, and is now in the possession of his descendants. It was for long the headquarters of the Whig party.

HOLLANDER, Bernard, British physician. Born in Vienna, 1864, he settled in London in 1883. In 1899 he was naturalized, and soon made a reputation as a specialist on nervous and mental disorders. He helped to found the Ethnological Society, and put forward a scientific system of phrenology. He collected a great number of facts about the working of the brain, and wrote much for scientific journals about its functions. Among his works may be mentioned *Crime and Responsibility* (1907); *The Insanity of Genius* (1913); and *Seeing Ourselves in the Light of Modern Psychology* (1931).

HOLLAR, Wenzel or Wenceslaus, a Bohemian engraver, born in Prague about 1607, died in London 1677. He accompanied the Earl of Arundel, the British Ambassador to the German Emperor, to London, who employed him to engrave some of the pictures of his collection. Among his numerous works, which are esteemed for their delicate, firm, and spirited execution, and which number some 2,740 plates.

are a set of twenty-eight plates, entitled *Ornatus Muliebris Anglicanus*, representing the dresses of Englishwomen of all ranks and conditions in full-length figures; Holbein's *Dance of Death*; and etchings from the works of Titian and Van Dyck.

HOLLOWAY, Thomas, born 1800, died 1883; proprietor of the popular pills, ointment, &c. He founded a sanatorium or asylum for the insane, and hospitals for incurables and convalescents, at Egham, Surrey, 1873; and also at the same place the **Royal Holloway College,** designed to supply the best and most suitable education for women of the middle classes. The college, which was opened by Queen Victoria in 1886, contains a collection of pictures of the value of £100,000. The total cost of the two institutions was about a million sterling

Holly

HOLLOWAY, district of London, in the Borough of Islington, about 3 miles N. of the city. Here are the Northern Polytechnic Institution, the prisons of Pentonville and Holloway, and the Caledonian Market.

HOLLOW WARE, the name given to all classes of vessels used for general household purposes, cooking, &c. These vessels are made of cast or wrought iron, steel, copper, brass, nickel, aluminium, &c. For purposes other than cooking the articles are generally galvanized, as in the case of buckets, &c., to protect the metal from rusting and corrosion, or enamelled, as in the case of pans, &c. Cooking-utensils are frequently made of cast iron or pressed steel, and may also be enamelled or tinned. Many cheap articles are made of thin tinned steel sheet, and better-class articles are made of the same material fitted with copper bottoms. Formerly copper and brass were largely used in the manufacture of cooking utensils; these have to be kept scrupulously clean, owing to their tendency to form the poisonous substance known as verdigris.

Metallic nickel makes an ideal material for the manufacture of cook-ing-vessels, but is expensive; it was largely used on the Continent for this purpose before the European War, especially in Austria. Aluminium is also now largely used and has many advantages; for example, culinary utensils made of aluminium are light, are absolutely free from verdigris met with in copper or brass articles, rust met with in iron and steel articles, and the chipping difficulty met with in enamelled goods. Cast aluminium utensils are generally used for the heavy wear met with in hotels, restaurants, &c., whereas wrought vessels are used for general household purposes.

HOLLY (Ilex), a genus of plants of the ord. Aquifoliaceæ, embracing a number of evergreen trees or shrubs. The common holly (*I. aquifolium*) is common in Britain and the continent of Europe. It is a handsome, conical evergreen tree, growing to the height of 20 or 30 feet. Its leaves are dark-green, shining, and leathery, abundantly armed with prickles on the lower branches, but free from them on the upper, or on very old trees. The flowers are white, appearing in May; the fruit is red, ripening in September, and remaining on the tree all the winter. A good many varieties are known, distinguished by the shape and colour of the leaves, which are sometimes spotted or edged with yellow, &c. It is excellently adapted for hedges and fences, as it bears clipping. The wood is hard and white, and is employed for turnery work, knife handles, &c. The bark yields a mucilaginous substance, from which birdlime is made.

Among the Romans it was customary to send boughs of holly to friends, with new-year's gifts, as emblematical of good wishes; and it is used to decorate houses at Christmas. Some have assumed that the name 'holly' is equivalent to 'holy tree,' being derived from the custom of using the branches and berries of the tree for the decoration of churches at Christmas. The American holly (*Ilex opaca*) is widely diffused throughout the United States. It sometimes attains the height of 80 feet, with a trunk 4 feet in diameter. The *I. glabra* is another species of holly, inhabiting the coast regions of the United States. Its leaves furnished the 'black drink' which used to hold an important place in Indian ceremonies. The *Yerba maté* or Paraguay tea-plant is a species of holly (*I. Paraguayensis*).

HOLLYHOCK, a biennial plant (*Althœa rosea*), nat. ord. Malvaceæ. It is a native of China, and is a frequent ornament of gardens. There are many varieties, with single and double flowers, characterized by the tints of yellow, red, purple, and dark purple approaching to black. It reaches a height of 8 feet or more.

HOLLYWOOD, centre of the American film industry. It is in California, W. of Los Angeles, and has a beautiful climate and surroundings. *See* LOS ANGELES.

HOLME LACY, village of Herefordshire, on the Wye, 4½ miles from Hereford. Here is Holme Lacy House, long the seat of the Scudamore and Stanhope families, represented by the Earl of Chesterfield. Built in the 17th century it is now the property of the county council of Herefordshire.

HOLMES (hōmz), Oliver Wendell, American essayist, poet, and physician, born at Cambridge, Mass., 1809, died in 1894. He was educated at Harvard University, began the study of law, but in a short time relinquished it for that of medicine. In 1839 he became professor of anatomy and physiology in Dartmouth College, N.H., but resigned after two years' service in order to devote himself to practice in Boston.

In 1847 he was appointed to the chair of anatomy at Harvard, a position which he filled till 1882. He was a voluminous writer both in prose and verse, and shone as a prominent figure in the famous group associated with *The Atlantic Monthly.* His chief works, besides several volumes of poems, and treatises on medicine, are: *The Autocrat of the Breakfast Table, The Professor at the Breakfast Table,* and *The Poet at the Breakfast Table*; *Elsie Venner, The Guardian Angel, A Mortal Antipathy,* and *Emerson* (in American Men of Letters Series). A visit to Europe in 1886 produced a charming record, *Our Hundred Days in Europe.* —BIBLIOGRAPHY: J. T. Morse, *Life and Letters of Holmes*; W. Jerrold, *O. W. Holmes*; L. W. Townsend, *O. W. Holmes.*

HOLMFIRTH, market town and urban district of Yorkshire (W.R.). It is 6 miles from Huddersfield, and a centre of the woollen industry. Pop. (1931) 10,407.

HOLM-OAK(*Quercus Ilex*), a shrub-like tree, native of the Mediterranean countries, with holly-like leaves. In its native countries it attains a considerable size and age, but in Britain it forms an ornamental evergreen bush of from 20 to 30 feet high, seldom becoming single-stemmed.

HOLOCEPHALI. *See* CHIMÆRA.

HOLOGRAPH (Gr. *holos,* entire, and *graphein,* to write), any writing, as a letter, deed, will, &c., wholly written by the person from whom it bears to proceed. In Scots law a holograph deed is valid without the signatures of witnesses, but in English law every deed, whether holograph or not, must have the names of two witnesses attached to it to render it valid.

HOLOPTYCHIUS (-tik'i-us; Gr. *holos,* entire, and *ptyx,* fold), a genus of fossil ganoid fishes occurring in the Upper Red Sandstone. The head was covered with large plates, and the body with bony scales, with their exposed surfaces roughly grooved. The pectoral fins were long, and the jaws were armed with pointed teeth, of unequal size. A fine Scottish example is more than 2 feet long.

HOLOTHURIA, the type of a class of Echinoderms, the Holothurioidea or sea-cucumbers. These are typically cylindrical in form, and covered by a leathery skin in which scattered calcareous plates are embedded. Longitudinal rows of tube-feet are commonly present. They have the mouth surrounded by branching tentacles; a long convoluted alimentary canal; respiratory organs near the anus, and generally in the form of two branching arborescent tubes ('respiratory trees') into which the water is admitted.

They are capable of great extension in length, and of extraordinary reproduction of parts, even of vital organs. The young undergo a metamorphosis during development. Remarkable deep-sea forms (Elasipods) are known, in which the body is bilaterally symmetrical; and there is one free-swimming species (Pelagothuria). In some cases (Synapta) tube-feet are absent, and the calcareous plates are shaped like wheels and anchors. Trepang or bêche-de-mer consists of the dried bodies of various holothurians abounding in the Malayan seas.

HOLST, Gustav. English composer, born at Cheltenham, 21st. Sept., 1874. The son of a musician of Swedish extraction, he became at an early age an organist and choirmaster, and later studied under Stanford at the Royal College of Music. From 1903 he was music master at various schools, among them Edward Alleyne School, Morley College and St. Paul's Girls' School, Brook Green, for which much of his early music was composed. His compositions include *The Planets,* an orchestral suite; the *Hymn to Jesus*; *Ode to Death*; *The Cloud*; *Egdon Heath*; *Hammersmith*; *First Choral Symphony.* His opera *The Perfect Fool* was produced at Covent Garden in 1923.

HOLSTEIN. *See* SCHLESWIG-HOLSTEIN.

HOLSWORTHY, market town and district of Devonshire, 46 miles from

Exeter. A horse fair is held here in July. In 1819-26 a canal was made from Holsworthy to Bude, but it is not now used. Pop. (1931) 1,403.

HOLT, town of Norfolk, 9½ miles from Cromer. There is a grammar school founded in 1555 by Sir John Gresham, who was born here. It is now a large public school with fine modern buildings, and is controlled by the Fishmongers' Company. Pop. 2,249.

There are other Holts in England. One is a village in Wiltshire, 100½ miles from London. Pop. 987.

HOLY ALLIANCE, a league concluded at Paris, 26th Sept., 1815, between Alexander I, Emperor of Russia, Francis of Austria, and Frederick

The Holy Carpet. Procession in Cairo

William III of Prussia, and signed with their own hands, without the countersignature of a minister. It consisted of a declaration, that, in accordance with the precepts of the gospel of Jesus Christ, the principles of justice, charity, and peace should be the basis of their internal administration, and of their international relations, and that the happiness and religious welfare of their subjects should be their great object.

Its real aim, however, was to maintain the power and influence of the existing dynasties. It was offered for signature to all the European Powers except the Pope and the Sultan of Turkey, and accepted by all except Britain. The document was drawn up by Tsar Alexander I, and was signed by the three rulers.

The Tsar was inspired by the Baroness von Krüdener, and, as far as he himself was concerned, the Holy

Alliance was the scheme of a pietistic idealist, but it was used by Metternich, and afterwards by Russia and France, as an instrument of reactionary policy. The events of 1848 broke up the Holy Alliance.—Cf. A. S. Rappoport, *The Curse of the Romanovs* (with bibliography).

HOLY CARPET (Ar. *Kisweh*), outer covering of the Kaaba (q.v.). It is manufactured at Cairo, and sent with a caravan of pilgrims to Mecca. The holy carpet is made of coarse black brocade, with inscriptions from the *Koran* interwoven in it in silk of the same colour. Across each side it has a large band covered with inscriptions worked in gold. The carpet is presented annually to the Shrine, remains on the Kaaba for a year, and is then cut into pieces and sold to the pilgrims at exorbitant charges.

HOLY COAT OF TRÈVES, a relic preserved in the cathedral of Trèves, and said to be the identical seamless coat worn by our Saviour at his crucifixion, and for which the soldiers cast lots. It was the gift of the Empress Helena, by whom it was discovered in her visit to Palestine in the fourth century. It has been exhibited to vast numbers of pilgrims at irregular intervals, for the last time in 1891, when it was seen by nearly two million pilgrims. The same claim is made for several coats kept in other places.

HOLYCROSS, ruined abbey in Tipperary, Irish Free State. It is on the Suir, 4 miles from Thurles, and was founded in 1182.

HOLY FAMILY, in art, representations of the infant Saviour and his mother, accompanied by one or more members of his family. The earliest composition is that in the catacomb of St. Calixtus in Rome. During the Middle Ages other figures, such as St. Anna, St. Joseph, and John the Baptist, were added to those of the Virgin and the Saviour.

The Madonna and Child was a favourite subject of the artists of the Italian Renaissance. Among the painters of the Holy Family are: Raphael, Correggio, Giulio Romano, Leonardo da Vinci, Michael Angelo, Dürer, Rubens, and Murillo.

HOLY GHOST. *See* HOLY SPIRIT.

HOLY GHOST, Order of, an order of male and female hospitallers founded by Guy, son of William, Count of Montpellier, towards the end of the twelfth century, for the relief of the poor, the infirm, and foundlings. After the middle of the eighteenth century it was united with the order of St. Lazarus by Clement XIII. This was also the name of the principal military order in France instituted in 1578 by Henry III, abolished in 1789, revived at the Restoration, and definitely abolished on 10th Feb., 1831, by Louis Philippe.

HOLY GRASS (Hierochlöe), an odoriferous genus of grasses belonging to the Phalarideæ, and consisting of several species spread over the cold parts of both hemispheres. The *H. borealis*, or northern holy-grass, is found in Scotland, Iceland, and throughout Northern Europe, Asia, and America, and occurs also in New Zealand. It owes its name to the practice adopted in some parts of Germany of strewing it before the doors of churches on festival days.

HOLYHEAD, an island, urban district, and seaport town of North Wales, in the county of Anglesey. The island is about 7 miles long, and 5 miles broad at the widest part, is situated off the west side of Anglesey, and is connected with the mainland by a causeway. The town is on the north-east side of the island, and owes its prosperity to the railway and steamboat traffic between England and Dublin. The harbour of refuge (Victoria Harbour), opened in 1873, is formed by a breakwater which is 7,860 feet in length, and was built at a total cost of £1,500,000. Pop. (1931), 10,707.

HOLY ISLAND, or LINDISFARNE, an island off the north-east coast of England, 11 miles south-east of Berwick. It is 1¾ miles from the mainland, with which it is connected by a narrow neck of sand, traversable at low water. It is of an irregular form, about 2¼ miles in length, and about 1½ miles in breadth at the broadest part.

The village of Lindisfarne on the south-west is much resorted to by summer visitors, but the great object of interest is the extensive ruined abbey of Lindisfarne, founded in A.D. 635 by Oswald, King of Northumbria, destroyed by the Danes, and restored by the Normans in 1082. The castle, on a rock 90 feet high, also dates from an early period. Pop. (1931), 586.

HOLY LEAGUE, a term applied to several political alliances formed in Europe. The principal leagues were the following: (1) The alliance formed in 1510 by Pope Julius II, Ferdinand V of Spain, and the Republics of Switzerland and Venice against Louis XII of France; it was dissolved in 1513. (2) The alliance formed in 1571 by the Pope, Spain, and Venice against the Turks. (3) The coalition formed in 1576 at Péronne, in France, by the Pope, Spain, the Guises, and the Parliament of Paris, with the object of preventing Henri of Navarre from ascending the throne of France. This league lasted till 1593, when Henri embraced Catholicism. (4) The Holy League (also known as the Catholic League) formed by the Catholic states of Germany in 1609 against the Protestant Union.

HOLYOKE, a city of Hampden, county Massachusetts, on the west bank of the Connecticut River. It is a prosperous manufacturing place, its rise dating from 1849, when a dam constructed across the river supplied it with extensive water power. A larger dam was built in 1900. It has manufactures of paper, cotton, wool, and wire; and machine works. Pop. (1930), 56,537.

HOLY ROMAN EMPIRE. The political institution known as the Holy Roman Empire was founded in A.D. 800, and came, formally, to an end in 1806. It was a revival of the ancient Roman Empire which claimed authority over the whole civilized world. The Roman Empire, before it fell in Western Europe, had been divided into two rival powers at Rome and at Constantinople; the Western Empire was destroyed by barbarian invasions in the fifth century, and the Eastern Empire survived until it was destroyed by the Turks in the fifteenth century.

The Holy Roman Empire represented the ancient Western Empire, and its revival was a tribute to the impression made upon men's minds by the power of 'eternal Rome' and by the supreme authority which had been exercised by the Emperor.

When the King of the Franks, Charles the Great, came to dominate Europe in the end of the eighth century, he was fascinated by the ancient ideal of one great secular Power, acting as the partner and the protector of the Christian Church in the government of the world. The Church, as represented by the Papacy, was threatened by many enemies, and in 800 Charles led a Frankish army to the support of the Pope.

On Christmas Day he was crowned in St. Peter's Church by the Pope, as Charles Augustus, an incident which is regarded as the most important European event of the early Middle Ages, and was acclaimed by contemporaries as likely to bring peace and good order to a troubled world.

Charles considered himself to be Emperor by divine appointment, and believed that he held a divine commission to rule the nations and protect the Church. He did not admit that the imperial dignity had been conferred on him by the Pope or by the Roman populace which acclaimed his coronation, and he asserted the right of naming his successor.

During his lifetime, his theory of an Empire, holy and supreme, was realized, but after his death, in 814, his descendants quarrelled among themselves, and the titular Emperor ceased to exert any authority outside the regions under his own immediate rule. Further, personal rivalries for the imperial title gradually gave to the Papacy the right of choosing the Emperor, and from the coronation of Charles the Fat, in 881, the imperial office was the gift of the Pope.

In the end of the ninth century there was a new series of barbarian invasions, and the Carolingian Empire was destroyed by Saracens, Norsemen, Danes, Wends, and Hungarians, but memory clung to the imperial institution as the hope of mankind, and when a great German ruler arose in the person of Otto the Great, who became King of the East Franks in 936, he repeated the experiment which had been tried by his famous predecessor. The Pope, the worthless John XII, appealed to Otto for aid, and on 2nd Feb., 962, he was crowned Emperor amid the plaudits of a generation which trusted in the beneficent co-operation of a Universal Empire and a Universal Church.

Papacy and Empire were to be interdependent, and Pope and Emperor were to be the Vicars of God upon earth, the one in matters spiritual and the other in matters temporal. The canon law of the Church was to be the complement of the civil law of the Empire, and Church and Empire were believed to be but two sides of one divinely appointed ordinance for the well-being of human society.

The theory assumed the harmony of the two Universal Powers, and the hold which it had on men's minds is proved by the persistence with which it was cherished, in spite of the fact that this essential harmony was never attained.

Otto I began his rule as Emperor by trying and deposing John XII, and he obtained a recognition of a claim that the election of a Pope required the imperial confirmation. The disputes between the Papacy and the Emperor did not, however, become vehement under the Saxon Emperors —Otto I and his successors, Otto II (973–983) and Otto III (983–1002)— partly because of the weakness of the Papacy during these years, and partly owing to the friendship between Otto III and the reforming Popes, Gregory V and Sylvester II.

The Saxon line ended with Otto II, whose successor was a Bavarian, Henry II. He also remained on good terms with a reforming Pope, Benedict VIII, and his main interest, unlike that of the Ottos, was in Germany, not in Italy. These were the two regions which, for practical purposes, formed the Empire, and the attention of the Emperors was usually concentrated on one or the other of them.

There were shadowy claims to imperial authority over Hungary, Denmark, France, and even England, but the first three of these countries soon insisted on their independence, and the only claim to any control over England was an arrangement made, at a later date, between Richard I, as a prisoner, and the Emperor Henry VI. The Holy Roman Empire may be said to have reached the height of its power under Henry II and his successor, Conrad II (1024–9), a Franconian, who conciliated the powerful ecclesiastics who were engaged in what is known as the Clugniac Reformation of the Church.

The reign of his son and successor, Henry III, affords the last illustration of the successful operation of the Imperio-Papal theory of government, but it was successful only because the Emperor was able both to nominate Popes and to use them as his political agents in Italy, and also to gain the confidence of the reforming party in the Church.

When Henry III died in 1056, the Empire had been weakened by the rise of the Norman power in Southern Italy, and the Papacy could use the Normans against the Emperor. It found another potent ally in the Countess Matilda of Tuscany, and was ready to enter upon a struggle to shake off the imperial authority. The conflict came in the reign of Henry IV (1056–1106), which marks the turning-point in the history of Empire and Papacy.

In 1059 the Church claimed that the nomination of a Pope belonged to the College of Cardinals, and about the same time the ecclesiastical objection to the investiture of bishops by secular princes (see INVESTITURE) brought about a serious dispute. Henry was involved in a civil war caused by the rebellion of the Saxons against his rule; Pope Gregory VII (Hildebrand) excommunicated him in 1076, and Henry summoned an ecclesiastical Synod which deposed the Pope.

At Canossa, in 1077, Henry went through a humiliating submission and received the Pope's absolution, but the conflict continued. In 1080 Henry created an Anti-Pope, and had himself to face an Anti-Emperor, but he subdued his Saxon enemies, and in 1084 he captured Rome and was crowned by the Anti-Pope, while Gregory VII held out in the castle of St. Angelo until his Norman allies came to his aid.

They sacked the city, and Gregory

had to flee to Salerno, where he died in 1085. Henry survived until 1106, but the rest of his reign was occupied in conflicts with the Papacy, with his German subjects, and with his own son, who reigned as Henry V (1106–25), and in 1122 closed the Investiture controversy by the Concordat of Worms.

The next two reigns, those of Lothar II (1125–38) and Conrad III (1138–52) form an interlude in the long struggle between Empire and Papacy. They witnessed the growth of great ruling Houses in Germany, possessed of rival ambitions, and the development of an Electoral College of princes for the nomination of the Emperor. Conrad III was the first of the Hohenstaufen dynasty, and was succeeded by his famous nephew, Frederick I (Barbarossa), who speedily became involved in a new quarrel with the Papacy.

Under Henry IV the causes of quarrel had been definitely religious, but in the time of Frederick I they were political, for the Papacy, which had been enriched by the inheritance of Matilda of Tuscany, entertained great territorial ambitions, and was creating an independent Papal State which included the whole of the middle of Italy.

Frederick's first antagonist was the only English Pope, Hadrian IV, who claimed that the Empire was a fief held by the Emperor from the Pope. Hadrian found allies not only in the Normans but also in the Lombard Republics, which believed that their interests were threatened by the policy of the Emperor; but he died in 1159 just as war seemed likely to break out. There was a disputed election, and the quarrel between Pope and Anti-Pope involved the question of the predominance of the Empire in Europe.

Frederick invaded and conquered the north of Italy, but the Lombard League ultimately drove him out in 1168, and in 1176 he was defeated at Legnano and compelled to acknowledge his enemy, Pope Alexander III. He strengthened his position by the Peace of Constance in 1183. By that time attention had been diverted to the Holy Land through the capture of Jerusalem by the Seljuk Turks in 1180, and Frederick died while leading the first armies of the Third Crusade.

The short reign of his son, Henry VI (1190–7), was notable for his marriage with the heiress of the Norman Kings of Sicily, an alliance which menaced the territorial power of the Papacy. When Henry died, he left a small boy, afterwards Frederick II, who was crowned King of Sicily.

The great Pope, Innocent III, was bent on the establishment of a Papal State, and was determined to prevent the union of Sicily and the Empire, and this became the main object of Papal policy. There was a disputed imperial election between Philip of Suabia and Otto IV, the son of Henry the Lion, a Saxon noble who had played a great part in the reign of Frederick Barbarossa. Philip was murdered in 1208, and Otto, who had been supported by Innocent III, quarrelled with the Pope and allied himself with his cousin, King John of England, but he was defeated at Bouvines in 1214 and died soon afterwards.

Frederick then became Emperor at the age of twenty, and his reign (1215–50) was spent in constant conflict. Educated among Greeks, Normans, Lombards, and Saracens, he was a man of wide culture and sympathies, and he encouraged art and founded the University of Naples. His political aims were the incorporation of Sicily in the Empire and the destruction of the temporal power of the Papacy in Italy. These were the real questions at issue, but the actual quarrel with the Papacy arose over his failure to fulfil his solemn vow to go on a Crusade.

In 1227 he was excommunicated by the Pope for not going, and when he went, in the following year, the excommunication was renewed, and although he succeeded in obtaining the cession of Jerusalem to the Christians, the ban was not removed until 1230. The Papacy continued to be on the side of the enemies of the Empire in Italy and in Germany, and the imperial authority was greatly weakened by another struggle with the Lombard League.

The reign of Frederick II, 'the Wonder of the World,' ended in failure, and the Empire fell with him. His son, Conrad IV, had a brief and troubled reign, and there followed an Interregnum (1256–73), during which there was no recognized Emperor.

The failure of the great House of Hohenstaufen proved the impracticability of the imperial ideal, and though the name was revived, the Holy Roman Empire really ceased to exist. After the Interregnum the Empire was essentially a German Empire, though it retained the old name and was ready to advance the old pretensions. As a German Empire it had a chance of a great future, for the local rivalries of the German princes would not allow of any attempt at German unity except under an Emperor whose title satisfied German arrogance by its claim to supreme authority all over the Western world.

In 1273 Rudolf, Count of Habsburg, was elected Emperor by the German princes, and the House of Habsburg entered upon its long career of aggrandizement. Rudolf I (1273–91) was merely a German ruler, with much less actual power than the sovereigns of France or of England, and his aim was to create a great imperial territory in Germany in order to provide support for his titular authority.

He abandoned the old imperial claims to Italy and made an alliance with the Pope, and after a war with the Bohemians he was able to secure the fiefs of Austria, Styria, and Carinthia for his own family. He failed to obtain a hereditary status for the Empire, and his immediate successor was Adolf of Nassau (1292–8), but, on

Sigismund—1437. King of Hungary

Adolf's deposition, Rudolf's son, Albert of Austria (1298–1308), was elected.

He failed to protect the Empire from the growing power of France, and French influence over some of the German princes brought the Empire into the House of Luxemburg, in the person of Henry VII (1308–13), who tried to restore the imperial power in Italy and died in his Italian expedition. The election which followed was disputed between Lewis IV of Bavaria (1313–47) and Frederick of Austria, but Lewis overcame his rival and renewed his predecessor's attempt in Italy. He was at first successful, and was crowned in 1328 at Rome, where he deposed Pope John XXII, but he was not strong enough to hold the country, and the end of his reign was unfortunate in Germany.

After his failure the Empire passed

again to the House of Luxemburg, and Charles IV (1347–78) abandoned the Italian claims and devoted himself to Germany. By the famous Golden Bull of 1356 he settled the method of election to the Empire and attempted to lay the foundation of German unity. He was himself King of Bohemia, and he increased the territorial possessions of his House, but his later years were troubled, and he weakened his son and successor, Wenzel (1378–1400), by dividing his territories among his family.

Wenzel found it impossible to maintain the authority of the Empire against his opponents in Germany and Bohemia, and a schism began with his deposition in 1400. It was healed by the election of Sigismund (1411–37), King of Hungary, whose reign was occupied by the Hussite wars and by an attempt to conquer Bohemia.

After Sigismund's death the Empire passed permanently into the House of Habsburg. The first of the continuous Habsburg line, Albert II, Duke of Austria, and King of Hungary and Bohemia, died a year after his election as Emperor, leaving a posthumous son, whose title was acknowledged in Austria and Bohemia. His successor as Emperor was a cousin, Frederick III (1440–93), who attempted with the help of the Papacy to recover Austria, Hungary, and Bohemia.

His long reign was almost uniformly unfortunate, but his son Maximilian made a marriage with the heiress of the large dominions of the Duke of Burgundy, and at the end of his life he was able to regain Austria and to make an arrangement by which Hungary and Bohemia were ultimately to pass to the Habsburgs.

With the reign of Maximilian I (1493–1519) began an attempt to reform the Constitution of the Empire. The Electoral Princes formed the first chamber of the Diet or governing body, and there were other two chambers, composed respectively of princes, clerical and lay, and of the representatives of the imperial cities. The Diet, with the sanction of the Emperor, could pass legislation and punish offenders with the 'ban of the Empire,' but its internal jealousies rendered it ineffective, and, at the best, the authority of Emperor and Diet had little weight in the independent states which formed the Empire.

At the Diet of Worms, in 1495, some of the Electoral Princes proposed a scheme for enforcing the imperial authority, but combined it with conditions which would have created a check on the Emperor by the action of a Central Council; Maximilian refused the demand, and some lesser reforms were attempted. His great position in

Europe increased the prestige of the Empire, but during his reign the Swiss Confederation, which had been loosely connected with the Empire, succeeded in vindicating its independence.

His grandson and successor, Charles V (1519–56), was not only Emperor and Duke of Austria. As the grandson of Maximilian's wife, he inherited Burgundy and the Low Countries, and from his mother, Joanna, daughter of Ferdinand and Isabella, he also inherited Spain, Naples, and the Spanish colonial dominions. His vast possessions and the influence which he acquired in Italy by force of arms revived for a time the old greatness of the Holy Roman Empire, which seemed to have an opportunity of becoming again a European, and not merely a German, political institution.

His power in Germany was lessened by his grant to his brother Ferdinand both of Austria and of the Habsburg claims on Hungary and Bohemia, and in his time Germany was torn asunder by the Reformation, the Peasants' War, and the War of the League of Schmalkalde. Charles identified the Empire with the cause of the Roman Church, and failed in his effort to repress Protestantism and establish religious uniformity, and he left the German Protestants the enemies of the imperial authority.

On the abdication of Charles V his son, Philip II, became the ruler of Spain and the Netherlands, but the new Emperor was Charles's brother, Ferdinand I (1556–64), who was already King of Hungary and Bohemia, and the Empire again became definitely German. The religious question had been partially settled at the end of the reign of Charles by a compromise known as the Peace of Augsburg (1555), and neither Ferdinand nor his son, Maximilian II (1564–76), made any attempt to disturb it.

But two great forces were at work which were ultimately to bring about a struggle that profoundly modified the position of the Empire. By the date of the accession of Rudolf II (1576–1612), the influence of the counter-Reformation had become very powerful, and, on the other hand, the Peace of Augsburg had made no provision for the recognition of Calvinism, which was strong in Western Germany.

Rudolf was a weak ruler and was deposed, and Matthias (1612–9), the brother who succeeded him, was old and childless. Before his death he arranged for the succession of his cousin, Ferdinand, Duke of Styria, alike to the hereditary possessions of the Habsburgs and to the elective crowns of Hungary and Bohemia. He was successful in obtaining the necessary recognition from the Estates both of Hungary and of Bohemia, but the Bohemian Protestants feared the rule of an heir who was known to be a strong Catholic, and in 1618 occurred the Bohemian Revolution which was the beginning of the Thirty Years' War.

At first the Empire under Ferdinand II (1619–37) seemed likely to be able to repress the German Protestants, for the division between Lutherans and Calvinists was acute, but the intervention first of Sweden and then of France turned the scale, and in its last stages the war was rather a duel between France and the Empire than a religious war in Germany.

By the Treaty of Westphalia (1648) the Empire became distinctively Austrian, and the attention of Ferdinand III (1637–57) and his successors became more and more occupied by imperial interests in the east of Europe. In the west the Emperor had to face not only the growing power of France but also a new rivalry from the northern state of Brandenburg-Prussia. In the east a more immediate danger came from the revival of the power of the Turks, who, in the course of the long reign of the Emperor Leopold I (1658–1705), invaded Austria and besieged Vienna in 1683; the city was saved by the Polish hero John Sobieski.

Leopold also took part in the European opposition to the aggrandizement of France under Louis XIV, but the essential weakness of the Empire was illustrated by the circumstance that some of its western states, and especially Bavaria, were sometimes in alliance with the French. The Emperor took a part in the War of the League of Augsburg, which was formed in 1686 and greatly strengthened by the accession of William III in England and Scotland in 1689, when it became the Grand Alliance.

The War of the Spanish Succession was fought to place Leopold's younger son, the Archduke Charles, on the Spanish throne, but by the close of the war he had succeeded his brother, Joseph I (1705–11), as Emperor, and his allies had no wish to revive the union of the Empire with Spain.

By the Treaties of Utrecht, Rastadt, and Baden (1713–4), the Emperor received Naples, the Milanese, Sardinia, and the Netherlands as compensation for his claims. This arrangement emphasized the practical disruption of the Empire which had been produced by the Peace of Westphalia. It became, in fact though not in name, an Austrian Empire with a formidable German rival in the new Kingdom of Prussia, and the territories in the Netherlands and in Italy were not states of the Empire but Austrian possessions.

Under Charles VI (1711–40) Austria was engaged in the Turkish War, which had continued almost without interruption for half a century, and in various European struggles, and his later years were occupied in an attempt to secure the 'Pragmatic Sanction,' an agreement by which his daughter, Maria Theresa, was to succeed to his territories.

The Empire was greatly weakened by the war which followed the death of Charles VI, for Frederick II of Prussia advanced some ancient and dubious claims to the province of Silesia, a dependency of Bohemia, and wrenched the greater part of it from the queen, an event which led to the Austrian Succession War in Europe. After a short reign of Charles Albert of Bavaria as Charles VII (1742–5), the imperial crown was given to Francis I (1745–65), the husband of Maria Theresa, and was ultimately restored to the Habsburg House in the person of her son Joseph II (1765–90).

The Austrian Succession War was closed by the Treaty of Aix-la-Chapelle in 1748, by which the Emperor and his wife acknowledged the cession of what was thenceforth Prussian Silesia, and an effort to recover it in the Seven Years' War was unsuccessful. Both Maria Theresa and Joseph II made important constitutional reforms in the Empire, but these related solely to the Austrian territories, with which the imperial authority had become almost entirely identified.

Joseph increased the Austrian possessions by the first Partition of Poland (1772). He died a year after the French Revolution began, and in the last months of his life the revolutionary ferment spread to the Austrian Netherlands, where a republic was proclaimed. His successor, Leopold II (1790–2), espoused the cause of Louis XVI, and his son Francis II, the last Holy Roman Emperor, began the war against revolutionary France.

In the course of the long struggle the position of the traditional Empire became farcical, for out of its component states new kingdoms and electorates were created and old ones ceased to exist. When, in the summer of 1806, Napoleon, as Emperor of the French, formed with Bavaria, Württemberg, and other states which had belonged to the Empire, the Confederation of the Rhine, these states renounced their nominal allegiance to the Holy Roman Empire, and Francis resolved on its formal dissolution.

In his deed of abdication (6th Aug., 1806) he recognized what had long been the fact by describing the dying institution as the 'German Empire,' and he took the title of Emperor of Austria, and repudiated any power or responsibility outside his own territorial dominions. The Holy Roman Empire had lasted, with some interruptions, for 1,006 years, but from the death of Frederick II, in 1250, the old ideal which inspired the name had ceased to have any practical significance; it had been a German Empire from 1273 and an Austrian Empire since 1648.

After the fall of Napoleon its revival was suggested, but it would have accentuated the rivalry of Prussia and Austria, and the idea was abandoned. It had long lost its ancient prestige, and contemporaries thought of it, in the words of Voltaire, as "neither Roman, nor holy, nor an empire."— BIBLIOGRAPHY: Viscount Bryce, *The Holy Roman Empire*; H. Fisher, *The Mediæval Empire.*

HOLYROODHOUSE, PALACE AND ABBEY OF, in Edinburgh, at the east end of the old town. The abbey church, founded in 1128 by David I, containing the royal vault, with the ashes of numerous members of the Scottish royal race, is now mostly in ruin. The palace is a large quadrangular building of hewn stone, with a court within surrounded by a piazza.

It was erected in successive parts from 1501 to 1679, contains the private royal apartments in modernized condition, the rooms associated with the events in the reign of Mary Queen of Scots, such as the murder of Rizzio, and a gallery 150 feet long, in which are portraits of all the Scottish kings, most of them imaginary.

Until 1880 the abbey and its precincts possessed the privilege of sanctuary for insolvent debtors. The King Edward memorial at Holyroodhouse includes ornamental gates and a statue. The palace is used by royalty as an occasional residence.

HOLY SPIRIT, or HOLY GHOST. 'Ghost' is the old English term for 'spirit,' which is rightly substituted for the older term in the Revised Version of the English Bible. God's 'Holy Spirit' is mentioned twice in the later sections of the Old Testament (*Is.* lxiii, 10, 11; *Ps.* li, 11), and in both places it is an equivalent for the sacred presence of God in the community, which is outraged by sin.

'*The* Holy Spirit' is a New Testament expression, which also denotes the relation of God to His people, not to nature, but which assumes special prominence in connection with the person and work of Jesus Christ. It denotes the power of God over human personality, personified often until 'the Holy Spirit' occupies a position which the later Church defined as trinitarian, i.e. the unity of God is revealed in the Father, the Son, and the (Holy)

HOLYROOD PALACE

Above—Holyrood Palace with Abbey ruins on left.   *Below*—Front of Palace with Queen Mary's rooms on left

Spirit, who are neither three aspects nor three individuals.

In the New Testament the Holy Spirit is represented as the divine power which operates at the birth of Jesus, the Son, which inspires Him at His baptism for His work, and continues to inspire Him against the powers of evil, as a prophet and as a conqueror of demons. But it is only after His death and resurrection that the Holy Spirit is given to His people.

The sphere of the Spirit's work is now the Church, or fellowship of those who believe in God through Jesus Christ; it completes the spiritual presence of the Lord in various ways: by (i) awakening the mind and conscience; (ii) by regenerating the nature of the believer; (iii) by uniting him to the Lord; (iv) by inspiring to prayer, hope and service; and (v) by binding believers together in unity.

Many supernatural phenomena are associated with the Holy Spirit, especially in the earlier books of the New Testament; miracles and ecstasy are described as accompaniments of the Spirit in the primitive Christian society. But there is a tendency, particularly in St. Paul's epistles and in the *Gospel of John*, to lay deeper stress upon the inner, spiritual experience, to emphasize faith and love as the supreme manifestations of the Spirit, and to minimize the intermittent phenomena. Its manifestations are sought in (i) Scripture, which is viewed as the speech of the Holy Spirit, and in (ii) the sacraments of baptism and the Lord's Supper.

The former bring out the anticipations of Christ in the past (the Old Testament being regarded as an inspired prediction of Christ); the latter emphasize the present power of the Spirit as regenerating, illuminating, and sustaining the Christian life. But the Holy Spirit is also viewed as the pledge of future bliss, for the possession of this gift of God guarantees the future and final perfection of the believer.—BIBLIOGRAPHY: H. B. Swete, *The Holy Spirit in the New Testament*; W. T. Davison, *The Indwelling Spirit.*

HOLY SPIRIT PLANT, an orchidaceous plant (*Peristeria elata*) of Central America, known also as the *dove-plant*, from the resemblance of the united stamens and pistil of the flower to a dove hovering with expanded wings, somewhat like the conventional dove seen in artistic representations of the Holy Ghost. It has a spike of almost globose, sweet-scented flowers of a creamy-white, dotted with lilac on the base of the lip.

HOLYTOWN, town of Lanarkshire. It is 11 miles from Glasgow, and 389 miles from London by the L.M.S. Rly. Here are iron mines and collieries, also iron and steel works. Pop. 20,669.

HOLY WATER, in the Greek and Roman Catholic Church, salted water which has been consecrated by prayers, exorcism, and other ceremonies, to sprinkle the faithful and things used for the Church. It is placed at the door of churches, so that worshippers may sprinkle themselves with it as they enter, and it is used in nearly every blessing which the Church gives. Sprinkling the people with holy water seems to date from the ninth century, and it is considered efficacious not from any virtue of its own, but from the effect of the Church's prayers at the time of using.

HOLY WEEK, or **PASSION WEEK,** is that which immediately precedes Easter, and is devoted especially to commemorating the passion of our Lord. The days more especially solemnized during it are Spy Wednesday, Maundy Thursday, Good Friday, and Holy Saturday. It is an institution of very early origin, and is known as Great Week, Silent Week, or Penitential Week. Spy Wednesday was a name given in allusion to the betrayal of Christ by Judas Iscariot. Maundy or Holy Thursday specially commemorates the institution of the Eucharist.

HOLYWELL, a market town in Flintshire, North Wales, on the estuary of the Dee, 17 miles s.w. of Liverpool. It takes its name from the well of St. Winifred, one of the most copious springs in Britain, long a famous resort for the supernatural cure of bodily disease and infirmity. The well is covered by a small Gothic building of early date. Near the town are coal- and lead-mines, and quarries. Pop. (1931), 3,423.

HOLYWOOD, watering place and urban district of Co. Down, N. Ireland. It i. 4 miles from Belfast, on Belfast Lough, and has the usual seaside attractions for visitors. Pop. 4,827.

HOMAGE (O.Fr. *homage*, Lat. *homo* man), in feudal law, a formal acknowledgment made by a feudal tenant to and in presence of his lord on receiving the investiture of a fief or coming to it by succession, that he was his vassal. The tenant, being ungirt and uncovered, kneeled and held up both his hands between those of the lord, who sat before him, and there professed that "he did become his man, from that day forth, of life and limb, and earthly honour," and then received a kiss from his lord.

HOMBURG VOR DER HÖHE, a town of Prussia, province of Hesse-Nassau, 9 miles N.N.W. of Frankfort-

It is much frequented on account of its mineral springs and bathing establishment, to which gaming-tables were formerly attached, but were suppressed in 1872. The waters are of two classes, those of three springs being purgative, and used for complaints of the stomach, liver, kidneys, &c.; those of the remaining two containing iron, and being used as a tonic. *Homburg hats* originated here. Pop. 14,344.

HOME, Henry, a Scottish lawyer and author, born 1696, died 1782. He studied law at Edinburgh, and was called to the Bar in 1724. He soon acquired reputation by a number of publications on the civil and Scottish law. In 1752 he became a judge of session, and assumed the title of Lord Kames.

In addition to his legal works he published *Essays on British Antiquities*; *Essays on the Principles of Morality and Natural Religion*, in which he advocated the doctrine of philosophical necessity; *Introduction to the Art of Thinking*; and his best-known work, *Elements of Criticism*, in which, discarding all arbitrary rules of literary composition, he endeavoured to establish a new theory on the principles of human nature. In 1776 he published the *Gentleman Farmer*, and in 1781 *Loose Thoughts on Education*.

HOME, John, Scottish clergyman and dramatic poet, born at Leith 1722, died at Edinburgh 1808. He studied for the church, and was appointed to the parish of Athelstaneford, vacant by the death of Blair, author of *The Grave*. His tragedy of *Douglas* was performed at Edinburgh in 1756, and at Covent Garden (with Peg Woffington in the cast) in 1757, and attained a wonderful popularity.

The production gave great offence to the Church as a body; the author was threatened with ecclesiastical censures, and in consequence resigned his living, and ever after acted and appeared as a layman. He retired into England, obtained the protection of the Earl of Bute, and received a considerable pension. His other plays, *The Siege of Aquileia*, *The Fatal Discovery*, *Alonzo*, and *Alfred*, are absolutely forgotten, a fate which their mediocrity deserves. His *History of the Rebellion of* 1745–46 (4to) also disappointed public expectation.

HOME OFFICE, THE, as it exists to-day, dates from 1782, when it was formed from the 'Southern" Secretaryship of State, which had, from 1688, controlled the relations of Great Britain with Ireland, the Colonies, and the countries of Southern Europe. The Home Office continued to be entrusted with Irish and colonial affairs until 1801, and it administered the militia up to the time of the Crimean War; it is now concerned entirely with domestic affairs as a "Ministry of the Interior," but many of the matters of policy and administry which fall, in other countries within, the competence of such a Ministry are dealt with not by the Home Office but by other Ministries such as the Ministry of Health, and the Ministry of Labour.

At the present time the Secretary of State for the Home Department is charged with the maintenance of order and the repression of crime in England and Wales. In his hands lie the supervision and control of English and Welsh prisons and convict establishments; he is also responsible for the administration of the Factory Acts, the Coal and Metalliferous Mines Acts, Poor Law Acts, Reformatory and Industrial School Acts, Explosives Acts, Inebriates Acts, Vivisection Acts, Prevention of Cruelty to Children and to Animals Acts, the Burial Acts, and the Licensing Laws. Further, this minister, always of course, as a Secretary of State, a member of the Cabinet, is the proper channel for addresses to the Crown and the replies to such; and it is through him that the sovereign's communications by way of proclamations or formal announcements are made to the nation.

Finally, it is on the 'advice' of the Home Secretary that the Crown exercises, or declines to exercise, its prerogative of remitting the death sentence; there being thus laid upon a single man a grave responsibility which many think would be better shared among several persons; though the Home Secretary, in practice, usually consults privately the judge who tries a capital case. The Home Secretary is assisted in his work by both permanent and parliamentary under-secretaries, numerous assistant secretaries, and an extensive staff of inspectors and other officials attached to the various departments under his control. The salary is £5,000 a year, and the present holder of the office (1933), is Rt. Hon. Sir John Gilmour, Bt., D.S.O.

HOMER ('Oμηρος) the name attached as that of their (traditionally blind) author to the two great Greek epics, the *Iliad* and the *Odyssey*, and also to certain minor poems, the *Homeric Hymns*, a collection of poems addressed to various divinities, the *Margites* (The Madman), which, from the fragments which remain, appears to have been a mock-heroic epic, another mock-heroic epic the *Batrachomyomachia* (The Battle of the Frogs and the Mice), and a collection of epics dealing with the Trojan War and known as the *Cyclic Poems*, of which.

only small fragments remain. These minor poems are of comparatively small account; their connection in authorship with the *Iliad* and *Odyssey* is, to say the least of it, very doubtful; and it is the two great epics which are here mainly to be considered.

The *Iliad* deals with an episode of the Trojan War, the wronging of Achilles, the greatest of the Greek warriors, by Agamemnon, the supreme leader of the host, in the matter of the captive maiden Briseis, the wrath which Achilles thereupon conceives, and the consequences and final appeasement of his wrath. The Greeks

Homer

suffer disaster through his withdrawing himself from the fight; Patroclus, his bosom friend, is slain by the Trojan champion, Hector, son of Priam, the king; he is roused to slay Hector in revenge, and the poem ends with the ransoming of Hector's body by his father.

The *Odyssey* tells of the wanderings and adventures of Odysseus (Ulysses) in the course of his return to Ithaca after the capture of Troy, and of what had meanwhile gone forward in his house, where Penelope, his wife, was beseiged by suitors; and finally relates howOdysseus and his son Telemachus, whom he had left an infant when he set out for Troy, encountered and slew the suitors, and how husband and wife were reunited. The capture of Troy is incidentally related. The *Iliad* breaks off before that point is reached.

Herodotus, the historian, who flour-ished about 440 B.C., speaks of Homer as having lived about 400 years before himself; and for long a personal Homer, the author of all the poems above mentioned, appears to have been taken for granted, dates varying between limits not very far from each other being assigned to him, and seven cities contending for the honour of having been his birth-place.

About the third or second century B.C. a school of Homeric critics, among whom the most eminent was Aristarchus, existed at Alexandria; and the result of their criticism was that the authorship of Homer was confined to the *Iliad* and the *Odyssey*, the other poems being regarded as not genuine. Among these critics, however, some appear to have gone a step further. A sect known as the Chorizontes ('Separators') held that the *Iliad* alone was to be assigned to Homer, and that the *Odyssey* was the work of another author. Their views produced little or no effect.

There the ancient scrutiny of Homeric authorship may be said to have stopped; and it was not till what may almost be called our own time that the matter was reopened. Robert Wood in his *Essay on the Original Genius of Homer*, published in 1769, appears to have been the first fully to realize the importance of the question whether the art of writing was practised at a date to which the composition of the epics could be assigned.

He answered this question in the negative; and this answer was the keystone of the theories of Friedrich August Wolf, who in his *Prolegomena ad Homerum*, published in 1795, maintained that poems forming the basis of the epics were put together from older pieces of various authorship by a poet of commanding genius whom he often calls 'Homer'; that, writing being unknown, or at any rate not yet employed for literary purposes at the time of the putting together of the poems, the poems were for long transmitted by memory and oral recitation; that in the course of transmission alterations and additions, deliberate or accidental, were made; that the poems were not written down till about 550 B.C., and after being written down suffered still further changes deliberately made by 'revisers' or critics until they attained their present state; and that the artistic unity seen in the epics as we possess them is due not so much to 'Homer' as to later artificial treatment.

In asserting that the epics were not written down before 550 B.C., Wolf chiefly relied on a doubtful and vague tradition to the effect that a definite text was first settled from scattered materials and committed to writing at

Athens in the time of the tyrant Pisistratus (died 527 B.C.). This tradition occurs first in Cicero (106–43 B.C.), and is found in no Greek author before Pausanias (*floruit c.* 180 B.C.); and the evidence for it is inconclusive, though, of course, rejection of the tradition does not necessarily imply rejection of Wolf's thesis as to the date at which the use of writing might be presumed.

J. G. J. Hermann (1772–1848) developed Wolf's views with a tendency to make 'Homer' more influential than Wolf had done. He held that the primitive poet had settled the main form and the limits of the poems, and that those who came after him confined themselves to retouching, recasting, and engrafting new work, without seriously affecting the main features of that on which they worked. G. W. Nitzsch (1790–1861) gives 'Homer' still further influence, conceiving that, working on old materials (as great poets so often have done), he made them his own, and produced the epics substantially as we have them.

On the other hand, K. K. F. W. Lachmann (1793–1851) tended to minimize the influence of 'Homer.' He split up the *Iliad* into no fewer than eighteen separate and originally independent 'lays' by various hands strung together by the primitive poet. He was followed on similar lines by others, such as Köchly, but these dissectors do not agree as to the points of dissection, and for the most part each produces a different set of 'lays.'

George Grote (1794–1871), while largely agreeing with Nitzsch, conceived the *Iliad* as having been originally a comparatively short poem, an *Achilleid*, dealing solely with the wrath of Achilles, and as having been expanded to its present dimensions by a later poet whom he regarded as the true Homer.

Other scholars, such as W. Christ, W. D. Geddes, and Dr. Walter Leaf, have each in his own way continued the analysis of the *Iliad* on the general lines of Lachmann; but other scholars, such as the late Andrew Lang, have strenuously maintained that the epics were composed substantially in their present form by a single poet, though they, of course, admit that minor changes in the text must have taken place in the course of the long transmission.

It will be noticed that the scholars who question the unity of authorship have devoted their chief attention to the *Iliad*, which from the nature of its plan is of comparatively loose structure. Attempts have been made to split up the *Odyssey* also; but these cannot be said to have been successful. The plot of the *Odyssey* is, in fact,

of the most ingenious and closely-knit construction; and while it is, of course, possible to attribute different parts of the poem to different hands, just as we might deal with a modern novel in which plot and subplot are interwoven, it is on the face of it far more probable that the cunningly-contrived structure is the work of one brain. There is, too, another consideration which does not seem to have been fully kept in view. There is no good reason to suppose that the *Cyclic Poems*, of which mention is made in the beginning of this article, are of later, or at any rate of much later date than the *Iliad* and the *Odyssey*.

Now these epics were evidently, at least in some cases, comparable in length with the two great epics, and must reasonably be considered to have been composed, and, as they were known down to comparatively late times, to have been transmitted, much as these were. All the epics must be treated in the same way; and treatment which is avowedly exceptional becomes increasingly open to objection as it is more widely applied.

Such, in brief, was the state of the Homeric question up to the time of the discoveries made in Crete from 1900 onwards by Sir Arthur Evans and his followers. These discoveries have completely changed our conceptions of the early history of the Ægean area. Formerly the men of the age to which the epics were assigned were regarded as more or less rude, as standing at the beginnings of civilization. We now know that they looked back over a space of civilization at any rate as great as the space which lies between us and them.

In Wolf's theory the fundamental proposition was his denial that the literary use of writing could be assumed for any age to which the epics could be assigned. We now know that the art of writing was practised long before any date which can possibly be fixed for them; and it may confidently be assumed that if at the place and date of their composition the art of writing was felt, as it certainly would be, to be useful for literary purposes, it would be practised.

It may, in fact, safely be said that if Wolf could have viewed Homer as we can view him, his theories, and the theories of those who followed him, would have been entirely different. He could point to the external evidence, such as it then was, as supporting him, and could invoke it in aid of his attempt to assign to the epics from the internal evidence an origin in conflict with all analogy.

Now the external evidence strongly supports those who regard the epics as having been produced as all other great epics have been produced, as having been the work of a conscious artist working more or less in the manner predicated by Nitzsch on materials furnished to him by pre-decessors.

There seems to be no serious objec-tion to our supposing, in one of the cities of Asia Minor (say Smyrna), somewhere about 800 or 700 B.C., the existence of a great poet named Homer writing his epics in a period of poetical activity in the midst of fellow-poets whose works are partially represented by the *Cyclic Poems.*

So far as extant remains show, the poets of the age would seem to have taken their themes from stories about or connected with the Trojan War (which may be regarded as actually historical); but, of course, many poems on other themes may have perished. It is perhaps not entirely fanciful to picture a period of epic activity at Smyrna not unlike the period of dramatic activity in Elizabethan London.

At any rate, opinion seems now to be moving in the direction of a per-sonal Homer composing and writing down his epics substantially in the form in which we have them, though the text must from obvious causes have suffered a certain measure of corruption, and must have been added to or mutilated here and there by editors or copyists. But not a few still maintain the older views.

Our text of Homer rests on a large number of manuscripts dating from the tenth century A.D. onwards. These manuscripts differ remarkably little among each other; and there is good reason to suppose that the text which they furnish approximates very closely to that current in Athens in the time of Pericles. Beyond that the stream of testimony dries up; and we cannot tell how nearly that text approximated to the original text. That there were differences is certain, if only on account of the change in the alphabet which in the meantime took place.

The best modern text of the *Iliad* and *Odyssey* is that published at Ox-ford by the Clarendon Press in its series of classical texts. For English readers the best editions with com-mentaries are the *Iliad* by Dr. Leaf, second edition, 2 vols., 1900–2, and the school edition of the *Iliad* by D. B. Monro, also in 2 vols., originally published 1884–8; the *Odyssey*, books i–xii, by W. Walter Merry and James Riddell, second edition 1886, and the *Odyssey*, books xiii to xxiv, by D. B. Monro, 1901.

The best English prose translations are the translation of the *Iliad* by Lang, Leaf, and Myers, and that of the *Odyssey* by Butcher and Lang.

Translations in verse are numerous. That of both epics by Pope, though it is not at all like Homer, has at any rate the merit of being readable, a characteristic shared by few or none of the others. Jebb's *Homer: an In-troduction to the Iliad and the Odyssey* should be referred to.

HOME RULE, a term invented in 1873 to designate the Irish demand for self-government, which took the form of an organized 'Home Rule' movement in 1870. The struggle for self-determination on the part of Ire-land ranged over a period of seven and a half centuries. From 1172, when Henry II received the homage of the chief Irish kings at Dublin, a bitter feud was waged with England. The story is one of struggle, repression, and fierce resolve, which, in the final fifty years, almost dominated English political life. The country was not conquered at the outset, and guerrilla warfare ended in some form of inde-pendence during the Wars of the Roses.

In 1495 Poynings' Act was passed, making Irish laws dependent on the sanction of the King and the English Privy Council. But revolt continued, intensified by the 'plantation' policy which settled Scottish and English families in Ireland, mainly in the North, and by the efforts to introduce Protestantism after the Reformation.

Cromwell and his son-in-law, Ireton, subjugated the land between 1649 and 1656, when many Irish families were forcibly removed beyond the Shannon. The Irish rallied to the cause of James II at the English Revolution of 1688, but they were defeated at the battle of the Boyne in 1690, and the history of the subsequent century is one of penal laws against the Roman Catho-lics, who were also excluded from the Irish (Grattan's) Parliament, which existed from 1782 to 1800. A rebellion in 1798 was not suppressed until 1800, and on the first day of the following year a legislative union with Britain was effected by the passing of identical statutes by the Parliament at West-minster and the Irish Houses of Parliament at Dublin.

By this Ireland was united to Great Britain, and was given 100 seats in the House of Commons and 34 in the House of Lords. Almost immediately, however, the struggle for separation was resumed. After Catholic emanci-pation was brought to its fulfilment by Daniel O'Connell, a 'Young Ire-land' movement was inaugurated, but famine depopulated the land, dis-content grew, and armed risings followed.

Then came the Tenant Rights movement, the Fenians (which origin-ated among the Irish-Americans, at

Chicago about 1860) and many secret societies, with riots, and much bloodshed; Fenians in the United States made raids into Canada, there were outrages in England, and wholesale arrests. In 1870 Isaac Butt, the leader of the Irish Party in the House of Commons, inaugurated the Home Rule movement. A motion in its favour, brought up at Westminster in 1874, was rejected by 458 to 61.

Charles Stewart Parnell, who succeeded Butt as leader of the Irish Nationalists, forced the question to the front by persistent obstructive tactics in Parliament, while outside the 'land war' was intensified. Inside the Home Rule movement the 'physical force' party gained the ascendancy over the constitutionalists, and a group of the extremists, called the 'Invincibles' assassinated Lord Frederick Cavendish, the Irish Secretary, and T. H. Burke, the Under-Secretary, in Phœnix Park, Dublin, in 1882; the Clan-na-Gael Society, as some of the Fenians called themselves, adopted a terrorist policy; there were dynamite outrages, which included an attempt to blow up the Houses of Parliament and the Tower of London in Jan. 1885; there were moonlighting crimes, cattle maiming, boycotting, a no-rent campaign, and a general state of unrest in Ireland.

Coercion Acts were passed after acrimonious debates in which Irish members were suspended. Gladstone introduced the first Home Rule Bill in 1886. It was defeated, and completely altered British party politics by dividing the Liberal Party, Joseph Chamberlain, Lord Hartington (afterwards Duke of Devonshire), and other prominent Liberals seceded and formed the Liberal Unionist Party, which in due course fused with the Conservatives and became the Unionist Party.

With the Unionists in power, Arthur Balfour, as Irish Secretary, was given a free hand to restore order in Ireland. An unexpected new complication was a divorce suit in which Parnell was the co-respondent. The Nationalist Party was split in twain, 30 remaining faithful to Parnell and 54 forming themselves into an Anti-Parnellite group. Parnell died in 1891, and was succeeded by John Redmond.

Two years later Gladstone was returned to power again, and in 1893 introduced a second Home Rule Bill, which differed from the previous measure by retaining eighty Irish members in the Imperial Parliament. It passed the Commons, but was rejected by the Lords by a majority of 378. Following this, Home Rule receded for a time and a policy of humane administration did something, along with land legislation, to appease Irish opinion. Gladstone died, the Liberals were out of office for over ten years, the Boer War monopolized attention, and following it Chamberlain introduced his policy of Tariff Reform, which became the dominating political question.

When the Liberals were returned to power again in 1906 Ireland was relatively peaceful and prosperous, but it was not until 1912 that the Liberal party, faithful to its Gladstonian policy, endeavoured to satisfy the Irish demand for self-government by bringing in a Home Rule Bill. The Liberal Government, however, had first to deal with the Lords' veto which blocked the passing of the measure, and after a bitter struggle the Peers were compelled to pass the Parliament Act of 1911. Under this their veto is limited to two sessions; in the third they are ignored if the Commons pass a measure the third time.

The Home Rule Bill introduced by Mr. Asquith, the Premier, in 1912, met with fierce opposition in Ulster, which is mainly Protestant. A covenant of resistance was signed, among others, by Sir Edward (afterwards Lord) Carson, and prominent Unionists, and a volunteer force was raised; there was a serious 'mutiny' among the officers at the Curragh, and a determined attempt was made by the leaders of the Unionist party to prevent the Bill becoming operative. A conference of the leading statesmen held, on the King's summons, at Buckingham Palace, failed to compose the differences between the two parties. As the Nationalists also recruited volunteers, and there was gun-running by both the Ulster and the Irish nationalists, the crisis assumed a most menacing aspect. In 1914, when, after a third passing by the Commons, the Home Rule Bill was bound to become law, the prospect of civil war in Ireland was serious.

The European War gave the Home Rule movement its most dramatic and tragic turn. The Bill was passed with a proviso that it was not to come into force until after the war. On Easter Monday, 1916, rebellion broke out in Dublin. It was organized by the Sinn Fein ('Ourselves Alone') Party and assisted by Germany, who sent Sir Roger Casement, an ex-British consul, who had tried to raise a German-Irish regiment from among British war prisoners in Germany, to land arms in Ireland. Casement was arrested on landing, tried for high treason and executed, the rebellion, which had proclaimed a republic, was suppressed in a week, and the leaders tried by court-martial and shot.

Sinn Fein, however, continued to flourish, the passing of an Irish Conscription Bill in 1918 was bitterly resented, and at the general election at the end of that year, after the Armistice, a totally new situation was created by the election of seventy-three Sinn Feiners who refused to sit in the British House of Commons, constituted themselves an Irish Parliament under the title of Dail Eireann and declared Ireland an independent republic with De Valera as president.

A terrible campaign of outrage and reprisal followed; the country was plunged into virtual civil war. To meet the situation, the Home Rule Act of 1914 was repealed in 1920, and a new Act passed, giving Ireland two Parliaments, one for the south and west and the other for the six northern counties of Ulster, where the hostility to Home Rule and an All-Ireland Parliament was intensified.

The campaign of outrage and reprisal in which the Coalition Government at Westminster vied with Sinn Fein in ruthlessness, was at its height when King George V and the Queen visited Belfast to open the Northern Parliament on 22nd June, 1921. In his speech, the King made a solemn appeal for conciliation, and that marked the great turning-point in Irish history. David Lloyd George, the Prime Minister, issued invitations to a conference, a truce was declared, and, after preliminary disappointments, discussion between the Sinn Fein leaders and representatives of the British Government began in London on 11th Oct., 1921.

Proposals were rejected by each side, Sinn Fein insisting on an All-Irish Parliament, and Sir James Craig, the Ulster Premier, refusing it. Just when it seemed that the negotiations would prove futile, an agreement was reached at the Premier's residence, 10 Downing Street, London, just before 3 a.m. on Tuesday, 6th Dec., 1921.

This made Ireland a free state on terms of Dominion Home Rule, leaving Ulster the option of remaining out if she preferred to do so. A week later a special session of Parliament approved the treaty with only 58 dissentients in the Commons and 47 in the Lords. After several days of acrimonious debate in which much Celtic eloquence was heard, An Dail Eireann ratified the treaty on Saturday, 7th Jan., 1922, by the narrow majority of 7 (64 to 57).

The Sinn Fein party was split in two, one section under Mr. Griffith, who was elected President of Dail Eireann on 10th Jan., 1922, being in favour of the Irish Free State, and the other section under Mr. De Valera being content with nothing less than a

republic and complete separation from Great Britain. Sinn Fein gained control over the Cosgrave party in the Elections of 1932 and Mr. De Valera proceeded to carry out his policy of withholding payment of the land annuities claimed by the British Government, and of abolishing the oath of allegiance to the British Crown taken by deputies in Dail Eireann. These decisions, alleged by the British Government to be a violation of the Treaty of 1921, were met by a tariff on British imports from the Irish Free State; a measure to which the De Valera Government promptly replied by raising Irish Free State tariffs against British goods. The Irish Free State is now to all intents and purposes an independent republic, but it is still held to be largely within the British Commonwealth of Nations.—BIBLIOGRAPHY: A. J. Balfour, *Aspects of Home Rule*; E. Childers, *The Framework of Home Rule*; F. Hackett, *Ireland: A Study in Nationalism*; M. Macdonagh, *The Home Rule Movement*; J. E. Redmond, *Home Rule*.

HOMICI'DAL MANIA, a term applied to the action of an insane person who displays a sudden irresistible impulse to destroy life. It is often independent of hatred towards the victim, but as a rule it is due to a mental conflict which destroys the patient's power of controlling his impulses. Hence some trivial or imagined insult may be sufficient to excite the patient to action.

HOMICIDE (Lat. *homo*, man, and *cædere*, to kill), the killing of one man or human being by another. In law, homicide is of three kinds—Justifiable, Excusable, and Felonious; Justifiable, when it proceeds from unavoidable necessity, as where the proper officer inflicts capital punishment, where a person is killed to prevent him committing a forcible and felonious crime, where an officer of justice kills an offender who assaults or resists him and who cannot otherwise be captured, or where persons are killed in the dispersion of rebellious or riotous assemblies.

Excusable; when it happens from misadventure, as where a man in doing a lawful act by accident and without negligence kills another, or in self-defence, as where a man kills another in defence of the life of himself, his wife, children, parent, servant, &c.; Felonious, when it proceeds from malice, or is done in the prosecution of some unlawful act, or in a sudden passion, or without justification or excuse. Self-murder also is felonious homicide. Felonious homicide comprehends murder and manslaughter.

In Scots law manslaughter gets the name of *culpable homicide*. *See* MAN-SLAUGHTER; MURDER.—Cf. Stephen, *History of the Criminal Law of England*.

HOM'ILDON, BATTLE OF, a battle fought in 1402 between the Scots under Archibald, Earl of Douglas, and an English force under Hotspur and the Earl of March, at Homildon Hill, near Wooler. The Scots were utterly defeated.

HOMILET'ICS, the art of preaching that branch of practical theology which teaches the principles of adapting the discourses of the pulpit to the spiritual benefit of the hearers, and the best methods which ministers of the gospel should pursue for instructing their hearers by their doctrines and example. The earliest Christian writer on homiletics is St. Augustine (*De Doctrina Christiana*).

HOMILY, a discourse or sermon read or pronounced to an audience on some subject of religion; a discourse pronounced in the church by the minister to the congregation. The ancient homily was sometimes simply a conversation, the prelate talking to the people and interrogating them, and they in turn talking to and interrogating him. In modern use a homily differs but little from an ordinary sermon, the idea of simplicity, however, being always attached to it. The earliest existing examples of the homily are those of Origen in the third century.

In the schools of Alexandria and Antioch this form of discourse was sedulously cultivated, and Clement of Alexandria, St. Dionysius, and Gregory Thaumaturgus are among the names most eminent in this department. It was in later centuries, however, and in the hands of Athanasius, Gregory of Nyssa, and Gregory of Nazianzus, Basil, Cyril of Jerusalem, and Cyril of Alexandria, and especially of Chrysostom, that the homily reached its highest excellence. Augustine and Gregory the Great were among the Western composers of homilies.

In the Church of England, after the Reformation, two official books of homilies were issued. These were called *The First* and *Second Books of Homilies*, and the former, ascribed to Cranmer, appeared in 1547; the latter, said to be by Jewell, in 1563. They were originally meant to be read by those of the inferior clergy who were not qualified to compose discourses themselves.

HOMOCER'CAL (Gr. *homos*, same, *kerkos*, tail), a term applied in the case of bony fishes which have externally symmetrical tails. *See* HETERO-CERCAL.

HOMŒOP'ATHY, a word of Greek origin, meaning, literally, 'like suffering.' A system of therapeutics built upon the law that likes are cured by likes, discovered by Hahnemann, and elaborated in his various works, the chief of which are *Organon of Medicine* (Everyman's Library) and *Chronic Diseases*. He was famous as a linguist and translator, a great chemist, discovered soluble mercury, and was the first physician to treat lunatics on the humane non-restraint principle.

The law of similars in practice demands no experimentation on the sick, but detailed and careful provings of drugs on the healthy. A drug given to persons in health consistently produces a sickness peculiar to itself. The totality of the symptoms produced gives the complete drug-disease picture, and the similarity between the drug picture and the symptoms of the sick individual determines its applicability as the curative remedy.

The closer the similarity between the drug and disease pictures, the greater the sensitiveness of the patient's reaction to the remedy. The virus gives the outline, but the individual creates the colouring of the disease picture.

In the homœopathic system the sick individual is treated, and not the disease as labelled by the 'authority of the day.' Individualization is the key-note to successful homœopathy. To sift out the uncommon and peculiar symptoms that are part of the personal recuperative effort of the patient from the symptoms that belong to the nature of the disease is to individualize the sick person and the similar drug.

Hahnemann says: "Without the most minute individualization, homœopathy is not conceivable." It is the reaction of the drug that is desired, and, consequently, the minuter the dose which will produce the desired effect without first aggravating the trouble, the speedier the cure.

Hahnemann discovered that by repeated triturations and succussions the power of the remedy was enhanced. These attenuations he called 'potencies.' The greater the subdivision the more the potency increases, and the higher the potency the deeper the reaction. Even an inert substance like silica, treated thus and given to the healthy, produces symptoms of sickness, and is proven as a valuable remedy.

Science verifies that a substance such as gold can be subdivided and a colloid produced. Such colloids have a profound effect on the vital economy. Physics and physiological chemistry are proving the great power of the minute. Physics has passed from mass to molecule, from molecule to atom, from atom to electron, and powers undreamed of before are disclosed. Homœopathic remedies are not mere dilutions but potentizations. Homœopathy creates a new orientation in medicine.

HOMOIOUSIANS, a sect of Arians, followers of Eusebius, who maintained that the nature of Christ is not the same with, but only similar to (Gr. *homoios*, like), that of the Father, as distinguished from the Homoousians, who maintained that he was of the same nature.

HOMOLOGY. Term in biology referring to the common origin of organs or parts of a plant or animal organism. Thus the arm of a man, the wing of a bird, and the foreleg of a dog are homologous structures, al-

Homoptera. One of the Cicadas (under side)

though in each case the function is different.

HOMOOUSIANS (Gr. *homos*, same, *ousia*, being nature), the orthodox party in the Church during the great controversy upon the nature of Christ in the fourth century, who maintained that the nature of the Father and the Son is the same, in opposition to the *Homoiousians*, who held that their natures were only similar.

HOMOPLASY, in biology, similar structural characters presented by different groups of organisms which have been adapted to the same kind of environment, and which have been independently acquired, so that they do not prove relationship. A great many desert plants, for instance, are markedly spiny and devoid of thin flattened leaves.

Aquatic animals, belonging to diverse groups, are often of similar shape; and creatures that live in thick undergrowth tend to be elongated and cylindrical, with limbs reduced in size

or absent, e.g. snakes and snake-like lizards. Such resemblances are often expressed by using the term 'convergence of characters.'

HOMOP'TERA, one of the sections into which the order of hemipterous insects has been divided, the other section being the Heteroptera. The insects of this section have the wing-covers generally deflexed, of the same consistence throughout, the antennæ mostly short and terminated by a bristle, and the body convex and thick. To this section belong the aphides, cicadas, lantern-flies, &c.

HOMOTAX'Y, in geology, the sequence of fossil faunas in the same order in widely separated regions of the globe.

HONAN', an inland province of China, named after a city of the same name, now little but a scene of ruins. The province has an area of 67,954 sq. miles. It is generally level, and is watered by the Hwang Ho and its affluents. The soil is fertile and carefully cultivated; the forests in the west supply timber; and mines yield tutenag or Chinese copper, cinnabar, and mica. Honan suffered severely from the inundation of the Hwang Ho in 1887; capital, Kai-feng. Pop. 35,289,752.

HONDO, the name given by the Japanese to the chief island in their empire; the official name is Honshiu. In many geographical works Nippon or Niphon is the distinctive appellation of this island, but by the Japanese themselves that name is applied to the whole country. *See* JAPAN.

HONDURAS, a Central American republic with a coast-line of 400 miles on the Atlantic and 60 miles on the Pacific. It is bounded on the west by Guatemala, south by Salvador and the Pacific, east by Nicaragua, and north by the Atlantic. It has an area of 44,275 sq. miles, and a population of (1930), 859,761. Honduras is mountainous, richly timbered, and well watered (the main rivers are the Chamelicon, Ulua, and Choluteca). There are some extremely fertile valleys, and the Comayagua Plain is very productive.

The capital is Tegucigalpa, the chief ports are Amapala (the only one on the Pacific), Puerto Cortez, La Ceiba, Omoa, Tela, and Trujillo (all on the Atlantic); and the other towns are Pespire, Nacaome, La Esperanza, Santa Rosa, Choluteca and San Pedro Sula. Roatan is the port of entry for the Bay Islands. The climate is hot on the coasts, but is elsewhere temperate and healthy.

The mineral wealth of Honduras is great but almost unexploited. The value of gold and silver exported in 1931 was £304,000. Much silver is found, and gold, coal, oil, and lignite are worked, but on a very small scale. The chief product is the banana, while the coco-nut is also valuable. Coffee, maize, tobacco, and the sugar-cane are also grown, and vegetable oils form an important export. Ex-cellent cattle are reared, and a certain amount of mahogany, cedar, and ebony is cut. Straw hats and cigars are manufactured. 6,947,378 cigars were exported in 1931.

In 1931, 28,960,948 branches of bananas were exported, the total value of exports being £4,005,517 and of imports £2,058,284. Roman Catho-licism is the prevailing religion (though there is complete toleration), and education is free and compulsory. There is a university at Tegucigalpa, also a school of jurisprudence at Comayagua. The language spoken is Spanish. Good roads are few, but gradual improvement is taking place. In 1931 there were 361 miles of motor roads. The principal towns are linked up by air service. The Re-public has six wireless stations. In 1932 the gold lempira became the unit of currency, in place of the silver peso, which is being withdrawn from circulation; its value is that of 50 cents, U.S. currency. In 1932 there were 1,149 miles of railways.

Constitution and Government. The republic declared its independence of Spain in 1821, and is at present governed by a Constitution approved in 1894, and re-written in 1924. The executive authority is vested in the President and the Cabinet, while the legislature consists of one chamber, the Congress of Deputies (43 members). —BIBLIOGRAPHY: A. H. Keane, *Cen-tral and South America* (Stanford's Compendium); Pedro Rivas, *Dic-tionary of Honduras*; *The South American Handbook*.

HONDURAS, BAY OF, a wide inlet of the Caribbean Sea, having on the south Guatemala and Honduras, and on the west British Honduras and Yucatan.

HONDURAS, BRITISH, a British Crown colony of Central America, bounded by Yucatan, Guatemala, and the Bay of Honduras. The area of 8,598 sq. miles includes Albion Island and numerous *cayes* (islands) with a total area of 238 sq. miles. The coast is low and swampy, but the land rises toward the interior, being flat in the north and mountainous in the south. The climate is fairly healthy.

There are numerous rivers which provide the principal means of trans-port. The chief are the Belize, Hondo, Sibun, and Sarstoon. There are exten-

sive forests (the main wealth of the country), the principal timbers being cedar, mahogany, pine, iron-wood, and logwood. Sugar-cane, coffee, bananas, coco-nuts, tobacco, &c., are cultivated.

The principal exports are timber, bananas and other fruits, and tortoise-shell, the total value in 1931 being 2,911,066 dollars. In the same year imports amounted to 4,435,358 dollars. There are 25 miles of railway track and 30 miles of metalled roads. The unit of currency is the dollar and the chief bank is the Royal Bank of Canada.

The chief town is Belize (Pop. 1931, 16,687), which was devastated by a terrible hurricane in 1931. Honduras became known to Englishmen in 1638, but it was not till 1798 that Spanish opposition was finally quelled. In 1862 Honduras was made a colony subject to Jamaica, and in 1884 its independ-ence was declared.—A. B. Dillon, *Geography of British Honduras.*

HONE, William, English antiquary, born 1780, died 1842. He began life in a law office, and became imbued with free-thinking opinions. In 1800 he abandoned the law and made ventures as a writer, bookseller, and publisher, which were all failures. In 1817 he was prosecuted by Govern-ment for the publication of alleged irreverent parodies and lampoons, which he defended himself with great acuteness, and was acquitted.

He subsequently had a large sum subscribed for him as a champion of the freedom of the Press. He grad-ually abandoned free-thought and the writing of satires for religion and antiquarianism. His chief publica-tions are: *The Political House that Jack Built* (1819), *The Man in the Moon* (1820), *The Every-day Book* (1826), *Table-book* (1827–8), and *Year Book* (1829), perfect mines of anti-quarian lore.

HONE, the name given to several varieties of slaty stones employed in whetting knives, razors, or other edge-tools. They are usually pieces of hard close-grained clay-slate, con-taining minute particles of quartz, with a uniform consistence. The best-known varieties are the Ayr stone, so called from being found in the River Ayr, in Scotland; the Charnley Forest stone, found in Leicestershire; the German hone, the Canada oil-stone, and the Turkey oil-stone.

HONEY, a vegetable product, with saccharine properties, collected by bees from the blossoms of flowers, and deposited in the cells of their combs. The best is clear and transparent, and solidifies when kept for some time into a granular, white mass. Some varieties of it are dark-yellow or brownish in colour. Spring honey is considered better than summer honey and the latter than that of autumn.

Virgin honey is taken from hives in which the bees have never swarmed, and it is of a white colour. *Yellow* honey is extracted from all sorts of combs. The flavour of honey largely depends on the plants from which it is collected. Honey is obtained in large quantities in many countries, partly from wild bees, but chiefly from those kept in hives. In addition to its ordinary domestic uses, it is employed medicinally as a promoter of expectoration, to sweeten certain medi-

Honey-Eater (*Meliphagidae*)

cines, to make a gargle with vinegar, &c. It is also used in making mead.

Honey was held in very high esteem and was valued by the ancients. The Hebrews defined the Promised Land as "a land flowing with milk and honey." It was used for sweetening purposes throughout the Mediterranean area until the introduction of sugar. The ancient Egyptians made sweet beer from honey, and also used it for embalming the dead. Honey was also used as an article of barter in Ceylon and East Africa.

HONEY-ANT, an ant, species of Myrmecocystus, inhabiting the United States and Mexico, and living in communities in subterranean galleries. In summer a certain number of individuals are fed by the workers with a kind of honey obtained from oak-galls, until their abdomens become so distended as to appear like small pellucid grapes. Later in the season, when food is scarce, these 'honey-pots' are devoured by the others, and they are also dug up and eaten by the inhabitants of the country.

HONEY-COMB, a waxen cellular structure formed by bees for storage of honey and eggs. The wax is secreted by the insect in the form of small and thin oval scales in the folds of the abdomen. The comb is composed of a number of cells, most of them exactly hexagonal, and arranged in two layers placed end to end, the openings of the layers being in opposite directions. The comb is placed vertically, the cells being therefore horizontal. The sides of the cells are very thin, and yet the whole structure is of considerable strength. The cells are closed by waxen lids after honey has been stored or eggs deposited in them. Queens are reared in irregular acorn-shaped queen-cells.

HONEY-DEW, a sweet saccharine substance found on the leaves of trees and other plants in small drops like dew, but in reality deposited by aphides. Different kinds of manna are the dried honey-dew or saccharine exudations of certain plants.

HONEY-EATER, the name given to a number of perching birds forming the family Meliphagidæ, and native to the Australian region. They feed on fruit, buds, and the nectar of flowers. They have long curved sharp bills, with tongues terminating in a pencil of delicate filaments, to enable them the better to extract the juices of flowers. Among the species are the wattled honey-eater (*Anthochæra mellivora*), soldier bird (*Myzomela sanguinolenta*), cobbler's awl (species of Acanthorhynchus), friar birds (species of Philemon), and bell birds (species of Anthornis and Manorhinus).

HONEY-GUIDE, a name given to the cuckoos of the genera Indicator and Prodotiscus, which, by their motions and cries, conduct persons to the nests of wild honey-bees. They are natives of South Africa and South Asia, and with the barbets (which also range into tropical America) make up the family Capitonidæ, allied to toucans and woodpeckers.

HONEY-LOCUST, SWEET LOCUST, or **BLACK LOCUST** (*Gleditschia triacanthos*), a forest tree belonging to the United States, nat. ord. Leguminosæ. The leaves are pinnated, divided into numerous small leaflets, and the foliage has a light and elegant appearance; the flowers are greenish, and are succeeded by long, often twisted pods, containing large brown seeds, enveloped in a sweet pulp. This tree is especially remarkable for its formidable thorns, on which account it has been recommended for hedges. The *G. monosperma*, a tree resembling the last in general appearance, grows in swamps in Illinois and south-westward. The wood is inferior in quality.

HONEYSUCKLE, or WOODBINE, genus Lonicēra of Linnæus, nat. ord. Caprifoliaceæ. The common honeysuckle of Britain, *L. periclymēnum*, a twining shrub, with distinct leaves and red berries, is indigenous in Great Britain; but two others have been naturalized, *L. caprifolium*, distinguished by its upper leaves being united in a cup; and *L. xylosteum*, with small, yellowish, scentless flowers, and scarlet berries.

L. sempervirens (trumpet-honey-suckle) is also cultivated in Britain on account of the beauty of its flowers. The honeysuckle family is represented in North America by nine different species. *Australian honeysuckle* is a name given to *Banksia australis* and other species of the Protea family, from their flowers being filled with a sweet liquid.

HONFLEUR (on-*fleur*), a seaport of France, department of Calvados, on the estuary of the Seine. It is a town of old buildings and narrow streets, and although the rise of Havre has injured its commerce, it still has a trade in agricultural and dairy produce, and some manufactures in connection with shipping and fisheries.

On the hill above the town is the chapel of Notre Dame de Grâce, much frequented by sailors and filled with their votive offerings. Honfleur was long in possession of the English, and was of considerable strategical importance during the Hundred Years' War. Pop. 9,298.

HONG KONG, an island on the south-eastern coast of China at the mouth of the Canton River. It is 11 miles long, has an area of rather more than 32 sq. miles, and is broken by abrupt ridges rising in Victoria Peak to a height of over 2,000 feet. The narrow straits between the island and the mainland form a magnificent harbour on the south shores of which, and in terraces round the Peak, is the city of Victoria. The island is well watered, and, though once barren, is now covered with luxuriant vegetation. Hong Kong was ceded to Britain in 1841 and became a Crown colony.

Hong Kong Harbour

In 1860 the opposite peninsula of Kowloon (2¾ sq. miles) on the mainland was ceded by the Chinese, and in 1898 a further area (356 sq. miles) including Deep Bay and Mirs Bay was leased to Britain for 99 years. The total area of the colony is 391 sq. miles; the civil population in 1931 was 840,473; Chinese population, 821,104.

The chief industries are sugar-refining, ship-building and repairing, deep-sea fishing, and tobacco manufacture. There are several native industries, and much of the land in the leased territory is cultivated by Chinese. The island by reason of its position is a Chinese emigration and immigration depot, and is a trade distributing centre.

Hong Kong is a free port, the harbour is one of the busiest in the world, the tonnage entered and cleared (excluding the coasting trade) being 40,511,650, tons.

In 1931 the value of exports was £25,733,065, and of imports £36,142,983. The Chinese tea and silk trades are largely in the hands of Hong Kong merchants, and other exports are antimony, bamboo, cassia, coir, ginger, wood and vegetable oils, rice, tobacco, and soy. There is an electric tramway (9¼ miles), and a cable tramway (up Victoria Peak) in Hong Kong, while in Kowloon there is the British section of the Canton Railway (22 miles). The wireless telegraph service is controlled by the Public Works Department, there is also a military and naval wireless station.

Hong Kong is a military station, and is the head-quarters of the China Squadron. It is also the head-quarters of the Hong Kong and Shanghai Banking Corporation.

There is a residential teaching university on the island. Education is not compulsory.—BIBLIOGRAPHY: *Oxford Survey of the British Empire* (Vol. II); and various official reports.

HON'ITON, a borough and market town of England, in Devonshire, on the Otter, long celebrated for the manufacture of a special variety of lace. There is an agricultural trade and beer is brewed. The town has a Fair dating back to 1221. It was a parliamentary borough till 1868, and now gives name to a parliamentary division of the county. Pop. (1931), 3,008.

HONLEY, urban district of Yorkshire (W.R.). Near Huddersfield; it is 185 miles from London by the L.N.E. Rly. Woollen goods are manufactured. Pop. (1931), 4,611.

HONOLU'LU, the capital of the Hawaiian or Sandwich Islands, on the Island of Oahu, annexed in 1898 by the United States. It is electrically lighted, and has a tramway system. There is a fine natural harbour, very much improved, and now admitting the largest vessels afloat. Pop. (1930), 137,582.

HONORIUS, Flavius, son of Theodosius the Great, born A.D. 384, died 423. After the division of the empire, A.D. 395, Honorius received the western half, but, on account of his youth, Stilicho was appointed his guardian. The principal events of his reign are the adoption of rigorous measures against paganism in 399; the invasion by Alaric in 400–403; and another irruption of barbarians under Rhadagaisus, 405–406.

Both invasions were repelled by Stilicho, who was assassinated at Ravenna in 408. Alaric marched on Rome and plundered it in 409, while

Honorius shut himself up in Ravenna. Some of the finest provinces of the empire, Spain, Gaul, and Pannonia, were lost in this reign.

HONOURABLE, RIGHT HONOURABLE, and MOST HONOURABLE, titles given in the United Kingdom to peers, their families, and certain public functionaries. Marquesses are styled 'Most Honourable,' Earls, Viscounts, Barons, and Privy Councillors 'Right Honourable.' 'Honourable' is the courtesy title of the younger sons of earls and all the children of viscounts and barons, as well as of Maids of Honour and Judges of the High Court. In America the Governors of states, judges, members of Congress, and others holding offices of dignity and trust, are styled 'honourable.'

HONOURS, MILITARY, compliments or salutes paid by troops to royalty, officers of rank, &c., or given at funerals to all grades of the army. Honours of War are stipulated terms granted to a garrison surrendering, in consideration of a brave defence, &c. Sometimes the vanquished are allowed to march out with their arms, drums beating, and colours flying; or they may be permitted to deposit their arms and stores, and return to their own country on parole.

HONSHU. *See* JAPAN.

HONVÉD, the name applied to the Hungarian national champions, under the earlier kings. The word disappeared afterwards, but was revived in 1848, when it was applied to the patriotic army during the war with Austria. It was afterwards applied to the Hungarian militia.

HOOCH, or **HOOGH** (hōh), **Pieter de,** Dutch genre painter, born at Rotterdam about 1632, died about 1681. He was peculiarly successful in depicting scenes, illuminated by sunlight, of Dutch domestic life. His earlier work, influenced by Rembrandt's first manner, is remarkable for its harmonious, rich colour, and puts him in the front rank of the smaller Dutch masters. His later work is more mechanical and mannered. He produced comparatively little work, but is well represented in the National Gallery and the Wallace Collection.

HOOD, Alexander, Viscount Bridport, brother of Samuel, Viscount Hood, born 1727, died 1814, was also an admiral. He commanded under Lord Howe in the Channel Fleet in 1794; defeated the French off L'Orient, 1795; and was created Viscount Bridport, 1801.

HOOD, Robin, English outlaw and legendary hero. The earliest allusion to Robin Hood is to be found in Passus V of *Piers the Plowman* (B text), which was written about 1377. A large number of old ballads deal with the Robin Hood legend; most of these ballads date from the fifteenth century. There are three different theories advanced to explain the origin of the Robin Hood cycle of ballads: (1) Robin Hood was a real man, the greatest of outlaws. He may have lived in the reign of Edward II, and been an adherent of Thomas, Earl of Lancaster, in the insurrection of 1322. (2) Robin Hood is the central personage of a sun-myth, or is to be identified with the Teutonic god Woden. (3) Robin Hood was originally the name given to a mythical forest elf (cf. Robin Goodfellow), and then given, like the Irish Rory o' the Hills, as a generic name to any outlaw chief who lived in the forest and defied the unpopular game laws. The last of these three theories is the most probable.

A good deal of research into records has failed to bring to light any evidence that Robin Hood was a real historical person. Nor can much be said for the theory that he is to be identified with the sun or with Woden. It is much more likely that the name was given to a succession of captains of outlaws; one of them, perhaps the earliest, may have been an outstanding man, and in that sense there may have been a real Robin Hood.

The Robin Hood cycle is very closely connected with Sherwood Forest and with Nottingham. Adam Bell, Clym of the Clough, and William of Cloudislee performed in Cumberland feats similar to those of Robin Hood. The cycle of ballads grew and grew; Robin's company originally contained Little John, Much the miller's son, William Scathlock, and others; in the early sixteenth century Friar Tuck was added to the company, while a love-interest was supplied by Maid Marian. By a later sophistication Robin Hood was represented as being the Earl of Huntingdon in disguise. In those days a title was an almost essential adjunct to a hero. The later ballads have not the freshness and charm of the earlier ones.

Robin Hood was essentially the hero of the yeoman class, as King Arthur was that of the upper classes. He was a typical middle-class Englishman, an unerring marksman, an expert with the quarter-staff, and had a rough, boisterous sense of humour. Above all he defied the oppressive forest-laws, as every middle-class Englishman wished to do, and he aided in the redistribution of wealth, which every middle-class Englishman wished to see redistributed.

The Robin Hood ballads are among the best of their kind. They are redolent of the greenwood, and of careless, happy life in the country. It is always the month of May in the ballads, and the freshness of a May morning seems to pervade them. They have given pleasure to innumerable people, especially boys. They have inspired many poets, as Drayton, Jonson, and Tennyson, and some prose writers, as Scott and Thomas Love Peacock. They appeal straight to the spirit of youth and the love of open-air adventure that lives in all of us, even in the most elderly city-dweller.—BIBLIOGRAPHY: J. Hunter, *Great Hero of the Ancient Minstrelsy of England, Robin Hood*; F. J. Child, *English and Scottish Popular Ballads*; J. Ritson, *Collection of Ballads concerning Robin Hood.*

HOOD, Horace Lambert Alexander a son of the 4th Viscount Hood, became head of the naval college at Osborne in 1910. In 1914 he took command of a ship and in the Battle of Jutland he went down in the *Invincible* when in command of a squadron of battle cruisers, 31st May, 1916.

HOOD, Sir Samuel, cousin of the above, born 1762, died 1814, was present at the battle of the Nile, 1798; captured Tobago and the Dutch settlements in Guiana, 1803; and defeated the French squadron off Rochefort in 1806.

HOOD, Samuel, Viscount, a British admiral, born 1724, died 1816. He joined the navy as a midshipman, in 1740, and attained the rank of post-captain in 1759. Having become rear-admiral, he preserved the Island of St. Christopher from being taken by de Grasse, assisted in the defeat of de Grasse by Rodney in 1782, and was rewarded with the title of Baron Hood of Catherington in the Irish peerage. In 1793 he commanded against the French in the Mediterranean, and captured Toulon and Corsica. In 1796 he was made an English peer, with the title of Viscount Hood.

HOOD, Thomas, an English poet and humorist, of Scottish extraction, born at London 1799, died 1845. During a residence at Dundee, and while only fifteen or sixteen years of age, he contributed articles to a local paper and magazine. In 1821 he became sub-editor of *The London Magazine,* and in 1826 appeared his *Whims and Oddities,* which was followed by *National Tales* and a volume of serious poetry. From 1829 to 1837 he conducted *The Comic Annual.* At the same time his pen was employed on other subjects, and he published *The Epping Hunt*, a comic poem, ridiculing Cockney sportsmen; *Eugene Aram's Dream*, inserted in *The Gem*, of which he was for a short time editor; and *Tylney Hall*, a novel. In 1837, on the termination of *The Comic Annual*, he commenced a monthly periodical entitled *Hood's Own*, which consisted chiefly of selections from the former work.

His health now began to fail, and with a view to its recovery he paid a visit to the Continent. While there in 1839 he published his *Up the Rhine*, which, based on the lines of *Humphry Clinker*, was very popular. Shortly after his return he undertook the editorship of *The New Monthly Magazine*, and continued it till 1843. His principal contributions to it he published separately, under the title of *Whimsicalities*. His last periodical, entitled *Hood's Magazine*, was commenced in 1844; but his health shortly afterwards completely broke down, and his death occurred in the following year.

It was during his last illness that he contributed to *Punch*, *The Song of a Shirt*, *The Bridge of Sighs*, and *The Lay of a Labourer*. Hood is unrivalled as a punster, and he possesses a singular power of combining the humorous with the pathetic. He had the satisfaction of knowing that the pension of £100 conferred upon him on his last illness by Sir Robert Peel was to be transferred to his wife. *Memorials of Thomas Hood*, by his daughter, were published in 1860.— Cf. Walter Jerrold, *Thomas Hood: his Life and Times*.

HOOD, Tom, son of the great humorist, and a miscellaneous writer, born 1835, died 1874. He studied at Oxford, and during his residence there he wrote *Pen and Pencil Pictures*. In 1861 appeared his *Daughters of King Daker, and other Poems*. In 1865 he became editor of *Fun*, which became very popular under his management. His talents, although similar to those of his father, were less brilliant.

HOODED SEAL (*Cystophŏra cristāta*), a species of seal, the male of which possesses a movable, inflatable muscular bag, stretching from the muzzle to about 5 inches behind the eyes. The prevailing colour is dark-grey with spots of deeper tint—the head and limbs being uniformly black. Its usual range extends in America southwards to Newfoundland, and in Europe to Southern Norway.

HOOFS, the horny tissues which constitute the external part of the feet of certain animals, mostly herbivorous. They may be regarded as homologues of the toe-nails of other animals. They are composed of epithelial cells, agglutinated and dried, and of intercellular substance and cell contents. Chemically they consist of keratin.

HOOGE, a village of Belgium, in the province of West Flanders. Situated on the Ypres-Menin road, it was the head-quarters of Earl French (then Sir John) during the first battle of Ypres. The village was taken by the Germans in May, 1915. The site of Hooge was retaken by British troops in July, 1917, and the region finally cleared in Sept., 1918.

HOOGHLY RIVER. *See* HUGLI.

HOOK, Theodore Edward, novelist and journalist, born 1788, died 1841, was the son of James Hook, a musical composer. After leaving Harrow he helped his father with the libretto of a comic opera, *The Soldier's Return*, instead of reading for Oxford. For some years Hook led a life of gaiety in London, and became notorious for practical jokes and similar escapades. In 1812 he was appointed Accountant-General and Treasurer of the Island of Mauritius; but, owing to his gross carelessness, a serious deficiency in the Treasury accounts was discovered, and in 1818 he was sent home under arrest, but no proceedings were taken against him.

From 1820 to 1841 he was editor of *John Bull*, and at intervals from 1824 to 1828 he published his *Sayings and Doings*, while in 1836 he became editor of *The New Monthly Magazine*. His other principal works are *Life of Sir David Baird*, and a series of novels, among which may be mentioned: *Love and Pride*, *Jack Brag*, *Gilbert Gurney*, *Gurney Married*, *Precepts and Practice*, and *Fathers and Sons*. Hook was satirized by Thackeray in *Vanity Fair*, and by Disraeli in *Coningsby*.—Cf. R. H. D. Barham, *Life and Remains of Hook*.

HOOKE, Robert, an English mathematician and natural philosopher, born 1635, died 1703. He is chiefly known as the discoverer of *Hooke's Law*, which he stated in the form " Ut tensio sic vis"; the meaning being that in elastic bodies stress is proportional to strain. In 1664 he became Cutlerian professor of mechanics to the Royal Society, and in 1664 professor of geometry at Gresham College. He partially anticipated the Newtonian theory of gravitation and the undulatory theory of light, and invented or materially improved many scientific and mechanical instruments.

HOOKER, Sir Joseph Dalton, British scientist, second son of Sir

William Jackson Hooker, born at Halesworth, Suffolk, 30th June, 1817, died 10th Dec., 1911. He studied medicine at the University of Glasgow, where he took his degree in 1839. His first botanical work began in his father's herbarium, but in 1839 he accompanied Sir James Ross's Antarctic expedition in the *Erebus*, and published an account of tne flora of the sub-Antarctic and south temperate regions. His desire to acquire more knowledge of the flora of Oriental tropics made him lead a botanical expedition to North India in 1848.

He was appointed assistant director of Kew Gardens in 1855, and succeeded his father as director in 1858, retaining this post till 1885, when he retired. Hooker was an intimate friend of Darwin, and it was through his and Sir Charles Lyell's influence that Darwin was induced to publish his first statement of the theory of natural selection. Knighted in 1877, Hooker received the Order of Merit in 1907. His works include *Genera Plantarum* and *Flora of the British Isles*.

HOOKER, Richard, English ecclesiastical historian, born 1553, died 1600. He went up to Oxford, a..d became a Fellow of Christ Church in 1577. In 1579 he was appointed deputy professor of Hebrew; took orders in 1581, and was made preacher at Paul's Cross. About this period he was induced to marry the daughter of Mrs. Churchman, who had charge of the dwelling set apart for the preachers —a marriage which proved the reverse of happy.

In 1584 he became rector of Drayton Beauchamp, and in 1585 Master of the Temple. In 1595 he received the living of Bishopsbourne, in Kent, where he ended his days. His *Ecclesiastical Polity*, published at various dates, and written in defence of the Church of England, is no less remarkable for learning and extent of research than for the richness and purity of its style, which entitles its author to be regarded as one of the classics of the Elizabethan age.— BIBLIOGRAPHY: Izaak Walton, *Life of Richard Hooker*; Vernon Staley, *Life of Richard Hooker*.

HOOKER, Sir William Jackson, a celebrated botanist, father of Sir Joseph Hooker, born 1785, died 1865. From 1821 to 1841 he was professor of botany at Glasgow University; he was knighted in 1836; and became director of Kew Gardens in 1841. He wrote, among other works, *The British Jungermanniæ, Icones Plantarum*, and *A Century of Orchidaceous Plants*.

HOOKE'S JOINT, or UNIVERSAL JOINT, a device for transmitting a continuous rotational motion from a shaft A to another B which is not parallel to A (see fig.). The angular velocity ratio is not constant. It varies during each revolution from a maximum value, $\sec\theta$, to a minimum value $\cos\theta$, where θ is the acute angle of inclination of the shafts. There are two maximum values and two minimum values per revolution. If a constant angular-velocity ratio is required, a double Hooke's joint can be used.

This consists of two Hooke's joints coupled by an intermediate idle rod. It is essential that the lines through the joint pins on the intermediate rod, at each end, shall lie in the same plane. If this is not the case, the irregularity in the angular-velocity ratio is worse with the double joint than with the single one. A kind of

Hooke's Universal Joint

hydraulic Hooke's joint is to be found in the Williams-Janney gear.

HOOLIGAN, a term first applied towards the end of the nineteenth century to a gang of young ruffians under the leadership of one Hoolly or Hooligan, whose terrorizing exploits extended over the Southwark district, London. The gang became known as the Hoolly gang, or the Hooligans. Spreading over Europe, the term is now applied to all gangs of ruffians and street rowdies. The Parisian *apache* and the Australian *larrikin* are counterparts of the hooligan, although the latter is less associated with crime than the two former.

HOOP-ASH (*Celtis crassifolia*), an American tree of the ord. Urticaceæ, found in the forests of Ohio and in the Western States. It is a fine tree, attains a height of 80 feet, and is employed for making charcoal. Its fruit is round, and in size nearly equal to a pea. *See* HACKBERRY *and* NETTLE-TREE.

HOOPER, John, an English reformer, born 1495, burnt 1555. Having studied at Oxford, he joined the Cistercian order; but by the year 1539 he had adopted the reformed opinions, and withdrew to the Continent on the imposition of new articles of faith by Henry VIII, and lived at Zürich. In 1547 he returned to England, and took an active share in the Edwardian Reformation. In

1550 he was nominated Bishop of Gloucester, but declined consecration until certain vestments and ceremonies were dispensed with in his case. On the accession of Queen Mary, in 1553, Hooper was deprived

Hoopoes (*Upúpa epops*)

and imprisoned, and in 1555 burnt at Gloucester, near his own cathedral. His works consist chiefly of *A Godly Confession and Protestation of the Christian Faith, Lectures on the Creed, Sermons on the Book of Jonah, Annotations on the Thirteenth Chapter of the Epistle to the Romans,* and expositions of several psalms.

HOOPOE (Upŭpa), a bird forming the type of a family (Upupidæ) related to that including the hornbills. The European hoopoe (*U. epops*) is about 12 inches long; it has a fine crest of pale cinnamon-red feathers, tipped with black; upper surface on the whole ashy-brown; wings black, the coverts having white bars; throat and breast pale fawn; abdomen white, with black streaks and dashes. It has a very wide range though Europe, North Africa, and Asia to Japan.

It is a ground-feeder, preying chiefly on insects, and seems to delight in filth; it nests in cavities of trees or walls, and its eggs vary from four to seven. The hoopoe utters a loud double or treble *hoop.* whence its name. A well-known Arab legend describes the endowment of this bird by Allah with a golden crest, afterwards converted into feathers in answer to the petition of the persecuted wearer.

HOORN (horn), a seaport of the Netherlands on a small bay of the Zuider Zee, 20 miles N.N.E. of Amsterdam. The trade is extensive, more especially in cheese, and there is some shipbuilding and other industries. Pop. 12,026.

HOOVER, Herbert Clark, thirty-first President of the United States, born in 1874 at West Branch, Iowa, where his father, a Quaker, worked a farm. Educated at the Leland Stamford University, he went to California, became a mining engineer, and went out to Western Australia and China. During the siege by the Boxers in 1900 he was in Tientsin, where he defended not only his European fellow-workers, but also the Chinamen in his service.

Hoover became famous during the European War, first as chairman of the American Relief Committee in London, and Commissioner for Relief in Belgium, and afterwards, when America entered the war, as Food Controller. Thanks to his energy and wise administration, his country was able to provide a surplus for feeding Europe. Director of European Relief, he became Secretary of Commerce in 1920 under President Harding, and was appointed to superintend the relief to be sent to famine-stricken Russia. He was President of the United States from 1929 to 1933, elected by a popular vote of 21½ millions against 15 millions cast for his Democratic opponent Gov. Alfred E. Smith, a poll which gave Mr. Hoover 444

Hoorn—17th century building

votes in the Electoral College against Governor Smith's 87. Mr. Hoover's administration encountered serious difficulties from its first day, owing mainly to the 'break' in the extending boom which marked the whole period of Mr. Coolidge's administration. As a consequence Mr. Hoover's popularity rapidly waned. He displayed much less vigour and initiative as president than he showed as Secretary of Commerce, and the Republican party departing from the precedent of recent years, only very reluctantly nominated him for a second time. In the 1932 presidential election he was handsomely defeated by Mr. Franklin D. Roosevelt (q.v.) and retired to his home in California.

HOP (*Humŭlus Lupŭlus*), a plant of the nat. ord. Moraceæ, a native of Europe, and perhaps of the United States, where it occurs wild. The root is perennial, giving out several herbaceous, rough, twining stems, with large lobed leaves; the fertile flowers are green; the fruit is a catkin, and the plant is cultivated for the sake of the catkins, which are employed to communicate to beer its aromatic bitter flavour. The young shoots are sometimes boiled and eaten like asparagus; the fibres of the old stems make good cords. The cultivation of the hop is more carefully attended to in England than in any other country, Kent being the chief county in which it is grown; but the plant is also extensively reared in other parts of Europe, as also in North America, Australia, New Zealand, &c.

The use of the hop catkins depends upon a peculiar bitter substance which they contain, called *lupulin*, which is a yellow powder, containing a bitter principle and a volatile oil. The lupulin constitutes from 10 to 12 per cent by weight of the catkin, and the bitter principle forms from 8 to 12 per cent of the lupulin. Having tonic, stomachic, and narcotic properties, hops are often used medicinally. Pillows stuffed with hops are used to induce sleep.

HOP-CLOVER (*Trifolium procumbens*), a plant of the ord. Leguminosæ, distinguished from other species of clover by its bunch of yellow flowers, which wither to the bright brown of a strobile of hops.

HOPE, Anthony, pseudonym of Sir Anthony Hope Hawkins, British novelist, born in London 9th Feb., 1863. Educated at Marlborough and at Balliol College, Oxford, where he graduated with high classical honours; he studied law and was called to the Bar in 1887, but devoted his activities to literature. Some of his first books, *A Man of Mark* and *Sport Royal*, attracted attention, but he became generally known only after the publication of his *Dolly Dialogues* (1894), a delightful and brilliant work which first appeared in *The Westminster Gazette*.

The *Prisoner of Zenda*, his first romantic novel (1894), met with an immediate success. Other works are:

The *Chronicles of Count Antonio* (1895), *Rupert of Hentzau* (1898), *Simon Dale* (1898), *Quisanté* (1900), *Mrs. Maxon Protests* (1911), *A Young Man's Year* (1915), *Beaumaroy Home from the Wars* (1919), *Little Tiger* (1925), *Memories and Notes* (1927). He also wrote some plays. He was knighted in 1918. Hope is a master of dialogue, and his works are distinguished both by command of plot and a sense of humour.

HOPE, Thomas, an English writer and art patron, born 1770, died 1831. He inherited great wealth, and devoted much of his time while young to extensive travels in various parts of Europe, Asia and Africa. His principal works are: *Household Furniture and Internal Decorations*; *The Costume of the Ancients*; *Anastasius, or Memoirs of a Modern Greek*, a novel displaying remarkable descriptive powers and a minute accuracy in the accounts of Eastern life; and *An Historical Essay on Architecture*.

HOPE, town of Flintshire. On the River Allen, it is connected with Chester by the L.M.S. Rly., and is 188 miles from London. Offa's Dyke passes near, and Roman remains have been unearthed. Pop. 4,800.

HOP-FLEA (*Haltica concinna*), a beetle which belongs to the same genus as the turnip-fly, and which devastates hop plantations. These insects eat up the young shoots, and even after the hop stems have grown 8 or 9 inches long they will devour every leaf and head.

HOP-FLY (*Phorodon humŭli*), a species of plant-louse very destructive to the hop. The winged female is green, with a black head and bands and spots of black on the body; the legs and wings are long. A few winged females make their first appearance about the middle of May, and wingless myriads by the middle of June. The insects suck the under side of the upper leaflets, and there deposit their young on the most succulent part of the plant.

Myriads perish by means of ladybirds and other insects, as well as by their extreme susceptibility to atmospheric changes. Winged males and females are produced in autumn, when the fertilized eggs are laid on the branches of damson trees. In spring these hatch out into winged females that migrate to the hop.

HOPKINS, Edward John, British composer and organist, born at Westminster 30th June, 1818, died 9th Feb., 1901. He was a chorister in the Chapel Royal from 1826 to 1834, then organist at Mitcham Church, Surrey, and in 1843 was appointed organist at the Temple Church, **London,** retaining this post till 1898, when he retired. Hopkins raised the musical service to a high degree of perfection, and published *The Organ: its History and Construction.* He also issued a *Book of Responses,* and *The Temple Psalter.*

HOPPNER, John, English painter, born in 1758 in London, of German parents, died 1810. He studied at the Royal Academy schools, and first exhibited at the Academy in 1782. Under the patronage of the Prince of Wales, he soon acquired a lucrative practice as a portrait painter. He was elected A.R.A. in 1792 and R.A. in 1795. The chief rival of Lawrence, he painted most of the prominent

John Hoppner

men and women of the day, **especially** those in the circle of the Prince of Wales.

Among his more important works are portraits of the Prince of Wales and other members of the royal family (in the Royal Collection), and portraits of Pitt, Canning, and Grenville. He is adequately represented in the Tate Gallery and the National Portrait Gallery. Despite his vogue in the sale-room, Hoppner is little more than a facile, fashionable portrait painter, whose style imitates that of Reynolds, with occasional borrowings from Gainsborough.

HOR, or JEBEL HAROUN, a mountain of Arabia Petræa, south-east of Palestine, forming part of the range of Seir or Edom, and the scene of the death of Aaron; height, 4,580 feet.

HORACE (Quintus Horatius Flaccus), Roman poet, was born on 8th Dec., 65 B.C., and died on 17th Nov., 8 B.C. His father was a freedman, who earned a fairly comfortable livelihood as a collector of taxes; of his mother we know nothing, which makes it probable that she died during the poet's childhood or infancy. Horace always speaks of his father in the most glowing terms of affection and reverence, and attributes much of his success in after life to his father's wise guidance and good example.

His father was a strong believer in a liberal education, and did not consider the local country school good enough for his son; he took the boy to the best school in Rome, and afterwards sent him, when aged about seventeen, to the University of Athens. Horace was probably at Athens when Julius Cæsar was murdered (15th March, 44 B.C.), and soon after in an outburst of Republican zeal, joined the army of Brutus. Owing to a shortage of officers, he was soon given a senior commission, being appointed *tribunus militum,* a rank more or less equivalent to our lieutenant-colonel.

He was present at the battle of Philippi, and took part in the general flight of the Republican forces. He was not designed by nature to be a soldier, but there is no reason to suppose him more inefficient than the majority of amateur soldiers. Several of Horace's own allusions to his flight are jocular in tone, which is not the tone assumed by a coward; and he probably would not have emphasized the fact that he dropped his shield had not that same accident happened to Alcæus, whose metre and style Horace imitated.

He returned to Italy to find his property confiscated and his father dead. He managed to scrape together enough money to purchase for himself an underclerkship in the Civil Service, and by strict economy he was able to live on his salary. He eked out his livelihood by means of writing verses, and he made the acquaintance of other poets and literary men, among whom were Virgil and Varius. In 38 B.C. they introduced him to Mæcenas, the minister of Augustus, who became his life-long friend and patron. Mæcenas presented Horace with a Sabine farm, which made the poet able to leave his Civil Service appointment.

From this time Horace divided his time between Rome and his Sabine farm; it is the delight in both city and country life that gives Horace's poetry some of its unique qualities. Mæcenas introduced Horace to Augustus, who offered him a post as private secretary, which the poet, wise in his generation, declined.

Meanwhile he was slowly producing poems of various kinds. The first book of his *Satires*, ten in number, appeared in 35 B.C. In some of these Horace shows himself somewhat immature; he imitated freely the early satirist Lucilius, whom he abused equally freely. There is rather an unpleasant undertone of vulgarity and bitterness in the earlier book of *Satires*. A collection of poems, in iambic and composite metres, known to us as the *Epodes*, was published about 30 B.C. These poems, which follow Archilochus, the Greek satirist, as a model, are not pleasing; many of them are scurrilous personal lampoons. They may perhaps not be meant very seriously; it has been suggested that there is a tone of parody about them.

Horace developed late, and it was not until the publication of the second book of his *Satires* (29 B.C.) that he attained maturity. The advance on the first book is most striking; Horace shows himself as a polished man of the world, a master of quiet humour, and a great literary stylist. His mastery over metre is no less remarkable; he has as perfect command over the satirical hexameter as Virgil has over the stately heroic hexameter. Horace possessed to an almost unequalled degree the faculty of being able to write about himself without being tedious. Most of these satires are about himself, yet none are egotistic.

In 19 B.C. Horace produced what may be considered his greatest work, the first three books of his *Odes*. These poems are perhaps as well known as any poems in the world; almost every line of them has become proverbial. It is easy to criticize them: it is plain that Horace has not got the fire of Shelley or Catullus, and that there was no 'unpremeditated art' about him. His love poems do not ring true. Some of them may be simply translations from the Greek. Yet the value of the *Odes* is great. For choice language and for clothing commonplace thought in an unforgettable form they are unequalled.

Horace is the poet of those who do not as a rule love poetry; he is a matchless master of language; he is a skilful adapter of Greek metres. In some of his Roman odes he is even more than this; his love for Rome was much deeper than his love for Chloe, and there is no loftier patriotic poetry in the world than the opening odes of the third book. Soon after the publication of the *Odes* Horace published the first book of his *Epistles*, where we see the wise author of the *Satires* mellowed by the passage of time.

In the *Epistles* Horace reveals himself most clearly, and brings this branch of his art to perfection. He had by this time attained a position at court not unlike that of Poet Laureate, and in 17 B.C. he was commissioned to write an ode to be sung at the secular games (the *Carmen Seculare*). It is a dignified composition, but does not rise much above the level of official verse.

The fourth book of the *Odes*, published probably in 13 B.C., may be regarded as a semi-official publication, some of the poems celebrating the victories gained by Drusus and Tiberius. The second book of *Epistles*, consisting of two only, deals mainly with literary criticism, as does the *Epistula ad Pisones*, usually known as the *Ars Poetica*. The *Ars Poetica* gives rules for writing tragedies, a form of composition which Horace never attempted, and which he discusses with rather less than his ordinary good sense. This poem was treated by later critics almost as if it had been divinely inspired; Boileau, for example, allowed no appeal from the authority of Horace. Horace died somewhat suddenly in his fifty-seventh year.

There is no writer, ancient or modern, whom we feel we know so intimately as we do Horace. He tells us all about himself; even his personal appearance is familiar to us. He was small, with dark eyes and dark hair, which went grey in front; he was inclined to be stout, and had weak eyesight. Horace is one of the best loved of all authors. In the days when there were gentlemen, it was part of a gentleman's education to know his Horace by heart. When Latin was understood in the House of Commons, debates were frequently enlivened by Horatian quotations.

His popularity is partly due to his exquisite choice of language, that which Petronius called "Horati curiosa felicitas," and which makes him the most quotable of authors. It is, however, due more to those qualities which make him the most companionable of poets—it is due to his *Satires* and *Epistles* even more than to his *Odes*. We cannot always be on the heights with Æschylus and Dante and Shakespeare. Horace is the poet of the workaday world, the greatest of all the second class of poets. No other poet who is so essentially national and 'of an age' has managed also to become 'for all time.'

BIBLIOGRAPHY: (Editions): Bentley's edition of 1711, while admitting conjectural emendations too freely, marked an epoch in the study of Horace. There is a good edition by J. C. Orelli, and another by E. C. Wickham. There are useful editions for ordinary students by J. Gow and by T. E. Page (*Odes*), A. Palmer (*Satires*), and A. S. Wilkins (*Epistles*). (Critical dissertations): W. Y. Sellar, *Horace and the Elegiac Poets*; H. E. G. Patin,

Études sur la poésie latine. (Translations): Of making many translations of Horace there is no end, the reason being that he is untranslatable. The best complete translation is that by J. Conington; C. S. Calverley has translated some few odes in his own inimitable way. The translation by Sir Theodore Martin has not much to recommend it; neither has that which used to be considered the standard one, by Philip Francis (published 1742–6).

HORÆ, in classical mythology, the goddesses of the seasons and the order of nature. At Athens they were originally two: Thallo and Carpo. Elsewhere they were at first three: Thallo, Carpo, and Auxo, and afterwards increased to four. They are represented as maidens carrying the different products of the seasons.

HORÆ CANONICÆ, or simply **HORÆ**, in the Roman Catholic Church the canonical or appointed hours at which certain hymns and devotions, themselves termed *Horæ* or *Hours*, are performed in monasteries. *See* CANONICAL HOURS.

HORAPOLLO, the alleged author of a work on Egyptian hieroglyphics supposed to have been translated from the Egyptian into Greek. By many authorities the book is considered to have been written about the fifth century and translated as late as the fifteenth.

HORATII, three Roman brothers, who, according to tradition, in the reign of Tullus Hostilius engaged three Alban brothers (the Curiatii), in order to decide the supremacy between Rome and Alba. Victory went to Rome, and the sole surviving Horatius was triumphantly conducted back to the city. But his sister had been betrothed to one of the Curiatii, and her demonstrative grief so enraged Horatius that he stabbed her. For this he was condemned to death, but his father and the people begged him off.

HORATIUS COCLES, a hero of ancient Rome. The Tarquins having, after their banishment, sought refuge with the Etrurian king Porsenna, the latter advanced against Rome (507 B.C.) to restore them. According to tradition, Horatius Cocles, along with two companions, held the Sublician bridge against the enemy, while the Romans broke it down behind them. When this was nearly finished, he sent back his two companions, and as the bridge fell he plunged into the Tiber with his armour and safely reached the opposite bank.—Cf. Macaulay, *Lays of Ancient Rome.*

HORBURY, a town (urban district) of England, W. Riding of Yorkshire, 3 miles south-west of Wakefield, with manufactures of woollen goods. Pop. 7,509.

HÖRDE (*heur'dè*), a town of Germany, in the Prussian province of Westphalia, on the Emscher, a centre of the iron manufacture, and having large coal-mines. Pop. 34,694.

HORDER, Lord, English physician. Thomas Jeeves Horder was born 7th Jan., 1871, and received his medical training at S. Bartholomew's Hospital, London. He joined the staff there and soon became known as a consultant, his patients including members of the royal family. He served at the front in the Great War, was knighted in 1918 and in 1923 was made a baronet. He was raised to the peerage in 1933. He has been actively interested in Cancer Research and is the author of technical books on Diagnosis, &c.

HOREB (Ar. *Jebel Mûsa*, Mountain of Moses), a mountain belonging to the same ridge as Mount Sinai, where is still pointed out the rock from which water issued at the blow of Moses.

HOREHOUND (*Marrubium vulgāre*), a labiate plant, with whitish, downy leaves and stem; flowers small, nearly white in crowded whorls, possessing an aromatic smell and bitter flavour. It is a popular remedy for coughs and colds, usually as an infusion. It is a native of Britain and Europe generally. Black horehound (*Ballōta nigra*), also a labiate plant, is a malodorous and unattractive weed.

HORI'ZON, in ordinary speech the line where earth and sky seem to meet, or the circle which bounds that part of the earth's surface visible to a spectator from a given point. This is termed the *sensible, visible,* or *apparent horizon,* as distinguished from the *rational* or *true horizon,* an imaginary great circle, parallel to the sensible horizon, whose plane passes through the earth's centre, whose poles are the zenith and the nadir, and which divides the celestial sphere into upper and lower hemispheres.

In observations with the sextant on land, or at sea, when the horizon is observed, a small basin containing mercury may serve as an *artificial horizon.* The observer then measures the angle between the sun or star and the image of the sun or star in the basin of mercury, and it is easily seen that half this angle is the altitude of the object. In geology, the term is applied to any well-marked formation which suffices as a starting-point from which to study the rest.

HORLEY, market town of Surrey. It is on the Mole, 24¾ miles from London and 5 miles from Reigate, on the S. Rly. Pop. 6,100.

HORN, HOORNE, or HORNES, Philip, Count van, a Flemish soldier and statesman, born 1518, beheaded in June, 1568. He was the son of Joseph de Montmorency-Nivelle, and of Anne of Egmont, and stepson of John, Count van Horn, who constituted him and his brother his heirs on the condition of assuming his name. Philip gradually rose to be Governor of Gueldres and Zutphen, Admiral of the Fleet, and Councillor of State. He fought at St. Quentin in 1557, and Gravelines in 1558, and in 1559 accompanied Philip to Spain. On his return he joined the Prince of Orange and Egmont in resistance to Philip. On the arrival of Alva at Brussels he was arrested, in Sept., 1567, on a charge of high treason, and he and Egmont were beheaded.

HORN, a general term applied to all hard and pointed appendages of the head, as in deer, cattle, &c.; but as a term denoting a particular kind of substance nothing should be called horn which is not derived from the epidermis or outer layer of the integument, whether on the trunk, hoofs, or head. Horn is a tough, flexible, semi-transparent substance, most liberally developed in the horns of bovine animals, but also found in connection with the 'shell' of the tortoise, the nails, claws, and hoofs of animals, the beak of bird and turtle, &c. Horn is softened very completely by heat, so as to become readily flexible, and to adhere to other pieces similarly softened. True horn consists principally of an albuminoid substance, *keratin*, with a little gelatine and phosphate of lime.

In some species of animals the males only have horns, as for instance the stag. In cattle both male and female have horns, though there are also hornless, or polled cattle. Horns differ widely in the case of different animals. Thus the antlers of deer consist of bone, and are deciduous; those of the giraffe are independent bones, with a covering of hairy skin; those of oxen, sheep, and antelopes consist of a bony core covered by a horny sheath.

The horns of the rhinoceros alone consist exclusively of horny matter. The horns of oxen, sheep, goats, and antelopes are never shed, except in the case of the prong-horned antelope. The number never normally exceeds four, and in the case of deer the antlers are usually branched.

The various kinds of horns are employed for many purposes. The ones mostly used in the arts are those of the ox, buffalo, sheep, and goat. Deer antlers are almost invariably turned into handles for knives, sticks, and umbrellas. Horns which furnish true horn can be softened by heat (usually in boiling water), cut into sheets of various thickness, which sheets may be soldered or welded together at the edges so as to form plates of large dimensions, and polished and dyed so as to imitate the much more expensive tortoise-shell. Clippings of horn may be welded together in the same manner, and made into snuff-boxes, powder-horns, handles for umbrellas, knives, forks, &c.

As horn has the valuable property of taking on and retaining a sharp impression from a die, many highly ornamental articles may be turned out. Combs for the hair are made from the flattened sheets, and out of the solid parts of buffalo horns beautiful carvings are made.

French Horn

HORN, ENGLISH. See COR ANGLAIS.

HORN, FRENCH (Fr. *cor de chasse*, Ger. *wald-horn*), a musical instrument, originally formed, as the name denotes, from the horn of an animal. The name includes a large family of wind-instruments, many of which have fallen into disuse. The French horn, or simply *the horn*, consists of a metallic tube of about 10 feet in length, very narrow at top, bent into rings, and gradually widening towards the end whence the sound issues, called the *bell*. It is blown through a cup-shaped mouthpiece of brass or silver, and the sounds are regulated by the player's lips, the pressure of his breath, and by the insertion of the hand in the bell of the instrument.

As a simple tube, unprovided with holes, the horn yields only the generating note, and of course would be confined to one key; but by means of *crooks* the tube can be lengthened, and transposed into any key. By inserting the hand into the bell, which flattens a note, the sounds which are wanting are produced. The compass of the instrument is three octaves.

Music for the horn is always written on the key of C, an octave higher than it is played, with the key of the composition marked at the beginning of each movement; thus 'corni (or horns) in D' directs the performer which crook he must use to play the notes in the key indicated. The bugle, cornet-a-piston, and sax-horn are allied in-

Crested Hornbill

struments.—Cf. J. Blaikley, *The French Horn*.

HORNBEAM (*Carpīnus Betŭlus*, nat. ord. Cupuliferæ), a small bushy tree common in Britain, and often used in hedges, as it stands cutting and in age becomes very stiff. The wood is white, tough, and hard, and is used in turnery, for cogs of wheels, &c. The inner bark yields a yellow dye. The American hornbeam (*Carpinus americāna*) is a small tree sparingly diffused over the whole of the United States. The wood is fine-grained, tenacious, and very compact.

HORNBILLS, a remarkable family of birds (Bucerotidæ), mostly confined to Africa and Southern Asia, but also ranging into the Australian region, though not into Australia; akin to the kingfishers and the hoopoes, remarkable for the very large size of the bill,

and for an extraordinary horny protuberance by which it is surmounted, nearly as large as the bill itself, and of cellular structure within. The rhinoceros hornbill (*Bucĕros rhinoceros*), native to the Malay Peninsula and Indo-Malay islands, is almost the size of a turkey, of a black colour, except on the lower part of the belly and tip of the tail, which are white. It has a sharp-pointed, slightly-curved bill, about 10 inches long, and furnished at the base of the upper mandible with an immense appendage in the form of an inverted horn.

The skeleton though bulky is very light, being permeated with air to an unusual degree. During incubation the female is plastered up in the hollow of a tree and fed by the male through a small aperture left for the purpose. The hornbills are of arboreal habits, and feed on fruits; but in captivity they take small reptiles, and the Abyssinian species even attacks snakes.

HORNBLENDE (-blend), the typical member of the *amphiboles*, one of the most abundant and widely diffused groups of minerals, occurring principally in igneous rocks. The amphiboles are also important constituents of several species of metamorphic rocks. In colour hornblende exhibits various shades of green, often inclining to brown and black; it is nearly transparent in some varieties, but is commonly opaque; hardness a little less than that of felspar; specific gravity, 3·00. It is an aluminous magnesium iron silicate, with some calcium, and often arises from slow processes of change in augite, the corresponding pyroxene. The prism angles in hornblende, as in the amphiboles generally are 124° and 56°, as against 87° and 93° in the pyroxenes (*see* AUGITE). Hornblende containing sodium connects this mineral with the blue species *glaucophane* and *riebeckite*. Glaucophane is common in schists in the Western Alps of Italy.

HORNBOOK, in former times the first book of children, or that in which they learned their letters: so called from the transparent horn covering placed over the single page of which it usually consisted, the whole being fixed to a wooden frame with a handle. It generally contained the alphabet in Roman and small letters, several rows of monosyllables and the Lord's Prayer. The alphabet was usually prefaced with a cross, or was printed in the form of a cross; hence the term Christ-cross row, corrupted into *criss-cross* row, applied to the alphabet, and by extension to the hornbook. The first hornbook was made about 1450. It is referred to in Shakespeare's

Love's Labour's Lost, v. 1.—Cf. A. W. Tuer, *History of the Hornbook*.

HORNCASTLE, a town of England, county of Lincoln, 21 miles east of the city of Lincoln. There is a considerable trade in corn and wool, and one of the largest horse-fairs in the United Kingdom is held annually in August. Pop. (1931), 3,496. Horncastle is one of the parliamentary divisions of Parts of Lindsey.

HORNCHURCH, urban district of Essex. It is 2 miles from Romford, on the L.M.S. Rly. The industries include the making of agricultural implements and brewing. There is an R.A.F. aerodrome here. Pop. (1931), 28,417.

HORNE, Henry Sinclair Horne, Baron, British soldier, born at Caithness, 19th Feb., 1861. Educated at Harrow and the Royal Military Academy, Woolwich, he obtained a commission in the Royal Artillery in 1880. He served in the South African War (1899–1902), and became a lieutenant-colonel in 1905. When the European War broke out, he went to the front as commander of an artillery brigade, was in Gallipoli and Egypt, where he defended the Suez Canal, and in 1916 commanded the 1st Army. Knighted in 1916, he was raised to the peerage in 1919 as Baron Horne of Stirkoke, county of Caithness, and received a grant of £30,000. He died in 1929.

HORNE, Richard Hengist, poet, dramatist, and miscellaneous writer, born 1803, died 1884. He was educated for the army at Sandhurst, entered the Mexican navy, and served during the war between Mexico and Spain. In 1828 he began his literary career, and produced several tragi-comedies of an ironical and satirical kind, and a large quantity of miscellaneous work. In 1843 he made his historic appeal to public judgment by publishing his epic *Orion* at one farthing.

In 1844 *A New Spirit of the Age*, a critical work in which he was assisted by Miss Barrett (Mrs. Browning) and Robert Bell, appeared. In 1852 he took to gold-digging in Australia, still keeping in touch with his literary work. Of his many writings, the best known are: *Orion, Cosmo de Medici, The Death of Marlowe*, and *Prometheus*.

HORNE, Rt. Hon. Sir Robert Stevenson, British lawyer and politician, born 28th Feb., 1871, the son of a minister of the Church of Scotland. Educated at George Watson's College, Edinburgh, and at Glasgow University, he was for some time lecturer in philosophy at the University College of North Wales, and in 1896 was called to the Scottish Bar. Assistant Inspector-General of Transportation in 1917, he was transferred to the Admiralty, where he became Director of the Labour Department and subsequently Third Civil Lord. He entered Parliament in 1919 as member for the Hillhead division of Glasgow (which he still represented in 1933), was Minister of Labour, 1919 to May, 1920, and President of the Board of Trade, May, 1920, to April, 1921, when he became Chancellor of the Exchequer, leaving office when the Coalition broke up in 1922. In business he became associated with several railway, banking and other companies.

HORNED-OWL, a familiar name applied to several species of owls having two tufts of feathers on the head supposed to resemble horns. *See* OWL.

HORNED-SCREAMER (*Palamedea cornúta*), a South American bird rang-

Horned Screamer

ing from Guiana to Peru, and the type of a special family (Palamedeidæ) related to ducks and geese. A long, slender, movable horn of yellowish-white colour projects from its forehead. Its voice is loud and shrill, and is uttered suddenly and with such vehemence as to have a very startling effect.

HORNED-TOAD, a name given to a genus of lizards (Phrynosóma), of toad-like appearance, found in North America west of the Mississippi and in Central America. There are about a dozen different species, all more or less covered with spine-like scales.

HORNET, an insect of the genus Vespa (*V. crabro*), much larger and stronger than the ordinary wasp. It is very voracious, feeding on fruit and honey, and preying on other insects. They form their nest of a kind of paper-work in hollow trees and walls, and are able with their sting to inflict a painful wound, usually accompanied by considerable swelling.

HORNING, in Scots law, a writing commanding a debtor in the sovereign's name to pay within a certain time under pain of being 'put to the horn' and declared a rebel with three blasts of the horn.

HORNSEA, urban district and watering place of Yorkshire (E.R.). It is about 19 miles from Hull, on the coast between Spurn Point and Flamborough Head, on the L.N.E. Rly. Near is **Hornsea Mere,** a lake covering about 400 acres. Pop. (1931) 4,450.

HORNSEY, a municipal and parliamentary borough of North London, in the county of Middlesex. It includes the districts of Harringay, Crouch End, Muswell Hill, and Finsbury Park. In olden times there was a royal park which is mentioned by

Horned Toad

Shakespeare in *Henry VI*. It returns one member to the House of Commons. Pop. (1931), 95,524.

HORN SILVER ORES, so called because they have a resinous horny appearance, a group of sectile ores ranging from *chlorargyrite*, silver chloride, which is colourless, through species containing bromine and iodine to *iodyrite*, silver iodide, which is yellowish to brown. *Cerargyrite* is a mineral name used to cover the whole group.

HOROLOGY, science dealing with the principles and construction of timepieces. Wheel clocks came into use about the 12th century, portable clocks in the 14th, and watches with a coiled spring a century later. The introduction of the pendulum in the 17th century, followed by the first escapement, was an important step and since that time steady progress has been made.

HOROSCOPE (Lat. *horoscopium*, Gr. *horoskopion*, from *hora*, hour, and *skopein*, to view), in astrology, a scheme or figure of the twelve houses, or twelve signs of the zodiac, in which is marked the disposition of the heavens at a given time and place, and by which astrologers formerly told the fortunes of persons, according to the position of the stars at the time of their birth. To each of the houses was assigned a particular virtue of influence. The ascendant was that part of the heavens which was rising in the east at the moment; this was the first and most important house, or house of life, and contained the five degrees above the horizon and the twenty-five beneath it. Other houses were those of riches, marriage, death, &c. See ASTROLOGY.

HORSE (*Equus caballus*), a well-known mammal belonging to the family Equidæ, ord. Ungulata (hoofed animals), and subdivision Perissodactyla (odd-toed); characterized by an undivided hoof formed by the third toe and its enlarged horny nail, a simple stomach, a mane on the neck, a broad flat tail, a hard bare patch (chestnut) on the inner side of each limb, and by six deeply-pitted incisor teeth in each jaw, seven grinding teeth (the first much reduced and often absent) on either side of both jaws, and by two small canine teeth in the upper jaw of the male, rarely in the female. The family includes also the asses and zebras, and ancestral types appear to have been at one time common in both the Old World and the American continent.

No horses existed in America when it was discovered by Columbus, the ones now found in a wild state there being descendants of those introduced by the Spaniards. But a number of fossil species have been described from America—one of them standing only two and a half feet in height. The stages in the evolution of the horse are illustrated by a series of extinct types. The earliest of these were small swamp-dwellers with simple teeth and five-toed plantigrade feet. Then came an animal only about the size of a fox, and having four separate digits or toes on the fore-foot and three on the hind. Subsequent forms show how the third toe developed at the expense of the others till eventually a form identical with the common horse appeared. There was at the same time increase in size, the body was lifted more and more off the ground, and the teeth became more complex.

All these changes were adaptations to life on the grassy plains that gradually replaced primeval swamps. It is doubtful whether the horse is now anywhere to be found in its native state, the wild horses of the steppes of Tartary and other regions of the

Old World being possibly descendants of animals escaped from domestication. Probably the only really wild horse now existing is a small form (*Equus przewalskii*) indigenous to Central Asia.

The horse was probably first domesticated in Asia, and it varies much in form, size, and character with the climate and nature of the district it inhabits. Arabia produces perhaps the most beautiful breed, which is also swift, courageous, enduring, and persevering. As bred in Britain the horse has attained high perfection.

Two breeds—namely, the large, powerful, black breed of Flanders, and the Arabian—have contributed more than all others to develop the present British varieties from the original, comparatively light-limbed, wiry race found by Cæsar. The former laid the foundation of size, strength, and vigour for draught-horses and for those anciently used in war, while the latter conferred speed and endurance.

The ladies' palfrey is largely derived from the Spanish genet, a small, beautiful, fleet variety of the Moorish barb. The hunter, characterized by speed, strength, and endurance, represents the old English, Flemish, and Arabian breeds. The race-horse has less of Flemish and more of Arabian blood. Other leading varieties are the Shires, Clydesdales, and Suffolk Punches, chiefly of Flanders blood, and the best for draught and agriculture; and several varieties of ponies, as Galloway, New Forest, Shetland, &c. Carriage, riding, and other horses combine the above breeds in varying degrees, as speed, strength, size, &c., are required. Horses are said to have 'blood' or 'breeding' in proportion as they have a greater or less strain of Arab blood.

At the age of two years the horse is in a condition to propagate. The mare carries her young eleven months and some days, continues to breed till the age of sixteen or eighteen years, and lives on an average between twenty and thirty years. The various species of the horse family have been artificially crossed by man, and are found to be fertile with each other; the offspring, however, are generally sterile.

The horse is, strictly speaking, an herbivorous animal, and is more scrupulous in the choice of his food than most other domestic quadrupeds. The staple diet on which horses are kept consists of oats and hay, with beans added for animals subjected to heavy work. As a substitute for, or an addition to the regular food, bran, linseed, and carrots are used.

The age of a horse can be told by the marks on its teeth, which change a little yearly until the animal is about nine years old, after which period it is difficult to determine the age by mark. In some countries the flesh of the horse is used as food; the hide is made into leather; and the hair of the mane and tail is used for making haircloth, for upholsterers' stuffing, &c.—BIBLIOGRAPHY: Sir W. Flower, *The Horse : a Study in Natural History*; J. Wortley Axe, *The Horse : its Treatment in Health and Disease*; R. F. Meysey-Thompson, *The Horse : its Origin and Development combined with Stable Practice*; C. Richardson, *The New Book of the Horse.*

HORSE, MASTER OF THE, one of the great officers of the British court. He has the management of all the royal stables and bred horses, with authority over all the equerries and pages, coachmen, footmen, grooms, &c. In state cavalcades he rides next behind the sovereign.

HORSE-ARTILLERY is designed to work with cavalry and support it in the fight. Though not quite as mobile as cavalry themselves, horse-artillery is the most mobile of all artillery. It possesses marked advantages in this respect over field-artillery, and can cover long distances in a minimum of time, and travel over ground which would prove impassable to heavier guns. Strict march discipline and a high degree of horse-mastership are necessary to enable horse-artillery to keep pace with cavalry.

Horse-artillery is employed to supplement the fire-power of cavalry, whether that arm is acting mounted or dismounted. It is equally capable of supporting infantry or other arms. In the British service the officers are specially selected in each rank from the field-artillery, returning again to the latter on promotion. The men are taken from recruits especially selected for smartness and intelligence.

Horse-artillery is at present horse-drawn (in the British service each gun and wagon by teams of six horses), though these may possibly be to some extent replaced in the future by tanks or some form of light mechanical traction.

The gun travels and shoots off its own pair of wheels, and is quick to come into action. When travelling, the trail of the gun is hooked on to a two-wheeled 'limber.' The total weight behind teams, including the limber, should not generally exceed 1¾ tons.

Many nations (e.g. Germany in 1914) consider that the difficulty of supplying two different rations of ammunition on the battlefield is a bar to the introduction of a special horse-artillery gun, and use the same gun as in field-artillery, lightening as far as possible and using a light limber. Other nations (e.g. Great Britain) have a specially light gun.

HORSE-ARTILLERY ARMAMENT

Country.	Calibre of Gun.	Weight of Shell.	Remarks.
British Empire	3 in.	12½ lb.	—
France..	2·95 in.	16 lb.	Similar to field-artillery gun.
Italy ..	2·95 in.	14¼ lb.	Similar to field-artillery gun.
Russia..	3 in.	14¾ lb.	—
Germany	3·03 in.	15 lb.	Similar to field-artillery gun.
Japan ..	2·95 in.	14¼ lb.	—

HORSE-CHESTNUT, a handsome genus of trees or shrubs (Æsculus) belonging to the nat. ord. Sapindaceæ, having large opposite digitate leaves, and terminal panicles of showy white, yellow, or red flowers. Æ. Hippocastánum (the common horse-chestnut) is familiar to everyone. The seeds are large and farinaceous, and have been used as food for animals; they are bitter, and the bark also is bitter, astringent, and febrifugal. The tree is said to have been brought from Constantinople to England in the beginning of the sixteenth century, and is supposed to be a native of Northern Asia. Three other species are found in North America, where they are popularly known under the name of Buck-eye.

HORSE-FLY, the Hippobosca equina, a winged species of the family Hippoboscidæ, parasitic on the horse.

HORSE GUARDS, or under the present official designation 'The Royal Horse Guards (The Blues),' were raised by Charles II in 1661, the first muster parade taking place at Westminster in February of that year. The Earl of Oxford was the first Colonel. During the 260 years of its existence the title of the regiment has been considerably varied from time to time. Starting as the Royal Regiment of Horse, the word Guards was soon added, and a little later it was known as the 'Blew' Guards. Then, after several other variations of title had been used, it became the 'Oxford Blues,' and is at the present time invariably known as 'The Blues,' though its full official title is as above.

The Army List gives the uniform as "Blue, facings scarlet, plume red." Their cloak or overcoat is red instead of the more usual blue. In 1684 a contemporary publication quoted in

Packe's History of the 'Blues' describes the uniform as follows: "The private men are distinguished by their carbine belts with gold upon buff with a red edging; hooses and holster caps with the royal cypher embroidered upon blew, coated and cloaked blew, lined red. . . ." The arms at this period were a sword, carbine, and two pistols, horse and arms being provided by the troopers themselves. The well-known cuirasses still worn in full dress were first taken into use for ceremonial purposes in 1821.

The battle-honours borne by the regiment are: Dettingen; Warburg; Beaumont; Willems; Peninsula; Waterloo; Tel-el-Kebir; Egypt, 1882; Relief of Kimberley; Paardeberg; South Africa, 1899–1900. The height for recruits of The Blues should be between 5 feet 11 inches and 6 feet 1 inch, and the age between eighteen and twenty-five.

The appointment of Colonel (not to be confused with that of the actual commanding officer of the unit, who is a regimental lieutenant-colonel) of the Blues, in common with that of the

Badge of Horse Guards

two regiments of Life Guards, is conferred on distinguished officers of the highest rank, and carries with it the duty of serving as Gold-Stick-in-Waiting at court. In the case of the Blues this honour was granted in 1820, in which year, by the king's command, the Blues were admitted to the " position and full privileges of the

Household Cavalry," formerly only possessed by the two regiments of Life Guards.

The duties of Gold- and Silver-Stick were, according to a writer of 1743, to attend week by week "on the king's person on foot wheresoever he walks from his rising to his going to bed: and this is performed by one of the four captains, who always waits immediately next to the king's own person, before all others, carrying in his hand an ebony staff or truncheon with a gold head engraven with His Majesty's cypher and crown. Near him also attends another principal officer with an ebony staff and a silver head. . . ."

The duty of Silver-Stick is now performed by regimental field officers other than the colonels of the regiments of Household Cavalry. At the present time H.M. the King is Colonel-in-Chief of the Blues, and Field-Marshal Sir W. R. Robertson Colonel.

HORSENS, a seaport in Denmark, east coast of Jutland, on a fiord of the same name, 25 miles s.w. of Aarhuus. It has manufactures of tobacco and a good general trade. It is the birthplace of Vitus Bering, the discoverer of Bering Strait. Pop. (1930), 28,363.

HORSE-POWER, a unit of rate of doing work, or of supplying energy. An engine which is developing 33,000 foot-pounds of energy per minute is said to be working at 1 h.p. The horse-power is therefore in all cases found by dividing the number of foot-pounds of work done per minute by 33,000. The term was introduced by James Watt, and was intended to represent the ordinary rate of working of a good horse. Later experiments have shown that the output of the best horses does not exceed $\frac{4}{5}$ h.p. *Indicated horse-power* is the power delivered by the steam to the piston of a steam-engine, or by the hot gases to that of a gas-engine.

The power is measured by means of an indicator (q.v.), which draws a diagram showing the work done on the piston at each stroke. *Brake horse-power* is the horse-power output at the shaft of a steam-engine or an electric motor. This output is frequently measured and absorbed by applying a friction brake to a pulley on the shaft. The *horse-power hour* is a unit of energy equal to the work done at 1 h.p. in one hour. 1 h.p. = 746 watts. 1 h.p. hour = 0·746 kilowatt-hour, i.e. 0·746 kelvin. *See* DYNAMOMETER; UNIT.

HORSE-RACING. Whilst historical evidence is to hand of equestrianism having been established in this country before the Roman conquest, the earliest mention of race-horses is in the ninth century. In the reign of Henry II races were frequent exhibitions, but it was not until the time of James I that public races were to any considerable extent established, the best of which were called 'Bell courses' on account of the prize being a bell, from which circumstance has arisen the expression 'bearing the bell.'

James I built stables at Newmarket, which were rebuilt by Charles II, and again in the middle of the last century by the Rothschilds. The restoration of Charles II gave a great impetus to horse-racing, and the reward of bells was superseded by that of silver cups.

From James I onwards racing has indeed been the sport of kings. Most reigning monarchs have not only patronized the sport, but as actual owners have contributed to the democratic spirit of sport by competing enthusiastically in the more important events. Queen Anne at York in 1712 ran horses in her own name. The late King Edward VII, who as Prince of Wales won the Derby with Diamond Jubilee in 1900, was again successful with Minoru in 1909.

Horse-racing of some kind or another is practised in this country throughout the entire year. The varieties are flat-racing, steeple-chasing, hurdle-racing, and trotting matches. It will be convenient to dismiss the last named first as a variety which, whilst exceedingly popular in America, has never captured the fancy in this country and is patronized by very few enthusiasts.

The late Walter Winans, who died whilst actually driving in a trotting match, was exceedingly well known in this connection. A horse has trotted over 20 miles within an hour, and under exceptionally advantageous conditions in America has completed a mile in 1 minute 54$\frac{3}{4}$ seconds, but such speed has not been approached in this country.

A few general principles relating to race-horses will form a convenient introduction to the consideration of flat-racing. Flat-races are confined first to horses of a certain age, e.g. two-year-old or three-year-old, some for colts and fillies, or for fillies only. In these races the only handicap is what is known as sex allowance in racing parlance; thus colts carry 9 stones, fillies 8 stones 10 pounds.

The principal two-year-old races are the Woodcote Stakes at Epsom, the July Stakes, Middlepark Plate, and Dewhurst Plate run at Newmarket, the Coventry Stakes at Ascot, and the Champagne Stakes at Doncaster. All these races are open to colts and fillies, and the winners of the classic events in the following year are generally found among the runners. Two-year-olds cannot run in a race exceeding 6 furlongs until September. It must be observed that the age of a race-horse dates from the 1st of January, no matter the day of birth; so that foals born in May are yearlings on the 1st of January following, although really only seven months old.

To proceed to three-year-old races, there are five classic events—three open to colts and fillies, and two to fillies only. The three former are the Derby (1½ miles) at Epsom, the Two Thousand Guineas (1 mile) at Newmarket, and the St. Leger (1¾ miles) at Doncaster. The races for fillies only are the One Thousand Guineas (1 mile) at Newmarket, and the Oaks (1½ miles) at Epsom.

The Derby, 'the Blue Riband of the Turf,' is unquestionably the greatest sporting event in the world. It has been won only twice in the history of the race by French horses, viz. Gladiateur in 1865 and Durbar II in 1914. Recent winners of the Derby were Blenheim (Aga Khan) in 1930, Cameronian (Mr. J. A. Dewar) in 1931, April the Fifth (Mr. T. Walls) in 1932, Hyperion (Lord Derby) in 1933. The record time for this race is 2 minutes 34 seconds by Hyperion in 1933, but this, of course, does not mean that no faster horse has won the race, as many conditions affect the time. (Incidentally it may be noted that the record for 1 mile is 1 minute 33½ seconds at Lingfield in 1920.)

Whilst the form of every horse competing is intimately known and favourites predominate among those placed, it is interesting to note that three times in the history of the race the winner has been a 'rank outsider,' starting with odds of 100 to 1 against. As would be expected, many Derby winners are successful in the other classic races of their year. Although the Derby was not run during the years 1915 to 1918 inclusive, it was regarded as essential in the interests of horse-breeding to preserve the sport by a substitute race held at Newmarket, and the same procedure was adopted in the case of the other classic events.

As regards handicap events, these are arranged on two plans. The first is weight for age, and is based on the principle that a three-year-old improves a stone up till the age of four, so that in April a three-year-old carries 7 stones 8 pounds over a mile, a four-year-old 9 stones; in October the latter still carries 9 stones, the former now 8 stones 7 pounds. Naturally this system of handicapping leads to discrepant results, as horses do not improve automatically with age.

The principal three-year-old weight-for-age races are the Ascot Gold Cup (2½ miles), the Hardwick Stakes (1½ miles), both at Ascot, the Eclipse Stakes (1¼ miles) at Sandown, the Goodwood Cup (2½ miles) at Goodwood, the Doncaster Cup (2 miles) and the Jockey Club Stakes (1¾ miles) at Newmarket. Entries for these races are made two or more months before the event; for the classic events entries are made when the horses are yearlings.

The other system of handicapping is an attempt to offer an equal chance to all competing by inflicting the handicap of weight according to the horse's previous or estimated form. It is clear that on this account a great deal of opportunity is afforded to backers to study the previous form of a horse and its opponents, and estimate its chances in a subsequent race, bearing in mind its present handicap. The weights, as a rule, run from 9 stones down to 6 stones; the principal handicaps are the Cesarewitch (2½ miles), the Cambridgeshire (1 mile 1 furlong), both at Newmarket, the Lincoln Handicap, the City and Suburban, the Chester Cup, the Jubilee Cup, and the Manchester Cup, and a large number of others too numerous to mention.

Steeple-chases and hurdle-races are more usual in the winter months, the most important of all being the Grand National at Aintree, near Liverpool. This is over a course of 4 miles 1,000 yards with thirty jumps, the water-jump being 15 feet wide; yet such is the stamina of the steeple-chaser stock that the average winning time is as little as 10 minutes 13 seconds.

The chief racing meetings other than Newmarket and Epsom are Goodwood, which is a curiously private affair, the whole *mise en scène* belonging to the House of Richmond, the reigning representative of which can exercise his prerogative to permit the races to be run; Ascot, Sandown Park, Doncaster, and Chester. There is a big social element in these meetings, particularly Ascot and Goodwood.

The rules guiding flat-racing in Britain are framed by the Jockey Club, a body with absolute power, founded in 1750. A French Jockey Club performs the same function in France, where the principal races are the Prix de Diane (the French Oaks) and the Prix du Jockey Club (the French Derby), run in the spring at Chantilly, which is regarded as the Newmarket of France and is 25 miles from Paris; the Grand Prix de Paris, run at Longchamps in the Bois de Boulogne in June; and the Grand

Steeple de Paris, run at Auteuil, also in the Bois de Boulogne, in June.

Frequent meetings are held at Longchamps, Auteuil, St. Cloud, Maisons-Laffitte, &c.

The biggest price ever paid for a race-horse is 47,000 guineas (paid by Lord Glanely for Solario in July, 1932), but £30,000 has been paid on several occasions. The lightest jockey on record weighed only 2 stones 1 pound, an impossibility since 1860, when the minimum was fixed at 5 stones 7 pounds, and in any case the Education Act prevents boys under twelve from being engaged in a racing stable.

Even to the present day the reputation survives of Eclipse (foaled in 1764) as the fastest horse on record, although the speed attributed to this animal and to Flying Childers (1715) seems incredible in the light of accredited modern achievements.

The breeding and training of thoroughbreds is too complicated a subject to justify more than a passing mention. The recognition of certain strains and the suitability of admixture with others is an art which perhaps rests upon an empirical rather than a scientific basis, and many disappointments ensue as a consequence. In the same way many surprises are in store for a trainer.

Horses are not the mere machines which the general public is inclined very often to suppose. Some horses come to maturity very slowly and do not show any striking form until their fourth or fifth year; others reach maturity very quickly and are best as two-year-olds; others, again, seem at a critical period to find their form suddenly. And in these respects highly experienced trainers, like everybody else, are prepared for mistakes in either direction.

A feature of all horse races is the betting through bookmakers or by means of the totalisator, an electrically-worked machine which automatically records the number of bets on a given horse, and the amount of money that the winners receive.—BIBLIOGRAPHY: Sir John Dugdale Astley, *Fifty Years of Sport at Home and Abroad*; A. E. T. Watson, *The Racing World and its Inhabitants*; Finch Mason, *Heroes and Heriones of the Grand National*; T. A. Cook, *History of the English Turf*.

HORSE-RADISH (*Cochlearia Armoracia*), a cruciferous plant inhabiting the temperate parts of Europe, in moist situations. The root is cylindrical, whitish in colour, and forms a well-known condiment, possessing a pungent taste and odour. It is also employed medicinally, as a stomachic,

diaphoretic, and diuretic, and externally as a rubefacient.

HORSE-RADISH TREE, an Indian tree (*Moringa pterygosperma*) having pinnate leaves and long three-valved pod-like capsules, from which an oil called *ben-oil* is obtained. The fresh root has a pungent odour and warm taste, much like that of a horse-radish.

HORSESHOE, a shoe for horses, consisting commonly of a narrow plate of iron bent into a form somewhat resembling the letter U, so as to accommodate itself to the shape of the horse's foot. Horseshoes do not appear to have been known to the ancients, though there are a few references to shoes for mules (e.g. Catullus, *Carmen*, xvii, 26). Xenophon, Vegetius, and others mention various processes for hardening the hoofs so as to make them stronger, but say nothing of any protection like the horsehoe.

Iron horseshoes are mentioned as being in use in Europe in the ninth century of our era. They seem to have been introduced into England by the Normans. The belief in the horseshoe as a protection against evil spirits is widely spread in Germany, Scandinavia, Great Britain, and the United States. This belief is referred to by Butler in *Hudibras*: "Chase evil spirits away by dint Of sickle, horse-shoe, and hollow flint."

HORSESHOE VETCH (*Hippocrepis comosa*), a British leguminous herb, characteristic of chalky soils. It is not unlike bird's-foot trefoil, but the pods are very distinctive, being composed of many one-seeded joints, each curved into the shape of a horseshoe.

HORSE-TAIL, the general name of plants of the genus Equisetum, nat. ord. Equisetaceæ. The cuticle abounds in silica, on which account the stems of some species are used for polishing wood. *E. hiemāle*, the greater rough horse-tail or Dutch rush, is best fitted for that purpose, and is largely imported from Holland. Several species are natives of Britain.

HORSE-TAIL, among the Turks and other Eastern nations, the tail of a horse mounted on a lance, and used as a standard of rank and honour. The three grades of pashas were distinguished by the number of tails borne on their standards, three being allotted to the highest dignitaries or viziers, two to the governors of the more important provinces, and one to those of less important districts.

HORSFORTH, a town of England, West Riding of Yorkshire, on the Aire, 5 miles north-west of Leeds, with woollen manufactures, &c. (Urban district), Pop. (1931), 11,770.

HORSHAM, a town of England, in the county of Sussex, on a branch of the River Arun, 37½ miles s.s.w. of London, and 23 miles N.W. of Brighton, giving name to a parliamentary division of the county (Horsham and Worthing). Christ's Hospital, removed from London in 1902, is here. Pop. (1931), 13,579.

HORSHAM, town of Victoria, Australia. A railway junction, it is about 200 miles from Melbourne, and is the principal town of a sheep farming area. It is on the Wimmera river and has irrigation works. Pop. 4,700.

HORSLEY, Samuel, English bishop, born 1733, died 1806. He was educated at Cambridge, and in 1759 became rector of Newington Butts. In 1767 he was chosen a Fellow of the Royal Society, of which he was appointed secretary in 1773.

After several charges he was appointed in 1788 Bishop of St. David's, from which he was translated to Rochester in 1793, receiving at the same time the deanery of Westminster; and finally to St. Asaph in 1802, when he resigned his deanery. Dr. Horsley was the greatest theological controversialist of his day, and is famous for his controversy with Priestley on Unitarianism. He published numerous sermons, and several works on Biblical criticism, besides editing an edition of Sir Isaac Newton's works.

HORSLEY, Sir Victor Alexander Haden, British surgeon and neurologist, born at Kensington 14th April, 1857, died in Mesopotamia of heat stroke 16th July, 1916. He studied medicine at University College Hospital, London; was professor superintendent of the Brown Institution from 1884 to 1890; Fullerian professor at the Royal Institution from 1891 to 1893; professor of pathology, University College, from 1893 to 1896; and professor of clinical surgery at University College Hospital.

A specialist in facial surgery, he was surgeon to the National Hospital for Paralysis and Epilepsy from 1886 to 1916. He was knighted in 1902. During the European War he went to Mesopotamia in 1916, where he served as consultant to the British forces. He was one of the leaders of a medical movement against alcohol, and a champion of women's suffrage. His numerous works include: *Brain Surgery, Hydrophobia and its Treatment, Experiments upon the Functions of the Cerebral Cortex,* and *Alcohol and the Human Body* (with Dr. Mary Sturge).

HORTA, a town in the Island of Fayal, one of the Azores, on the shores of a small bay between two rocky headlands. It has a good harbour and exports wine, oranges, and grain. Pop. 6,057.

HORTENSIUS, Quintus, Roman orator, born of an equestrian family 114 B.C., died 50 B.C. He held many military and civil offices, and was elected Consul for the year 69 B.C. In the previous year he had been engaged to defend Verres during the famous prosecution in which Cicero acted for the accusers. Hortensius continued to maintain a generous and friendly rivalry with Cicero, acknowledging his superior oratorical powers without jealousy. His speeches are all lost.

HORTHY, Nicholas, Hungarian leader. Born 18th June, 1868, of a noble family, Nicholas Horthy de Nagybanya was educated for the navy, which he entered about 1884, and rose to command some cruisers during the Great War. He was given command of the Austro-Hungarian fleet in 1918 and made an admiral. During the troubles in Hungary that followed the War, he collected a force that drove the Bolshevist Bela Kun and his followers from the country and restored order. He was chosen regent in March, 1920, and held that position for the next 12 years.

HORTICULTURAL SOCIETIES, societies formed for the encouragement of both the art and the science of the cultivation of garden plants. The Royal Horticultural Society of London, the first of its kind, was founded by Sir Joseph Banks and others in 1804. It has about 13,000 members, associates, and fellows, and its research station is in the gardens at Wisley, Surrey, presented in 1903 by Sir Thomas Hanbury.

HORTICULTURE (from Lat. *hortus,* garden, and *colere,* to till), or **GARDENING,** includes, in its most extensive signification, the cultivation of esculent vegetables, fruits, and ornamental plants. It may be regarded as a specialized branch of agriculture, and in so far as it is concerned with flowers and shrubs differs from this in being of non-utilitarian character. In large gardens there are generally separate departments for flowers, fruits, and vegetables; but in small gardens they are usually more or less combined.

A garden should be either on a level, but admitting of effectual drainage, or on a gentle slope, preferably on the lower portion of a slope facing the sun. It should be well sheltered, either naturally from situation, or artificially by means of plantations, or walls. The character of the soil is of much importance. A good loam, or a sandy loam mixed with humus, is the best. The former is better fitted for fruit-trees, but for early crops the sandy loam is desirable. Whilst the greater part of a garden should consist of such soil, either naturally or artificially formed, it is useful to have a portion stronger and another much lighter in order to suit the requirements of different plants.

The nature of the subsoil is also important. The best is a dry bed of clay overlying sandstone. Digging, ploughing, and pulverizing the soil, and exposing the surface to the action of the summer sun and the winter's frost, are highly useful operations, by which the tenacity of stiff soils is overcome, weeds and insects are destroyed, and a quantity of air is admitted into the ground.

Nutritive matter is frequently supplied to plants in the form of manure, either organic or inorganic. After the soil is properly dry and pulverized, the seeds are deposited, and this should always be done in dry weather, for a dry soil is especially requisite for covering in the seeds. Watering is often necessary as a means of nourishment to growing plants, especially as a support to newly-transplanted vegetables, and for cleaning the leaves and destroying insects. The methods of propagating plants are various. For an account of the processes of budding and grafting see these articles. Another mode of propagation is that by means of cuttings, or shoots cut off and planted in the soil, where they take root. This process is exceedingly simple and easy in the case of many trees, as the willows and poplars; but requires some management in the heaths, myrtles, and other shrubs. When it is a question of producing new varieties, whether of vegetables or flowers, artificial cross-pollination is largely employed. Desirable 'sports' are also carefully picked out, and made the starting-point for new races. In growing ornamental plants and flowers and exotic fruits, plant-houses of various kinds are necessary. These comprise the numerous forms of conservatory, plant-stove, greenhouse, pits, and frames. The tools, implements, and machinery used are very various. The subject is now taught in agricultural colleges, and excellent textbooks, such as Thompson's *Gardener's Assistant*, exist.— BIBLIOGRAPHY: L. H. Bailey, *Standard Cyclopædia of Horticulture*; W. P. Wright, *Illustrated Encyclopædia of Gardening*; K. L. Davidson, *Gardens Past and Present*.

HORUS, the Latinized name of two Egyptian divinities. The elder was the son of Seb (identified by the Greeks with Kronos) and Nu (Rhea) and brother of Osiris. The other was the son of Osiris and Isis. On the death of Osiris he was his avenger, defeating the serpent Typho, and enabling Isis to thwart his wicked designs. Both the elder and the younger Horus were regarded as symbols of the sun.

HORWICH (ho'rich), a town (urban district) of England, in South Lancashire, 5 miles west by north o. Bolton, with cotton mills, dyeworks, railway works, collieries, quarries, &c. Pop. (1931), 15,680.

HOSANNA, a word composed of two Hebrew words occurring in *Psalm*

The God Horus

cxviii, 25, *hoshia-na*, signifying 'save now.' The psalm was sung on joyful occasions, and particularly at the Feast of Tabernacles. The phrase is used as an exclamation of praise to God, or an invocation of blessings. *Hosanna* is the cry with which Jesus was greeted at His last entry into Jerusalem.

HO'SEA, the first in order among the minor prophets of the Old Testament, but probably the third in order of time, flourishing about 750 B.C. Nothing is known of his life, except that he was the son of Beeri, and that his ministry belonged to the reigns of Uzziah, Jotham, Ahaz, and Hezekiah,

Kings of Judah. The nation generally and the ten tribes in particular are reproved, exhorted, and threatened in his prophecy. He predicts the approaching exile of his countrymen, and their subsequent return and greater prosperity.

HOSHANGÁBÁD, chief town and head-quarters of district of the same name, Central Provinces of India, on the Narbada. It is a chief seat of the British piece-goods trade, and does business in cotton and grain. Pop. 12,084.—The district has an area of 3,681 sq. miles, and a pop. of over 450,000.

HOSHIARPUR, chief town and seat of administration of district of same name, Punjab, India. Pop. 21,285.—The district has an area of 2,247 sq. miles, and a pop. of about 920,000.

HOSE refers to footwear used by ladies, the term half-hose being given to the socks worn by men. The chief divisions of the trade are as follows: *Seamless* hose are produced on circular machines and made automatically from start to finish, the toes and heels being worked in pocket form, and when the machine completes the article, all that is necessary is a short joining of raw loops across the toe. *Full-fashioned* hosiery is produced on flat machines where the article is made in a flat piece at double width, and the fullest interpretation is given to the shape of the article, narrowing in from calf towards the ankle and giving a heel and toe of adequate roominess.

By this system it becomes possible to make articles exactly to the required size and shape, but the flat piece has afterwards to be seamed down the back of the leg and along the foot. In regard to making the foot, there is the *French* style of foot, where a seam or join is made along the bottom of the instep, which creates a raised part due to the seaming thread at the part of the foot which is usually rather sensitive.

The *English* foot has the join made along each side of the foot, and the sole portion is thus left plain and gives greater comfort to the wearer. Certain types of hosiery, notably half-hose, are made with the top part in ribbed stitch to give a greater grip on the leg and keep the article in position, and till recently this has been made on a separate machine from the hose proper, having to be transferred or joined. Recent important improvements have made it possible for the rib top and the plain leg and foot to be made entirely automatically on one and the same machine. In the case of full-length hose the top is made

in two-ply fabric folded over, and this can be automatically turned and joined to the hose in the machine under the term of 'automatic welt.'

In the case of such materials as silk and artificial silk, it is now possible to make the heel, toe, and under part of the foot in a thicker count of woollen yarn, whilst the top of the foot and the leg are of silk. This is a much-valued improvement because the thicker yarn at the heel and along the sole of the article gives a much longer period of service, and the use of more expensive materials at those places is obviated. A type of hosiery recently introduced has the top of elastic material, making the use of stocking-suspenders unnecessary.

HOSE-PIPING, a heavily woven circular or seamless pipe, used extensively by the members of fire brigades and the like for conveying water to extinguish the fires of burning buildings. It is made invariably of linen or flax yarns, and woven on the double plain principle of weaving to obtain the circular section of cloth. Such fabrics are made both in hand looms and in power looms, the hand-made article being generally admitted to be the best, because the weft is beaten up both with the shuttle in the shed and out of it, and the renewals of weft are arranged for the ends to overlap each other.

Special types of looms, shuttles, and reeds are made for the weaving of hose-pipe, and the finished product must obviously be perfect if it is capable of sustaining the usual high pressure of water (500 to 1,000 lb. per square inch) from the mains. Both warp and weft yarns are level, multiple-ply, twice boiled, and beetled to ensure strength and flexibility. After the cloth is woven, it is steeped in a bath of copper sulphate, during which a shrinkage takes place; it is then dried in an artificially heated room. When the necessary unions and nozzles are fitted to the ends, the fire-hose is ready for use.

HOSIERY, a term which originally referred to the making of footwear, which was the first branch to be taken up in the knitted stitch. In recent years there has been a great extension of the use of this fabric for underwear, outer-wear, and intermediate garments, and all these various branches are loosely included under the generic term of hosiery. These extended uses of the knitted fabric have been made possible by the great improvements made in knitting machinery, where the original plain stitch has been elaborated so that fabrics of the most fancy description are produced.

Attachments have been made to

underwear and hose machines which make it possible to produce very intricate open or lace designs on garments intended for evening wear; shirtings have been greatly enhanced in their appearance by the use of vertical and horizontal stripes, and the Jacquard attachment has been adapted to producing lace and striped effects with the freest kind of floral patterns. The plain stitch in itself is often too thin and light for many purposes, but the devices added to most knitting-machines make it possible greatly to increase the weight and thickness of the fabric, thus achieving greater warmth and giving the fabric a much wider application than its use for footwear and underwear.

Fleecy-backed fabrics are largely employed for garments where a bulky handle and a soft brushed effect is required inside. There has recently been a great advance in the fine textures which can be produced on the knitting-machine, and the latest developments lie in the direction of the use of fine pure silk and artificial silk.

Hosiery-trade production is proving more and more a serious rival to the older industry of weaving, owing to the ease with which the fabric can be produced, and also to the fact that most manufacturers are in direct touch with the public and produce the garments ready-to-wear. The trade in knitted novelties such as knitted caps, ties, scarves, and vests is assuming ever larger proportions, and now forms a staple part of the clothing production of each season. The rawness with which the knitted stitch was formerly associated for certain classes of goods has been largely eliminated by the perfection of our present-day brushing machines, which can produce a nap on cotton goods to give them an appearance approaching wool; in woollen goods very elegant effects can be produced from long-fibred yarns worked in fancy colours, where the fibre is drawn to the surface to obscure the rawness of the loops and give a desirable *mélange* to the colour scheme.

The small-diameter knitting-machine has been greatly developed for the production of knitted ties, and a promising branch is that of making narrow tubular fabrics suitable for edging garments to enable them to keep their shape in wear; these can also be used with good effect as decorative agents in many types of garments.

An increasing trade is being done in knitted fabrics cut into costumes and blouses, and the material for this work is now sold in web form ready to be cut into garments similar to woven cloth; great advances have been made in trimming these gar-

ments so as to prevent abnormal stretching of the fabric during wear. The knitted stitch lends itself to the production of open gauzy textures, often used for indoor wear and for intermediate garments, calculated to increase the heat-retaining power of ordinary woven clothing.

HOSPITAL (Lat. *hospitalis*, pertaining to a host or entertainer), an institution for the treatment of disease and injuries, to which may be added the even more important functions of training doctors and nurses, and the prosecution of medical research. The term *infirmary* is sometimes used in a similar sense, but there is a tendency in Britain to restrict it to rate-supported institutions. Hospitals take origin from very remote times, and long before the Christian era a commencement in this direction was made in Greece, Egypt, and India. At a later period a number of them were founded in Bagdad by Harun-al-Rashid (A.D. 763–809).

In England a leper asylum was erected in London in 1118; St. Bartholomew's Hospital dates from 1123, and St. Thomas's from 1200. The last two institutions were the only metropolitan hospitals at the beginning of the eighteenth century, and the provinces were at that time still more backward in provision for the sick.

There are now over a dozen great general hospitals in London, making provision for cases of all kinds, and possessing more or less adequate arrangements for training and research; and a large number of smaller institutions, many of them devoted to special diseases, or meeting the medical requirements of women and children. The provinces are also, for the most part, well provided with hospitals, those in the more important centres having medical schools attached and engaging in medical research. The hospital system has also been adequately developed throughout the British Empire and in many foreign countries.

On the Continent and in the United States it is usual for hospitals to be subsidized and administered either by the State or by municipalities. This method not only prevents the work from being hampered and restricted by financial difficulties, but also enables an ordered system to be adopted for the convenience of the whole community, while at the same time economizing energy.

The doctors and nurses trained at one of our great general hospitals attain a higher standard from year to year, and the atmosphere of medical research prevents instruction from becoming sterile and stereotyped.

But the maintenance of the voluntary system will prove difficult if not impossible unless the finances of our hospitals are put on a thoroughly sound footing, and at the present time (1933) expenditure is in most cases far in advance of the income derived from endowments, grants, payments, subscriptions, and donations.

Hospitals were established at a time when the distinction between classes was very sharply marked, and their object was to relieve the sufferings of the extremely poor. Large numbers of patients do not now come under that category, and these are now required to contribute towards the cost of maintenance according to their means, the medical treatment remaining free. It is found that patients are not only willing but anxious to do this, and those among the professional and middle class unable to afford specialist treatment are availing themselves in increasing numbers of the facilities offered by hospitals, it being no longer a question of receiving 'charity.'

Some hospitals even have 'paying wards,' where the patient remains under no material obligation and greater privacy is secured than in ordinary wards. Payments by patients, however, though easing the situation, do not remove the necessity for a very large increase in subscriptions and donations, especially as it will always be necessary to provide for those unable to make even a small contribution.

King Edward's Hospital Fund, founded in 1897, has proved a great financial boon to London hospitals, and has also been a valuable check on methods of administration, for the conditions attached to grants and the comparisons made between institutions have undoubtedly promoted rigid economy in no small degree.

Those possessed of large means can do much for hospitals by endowing professorial chairs, research laboratories, wards, and beds; and it seems an anomaly that such endowments, when taking the form of bequests, should be subject to legacy duty. Valuable contributions are also made by such voluntary associations as the Hospital Sunday Fund and Hospital Saturday Fund, British Charities Association &c.; but by far the most important source of income consists of annual subscriptions given by firms and individuals, and of regular collections organized by employees.

In this respect a provincial city or town is fortunately situated, for it is a co-ordinated community in which co-operation is easily possible and conflicting claims are not too numerous. Leicester, for example, has been able to run its own medical services by well-organized concerted action. London, however, presents a gigantic problem for solution, and one of unique difficulty.

It may be that in course of time we shall see the metropolis properly organized into districts, each with its own great general or key hospital, associated with smaller institutions of more specialized kind. Much waste of force and overlapping would thereby be avoided.

We may take as an example the great and wealthy borough of St. Marylebone. For this the general hospital is the Middlesex Hospital (founded in 1745), with a flourishing medical school, cancer research laboratories, and the Bland Sutton Pathological Institution. There are also nine smaller hospitals of special character. Taken together, these ten institutions provide a complete system of medical services, which could easily be maintained and extended by the abundant resources of the borough.—BIBLIOGRAPHY: Sir H. Burdett, *Hospitals and Asylums of the World* (with supplements); Sir Douglas Galton, *Healthy Hospitals*; *Annual Reports* of individual hospitals.

HOSPITAL FEVER is fever arising in hospital on account of insanitary or septic conditions. It was at one time very common in hospitals, but is now extremely rare. Up to the middle of last century this name was also used for many cases of typhus fever.

HOS'PODAR, or GOSPODAR, a title of dignity formerly borne by the vassal princes of Moldavia and Wallachia from the fifteenth century to 1866, and in earlier times by the princes of Lithuania and the kings of Poland down to John Sobieski. The word is connected with *gospod* and *gospodin* in the various Slavonic languages, and meaning *master*.

HOST (Lat. *hostia*, a sacrificial victim), a term used for the bread (or wafer) and wine in the eucharist, as containing the body and blood of Christ. As the wafer alone is given to laymen in the Roman Catholic Church, as containing both the body and blood of the Redeemer, the term *host* is usually applied to the consecrated wafer. See ELEVATION; MASS; TRANSUBSTANTIATION.

HOSTAGE (O. Fr. `ostage`, Fr. *ôtage*), a person left as pledge or surety for the performance of the articles or conditions of a treaty. The taking or giving of hostages is now scarcely known in the relations of modern communities, but was formerly almost universal, and many questions in the law of nations arose out of the practice. If the stipulated terms were observed, the hostages were returned on each side, but if the terms were violated or evaded, the hostages might be put to death.

HOTCHKISS-GUN, a small machine gun used by cavalry and tanks. In action the Hotchkiss is easily concealed, and can be used in much the same way as an ordinary rifle, the calibre and ammunition used being the same. Normally three men form the gun detachment for firing purposes, but on emergency it can be worked by one man, and, carried dismounted, can hardly be distinguished from a rifle at a distance of a few hundred yards. It is, in fact, an automatic rifle, and its 'effective' range, i.e. from 1,400 to 600 yards, is considered to be the same as that of a Lee-Enfield. Its weight is 27 pounds, and it is therefore considerably lighter than an ordinary machine-gun, and consequently not so steady when firing.

The gun consists of two main portions, called respectively the stationary and the moving portion. Roughly speaking, the stationary portion consists of the barrel (herein differing from the Vickers-Maxim machine-gun), the body, the trigger mechanism, the cocking-handle, and the butt; while the moving portion comprises the piston-rod, the breech-block with firing-pin, the feed-piece, and the recoil spring. To load the gun the cocking-handle is brought into operation, and one end of a metal 'feed-strip' containing thirty cartridges inserted into the feed-piece. Then the pressure on the trigger sets the mechanism in motion, and the gun is fired.

After this two main forces act on the mechanism: the gases generated by the explosion of the cartridge working in a controlled direction act on the head of the piston-rod and force it back; this piston-rod is placed underneath the barrel, and in its backward journey it engages with a part of the feed-piece and moves it to the left, bringing a fresh cartridge into position; the piston-rod also acts on the breech-block and prepares it for firing.

When the piston-rod has reached its farthest back position, the recoil-spring takes charge and forces the piston-rod forward. In its forward journey the piston-rod again engages with the breech-block, which in its turn forces the cartridge presented by the movement of the feed-piece into the chamber, the firing-pin being released at the same moment and exploding the cartridge. The empty case of the preceding round is auto-matically withdrawn, and ejected through an aperture on the left of the gun during the first or backward movement of the piston-rod.

The mechanism of the gun is so arranged that by a simple adjustment it can be used for single shots or for continuous fire. In the former case the trigger must be pressed for each shot, while in the latter it is only necessary to retain a pressure on the trigger and the gun will fire as long as there are cartridges in the feed-piece.

Normally the gun is carried on a pack-horse led by a mounted man, while three other mounted men form the gun detachment proper. When necessary, the pack-horse can be dispensed with and the gun carried on the horse of one of the detachment. It can also be carried on a specially-fitted bicycle. When carried normally, the pack-horse also carries 1,200 rounds of ammunition and certain spare parts; more ammunition, making up a total of some 2,000 rounds all told, is carried on the horses of the detachment.

HOTCHPOT. in English law, a term applied to the act of a claimant on a fund, who, in order to be entitled to a share, brings into account payments previously made to him. Thus if a daughter A has received £2,000 from her father as a marriage portion, and a son B £3,000 to commence business, and if thereafter the father dies intestate leaving £10,000 and another child C, then if A and B desire to share in the estate they must bring into hotchpot the £5,000 they have received. The share of each child is then £5,000, of which A has already received £2,000 and B £3,000. A, therefore, now receives £3,000, B £2,000, and C £5,000.

HÔTEL DE VILLE, the French name for a town hall. The old Hôtel de Ville in Paris, begun under Francis I and completed under Henri IV in the sixteenth century, was destroyed in 1871 during the Commune. It was replaced by a new building, erected by the architects Ballu and de Perthes, which is one of the finest examples of modern architecture. It is in the French Renaissance style and rect-angular in shape. Its imposing façade is enriched with allegorical groups and statues typifying French cities.

HOTTENTOTS, a peculiar African people, supposed to be a cross between the Bushmen (the primitive aboriginal race of South Africa) and the Bantu negro. The most obtrusive evidence of the Bushman element is provided by the colour of the skin and the peculiar hypertrophy of the buttocks known as steatopygia. In former times they and the Bushmen are supposed to have occupied Africa as far north as the Victoria Nyanza; but they have gradually been pushed to the south by the Bantu and then north-west by the European settlers at the Cape.

When young they are of remarkable symmetry; but their faces are ugly, and this ugliness increases with age. The complexion is a pale olive, the cheek-bones project, the chin is narrow and pointed, and the face consequently is triangular. The lips are thick, the nose flat, the nostrils wide, the hair woolly, and the beard scanty.

When the Dutch first settled at the Cape in the middle of the seventeenth century, the Hottentots were a numerous nation, of pastoral and partially nomadic habits, and occupied a territory of 100,000 sq. miles. At the present day this race is nearly extinct within the wide territory which formerly belonged to it, having been entirely hunted out and dispersed by the Boers. Amongst the offshoots of the Hottentot race are the Griquas, descended from Hottentot mothers and Dutch fathers, giving name to the districts Griqualand East and West. They are semi-civilized, and have towns or villages.

The Koras or Korannas, about the middle of the River Orange, are favourable specimens of the Hottentot race. They are taller, stronger, and more cleanly than the tribes farther west. Other tribes are the Gonas or Gonaquas, much mixed with the Amakosa Kaffirs; the Namaquas, dwelling towards the mouth of the River Orange; the Hill Damaras, farther north. The Bosjesmen or Bushmen are a more primitive people than the Hottentots. Dr. Robert Broom is inclined to regard the Korannas, Bushmen, and Hottentots as distinct races, of which the Korannas are the most primitive. The language of the Hottentots is peculiar, consisting of a system of clicks or clucks.—BIBLIOGRAPHY: P. Kolben, *The Present State of the Cape of Good Hope*; Sir John Barrow, *Travels into the Interior of South Africa*; E. Holub, *Seven Years in South Africa*; G. W. Stow, *Native Races of South Africa*.

HOUDINI, Henry. American entertainer. Born in Wisconsin, 6th April, 1873, he became a locksmith. His extraordinary skill in freeing himself from handcuffs, locks and other impediments soon led him to give exhibitions on the variety stage in London, New York and elsewhere. He died 31st Oct., 1926. In 1931 a book, called *Houdini's Escapes*, explained how some of his feats were performed.

HOUGHTON (hō'tun), **Richard Monckton Milnes,** Lord, only son of Robert Pemberton Milnes, of Fryston Hall and Great Houghton, was born in Yorkshire in 1809, and died in 1885. Educated at Cambridge, he made some reputation as a writer of verse, essays, memoirs, &c., but it was rather his social and conversational powers, and his kindly patronage of literary aspirants, than the merit of his writings which gave him his prominent position in London society. In 1837 he entered Parliament as member for Pontefract, at first as a Tory, but afterwards as a supporter of Russell and Palmerston.

He was an active member of numerous learned societies and institutions, president of the Royal Society of Literature, trustee of the British Museum, and foreign secretary of the Royal Academy. The best-known work by Lord Houghton is his *Life of Keats* (1848), in which he finally removed many popular misconceptions about the poet.

HOUGHTON, village of Norfolk. It is famous for its hall and its associations with the Walpoles. Sir Robert Walpole, who was born here, built the enormous hall. Houghton is now the seat of the Earl of Rocksavage, but the pictures collected by Walpole have been sold. In the park is the village church, which contains the tombs of Walpole and his famous son, Horace.

HOUGHTON-LE-SPRING, a market town of England, in the county of Durham, 6¾ miles N.E. of Durham. Its prosperity depends on the numerous coal-mines in the neighbourhood. Bernard Gilpin was rector of the parish from 1556 to 1583. Houghton-le-Spring gives name to a parliamentary division of the county. Pop. (1931), 10,492.

HOUND (*Canis sagax*), a name given generally to hunting dogs; but restricted by scientific writers to such as hunt by scent, a definition which excludes the greyhound. Amongst the varieties are the bloodhound, stag-hound, foxhound, harrier, and beagle. Hounds are distinguished not only by their fineness of scent, but by docility and sagacity. Of the rough-haired and smooth-haired varieties the former manifest the greater affection for man.

HOUNSLOW, a town of England, in Middlesex, 9 miles south-west of Hyde Park Corner, London. There are many market gardens. The adjoining Hounslow Heath, once notorious for the highway robberies committed on it, is now entirely enclosed, and is the site of cavalry barracks and powder-mills. Pop.

(Heston and Isleworth urban ditricts, 1931), 75,446.

HOU-PE, HU-PEH, or **HOO-PE** (North of the Lakes), a central province of China. It is intersected by the Han-Kiang and the Yangtze Kiang, and is considered one of the most fertile parts of the republic. Area, 71,428 sq. miles; pop. 28,616,576.

HOUR, the twenty-fourth part of a day. In most countries the hours are counted from midnight to midday, and twelve hours are twice reckoned. Some Continental and British foreign military time is reckoned as 24 hours, one day; e.g. 8 a.m. is written 0800 hours, and 9 p.m. would be stated as 2100; 9.30 p.m., 2130 hours, &c. See DAY; TIME.

HOUR-GLASS, an instrument for measuring time, consisting usually of two hollow bulbs placed one above the other, and having a narrow neck of communication through which a certain quantity of dry sand, water, or mercury is allowed to run from the upper to the lower bulb, the quantity of sand being adjusted so as to occupy an hour in passing from one bulb to the other. The hour-glass was commonly used in churches during the sixteenth and seventeenth centuries to regulate the length of the sermon.

HOURIS (hou'riz or hŏ'riz), the 'black-eyed' nymphs of Paradise, whose company, according to the *Koran*, is to be one of the rewards of the faithful. They are described as most beautiful virgins, endowed with perpetual youth, and subject to no impurity. They are made not of clay, but of musk, saffron, incense, and amber. They dwell in beautiful gardens, by flowing streams, and the very meanest of the faithful will have at least seventy-two of them. Later Mahommedan theologians endeavoured to give an allegorical explanation of the houris.

HOUSE. In point of law, the common expression, "an Englishman's house is his castle," is in most instances true. Except where there has been a criminal offence, an Englishman can hold his house against all comers. No bailiff can break open his door to arrest him, or to seize his goods for debt, nor can any court give him this power; but if a bailiff is once permitted to enter he cannot be expelled. Scottish law does not give the householder such a strong position. A Scottish court can give a messenger permission to force a door, and arrest or distrain as may be wished. Breaking into a house by night with the intent to rob is *burglary*.

HOUSE, Edward Mandell. American politician. Born at Houston, Texas, 26th July, 1858, he was educated at Newhaven and at Cornell University. He played an active part in the public life of Texas where he lived as a planter for over 30 years. Known as Colonel House, he became through his attachment to President Wilson, an influential figure in the political life of America, but never held office. He became associated with Wilson as confidential adviser when the latter was governor of New Jersey, and continued to serve him on very important missions during Wilson's presidency, including negotiations with regard to the Panama tolls and the Pan-American pact with the A.B.C. republics of Latin America (Argentine, Brazil, and Chile). In 1914, as an intimate friend of President Wilson, he was sent to Europe to collect information and in 1917, when the United States entered the war, he represented his country in Paris. He attended the Peace Conference, when the breach of his relations with Wilson began. He retired into private life after Wilson's death. In 1926–28 there appeared *The Intimate Papers of Colonel House.*

HOUSEBREAKING, in English law, is the crime of breaking and entering into a house or other building with intent to commit a felony therein or breaking out of such a place if a felony has been committed. 'Breaking and entering' are constituted by forcibly picking a lock or smashing a window or by any mode of entry without force, which, however, necessitates displacing some part of the building, e.g. lifting a latch. Housebreaking is punishable by 14 years' penal servitude. Breaking into a dwelling-house by night (i.e. between the hours of 9 p.m. and 6 a.m.) is burglary.

HOUSE-FLY. See FLY.

HOUSEHOLD SUFFRAGE, suffrage based on the occupancy of a house or a distinct part of a house. For the details governing franchise qualifications, *see* REPRESENTATION OF THE PEOPLE ACT.

HOUSELEEK (*Sempervivum tectōrum*, nat. ord. Crassulaceæ), a succulent plant, common in Britain, and growing on old walls, the roofs of cottages. &c. The stem rises to the height of 8 or 10 inches, and bears a few purplish flowers, which have twelve or fifteen petals. The leaves are sometimes applied to bruises and old ulcers.

HOUSEMAID'S KNEE, acute inflammation of the bursa or sac between the knee-pan and the skin, so called because it is common amongst housemaids from their kneeling on hard floors. But it may occur in anyone whose knee is exposed to repeated irritation. It usually develops suddenly, and the knee becomes hot, swollen, and tender. It is treated like other local inflammations by rest and fomentations in the early stages. But if neglected it may result in the formation of an abscess, which is liable to involve the bone or even the joint.

HOUSE OF COMMONS. *See* PARLIAMENT.

HOUSE OF LORDS. *See* PARLIAMENT.

HOUSING. The problem of housing existed long before the European War of 1914–8, and its origin may be found in the industrial revolution which, beginning in the later part of the eighteenth century, led to the sudden growth of small villages into industrial centres with large populations.

To accommodate these masses, houses were erected without regard to any plan or system. The result was overcrowding, congested housing, and insanitary conditions.

Legislation for housing reform dates from the middle of the nineteenth century. The earlier measures were mainly of a negative character, and gave public authorities power to proceed against the owners of bad property for the removal of nuisances. Then in 1874 they were allowed to grant or lease land for the erection of workmen's dwellings, and in the following year, under the Cross Act, authority was given to them to undertake large housing schemes.

The Housing of the Working Classes Act of 1890 followed. Part I of the Act deals with great clearance and re-housing schemes to be carried out by local authorities; Part II provides for the improving and suppression of the insanitary conditions of single houses or small slums; Part III gives local authorities powers to acquire land by compulsory purchase and contract loans for the erection of new dwellings. Little use was, however, made of the powers given until after 1900.

The Housing and Town Planning Act of 1909 extended the powers already given, and strengthened the hands of the Government for enforcing execution of the Housing Acts.

In the earlier attempts at dealing with the problem of housing nothing was done in the way of laying down rules to guide the development of sites. It was only after 1890, and still more after the Act of 1909, that 'town planning' really came to the fore.

Port Sunlight was started in 1887, and Bournville developed from 1894 onwards. In 1903 the first 'garden city' was started at Letchworth, and in 1904 the Hampstead Garden Suburb was established. The Acts of 1909 and of 1931 (The Town and Country Planning Act of 1931 particularly) gave further encouragement to this movement. *See* GARDEN CITIES; INDUSTRIAL VILLAGES.

One consequence of the European War was that the housing problem was much accentuated, for building stopped almost entirely for five years.

An Act was passed by Dr. Addison (then Minister of Health) in July, 1919, which placed on local authorities an obligation to see that provision was made for the whole working-class needs of their district, their liability being limited to the produce of a penny rate, any additional deficit to be met by the State.

A minimum standard of accommodation had to be provided. Model plans of houses were issued by the Ministry of Health as a guide to local authorities and architects to the type of accommodation and general arrangement to be adopted. Architects were encouraged to suggest alternative types of plans, especially those which could be adopted at economical prices.

Model specifications for houses, streets, by-roads, &c., were also prepared, but variations suitable to local needs were permitted. The number of houses to the acre was in the first instance limited to twelve, but in some cases up to twenty houses per acre were sanctioned. Local authorities were required to prepare housing schemes and submit them for approval to the Ministry of Health. The Government passed legislation to secure that the necessary land should be acquired on the most economical basis.

Progress was, however, slow. Local authorities hesitated to proceed with building owing to the excessive cost involved. The price of each house was abnormally high for many reasons. Building materials had risen greatly in price and continued to rise.

By the end of 1919 the actual number of houses started was negligible, and the Government had to offer further inducements. Before the European War 95 per cent of working-class dwellings were built by private enterprise, which stopped during the war.

In order to encourage resumption of private building the Government offered a subsidy of £150 on the average to anyone who built a house of an approved type within twelve months. (The period was subsequently extended and the amount of the subsidy increased to £260 for a five-roomed house.) Powers were also given to local authorities to prevent 'luxury' building and an agreement was made with employers in the building trade that a certain proportion of work undertaken by them should be on housing schemes.

Still little advance was made. In order to remedy the shortage of labour steps were taken to introduce 'dilutees' into the building trade. To this the trade unions were strongly opposed. They were not prepared to admit unskilled men with a few months' training to work alongside skilled craftsmen. All attempts at negotiation failed and finally the Government agreed with the employers to enforce the introduction of 50,000 ex-service men into the ranks of building-trade labour.

On the labour side of the problem interesting experiments were also made in the form of the employment of labour direct by local authorities, who endeavoured to dispense with the services of contractors; and the organization of the Building Guild, which was started in Manchester, and whose object was to enable groups of building-trades workers to contract with local authorities direct for the building of houses, the saving which it was hoped would be made by the elimination of the contractors' profits to be devoted partly to reducing cost and partly to improving conditions of employment. The Addison scheme produced 175,000 builders in England and Wales.

The Chamberlain Housing Act of 1923 was intended merely to encourage private enterprise, and provided an annual subsidy over a period of 20 years, while the Wheatley Housing (Financial Provisions) Act of 1924 aimed at the production of working-class houses at a rent within the reach of working people. It increased the subsidies for houses in agricultural areas to £12 10s. per year for 40 years and to £9 in other areas. A Housing Act of 1925 presented in consolidated form the existing permanent law regarding the housing of the working classes. The subsidy was reduced in 1926 and again in 1928. As a result there was a fall in the number of houses built, and the standard of housing also declined. To stimulate building again the Labour Government when it took office in 1929 immediately passed an Act to prevent further cuts in the Wheatley subsidies then about to be made. In 1930 two new Acts for England and Scotland, introduced a new principle by providing subsidy for 40 years towards the cost of new houses which displaced slum dwellings, the subsidy depending not on the number of houses built, but upon the number of persons rehoused. Slum-clearance schemes under previous legislation had provided a great quantity of houses and the 1930 Act opened up a prospect of steady improvement, as local authorities covering about ⅗th of the population of England and Wales prepared programmes for the provision of about 340,000 houses by these authorities in the next five years. A Rural Housing Act was also passed by the Labour Government in 1931 which provided a State grant of £2,000,000 for the provision of 40,000 working-class houses in rural areas.

The Housing (Financial Provisions) Act, 1932, initiated by the National Government greatly reduced these housing programmes and slowed down the rate of progress. The 1932 Acts brought all subsidies to an end, except in respect to slum-clearance schemes under the 1930 Act, and left to private enterprise the various tasks of building houses; a State guarantee being provided in respect of advances made by Building Societies to individuals for the building of working-class houses; standards of housing have been lowered.

HOUSMAN, Alfred Edward, English scholar and poet. Born 26th March, 1859, he was educated at Bromsgrove School and S. John's College, Oxford. Professor of Latin in University College, London, from 1892, he was in 1911 made Fellow of Trinity and Professor of Latin at Cambridge. He has published two volumes of unique poetry, *The Shropshire Lad* (1896), a series of 63 ballad-like poems on country life, and *Last Poems* (1922), both marked by their flawless style, economy of diction, melody and unflinching realism. He has also edited some volumes of classical works.

HOUSMAN, Laurence, British novelist, poet, and artist, born 18th July, 1865. He studied art at South Kensington, and began his career as an illustrator. He illustrated George Meredith's poem *Jump-to-Glory Jane,* Shelley's *The Sensitive Plant,* and Christina Rossetti's *Goblin Market.* As a poet, Housman is a mystic, and the influence of Rossetti is clearly noticeable in his poems. Housman also wrote symbolical and allegorical tales, novels, and plays. His works include: *A Farm in Fairyland* (1894); *Gods and their Makers* (1897); *An Englishwoman's Love-Letters* (1900), which, published anonymously, met with great success; *Bethlehem* (1902); *Prunella* (1906); *Lysistrata* (1910); *The Royal Runaway* (1914); *The*

Sheepfold (1918); *Ploughshare and Pruning-hook* (1919); *Trimblerigg* (1924); *The Duke of Flamborough* (1928); *Palace Plays* (1930).

HOUSSA, or **HAUSA** (hous'a), a people of Africa, in the Sudan, between lat. 11° and 14° N., and long. 4° and 11° E. They are negroes with much admixture of other races, such as Tauregs, Berbers, &c. The country of the Houssas, or the Houssa States, is included in Northern Nigeria, is generally fertile, and skilfully cultivated.

It was brought under the rule of the Fellatahs, who subjected the natives, the Hausana or Houssas. They are intelligent and lively, expert weavers as well as agriculturists, and well acquainted with tanning and working in iron. Their language is rich and sonorous, and has become the general medium of commercial intercourse in Central Africa. They are Mahommedans. The country contains Gando and other large towns.—BIBLIOGRAPHY: C. H. Robinson, *Hausaland : Fifteen Hundred Miles through the Central Soudan*; *Hausa Dictionary*.

HOUSTON, a town of the United States, in Texas, capital of Harris county, at the head of steamboat navigation in Buffalo Bay, 48 miles north-west of the important seaport of Galveston, and the great railway centre of the state. There are many churches and schools including the Rice Institute. It stands in an excellent grazing district, and contains iron-foundries, cotton-presses, machine-shops, and other industrial establishments. It is a great shipping port for cotton. Pop. (1930), 292,352.

HOVAS (more correctly the Antimerina), one of the elements of the population of Madagascar, characterized by a strong infusion of Malay blood.

HOVE, a borough and wateringplace of Sussex, England, practically joined to Brighton. It has all the attractions of a first-class holiday resort, and is extremely popular. Here the Sussex Cricket Club has its grounds. The area of the borough was extended in 1928. Pop. (1931), 54,994.

HOVEDEN, Roger de, an English historian, who probably received his name from Hoveden or Howden, in Yorkshire. The exact dates of his birth and death are unknown, but he flourished in the reign of Henry II, and, entering the Church, was for some time professor of theology at Oxford.

After the death of Henry he applied himself to compiling in Latin a general history of England entitled *Chronica*, commencing at 731, the period at which Bede finished, and bringing down affairs to 1201. An English translation by H. T. Riley has been published in Bohn's *Antiquarian Library*.

HOVER-FLY, a member of the family of the Syrphidæ, popularly known as hoverers, hawk-flies, and drone-flies.

HOW'ARD, the patrician house that has been for centuries at the head of the English nobility. The first of the family of whom anything is certainly known is Sir William Howard, Chief Justice of the Common Pleas under Edward I and Edward II. His grandson, Sir John Howard, possessed extensive property in Norfolk, and was also sheriff of the county.

His grandson, Sir Robert Howard, by marrying the co-heiress of the Mowbrays, Dukes of Norfolk, greatly increased the family possessions, and enhanced the family importance. Their only son, Sir John Howard, distinguished himself in the wars with France in 1452–3, and in 1470 was created Lord Howard, and made Captain-General of the Royal Forces at Sea.

Adhering to the fortunes of Richard III, he was in 1483 created Duke of Norfolk, and elevated to the high dignity of Earl-Marshal of England, but two years after he was killed at Bosworth Field, and his blood and honours were attainted by Parliament, 1485. A like attainder was decreed against his son Thomas, who had been created Earl of Surrey by Richard. Thomas, however, was restored to his titles and possessions, manifested high military talent, and distinguished himself, especially by his defeat of James IV of Scotland at Flodden in 1513.

His son Thomas, third Duke of Norfolk, obtained distinction both as a naval and military commander, and became High-Admiral of England. But in spite of his services both at home and against the Scots and the French, Henry VIII at last condemned him, on slight grounds, to suffer the death of a traitor.

The death of Henry prevented the execution, and he was reinstated in his rank and property by Queen Mary, and died in Aug., 1554. By his marriage with a daughter of Edward IV he became the father of the illfated and accomplished Henry Howard, Earl of Surrey, the best English poet of his age. (*See* SURREY, EARL OF.) Thomas, fourth Duke of Norfolk, entertained the project of marrying Mary Queen of Scots, which led to him being convicted of high treason, and beheaded in 1572. The attainder was reversed and the family honours restored, partly by James I and partly by Charles II.

The ducal House of Norfolk has thrown out many branches which have enjoyed, or still enjoy, the earldoms of Carlisle, Suffolk, Berkshire, Northampton, Arundel, Wicklow, Norwich, and Effingham, and the baronies of Bindon, Howard de Walden, Howard of Castle Rising, and Howard of Glossop.

As connected with this noble family we may mention Lord Howard of Effingham, who defeated the Spanish Armada in 1588; Catherine Howard, one of the ill-fated consorts of Henry VIII; and Sir Thomas Howard, who died in the Tower a prisoner, for having aspired to the hand of the Lady Margaret Douglas, daughter of Margaret, Queen-Dowager of Scotland, and niece of Henry VIII. "The blood of the Howards" has become proverbial, as expressive of ancient lineage combined with high rank.—Cf. Brenan and Statham, *The House of Howard*.

HOWARD, John, English philanthropist, was born in 1726, and died in 1790. His father, a wealthy London tradesman, died when his son was about nineteen years of age, and left him an immense fortune. In 1756 Howard undertook a voyage to Lisbon to view the effects of the recent earthquake. The vessel in which he embarked being captured, he was consigned to a French prison. The hardships he suffered and witnessed previous to his release first roused his attention to the subject of his future researches.

In 1773 he resolved to devote his time to the investigation of the means of correcting the existing abuses in the management of prisons. With this view he visited most of the English county jails and houses of correction, and in March, 1774, he laid the result of his inquiries before the House of Commons, for which he received a vote of thanks. In 1775 and 1776 he visited many of the Continental prisons, as well as those of Scotland and Ireland; and the substance of his investigations appeared in a work he published in 1777 (*State of the Prisons in England and Wales, with an Account of some Foreign Prisons*).

This work was supplemented by his experiences of foreign prisons (1778–83). In 1789 he published an *Account of the Principal Lazarettos in Europe*, with notes on Continental and British prisons and hospitals. In the same year he made a final journey through Germany and Russia, when prisons and hospitals were everywhere thrown open for his inspection as a friendly

monitor and public benefactor. He died of fever at Kherson in South Russia.

HOWDEN, market town of Yorkshire (E.R.). It is 21 miles from Hull, on the L.N.E. Rly. There is an aerodrome here. Roger of Hoveden, who wrote a chronicle of English history from 732 to 1201, was born here. Pop. 2,052.

HOWDENSHIRE, one of the three parliamentary divisions of the East Riding of Yorkshire.

HOWE, Elias, an American inventor, was born in Spencer, Massachusetts, in 1819, died at Brooklyn in 1867. He constructed a sewing-machine in 1846, and was for several years involved in expensive and harassing lawsuits to establish his right to reap the benefits of his own ingenuity. He received the gold medal and the cross of the Legion of Honour at the Paris Exhibition of 1867.

HOWE, Richard, Earl Howe, English admiral, was the second son of Emmanuel Scrope, second Viscount Howe, and was born in 1725, died 1799. He joined the navy at the age of fourteen, and served under Anson till 1745, when, though only twenty years of age, he obtained the command of the *Baltimore* sloop of war, in which he took part in the siege of Fort William, during the last Jacobite rebellion. In 1758 he reduced Cherbourg, and in the same year succeeded to the title of Viscount Howe. Having greatly distinguished himself on many occasions, and risen to be Vice-Admiral of the Blue, he was in 1782 created an earl.

In the course of the same year he sailed to the relief of Gibraltar, which he effected in spite of the combined fleets of the enemy. In 1783 he accepted the post of First Lord of the Admiralty, which, with a partial intermission, he continued to hold until 1793, when, on the breaking out of the war with France, he took the command of the British fleet, and bringing the enemy to an action on 1st June, 1794, he obtained over them a decisive victory, for which he received the thanks of Parliament and other honours. In 1797 Lord Howe exerted himself with great success to quell the mutiny among the seamen at Portsmouth.—Cf. Sir J. K. Laughton, *From Howard to Nelson—Twelve Sailors*.

HOWELLS, William Dean, an American novelist, born at Martinsville, Ohio, in 1837, died 11th May, 1920. He learned the printer's trade with his father; was afterwards assistant editor on the *Ohio State Journal*;

published a life of Abraham Lincoln and a volume of poems; and was appointed in 1861 United States Consul at Venice. On his return to America in 1865 he joined the staff of the *Nation*, became afterwards editor of the *Atlantic Monthly* (1871–81), but made himself known chiefly as a writer of novels. Amongst his works are: *Venetian Life* (1866); *Italian Journeys* (1867); *A Chance Acquaintance* (1873); *A Foregone Conclusion* (1874); *The Lady of the Aroostook* (1879); *Dr. Breen's Practice* (1883); *A Modern Instance* (1883); *The Rise of Silas Lapham* (1885); *Indian Summer* (1886); *The World of Chance* (1893); *The Landlord of the Lion's Head* (1897); *Their Silver Wedding Journey* (1899); *Heroines of Fiction* (1908); *My Mark Twain: Reminiscences and*

Howitzer, B.L. 9·2-inch howitzer in firing position

Criticisms (1910); *The Vocation of the Kelwyns* (1920).

HOWITT, Mary, English writer, born 1799, died in 1888. She was the daughter of Mr. Botham, a Quaker, and was married in 1823 to William Howitt. Mary Howitt wrote a number of hymns and ballads, several volumes in prose and verse for children, and translated Miss Bremer's works and H. C. Anderson's *Improvisatore*.

Amongst her writings for the young may be mentioned *The Children's Year*, *The Dial of Love*, and *A Treasury of Tales for the Young*. In conjunction with her husband, she also wrote *The Literature and Romance of Northern Europe*, and *Ruined Abbeys of Great Britain*. Six years before her death she joined the Roman Catholic Church. In 1879 she received a Civil List pension of £100.

HOWITT, William, born in 1792 of a Quaker family, died in 1879. He began early to publish verses, and in conjunction with his wife (*see* above article) published shortly after their

marriage a volume of poems—*The Forest Minstrel* (1823). In 1831 appeared his *Book of the Seasons*, in 1834 his *History of Priestcraft*, and in 1838 his popular *Rural Life in England*.

In 1840 the Howitts settled at Heidelberg, and devoted themselves to introducing the literature of the north, especially of Sweden, to English readers. *Student Life in Germany* appeared in 1841, *Rural and Domestic Life in Germany* in 1842. In 1847 Howitt published his *Homes and Haunts of the British Poets*, and, after a visit to Australia, his *Land, Labour, and Gold*; and *The History of Discovery in Australia*. He also wrote a *History of England*. Afterwards both Howitt and his wife became converts to spiritualism.

HOWITZERS are artillery weapons of comparatively low muzzle velocity, but with a high trajectory. To obtain this high trajectory at all ranges it is necessary to have varying charges. These charges are small compared with those of guns; howitzers are therefore short-barrelled weapons with great shell power compared to guns of similar weight. Their range is less than that of guns of similar calibre.

The steep angles of departure and descent make them especially suitable for employment in close or mountainous country, and to engage targets that are in ground 'dead' to guns with a flat trajectory.

Their great shell power renders them specially adapted for the destruction of strong points—batteries, entrenchments, fortifications, &c.

Owing to the low velocity of their shell, shrapnel cannot be fired effectively from howitzers, but high-explosive shell with instantaneous fuse makes them effective weapons against troops in the open.

Howitzers are generally classed as follows: (1) Pack howitzers carried on mules, ponies, &c., are invaluable in mountainous or enclosed country, or for the close support of infantry. (2) Field-howitzers form the bulk of the howitzers with a field-army. (3) Medium howitzers for the destruction of stronger works, and for counter-battery work. (4) Heavy and super-heavy howitzers for the destruction of strong defences, fortifications, &c. The Germans used a 17-inch howitzer to reduce the fortresses of Namur and Maubeuge.

Field-howitzers are at present horse-drawn, though horses are likely to be replaced in the future by some form of light mechanical tractor. Medium howitzers are sometimes horse-drawn and sometimes mechanically drawn. Heavy and super-heavy howitzers are all drawn by some form of mechanical transport, or are mounted on railway mountings.

HOWLER MONKEY (Mycētes), a genus including six species of Central and South American monkeys, characterized by a remarkable loudness of voice, which is due to the presence of a large chamber within the hyoid bone and the enlargement of the ventricles of the larynx. In the tropical forests of America their hideous howls (probably meant to alarm their enemies) may be heard during the night more than a mile away. They are prehensile-tailed, large, and heavy of body, with a high pyramidal head flattened on the summit.

HOWRAH, a town of India, on the right bank of the Hugli, opposite Calcutta, of which it is practically a suburb, and with which it communicates by a floating bridge. It has large dockyards, jute and sawmills, and various manufactories. Pop. 222,488.

HOXTON, district of London. In the N.E. of the city, it is in the borough of Shoreditch. It includes De Beauvoir Town. The chief industry is cabinet making.

HOY, an island of the Orkneys, Scotland, separated from the mainland of Scotland by the Pentland Firth, and from the largest island of the Orkneys, known as Mainland, by the Sound of Hoy. It is about 13 miles long and 6 miles broad; mountainous and heathy, but with fertile

Red Howler Monkey

tracts. It has an excellent harbour, Long-Hope. At the south-west of the island there is a detached pillar of rock 450 feet high, known as the Old Man of Hoy. Other natural features are the Dwarfie Stone, mentioned by Scott in *The Pirate*, and Ward Hill (156 feet), which is of interest to botanists. Pop. (1931), 264.

HOYLAKE, an English watering-place in Cheshire, at the entrance of the Dee estuary, with one of the championship golf-courses, race-course, and various attractions for visitors. It forms part of the urban

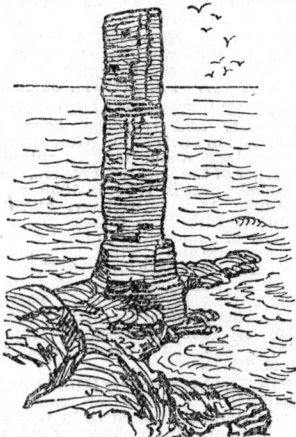

The Old Man of Hoy

district of Hoylake and W. Kirby. Pop. (1931), 16,628.

HUBER, François, a Swiss naturalist, born in 1750, died in 1831. Notwithstanding the loss of his eyesight, he was able, by the help of his wife and his reader and amanuensis, to make observations and deductions which constitute decidedly the most important contribution by any one man to our knowledge of bees. His first work was published in 1792 under the title of *Lettres à Ch. Bonnet*. Four years after his *Nouvelles Observations sur les Abeilles*, practically a new edition, enlarged and amended, of the other, appeared. His son Pierre also assisted his father, and himself published important observations on ants.

HUBERT, ST., the Apostle of Ardennes, a saint of the Roman Catholic Church, the patron of huntsmen, and the healer of hydrophobia. He was of a noble family of Aquitaine. While hunting in the forests of Ardennes he had a vision of a stag with a shining crucifix between its antlers, and heard a warning voice. He was converted, entered the Church, and eventually became Bishop of Maestricht and Liége. He worked many miracles, and is said to have died in A.D. 727 or 730.

HUBERTUSBURG, formerly a hunting seat of the Electors of Saxony, in the Leipzig district, now enlarged and divided into portions, used respectively as a public prison, a hospital, a lunatic asylum, &c. Here the Peace of Hubertusburg, ending the Seven Years' War. was signed on 15th Feb., 1763.

HUBLI, or **HOOBLY,** a town of India, in Dharwar district, Bombay Presidency, a great centre of the cotton trade. Pop. (1931), 69,206.

HUC (ük), **Evariste Régis,** French missionary and traveller, born in 1813, died in Paris 1860. After studying theology, about 1837 he entered the order of the Lazarist Fathers, was ordained priest in 1838, in 1839 went to China as a missionary, and in company with Père Gabet, made a journey of exploration in the interior of the empire and of Tibet. After this he returned in broken health to France, where he published *Souvenirs d'un Voyage dans la Tartarie, le Thibet, et la Chine pendant les Années* 1844, 1845, *et* 1846; *L'Empire Chinois* (1857); and *Le Christianisme en Chine* (1857).

HUCKNALL, formerly **HUCKNALL TORKARD,** a town of England, Nottingham, 6 miles north by west of Nottingham, with a church, restored in 1873, in which Lord Byron is buried. Coal-mining and other industries are carried on. Pop. (1931), 17,338.

HUDDERSFIELD, a borough and manufacturing town, in the West Riding of Yorkshire, England, 15 miles south-west of Leeds. The plan of the town is very regular, and the houses are well built. Amongst its institutions are two colleges for higher education and a technical school. The town is the chief centre of the fancy woollen trade. Broadcloths, doe skins, and trouserings are also manufactured, and there are manufactories of steam-engines and machinery. It sends a member to Parliament. Pop. (1931), 113,467.

HUDSON, Henry, English navigator, date of birth unknown. He sailed from London in the year 1607 in a small vessel, with only ten men and a boy, to discover the North-East Passage, and proceeded beyond the 80th degree of latitude. In a second voyage he landed at Novaya Zemlya, but could get no farther eastward. In 1609 he sailed for North America, and discovered the Hudson River, which he ascended about 50 leagues.

In 1610 he sailed in an English ship named the *Discovery*, and discovered Hudson Strait and Hudson Bay, where he wintered; but his crew, after suffering many hardships, mutinied and set him adrift in a boat along with his son John and seven of the most infirm of the crew, none of whom were ever again heard of. Hudson published *Divers Voyages and Northern Discoveries* (1607), and a *Second Voyage* (1608).—Cf. Edgar M. Bacon, *Henry Hudson : his Times and his Voyages.*

HUDSON, a town and port, United States, in the state of and 116 miles north of New York, on the left bank of the Hudson. It has large iron-smelting works, foundries, and breweries. Pop. 12,337.

HUDSON BAY, or **HUDSON'S BAY,** an extensive bay, or rather an inland sea, Dominion of Canada, extending between lat. 51° and 64° N., and long. 77° and 95° W.; length, north to south, about 800 miles; greatest breadth, about 600 miles. Hudson Bay is navigable for four and a half months in summer (from middle of June to end of October), being obstructed by drift-ice during the rest of the year.

There are many islands, reefs, and sand-banks. The shores on the east are high and bold; but those on the west, especially towards the south, are low and level, and much of the land there is favourable for stock and dairy farming. There is a considerable summer fishery. Churchill and Port Nelson are the two chief settlements.

HUDSON RIVER, a river in the United States. It rises, by two branches, in the northern part of the state of New York, in the Adirondack Mountains, about lat. 44° N. Two small streams unite to form the river, which is afterwards joined by the Schroon and Sacondaga. At Glen's Falls it has a fall of 50 feet, after which it runs almost due south to its mouth in New York Bay. Its whole course is about 315 miles; it is navigable as far as Hudson, 118 miles, for the largest vessels. The banks of the Upper Hudson are high and rocky, and the scenery very picturesque.

HUDSON'S BAY COMPANY, an English trading company, chartered 2nd May, 1670. It had long a monopoly of the trade throughout the whole territory of North America whose streams flow into Hudson Bay, and at one time as far westward as the Pacific, with rights of governing and making war.

In 1870 its authority was transferred by Act of Parliament to the Crown, and its territories incorporated in the Dominion of Canada, but it received a money indemnity and valuable tracts of land (c. 18,000,000 acres), which have yielded it a large revenue. It then became a limited liability company. Its trade in furs is still very large. During the European War the company lost over one hundred steamers, which were sunk by German submarines. Its headquarters are in London, and it has large stores at Winnipeg and elsewhere. *See* FUR AND FUR TRADE.

HUÉ, the capital city of Annam, on the River Hué, walled, fortified, and garrisoned by French troops who occupy the Mang-Ca or citadel. (*See* ANNAM.) The circumference of the walls is upwards of 5 miles. The city has a considerable trade, and since 1906 a railway connects it with Hanoi. Pop. (1931), 31,885.

HUELVA (ṇ-el'vá), a seaport town of South-Western Spain, capital of the province of same name in Andalusia. It has wide and well-built streets. There are manufactures of matting, ropes, sails, &c.; a large trade in the exportation of copper ore, also in fruits and wine. The fisheries, mainly sardine and tunny, are productive. Pop. (1931), 45,915. —The province of Huelva is mountainous and well wooded in the north, and contains celebrated copper-mines (Tharsis, Rio Tinto). In the south it is comparatively level, and has a rich alluvial soil. Area, 3,913 sq. miles; pop. (1931), 357,503.

HUERTA, Victoriano, Mexican sol-

Hudson River

HUE AND CRY, in English law, the pursuit of a felon or offender, with loud outcries or clamour to give an alarm. This procedure may be taken by a person robbed, or otherwise injured, to pursue and get possession of the culprit's person, or by an officer of justice. At common law, a private person who has been robbed, or who knows that felony is committed, is bound to raise hue and cry.

This is generally done by informing the nearest constable; and this process is still recognized by the law of England as a means of arresting felons and breaking open doors without the warrant of a justice of the peace. The same name is also applied to an official paper circulated to announce the perpetration of offences.

dier and Provisional President of Mexico, born in 1854, died 10th Jan., 1916. He entered the army as a boy, and eventually attained the rank of brigadier-general (1902), after suppressing an Indian revolt in Yucatan. He came into prominence in 1911, served under President Porfirio Diaz, and after the latter's resignation he entered the service of Madero, but in Feb., 1913, he suddenly deserted the President and combined with General Felix Diaz to make Madero a prisoner. After Madero's murder (23rd Feb., 1913), Huerta was himself elected Provisional President. Popular feeling, however, being against him, he resigned in 1914 and went into exile, where he died.

HUESCA (ṇ-es'ká; ancient OSCA), a town of Spain, capital of the province of Huesca, on the Isuela. It is beautifully situated on an eminence in a fertile plain, has well-paved streets, a magnificent Gothic cathedral dating from the thirteenth century, an ancient royal palace, and a celebrated bull-ring. Pop. 12,000.— The province of Huesca is mountainous in the north, but has much fertile land in the south. Area, 5,848 sq. miles; pop. 252,584.

HUET (ü-ā), **Pierre Daniel**, a French critic and classical scholar, was born at Caen, Normandy, in 1630, died in 1721. He was educated at the Jesuits' College of Caen; afterwards went to Paris; accompanied Bochart to the court of Queen Christina of Sweden; was appointed in 1670 sub-preceptor under Bossuet to the dauphin, and

Huesca

superintended the celebrated 'Delphin Series' (*in usum Delphini*) of the Latin classics.

After the completion of his tutorship, having taken holy orders, he was made Abbot of Aulnai, and subsequently nominated Bishop of Soissons, which see he exchanged for that of Avranches, but afterwards retired to an establishment of the Jesuits at Paris, where he died. Amongst his writings are: *Carmina Latina et Græca*; *De Interpretatione*, a treatise on translation; *Sur l'origine des Romains*; *Censura Philosophiæ Cartesianæ*; and *Histoire du commerce et de la navigation des anciens*.

HÜGEL, Friedrich, Baron, Austro-English author, born at Florence, May, 1852. Educated at Florence and Brussels, he became deaf in 1871, as a result of typhus fever, and was unable to do any sustained mental work for some time. He settled in England in 1871, and afterwards devoted his life to the study of Biblical criticism, and to philosophy and psychology as applied to religious experience.

After the death of Lord Acton, von Hügel became the foremost representative of Catholic scholarship in Great Britain. He wrote: *The Papal Commission and the Pentateuch* (with Professor Charles Briggs, 1906); *The Mystical Element of Religion* (1908–9); *Eternal Life* (1912–3); *The German Soul* (1916); besides contributing numerous articles on philosophy of religion to English, American, French, and Italian reviews. He died in 1925.

HUGGINS, Sir William, English astronomer, born 1824, died 1910. Educated at City of London School and privately, he early devoted himself to scientific pursuits, especially astronomy, and erected an observatory at Tulse Hill, a few miles south of London. Much of his work was connected with the spectroscope in its applications to astronomy and especially as a means of determining physico-chemical nature of the stars, comets, nebulæ, &c., and of ascertaining and measuring their motions. He was also highly successful in applying photography to the study of the stars and their spectra. Elected a Fellow of the Royal Society in 1865, he was president of the society from 1900 to 1905, and had other honours conferred upon him, being created K.C.B. in 1897.

HUGGLESCOTE, town of Leicestershire. It is a mining centre, 5½ miles from Ashby de la Zouche and 113 from London, on the L.M.S. Rly. Pop. 6,475.

HUGHENDEN (hū'en-den), or **HITCHENDON**, a parish and village of England, in Buckinghamshire, a short distance north of High Wycombe, with a church containing the tomb of the Earl of Beaconsfield, and a statue of him erected by Queen Victoria. Pop. 2,523.

HUGHES, Charles Evans, American politician. Born 11th April, 1862, the son of a Baptist minister, he was educated for the Law and began to practise in New York. From 1891–93 he was Professor of Law at Cornell University. In 1907 he was chosen Governor of New York, and three years later was made a judge. A candidate for the Presidency in 1916, he was beaten by Wilson. From 1921–25 he was Secretary of State under Harding and presided over the Armaments Conference at Washington in 1921. He became Chief Justice in 1930.

HUGHES, David Edward, inventor of the printing telegraph and other electrical instruments, born in London in 1831, died in 1900. He spent his early life in America, and there, in 1855, patented his printing telegraph, which was at once adopted in the United States, some years later in France, which he visited in order to secure its adoption, and by 1876 practically in every European country. Other inventions of his were the microphone and the induction balance. He left a large fortune, which he bequeathed chiefly to four London hospitals.

HUGHES, Richard. English writer. Born in 1900 he was educated at Charterhouse and Oxford. In 1922 his first play, *The Sisters' Tragedy*, was produced. He also wrote *A Comedy of Good and Evil*, several plays for broadcasting purposes, and many poems. In 1929 his successful novel, *A High Wind in Jamaica*, was published, and in 1931 *The Spider's Palace, Children's Stories.*

HUGHES, Thomas, an English barrister, author, and philanthropist, born at Uffington, Berkshire, in 1822, died in 1896. He was educated at Rugby under Dr. Arnold, and afterwards at Oxford. In 1848 he was called to the Bar, and in 1869 became a Queen's Counsel. He is widely known by his story *Tom Brown's School-days*, a picture of school life at Rugby, published in 1856.

It was followed by *Tom Brown at Oxford* (1861), *A Layman's Faith* (1868), *Alfred the Great* (1869), *The Manliness of Christ*, and other writings. He was one who devoted much time to the social elevation of the working-class, encouraging in particular the co-operative system. From 1865 to 1868 he was member of Parliament for Lambeth, and from 1868 to 1874 for Frome. He was afterwards a county-court judge.

HUGHES, Rt. Hon. William Morris, Australian statesman, born in Wales 25th Sept., 1864. Educated at Llandudno Grammar School, he went to Australia in 1884, was employed as a sheep-drover for some time, and in 1890 settled in Sydney. Here he organized the wharf labourers during a strike, and became secretary of their Union. Entering politics as a member of the legislative Assembly of New South Wales in 1894, he resigned his position in 1901 on becoming member of the Federal Government.

He was Minister for External Affairs, and Attorney-General in various Labour administrations from 1908–15, when he succeeded Andrew Fisher as Prime Minister. He broke with the extreme section of the Labour party when he was defeated on the subject of conscription, and formed a coalition with the Liberals. From that time until 1923 he remained Prime Minister of Australia. In 1918 he represented the Common-

wealth at the Imperial War Cabinet, and attended the Peace Conference in Paris in 1919. He was made a Privy Councillor in 1916. In 1929 he published a *Review of Empire Relations.*

HUGLI, or **HOOGHLY** (hōg'li), a river of India, in Bengal, one of the Ganges mouths, formed by the Bhagirathi and the Jalangi, about 55 miles above Calcutta. It is 15 miles wide at its mouth, but much encumbered by shoals. At Calcutta it is about a mile wide, and has rapid and violent tides. The south-west monsoons produce a 'bore' in the Hugli, that is, a tidal wave which

Victor Hugo

rushes up the river at the rate of 15 or 20 miles an hour. Ships drawing 26 feet ascend as far as Calcutta. In 1931 a tunnel under the river was opened. Total course, about 200 miles.

HUGLI, a town of India, in Bengal, on the Hugli River, 22 miles north of Calcutta. It was founded by the Portuguese in 1537. It was made the seat of a British Factory in 1676, but declined in importance as Calcutta rose. An important iron railway bridge connecting the East India railway system with that of the Eastern and Northern Bengal railway crosses the river near the town. Pop. 29,938.

HUGO (ü-gō), **Victor Marie,** a French poet and novelist, born 26th Feb., 1802, at Besançon, where his father, then Major Hugo, was stationed in command of a brigade, died 2nd May, 1885. His father having entered the service of Joseph Bonaparte, King of Italy, and afterwards of Spain, Victor's earlier years were partly spent in those countries, but in 1812 he went with his mother to Paris. At the age of twelve he was already writing verses, and in 1823 his first novel, *Han d'Islande*, appeared, followed in 1825 by *Bug Jargal*. In 1828 a complete edition of his *Odes et Ballades* appeared.

In all these writings Hugo's anti-classical tendencies in style and treatment of his subject had been very visible, but the appearance of his drama *Cromwell* (1827), with its celebrated preface, gave the watch-word to the anti-Classical or Romantic school. *Cromwell* was too long for representation, and it was only in 1830 that *Hernani*, over which the great contest between Classicists and Romanticists took place, was brought on the stage. Other dramas followed —*Marion Delorme* (1831), *Le Roi s'amuse* (1832), *Lucrèce Borgia* (1833), *Marie Tudor* (1833), *Angelo* (1835), *Ruy Blas* (1838), *Les Burgraves* (1843).

During those years he had also published a novel of the fifteenth century, *Notre Dame de Paris* (1830), and several volumes of poetry, *Les Orientales* (1829), *Les Feuilles d' Automne* (1831), *Les Chants du Crépuscule* (1835), *Les Voix intérieures* (1837), *Les Rayons et les Ombres* (1840). The poetry of this period has a melody and grace superior perhaps to any that he afterwards wrote, but wants that deep and original sense of life which is characteristic of his later poems.

During the same period he also wrote his critical essays on Mirabeau and Voltaire, and a number of articles for the *Revue de Paris*. In 1841, after having been twice previously rejected, he was elected a member of the French Academy; shortly afterwards he made a tour in the Rhineland, of which he wrote a brilliant and interesting account in *Le Rhin*, published in 1842. In 1845 he was made a peer of France by Louis Philippe.

The revolution of 1848 threw Hugo into the thick of the political struggle. At first his votes were decidedly Conservative, but afterwards, whether from suspicion of Napoleon's designs or from other reasons, he became one of the chiefs of the Democratic party.

After the *coup d'état*, 2nd Dec., 1851, he was one of those who kept up the struggle in the streets against Napoleon to the last. He then fled to Brussels, where he published the first of his bitter satires on the founder of the Second Empire, *Napoléon le Petit*.

In the following year (1853) the second, the famous volume of *Les Châtiments*, a wonderful mixture of satirical invective, lyrical passion, and pathos, appeared. Hugo now went to live in Jersey, was expelled along with the other French exiles in 1855 by the Government of the Island, and finally settled in Guernsey. It was in the comparative solitude and quietness of the Channel Islands that he wrote most of the great works of his later years, *Les Contemplations* (1856), *La Légende des Siècles* (first series 1859), *Chansons des Rues et des Bois* (1865), and his celebrated series of social novels, *Les Misérables* (1862), *Les Travailleurs de la Mer* (1866), and *L'Homme qui rit* (1869).

In 1870, after the fall of the Empire, Victor Hugo returned to Paris, where he spent the remaining years of a remarkably vigorous old age in occasional attendances at the Senate, and in adding to the already long list of his literary works. Amongst these latest productions we may mention: *L'Année terrible* (poems on the war, 1872), *Quatrevingt-treize* (1872), *L'Art d'être grand-père* (1877), *L'Histoire d'un Crime* (1877), *Le Pape* (1878), *Les Quatre Vents de l'Esprit* (1881), *La Légende des Siècles* (last series 1883), and *Torquemada* (1882). A complete edition of his works was published in 58 volumes between 1885 and 1902.— BIBLIOGRAPHY: Sainte-Beuve, *Portraits Contemporains*; C. Renouvier, *Victor Hugo le philosophe*; T. Legay, *Victor Hugo jugé par son siècle*; A. F. Davidson, *Victor Hugo : his Life and Work*; F. T. Marzials, *Life of Victor Hugo*; J. Claretie, *Victor Hugo : Souvenirs intimes*; Mme Duclaux, *Victor Hugo.*

END OF VOLUME V